By the same author

The Spanish Civil War
Cuba or the Pursuit of Liberty
The Suez Affair
John Strachey
Goya and 'The Third of May 1808'
Armed Truce
An Unfinished History of the World
Ever Closer Union

CONQUEST

Montezuma, Cortés, and the Fall of Old Mexico

Hugh Thomas

A Touchstone Book
Published by Simon & Schuster
New York   London   Toronto   Sydney   Tokyo   Singapore

TOUCHSTONE
Rockefeller Center
1230 Avenue of the Americas
New York, New York 10020

First Touchstone Edition 1995
Originally published in 1993 in Great Britain
by Hutchinson, London

TOUCHSTONE and colophon are registered trademarks
of Simon & Schuster Inc.

Manufactured in the United States of America

1 3 5 7 9 10 8 6 4 2

Library of Congress Cataloging-in-Publication Data
Thomas, Hugh, date.
Conquest: Montezuma, Cortés, and the fall of Old Mexico /
Hugh Thomas.
p. cm
Includes bibliographical references and index.
1.Mexico—History—Conquest, 1519-1540. 2.Montezuma II,
Emperor of Mexico, ca. 1480-1520. 3.Cortés, Hernán,
1485-1547. I.Title. F1230.T48 1994
972'.02-dc20   93-30474
                                                          CIP

ISBN 0-671-70518-0
ISBN 0-671-51104-1 (Pbk)

This work is dedicated in gratitude to all my friends in Seville and in Mexico

Contents

Illustrations

Preface

This book tells how a small party of well-led adventurers fought against a large static monarchy. It is also a study of a clash between two empires. Both were imaginative and inventive. Though different, they had some things in common: they held many things sacred, they had conquered others, they loved ceremonial. Both were by most modern standards cruel, but cultivated. Both intermittently dreamed of conquering what they thought of as "the world". Both were possessed by powerful beliefs which their leaders looked on as complete explanations of human life.

The Spanish invasion of Mexico was a continuation of the conquests which began in 1492 after Columbus' first journey. Hernán Cortés, the Spanish commander, had lived in both Hispaniola and Cuba. All the members of his expedition had been for a time in those islands. A few of them had been elsewhere on the mainland, near Panama, before they went to what is now Mexico.

The peoples of Mexico were in 1519 ruled by a monarchy of greater sophistication than were the little chieftainships of the Caribbean before Columbus. The Aztecs – or, as I prefer to call them, the Mexica (the reason is explained in the Notes, p. xix) – had many qualities. They were well organised. Old Mexico was very like a state. One conquistador thought that their houses were superior to those of Spain. Upper-class Mexicans wore embroidered clothes. Their craftsmen made jewellery which astonished the Europeans. Being largely urban, they could provide something like universal education: at least to boys who were the children neither of serfs nor of slaves.

In the sixteenth century, the Spaniards still generally used the Roman system of numbering, including their fractions, rather than the more helpful decimal which the Arabs, thanks to the Hindus, had introduced many years before. The Mexicans had the vigesimal method, as well as the zero, which enabled calculations on a more accurate basis than was possible in Europe.

A controversy about the ethics of the Spaniards' imperial mission had been engaged even before the discovery of Mexico, because of the soul-searching of several Dominican friars who had seen the empire in the Caribbean. The arguments seem today remote and dry. Yet no other European empire, neither the Roman, the French, nor the British, entered upon such discussions about the purposes of their expansion. The arguments continued. In 1770, the Marquis of Moncada sent a friend in France a beautiful ancient painted book, probably from Puebla, now known as the Map of Quinatzin. He wrote, "You will judge for yourself if they [the Mexicans] were barbarous at that time when their country, their goods and their mines were stolen from them; or whether we were".[1]

The morality of the Mexica is suggested by a passage in the Florentine Codex: where it is shown that, at least in theory, they admired many of the things which Christian gentlemen were supposed to in Europe: "thrift, compassion, sincerity, carefulness, orderliness, energy, watchfulness, hard work, obedience, humility, grace, discretion, good memory, modesty, courage and resolution"; while they despised "laziness, negligence, lack of compassion, unreliability, untruthfulness, sullenness, dullness, squandering, deceit, pilfering", and even "agitation, disrespect and treachery".

One element in the practices of the ancient Mexicans caused them to seem even to Spanish friars to be barbarians, and therefore in special need of salvation. That was human sacrifice. For Spaniards in Mexico, the evidence of human sacrifice removed all doubts about the morality of the invasion mounted by Cortés, at least until the conquest was over.

Today we are all, as it were, Gibbonians. Different modes of worship seem to most of us as equally true, to our philosophers as equally false, and to our anthropologists as equally interesting. Every culture, Jacques Soustelle (author of a masterpiece about the daily life of the Mexica) reminded us, has its own ideas of what is, and what is not, cruel; adding that human sacrifice in old Mexico was inspired neither by cruelty nor by hatred: it was "a response to the instability of a continually threatened world". Every people, it is now generally supposed, has its own right to conduct itself as its national customs provide.

Still, even now one would have to have a strong stomach to accept with a purely anthropological judgement all the manifestations of human sacrifice: not just the tearing out of the hearts of prisoners of war or slaves, but the wearing by priests of the skins of the victims (inside out) as a ceremonial uniform, the occasional throwing of victims into a fire, the incarceration or drowning of children, and finally the ceremonial eating of the arms and legs of the victims. How can we judge the Matlatzinca, who sacrificed people by slowly crushing them in a net? Are we really content to see the victims as "bathers in an early dawn"? Babies in arms, "human standard-bearers", were brutally made to cry, to ensure that the god of rain, Tlaloc, seeing the tears, made no mistake about the nature of what was required. Later on, the Anglo-Saxons in North America seized upon the action of scalping as a justification of conquest. The conquistadors judged human sacrifice similarly. Whether it should be described as a good reason for the conquest would take us into detail inappropriate for a preface.

Neither Cortés nor Columbus, nor any other conquistador, entered a static, timeless and peaceful world of innocents. The Tainos whom Columbus encountered seemed happy. But they had themselves once come to the Caribbean islands as conquerors and had driven out, or rather had driven into the west end of Cuba, the primitive inhabitants, the so-called Guanahatabeys (also known as Casimiroids). They themselves were menaced by the Caribs who, coming from the South American mainland, had been fighting their way up the lesser Antilles. The Caribs had already conquered the so-called Igneri culture in what are now called the Windward Islands, and were beginning to threaten the Leewards, perhaps even Puerto Rico.

The Mayas in Yucatan whom Cortés and his fellow conquistadors visited, and whom expeditions led by the Montejo family eventually conquered, have now been shown to have been warlike even during their golden age. The Mexica were the successors of several warrior peoples who had ruled in the Valley of Mexico. Their own empire had been established by military conquest. The Spaniards in their opposition to old Mexico were given decisive support by Indian allies, who hated the Mexica. The Spanish were, of course, conquerors, as were, in their day, the Vikings, the Goths, the Romans (whom they admired), the Arabs, the Macedonian Greeks, the Persians, to mention only a few of those who preceded them; or the English, the Dutch, the French, the Germans and the Russians, to mention some who followed them. Like most of those other warriors, and like those, principally other Europeans, who would come after them, they carried ideas with them.

The Spanish had unbounded confidence in their own qualities, in the political wisdom of their imperial mission, and in the spiritual superiority of the Catholic church. "O what great good fortune for the Indians is the coming of the Spaniards," the historian Cervantes de Salazar would say in 1554, "since they have passed from this unhappiness to their present blessed state".[2] "O, the strange bestiality of these people," the Dominican friar Durán would write, towards the end of the century, "in many things they have good discipline, government, understanding, capacity and polish but, in others, strange bestiality and blindness."[3] The declared aim of the conquistadors was to end the bestiality and build on the capacity. Cortés and his friends did not mean to destroy old Mexico. Their purpose was to hand it over, as a present, a "precious feather", as Mexicans, who used many such metaphors, would have said, to the Emperor Charles V, the most reliable "sword of Christianity".

Europeans in the sixteenth century knew nothing of those ideas which render our sentiment of justice timid and hesitant, wrote the great Dutch historian Huizinga: doubts as to the criminal's responsibility, the conviction that society is the accomplice of the criminal, the desire to reform, rather than inflict pain: these notions existed among neither the Castilians nor the Mexicans. Thus Soustelle, a great friend of old Mexico, was right when he admitted in an interview in the 1960s that "the Spaniards could not have acted otherwise. And we mustn't forget the efforts which some Spaniards made to record and defend; or that they made possible the society in which Indian life was to re-awaken."[4]

One friend, on reading an early draft of this book, suggested that to give Cortés the benefit of the doubt on several occasions was to allow oneself tolerance towards the memory of Himmler in 1942. We can all see what he generously meant. Yet two of the best scholars of modern Mexico, Miguel León-Portilla, the great Mexican historian, and Rudolph van Zantwijk, the Dutch anthropologist, talking of the military life which the ancient Mexicans extolled, have dared to compare *them* with the Nazis.[5] All such comparisons are interesting. Yet to read into the past the morality of our time (or the lack of it) may not make the historian's task any easier.

It may be said that this is a subject which has been recorded before; in the United States, incomparably, by the great Prescott, in Europe by Salvador de Madariaga, and in Mexico by Carlos Peyrera. I need not devote attention to every one of these and other writers who have written of this subject. Most people who write of interesting subjects of long ago have predecessors. Did not Wilde think that the only thing to do with history was to rewrite it? Both Peyrera and Madariaga wrote biographies of Cortés. So more recently have José Luis Martínez and Demetrio Ramos. That is not what I intended. Prescott is a different matter.

Prescott was a marvellous man. He wrote magnificently. Who can forget his description of how a modern traveller, standing on top of the pyramid of Cholula, can see several hundred churches where Cortés could in 1519 have seen the same number of temples? Prescott's book was used as a guide by United States officers in the Mexican War of 1848: an astonishing achievement for any historian, even more so for one who was almost blind. It is moving to read of Prescott's decision to make himself a historian, his victory over so many physical handicaps, and his "nocto-graph", which he devised so as to be able to write; of his imaginings, in letters to Fanny Calderón de la Barca, as to how the country looked outside

Texcoco; and of his delightful conversation, in his house on Beacon Street, Boston – a residence still to be admired. It is fine to hear of his morning rides, his triumphant visit to London, his philanthropy, his generosity, and his charm as a man. Yet Prescott published his work on Mexico in 1843, a hundred and fifty years ago. His history stands as a monument of its own, to be admired as part of its age, as if it were a neo-Gothic cathedral. The tone is of another era.

In Prescott's cathedral, some of the stonework also seems less secure than it once did. For there are some matters where a modern historian has an advantage over the great Bostonian. Since 1843 much new material has been found. To take only one example: Prescott regarded the long enquiry into Cortés' conduct of affairs, the *juicio de residencia*, which began work in 1529, and to the study of which I myself have devoted many worthwhile hours, as beneath his attention. Yet Prescott only knew a summary of the charges (the *pesquisa secreta*). Even that, he seems to have thought, contained "a mass of loathsome details such as might better suit a prosecution in a petty municipal court than that of a great officer of the crown".[6] This judgement is mistaken, even if one takes Cortés' point of view.

The 6,000 manuscript pages of the *residencia*, though often repetitious, tedious and irrelevant, contain information on almost every aspect of the conquest and its aftermath. They cannot be merely dismissed. They raise the number of eyewitness accounts of what happened from ten or so (Cortés himself, Bernal Díaz, Fr. Aguilar, Andrés de Tapia, "the Anonymous Conquistador", and one or two identified people who talked to the historians Cervantes de Salazar, Bartolomé de Las Casas and Fernández de Oviedo) to over a hundred. How often the transcribed report of the *residencia*, in its difficult *procesal* hand, has a witness being asked how he knew such and such: "he replied," the text enticingly reads, that he "was there and saw it all"!

Much of this material is fragmentary and biased, either for or against Hernán Cortés. All the same it is testimony made on oath, in Mexico, between 1529 and 1535, by participants in the great expedition. Some of these statements were published in the nineteenth century, though after Prescott had finished his work. A little more has been published since (for example, by José Luis Martínez, in his most helpful volumes of *Documentos Cortesianos*). But many folios of unpublished and, so far as I can see, unconsulted documents have remained in the Archivo General de Indias in Seville. I have studied them.

Much other relevant material has also come to light since Prescott wrote. I have examined the *juicio de residencia* of 1524 against Diego Velázquez, Cortés' one-time superior, the Spanish governor of Cuba, also to my knowledge never used. I have also looked at papers relating to Cortés' master boat-builder, Martín López, collected by G. L. R.

Conway (and rather curiously distributed by him in Washington, Cambridge and Aberdeen). There is in the Archivo de Protocolos in Seville unpublished material relating to Cortés, including a letter to the master of the ship which took him to Mexico, as well as a document which suggests that Cortés left Spain for the first time two years later than has been generally supposed. At the great national archive in Simancas there are papers relating to the life of Cortés' birthplace, Medellín, in the 1480s and 1490s, suggesting that the conquistador's childhood was passed in a most explosive society. There are available, too, numerous unpublished statements of services by conquistadors, as well as testimonies in other lawsuits, made so frequently in the middle years of the sixteenth century that it seems that testifying about the past must have been the main activity of conquistadors once the conquest was over.

At the same time, many scholars have written monographs which, taken altogether, and considered alongside the new material which I have unearthed, should change our picture of Spain and its empire in the early sixteenth century.

There is another side to this: Prescott, like most people of his generation, was a little disdainful of the indigenous culture of old Mexico. "I have had hard work in dressing up the remains of Aztec civilisation," Prescott wrote in 1840 to a French friend.[7] But here too the situation has been transformed. Prescott was a contemporary of John Lloyd Stephens and Frederick Catherwood. Their work demonstrating that Maya civilisation was in many ways comparable to that of ancient Greece appeared only in 1841 and 1843, while Prescott was actually at work. The world of old Mexico, in respect of both Yucatan and the Valley of Mexico, has since then been illuminated by the discovery, and publication, of much new primary material. An immense secondary literature, the work of innumerable scholars in many disciplines (anthropology, archaeology and the social sciences, as well as history, literature and even archaeo-astronomy) has grown up.

I should perhaps say here that I have treated the works of Fr. Diego Durán, Fr. Sahagún, Fernando Alvarado Tezozomoc and Fernando Alva Ixthlxochitl (see Sources) as historians of the first importance.

I record my gratitude for the help of numerous people: first, to Teresa Alzugaray, a specialist in *procesal* handwriting, who made light of work which, had it been left to me, would have taken me a lifetime. It was said of the Spaniards that their war with Granada would have lasted ten years beyond 1492 if they had not possessed cannon. Señorita Alzugaray has thus been my culverin. Her transcriptions, under my direction, of documents in the Archivo General de Indias, the Archivo de Protocolos de Sevilla, the Archivo General de Simancas, and elsewhere, have been invaluable.

I thank Nina Evans, the superintendent of the Reading Room of the

British Library, and her wonderful staff, for their trouble; Rosario Parra, until recently Director of the Archivo General de Indias, Seville, and her staff; Douglas Matthews, Librarian of the London Library, who also made the Index; the Cambridge University Library; the Bodleian Library; Professor Nicholas Mann and the staff of the Warburg Institute; the library of the Institute for Pre-Colombian Studies at Dumbarton Oaks, Washington DC (Bridget Toledo); Dr James Billington, the Librarian of Congress, and Everette Larson and the staff of the Hispanic Division; Isabel Simó, Director of the Archivo Histórico Provincial in Seville; Antonio López Gómez, Librarian of the Real Academia de la Historia, Madrid; Enriqueta Vila, until recently Director of the *Anuario de Estudios Americanos*; Antonio Sánchez González, Director of the Archives, Casa de Pilatos; Roger Morgan and David Jones, Librarians of the House of Lords; and the Directors of the Archivo Histórico Nacional, Madrid; of the Archivo Nacional, Simancas (including Isabel Aguirre); Jaime García Terres, Director of the Biblioteca de México; Dr. Judith Licea, Co-ordinator of the Biblioteca National de Mexico; Manuel Ramos, Director of the Biblioteca de CONDUMEX, Mexico; and Licenciado Leonor Ortiz, Director of the Archivo General de la Nación, Mexico.

My work, like that of everybody working on the history of the discovery of America, has been made much easier by the provision by *Historia 16* of a new, admirably printed collection of most of the basic Spanish and indigenous texts, many of them excellently introduced by Dr Germán Vázquez.

I should like to thank several people, other than those directors of libraries, etc., already mentioned, with whom I have had conversations on the theme of this book. These include Professor José Pérez de Tudela, who enabled me to consult the Juan Bautista Muñoz and Salazar collections in the Real Academia de la Historia, Madrid; María Concepción García Sáiz, of the Museo de América, Madrid; Homero and Betty Aridjis; Professor John Elliott; Professor Juan Gil; Professor Francis Haskell; Professor Miguel León-Portilla; José Luis Martínez; Professor Francisco Morales Padrón; Professor Mauricio Obregón; Professor Julian Pitt-Rivers; Marita Martínez del Río de Redo; Guillermo Tovar de Teresa; Professor Consuelo Varela; Professor Edward Cooper (genealogy and Medellín); Dr Richard Emanuel; Mr Howard Philips (glass); Felipe Fernández-Armesto (especially ballads); Mr Joel McCreary (sacred mushrooms); Owen Mostyn-Owen (comets); Conchita Romero (portable altars); Sir Crispin Tickell (volcanoes); and Zahira Véliz (sixteenth-century iconography).

I am, too, most grateful to my son, Isambard, for his invaluable help with my computer; to my wife, Vanessa, for reading the manuscript at an early stage and reading the proofs; to Oliver Knox and Jane Selley for their work on the proofs; and to the Duke and Duchess of Segorbe, for having me to stay in Seville while working in the Archivo General de Indias. Many have written of that Archivo. Irene Wright even wrote a poem. The obligation to study there has once more shown how duty and pleasure can be combined. I am grateful, too, for their enthusiasm and support, to: Gillon Aitken and Andrew Wylie; Carmen Balcells and Gloria Gutiérrez; Anthony Cheetham, then of Random Century; Simon King and Anthony Whittome of Hutchinson – the latter a most generous, considerate and patient editor; and Michael Korda of Simon and Schuster, as encouraging as he was imaginative. I also thank Mrs Susan Eddleston, of Coutts and Co., for her backing.

HUGH THOMAS
1 August 1993

I am grateful to the University of Utah Press, Charles Dibble and Arthur Anderson for their translation of the Florentine Codex. I have on occasion changed a word of this translation in which case I have removed the inverted commas round the passage concerned. Occasionally I have used Angel Garibay's translation of the Codex and re-translated accordingly. I am also grateful to John Bierhorst, the late Irene Nicholson and Miguel León-Portilla, and of course indirectly the late Angel María Garibay, for their translations of verses originally in Nahuatl. I am grateful to the heirs of the late Thelma Sullivan for the translation quoted on page 317.

I am similarly grateful to Anthony Pagden for use of his translation of Cortés' letters to Charles V; to Doris Heyden and F. Horcantes, for their translations from Fr. Durán's *Historia de las Indias*; Fr. Francis Speck SJ, for his translation of Motolinía's *Historia de los Indios*; Benjamin Keen, for his translation of Zorita's *Relación de los señores de la Nueva España*; L. B. Simpson, for his translation of López de Gómara's *La conquista de México*; and the late Rita Hamilton and the late Jane Perry for their translation of *The Poem of the Cid*. References to these works in the notes are always to Spanish editions. I have often varied the translations or made my own. Bibliographical details of all these publications can be found in the Sources. Finally, Genealogy III, "Cortés and his relations", owes a great deal to Edward Cooper's work in his *Castillos Señoriales en la Corona de Castilla*.

Notes

1 I refer to the people usually called Aztecs as the Mexica (pronounced "Mesheeca"), the word by which they called themselves. Neither Cortés, nor Bernal Díaz, nor Fr. Bernardino de Sahagún used the word "Aztecs". "Aztec", from Aztlan, was not a word used in the sixteenth century (though it may have been in the thirteenth). It was made popular by the Jesuit scholar, Francisco Javier Clavijero, in the eighteenth century, and then by Prescott. In this matter I follow R. H. Barlow, "Some remarks on the term 'Aztec Empire' ", *The Americas*, I, 3 (January 1945).

When I refer to the Mexica I mean the people as such. If I speak of Mexicans I mean identifiable individuals.

To those who will say that the use of the word "Mexica" confuses the present Mexicans with their indigenous predecessors, I would reply that those who have recently been in control of Mexico, whether white, *mestizo* or Indian, have maintained themselves by insisting that they are the heirs of the ancient indigenous peoples.

2 I have spoken of the capital of the Mexica as "Tenochtitlan", the name most frequently used in the sixteenth century. The Mexica often called it "Mexico", sometimes "Mexico Tenochtitlan" or, if they were referring to Tlatelolco, "Mexico Tlatelolco". They frequently called themselves the "Tenochca", that is, residents of Tenochtitlan, and the "Tlatelolca", the residents of Tlatelolco. I have eschewed those usages, except where essential, as, for example, in Chapter 35.

3 I have usually spoken of the conquistadors as Castilians, sometimes as the Spaniards. Similarly I refer often to the King of "Spain" as the King of

Castile. "Spain" was increasingly in use, not least because of Cortés' designation of what became his conquest as "New Spain".

4 I have throughout used the modern calendar for dates, and, as a rule, modern geographical names.

5 I have called the Emperor of Mexico in 1518 by his to us familiar name of Montezuma. Sahagún spoke of "Motecuçoma", the Codex Aubin had "Motecucoma", and the Codex Mendoza "Motecuma". Cortés spoke of "Mutezuma", the Church translated the Emperor as "Motevcçuma" ("*dominus Motevcçuma, cum 17 aut 18 annis regnaret . . .*"), and the modern Spanish form is "Moctezuma".

6 I have permitted myself many other anglicisations of both place names and personal names, depending on usage. Thus I have Saragossa, Corunna, Navarre, Seville, Havana; Ferdinand, Charles, and Philip, but, all the same, Juana, Pedro and Juan, where the individuals concerned are not kings, and even Juana rather than Joanna for the queen of that name.

1
Ancient Mexico

I

Harmony and order

"The fashion of living [in Mexico] is almost the same as in Spain with just as much harmony and order . . ."
Hernán Cortés to Charles V, 1521

T HE BEAUTIFUL POSITION of the Mexican capital, Tenochtitlan, could scarcely have been improved upon. The city stood over seven thousand feet up, on an island near the shore of a great lake. It was two hundred miles from the sea to the west, a hundred and fifty to the east. The lake lay in the centre of a broad valley surrounded by magnificent mountains, two of which were volcanoes. One of these was always covered by snow: "O Mexico, that such mountains should encircle and crown thee," a Spanish Franciscan would exult a few years later.[1] The sun shone brilliantly most days, the air was clear, the sky was as blue as the water of the lake, the colours were intense, the nights cold.

Like Venice, with which it would be insistently compared, Tenochtitlan had been built over several generations.[2] The tiny natural island at the centre of it had been extended to cover 2,500 acres by driving in stakes, and throwing mud and rocks into the gaps. Tenochtitlan boasted about thirty fine high palaces made of a reddish, porous volcanic stone.[3] The smaller, single-storey houses, in which most of the 250,000 or so inhabitants lived, were of adobe and usually painted white.[4] Many of these had been secured against floods by being raised on platforms. The lake was alive with canoes of different sizes bringing tribute and commercial goods. The shores were dotted with well-constructed small towns which owed allegiance to the great city on the water.

The centre of Tenochtitlan was a walled holy precinct, with numerous sacred buildings, including several pyramids with temples on top.[5] Streets and canals led away straight from the precinct at all four points of the compass. Nearby stood the Emperor's palace. There were many minor pyramids in the city, each the base for temples to different gods: the pyramids themselves, characteristic religious edifices of the region, being a human tribute to the splendour of the surrounding volcanoes.

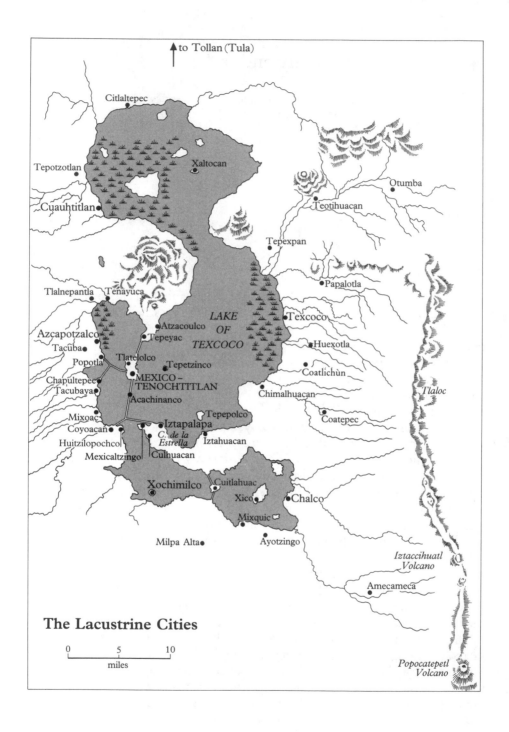

↑ to Tollan (Tula)

Citlaltepec

Tepotzotlan

Xaltocan

Otumba

Cuauhtitlan

Teotihuacan

Tepexpan

Papalotla

Tlalnepantla   Tenayuca

LAKE
OF
TEXCOCO

Texcoco

Azcapotzalco
Tacuba

Atzacoulco
Tepeyac

Huexotla

Popotla

Tlatelolco

Tepetzinco

Coatlichùn

Chapúltepec
Tacubaya

MEXICO –
TENOCHTITLAN

Tlaloc

Acachinanco

Chimalhuacan

Mixoac
Coyoacan

Tepepolco

Iztapalapa

Coatepec

Huitzilopochco

C. de la
Estrella

Iztahuacan

Mexicaltzingo   Culhuacan

Xochimilco

Cuitlahuac

Xico

Chalco

Mixquic

Milpa Alta

Ayotzingo

Iztaccihuatl
Volcano

Amecameca

The Lacustrine Cities

0   5   10

miles

Popocatepetl
Volcano

Tenochtitlan's site made it seem impregnable. The city had never been attacked. The Mexica had only to raise the bridges on the three causeways which connected their capital to the mainland to be beyond the reach of any plausible enemy. A poem demanded:

> Who could conquer Tenochtitlan?
> Who could shake the foundation of heaven . . .?[6]

Tenochtitlan's safety had been underpinned for ninety years by an alliance with two other cities on, respectively, the west and east sides of the lake – Tacuba and Texcoco. Both were satellites of Tenochtitlan, though Texcoco, the capital of culture, was formidable in its own right: an elegant version of the language of the valley, Nahuatl, was spoken there. Tacuba was tiny, for it may have had only 120 houses.[7] These two places obeyed the Emperor of the Mexica in respect of military affairs. Otherwise they were independent. The royal houses, as there is no reason not to call them, of both were linked by blood with that of Tenochtitlan.[8]

These allies helped to guarantee a mutually advantageous lacustrine economy of fifty or so small, self-governing city states, many of them within sight of one another, none of them self-sufficient. Wood was available for fire (as for carved furniture, agricultural tools, canoes, weapons, and idols) from the slopes of the mountains; flint and obsidian could be obtained for some instruments from a zone in the north-east; there was clay for pottery and figurines (a flourishing art, with at least nine different wares) while, from the shore of the lake, came salt, and reeds for baskets.

The emperors of Mexico dominated not only the Valley of Mexico.[9] Beyond the volcanoes, they had, during the previous three generations, established their authority to the east as far as the Gulf of Mexico. Their sway extended far down the coast of the Pacific Ocean in the west to Xoconocho, the best source of the much-prized green feathers of the quetzal bird. To the south, they had led armies to remote conquests in rain forests a month's march away. Tenochtitlan thus controlled three distinct zones: the tropics, near the oceans; a temperate area, beyond the volcanoes; and the mountainous region, nearby. Hence the variety of products for sale in the imperial capital.

The heartland of the empire, the Valley of Mexico, was seventy-five miles north to south, forty east to west: about three thousand square miles; but the empire itself covered 125,000 square miles.[10]

Tenochtitlan should have been self-confident. There was no city bigger, more powerful, or richer within the world of which the people of the valley were informed. It acted as the focus for thousands of immigrants, of whom some had come because of the demand for their crafts: lapidaries, for example, from Xochimilco. A single family had ruled the city for over a century. A "mosaic" of altogether nearly four hundred cities, each with its own ruler, sent regular deliveries to the Emperor of (to mention the most important items) maize (the local staff of life) and beans, cotton cloaks and other clothes, as well as several types of war costumes (war tunics, often feathered, were sent from all but eight out of thirty-eight provinces).[11] Tribute included raw materials and goods in an unfinished state (beaten but not embellished gold), as well as manufactured items (including amber and crystal lip plugs, and strings of jade or turquoise beads).

The power of the Mexica in the year 1518 or, as they called it, 13-Slate, seemed to rest upon solid foundations. Exchange of goods was well established. Cocoa beans and cloaks, sometimes canoes, copper axes, and feather quills full of gold dust, were used as currency (a small cloak was reckoned as worth between sixty-five and a hundred cocoa beans).[12] But payments for services were usually made in kind.

There were markets in all districts: one of these, that in the city of Tlatelolco, by now a large suburb of Tenochtitlan, was the biggest market in the Americas, an emporium for the entire region. Even goods from distant Guatemala were exchanged there. Meantime, trade on a small scale in old Mexico was carried on by nearly everyone, for marketing the household's product was the main activity of family life.

The Mexican empire had the benefit of a remarkable lingua franca. This was Nahuatl: in the words of one who knew it, a "smooth and malleable language, both majestic and of great quality, comprehensive, and easily mastered".[13] It lent itself to expressive metaphors, and eloquent repetitions. It inspired oratory and poetry, recited both as a pastime and to celebrate the gods.[14] An equally interesting manifestation was the tradition of long speeches, *huehuetlatolli*, "words of the old men", learned by heart (as was the poetry) for public occasions, and covering a vast number of themes, usually affording the advice that temperance was best.

Nahuatl was an oral language. But the Mexica, like the other peoples in the valley, used pictographs and ideograms for writing. Names of persons – for example, Acamapichtli ("handful of reeds") or Miahuaxochitl ("turquoise maize flower") could always be represented by the former. Perhaps the Mexica were moving towards something like the syllabic script of the Maya. Even a development on that scale would not have been able to express the subtleties of their speech. Yet Nahuatl was, as the Castilian philologist, Antonio de Nebrija had, in the 1490s, described Castilian, "a language of empire". Appropriately, the literal translation of the word for a ruler, *tlatoani*, was "spokesman": he who speaks or, perhaps, he who commands (*huey tlatoani*, emperor, was "high spokesman"). Mexican writers could also express elegiac melancholy in a way which seems almost to echo French poetry of the same era:

I am to pass away like a faded flower
My fame will be nothing, my renown on earth will vanish.[15]

Nahuatl, its foremost modern scholar has passionately said, "is a language which should never die".[16]

Beautiful painted books (usually called codices) recorded the possession of land, as of history, with family trees and maps supporting the inclination of the ancient Mexicans to be litigious. The importance of this side of life can be gathered from the 480,000 sheets of bark paper regularly sent as tribute to "the storehouses of the ruler of Tenochtitlan".[17]

The politics of the empire were happily guaranteed by the arrangements for imperial succession. Though normal inheritance customarily passed from father to son, a new emperor, always of the same family as his predecessor, was usually his brother, or cousin, who had performed well in a recent war. Thus the Emperor in 1518, Montezuma II, was the eighth son of Axayácatl, an emperor who died in 1481.[18] Montezuma had followed an uncle, Ahuítzotl, who had died in 1502. In the selection of a new ruler, about thirty lords, together with the kings of Texcoco and Tacuba, acted as an electoral college.[19] No succession so decided seems to have been challenged, even if sometimes there had been rival candidates.[20] (Vestiges of this method of election can be detected by the imaginative in modern methods of selecting the President of Mexico.)[21] Disputes were avoided since each election of a ruler was accompanied by the nomination of four other leaders, who in theory would remain in their places throughout the reign of an emperor, and of whom one would become the heir.[22] No doubt the actual duties of these officials ("Killer of Men", "Keeper of the House of Darkness") had become detached from the titles just as the "Chief Butler of the King" had ceased in Castile to have much to do with the provision of wine. The system of succession varied in nearby cities: in most of them, the ruler was hereditary in the family of the monarch, though in some places the kingship did not always fall to the eldest son. In Texcoco primogeniture was the rule.[23]

It is true that the deaths of the last three emperors had seemed a little odd: Ahuítzotl died from a blow on the head when fleeing from flood waters; Tizoc was rumoured to have been killed by witches; and Axayácatl died after defeat in battle. Yet there is nothing to prove that in fact they did not die from natural causes.[24]

The Mexican emperor stood for, and concerned himself with, the external face of the empire. Internal affairs were ultimately directed by a deputy emperor, a cousin, the *cihuacoatl*, a title which he shared with that of a great goddess, and whose literal translation, "woman snake", connected him with the feminine side of divinity. The word gives an inadequate picture of his multifarious duties. Probably in the beginning this official was the priest of the goddess whose name he had.

The internal life of Tenochtitlan was stable. It was in practice managed by an interlocking network of something between a clan, a guild and a district, known as the *calpulli*, a word about whose precise nature every generation of scholars has a new theory, only agreeing that it indicated a self-governing unit, and that it held land which its members did not own, but used. It was probably an association of linked extended families. In several *calpultin* (that being the plural style) families had the same professions. Thus featherworkers mostly lived in Amantlan, a district which may once have been an independent village.

Each *calpulli* had its own gods, priests, and traditions. Marriage (celebrated in old Mexico with as much ceremonial as in Europe) outside the *calpulli*, though not impossible, was unusual. The *calpulli* was the body which mobilised the Mexica for war, for cleaning streets, and for attending festivals. Farmers of land which had been granted by the *calpulli* gave a proportion of the crops (perhaps a third) to that body for delivery to the imperial administration. Through the *calpulli*, the farmer heard the requests, or the orders, of the Emperor.[25] There were perhaps as many as eighty of these in Tenochtitlan. Earlier, the leader, the *calpullec*, had apparently been elected but, by the fifteenth century, that office had become hereditary and lifelong. He too had a council of elders to consult, just as the Emperor had his more formally contrived advisers.

The most powerful *calpulli* was that in the suburb known as Cueopan, where there lived the so-called long-distance merchants, the *pochteca*. These had a bad name among Mexica: they seemed to be "the greedy, the well-fed, the covetous, the niggardly . . . who coveted wealth". But they were officially praised: "men who, leading the caravans of bearers, made the Mexican state great".[26] Knowing that they were the object of envy, they were secretive. They served the Mexica as spies: telling the Emperor the strengths, the weaknesses and the wealth of the places which they saw on their journeys.[27]

These merchants, who imported Tenochtitlan's raw materials, as well as the luxury goods from both the temperate zone and the tropics, antedated the empire in their organisation.[28] Much of their work consisted of the exchange of manufactured objects for raw materials: an embroidered cloak for jade; or a gold jewel for tortoiseshells (used as spoons for cocoa). These great merchants lived without ostentation, dressed badly, and wore their hair down to their waists. Yet they had many possessions. They were even referred to by the Emperor as his "uncles"; and their daughters were sometimes concubines of monarchs.

Important though the merchants were, the supremacy of the Mexica in the valley and beyond had been won by their soldiers. These warriors were both well organised and numerous: the rulers were said to have waited till their population was large before challenging the Tepanecs, to whom they had previously been subject, in 1428.[29] Boys in Mexico were prepared for war from birth in a way which both Spartans and Prussians would have found congenial. At baptisms (the process of naming a child included the use of water sprinkled on the infant, and the placing of water over the heart, so the Christian word is appropriate) the midwife, taking the male child from the mother, would announce that he "belongs to the battlefield, there in the centre, in the middle of the plains". Male children's umbilical cords were buried in places facing where the enemy might be expected. "War is thy desert, thy task . . ." the midwife would tell the newborn boy, "perhaps thou wilt receive the gift . . . [of] the flowered death by the obsidian knife" (that is, by sacrifice, as a prisoner of war).[30]

The weapons of war were present too at christenings: the bow and arrow, the sling, the stone-headed wooden spear. Those weapons, along with the club and the *macuauhuitl*, a two-edged sword of black obsidian blades set in oak (they cut "like a razor from Tolosa", one conquistador would say), had given these armies their victories.[31] The sign (glyph) for government in Nahuatl was a depiction of a bow and arrow, a round shield (of tightly arranged feathers on a wooden, or cane, backing), and a throwing stick (*atlatl*, used to launch spears – at fish as well as at men). The best cloaks and the richest jewels were obtained as prizes for valour, not by purchase. Any male who failed to respond to the call to go to war lost all status, even if he were the son of the Emperor ("he who does not go to war will not consort with the brave" was a Spanish chronicler's formulation of the principle).[32] Promotion in the army (and hence a social rise generally) depended on capturing a specific number of captives: an event consummated by special insignia. Membership of the knightly orders, the "jaguars" and the "eagles", was a supreme distinction obtained by the brave.

The costumes of these orders, and indeed all the war costumes, ridiculous though they seemed to Europeans, were intended to terrify, by playing on the nerves of enemies. Full-feathered constructions on bamboo frames were strapped to captains' backs, while feather-decked heads of animals, sometimes worn as part of a full animal skin, completed the psychological warfare of armies whose first aim was to inspire fear, and so secure surrender without conflict. The colossal Mexican sculptures, such as that of the great Coatlicue, for which there was no precedent in earlier empires in the valley, had the same purpose. There had been so many conflicts that war, not agriculture, seemed the main occupation of the ancient Mexica: "if war is not going on, the Mexica consider themselves idle," the Emperor Montezuma I had remarked.[33] For, as poets insisted, "a battle is like a flower".[34] It must sometimes have looked like that.

The commitment of the population to war makes credible the estimates given by historians of the late sixteenth century for the size of the Mexican armies. Thus Axayácatl, the rash poet-emperor who lost a war against the Tarascans, was said to have had 24,000 men with him. His successor but one, Ahuítzotl, who tried to absorb far-off Tehuantepec, was believed to have had an army of 200,000, gathered from many cities. Tenochtitlan during this campaign was said to have been empty save for women and children.[35]

These forces, organised in legions of 8,000 men, divided into companies of 100, and co-ordinated by the *calpultin*, maintained peace, and imperial rule, by the constant threat, and sometimes the use, of terror. No doubt references in codices to decisions "to wipe out all traces" of such and such a place were often exaggerated. But since successful wars ended with the burning of the enemy's temple (which had the benefit of enabling the destruction of the armouries which were usually close by), brutality must have occurred. Mexican leaders often arranged to persuade their own people that conflict had been forced upon them.[36] There were many small wars, or shows of force, for the empire was so large, the terrain so rugged, that the armies of Tenochtitlan were constantly on the move, putting down rebellions, as well as conquering new cities.

This Mexican era of continuous conquest had begun about 1430. The instigators were the first emperor, Itzcoatl, and his curious nephew, and general, Tlacaelel, who was also *cihuacoatl*. Previously, the Mexica had seemed to have been just one more small tribe of demanding people in the valley. But as a result of the efforts of these two men, the Mexica had transformed themselves into "a chosen people", with a mission, whose purpose was to give to all humanity the benefits of their own victory.[37]

A special people needs a special training. That was possible since most of the Mexica lived in a city and therefore their children could easily be sent to schools. The upper class sent their sons to rigorous boarding academies, the *calmécac* ("houses of tears"), which, in their cultivation of good breeding, their design to break boys' loyalties towards their homes, and their austerity, bore a definite resemblance to public schools in England during the reign of Victoria (boys aged seven were urged not to look "longingly to thy home . . . Do not say 'my mother is there. My father is there' ").[38] Attention was paid to "character": the preparation, it was said, of a "true face and heart". But there were classes too in law, politics, history, painting, and music.

The children of workers received vocational training in the more relaxed *telpochcalli*, the "houses of youth" established in every district. The teachers were professionals, but priests played a part. From these institutions, children could go home frequently. Yet they, like those in the *calmécac*, received ample instruction in morality and natural history through homilies which they often learned by heart, and of which some survive. "Almost all," wrote a good observer in the 1560s, "know the names of all the birds, animals, trees and herbs, knowing too as many as a thousand varieties of the latter, and what they are good for."[39] A strong work ethic was inculcated: and children were told that they had to be honest, diligent and resourceful. All the same, preparation for combat was the dominating consideration where boys were concerned: above all, single combat with a matched enemy.

In both educational institutions, food was provided by children or their parents, but the teachers were supplied by what it is probably permissible to call the state.[40] Girls received training as housewives and mothers.

The commitment to fighting for male children was marked by a custom whereby, at the age of ten, a boy had his hair cut with only one lock left on his neck. He was not permitted to have that removed till, at the age of eighteen, he had taken a prisoner in war. Then he could grow his hair, and embark upon a competition, which lasted throughout his early manhood, to achieve other benefits, by capturing more prisoners.[41]

Another mark of serenity in Tenochtitlan was that there seemed to be no tensions between religion and civil government. Indeed, the very idea would have seemed incomprehensible. The monarch had supreme religious duties. His responsibility, like his palace, was distinct from that of the priesthood. He had civil duties. His judges and their officials administered a civil law. Yet he had a mandate which he considered came from the gods. He used that to preserve society by playing on his people's sense of natural obligation, rather than by imposition. For all citizens accepted that the reason for their being was to serve the gods.

In the early sixteenth century, no Mexican questioned the central myth of the people, the Legend of the Suns. According to this, time on earth had been divided into five eras. The first of these, known as "4-Tiger", had been destroyed by wild animals; the second, "4-Wind", by wind; the third, "4-Rain", by fire; and the fourth, "4-Water", by floods. The last, the fifth age, that of the Mexica, known as "4-Motion", would, according to myth, one day culminate in a catastrophe brought on by terrifying earthquakes. Monsters of the twilight would come to earth. Human beings would be changed into animals: or, possibly, turkeys.[42]

In order to stave off that bleak day, the god Huitzilopochtli (whose name meant "Hummingbird on the left", or "of the south"), who incarnated the sun (as well as war and the chase), the virginally conceived child of the ancient earth goddess Coatlicue (literally, "serpent skirt"), had, every morning, to put to flight the moon (his sister Coyolxauhqui, whose name meant "her cheeks are painted with bells") and the stars (his brothers, the Centzonuitnaua, "the four hundred southerners"). That struggle symbolised a new day. It was assumed that Huitzilopochtli would be carried into the middle of the sky by the spirits of warriors who had died in battle, or on the sacrificial stone. Then, in the afternoon, he would be borne down, by the ghosts of women who had died in childbirth, to the sunset, close to the earth.

To carry through this ceaseless work, Huitzilopochtli had, by extraordinary convention, to be given nourishment, in the shape of human blood ("most precious water").

Huitzilopochtli may once have been a real chief who had been deified after his death.[43] He may not even have been known till the Mexica, after a peregrination, reached the valley. In those early days, other deities such as the earth goddess, Coatlicue (Huitzilopochtli's mother), or the god of rain, Tlaloc, were far more important than he. But the role of Huitzilopochtli had grown with the empire. He was more and more represented in fiestas where previously he had had no place. He seemed to be the central deity.[44]

The Great Temple, at the geometric centre of Tenochtitlan, symbolised the place of gods in the minds of the people. Each profession had, however, its own deity. Important professions had their own sanctuaries in each of the city's four quarters. Every common food, above all maize, also had its god, or was expressed as a deity. Agricultural tools were not only revered, but thanked, with food, incense and *octli*, the fermented juice of the cactus (now known as *pulque*).

Priests were ascetic celibates of high standing. Two high priests commanded them: one to serve Huitzilopochtli, the other to care for the interests of the still very important deity, Tlaloc, god of rain. Both were named by the Emperor.

Priests had many responsibilities. They acted as watchmen as, nightly, they patrolled the hills round the city, and looked at the heavens to await the periodical reappearance of the planets. They sounded the hours, and inaugurated battles with conch shell trumpets. They guarded the temples, and preserved the people's legends. Their bodies dyed black, their hair long, their ears tattered by offerings of blood, priests were immensely influential.[45]

The Emperor, meantime, was considered a semi-divine figure, to whom even the priests looked up. Both Montezuma II, Emperor in 1518, and his predecessor, Ahuítzotl, had been high priests in early life. Mexico was not a theocracy. There was no public cult of the Emperor's person. Yet religion governed all. The average Mexican's home of adobe and thatch was bare. It rarely had more than a sleeping mat and a hearth. But it always had a shrine, with a clay figurine, usually of the earth goddess Coatlicue.

The priests served perhaps 200 major deities, perhaps 1,600 in all. Figures representing these gods were to be seen everywhere, at crossroads, in front of fountains, before large trees, on hilltops, in oratories, sometimes made of stone, sometimes of wood, baked clay, or even seed, some big, some small. The leading deities, such as the ubiquitous Huitzilopochtli, the capricious Tezcatlipoca, the rain god Tlaloc, and the normally humane Quetzalcoatl, were the real rulers of the Mexica.[46]

There may appear to the modern enquirer to be ambiguities about the role of certain gods. For example, one account describes the sun, fire, water and the regions beyond the heavens as being seen to have been created by four separate deities. Another suggests that the mother-father, Ometeotl, God-Goddess, god of the positive and negative at the same time, was responsible. The gods of Mexico seem to have been the rain, the sun, the wind, fertility, themselves – not just the inspirers of those things. Different interpretations of these complexities divide scholars, partly since the Mexican religious world was all the time changing: the old gods of the Mexica as nomads were still being superimposed upon deities already established in the valley.[47] Though often seeming contradictory to us today, Mexican religion at the time inspired no controversies.

Then a recent king of Texcoco, the long-reigning poet Nezahual-coyotl, with a group of cultivated courtiers, had apparently been drawn to the potentially explosive idea of a single "Unknown God", Ipalnemoani, a deity who was never seen and who was not represented by portraits:

> My house is hung with pictures
> So is yours, one and only God,

Nezahualcoyotl had written, in one of his many moving poems.[48] This poet-king's eloquent devotion to the god Tezcatlipoca, "smoking mirror", might seem to foreshadow the coming of a single inspiration: "O lord, lord of the night, lord of the near, the night and the wind," Mexicans would often pray, as if, in moments of perplexity, they required a unique recipient of supplication. Even if Nezahualcoyotl's poems are dismissed (as they sometimes are) as the skilful embroideries of his descendants, the Mexica plainly accepted that there was a grand supernatural force, of which all other gods were the expression, and which assisted the growth of man's dignity: one divine poem talked of precisely such a person.[49] This force was the combination of the Lord of Duality, Ometecuhtli, and his lady, Omecihuatl, the ancestors of all the gods, who if almost in retirement, still decided the birth date of all beings. They were believed to live at the top of the world, in the thirteenth heaven, where the air was "very cold, delicate and iced".[50]

In the remote past, in the nearby lost city which the Mexicans called Teotihuacan, "place where gods are made", there may even have been a cult of the immortality of the soul. There had thus been those who had said, "When we die, it is not true that we die. For still we live. We are resurrected. We still live. We are awakened. Do thou likewise."[51]

Yet Nezahualcoyotl's "Giver of Life" was not the focus of a major cult. The handsome, empty temple to him in Texcoco was not copied. Nor did Nezahualcoyotl abandon his belief in the traditional gods. There seems to have been no contradiction between Nezahualcoyotl's stress on the Divine Giver and his acceptance of the conventional pantheon.[52]

There was also in Mexico a semi-sacred profession separate to the priesthood, containing men dedicated to private rites, principally fortune-telling, miracle-healing, and interpreting dreams. These were as ascetic and dedicated as the priests. But they were able to transport themselves into states of mind incapable of being reached by ordinary men and women, finding the answer to all problems by placing themselves in a state of ecstasy, itself often obtained by drinking *pulque*, smoking tobacco, eating certain mushrooms (sometimes with honey, to constitute the "flesh of the gods"), or the seeds of morning glory, the datura lily, and the *peyote* cactus. The mushrooms, to the Mexica the most important of these plants, came from the pine-covered slopes of the mountains surrounding the valley. Others were brought to Mexico as tribute. Through their use, men thought that they could be transported to the underworld, to heaven, or to the past and to the future. (Conventional priests also used mixtures of these sacred plants, in the form of a pomade, when they talked to the gods.) These things may have been employed by the Mexica in their nomadic stage. They were certainly the special delight of their remote cousins, the surviving Chichimecs.[53]

Neither the priests nor these divines should be confused with magicians and sorcerers. The tricks of these men included the art of seeming to change themselves into animals, or to disappear. They knew all sorts of magic words or acts which could "bewitch women, and turn their affections wherever they chose".

Finally, in the Mexican divine scheme of things, there was the sun. Like most societies of that era, including most in the old world, the heavenly bodies dominated life. The ancient Mexica were not the only people to follow the movement of the sun meticulously, to note down what they observed, to predict eclipses, to plan their buildings for effective observation, or for astronomically satisfying angles. Indeed, the Mayas in Yucatan, in their heyday in the sixth century AD, had been more remarkable in their persistence, and knowledge. They had "a long count" of years which the Mexica did not. Their mathematics had been more complex. Mexican hieroglyphs were also more pictorial and less abstract than Maya ones. All the same, the Mexican priests who interpreted the calendars and, with two notched sticks, the heavens, were mathematicians of skill and imagination. Most cities of the size of Tenochtitlan

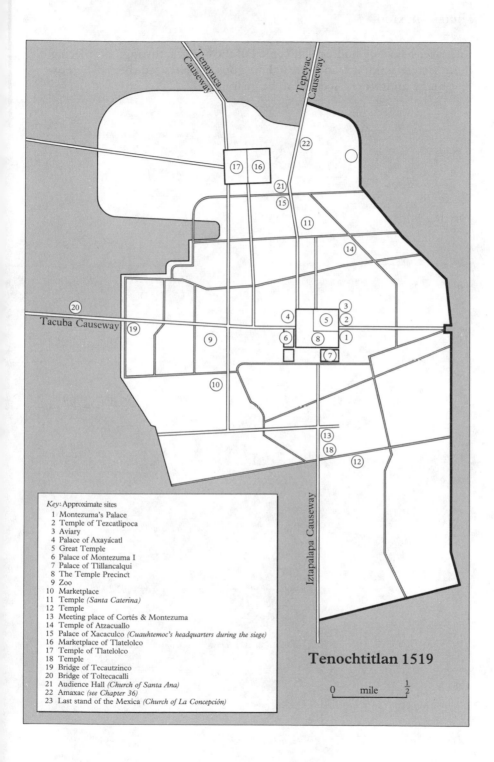

Tenochtitlan 1519

Tenayuca Causeway

Tepeyac Causeway

22

17 16

21
15
11
14

20
Tacuba Causeway
19

3
4 5 2
6 8 1
7
9

10

13
18
12

Iztapalapa Causeway

Key: Approximate sites
1 Montezuma's Palace
2 Temple of Tezcatlipoca
3 Aviary
4 Palace of Axayácatl
5 Great Temple
6 Palace of Montezuma I
7 Palace of Tlillancalqui
8 The Temple Precinct
9 Zoo
10 Marketplace
11 Temple *(Santa Caterina)*
12 Temple
13 Meeting place of Cortés & Montezuma
14 Temple of Atzacuallo
15 Palace of Xacaculco *(Cuauhtemoc's headquarters during the siege)*
16 Marketplace of Tlatelolco
17 Temple of Tlatelolco
18 Temple
19 Bridge of Tecautzinco
20 Bridge of Toltecacalli
21 Audience Hall *(Church of Santa Ana)*
22 Amaxac *(see Chapter 36)*
23 Last stand of the Mexica *(Church of La Concepción)*

Tenochtitlan 1519

0   mile   ½

forget the heavenly bodies. The capital of the Mexica, through the placing of its sacred buildings, and through its gods, emphasised them. Thereby "harmony and order" seemed to be guaranteed.

2

Palace of the white sedges

"Behold Mexico, palace of the white willows, palace of the white sedges!
And you like a blue heron, above her, you open your wings.
You come to her flying.
Beautifully, you open your wings and your fantail.
These are your subjects, they who rule throughout the land, everywhere . . ."
Angel María Garibay, *La Literatura de los Aztecas*, tr. Bierhorst

THOUGH APPARENTLY STABLE, the Mexican empire had taken shape recently enough for its leaders to be conscious, in a world which venerated the past, of its relative youth. A few generations before, the Mexica had seemed just one more tribe of intruders which, famished and "uncouth", had, about 1250, descended from the north in search of good land in the fertile valley.[1] With difficulty, they had found themselves a home where (probably about 1345) they had begun to build their city – on a spot where, legend insisted, an eagle had been observed sitting on a cactus (Tenochtitlan meant "place of the fruit of the cactus"). There were arguments as to whether the Mexica had originally come from the island Aztlan ("place of the white heron"), in a far-off lake, or from Chicomoztoc ("the seven caves"); and where those places were. No one disputed that they had arrived recently.

Many places even in the valley had been independent of the Mexica until within living memory: thus Chalco, on the east of the lake, and once the centre of a little empire of its own, with twenty-five dependent towns, had only succumbed to the Mexica in 1465. Such seemingly traditional things as the customary war costume dated only from the Emperor Axayácatl's victory in the Huaxtec region in the 1470s.[2]

The Mexica were proud of their recent achievements. Twenty-five years before their victorious war against the Tepanecs, even the King, Acampichtli, had scarcely enough to eat. Now in 1518 his descendant the Emperor Montezuma dined regularly off a hundred dishes. In the days of Acampichtli, the Mexica had been able to offer only a modest tribute to the Tepanecs: frogs, fish, juniper berries, willow leaves. Now they themselves regularly received riches which made those lakeside products seem perfunctory. In the old days, the Mexica had dressed in clothes made of maguey fibre; but now their upper class wore robes of long quetzal feathers, and very elaborate cloaks of white duck feathers, embroidered skirts, and necklaces with radiating pendants and huge objects of greenstone[3] – which the Mexica considered more beautiful than gold (indeed the word for it, *chalchihuite*, meant not only the stone but anything beautiful). The Tepanecs had once controlled the modest aqueduct of reeds and clay which brought water to Tenochtitlan from a spring at Chapultepec ("hill of the grasshopper"). Now the Mexica had one of stone with two channels (used alternately, to allow cleaning), which they managed for themselves. Inventive people such as the Totonacs and Huaxtecs on the coast had made sculptures in terracotta. The Mexica, learning from them, did the same in rock. Above all, the Mexica had in the mid-fifteenth century built a colossal city, bigger than any in Europe with the possible exception of Naples and Constantinople, on what had been, only a hundred and fifty years ago, a few huts on a mud bank. Is it surprising that something like patriotism was well established?

Another achievement which seems remarkable was that crime in old Mexico was limited, whether because of a general acceptance of the mores of society or as a consequence of harsh penalties. Strict judges sitting in regularly constituted tribunals administered equitable if severe punishments through officials whose task was to maintain order, arrest suspects, and carry out sentences. These judges had a messenger service of "the greatest speed, whether it was by day or night, travelling through rain, snow or hail".[4] Certain cases would go for judgement to the Emperor or the *cihuacoatl*.[5] The law did not favour noblemen. Indeed, they were supposed to be punished more severely than commoners in respect of most crimes. Monarchs considered their own families bound by laws: King Nezahualpilli of Texcoco had a favourite son put to death on the suspicion of adultery with one of his wives.[6] Weakness by a judge was harshly punished. The law provided that, whenever a crime was committed, the principals in the place concerned were responsible for delivering the offender within a certain time; otherwise, they would have to pay the penalty reserved for the criminal.[7] Most punishments, such as breaking of heads with cudgels, were carried out in public. The death penalty was used for almost every crime considered a felony in modern society. Naughty children met a series of progressively more unpleasant retributions: a disobedient nine-year-old would be bound hand and foot, and have maguey spikes thrust into his shoulders; at ten, he would be beaten.[8] Save at certain festivals, neither the young nor the ordinary workers were allowed to touch *pulque*, the only Mexican alcohol. Drinking was punishable by death on the occasion of the second offence. Those over seventy, providing they had grandchildren, could, however, drink more often; at festivals, as much as they liked.

A clear distinction existed among the Mexica between good and bad.

Thus the Florentine Codex, an admirable summary of what occurred in old Mexico in almost every sphere, tells in detail what a good father would do ("he regulates, distributes with care, establishes order") and how a bad one would behave ("he is lazy, uncompassionate, negligent"). Similar distinctions were made in the same text between good and bad mothers, children, uncles, aunts, down to great-great- grandparents and mothers-in-law ("the bad mother-in-law is one who . . . delights in the misfortune of others, who alienates people, who is disloyal").[9] The good magistrate and the bad magistrate were carefully distinguished too: the latter, for example, was described as a "shower of favour, a hater of people, an establisher of unjust ordinances, an accepter of bribes, an issuer of corrupt pronouncements, a doer of favours".[10]

Stability was further strengthened by the tradition whereby most people remained in the same profession as their fathers: the feather-workers (the most respected of craftsmen) were children of feather-workers, the goldsmiths of goldsmiths.

Most Mexicans were obedient, respectful, disciplined. There were no beggars. The streets were clean, the houses were spotless. Women's lives were spent weaving cloths. For them the spindle, the weaving frame, the loom, the skeins of thread and the straw mat marked, with the family, the boundaries of life. Such discipline was easily accepted in return for the benefits of order. Individuals scarcely existed outside the collectivity. The German newssheet, *Neuwe Zeitung von dem Lande das die Spanien funden*, of 1521, thus exaggerated only slightly when, as a result of reports sent from the New World, it told its readers in Nuremberg that "if the King tells the people to go into the forest to die there, they do".[11] To secure such order, "the nation had a special steward for every activity. Everything was so well recorded that nothing was left out of the accounts. There were even officials in charge of sweeping."[12]

The standing of women was at least comparable to what it was at that time in Europe. Thus a woman could own property, and go to law, without the approval of her husband. Women played a part in commerce, and they could become priestesses, though they never reached the highest level. As in Europe, a man's right to office was affected by his mother's or his wife's status, office was sometimes transmitted through a daughter's son and, occasionally, a woman would hold a title. All the same, daughters were often given away as presents; and, one formal instruction for married women ran, almost as if in Castile: "when your parents give you a husband, do not be disrespectful to him . . . obey him".[13] Though in the early nomadic days of the Mexica, monogamy had been normal, the rulers by the sixteenth century had many concubines as well as a chief wife, or queen.

The Mexica were tolerant of the other peoples, such as the Otomí, who lived among them. These had their own religion, culture, language, even their own calendars (slightly different from those of the Mexica). But tribal hatreds did not seem to exist within the Mexican body politic.

Nor, at least on the surface, did there seem to have been serious disputes about property (though there have been many feuds among historians about the nature of its holding). The land of the city – both inside it and on the further shore of the lake – was divided between the *calpultin*, the nobles, the temples, and the government. Conquered land was a reward for services to those who had fought.[14] Agriculture of course varied from zone to zone. The dependent cities in the fertile low land near the sea enjoyed two crops a year. The Valley of Mexico usually had one crop only. But that latter basin had at its heart a most unusual feature: the "floating gardens", the *chinampas*, intensely cultivated artificial islands built of mud, in practice usually rooted to the bed of the lake by willow trees, though some nursery beds were begun on floating rushes, or weed.[15] (These had begun about AD 1200, in the lakes of Xochimilco and Chalco. They had recently been extended to Tenochtitlan itself.) These fertile acres had permanent irrigation through seepage, and, hence, could be continuously cultivated, unaffected by drought.[16]

In these *chinampas* the Mexica produced about 100 million pounds of maize a year without fallowing, as well as much fresh fruit, vegetables and flowers.[17] Fire-hardened oak spades and digging sticks made possible the cultivation of the fertile swampy land near the lake, and that on the "rough sierras" too.[18]

Most land near the lake was ingeniously irrigated, and so could be continually cultivated. This land, outside the *chinampas*, was regularly allowed to lie fallow, and excrement of all sorts, including human, was used for manure. The land had been originally cleared by felling trees or, more often, girdling them, then burning the branches.

The average farmer in old Mexico – the average man, that is – had as hard a life as any peasant in Europe. It was, too, the same kind of life: the Florentine Codex says that he was bound to the soil, prepared it, weeded it, levelled it, made furrows in it, set the landmarks in it, thinned out the maize, harvested it, and winnowed it.[19]

The main crop was, above all, maize, grown at all heights. Almost as important were amaranth and sage. Beans, chilli peppers and squashes were also widely grown. The sweet potato was produced on the coast. Cacti were cultivated, for many purposes: the sap was drunk as a syrup, and was made into the alcoholic *pulque*; and the needles were used for sewing, and blood-letting. Turkeys, muscovy ducks, little dogs and bees were domesticated.[20] Almost everything which moved was eaten. So was scum from the lake.

Agriculture was not left to chance. Here we see signs of state intervention. For inspectors appointed by the Emperor ensured that a centrally agreed pattern of cultivation was carried out: a policy which had probably been introduced only recently, when the growth of population began to cause pressure on land.[21] Drought and famine had always led to intervention. If the harvest were bad, the Emperor would order not only sacrifices, but the special planting of maguey cacti and prickly pears.

There were thus four main sources of food for Tenochtitlan: *chinampa* agriculture for vegetables, fruit and some maize; maize locally grown on land on the lakeshore and elsewhere; game and fishing; and tribute.[22] Much of the last item, it is true, was given as payment to judges and officials for their services, and to add to the reserves.

The upper classes of Mexico ate diversely. The poor perhaps survived on two and a half to three and a half pounds of maize a day, made into tortillas. They would have beans and vegetables cooked with peppers: and, on feast days, a slice of dog or, occasionally, venison. The availability of the latter, and the time which the poor farmer or townsman could afford to to secure it, had diminished since Tenochtitlan had grown so much.[23] All the same, an enterprising family could still find much free food: a larger variety, certainly, than enjoyed by the modern Mexican, for it included fish, weasel, rattlesnake, iguana, insects, grasshoppers, lake algae, worms and over forty kinds of water fowl. Thus consumption compared well with that of the then population of Europe. Those who later thought that the Mexica ate very badly must have been making a partial judgement on the basis of subsequent events.[24]

Family life, meantime, was cemented by elaborate formal courtesies as well as by ceremonies at important occasions: pregnancy and birth; baptism, marriage and death. Each had their poems, their dances, their rhetoric. Fathers' advice to sons recalls that of Polonius: "revere and greet your elders . . . do not gossip . . . if you be rude, you will get along with none . . . console the poor", and, "Do not stay too long in the market place nor in the bath, lest the demon gain mastery over you."[25] The institution of marriage was protected. Though the Emperor, members of his supreme council, noblemen, and successful warriors could, as we have seen, have concubines, adultery (defined as sexual relations between a man and a married woman) was punishable by death (both parties were often thrown into the river or to the vultures). The highest in the land might be punished if their adultery became publicly known.[26] The Florentine Codex's description of a prostitute would not have sounded ill on the lips of Calvin: for "badness" in women was associated with dissolute behaviour, pride, excessive interest in carnal relations, and gaudy clothes.[27]

Beauty was prized. Old men spoke of children as "a jewelled necklace", "a precious feather" or "a precious stone bracelet". A good nobleman might be compared to "a precious green stone", or a "bracelet of fine turquoise".[28] Metaphors reflected reality. Thus goldsmiths produced jewels of gold leaf which matched the contemporary achievements of the Europeans.[29] The observant, if passionate, friar, Motolinía, thought that these men were superior to "goldsmiths in Spain, inasmuch as they can cast a bird with a movable head, tongue and feet and, in the hand, they place a toy with which they seem to dance".[30] The wood carvers, the manuscript painters and lapidaries, workers in alabaster, turquoise and rock crystal, were equally skilled.[31] Silversmiths combined with goldsmiths to make objects half in gold, half in silver. Mosaics were contrived of turquoise and pearls. The featherworkers too produced mosaics which had no equivalent in Europe.

The craftsmen who produced these marvels with rudimentary equipment had remarkable ingenuity, as well as sure eyes. Mexican art was also distinguished by both relief and fully carved sculpture, which enabled the Mexica to commemorate great men, great deeds, and good gods, as well as to ward off devils and frighten enemies.

Two calendars gave continuity to the Mexicans. These had been taken over from earlier civilisations in the Valley of Mexico. First, there was the *tonalpohualli*, a count of 260 days grouped into twenty thirteen-day weeks, each day named and indicating special fortunes for those born on it. Second, there was the *xiuhpohualli*, based on a solar year of 360 days divided into eighteen months; the extra five days which made up a 365-day year (long ago realised as the appropriate measure) were "useless fillings", dedicated to no god: unfortunate occasions on which to be born.

Special divines interpreted these calendars. These men not only gave the infant his name, but predicted with certainty the kind of life which he or she might expect to have. These predictions were self-fulfilling: they affected the conduct of the child's parents towards him, and the child himself, so that it was almost impossible to triumph over such expectations. A good day on which to be born was 4-Dog. But little could be done for anyone born on 9-Wind.[32] There were also some mediocre days: neither good nor bad. The calendars indicated whether a good time had come to start on a journey; when war should be declared; and, of course, when to begin the harvest.

After fifty-two years in Mexico, a new century (so to speak) was begun. The ceremony marking this occasion, the "binding of the years", was solemn. It was awaited with trepidation. The most recent such event, the fourth since the foundation of the city, had been in 1507. New fire had been carried as usual from a sacred hill. Continuity was assured. Those "who were there watching then raised a cry which rose to the heavens with joy" that the world had not ended.[33]

The Mexica had also achieved what every successful people tries to do: they had established a grand history for themselves. Not only had they produced a heroic account of their early journeys; but they had secured the acceptance by their neighbours that they, the Mexica, were the true heirs of the last great people of the valley, the Toltecs, whose capital had been at Tula (or Tollan), some forty miles north of the lake, and who had been overthrown by nomads in the late twelfth century. The Mexica ensured this inheritance by choosing, as king, in the late fourteenth century, Acampichtli, son of a Mexican warrior and a princess from the nearby city of Culhuacan, six miles from Tenochtitlan, whose ancestors were supposed to derive from the kings of Tollan. Acampichtli is said to have had twenty wives, all daughters of local lords, for the purpose of engendering a Mexican nobility with Toltec blood. He seems to have been successful.[34]

There was good reason to admire the memory of Tula. The Toltecs had been fine craftsmen in featherwork, precious stones, and gold. They had apparently invented medicine. They had discovered the art of mining, and treating, precious metals. The Toltecs had also been clever farmers, knowing, it was said, how to bring three crops a year from soil which later produced one. Legend insisted that with them cotton grew in different colours, so that dyeing was unnecessary.

Nothing was more important for the Mexica than to have so successfully captured the Toltec heritage. For they assigned all fine achievements to Toltec initiative. Thus they said that "the true artist works like a true Toltec"; "the good painter is a Toltec, he creates with red and black ink";[35] and "the Toltecs were wise . . . all good, perfect, wonderful, marvellous their houses were beautiful," tiled in mosaics, smoothed, stuccoed".[36] In practice, however, the Mexica surpassed the Toltecs in artistry as they did in political achievements. The institutions of Tenochtitlan in the early sixteenth century were a combination of Toltec and ancient nomadic Mexican practices, and probably the better for it.

These Mexican re-interpretations of history had been accompanied by a "burning of books" about the past by the Emperor Itzcoatl. Those works could scarcely have been stylish, numerous, or profound. But in place of whatever they contained, the new men created the central myths of Mexico. Old books had presumably given a different picture of Mexican history to what the new rulers wanted to have known. Perhaps the Mexica had taken part in the sacking of Tollan: something which by 1428 they would not have wished to commemorate.[37] Anything which suggested that the Mexica had been motivated to set off on their travels by anything so prosaic as a shortage of water in their previous humble dwellings would have been excised. Probably it was now that, to the Toltec myth that all existence had been marked by four ages of four suns, there was added the legend of a fifth sun, that of the Mexica.[38] Itzcoatl probably also took the opportunity to destroy such records as there were which described how, in the past, his own office as emperor had once been in some ways inferior to that of the *calpultin*. These developments can no doubt be seen as an acceptance of the valley's customs by a previously nomadic tribe.[39] But it may also be seen as one more "noble

23

lie" which a group of leaders sets out to propagate in order to inspire their people with a version of history which bears only a tenuous relation to truth.

Mexican life was, finally, bound together, as was that of all the cities of the valley, by a busy, regular programme of festivals, big and small, on which an enormous amount of time, energy and resources was expended. These meticulously arranged ceremonies, associated with the different months of the year, were mostly intended to assure the abundance of rain and the success of agriculture. There were movable feasts too. The main gods were also separately honoured on other special days. Then there were rejoicings to mark inaugurations of new buildings, coronations, the successful conclusions of wars, and the deaths of kings. There were festivals to obtain rain during drought. The Mexica were considered austere by some who paid them tribute, such as the Otomí, who looked on them as prudishly hostile to both nudity and adultery. All the same, the Mexica were without rivals in the amount of time which they devoted to celebration. In the past many ceremonies had been modest, as they continued to be in small places. But in Tenochtitlan under the emperors they had become flamboyant.[40]

These occasions were marked not only by songs and dancing, accompanied by music from drums, flutes, conch shells, and rattles,[41] but by processions – in which the participants dressed in feathers, in dramatic cloaks, in masks and wigs, in jaguar skins, in some circumstances even in the skins of human beings. Those celebrating painted their faces extravagantly. There were theatrical battles between mock gods and mock soldiers. Flowers were important too: for the Mexica "the smelling of flowers was apparently so comforting that they even staved off hunger by so doing".[42] Hallucinogens, as used by wizards and fortune-tellers, played a part. "Whenever there was singing or dancing," ran one text, "or when the mushrooms were to be eaten, the ruler ordered the songs to be sung."[43]

Blood-letting was of great importance: even on ordinary days, emperor and clown, priest and warrior, regularly, with needles from the maguey cactus, took blood from their tongues, or from the lobes of their ears, in acts of self-mutilation in the service of the gods. Sometimes blood would be obtained by passing straws through a hole made in the tongue, the ears, even (by priests) the penis.

At festivals there were other offerings: sometimes of animals or birds, especially quail; but, on an increasingly large scale, human beings, as a rule prisoners of war, or slaves especially bought for the purpose. Most of those sacrificed were men, though boys and girls sometimes took the main parts in these astonishing, often splendid, and sometimes beautiful barbarities.

This form of sacrifice had probably started in the region of Mexico as soon as human settlements began to be made: at, for example, Tehuacan,

120 miles south-east of Mexico, in about 5000 BC. (The Valley of Mexico began to have settled inhabitants practising agriculture about 2500 BC, and had sophisticated calendars by 300 BC.)

The Mexica had probably made human sacrifices on a modest scale before they broke free from the Tepanecs in 1428: in order to please the gods and so, by enabling an elaborately adorned priest to hold up at dawn a bleeding heart (spoken of in these circumstances as "the precious cactus fruit") to the sun ("the turquoise prince, the soaring eagle"), to postpone for another twenty-four hours the catastrophe of a dark world. The normal procedure was for the victim to be held down on a stone block by four priests. His heart would be plucked out professionally by a chief priest or even the monarch, using a flint knife. The heart would be burned in a brazier. The head would be cut off and held up. The limbs would be ritually eaten, with maize or chilli, by noblemen and successful warriors. (Possibly this Mexican upper class came to enjoy the taste of flesh which they ceremonially ate.)[44] The torsos would be thrown away, or given to animals in one of the zoos. This remained the classic method of sacrifice, though there were variations, involving shooting by bows and arrows, by the use of gladiatorial combat of a rather limited kind, or the offering, in certain circumstances, of children.[45]

Up till the middle of the fifteenth century, even among the Mexica, human sacrifice may have been confined to the slave or captive who had been selected to impersonate a deity, live and be dressed like him for a time, and then be killed, with fitting ceremony. Perhaps, as suggested in a text of the 1540s, a people victorious in war might sacrifice one slave (their "best slave") to give thanks.[46] But from the 1430s onwards, when the Mexica embarked on their drive to empire, sacrifices were ever more frequent.

This was probably the consequence of the long domination of Tenochtitlan by Tlacaelel, the *cihuacoatl*, or deputy, to four emperors, including his uncle Itzcoatl.[47] He stressed the ever greater role of Huitzilopochtli to the exclusion of other gods. He was the architect of Mexican military expansion. He inspired Itzcoatl's burning of books.[48]

The increase in sacrifice was on so lavish a scale that the author of one codex believed (wrongly) that, before 1484, there had been no offerings of human beings at all, only of quail or animals.[49] The innumerable prisoners who died on fourteen pyramids over four days, with long lines of victims stretching from the site of the temple in four directions, as far as the eye could see, at a festival in 1487 to mark the inauguration of the new temple to Huitzilopochtli in Tenochtitlan, had no precedent. No evidence exists which enables anything more realistic than a good guess.[50] A conquistador, Andrés de Tapia, estimated the number of skulls hanging on the rack in Tenochtitlan at 136,000.[51] But a modern ethnologist has pointed out that, from Tapia's own measurements, there

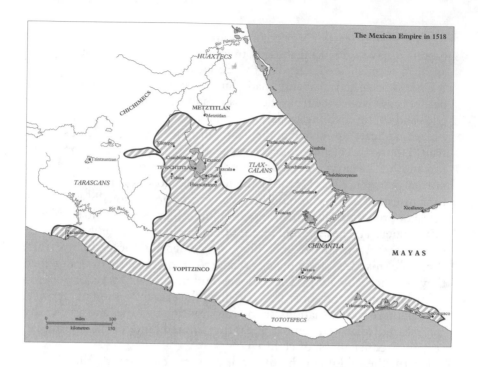

could not have been more than 60,000 at most, and probably many fewer, since the rack could not have filled the space described.[52] Probably that ratio of reduction is one to be applied to most estimates of the sixteenth century. Perhaps the chronicler Fr. Diego Durán was nearer the usual figure when he explained that, at the funeral of King Axayácatl in 1479, fifty or sixty hunchbacks and slaves were offered.[53]

All the same, the blood of sacrificed victims was regularly spattered, as if it were holy water, over the doors, pillars, staircases and courts of Mexican temples and houses. As captives became scarce because of the decline in victorious wars, previously conquered places offered slaves, or even common people, as if they were tribute: particularly children.[54] By the early sixteenth century, the Mexica's own poor had begun to offer their children as victims. (Children anyway were needed for several of the festivals to Tlaloc, the rain god.)[55]

Mercy was as foreign to the Mexica as it had been to the ancient Greeks. What after all are life and death but two sides of the same reality? as the potters of Tlatilco suggested when they made their double faces, one part alive, the other a skull.[56] Was not death a handing-over of something which everyone knew had one day to be transferred? (The Nahuatl word for sacrifice, *nextlaoaliztli*, meant literally an "act of payment".) Were not boys educated to look on the "flowery death" by the "obsidian knife" as the honourable way to die (along with the more infrequent death on the battlefield, and, in the case of women, childbirth)? The gods had no interest in those who died from normal diseases, or of old age. Those who suffered under "the obsidian knife" were assured a place in a better afterlife – in Omeyocan, the paradise of the sun – than those who died conventionally (in practice a flint knife was used for sacrifice, for obsidian is brittle: but the latter stone was used as a metaphor). Ordinary souls were supposed merely to go to Mictlan, grey underworld of annihilation. Those sacrificed were often given the benefit of hallucinogenic doses in order to make them accept their fate; or, at least, a good drink of *pulque*.[57] It must be doubtful, though, whether all were so well looked after.

Fr. Durán wrote in the 1550s: "many times did I ask Indians why they could not have been content to offer quail, turtle doves, or other birds", to receive the answer that those were "offerings of the poor; while to offer prisoners of war or slaves was something suitable for great lords and knights".[58]

Enemies and friends alike of the Mexicans found acceptable this shedding of blood, and the ritual eating of the sacrificed victims' limbs. The population seems to have been spellbound by the drama, the beauty and the terror of the event. Yet there are just one or two hints that there was disquiet, at least, at the increase in the scale of the sacrificial procedure. Thus the visiting rulers who went (secretly) to Tenochtitlan for the opening of the new temple are said to have been shocked by the scale of what they saw.[59] (That was partly, no doubt, the intention.) Nor is it easy to accept that the poor were happy that their children should be sacrificed. The cult of Quetzalcoatl at Cholula must have been a focus of enmity to sacrifice, for that god was against this kind of offering. Disputes over human sacrifice may have first divided and then destroyed the Toltecs. Hostility to the increase of sacrifice in Tenochtitlan may, too, have been one motive for the revolt of the Tlatelolca in 1473: the King of the city, Moquihuix, is said to have sought help from other cities on the ground that the Tenochca were waging wars in order to keep their priests happy with captives for victims.

The achievements of the Mexica should not be overshadowed by consideration of this to us unacceptable side of their practices. Human sacrifices have, after all, been carried out in innumerable places in the West. Brazilian tribes also sacrificed prisoners of war (to symbolise revenge). The Caribs of the Windward Islands ate slices of enemy warriors' flesh in order to acquire their prowess. Yet in numbers, in the elevated sense of ceremony which accompanied the theatrical shows involved, as in its significance in the official religion, human sacrifice in Mexico was unique.

3

I see misfortune come

"I see misfortune come, it shudders in the temple.
Shields burn, it is the place of smoke, there where the Gods are created.
I see misfortune come, it shudders in the temple."
Warrior song, tr. Irene Nicholson, *Firefly in the Night*

"LOOSELY KNIT EMPIRE", "confederation", "mercantile economy backed by military force", whatever name is given to old Mexico in a table of the political enterprises of history, it seemed an overpoweringly formidable undertaking to its neighbours and tributaries.[1] Yet despite the grandeur of the wonderful city, the near-universal education, the remarkable attitudes to law, the poetry, the military successes, the artistic achievements, and the brilliant festivals, there were certain anxieties in Tenochtitlan.

These came not, of course, from the absence of the wheel, of the arch, of metal tools, of domestic animals for traction, nor even of proper writing. Nor was there any difficulty caused because men had sandals and women went barefoot. Perhaps the festivals had begun, in several ways to sacrifice too many people, or even to rely excessively on the "divine mushroom". If so, these were not matters for despair.

The first concern derived from the fact that the Mexica had constructed their history on a myth of eventual cataclysm. This myth, as has been seen, suggested that the world had already been through four eras, lit by four separate suns. The existing time, that of the Fifth Sun, would, everyone knew, one day come to an end.

The general acceptance of that legend, comparable to the Norse fear of the terrible day when Odin would meet the wolf, was one reason for pessimism among the Mexican upper class, despite their wealth, luxurious life, success, and power. Though the Mexica certainly were dominated by a cyclical calendar, their universe did not seem static. On the contrary, it was dynamic. Divine content might be followed by divine calamity.

The Mexica and the people in their dependent polities lived, too, with the memory of the ruin of past cities. In particular they lived, as we have seen, in the shadow of Tollan. The people of that civilisation, the Toltecs, immaculate in their blue sandals though they had seemed, had been overthrown. Even their gods had been dispersed. If such superior people could be ruined, what hope of immortality could there be for the Mexica?

Nor was Tollan the only great place to have vanished. The Mexica knew nothing of the glories of the Mayas in Yucatan in the fifth and sixth centuries. Palenque and Tikal were as unknown to them as they were to Europeans.[2] But everyone in Tenochtitlan knew that, ten miles from the shores of the lake to the north-east, there had once been another city, Teotihuacan, whose mysterious pyramids, now covered in brushwood, were a byword for their size. Nobody knew (nor knows) what people had flourished there, nor what language they had spoken. But the name of that ruin (the word meant "city of the gods") was recalled as a reminder of the ephemeral nature of greatness: "there in Teotihuacan" was a frequently used phrase indicating the past.[3] Remarkable for its mural paintings, its fall had been more complete, perhaps more sudden, than that of Tollan. It had been in truth far grander than Tollan, if the remains to be seen at Tula indicate anything. Its eclipse had affected those who came after it as if it had been the fall of Rome. The comparison is not extravagant. Teotihuacan, at its height, probably had a population larger than Tenochtitlan's. Its size, sculpture, painting, architecture, its special districts reserved for diverse crafts, made it, at the time of its collapse in AD 650, without an equivalent in the world save in China. In 1518, the Emperor of Tenochtitlan and his priests went there every twenty days to make sacrifices.[4]

There was thus a concern among the Mexica with the possibility of catastrophe. When they assumed power, the emperors of the Mexica were called upon to address their citizens in grand terms, which ritualistically anticipated the worst. They asked, amongst other things, "What will result when . . . [the] lord of the near, of the nigh, makes thy city a place of desolation? What will result when it . . . lieth abandoned? . . . And what will result when filth, when vice, have come upon me? What will result when I have ruined the city? . . . What will happen when I cast the common folk into the torrent, cast them from the crag?" At those same imperial inaugurations, a nobleman was called on to demand: "Wilt thou fear the declaration of war . . . will perhaps the city be shot with arrows? Will it be surrounded by enemies? . . . Wilt thou fear that perhaps the city will crumble, will scatter? . . . Perhaps there will be . . . tremors" and the city be abandoned? Will it be darkened? Will it perhaps become a place of desolation? And will there be enslavement? . . .[5]

King Nezahualcoyotl of Texcoco had written many poems which breathed an air of the evanescence of human achievement. His most famous one included the injunction:

Ponder this, eagle and jaguar knights,
Though you are carved in jade, you will break;
Though you are made of gold, you will crack;
Even though you are a quetzal feather, you will wither.
We are not forever on this earth;
Only for a time are we here.[6]

Rulers would ritually tell their daughters: "Difficult is the world, a place where one is caused to weep, a place where one is caused pain. Affliction is known. And the cold wind passeth, glideth by . . . it is a place of thirst, . . . of hunger."[7]

Still, ritual anxiety about the long-term future is often combined with short-term resolution, pride, and aggression. It was so in the case of the Mexica: a fact which made them not unlike those Europeans who, despite a reasonable fear of hell, would shortly make an impertinent appearance on the eastern shores of the Mexican empire.

A second concern was that the Mexica never forgot that they were newcomers. They had rewritten the history of their past, it is true. The reality of what had happened to them before 1428 (when Itzcoatl had burned the old histories), much less before 1376 (when Acampichtli was said to have come to the throne), was, and is, impossible to know. The Mexica had captured the Toltec heritage. But they knew that originally they had been a nomadic tribe which had descended on sedentary peoples of higher culture than they.

The completion of a great city in which their god Huitzilopochtli sat by the side of the rain deity Tlaloc, the assumption of power of a royal house with Toltec origins, and the successful effort to create a nobility with Toltec blood should have removed the Mexican sense of inferiority. It seems not to have done.

There were also some material reasons for concern. The first was that the climate made the economies of all the cities of the valley, but of Tenochtitlan especially, uncertain. Rain fell only between July and November. Every winter, between November and February, was a crisis. An early frost could, of course, ruin harvests. Droughts were also not infrequent. Stores of maize were kept against such occurrences. But there had been times when the crises had been prolonged. In the 1450s, within the living memory of old men, drought had caused famine for several years. A freak snow storm sank many *chinampas*. The reserve of food had been inadequate. Thousands died.[8]

Then the lake was subject to storms which could in a short time fill the basin with too much water and which took a long time to drain. In 1499 there had been a major flood, because of an unwise decision. Much of Tenochtitlan had been lost. The Emperor, Ahuítzotl, whose policies on the supply of water had partly led to the disaster, was discredited. A new city was built. It was more beautiful than its predecessor. But the event constituted a reminder of the ease with which a civilisation built on a lake could fall.

Harvests were also adversely affected by rigid attention to interpretations of the calendar. Fr. Durán recalled that he once "asked an old man why he sowed beans so late, since there was hardly a year when they were not caught by frost. He told me that everything had its number, its reason, and its special day . . . In many places, they would not gather the harvest even though it was lost, until the old men told them that it was time . . ."[9]

Another difficulty was that the economy of Tenochtitlan had begun to depend on tribute. The population had in the last hundred years grown greatly.[10] So local maize was in increasingly short supply. At the same time, a substantial proportion of the population of Tenochtitlan was now engaged in services and crafts: as sandalmakers, sellers of fuel, weavers of mats, potters, carriers; or, as featherworkers and goldsmiths, making use of raw materials which reached them by trade.[11] Supplies of obsidian, previously secured from inside the valley, and salt (much sought after), from the lakeshore, were also becoming scarce, as were those of easily obtainable game and wood.

So the extra supplies made available by tribute had started to seem necessary. But there was more to the problem than that. The pampered official class now found it essential to have tropical fruit and cocoa. Noblemen could not do without their annual 15,000 jars of honey, not to speak of their regular supply of over 200,000 cotton cloaks of different sizes.[12] The Emperor also needed some of these things, in a society without money, to compensate officials for services. To begin with, such "payments" had been in land. But there was now less of that to be come by. The festivals too, which had become ever more grandiose, needed luxuries, both as presents for the gods, and as decorations for the participants. The schools, temples and courts had to be sustained; the officials, public works, the professional soldiers and also the stewards who supervised the collection of tribute all had to be compensated. The Mexica needed colour. Tribute, with its supplies of cochineal and other dyes, made it possible.[13] Even the waging of wars required the war tunics and weapons imported as tribute.

So the maintenance of what had come to be thought of as normal life depended on the thousands of bearers, *tamemes*, who, with carefully made backpacks, trundled their way across the mountains, and along the river beds, with the tribute from the subject cities: trains of men which must have made a fine sight *en route*, for they brought decorative birds, winged insects, flowers, and wonderful feathers, as well as prosaic things such as fruit, beans, cocoa beans, honeycombs, cloaks, cotton armour, and bows and arrows – not to speak of pretty girls and boys for sacrifice.

Travelling fifteen miles in five hours each day, and carrying loads of fifty pounds, the bearers compensated for the absence of animals of traction as of wheeled vehicles[14] (the American horse was long extinct; cattle had never existed; and wheels were confined to toys).[15] The most exotic items of tribute (jade, precious quetzal feathers, gold, copper) came from the furthest and most recently conquered peoples. Some cities provided Tenochtitlan with personal service. Others sent people to act as audiences at festivals. In some places, the best lands were farmed for the benefit of the Mexica. All these offerings were carefully recorded on paper made from the inner bark of the wild fig tree (*amatl*).[16] Though important towns had to suffer Mexican stewards (*calpixque*), and though there were some garrisons, the tributary system avoided the cost of a centralised empire. Provided the right city dispatched the right goods at the right time, it was left alone to govern itself. Yet many subject territories found the demands onerous. Many were restless and resentful. A few were ready for rebellion.

Another cause for disquiet should have been an increasing stratification of Mexican society. In the early days most heads of families seem to have been concerned in the election of a monarch. Now the electoral college was confined to grandees. The attitude of the monarch to his subjects was expressed in the wording of his invitation to the leaders of other cities to come to Mexican festivals. They were to do so in private, since "they did not wish the common people . . . to suspect that kings and rulers made alliances, reached agreements and found friendships at the cost of the life of the common man".[17] Secret alliances secretly arrived at were the rule.

Then the fifteenth century had seen the deliberate creation, it will be remembered, of a class of nobility, *pipiltin*, most of whom were descended from King Acampichtli.[18] Several later kings had had vast families by numerous wives. No doubt the chroniclers exaggerated when they said that Nezahualpilli, King of Texcoco, who died in 1515, had one hundred and forty-four children; but, with a well-tended harem, anything is possible. The power of these half-royal nobles was increased by the distribution of conquered land, together with those who worked it, directly to them, enabling them to bypass, in their loyalties, the traditional clans of Tenochtitlan, the *calpultin*. Perhaps they acquired a rigid approach from those whom they conquered: when Maxtla, King of Azcapotzalco, put a price on the head of Nezahualcoyotl, of Texcoco, then a fugitive, he offered land to anyone who captured him, "even if he were a plebeian".[19]

The Emperor in the 1460s, Montezuma I, consolidated the stratification by introducing a series of rules of conduct, "sparks of a divine fire", as they were improbably named, to ensure that "all might live within their status".[20] These established demarcations between monarchs and lords, lords and high officials, high officials and lower ones, lower officials and ordinary people. There were distinctions between an upper class of grand lords and a lower class of inferior ones. Differences of dress and forms of address were accentuated: noblemen now wore embroidered cotton cloaks and loincloths, golden sandals, earrings, and labrets. Ordinary people could not wear cotton, but had to be content with clothes made from maguey fibre. Their cloaks had to stop at the knee. They could not wear sandals in the presence of superiors. Noblemen alone could build houses with two storeys, only nobles could drink chocolate, while ordinary families were obliged to use earthenware rather than painted or glazed pottery as bowls and plates.[21]

Perhaps these rules were not kept to. Commoners who distinguished themselves in war were rewarded with grants of land, or released from payments of tribute. They might even wear cotton. All the same, opportunities for prowess were easier for the nobility, whose members alone were allowed to use swords, the weapons likely to lead to feats of arms. Further, if a family were not directly descended from the Toltecs (through Acampichtli), it could never be assimilated into the upper class. Mobility of every kind was condemned: "Where a man's father and ancestors had lived, there must a man live and end his days."[22]

The Emperor Montezuma II took these discriminations further. All officials, and even all priests, were henceforth to come from the highest class – in practice, members of the large extended royal family.[23] Even within that great family, offices tended to become hereditary. Quite logically, from his own point of view, Montezuma II closed the special schools, the *calmécac*, to all but the highborn. Previously, promising boys of humble birth could aspire to become priests and thus join one of those austere establishments.

The social structure, therefore, in 1518, seemed more rigid than it had been. This presumably appeared natural to people governed by the calendars as to when to do such and such: "If chilli were not sown on a certain day, squash on another, maize on another, and so forth, people thought that there would be great damage."[24] The calendars thus encouraged people to be content with their lot. The ancient Mexicans "were set against all form of change and renovation", wrote a famous modern scholar, "a will to the immutable was engraved in their style of culture . . . in their art . . . [and] a tendency to repeat the same forms is noticeable".[25]

The isolation of the Emperor was in 1518 greater than ever. Montezuma II had more attendants and guards, jugglers and acrobats, jesters and dancers than his predecessors. After him in order of precedence came the principal advisers, the inner royal family, the senior administrators and the nobility, *pipiltin*, of whom the grandest twenty-one families had imposing titles. They had splendid palaces, where they gave feasts and listened to young men reading poems, or to elderly men discussing the wisdom of the ages. They lived from the produce of land outside Tenochtitlan. Their ancestors had built, or inspired the building of, the great city. They now counted on its size and imposing edifices to overwhelm psychologically both visitors from other cities and the poorer members of their own people.

The main difference within old Mexico (a remarkable similarity to Europe) lay between the tribute-payers and the fiscally exempt. The latter class included nobility, priests, and children, minor or local administrators, priests, and teachers. It also included the leaders of the *calpultin*, and those common men who, through military prowess, had begun to ascend the slippery pole of social advancement. It embraced the craftsmen, the merchants and some farmers.

Within this exempt class, the differences were a matter of interest groups. In comparison with the priests, the merchants could not be said to be superior or inferior. They were powerful in their own right. Both merchants and craftsmen operated as families, on a small if effective scale. All professional, full-time workmen, once they were organised in guilds, seem to have become hereditary (some, such as the manuscript painters, may have been ethnically different).[26] Most noblemen also had some craft or activity: "nobody has seen anyone living on nobility alone", a head of a great family said to his sons.[27]

Among the Mexican masses who did pay tribute or had duties there were also categories: first, the labourers, or commoners, *macehualtin*, who participated in *calpultin*. A *macehual* had the use of specified land which he could pass on to his children. In certain circumstances he could sell it. Even though he might for part of his time do good work as a craftsman, if he did not keep his land cultivated, the *calpulli* could in theory take it from him. He was obliged through his *calpulli* to serve in the army, participate in public works, take part in festivals, and above all pay tribute: much the same as a tax.

Macehualtin formed the bulk of Mexican society. Nothing suggests that they were resentful at their lot. Presumably those in Tenochtitlan knew that they were favourably placed in comparison with their equivalents in dependent cities. What impressed an observant Spanish judge, though, among those Mexicans whom, many years later, he saw working on public works, was the "merriment and great rejoicing" which went on. "It is well known that Montezuma gave tasks to Indians in order to entertain them," was the comment of another witness.[28]

Less clearly differentiated were the *mayeques*, a class comparable to European serfs, being neither slave nor free. They were men, or families, who worked on other people's land, particularly noblemen's land. They may have been more a profession than a class and accounted for a third of the population.[29] They were probably descendants of earlier, or conquered, populations; or children of slaves: poor people, compared to "bumblebees" or "hornets" on the edge of feasts, waiting for a charitable distribution of maize stews. On lakeside properties, their services seem often to have been part of the original grant of land.[30] They were subject to the laws of the Mexica, and were obliged to fight in their wars. But they could not participate in communal activities. Perhaps their standard of living, and their capacity for individual decision, was not much less, if less at all, than that of the *macehualtin*. Yet "they were, and are, so subservient," wrote a Spanish official in 1532, "that even if they are about to be killed or sold, they do not speak . . ."[31]

Finally, in the classification of these ancient Mexicans, there were a few real slaves, *tlatlacotin*, who were in a way more favoured than their European counterparts, since they could own property, buy their liberty, and marry free women or men. Their children were born free. If they escaped into the royal palace, they became automatically free. But there was one serious disadvantage: they could be sacrificed. Some have even suggested that they were mostly sacrificed, having often been bought in the market at Tlatelolco for that purpose.[32]

Many of these slaves were *macehualtin* who had committed crimes or who had failed to meet levies for tribute; peasants who had become slaves when sold by families who needed food; or prisoners awaiting sacrifice. Some too were people who had made themselves slaves voluntarily, to escape the responsibilities of normal life. Slaves played a minor part in the economy in the Valley of Mexico, though a greater one in the subtropical east.

The contrast between the poverty and the riches at the two extremes in Mexican society seems to have been every year more remarkable. Witnesses told Fr. Sahagún how the Emperor's palace, the *tecpan*, was "a fearful place, a place of fear, of glory . . . There is bragging, there is boasting; there are haughtiness, pride, presumption, arrogance. There is self-praise, there is . . . gaudiness . . . it is a place where one is intoxicated, flattered, perverted." The eagle and jaguar knights flaunted themselves.[33] Meantime, the poor probably ate less well than they had used to: there was a greater dependence on maize, less often varied with game. Perhaps they had begun to take refuge in the only way open to them: drink. For despite the heavy punishments for drinking, *pulque* was, all the same, more and more consumed, by lords and poor alike. The Florentine Codex contains a vivid picture of the evils resulting – a temptation to which those born on the day called 2-Rabbit were, it was said, especially prone; or doomed.[34]

Old men in Mexico probably thought that what was disturbing in the Tenochtitlan of their day was less this contrast between the classes than the decline in the power of the *calpultin*. These clans had managed society in the primitive days. Membership of them had made it possible for ordinary men and women to feel part of the collectivity. *Calpultin* still performed essential services. Yet these seem to have been carried out in the early sixteenth century more as if they were lessons learned by rote than out of a willing collaboration with the state, a newfangled thing with disagreeable pretensions. There was a conflict between *calpultin* and government, since the Emperor increasingly conducted himself as if he were the authority which granted land, while the lore of the *calpultin* was that it was theirs in the first place. Meantime the determining matters in Mexican society, the management of appeals for rain, and the interpretation of the calendar, were of course in the hands of the administration or of the priesthood.

The Mexica also had some political problems. For example, forty years before, Tlatelolco ("earth-hillock"), then a semi-independent mercantile city, a mile to the north, on an island linked to Tenochtitlan by several broad causeways, whose population was also Mexican, but who had enjoyed a separate line of monarchs, had made a bid for full independence. The acute stage of the crisis derived from a quarrel of the sort which could have led to a war in Europe: the King of Tlatelolco, Moquihuix, tired of his wife, Chalchiuhnenetzin, a sister of the Emperor of Mexico (she was too thin, her breath was bad). Mexican honour was outraged.[35] Tlatelolco was invaded and defeated. The last king of Tlatelolco jumped off the Great Temple in the marketplace when he saw that defeat was inevitable. It, and its subject cities, were incorporated into Tenochtitlan as a fifth "quarter" of that city. Its inhabitants, though a branch of the Mexica, thenceforth paid tribute to a "military governor", Itzquauhtzin, a brother of the Emperor, who was still in office in 1518. Its famous market was divided up between the victors. But the Tlatelolca were bitter. They warmly, if secretly, welcomed any difficulty for Tenochtitlan.[36]

The Mexica had also had their military setbacks. Under a rash emperor, Axayácatl, they had in 1479–80, been defeated, a hundred and thirty miles to the north-west, by the Purépecha (a people known to the Spaniards as Tarascans).[37] Those worshippers of the little green hummingbird maintained a small empire of some twenty cities (roughly coterminous with the modern Mexican state of Michoacan). They were the only people of the region to possess such metallurgical techniques as cold-hammering, casting, soldering, and gold-plating. This enabled them not only to produce remarkable copper masks, copper bells shaped as turtles, fish with gold bodies and silver fins, and lip plugs of laminated turquoise, but to make copper weapons. Their political life was less complex than that of Mexico, their capital city Tzintzuntzan far smaller, their clothes less sophisticated. But their metallurgy was superior. The Mexican soldiers in consequence had in battle against them died in hundreds, "like flies which fell into the water".[38]

Undisciplined nomads of the north whom the Mexicans called the Chichimecs were also unconquered. (The word *chichimec* meant people with lineage (*mecatl*) of dogs (*chichi*), men who ate meat raw and drank the blood of the animals which they killed.)[39]

The Mexican empire seemed too to have reached its limits. Successive monarchs had extended the frontiers, partly out of the need to guarantee resources from the temperate or hot zones, partly for the same reasons as most empires have expanded: it is difficult to draw a halt to the habit of aggression. But further major wars were difficult to conceive. The expeditions of the Emperor Ahuítzotl, at the end of the fifteenth century, towards what is now known as Central America, had made the populace restless at the idea of distant conflicts. Soldiers after all were not professionals: they were most of the time farmers with fields to tend. It was true that the Mayas in Yucatan had not been conquered. But Yucatan was far. The Mexica preferred to trade with them. It was also hard work to bring home prisoners from a great distance.[40] The Tarascans blocked further advances in the north. For a people primarily organised for war, it was unnerving to find that there were no more worlds to conquer.

The Mexica had come to lay weight on a strange stratagem to meet some of the consequences: "wars of flowers". There were certain cities just over the mountains to the east, which the Mexica had found it difficult to defeat. These were Cholula, Huexotzinco, Atlixco, Tliliuhquitepec and, above all, Tlaxcala. These cities would be allowed a token independence. Their people might even be allowed to assume that the independence was total. But their leaders would permit a "military fair" (the expression of Tlacaelel, the long-living *cihuacoatl*, the deputy emperor) to be staged: let a convenient market be sought where the god may go with his army to buy victims and people to eat, as if he were to go to a nearby place to buy tortillas.[41] The Mexica would gain experience of war. The battles would be good propaganda. Prisoners would be obtained for the sacrificial stones.

The cities concerned collaborated, to save themselves from absorption, in a design which by 1518 had lasted, off and on, about seventy years. These strange conflicts were marked by setting aside a special day for the battle in a previously selected place. The fight would begin with the burning of a pyre of paper, and the distribution of incense between the armies.

Such wars for display, as a kind of game or even a sacrament, were not new in the fifteenth century. The Mexica had fought just such a war (in which no one had died) with Chalco in 1375. Perhaps they had been begun in the days of Teotihuacan. But the scheme was elaborated extravagantly.[42]

By 1518 this convention had almost broken down. Partly that was because the Mexican appetite for prisoners was difficult to contain. Partly it was because the cities beyond the volcanoes did not establish a *modus vivendi* between themselves. Several wars between them were the reverse of theatrical. Their conflicts with the Mexica seemed also to be becoming serious: particularly those of the Tlaxcalans. In 1504, for example, the latter defeated the Mexica in a "flowery" engagement which turned into a genuine war. Much the same happened two years later in respect of a Mexican war with Huexotzinco. Thousands of Mexicans were captured. A Mexican army returned humiliated to Tenochtitlan. The Mexica next imposed sanctions on Tlaxcala: there would be no trading in cotton, nor in salt. That was serious for Tlaxcala since the Mexica had recently completed the process of making dependencies out of all the territory surrounding them, including the tropical land to the east. The Tlaxcalans, led by old and experienced lords, held out. Real hatred of the Mexica, not a "flowery" kind, grew in their city. This was the worse, no doubt, since the Tlaxcalan leaders must have feared that, had the Mexica given them their full attention, they could probably have crushed them.

Tlaxcala soon defeated Huexotzinco in a serious engagement. Huexotzinco swallowed its pride and asked the Mexica for help. The Mexica gave their leaders sanctuary at Tenochtitlan. A Mexican army occupied Huexotzinco. Another battle was fought with Tlaxcala in 1517. On this occasion, the Mexicans at least did not lose. The people of Huexotzinco went home. But the return seems to have been made possible by an arrangement between that city and Tlaxcala, whose bitterness and self-confidence were alike enhanced. The Mexica also offended the people of Huexotzinco by insisting, as a return for their help, that Camaxtli, the special goddess of Huexotzinco, should be installed in their newly opened temple in Tenochtitlan for conquered deities.

Another difficulty concerned the relation of the Mexica with their ally Texcoco, the cultivated city on the east side of the lake. Though much smaller than Tenochtitlan, it boasted beautiful palaces, lovely gardens, interesting temples, and a prosperous agriculture in fields nearby. Several irritants harmed relations. Thus Nezahualpilli, King of Texcoco, infuriated the Mexica in 1498 by executing his young Mexican wife for her adultery (she was a sister of the future Mexican emperor, Montezuma). She was garrotted in public "as if she had been a plebeian".[43] Then Nezahualpilli was offended by the Mexica: he had been a friend of the ruler of Coyoacan whom the late Emperor Ahuítzotl had murdered for giving him advice about the water supply (it had been the right advice). Nezahualpilli next distressed the Mexica again by acting as permanent host to Macuilmalinal, the Emperor Montezuma's elder brother, who had been passed over in the election for the empire and who then married one of his, Nezahualpilli's, daughters. The Mexica responded in a cold-blooded fashion. They devised a "flowery war" for Texcoco with Huexotzinco. Macuil-malinal, however, allowed himself to be killed in action – defying the convention that it would be better to accept death on the sacrificial block. A son of Nezahualpilli was also captured and sacrificed. Nezahualpilli died of grief, perhaps by suicide.

That monarch left an uncertain heritage. To begin with, the succession was unclear. The late king had many children but none by his "legitimate wife". He himself had had executed his eldest son by that lady, Huexotzincatzin, an "outstanding philospher and poet", for making advances to his own favourite concubine, "the lady of Tula".[44] The electors of the new *tlatoani* were the lords of the Texcocan towns and the Mexican emperor. The latter supported his nephew, Cacama, an "illegitimate" son of the late king by that sister of his own whom Nezahualpilli had executed. His vote was the determining one. But another son, Ixtlilxochitl, a brother of Cacama, refused to accept that decision. He raised a rebellion in the mountains. Civil war thereupon began in territory close to the lake. It was sporadic, but it seemed serious. Ixtlilxochitl conquered several towns. A compromise was reached. Cacama was to be looked on as King. But Ixtlilxochitl would be considered lord of the cities which he had captured. Texcoco remained an ally of Tenochtitlan. But it could not be looked upon as so committed a one as had been the case in the past. Trouble so near at home seemed yet one more peril facing the proud Mexica.

4
Not with love but with fear

"Montezuma said to the Marquis of the Valley when he saw him giving a
present to some Indian that . . . these people did not like being treated with
love but with fear."
Jerónimo López to Charles V, 1544

THE MEXICA HAD a trading outpost at Xicallanco, on the edge of a lagoon far down the Gulf of Mexico which might have been regarded as the lodge gate to Yucatan. From there, about 1502, they heard rumours of the appearance of bearded white men on the Caribbean coasts beyond Yucatan. The strangers sounded as if they were men of peculiar ferocity. Stories may have reached Mexico of what had recently been happening in the larger islands of the Caribbean: which (though this is to anticipate) would not have needed to be exaggerated to be frightening. A canoe of natives from the island of Jamaica was lost off Yucatan, with one or two survivors, about 1512. Those people would have had unpleasant stories to tell: or to indicate with signs, since the Maya language was quite different from that of the people of Yucatan or of Mexico.[1]

A trunk was then brought to Tenochtitlan from the Gulf of Mexico. It had been washed up on the shore. Inside were several suits of clothes, some jewels and a sword. Whose possessions were they? No one had ever seen anything like them before. The Emperor Montezuma divided the contents between the kings of Tacuba and Texcoco.[2] A little later a message came from Yucatan, probably sent by a Mexican merchant. It was a folded manuscript. This depicted three white temples at sea floating on large canoes.[3]

Montezuma asked his chief advisers what to do. They were not as perturbed as he was. They recommended further consultations with the god Huitzilopochtli. He then consulted the priests. Forewarned, they were noncommittal. Montezuma punished some of them.[4]

Then merchants from Xicallanco seem to have sent more reports of strange new men. This probably confirmed stories from other Mexican outposts farther south down the isthmus of Central America.[5] The

Mexica would thus perhaps have heard of a colony of white men which had been established in 1513 only a thousand miles (as the crow flies) south-east of Yucatan, in Darien.[6]

It was also, later, reported that in Mexico, after about 1502, a series of phenomena were observed which seemed to presage difficult times. First, for example, a tongue of fire in the sky, presumably a comet of unusual brilliance, was said to have been seen every night for a year. Then the thatched roof of the temple of Huitzilopochtli caught fire on top of the great pyramid: the flames could not be put out. Another temple, that of a more ancient deity, Xiuhtecuhtli, the god of fire (also known as the lord of the turquoise and even as the father and mother of the gods),[7] was destroyed by what was described as a noiseless thunderbolt. This was especially alarming, since fire, expressed by family hearths and braziers before temples, was looked upon as one of the great achievements of the gods. Then a comet was said to have fallen sharply in the sky, to have divided into three, and to have scattered sparks throughout the Valley of Mexico. The water of the lake foamed for no reason; many houses built next to the water were flooded. Cries were reported to have been heard at night from a woman who was never identified: she cried, "O my beloved sons, we are all going to die"; and "My beloved sons, where shall I hide you?" Some strange, two-headed people were then said to have appeared. They were taken to Montezuma's special zoo for human beings, where misfits were kept. There they vanished.

The most famous tale of this time is the most esoteric: some fishermen were said to have found a bird like a crane, of an ashen colour. They showed it to the Emperor, who saw a mirror on its head. In the mirror, he observed the heavens and the stars, and then a number of men riding on deer, approaching as for war. The Emperor is said to have summoned specialist wise men. He asked them for their interpretation. But when they looked, the vision, the mirror, and the bird had all disappeared.[8]

All these predictions were said to have occurred in the Valley of Mexico. There were believed to have been similar portents among the Tarascans, to the north-west, as on the other side of the mountains, in Tlaxcala. Even in Yucatan, a prophet known as Ah Cambal was later recalled for having publicly announced that the people would "soon be subject to a foreign race".[9]

The King of Texcoco, the learned Nezahualpilli, was still alive when these things were said to have been observed. He had a reputation of being the best astrologer in the land. Perhaps relishing the opportunity to cause fear in a man who had humiliated Texcoco, he told the Emperor in Tenochtitlan that the brilliant comet suggested that terrible, frightful things would come. In all their lands, there would be great calamities . . . Death would dominate the land.[10] The Emperor said cautiously that his own soothsayers had predicted otherwise. Nezahualpilli suggested that the two of them should hold a series of ritual ball games to decide whose advisers were right. The Mexica were great gamblers. So the Emperor agreed. Nezahualpilli bet his kingdom against three turkeys that his men had predicted well. The Emperor accepted the bet. He won the first two games. But he lost the next three.[11]

Nezahualpilli also apparently predicted that the Triple Alliance (between the three main cities around the lake) would never win another war of flowers; and that the Mexican empire would be destroyed.[12] He insisted on his deathbed in 1514 that he had been told by fortune-tellers that the Mexica would soon be ruled by strangers.

People in old Mexico were often influenced by far less dramatic events than these. Unaccustomed noises or sights of any kind, from the cry of an owl to the sight of a rabbit running into a house, suggested calamities. The call of a white-headed hawk (identified with the sun) might have several interpretations. Anyone whose path was crossed by a weasel might expect a setback.[13] The Mexica spent a great deal of time speculating about the significance of such things. This should not be a matter of surprise.

It has been represented that the "portents" never occurred and that the interpretations in consequence were invented later. Machiavelli, in his *Discorsi*, in these very years (1515–18), remarked: "Both modern and ancient examples go to show that great events never happen in any town or in any country without their having been announced by portents, revelations, prodigious events or other celestial signs."[14] He was writing in Italy: by most standards the most civilised country in Europe. Yet even there, popular imagination, we are told, saw warring armies in any unusual formation of clouds. 1494, the "unlucky year which forever opened the gates of Italy to the foreigner", was said to have been ushered in by many prophecies of misfortune.[15] In all Italian families horoscopes of children were drawn up as a matter of course. Not unlike the Mexica, even the sophisticated Florentines looked on Saturday as a fateful day when everything good or bad had to happen. Leo X, the brilliant humanist who was Pope in 1518, thought the flourishing condition of astrology to be a credit to his pontificate. King Ferdinand the Catholic of Aragon, the model of a modern monarch, listened to prophecies which, accurately as it happened, predicted his acquisition of Naples. In Europe, also, monsters were considered to indicate divine anger: Montaigne, in his essay "On a monster child", wrote (later in the century) that he had seen a child aged fourteen months who was attached below the breast to another child with no head. He said, "This double body and these sundry limbs all depending on a single head could well provide us with a favourable omen that our king will maintain the sundry parties and factions of our state in unity . . ."[16]

In a spirit of scepticism engendered by such correspondences between the old world and the new, some have argued that these portents in Mexico were artfully devised in the 1530s or 1540s on the ground that simple people find catastrophes easier to bear if it can be argued that they have been foretold.[17]

Yet most of these phenomena in Mexico were unsensational. Assuming that one or other of them occurred at all, they might have been forgotten had the Mexican empire subsequently prospered. The unusual glare could have been caused by zodiacal light, or even an aurora borealis. Storms on the Lake of Mexico which caused water to foam were not infrequent. Fires on thatched roofs on the top of pyramids should have been expected since braziers were nearby. The two-headed beings could have been Siamese twins. If they existed, they might easily have been secretly murdered. Both they and the bird with the mirror sound as if they were figments in the imagination of someone who had eaten sacred mushrooms.[18]

Finally, comets and eclipses were in fact seen in these years: there was a comet in 1489; a total eclipse in 1496; and another comet in 1506.[19] This last was sighted in China in July of that year, subsequently in Japan, and then in Spain, where it was thought to have foreshadowed the death of King Philip the Beautiful. In China the comet seemed to be like a pellet, with a "darkish white" colour and faint rays. It had no tail to begin with. The Japanese also recorded it, and described it as "a large sphere with a bluish tint". It started in the constellation of Orion but, because of the time of the year and the layout of the heavens at that time, the comet would have been close to the sun and so only just visible before sunrise and after dusk. As it drifted westwards, it would have become visible longer into the night. It would have been a spectacular sight by mid-August. It would have appeared every day further and further to the north, would have vanished in the west, and would have developed a long nebulous tail pointing to the south-east.[20] The Mexica would have been certain to have drawn some sensational conclusion from this.

The most likely interpretation of the story of these portents is that some, if not all, of them occurred; that given that rumours of atrocious happenings in Panama and the Caribbean had reached Tenochtitlan, gloomy conclusions were instantly drawn; that though they may have been temporarily forgotten, both the portents and the interpretations were recalled in 1519; and that clever Mexicans and friars, writing later of the Mexican empire, were happy to link those memories with what they knew occurred in Europe, adding picturesque details drawn from European classics. (The Spanish friars who told the story of the portents, such as Fr. Olmos, Fr. Motolinía, and Fr. Sahagún, were all born about 1500, and would have remembered the comet of 1506 from their Castilian childhoods.) Stories of men riding on "deer" may have reached Mexico from Darien.

The Emperor of the Mexica in these years seemed well equipped to deal with all these difficulties. Montezuma II (his name meant "he who angers himself") was the fifth ruler since his people had broken away from subjection to the Tepanecs; and the eighth since the royal house had been established at the end of the fourteenth century. He was a son of the rash Emperor Axayácatl, who had lost the war against the copper-armed Tarascans. He came to the throne, or the sacred "mat", in 1502, and in 1518 was about fifty years old. He was referred to as Montezuma "Xocoyotzin", "the Younger", in order to differentiate him from his namesake, his great-grandfather, the conqueror who had ruled in the mid-fifteenth century.[21]

Montezuma II is one of the few Mexica of those days whom modern readers can see in the round. Most of the others remain two-dimensional, dominated by their offices, their unpronounceable titles often confounded with their difficult names, and hidden in the anonymity of the collective splendour. Montezuma was, like most Mexica, dark and of average height. His hair was wavy, his nose aquiline. He was well proportioned, spare, with a large head and somewhat flat nostrils. He seemed astute, wise and prudent; and in speech sharp, firm and eloquent. "When he spoke, he drew the sympathy of others by his subtle phrases and seduced them by his profound reasoning . . ." His subjects thought him the most eloquent of their rulers.[22]

Again like most Mexica, he was courteous: "as polite as a Mexican Indian" was a well-known phrase in Spain in the seventeenth century. That courtesy was necessary. Government depended on personal communication; and Montezuma spent most days in consultation. The leaders of the community and their servants would cram the palace, even spill out into the street. When they achieved their audience with the Emperor, they would speak in a quiet voice, without raising their eyes to his. That was an innovation. But, as with many new traditions, it was scrupulously maintained. When Montezuma answered, it was in a voice so low that he did not seem to be moving his lips. When he went into the city, to the temple or to visit one of his secondary palaces, he would be greeted with an extravagant respect: "None of his predecessors attained a fourth part of his majesty," commented the author of the Codex Mendoza. Most people, when they went to see him, would approach him with bare feet. Fr. Durán asked an old Indian in the 1560s what he looked like. The Indian replied that, though he had lived in proximity to the ruler, he did not know, since he had never dared to look.[23]

Montezuma was a successful general before he came to the throne. As earlier mentioned, he had also been for a time chief priest. Though he could laugh, even giggle helplessly, and appear kind, he had a name for being inflexible.[24] That seemed an advantage. He was said to have had seven corrupt or procrastinatory judges jailed in cages and then killed.[25] Montezuma believed that the way to rule was to inspire people "with fear, not affection".[26] His predecessor Ahuítzotl had often acted without consultation of the Supreme Council. Montezuma did the same. He carried out his official duties with solemnity. He seems to have been a stickler for accuracy: thus the festival of the month Tlacaxipehualitzli was supposed to take place when the sun, at the equinox, could be seen in the middle of the Great Temple. Because that edifice was a little out of alignment Montezuma wanted to pull it down and rebuild it.[27]

He wanted to tighten all rules. For example, he had not only insisted that all official appointments be performed by nobles; he had the old office-holders killed for fear that they might pass on news of what had happened in the past. But it is fair to say that different people held different views: thus Fr. Durán, who talked to survivors of Montezuma's court, said that he was "modest, virtuous and generous, and with all the virtues which one could look for in a good prince".[28]

The Emperor maintained a guard composed of provincial lords, as well as many armed men ready for any emergency. At meals, he would be waited upon by a large number of boys.[29] Montezuma would choose a few mouthfuls from the innumerable dishes, while handing on titbits to those wise men who sat with him. He might then be amused by jugglers, jesters, dwarfs and hunchbacks, or listen to music: there were instruments enough to have filled his palace continually with music had he so wished, as had occurred in the days of Ahuítzotl.[30] Montezuma had a large family: a legitimate wife (Teotalco, a princess from Tula), and several other important wives (one being the daughter of the King of Tacuba; one the daughter of the ruler of the small city of Ecatepec; and one his cousin, the daughter of the cihuacoatl Tlilpotonqui, Tlacaelel's heir).[31] But he also had numerous concubines. Estimates of his children vary from nineteen to a hundred and fifty, though from his chief wife he was said to have had only three daughters.[32] He changed four times every day into separate tunics, none of which he ever wore a second time. His retreats every two hundred and sixty days to the Quauhxicalco, "the house of the ceremonial blood dish", afforded him good opportunities for sober reflection.[33]

Montezuma's reign, though marked by increased inequalities, had had several successes. The conquest of Soconusco, for example, had enabled the realm to be provided for the first time amply with green quetzal feathers: "The craft of feather design," reported the Florentine Codex, came to fruition in his time.[34] He had defeated as many cities as his predecessor, the "conqueror" Ahuítzotl. Many of them were in the fertile coastal region near what is now Veracruz. The rebuilding of

Tenochtitlan after the flood caused by Ahuítzotl's mistakes had been a triumph. Montezuma was responsible for many of the famous works of art (particuarly in stone) which are looked upon as characteristic of the Mexican civilisation.[35] He had taken the initiative in establishing a temple of other cities' gods.[36] It was probably under Montezuma that rules were introduced making it obligatory to cultivate land.

Having been high priest, Montezuma knew the sacred calendars well. Failing to secure good advice from his counsellors and the priests as to what to do about the mysterious news from the sea, and the "portents", he sent for magicians. Their responsibilities were, it will be remembered, different from those of the priests. They operated under the authority of the mischievous god Tezcatlipoca, and used all kinds of hallucinatory plants to assist them in their divinations. Montezuma was said by his grandson, the historian Tezozomoc, to have asked: "Have you seen strange omens in the sky? Or on the earth? In the caves under the earth or in the deep lakes?" Had they observed strange weeping women? Or unusual men? Visions or phantasms?[37]

The magicians said firmly that they had seen nothing of this sort. They could give no advice. Montezuma told his majordomo: "Take away these scoundrels, and lock them up in Cuaulhco prison. They shall talk to me tomorrow." It was done. Next day, Montezuma called for the major-domo and ordered him to ask the magicians again what they believed was going to happen: "Whether we are going to be struck down by sickness, by hunger, by locusts, by storms on the lake, or by droughts, and whether it will rain torrentially. Let them tell me if we are menaced by war, or if we must expect sudden deaths, or deaths caused by wild beasts. They must not hide the facts from me. They must also tell me if they have heard the voice of the earth goddess Cihuacoatl for, if something unpleasant is going to happen, she is the first to predict it." (Cihuacoatl, "woman snake", who so curiously lent her name to the deputy emperor, was the leading deity of the nearby city of Culhuacan.)

The magicians were not helpful. One told the majordomo when he went to the prison: "What can we say? The future is already determined. What has to come, will come." No one could have quarrelled with that conventional statement. They are also supposed to have added: "A great mystery will come to pass. It will come quickly. If this is what our lord Montezuma wants to know from us, so be it. Since it is bound to happen, he can only await it."[38] (The *Historia de los Mexicanos por sus pinturas*, a document of the 1530s, probably written by a Franciscan, stated that Montezuma was told by these wizards that the omens indicated that he had to die.)[39] Yet another magician, presumably informed about Spanish activities in Central America, said that he foresaw men "with beards coming to this land".[40]

The majordomo returned to Montezuma. When he heard of the gloomy predictions, he was alarmed. These men seemed to be agreeing with the predictions of the late King Nezahualpilli. He is said to have asked the majordomo: "Ask whence the danger will come, whatever it is, from the sky or the land, from what direction, what place and when." The question may have seemed superfluous, for the news of the bad bearded men came from the south and the west.

The majordomo went back to the Cuaulhco prison. When he unlocked the doors, nobody was there. He returned to Montezuma and said: "My lord, command that I be cut to pieces or whatever else you wish, for you should know that, when I reached the prison, there was no one there. Yet I had special guards at the prison, trustworthy men, whom I have known for years. None of them heard the magicians escape. I believe that they flew away, for they know how to make themselves invisible. They do that every night and can fly to the ends of the earth".

Faced with such a mass escape, Montezuma embarked on a prescription: he ordered the elders in the places where the magicians lived to seize those men's families, kill them, and destroy their homes. This was apparently done. But the magicians did not reappear.[41]

Montezuma put similar questions to some randomly chosen ordinary citizens: he received similar disturbing answers. Some people said that they had dreamed of waves sweeping into Montezuma's palace, of the Great Temple in flames, of lords fleeing to the hills. Perhaps they were recalling stories about the end of the Tepanec capital of Azcapotzalco about ninety years before. Perhaps too they were subject to hallucinogenic delusions. Montezuma imprisoned these unwisely candid dreamers. It was said that he had them starved to death.[42]

No doubt Montezuma had recourse to conventional divines: including those consulted about the meaning of certain birthdays. We picture them gazing nervously into mirrors of obsidian or jars of water, tying and untying knots, perhaps casting kernels of maize on to the pages of holy books. They too showed themselves inadequate.

Montezuma considered building a new, colossal shrine to Huitzilopochtli. Perhaps that would ward off all evils. He consulted the lord of Cuitláhuac, a small city on the lake whose ruler was said to descend directly from the god Mixcoatl. That potentate bravely replied that that plan would exhaust the people and offend the gods. Montezuma is said also to have had him executed, with all his supposedly holy family. He abandoned the idea of a new temple, though, and turned his attention to trying to bring down a colossal new sacrificial stone from the mountains above Chalco.[43]

Montezuma's reaction to the suspicious activities on the coast, and the apparent predictions of the end of his empire, was thus to embark on a frenzied witch-hunt, the reports of which, inadequate though they may be, indicate the freedom enjoyed by the Emperor of the Mexica to carry out all kinds of arbitrary brutalities, even outside the city of Tenochtitlan, if he thought them even momentarily in the public good.

In the spring of 1518 a common labourer came to the imperial court. He was unprepossessing, for he was not only dressed roughly, but he was said to have had no ears, no thumbs, and no big toes. He came from Mictlanquauhtla, near the eastern sea: an unpromising beginning, for the word indicated "wood of hell".[44] This individual brought the news that he had seen "a range of mountains, or some big hills, floating in the sea". Montezuma told his majordomo to put the man in prison and keep him under watch. He ordered one of his four chief advisers, the "Keeper of the House of Darkness", the *tlillancalqui*, perhaps his nephew, to go to ask the Mexican steward near the sea if there were something strange on the water; and, if there were, to find out what it was.[45]

The *tlillancalqui* and a servant, Cuitlalpitoc (probably a slave), set off for the coast. They were carried in hammocks by experienced bearers. They went first to Cuetlaxtlan, the only place near the coast which had a Mexican steward. It had a small Mexican colony, deriving from emigration during the famine at Tenochtitlan of the 1450s. The steward, Pinotl, told the emissaries to rest. Some of his people would go and see what there was to see.

The people concerned came back to say that the news was true: two towers, or little hills, were to be seen on the sea, moving backwards and forwards. The agents of Montezuma insisted on going to look for themselves. In order not to expose themselves, they climbed a tree near the shore. They saw that the deformed peasant had told the truth. There certainly were mountains on the waves. After a while, they saw a number of men coming towards land in a small boat, to fish. They had hooks and a net: methods of fishing familiar to the Mexicans. But they heard unfamiliar talk and laughter. The *tlillancalqui* and Cuitlalpitoc later saw the boat returning to one of the objects in the sea. They themselves climbed down from the tree, returned to Cuetlaxtlan, and made their way quickly to Tenochtitlan.

When they reached that capital, they went directly to Montezuma's palace. After the usual greetings, the *tlillancalqui* is reported to have said: "It is true that there have come to the shore I do not know what kind of people. Some of them were fishing there with rods; others, with a net. Until very late they were fishing. Then they got into a canoe and went back to the thing on the sea with the two towers, and went into it. There must have been about fifteen of them, some with red bags, some blue, others grey and green . . . and some of them had red handkerchiefs on their heads and others, scarlet hats, some of which were very big and round, in the style of little frying pans, against the sun. The skins of these people are white, much more so than our skins are. All of them have long beards and hair down to their ears."[46]

Montezuma was dismayed. Mexican Indians were usually beardless and did not need to shave. Except for the priests, they as a rule cut their hair short. A white skin was also rare. Its possession usually led to the person concerned being sent to the Emperor's human zoo for oddities.

Montezuma gave orders for craftsmen to set about making a series of fine gold and feathered objects, bracelets for both feet and wrists, fans, and chains. These were to be presents for the foreigners. Among them were two large wooden discs covered with gold and silver, representing the calendars used in the Valley of Mexico. But no one was to know of these commissions. Montezuma also ordered the peasant from "the wood of hell", who had brought news of these events, to be freed from prison. No one seems to have been surprised to find that, like the magicians of a year previously, he had escaped. Perhaps he had been quietly murdered to stop him from talking.

Montezuma gave orders for a watch to be kept on all parts of the coast.[47] He asked the *tlillancalqui* and Cuitlalpitoc to return there. They were to take presents for the leader of the visitors. The two discs were not finished, and so were not sent. But an ample treasure was soon ready. The Mexicans set off for Cuetlaxtlan. Some food was prepared there and taken to the coast. The emissaries realised this time that the mysterious objects in the water were boats: of a size which they had not previously imagined was possible. They had themselves rowed out to them, and kissed the prows of the ships in respect: They carried out "the earth-eating ceremony at the prows of the boats."[48]

The people on one of the ships called out to them through an interpreter, whose skill must have left much to be desired: "Who are you? Where is your home? Where have you come from?"

They replied: "We have come from Mexico."

"If in truth you are Mexican, what is the name of your ruler?"

"Our lord's name is Montezuma."

The Mexicans then offered the strangers their presents: cloaks – one with a design of the sun on it, with a blue knot; one with the design of a jar, with an eagle on it; one "with the wind-jewel . . . one with the turkey blood design"[11]; one with a mirror; and one with a serpent mask.[49] The strangers gave the Mexicans some less impressive objects, including some ships' biscuits, some bread (presumably made from cassava) and necklaces of green and yellow beads. The Mexicans expressed pleasure which the strangers assumed was naivety rather than, as was no doubt the case, politeness. Mexicans had their own beads: jade ones were an item of tribute paid by Soconusco to the Mexica, and were often put in the mouth of dead bodies to pay for the soul's journey in the underworld. But any green necklaces were welcome in a society for whom that colour, either in birds' feathers or in stone, was especially pleasing.[50]

The *tlillancalqui* proposed eating. The strangers warily suggested that they would like the Mexicans to begin. They did so. There was joking over the turkey stew, the maize cakes, and the chocolate. The Mexicans drank some wine. Like most Indians when they drank it for the first time, they liked it.[51] The strangers then said: "Go in peace. We go first to Castile, but we shall not delay in returning to Mexico."

The Mexicans returned to land, and swiftly made their way to Tenochtitlan. Their report to Montezuma ran along the following lines: "O our lord . . ., mayest thou destroy us! for behold this we have seen, behold, this we have done, there, where thy grandfathers stand guard for thee before the ocean. We went to see our lords . . . in the midst of the water. All thy mantles we went to give to them. And behold they gave us of their noble goods." And they told him what the strangers had said.[52]

Montezuma replied: "You have suffered fatigue. You are exhausted, rest." These words were formal ones of greeting. He added, "No one shall speak anything of this, no one will spread the news, you will keep it to yourself."

The Emperor then examined the presents. He liked the beads. He ate one of the biscuits. He said that it tasted of tufa rock. He weighed a piece of rock and another of the biscuits against each other, and naturally found that the rock weighed less. Montezuma's dwarfs ate some of the bread given by the visitors. They found it sweet. The remains of the biscuits and the rest of the bread were taken solemnly to the temple of Quetzalcoatl in Tula.[53] The beads were buried at the foot of the shrine to Huitzilopochtli in Tenochtitlan. Montezuma talked with his senior counsellors: probably all the thirty members of the Great Council. They agreed that the only thing to do was to keep a close watch on the coast.[54]

The mysterious visitors, the givers of the beads and the hard biscuits, left the coast. The few Mexicans who had known of the strangers' arrival were threatened with death should they speak of it. The authorities in Tenochtitlan sought to discover what had been said in the past about such mysterious arrivals. For they found it hard to imagine anything without a precedent.[55] But here their own past policies hampered them. Tlacaelel and Itzcoatl had burned the Mexica's own histories at the beginning of the people's imperial adventure. Texcoco still had much historical material. But the relations between the two cities were not what they had been. Montezuma ordered his court artist to paint a picture depicting what had been seen at the coast. He showed it to his archivists. None of them had seen anything like these ships, with their great sails, their rigging, and their extraordinarily high poops. Some magicians of Malinalco are then said to have prophesied the arrival of one-eyed men, others foresaw the coming of men with the bodies, below the waist, of snakes or fish. One old man, a certain Quilaztli, who lived in Xochimilco, had a library of old, pre-imperial codices. He was said to have seen similarities between one of these documents and what had been seen on the coast. The men on the sea, he thought, were not strangers. They were people long dead, returning to their own land. They might have left for the moment but they would, he thought, be likely to be back in two years. Quilaztli was transferred to live in Tenochtitlan. But Montezuma was ever more gloomy.[56]

A year passed. Montezuma became once more immersed in his imperial duties. His favourite concubine brought him a new son, the court hunchbacks danced, the dwarfs sang, the jesters made their master laugh. Jugglers lay on their backs and, with their feet upwards, spun balls round in the air. The regular programme of sacrifices continued. There was the dancing and the music of flutes and drums; the dressing-up and the painting of faces; the singing, the collecting of flowers and, no doubt, the uncontrollable laughter caused by the eating of sacred mushrooms. The priests kept the fires burning in the great temples. Another year's tribute came in on the backs of patient bearers. Merchants brought back beautiful long green feathers of the quetzal bird and rumours of war from the Pacific. Workers in precious stones rejoiced that Montezuma had conquered the territories where there was good sand with which to polish their raw material. Ordinary men and women, *macehualtin* and *mayeques*, pursued their regular pattern of work, celebrated pregnancy and childbirth, educated children, sought to instil moral codes, died, and descended to Mictlan, that place of gloomy emptiness to which everyone who had lived an unadventurous life expected to go. Poems were composed at Texcoco by courtiers mourning the brevity of life and the decay of empires. The Emperor made fine speeches about his forebears. He almost forgot the strangers of 1518.

But the strangers did not forget Mexico. As they had promised, the next year, "Year of One Reed", 1519, they came again.

II
Spain of the Golden Age

5
The golden years begin

"O King Don Fernando and Doña Isabel
With you the golden years begin . . ."[1]
Song of c.1495 by Juan del Encina

THE MEXICA WERE right to be apprehensive at the sight of the foreigners. For they were, of course, Spanish conquistadors. Had Montezuma known precisely how these men had conducted themselves in the Caribbean during the previous quarter-century, he would have been aghast. Yet though the Mexican rulers were aware of the importance of espionage in war, they had no knowledge of the archipelago which lay only seventy miles off their eastern seaboard. They had no boats beyond canoes which were incapable of making long voyages by sea; or indeed, any voyages, apart from short ones along the coast or on lakes and rivers. The Mayas and some other peoples on the coast of what is now known as the Gulf of Mexico may have had primitive sails. But they did not seek to leave the coast.[2]

"We are capable of conquering the entire world," the sinister fifteenth-century *cihuacoatl*, Tlacaelel, is supposed to have told Nezahualcoyotl, King of Texcoco.[3] A hint of the same rhetorical ambition was conveyed to those rulers who were obliged to visit Tenochtitlan on the occasion of the inauguration of the great new temple to Huitzilopochtli: "The enemies, guests and strangers were bewildered, amazed. They saw that the Mexica were masters of the entire world, and they realised that the Mexica had conquered all the nations and that all were their vassals." "Are not the Mexicans masters of the world?" Montezuma is said to have once demanded.[4] But this "world" ended at the Gulf of Mexico. It scarcely extended to Yucatan. The Mexica traded in the Gulf of Honduras, even as far south as what is now Costa Rica and Panama. They had some cultural influence there.[5] They may have learned the art of casting metal from Colombia, and obtained emeralds from there.[6] But no Mexican seems to have coveted those territories as colonies. For the ancient Mexicans the earth was a flat disc surrounded by water, or perhaps a giant crocodile swimming in a sea covered by water lilies. Of that earth, Tenochtitlan, an island city surrounded by a lake, was a microcosm.[7] To investigate too far was unnecessary.

One reason for this lack of interest is explained by the north–south current between Cape Catoche, as it is now known, in Yucatan, and Cape Corrientes, in Cuba. The one hundred and twenty-five miles between the two were as a rule crossed only by accident, and in bad conditions.

Such contacts as there were had modest consequences: as indicated earlier, a few Jamaican castaways were a little later found in Yucatan; some beeswax, known to have come from Yucatan, was discovered in Cuba in the early sixteenth century; and some Maya pottery also reached Cuba.[8] There were some other infrequent crossings, though the only authenticated one seems to have been in 1514 in circumstances still not fully explained. The argument that the people of Hispaniola took their drum from the mainland does not seem proven.[9] The Caribbean had derived its population from the north of Venezuela via the Lesser Antilles, not across this strait.[10]

The native population of the Caribbean also seemed ignorant of the Mexica. Their lack of a high culture was, of course, not the determining element in the Mexicans' lack of interest in them. For the Mexica lived in a cocoon of self-preoccupation. Montezuma II is said to have been curious about nature. But like everyone else in his realm, he was unconcerned about human beings.

The Castilian activity in the western Caribbean, which had been reported in Tenochtitlan, is easily identified. In 1502 Columbus himself, on his fourth voyage, had touched at several places in Central America. His first stop, and furthest point north, was one of the Bay Islands in the Gulf of Honduras, three hundred miles south, as the crow flies, from Yucatan. Here, Columbus came on a large canoe manned by men who were probably Jicaque or Paya Indians. They seem to have been on their way from trading in Yucatan. The canoe carried cacao beans (which the Admiral thought were almonds), obsidian, copper bells and axes from Michoacan, as well as coloured cotton goods. Columbus was presented with some long swords, with sharp stone blades, which sound as if they were Mexican. He accepted some *pulque*: the fact that the inhabitants of *tierra firme* had alcohol helped to convince the Spaniards of their superiority to the abstemious islanders. Columbus also became the first European to eat turkey. He exchanged some goods.[11] The embroidered clothes of some of the twenty-five Indians on board, and the quality of their cottons, confirmed to the Spaniards that, somewhere inland, there was a more sophisticated world than anything which they had met in the Antilles.[12] But Columbus did not sail on west with these Indians, as they invited him to; he wished to follow the wind south; and, for a few years, no further European enquiry was made in the direction in which the Indian canoe had disappeared.

Then in 1508 the two stars of Spanish maritime enterprise at the time, Vicente Yáñez Pinzón, a native of Palos, who had captained the *Pinta* on Columbus' first voyage, and Juan Díaz de Solís, from Lepe, another little port between Huelva and Seville, set out to look for a route which would take them west from the Caribbean to the Spice Islands. They made landfall at Honduras, not far from where Columbus had turned south in 1502, and then sailed north. Yáñez Pinzón and Díaz de Solís could find nothing like a strait. They probably sailed along the coast of Yucatan, they perhaps reached Tabasco, they may have reached what is now Veracruz, or even Tampico. They were certainly the first Europeans to see the coastline of what has become known as "Mexico". But they did nothing about what they had seen.[13]

Two years later, Martín Fernández de Enciso, later a famous geographer, with Francisco Pizarro, the future conqueror of Peru, and Vasco Núñez de Balboa, the "first *caudillo* of the New World", founded a European settlement on the mainland of the Americas, at Darien, in what is now Panama. In 1511, several men from a convoy returning from there to the main Spanish entrepôt at Santo Domingo were shipwrecked off Yucatan. Two of these were still alive in 1518. They were in Maya hands. These men were Gerónimo de Aguilar, a priest from Écija, between Seville and Córdoba, and Gonzalo Guerrero, from Niebla, near Palos. Once these men learned Maya, as they did, they presumably became a good source in Yucatan and eventually perhaps, through translation, in the Valley of Mexico, about the Spanish activities. Next, a Spanish expedition, on its way back from the discovery of Florida, led by Juan Ponce de León, apparently landed in 1513 in Yucatan.[14] Distressed by his failure to find the Fountain of Youth, he thought that he had reached Cuba. This stop on his journey did not, however, register in the minds of his compatriots, though his pilot, Antonio de Alaminos, another native of Palos, had travelled with Columbus on his fourth voyage, and later recalled what had happened. Several Maya texts recorded this landing.[15]

In 1515 there was another well-documented communication between Castile and Mexico. A judge named Corrales in the Spanish colony of Darien reported that he had met a "fugitive from the interior provinces of the West". This man, seeing the judge reading, started with surprise. He asked, through interpreters, "You also have books? You also understand the signs by which you talk to the absent?" He examined the book which Corrales was studying and saw that the letters were not the same as those signs to which he was used. He then said that, in his country, "the towns were walled, the citizens normally wore clothing, and they were governed by laws".[16] He was presumably talking of Yucatan, but it could have been Mexico.

✣

The Spaniards involved in all these voyages were mostly Andalusians, Castilians, or Extremeños (from Extremadura).[17] Most of the leaders were members of the minor nobility, hidalgos, who, though they probably had little money, were certainly "not reared from behind the plough".[18] They were often younger sons (or younger sons of younger sons) forced, by the size of their parents' families, to find a career in order to live, and had been obliged to choose between church, the sea or the court (*iglesia, mar o casa real*). They were men driven by several motives: to become rich; to become famous – by which they meant they wished to distinguish themselves in the service of the King or of God (and to become recognised for it); and to extend the dominions of Christianity.

Among the rest of the volunteers, an increase in sheep rearing and cattle farming in Castile, and especially Extremadura, and the consequent decline in the acres devoted to arable agriculture, had stimulated emigration. An economic crisis in Spain between 1502 and 1508 was another encouragement.[19] "The poverty is great," wrote an Italian, the historian and diplomat, Guicciardini, in 1512. "Hunger and disease are never wanting," a conquistador from León, Diego de Ordaz, would write in 1529.[20] A simple desire for freedom, not only from the poverty of Castilian country life, but from obligations to lords, bishops, and the still powerful military orders, was also a motive. The historian, missionary, propagandist and bishop, Bartolomé de Las Casas, described meeting in 1518 an old man aged seventy who wanted to emigrate. He asked: "You, father, why do you want to go to the Indies, being so old and tired?" The answer was, "By my faith, sir, to die and leave my sons in a free and happy land."[21]

Andalusians, and to a lesser extent Extremeños, had, of course, been living on the frontiers of Christian Spain with Islam for centuries. Nearly all the Christian families of Seville had been immigrants after the liberation in the 1240s: and so Andalusia had afforded a demographic rehearsal for the colonisation of America. At the same time, Seville, the biggest city in Spain (though probably a mere quarter of the size of Tenochtitlan), was still (indeed, was every year more) a melting pot of Castilian peoples. Merchants from Burgos, the great wool-exporting city of the north, usually had representatives in Seville. So did the Genoese, the entrepreneurs of the age. Seville was the home of the far from negligible late medieval Spanish navy, and had been the city most enterprising in trading with Africa, for gold as for slaves. In the neighbourhood of Seville, along the coast towards Portugal, there were several small, newly thriving ports, such as Lepe, Palos, Moguer and Huelva, whose citizens had become accustomed to the sea. This part of the realm was full of men who contemplated journeys to the New World with zest; and would be happy to sell a passage to it for about eleven or twelve gold ducats (for, of course, the journey was not free) to anyone able to pay.[22]

The philosophy of the discoveries, the emigration, and the colonisation was Christianity. Ferdinand and Isabel, King and Queen of a new, if precariously united, Spain, had conquered Granada in 1492. They had been hailed by the Pope not only as the "Catholic kings" but as "athletes of Christ". The primate of Spain, Cardinal Ximenez de Cisneros, likened himself, not wholly inappropriately, given his fighting spirit, to a new Joshua.

The discoverers of America, from Columbus onwards, presented their findings as new triumphs on behalf of God. In this, the Castilians were supported, as were all who, from the mid-fifteenth century onwards, had left Europe with similar ambitions, by papal authority. For the bull *Dum Diversas* of 1452 had authorised the King of Portugal "to subdue Saracens, pagans, and other unbelievers inimical to Christ, to reduce their persons to perpetual slavery and then to transfer for ever their territory to the Portuguese Crown". When discoveries began to be made, in the 1490s, under the auspices of the Spanish Crown, the Pope was Alexander VI, who, as Rodrigo Borgia, came of a family of lesser nobility from Játiva, near Valencia. He had reached the throne of St Peter in August 1492, the same month that Columbus embarked on his first voyage. He was under an obligation to the Catholic kings for their help in securing his election. Hence he gladly issued new bulls which were helpful to Castile. The most famous one, of 4 May 1493, gave the Catholic kings dominion over all the lands which they discovered three hundred miles to the west of the Azores, on condition that they converted to Christianity the peoples whom they found.

The militant Christianity which characterised Spain in the late fifteenth century had several springs: there was a millenarian expectation that the monarchy could revive the Christian presence in Jerusalem; there was a revived threat from Islam which, for the first time, had in those years become a maritime power in the Mediterranean (the menace of Islam had previously seemed to derive from its cavalry); and there was renewed anxiety about what was curiously perceived at the time as the growth of Judaism.

The need to meet the threat of Islam, and the requirement to prevent the spread of Judaism, was the culmination of the Spanish Crown's desire to create a Catholic monarchy which would act as the sword of Christendom. The imperial mission would be a cement to keep the newly unified kingdom together.

Both the anti-Islamic and anti-Judaic drives came to a head in 1492 with, first, the surrender of the city of Granada in January, bringing the *Reconquista* to a triumphant conclusion; and, secondly, the decree in March expelling Jews from Spain unless they converted to Christianity.

These events were surprising. Islam and Christianity had for generations lived side by side in Spain. Christian heroes, including the greatest one, El Cid Campeador, had fought for Moorish kings against Christians. Even his title, "El Cid", was a corruption of an Arab expression. In Christian Spain the dominant architecture was still the Moorish (or *mudéjar*) style of Islamic Spain.

The Jewish minority of Castile was at the same time intellectually alive, providing in some cities not only the tax gatherers but the chief taxpayers too. Jews were clerks and craftsmen, as well as poets. When converted to Christianity, they made admirable theologians, mystics, friars, even bishops. But the consensus had broken down. Ever since the late fourteenth century, Spain had been marked by suspicion. People feared that the church had been penetrated by secret Jews; had not the prior of the Jeronymite monastery of La Sisla near Toledo even celebrated the feast of the Tabernacle?[23] The Spanish Inquisition was set up in 1481. City after city in Castile passed ordinances against Jews. *Autos de fe* may have caused the burning of eight hundred converted Jews in the 1480s in Seville alone, and the imprisonment of several thousand others. The policy of the Crown was not to punish Jews. It was to cut off "the new Christians", the *conversos*, from the temptation of remaining in touch with Judaism. But an unexpectedly large number of Jews refused to convert to Christianity. The Jews were, to begin with, astonished to think that they could be attacked: "Are we not the principal men in the city?" asked a leader of the community in Seville.[24]

If the homeland was thus in difficulty, all the more reason for Castilians abroad to act as the sword of Christianity itself.

Yet if Christianity was the ideology behind the expansion of Spain, most of the leaders were also driven by earthly motives. They wished to rise in status, to become noblemen, to attract the attention of the monarch and the court.

In these ideas their imaginations were excited by both old songs and new publications. Thus most leading conquistadors would have learned in their childhood frontier ballads, sung for Andalusian knights in praise of military values. Sometimes these would tell of the Moor Gazul, or of half-forgotten local heroes of the territory between Seville and Ronda, endlessly skirmished over in the fourteenth or fifteenth century. Sometimes the theme would be the Cid, the mysterious victor of the late ninth century, or Pedro Carbonero, a more recent Christian knight who improvidently had led his men into Moorish territory. At other times Charlemagne, Alexander, Caesar, even Hannibal, or other classical personalities who had made the curious transition from being well-documented historical figures to ones of myth, would inspire a whole cycle of stories.[25] How sweet to cross the Rubicon! How noble to fight in two continents as Alexander had done! But usually the allusion derived from a ballad, not from a reading of Plutarch.

The men in the ships seen by Montezuma's messengers in 1518 near what is now Veracruz were those who, born between 1480 and 1500, were, too, a first generation of readers for whom printed texts could be not just an instruction; they could give entertainment, even delight.[26] Readers to begin with felt themselves transformed by the mere act of holding these "almost divine instruments".[27]

Thus there were now to be found printed versions of many ballads. From now on, too, there would also be romances which, from the publication of *Tirant lo Blanc* in 1490 to that of *Amadís de Gaula* in 1508, would recount extraordinary stories to this, the first generation of mass novel readers. *Amadís de Gaula*, the most successful printed book of the early sixteenth century in Spain, though written far earlier, accompanied conquistadors as much as did prayerbooks and books of hours. Sometimes these novels too would form the themes of ballads. These writings are now remembered because Cervantes in *Don Quixote* made fun of them. At the time they satisfied a deep need.

Further, sailors and conquistadors of the "generation of 1500" were easily made conscious, through printing, of innumerable fantastic expectations, to be found in the works of Sir John Mandeville and others, about men with two heads, Amazons, and the Fountain of Eternal Youth which would revive the fading sexual powers of elderly men, and which even rational people would expect to find in the Americas beyond the next cape.

Some of the most famous place names of the Americas derive from these romances: the river Amazon; California was an island in *Sergas de Esplandián*, a sequel to *Amadís de Gaula*: Patagonia occurs as a country in the romance entitled *Palmerín de Oliva*; while the name "Antilles", as used for the islands of the Caribbean, derives from Atlantis, the myth of which much excited sailors of the fifteenth century.

Another influence on Castilians in the early sixteenth century was more genuinely that of antiquity. One conquistador, Francisco Aguilar, who may have been among those seen by Montezuma's messengers at the coast, subsequently became an Augustinian monk. He wrote in the 1560s that, from his childhood onwards, he had been "concerned to read and study histories of Greek romance and Persian antiquity".[28] In consequence of this fashion any formal piece of writing would be decked out with quotations from Cicero and Caesar, whether or no the writer had read the authors in question; or whether, as was as likely, he had found the reference in a collection of old sayings such as that of the Marquis of Santillana, whose book of proverbs which "old women repeat by the fireside" had been immensely successful when it first came out in print in Saragossa in 1488.[29]

Then there was yet another inspiration: Spain! The surrender in

January 1492 of Granada unleashed what seems, even in the limited circumstances of the time, to have been an era of genuine patriotism. The conquest of Granada itself was described as "the most distinguished and blessed day that there had ever been in Spain". Fr. Iñigo de Mendoza, a popular satirist at the court, declared that he became aware in those years of a will to empire.[30] The humanist philologist Antonio de Nebrija, tutor of both public servants and noblemen, published in 1492 his Spanish Grammar: the first for any language other than Latin (for which he had produced a comparable work). It was written, said the author, in order to make Castilian a fit language for the historical narratives which would surely be written, so that the deeds of her great kings would be remembered for ever.

These memories invigorated the imagination of the conquistador who, riding or tramping through remote jungles, or trapped in faraway creeks, allowed a vision of the homeland to inspire him; and the homeland as one nation, not a confederation of León, Castile, Andalusia and Aragon. He would, if a leader, christen some improbable village of a few huts covered by palm roofs with the name of his *pueblo*; and would give to a bigger city, full of sceptical Indians, the name Sanlúcar, or Valladolid, or even Seville. In combat in tropical swamps he would shout some medieval battlecry such as "*¡Santiago y cierre España!*" at a time when such cries were out of date at home.

The commercial motives behind Spanish and Portuguese expansion were important. Bartolomeu Dias was looking for spices as well as "the kingdom of Prester John" when in 1497 he sought the sea route to India. In the New World, commerce, in the twenty-five years after Columbus' first journey in 1492, had come to mean primarily the pursuit of gold. If the Mexica looked back to Tollan and the Toltecs, the Castilians were drawn to that earlier golden age which marked their eleventh century: the time of El Cid, who found such stores of that precious metal when he conquered Valencia ("The gold and the silver, who can count it?" ran a line in the *Song of the Cid*).[31] Fixed tributes in gold were for years paid by Muslim rulers to Christians in return for peace. But in the fifteenth century Spanish and European demand for gold increased. All monarchs wished to copy the Florentines, and use gold for coins. Gold was demanded for chains across velvet robes, and to embellish altars and the dresses on effigies of the Virgin. Gold thread was needed for tapestries.

Nor did the romances of chivalry forget the pursuit of gold. Thus Gasquilan, King of Sweden, in *Amadís de Gaula*, had on his shield "a griffin grasping a heart in his talons, wrought in gold, and fastened to the shield with golden nails . . ."[32] Yet before the discovery of America, the gold of Europe itself mostly came from West Africa: the Upper Volta, the Upper Niger, and the Senegal rivers.

The pursuit of new sources of this metal became an obsession. For riches, in the luminous words of Huizinga, had not yet acquired "the spectral impalpability which capitalism, founded in credit, would give later: what haunt[ed] the imagination was still the tangible, yellow gold".[33] Columbus thought that a man with gold could do what he liked in the world: "He can succeed in bringing souls to paradise."[34] Before his first voyage, he had even promised the sailors of Palos that, if they would only follow him, they "would all have houses with tiles of gold".[35]

The Spain of Ferdinand and Isabel seemed to later generations to have been a golden age in a political sense. "We have discovered that the new state [which we are seeking] is nothing other than the Spanish state of the Catholic kings," wrote a Carlist politician in the 1930s.[36] The legend began at the time. The phrase "the golden years" was coined in 1495 by the playwright Juan del Encina.

In some ways, this identification of the reign of Ferdinand and Isabel with the picture of Spain at its zenith is true. Aragon (with Catalonia) and Castile were brought together for the first time. The union was a conscious work of art in true Renaissance style, by the majestic Queen Isabel and her prudent husband, Ferdinand. Their symbol, the yoke or knot of Ferdinand, and the arrows of Isabel, with the motto, "*Tanto Monta*", literally "Each as good as the other", expressed the nature of the new association (though Castile was always to be the politically dominant partner).[37] The victory over Granada had certainly been a triumph. Spain, hitherto merely a geographical expression, genuinely came into being, and not just in the minds of the conquistadors. For good or evil, Jewish and Moorish Spain ceased to exist as separate sources of loyalty. Noblemen were obliged to see the benefits as well as the responsibilities of the sovereign state: a consummation symbolised by the Crown's seizure of the masterships of the overbearing knightly orders of Santiago, Alcántara and Calatrava. The government's finances were reinvigorated. A monetary reform was carried through in 1497. The creation of the Holy Brotherhood in 1476 gave Castile the beginnings of a police. A supreme tribunal was established in Valladolid. The Crown was henceforth usually (rather than, as theretofore, sporadically) represented in large cities by a *corregidor*, or co-council member, whose appointment marked the beginning of administrative centralisation. The Council of Castile was made effective as the supreme organ of power. The national endeavour received artistic commemoration: first under Flemish, then Italian, influence. Spain was also beginning, in a hundred small ways, to receive the spirit of humanism from Italy, with the famous Mendoza family as the triggers of cultivated change. Despite King Ferdinand's authoritarian instincts, the two kingdoms over whose affairs he presided began, even if incompletely and partially, a cultural awakening. Had not

Queen Isabel herself learned Latin? Were not scholars beginning to be prized as much as warriors? Were not even Spanish noblemen seeing the point of education and entrusting their sons to the attention of Italian humanists such as Lucio Marineo and Peter Martyr?

But though the energy and the achievement were undoubted, the unity was fragile. The artistic innovations, the sculpture of a Berruguete, the Latin of a Nebrija, were bright spots on the surface of a still medieval, half-Moorish country. The kingdoms were held together only at the top and by a common foreign policy. The culture, however brilliant, was on the surface. Beneath, everything was divided. The measures against secret Jewry led to a profound intolerance which prevented the emergence of a real Spanish Renaissance. The court was especially fragmented. Friends of King Ferdinand intrigued against old supporters of his dead son-in-law, King Philip the Beautiful. Ferdinand's Aragonese civil servants were widely hated. Big cities and small had consuming family disputes, such as that in Seville between the Ponce de León and the Guzmán families, or in Trujillo between the Altamiranos and the Bejaranos. Some noblemen believed that the Infante Ferdinand, a son of Queen Juana, who had been brought up in Spain and spoke Spanish, should be King instead of his elder brother, the French-speaking Charles, with his Burgundian ways and international, imperial ambitions. Both aristocrats and bourgeoisie despised and feared King Charles' Flemish courtiers.

Political agitation was also to be seen in the cities of Castile. This was in theory an expression of the municipalities' concern about the King's foreign interests. In practice it was soon to be directed by uncontrollable, popular, even democratic movements, upon which family feuds became superimposed. Just men, such as the Dominicans, disposed to be tolerant to the Indians in the Caribbean, distrusted the Jewish *conversos*. The Dominicans dominated the Holy Office, the Spanish Inquisition. Erasmus' works swept into Spain in 1516 to conquer intellectual life in a way which increased the risk of political as well as religious combustion.

It is thus ironically fitting that even the Crown should have been divided: between, on the one hand, the tragic Juana, in 1518 in her ninth year of confinement as mad, in the black castle of Tordesillas; and, on the other, her son Charles, who acted in her stead, but seemed too young, and too influenced by too many foreign interests, to give to Spain the patriotic direction which, under Ferdinand and Isabel, it had been coming to expect. Yet conquistadors, writing home from their tropical New Sevilles and New Santiagos, would address them, the imprisoned and the free, the unbalanced mother and the inexperienced son, as co-equal monarchs of vast power.

The Castilians who were met by the *tlillancalqui* and his slave in 1518 were mostly men who had come to the Caribbean in the last few years as a second generation of colonisers. They had travelled out, as paying passengers in search of fame and fortune, in one of the two hundred or so ships which had left Spain for the Indies between 1506 and 1518.[38] Their mentors, the first generation, had, however, presided over, though they had not instigated, a major tragedy.

At first, in 1492, the Castilians who followed Columbus thought that they had discovered paradise in the West Indies. The local inhabitants, the Tainos, were skilled weavers, potters and carvers of shell, bone and stone. They sometimes inlaid their carvings with beaten gold and shells. They could not cast metal, and were militarily negligible. But their agriculture was successful. They cultivated cassava, sweet potatoes and, to a lesser extent, maize, edible tubers, beans, peppers, peanuts and cashews. They gathered fruit. They smoked tobacco for pleasure. They made pottery and, like the Mexica, played games with rubber balls. Hunting and fishing thrived. They lived in wooden houses ranged in large villages of a thousand to two thousand people, and traded by canoe with peoples in the Lesser Antilles and even in South America. Their deities, *zemis*, seemed mild, the lord of cassava and the goddess of fresh water being prominent. Peter Martyr (a well-informed courtier from Lake Maggiore who had come from Italy to Spain in the train of the Mendoza family) described glowingly the Indians whom Columbus met: "Amongst them the land belongs to everyone, just as does the sun and the water. They know of no difference between the *meum* and the *tuum*, that source of all evils. It requires so little to satisfy them that, in that vast region, there is always more land to cultivate than is needed. It is indeed a golden age, [for] neither ditches nor hedges nor walls enclose their domains; they live in gardens open to all, without laws and without judges."[39]

On his second journey, in 1493, Colombus took an expedition of nearly 1,500 to set up a colony in La Isla Española, or "Hispaniola". It included two hundred volunteers who were "gentlemen and craftsmen"; and, among the gentlemen, twenty knights who conducted themselves with undisciplinable arrogance. The goal was to build a trading factory, such as the Portuguese had created in West Africa. These conquistadors expected to remain only a few years before returning home rich. The hard work was to be done by the Tainos.

Spain's initially friendly relations with these Indians in Hispaniola soon ended. The conquistadors seduced women, enslaved men, imposed unjust punishments, and insisted on being provided with gold. The Taino chiefs protested. They were overthrown, transported or killed. Consequent Indian "rebellions" were followed by pacification. The Spaniards also fell out among themselves: Columbus and his brothers were no good at administration. In 1500 the tyranny of "the pharaoh", as Columbus had come to be known, was ended by the Crown. The

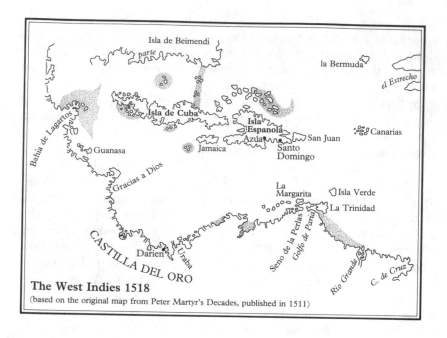

The West Indies 1518
(based on the original map from Peter Martyr's Decades, published in 1511)

Columbus brothers were replaced by officials: first Francisco de Bobadilla, majordomo to the King, a success in the war against Granada, and a brother of the Queen's best friend, Beatriz, Marchioness of Moya; then an able administrator, Fr. Nicolás de Ovando. They were effective. Bobadilla sent Columbus home in chains for mismanagement. Ovando created something like a successful colony.[40] He was high-minded and persistent, if cold and stony-hearted. He broke the native revolts. He created order among the colonists. He introduced European crops. He divided the island into seventeen municipalities, to one of which every settler had to belong. He made these town councils the heart of his administration: a decision which permanently influenced the Spanish empire towards an urban history. As *Comendador de Lares* of the Order of Alcántara, which had worked well in Extremadura, he knew the benefits of the *encomienda*, a system based on the handing-over of a specified number of the conquered population to the care of a single landowner. So following earlier attempts by Columbus to do the same in a more *ad hoc* fashion, he sought to transfer what had been done in Spain to the Indies. He thus founded the colonial version of the *encomienda*, a word which has been misunderstood as much as it has been attacked.[41]

But Ovando was harsh. One of his monuments was the massacre of Xaragua, where, in 1503, Anacaona, the native queen of the west of the island, was tricked into accepting an invitation to dine. She was hanged while her chief followers were burned alive. The pretext was that a native revolt was planned and that the Spaniards barely acted in time. The story may have been true. But that scarcely justified the reaction.[42]

Columbus being dead, his son Diego Colón, who had been brought up at the Castilian court, came out in 1509 to succeed Ovando as Governor.[43] As children in Valladolid he and his brother remembered being shouted at: "There go the sons of the Admiral of the Mosquitoes, who discovered lands of vanity and delusion, the grave of Castilian gentry."[44] Diego Colón's intentions towards the Indians were an improvement on Ovando's. But he could not impose his will on the settlers who were by then established as petty monarchs on large properties. The second Admiral – Diego Colón had inherited the title from his father – ruled ineffectually if benignly till he was succeeded in turn in 1516 by the curious experiment of a board of four Jeronymite friars.

The Indian population of Hispaniola, meantime, which may have been over 100,000 in 1492, dropped to about 30,000.[45] Traditional agriculture had been based on the cultivation of cassava and the sweet potato. Those crops declined because of the demands of the conquerors for precious metals. There was soon not enough food: indeed, not enough for the conquerors. Many Tainos died of hunger. The execution, or flight, of traditional rulers caused the survivors to abandon hope. Many of those who died did so by being worked to death. The collapse of the Taino population was completed by the association of many Taino women with the Spaniards. Assimilation thus played a part, perhaps a more important part than is usually realised, in the eclipse of the native culture.[46] All the same, there certainly was a demographic catastrophe.

The Spaniards did not limit themselves to Hispaniola. That island became the base for other expeditions. These resulted in the capture of Puerto Rico and Jamaica, in 1508 and 1509 respectively. The conquerors were Juan Ponce de León and Juan de Esquivel, the first a bastard son of the best-known family in Seville, the second from a less famous family of the same city. Cuba was circumnavigated in 1509–10 by Sebastián de Ocampo.[47] It was then invaded by Diego Velázquez, from Cuéllar, near Valladolid, in 1511. The leaders of these expeditions were all survivors of that famous company of "gentlemen" who had travelled out to the Indies on Columbus' second voyage.

Several temporary colonies were established too on the mainland, in what had become known as Little Venice, Venezuela (where the regime of the German Fuggers soon demonstrated that northern Europeans were no better at managing hostile Indians than Castilians were). Florida was found, but not colonised, also by Ponce de León, on Easter Sunday (*Pascua Florida*) 1513. A settlement was made, as has been indicated, on the mainland of Central America. This territory was hopefully called Castilla del Oro: it was supposed from some trifling discoveries there that gold would be forthcoming in quantity. Far to the south, meantime, that same Juan Díaz de Solís from Lepe who had voyaged along the coast of Mexico in 1508 discovered the river Plate in 1515.

Most of these discoveries had their black moments: where Hispaniola had Xaragua, the occupation of Cuba had its massacre at Caonao. A general rising of natives in Puerto Rico occurred in 1511 as a result of the harshness of Cristóbal de Sotomayor, a lieutenant to Ponce de León. It failed, though Sotomayor and his son were killed. Meantime everywhere in the Caribbean, the Indian population declined almost to nothing in the course of two generations.

First, as in Hispaniola, traditional agriculture was destroyed: the first Governor of Cuba, Diego Velázquez, told the King in 1514 that the handful of pigs which he had brought to that island four years earlier had already turned into 30,000.[48] Ferdinand, the wealth of whose kingdom depended as much on its five million sheep as its four million inhabitants, presumably approved. In fact both Hispaniola and Cuba went through a more radical version of a depopulation which had been happening in Castile: men gave way to animals. Wild cattle, wild horses and even wild dogs did untold damage.

Then there was the search for the precious mineral which everyone coveted. "Let us be strictly truthful," wrote Peter Martyr to the Pope, "and add that the craze for gold was the cause of their [the islands'] destruction. For these people were in the past accustomed, as soon as they had sown the fields, to play, dance, sing and chase rabbits. But now they have been set to work mercilessly . . . extracting and sifting gold."[49] In Cuba those who did not succumb because of "the cruelty and avarice of the colonist", the continuous hard labour, and the shortage of food, sometimes killed themselves, while their wives practised abortion.[50]

The Bahamas and, to a lesser extent, the Leeward Islands, as well as the little islands off the coast of South America such as Curaçao and Aruba, were ruined in a different manner. These "useless islands", in Ovando's haughty phrase, were depopulated as a result of a slave trade to compensate for the demographic losses in the larger colonies. The few indigenous people were replaced by cattle. The exceptions were the Windward Islands, where the Caribs, who were used to fighting, held out successfully; and the island of Margarita, off Venezuela, which was out of bounds to slave traders because of the discovery there of pearls.

The imported and enslaved Indians did not adapt very well. Out of 15,000 taken to Hispaniola, all but 2,000 died within ten years.[51]

Part of the trouble was that all these expeditions of discovery were private ventures. Columbus' first and second voyages had been financed by the Crown. Pedrarias de Ávila's journey of 1514 to the Castilla del Oro had also been paid for by the King, though everyone was expected to live at their own cost after they had arrived. All other expeditions were financed by their captains. The need to recover their outlay perhaps explains, though it scarcely excuses, how well-mannered Castilian gentlemen such as Juan de Ayora, a judge and veteran of the Italian wars, would threaten Indian chiefs in Darien with being burned alive or thrown to the dogs unless they quickly brought gold.[52]

The Spanish Caribbean in 1518 thus seemed a ruined place. The Indians washed for gold and died young, while the Spanish fed livestock, seduced the native women and read romances. The Crown seemed uninterested, except where profit could be obtained to finance the royal adventures in Italy. King Ferdinand, in sole control of Castile after the death of first his queen Isabel in 1504 and then his son-in-law Philip in 1506, allowed his civil servants to approve Caribbean autocracies such as even the sleepiest Castilian town would not have tolerated for a moment. Those domestic officials, always ill-paid and therefore corrupt, were avid for fortunes from those Indies which they did not choose personally to visit. They allowed the tropical autocrats a free rein, provided that they at home could enjoy bizarre titles indicating Cuban or Puerto Rican responsibilities, and provided that products were sent home which could be turned into money; especially gold.[53]

The great Bishop de Las Casas later made much propaganda out of the collapse of the population in these islands. His *Short Account of the Destruction of the Indies* was one of the most successful polemics in history.[54] But by exaggerating the original numbers of the inhabitants, as he did, he damaged his cause. The world was left after reading him with the impression that the conquistadors killed directly three million people in Hispaniola, and only modestly fewer in the other islands. The facts are less dramatic, though they are certainly tragic: the native population did disappear. Perhaps 200,000 people died in the four large Caribbean islands in a quarter of a century. They did so from overwork, fear, and loss of faith in the future, not from Spanish steel. Nor at this stage did European diseases seem to have been decisive.

There was, however, hope for change. This did not derive from the movement in several colonies to render genuine the work of the *procuradores*, or city representatives, such as would lead to a near revolution in 1520 in Castile itself; though some such local leaders did seek to assert themselves as spokesmen of their communities. No, the ray of light in the Caribbean was provided by the efforts of a few remarkable churchmen.

6

The Pope must have been drunk

Comment of the Cenú Indians when being told that Alexander VI had
divided the world between the Portuguese and the Spaniards, c.1512

COLUMBUS BELIEVED THAT he was led to his discoveries by God.
There is even a suggestion in his writings that one of his aims might
have been not to reach China, but Jerusalem, from the rear.[1] The
most ruthless of the conquistadors lived in fear of hell. Even the conquest
of Cuba was saluted as a religious triumph. Thus it is logical, if
surprising, that the Spanish Caribbean in 1518 should in theory have been
managed by four Jeronymite priors who, for two years, had been
formally the Crown's commissars of the Indies. They were not exactly
royal governors. They were supposed to gather information, and then
both recommend, and carry out, reforms. They lived in Santo Domingo,
then the headquarters of Castilian operations in the Americas.

The designation of the Jeronymites to a place of political power in the
West Indies can be traced to the coming of Dominican friars to Santo
Domingo in 1510. These were led by Fr. Pedro de Córdoba, a man
"endowed with much prudence and an exceptional gift for teaching . . .
he it was who, with his religious fervour, turned the natives away from
their primitive beliefs." That fervour created trouble among the hard-
faced colonists. If the natives could become Christians, they obviously
could not be treated as savages. One of Fr. Pedro's colleagues, Fr.
Antonio de Montesinos, took the matter further, in a sermon on the first
Sunday of Advent 1511. Using as a text the insistence of St John the
Baptist in the Gospel of Saint Matthew that he was "a voice crying in the
wilderness" ("*Ego vox clamante in deserto*"), he told his appalled
congregation that they were living in mortal sin because of their
treatment of the Indians. "Are they not men? Do they not have rational
souls? Are you not obliged to love them as you do yourselves? On what
authority have you waged a detestable war against these people?"[2]

The colonists called for the return to Spain of the Dominicans. Fr.

Montesinos outmanoeuvred them by going home himself to plead the cause of the natives. He at first gained no hearing. But a debate was eventually joined. A theologian, Matías de Paz, in his *Concerning the Rule of the King of Spain over the Indies*, argued that Christian princes were not entitled to make war on infidels purely out of a desire to dominate or to capture their wealth. The spreading of the Faith could be the only justification for such conflicts.[3] A meeting was held at Burgos to discuss the matters arising. King Ferdinand was present. Fr. Montesinos found himself arguing against a skilled polemicist, Juan Palacios Rubios, a university professor of distinction, who defended the conquistadors.[4] Palacios Rubios argued that the founding charter of the Spanish empire in the New World was the donation of the Indies to the Catholic kings by Pope Alexander VI. So far as the issue raised by Fr. Montesinos was concerned, he cited Aristotle's *Politics*. Aristotle had discussed whether certain peoples were "slaves by nature".[5] That discussion had interested thinkers in Europe in the late fifteenth century. It had enabled them to contrast freedom in the West with subjection in Turkey. Palacios Rubios argued that the natives in the Indies were so barbarous as to be natural slaves, if anyone were. They were in need of correction.[6] Yet the Italian philosopher Pico della Mirandola had caused one of his characters, in a dialogue, to say that "he who looks closely will see that even the barbarians have intelligence – not on the tongue, but in the heart".

The consequence of this discussion was the adoption of the Laws of Burgos (27 December 1512), the first legal approach to "the Indian question". The most important provision in it was that Indians were to be made Christians. They were to be assembled in villages, taught the creed, the Lord's prayer and the *Salve Regina*, how to pray and how to confess. They were to be given Christian baptism and Christian funerals. The sons of chiefs were to be educated in their teens by Franciscans. A special teacher, a certain Hernán Xuárez, was to go to the Caribbean to teach Latin grammar. Natives who worked for wages were not to be ill-treated. Every town was to have an inspector to ensure that the settlers conducted themselves humanely.[7] There were some less philanthropic provisions. The *naturales* (natives) were forbidden to dance. Church-going was compulsory. Old houses were to be burned, to prevent sentimentality. A third of all Indians were to work in the mines. Despite these and other such clauses, these laws began an intellectual revolution. The practical consequences were more uncertain.

A further Spanish discussion was held in 1513 at the Dominican convent of San Pablo, in Valladolid. Some provisions supplementary to the Laws of Burgos were passed. Martín Fernández de Enciso, a geographer who had been among the founders of the colony at Darien, expounded the thesis that the Indies had been given to Spain (by the

Pope), just as Canaan had been given to the Jews (by God). The Spaniards, he insisted, could, therefore, treat the Indians as Joshua treated the citizens of Jericho.[8] King Ferdinand then commissioned a new proclamation to be read formally aloud by conquistadors on the occasion of new conquests. That procedure, he hoped, would at least legalise the position.

That document was the *Requerimiento*, the Requisition, drafted by that same professor Palacios Rubios who had argued with Fr. Montesinos at Burgos.[9] There were medieval precedents. Indeed, the thing may have had its origin, like many other instances of Castilian chivalry, in the Muslim practice of challenging opponents before a battle to embrace the true faith or to die. A similar declaration had been used in the Christian conquest of the Canary Islands. But the new document was more all-embracing. It began with a short history of Christendom up till the "donation" of Alexander Borgia. It called upon Indians to accept the authority of the Spanish Crown as the temporal representative of the papacy. Palacios Rubios, a realist, described the document as intended to "calm the conscience of the Christians". He could see the macabre side of reading on, for example, a tropical beach, a document of this nature before Indians who could understand neither the language nor the concepts presented.[10] Bishop de Las Casas said that he did not know whether to laugh or to weep when he heard of the instruction.[11] Fernández de Enciso once described reading the *Requerimiento* to two chiefs of the Cenú in what is now Colombia. The chiefs accepted that there might be one God, and that He might rule earth and sky, but they thought that "the Pope must have been drunk" when he gave to the Catholic kings so much territory which belonged to others.[12]

This text was first read in seriousness by Rodrigo de Colmenares on the shores of Panama, in the presence of the future historian of the Indies, Gonzalo Fernández de Oviedo, in 1514.[13]

A serious argument about the legality of empire was now joined in Spain. But it might not have been taken any further, and there might never have been an ecclesiastical government in Hispaniola, had it not been for another Dominican monk of persistence, courage, humanity, and eloquence: Fr. Bartolomé de Las Casas. Las Casas had faults: he was, as has been seen, inclined to exaggeration, and he quarrelled with everyone. He was at the same time naive and overweening. But of his generosity of spirit and his determination there can be no doubt.

Las Casas was a native of Seville, as were so many of those involved in the tale of Spanish expansion. His father, Pedro de Las Casas, went to Hispaniola as one of the "gentleman" colonists on Columbus' second journey in 1493. The family may have been Jewish in origin.[14] When Pedro de Las Casas went back disillusioned to Seville in 1498, he brought with him a slave whom he was later obliged to return in consequence of a decision of the Queen. (She remarked: "What power of mine does the Admiral hold to give my vassals to anyone?")[15]

The Las Casas family retained property in Hispaniola. It was therefore logical that Bartolomé, aged eighteen, should have gone out with Ovando in 1502 to that island, in a great fleet of thirty ships, with another 2,500 men and women. This was the first time that people went to settle, as they supposed permanently, in the New World, as opposed to going out to make a fortune and return. After a while, to the astonishment of his friends, Las Casas went to Rome to be ordained a priest in 1506. He returned and was the first man to give his first mass in the New World.[16] In 1510, he went as chaplain to a reinforcement of Spanish soldiers in Cuba to assist the governor there. His presence at the burning of the chief Hatuey perhaps turned his attention to the sufferings of the Indians.[17] He took part in the subjugation of central Cuba: "I do not remember with how much spilling of blood he marked that road," Las Casas later wrote of his commander, Pánfilo de Narváez.[18] But though these experiences distressed him, his protest was delayed. For a year or two, priest or no, he managed an estate, presumably an *encomienda*, on the river Arimao near Cienfugos in Cuba. Las Casas maintained a fish farm. But in 1514, he renounced this property, preached passionately to his neighbours, on Whit Sunday, much as Montesinos had preached in Santo Domingo, returned to Spain, and devoted his life thereafter to the sufferings of the Indians.[19]

The King saw Las Casas in Plasencia, where he had gone for the marriage of a bastard granddaughter. He promised to help Las Casas when he reached Seville. But Ferdinand was not put to the test. He died in a farmhouse before he attained his destination. Las Casas went next to see the Regent, the octogenarian Cardinal Archbishop of Toledo, Ximénez de Cisneros. Cisneros would remain Regent for two and a half years, until the arrival in September 1518 of the late King's young Flemish grandson, who would become eventually the great Emperor Charles V, but was, for the time being, merely the improbable young Charles I, King of Spain. Because of the survival of his mother, Juana, Charles had an uncertain claim to the royal dignity.[20]

Ximénez de Cisneros, reformer of the Spanish Franciscans, inspiration of the first polyglot Bible, founder of the University of Alcalá de Henares, patron of the arts (especially in the cathedral of Toledo), inquisitor-general, and commander-in-chief of a North African expedition in 1509, was one of the greatest men of his age.[21] Las Casas once asked with what justice could the enslavement of the Indians be accepted. "With no justice," Cisneros fiercely answered, "for are they not free? Who can doubt that they are free men?"[22] Yet for all his wish to be kind to Indians, Cisneros had been the hammer of the Moors. Nor, like the great Isabel, his benefactress, was he tolerant of Jews.

Las Casas presented a powerful memorandum to Cisneros. He suggested that the Indians in Hispaniola should be asked to work for wages, not as slaves. They should be gathered into new villages and provided with churches and hospitals. Castilian farmers rather than adventurers should be encouraged as settlers. Each new farm would take under its wing a prescribed number of Indians, who would be instructed in European agriculture. A third only of the Indians between twenty-five and forty-five should at any one time work for the Castilians; then only for two months and at no more than sixty miles from home.

Fortresses would be established three hundred miles apart along the north coast of South America. Their purpose would be to act as centres of peaceful trade, comparable to the places which the Portuguese had set up in Africa. Each would have allocated to it a bishop, supported by friars. A special colony, Las Casas imaginatively proposed, should be set up at Cumaná in Venezuela to be staffed by a new knightly order, the "knights of the golden spur", on the model of the old orders of Santiago or Alcántara. They would trade with the Indians. Further *entradas*, expeditions, into the hinterland of Indian territory would be prohibited. Finally, the slave trade in Indians in the Caribbean would be ended. If slaves were needed – this was a suggestion which Las Casas later regretted – they should be brought from Africa.[23] Cisneros was convinced. At eighty, he was easier to impress with ideas than are most men of thirty.

Cisneros sent out three Jeronymite friars – Fr. Luis de Figueroa, Fr. Bernardino de Manzanedo and Fr. Alonso de Santo Domingo – to Hispaniola to act as commissioners (*comisarios*) in the place of Diego Colón (to these three, Fr. Juan de Salvatierra was later added). The Cardinal never had any doubts about the benefits of churchmen in power, though the Jeronymites, after several generations of growing influence since their foundation at the end of the fourteenth century, had been somewhat shaken by the discovery that they had been penetrated by Jewry. Cisneros chose the order to avoid making trouble between the Franciscans and the Dominicans; Las Casas chose the men. As "religious persons in whom there could be no spirit of greed",[24] the priors were to carry out a full investigation of the Indian problem, to seek to end the system of *encomienda*, and to explore the idea of Indian self-government. Alonso de Zuazo, a fair-minded judge from Segovia (or near it), was to carry out a judicial enquiry (*residencia*) into what had occurred in recent years.[25]

The priors arrived in December 1516, Zuazo in April 1517. All five worked hard. They visited the mines and the villages, which they found sadly empty: Zuazo wrote that, unless something were done, in a few years there would be nobody left. There were already as "few [natives] as grapes after a harvest".[26] The priors asked questions.[27] Their first report was that the island lacked both Indians and Spaniards. Their second echoed, strongly, Las Casas' demand for African slaves.[28] They believed that sugar, cotton, lumber and cassia might substitute for gold as an export. Wives, suggested Zuazo, were also needed for the Spanish settlers. Only thus would the colonists feel that they had a home there. The islands should be treated as if they were the Azores or Madeira: permanent places of residence. Immigration should be unlimited. People should be encouraged to come from everywhere in Spain, not from just the "needle's eye of Seville".[29]

Of these men, the strongest character, and the noblest man, was the judge Zuazo. He was brave, imaginative and, at least at that stage of his life, honest. Fr. Luis de Figueroa turned out to be as ambitious as any Aragonese civil servant. Fr. Santo Domingo and Fr. Salvatierra were old, grey and weak. Fr. Manzanedo was well intentioned and eloquent, but as ineffective as he was ugly. None of them knew how to behave when faced, so far from home, with brutal adventurers, insolent colonists and dying Indians. They longed to return to their fashionable monasteries in Castile. They even received praise from the corrupt treasurer, Miguel de Pasamonte, who had survived every change in Santo Domingo for ten years.[30] No condemnation could have been more damning. They only found one Indian in the whole of Hispaniola whom they defined as "ready for liberty". The rest were to be gathered into villages or towns under Spanish administrators and priests. Las Casas had come back to Hispaniola as "protector of the Indians". But he had quarrelled with his protégés and returned to Spain to denounce them. His ideas of reform were undercut by the continuing fall of the population. There was almost nothing which anyone could do by then.[31] In August 1518 the new king removed judicial questions from the control of the priors. In December he would transfer all their authority to a judge, Rodrigo de Figueroa, one of whose tasks was to carry out an enquiry. Power passed to him formally in December 1518. But he did not arrive in Santo Domingo till August of the next year. Till then, theocracy struggled on.[32] Conquistadors continued to come out from Spain. But they looked after cattle with little help from the Indians.

Of the other Spanish rulers in the Caribbean, the outstanding man was Diego Velázquez, the *Caudillo* (leader) of Cuba. He was a fair-haired giant, with an amiable face, turning to fat.[33] He came from a noble family long established at Cuéllar, an old city in Castile lying halfway between Valladolid and Segovia. The door of his family's later ramshackle palace could until recently still be seen in the steep Calle San Pedro running down from the main square. Cuéllar lay in the shadow of the castle of Albuquerque. That colossal pile was the seat of the famous Beltrán de la Cueva, Duke of Albuquerque, the favourite of Enrique IV, to whom the town, previously royal, had been presented about the time of Diego Velázquez's birth in 1464. Among Diego's brothers, Antón had followed him to Cuba; Cristóbal was captain of the Castilian militia; and a third, Juan, was also a conquistador in the Caribbean. A cousin, another Juan Velázquez, having been treasurer to the now dead Infante Juan, was at this time one of the two chief accountants, *contadores mayores*, of Castile (Iñigo de Loyola had been brought up in his house in Arévalo, of which city he was governor). Another cousin, Sancho Velázquez de Cuéllar, had been a member of the first national council of the Inquisition in 1484.[34]

Diego Velazquez's home city, Cuéllar, was famous in the 1470s, when the Governor had been a boy, for a rabbi whose eloquence drew not only Jews but old Christians to his sermons in the synagogue. Cuéllar, today seemingly remote, was, in the late fifteenth century, close to the centre of many complicated political negotiations. It was a day's ride from Segovia, the favourite city of Enrique IV. Arévalo, the childhood home of Queen Isabel, was no distance. The great battles of the time had been fought nearby: at Valladolid, Torquemada and Olmedo.[35]

Diego Velázquez probably served in the Granada campaigns in the 1480s. From them he emerged "poor and ill".[36] Then, at the age of twenty-eight, he accompanied Columbus on his second voyage in 1493.[37] He became a member of the household of the Admiral's brother, Bartolomé Colón. Before long, he was one of the richest men in Hispaniola. Ovando, the Governor, and a man on whom Velázquez later modelled himself, named him his lieutenant in the wars against the Indians in the west. He was one of the two captains in charge of the disgraceful massacre of Xaragua in 1503. Ovando made him Governor of all the "cities" of western Hispaniola: poor places, with wooden houses with straw roofs, roads of mud, and wooden churches and makeshift town halls.[38]

From west Hispaniola it was an easy step to Cuba. The ostensible reason for the Spanish invasion of it was that Hatuey, a chief in Hispaniola, had fled there after Xaragua. In 1511, some weeks before Fr. Montesinos' famous sermon, Velázquez assembled about three hundred and thirty conquistadors, with some supporting Indians, at the little port of Salvatierra de la Sabana. They crossed the strait now known as the Windward Passage. Velázquez established himself at Baracoa – Nuestra Señora de la Asunción, as he renamed it – at the far east end of Cuba.[39]

Cuba was less populated than Hispaniola, even though it was far larger. The Tainos who lived there were, however, related to those of that first Spanish outpost, whose ball games, customs and language they shared. Like the people of Hispaniola, their staple crop was cassava. But their tree-covered plains were less suited to extensive cultivation with the digging stick than was Hispaniola. Their main food was green turtle, caught by suckerfish, sometimes held till needed in large corrals (similar to that once owned by Las Casas on the river Arimao). The natives also hunted, in the forests of mahogany and tropical cedar, innumerable parrots, doves and pigeons. According to Las Casas, one could then walk the entire length of the island (1,000 miles) under trees. Certainly, at that time four-fifths of the island was covered by jungle.[40]

The Cubans offered little resistance to the Spanish: the only chief who did so was that same Hatuey who had fled from Santo Domingo. He is said to have refused baptism before being burned alive. Had he agreed to become a Christian, he would merely have been executed with a sword. But he was told that, if that were to happen, he would spend eternity with the Castilians; an eventuality which he wished to avoid.[41]

The conquest of Cuba was carried through thoroughly. Velázquez's chief lieutenant was Pánfilo de Narváez, a near neighbour of his in Castile. He came from Navalmanzano, fifteen miles south of Cuéllar, on the way to Segovia. He had played a part in the conquest of Jamaica. Now he slashed his way with fifteen crossbowmen and a few arquebusiers across the southern part of the island. The people fled and neglected cultivation.[42] As in Hispaniola, many native women became associated intimately with the conquerors.

Within a few years Velázquez and his lieutenants had founded seven townships in Cuba, all of which survive – though it would be hard to argue that the firm beginnings laid by Velázquez ensured that.[43] In 1518 none of these places had houses of stone, the churches (if there were any) being of wood, with roofs of palm leaves.[44] The main city had been, first, Baracoa, on the north side of the far east tip of the island. But the Castilian headquarters soon passed to Santiago de Cuba, a site with a fine harbour on the south coast, and also not far from the easternmost point.

Cuba was first christened "Juana" after the Queen of Spain. But that name soon seemed unfashionable since the Queen was in semi-captivity. So it became "Fernandina" after the King. That designation did not last either – though it was still being used in the 1520s. The island recovered its indigenous name, Cuba, soon after the native population had been destroyed.

Gold was found in Cuba in several streams in the central mountains. For some years, there were considerable returns for the settlers near the two new towns of Trinidad and Sancti Spiritus. The local population, overworked and leaderless, followed that of Hispaniola into unpitied extinction.

Despite his role in the massacre at Xaragua, and the burning of Hatuey, Velázquez was far from being the most brutal of the conquistadors. Indeed, one witness at a later enquiry into his actions, a Basque shipmaster, Juan Bono de Quejo, testified that he was a good Christian as well as a good servant of their Majesties, who treated his Indians well.[45] Though concerned to make Cuba prosperous, he had resisted a division of the Indians in Cuba into *encomiendas* along the lines of what had happened in Hispaniola until it seemed that there was no alternative. He thereafter did what he could to limit the size of *encomiendas* to two hundred Indians. He had, Las Casas admitted, a happy temperament. His talk was all about pleasure. Conversation with him had the style of banter between undisciplined youths. He enjoyed banquets.[46] Although he had a bad temper, he was not vindictive. He pardoned most things once his angry mood had passed.[47] All the same, he was proud of his family (though he had no children), and he knew how to maintain his dignity if it were necessary.

The tropics had become home for Velázquez. He was by 1518 accustomed to the local foods: green turtle, cassava bread, cotora birds, iguana. He owned or had interests in ten haciendas in different parts of the island, some of which he held in association with the well-known Genoese merchants of Seville, Juan Francisco de Grimaldo and Gaspar Centurión.[48] He remained on good terms, by means of letters, with the authorities in Spain. They in turn looked on him favourably, as a counterweight to Diego Colón, whom they were always seeking to make uncomfortable; and to whom Velázquez was both indebted and disloyal.

Velázquez's wife, his cousin María del Cuéllar, had died in Baracoa in 1512 soon after their wedding. It was said thereafter that the Governor aspired to marry one of the nieces of the powerful Bishop of Burgos, Juan Rodríguez de Fonseca. The idea was just a tropical tease: the sort of fancy with which the Governor would entertain his friends in the evenings in his improvised palace as to what he would do when he returned to Castile: which everyone knew that he never would. (Both the Bishop's nieces, María and Mayor, had anyway married.)

These discussions in Santiago had the character of a *tertulia*. The Spaniards would smoke tobacco: the first Europeans, perhaps, to take full advantage of the charms of that famous Cuban product (the Spanish colonists began to cultivate tobacco themselves about 1520).[49] Present often would be the Governor's cousin, Antonio Velázquez Borrego, though he left in 1516 for Spain as *procurador general*, or representative of the colony. There would be other cousins and nephews from the huge Velázquez clan: Juan, another Diego, another Antonio, and Bernardino, all men born in far-off Cuéllar, their memories full of stories of when that city had been so close to the court of Spain. There would be the Governor's father-in-law, Cristóbal de Cuéllar, the treasurer of Cuba, who was known to be a little slow about handing over the King's share of Cuban gold, but who had interesting tales of the days when he had been cupbearer to the long-dead Infante Don Juan (said to have died from excessive lovemaking in the first months of his marriage).[50] Cuéllar, who had come to the Indies as chief accountant to Ovando (another sometime member of the Infante's circle) in 1502, was wont to say that his service to that prince, in a brilliant and self-indulgent circle, was something which would give him "two or three tumbles in hell at the right time".[51] Perhaps he explained why that court had been so especially friendly to Columbus, both before and after his first voyage. There would be Velázquez's secretary, Andrés de Duero, a tiny man from Tudela del Duero, a small town on the Cuéllar side of Valladolid, and his accountant, Amador de Lares, a native of Burgos who was shrewd if illiterate. The former was usually silent; the latter talkative and astute. He too would hold the floor with stories – of the years when he had been steward (*maestresala*) to the "Great Captain", Gonzalo Hernández de Córdoba, in Italy.[52] Another member of Velázquez's tropical court was Manuel de Rojas, also a Cuellerano, married to Velázquez's niece Magdalena, and brother of that Gabriel de Rojas who would one day be famous in Peru (Rojas had lived practically next door to the Velázquez family in Cuéllar).[53] The Governor's jester, Francisco Cervantes, would say provocative things or quote lines from romances in a disconcertingly appropriate manner. Velázquez himself might recall the time when he had ridden over to Seville from Granada to take part in Columbus' second voyage. He surely talked sometimes of what it had been like to work with the Admiral, as Columbus always called himself. Sometimes at the *tertulia* there would no doubt be an ex-secretary of the Governor, the magistrate of Santiago, an obsequious, clever and unpredictable settler from Medellín, in Extremadura: Hernán (or Hernando) Cortés, who had made money from gold on the Duabán river. .

The native population in Cuba was meantime declining as fast as that of Hispaniola. Only about fifteen settlers had more than a hundred Indians, but for the moment there were servants enough.[54] Amador de Lares had begun to bring in a few black slaves from Africa to compensate for the shortage.[55] Wine, olive oil, flour, vinegar, and leather shoes, even satin and damask, would come in shipments from Seville, making money for merchants of that city or of Burgos, and for the Governor too, since he owned the best shop in Santiago.[56] (Actually Velázquez did not legally hold the title of Governor: he remained Diego Colón's lieutenant governor for the island of Cuba, and the distributor (*repartidor*) of Indians there: a junior status which he was in constant hope of changing.)

Second in importance among the Caribbean rulers in 1518 was Francisco de Garay, the Basque *Caudillo* in Jamaica, an island which for a time was known by the name of "Santiago".[57] Like Velázquez, Garay had also come to the Indies from Spain (in fact as a notary) with Columbus in 1493. He became even closer to Columbus than Velázquez had done, for he married the Admiral's sister-in-law, Ana Muñiz.[58] Also like Velázquez, Garay made himself rich in Hispaniola: an Indian woman in his employment, resting for lunch, had found, on the side of the River Ozama, a big lump of gold weighing thirty-five pounds. That led Garay to found the so-called New Mines, which he and an Aragonese friend,

Miguel Díez de Aux, cleverly exploited. The undertaking made both rich. Garay was still the only man, apart from officials, to have a house of stone in Santo Domingo.[59]

After a few years, Garay became restless. Most conquistadors liked variety. He tried, therefore, to capture – or, as he put it, "discover the secret of" – the island of Guadalupe (Columbus had firstly discovered and so named it, just as he had given names to most of the Lesser Antilles). But Garay was repelled by Caribs, who were better fighters than the Tainos. He then traded pearls. Some years later, he was named Governor of Jamaica, to succeed Juan de Esquivel, the first Spanish *caudillo* there.[60] Esquivel had built two towns, Santa Gloria and Sevilla la Nueva, but allowed imported livestock to run wild all over the island. Once more, the native agriculture was ruined. By the time that Garay went to Jamaica in 1515, the population had already begun the major decline which marked the other islands of the Spanish empire. Though Peter Martyr regarded him as "the best of the governors of the New World", and though Las Casas conceded that he was "an honourable man", Garay was not the man to reverse this decline. Probably it was by then impossible. He too built two towns, Melilla and Oristán, he pioneered the eating of potatoes, and he lived an idyllic existence on an island which still seemed "Elysian".[61]

Puerto Rico need not delay us long. The first conquistador had been that brave and swashbuckling bully, Juan Ponce de León, who had also come out as a "gentleman" in 1493 with Columbus.[62] As with others on that expedition, noble birth and experience in fighting against Granada did not prevent him from being preoccupied by money. He and Esquivel (later Governor of Jamaica) conquered east Hispaniola. Ovando then permitted Ponce de León to establish a property there, at Salvación de Higuey. Ships passing bound for Spain would stop at his harbour to buy cassava bread. He crossed the narrow Mona Passage to Puerto Rico in 1508. He was initially well received by the *naturales*. The subsequent conquest was simple, marked by the achievements of his dog Becerillo, who, with his terrifying red hair and black eyes, became renowned for his skill in distinguishing by smell between friendly and enemy Indians.[63]

The barbarities of Ponce de León aroused rebellion among the natives. But though they were supported by the Caribs from the island of Santa Cruz nearby, they were no match for the conquistadors. Ponce de León settled in Puerto Rico. He made money. But he tired of administration. He enjoyed great journeys. He returned to Spain to persuade the King to give him a licence to seek the Fountain of Youth. That unique source of happiness, which figured in many popular romances, was believed to exist in what is now known as Florida. Ponce then set off on a series of adventures. He was, in consequence, as has been seen, the first European to touch at Yucatan. He (or his pilot Alaminos) was also the first

European to report the existence of the Gulf Stream. Back in Puerto Rico, he gave way to a grave lawyer, Sancho Velázquez, probably a cousin of the Governor of Cuba, whose mission was to investigate the achievements and errors of his predecessor over the last ten years.[64] Ponce busied himself with organising a new expedition to Florida. Once again, the Indians died overworking in streams looking for gold, carrying the Spanish baggage, or growing food for them in a country whose cultivated areas were suffering from the ravages of wild cattle.

The last of the *caudillos* of the Caribbean in 1518 was Pedrarias – properly Pedro Arias – de Ávila, who was ruler of the one Spanish colony already established on the mainland, at Darien in Castilla del Oro, a territory approximately coterminous with what is now Panama. It was given its encouraging name by King Ferdinand in 1513 because it was reported that there were "rich rivers of gold" there: thus fulfilling an ancient fairy tale.[65] Pedrarias was the brother of the Count of Puñonrostro. His *converso* family had been important in Segovia for several generations.[66] His grandfather, Diego Arias, had been treasurer to King Enrique IV. His uncle had been that Bishop of Segovia who had established Spain's first printing press. Pedrarias had as many nicknames as his cousins had titles: "the Gallant", "the Jouster", "the Courtier". Like some of his fellow *caudillos* in the Caribbean, he had fought against Granada; and probably he had fought in many of the civil wars of the 1470s, for he was in 1518 a man of seventy-eight. He led out to the isthmus in 1514 an expedition with many gentlemen of fortune: "the most splendid group of men who had ever left Spain", it was thought, since they were "dressed in silk and brocade"; though those things served them little in their fight against heat, mosquitoes and sickness.[67] These men had been attracted to this expedition because they had been led to suppose, so Las Casas said, that in Darien one fished for gold with nets.[68] Pedrarias had been ordered to take over the government of Darien from Vasco Núñez de Balboa, who as interim governor had seemed too self-assured to be acceptable to a suspicious royal authority. Balboa might have been the first European to see the Pacific – in 1513. But he was also the first rebel of the New World.

Pedrarias established himself successfully, at a high cost. He antagonised the native Indians by methods which Balboa had eschewed: for example, his pacification of the region was marked by a brutal use of dogs. It was from then on that the expressive word *aperrear*, to throw to the dogs, began generally to be used.[69] The Indians were so estranged that it was soon said that "no Christian dares to go a league from town except in company".[70] The gifted Balboa was imprisoned, being executed for rebellion in January 1519 – the first time that a European was done to death by a compatriot on the American mainland. "The Gallant" himself lived on at Darien, organising expeditions into the interior in order to obtain slaves to sell to Hispaniola (or to give his underemployed countrymen something to do), hated by the Indians, feared by his own men and joylessly exerting a supreme power which was no less despotic because it was on a tiny scale and exercised by a resourceful septuagenarian in a steamy backwater.[71]

This picture of the governance of the Caribbean in 1518 omits one element: the survival of Diego Colón as a contender for power. Though he had left Hispaniola in 1515 as Governor, he still aspired to a hereditary viceroyalty over the entire Caribbean. Dull, tenacious, well connected through his marriage to María de Toledo, a niece of the Duke of Alba, Diego Colón, "the Admiral", as he liked to be known, was in these years constantly haunting the court but often ignored by it, a living ghost of great voyages past, a reminder that even then, as later, the achievement of his father was impossible to measure appropriately.

This new empire was neglected in Spain itself. Isabel the Catholic had succumbed to the charm of Columbus' vision. She even interested herself, if sporadically, in the welfare of "her" Indians. But her husband Ferdinand never did so. His plans were ambitious but they were Mediterranean plans. His chief interest in the Indies was to secure the maximum income from them. The late Queen had left him half the income which the Crown of Castile received from the Indies. But everyone knew that the islands were in decline. For though no book could after 1501 be published in Spain without official approval, there was no censorship of private reports from the New World. In 1511 it was even declared that no official was to prevent anyone sending to the King or anyone else letters and information which concerned the welfare of the Indies.[72] The few Spaniards who were interested in Columbus' heritage were therefore well informed.

Through much of his reign, Ferdinand was happy to leave the affairs of this empire in the safe, experienced hands of Juan Rodríguez de Fonseca, the Bishop of Burgos – and after 1511 titular Archbishop of Rossano in Naples – who had once, years before, been a protégé of the late Queen Isabel.[73]

Fonseca was feared in his time, despised afterwards. Peter Martyr described him as a man "of illustrious birth, genius and initiative".[74] He came from a family of bishops and loyal servants of the Crown: a "link in a priceless chain", wrote a later enthusiast.[75] Thus his father, Fernando, had been *corregidor* of Burgos and had been killed at the Battle of Olmedo by the Duke of Albuquerque, apparently in person, fighting for the Catholic kings. His brother Antonio was captain-general of Castile: in effect commander-in-chief of the royal armed forces. Three generations of Fonsecas had been archbishops of Santiago de Compostela: one being Bishop Juan's uncle, the second his cousin, the third (the archbishop in 1518) that cousin's bastard son. These connections enhanced Fonseca's value to the Crown: monarchs respect the principle of birth even when those concerned are churchmen and bureaucrats rather than noblemen. Fonseca was loyal, experienced, tireless, hard and intelligent: he had once been a pupil of the humanist Nebrija.[76] He organised Columbus' second voyage, with all its "gentlemen volunteers", very well, and in a short time. He also managed the Great Captain's first expedition to Italy. He seemed better at "arming warships than in hearing masses",[77] but then much the same had been said of Cisneros. It was Fonseca who insisted that trade with the Indies should be concentrated in Seville; who arranged a special postal service which took letters from Seville to the court quickly; and who, in 1503, organised the Casa de la Contratación, a regulating body for Atlantic trade, which operated from a suite of rooms in the Alcázar in the heart of that city. Naturally, protégés of his own, Sancho de Matienzo, a native of Aguilar de Campo, whom he had met when both were in the chapter of the cathedral of Seville, and Juan López de Recalde, a Basque from Vizcaya, were, respectively, the treasurer and accountant. (Matienzo was "Abbot of Jamaica", an island which he had no intention of visiting but which he hoped would one day produce gold for him: as indeed it did.)[78] The Casa's chief task was to ensure that the tax, the Royal Fifth, was levied on all profits made by subjects of the Spanish Crown in the New World. But it also acted as a trustee of those who died in the Indies. It fitted out the few fleets which sailed at the cost of the Crown. It licensed navigation, it checked all cargoes in and out, it enforced limits on size of ships in the interests of safety. It commissioned charts and established a school of navigation. Fonseca carried out an investigation of the Casa de la Contratación in 1511. When he reorganised it, with a tiny staff (there was only one porter), he gave it judicial as well as executive powers. He did not forget to equip it with a prison.[79]

Though unimaginative, and opposed to anyone original having anything to do with the Indies, Fonseca was interested in the arts, of which he, like others of his family, was a generous patron. He used his frequent diplomatic missions to Flanders, for example, to bring back paintings; even painters.[80]

Fonseca was a symbol of continuity. In 1518 he was still the individual on the Council of Castile who dealt with the affairs of the empire: in reality, minister for the colonies in all but name. Imperial treasurers and governors fawned on him. He was slowly turning the *ad hoc* committee of the council which dealt with the Indies into a special council of its own, that of the Indies proper: an institution which, once founded, would last over two hundred years.[81] Fonseca was also a protector of *conversos*, whether Jewish or Muslim: the first including his bland, devious, corrupt but able chief secretary from Aragon, Lope de Conchillos;[82] the second including Miguel de Pasamonte, also an Aragonese who, formally the treasurer of Hispaniola, was in practice the financial dictator of the Caribbean.[83] But Fonseca did not exercise such protection out of kindness. On the contrary, it was because he needed competent and loyal men who would be compliant, since they knew that their fortunes, perhaps their lives, were in his hands.

Fonseca's deceptively benign, calm features, then forty years old, as the donor in the picture of the Virgin of la Antigua in the cathedral of Badajoz, or the fifty-year-old donor in a triptych in the cathedral in Palencia, depict the face of the perfect civil servant certain to quarrel with adventurers.[84] He once unwisely wrote to Antonio de Guevara, the author of *The Golden Book of Marcus Aurelius* (another very popular book in Spain), asking what people were saying of him at court. The reply was honest if complicated. Guevara wrote: "All say that you are a very solid Christian but a very peevish [*desabrido*] bishop. They also say that you are fat, prolix, and as careless in respect of the contracts which you have in your hands as you are indecisive with the petitioners who appear before you. They say that many of the latter return to their homes exhausted, with their suits still unsettled. They add that you are bullying, proud, and impatient, if high-spirited . . . Others admit that at least you are someone who deals in truth . . . and that a liar is never your friend. They say that you are direct in what you do, and both just and moderate in your sentences and in how they are executed. They also say that you have no passion nor affection where justice is concerned . . . But I would add myself that there is no virtue more necessary in a man who governs a republic than patience . . ."[85]

Fonseca had passed difficult days during the regency of Cardinal Ximénez de Cisneros. Cisneros did not like him. He did not dismiss him. But he pushed him into the background. Fonseca's long-serving secretary, Lope de Conchillos, was forced to retire. But when Cisneros died, in October 1517, and the new King Charles came to Spain, Fonseca recovered his position, so that, as the Governor of Cuba well knew, at the time when the first Castilian expedition touched the Mexican coast, he remained the dominant influence on policy towards the Indies.

7

Better lands have never been discovered

*"In all the islands of Santo Domingo and in Cuba and even in Castile, the
fame of it arrived and they said that, in all the world, better lands have never
been discovered . . ."*
Bernal Díaz, on Yucatan, c.1518

THE GOVERNOR OF Cuba, Diego Velázquez, wrote to King
Ferdinand in Spain, on 1 April 1514, to say that he had been "told
by chiefs and Indians that, on occasion, certain Indians had come
from the islands beyond Cuba towards the side of the North navigating
five or six days by canoe and . . . there gave news of other islands that lie
beyond".[1]

No other news exists of these Indian expeditions. How recently had
they come? Were they Mexicans or Mayas in search of information? To
confirm rumours of bloodshed? Did they perhaps take back the reports
on which the Mexica built a legend of fear? Were the expeditions
deliberately contrived or did they reach Cuba by accident? How did they
travel? The answers to these questions are unclear, partly because they
have never been put. But the fact is that the eastern coast of the Mexican
empire was at that time exactly "five or six days by canoe" from northern
Cuba, and the report, for which there is no other evidence, suggests that
there must have been some expedition by the Mexica or the Mayas.

Velázquez naturally wished to investigate. But for the moment he did
not do so. Such maritime initiatives as he carried out in those days were
raids for slaves to make up for the shortage of labour from which he, like
the settlers in Hispaniola, was beginning to suffer: from the Bahamas;
from his friend Pedrarias in Panama; or sometimes from the Bay Islands,
a tiny archipelago off the coast of Honduras. Some of those slaving
expeditions had brought difficulties: in 1516 Indian captives from
Nicaragua staged a rebellion against the Castilians on the south coast.[2]

At that time, the idea still predominated that Central America and
what was known of North America were outlying parts of, or islands off,
Asia. A map of the world of the geographer Waldseemüller shows North
America as "Asiae Partis".[3] Even for someone so easy-going as

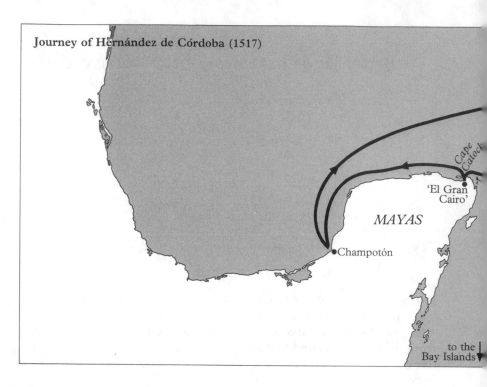

Journey of Hernández de Córdoba (1517)

'El Gran Cairo'

Cape Catoch

MAYAS

•Champotón

to the
Bay Islands

Velázquez, it was difficult to rest tranquil while no one knew exactly
what lay between that Cape Gracias a Díos, where Columbus had turned
south on his last voyage, and Florida. Pinzón and Díaz de Solís, and then
Ponce de León, might, separately, have sailed along part of the coast of
Mexico. But it was unclear where they had been. Was there a strait to the
"Southern Sea", as the Pacific was known (till Magellan opened the
way into the latter ocean in 1520)? It seemed probable, for Balboa had
shown that the isthmus was narrow when he first saw the Pacific. It was
known that to the far west of Cuba there was a long, east-facing coastline.
But there was an uncertain hinterland.

In the end, the initiative to find out what lay beyond the west end of
Cuba was taken by three of Velázquez's friends: Francisco Hernández de
Córdoba, Lope Ochoa de Caicedo, and Cristóbal de Morante. They
were conquistadors established in Sancti Spiritus, about forty miles from
the sea in the centre of the island. The first two came originally from
Córdoba, while Cristóbal de Morante was from Medina del Campo.
Hernández de Córdoba may have been remotely related to the "Great
Captain", the hero of the Spanish wars in Italy, but that family was an
enormous one. Had there been a close connection, it would have been
known in the Caribbean: the admiration for that commander was such
that Francisco Pizarro, now in Darien, always wore white shoes and a
white hat, simply because the famous general had done so.[4]

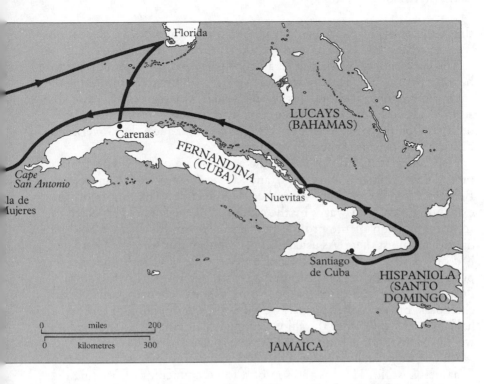

These three men financed two ships, *naos*,[5] and Diego Velázquez himself paid for (or lent money for) a third, a brigantine.[6] Hernández de Córdoba, a soldier, was intelligent but lacked subtlety. They carried one hundred and ten men with them – among them several who had set off from Spain with Pedrarias in 1514 for Castilla del Oro, and had then gone, disillusioned, to Cuba where, in the case of some, there was further disappointment: the Governor had promised to give them Indians, "when there were any to spare". But there were now none available. After being in Cuba for three years, without prospects, they were ready for a new adventure. The prime purpose of the expedition, above all in the mind of Governor Velázquez, was to find slaves. But those who directed the little armada wanted also "to find new lands and new employment".[7] To that end, the planners hired the "clever and experienced" Antonio de Alaminos of Palos as their pilot. He had, of course, been to that coast before, with both Columbus and Ponce de León. He had just come back from Spain on the *San Sebastián*, the ship which he piloted for Hernández de Córdoba.[8]

The other two pilots were Pedro Camacho, from that village of Triana just across the river from Seville which had given so many seamen to the cause of discovery; and Juan Álvarez, "*el manquillo*", the lame, who came from Huelva. Hernández de Córdoba captained one of the two *naos*. The other was captained by Francisco Iñiguez, receiver in Cuba of the revenues of the King. Being from Santo Domingo de la Calzada, he was one of the few Navarrese to seek his fortune in the Indies.

The Governor of Cuba played a major part; and it was important to have his permission. The Crown had in 1513 prohibited the mounting of such expeditions without royal approval.[9] Velázquez had already secured a licence for expeditions of this kind from the Jeronymite priors in Santo Domingo: in December 1516, Antón Velázquez, the Governor's brother, had procured the right document.[10]

Hernández de Córdoba had all the appropriate officers with him: a priest, Fr. Alonso González;[11] and a *veedor*, or royal inspector, Bernardo Iñiguez, perhaps a brother of Francisco. The sailors on the expedition were paid wages by the captain. But the soldiers expected to receive a portion of the profits: perhaps a two-thirds share would be divided amongst them. As usual in expeditions of this sort, the Castilians had on board a supply of food and water for the voyage: some beef or pork pickled in brine; salt fish; perhaps sardines and anchovies; cassava flour; probably sun-dried bacon, some onions, cheese, garlic, dried chickpeas, biscuits salted against weevils; and a daily ration of one and a half litres of wine. Once the ships had made landfall, the conquistadors were expected to live from what they could get.

Among those on board one of the *naos* was the future historian, Bernal Díaz del Castillo. He was the son of a town councillor of Medina del Campo, the great city of commerce and notaries, and the home of Cristóbal de Morante. According to his own account, Díaz had been among those who left Spain to go to Darien with Pedrarias.[12] Dissatisfied with his prospects, he had gone to Cuba, where he had high hopes. He claimed to be related to Diego Velázquez[13] (Medina del Campo is only thirty miles from the home of the Velázquez family). But Velázquez had many relations. At a loose end, Bernal Díaz jumped at the prospect of taking part in a new expedition.

Hernández de Córdoba's three ships set out from Santiago on 8 February 1517. They first turned east. Rounding the far eastern point of Cuba, they travelled westwards along that island's north coast, stopping briefly at Puerto Príncipe (now Nuevitas), Axaruco (Boca de Jaruco), then, after six days of sailing, at Cape San Antonio, on the far west of the island, in order to pick up wood and water. The chief pilot, Alaminos, apparently then persuaded Hernández de Córdoba to head due west, not south-west to the Bay Islands. He said that he knew, from having been there with Columbus (and Ponce de León), that, in the west, there was a rich land. But in the Bay Islands there was nothing. Even slaves were hard to come by there. His captain agreed to follow his recommended route.[14] This suggests that a major initiative, from which much would follow, was proposed by a professional technician, not a gentlemanly leader.

The expedition found land when they had travelled between a hundred and fifty and two hundred miles, after precisely six days of sailing: those six days of which Velázquez had spoken when talking of the mysterious Indians' journey.[15] This was probably the island later called the Isla de Mujeres because statues of goddesses were found there, dressed only from the waist down. Both the island, like others nearby, and Yucatan, were flat. Land cannot be seen by ships until they are close. Both territories were covered with trees, though a recent hurricane had destroyed the tallest of them. It was hot at all seasons of the year. The place was full of birds: "On the sea," wrote Bishop de Landa fifty years later, "the variety and multitude of the birds" was remarkable, as was also the beauty of each one of the species. There were "birds as big as brown ostriches, and with larger beaks. They move on the water hunting the fish and, when one is seen, they rise in the air and launch themselves with great force upon the fish. They never make a mis-stroke and, on making the dive, continue swimming and swallowing the fish, without any preparation."[16]

The Castilians moved on towards what they considered to be the "main island" of Yucatan. Five large canoes, possibly with sails, full of Maya Indians, came out to meet them.[17] The Mayas were good makers of canoes, though it was a sphere in which they were less accomplished than the Tainos and the Caribs (who made vessels capable of carrying a hundred and fifty people in hollowed-out ceiba tree trunks). The Castilians made signs of peace by waving cloaks. The canoes drew alongside. The Mayas were wearing cotton shirts, loincloths and sandals of dried deerskin. So the Europeans knew these men to be superior to those of the Caribbean, who as a rule wore nothing. Alaminos would have remembered Columbus making a similar judgement fifteen years before.

Other aspects of Maya life must have seemed less admirable: the hair of the people was grown long, ringed with a tonsure; their faces and bodies were often painted, or tattooed, red; their ears were usually pierced for earrings and much tattered by the habit of extracting blood from the lobes as a sacrifice; their chins were beardless; they often had bow legs, due (it was said) to having been from infancy carried on their mothers' hips. Their frequent cross-eyes were considered a sign of beauty and were artificially encouraged in childhood.[18]

Some thirty Indians came on board Hernández's flagship. The Castilians offered them some of the presents which expeditions of that kind always took with them: green glass beads, silk, woollen clothes, and copper bells, as well as bacon and cassava bread.[19] These the Mayas gratefully acknowledged. As suggested earlier, when discussing the Castilian gifts to the Mexica near Veracruz, it is hard to believe that they were impressed, for "they themselves made far more brilliant objects".[20]

The following day a chief came with another twelve large canoes, apparently saying "*Ecab cotoch*", which meant "We are from Ecab" – Ecab (or Ekab) being the name of that small Maya kingdom where the Spaniards had landed. The Castilians therefore named the point where they had made landfall "Cape Catoche": a name which it retains.[21] Hernández de Córdoba realised that he had reached new land rather than an extension of something well known.[22] But he still thought that the territory was probably an island.[23] With no interpreters, communications were presumably by signs. Probably there were some Cuban Indians on board one or other of Hernández's ships. But the Taino language was almost as far from Maya as it was from Castilian.

Maya civilisation was then in decay. True, there were organised cities, priests, a dominant religion, and a pantheon of gods similar to that which existed in Mexico. Mayan writing, with its eight hundred or so hieroglyphs, was much the most elaborate in the Americas.[24] Their version of paper, a bark cloth, made like that of the Mexica from the wild fig tree (occasionally from deerskin), was superior in texture and durability to the Egyptians' papyrus.[25] There was a lively commercial class, and much trade with Mexico, as well as with other peoples both to the north and to the south. The Mayas produced salt, a much prized product. They also exported both slaves and cotton cloth. In exchange they imported cacao, obsidian, copper, gold and feathers, mostly through what is now Tabasco. Mexican merchants from Xicallanco and Potonchan often travelled to the eastern coast of Yucatan. Mexicans had a warehouse on the nearby island of Cozumel.[26] Remarkable featherwork, fine pottery and a little work in gold were made by skilled craftsmen. The Mayas retained a strong sense of time, as shown by their calendars. The peasants, though apparently in most respects free, were obliged to give service to the upper classes as well as to support religious and communal activities. Human sacrifice was practised, though not on the scale of that among the Mexica.[27]

But the people were divided into about sixteen separate entities. Wars among them were constant, often over access to fresh water. Three tribes led by three families were the main disputants: for example, the Chel, living by the coast, would not trade fish and salt with the Cocom family. The Cocom, in the interior, would, in turn, not allow the Chel access to game or fruit.[28] There was no imperial centre. A few settlements could be called towns. But houses were mostly scattered and rural. The classical age of Maya culture had after all ended in the tenth century AD. Its successor civilisation, a silver age, inspired by emigrant Toltecs, had been ruined by AD 1200. The sacred centres of, for example, Palenque and Chichen-Itza had been overgrown by forest. It is true that the languages spoken in the region – Chontal, Chol and Chorli – were dialects of the same tongue. Yucatec, though a different language, was so similar to Chontal that merchants from any of these areas could communicate easily with one another.[29] But no one could paint or sculpt with the skill that had been shown in the ninth or eighth century. Even a literate Maya of 1517 could not read an inscription of the classical era. Yet though people looked back, not forward, they had forgotten most of their history. The experience of the Mayas is one more reminder that any interpretation of human evolution based on the idea of unilineal progress forwards (or upwards) is an illusion. Peoples decline as well as rise.

The population of Yucatan at the time of this first Spanish expedition is as difficult to estimate as that of Hispaniola, Cuba and Mexico. A figure of 300,000 would seem possible.[30]

The Maya leader at Cape Catoche invited the Spanish to land. Hernández de Córdoba agreed to do so, apparently after asking the advice of his men.[31] They went to the shore in small boats, taking crossbows and arquebuses with them. They were amiably received. They asked the name of the place where they were. The Spanish thought that the Indians replied "Yucatan". But they probably said, in answer to some other question, "*Ciuthan*", which merely means "They say so" in Maya. (There are at least four alternative derivations of the word "Yucatan": first, that the word comes from "*U yu tan*", an expression of astonishment at hearing the barbarous language of the Spanish; second, that it is a corruption of "*Tectetan*", "I do not understand you"; third, that it indicates in Maya "mounds [*tlati*] of yucca"; and last, that it is a corruption of a word which indicates a common language.)[32] The Castilians christened the whole island, as they thought it to be, "Santa María de los Remedios", after the Virgin of that name in the cathedral of Seville.

Hernández, in the name of the King of Castile, took possession formally of the territory. He had a statement to that effect, either the famous *Requerimiento* or some similar document, read out in the presence of a clerk.[33] It is not recorded whether the Mayas listened. Certainly they could not have understood. The expedition then moved inland. The beauty of the forests was probably no surprise to those who had lived in Cuba and Santo Domingo. But the vegetation seemed even more lush than it was in Cuba. The adventurers would have been attended by innumerable birds – some singing, some hammering; and by some birds of prey.[34] There would have been continuous noise in the undergrowth: of deer, hares, weasels, moles, perhaps of foxes – as well as more rare beasts such as tapirs, Yucatec badgers and little skunks, which defended themselves against their enemies by loosing a foul urine whose smell nothing could tolerate.

Despite their welcome, the Castilians had no sooner entered the forest than they were attacked by a group of Maya soldiers in cotton armour, wielding all the customary weapons of the region: missiles and darts, arrows, stones by special slings.[35] It is unclear from where these warriors came, nor whether they wore the costumes of feathers which all the Indians of Central America and Mexico used; indeed loved. They seem, though, to have come from the very people who had just welcomed the Castilians, and who would shortly receive them again as guests. Fifteen of the expedition were wounded. Yet, whatever their origin, as had happened so often before, in conflicts in the Caribbean, the European swords, crossbows (they had fifteen of them) and arquebuses (of which they had ten) put the attackers to flight. Fifteen Indians were said to have been killed. It was here that the Indians of what is now Mexico first heard, saw, and smelled gunpowder, which caused them to think that "a thunderbolt had fallen from heaven".[36]

Moving on, Hernández de Córdoba soon found a fortified town on the banks of a river which they had already observed from the sea. Here were "houses with towers, magnificent temples, regular streets and market-places" – and presumably pyramids.[37] This was the first time that the Spaniards had seen stone buildings built by *naturales*. This place must have been close to the small modern town of Porvenir. The Spanish christened it Great Cairo, "El Gran Cairo", since, though none of them could have been to the capital of Egypt, all would have associated pyramids with that city. Perhaps some members of the expedition had read, or had heard of, *Legatio Babylonia*, the account by Peter Martyr of his embassy to Cairo in 1498. That book had been published by Cromberger in Seville in 1511. There were also a few so-called Levantine sailors (*marineros levantiscos*) on the expedition: these may have been Greek.[38]

The Castilians remained at "Great Cairo" several days as guests of the Mayas. They must have slept in long rooms in houses covered with thatch, the roofs dropping low against both rain and sun, the walls whitewashed, with no doors: an open loggia was usual. The beds were probably built on bundles of dry grass or sticks and covered with cotton mats.[39] The visitors no doubt observed with amazement a number of crosses which the Mayas worshipped as rain goddesses.[40] Could it be, they asked, that Christians had been to Yucatan before? They continued to be impressed too by the fact that these *naturales* wore clothes: even if the loincloths, hip-cloths and cloaks of the Mayas were, because of the heat, more exiguous than those which they later saw in Mexico.[41] The Spaniards would have observed the labour performed by women – in most communities they made tortillas twice a day: a pleasing similarity to life at home.[42]

There was probably at least one feast with the Mayas. This would have been an elaborate carouse, with the Indians becoming drunk on *pulque* in a way that the Castilians probably did not recognise for what it was. Hard liquor was rare in Spain at that time except in apothecaries' shops and certain monasteries, where a fine liqueur was already made.[43] Various sherries were, however, probably taken on some Castilian ships: for example, manzanilla.

The Mayas spent a great deal of energy on banquets. There would have been dancing to drums, trumpets, tortoise shells, whistles of cane or deer bones, conches and reed flutes.[44]

The Mayas, courteous as hosts, as was normal among them, soon tired of the Spanish presence. "Visitors who prolong their stay are never welcome," Peter Martyr once wisely commented.[45] The one hundred and ten Castilians, after all, ate a great deal: principally maize in various types of preparations, but also vegetable, game and fish stews, often with sauces of pepper. They probably drank cocoa. They also used a great deal of water, which was more difficult to come by in Yucatan than on the Caribbean islands.

Hernández de Córdoba ordered a re-embarkation. He took with him a number of small discs of gold and silver, some other gold and copper objects, several effigies of gods, and some pottery. Whether he and his men stole these things or whether they were given them is unclear. The objects themselves are lost. The gold ones would have been melted down in Spain in the generally accepted philistine style of the day. But the treasures from Yucatan were evidently elaborate enough to lead to a train of reactions which, in Cuba and then in Castile, led to a transformation in the history of the world. Actually, there was no gold in Yucatan. It was imported from lower down Central America as well as from Mexico, even if it was worked, elaborately, by Maya craftsmen.[46] One or two Mayas wore golden earrings or labrets. Golden objects were thrown into the famous *cenote*, the natural well at Chichen-Itza, to the benefit of later generations.

Hernández de Córdoba also took with him two cross-eyed Indians who were respectively nicknamed "Old Melchor" and "Little Julián". The plan was to make these prisoners into interpreters (it does not seem that they became Christians). The need for interpreters had always been recognised in the Caribbean: just as it had been in medieval Spain which had boasted of many great translators.[47] Hernández de Córdoba was acting thus in an entirely expected manner, though he could scarcely have understood that cross-eyes were considered a sign of beauty. This scheme did not work very well: "Melchor" was a fisherman, with a limited vocabulary even in Maya; "Julián" suffered depression at being away from home.

They sailed on west, close enough to the coast to see that "men and women came from all directions with their children to look at . . . the great size of the floating hulls." The Spaniards likewise saw, with amazement, temples on pyramids resembling fortresses which stood near the shore. They threw overboard the bodies of two soldiers who had died of wounds incurred in the engagement near El Gran Cairo: the first casualties of Spain in what is now Mexico.[48] Hernández de Córdoba decided to anchor next near what is now Campeche, about three hundred miles from Cape Catoche, and a hundred miles after the coast had turned south into the Gulf of Mexico. The Castilians saw what seemed a large town. Hernández de Córdoba decided to try to take on water. A detachment went ashore in boats, leaving the ships some way out.

They found a good pool of drinking water and filled their casks. While that was happening, fifty Indians came out from their town and invited the Castilians to look at it. They did so, in "good formation". They were then shown several temples in which some dead snakes had been draped before an altar clotted with blood. There were evil-looking idols. These temples were attended by priests, dressed in long white cotton robes, with long black matted hair "like a horse's braided mane".[49] They reeked of blood. Gathered around were many soldiers in cotton armour, as well as some women who seemed friendly. According to Peter Martyr they were offered a banquet, the menu being elaborate: turkey, quail, partridge and several sorts of duck.[50] But the Castilians were left with the impression that they had been led to the temples so that they could see that sacrifices had been recently made, to ensure a Maya victory over them. Around the temple, firewood had been piled up. The priests fumigated the Castilians with incense, perhaps because these conquistadors smelled heavily of sweat and dirt in a way which would have been inconceivable among the Mayas.[51] The priests showed by signs that the conquistadors should leave before they began to burn the firewood, or else they would be attacked. Hernández de Córdoba then sensibly did withdraw and re-embark, having called the town which they had just visited "Lázaro", since they had arrived there on St Lazarus' day. No one opposed him. But the expedition seems to have been seriously frightened.[52]

They continued, but encountered high winds. So, having travelled only a short distance in six days, they dropped anchor again about three miles offshore, close to another Maya settlement, near the modern town of Champoton.[53] Once again the Castilians were impressed to see houses of stone. They also saw well-cultivated plantations growing maize. They looked for water and were told by some Mayas that there was a spring the other side of a hill. The information seemed suspicious, for they saw Indians painted black and white. Since they were also carrying weapons, the Castilians rightly took this to be war paint. So the expedition took water from another place, but obtained too little of it. While they were doing so, a large force of Indians came up, not only painted in black and white, but with several wearing feathered crests. The Indians asked by signs where the Castilians came from. Did they by chance come from where the sun rose? The Castilians said that they did indeed. The Mayas' question may have been a roundabout way of asking whether they came from the Caribbean, where it might have become known that terrible events had occurred in the previous twenty years. The Indians went off and the Castilians most unwisely settled down for the night on shore: something which they were probably formally forbidden to do by their instructions.[54]

They did not sleep well. All night they heard the noise of preparation for battle, the beating of drums, the playing of flutes, the shouting of commands. The Maya chief, Mochcouoh, was an intelligent man. He realised that an immediate strike against these newcomers was essential: (it also suggested that he must have considered that the newcomers were barbarians, not gods).[55] When daylight came, the Indians were seen to have surrounded the Castilians on all sides. Their leaders adorned with feathers, and prefacing the battle with a deafening war cry made by beating their mouths with their hands, the Mayas immediately launched an attack. It was well directed. The Mayas used both stone-headed and copper-headed axes for agriculture, but they turned these to military use when necessary. This was a major technological contrast from what prevailed in the Caribbean.[56]

Within a very short time, over twenty conquistadors were dead. Most of the rest were wounded. Hernández de Córdoba himself was said to have received thirty-three wounds.[57] The damage was done by stones cast by slings, by arrows, or by the obsidian-edged swords which the Indians used in hand-to-hand fighting. This was the first Castilian defeat in a pitched battle in the New World.

Two of the expedition, Alonso Bote and an old Portuguese, were captured and the Castilians presumed that they were soon sacrificed.[58]

The battle probably arose from the Spanish seizure of the local water which, as earlier noticed, was in much less good supply in Yucatan than the Castilians supposed. The battle must have shown to the Spaniards the effectiveness of the Mayas' swords, the superiority of their bows and arrows to those of the Caribbean islanders, and the store which these people placed in psychological warfare waged with feathered costumes and war paint.

Hernández de Córdoba ordered a retreat to the boats – a manoeuvre which he accomplished with difficulty. The surviving members of the expedition nearly sank these craft through overcrowding. Some had to swim to safety.[59] After they had treated the wounded, Hernández, with half his expedition dead, decided to return to Cuba. He abandoned the third ship, the brigantine, which had for some time been in a bad way. Before leaving they again looked for fresh water but unfortunately filled their casks with what turned out to be salt water. They then made for Cuba via Florida, which the pilot Alaminos knew from having been there with Ponce de León – though it made the journey longer. There they at last found fresh water, but were attacked by Indians with long bows and arrows in canoes. Several of the Castilians were injured, including

Alaminos. A certain Berrio, one of the few men not to have been injured at Champoton, suffered the fate which the Spaniards came to know had at all costs to be avoided: capture. But twenty Indians were said to have been killed. From there, the two ships of this ill-fated expedition limped back to the Bay of Carenas, whose port is now the modern Havana. They had been away about two months.

Hernández de Córdoba struggled to Santiago to report to Diego Velázquez. Velázquez made clear that he was going to send another expedition to Yucatan under another commander. Hernández vowed to go to Spain to complain to the King. But death caught up with him first. He died of his wounds apparently at his house in Sancti Spiritus.[60] His surviving comrades also went to Santiago and, despite their losses, were enthusiastic. They were quick to tell Diego Velázquez that they "had discovered a new land and that it was very rich".[61] They had seen good stone buildings, fine cotton goods, signs of an agriculture superior to anything in the Caribbean, and people wearing clothes. The little gold objects which they brought with them showed such workmanship that it was soon said that "better lands have never been discovered".[62] Fr. González also brought back some pottery figurines. Some seemed to depict obscene images, by which was meant acts of sodomy. Thereafter many Castilians, nothing like so steeped in humanism as their leaders gave out, looked on the *naturales'* priests as all liable to be homosexuals. The comment was misjudged. The Florentine Codex is full of fierce condemnation of such people.[63]

Diego Velázquez questioned the cross-eyed prisoners, "Little Julián" and "Old Melchor", as to whether there were gold mines in their land. They replied in the affirmative, though there were actually none in Yucatan.[64] They also told Velázquez the astounding news that there were several Christians, perhaps six, in the power of certain chiefs of Yucatan.[65] Probably these Mayas thought that these answers would lead to the promotion of a new expedition, and so enable them to escape and return home.

Bernardino de Santa Clara, a leading *converso* settler of Cuba, wrote to his friend, Francisco de Los Cobos, secretary to the King, about the marvels, the riches, and the size of the population which had been discovered on this new island of Yucatan. He hoped that Los Cobos would help Velázquez to receive a licence to exploit the discovery.[66] So, therefore, everyone in Spain could have known the news soon. Most people there were, however, too preoccupied by the recent arrival of the new young King Charles and his Flemish courtiers to realise the significance of what was reported.

8

What I saw was so splendid

"I do not know what more to say of these people because what I saw was so
splendid that one could scarcely believe it."
Fr. Juan Díaz of the land near Vera Cruz, 1518

THE GOVERNOR OF Cuba, Diego Velázquez, instantly understood
the importance of the unsuccessful journey of Hernández de
Córdoba. He quickly sent one of his friends, Juan de Salcedo, back
to the Jeronymite fathers in Santo Domingo. Salcedo told the friars that
Velázquez had dispatched a fleet to Yucatan and that he had discovered a
rich land; but that the natives had not let his people into the interior. The
Castilians were, therefore, unable to penetrate the secret of it. The
naturales had even fought. The Castilians had to re-embark, though not
before they had seen that the people customarily carried many rich things
of gold. So Velázquez asked the priors to extend their permission to him
to explore the coasts where Hernández de Córdoba had been, and to
trade in gold and pearls. Such an undertaking, he insisted, would lead to a
valuable share of the profits being available for the Crown: presumably,
as was usual in the circumstances, a fifth.[1]

Velázquez also sent another friend, Gonzalo de Guzmán, to Spain
to ask of the Crown a special concession which would enable him to
benefit from any new discoveries which he would make. He was to
ask that the title *adelantado*, or proconsul, be given to Velázquez in
respect of Yucatan. Guzmán, who had become treasurer of Cuba,
was no doubt, like many conquistadors, an impoverished member of a
great cousinhood – in his case, that of Guzmán, Dukes of Medina
Sidonia, the family which disputed the leadership of Seville with the
Ponces de León. No doubt he was an effective manager of Velázquez's
interests at court. Just in case he might be, however, inadequate, the
Governor also sent his personal chaplain, Fr. Benito Martín, to Spain
to assist him.[2]

The double request for approval, one to Santo Domingo, the other to
Spain, shows Velázquez's political shrewdness. He no doubt guessed

97

that, after the death of Cardinal Ximénez de Cisneros, the days of the friars' power would soon come to an end.

A Mexican historian about fifty years later argued that Velázquez had a great desire to "conquer and populate these new territories because he wished first to spread our Holy faith; and, second, to gain honour and wealth".[3] As to the first aim, there is no evidence for it. Velázquez had cheerfully fought his way through Hispaniola in his late twenties and through Cuba in his forties without much consideration of the *naturales*. He was not a sadist but, if the Indians had souls, it meant little to him.

Yet the Governor was ambitious. He wanted, in particular, to break free from the formal jurisdiction of Diego Colón. Bartolomé Colón, the first Admiral's brother, had been for a time *adelantado* in Hispaniola. Ponce de León had been so in Florida. If he, Velázquez, were to gain that title in respect of Yucatan, it would give him the authority which he coveted. It was a title invented in the middle ages for a commander allocated political control of the territory which he had conquered. There had also been *adelantados* for Jewish populations. The word had come to be associated almost as a title with certain families. For example, the Fajardos had ruled Murcia as *adelantados* with, to the court, a perturbing independence. Velázquez thought that such a nomination would crown his career.

Though, like most conquistadors, Velázquez coveted fame, riches and power, he wanted those palms without dust. He had no wish to go himself to these new islands in the west. He wanted to send others to bring back the prizes for him. To ensure this he was even prepared for deceit. Thus he told the pious fathers in Santo Domingo that it had been he who had financed the voyage of Hernández de Córdoba, even if he may have had only a quarter share in the expedition.[4]

The reply from the priors naturally came quicker than that from the King. Advised by allies of Velázquez such as Miguel de Pasamonte, they gave their approval. Without waiting for the answer from Castile, Velázquez began to make plans for a second expedition to Yucatan. On this occasion, he himself financed the four ships, while the captains contributed the provisions. As usual in Caribbean expeditions, cassava bread and salt pork were the chief stores. A suitable quantity of beads, scissors, and looking glasses were also taken for exchange with the *naturales*.

The new captain appointed by Velázquez was his nephew, Juan de Grijalva, who, like the Governor himself, came from Cuéllar.[5] He was a "charming young man, beautiful to look at and very well mannered", without a beard,[6] "a person inclined to virtue, obedience and good manners, and very obedient to his superiors". He was about twenty-eight when he accepted the command. He had gone quite young to Santo Domingo, in 1508. Then he accompanied Velázquez to Cuba in 1511.

Velázquez had given him an *encomienda* with thirty-four Indians.[7] In 1517 he apparently took part in a disgraceful slaving enterprise to Trinidad under the Basque shipmaster, Juan Bono de Quejo.[8]

Grijalva took a fleet of four ships: two *naos*, both confusingly called *San Sebastián*; a caravel called *La Trinidad*; and a brigantine, the *Santiago*. The force was about two hundred men.[9] The pilots included those who had travelled with Hernández de Córdoba: namely, the famous Alaminos, Juan Álvarez the lame, and Pedro Camacho from Triana. The pilot on the brigantine was Pedro Arnés de Sopuerta. Grijalva, like Hernández, had a chaplain: Fr. Juan Díaz, a thirty-eight-year-old Sevillano. The royal inspector (*veedor*) of the expedition, Francisco de Peñalosa, was a Segoviano, while the treasurer, Antonio de Villafaña, came from Zamora.[10] Grijalva took with him as interpreter the depressed cross-eyed Yucatec, "Julián", captured the previous year by Hernández de Córdoba. But he left behind his silent colleague "Melchor" in Cuba.

The captains under Grijalva were Castilian gentlemen such as he was himself, of reasonable family but no money: Pedro de Alvarado, Francisco de Montejo, and Alonso de Ávila. The first came from Badajoz; Montejo was a native of Salamanca; while Ávila was from Ciudad Real. All were hidalgos, that is, minor members of the nobility, with coats of arms. Like Grijalva himself, these were all men who, had it not been for the opportunity offered by the Indies, would probably have lingered about the court, hoping to catch the eye of more prosperous cousins or even of the King himself. They might also have been implicated in the innumerable brawls for which their countryside in the previous generation had become remarkable. Earlier they would, given their temperaments, have no doubt sought their fortunes in the constant frontier wars which had for so long been available as a field of combat to ambitious men of knightly families in Castile.

Alvarado, the most famous of these men, was in his middle thirties, and was well proportioned, cheerful, winning, good-mannered and handsome. He was also brave, impulsive, and cruel. He appeared always to be smiling. He was a good if indiscreet talker. He liked rich clothes and wore both a gold chain round his neck and rings on his fingers. He was a fine horseman. In his youth, he had been known for escapades: he had walked across a dangerous stretch of scaffolding over one of the highest windows of the Giralda in Seville.[11] He came from a family which had distinguished itself as *comendadores* of the Order of Santiago, to which both his uncle Diego and his grandfather had belonged, and of which indeed his uncle had once been briefly, if in irregular circumstances, grand master. He had himself been ironically known in both Santo Domingo and Cuba as "*el comendador*", from the fact that he often wore his uncle's white cloak with the red cross – a garment to which he had (as yet) no right.[12] Montejo on the other hand seemed more a man of business than one of war, yet he was extravagant, open-handed, cheerful, and liked merriment, being also an excellent horseman.[13] This first journey to the territory of the Mayas must have made a great impression on him, for he was the future conqueror of Yucatan. Like most conquistadors he had lived for some time in Seville, where he had an illegitimate son by a well-born lady, Ana de León, daughter of a well-known lawyer, Licenciado Pedro de León. That son was already in Cuba and would one day become lieutenant to his father. Montejo had been in Panama with Pedrarias, and taken part in that expedition against the Cenú where the geographer Fernández de Enciso had had such a sophisticated exchange with the chiefs. He is said to have invested heavily in the expedition of Grijalva.[14] Finally among these captains, Alonso de Ávila was brave and not only articulate but frank to the point of indiscretion, and "somewhat given to turbulence". He was definitely a man born to command rather than to obey but, when given command, could seem both jealous and quarrelsome.[15] All three captains were in their middle thirties, a little older, that is, than their "general", Grijalva. The four leaders supplied most of the fleet's supplies from their own properties.[16]

One innovation was the equipment of Grijalva's ships with one or two pieces of artillery. These were probably culverins, guns able to fire a twenty-pound ball about four hundred yards horizontally. These weapons had had a decisive effect in the Spanish wars against Granada. The heavy bombardments knocked down big walls. Lighter guns prevented the defenders from repairing them. No doubt Grijalva insisted on taking them after hearing what had happened to Hernández de Córdoba, who had had no such weapons. Grijalva had also about twenty arquebusiers. He seems to have taken a few dogs but no horses. There were considerable difficulties in carrying horses on board these small ships, and Grijalva had no plan to establish a colony in any new territory which he might find.

Velázquez's instructions to Grijalva have not survived. Probably the new captain was told simply "to trade and leave in peace the people amongst whom he went".[17] He may not have received any instructions as to whether or no to make settlements. Bernal Díaz wrote, however, that he was led to assume that, if it seemed advisable to form a settlement, he should do so.[18] Perhaps Velázquez expected him to go further than, or even to ignore, his instructions, if it seemed right to do so, thereby founding a place where a springboard might be established for the Governor's own later, grander expedition.

The little fleet set off from Santiago at the end of January 1518.[19] They first travelled, as Hernández de Córdoba had done, along the north coast of Cuba, stopping at Boyucar in what is now the Bay of Matanzas to pick up men and sailors. For reasons of hygiene all the soldiers' hair was cut short, in Venetian style: the first time that such an order had been given. Previously the Spanish had worn pigtails.[20]

Grijalva and his men moved on to Cape San Antonio. By that time they had lost their brigantine. They are said to have found a note in a tree, which said that the crew had turned back because they had run out of food. But another, similar, ship, the *Santa María de los Remedios*, joined them, so that the expedition still constituted four ships in all.[21]

They left Cuban waters at the end of April 1518 and, as expected sighted land after a week. This was the island of Cozumel, fifteen miles off the coast of Yucatan. The name derived from "*Ah-Cuzamil-Peten*", "Swallow Island" in the Maya tongue. It is thirty miles long by twelve miles at its broadest point. The population may have been 2,000 to 3,000 in 1518.[22] The island was without streams: water came from wells. It was not a place at which Hernández de Córdoba had touched. It was 3 May, the day of Santa Cruz. So Grijalva gave the island that name.[23]

Cozumel was an important centre of pilgrimage. For there was the shrine to Ix Chel, lady of the rainbow, patroness of medicine, a goddess of weaving, procreation and illicit love. To some people she also stood for the moon. Ix Chel was especially venerated by the Chontal Maya, whose main centre at this time was the province of Acalan, on the west of Yucatan. Its royal family came from Cozumel. Ix Chel was represented by a hollow idol of burned clay, from which, as at Delphi and elsewhere in Greece, a priest would customarily answer those who asked questions. The goddess was offered incense, bread, and fruit, as well as the blood of quail, dogs and, sometimes, men.[24]

When the Spanish arrived offshore they could see houses and pyramids such as had been seen by Hernández de Córdoba in Yucatan. It seemed "a very towered land".[25] A delightful scent was wafted by a soft breeze from the island to the fleet. This came from the large number of rockroses whose white flowers produce an aromatic resin. The expedition was then probably close to the town now called San Miguel. Grijalva named it "San Juan ante Porte Latinum", since it was 6 May, that saint's day. (That echo of Rome did not, however, survive.) Two canoes came out, each carrying three Mayas. Keeping their distance, they indicated that their chief would appear the next day: which he did. The chief came in one of the same canoes. He stepped on board Grijalva's vessel. Making use of the interpreter Julián in a no doubt primitive way, he invited Grijalva to land. Grijalva presented to the chief some Spanish shirts and "some good wine from Guadalcanal", a *pueblo* high up in the Sierra Morena on the borders of Extremadura and Andalucía. The historian Oviedo said that everywhere in the Indies "once they have tried this, the people desire it more than anything else. They drink it till they fall on their backs if they are given enough."[26] Grijalva asked what had

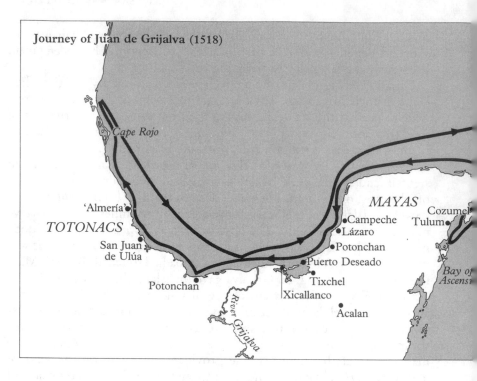

Journey of Juan de Grijalva (1518)

Cape Rojo

'Almería'
TOTONACS
San Juan
de Ulúa

Potonchan

River Grijalva

MAYAS
Campeche
Lázaro
Potonchan
Puerto Deseado
Tixchel
Xicallanco
Acalan

Cozumel
Tulum

Bay of
Ascensi

happened to the two men left behind by Hernández de Cordoba (Bote and the old Portuguese). The Mayas said that one of them was still alive, the other dead. But nothing more seems to have been done for them.

Next day, after some further sailing, Grijalva landed with a hundred men on another point of Cozumel, where they had seen a high white tower, and whence they had heard the beating of drums. Here were several stone houses and temples with skilfully decorated towers on pyramids. The streets were paved with stone, in a concave style, a gutter in the middle. Much impressed, Fr. Juan Díaz added that the houses were such that "they might have been built by the Spaniards".[27] That priest was also interested in the beehives – much as in Spain, he reported, if smaller. The conquistadors also saw more of the mysterious crosses, "ten palms high", used as an object of devotion to the god of rain, which had so excited Hernández de Córdoba's men.[28]

The Spaniards expected that they would be attacked but, when they reached the tower, they found no one. The population had fled into the interior of the island. The only people left behind were two old men to whom Grijalva spoke, not very successfully, through Julián. They also found a woman from Jamaica who had been wrecked on the island with another ten Jamaican Indians. All save her had been sacrificed to Ix Chel.[29] She surely had passed on to the Mayas something of what she had observed among the Castilians in the Caribbean.

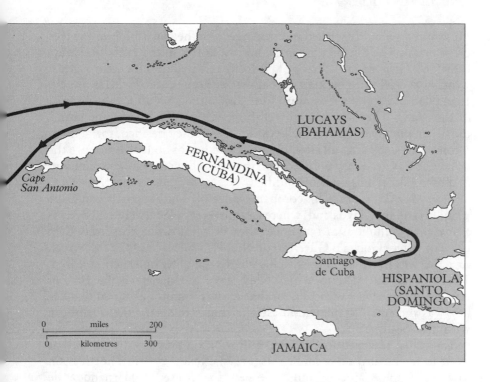

Grijalva, with his standard-bearer (*alférez*), Vázquez de Tapia, a gentleman from Oropesa, and the chaplain Juan Díaz, climbed the eighteen steps of a white pyramid.[30] It was between a hundred and forty and a hundred and eighty feet in circumference. At the top, they found, as usual in Mexico and Yucatan, a platform on which stood another small temple, in which were bones and idols.[31] This was the main centre of the cult of Ix Chel. On top of it Vázquez de Tapia raised the flag of Spain: perhaps the famous *Tanto Monta*, specially designed by the linguist Nebrija, with its yoke and arrows. The lions and the castles of that emblem waved bravely. The notary, Diego de Godoy, a man from Pinto near Toledo, then read out the famous *Requerimiento*, though there did not seem to be anyone to hear it.[32] A copy of it was attached to the side of the tower.

When this ceremony was completed, Grijalva observed three Maya leaders approaching. One of them was old and had had his toes cut off: because, it later transpired, of a narrow escape from a shark.[33] He carried a pot of liquid balsam. This was not, however, for Grijalva, nor even for the King of Castile, but for the gods of Cozumel. While offering it up, the old man sang in a high voice. He took no notice of the Castilians. Grijalva ordered Fr. Díaz to hold a mass. The Indians, in no way discomfited by hearing a Catholic service in those precincts, now did offer presents: turkeys, honey, and maize. Grijalva said that he did not need such things.

He wanted gold. He wished to exchange what he had with him for that great metal. The Mayas were noncommittal. But in the friendliest way, they took Grijalva and a dozen of his followers to dine with them – a feast which was celebrated beside a well in a stone house roofed with straw. Fr. Juan Díaz and about ten conquistadors, meantime, set off for the interior of the island. They saw several well-built villages, and also some farms, mostly maintained for keeping bees. The bees, they decided, formed not a comb but small sacs, all close together and full of honey. To secure the honey, it was necessary only to open the sacs, allow the liquid to run out, and then take it away when solidified.[34]

On 7 May Grijalva and his company sailed off south towards that Cape Trujillo (and that Bay Island) where Alaminos recalled that he had been as a boy with Columbus in 1502. Had they only known it, they were then close to where Gonzalo Guerrero of Niebla, a survivor of the shipwreck of 1510, was living happily with his chief's daughter and their children. They found an inlet, to which they gave the name of the Bay of Ascension, since it was the day of that feast. Alaminos assumed that the bay was the entry to the famous strait which connected the Caribbean with the "Southern Sea".

They then returned to Cozumel and took on board water, as well as some food and also a few edible rats (utías). Next they sailed north again towards Cape Catoche, and followed the route of Hernández de Córdoba along the east coast of northern Yucatan. On the way, they saw several places with tall towers and houses built of stone, as well as huts with palm leaves as roofs. One of these places, perhaps it was Tulum, seemed to Fr. Díaz, with its buildings on pillars, "as big as the city of Seville".[35] At that time Tulum was a centre of the coastal trade and probably did bustle with activity. On another headland there was a "very beautiful tower believed to be inhabited by women without men . . . probably of the Amazon family".[36]

The next spot at which Grijalva anchored was a little beyond Campeche near Champoton: the place which Hernández had named Lázaro. On 26 May, most of the Castilians landed in boats, with three cannon and several arquebuses. They were well received, invited to enter the town, and then asked to leave. The Castilians and the Mayas talked through the services of Julián the interpreter. Grijalva as usual requested gold. The Mayas said that they had none. They repeated their demand to their visitors to leave. They knew, of course, of the battle of the previous year a little way along the coast, and must have felt confident of victory should there be fighting. Grijalva asked for water. He was shown wells. Having filled his casks, he decided to spend the night there. The Mayas brought Grijalva a cooked turkey, some maize and some vegetables. The captain again demanded gold. This time he was brought a mask of gilded wood and two gold plates. The Mayas repeated their request to him to leave. They said that they did not want him to take any more water. But the Castilians decided to sleep where they were. Three thousand suspicious *naturales* were not far away. The night was disturbed by the piercing noise of drums and conch trumpets. It must have seemed to those of the expedition who had been with Hernández de Córdoba that events were taking an alarmingly familiar turn. Several of the Castilians would have preferred to face the enemy there and then. But Grijalva refused to attack; and "all the men were desperate because Grijalva would not let them fight". Several Indians, meantime, visited the Spanish camp that night. Some even danced to a flute played by one of Grijalva's men. The combination of Indian friendliness and menace was unnerving.[37]

When day came, the Indians were seen to be painted in the black and white colours of war. A Maya chief placed a torch of incense between his men and the Castilians, and said, as translated by Julián: "Behold this torch which we will light and place between our armies. If you do not make haste and retreat before the torch is burned, you will die. We do not want you as guests." This action, of course, was similar to what had occurred with Hernández de Córdoba. The Castilians did not withdraw. A battle was joined.

Grijalva conducted himself more intelligently than his predecessor had done, using psychological methods as well as superior technology to sustain his position. Thus he placed cannon in one of the towers of a temple, by which previously the Spaniards had been so impressed. The Mayas were frightened by the noise of these guns. Three of them were killed by either fire or crossbows. One version of Fr. Díaz's memoir reported that several Indians were stabbed and later buried alive.[38] The Castilians, beset suddenly by locusts, mistook them for arrows.[39] The Mayas withdrew at finding matters difficult, having killed at least one expeditionary, Juan de Guetaría, a Basque captain of some importance. About forty Castilians, including Grijalva himself, were wounded: he was said to have lost one or two teeth.[40] Next day another squadron of natives approached. Grijalva, speaking to them through his interpreter, said that he did not wish for war, nor even gold, only wood and water. The Maya gave him another mask of gilded wood. The majority of the Castilians seem to have wanted to stay and avenge Guetaría. But Grijalva wisely insisted on embarking. He sailed that night. Just before he did so, a Maya came to say that, if Grijalva desired it, he could guide them to a place where there were people similar to themselves, with large ships, good swords and strong shields. The chief difference between them and the Castilians was that the former had enormous ears. Much to the annoyance of his men, Grijalva dismissed this offer. He was one of the few conquistadors who was not influenced by such tales. The ease with which the Mayas impressed the Castilians with these tales is explained by the fact that they themselves had similar myths: there was apparently even in their legends a territory inhabited by what sound like Amazons: a place in the west "where it is said there only lived women".[41]

The fleet now sailed on beyond the point where Hernández had turned back. But it was not quite new land to everyone, since the pilot Alaminos had been along that way with Ponce de León in 1513: how far he remembered it is unclear.

Their next stop was at a good port on the narrow opening to a large lagoon. This was where Alaminos supposed a channel would lead back to the Bay of Ascension. They in consequence christened the water "la Laguna de Términos".[42]

Grijalva allowed his men to stay nearly two weeks in this haven, careening one of the ships, and eating the delicious fish of the lagoon. They called the place "Puerto Deseado", the Desired Port, because they had not previously found a good port at all.[43] It was in the position of what is now Puerto Real. The area was deserted. But they saw the ruins of Tixchel, a former outpost of the Acalan people.[44] They could also see in the distance the commercial capital of the area, Xicallanco, on the site of the modern Cerrillo, a place of Chontal Maya-speaking people, if ruled by Mexican merchants.[45] As before, they observed temples. They saw what they thought were fishermen with golden fishhooks. Presumably they were copper, though sometimes gold ones were known in Colombia and Ecuador.[46] They would have seen some of the herons for which the lagoon was famous. Here they by mistake left behind, among the rabbits of Tabasco, a mastiff bitch (reunited with her European masters the following year).[47] They also seized, and baptised, four Indians to act as interpreters since Julián could not understand Chontal. One of these new captives was named "Pedro Barba" after his Spanish godfather, one of Grijalva's captains.

About 8 June, the Spaniards moved on to the mouth of the river Tabasco which they rechristened the Grijalva – a name which it retains. There was a good harbour there. The current of the river carried drinkable water some miles out to sea. Grijalva and most of his expedition went up the river in small boats. Here again they saw a large number of Indians, armed, several carrying gilded shields. These were Chontal Mayas, probably from Acalan, in the foothills of the mountains of Chiapas. Some of them came out in a canoe, and asked Grijalva what he wanted. The answer was that he wanted to trade. He gave them some strings of his popular green beads, as well as some mirrors. Shortly afterwards, a chief came aboard Grijalva's flagship. He paid homage to that captain by having him dressed in a breastplate and bracelets of gold, as well as with a golden crown of delicate leaves, and by giving him shoes of a kind of lace, also ornamented in gold. Grijalva, in polite reply, ordered the chief to be dressed in Spanish clothes: a green velvet doublet, pink stockings, espadrilles, and a velvet cap. The native chief said that he wanted to take the name of Grijalva. Grijalva expressed enthusiasm for the suggestion. He added that he and his men desired to be friends, and would exchange some of his ornaments for more of the *naturales'* gold. Yet no more of this was forthcoming. There were many other presents given.[48] There was a banquet and more promises of trading. Several of Grijalva's friends wanted "to enter the territory" and look for gold on their own, but the captain prevented it. That was sensible. The region was not a gold-producing one. The gold possessed by these Mayas had been traded, not mined. The chief did offer to exchange a captive (perhaps Pedro Barba) for his weight in gold. Grijalva refused to wait, understandably fearing a trick (there can be no other explanation).[49]

Grijalva talked to the Indians through a double translation. He spoke to Julián, who by now knew some Spanish and who in turn spoke to "Pedro Barba", who talked both Yucatec and Chontal Maya.

Grijalva now began to sail on north-westwards. In the next few days his expedition stopped at several places: at the mouth of the river Tonalá, and at the site of what is now Coatzacoalcos. Local Indians offered more jewels and ornaments. At Coatzacoalcos, the local chief gave a dinner for Grijalva and established his followers in attractive cabins with green branches overhead. Grijalva was offered a twelve-year-old boy as a slave. Once again he refused this present.

This region, known as Tabasco, was prosperous from the local production of cacao, prized both in itself as providing a chocolate drink, and for the beans which were the currency of the Mexican empire. The region also served as a source of tanned jaguar skins, carved tortoise shells, and the green stone (*chalchihuite*) which was so much appreciated in Mexico. These things were produced in the foothills of the mountains of Chiapas and brought down to the coast on the river Usamacinta. In return, the Mexica offered gold, copper, dyed rabbit skins, obsidian and slaves: the latter being useful in a place which enjoyed continuous cultivation.

The journey continued towards the site of what has since become Veracruz. Grijalva had some difficulties with one of his captains, Pedro de Alvarado, who annoyed him by making a long detour of his own up a beautiful river, the Papaloapan (which was subsequently called the Alvarado after him).

The expedition continued along the Mexican coast. Francisco de Montejo, the aristocratic Salamantine, sailed close to the shore in a brigantine. The others kept a little further out to sea. All the way along this stretch of the continent were numerous Indian habitations. While the Castilians continued to be surprised by the sight of temples, the Indians were again astonished by that of ships.

About 17 June, Grijalva reached an island a mile and a half long by three-quarters of a mile broad, a short way from the coast at Veracruz.

When they went ashore, they saw two stone temples on pyramids. On climbing one of these, they found at the top a marble puma. A basin stood before it. In this there was blood, which they judged (on what evidence is obscure) had been there for eight days. There was an idol, probably of the mischievous god Tezcatlipoca. Before this effigy, they found cloths, a fig tree, four dead Indians (two being children), and a number of skulls and bones. There was much dried blood on the walls. The Castilians met a local Indian to explain the meaning of these things. He nearly died from fear on the way to his meeting with Grijalva, but was able to explain the technique of human sacrifice.[50]

This was the first full description given to the Castilians of the kind of offerings practised by the Mexica and their dependants. It made a sombre impression. They therefore called the place the Island of Sacrifices. Among the other buildings on the island was an arch which they thought as impressive as the Roman one at Mérida in Spain.[51] Archaeological evidence suggests that the two temples on the island were to Quetzalcoatl and Tezcatlipoca respectively.

The Castilians from their boats next day saw two white banners being waved on the mainland. So Grijalva sent Montejo to the shore in a small boat with about forty men, including the arquebusiers and crossbow-men, as well as an interpreter (either Julián or Pedro Barba), to discover what they wanted.[52] On arriving, the Indians gave them many pretty coloured cloaks. Having accepted these, Montejo naturally asked them if they had gold. They said that they would bring some in the evening. With that, Montejo returned to the ships. In the evening, some Indians came out to the fleet in a canoe. They merely brought more cloaks. Their leader said that they would bring gold another day.

Next day the Indians reappeared on the sand dunes opposite the Island of Sacrifices, again waving white banners. They called to Grijalva, who this time landed himself with a few of his captains. He was warmly received by a local chief and his son, being asked to sit in a hut with newly cut branches as its roof.[53] Grijalva was offered sweet-smelling incense, and tortillas to eat. He was also presented with some cotton cloaks of differing colours. Grijalva was now outside an Indian town called Chalchicueyecan situated near the modern port of Veracruz. It was said to have had five hundred houses. One report, improbably, says that it had a wall round it.[54] In the distance, Grijalva could see the snow-capped peak of Mt. Orizaba.

These *naturales* treated the Spanish with extravagant respect. This was a contrast with the manner with which they had been welcomed by the Mayas, who in Yucatan had seen the Spaniards as a potentially dangerous new breed of conquerors (perhaps from having learned something about Spanish activity in the Caribbean). These new people were Totonacs, who were among the Mexica's most reluctant tributaries.

The Totonacs had come down to the coast from the mountains in the north of the modern state of Puebla about the beginning of the Christian era. One tradition was that they had built the temples of the sun and moon at Teotihuacan. There is a possibility that they were the people who inspired an elaborate culture in the region of Veracruz, its greatest achievement being the centre of ceremonial games at El Tajín. The people of Veracruz, whether Totonac or not, about AD 700 had made fine terracotta heads, for both burials and shrines. The sculpture of Veracruz, both in moulded terracotta and in stone, probably influenced the Mexica. The Totonacs also produced vanilla (if not on the scale that they did later). This was already used to flavour chocolate. They had numerous curious myths; among them, the belief that in the past fish had been men.[55]

The Totonacs formed a dozen or so small principalities, most of which had been conquered in the mid-fifteenth century, first by the Texcocans, then by Montezuma I. Some of these polities, however, survived independently until the time of the conqueror Ahuitzotl. Then, as was usual with their conquests, the Mexica did not overthrow the local principalities: they exacted tribute.

In this instance, the Mexica took substantial deliveries of the fine cotton clothing for which the region was known: twice a year, the Totonacs had to send 400 women's blouses and skirts; 400 small cloaks, with black and white borders; 400 half-quilted cloaks; 400 large cloaks four *brazas* big (a *braza* being six feet); 400 white cloaks, also four *brazas* big; 160 "very rich cloaks for lords"; and 1,200 black and white striped cloaks. Once a year, the province had to deliver two warrior's costumes with shields, one necklace of green stones, 400 quetzal feathers, two lip plugs of crystal with blue and gold mounts, twenty light amber lip plugs mounted on gold, one hair ornament of quetzal feathers and 480 pounds of cacao beans (in twenty "loads").[56] Some of these things had to be obtained by trade from elsewhere. Beautiful local birds, the cotinga, the roseate spoonbill, and the Mexican trogon, were also caught and their feathers extracted for the benefit of the overlords. The dimension of these burdens explains the warmth of the Totonacs' welcome to Grijalva. Their resentment may have been the greater because they considered the Mexica new rich people in an ancient environment. The Mexica on the other hand looked on the Totonacs as the embodiment of an easy life, where women wore well-woven clothes with flair, and where sexual freedom was greater than it was in the austere highlands.[57]

There were several garrisons of Mexicans in the region: at Actopan, Nauhtla and Tizpantzinco just inland to the north, and at Cuetlaxtlan in the south. The tribute from the Totonacs was in some cases sent to those garrisons and then taken back to Tenochtitlan; in other instances it was delivered direct to the Mexican capital. One place, Tlacotlalpan, on the river Papaloapan, in the next-door province of Tochtepec, had a lord appointed by the Emperor in Tenochtitlan. This was unusual in the Mexican empire whose rulers, as we have seen, preferred indirect to direct rule.

The Totonacs were cultivated people. They were known for their coloured embroideries. They were tall, and usually had good skins, with long heads. They were good dancers. They used fans against the heat, often looked at themselves in mirrors, and wore beautiful sandals. They hung elaborate decorations on their lips, their noses and their ears – with holes through those orifices big enough for large jewels to pass through. The labrets of the Totonacs in particular disgusted the Spanish: sometimes they were blue and sometimes gold, but they always had the alarming effect of dragging the lower lip down so that the teeth showed. Every day before work, the Totonacs burned incense, and sometimes cut their tongues or ears in order to obtain blood to sprinkle in the main temples, and also on food before it was eaten. Human sacrifices were celebrated, but apparently exclusively of prisoners taken in war.[58]

This region was hot, unhealthy but fertile. The north was dry and the south, below the modern Veracruz, wet. A wave of immigration to this coastal territory arrived during the famines in central Mexico in the early years of the sixteenth century.[59] Thus some of those Indians seen here by the Castilians may not have been long in the region.

The Totonacs had their own "barbarous" language, as the Mexica thought it. But some spoke Nahuatl. Their distinguishing mark was the special importance which they gave to a dance of "*voladores*" whereby men would climb to the top of a high pole, dance there on a platform, and then swing upside down in fifty-two expanding circles (fifty-two to recall the years in a Mexican "century"), their legs attached by a rope tied to the top of the pole. The main city of the Totonacs was Cempoallan, twenty miles from where Grijalva had landed. It had a population of several thousand gathered around a ceremonial centre.[60]

The Castilians stayed ten days at Chalchicueyecan: or rather off it, since they slept on their ships. Every day they landed and the Indians provided new branches to keep the heat from them. The chief showed the visitors "such affection that it was a marvellous thing".[61] The Castilians nicknamed him "Ovando" – because he looked like that great governor. He and his son talked easily to the newcomers as if they had known them for years, and as if the problem of translation did not exist. The Totonacs were in no way shy. Grijalva kept saying that he needed gold. The Totonacs therefore brought some in bars. Grijalva said that he wanted more than that. The next day they brought him a pretty gold mask, a figure shaped as a man, with a smaller mask of gold, and even something like a tiara – "like that of the Pope, in gold" – as well as other golden objects.[62] Grijalva then said that he really wanted gold for melting down. The Totonacs said that they would get some gold dust from the hills where they were accustomed to send people during the day. They would come back at night with a pipe of it the same size as a finger. They also described their methods of finding gold in the streams, and how they turned it into bars or plate.

During all this time the relations between the Castilians and the Totonacs seem to have been excellent. Even ordinary soldiers were constantly offered presents by their hosts. Food was delivered every day. Tobacco was smoked: no doubt some of the Castilians had already participated in that ritual in Cuba. The visitors were also made aware of the importance of the "great city of Mexico";[63] as of the resentment felt by the coastal people for it. It was now that the *tlillancalqui*, Montezuma's emissary, made contact with Grijalva in the way mentioned in Chapter 4. Perhaps some of Montezuma's anxiety at hearing of the Castilian arrival was due to the news of the good relations that the visitors had established with his tributaries.

The Franciscan monk, Fr. Toribio de Benavente, known as Motolinía, who reached this territory in 1524, would in the 1530s write how at the beginning the Castilians inspired "wonder and admiration. To see a people arriving by water, which was something which they had never seen nor heard of happening, in a costume so strange, being so intrepid and so animated, and so few of them to enter this territory . . . with such authority and daring, as if all the natives were their vassals . . . they called the Castilians *teteuh*, which is to say gods, and the Castilians, corrupting the word, said *teules*."[64]

The effect was twofold. If the Totonacs admired the Castilians (partly for strategic reasons, due to their hope of help against the Mexica), the Castilians used superlatives in writing home: "We believe this land to be the richest in the world in stones of great value," wrote Fr. Díaz.[65] During these days of conversation, Grijalva was evidently told that the Mexica had an empire of which the place where they were talking was part; and that they had "a political life", with "laws, ordinances and courts for the administration of justice".[66] He was given to understand that the Mexica were ingenious, as shown by their golden vases and elaborate cotton cloaks. He was even also told, it seems, that they worshipped before a large marble cross, on the top of which stood a crown of gold. On that, he was apparently assured, there had once died one who was more lucid and shining than the sun itself. This story was obviously an invention, probably deriving from the desire to please of the interpreter.[67] Grijalva seems too to have formed the impression that the Totonacs were circumcised – a mistake caused by a failure to realise that all the priests of the region drew blood from their penises as a form of self-mortification and as an offering. "Probably there were Jews and Moors nearby," Fr. Díaz commented sententiously.[68]

Now, as well as being well received, the Spaniards could see how rich the soil was where they had landed. Several of them, therefore, thought that it would be sensible to establish a colony there. There was a long conversation between the captains. Grijalva was the commander of the expedition. But it was essential for someone in his position to discuss critical matters with his followers. After all, they had committed themselves unpaid, as free men, to work under him in the hope of eventual profit. Grijalva was against the idea of colonisation.[69] He thought that he had too few men, for thirteen had died of wounds received at Champoton. His supply of cassava bread (on which the Castilians had come to rely, even if they were given maize tortillas by the Indians) was going mouldy. The mosquitoes caused a lot of trouble. Grijalva said that Diego Velázquez had not given him permission to found a settlement. Two other captains, Alvarado and Alonso de Ávila, argued that, though that was true, it was also the case that he had not forbidden him to do so. Grijalva's chaplain, Fr. Juan Díaz, complained that the captain merely lacked the sense of adventure to try and take over the territory.[70]

All the same Grijalva read out the *Requerimiento* to the people of Chalchicueyecan, and claimed the land in the name of Queen Juana and King Charles of Castile.[71] (A new *Requerimiento* was necessary because the Castilians now believed themselves to be on the territory of a continent, not an island such as "Yucatan": a judgement which they arrived at from observing the size of the rivers and the height of the distant mountains, as well as the variety and richness of the languages.) They named the place where they had landed "San Juan de Ulúa": "San Juan" because the day of the naming was that of St John, 24 June: "Ulúa", because of a confusion of language frequent at that time: when the Spaniards asked the Indians where they were, the reply was "Culhúa", one of the names used by the Mexica. They misheard.[72] At that time, the Castilians had no interpreters since neither Julián nor Pedro Barba knew Nahuatl, while a Nahuatl-speaking Indian boy, "Francisco", who had been captured along the coast to translate, had as yet learned little Spanish.

Before the expedition set off again, Grijalva decided to send Alvarado back to Cuba to show to his uncle Velázquez some of the things which he had obtained and to take home some of the sick sailors. Alvarado, though keen on adventure, accepted – allegedly because (so he said) he was himself not very well; second, because he was in love with an Indian girl in Cuba;[73] and third, probably most important, because he chafed under the unenterprising leadership of Grijalva.

Alvarado returned to Cuba with most of the gold which Grijalva had been given – between 16,000 and 20,000 pesos' worth of it – and many other objects of beautiful workmanship but which seemed then "of little intrinsic value";[74] by which the Spaniards meant that, if they were melted down, they would be worth little. Grijalva wrote a letter to his uncle describing his voyage. Other captains did the same to their own families. Presumably they reported that the most sought-after Castilian objects in the new territory were glass beads, of which Grijalva had disposed of 2,000; pins and needles, of which he had given away 2,000 and 1,000 respectively; and, finally, scissors and combs, which were even more liked, though he had had with him only six pairs of the first, twenty of the second.[75]

After Alvarado left, the rest of the Spaniards re-embarked, the Totonacs weeping to see them go – perhaps out of politeness, more likely because they had hoped for their help against Montezuma. Grijalva was given a girl "so finely dressed that, had she been in brocade, she could not have looked better".[76] Fr. Díaz wrote: "I do not know what more to say of these people because what I saw was so splendid that one could scarcely believe it."[77] One conquistador, Miguel de Zaragoza, was left behind by mistake. He lived with the Totonacs, apparently in hiding.[78]

The expedition then continued up the coast towards the north, past what is now Tuxpan. A town on the coast was christened Almería after the city in Spain which they thought that it resembled (though it has in practice always retained the Totonac name of Nauhtla). Off a river which they named the Río de Canoas (the modern Cazones), they experienced a maritime attack by Indians. These must have been Huaxtecs, coming from yet another city which the impressionable Fr. Díaz thought was no less grand than Seville "in size and stone".[79] Some of these *naturales* sallied out at the mere sight of the Spaniards, in rather more than a dozen canoes, with bows and arrows. Montejo's ship had its cables cut by copper axes. These Indians must have had some kind of commercial relation with those of Michoacan. But Grijalva's cannon frightened the attackers. Indeed, the cannon, or the crossbowmen, are said to have killed four of them and sunk one of the canoes. The Indians fell back and their attack was subsequently thrown off.[80] Some conquistadors wanted to land and capture the town. Once again, Grijalva refused permission for an adventurous idea.

Somewhere near the modern Cape Rojo, the fleet found it difficult to make headway against the wind. Alaminos recommended a return to Cuba. In addition, one of the ships was leaking. The rainy season had begun. Two of Grijalva's captains, Montejo and Ávila, said that the men were tired of seafaring. So the expedition did turn back. But it made slow progress. They rested for a time at the mouth of the river Tonalá, where a port was named San Antonio, and where the leaky ship was satisfactorily careened.[81] Some of the Castilians again wanted to stay in that place and to colonise it. But Grijalva again refused. While they were there, there were further interesting contacts with the local Indians, who brought them much valuable material, including some more hatchets of copper which they took for gold (until they became covered with verdigris).[82] Now it seems the chronicler Bernal Díaz planted the first oranges of the Americas – or so he later claimed: an action which, it may be argued, in the long run compensated for a thousand injustices.[83]

Grijalva set off again, but another setback occurred: the flagship *San Sebastián* was damaged as it crossed the bar. More repairs were needed. The conquistadors whiled away the extended time of waiting for the work to be done by some modest exploration. The inspector, Peñalosa, with Fr. Juan Díaz, observed a human sacrifice on top of a local pyramid. Some of the Cuban Indians entered the forest: "Had we had a resourceful captain," Fr. Díaz complained, thoroughly disillusioned, "we should have got over 2,000 castellanos out of this. But with Grijalva in command, we could not carry out barter, nor settle the land, nor do anything good."[84]

The fleet afterwards passed by the Laguna de Términos, at its western end near Xicallanco and the Isla de Carmen. The fleet also stopped at Champoton, where Hernández de Córdoba had had his battle with the Mayas. The Indians there again prepared for war, but Grijalva sailed off quickly and avoided conflict. Touching near Campeche and Cape Catoche on 21 September, he then set off across the Yucatan channel for Cuba. They arrived at Mariel, a little to the west of what is now Havana, on 29 September, and reached Matanzas on 4 October, disembarking there on the 5th. Grijalva stopped to rest for some days at one of Velázquez's farms at a place newly christened Chipiona, presumably after the lighthouse at the mouth of the Guadalquivir which was the last thing most conquistadors saw of Spain on their way out to the Indies.[85] Many of the expedition went straight back to their homes in Sancti Spiritus and Trinidad. It was several weeks before Grijalva reached Santiago. By the time that he did get there, much had happened.

Grijalva's expedition was never regarded highly by the conquistadors who came after him. Cortés, for example, in a later questionnaire about his own exploits, said that the captain returned from San Juan de Ulúa without having seen any town of that territory and "without having done anything at all".[86] The judgement is unfair. Grijalva extended the knowledge that the Spanish had of the American mainland. He reached Cape Rojo, a thousand miles north from the furthermost point seen by Hernández de Córdoba. He brought back to Cuba the first news of the great monarchy of Mexico. He established good terms with the Totonac Indians, and returned to Cuba with some interesting pieces of gold and other precious objects. He initiated the technique of using two interpreters, one from Spanish into Chontal Maya, another from that tongue into Yucatec. He was cautious, he had no personal magnetism, and he was unlucky. Yet his uncle Velázquez seems to have made a profit out of the voyage.[87]

That governor had been busy in Cuba since the return of Pedro de

Alvarado. He had been much impressed by the treasures which the captain had brought. For several days indeed he did nothing but embrace him.[88] He sent some of the objects home to Spain to his representative at the court, Fr. Benito Martín, for him to show to the King and Bishop Fonseca. He knew that the Bishop would be delighted by the sight at last of rich objects from the Americas.[89]

Alvarado did not serve his late captain Grijalva well. He had been angry at the reprimand which Grijalva had given him when he sailed into the river which now bears his name. He complained that Grijalva had been reluctant to found a colony. Nor had he sought to "find the secrets of the territory".[90] Velázquez was angry. He decided that obviously he had sent out a booby (*bobo*) as captain.[91] That was unjust, since Grijalva had carefully followed his instructions.

All the same, Velázquez had begun to worry lest Grijalva were lost, and dispatched a search party to find him. This was led by Cristóbal de Olid, an Andalusian member of his household, a native of either Baeza or Linares (though of a family which probably came originally from Olite in Navarre), a coarse individual but a fine fighter. Provided he was kept as a second-in-command, he was "a Hector in single combat", as Hernán Cortés described him – though not till after Olid had died.[92] Olid impressed his friends as being as brave on horseback as on foot. He was a strong, tall, broad-shouldered man, with a ruddy complexion and, though he had good features, his lower lip crinkled as if it were cleft.[93]

Olid took a single ship across to Yucatan. He went to Cozumel and took possession of it in the name of King Charles and Queen Juana, not knowing that that formality had already been gone through by Grijalva. He then turned towards Yucatan, along the route made familiar by Hernández de Córdoba. But in the Yucatan channel he met a heavy gale and lost his anchors. It was "the season for cyclones". Olid landed near the Laguna de Términos where he found traces of Grijalva's recent stay. But he himself decided to return to Cuba because of his own difficulties. He reached Cuba a week before the return of the expedition which he had failed to find.

9

A great Lord born in brocade

"Finally, Cortés there showed himself as a great Lord and as if he had been born in brocade and with such authority that no one dared to show him anything but love."
Bartolomé de Las Casas, *Historia de las Indias*

THE UNEXPECTED RETURN of Pedro de Alvarado from the new lands inspired the Governor of Cuba, Diego Velázquez, to seek to profit further from the discoveries in Yucatan and "Ulúa". His first move, as a responsible official, was to give the new "island" of Yucatan a name. He chose "Carolina", after the young King:[1] a christening quickly forgotten. His second move was to think of organising yet another expedition, even before Grijalva had returned.

Velázquez wanted someone to lead the new venture who would, first, show more imagination than Grijalva; and, second, be able to finance part, or even all, of the expenses. But he did not want it to be a great armada of conquest. That would be led by himself when he had authority from Spain. The third expedition would be a holding operation, to prevent Diego Colón or some adventurer from stealing the opportunity. It was, therefore, a difficult task to find the right person to lead it. No wonder that Velázquez made, at least from his own point of view, a mistake.

He first thought of appointing another nephew to help: Baltasar Bermúdez, a native of Cuéllar, who had married Iseo Velázquez, his niece. Bermúdez rejected the commission, saying that his costs, say three thousand ducats, would be greater than the profit.[2] Another suggestion was Vasco Porcallo de Figueroa, an Extremeño and cousin of the Count of Feria, who had established a ranch near Trinidad. The Porcallos were a family of minor nobility from Cáceres; the Figueroas were grander.[3] Velázquez rejected him on the ground (ironically, in the circumstances) that he seemed an uncontrollable person who would not respect Velázquez's own position as the supreme commander. It was as well, though, that the appointment did not go through: Vasco Porcallo was sadistic (in 1522 he was charged with mutilating his Indians by cutting off their private parts).[4]

Other candidates for the command included various members of Velázquez's close family, such as his cousins Bernardino Velázquez and Antonio Velázquez Borrego. All these gentlemen from Cuéllar or Segovia rejected the idea. They were happy on their properties in Cuba. Some of those who had returned from the new territory with Alvarado were in favour of offering Grijalva another opportunity.[5] But Velázquez was too irritated with him for that.

In the end, Velázquez, on the advice of Amador de Lares (his accountant) and Andrés de Duero (his secretary), nominated a man who had been his protégé for over ten years, a nephew, indeed, in all but name: the young magistrate of Santiago, Hernán Cortés. Both Lares and Duero thought that they could share in the profits of the new expedition.[6] So Lares, though (as will be recalled) he could neither read nor write, signed a letter to Cortés asking him to go to Santiago to see the Governor.

Cortés was at this time on his property at Cuvanacan on the Duaban river, prospecting for gold in the company of a friend of his, a Sevillano whom he had known in Hispaniola, Francisco Dávila.[7] Cortés accepted the invitation. A fortnight later, Dávila had a letter from Cortés, telling him that Velázquez had asked him to lead a new expedition to Yucatan, and that he had accepted.[8]

Cortés seems to have been born in 1484, and so was at that time thirty-four: the right age for leading an expedition. He had been in the Indies for about twelve years, having reached Santo Domingo aged twenty-two in 1506.[9]

Hernán Cortés was descended from some of the most turbulent families, in the most undisciplined of towns, Medellín, in Extremadura, the wildest part of Castile. He was an offspring of an immense extended family of hidalgos of that region, with which almost all those who went to America from there had some connection. His father, Martín Cortés, is usually described as an infantryman: a poor soldier who, though a gentleman, a hidalgo or minor nobleman, could not afford to buy a horse to take him to war.[10] But Cortés' chaplain and biographer, Fr. López de Gómara, said that Martín Cortés had at one time served in a company of horse under "a relation, Alonso de Hinojosa" – probably a native of Trujillo. That author usually wrote what his patron told him. Yet the information may be true: Martín Cortés fought in several wars.

These conflicts were for the most part private ones, in which one noble family of Extremadura fought another for control of castles, land, and cattle: often the fighting was between two branches of the same family. These quarrels matured, it might be said, into real civil war in the 1470s, when they became struggles between the Catholic kings and their faction of the nobility, and the Portuguese-backed candidate in the 1470s, "La Beltraneja", Isabel the Catholic's niece, and her supporters. Outside the towns, meantime, "everything was robbery and murder", there were no bridges over the rivers, and no one travelled unless in an armed band.

Martín Cortés seems to have been the bastard son of a certain Rodrigo de Monroy, whose resounding patronymic he, and later Hernán Cortés, took as a second surname.[11] The Monroys were a family which counted for much in Extremadura, with their two castles, Belvís and Monroy, their violent disputes, and their continuous production, generation after generation, of unruly warriors. Rodrigo's father, Hernán Rodríguez de Monroy, had conquered Antequera from the Moors in the royal interest: an almost unique public service in a family used to private war. Martín Cortés' mother, María Cortés, may have left her son a small property in Medellín; hence the surname.

Martín Cortés served for a time with his father's first cousin, the most dramatic member of this family, "El Clavero" Monroy, "The Keeper", so called since he had held that honorific post in the great knightly Order of Alcántara. El Clavero, literally the man who held the keys of the castle of the order, was an individual of legend. Physically "a Hercules", it was said that no horse could carry him. Two swordsmen were quite incapable of dealing with him. Some defect of the eye made it possible for him to see better in the dark than in the day. By 1480 he had been fighting continuously for almost fifty years, sometimes against the Crown, usually against his family, even his own brothers. Once, weighed down with chains, he scaled the wall of the castle of Magacela, fifteen miles south-east of Medellín, where a cousin had imprisoned him. Though he broke both legs and many other bones in escaping, it took hard fighting to recapture him. He once seems to have planned to hand over Extremadura to Portugal. After the recovery of the royal peace in the 1480s, El Clavero left for Lisbon where he lived out the rest of his life in angry exile.[12]

Martín Cortés, however, like his uncle, Hernán Monroy, "El Bezudo", "Blubberlips", as well as his own lord, the Count of Medellín, and some other hidalgos from the town,[13] went on to fight in the last stages of the royal war against Granada. He then settled down in Medellín, some twenty miles west of the old, and at that time ruined, Roman capital of the province, Mérida. Medellín had also been a Roman town, having been founded by Metellus Pius in the first century BC: hence its name. Roman memories must have been more evident then than they are now: the remains of a theatre, some villas, and a bridge could all be seen. Though now remote, Medellín was in those days on the most used route north to Valladolid and Guadalupe from Seville.[14] It lay in the centre of a fertile valley.

Martín Cortés probably inherited from his mother his mill on the banks of the pretty river Ortigas (a tributary of the Guadiana), some beehives just to the south of Medellín, and a small vineyard in the valley of the river Guadiana. He also had some fields which grew wheat. These properties produced about five hundred pounds (twenty *arrobas*) of honey, eighty gallons (also twenty *arrobas*) of wine, and about sixty hundredweight of wheat – bringing in the tiny sum of five thousand maravedís a year – a sum which, had it constituted his entire income, would have placed him in the class of misery.[15] But Martín Cortés also had a house in the main square of Medellín (in which Hernán Cortés was born) and some other buildings in the place from which he drew rents. With its partly urban, partly rural character, this property was typical of that time. It enabled Martín Cortés to play a part in the town as councillor (*regidor*), and even chief spokesman (*procurador-general*).[16]

Bishop de Las Casas knew Martín Cortés. He wrote that he "was rather poor and an old Christian" – that is, neither Jew nor Moor – adding "and, they say, a hidalgo" – a scarcely reassuring statement of lineage which, however, was certainly true.[17] The Monroys might be rebels but they were undoubtedly aristocrats: while illegitimacy, by the custom of Castile, did not prevent the inheritance of *hidalguía*, assuming that the male line was concerned. Nor did illegitimacy cast a stigma: both the Count and the Countess of Medellín, the lords of Cortés' town, were bastards, as were the commander of Spain in the war against Granada, Rodrigo Ponce de León, Marquis of Arcos, and his brother Juan, the discoverer of Florida. Any hidalgo could grant a bastard son *hidalguía* if he guaranteed him a minimum of five hundred sueldos: a modest sum. To be a hidalgo by then meant no more than having an exemption from certain taxes.

Several people also testified, in a suit in 1525, when Hernán Cortés was making a petition in Valladolid to become a knight of the Order of Santiago, that Cortés' parents were hidalgos; and he thus had the right to a coat of arms (in fact, the arms of the Rodríguez de Varillas, a noble Salamanca family, from whom the Monroys descended in the male line).[18]

Cortés' first biographer, the Sicilian humanist Marineo Siculo, gave him, without evidence, an Italian (noble) ancestry: thereby betraying the prejudice of a happy age when Italian blood was considered a mark of distinction.[19] That was not so, even if his hero may have had Italianate ambitions.

The surname Monroy sounds grand. There were two large Monroy castles in Extremadura; yet there was also a family of biscuit-makers so called in Triana.[20]

In that same enquiry as to whether Cortés was worthy to become a Knight of the Order of Santiago, Cortés' paternal grandparents were not mentioned, except indirectly by a certain Juan Núñez de Prado, who said that he assumed that they came from Salamanca, but could not name them.[21] That is why the suggestion of illegitimate birth for Martín Cortés seems certain.²² (Núñez de Prado, then aged eighty, would have known all about the Monroys, for he had married one.)

Hernán Cortés presumably learned about the art of soldiering from his father and, at some point, he became an excellent horseman, whether or not Martín rode a horse in his wars. Soldiering in those days would have included the technique of early artillery as well as some elementary methods of discipline.

Hernán Cortés' mother, Catalina, came from as interesting a family as his father. Her father, Diego Alfon Altamirano, was a notary and, for a time, a majordomo too, in the service of Beatriz Pacheco, Countess of Medellín.²³ He, too, was a notary of the King, which title gave him a semi-official position as one whose learning was respected, probably being the possessor of a degree from Salamanca. Most of the life of Medellín must have been known to him, since he would have been the lynchpin of administration, even if he did act, as was natural in a town ruled by a count, on behalf of his master. Like Martín Cortés, he played a part in the local politics of Medellín, though not as a councillor, rather as a magistrate (*alcalde ordinario*).²⁴ His wife was Catalina Pizarro.

Both the Altamiranos and the Pizarros derived from the nearby city of Trujillo, some forty miles to the north. The dozen or so hidalgo families of Trujillo and Medellín intermarried often. Thus Catalina Pizarro was related to the conqueror of Peru²⁵ (when Hernán Cortés received his commission from Velázquez, Francisco Pizarro was still living ruthlessly in Castilla del Oro: he commanded the troop of soldiers which, that same month of October 1518, arrested Núñez de Balboa, that other capable and imaginative Extremeño conquistador, probably born in Jérez de los Caballeros). Members of the families of Pizarro ("as proud as they were poor", wrote the historian Oviedo)²⁶ and Altamirano would frequently figure in Cortés' career, often a support in difficult times. But at the time of Hernán Cortés' birth, the two families were members of different parties in Trujillo: the Altamiranos, an enormous cousinhood, were indeed leaders of one faction; the Pizarros were supporters of another, the Bejaranos. The matters at dispute had begun by being concerned with the control of municipal offices, though different attitudes to the state sheep monopoly, the Mesta, were also important. But those disputes were half forgotten; recent brawls, insults, and murders were the points at issue. A marriage between the families would have been as provocative as one between Capulets and Montagues. Perhaps that is why the grandparents of Hernán Cortés moved to Medellín.²⁷

But Medellín, with its two-and-a-half thousand or so residents, could scarcely have been a restful place.²⁸ It was on the boundary between territories controlled by the two great knightly orders, Santiago and Alcántara. The city itself was dominated by its castle which, in the days of Cortés' infancy, was run by the fierce Countess of Medellín, Beatriz

Pacheco, a bastard daughter of King Enrique's favourite, the Marquis of Villena. That connection had made Beatriz a strong advocate of La Beltraneja in the civil wars, an enemy of the Catholic kings and an ally of El Clavero. The Countess maintained a long siege against the royal forces in 1479. Medellín and Mérida were the two last towns of any size to continue to recognise La Beltraneja as Queen of Castile.[29] When Beatriz's husband, Count Rodrigo, died, he left instructions in his will that their son should not be brought up by his widow. The Countess promptly shut up this heir in a Moorish well (*aljibe*), from which he was later rescued by the citizens of the town. He was converted by the experience into a "veritable hyena", a passionate opponent of everything for which his mother stood. Even so, after her death, disputes between the new Count and the town continued, Martín Cortés taking part against the Count. His father-in-law, Altamirano, must have had a hard time, whether he was primarily a lawyer or a majordomo. The thefts, murders, illegal imprisonments, brawls, acts of menace, and improper occupation of lands in Medellín during the childhood of Cortés are amply recorded in the innumerable cases brought to the King's court.

Medellín depended for such wealth as it had on the cultivation of wheat and flax. The Jeronymite monastery of Guadalupe, some fifty miles to the north-east, used its pasturage. The Order of Alcántara employed the richer lands of the nearby valleys of the Serena, and needed to be on good terms with whoever controlled Medellín. The Count of Medellín, deeply indebted in consequence of the military pretensions of his forebears, sought, on many occasions, to compensate for economic distress by the use of arms. The town was against him, its champion being Juan Núñez de Prado, to whom the Cortés family gave their loyalty, and who had his own designs on the lands, if not the title, of the Count. In the early years of the sixteenth century the party opposed to the Count began to be used by the Duke of Alba who was determined to extend his influence in the region.[30]

Medellín in Cortés' childhood, like many towns of similar size, was a city of three cultures: Christian, Muslim and Jewish. The dimensions of each population remain a matter for speculation, but in Extremadura as a whole the last two sections of the population accounted together for as much as a third of the total.[31] The Castilian liberation of the town had, after all, only been in 1235, the Christian population were almost all immigrants since that time, while several Moorish families had remained. The Jewish quarter numbered sixty or seventy families: say two hundred and fifty people. It was an important city for Spanish Jewry: in 1488, for example, only nine towns in Castile contributed more taxes to the prosecution of the war against Granada.[32] The young Cortés would therefore have been brought up in the sight of a mosque and a synagogue next to the Christian churches of Santiago (so called for the order which had liberated the city) and San Martín, whose cult was in those days highly developed.

Most of the Jews left in 1492, when the young Cortés was seven years old, with about ten thousand from all Extremadura, for Portugal; whence they were no doubt expelled again in 1497.[33] The sudden departure in ignominy of this large and well-established minority was one of the main events of Cortés' childhood. A few slaves, some Turkish, some African imported from nearby Portugal, were probably also to be found in Medellín. Black slaves were seen everywhere in Spain in those days.[34] The fact of observing peoples other than the Christian must have played a major part in the formation of Cortés' imagination, and of his attitude towards the new societies whom he would meet in the New World.

The nearest place of culture to Cortés' birthplace was Zalamea de la Serena, twenty-five miles to the south, where Juan de Zúñiga, last independent grand master of the Order of Alcántara, Monroy's successor, patron of the great philologist, Antonio de Nebrija, maintained an elegant if bucolic court.[35] There, between 1487 and 1490, Nebrija wrote his *Isagiogicon Cosmographicae*. There too, in 1486, Abraham Zacutus, the last great Spanish Jewish thinker, raised astrology almost to the level of science, with his work *El Tratado de las influencias del Cielo*. (His tables closely resemble the cyclic "Venus tables" of the Maya.)[36] Zalamea, like Medellín, was then on the main route between Seville and Valladolid. Perhaps some sense of the opportunities of the lands beyond the Atlantic was, after 1492, brought by word of mouth to Cortés, either from there or from along the river Guadiana, which flowed from Medellín to join the sea not far beyond Huelva; or perhaps Portugal was the source of the information that beyond the sea lay the prospects of gold and preferment. Some of the two hundred "gentlemen volunteers" who accompanied Columbus on his second voyage were probably from Extremadura, even one or two from Medellín (for example, Luis Hernández Portocarrero).

Cortés wrote many letters in later life but he scarcely mentioned his childhood in them. Almost the only known anecdote about that time is that his life was despaired of at birth, and that he was saved by a wet nurse, María Esteban, from Oliva, a tiny place to the south of Medellín in the Sierra de la Garza. She attributed her achievement to San Pedro: hence Cortés' later loyalty to that saint.[37] He is said to have been sickly until his teens. He was also an only child. Both conditions must have made difficulties for him in a society dedicated to martial arts and urban brawls. Perhaps his physical weakness led his parents to wish him to be educated. They are said too to have wished him to become a page. But they did not find a suitable niche for him at the castle of Medellín. So instead he became an acolyte in one of the churches, probably San

Martín.[38] In these youthful, even childish, religious preoccupations, the future conquistador gained some of that feeling for the liturgy, and that knowledge of the art of preaching, which would make him a most effective proselytiser.

Although there is little record of Cortés' childhood, he must, given his connection with the Altamiranos, have lived in more literate circumstances than did most conquistadors from Extremadura.

Cortés left Medellín in his teens. In later life he favoured people who came from that city (for example, Rodrigo Rangel, Alonso Hernández Portocarrero, a cousin of the Count of Medellín, Gonzalo de Sandoval, Alonso de Mendoza and Juan Rodríguez de Villafuerte – the last-named in defiance of the evidence about his modest capacities). When he was in a position to give presents on a lavish scale Cortés would send some both to the Count of Medellín and to his grandson. He gave the name of Medellín to a town in Mexico and sent money for a chapel dedicated to St Anthony in the Franciscan monastery there.[39] He surrounded himself by choice with Extremeños: and Pedro de Alvarado, born in Badajoz, became his closest confidant. But Cortés never sought, when he became famous, to build a palace in his home town. He even made over his family's property to a cousin, Juan Altamirano.[40] The Pizarros, on the other hand, bought extensively in Extremadura after their conquest of Peru, even buying land worth 1.6 million maravedís in Medellín itself.[41] The explanation for Cortés' withdrawal from his native city must be that he did not wish to resubmit himself to the feudal jurisdiction of such an eccentric, demanding and unpredictable lord as the Count of Medellín had continuously shown himself to be. Martín Cortés after all had sided with the Count's enemies such as Juan Núñez de Prado.[42] The Count was also a political ally of Cortés' enemy, Pedrarias, the Governor of Castilla del Oro (he was his brother-in-law).[43] In Trujillo, a city owned by the Order of Santiago, the Pizarros were already a dominant family in one of the two contending factions, and there was no outstanding lord – though it was just as disturbed as Medellín: Juan Núñez de Prado killed a supporter of the Count of Medellín there in a brawl in 1510.[44]

Cortés went in 1496 at the age of twelve to Salamanca. This was the city in which his father was supposed to have been born. It had certainly long been associated with the Monroys, as with the Rodríguez de Varillas family. An epitaph in a chapel in the cloister of the old cathedral requests God to give to the Monroys "as great a part in heaven as by their persons and ancestors they merited on earth".[45] Cortés apparently lived in Salamanca for two years, with an aunt (his father's half-sister), Inés de Paz, and her husband, Francisco Núñez de Valera, a notary, like Diego Altamirano.[46] Cortés is said to have studied Latin and grammar, either with him or in classes elsewhere, as a preparation for the law, thus following in the footsteps of his maternal grandfather.[47] There is no record of his having attended the university, but that "nursery of scholars and gentlemen" (as it was overgenerously described by the Italian humanist Lucio Marineo Siculo, already professor of poetry there) was at the time strongly Extremeño in character.[48] Probably Cortés went to some classes. Universities in those days were not the tight bureaucratic enterprises that they later became. Diego López, of Medellín, testified in 1525 that "he had once studied in the same class [estudio]" as Cortés.[49]

Las Casas, who did not approve of Cortés but knew and, to some extent, admired him, described him as having been a bachelor of law, as well as being a good Latinist (and Latin speaker).[50] The conquistador later displayed knowledge of law, though he certainly had no degree in it: even if the records were faulty, he could not have become a bachelor in a mere two years.[51] Cortés' knowledge of the classics did not seem substantial, but it existed: Las Casas should have been a good judge, for he spoke Latin fluently.[52] Marineo, the Sicilian professor of poetry whose Latin must have been better than that of Las Casas, was enthusiastic: "He took great pleasure in the Latin language"[53] (Marineo knew Cortés in the late 1520s). Cortés' various classical allusions in his conversation and letters may, however, easily have derived from one of the new books of proverbs. Certainly most of Cortés' favourite sayings – such as "Fortune favours the Brave" ("Fortes Fortuna adiuvat"), originally from Terence's play, Phormio, and "A kingdom divided against itself cannot stand", from the Gospel according to St Mark – can be found in Erasmus' Adagio or other such volumes. Perhaps Cortés heard people quoting from them. It was then very fashionable to cite quotations: Fernando de Rojas, in his wonderfully racy dialogue, La Celestina, published in 1499 in Burgos, caused even the maids to quote Horace. Cortés perhaps saw the book: Rojas was at Salamanca in Cortés' days there.

Cortés later impressed people as liking to read "when he had time". But "he was more inclined (when young) to arms"[54] – and to gambling: a habit which never left him.

These interests suggest why it was that, unlike another clever, ambitious boy from Extremadura, Juan Martínez Siliceo, born near Llerena in 1486 of humbler parents, also old Christians, Hernán Cortés never thought of the church as a career (Siliceo, born Guajirro, would become an unbending archbishop of Toledo in the 1540s).

No doubt, among the chess-playing and guitar-picking Latinists, several thousand strong, Cortés picked up something of the lively atmosphere which marked those years in Salamanca. Several professors were trying to dismantle what, after a visit to Italy, Nebrija called medieval "barbarism".[55] Nebrija himself had gone to Zalamea but his disciples were busy. Peter Martyr held an audience of students there entranced in 1488 by a lecture of three hours on the second satire of

Juvenal. Lucio Marineo, the first Italian to talk in Spain about the Renaissance, was seeking to revive Latin as a living language.[56] (The rule in Salamanca was that Latin should be talked at all times but it was the first of many such rules to be continuously broken.) Nebrija's famous parallel between the greatness of the Spanish language and the nation itself must have been known to Cortés, if only because a new college, with a great domed library, had just been inspired by Nebrija in Salamanca.[57] Some sense of national grandeur must have been communciated. It was in Salamanca, just before Cortés arrived there, that Juan del Encina, "the father of Spanish Renaissance drama", published his verse about the Catholic kings, quoted as a title to Chapter 5.

In 1501, aged seventeen, Cortés returned to Medellín. He had been kindly treated by his aunt, and twenty-five years later he wrote her one of his few surviving informal letters, saying that he had never forgotten her "kindnesses and endearments".[58] His parents are said to have been angry at his homecoming. They had hoped that he would have had a career in the law, as his grandfather Altamirano had done, perhaps in the royal service as one of those new *letrados*, university-educated civil servants, whom the Catholic kings were known to like, since they had no inherited power; and who had many opportunities for making money, since anyone wanting the royal favour had to make a private payment to an official. The Cortés family had a distant connection with just such a person in Lorenzo Galíndez de Carvajal, already on the brink of a great career as a royal counsellor (only twelve years older than Hernán Cortés, he was half-first cousin to Martín Cortés' grandfather, Rodrigo de Monroy).[59]

Cortés was, however, determined on a life of action. But he seems to have vacillated between going to the Indies and going to fight in the Spanish wars in Italy under the legendary "Great Captain", Gonzalo Hernández de Córdoba, who was then launching the Spanish infantry on a hundred and fifty years of victories. The temptation of Italy must have been considerable, because of the Extremeños who were going there, including some of his father's relations. A powerful fleet had left Málaga in 1501 for Italy, with several famous men on board: the "Samson of Extremadura", Diego de Paredes, (of whom Cervantes would cause Sancho Panza to speak preposterously in *Don Quixote*);[60] Cortés' mother's cousin, Gonzalo Pizarro, father of the conqueror of Peru; and Cortés' own uncle, his father's legitimate brother, Pedro de Monroy.[61]

For reasons on which he never dwelt, but which no doubt had something to do with family connections, Cortés chose the Indies. He arranged to accompany the expedition which was planned to leave next year with Fr. Nicolás de Ovando, *Comendador de Lares* in the Order of Alcántara, who, also from Extremadura (his family came from Brozas, on the road to Alcántara from Cáceres), was yet one more distant relation, through the Monroys. In addition, a sister of Ovando had married a brother of the Cortés family's friend and champion, Juan Núñez de Prado.[62] Then Hernando de Monroy was quartermaster with Ovando's expedition: he must have been another cousin.[63] Ovando planned to take with him numerous Extremeños; while his secretary was Francisco de Lizaur, from Brozas, who would have known all about Cortés' ancestry, if not his character.

Cortés set off for Seville where Ovando was making his plans for his expedition of thirty-two ships, which was intended to rejuvenate Hispaniola after its depredation by "the Genoese", with pigs, chickens and cows, sixty horses and mares, not to speak of thirteen Franciscans.

Seville, with about 40,000 inhabitants, was then the largest city in Spain. It was the capital of Spanish maritime enterprise, "a veritable Babylon". Italian sailors, German printers, slaves from Guinea brought by Portuguese merchants, and descendants of earlier waves of African slaves all crowded into the city. Long-established Genoese merchants had infected the Sevillano aristocracy with a zeal for enterprise which contrasted with the parochial rivalries of towns such as Medellín. The Genoese were rivalled by the merchants of Burgos, who sold goods of all sorts, much of it coming from the Low Countries, bought with the profits from the sale of Castilian wool. The new, still unfinished cathedral was then the biggest in Christendom, the port the best in Spain, the pontoon bridge across the Guadalquivir to Triana ingenious. Abundant water was brought by a Roman aqueduct from Carmona, there were many paved streets, marble (and much frequented) steps lay round the cathedral, and there were well-maintained patios in the houses, innumerable fountains, flowers and trees. The public baths of Seville (frequented by women in the day, men at night) must have seemed astonishing to an Extremeño. The Sevillanos were as proud of their white soap, made in Triana, as of their olive oil and their oranges. Cortés would have been as impressed as the Venetian Andrea Navagero was a few years later by Seville's broad streets.[64] Yet those roads were usually deep in filth, and crowded with vagrant children, while the river, though the artery of wealth, was foul, and plague was frequent.[65] Cortés would have seen also the great palace of the Dukes of Medina Sidonia, and the Moorish castle at Triana where those accused of Judaism were held (probably twenty prisoners when he was there). Perhaps he witnessed an *auto de fe*, outside the walls in the field of San Sebastián.[66] The King and Queen were in Seville in January 1502, while in the spring there was a forced expulsion of the resident Moors.[67]

From his later devotion to her, Cortés seems to have developed a special respect in the cathedral for the Virgin of los Remedios, whose beautiful features, with slanted eyes in Sienese style (she was painted about 1400), occupied, then as now, a place of honour on the west side of the choir. But he would have realised the generally greater appeal of the

Virgin of la Antigua, in a side chapel of the same great church, an inspiration for the names of innumerable ships (Ovando's flagship among them), islands, and cities in the Americas: including the first city founded on the American mainland, La Antigua, in Darien.

But Cortés did not leave with Ovando after all. Waiting for his ship, he hurt himself in a somewhat obscure way, falling from a wall while trying to climb into (or perhaps out of) a girl's window.[68]

While recovering, Cortés also caught a variety of malaria known as *cuartanas*, that is, a fever which returns every four days. Seville was full of such infections. Perhaps he was fortunate: Hispaniola was even less healthy and, out of two and a half thousand Castilians who travelled with Ovando, a thousand soon died, and another five hundred became very ill.[69]

With no further great expedition to the Indies planned, Cortés again toyed with the idea of going to Italy. He apparently set off for Valencia, whence he expected to take ship for Naples.[70] That city was then the main port of Spain, "the capital" of Spanish commerce, and, because of political troubles in their own city, many merchants from Barcelona had removed there.[71] Being geographically close to Italy, it was a centre for Italian ideas, among them that humanism which was expressed in attention to the classics. Italian and German architects and sculptors had been working in the city, as had Flemish painters. The beautiful Lonja, with its next door Consulado del Mar, had just been finished. The Estudi General had been recognised as a university in 1500, the "anti-barbarian" Nebrija was as much studied in Valencia as in Salamanca, and soon the young Joan Lluís Vives, the Valencian-born philosopher, would draw together all the main threads of Spanish humanism in a powerful series of original works. But an observant visitor such as Cortés would probably have been as much impressed by the women, who were "the most beautiful, luxurious and agreeable that one can imagine", as by the variety of fine cloths, damasks and brocades which were made in Valencia, in particular the famous *"draps d'or"* or *"damasquís d'or"*, made of silk and threads of gold.[72]

Had he gone to Italy, Cortés might have participated in the Great Captain's triumph at Cerignola in April 1503. He might even have joined the sanguinary pack of Spanish bodyguards who attended that great Valencian, César Borgia. But Hernán Cortés seems again to have hesitated. Instead of going to Naples, he is said to have spent some time as a mere wanderer, on the loose, *"a la flor del berro"*, in the words of his biographer López de Gómara.[73] This interlude (bearing in mind that Cortés seems not to have left for the Indies till 1506, not 1504 as has been generally supposed) must have lasted for two years. Perhaps it was now that he visited cities such as Granada, of whose still fine silk market he would later seem to have a vivid knowledge.[74] Then, according to another biographer, Suárez de Peralta, his nephew, he spent another year, perhaps more, in Valladolid, a city only a little smaller than Seville (it had about 35,000 inhabitants). Perhaps Cortés' Salamantine uncle, Núñez de Valera, was responsible for finding a place for him in the office of a notary, or *escribano*, where he learned how that work, so important in deciding policy in the Indies, was performed. No doubt he also saw how well notaries were rewarded.[75] It must have been then that he made himself familiar with the main code of Castilian law, the *Siete Partidas*, the great compilation of the thirteenth-century king, Alfonso el Sabio (recently printed for the first time), of which he would later show considerable knowledge.[76] At that time, the office of notary was not so much a learned profession as one in which an experienced writer dictated contracts, wills, writs and other legal documents. A degree in law was desirable but not essential.[77]

These years in Salamanca and Valladolid, as well as the shorter stay in Seville and, perhaps, Valencia, were important for the young Cortés in ways other than intellectual. He observed the great world. Salamanca was one of the cities given to the short-lived heir of the Catholic kings, the Infante Juan, on his marriage in 1497. It was there that the Infante had so sadly died. There was also an active commerce in drapery, silk, textiles, and tanneries. Valladolid was even more royal in character, the nearest thing Spain then had to a capital. There, in 1496, the doomed Infanta Juana had been married by proxy to the philandering Flemish Prince Philip the Beautiful (*el hermoso*). There, the Court of Appeal for northern Spain had been established. Imposing new buildings were being erected: the Dominican College of San Gregorio, the Convento de San Pablo, and Lorenzo Vázquez de Segovia's Colegio Mayor de Santa Cruz, with its Italianate façade, were all built in the 1490s. The silversmiths of Valladolid were every year more famous. There was much money about: Charles V, when he entered Valladolid in 1517, was greeted by the burghers of the city in brocades, wearing great chains of gold, some being worth six thousand ducats and, no doubt, made from American gold.[78] In both Salamanca and Valladolid, Cortés would have learned of the importance of Juan Rodríguez de Fonseca, at that time still Bishop of Badajoz, whose power as minister for the Indies in all but name was everywhere growing. Perhaps the young Cortés saw, or even met, the Bishop, or his assistants, Conchillos and Los Cobos, discreet and clever men soon to rise in the zones of power.[79]

Surely in these years Cortés developed his ambitions: or, rather, set for himself a goal as to how to live, in a style very different from that of the average son of a poor hidalgo from Medellín. For he would have learned how Bishop Fonseca gave money to Flemish painters, Castilian chapels and important monasteries. He would have learned too, at one remove, of course, of that "sumptuousness" which, as the German traveller

Thomas Münzer put it, was displayed by great Castilian noblemen such as the Count of Benavente or the Mendoza family.[80] Columbus had been impressed by the way of living of Alfonso Enríquez, Admiral of Castile, Ferdinand the Catholic's uncle. Perhaps Cortés' craving for glory derived from some similar observation. Perhaps too he read the new edition of Julius Caesar's *Gallic War* or Enrique de Villena's edition of *The Twelve Labours of Hercules*, published in Burgos in 1499. With him as with others of his generation, the ambition which he developed seems not to have been just an extreme case of egotism; it was something more daemonic, involving, as Burckhardt would put it in his study of the Italian Renaissance, a full surrender of the will to the purpose, as well as the use of any means, however harsh, to achieve his end. Cortés aspired not simply to be rich, but to live as a king, to give away presents like a bishop, to have a title, and to be known as "Don", a then rare distinction granted even to few noblemen. "I look on it as better to be rich in fame than in goods," he would one day write to his father.[81] Las Casas later wrote of Cortés that he behaved "as if he had been born in brocade"; as if he too had been a grandee of Valladolid.[82]

These were in most ways traditional Spanish medieval ambitions, as expressed in innumerable ballads and romances, of the sort which were read to "good old knights" when dining, or when they could not sleep. Nobody is more proud of his descent than someone who, like Cortés in 1506, has scarcely a maravedí to his name. The memory of the Rodríguez de Varillas coat of arms, with its gold bars and silver crosses of Jerusalem, must have seemed both an inspiration, and a commentary on Cortés' poverty.[83] The recollection of El Clavero, of Juan de Zúñiga, of the Bishop of Badajoz, even of the Count and Countess of Medellín, whom Cortés must have seen in their castle, probably played a part. Historians have disputed as to whether the Middle Ages or the Renaissance dominated in Cortés' approach to his self-appointed tasks in the Indies. Certainly the values of the first seen through the lens of ballads and experience in Extremadura coloured Cortés' intellectual outlook. Like most conquistadors of his generation, he saw the Indians of the Caribbean and its littoral as if they were new Moors, to be converted and subjected. But Cortés' experience in Salamanca and Valladolid seems to have given his purposes a Renaissance edge. Although he may not have heard of him, he would have agreed with Alberti who, in *The Family*, argued that the end of education was to create a man who prizes "the beauty of honour, the delights of fame and the divineness of glory".[84]

In the summer of 1506, Cortés, aged twenty-two, was again in Seville. After working there for some weeks in another notary's office, he finally did embark for the Indies, travelling from Sanlúcar de Barrameda, the salt-famous port at the mouth of the Guadalquivir, on a ship carrying merchandise for Hispaniola.[85] Cortés agreed, before the notary Martín Segura, to pay eleven golden ducats to Luis Fernández de Alfaro, for his passage and maintenance on board the *San Juan Bautista*, a *nao* of one hundred tons, like most of the vessels then used on the Atlantic route.[86] Fernández de Alfaro, a sea captain, had already founded a company of ships trading to the Indies. He soon became a merchant, with whom Cortés would later have many important business dealings. But Cortés in the end did not sail on one of his ships, presumably because that year he went not to Santo Domingo but to Puerto Plata, on the north coast of Hispaniola. Cortés' captain was Antonio Quintero, of Palos, who sailed on the *Trinidad*.

Sweating, hunger and hard work

"With the 2,000 castellanos that the Indians extracted from the mines that Dìego Velázquez had given him, with immense sweating, hunger and hard work, he began to dress himself up and to spend lavishly."
Bartolomé de Las Casas, *Historia de las Indias*

ORTÉS LEFT NO account of his voyage to the West Indies. But it is to be assumed that, like most journeys of that time, the ship stopped for water and some provisions in the Canaries, no doubt at Las Palmas, "land of many sugar canes", the first Castilian stepping stone to overseas empire. His captain, Quintero,[1] afterwards broke away from the other ships with which he was sailing, met bad weather, and arrived in Santo Domingo discomfited.[2]

The journey could hardly have been different from what transpired when a Dominican friar crossed the Atlantic forty years later: "The ship is a very strong and narrow prison from which no one can flee, even though there are no chains . . . the heat, the stuffiness, and the sense of confinement are sometimes overpowering. The bed is ordinarily the floor . . . Add to this the general nausea and poor health, most passengers go about as if out of their minds and in great torment . . . There is a terrible smell, especially below deck, which becomes intolerable throughout the ship when the pump is functioning – and it is doing that four or five times a day . . ." The dirt was appalling, the only lavatory – slung over the side – dangerous, the only meat was bacon, the thirst of everyone usually overpowering. Prayers to San Telmo, patron of sailors, Camoens' "living light which sailors hold as sacred", usually proved ineffective in preventing illness.[3]

Yet there were also probably cock-fights, dice and cards, plays and dances, prayers, the simulation of bullfights; singing, the reading aloud of romances, and the reciting of ballads; and the observation of the stars.

Arrived in Santo Domingo, Cortés grandly gave the impression that he supposed that "he had only to arrive to be weighed down with gold". He told those whom he met that he wanted to mine. The Governor, Ovando, was away, no doubt with his Extremeño secretary, Lizaur, while Hernando de Monroy, the quartermaster of the colony, on whose help Cortés may have hoped to rely, had died. But one of Ovando's friends, a certain Medina, told Cortés that, to find gold, one needed to be prepared to work hard, as well as to have luck.[4] Still, Cortés soon became a friend of the secretary, Lizaur. That connection must have greatly helped him.[5]

Governor Ovando certainly favoured Cortés: perhaps because he was a distant relation, perhaps because he was a Monroy, perhaps because he seemed both clever and ready for anything, or, merely because he was an Extremeño. In those days, blood connections were the determining ones in most affairs. Ovando was acting as everyone did. First, he sent Cortés on an expedition to Xaragua, in the western part of the island. This was many months after the massacre by Diego Velázquez and Juan de Esquivel of Queen Anacoana and her chief followers. But the memory of those events must have lingered. Perhaps it afforded a brutal lesson for Cortés. Absolute ruthlessness, he could have been forgiven for deciding, sometimes pays absolutely.[6] Subsequently, Gonzalo de Guzmán, a settler who later became Diego Velázquez's deputy in Cuba, offered Cortés work on his sugar mill, one of the first to be established in the New World, though what kind of work is unknown. Later still, Ovando made him notary, *escribano*, in the new town of Azúa de Compostela, founded on a sheltered bay on the south side of the island, sixty miles to the west of Santo Domingo, where Columbus and his ships had taken refuge from the hurricane of 1502. He also seems to have obtained some Indians and an *encomienda* in the Indian settlement of Daiguao.[7]

Cortés would never again live in one place as long as he lived in Azúa, but it is hard to know what his life was like there. It was not a city of consequence. Nor is Cortés' name to be found in documents concerning the difficulties which the island encountered in those days. He gained a reputation, but more as a dissolute gallant than a Latin-speaking lawyer. He had brawls, one of which left a scar on his chin. Yet everything which happened in the town must have been known to him, for in the Indies, as in Extremadura, the notary was the essential recorder of all events. Cortés was now already carrying out his grandfather Altamirano's role, in colonial circumstances. But he had dreams of far greater things, as is suggested by a story which relates how he sketched a wheel of fortune, and told his friends that he would "either dine to the sound of trumpets or die on the scaffold".[8] Francisco de Garay, another "alchemist of ink", as the historian Oviedo would describe lawyers, had recently done spectacularly well with his mines, and would soon embark on a career as proconsul.[9] Cortés aspired to do the same.

Cortés saw the tragic decline of the population of Hispaniola. He realised that he ought to move. So he thought of going to Darien in 1509 in a new expedition of several hundred men with Diego de Nicuesa, but he developed an infirmity in his right leg, so he withdrew at the last moment.[10] Once again the setback was providential: the expedition of Nicuesa, a protégé of the powerful Lope de Conchillos, ended in shipwreck.

The population of Azúa could not have numbered more than about seven hundred and fifty.[11] A map of Hispaniola, commissioned in 1508 by Ovando from a pilot, Andrés de Morales, shows Azúa with what looks like a stone church, but it must have been a mere converted *bohio*, or Indian hut.[12] Such was anyway the gloomy report of Judge Zuazo in 1518: "I want to undeceive your Majesty, that unless it is a question of the city of Santo Domingo, where there are houses of stone . . . all the others have houses of straw . . . like a poor village in Spain."[13] At least sugar began to be planted there while Cortés was clerk: a compensation of a kind. This enterprise flourished after Cortés left, one property being converted by the Genoese merchant Jácome de Castellón into a successful mill.[14]

Cortés, meantime, joined Diego Velázquez in his conquest of Cuba. Velázquez had been the lieutenant governor in military control of Azúa, so he had had the opportunity to see how the young Extremeño was developing. In Cuba, along with the treasurer, Cristóbal de Cuéllar, who would soon be Velázquez's father-in-law, Cortés was responsible for seeing that a fifth of profits obtained, from gold to slaves, was sent back to the King in Spain.[15]

Cortés, like Las Casas, was probably present at the burning of the chief Hatuey. If so, that experience too must have been another education in brutality. He probably accompanied Velázquez in his first drive through Cuba, in search of places in which to found towns. He is said to have had built the first foundry and the first hospital in Cuba.[16] He must afterwards have seen the reports, *relaciones*, which Velázquez sent to the King about his achievements.[17] Probably he helped to draft them. After the conquest, the Governor made Cortés his secretary and gave him an *encomienda*, jointly with Juan Suárez, a settler who had recently come with his family from Granada.

Cortés first established himself in Cuba in the new settlement of Asunción de Baracoa, Velázquez's first capital on the island. He was both the first notary there, and apparently the first man to own cattle in Cuba. But his real interest was still gold. He soon discovered that essential source of human happiness about 1512 at Cuvanacan, where he and his Indians panned the river successfully. He accumulated some wealth, established a hacienda, and had a daughter by an Indian girl, christened Leonor Pizarro. Governor Velázquez stood godfather.[18]

In 1514, when he was thirty, Cortés had the first of his quarrels with his benefactor, the Governor. Cortés allowed himself to associate with a group of discontented settlers who wanted Velázquez to apportion Indians on a larger scale than he had been doing. Cortés was chosen to lead this group, for he seemed to be the most daring of the people close to the Governor. In consequence, Velázquez not only dismissed Cortés from being his secretary, but ordered him to be sent to Santo Domingo under arrest. In the end, the Governor was prevailed upon to pardon his secretary and, indeed, seems to have given way over the question of grants of Indians.[19] By that time the system of the *encomienda* seemed to the settlers the only way to manage a colony. Given the destruction of the traditional polity, they may have been right.

The following year another difficulty arose. Cortés' fellow *encomendero*, Juan Suárez, brought from Santo Domingo both his mother, María de Marcayda, and his three sisters, who had originally come to the Indies as ladies-in-waiting to the new vicereine, María de Toledo, wife of Diego Colón and niece of the Duke of Alba. The Suárez family were poor, but they claimed to be distantly connected with the Dukes of Medina Sidonia and the Marquises of Villena. "La Marcayda", the mother, was a Basque; her husband, Diego Suárez Pacheco, was originally from Ávila.[20] The family had moved to Granada after its conquest. They left Santo Domingo for Cuba in the train of Diego Velázquez's bride (his cousin María de Cuéllar, daughter of his treasurer, Cristóbal de Cuéllar; she died a week after her wedding). Cortés courted Catalina, one of these three girls, promised to marry her, seduced her, and then showed himself reluctant to go through with his commitment.[21]

Catalina had no property, and scarcely enough money to dress herself. Her brother had to buy some of María de Cuéllar's dresses for her when they were put up for auction.[22] She theatened to sue Cortés for breach of promise. That caused another rift between Cortés and Velázquez, who had become fond of one of Catalina's sisters. Juan Suárez, with Antonio Velázquez (cousin of the Governor) and Baltasar Bermúdez (Velázquez's first choice to be the commander of the third expedition to Mexico), tried to persuade Cortés to marry Catalina. He continued to refuse. The Governor put Cortés in gaol. He broke out and had further picaresque adventures. He took sanctuary in a church. He was then arrested by the *alguacil*, the town constable, Juan Escudero, and was put in irons (an action which Escudero would later rue). He made a further escape, this time in disguise. Cortés was eventually reconciled with Velázquez. Las Casas recalled Cortés at that time as "downcast and humble, hoping for a smile from the least important of Velázquez's servants".[23]

Cortés next accompanied Velázquez on a small expedition to put down certain "rebels" in western Cuba. On his return, he narrowly avoided being drowned in the Bocas de Bany, while inspecting some of his land at Baracoa. He did not return to being secretary to the Governor. But he did marry Catalina. The forgiving Velázquez was a witness at the wedding. There were no children. Catalina was later said by Cortés (and several others) to have often been ill, with a bad heart, and to have been lazy.[24] In the years before 1518, all the same, Cortés seemed as happy with her "as if she had been daughter of a duchess".[25] He lived well, and spent a lot on his wife, as he did on the guests who, because he was a good talker, gathered in his house.[26] He worked hard in his pursuit of gold: "immense sweating, hunger and hard work" was how Las Casas described life in his mines.[27] In a lawsuit in 1529 he talked of having a hacienda on the river Duabán, "than which there was none better on the island". As a result he made money: how much it is difficult to say; Sepúlveda, the historian of Charles V, says that it was "a great fortune".[28] It was certainly large enough for Velázquez to think that Cortés could afford to pay for much of the new fleet destined for the west. Like Velázquez, Cortés moved from Baracoa to Santiago de Cuba, which became the headquarters of government in the island. He so re-established himself in the favours of the Governor that he became chief magistrate, *alcalde*, of Santiago, in which position he seems to have overawed many with whom he came into contact.[29] In 1517, he returned to Santa Domingo, with another Extremeño, Diego de Orellana, probably a distant relation, as *procurador* to ask permission for Grijalva's expedition.[30]

Hernán Cortés in 1518 was known to be resourceful, capable, and good with words, in both speech and writing. He talked well: always having the right expression for the occasion, and agreeable in conversation. In his way he was already experienced in politics. He had that capacity of all successful men of being able to conceal his real intentions until the pear which he coveted was ready to fall. Las Casas described him as prudent.[31] He never lost his temper.

These qualities of restraint sat strangely with his turbulent reputation of being often at loggerheads with Velázquez. There were other contrasts. Thus Cortés went to mass devotedly and prayed often. But he seemed, later, at least, almost to collect women.[32] In 1518, though, the Governor had judged his talents well enough to know that he would make a good leader. He was evidently very observant. He could also sound almost as enthusiastic about the sight of new territory as Columbus could. But his comments were always directed towards specific ends. Cortés' endeavours would be aimed to attract the attention of the King of Castile, to attain honours as well as riches, letting him conduct himself as a Renaissance prince, giving away presents to churches and monasteries: a man "born in brocade" indeed.

The weakest side of Cortés seemed to be the military one: he had never commanded men in battle. His experience of fighting was confined to one or two discreditable incidents in Santo Domingo and Cuba, under the command of Velázquez. But having seen Cortés in the circumstances of those little engagements, Velázquez had presumably noted his coolness of nerve. Velázquez did not expect him to encounter battles on a scale larger than those fought by Hernández de Córdoba or Grijalva.

Cortés, too, seemed clever. He may or may not have enrolled at the university in Salamanca. But he had plainly learned there or at Valladolid enough to be able to pass as a well-read man. He must have been among the few people in Cuba, apart from priests, who could read Latin. His work as a notary at Azúa and in Cuba was obviously important: he would always be aware of both the legal complexities and possibilities of any position which he had adopted. Grandees such as Velázquez often misjudge such persons as Cortés, either under- or over-estimating their qualities, as well as supposing them to be certain to be subordinate.

Velázquez certainly misjudged Cortés. That was because Cortés had grown up in his shadow, as his secretary, follower and adviser. To people around Velázquez, Cortés was "Cortesillo": a difficult man, even a ninny.[33] The Governor would use the word *criado*, servant, to describe their relations in correspondence, for example, in letters to Bishop Fonseca;[34] though the word *criado* at that time meant something more than just a servant. It indicated a member of the household: someone who shared the daily life of his master, and knew of his political engagements and private affairs.

In physique, Cortés was "of medium stature, somewhat bent, without much of a beard".[35] He had "a deep chest, no belly to speak of and was bow-legged. He was fairly thin."[36] Such other evidence as exists suggests that he had a small head and was short: about five feet four.[37]

His colouring is a puzzle. Everyone agrees that his face was pale. The only painting made from life, a watercolour by an artist from Augsburg, Christoph Weiditz, who visited Spain in 1529, shows Cortés' hair and beard as fair.[38] A formal medal made at the same time throws no light on the matter, though it certainly shows Cortés as Las Casas said that he was: "learned and prudent".[39] Perhaps that was because he was then recovering from an illness. The next year, 1530, Cortés' first biographer, the humanist Marineo Siculo, wrote that his hair was "rather red".[40] Fr. López de Gómara, his chaplain in the 1540s, seems to confirm that by saying that "his beard was fair, his hair long".[41] The Mexican indigenous commentators imply that most of the Castilians had fair hair, even if some were dark. But Bernal Díaz, who saw Cortés most days for two and a half years, wrote that Cortés' beard was "dark and his hair the same as his beard".[42] Probably the truth is that Cortés' hair was brown, with some reddish tints.

Diego Velázquez told Cortés that Grijalva (who was not yet known to have returned) had been a failure. He asked Cortés to go back to the new territory because Grijalva seemed to be in difficulty. The "islands" of Yucatan and San Juan were rich, unlike Castilla del Oro, Pedrarias' poor fief on the isthmus. Cortés could expect to obtain much gold. The expedition would make him famous. In addition, he, Velázquez, would provide Cortés with two or three ships. Cortés would have to find the money for other vessels, and indeed for everything else. Velázquez may have chosen Cortés because he thought that more people would rally to him than to anyone else.[43]

Cortés accepted the commission. Velázquez then named him "captain and principal *caudillo*" of the expedition.[44] He gave him a detailed instruction on 23 October.[45] This, drafted by Andrés de Duero, but perhaps corrected by Cortés himself, later inspired controversy, for Velázquez would claim that Cortés had ignored his orders.[46]

It was a long and, in some ways, a contradictory document. A preamble rehearsed the background to Grijalva's expedition. This section spoke of the need to "populate and discover" (*poblar y descubrir*) new territories. That was really a licence to colonise. But the instruction itself, as opposed to the preamble, envisaged a journey of discovery and modest trading – modest, since private trading was excluded.

The instruction proper said that the principal purpose of the expedition was to serve God. Blasphemy and sleeping with native women were, therefore, not allowed. Those women were not to be teased, much less seduced. The playing of cards was banned. Cuban Indians were not to accompany the expedition. The fleet was to keep together and travel west along the coast much as Grijalva was known to have done. Any Indians encountered had to be well treated. The natives of Cozumel were to be told of the power of the King of Spain and how he had placed the islands of the Caribbean under his control. They were to hear the famous Requisition, the *Requerimiento*, or a version of it, placing them also under the rule of Charles V, in return for protection. Indeed everywhere that Cortés landed he was to take possession of the place in the name of the Crown of Castile, doing so in the most solemn way possible. A notary, *escribano*, was, of course, to be present on these occasions. The assumption was that Cortés would keep touching at islands. The idea that there was a great empire to be treated with was not envisaged.

The Indians of Yucatan were to be told how Velázquez had been distressed to hear of the battle between Hernández de Córdoba and the people of Champoton. Cortés was also to find out what the crosses on Cozumel really signified. He was to discover, too, in what the *naturales* of Yucatan and elsewhere believed, and whether there were churches and priests. Cortés was to point out that there was only one God. He was to seek news of Grijalva, as of Cristóbal de Olid, who had gone to look for him. He was also to seek news of those Christians who, as the cross-eyed Mayas had reported, were said to be prisoners in Yucatan: among them, perhaps, there might be Diego de Nicuesa, that conquistador who had been lost in 1510 on a voyage from Darien to Santo Domingo and who had been a friend of Velázquez.

A royal treasurer and inspector (*veedor*) were to be appointed to collect and catalogue the gold, the pearls and the precious stones which might be exchanged with the Indians. These objects were to be put in "a box with three locks" of which Cortés and the two officials would have one key each. They were to collaborate with the inspector of Grijalva's fleet, Francisco de Peñalosa, should the two expeditions meet.[47] If Cortés needed to collect wood or water, the landing party should always be led by a person in his confidence. On no account was anyone ever to sleep on shore. Cortés was to report about the vegetation and the agricultural products of the new land. He of course had to find out about the gold available there. Velázquez had received from Grijalva, through Alvarado, presents of gold: dust, objects, and plate. That Governor wanted to know whether that gold had been smelted near the coast by the Totonacs or if they had received it in that form from somewhere else. If so, where? Cortés was to send back a ship as soon as possible with news; as well as any gold or other treasure obtained.

There were some romantic orders: Cortés was to find out the whereabouts of Amazons, of which there had been much talk; and whether it was true, as the strange Maya had told Grijalva (and as Alvarado must have passed on), that there were people there with huge ears, and even some with faces of dogs. This last concern was then still a preoccupation: both the great Pliny and Solinus, who summarised his work, had devoted much time to discussing that type of anthropological enormity; and, in *Le Livre des Merveilles* of the Duke of Berry, men of that nature were depicted in the land of Pitan among the pygmies. They lived on the smell of fruit.[48] Neither of the two previous expeditions had reported such people: Velázquez and his clerks drew on their memories of books.

There was, as in most such instructions, a clause which gave Cortés such powers as he might need in order to carry out actions not specifically covered by the earlier paragraphs. Another paragraph gave him legal authority to act as judge in any criminal case which might arise.

Probably neither party to the document expressed their real feelings when they signed it: Velázquez looked on the expedition as a holding operation; Cortés, judging from the zest with which he mounted his preparations, had from the earliest moment the grandest designs. Like most such papers, it constituted a contract (*capitulación*) giving state authority for a private venture. The Crown gave approval, subject to certain conditions. Everything else depended on the expeditionaries.[49]

The document was handed to Cortés at a little ceremony in Santiago. The Governor had still heard nothing from Spain in reply to his request the previous year for the title of *adelantado* of Yucatan. So he still had to sign as deputy to the Admiral and commander-in-chief, Diego Colón. Those present were Alonso de Parada, the public notary in Cuba and adviser to Velázquez; Alonso de Escalante (whose house in Santiago was used as a foundry); Vicente López, an assistant notary; and Velázquez's secretary, Andrés de Duero, as well as Cortés and Velázquez himself.[50]

There are some curiosities about the instruction. The most important of these is that Grijalva had been back in Cuba at Velázquez's property, Chipiona, since 30 September, and in Matanzas, a good port, since 8 October. Velázquez, despite his orders to Cortés to look for him, must have known it by about 20 October. Probably even before his instruction to Cortés, he had written to Grijalva, asking him to send his ships and men in great haste to join the new expedition.[51] It is, however, not clear that Cortés was told by Vélazquez of Grijalva's return, since a later statement says that he heard of it only after he had left Santiago de Cuba, about 10 November.[52] (One can discount the remark of the historian Sepúlveda that Grijalva arrived in Santiago on 1 November.)[53]

The explanation must be, first, that Velázquez wanted at all costs to press ahead with the new expedition, because he was afraid that someone else in Hispaniola really might embark on a similar venture.[54] Antonio Sedeño, the chief accountant of Puerto Rico, had sent an expedition of three ships and a brigantine to Honduras that very year. It had been lost in a storm, but it must have constituted a warning to Velázquez.[55]

The second explanation was that the Governor wanted to be the first to find the strait which divided the "island" of Yucatan from the "mainland", where "the Gallant" Pedrarias de Ávila had established himself as governor. The general impression which Velázquez, Grijalva, Cortés, Alvarado and others in Cuba had at that time was that, to the west, they were facing a long line of coast, divided by a strait from some large islands (Yucatan, Ulúa). But beyond the strait they believed that there lay an unknown territory. Perhaps China or India really was close by. Magellan had not yet demonstrated the great size of the "Southern Sea" (the Pacific). Even after he had done so, the connections between the different lands were still falsely seen: China and India were shown in a map in an edition of Ptolemy's *Geography* in 1548 as attached to Mexico.[56] Columbus in 1502, and Hernández de Córdoba and Grijalva in 1517 and 1518, had found that the people were more civilised in these places than they were on "the islands". So perhaps Cortés and Velázquez were secretly in agreement that the journey would be a more serious adventure than the instruction of 23 October offered, being privately designed to establish relations with the lands for which Columbus had been looking.[57]

Having received his orders, Cortés immediately busied himself looking for both men and ships, and buying provisions. He appealed for the former through announcements by the town crier.[58] He did not build any ships, though permission to Cuban residents to do so had recently been given by the Crown:[59] he thought that he had no time. He bought rations on credit, some five or six thousand castellanos' worth, from the shopkeeper in Santiago, Diego Sáinz. In addition, he borrowed another six thousand castellanos from many friends, including an unknown amount from Velázquez himself.[60] He showed generosity: many who signed up with him dined continually at his table.[61]

Cortés' next move was to secure the collaboration of Pedro de Alvarado, restless after his return from the new territories the previous month. The enthusiasm of that conquistador for a new voyage, and his willingness to finance his own ship, horses and men,[62] suggests that his reasons given for coming back were fraudulent. He surely came home because, having seen some of "the secrets of the land", he wanted a more imaginative leader than Grijalva had shown himself. Perhaps Cortés and Alvarado had known each other in childhood, for Alvarado's father, Gómez de Alvarado, may have once lived in Medellín.[63] Cortés and Alvarado surely had prolonged discussions about the significance of Grijalva's discoveries, the nature of the mysterious empire in the mountains behind San Juan de Ulúa, and the truth about human sacrifice. Alvarado's impetuous approach may have attracted Cortés: the charm that a rash man often has for a prudent one. Perhaps too, Alvarado had seen how enthusiastic the Totonacs had been towards the Castilians.[64] He may even have realised how that enthusiasm might be tapped to inspire a campaign designed to overthrow the Mexican empire. That would explain the unquestioning support which Cortés always after-wards showed for Alvarado, even when he did not deserve it. It would explain too why Cortés, a cautious man, was persuaded suddenly that here was the great opportunity which the goddess Fortune had reserved for him, and why he invested everything he had in the expedition.

The scale of Cortés' operations began to worry Velázquez. There seemed no relation between the instructions and the outlay. Cortés seemed to be "doing what he liked".[65] He began to live as if he were a king. His deportment changed. He even dressed differently, as befitted, as he thought, a leader of men, in a hat with a plume of feathers, with a medallion of gold, and a black velvet cloak with golden knots.[66]

Velázquez had begun by going down every day to the port in Santiago to see how the preparations for the expedition were going. But once he became worried, he kept away. Baltasar Bermúdez, and two of the many members of the Velázquez family then in Cuba, began to regret that they had themselves not accepted the Governor's earlier suggestions that they should lead the enterprise. They sought to poison the Governor's mind against Cortés. Velázquez's jester, Cervantes, teased his master that he had chosen the wrong man to command the fleet and that Cortés would make off with it.[67] Velázquez told Cortés of the joke. Cortés gravely said that "Franquescillo" was merely a mad jester. Duero said that some relation of Don Diego must have paid the jester to talk so. In the end the jester himself decided to join Cortés' expedition.[68]

Not much more than two weeks after being asked to direct the expedition, Cortés had three ships (one was a brigantine) and about three hundred men. The work and concentration of effort which made this possible seriously perturbed the Governor. Usually such expeditions took months to plan. That official began to wonder whether his jester might not have been right in his prediction. He thought of changing Cortés for someone else. Cortés, learning of Velázquez's private thoughts, hastened his preparations even more.[69] He believed that, even if everything went well, Velázquez would not maintain his side of the bargain to share the profits.[70] Had the Governor made up his mind to dismiss Cortés, he could have done so then: he was all-powerful in Cuba, and "adored" by the Spanish colony.[71] Yet people meanwhile continued to flock to Cortés' standard: some came specially from Hispaniola, such as Francisco Rodríguez Magariño, constable of Puerto Real on the north side of that unhappy island.[72] Cortés was probably in special haste since he feared that any day royal approval of Velázquez as *adelantado* of Yucatan would arrive from Castile: a nomination which Velázquez might seek to act upon immediately and which would have seriously complicated everything.[73]

Velázquez eventually made up his mind to relieve Cortés of his commission. But he did not want to face his ex-*criado* himself. Instead he told Amador de Lares to go to Cortés and say that he, the Governor, would reimburse him for what he had spent if he would cease his preparations. He also tried to prevent Cortés from buying any more food. That was easy enough since he himself controlled the biggest seller of wines, oil, vinegar, even clothes in Cuba.[74] Cortés appeared to take no notice. Then at last Velázquez nerved himself to cancel Cortés' orders and to transfer the authority which he had given to him to a certain Luis de Medina. But (according to a nephew by marriage of Cortés) Cortés' brother-in-law, Juan Suárez, on a lonely road stabbed the messenger whom Velázquez was sending to Medina and threw his body into a ravine. The papers appointing Medina were taken immediately to Cortés.[75]

Cortés realised that he would do well to leave Santiago as soon as possible. His captains and friends agreed. So he sent certain of his servants, armed, to Fernando Alonso, the director, *obligado*, of the city's slaughterhouse to say that he wanted to buy all his meat. Alonso demurred: he had a contract to feed the town. Cortés' men seized it all, not leaving a single pig, cow or sheep. Alonso went to Cortés and said, "for the love of God", could he not have at least some of the meat back because "if he did not provide for the people, he would be fined". Cortés gave him a gold chain with an emblem in the shape of a thistle, which he took off his own neck and handed to him, presuming that that would cover the fine, as well as the cost of the meat.[76] How the city dined for the next few weeks is not recorded.

Cortés' next call was on the accountant, Amador de Lares. He told him that he wanted to leave immediately with the ships which were ready. Could Lares register those vessels there and then? He did so, though how he combined that action with loyalty to Velázquez is hard to see. Perhaps, though, the *alguacil mayor* (constable), Gonzalo Rodríguez de Ocaña, took the decision.[77] Cortés went on board his flagship. He left his wife, his mines, and his house without much concern. His only interest was now the expedition.

The disgruntled butcher, meantime, told Velázquez what had happened. The Governor rose from his bed at daybreak, and went to the quay. Cortés, flanked by armed men, had a conversation with him from a small boat. Velázquez said: "How is this, my friend [*compadre*], that you are setting off in this way? Is this a good way to say goodbye to me?" Cortés replied: "Forgive me, but these things have all been thought about some time before they were ordered. What are now your orders?" Velázquez, shaken by the insubordination, made no reply. Cortés instructed his captains to set off.[78] He (and they) knew from experience that Velázquez, though quick to anger, was also quick to forgive. Perhaps Cortés hoped for a tacit acceptance of his behaviour. It was 18 November 1518.[79]

III
To know the Secrets of the Land

11

A gentlemanly pirate

"All this was told me by Cortés himself, with other things relating to it, after
he was made a marquis, in the town of Monzón, where a parliament was held
by the Emperor in 1542, laughing and mocking and with these formal words:
'By my faith, I carried on over there as if I had been a gentlemanly pirate.' "
Bartolomé de Las Casas, *Historia de las Indias*

CORTÉS LEFT SANTIAGO with six ships. He left a seventh one behind being careened. He did not have much food – being especially short of bread. He therefore stopped at the small port of Macaca (probably the modern Pilón) on Cape Cruz. He there picked up a thousand rations of cassava bread from his friend, Francisco Dávila, who had a property there. Cortés seems to have obtained some supplies from a royal farm there, too. He sent a ship to Jamaica for wine, eight hundred flitches of bacon, and two thousand more rations of cassava bread.[1]

Cortés next stopped at Trinidad, the little settlement founded in the centre of Cuba, not far from where, a few years before, Las Casas had had his farm. Here the magistrate was Francisco Verdugo, who had married Inés, a sister of Velázquez. He was a hidalgo of Cojes de Iscar, a village a short distance from Cuéllar.[2] Just as Cortés arrived, Verdugo received a letter from the Governor requiring him to delay the armada. Velázquez had decided to replace Cortés with Vasco Porcallo de Figueroa. Similar letters were received by the captains of two of Cortés' ships, Francisco de Morla and Diego de Ordaz. The first, who came from Jerez, had been steward, *camarero*, to Velázquez. The second, Ordaz, came from Castroverde de Campos in León. His first adventure in America had been in Colombia in 1510, with the disastrous expedition of Alonso de Ojeda when the cartographer, Juan de la Cosa, had been killed by a poisoned arrow at the battle at Turbaco, prior to a disgraceful massacre of Indians. Ordaz had taken part in the conquest of Cuba. He was famous for having been left behind by his brother Pedro in a swamp.[3] In 1518 he had probably been asked by the Governor to join Cortés in order to prevent mutiny on Cortés' expedition – by its commander most of all. His mother was a Girón, a grand family, and he was connected by blood to Velázquez, as were most of that Governor's officials.[4] In 1518, he was nearly forty, he had a slight stammer, a thin black beard, rode badly, but had a strong face. On this expedition he financed his own ship of sixty men, with meat, cassava bread, wine, chickens and pigs. Though he was a poor horseman (and would often remain in command of foot soldiers), he was literate, being an excellent, often caustic, letter-writer.[5] Like several other leaders of Cortés' expedition, Ordaz seems to have been involved in various disputes over debts (perhaps in respect of the pearl trade) which made it desirable for him to leave Cuba.[6]

Cortés heard of these letters of Velázquez and, using powers which nobody previously knew him to possess, not only persuaded Ordaz and Morla to continue to collaborate with him but prevailed upon the first to arrange with Francisco Verdugo to provide the fleet with some horses, several loads of fodder, and more bread. One of Velázquez's messengers, Pedro Laso, was even persuaded to enlist in Cortés' fleet. This was an early example of Cortés' skill with words which would be one of his most formidable weapons. Years later, Verdugo explained that he had given Cortés these goods since Velázquez had asked him to.[7] No doubt that meant that he was obeying an earlier request of the Governor's, and turning a blind eye to his latest one.

Cortés then sent Ordaz with a brigantine, the *Alguecebo*, to seize a ship which he had heard was on its way carrying provisions to Darien. Ordaz was successful. He secured the load of four thousand *arrobas* of bread and fifteen hundred flitches of bacon or salted chicken. The owner, a merchant of Madrid, Juan Núñez Sedeño, who was on board, with a mare and a colt, decided to throw in his lot with Cortés.[8] Talking of these incidents to Las Casas years later (in Spain in 1542), Cortés admitted, "By my faith, I carried on over there as if I had been a gentlemanly pirate."

Cortés was involved in at least one non-piratical activity: his page, Diego de Coria, saw him writing for the first eight nights after leaving Santiago. What was he working on? Letters to Spain? To his father and to the judge, Licenciado Céspedes, telling them what he was planning? Or to merchants in Hispaniola or Seville, forewarning them of their new opportunities?[9] The page never knew.

Some of those who had been on Grijalva's expedition joined Cortés at Trinidad. From there, Cortés sent down some messages forty miles away to Sancti Spiritus, from where he was joined by others who had farms in the neighbourhood. These included one of the most important members of the expedition: a fellow citizen of Medellín, Alonso Hernández Portocarrero, a cousin of the Count of that city.[10] Though this conquistador could scarcely speak without swearing,[11] and though his military qualities were unproven, Cortés was evidently pleased to have with him a grandee from his own *pueblo*. Portocarrero was also a nephew of Judge Céspedes. He had a small farm and a hundred and fifty Indians in Cuba.[12] But he could not have been rich, for Cortés bought him a horse by selling the gold tassels from his own velvet cloak. He also recruited at Trinidad two other men from Medellín, Rodrigo Rangel and Gonzalo de Sandoval. The latter was only about twenty-one years old. When about fourteen, he had been a page to Velázquez. His capacity for endurance would make him in the end the most successful of Cortés' captains. All of them (and there were others) contributed whatever they could from their properties, particularly cassava bread and smoked ham.[13] Much of the latter was now available since, by that time, the wild pigs of Cuba were prospering as much as they did in Extremadura.

By now at last Cortés had learned of Grijalva's return: he heard of it when at Macaca.[14] Grijalva had with him many interesting and beautiful gold objects beyond what Alvarado had brought.[15] He also had his girl slave, with her splendid ornaments, several men and, surprisingly for someone so apparently rational, some tantalising information about Amazons. All this made Velázquez even more concerned to bring Cortés' imminent expedition to a swift end.

But from Trinidad Cortés sailed on to the little port of San Cristóbal de la Habana on the south coast of Cuba. It was at that time in the process of being transferred fifty miles across the island to the north coast, where it now stands, apparently because the harbour was better there, and perhaps because one of Velázquez's relations, Juan de Rojas, had land there.[16] On the way, Cortés became lost in the dangerous archipelago which Velázquez had christened Los Jardines de la Reina, the Gardens of the Queen. His flagship ran aground and it took some days to be freed. Pedro de Alvarado and his brothers and some other conquistadors who had been to "the new land" with Grijalva separately made their way to Havana. These included Francisco de Montejo and Alonso de Ávila, among the captains of that journey, and also Cristóbal de Olid, the "Hector of single combat", who earlier on had gone in search of Grijalva.[17] These conquistadors whiled away the time of waiting for their leader considering the pleasing topic as to which of them should succeed Cortés should he turn out to be lost for ever.[18]

Havana, then a new city, was loyal to Velázquez. Most of its few settlers refused to help Cortés. But all the same, Cortés stayed in the house of Pedro Barba, who had also journeyed with Grijalva (he had given his name to the Mayan interpreter) and was in command of the town. Cortés displayed his banner in the street. He also had his expedition announced by the town crier. In consequence, he gained the backing not only of one or two more adventurers, but also of Cristóbal de Quesada, collector of tithes for the bishop, who declared himself willing to assist. So did Francisco de Medina, the collector, on the Crown's behalf, of the tax known as "la cruzada" ("the bull of crusade", in theory a voluntary contribution to the expenses of the war against Islam, but now an ordinary tax extended to the New World). These two sold Cortés another five thousand rations of bread, two thousand flitches of bacon, and many beans and chickpeas, as well as wine, vinegar and six thousand loaves of bread made from cassava – one of the few Caribbean products which the Castilians deigned to eat: wisely, for it lasted much longer without deterioration than bread made from wheat.[19]

Yet one more intimate of Velázquez, Gaspar de Garnica, appeared by ship in Havana. He brought another letter for Cortés from the Governor. It required him to wait. Garnica carried other letters from Velázquez for his cousin Juan Velázquez de León, who had joined Cortés at Trinidad, and for Diego de Ordaz. Fr. Bartolomé de Olmedo, a Mercedarian who had agreed to accompany Cortés, received a letter from a fellow friar in Velázquez's circle.[20] All these communications asked their recipients to delay Cortés. The letter to Ordaz even requested him to seize Cortés and bring him back a prisoner to Santiago. Ordaz asked his commander to dine on the caravel in which Garnica had come. But Cortés suspected a trap. He feigned a stomach ache.[21] Garnica wrote to Velázquez that he had not dared to seize Cortés, since he was too popular with his soldiers.[22]

Velázquez, in fact, seemed close to forgiving Cortés. In early December 1518, two weeks after the latter had left Santiago, Andrés de Tapia, a pale man with a thin beard, who had once worked in Seville as a groom to Columbus, came to see the Governor, perhaps from Hispaniola, and told him that he wanted to serve with Cortés. Velázquez, greeting Tapia affectionately, as if he had been his nephew, said: "I do not know what Cortés' intentions really are towards me, but they must be bad, because he has spent everything that he had and is in debt. He has taken my officials into his service as if he were one of the lords of Spain. In spite of that, I wish you would go with him. It is not fifteen days since he left this port, and you can soon catch him up. I will help you and one or two others who also want to go with him."

Velázquez then gave Tapia and his companions a loan of forty ducats to help them buy clothes in a shop which belonged to him. They would, they thought, have found the same goods elsewhere for a quarter of that.[23] But they nevertheless set off and joined Cortés at Havana. Perhaps Velázquez's atttitude derived not from his forgiving nature but because by then he had received Grijalva. He had bitterly upbraided him for not breaking his instructions and going ahead to settle the new country.[24] It was perhaps difficult to be disillusioned with Grijalva at the same time as being angry with Cortés.

Velázquez had another visitor: Juan de Salcedo, who had taken part in the expedition of Grijalva. He rode the long distance from Havana to Santiago. There, Velázquez asked him: "What shall I do? The truth is that I sent Hernán Cortés with a fleet to the new land with instructions to find Grijalva, not to settle there. What do you advise me to do?" Salcedo knew Cortés well, for he had married Leonor Pizarro, the Cuban girl by whom Cortés had earlier had a child. He replied to Velázquez: "I suggest you go yourself." Salcedo went to the Jeronymite priors in Santo Domingo. He secured a permission for the Governor to settle the new land.[25] The poor priors were then living on sufferance. Their powers had been taken from them. But until their successor Figueroa arrived the following August they were in authority. Their inclination was to approve everything they were asked.

But Velázquez was in as weak a position as ever, since it would have been impossible for him to have gathered a new fleet quickly to sail either against or in collaboration with Cortés. Cortés was evidently not to be dissuaded. He had invested his fortune in the enterprise, as had some others.

The question of how much of the costs of the expedition were paid by Cortés or by Velázquez is, at this distance of time, a matter of judgement rather than of analysis, since so many contrary things were later said. Velázquez, in his will, said that he had offered to pay a third of the costs, assuming that Cortés would pay another third, and that the volunteers would find (and share the profits from) the final third.[26] A letter the following year from Cortés' friends, probably drafted by Cortés himself, admitted that Velázquez had indeed paid a third.[27] Pedro de Alvarado, as has been seen, claimed to have paid for one *nao* and its equipment. So did Ordaz. Cortés himself claimed that he paid "nearly two-thirds" of the costs, including the wages of the sailors and the pilots.[28] But several witnesses at Cortés' enquiry in 1520 went further and said that "everyone knew that the cost was borne by Cortés".[29] Years later, the polemicist Sepúlveda, in his *De Orbe Novo*, wrote, after talking to Cortés himself, that the two men had agreed to pay half each.[30]

The safest judgement in the matter would seem to be to echo the testimony of the pilot, Antonio de Alaminos, an honest man who, in 1522, stated that Cortés and Velázquez financed the fleet between them, with Cortés paying the larger share.[31] Cortés, however, probably did not put up in cash more than a third of the money needed: say 6,500 pesos. He said in 1520 that his costs came to about 20,000 pesos, of which he had borrowed three-quarters. But in 1529 he reduced the estimate to 12,000 castellanos, half of which, he admitted, he had borrowed. Many settlers in Cuba felt in consequence that they had a share in the undertaking.[32]

This expedition, like most in those times, was an adventure of private enterprise. The model, like most things in the history of the establishment of the Spanish empire, derived from medieval practice. The Crown had (indirectly) given permission; and the Crown's governor had nominated the commander. The commander was responsible for fitting things out. Those who volunteered for the journey were on it because they hoped to make their fortunes. Only the forty or fifty sailors and the five pilots were paid – by Cortés. The soldiers, whether captains or humble infantrymen, lived, as usual, on expectations. Yet once they had agreed to join the "army" of the *Caudillo*, they assumed the obligation under pain of death not to abandon it.[33]

Cortés held a muster of his expedition just short of the extreme west point of Cuba, at Cape Corrientes. In this at least he was following his instructions.

He now had eleven ships. But only four were of substance – the flagship, *Santa María de la Concepción*, a *nao* of a capacity of a hundred tons, and three others with a capacity of sixty to eighty tons.[34] The rest were small open ships or brigantines. All the bigger ships, and perhaps some of the brigantines, would have been built in Spain. One of the *naos*, that captained and apparently paid for by Pedro de Alvarado, failed to be present at the muster.[35] Cortés decided to sail without him. Another ship which Cortés had bought was, it may be remembered, still being careened in Santiago.

Counting the men who later sailed with Alvarado, Cortés had with him about five hundred and thirty Europeans, of whom thirty were crossbowmen. Twelve had arquebuses.[36] These last were men who belonged to a different order of society from the captains or the infantrymen. Yet they were as important as the captains. There had been *condottieri* in Italy who had opposed their introduction: Paolo Vitelli had put out the eyes and cut off the hands of captured German *schiopettieri*, because he thought it unworthy that a knight should be laid low by common men with guns. Cortés had no such reluctance to use modern technology. He also had fourteen pieces of artillery of the same type that Grijalva had taken: probably ten culverins of bronze, with four falconets.[37] But Cortés probably also had with him some breech-loading cannon, lombards, such as were often found then on ships. These could sustain a higher rate of fire than the other muzzle-loaders.[38] These weapons, most of which had names (San Francisco, Juan Ponce, Santiago and so on), were in the hands of specialists: Francisco de Mesa; a Levantine named Arbenga; Juan Catalan, one of the few Catalans to be found in the Indies; and Bartolomé de Usagre, from his name an Extremeño. The captain of this little unit of artillery was Francisco de Orozco, "who had been a good soldier in Italy":[39] the magical experience which was supposed to guarantee everything. Similar responsibilities in respect of the crossbowmen went to Juan Benítez and Pedro de Guzmán, masters in the art of repairing those weapons.

There may have been as many as fifty sailors, many of them, as was common in those days on Spanish ships, foreigners – Portuguese, Genoese, Neapolitans, and even a Frenchman.[40]

About a third of Cortés' expedition probably originated in Andalusia, almost a quarter from Old Castile, and only sixteen per cent from

Birthplaces of the Conquistadors

BADAJOZ
Pedro de Alvarado
& his brothers

BURGOS
Pedro de Maluenda
Gerónimo Ruiz de la Mota

BURGUILLOS DEL CERRO
Leonel de Cervantes

CÁCERES
García Holguín
Gutierre de Badajoz
Juan Cano

CASTROVERDE DE CAMPOS
Diego de Ordaz

CIUDAD REAL
Alonso de Ávila

COJECES DE ISCAR
Fco. Verdugo

CÓRDOBA
Fco. Hernández de Córdoba
Lope Ochoa de Caicedo

CUÉLLAR
Diego Velázquez
Juan Velázquez de León
Juan de Cuéllar
Juan de Grijalva
Baltasar Bermúdez

ÉCIJA
Gerónimo de Aguilar

ENCINASOLA
Fco. de Flores

FONTIVEROS
Juan de Salamanca

FREGENAL DE LA SIERRA
Juan Jaramillo

GIBRALEÓN
Alfonso Penate

ILLESCAS
Pedro Gutiérrez de Valdelomar

JEREZ DE LA FRONTERA
Fco. de Morla

MADRID
Juan Núñez Sedeño

MEDELLÍN
Hernán Cortés
Gonzalo de Sandoval
Alonso de Mendoza
Alonso Hernández Portocarrero
Juan Rodríguez de Villafuerte

MEDINA DEL CAMPO
Bernal Díaz del Castillo
Cristóbal de Morante
Cristóbal de Olea
Fco. de Lugo (Fuencastín)

MEDINA DE RIOSECO
Fco. de Saucedo 'el pulido'

NAVALMANZANO
Pánfilo de Narváez

NIEBLA
Gonzalo Guerrero

OLIVA
Fco. Álvarez Chico

OLMEDO
Fr. Bartolomé de Olmedo

OROPESA
Bernardino Vázquez de Tapia

PINTO
Diego de Godoy

PLASENCIA
Andrés de Tapia

SALAMANCA
Fco. de Montejo
Juan de Salamanca
Bernardino de Santa Clara

SANLÚCAR DE BARRAMEDA
Luis Marín
Alonso Caballero

SAN SEBASTIÁN
Juan Bono de Quejo

SEVILLE
Martín López
Fr. Juan Díaz
Juan de Limpias
Cristóbal de Tapia

TIEMBLO
Cristóbal del Corral

TORDESILLAS
Julián de Alderete

TORO
Diego de Soto
(Bishop Rodríguez de Fonseca)

TUDELA DE DUERO
Andrés de Duero

VALENCIA DE DON JUAN
Cristóbal Flores

ZAMORA
Antonio de Villafaña
Antonio de Quiñones

Extremadura. Seville and Huelva were far the most frequent birthplaces of the men concerned.[41] But as so often, many commanders were Extremeños. A few Spanish women also travelled: these were two sisters of Diego de Ordaz, three or four maids, and one or two women who went as housekeepers.[42] The exact role of these particular *"conquistadoras"* – the word was used by Andrea del Castillo, Francisco de Montejo's daughter-in-law, in a subsequent enquiry – is unclear. But no doubt that lady was correct when she said that, when women of her quality did take part in these engagements, their work was considerable.[43] One or two of these women certainly later fought effectively.

The pilots with Cortés were the same as those who had served with Hernández de Córdoba and Grijalva: Alaminos, Juan Álvarez the lame, Pedro Camacho and Pedro Arnés de Sopuerta. Cortés had two churchmen: Fr. Juan Díaz, the Sevillano who had been with Grijalva; and Fr. Bartolomé de Olmedo, a Mercedarian friar from Olmedo, a town no distance from Valladolid and Cuéllar. He was a man of good sense whose advice to Córtes (usually to be patient) would be invaluable. Of a merry disposition, he sang very well. Still, he had enemies who said that he was more interested in gold than in souls.[44] Olmedo was well educated, having probably studied at the University of Valladolid, and had spent some time in the *conventos* of Segovia and Olmedo. Being more worldy than Díaz, as well as having much better judgement, his influence was far more important. All the same, the spiritual work of both these men was considerable: they enabled the captains of the expedition to hear mass, particularly Cortés, who, whatever his private reflections, was publicly on his knees most days, as even his enemies testified.[45]

There were a dozen men with some kind of professional training, though only one doctor, Pedro López. There were several notaries, whose services Cortés later would use indiscriminately. Perhaps there were half a dozen carpenters. Apart from the sailors, there were a few Greeks, Italians, some Portuguese, and several other foreigners.[46]

Despite Velázquez's prohibition, there were with Cortés several hundred Cuban Indians, including some women, as well as a few African freemen and black slaves.[47] (It is possible that Juan Garrido, a free black African who had become a Christian in Lisbon, later famous as the first man to grow wheat in Mexico, was among these.)[48] One citizen of Cuba said later that he thought that every one of Cortés' expedition had two Cuban servants.[49] The fisherman "Melchor", one of the cross-eyed Mayas captured in Yucatan by Hernández de Córdoba, accompanied the fleet (though his comrade, the melancholy Julián, who had accompanied Grijalva, had died). "Francisco", the Nahuatl-speaking Indian who had been captured by Grijalva, was also on board Cortés' ship.

Sixteen horses were loaded: the important innovation of this voyage.

These were, as Piedrahita, the historian of the conquest of Nueva Granada, would put it, "the nerves of the wars against the natives".[50] Those taken by Cortés were probably the same breed as those which a later Diego Velázquez painted in his equestrian portraits: sturdy, short-backed, legs not too long, strong enough to carry a man in armour and a heavy, comfortable Moorish saddle. For the riders would have ridden *à la gineta*, that is with stirrups long, a powerful bit and a single rein. The legs of the riders would have pressed back, the heads of the horses turned by pressure at the neck, not at the mouth.[51] On the crossing from Cuba to Yucatan these horses would have been hoisted on to the decks by pulley and remained there for the voyage. The horses were expensive: each one cost at least three thousand pesos: even an African slave cost less. No doubt some of the horses were descendants of those carried to Hispaniola by Columbus on his second voyage. The names of some of them were recalled by Bernal Díaz: El Rey ("the King"); Roldanillo ("little Roland"); Cabeza de Moro ("Moor's head").

There were also numerous dogs – presumably either Irish wolfhounds or mastiffs, the difference in breeds being then obscure. Dogs had fought effectively, and had been used brutally, in establishing other parts of the Spanish empire, as they had in the wars against the Moors. Cortés would not have dreamed of depriving himself of their use. His father might have told him that a dog, Mohama, had fought so valiantly at Granada that he received a horseman's share of the spoil. Indeed, the use of dogs in war in Europe was common. Henry VIII would soon send four hundred mastiffs to Charles V for use against the French, some of them wearing light armour. In the conquest of Puerto Rico, Ponce de León's dog Becerrillo ("little calf") had played an important part, with his "reddish fur and black eyes". Becerrillo's son, Leoncillo ("little lion"), had been with Balboa when he first saw the Pacific.[52]

The captains on the expedition presented some political difficulties to Cortés. Several were more experienced than he in wars in the Indies. Others were close friends of Diego Velázquez. Most prominent among these last was, of course, Diego de Ordaz, whose equivocal role at Havana had already distinguished him. Other "Velázquistas", as they came to be known, were Francisco de Montejo, the Salamantino commander of one of the four *naos*; Francisco de Morla; and Juan Velázquez de León. The latter, a strong fighter with a well-kept curly beard, and a harsh voice which stuttered, was a spirited man, very grand in his ways, whose attachment to his kinsman, the Governor, had slackened when he did not receive a good grant of Indians.[53]

There were also men who would rarely say a good word for Cortés. The most prominent of these was Juan Escudero, that constable, *alguacil*, of Asunción de Baracoa who had seized Cortés in 1515 and imprisoned him during one of his rows with the Governor.

At the same time, the *Caudillo*, to use Velázquez's word for him, had some dedicated friends. Most were Extremeños. These included Alonso Hernández Portocarrero and Gonzalo de Sandoval, who came from Medellín; Juan Gutiérrez de Escalante, who had been with Grijalva; Alonso de Grado, "a man of many graces but not much of a soldier",[54] an *encomendero* on a small scale in Hispaniola, who had been born in Alcántara; and, above all, Pedro de Alvarado and his four brothers, who, from the beginning of the journey, were the strongest backers of the new *Caudillo*. Two Castilian supporters of Cortés were Francisco de Lugo, a bastard son of Álvaro de Lugo, the lord of Fuencastín, near Medina del Campo,[55] and Bernardino Vázquez de Tapia, Grijalva's standard-bearer, who could also be counted at this time in this category. But these men compensated neither in seniority nor in numbers for the friends of the Governor. Thus Cortés had to make a practice of attempting to win over the first group, by promoting and seeking to inspire them without losing his own friends. It was a delicate task.

Cortés' tasks was made easier by the fact that he had established by this time a household of his own, modelled on the kind of staff that the Count of Medellín or some other Extremeño baron would have had, though Ovando and Velázquez would have had the same: Cristóbal de Guzmán was master of his household; Rodrigo Rangel was chamberlain (*camarero*); and Joan de Cáceres, a man of experience who was nevertheless illiterate, was his majordomo.[56] The first of these was from Seville, the other two Extremeños. Rangel was from Medellín. People noticed that Cortés, having "established a household, lived as a lord". All the same, for some time more he remained, in the memory of Juan Núñez Sedeño, "almost as a companion" to the rest of the expedition.[57]

As for the rest, another witness, Fernando de Zavallos, said in a lawsuit in 1529 that the expedition was composed of "young men . . . in needy circumstances and easily dominated by [Cortés]".[58] Youth was certainly a factor: the majority of the expeditionaries must have been in their early twenties.[59] Diego de Vargas told an enquiry in 1521 that: "Among those with Cortés, there were those who said that they were rich, and those who did not have as much as they wished, and there many poor and indebted among them."[60] The backbone of Cortés' army was undoubtedly composed of the second of the two groups: men who wanted more money and were prepared to go to a lot of trouble to find it. Most would have come out to the Indies, either to Cuba, Hispaniola, or Tierra Firme, since 1513. But some would have been elderly survivors of the early expeditions to Hispaniola, and perhaps there were some with clipped ears or noses – indicating that they had once been convicted robbers in Castile. Several expeditionaries (Cristóbal Martín de Gamboa, Joan de Cáceres) had first gone to the Indies with Ovando in 1502, and had taken part in the conquest of Cuba.[61]

On board there was enough bread, smoked or salted meat, bacon, salt, oil, vinegar and wine to last the five hundred or so men for a few weeks. The maize, chillis and yucca were no doubt looked on as a reserve. Fresh water was carried in barrels, though they often leaked, because the European wood from which they were usually made did not survive the tropics well (very soon, water, like wine, began to travel in earthenware jars).[62] No more water was taken than was estimated would last the crossing to Yucatan.

The weapons, apart from the cannon, arquebuses and crossbows, and the ammunition needed, were mostly swords and lances. Cortés had intelligently ordered cotton armour for use against arrows, such as he had learned was favoured for its lightness by the Indians in Yucatan. This had been made for him near Havana, where cotton was available and where Cuban Indian women were adept at weaving.[63] But those who considered themselves, or were, of knightly class had brought the traditional steel helmets, breastplates and bucklers which, heavy as they were, made, as Cortés had discovered from stories from men on the earlier expeditions, a strong impression on their opponents. He must have had many spare parts: not just for the soldiers, but for the horses who required spare bridles, saddles, stirrups and of course horse-shoes, a surprisingly expensive item.

A final cargo consisted of the presents which the conquistadors took to give to the Indians: the same things which Hernández de Córdoba and Grijalva had taken, including glass beads, bells, mirrors, needles, pins, leather goods, knives, scissors, tongs, hammers, iron axes, as well as some Castilian clothes: handkerchiefs, breeches, shirts, capes, and stockings. Some of these objects such as scissors were of real interest to people who had not reached the age of iron, much less that of steel, yet whose capacity to adapt and learn about new technology was soon shown to be remarkable. Most of these things probably came originally from Germany, Italy or Flanders, though perhaps there were oyster shells from the Canaries, and there were, as will be seen, one or two pearls from what is now Venezuela.

According to Cortés' chaplain, López de Gómara, Cortés started the expedition to Mexico with a speech. Perhaps he did, though it is hard to believe that he made the full-blooded appeal to the desire for fame and fortune which that author, well versed in the oratory of the later Italian Renaissance, published. The speech, according to López de Gómara, purported to say that the expedition would win for the conquistadors "vast and wealthy lands", kingdoms "greater than those of our monarchs", and "great rewards wrapped around with hardships".[64] Had Cortés spoken so directly, the friends of Velázquez under his command might have overthrown him there and then. Still, Cortés would probably have known that modern generals often made speeches to their assembled troops. But it is uncertain to whom Cortés could have spoken. Merely his own ship's company? Or to his captains, especially carried over from their ships to hear him?

Cortés all the same permitted his men to have an inkling of what he was privately thinking, by displaying, on a banner which he flew from the masthead of his flagship, and which he had had prepared in Santiago, a blue cross and a slogan in Latin: "*Amici, sequamur crucem, et si nos fidem habemus, vere in hoc signo vincemus*", which, being translated, might be said to read, "Friends, let us follow the cross and, if we have faith, let us conquer under this banner".[65] To those who had been educated, or who wished to be thought educated, this motto of course recalled the sign of the cross which, in legend, appeared to the Emperor Constantine's army before the battle of the Milvian bridge. But the instructions of Diego Velázquez had not mentioned a battle, much less the need to win it. Quite possibly Cortés, if advised by the Mercedarian friar Bartolomé de Olmedo about the Latin, recalled the slogan from a ballad. Some of Cortés' admirers may have been less than delighted by the appeal to religion: Gonzalo de Sandoval, for example, was always giving the impression he had "reneged on divine Providence" and was incessantly "speaking ill of Our Lord God and his blessed Mother".[66] If he were going to fight, he would do so for Castile.

The subject of Cortés' religious beliefs baffles all but the fortunately simple who, like the first historian of the Mexican church, Fr. Mendieta, believe that Cortés was chosen by God to carry out His purposes. The evidence is as conflicting as that relating to the colour of his hair. "Even though he was a sinner, he had faith and did the work of a good Christian," wrote the Franciscan priest Motolinía, who knew him well (being his confessor) in later life, adding that "he confessed with many tears and placed his soul and treasure in the hands of his confessor".[67] His favourite oath was "by my conscience". Yet Diego de Ordaz, who saw him most days for the next eighteen months, would write in 1529 that Cortés had "no more conscience than a dog".[68] He was "addicted to women in excess", greedy, and loved the "worldly pomp" of which he would speak disdainfully in his will; yet he preached well, prayed often, and usually wore a gold chain with a picture of the Virgin on one side and John the Baptist on the other.[69]

The truth seems to be that, though a sincere Christian, Cortés was quite able to combine Christian beliefs, and actions, with a realisation that these things were useful. The motives of Cortés, like those of Columbus, were inextricably mixed: above all, no doubt, he wanted glory, he also wanted wealth and, where appropriate, or convenient, he also wanted to serve God. "For God and Profit" was the slogan of the merchant of Prato, Francesco Datini. The Roman Church before the Counter-Reformation, and before the establishment of the Jesuits, was a more relaxed enterprise than it subsequently became. Cortés forgave Sandoval and Portocarrero for blasphemy since they were intimates; but he ostensibly punished others for the same crime (Cristóbal Flores, Francisco de Orduña). He gambled. He loved, as a show above all, the material things of life, of which he had seen too few in his childhood. He liked having a court of assistants. He would contemplate any tactic, even one which might (given his time) have been with justification called Machiavellian. These things show his priorities. But he naturally developed as his expedition gathered strength. He probably became more God-fearing as he faced more and more challenges. The Church often afforded a convenient pretext for action – more so (though this is to anticipate) than was the case in respect of other conquests in the Caribbean, for the obvious reason that the religions of old Mexico and its subordinate territories were more formidable than those of the West Indies. Christianity, after all, was the philosophy of Cortés' expedition, even if it was decorated with Castilian honour. It was the morality which offered morale, the sense of community which sustained the individual in battle, and the faith which might even comfort prisoners who would meet their death on the sacrificial stone.[70]

The departure of five hundred men left Cuba exposed. It seems doubtful whether the whole Castilian population of the island could in 1518 have been more than a thousand males. In Baracoa there were only one or two Castilian households remaining.[71] Had the indigenous population had a leader, or had the French been as willing then to attack the Spanish empire as they already were beginning to be to attack ships on the high seas, Velázquez would have been hard pressed to protect his little kingdom.

Cortés sent a respectful letter of goodbye to that proconsul before he left.[72] But neither respect nor obedience were in his heart. Cortés kept his own counsel. He never allowed himself to talk about his intentions before he left Cuba. The evidence is, though, that he intended to colonise and conquer, as well as to discover (*poblar* as well as *descubrir*). Bernal Díaz recalled him saying so before he left Santiago.[73] No one, after all, takes horses and cannon if they are going merely to trade.

So it was that the third Castilian expedition finally set off for Yucatan on 18 February 1519.

The advantage of having horse and cannon

"The advantage of having horse and cannon is very necessary in this land, for it gives force and advantage to few against many"
Fr. Motolinía, letter to Charles V, 1555

A S SOON AS his expedition was under way, Cortés dedicated it to his patron saint: San Pedro, who, he believed, had saved his life as a child in Medellín. He ordered the masters of the ships to keep his flagship in sight. He had a lantern hung on the stern of that vessel as a beacon. Should there be bad weather, the good harbour of the island of Santa Cruz, Cozumel, would be the place of rendezvous. It was by now well known to the pilots.[1]

Cortés caused the fleet to make for that point for two reasons: first, it was the shortest way to the "island" of Yucatan; secondly, he took seriously his instruction to try and find the Christians believed to be held captive there.

Bad weather began instantly. The ships were separated during their first night at sea. At dawn the next day, Cortés lacked five ships, in addition to the continuing absence of Alvarado. Francisco de Morla found that his ship had lost its rudder. He dived into the sea himself to retrieve it.[2] Cortés arrived at Cozumel to find several of his ships already there. First to arrive had been the *San Sebastián*, with Alvarado. That captain insisted that he had reached the muster point in Cuba before Cortés. But bad weather had forced him out to sea.[3]

When Cortés and his men landed, they found, as Grijalva had done, that the inhabitants of the coastal villages had fled into the interior. This was not only from natural timidity: for Alvarado had been enjoying himself at the local people's cost. He had seized turkeys, men, women, and ornaments from the temple.[4] Cortés reprimanded him: that was "no way to pacify [*apaciguar*] the country".[5] Alvarado denied that he had done anything unusual. When his men had arrived, they had found no Indians. So they had helped themselves to the food which they found in the deserted houses. Cortés had Alvarado's pilot Camacho briefly imprisoned for having failed to make the rendezvous.[6]

Cortés, in his reproof, again showed his hand, for his orders from Velázquez had said nothing about pacifying anyone.

In the next day or two, nine of the ten ships with which Cortés had left Cuba assembled at Cozumel. The exception was that captained by Alonso de Escobar. That vessel seemed lost for good.

Cortés himself looked at the Indian villages on Cozumel. Perhaps a third of his men had been to the island with Grijalva but, for himself and the rest, the temple to the lady of the rainbow, Ix Chel, with its thatched sanctuary on top of a many-stepped pyramid, characteristic of the whole region, was a novelty. So was the curious honey, the unexpected fruits, the new vegetables, and the sea birds. On their arrival the Castilians also found "beds of native cotton called hammocks", *hamacas* – a word unknown to Cortés before, though Hernández de Córdoba and Grijalva must have seen them, and probably slept in them. He and his friends also observed a wealth of interesting ornaments "and, most Holy Father, books", as Peter Martyr put it in a letter to the Pope, after he had talked to members of this expedition the following year.[7]

These "books" were beautifully painted picture series made from bark, smeared with bitumen, and stretched into sheets several feet long. They must have seemed closer to the old-fashioned illuminated manuscripts of Europe than to the new printed works with which Cortés' generation was becoming familiar.

A woman (probably the wife of a chief) was found, with her children and servants. She had stayed behind when the populace fled. Cortés gave her some clothes and other *"cosas de Castilla"*.[8] To the children he gave toys; to the servants, scissors and mirrors. Through the unsatisfactory interpretation of Melchor, Cortés asked her to invite the chiefs and other islanders to return. He promised that they would be well treated.[9] They did come back. Cortés ordered that, so far as possible, the things stolen from their houses by Alvarado's men before he had arrived should be restored to them. In response, the chief of the island arranged with his people to give food to the Castilians; fish, bread and honey. There was a ceremonious greeting between the leaders. The Indians burned resin in the main courtyard before the temple: a smell like incense.[10]

Cortés was so friendly that the Mayas of Cozumel listened to him with attention as he explained to them, through Melchor, the odious character, as he saw it, of human sacrifices. They asked him to what law they should then submit. Cortés replied that there was one God, the creator of heaven and earth, giver of all things.[11] Interrupting an indigenous ceremony, he arranged for a mass to be held and told his astonished hearers that he wanted to break their idols and provide them with a better law and better things to worship.[12] The idols in their temples, he insisted, were evil. They would, in his opinion, lead their souls to hell. He asked them to put up an image of the Virgin Mary

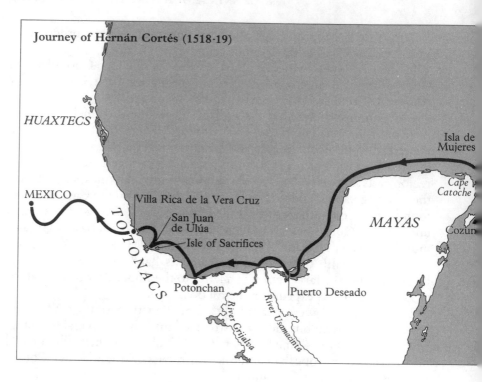

Journey of Hernán Cortés (1518-19)

HUAXTECS

Isla de Mujeres

Cape Catoche

MEXICO

Villa Rica de la Vera Cruz

San Juan de Ulúa

Isle of Sacrifices

TOTONACS

MAYAS

Cozun

Potonchan

Puerto Deseado

River Grijalva

River Usumacinta

in place of their idols. That action, he argued, would be sure to bring them good harvests, and to save their souls.[13]

This was the first time that Cortés had tried his hand at sermons to the *naturales*. It was a most successful beginning to what became for him an important activity. Perhaps he was advised what to say by Fr. Olmedo. But perhaps his years as an acolyte at the church of San Martín in Medellín had taught him something of the art of preaching and recorded in his memory the subjects of sermons. His hearers were probably much more impressed by the candles than by the words of the preacher (they are reported to have been "pleased and astonished" by the former).[14] At all events, they did nothing when Cortés ordered some of his men to roll the idols down the steps of the temples; though he seems for the moment to have left alone the hollow idol through which priests in the past had been wont to speak to the faithful.[15] The Indians were similarly speechless when Cortés had built a Christian altar and put on it an image of the Virgin Mary (probably from a portable altar on a ship). Apparently they hung this Virgin with native clothes.[16] Two carpenters, Alonso Yañez and Álvaro López, built a cross, which an Extremeño, Martín Vázquez, placed on top of the high tower of the main pyramid.[17] The Mayas also put an image of the Virgin in their boats.[18] While the Castilians stayed, there were apparently no sacrifices of human beings (or so they believed).[19] But there were anyway fewer such sacrifices among

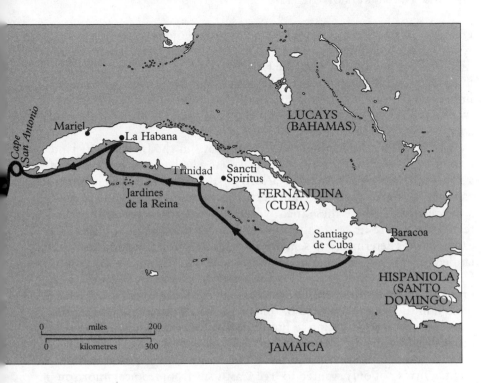

the Mayas than the Mexica. Partridges, quails and dogs suffered instead. Perhaps the Mayas thought that the new Christian cross was in some way an act of homage to their own whitewashed structure which both Hernández de Córdoba and Grijalva had observed with amazement (and which Cortés also saw).[20]

This slight acquaintance with the natives of Cozumel confirmed to Cortés what Alvarado and others must have told him: namely, that these people were superior in civilisation to the Indians whom he had known in both Hispaniola and Cuba. Some echoes of the controversy in Spain as to whether the Indians of the New World were slaves by nature would, of course, have reached Cortés. He must have seen instantly that the Indians of the "new islands", brown, ignorant and idolatrous though they might be, were human beings who could be "raised to the dignity of children of God, brothers and sisters of Christ, and heirs to His glory".[21] This sense of religious purpose was surely enhanced by his realisation of the nature of Maya religion and of the incidence of human sacrifice. Politically and technologically superior though these *naturales* were, their religion made them seem evil. So Cortés was the more inclined to recall that instruction of Velázquez which insisted that the "first motive which you and your company have to carry with you is to serve our Lord God and increase the dimension of our holy Catholic faith".

The relations between the Mayas and the Spaniards were good. Cortés enlarged often on the desirability of the people of the island accepting King Charles as their suzerain.[22] Perhaps Cortés was remembering medieval precedents as to how the King of Castile had conducted himself in relation to Moorish lords. The Mayas for their part were much impressed by the Castilians' beards and the colour of their skin.[23] They were not shown the horses, for those secret weapons were left on the ships.

After a while, the Mayas told Cortés that "in the [next-door] land known as Yucatan, there were two Christians who had been carried there a long time ago in a boat, and a lord of that land had held them as captives".[24] The *Caudillo* tried to persuade the chief of Cozumel to send a messenger to where these men were. But that potentate said that he feared that, were he to do that, his messenger would be captured and eaten. Cortés determined to send his own messengers. Some Mayas were landed for this purpose in Yucatan by Juan de Escalante, one of Cortés' friends, from his brigantine. Ordaz acted as an escort, in two more brigantines, with fifty men. The messengers carried a letter from Cortés hidden in the hair of the head of one of them. The letter stated that the *Caudillo* had arrived with five hundred and fifty Spaniards in order to discover and settle these lands.[25]

After a week, these men had not come back. This was a disappointment. Cortés not only wanted to free Castilians from tropical imprisonment. He guessed that a Spaniard who had been living for some years with the Indians would turn out to be a much better interpreter than Melchor or Julián, whose lack of Castilian was a serious weakness. A good interpreter, he must have known from memories of the wars with the Moors, was worth his (or her) weight in gold.

Once Escalante and Ordaz had returned, Cortés arranged, all the same, to leave.[26] The expedition took with them some honey and wax, and bade goodbye with regret to the sweet-scented island of Santa Cruz, as they called Cozumel. They made first for that other smaller island, the Isla de Mujeres (discovered, and named, by Hernández de Córdoba). The day they arrived was, in Spain, as they recalled with a sudden twinge of homesickness, the first day of carnival.[27] Cortés had gone there only to see the place. He was about to set off again for Cape Catoche when Juan de Escalante signalled by cannon that his brigantine had sprung a leak. This was an important supply ship. It had on board most of the bread brought from Cuba. Cortés decided to go back to Cozumel and mend the vessel there, since the *naturales* had been so friendly. When they did so, the Spaniards were glad to find their image of the Virgin still in place.[28]

Several days passed in the repair of the ship. They took on water again. On 12 March, they were once more ready. All the expedition re-embarked save for Cortés and about ten others. These commanders stood on the shore waiting for the little boats to take them to their ships. Then came a contrary wind which delayed them again. So they spent another night on the island. The next day was a Sunday. Cortés insisted on hearing mass before he left. After this further delay, they saw a canoe coming towards them from Yucatan. Cortés told Andrés de Tapia to investigate. The canoe carried "three men naked except that their private parts were covered. Their hair was tied as women's hair is tied, and they carried bows and arrows. They made signs that the Castilians should not be afraid and reached the shore." One of them came forward, asking in Spanish, "Gentlemen, are you Christians? Whose subjects are you?" One of Tapia's men, Angel Tintorero, said that they were Castilians, and were subjects (*vasallos*) of the King of Castile. The other joyfully asked them, weeping, to give thanks to God. He himself did so.[29] This was Gerónimo de Aguilar, one of those men whom the people of Cozumel had told them were still alive in captivity, and whom Cortés had been instructed to seek. He had received the *Caudillo*'s letter.

Aguilar was then about thirty years of age. He was a native of Écija in Andalusia, between Seville and Córdoba, one of the hottest places in Spain. He had taken minor orders before his great adventure began nine years before. Aguilar's mother in Écija, hearing that her son was probably the prisoner of cannibals, refused to eat meat, and became crazy at the sight of anything frying, in the fear that it might be a part of Gerónimo. "That is the flesh of my son," she would cry. "Am I not the most unhappy of mothers?"[30]

In the spring of 1511, Aguilar explained, he had been on a ship under a conquistador named Valdivia, making its way from Darien to Santo Domingo. The purpose had been to report to the Governor in Santo Domingo the interminable quarrels in Darien between Diego de Nicuesa and Núñez de Balboa. The ship struck shoals off the Víboras, the Vipers, some islands near Jamaica. Aguilar set off in a boat with Valdivia and about twenty others. There was neither food nor water, and only one pair of oars. They were caught in a current which ran fast to the west. After privations, they were cast ashore in Yucatan. Half their number were by then dead.[31]

The Mayas captured the survivors, sacrificed Valdivia and four others, and ate their bodies at a fiesta. Aguilar and some others were put in cages to be fattened, as they supposed, for a subsequent banquet. They broke out of the cages and fled, being received by Xamanzana, another Maya chief. He sheltered them, but kept them as slaves. After some time, all died, except for Aguilar and Gonzalo Guerrero, a native of Niebla, a port some miles up the Río Tinto from Palos.

Aguilar managed, through the strength of his faith (he insisted), to keep himself from temptations in the forms of girls offered him by his hosts. He concentrated his mind by counting the days but, by the time he was liberated, he was three days out: he thought that it was a Wednesday, not a Sunday, when he met Tapia.[32] One account says that he always had with him a much-used Book of Hours: a collection of conventional prayers, with illuminated paintings.[33] He was more than ready to return to Spanish life. Gonzalo Guerrero was not. Aguilar had sent him Cortés' letter. But Guerrero now had a Maya wife, the daughter of Na Chan Can, lord of Chactemal, some hundred miles to the south, the only cacao-growing area of Yucatan. He had three children. He had had his nose and ears pierced, and his face and hands tattooed, as if he were an Indian.[34] He was ashamed of that. He also had a position with Na Chan as a military adviser.[35] Perhaps too he had unhappy memories of his home town, Niebla. The conquistadors might deplore the indigenous habits in the Americas. But would not the poet Juan del Encina describe how famine in Niebla had once reduced the population even there to cannibalism?[36]

It immediately seemed to Cortés that Aguilar might become the interpreter whom he needed. Aguilar spoke Chontal Maya. His Spanish was rusty, as might be expected, after eight years in the wilderness, and he never completely recovered it.[37] But he was nevertheless immensely useful. Aguilar's stories about human sacrifice among the Mayas must have cast a shadow over many conquistadors' enthusiasm, as well as strengthening their sense of Christian mission.

Córtes then gave orders to his fleet to set off once again. Before doing so, he again talked to the natives about the importance of salvation. For this homily he tested Aguilar as interpreter. The practice worked perfectly. The Castilians then completed the destruction of the local idols. The Mayas seemed distressed by Cortés' proposed departure. Cortés now saw how simple it was, relatively speaking, to impress these Indians: indeed, to inspire in them what seemed like affection. They, perhaps out of those natural good manners which had always been characteristic of the inhabitants of those territories, begged him to leave behind a preacher when he had gone. But Córtes had need of Fr. Juan Díaz and Fr. Bartolomé de Olmedo.[38]

The expedition set off back to the Isla de Mujeres where they took on both water and salt. They waited two days there for a favourable wind to take them past Cape Catoche. While waiting, they caught a shark which, on cutting it up, they discovered to have within its belly a typical haul of flotsam from the sixteenth-century Caribbean: three shoes, a tin plate, over thirty rations of pork, and a cheese.[39]

Once past Cape Catoche, Cortés continued along the route previously taken by Hernández de Córdoba and Grijalva, as by his own pilots. He kept a brigantine close to the coast, not only to look for the missing ship under the captaincy of Alonso de Escobar, but also to make some effort to find the "secrets of the territory". He considered stopping at Champoton to avenge the defeat of Hernández de Córdoba, but did not do so, on the advice of the pilots; they had remarked, on previous journeys, the shallowness of the water. After some days, the missing vessel of Escobar was discovered in the harbour which Grijalva had named Puerto Deseado. The pilot, Juan Álvarez "the lame", had led Escobar there, knowing from his previous voyage with Grijalva that they could probably survive on local products, even if they had no food on board. They had lived well, eating rabbits and some game: this being much assisted by the miraculous discovery of the mastiff bitch left behind by Grijalva.[40] That early European colonist of Yucatan had provided for herself for a year apparently without difficulty. Escobar's ship had so profited that its rigging, when Cortés discovered it, was shrouded in pelts of deer and rabbit.[41]

Cortés moved on to the mouth of the river Usamacinta. He named it the San Pedro and San Pablo. The fleet arrived next at the river Grijalva (or Tabasco), about 22 March.[42] Cortés said that he was going to land and get food and water.[43] But he was short of neither. Probably he was looking for gold, since it was there, as he must have been told, that Grijalva had been given a golden figure of a man.

Though this is a broad river, the pilots thought it unwise to take the big ships up it. Cortés accordingly went in with his brigantines and the boats attached to the caravels. He took with him two hundred men.[44] On the banks of the river, the Castilians saw many Indians assembled, in feathers, watching. Grijalva had conducted himself cautiously in the same place the previous year. So the natives, who were Chontal Mayas, showed no fear. A mile and a half up the river, the Castilians found a settlement which was alleged to have 25,000 houses, mostly built of adobe with straw roofs.[45] This figure is open to the usual suspicion of gross exaggeration, which marks all such estimates. It at all events impressed the Castilians as constituting a substantial town with houses of stone built by "architects of real talent".[46] This was Potonchan, an important commercial centre. It must have been approximately where the town of Frontera is now. But the river Grijalva has changed its course since the sixteenth century. Thus it is impossible to be sure of the site. It seems likely that the region produced rubber, used at that time for making both soles of sandals and balls. Just before they got to the town, the inhabitants came out in canoes towards them. They asked what Cortés wanted.[47]

Cortés, replying through Aguilar (who was able to talk effectively with them), said that he required food and would pay for it. He was, he said, a brother of that Grijalva with whom the Indians had established such good relations the previous year.[48] The Indians said that the Castilians should assemble the next day in the square in front of the town. This they did, after sleeping the night on the sandy river bank. Both sides sought to deceive: the Mayas had used the night to begin to evacuate their women and children; the Castilians, to take more men from their ships, including crossbowmen and arquebusiers, but not as yet the horses.[49]

In the morning, the Mayas brought eight turkeys, and maize enough for ten people. According to Juan Álvarez, who was present, they also brought a mask of gold and some other jewels. They told the Castilians that they should leave. Cortés refused and said that they had not brought enough food. He would also like a basket full of gold. The Indians replied that they wished neither for war nor for trade. They had no more gold.[50] If the Castilians did not leave, they would be killed. They promised to bring a little more food the next day. If Cortés needed water he could take it from the river. Cortés said that the river was salt. The Indians replied that fresh water could be obtained by boring holes in the sand on one of the islands.[51]

Three more days passed. The Castilians remained in their boats on the river. Cortés brought out yet more men from the anchored fleet. He also sent Pedro de Alvarado and Alonso de Ávila up the river on foot with fifty men each, to look for a crossing beyond the town.[52] Ordaz set off on another reconnoitre, and came upon, as he rather improbably put it, 30,000 Indians, to whom he read the *Requerimiento*. He was then saved by some other Castilians from being surrounded.[53] (Exaggeration of numbers in battle, and other things, was, as will be incessantly seen, a characteristic of the time: thus the historian Chastellain told how at the battle of Gavre, Charles the Bold, Duke of Burgundy, lost only five noblemen while the rebels of Ghent lost 20,000 to 30,000 infantrymen.)

On the fourth morning, the Indians again brought eight turkeys and maize enough for ten people. Cortés repeated that he wished to visit the town. He added that he wanted more food. The Indians said that they would think about the matter. The ensuing night they evacuated all their families and much property. They brought soldiers into the town: "All that night," said one conquistador, "the *naturales* kept a very good guard, with men watching, with many fires and horns."

Next day the Mayas brought a small supply of food in eight canoes. They insisted that they could bring no more, since the people had left the town, out of fear both of the strangers and of their great ships. Some of Cortés' men set out to try and find provisions. They were surrounded in the town and returned in disorder. Cortés, unimpressed, said that those who were ill should go back to the ships, while those who were fit should put themselves on a war footing. He told the next party of Indians to visit him that it was inhuman to let the Castilians die of hunger. If the Indians would allow him to enter the town, and feed his men, he would give them good advice.

The Indians said that they were in no need of advice and that they would certainly not receive the Castilians in their houses. Cortés said that if the Indians would only listen to him, they would prosper. He had to enter the town in order to be able to describe it to the greatest lord in the world, that is his king, who had sent him to see and visit that land.[54] He,

Cortés, liked doing good, but if the Indians did not want to help him do so, he could only commend their souls to God. In reply, the Mayas again said that the Castilians should go away and cease bullying them. If they did not leave, they repeated, they would all be killed. Cortés replied that he would enter the town that night, even if it irritated them. The Mayas merely laughed. Cortés then had a statement demanding an acceptance of the supremacy of the King of Spain read out by the notary, Diego de Godoy. He had, it may be remembered, performed that service twice for Grijalva, though not at Potonchan.[55]

This action had an undesired consequence. The Mayas immediately attacked with bows and arrows, and stones flung from their slings. They also walked knee-deep into the river in order to attack the conquistadors' boats.[56] At this, Cortés put ashore some of his cannon as well as most of his men. As the sun was setting, the Castilians fired the cannon at the Indians, who were naturally frightened. But they rallied. A battle then ensued. The Indians continued to shoot arrows and fling spears from their *atlatls*. They also used their swords with the brittle obsidian blades. They were probably more experienced in war than Cortés' expeditionaries, few of whom had ever fought in a real battle – at least not a battle against so many. Twenty Castilians were wounded. But within a short time, thanks to an attack from the rear by Alvarado and Ávila (who had found hidden paths through the marshes into the back part of the town), the four hundred or so Indians who had been left to fight were either dead, had been taken prisoner, or had fled.[57] The Castilians then moved into the centre of the town. They slept in the patio of the main temple.[58] Before that, as a sign of taking possession of the territory, Cortés made three cuts in the beautiful ceiba tree which stood in the square where all these events had been going on. Pedrarias had done the same when he had arrived in Castilla del Oro with a similar purpose, as some of those with him who had been with "The Gallant" (Vázquez de Tapia, Montejo, perhaps Bernal Díaz) must have told Cortés: a ritualistic act which would not have seemed far away from Maya practices.[59]

The only loss to the Castilians was the disappearance during the fighting of their old interpreter, Melchor. He used this opportunity to escape. Whether he ever rejoined his own people, and resumed his profession as a fisherman in Yucatan, is unknown. But he did tell the Mayas that they should attack the Castilians day and night, since the conquistadors were subject to the pains of death, just as other men were. (Aguilar gained this information the following day when he interrogated two prisoners with whom Melchor had spent the previous night.)[60]

This victory of Cortés at Potonchan afforded several lessons. First, the *Caudillo* was able to see how important the impact of artillery could be. To those who had seen Grijalva using cannon, this was no surprise.

Indeed Velázquez had employed these weapons in Cuba, and Cortés must have observed that. But for Cortés the important lesson was that, even with these more sophisticated people, the use of guns could have a shock effect out of all proportion to their lethal consequence.

Second, the Castilians could see that, in a battle between themselves and an overwhelming number of Indians, victory could be assured with little injury. It is impossible to say how many Indians there were. But the Castilians must have been outnumbered at least ten to one. This would give them the opportunity to live a legend reminiscent of their favourite romances. A tremendous fight could be engaged, many wounds suffered, the hidalgos could think that they were fighting as if they had been Hector or Roland, but, because of the nature of Indian weapons and of Indian tactics, the number of deaths would be tiny. Thus the age of the paladins in the ballads could be restored.[61] For the Indians fought – and their obsidian- bladed swords were made accordingly – in order to wound, not to kill. Wishing to capture not kill their enemies, they seemed to want to "impale themselves on the points of the Castilian swords so as to lay their hands on their owners", as Bernal Díaz commented in respect of a later contest.[62] A soldier could probably have killed three of the enemy in the time taken to capture one.[63]

Probably there was a third lesson: this was that the Mexican-style quilted cotton "armour" by which Cortés had been impressed even when still in Cuba was all that was really needed in battle against this kind of enemy with their brittle if sharp swords. Thereafter the Spaniards only used their full armour almost as the *naturales* used feathers: for psychological effect.

The day after the battle, 25 March, Cortés had the prisoners brought before him. He said that what had happened had been the Indians' fault since he had begged them to be peaceable. If they now wanted to go home, they could do so. Cortés added that he wanted to talk to their king. For he still had many things which he wished him to know. The prisoners left. The Castilians realised that the Mayas were reassembling for another attack. In consequence, Cortés sent out small forces of reconnaissance in all directions round the town. They brought back as prisoners all the Indians whom they saw. Cortés promised to treat them as brothers if only they would lay down their arms.

The following morning, twenty Indian leaders came. They greeted Cortés in the traditional style: touching the ground with their hands, then kissing them.[64] Their lord asked them to beg Cortés not to burn down the town, and to tell him that they would bring food. Cortés said that he had come intending to do good. After all, he knew the truth of many great mysteries about which, he was convinced, they would be pleased to hear.

Another day passed. The Mayas returned with some fruit, nothing else. They apologised that there was no more food. But, they said, the populace was now scattered. They were hiding out of fear. They said, however, that they would be pleased to accept some of Cortés' famous beads and perhaps some bells as presents. As for the lord of Potonchan, he had gone away to a distant fortress. Cortés dismissed these messengers, saying that the next day he would go with his army and seize what food he could. He advised the Indians to have ready a good supply. He does not seem to have given away any more beads.

The following day he sent out three companies of about two hundred and fifty men, led by Extremeños: Gonzalo de Alvarado (a brother of Pedro), Gonzalo de Sandoval, and Domingo García de Albuquerque, with some Cuban Indians for service.[65] They would seek maize in the fields. They were told to offer to pay for anything which they wanted and not to go more than six miles away.

One of these expeditions found a substantial number of fields of maize near a village called Centla. They were, however, guarded. The Indians refused to discuss a sale. A battle ensued. The Indians were infinitely more numerous than the Castilians, who were forced to retreat. They might all have died or been captured, had it not been for the help of their compatriots from the other companies, and from Cortés himself who, warned by some Cuban Indians, showed himself, in this potentially dangerous skirmish, extremely effective in hand-to-hand fighting with the sword.

Fighting began again the next day. In the meantime, Cortés had sent some wounded men back to the ships and had had brought out to him the rest of his army, and also, for the first time, most of the horses.[66] The Castilians found themselves in the fields fighting five large Maya squadrons.[67] Ditches dug for irrigation made it difficult to fight. Neither the crossbowmen nor the arquebusiers had much effect. Even when artillery was brought up, it was unsatisfactory: the Indians seemed to be learning quickly to conquer their fear of it. But the horses were another matter. Cortés and about a dozen horsemen (including some of his best men)[68] had a sensational effect. This derived as much from the sight and speed of these animals as from the ease with which the Spanish used them. The Indians really thought that they were dragons. As one of those present, Martín Vázquez, pointed out later, it was the first time that horses were used in a battle in the Americas.[69]

One successful Spanish mounted warrior was Francisco de Morla, who, on a dappled grey horse, caused much trouble to the Indians. They apparently thought that here was a centaur. Some equally credulous Castilians, who did not recognise Morla in his steel helmet and cuirass, thought that this knight was Santiago himself coming to assist them as he was reputed to have done so often in battles in Spain against the Moors. It seemed an excellent omen.[70]

The Indians eventually withdrew. This battle of Centla was thus in the end a signal victory for the Castilians. Despite everything, they had still lost no one killed, even if sixty were wounded, some badly; and even if, soon afterwards, another hundred were temporarily put out of action by the heat, or by a bad stomach caused by the water which they had drunk from one of the streams. The Indians said that they lost two hundred and twenty killed but it may have been more: even eight hundred.[71]

Afterwards, thirty Indians came forward "in good cloaks" with fowls, fruit and maize cakes. They asked leave to bury or burn the dead so that, as they said, they would not smell badly or be eaten by wild beasts. Cortés gave permission, providing the lord of Potonchan came himself to make the request. In consequence, this lord, or, more likely, someone purporting to be him, did indeed come. He brought more food and offerings. These last included some gold and turquoise objects. He also brought twenty women to cook for the conquistadors, since, he said, he had understood that there were none among them (presumably the few girls on the expedition had been left on the ships). Cortés accepted these gifts, including the women, whom he divided among his captains. This must have done wonders for Castilian morale. Cortés arranged for a horse to paw the ground menacingly and, being placed near a mare, to neigh. The frightened Mayas offered it not only turkeys but flowers. Cortés told the Indians that "the apostles were angry" that their troops had been attacked. For that reason he caused a cannon to be fired. This too had the desired effect of inspiring terror.[72]

Cortés put to these Mayas three questions. Where were the mines for gold and silver? Why had they denied him, Cortés, the friendship which they had offered to Grijalva? And why had so many of them fled from so few Europeans?

The Mayas answered that they had no mines. Gold, as it happened, did not interest them greatly. But inland, in Mexico for example, there were people who liked it. That kind of reply was a frequent ruse by Indians to persuade the Castilians to move on to another place. Grijalva, they continued, had had smaller ships and fewer people. He also had been interested in trading gold, not food. As for their defeat by such a small number, the Mayas admitted that the swords of their enemies had dazzled them. The wounds inflicted had often been fatal: a change from their own practice. The artillery had also astonished them. They had too been flabbergasted by the speed of the horses, whose mouths in particular had frightened them.

The Mayas also helpfully said that, though they had not understood everything that Cortés had said about the Christian God and the Emperor, they hoped to be better informed. They accepted that their idols, which the Castilians had said were evil, had to be destroyed. They had in fact already smashed some because they had deserted them in their hour of need. Such things were to be expected after a defeat: the Mexica always destroyed the temples of their enemies. As for being vassals of the King of Castile, they are said to have accepted the idea with enthusiasm. Whether they realised what they were saying must be doubtful: as later, on many other occasions, perhaps there was a confusion between "vassal" and "friend".[73] Cortés with equal enthusiasm anyway received them as vassals, in the presence of one of the notaries, Pero Gutiérrez, and afterwards purported to think of them as such,[74] as if they had been citizens of a small Moorish town conquered by the Castilian army (in which Martín Cortés and probably the fathers of many others present had served) on the way to Granada.[75]

Cortés afterwards permitted the Indians to return to the city, on the condition that they abandoned their human sacrifices and demons, "and henceforth lifted up their souls to Jesus Christ".[76] Cortés, whose preaching was as effective as it had been in Cozumel, then found it remarkably easy, even after hours of fighting, to give the captured Indians an elegant speech (*plática*), touching on the divine as well as the terrestrial, telling them that God was the master of all things, the rewarder of those who did good works and the scourge of those who did bad ones. In respect of temporal matters, there was the King of Castile, at whose command, he, Hernán Cortés, had come to those parts as "God's vicar".[77] Another altar and cross were put up by the carpenters. Several idols were smashed.[78]

The Castilians spent three weeks in Potonchan. They christened the town Santa María de la Vitoria, a name soon forgotten.[79] They left on Palm Sunday, 17 April. Before they did so, they did their best to reproduce that day as it was celebrated at home. There was a traditional procession, with branches of trees. The conquistadors carried round a picture of the Virgin Mary, and displayed their best ornaments. A cross was raised in the square where they had had their first difficult conversations with the Indians.[80] A mass was then said. Afterwards the Castilians embarked, carrying their branches. The Mayas were impressed. They probably joined in. Thus began that process of syncretic union which has made the Mexican church what it is.[81]

There was a final benefit gained from Potonchan. Among the women given by the chief to Cortés was a girl who knew both Chontal Maya and Nahuatl, the languages of Potonchan as well as of the Mexican empire. This knowledge enabled her to communicate first in Nahuatl with the Mexica and then in Maya with Gerónimo de Aguilar who would then talk to Cortés in Spanish. The consequent double translation took time. But the practice soon became of the greatest possible benefit to the Castilians.[82] It made possible a kind of communication on a quite different level from that which characterised discussions using Melchor or Julián – and, indeed, was on quite a different level from exchanges previously carried out in the Indies by the Castilians.

This girl was first presented by Cortés to his fellow citizen of Medellín, Alonso Hernández Portocarrero, probably at this time Cortés' chief friend after Alvarado. But after a while, the girl became Cortés' mistress.[83] She, like the other women given to Cortés by the lord of Potonchan, was christened. They were the first Mayas to accept such a thing. Each of them took Christian names. Presumably Fr. Díaz or Fr. Olmedo demanded, in the ceremony of baptism, if the girls renounced the devil and all his works. No doubt they replied in the affirmative.

This interpreter's original name was Malinali – which also was the name of the twelfth Mexican month. She now became "Marina". Her life had already been picaresque, to use a word which the Castilians had not yet invented. Her father had been lord, *tlatoani*, of Painala, a village about twenty-five miles from Coatzacoalcos. Her mother was apparently the ruler of a small place nearby, Xaltipan. Thus Marina's childhood must have been one of comfort. That condition changed when her father died. Perhaps for political reasons, her mother remarried another local ruler. She gave birth to a son. The mother and stepfather hoped that this boy would inherit the three lordships. The mother therefore sold the girl to some merchants from Xicallanco, the commercial port on the Laguna de Términos, and gave out that her daughter was dead. These Xicallanca sold Malinali to Maya merchants who, in turn, sold her to the people of Potonchan.

The Nahuatl which Marina had used as a child was that spoken in the southern marches of the Mexican empire. This dialect had certain differences from the language of Tenochtitlan. These explain why the Castilians, to begin with, misspelled many Mexican words.[84] Malinali was christened "Marina" by the Castilians since her real name sounded like that: "L" in Nahuatl is pronounced "R" in Spanish.[85]

Marina was clever and seemed sometimes humane.[86] Tradition says that she was "beautiful as a goddess".[87] That judgement is not immediately confirmed by the pictures of her in Mexican codices. But probably from Easter 1519, Cortés worked well with her (as late as July 1519 Cortés was regretting that he did not have interpreters to enable him to tell the truth of religion to the Totonacs, but they had a different tongue from those which Marina spoke).[88] The pair constituted a duet which often combined eloquence with subtlety, piety with menace, sophistication with brutality. After a while Marina learned enough Spanish for Cortés to be able to dispense with Aguilar as co-interpreter. All important communications between the Castilians and the Mexica would thenceforth pass through Marina. Neither her mistakes of translation nor her prejudices will ever be known. Her loyalty to Cortés seems to have been absolute. Her value was certainly equivalent to ten bronze cannon.[89]

Marina's impact must have been great on the Mexica and others to whom she talked, since usually a woman in old Mexico (as in old Europe, it may be said) "was one who went nowhere. Only the house was her abode."[90] A Mexican wife and mother was a manager who could be called upon to arrange a large household. She would have to ensure, if her family was of commoners, that there would be maize gruel (*atolli*) for breakfast; or, if it were a noble one, chocolate. Her lot was otherwise usually confined to weaving and grinding. Women were conventionally depicted in codices as kneeling, while men sat. Marina must thus have seemed to her compatriots to have the liberty of a prostitute.

Cortés sailed on and, passing the mouth of the river Tlacotalpan, reached the island which Grijalva had named the Island of Sacrifices, on Maundy Thursday, 20 April 1519. He and his men inspected the place which had so shocked Grijalva because of its relics of recent sacrifices. Several Indians came up to the brigantine of Juan de Escalante. They asked kindly after Grijalva, Pedro de Alvarado, and one or two others who had been on his expedition. Cortés should perhaps have felt a moment of gratitude to his predecessor for his intelligent diplomacy. But, on the brink of the decisive hour of his life, he had no time to spare for such niceties.

The fleet next anchored off its nominal destination, San Juan de Ulúa, where Grijalva had spent two happy weeks the previous year. As they prepared to land, Alonso Hernández Portocarrero gave an indication of what Cortés had in mind. He must often before have talked to Cortés about long-term plans. Looking at the shore, white and glistening in the sun, he said to Cortés: "It seems to me that those of us who have been twice already to this land are saying to you:

> Behold France, Montesinos,
> Behold Paris the city!
> Behold the waters of the Douro
> Which flow down to the sea.[91]

He added: "*I* say that you are looking at rich lands and may you know how to govern them well."

Portocarrero was quoting one of the romances in the cycle of Montesinos which had obviously been well known during the childhoods in Medellín of both these conquistadors. The allusions to Montesinos were fateful. In the ballad, that knight was the son of a certain Count Grimaltos and a daughter of the King of France. Grimaltos had been ruined by the villain Tomillas. Montesinos went to Paris in disguise to avenge the affronts. He played chess with Tomillas. Tomillas cheated. Montesinos seized the chessboard, and with it gave him a blow on the head, which killed him. Montesinos then revealed that he was the grandson of the King. All was forgiven: for "he who takes the King's commission is immune to dangers", the ballad continues.[92]

Cortés replied: "Let God give us that good fortune in fighting which he gave to the paladin Roland. After all, with you, and these other gentlemen, as leaders, I will easily learn how to manage things."[93]

We are to assume that, in this exchange, Cortés stood for Montesinos; Diego Velázquez for Tomillas. No doubt, as the anchors rattled down in the beautiful bay, with the stone-built white town seen by Grijalva glistening in the distance, Cortés would have uttered a prayer and, no doubt, recalled a proverb – one of those innumerable sayings which characterised the European nations in the fifteenth century: perhaps "The more Moors, the greater spoil"; or, if he preferred a classical allusion, "Sparta is yours; govern it; our lot is Mycenae".[94]

13

As much as where Solomon took the gold for the temple

"It seems to us that one should believe that in this land there is as much as where Solomon took the gold for the temple."
Cortés, of the land near Vera Cruz, 1519

O N MAUNDY THURSDAY 1519, the ships of Cortés' "blessed company", "*la santa compañía*", as Las Casas ironically named the expedition, lay off the island which Grijalva the year before had christened San Juan de Ulúa. This place was less than a mile from the Mexican mainland, close to the Totonac town of Chalchicueyecan, where the modern port of Veracruz now stands. Some Indians came out in canoes to visit the conquistadors. They had come from the new local Mexican steward, Teudile, whose headquarters were twenty miles away at Cuetlaxtlan. The steward, who had succeeded Pinotl who had been there the year before, wanted to know the purpose of the Spanish journey.[1] The visitors then paid Cortés many marks of respect, "as was their custom".[2]

Cortés explained through Aguilar and Marina also that the following day he would like to land and talk to their governor. He did not want that official to be in any way perturbed. But Cortés had many interesting things to say to him. He then gave the Indians some blue glass beads and some wine. As when they or their friends had drunk wine with Grijalva, they liked it very much. They asked for some to give to their governor. The coherence of the exchange suggests that the Indians who came must have been Nahuatl-speaking Mexicans. Marina could not speak Totonac.

The following day, Good Friday, having received neither approval nor hostility from the Indians, Cortés and about two hundred Castilians set off in boats and brigantines for the mainland. They took with them horses, artillery, Cuban servants, and a few dogs. Francisco Mesa, "the veteran of Italy", was there to place the guns in the best defensive position. They were probably breech-loading guns taken from the ships.[3]

On the shore the Spanish were well received, not by Mexicans but by

Totonacs. Francisco de Montejo had been the first to land when the expedition of Grijalva had reached the same place, but this time Cortés kept the honour for himself. One account (inspired by Cortés) says that the Spaniards were welcomed with "signs of love".[4] The Totonacs remembered Grijalva as benign, just as the Mayas at Potonchan had done. They perhaps had been thinking throughout the previous year of the Castilians as potential assistants in a war of liberation against the Mexica. So they enthusiastically gave Cortés food (beans, meat, fish, maize cakes, turkeys), cloaks, and some plates of copper and silver, the first deriving from the border province of Tepecualcuilco in the east, the latter probably the result of trading, since silver was not produced in Montezuma's empire.[5] The presentation of clothing must have seemed odd to the Castilians; but, in the empire of Montezuma, dress was "identity; even a god had to don his proper attire".[6] The Totonacs asked after some of those whom they had met with Grijalva: for example, Benito the tambourine player. That musician danced with the Indians, as he had done a year previously. They laughed and were pleased.[7] Cortés gave them presents for their chiefs: two shirts, two doublets (one of satin, one of velvet), some gold belts, two red berets, and two pairs of breeches. In matters of costume Cortés was for the moment not outdone. But of course such things would not have been received neutrally by the Indians. Red after all was the colour in which it was believed that the god Quetzalcoatl customarily painted his body.

The next day, Easter Saturday, one of Montezuma's emissaries arrived with an elaborate train of servants. This was a dramatic moment. The *Caudillo* was to meet a servant of the greatest monarchy in the Americas. But there was no special celebration. Apparently it was the slave Cuitlalpitoc who had been sent to the coast to report what was going on (an indication of the standing of slaves in old Mexico). He brought enough food for the entire expedition for several days, as well as more jewels. Cortés banned any member of his expedition from accepting or exchanging gold privately. But he had a table put just outside the camp where the Indians could come and trade officially. Every day thereafter the Totonacs as well as the local Mexicans came to offer Cortés interesting golden objects which, through his servants, he exchanged for his beads, looking glasses, pins, needles and scissors.[8]

On Easter Sunday, the steward Teudile came to salute Cortés in person. He brought with him a large number of men, unarmed but finely turned out in feathers and embroidered cloaks, and with many provisions. He came, he said, on behalf of Montezuma, who had heard of the new arrivals, and who had, of course, heard of the battle at Potonchan, as the Emperor himself later told Cortés.[9] Teudile presented Cortés with several good jewels and objects of featherware. He offered incense and straws dipped in his own blood. He and his entourage "ate dirt": that is, they put a damp finger to the ground and put it to their lips. Cortés by now realised that this implied respect for him and acknowledged the greeting. He gave Teudile a silk coat and a necklace of glass beads, as well as many other trinkets from Castile.[10] Teudile ordered his men to build several hundred huts for the visitors, with green branches and improvised roofs against the rain. It would soon, after all, be the rainy season. He also placed two thousand servants at Cortés' disposal.[11] This was the first indication that Cortés had that there was no shortage of labour in Mexico. But among the two thousand there were doubtless spies, priests, and sorcerers. Presumably these arrangements were made on Montezuma's suggestion. Hospitality was mixed with tactics. It was better to have the newcomers sleeping on land than in their ships.

Cortés asked his priests, Fr. Díaz and Fr. Olmedo, to hold a solemn mass. A cross was put up on the sand, the Spaniards told their beads, a bell rang, they recited the Angelus. Teudile and his companions looked on with interest. Why should these extraordinary men humble themselves before two pieces of wood? Then the Castilian leaders dined with Teudile, the combination of Marina and Aguilar making a halting conversation possible.[12]

Cortés explained that he, Cortés, was a subject of Don Carlos of Austria, King of Spain, and the ruler of the largest part of the world ("*el mayor parte del mundo*"). Don Carlos, having heard of Mexico, had sent him as his ambassador to relate several interesting things to Teudile's king.

Cortés' self-presentation of himself as the "ambassador" of his king was a skilful tactic, even if unjustified: the Mexica usually respected diplomats. Where, Cortés went on to ask, was Montezuma? When could he see him?[13]

Teudile's reply was that Montezuma was no less of a king than Cortés' monarch. He too was a great lord served by lesser lords. Teudile would send to Montezuma to find out his pleasure. In the meantime, he offered, in Montezuma's name, a chest full of gold objects, some beautifully worked white cotton cloths, and a good deal more food: turkeys, baked fish and fruit. Most of the gold treasures were probably designed to be worn: pectorals, rings, small bells, labrets. Cortés in return gave Teudile some more beads, an inlaid armchair, some pearls, and a crimson cap with a gold medal on it. The latter bore an equestrian figure of St George killing a dragon. Perhaps, therefore, it came from Valencia or Catalonia.[14] Teudile accepted these things on Montezuma's behalf with a good grace though without enthusiasm: Las Casas commented, surely rather harshly, that he gave the impression that he considered them "like excrement".[15] Cortés said that Montezuma might sit in the chair and wear the crimson cap when he himself came to visit him: an interesting suggestion. He would also like the Mexica to "set up in their city, in the temples where they kept the idols which they believed to be gods, a cross . . . and . . . an image of Our Lady with her precious son in her arms". If they did that, they would prosper. Cortés would arrange to have these objects of Christian veneration sent to Mexico.[16] He then asked how old Montezuma was and how he looked. Teudile replied: "He is a mature man, not fat but spare, small and thin."[17]

Cortés paraded his men in military formation to the music of drums and fifes. They staged a show of combat, swords flashing. Alvarado led a troop of horsemen to gallop along the beach, bells attached to their mounts' bridles. The lombard guns loosed several detonations. Teudile was overcome with admiration. When the artillery fired, he and his friends fell to the ground in fear. They were also impressed by the appetites of the horses.[18] The Mexicans may have continued to think of these animals as deer. But perhaps some folk memory may have reminded them that there had once been horses in the Americas. For, at certain fiestas, deer with manes and tails were sometimes modelled from amarynth seed.[19]

Cortés and Teudile had a famous exchange. The former asked Teudile if Montezuma possessed gold. He asked since he knew that that precious metal was good for a bad heart. Some of his men were ill with that complaint. Yes, Teudile replied, Montezuma did indeed have gold.[20] That exchange could not have been more dangerous for the Mexica.

Teudile, otherwise, showed himself an efficient servant of his emperor. He brought with him artists who carefully sketched on cloth their impressions of the visitors, as well as their horses, swords, guns and ships. He sent to ask Montezuma for more gold to give to Cortés and also dispatched Cortés' presents. These included a rusty but gilt helmet belonging to one of Cortés' soldiers. Teudile, seeing it, had said that it would greatly interest Montezuma, since it resembled what the god Huitzilopochtli was wearing in the Great Temple in Tenochtitlan. It must have seemed that it would help to enable Montezuma to identify the strangers, since gods in old Mexico were most recognisable by their headdresses. Cortés lent it to Teudile on the condition that it was returned by Montezuma full of gold dust. He wanted, he said airily, speaking more disingenuously perhaps than in the interests of comparative metallurgy, to know whether the gold in that country was the same as that which could be found in Europe.

Teudile then went home to Cuetlaxtlan, leaving a lieutenant in charge of the servants whom he had commanded to look after the Spanish expedition: to maintain for them several hundred huts; and regularly to give the visitors tortillas, beans, fish and meat, as well as grass for their horses.[21]

The report of Teudile reached Montezuma in a day and a half. The news was brought by messengers who had seen the intruders on the coast, rather than, as was usual in Mexican business, by relay (men stationed about five miles apart took messages onwards along accepted roads).[22]

It would be wise to assume that Montezuma had heard about all the activities of Cortés on the coasts of Yucatan: the speeches about the only true God, as about the great Spanish King; how the God's mother Mary had been commemorated in so many pictures; and how the visitors had shown such hostility to human sacrifice.

Montezuma received the new information from Teudile with alarm. If he had heard anything at all about the activities of the Castilians in Castilla del Oro and in the Caribbean (and, as earlier argued, it is likely that he had), he must have felt that the locusts swirling round Tenochtitlan, monsters of the twilight, were coming in ever smaller, nearer circles. One source says that Montezuma almost died of fright;[23] was filled "with dread, as if swooning. His soul was sickened, his heart anguished."[24] At first, it seems that he did not even want to hear what the messengers had to say. He did not know whether to dream or to eat. No one could talk to him. Almost every moment he sighed. Nothing gave him pleasure. No old source of delight counted any more with him. He kept saying: "What will happen to us?"[25] He wept: an action which was normal even among hard and brave Mexicans. Had not the iron-souled Tlacaelel done the same when Montezuma I died?[26]

Montezuma had a high sense of his own responsibilities. At his election, the elders would have said to him: Henceforth it is you who will now carry the weight and burden of this people . . . It is you, lord, who will for many years sustain this people and care for it . . . Consider, lord, that from now on you are to walk upon the high place along a very narrow path, which has great precipices to left and right . . . Be mild in the use of your power: show neither teeth nor claws.[27] Many passages of these speeches stress the role of the Emperor as the protector of his people. Obviously, this role was going to be severely tested.

Montezuma welcomed the messengers in the House of Serpents, which was part of his zoo. But he first made sacrifices of two captives. The messengers could, therefore, be sprinkled liberally with the victims' blood. Then he listened to their tales. The strangers' food, the messengers said, was like human food – it was white, and tasted sweet. This information confirmed that the strangers were the same people (or at least the same kind of people) who had come the previous year. These men, the messengers said, completely covered their bodies with clothes, except for their faces. Those faces were white. Their eyes were like chalk. Their hair was often fair. Sometimes, though, it was black and curly. Most of them had long beards. Their battle array was of iron, they clothed themselves for war in iron, they covered their heads with iron, iron were their swords, iron their crossbows, iron their shields and lances.[28]

Montezuma was frightened at the tale of how the cannon was fired, how it deafened the Indians, how the smoke smelled foul, and how, when struck by a cannonball, the hillside seemed to fall apart, while trees splintered and seemed to vanish altogether. As for "the deer" which bore the visitors on their backs, it was appalling to hear that they were "high as rooftops".[29] Then there were the dogs: these animals, Montezuma was told, were very large, and spotted like ocelots, with ears doubled over, great hanging jowls, blazing yellow eyes, gaunt stomachs, and flanks with ribs showing. They went about panting, tongues hanging out. Their barks astounded the Mexicans since, though they had their little dogs, they did not bark; they merely yowled (Mexican dogs, though kept as pets, were usually eaten; they were also sacrificed in order to escort dead souls through the underworld). Montezuma was distressed too to hear of the Spanish questions about what kind of man he himself was. That insolent curiosity suggested that the new arrivals might even be thinking of coming up to Tenochtitlan.[30]

The Emperor considered flight. He thought of hiding. His advisers made suggestions. He decided on Cincalco, "House of Maize", a cave on the side of Chapultepec known for its fresh and fragrant flowers. It was held to mark the way to a secret paradise within the hill which was presided over by Huemac, a long-dead ruler who, in ancient Tollan, had represented the common people against his rival, the aristocratic Quetzalcoatl. It was a place where many distinguished people went when dead.[31] Montezuma seems naturally to have thought that the spirit of Huemac would give him solace. But then he felt himself so weak as to be incapable even of deciding to hide. All he did was to leave one of his palaces for another. One source described him setting off to hide; but a priest saw him and told him that he, the Emperor, had to remain at his post. He vacillated.[32]

Montezuma's mood of panic communicated itself to the people. Everywhere there was a sense of fear, dread and apprehension. People went about with their heads hung low, greeting each other tearfully.

The grand difficulty was to identify the newcomers. Montezuma had to entertain at least four possibilities: the first was that they were a new group of invaders who, unlike the Chichimecs of the north, came from across the eastern sea in order "to rob and to conquer".[33] The messengers from Teudile, those who had talked with the Castilians, seem to have held that simple view. They thought that they were merely some new "powerful, cruel enemy".[34] This seems also to have been the judgement of the Mayas. Hence their determination to fight, against Hernández de Córdoba at Champoton, against Grijalva at Lázaro, against Cortés at Potonchan. Perhaps the Castilian "defector", Gonzalo Guerrero, had insisted to the Mayas on this harsh interpretation. But Montezuma was too deeply informed of the symbolic significance of things to have thought that for a moment. Nor were his relations with the Mayas such as to have received Guerrero's reports in an unvarnished form.

The second possibility was that the newcomers were the ambassadors of a great lord from far away, and had come in peace to trade, observe, and preach. No one in Mexico seems to have entertained this benign interpretation.

The Totonacs had a third suggestion. They thought that Cortés and his companions were "sent from heaven",[35] were "immortals";[36] definitely gods;[37] though, perhaps, not gods from anywhere in particular; not, for example, old Mexican gods returning after an exile: on the contrary, they were new gods, who had not previously had a place in the flowery pantheon. The fact that the Spaniards conducted themselves gaily, wilfully, and mercurially (though, with the Totonacs, in no way brutally) was no hindrance to this identification. Gods are not saints. Many local deities, like Greek ones, had a history of wayward behaviour. Thus the usually abstemious god Quetzalcoatl had been expelled from Tollan after being trapped into drinking too much, and then seducing his sister ("Bring me my elder sister Quetzalpetlatl," his blurred demand had been, "that we may be drunk together.")[38] Even the powerful Huitzilopochtli had stolen the clothes of the Mexica while they were bathing in Lake Pátzcuaro on their immortal journey south. Quetzalcoatl and Tezcatlipoca were always quarrelling. Nor were Mexican gods almighty: Quetzalcoatl could not save his escort of hunchbacks from being frozen to death when they crossed the sierra in the snow. Bernal Díaz seems to have grasped this characteristic of these deities (perhaps by mistake) when he remarked that these Totonacs "called us *teules*, which is their name for both their gods and evil spirits".[39] Perhaps the Totonacs were tempted to accept this interpretation by the thought that the newcomers might, though few in number, help them against the Mexica.

The word which Bernal Díaz seized upon did not seem to mean gods in a Christian, or even a Greek, sense. It indicated a notion of magical charging, possession of a vital fire, a sacred force, which could be physically expressed in a specific presence.[40]

Then there was, fourthly, the possibility that the Castilians were long-lost rulers, or even gods, returning; perhaps the bloodthirsty Huitzilopochtli, perhaps the generally humane Quetzalcoatl, or the mercurial Tezcatlipoca.[41]

Cortés, in a letter to the Emperor Charles V in September 1520, described how Montezuma, when he received him – this is to anticipate – did so as if he had been "a lost leader". The Mexica, Montezuma is supposed to have said, had themselves once been foreigners from distant parts. They had been led to the beautiful Valley of Mexico by a lord who later left for his native land. After a time, that lord returned. He found that the people whom he had led to the valley had married locally, had built houses, and did not want to follow him any more, nor to recognise him as a leader. So he again departed. Montezuma was then represented by Cortés as having said: "We always held that those who descended from him would one day come back to subjugate this land and take us as vassals."[42] Montezuma, Cortés also reported, said much the same thing later to his own lords. Cortés also talked of this prophecy when, some years later, he prepared a question for the official Spanish enquiry into his own doings.[43] Montezuma incidentally is supposed to have talked only of a lord returning; not explicitly of a god. But then there may have been a little verbal vagueness as to the difference between a god and a lord. Both were *teules*.

The first Spanish viceroy of Mexico, Antonio de Mendoza, in a letter of 1540 to his brilliant brother Diego, "last of the Spanish Renaissance men", apparently gave much the same story, with some differences (Diego was at that time Spanish ambassador to Venice). These were that the lost lord was none other than the god Huitzilopochtli; that he had come from the north, not the east; that he had established Tenochtitlan with four hundred men; and that he had left for Guatemala, then Peru. For many years, this story continued, Mexico had been left without a lord. Afterwards the Mexica had established the empire. Then when the Castilians came, they thought that Cortés "was Huitzilopochtli" coming back to claim his own.[44]

This interpretation must have received some support at the time from an examination of the Castilian helmet which Teudile had sent to Montezuma – if indeed it really resembled that on the head of Huitzilopochtli in the main temple of Tenochtitlan. The story might have gained extra force from the fact that Cortés' personal flag was blue: a special colour of Huitzilopochtli, which explains the high regard in which turquoise (and hence turquoise mosaic) was held.

After the 1540s this kind of story was told by every chronicler: thus the Florentine Codex, based on stories told by elders of Tlatelolco to Fr. Sahagún, explained (in the 1550s) that the first people who went to the Valley of Mexico were led by a god, and wise men. The latter told the people: "Our lord, the protector of all", the wind and night, says that you must remain. We shall go, leaving you here . . . "Our lord, the master of all, goeth still farther, and we go with him . . . When it is the end of the world", he will come to acknowledge you. So they "went . . . travelled to the east. They carried the writings, the books, the paintings . . . the song books, the flutes . . ."[45] A historian of the early seventeenth century, Ixtlilxochitl, descended from the royal family of Texcoco, wrote that, when Montezuma and the Mexica heard of the strange foreigners, they leapt to the conclusion that they were "sons of the sun, fulfilling the prophecies of their ancestors".[46]

Another possibility for Montezuma was that the intruders were captained not by Huitzilopochtli, the god who had led the Mexica to the Valley of Mexico, but by Quetzalcoatl, a name meaning the feathered (or plumed) serpent, a figure perhaps half historical, half god. He was a complicated deity.[47] For a human Quetzalcoatl had probably once been king, or priest, of the Toltecs. Perhaps he founded Tollan, perhaps he was a conqueror, perhaps he was that city's last king. At all events his story became fused with myth, his personality assuming the character of several deities. In Tollan, in myth, and perhaps in life, Quetzalcoatl stood for learning, culture and, in particular, opposition to human sacrifice: "Many times . . . certain sorcerers attempted to shame him into making human offerings . . . But he would not . . ."[48] A crisis occurred, Quetzalcoatl is supposed to have made a fool of himself, or was outmanoeuvred by enemies (the god Tezcatlipoca perhaps). He was expelled from Tollan, he travelled, he encountered difficulties, he went to the city of Cholula between the mountains and the coast, and he vanished on a raft of serpents into the eastern sea near Veracruz; though there is a possibility that he went also to Yucatan (symbolising a historically proven move of Toltecs to that zone, where they inspired the building of Chichen-Itza). Perhaps Quetzalcoatl in life was a religious innovator, destroyed by conservative forces, expressed by the myth of Huitzilo-pochtli and those concerned to propagate it. Perhaps Quetzalcoatl was a god of the valley whom the Emperor Itzcoatl and his partner Tlacaelel refused to accept because he was too benign. So they wrote him out of the histories. But Quetzalcoatl the irrepressible had come to express many things. He was sometimes seen as the wind, the spirit of regeneration, the solar light, the morning star, "warrior of the dawn": and, as the Codex Chimalpopoca put it,

> Truly with him it began
> Truly from him it flowed out.
> From Quetzalcoatl
> All art and knowledge.[49]

Whether or no he went there as a historical figure, the main place of worship of Quetzalcoatl in 1519 was Cholula, a city near Huexotzinco, beyond the volcanoes. There was apparently a statue of him there with a beard.[50] Many Toltecs are supposed to have emigrated, or fled, there. But there were minor temples to Quetzalcoatl in many places. In Tenochtitlan, he was the patron of the *calmécac*, the school of the upper class, whose pupils must be supposed to have heard his tale as a matter of course. In the fifteenth century an attempt had apparently been made to neutralise his appeal, by a technique reminiscent of twentieth-century totalitarian regimes: thus one of his names (Topiltzin) was given to the priests who officiated at the human sacrifices.

Quetzalcoatl therefore had a special, if complicated, relation with the Mexica, who looked back to Tollan with such respect. Montezuma II seems to have been interested in his legend, perhaps, even before 1519, perturbed by the occasional doubt that the Mexica might have made a mistake in handing over their fates to Huitzilopochtli. Was it possible that the people might have fared better had they given primary worship to Quetzalcoatl as the people of Cholula did? Montezuma established an unusually designed new round temple in the sacred precinct in Tenochtitlan to Quetzalcoatl in 1505 (most Mexican temples were square-edged; the circular form was for the benefit of the deity in his capacity as god of winds, since it was thought that circles would assist the current of air). The site provided a good spot from which to watch the sun rising between the two shrines on the top of the Great Temple. It was there, on the upper platform of the temple, that at sunrise and sunset a priest beat a drum in order to mark the beginning and the end of the day. Montezuma had also had made an especially beautiful greenstone box on which he himself, doing penance, and the god (with a beard) were both represented.[51] Perhaps Montezuma designed this to hold the sacred tools, sacrificial knives above all, which he thought of using in order to propitiate Quetzalcoatl.[52] A relief depiction of Quetzalcoatl, piercing his ear with a sharp bone, had been recently carved on a stony hillside outside Tollan itself, in a style which suggested that the sculptor was trying to represent him as a ruler of Tenochtitlan.[53]

The probability that there was some connection between Quetzalcoatl and the arrival of Cortés and the conquistadors must have seemed only too likely because 1519, "1-Reed" according to the Mexican calendar, was Quetzalcoatl's year. He had been born in 1-Reed, he had died (after an exact "century" of fifty-two years) in 1-Reed. Even in Europe such a coincidence would have seemed ominous, certainly impossible to ignore. But 1-Reed was also bad for kings. To quote from the Codex Chimalpopoca again:

> . . . They knew that, according to the signs . . .
> If he comes on 1-Crocodile, he strikes the old men, the old women;
> If on 1-Jaguar, 1-Deer, 1-Flower, he strikes at children;
> If on 1-Reed, he strikes at kings . . .[54]

Nothing was seen in Mexico as happening by chance. Though the Mexica (that is, their rulers and high priests) were good at adapting events in the past to appropriate calendrical moments, any surprising thing that year would in the first instance have been naturally associated with Quetzalcoatl.[55]

There were other indications which Montezuma, ex-high priest and master of the calendars, would have noticed. Thus it was always said that years with the sign of the Flint came from the north; those with the House, the west; with the Rabbit, the south; and those with the Reed, the east. The conquistadors had certainly come from the east. That too was where Quetzalcoatl, according to legend, had vanished on his raft of serpents.[56] It has been said that Cortés and his men dressed in black on their landing, because it was Good Friday: black was one of Quetzalcoatl's colours.[57] The reports that Cortés constantly criticised human sacrifice in speeches to Indian lords, Maya, Totonac, and Mexican, must have given further support the idea that he incarnated this complex deity.

The story that Montezuma thought that Quetzalcoatl, "white hero of the break of day", had returned was mentioned implicitly in 1528.[58] The report was echoed in the early 1530s,[59] then repeated by Fr. Motolinía.[60] Another letter from Viceroy Mendoza, this time to the historian Oviedo himself (he was in Santo Domingo collecting material for his history of the Indies), in 1541, denied having thought that the Mexica had been led by Huitzilopochtli. He knew that they had been led by a lord called "Quezalcoat".[61] Probably in fact there was a confusion, and Quetzalcoatl had always been intended. That deity was often talked of in the 1530s as having been an important influence on events.[62] By the 1550s Fr. Sahagún was saying firmly that Montezuma's emissaries at the coast thought that Quetzalcoatl had returned. He describes Montezuma as saying: "He has appeared! He has come back! He will come here to the place of his throne and canopy, for that is what he pronounced when he departed."[63] This causes the story to merge with the one that the Spaniards were the incarnation of a lost lord. Thereafter the legend became usual. For example, the Codex Ramírez insisted that "all the signs and news given by the Castilians suggested without doubt that the great emperor Quetzalcoatl had come, he who had for a long time gone away over the sea where the sun rose and who had allowed it to be said that in time he had to return."[64] Fr. Diego Durán describes first the mythical departure of Quetzalcoatl (whom he habitually calls Topiltzin); but says that Quetzalcoatl had himself prophesied that, in consequence of his own ill-treatment, strangers in multicoloured clothing would come from the east and destroy the Mexica.[65]

Yet another possibility is that Montezuma thought that the strangers were led by some other god: perhaps Tezcatlipoca, "Smoking Mirror", thought to be omnipotent in a way that other gods were not, the god who tricked Quetzalcoatl into leaving Tollan, the god who enjoyed cheating people out of their property, the god of "affliction and anguish", he who "brought all things down", and who "mocked and ridiculed men . . . he quickened vice and sin". Whenever he appeared on earth, he caused confusion. He was an arbitrary god. But he also stood for total power. At the same time, by one of those perplexing double identifications so favoured by the Mexica, he was also the eternally youthful warrior, the patron of the military academy, of the royal family, who could bring wealth, heroism, valour, dignity, rulership, nobility, honour.[66] He was said once to have created four hundred men – about the same number as those with Cortés – with fine women, especially to satisfy the sun's craving for human blood and hearts. As befitted a god whose emblem was an obsidian mirror, Tezcatlipoca was a master of disguise. He might appear as the naked seller of green chillis who seduced the daughter of Huemac; or the little old man with silver hair who went deviously to the house of Quetzalcoatl in Tollan. He was interested in riches. He was also associated with diseases of the skin. Most of what the Spanish would do in Mexico, such as desperately looking for gold, and later bringing smallpox, fitted his character.[67]

> He is capricious
> he likes to be coaxed
> he mocks us.
> As he wishes, so he wills,
> It is as he may want it:
> he puts us in the palm of his hand
> We roll about like pebbles . . .[68]

Given Montezuma's position as supreme ruler with religious duties, given his natural superstitiousness, and given that there was no action in Mexican life which did not have religious connotations, it is hardly odd that the Emperor, for a time at least, thought that the strangers by the sea might be gods of some kind.

All the possibilities were alarming. Tezcatlipoca, a bloody and restless god rather than a tranquil and tolerant one, was even less comforting a possibility than Quetzalcoatl. Montezuma seems to have hesitated between these judgements. Who would not have done the same in similar circumstances? Perhaps, being a clever man, he sensed that there was something deeply disturbing about the arrival of the Castilians; and what was disturbing had to be godlike. The life of the people, after all, revolved round religion. All actions, public or private, were touched by religious implications. The idea that the arrival of Cortés, after Grijalva, could have no such significance would have seemed as ridiculous to most Mexicans as the suggestion that he was not possessed by economic motives would have seemed to a Marxist.

Yet simpler, stronger, less theological members of Montezuma's family, such as his brother Cuitláhuac and eventually his cousin Cuauhtémoc, never seem to have had any doubts. Along with the Mayas, and indeed Montezuma's own emissaries, they seem to have looked on Cortés and his band of conquistadors as a group of criminals, political terrorists, as the twentieth century would have called them. They may have thought that Montezuma's suggestion that the newcomers were a reincarnation of Quetzalcoatl and his entourage was an excuse for procrastination about what to do.

Mexican legends with an unquestionably pre-conquest basis do not contain much about the idea of a lord or god returning to claim a lost territory. Almost the only indication is the story that at Xico, an island where the Toltecs were supposed to have moved after the fall of their capital, a few great heroes such as perhaps Nezahualcoyotl (and of course Quetzalcoatl) were sleeping till they were needed again. Still, the fact that nothing survived does not mean that it did not exist. Almost all the painted books of old Mexico were destroyed in the subsequent war. Mexicans lived in a world where they expected the repetition of past events. A proverb ran: "Another time it will be like this, another time things will be the same, some time, some place. What happened a long time ago, and which no longer happens, will be again, it will be done again as it was in far-off times: those who now live, will live again, they will live again . . ."[69]

A dragon's head for a "Florentine" glass

"The said principal lord came with many of the Indians and brought to the said captain Fernando Cortés a head like a dragon's, of gold . . ."
Juan Álvarez, in an enquiry in Cuba, 1521

"And Cortés sent by those messengers to Montezuma what our poverty could afford: which was a glass of Florentine ware, worked and gilded, with many trees and hunting scenes depicted . . ."
Bernal Díaz, in respect of 1519

ONTEZUMA DECIDED TO appease the mysterious visitors, whether or no they were gods. They were, first of all, to be given everything they wanted. He sent down to the coast more emissaries, with more elaborate presents. The chief emissary would again be Teoctlamacazqui the *tlillancalqui*, Keeper of the House of Darkness.[1] In conversation with this official, Montezuma seems to have been more distressed than he had been at the time of Grijalva's visit. He apparently surrendered to pessimism, by saying that he knew that his fate was sealed. Evidently the lord of all created things (Tezcatlipoca, "Smoking Mirror") was venting his ire against him. Montezuma asked the *tlillancalqui* to care for his children after his death. The Emperor is supposed to have added, "All of us will die at the hands of the [new] gods and those who survive will be their slaves and vassals. They are the ones to reign now, and I shall be the last ruler of this land. Even if some of our relations and descendants survive, they will be subordinates, like tax gatherers."[2] It was said that Montezuma was unable to control his tears.

Teoctlamacazqui, however, recalled how kind Grijalva had been. Neither he nor the other senior lords of the Mexica were as gloomy as was the Emperor. Montezuma refused solace. He hastened to send off his emissary to the coast. The unprecedentedly lavish presents which he took with him included offerings related to the legends of Quetzalcoatl and the god Tezcatlipoca: jewels of gold, quetzal plumes, obsidian, turquoise, necklaces of jade set in gold; golden bells and necklaces; gold models of ducks, lions, jaguars, deer and monkeys; and even arrows, bows and staffs of office, all in gold. There were numerous beautiful headdresses and fans of green feathers, some of which had gold attachments. There were also decorative cloaks, wigs, mirrors, shields, masks, jackets, sticks, earrings, diadems, breastplates, aigrets, and buskins, with bells.[3]

All were placed in baskets to be taken to the strangers. Montezuma said to his emissary: "Go, do not delay. Make reverence to our lord . . . Tell him that his lieutenant Montezuma has sent you here. Here is what he gives you in honour of your arrival in your home in Mexico." (The use of the phrase "his lieutenant" might mean what it says, namely that Montezuma accepted Cortés as his master; more likely, it indicated Montezuma's courtesy: "Your servant, sir" in old English did not imply inferiority.)

Montezuma also apparently gave another order. This suggested that he had not decided with whom he was dealing. According to Fr. Durán, he told his agent to "discover, with absolute certainty, if he really is the one that our ancestors called Quetzalcoatl. If he is, greet him and give him these presents from me. You must order the governor of Cuetlaxtlan to provide him with all kinds of food, cooked birds and game . . . Notice very carefully if he eats or not. If he eats and drinks what you give him, he is surely Quetzalcoatl, as he will be shown to be familiar with our food . . . Then tell him to allow me to die. Tell him that, after my death, he will be welcome to come here and take possession of his kingdom, as it is his . . . But let him allow me to end my days here. Then he can return to enjoy what is his . . . If, by chance, he does not like the food which you have given him," allegedly added Montezuma, "and if he is desirous of eating human flesh, and would like to eat you, allow yourself to be eaten. I assure you that I will look after your wife, relations and children . . ."[4]

Montezuma seems now to have taken another decision: to order the sculpting of his head in the hillside of Chapultepec just outside the city on the far side of the lake. This was a traditional action by Mexican rulers since the days of Montezuma I. They gave the commission when they sensed that age was beginning to take its toll.[5] The Emperor sat for the sculptors at the age of fifty-two: the same period as a Mexican calendrical cycle. Previous rulers had commissioned sculptures when they had reached that age.[6] The site of the carving would be not far from the entrance to the cave where Montezuma had thought of hiding. Perhaps he chose to be sculpted in order to give himself the capacity to do that. The dates on the sculpture mention 1-Reed, for 1519, but also 4-House, for 1509, the year when new fire, ceremonially, was brought.

When Teoctlamacazqui and his following arrived at the coast, they asked for Cortés. On this day Cortés was apparently back on the water. It will be remembered that he had been ordered by Velázquez not to sleep on the shore, for reasons of security. It was not a rule which he always followed, any more than the students of the University of Salamanca always spoke Latin as they were required to. But on this occasion he seems to have done so.[7] The messengers of Montezuma were taken to him by boat. The Castilians asked, through Marina and Aguilar: "Who are you? Where do you come from?" Thanks to Marina, they were able to communicate with the Mexicans. "We come from Mexico," was the emissaries' truthful answer. Whoever was talking to them from the ship (presumably Marina) then replied: "You may or you may not come from there. Perhaps you are teasing us."

One version of Sahagún's chronicle has the Mexicans announcing that they had come to their lord and king Quetzalcoatl. Whereupon (so this version goes on) the Castilians began to whisper and and ask each other: "What can this mean, when they say that their lord and king is here and that they want to see him?" Eventually (again this version continues) Cortés dressed as much like a king as he could and sat on a chair made to resemble a throne.[8] They permitted the Mexicans to come aboard. The Mexicans were greeted by Cortés. They kissed the deck before him. They offered ten slaves to be sacrificed before him. Cortés refused the proposal.[9]

The emissaries then apparently made the speech which Montezuma had requested: "Pray that the god will hear us. Your lieutenant Montezuma comes to give homage to you. He has the city of Mexico in his charge." They then dressed Cortés in the style of a Mexican deity.

The strange ceremony was to the Mexica a conventional one: as one conquistador present, Juan Álvarez, put it, it was "the custom among the leaders of those Indians".[10] Grijalva had experienced a similar greeting further down the coast, at Potonchan. The emissaries put a "dragon's head" of gold on Cortés' head, a rich cloak of feathers, with certain rings of gold and silver round the ankles, and green earrings, shaped like serpents, on both ears. They laid other ornaments at his side: a mirror of obsidian to be attached to his back; a tray of gold; a jar of gold; fans; and a shield of mother-of-pearl.[11] This does not sound exactly how Quetzalcoatl was usually dressed, but Álvarez was commenting inexpertly. A jaguar's head such as Quetzalcoatl was supposed to wear might easily look like a dragon's. The other adornments are similar.[12] Though Álvarez did not mention it, it seems certain that Cortés would have also been given some elaborate sandals, for extravagance in that department was a characteristic of the Mexicans; enabling the deity to differentiate himself from ordinary men in a striking fashion.[13]

Had Cortés known anything of the rites of Mexican religion he might have been perturbed, since sacrificial victims were often dressed in the garb of the god to whom they would be sacrificed. Cortés might have been a Renaissance man but he would not have envied the fate of that Sienese *condottiere* who was asked by his Machiavellian employers to have himself killed in order that he might be canonised.

The emissaries asked if there were other lords (*teules*) aboard. The Castilians pointed to Pedro de Alvarado, Cortés' chief confidant, who, with his dramatic fair hair, could look the part of a god, if a Nordic one. He was then similarly dressed. It was from this time that Alvarado became nicknamed by the Mexicans "Tonatiuh", the sun as expressed by its daytime power, a compliment in any country but an outstanding one in Mexico, where the sun was used in innumerable metaphors and expressions: "He moveth forward the sun a little" meant "He becomes a small child"; while "Now the sun is overturned" meant "A ruler is dead".[14] Perhaps too the designation meant a little more than a nickname. The *naturales* of Guatemala, where Alvarado later fought, are said to have found Alvarado so beautiful and so cruel that masks depicting him became a popular part of folklore.[15]

The Mexicans asked Cortés whether it was his intention to go to their capital – the great city where, they said, Montezuma ruled in his, Cortés', name.

Marina replied on Cortés' behalf that he kissed Montezuma's hands many times. She said that it was his intention to go to Tenochtitlan to see Montezuma and "enjoy his presence". But he had first to organise his affairs on the coast. He hoped for guidance as to the best way to Tenochtitlan. At this, the Mexicans insisted on bleeding themselves – probably from their ears or wrists. One of them offered Cortés some blood in a cup shaped like an eagle. Cortés became angry (or pretended to). He gave the Mexican some blows with the flat of his sword.[16] Disgusted, he began to behave as a bully. "Could these be all your presents?" "This is all we came with, O lord," the emissaries said. Cortés then ordered that all five should be placed in irons. This done, a lombard gun was fired off into the sea.[17] The emissaries, who were standing much too close to the gun for comfort, fell to the deck in shock. The crew picked them up, and revived them with some food and drink, including wine. Cortés continued to bully. "Listen," he said, "I have known and heard that you Mexica are very strong, exceedingly brave; tremendous people. It has been said that one Mexican can pursue, drive on, overcome, turn back even ten or twenty of his enemies. I wish to test you, to see how strong you are, how powerful." He gave them leather shields and steel swords. Then he said, "Early in the morning at dawn we shall fight and try our strengths. We shall joust in pairs, and see who falls."

The Mexicans were terrified at such a prospect. They said, "But this is not what your lieutenant Montezuma commanded us to do. We have only come to salute our lord. We cannot do what the lord asks of us. If we were to do such a thing, we would annoy Montezuma and he would punish us."

"No," Cortés said, "it must be as I say. I wish to marvel at your prowess. For it is known in Castile that you are very powerful and valiant [*muy gente de guerra*]. Now let us eat, and, in the morning, we shall fight."

With that, he allowed the Mexicans to go back to their canoes. Presumably he had no intention of jousting with the Mexicans. He was teasing them. Probably he wanted to observe how they would react to ruthlessness. But the Indians set off instantly for the shore. They rowed with energy. They were so keen to be back on the shore that those who did not have oars even paddled with their hands. When they reached the shore they did not stop before starting for Tenochtitlan. They had to pass through Teudile's town of Cuetlaxtlan. Teudile asked them to stay. "No," they said, "for we must go on as fast as we can. We must give the news to our lord . . . We must tell him what we have seen, which is terrifying – its like has never been seen before." They departed quickly.[18]

Arrived in Tenochtitlan the emissaries quickly told Montezuma what they had seen. The latter asked his supreme council to consult with him as to what should be done. Presumably, as on all important occasions, they met in the House of the Eagle Knights.[19] There, sitting on carved low benches with painted representations of richly dressed and armed figures, gathered Cacama, King of Texcoco, and Totoquihuatzin, the poet-king of Tacuba.[20] No doubt there were some of those "long, curious and elegant discussions" which usually characterised meetings of this nature.[21] The Emperor apparently said that, if these men who had arrived from the east were indeed the god Quetzalcoatl or his sons, they would be certain to come up and dispossess the present masters of the Mexican empire. They should, therefore, be kept out of the capital at all costs. If, on the other hand, they were, as they said they were, the ambassadors of a great lord from where the sun came, they should be received and heard. This argument, at first sight confusing, in fact clarifies Montezuma's approach: the Mexica would fight with gods; but they would be hosts to humans.

Montezuma of course was obliged to consult his supreme council, and the councillors were obliged to give their advice. It does not seem, though, that the Emperor had to follow the recommendation.[22] Still, the council's opinion could not be easily overridden. Here were the four most important advisers, one of whom was almost certainly the Emperor's successor. Here was the *cihuacoatl*, the deputy emperor, the chief priests, and some senior retired soldiers. Perhaps there were leaders of *calpullin*, perhaps there were judges. The total may have been thirty, or as few as twelve. Probably the membership varied.[23] One indication of the relation between emperor and council was shown by the Emperor Ahuítzotl's realisation that he had to apologise to the council of his day after he made the mistaken decision which led to the flooding of Tenochtitlan in 1501.[24]

No doubt there was discussion as to whether there was a real possibility that the Spaniards were gods. Perhaps there was a long discussion as to whether the newcomers had anything to do with Quetzalcoatl. It seemed that the matter could not be resolved. Presumably all the leaders of Mexico spoke. Perhaps the formality with which the Mexicans talked made it difficult to reach a decision. In the end, Montezuma asked his brother Cuitláhuac to speak. This prince was lord of Iztapalapa, a city on the south shore of the lake. "My advice," he allegedly said, "is not to allow into your house someone who will put you out of it." Cuitlahuac was seen as Montezuma's heir. He had been the commander of the expedition which had established Cacama on the throne of Texcoco. He had been the general who had reconquered the region of Oaxaca after a rebellion. Perhaps he had connections with the Mayas and the traders of Xicallanco, and so might have heard rumours of the way that Pedrarias and the other conquistadors had lived in Castilla del Oro.[25]

Cacama, King of Texcoco, who was of course a nephew of Montezuma, took a different view: "My advice," he apparently said, "is that, if you do not admit the embassy of a great lord such as the King of Spain appears to be, it is a low thing, since princes have the duty to hear the ambassadors of others. If they come dishonestly, you have in your court brave captains who can defend us." Cacama was by this time, however, more a puppet of Montezuma than the real successor of the poet-kings of Texcoco.

The Mexica were experienced in receiving guests. They often received foreign princes in order to demonstrate their grandeur and, on occasion, savagery. Vast numbers of people came to the markets, especially that at Tlatelolco, perhaps from remote parts. There were numerous lodgings for visitors. There were also in Tenochtitlan many "foreigners" – families, that is, who were not Mexican. The manuscript painters, for example, seem to have been descendants of a Mixtec group which had arrived in the Valley of Mexico in the fifteenth century.[26] Tenochtitlan had also received war refugees: some from Culhuacan who, in the fifteenth century, had settled in a south-eastern district of the capital. Some Cuauhquecholteca, also victims of wars with Tlaxcala, had established themselves near the great market of Tlatelolco.[27]

In the event, most of those present seem to have taken the view of Cuitláhuac: that they should do all they could to prevent the arrival of Cortés in Mexico. They should declare themselves willing to do anything which the visitors wanted. But they should insist that it was impracticable for Montezuma to meet Cortés. The Emperor would not go to the coast. Cortés should be sternly told that it would be impossible for him to come to Tenochtitlan, because the road was long, arduous and full of enemies of Mexico.[28] They also decided that it would be as well if the magicians of Mexico could be assembled and ordered to use "all their knowledge and power to harm, impede and frighten off the Castilians in order that they would not dare to come to Mexico".[29]

Montezuma to begin with acted on these recommendations. He arranged for more food to be sent to the Castilians, accompanied by expressions of regret that it was impossible to imagine any meeting between himself and Cortés. At the same time, he sent his "wizards and soothsayers" to the coast to see if they could work a spell over the conquistadors. Perhaps they could "blow them away".

The "wizards and soothsayers" were dependent on the god Tezcatlipoca. The success or failure of their mission would perhaps throw light on the identification of the newcomers. Montezuma did not hesitate to try to outmanoeuvre the Castilians even if they were gods. Human monarchs were not banned from trying to trip up immortals.

Teudile, the Mexican governor at Cuetlaxtlan, reappeared a few days later, about 1 May, at Cortés' camp. He again brought presents: white and coloured cottons; gold and featherwork; gold and silver jewels; and above all those two large gold- and silver-covered wooden discs or wheels which had been begun for Grijalva the previous year.[30]

The gold wheel was about six and a half feet in diameter, about two inches thick, and weighed about thirty-five pounds. The silver one was a little smaller and weighed less, perhaps twenty-four pounds. These discs depicted common Mexican emblems, standing for the Mexican cosmic era. Both had representations of animals. In the centre of the gold wheel there was the sun with a figure of a king on a throne; and, on the silver one, there was a moon, and the figure of a woman.[31] It would have been natural if this woman had been the earth monster often shown on such things, and often in contradistinction to Huitzilopochtli. But Spanish descriptions do not suggest that that was so. Both these discs seem to have been made by what in Europe would be called *repoussé* work, being placed on a wooden form.[32]

Though Montezuma gave to the Castilians many other things, these two great wheels were the most famous presents. Mexican thought was dominated by a sense of the duality of things. It was fitting therefore that they should be symbolically represented by two objects which seemed to stand for both the male and the female principles, by, let us say, Tonacatecuhtli, the sun, and Tonacacihuatl, the moon, the one symbolising what was perceived as masculine, luminous, celestial, active, airy; the other, the feminine, the night, the darkness, the passive, the lunar, the terrestrial.[33]

Teudile also brought turkeys, eggs, and tortillas, which, to the Castilians' disgust, he had sprinkled with the blood of recently sacrificed human beings. This was part of the policy of testing the newcomers to see who they were.[34] The Castilians made their reaction clear: they were nauseated. They spat. They closed their eyes tight. They shut their eyes. They shook their heads ... "Much did it revolt them. It nauseated them."[35] But they did eat some of the untainted offerings, such as sweet potatoes, yucca, guavas, avocados, carob fruit and cactus fruit.[36] They also accepted the gold, silver and featherware.

Teudile then gave Montezuma's reply to Cortés. Montezuma, he said, was delighted to hear news of the King of Castile. He said that he hoped that monarch would send him more of "these unusual, good, strange and never-before-seen men". Cortés could take whatever he needed to heal that strange sickness of his men which required gold for its cure. If there were anything in Mexico which Cortés wanted to send to his king, he had only to ask. But as for meeting Montezuma, it was impossible. Montezuma could not go to the sea. He had his duties in connection with the forthcoming ceremony of flowers, the festival of the month Tlaxochimaco. It would also be impossible for Cortés to go to Tenochtitlan. For the route was full of deserts, mountains, and enemies.[37]

Cortés gave Teudile a set of Spanish clothing. He must have by that time seen that the Indians enjoyed dressing up. He said that it was essential for him to visit Montezuma. If he did not, he would fall into disfavour with his king. He sent some more presents for Montezuma: a glass cup said (improbably) to have been of Florentine ware, depicting gilded trees and hunting scenes, as well as three shirts of Holland cloth – a textile much used for shirts throughout the sixteenth century.[38] Teudile said that he would pass Cortés' unappealing message back to Montezuma and left yet again. Before going, he tried to persuade the conquistadors to move inland; away from the mosquitoes on the coast, he said. But such a move would also have made it easier for the Castilians to be surrounded.

As soon as he had gone, Cortés was visited by about twenty Totonac Indians from Cempoallan, some twenty miles up the coast. These Totonacs seemed taller than those at the towns behind San Juan de Ulúa. They wore the (to the conquistadors) hideous lip ornament, or labret, of turquoise, which acted to pull down their lower lips disgustingly over their chins. The men had an interesting story to tell. They had come, they said, on behalf of their lord, who had maintained himself independent of Montezuma. That was not strictly true, since, though autonomous, he paid tribute to the Mexica. But Cortés was impressed by these Cempoallans' desire to distance themselves from the paramount power. He was delighted by their assertion that many peoples who had accepted subservience to Mexico as a result of military defeat during the last hundred years regretted it. The vassals of the Emperor of Mexico seemed to receive little from him, except vague promises of help in the event of famine. In addition, cities close to Mexico gained certain benefits from the provision of labour to work on public works. Their crops did better. But those arrangements had no effect on distant dependencies such as Cempoallan.[39] One consequence of submission to Tenochtitlan can be seen in what happened to Cuetlaxtlan. After conquest that city had been required annually to give ten lengths of cloth, some green stones and some skins of spotted jaguars. After a rebellion, they were forced to give much more: also once a year, another twenty lengths of cloth, a thousand small pieces of cloth, some snakes, white animal skins, and red and white stones.

Cortés was far from having definitely formulated his plans. But he found the news of resentments among the Indians reassuring.[40] He would have known that the Catholic kings' conquest of Granada had been rendered much easier by divisions among the Moors.

But if Cortés had taken heart from the evidence of these quarrels among the Indians, some disputes had also begun among the Castilians. That was partly because of the prolonged inactivity. Cortés himself had plenty to do. He and his friends on the expedition, Pedro de Alvarado and his three brothers, Portocarrero, Escalante, Olid, Lugo, with Ávila and the young Gonzalo de Sandoval, no doubt discussed how to deal with Montezuma's emissaries: when to be brutal, when to be courteous. They also no doubt talked about the long-term future, and entertained themselves with jokes directed against Diego Velázquez.

But some members of the expedition wanted to go home. Some, friends or protégés of Velázquez, believed that Cortés was on the brink of acting in a way for which he had no authority. These men included the Governor's kinsman, Velázquez de León, his ex-majordomo, Diego de Ordaz, Francisco de Montejo, and the one-time constable of Baracoa, Juan Escudero, Cortés' enemy since 1514, as well as Fr. Juan Díaz, the priest from Seville, who seems to have had a habit of falling out with commanders (he had had difficulties with Grijalva).

The first matter which arose to divide Cortés from these men, and to create two parties within the expedition, was that it was said that several soldiers had been seen bartering for gold with the Indians. Why did Cortés permit it? Velázquez had not organised this great expedition so that mere soldiers should carry off the gold. All the riches already gained, the friends of the Governor of Cuba thought, should be displayed, so that the Royal Fifth should be taken from it. Cortés at first agreed. He appointed a protégé, Gonzalo de Mexía, an Extremeño from Jerez de los Caballeros, to look after it.[41] This individual, who had a property in Trinidad in Cuba, was a fortunate man, since he had been spared by the Indians in Cuba in a rare setback for the conquistadors at a battle near a place which, because of the numbers of Castilian deaths, had become known as Matanzas, "massacres".[42]

The incident served to warn Cortés that he could not expect to have his own way on this expedition unless he organised his friends.

But before this matter came to a head, Montezuma's wizards had got to work. They had reached Cortés' camp with no difficulty. Presumably there were then so many Indian servants, both Mexican and Totonac, that entry presented no difficulty. The magicians tried all kinds of tricks. But they found that "if the Spaniards find a flea in their ear, they would kill it". There was another trouble: "The Spanish spend all night talking, and at dawn are on their horses again." Their flesh was also so tough that it was impossible to know where their hearts were. The men of magic returned to Montezuma with gloomy news: "We are not equal contenders. We are as nothing in respect of them."[43]

Soon after this, Teudile paid Cortés a third visit. He again brought cotton goods, some featherwork and four beautiful pieces of jade. But he told Cortés to leave the country since it would be futile for him to try and see Montezuma. Cortés said that he would stay until he had done so. Teudile, no doubt irritated, told him to insist no longer and left. He took away with him the two thousand or so Indians who had been attending the Spanish ever since his first visit. The provisions which the Mexica had been making available regularly to the Castilians also stopped. The expedition became short of food, for the cassava bread which they had brought had gone mouldy. Had it not been for shellfish caught in large numbers they might have been seriously hungry.[44]

Cortés assumed that a battle was being prepared. So he had all the clothing and other supplies put back on his ships. He sent Alvarado with a hundred soldiers, fifteen crossbowmen, and six arquebusiers into the interior to look for maize. About nine miles inland they came across a deserted village on a river with a large house in the centre of it decorated with gold. There was a temple there. In its shrine the Castilians again came across the evidence of recent human sacrifice: blood and flint knives. There and in one or two other empty villages they found ample provisions. Alvarado instructed his men by means of a crier not to touch anything but food. But the food they took.[45] Alvarado as usual allowed his men to conduct themselves roughly. He himself seized two handsome Indian women. He later explained: "If some town was burned or another was robbed, I did not see it, nor did I know of it, much less did I approve . . ."[46] Several witnesses in the *residencia* against Alvarado years later insisted, though, that Alvarado did conduct himself brutally. They alleged that there had been a move to proceed against Alvarado in consequence, but Cortés opposed it and so nothing happened.[47]

This repeated discovery of the evidence of human sacrifice concentrated the minds of the conquistadors. The practice had not been found among the Tainos in Hispaniola or in Cuba, nor even among the Caribs in the Lesser Antilles, though the latter had a (largely unjustified) name for cannibalism. The Portuguese had also found cannibals among the Tupinambá in Brazil. The Castilians in Mexico now realised the danger in which they would be if they were so unfortunate as to fall into the hands of the Mexica. This appreciation had a profoundly shocking effect, permanently souring relations with the Indians and causing the Castilians to adopt an unbending attitude in negotiations. Sacrifice was far from being merely a pretext for intervention. Aguilar (not the interpreter Aguilar), a member of the expedition, made this evident: "To my manner of thinking, there is no other kingdom on earth where such an offence and disservice has been rendered to Our Lord, nor where the devil has been so honoured."[48]

These things gave additional weight to those who argued that return to Cuba was desirable, since (as they said) the *Caudillo* had done what he had been asked to do: he had seen more of the crosses of Yucatan; he had freed a Castilian captive; he had travelled to San Juan de Ulúa; and he had obtained much more gold. Castilian knowledge of the nature of the Mexican kingdom was much increased.[49]

But there was also an alternative point of view headed by Cortés' friends. Cortés, before he had left Cuba, had openly discussed the idea of establishing a settlement. The scheme had considerable backing among many of those who were with him. The pilot Alaminos, not especially a supporter of Cortés, later said that "all the people with one accord required the said captain to settle the said land".[50] Portocarrero, who undoubtedly did back Cortés, would recall the same.[51] Many of these men who had come out to the Indies to make their fortunes had already been disillusioned in Castilla del Oro and Cuba, perhaps also in Hispaniola as well. "Yucatan" or "Ulúa" promised to compensate for those reverses of fortune. Their point of view was impossible to ignore. Perhaps it was more important than historians have realised.[52] Perhaps too they had gained the impression in Cuba that even Velázquez had really been in favour of colonisation.[53]

Cortés cleverly manipulated himself into a position of seeming to be influenced by the cautious. He even told friends who were pressing him to establish a settlement that he had no power to act.[54] Had not Velázquez instructed him to look for Grijalva and nothing else?[55]

Cortés allowed the friends of Velázquez to think that they had won him over to the idea of going home. He told them that he agreed that, since they were now almost without supplies, and had had instructions neither from Velázquez nor from the Jeronymite fathers in Santo Domingo to found a settlement, the sooner they embarked for Cuba the better. He ordered a general embarkation.

This led his friends, or rather the friends of the idea of staying, to protest. The Alvarado brothers, Portocarrero, Sandoval, Alonso de Ávila, Juan de Escalante and Francisco de Lugo accused Cortés of having misled them before they set out because, they said, while still in Cuba, he had talked of establishing a settlement. They called on him at once "in the name of God and the King" to found a colony, and to defy Diego Velázquez. After all, the Mexica would probably never let them land again, while, as soon as a good town had been built in this rich territory, settlers from Castile would compete with one another to be allowed to live in it. In that way, God and the King would be well served. Why could not those who wanted to go home do so? The adventurous spirits could stay. Cortés should also cease trading in gold as he had done up till then since, if he went on, the country would be ruined. Why should they, the loyal army, sit around and watch while he collected gold which would only be to his benefit and, worse, that of Diego Velázquez?[56]

Cortés appeared to hesitate. He gave out that he was making up his mind what to do. Yet at the same time he began privately to look for a suitable site for a colony.[57] He wanted this to have a good port. He did not think that the harbour at San Juan de Ulúa would be adequate in the long run: though Veracruz (as it later became) would, precisely in the long run, be one of the most important ports of the Americas. Cortés therefore sent two brigantines, with fifty men on each, up the coast to look for a better site. Francisco de Montejo, the leader of "the party of Velázquez", would be captain of one ship; Rodrigo Álvarez Chico, an Extremeño in his confidence, captain of the other.[58] The pilot Alaminos would be on board the first. Velázquez de León was also sent away on an expedition of three days into the interior.[59] Probably Cortés did not wish to decide whether to go ahead with a settlement until he had seen for himself just how prosperous the place was; then, as was said of him in a lawsuit some years later, "seeing the richness of the land and its availability, and the goodwill with which the natives received him", he made up his mind.[60] He thereupon sought a legal way of putting that decision into effect. Whether or no he had already conceived of the idea of moving on up to Tenochtitlan is uncertain. But certainly neither he, nor anyone else on the expedition, questioned the morality of establishing a colony in the territory of the Totonacs, or the Mexica. The notion that the Indian principalities (as opposed to Indian individuals) might have rights to the land had scarcely occurred to the Dominicans.

While Montejo and Velázquez de León were away, Cortés carried out what can only be described as a *coup d'état*. Their absence at that time was too convenient to be a coincidence. Probably most of the fifty men sent with Montejo were also friends of the Governor of Cuba. Cortés did, of course, want to know what there might be in the way of a harbour up the coast. But it was helpful not to have Montejo and Velázquez de León present at a moment of decision. For as a later enquiry against him would put the matter, during these days, "Don Hernando Cortés was elected *Justicia Mayor* and Captain General in these territories . . . by the magistrates [*alcaldes*] and councillors [*regidores*] of the town of Villa Rica de la Vera Cruz . . . until such time as His Majesty provided anyone else."[61]

This extraordinary development was apparently achieved in the following way. Cortés held a meeting. He told those who wanted positively to found a settlement in Mexico that, since he was more interested in serving the King than anything else, he would cease trading in gold as he had been doing up till then: though, by that activity, he had hoped to recover his outlay in fitting up the fleet. Then, with a show of reluctance, he agreed to found a city to be called Villa Rica de la Vera Cruz. The expedition would constitute its population. The name derived from the fact that the land was rich (*rica*); "*Vera Cruz*", the True Cross, would recall that they had landed there on Good Friday.

Cortés apparently next addressed his men in sensible terms: it was obvious, he said, that the indigenous people of Mexico were more civilised, reasonable, and intelligent than those in the Caribbean. There was evidently much more to the territory than what they had seen. They should build walls and fortifications, as the Portuguese had done in Africa (and as Las Casas had suggested should be done on the north coast of South America). When they had built the place, they could unload everything, and send their ships back to Cuba. They could trade with Cempoallan and other places known to be hostile to Mexico.[62] Each member of the expedition would become a citzen, *vecino*, of the new municipality, with a right to vote in elections for the municipal council. Cortés knew what he was doing. It had been in that style that Velázquez had founded Cuban towns. Cortés himself had often been the notary confirming the arrangements.[63] But he did something original also: having studied in Salamanca, and having worked both for and as an *escribano*, he believed that a case could be made for thinking that, in the absence of a properly constituted authority, authority would revert to the community, which would then be able to elect its own legal representatives.[64]

A number of people in Cortés' confidence were then named to be the first *alcaldes*, magistrates, and *regidores*, councillors, of this town. There seems to have been a vote, probably determined by a show of hands. Both Andrés de Tapia and Martín Vázquez, witnesses brought forward by Cortés at the enquiry against him in 1534, insisted that "the election of the officials was on the advice of all". Vázquez said that he "gave his vote and opinion".[65] Charles V's official historian, Juan Ginés de Sepúlveda, writing in the 1550s, talks expressly of there having been an "assembly".[66] In fact, either the officials were nominated by Cortés, or only names which Cortés approved were put forward. The idea of a real election surely did not come into question.[67] The names were safe ones, so far as Cortés was concerned. Thus the officials of the new town were nearly all Extremeños.[68] Portocarrero (born in Medellín) was one of the two chief magistrates (*alcaldes mayores*). Alvarado (born in Badajoz) and Alonso de Grado (born in Alcántara) were councillors (*regidores*). Another unconditional Cortesista, Francisco Álvarez Chico (brother of Rodrigo, and from Oliva near Medellín), was public spokesman (*procurador-general*), the young Gonzalo de Sandoval (born in Medellín), one of Cortés' new favourites, became constable (*alguacil*);

while Gonzalo de Mexía (born in Jerez de los Caballeros) was treasurer (he at that time was still on good terms with Cortés, though he would later become an enemy). The notary, *escribano*, Diego de Godoy, bore an Extremeño name, indeed one well known in Medellín, though he had been born in Pinto near Toledo. The only non-Extremeños were Ávila and Olid (born in Ciudad Real and Baena respectively); Escalante, probably from Huelva; and Montejo, from Salamanca, still up the coast on his journey of reconnaissance, who, in order to implicate him in the conspiracy, was named joint chief magistrate with Portocarrero.

All these men had titles (*alguacil, regidor, alcalde*) identical to those which they might have had had they been members of a similar council in faraway Castile. The councillors acting together were called the *regimiento*, the deliberative institution, in Villa Rica de la Vera Cruz as in Castile. Cortés had, of course, a memory of how such municipalities worked: his father Martín Cortés and his grandfather Diego Alfon Altamirano had once had offices with these names in Medellín. Alvarado, as well as being *regidor*, was named "captain-general for incursions inland [*entradas*]": a nomination which indicates Cortés' weakness for the chivalric, however imprudent. At this time, however, "Tonatiuh" seemed the most attractive of leaders. He was Cortés' confidant as well as in effect his deputy.[69]

Cortés was called on by the councillors of Villa Rica de la Vera Cruz to show them the instructions which Velázquez had given him. He produced the paper concerned. Having examined it, his colleagues – especially Alvarado, Escalante, Portocarrero, Grado, Olid and Ávila – decided that Cortés no longer had any authority to act. They declared his mission concluded. He, therefore, resigned his offices. But this resignation, even if legal, was a charade. For immediately afterwards, and assuredly by prior arrangement, the council nominated Cortés as chief justice (*justicia mayor*) of Villa Rica, as well as captain of His Majesty's armies (*capitán de las armadas reales*), until the King should decide otherwise.[70]

Cortés always referred to these nominations as an "election". He insisted that he did nothing in the way of settling (*poblar*) in Mexico until he had this authority from the new council. All his authority henceforth, he would insist, came from this body.

The character of the expedition now changed absolutely. Cortés had set off from Cuba, he said, to find Grijalva and had had no other intention. Then he saw what "a fine land Mexico was, and how both Our Lord God and the King would be so well pleased, and the royal taxes and rents so much enhanced, if there were to be a settlement". So on the authority of the new town council, he set about "populating" the place. He then had no need to obey Diego Velázquez.[71]

Cortés' enemies later denounced these actions as a rebellion. Cortés and those who agreed with him might have so arranged it that "they took over in the name of His Majesty". But since they were not prepared to use the powers which Velázquez had given to Cortés, they were acting illegally.[72]

Cortés' argument was different. Traditional Spanish medieval law, as summarised by the philosopher King Alfonso X, in *Las Siete Partidas*, "the Seven Chapters" of Spanish law, provided that a populace could form a municipal council.[73] All laws could also be set aside by the demand of the good men in a community. In Mexico this "community" was the expedition itself, in which Cortés' friends were in a majority and Velázquez's in a minority. It is true that, for the moment, "Villa Rica de la Vera Cruz" did not exist as an entity. But it would soon do so, in a primitive form.[74] Further, Cortés was setting out to achieve not just a new municipality but, as his friends (or perhaps really he himself) expressed the matter, in a letter to the King, a city in which there would be "justice": the first society in the Americas of which that could be said.[75]

None of the conquistadors since the first journey of Columbus had considered acting as Cortés was doing. Núñez de Balboa had allowed himself to think of independence from Castile. But he had not thought of asserting autonomy, as it were, while bypassing the governors in Santo Domingo and insisting on direct dependence on the Crown. In Cuba, Diego Velázquez had founded towns which developed their own identities. But he had consulted the authorities in Hispaniola before making his plans. Cortés would have known from his time in Salamanca and Valladolid of the provisions on these matters in the *Siete Partidas*. Perhaps a copy existed in Cuba or even in Villa Rica.[76] Still, legal arguments, though interesting, can be carried too far. A careful reading of another section of the *Siete Partidas* might have justified a conviction of Cortés for treason.[77] Perhaps an admission that Cortés knew that in truth he was breaking rather than keeping to the law was shown in the fact that he later was sometimes heard to say: "If laws have to be broken in order to reign, then let them be broken."[78]

Soon after the "artifices" (as the matter was described rather sharply by Peter Martyr) of Cortés' resignation and reappointment, Montejo and Alaminos returned from their journey to the north after twenty-two days at sea.[79] They had not been very successful. Almost immediately they left San Juan de Ulúa, they had been caught in a storm. They were carried a hundred and fifty miles up the coast. Then they were caught in countercurrents and flung back almost as far. They did, however, report that a small harbour by a cliff some forty miles to the north was a possibility for the new settlement.[80]

Montejo of course found the political situation, including his own position, transformed. As he told the Council of Castile the following year, in his absence the expedition had turned itself into a town.[81] Montejo too had been named a chief magistrate. Cortés, knowing that aristocrats can be bought as easily as commoners, apparently secured his collaboration with the "artifice" by a bribe of two thousand pesos.[82]

Once the council had elected Cortés to his grand positions they did something else unusual. They decided, in respect of the treasure which they expected would be found, that, after the King's Fifth had been taken, Cortés could take another fifth for himself.[83] The arrangement also meant that most of the gold which came into the possession of the Spanish had to be melted down. This is why there is so little original Mexican gold jewellery to be seen. Not for the last time, taxation caused philistinism.

Cortés later explained his system thus: "Till they had set up a settlement, they had no way of maintaining themselves, save by relying on what had been taken with them. [Cortés] . . . therefore would take what he needed for himself and his staff, while the rest would be valued at its right price and then distributed among the . . . men of the expedition." These men would either pay Cortés for what he provided (for example, a horse, a medicine, or a sword), or they would deduct the cost from what would be due to them from the booty at the end of the adventure. According to Cortés, they, the men of the expedition, also asked him to have the artillery and the ships valued so that he could be reimbursed. They wanted too to send for wine, bread, clothing, arms, horses and so on from Cuba. That, they said, "would be cheaper than if they had to depend on traders".[84]

Cortés brushed all these suggestions aside as details. He said that the expedition should feed and arm themselves at his cost. For the time being no one should think of paying for anything. The apparent generosity would in future inspire disputes, as generosity often does if the donor is reckless.

These exchanges between Cortés and the "men of the expedition" were of a limited nature. They were discussions between Cortés and members of the council. The rank and file were surely not implicated. Perhaps they did attend an "assembly". But if they did, it was no doubt a well-managed gathering. Some of the men later said that Cortés had "done what he should not have done. But they did not talk of it for fear of being hanged."[85] Others were more outspoken: Cortés, they said, should not have been chosen captain without their consent. They would prefer to return to Cuba rather than remain under his command. The *Caudillo* soothed these people's feelings with "a mixture of menaces and presents".[86] Probably he talked critically of the Bishop of Burgos, Juan Rodríguez de Fonseca, who could always be made to be a good whipping boy.

The *Caudillo* then decided to found Villa Rica de la Vera Cruz at the site, Quiahuiztlan, which had been recommended by Montejo. He set off for there. All the supplies and most of the artillery were embarked on the ships and dispatched to the proposed port by sea. Cortés himself led four hundred men, the horses and two small pieces of artillery (little falconets, probably) to that place by land.[87] Until their arrival, the expedition was a council without a town: an unusual state of affairs, though a town without a council is common enough.[88]

15
They received him with trumpets

"Afterwards the Marquis went to Cempoal and they received him with trumpets."
Historia de los Mexicanos por sus pinturas, c. 1535

THE FAILURE OF the magicians to unsettle the Spaniards of course disturbed Tenochtitlan. Once again Montezuma made no secret of his anxiety. So there were "consultations . . . formations of groups. There were assemblies of people . . . there was weeping . . . there was dejection . . . there were tearful greetings."

This panic passed. Accepting that the Castilians would probably carry out their threat and make for Tenochtitlan, Montezuma determined to dissuade them by planning all sorts of discomforts on the way: "He made himself resolute. He put forth great effort. He quieted, he controlled his heart."[1] As a consequence, he stationed on the roads messengers who travelled endlessly to bring him news of what was happening. At least he would be well informed.

The first important news which he must have received was that, on about 7 June 1519, Cortés had set off by land for Montejo's suggested harbour at Quiahuiztlan. Before leaving, he took possession of the new territory in the accustomed manner, causing the *Requerimiento* to be read out by the notary, Diego de Godoy. The fact that Grijalva had done the same a year before, in much the same place, did not disturb Cortés. He despised Grijalva.[2]

The journey to Quiahuiztlan was forty miles, or, as the crow flies, two days' march. It took much longer. For halfway up the coast lay Cempoallan, the seat of the Totonacs whose chief, an enemy of Montezuma, Cortés had determined to befriend.

On their first night after leaving San Juan de Ulúa the expedition slept on a river bank, probably the river now called Antigua on which the second Veracruz would one day be built.[3] They did this on the recommendation of Totonacs from Cempoallan. These Indians provided food of the now expected sort: turkey and tortillas. On the way they would no doubt have seen row upon row of well-planted fields of maize, "a type of chick pea", one conquistador commented, though he must have seen the plant in the West Indies.[4]

A hundred Totonacs from Cempoallan came to greet the Castilians. They also brought turkeys. Their lord regretted being unable himself to welcome Cortés. But he was, they said, too fat to move. The Spaniards were pleased at the thought of the prosperity which must lie behind such an incapacity. They thereupon ate the turkeys. That evening they made their way into Cempoallan. The surroundings seemed full of gardens and well-watered orchards.

This was one of the many places where the horsemen were at first supposed by the Indians to be one with their mounts, as if they had been centaurs. But the Spanish were the victims of a comparable fantasy. Several horsemen who went ahead were greeted at the gates of the city. They rejoined Cortés to say that they had seen houses covered with silver. Cortés told them to return and investigate but to show no surprise at that, nor indeed at anything: hidalgos from Castile were never supposed to find anything unusual. On examination, the silver turned out to be bright white paint gleaming in the sun.[5]

When Cortés arrived at the town the people "greeted him with trumpets": that is, the large perforated conch shells (known as *atecocoli*). He was also welcomed by the chief, who certainly appeared to be fat. His city was said to have in it 20–30,000 persons who were required to pay tribute to Mexico. That meant that the population was about 200,000. The first figure, if it bore any relation to the truth, must have included those living in dependent territory nearby.[6] Another contemporary estimate of the size of the city of Cempoallan was, however, 14,000.[7] That would seem more likely.

The chief, whose name appears to have been Tlacochcalcatl, asked the Castilians to stay. This was an invitation cheerfully accepted by the new *justicia mayor*. Hernández de Córdoba had similarly stayed in Yucatan. The visitors were lodged in a palace which had been emptied for them and which belonged to a rich and ugly widow, subsequently known to the Castilians as "Catalina" (like Cortés' mother and wife), a niece of the fat chief. Mats were provided for the Spaniards on which to sleep. Food was brought. The warmth of this reception was so remarkable that Cortés feared a trick. Taking no chances, he established his expedition as if this building had been a fortress, placing guns at the entrance and appointing a guard all night. Next day, Tlacochcalcatl visited them, gave them more food, and also some of the now usual presents of gold, cloaks and feathers. He invited the leaders to dine that night: a curious banquet it was, too, with "interesting soup and presents".[8] Several days then passed without the Castilians doing more than taking stock of the first town in the Mexican empire into which they had been invited.

Cortés went to make a formal call on the fat chief (as the Spanish consistently called him). He took fifty men, and a quantity of cotton goods as presents. The two talked through Marina and Aguilar, to whom two Nahuatl-speaking Totonacs had been added. The dialogue must have been in consequence slow. But Cortés was in no hurry. The chief explained the irritation of having to pay tribute to Montezuma. These Mexica, he said, were taking everything. They had first come with religious pretexts. Then they had seized all the arms in the country and had enslaved many people. Previously, the principality of Cempoallan had lived in "peace, quietness and liberty".

Perhaps in so arguing Tlacochcalcatl was being a little unfair. The fair-minded Spanish judge Alonso de Zorita would later argue that, in the Mexican arrangements for tribute, "there was a great deal of regularity and attentiveness to see that no one person was more heavily burdened than the rest. Each man paid little; and since there were many men it was possible to bring together great quantities of goods with little work and no vexation."[9] But then subject peoples never judge well the nature of their subservience.

The chief also talked of the strength of Tenochtitlan and how, being built on the water, it was thought impregnable. But the people of Tlaxcala and Huexotzinco, as well as the Totonacs, hated the Mexica. Ixtlilxochitl, the rival candidate for the throne of Texcoco, was also an enemy of Montezuma and, the chief thought, might help Cortés as well. The chief argued that if Cortés could make a league with these four peoples, Montezuma would be easily defeated.[10]

He was not quite accurate in this report. Tlaxcala and Huexotzinco, both in the temperate zone about two-thirds of the way to Tenochtitlan from Cempoallan, and about ten miles away from one another, were not in the same political position. Though both had been for a long time "enemies of the house", as the cities which had fought "flowery wars" with Tenochtitlan were known, Tlaxcala had certainly moved into open opposition to the Mexica. Huexotzinco, an enemy of Tlaxcala, was in a more ambivalent position.

All the same, Tlacochcalcatl's information was the most interesting news which Cortés had yet heard. The reason for the character of the welcome given by the chief was now obvious: he wanted a friend. The suggestion that the Castilians might ally themselves with the Totonacs and others against Montezuma gave Cortés for the first time an indication of how a serious onslaught against the Mexican empire might be made. For though he had aspired, for some time, to make a settlement on the coast, the idea of co-ordinating an alliance to fight Mexico itself seems not to have occurred to him before. The corpulent chief of Cempoallan, therefore, played a decisive part in Cortés' adventure. Perhaps he added one or two interesting tales such as, for example, how the people of

Cuetlaxtlan, the city of Teudile, had been reduced by the Mexica within living memory after a terrible rebellion, in which the people of the town had shut up the Mexican stewards in a house and set fire to it.[11] Cortés himself added that one of the reasons for his coming to this land was to soothe disputes and destroy tyrannies: a presentation of himself as leader of a Christian peacekeeping force even more remarkable than his other notion of being an ambassador of Charles V. Perhaps he was recalling occasions in Extremadura when a Crown representative intervened to settle disputes in Medellín with the Count.[12]

In visiting Cempoallan, the Castilians came upon a ceremonial precinct. It had its usual temple, staircase, pyramid, and palatial lodgings for priests. (Bernal Díaz irreverently thought that these local priests looked like Dominicans; or canons.) Several of these fine buildings can still be seen, if ruined and overgrown. Just outside there was an imposing skull rack, though holding fired clay models painted white, rather than real heads. One or two Spaniards may have observed a sacrifice in Cempoallan.[13] Cortés himself came across five slaves destined for sacrifice at an early date. He had them released.

Tlacochcalcatl was horrified. "You will ruin me and all this kingdom if you rob me of those slaves," he said. "Our infuriated gods will send locusts to devour our harvests, hail to beat them down, drought to burn them, and torrential rain to swamp them if we offer no more sacrifices." The Spaniards accordingly returned the slaves on the ground that it was better for the time being to maintain the friendship of this chief than ensure his enmity in future. The two priests on the expedition, Fr. Olmedo and Fr. Díaz, in particular insisted that "it was not yet time to suppress the ancient rites".[14]

Cortés and his expedition spent two comfortable weeks in Cempoallan.[15]

Then, about 1 June, the expedition moved on up the coast to Quiahuiztlan, which Montejo had suggested as the site of the first Castilian settlement on the Mexican mainland. The chief of Cempoallan offered Cortés bearers for the journey. He accepted. Henceforth, a very important matter, the expedition almost always had the assistance of about four hundred native porters. The Castilians very rarely thereafter had to carry their own equipment, their presents, their guns, their tents or their bedding. The benefit was incalculable.

There was already a little Totonac town at Quiahuiztlan on a hill overlooking the sea. When Cortés arrived, he found that, even though he himself had been delayed, his ships had not yet reached there. He therefore decided to enter the Totonac town, insisting that his horsemen ride up the steep path into the town without dismounting: as well as appearing never to be surprised, it was necessary for hidalgos to give the impression that they could do everything.

The chief of Cempoallan had alerted the town to the Castilians' arrival by messenger, and therefore the expedition was well received. The Castilians entered the square in the middle of the town, and the inhabitants showed great interest in the beards of the visitors: anything to do with adornment interested the Indians. Cortés sat down with the lord of the town in front of a brazier: the appropriate way to receive both gods and unexpected grandees. He was perfumed with incense. The lord, in welcoming him and explaining the local problems, remarked that he too, like the chief in Cempoallan, had been driven demented by the demands of the Mexican collectors of tribute. The Mexica even took their sons and daughters as servants or sacrificial victims. This lord did not make the mistake of thinking that the visitors, whether they were gods or not, were concerned only with principles. Excess of taxation was an equally acceptable subject of talk.[16]

At this moment, by an appropriate coincidence, a delegation of Mexican stewards of tribute (*calpixque*) arrived at Quiahuiztlan. These officials appeared in embroidered clothes, with their hair shining and drawn back. Each of them was carrying flowers, and smelling them, as they entered the square. Each carried a crooked stick. Among the Mexica, the smelling of certain flowers was restricted to the upper class, and no doubt these were in that category. Servants walking before these officials carried whisks to free them of the attention of mosquitoes and flies.[17] They walked straight past the Castilians without paying attention to anyone. The lord of Quiahuiztlan trembled.

Cortés and his friends were fascinated at the appearance of these grand bureaucrats. Cortés said amiably that he was certain that Montezuma would be delighted that the lord was receiving him and his friends. The lord of the town was less convinced of that. He went to arrange for the tribute collectors' reception in the usual fashion: with more flowers, turkey and chocolate. But Cortés detained him. He suggested to the lord that he should seize the stewards, tie them to poles, and imprison them in a room next to his own, to be guarded by his own men. The lord of Quiahuiztlan was aghast. But he did as he was asked.

During the night, Cortés carried out a devious trick. He ordered his guards secretly to release two of the stewards and bring them to him. He then required Aguilar and Marina to pretend to try and find out who they were. They declared themselves to be Mexican stewards. They added that they were surprised to have been treated so. Usually they were looked after very well. They thought that the Castilians must have encouraged the people of Quiahuiztlan to act so unwisely as to arrest them. They also feared lest their companions, the other collectors, might be put to death before Montezuma could be told of their plight. For the local people were barbarous. The stewards added that these people of the coast would rise against Montezuma if they had a chance:

a thing which would infuriate the Emperor, and give him the expense and trouble of suppressing them.

Cortés told the officials that he had freed them because he did not like to think of Montezuma's agents being mistreated. He personally liked what he had heard of Montezuma. He would be grateful if they could kindly go and tell the Emperor that he, Cortés, considered Montezuma his friend. He hoped that Montezuma would not spurn his friendship, as Teudile (as he thought) had foolishly done. He believed that Montezuma would be happy to see him, and become a brother of the King of Castile. Finally, he would do what he could to prevent the other collectors of tribute from being killed. Thereupon he released the two men. He had them carried in the darkness by sailors in a small boat up the coast to a point outside Totonac territory. Thence they returned to Tenochtitlan as fast as they could.

The lord of Quiahuiztlan was angry when, in the morning, he found that two of his prisoners had escaped. He would probably have had the remaining officials put to death had it not been for Cortés' intervention. Cortés said that they had probably only acted on superior orders. Therefore, because of "natural law" – perhaps he was remembering some saying of Aristotle picked up in a faraway lecture room at Salamanca – they should not be executed. Instead, Cortés offered to imprison them on one of his ships, which had just arrived offshore. That solution was accepted. The stewards were sent off in irons to a *nao*.

The success of the action against the Mexican officials gave heart to the people of Quiahuiztlan. A discussion followed in the town, presumably confined to the elders.[18] But there was at least an appearance of consultation which might perhaps not always have occurred in European cities before a rebellion against an emperor. The lord eventually announced that the town would be happy to rebel against Montezuma, provided Cortés would act as their captain. Whether that was what Cortés wanted at this moment is difficult to say. He might have preferred an ambiguous relation with Montezuma for a little more time. Still, he stated firmly that, if the Totonacs desired it, he would command and defend them, since he valued their friendship more than he did that of Montezuma. He asked how many men the lord of Quiahuiztlan could assemble. "A hundred thousand," was the encouraging reply.[19]

These occurrences filled Cortés with confidence. It was probably about now that he decided that, as soon as he could, natural law or no natural law, he would, with as many tributary enemies of the Mexica as he could gather, march up to Mexico. There is nothing to suggest that such a wild scheme, which certainly was straight from the pages of *Amadís de Gaula*, if anything could be, was in his mind before this.

Before he could do anything, however, in respect of this scheme, he had to finish founding his new town of Villa Rica. His fleet had by then arrived. So the expedition could move down to the coast and set about the laying out of that settlement. Before leaving Quiahuiztlan, he went through the quaint procedure of receiving the lord there as a vassal of the King of Spain, the notary, Godoy, again being present. The lord went through the ceremony without, it would appear, much quibbling about the exact use of words. He presumably supposed that he had now a powerful ally against the Mexica. Nor did it matter to him that Cortés rechristened his town Archidona (since, like the town of that name near Málaga, it was on a hill). It did not keep the new designation long.[20]

Villa Rica de la Vera Cruz was formally founded on 28 June 1519. The date was appropriate. For on that day, nine thousand miles away in Frankfurt am Main, Charles of Austria, who until then had been Don Carlos I of Spain, was finally, after unprecedented bribery, elected Emperor Charles V of the Holy Roman Empire. Cortés and his expedition would not, however, hear of that imperial transition for months.

The site of this first Villa Rica de la Vera Cruz is now not easy to distinguish. But it must have been on the coast near what is now Mexico's first nuclear plant, the Laguna Verde. The hills run close to the sea, sand dunes line the water's edge, and the breeze maintains a certain freshness. Cortés enjoyed himself laying out the plan for the main plaza of the new town, surrounded by the church, the town hall, the barracks, the slaughterhouse and, that essential companion of empire, the prison. There was also a plan for a fortress of stone. Cortés is even said to have helped to dig the foundations himself. Stocks too were placed in the plaza: a reminder that a civilised society was under construction.

Although none of the sources say so, the hardest work for this first city of New Spain – digging, cutting of trees for wood, making bricks – was probably mainly carried out by Cortés' or his captains' Cuban servants.

Some confusion was caused by the arrival of more, but grander, ambassadors from Montezuma. The leader of the mission was Motelchiuh, who had a military position in Tenochtitlan, as *uitznahuatl*. Two nephews of Montezuma were with him. They were accompanied by four old men as advisers, as well as by many servants to look after their personal needs. They said that they had come on behalf of Cacama, King of Texcoco, as well as of Montezuma.[21] They brought back the Castilian helmet which Teudile had liked and which Cortés had requested might be returned full of gold. It now contained gold dust. Montezuma had sent it to help to cure Cortés and his men of their sickness of the heart. The nephews said that the Emperor had decided that Cortés' kindness in saving the collectors of tribute had caused him to overlook his tactlessness in staying with such evil people as the Cempoallans. Montezuma sent some more presents, including clothes and feathers. The ambassadors also said that Montezuma was both ill and busy with wars and various negotiations. They could not say when a meeting would be possible. But they were sure that such a thing would be accomplished in the end. Until that happened, if Cortés really wanted to go up to Tenochtitlan, he should remember to travel slowly. Guides would be ready everywhere. Cortés would only have to watch out for his health.

Cortés received this delegation well, and had them lodged as best he could; which, given the circumstances of the new town, must have been much more humbly than they were used to. The Mexica would, of course, have been astonished at the evidence which they now had of the Spanish determination to remain in the country. Once again Cortés presented some of his apparently endless supply of green and blue glass beads to the Mexica. Again he asked Alvarado to arrange a display of galloping on the beach.

Cortés then sent privately for the lord of Quiahuiztlan. Through his tireless interpreters, he told that potentate that he ought now to look on himself as free from all duties of servitude to Montezuma. All the same, he hoped that he would not take it amiss if he, Cortés, were to release the remaining collectors of tribute, and hand them over to the ambassadors to take home to Mexico. The lord said that anything that Cortés, his new captain, suggested would be acceptable.

When the lord of Quiahuiztlan returned home, he spread the message throughout the province that a god or, at least, a lord, had arrived from the east to liberate the tributary towns from Mexico.[22] But at the same time Motelchiuh went home happily with the released tax-collectors. Cortés' diplomacy was paying off.

Cortés was soon called upon to live up to his commitment to support the Totonacs. The chief of Cempoallan sent a message to say that the Mexica had for some years kept a garrison at Tizapancingo, a hill town about twenty miles to the south-west.[23] When the tributary towns declared their freedom from Montezuma, the collectors had mostly fled there. It was believed that a Mexican army was being organised in that place to suppress the rebellion of Totonacs.

Cortés' reaction was instant. He set off immediately for the designated town, accompanied by most of the conquistadors, and his sixteen horses, together with a force of Totonacs gathered from Quiahuiztlan. Miguel de Zaragoza, the man who had stayed behind from Grijalva's expedition and remained hidden among the Totonacs till Cortés arrived, disguised himself as an Indian. Carrying two pails, such as Indian peasants often bore, he discovered the Indian dispositions.[24] The Mexica then came out to meet Cortés in full battle array: feathers, paint, shields, with conches. But they appear to have panicked at the mere sight of the Castilians and to have fled. The beards of the conquistadors seem to have caused as much fear as their horses. Small force though it was, Cortés' cavalry followed the Mexica and cut them off. The horses, however, were unable to climb the rock on which the town was set. Cortés and some others dismounted. They forced open the gates of the town with their swords and Cortés then entered Tizapancingo, disarmed the few Mexicans who remained, and handed them and the town to the chief of Cempoallan. He stipulated that no one should be killed and then withdrew to Villa Rica.

The speed of this victory greatly impressed the Totonacs and naturally had the effect of extending their rebellion against Mexico.[25] It also made Cortés even more self-confident; for it suggested to him and to his captains that the Mexica, despite their fame, had no special military qualities, no secret weapons, and little discipline.

On their way back to Villa Rica, Cortés and his men had to pass through Cempoallan. He used the opportunity afforded by his victory to insist on the destruction of the idols in the temples there. This was still opposed by Tlacochcalcatl. But Cortés threatened death to him and all his lieutenants unless the deed were done. Cortés gave the order to some fifty Spaniards to throw down the gods from their places on the top of the pyramid. They immediately did so. Bernal Díaz described how "when the chiefs and the people saw their idols broken and lying on the ground, they set up a miserable howl, covered their faces, and begged forgiveness of the idols that they were unable to protect them."[26] The lieutenants of Tlacochcalcatl began to attack the Spaniards. That chief intervened. Survival, he must have thought, was worth a mass. After some rather difficult moments, a conflict was avoided. The Cempoallans were astonished at the Castilian insistence. They were accustomed to seeing the gods of the defeated being destroyed. But victors, as they thought that they were themselves, never made such a concession. Victors or no, the Castilians (Bernal Díaz was among them) took great satisfaction in throwing these idols down the steps of the main temple, as well as forcibly persuading the priests to cut their hair. The long, black, dirty (often blood-caked) hair of the priests in Mexico unnerved the Castilians. They did not yet appreciate that the deliberate yielding of one's person "to dirt" meant the submission to sacred powers.[27]

The Castilians also set up, in the temple, a cross and a picture of the Virgin. They whitewashed the temple. Fr. Olmedo said mass. Subsequently Juan de Torres, an old and lame Cordobés, was appointed caretaker to the new shrine. But at the same time Cortés had four Indian priests have their hair cut and asked them to look after the altar and keep it clean. This astonishing occurrence passed without notice. But it was surely one of the most remarkable events in the history of Cortés' life. Here were Totonac priests who had not even been baptised, and who must have been presumed by Cortés to believe still in the devil, made responsible for a Christian altar.[28]

Here too it seems the Castilians first taught Mexican Indians an invaluable lesson: how to make candles. This was a contribution which the *naturales* may really have thought was worth a mass. The smelly, smoky torches which the Indians used did much damage. Fires were frequent. Candles were safer as well as more efficient.[29] This was an early example of adoption of European technology to the Indians' advantage.

The people of Cempoallan sought to adapt to the spiritual innovation of Christianity by absorbing it. No Mexican community minded receiving the Mother of God in their temple. A new god was usually welcome. The corpulent chief, to show that he was, on reflection, far from distressed permanently, also gave Cortés eight girls – eight girls of high rank. They were well dressed, and had gold necklaces and earrings. Cortés duly had them baptised. He gave them Christian names, and distributed them among his captains. The chief gave Cortés his own ugly niece, "Catalina". Cortés feigned pleasure. Portocarrero was apparently more pleased with "Francisca".

It is inconceivable that the Totonacs accepted the defeat of their own deities in any profound sense. No doubt the chief of Cempoallan and his advisers considered that freedom from Montezuma was worth a verbal concession which could easily be gone back upon.

On his return to Villa Rica on the coast on about 1 July, Cortés was delighted to find that reinforcements had arrived from Cuba: a caravel had reached the new town, with sixty men and several horses (including some mares) under the command of Francisco de Saucedo, known as *el pulido*, the neat (because of the pleasure which he took in arranging his appearance), a citizen of Medina de Ríoseco, a city which belonged to the great family of Enríquez (for whom Saucedo had once worked). It was the richest seigneurial city in Spain.[30] The boat in which Saucedo came was that one which Cortés had bought and left behind in Santiago for careenage. Saucedo, a friend of Cortés from Hispaniola, had been intended as one of the commanders of the original expedition. The most important of those who came with him was Luis Marín, a native of Sanlúcar de Barrameda, from one of the families there established of Genoese origin, who, despite a lisp, was a good talker. He soon also became an outstanding member of the little army led by Cortés.[31]

Though the reinforcement was welcome, the news which Saucedo brought was less so. This was that, in the spring, a letter had reached Cuba to say that the Council of Castile, meeting in Saragossa on 18 November, the very day that Cortés had left Santiago de Cuba, had agreed to give the Governor, Diego Velázquez, "a licence to seek, at his own cost, islands and mainland territory which had up till now not been discovered" – provided, of course, that they were outside the limits granted by the Pope to the King of Portugal. This licence spoke of land in the neighbourhood of Cozumel and Yucatan (referred to in Saragossa, following Hernández de Córdoba's christening of it, as "Santa María de los Remedios"). This nomination was as encouraging for Velázquez as it was the reverse for Cortés. Yet it gave Velázquez less than he had hoped. For he was still to regard himself as Deputy Governor of Cuba, lieutenant of Diego Colón, Admiral of the Indies. He was still subject to the *audiencia*, the supreme court of Santo Domingo. He had not received the title of *adelantado*. But he was to have numerous rights in Yucatan. The profits of the expedition were to go to him and his heirs. After he had found four islands, he would receive a twentieth of the profits perpetually. If gold were found, only a tenth was to be paid to the Crown, to begin with.[32]

Given the (for Velázquez) less than perfect solution, Fr. Benito Martín, the Governor's chaplain and representative in Spain, continued his negotiations, flatteries and, no doubt, briberies. He talked to Bishop Fonseca. He talked to those of the King's influential Flemish courtiers whom he could reach. He talked too to the important civil servants who worked in the Casa de la Contratación in Seville. Fr. Martín was an effective intriguer. By the time that Saucedo arrived in Villa Rica, Velázquez had been indeed granted the title of *adelantado*, so far as Yucatan and Mexico were concerned, though there was not to be any change in his title in respect of Cuba (thus his title became formally: "*Adelantado* Diego Velázquez, lieutenant of our governor of the island of Fernandina, captain and distributor of Indians").[33] But that eventuality had only occurred in May 1519. Velázquez did not yet know of this victory any more than Saucedo did.[34] Bishop Fonseca had in addition secured the nomination of a bishop for Cozumel in the shape of a confessor of his own, a learned Dominican monk, Fr. Julián Garcés, a Latin scholar. What value his wide scholarship would be to the people of Cozumel was obscure, for he had no immediate intention of visiting the place. Fr. Benito Martín had assured for himself what he assumed to be the lesser, if similarly absentee office of "Abbot of Culhúa".[35]

Saucedo *el pulido*'s news persuaded Cortés of the desirability of sending back direct to Spain his own delegation with news, offerings and petitions for the King.[36] The men whom the *Caudillo* chose to carry out these tasks were, first, his old friend Portocarrero; and second, his new friend, the still potentially untrustworthy Montejo. Portocarrero, as a man from Medellín, but also knowledgeable, through his family and connections, of the ways of the court (he was nephew of the prominent judge in Seville, Licenciado Céspedes, as well as being a cousin of the difficult Count of Medellín), could be trusted, though he had not distinguished himself in the fighting at Potonchan or Champoton. Cortés might miss his company in conversation, but not in combat. It was also sensible to think of removing Montejo from Mexico as the old leader of the friends of Velázquez, even if he had obviously seen the benefits which might accrue from the further penetration of the Mexican empire and even if he had become temporarily Cortés' ally. Montejo was an able man, with the capacity to think on a large scale, as his subsequent conquest of Yucatan would show. He had the imagination to see the benefits of Cortés' plans and could appreciate Cortés' leadership. But with his self-confidence, he might have been a disconcerting rival. At the same time, he could be expected to talk well at court. Cortés would send these men home on his flagship with the pilot Antonio de Alaminos. The principal aim of their mission was to gain the King's approval for what Cortés was doing.

Portocarrero and Montejo did not, however, return to Spain simply as messengers of Cortés. That would have been too simple a designation. They went as *procuradores*, representatives, that is, of the Council of Villa Rica de la Vera Cruz. The word was important. Members of the *cortes* (legislatures) of Castile or of Aragon were *procuradores* of their towns: not deputies.[37] Most substantial cities of Castile at that time sent two *procuradores* to the *cortes*. The cities of Hispaniola and Cuba also had their *procuradores*. They were accustomed to meet every year to discuss mutual problems, and also, sometimes at least, to name a *procurador-general* to formulate in person the requests which the settlers of the colony concerned wished to make to the King of Spain.[38] In giving his emissaries this name, Cortés was seeking to fit them, and his achievement, into an established pattern of behaviour. Yet the essential task of the *procuradores* at home was to vote taxes (*servicios*); the task of those of Villa Rica would be to secure recognition of their city.

Cortés sent papers and treasure with his *procuradores*. These papers included several letters to the King (and to poor mad Queen Juana, who was still in theory joint monarch of Spain with her son). While writing, Cortés probably discussed the position at home with some in his entourage who had come out to the Indies more recently than he. For such knowledge as the *Caudillo* had of the court dated from before 1506. He knew nothing at first hand of the curious treatment of Queen Juana; of the death of King Ferdinand; nor of the resentment in Castile against King Charles and his Flemish courtiers. Portocarrero, Montejo, Vázquez de Tapia (whose uncle had been a member of the Council of Castile, and who had other good connections), Velázquez de León, and, perhaps above all, Fr. Bartolomé de Olmedo must have helped him. But even they would have known nothing of the anarchy which in 1519 was threatening Castile in consequence of the demands of the Castilian muncipalities (*comunidades*).

The letters to the King seem to have been three in number: first, a joint letter from the Council of Villa Rica describing what had happened to the expedition so far;[39] second, a letter from the army in Villa Rica signed by most or all of those who had been under Cortés' command;[40] and third, a private letter from Cortés to the King. The first of these letters survives, the last two do not. Doubts have been raised as to whether the third ever

existed; or whether it was perhaps written and not delivered.[41] Probably
all the letters, including the first surviving one which was in theory from
the Council of Villa Rica, were written by Cortés.[42] For this letter "from
the municipality" has the same insinuating style that distinguishes
subsequent letters from the *Caudillo*, even if occasionally, artfully, it
uses the pronoun "we" to remind the reader of the putative authors.

The *procuradores* had too their own instructions: thirty-seven items in
a lucidly phrased paper which was no doubt also written by Cortés.[43]
This document survives.

The surviving letter from the municipality summarised the journeys of
Hernández de Córdoba and Grijalva in dismissive terms. It discussed
how the Council of Villa Rica de la Vera Cruz had formed itself, and how
it had nominated Cortés for the commanding offices. Both King Charles
and Queen Juana his mother were asked to confirm Cortés in those
positions. The letter demanded an official enquiry, a *residencia*, in short,
into the activities of Velázquez as Governor, on the grounds that he had
mismanaged his affairs. It besought the monarchs to make no concessions to that governor in future in the nature of an *adelantadamiento* or
new governorship. If such concessions had been already given (as of
course they had) they should be revoked. The letter said that the land was
as rich as that from which Solomon took the gold with which to build his
temple in Jerusalem, and that it had every kind of game, as well as lions
and tigers. It also dwelt on the disturbing practices of human sacrifice,
which, the letter implied, justified almost any action to secure protection
of the Indians. But the letter added that, leaving human sacrifice aside,
the Totonacs lived in a more political and rational way than other peoples
whom the conquistadors had seen in the Indies.[44] The conquistadors
thought that "the devotion, trust and hope" which these people had in
their own religions could be diverted so as to repose in the divine power
of the true God. If they would serve the Christian God with the "same
faith, fervour and diligence" as they served Tlaloc and other deities,
"they would work many miracles". (A completely contrasting letter had
been sent back to Lisbon by Pedro Vaz da Caminha in 1502 when he went
to Brazil with Amerigo Vespucci: there, he said, it was because the people
were of such innocence that they would make good Christians.)[45]

The letter of the municipality, for all its enthusiasm, insisted also that
all the people – presumably only the men – were sodomites: a statement
for which there was no evidence at all. The letter was addressed, in old-
fashioned terms, to both King Charles and Queen Juana: "very high and
powerful, most excellent princes, very catholic kings and lords" ("*muy
altos y muy poderosos excelentísimos príncipes, muy católicos reyes y
señores*"). But then it went on to employ the more modern term "Your
Majesties", using that term indeed as a synonym for "Highnesses".[46] It
explained that it was written so that the monarchs could get to know the

reality of the land in which they could establish a fief ("*feudo*") – an unequivocally imperial Castilian word even if one medieval by implication. No doubt the writer, or writers, of the letter emphasised the horrors of Mexican religion in order to justify an attempt at taking control of the land. But that does not mean that they were insincere in telling of their shock at the practices which they had discovered.

The second letter, from the army, is only known from allusions to it in other documents: but it apparently ended in triumphant terms, saying that Cortés' men were ready to die and hold the newly discovered territory, in the King's name, till the men concerned saw his reply to their letter.[47]

The third letter, Cortés' so-called "first" *Carta de Relación*, may, perhaps, one day be discovered in some neglected archive. Some impression can, however, be gained about what it may have said: for example, Cortés himself, in a letter of September 1520 to the King, recalled that, in it, he had promised to conquer, and pacify, the entire territory and "take or kill Montezuma dead or alive, but subject to your Majesty".[48] This was a clear admission that Cortés intended to move up to Tenochtitlan and in some way set about reducing the Mexican empire. Cortés also may have written about his intentions of one day turning his attention to the "Southern Sea".[49]

The instructions to the *procuradores* insisted on the zeal of Cortés to serve the King. They repeated that Velázquez should in no circumstances be given the title of *adelantado*. Such a nomination would be fatal to the King's interests. Cortés wanted permission to grant *encomiendas* to conquistadors, as had been done in Hispaniola and Cuba. But he proposed to treat the Indians better than his one-time benefactors Ovando and Velázquez had done in, respectively, Hispaniola and Cuba. He wanted the conquistadors – he used the word without apology – in Mexico to be free from duties on exports and imports for ten years (*almojarifes*), a concession often granted. The royal interest should similarly be limited to a tenth of the profits of the expedition for ten years, rather than a fifth (a concession, as Cortés would have known through Saucedo, recently made to Velázquez). Those who originally accompanied Cortés were to be given the right to tracts of land (*solares*) in the city of Villa Rica. Cortés wanted several other licences: to found hospitals and inspire *cofradías*, that is, religious brotherhoods; to buy and make slaves; and to melt down and mark gold, as well as to mark silver – usually a royal monopoly. Velázquez, he said, had spent nothing on the expedition: a statement which would not stand up to much analysis.

The instruction made clear that Cortés did not anticipate returning to Cuba. The presence of his wife in that island seems to have meant little to him. The allusion to treating the Indians well probably indicated Cortés' desires. He had with his own eyes seen the destruction in Hispaniola and

Cuba. From a practical point of view, he was intelligent enough to know that Indians who were well provided for would be likely to work rather than die.[50] He must have known something of the strenuous endeavours of Las Casas (an acquaintance from Hispaniola and Cuba) to secure changes on moral grounds to the treatment of the Indians.

Cortés also sent a letter via (and in fact addressed to) Juan Bautista, captain of the *Santa María de la Concepción*, asking for certain goods to be sent to him direct and empowering his father, Martín, to act on his behalf. This letter must have been accompanied by a verbal order to both the captain and the *procuradores* to enter into contact with those merchants whom he had known in Seville before leaving Spain and with whom he may have been in touch from Hispaniola and Cuba, such as Luis Fernández de Alfaro and Juan de Córdoba.[51] Cortés also asked the *procuradores* to give his parents gold and an account of his adventures.

Some private letters were sent back too: one of which, from a servant to his master in Spain dated 28 June 1519 from "New Seville", survives: a somewhat extravagant document, it gives a vivid impression of the enthusiasm which a minor member of the expedition at that time felt: "Yucatan" was said to be "the richest land in the world"; there was gold "without comparison"; there were many clothes of cotton "richly worked with figures sewn with a needle"; the women were beautiful, the beds covered with canopies, the palaces of the lords built of marble, the cities bigger than Seville, the gardens provided with wonderful tables for banquets; while the natives kept bees, ate peaches and worshipped idols. But it was still not known whether or no the territory was the mainland.[52]

In addition to the letters, Cortés sent the King of Spain and his mother Queen Juana a great deal of treasure.[53]

The Council of Villa Rica had ordered that all the treasure obtained – the cotton and featherwork, as well as the gold and silver – was to be gathered together in the plaza of the town: at that time presumably a sandy square facing the sea, with a few half-built wooden houses around it, and a wooden church under construction. The treasurers estimated that the gold and silver, measured by weight alone, would be worth about 22,500 pesos.[54] The featherwork and cotton goods, they intelligently thought, could not be valued.

Gonzalo de Mexía, treasurer of the army, and Alonso de Ávila, the treasurer responsible for the Royal Fifth, refused a distribution of profits among the expedition. Cortés, they said, had to be repaid first for financing the whole undertaking. Cortés brushed this loyal proposal aside in a lordly way. He proposed to give the King everything which had been gathered; anyway after his share as captain of the army had been deducted. Perhaps he had already taken what he wanted.

These ambiguities marked the beginning of an interminable series of arguments about how the booty in Mexico was to be shared. What seems then to have happened, at all events, is that the helmet full of gold dust, the wheels of gold and silver, the figurines, and most of the featherwork were packed to be sent to the King. Two brightly painted books, "folded in the style of cloth of Castile", as Bernal Díaz put it, were also dispatched – perhaps among several found by Cortés in a temple on the way to Cempoallan.[55] (These books were perhaps the so-called Codex Vindobensis Mexicanus, probably Mixtec in origin, now in the National Library in Vienna; and the Codex Nuttall, also called Zouche after its last private owner, now in London.)[56] Four Indian boys and two girls, all saved from sacrifice, probably at Cempoallan, completed the treasure to be sent to Castile.

Cortés realised how beautiful the treasures were. Of the jewels, he later wrote that they were "so realistic, in gold and silver, that no smith in the world could have done better; and in jewels so fine that it is impossible to imagine with what instruments they were cut so perfectly; and those in feathers were more wonderful than anything in wax or embroidery."[57]

But probably not everything which Cortés had received since he arrived in Mexico was handed over to the King. There was no mention, for example, of the gifts presented to Cortés at San Juan de Ulúa.[58] The lists of objects in different texts do not exactly concur.[59] The figures do not work out either: thus attached to the letter from the Council of Villa Rica was a receipt by the *procuradores* for the King's Fifth. This was for 2,000 castellanos. That implied that the total was 10,000 castellanos. But the total when it was displayed before the two treasurers was, as has just been mentioned, equivalent to 22,500 pesos, which amounted to 20,000 castellanos.[60] So the King seems to have only received a tenth, not a fifth, even of the declared goods.

The long list of goods sent (now in the Spanish archives) is dry but overwhelming. Thus: "Item: two collars of gold and stones, one of which, with a figure of a monster in the centre, has eight strings, and in them 232 red stones and 163 green stones; and hanging from the said collar and from the said border 27 golden bells, in the centre of which are four figures, made of large stones set in gold, and from each of the two in the centre hang simple pendants, and those at the ends have four pendants each. And the other collar has four strings with 102 red stones and 172 apparently green, and around the two green stones are 26 golden bells and, in the said collar, ten large stones set in gold . . . Also two other pieces of coloured featherwork which were for two pieces of gold which they wear on their heads, as if they were shells . . ." And so on for many lines of careful, handwritten script.[61] Perhaps one of those headdresses included that famous one, with its five hundred quetzal feathers standing three feet above a semicircular band, now in Vienna.[62]

Portocarrero and Montejo carried with them 4,000 pesos for their expenses, and a little less for Cortés' father: say 7,500 pesos in all. At the usual exchange of a peso being worth about 7.7 per cent less than a castellano, this would measure about 7,000 castellanos – which, with the Royal Fifth at 2,000 castellanos, would have amounted to almost the total value of the sum which was declared as having been found. However the matter is considered, about 10,000 castellanos (say 11,000 pesos) seem unaccounted for.

The two *procuradores* had both been *alcaldes mayores* of Villa Rica. So substitutes had to be found for them in those offices: Alonso de Ávila, the experienced captain from Ciudad Real, who had been on Grijalva's expedition, and whom Cortés came to respect, despite his intractable personality; and Alonso de Grado, from Alcántara in Extremadura, an *encomendero* of La Concepción, Hispaniola, whom Cortés at this time admired as a good writer and musician but whom he later mocked as a self-indulgent coward. Both had previously been *regidores*. Vázquez de Tapia now became a *regidor*.

Perhaps these nominations of yet more of Cortés' friends to the municipality, served to ignite a serious conspiracy. At all events, once the *procuradores* had been named but before they had sailed, the long-pending conspiracy of the "friends of Velázquez" came to a head.[63] Perhaps the news of what Cortés had put in his lost letter, namely that the *Caudillo* planned to try and capture or kill Montezuma, had become generally known. At all events, certain members of the expedition made clear that they had no wish to go on any *entrada* into the interior. They wanted to go back to their farms and families in Cuba. Friendship for Velázquez had given way, as a motive, to fear of the future.[64]

Cortés as usual managed this protest cleverly. He said: "Of course, let them embark." A well-known horseman named Morón was allowed to sell his horse. Cortés conducted himself as if he would really have liked to have given his enemies their freedom to go home. But in the circumstances he felt then that he could not do so. He revoked the permission. The council of the new city had determined, he said, that nobody should be allowed to leave. Everyone was needed.

Several friends of Velázquez now determined to challenge Cortés. They planned to seize one of the brigantines, kill its master, and make their way back to Cuba, in time for Velázquez to intercept Montejo and Portocarrero on their way to Spain. That would have meant that the treasure sent to the King by Cortés would have passed first to Velázquez: a fact which Cortés did not fail later to mention in a letter to Charles.[65] This plot was betrayed by a certain Bernardino de Soria.[66] Cortés arrested the conspirators. These were the priest Fr. Juan Díaz, Velázquez de León, Diego de Ordaz, Governor Velázquez's ex-page Escobar, and Cortés' old enemy, the ex-constable of Baracoa, Escudero. The plotters also included a pilot, Diego

Cermeño, and some sailors such as Gonzalo de Umbría, with Alfonso Peñate and his brothers, natives of Gibraleón (a town on the way to Huelva from Seville), who had agreed to sail the brigantine back to Cuba.

The *Caudillo* decided to make an example of the ringleaders in order to put an end to the plotting against him. He was surely encouraged to take a strong line by friends such as Alvarado and Sandoval. The two men on whom he picked as chiefs of the conspiracy were Escudero and Cermeño. It could scarcely have been a chance that the first of these was an old enemy: he had been constable in Baracoa and had arrested Cortés a few years before, when he was being pursued by Velázquez. These men were submitted to a court martial organised by the Council of Villa Rica, whose new chief magistrates, Ávila and Grado, were, of course, intimates of Cortés. Cortés anyway seems to have presided.[67] Escudero and Cermeño were condemned to be hanged. Gonzalo de Umbría was punished by having a part of his foot cut off – a most obscure sentence, occasionally inflicted on slaves, the details of which it does not seem possible to establish.[68] Peñate and his brothers were each given a hundred lashes. Fr. Juan Díaz was left under the impression that, had he not been a clergyman, he too would have been hanged. The others were held in the flagship under guard. Here they were imprisoned for several days till they made their peace with Cortés. Ordaz later said that in prison he thought that Cortés would cut off his head. But he did not do so, and later, perhaps out of gratitude, like several of these men, Ordaz became an unconditional supporter of the *Caudillo*.[69]

For some time an air of fear hung over the camp: the gallows on which Escudero had been hanged was still standing there a year later.[70] Juan Álvarez testified in 1521 that he, and many others, thought that Cortés should not have acted thus, but that they did not dare to speak, for fear of being also hanged.[71] One of the accusations against Cortés in the late 1520s was that those condemned had no chance to defend themselves;[72] while in 1521 it was said that those who judged the alleged malefactors were prejudiced, being those whom Cortés had chosen and who had "risen" against Velázquez with him.[73] Cortés' reply was that the conspiracy had been serious. To "steal a caravel" was a capital offence.[74] As commander of the expedition, he had the right to act as judge.

The *Caudillo* next proceeded with audacity to an action which took even his friends by surprise. He ordered the masters of nine of the twelve ships which were anchored off Villa Rica to sail their vessels on to the sands.[75] They were also told then to remove from the ships all the rigging, sails, anchors, guns, and other tackle (portable altars and Virgins too), for possible use in some new way. Cortés planned to use the wood, where possible, to build houses. He then announced that the ships had become unseaworthy – a judgement loyally sustained in a declaration by Portocarrero later in Spain.[76] Cortés probably had to pay the masters well for this action which of course was against their instincts.[77] These men and their sailors were then absorbed into his army.[78]

This course would, the *Caudillo* hoped, end all defeatist talk of going back to Cuba.[79] It would force even the most recalcitrant to support him, to see that they had now no alternative to entering the interior other than "dying like men".[80] Had Cortés not done this, he would perhaps "not have been able to take with him away from the port many of the people" who accompanied him on his journey into the interior.[81]

The ships' masters fulfilled their mission. All but three of the ships (one *nao*, two brigantines) were disabled: as Cortés himself put it later, the expedition "then had nothing to rely on, apart from their own hands, and the assurance that they would conquer and win the land, or die in the attempt".[82]

This action was a considerable risk for Cortés. For that reason, if for no other, he and his friends subsequently spoke of it in extravagant terms: his lawyer in his enquiry in 1529 called it "one of the most outstanding services – to God – since the foundation of Rome".[83] The scheme may have occurred to Cortés because much the same thing had been done some years before in Nicaragua: Gonzalo de Badajoz (possibly a brother of Gutierre de Badajoz, who was with Cortés), wanting to prevent the flight of eighty sailors from Nombre de Díos, had also sailed his ships on to the sands.[84]

The action was, as all who observed the thing agree, and as Cortés himself wrote, a grounding, not a burning. The famous usage – "the burning of boats" – with which the world is proverbially familiar, began to appear in print in the second half of the sixteenth century: the earliest reference being apparently a dedication of 1546 to Cortés (then still alive) by the historian Cervantes de Salazar in his *Dialogue of the Dignity of Man*.[85] The mistake perhaps derives from the fact that the early documents spoke of the boats breaking, *quebrando*; thanks to the bad handwriting of a scribe, Cervantes may have read the word as *quemando*, "burning".[86]

Cortés then made a speech at what may well have been another assembly of the army (Sepúlveda, the official historian, so described the meeting). He explained that the ships had been rendered useless by a wood-beetle known as the "*broma*". Whether any of his hearers pointed to the pun implicit in this deception is obscure (the word "*broma*" usually means a joke in Spanish.)[87] He then explained that now was the time for the journey to Mexico-Tenochtitlan (*la entrada de México*). This seems to have been his first public mention of this scheme. He said that he could not believe that anyone would be so pusillanimous as to estimate his life worth more than his, Cortés', own, nor so feeble in heart as to have any doubts about going with him. But if there were such, they could go back to Cuba on the one boat which did remain, with the blessing of God; though Cortés believed that, if they did that, they would soon become angry with themselves when they knew of the adventure which they were thereby missing. Shame (and fear of what Cortés' reaction might be) overtook the hesitant. They all agreed to follow Cortés to the death, praising him too, and, for a time anyway, nobody spoke of returning to Cuba.[88] The men to whom this appeal was made were, of course except for the sailors, all adventurers comparable to Cortés. They had fortunes to make.

The difficulty for Cortés was to explain what the expedition was going to do in Tenochtitlan. Joan de Cáceres at the enquiry against Cortés years later left the impression that most people thought that they were going to Tenochtitlan to see the sights.[89] That is not very probable, even though the Cid had once told his men that they had to keep moving:

> for we must live by our swords and lances.
> Otherwise in this lean land we could not survive.
> And in my opinion we must move on.

The Cid had also said:

> Hear me, my knights, and I will tell you the truth:
> He who stays in one place will see his fortunes diminish.

The mention of securing Montezuma "dead or alive" was presumably a serious commitment now that the *Caudillo* seems to have mentioned it in a letter to his king.

Probably Cortés himself thought that, in some as yet unrevealed way, he and his new allies and some others (the mysterious Tlaxcalans, for example) would be able, through diplomacy and courtesy, to win over Montezuma so that Cortés would be able to act as the latter's prime minister, an Álvaro de Luna to Montezuma's Juan II, rather than fight him. Perhaps, more adventurous still, he and Alvarado had conceived of the idea of capturing Montezuma, and then forcing him by duress to act in the Spanish interest; as the Cid had sometimes done with Moorish chieftains; or (to cite a Renaissance parallel) as Charles the Bold, Duke of Burgundy, had done in relation to King Louis XI of France at Péronne in 1468. Charles the Bold was, after all, the father-in-law of the Emperor Maximilian, the grandfather of Philip the Beautiful, and the great-grandfather of Charles V; the recollection may have been green in the memory of the court of Spain when Cortés had been at Valladolid. But if such a wild plan had occurred to him he would have kept it to himself.

Perhaps Cortés and Alvarado had, however, by now learned enough about Montezuma and his kingdom to know how they were likely to react to an armed Castilian arrival in Tenochtitlan. Thus Andrés de Tapia wrote, in his memoir, that Marina told Cortés that Montezuma and the Mexica looked on themselves as newcomers in the land which they now ruled; that they had established an empire under the pretext of preaching a religion; that they offered peace to those from whom they received tribute; and that they lived on an island in a lake.[90] This must have confirmed the information made available by the chief of Cempoallan. Perhaps by playing on the idea of the Mexican sense of being newcomers, he, Cortés, could in some way secure the acceptance of the supremacy of new strangers without a fight: victory without a battle being an aim of antiquity as well as of Clausewitz (and of Lenin).

Cortés would have realised that to conquer a great kingdom was, legally and morally, as well as strategically, a different matter from occupying an uninhabited island, or an island in the Caribbean with a tribal society, much less a beach-head such as all the conquistadors, from Columbus onwards, had at first established. In this respect, Cortés had learnt from the experience of Columbus, who seems to have given no thought as to what he would have done had he really reached Hangzhou. Would he have marched up to the Ming capital of Peking as Cortés was now planning in respect of Tenochtitlan?

Portocarrero and Montejo left for Spain on the only *nao* left, the *Santa María de la Concepción*. It was probably 16 July.[91] Montejo left behind, as well as his mistress (or perhaps ex-mistress) Marina, the interpretress, his natural son by his Sevillana mistress, Montejo *el mozo* the younger.

Cortés was now making his final arrangements for the *entrada*, the journey up to Tenochtitlan. He planned to leave his reliable friend Juan de Escalante at Vera Cruz as governor, with a hundred and fifty men, two horses and two arquebusiers. Escalante's main concern was to hold Vera Cruz against any new expedition which might be sent against Cortés by Diego Velázquez. The local Indians seemed a secondary danger.

Many of the men with Escalante were sailors from the ruined ships. Half were ill or old. The few Castilian women with the expedition seem also to have stayed with Escalante. The only persons of importance left behind were Francisco Álvarez Chico and Pedro de Ircio, who had arrived with Saucedo. The former, an Extremeño friend of Cortés, was declared the new *procurador* of Vera Cruz, in the absence of the two men who had gone to Spain. He demanded an assurance from Cortés that those left to guard the new town by the sea should share in the profits of the expedition. That was formally agreed. Ircio stayed behind since he had a bad leg, and because he bored all whom he met with stories of his time as steward to the intransigent (and shortly to be insurgent) Andalusian nobleman, Pedro Girón.

The arrangement whereby Cortés was to receive a fifth of the booty after the Royal Fifth had been taken was also confirmed.[92] This plan was later criticised. Surely it implied that Cortés was on the same level as the monarch? Yet had the arrangement been fairly carried out, the rank and file would have received sixty-four per cent of the total, rather than the one-third which they had earlier anticipated.[93] The lords of Cempoallan and Quiahuiztlan promised to provide food for the new town. They expressed pleasure that the Castilians wanted to give the name of "New Seville" to Cempoallan – though, as with Archidona for Quiahuiztlan, the renaming was soon forgotten.[94]

16

If I continue, shall I win?

" 'Tell me, O pilgrim knight:
If I continue, shall I win?'
'Don't go on, good king,
Good king, don't go onwards,
For Mérida is very strong' . . .
Thus spake Oliver;
So spake Roland.
'Thou liest, pilgrim knight,
Thou dost not tell the truth.' "
Story of the pilgrim from Mérida to Paris

ORTÉS AND HIS "holy company" set out for Tenochtitlan about 8
August 1519.[1] This comprised about three hundred Spanish
conquistadors.[2] These men were divided into companies of about
fifty each, captained by Alvarado, Velázquez de León, Olid, Ávila and,
the youngest and least tried, Sandoval, from Medellín. The standard-
bearer was Cristóbal del Corral. Cortés had about forty crossbowmen
and twenty arquebusiers. Most of the expedition wore armour and they
kept it on, over their jackets or tunics (sayos), their usual garments, even
to sleep.[3] But most of this was padded cotton armour, in the Mexican style.
Cortés took also probably a hundred and fifty Cuban Indian servants,
together with, most important perhaps, eight hundred Cempoallans and
other Totonacs led by a chief named Mamexi. "This was a great assistance,"
commented Joan de Cáceres, Cortés' majordomo, some years later, as well
he might, for they carried equipment, food and munitions, and hauled the
artillery (perhaps only three pieces).[4] It was a service in the tradition secured
by Columbus in Hispaniola, but it was not something which could have
been counted upon.[5]

The guns concerned seem to have been wrought-iron falconets, about
four feet long, able to fire balls or stones of two or three pounds. These
weapons may have included one heavier, bronze culverin, which fired a
ball between eighteen and thirty pounds in weight.[6] Cortés had
apparently arranged for some carts with wheels to be built by a carpenter,
Diego Hernández, a native of Saelices (now Sanfelices) de los Gallegos,
near Ciudad Rodrigo. These, the first wheeled vehicles of the Americas,
carried the guns till they broke down. Pulled by Totonacs, they were
doubtless nearly as surprising to the Indians as the horses.[7]

The Totonacs also built huts wherever the Castilians needed them for
overnight rests. They did all this "with a very good will, taking whatever

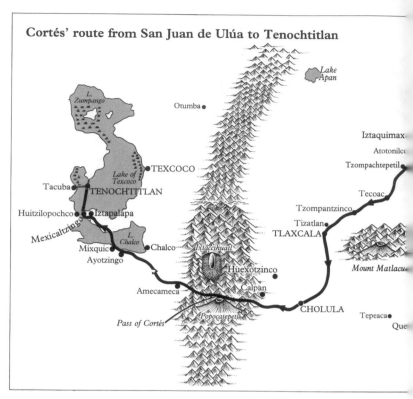

Cortés' route from San Juan de Ulúa to Tenochtitlan

job was offered".[8] (Usually Mexican armies travelled with one bearer per two soldiers.)[9]

Cortés had about fifteen horses but they were, of course, reserved for the "captains". His dogs "were many and gave great help to the Spaniards because they were well trained to fight".[10] Probably there were many Mexican spies with the army, perhaps long-distance merchants (*pochteca*). They would have travelled with the Totonacs. Certainly, Montezuma continued to be fully informed about Cortés' movements.

Cortés' chamberlain, Cristóbal de Guzmán, and his majordomo, Cáceres, carried a cloak and carpet on which their master could sleep after any meal, though these rests were sometimes under a tree, or in the shade of a hillside. Cortés slept little: he insisted extravagantly: "I shall not rest until I have seen Montezuma and observed the quality of this land."[11]

On his ship Cortés would have had with him one or two Venetian-made sand-filled hourglasses; there would have been no purpose in taking any inland.[12] But the *Caudillo* did apparently take a compass: it impressed the Indians, who thought that he saw the future in it.[13]

Cortés addressed the army once again before he set out. The speech as rendered by Bernal Díaz says that Cortés talked of how important it was to win every battle: "To conquer the land or die" was the slogan.[14] That expression must have been surprising to half the army, but they had no

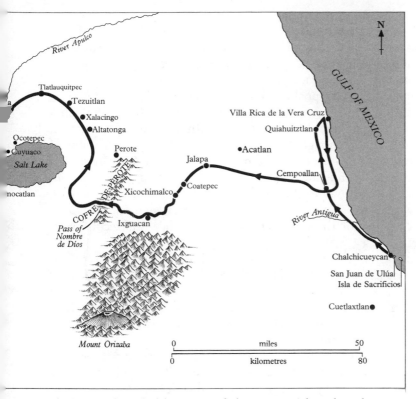

choice, and probably most of them no wish, other than to support the *Caudillo*. Cortés also apparently returned to the theme of ancient Rome. How many of his followers understood his comparison between himself and Caesar crossing the Rubicon, if he indeed made such an allusion, must be a matter for speculation. A ballad about Caesar crossing the Rubicon was probably the origin of Bernal Díaz's knowledge of the matter.[15]

Cortés also spoke of the religious purpose behind his advance into the hinterland. Would not God be served, he later wrote home, "if by the hands of your royal highnesses these people were introduced to, and instructed in, our holy catholic faith, converting the devotion . . . which they have for their gods into a regard for the divine power of the true God?"[16] Human sacrifice gave the expedition a pretext. It must have helped Cortés to secure the support of men who might have hesitated before any ordinary *entrada*. Cortés himself would have protested that Las Casas' mocking expression about the "holy company" had a meaning.

It was, of course, essential for Cortés to communicate with his men in this way since, though vested with powers by the "municipality of Villa Rica de la Vera Cruz", his control came from ancient custom. In the old days in Castile, a captain of a company acknowledged his duty to his commander, but he expected the commander to respect his dignity, and thus to consult him about major decisions. All expeditions such as

Cortés' consisted of free companies, united in pursuit of profit and disciplined only lightly by the commander. Not in jest did conquistadors refer to each other as comrades.[17]

The distance from Cempoallan to Mexico-Tenochtitlan is, as the crow flies, two hundred and fifty miles. The route is varied. The first stretch is flat, hot, tropical and humid, with fertile land. In the sixteenth century, it was heavily forested, though dotted with well-cultivated plantations of maize. The land then rises sharply beyond Jalapa to 6,000 feet. The climate becomes temperate. This region is towered over by two mountains, those known to the ancient Mexicans as Nauhcampatepetl, now known as the Cofre de Perote, and Citlatepetl, now Mount Orizaba. The first of these is over 13,000 feet high, the second over 18,000 feet.

The next stage of the journey is over a cold bleak plain. It was at that time dominated by a salt lake and by a third mountain, Matlalcueye (now known as Malinche), which rises to over 14,600 feet. Between that plain and the city of Tenochtitlan there lies a further chain of high mountains. Of these, the volcanoes Popocatepetl, a name which indicated "smoking mountain", and Ixtaccihuatl, which meant "mountain of the white woman", respectively nearly 18,000 feet and a little over 17,000 feet, can be seen from many miles away on the seaward side. The pass between the mountains is just under 13,000 feet. The land then falls away to the great lake of Tenochtitlan, whose height above the sea is 7,400 feet.

This route was, of course, unknown to Cortés. He had Mexican guides and also some from Cempoallan. The former are said to have deliberately led the Spanish through the most unpleasant routes.[18] Fr. Durán has an otherwise unsubstantiated story of Cortés being deliberately led at the beginning of his journey to the edge of a precipice.[19] Though there is no way of knowing whether that was true, it was certainly a strange decision to travel from Cempoallan by way of Jalapa and Tlaxcala: the salt lakes in what is now the east of the province of Puebla then constituted a much more formidable obstacle than they do today. Montezuma's messengers usually went by way of Cuetlaxtlan and what is now Orizaba.

Since Cortés travelled, on his own insistence, as an ambassador of the King of Spain, he could expect to be received in peace by the cities on the way, so long as he remained on the accepted roads. Even when he did so, the expedition would have found itself on tracks wide enough to permit only a single file. Mexican armies on a march would be provided with tortillas and toasted maize flour. The Indian camp followers provided similarly for the Castilians. The Mexica calculated that two quarts of water were needed per soldier per day. The route of the Mexican army was usually chosen to ensure that availability. Again the bearers must have expected that Cortés would have similar requirements.[20]

The territory between the coast and the capital was mostly under the control of the Mexica. They had, of course, a representative at Cuetlaxtlan, and also one at Acatlan, a Totonac town about fifteen miles north-east of the present city of Jalapa, as at Xicochimalco, the chief Nahuatl-speaking town in the region, about fifteen miles to the south of Jalapa. But beyond these Mexican towns there stood the interesting city of Tlaxcala, Mexico's chief enemy.

There were two other places of importance on the route between Cempoallan and Tenochtitlan: these were Huexotzinco and Cholula, at the foot of Popocatepetl and Ixtaccihuatl, the two great volcanoes, on the seaward side. Huexotzinco was another enemy of the Mexica, tradition-ally allied with Tlaxcala, though now on bad terms with her. But those old enmities and friendships had, as earlier noticed, altered.[21] Huexotzinco and Cholula had longer histories than Tlaxcala. But both had an equivocal relation with Mexico.

The region was politically charged. Both Huexotzinco and Cholula had played a part in the Mexican rise to power, for their support of Tenochtitlan had helped to achieve the defeat of Azcapotzalco in 1428. Cortés, like most generals, needed a historical, as well as a geographical, guide. The Cempoallans were not equipped for that role. But one of their guides recommended that Cortés travel by way of Tlaxcala. There, he thought, Cortés would be bound to find friends among those mortal enemies of Montezuma.[22] A Totonac leader, a certain Teuch, a prudent man, told Cortés that he had been once to Tenochtitlan as a boy. He thought that the Castilians were sure to be killed if they set out to fight the Mexica. All the same, if they did go, he would go with them.[23]

Cortés had to pass through this territory in the summer. Rain fell every afternoon. The paths were usually muddy. Rest was impracticable.

Montezuma's reaction to this new evidence of determination on the part of Cortés to come to Tenochtitlan was to sink into another bout of anxiety. According to his code, he could not prepare for war against the Castilians, since that implied all kinds of rituals, embassies, warnings to submit, presents of clubs and shields to the enemy, formal organisation and enlistment of soldiers by *calpultin*, with special duties allocated to stewards and majordomos. War entailed the careful preparation of an army, the establishment of priests at the head of columns carrying idols, the ordering of conscripted soldiers in long prearranged ranks, above all the keeping to the timetable of the season of war; which did not begin for several months yet. But Cortés was presenting himself as an ambassador, it seemed, not an enemy. So despite his doubts and instincts, Montezuma simply consulted beautiful books, talked with advisers, sacrificed, perhaps ate sacred mushrooms, and waited.

Cortés' expedition to Tenochtitlan had reached Cempoallan (New Seville), and was preparing to move on to Jalapa. A messenger from Juan de Escalante on the coast then brought word that some Castilian ships had appeared off Vera Cruz. This turned out to be a flotilla of four vessels under the command of Alonso Álvarez de Pineda. He had come on behalf of Francisco de Garay, the restless Governor of Jamaica, who continued to think that he had a future role on the mainland. Escalante made contact with these newcomers by having a man gallop along the beach in a red cloak. He was observed. Several men then put ashore in a small boat. Three were apprehended by Escalante's men. One of them, Guillén de la Loa, was a notary. He unwisely said that he had come from Álvarez de Pineda to present Cortés with certain documents which required Cortés to share Mexico with Garay.[24] Garay, still a very rich man, thanks to his gold in Santo Domingo, had his eye on the large territory to the north of Vera Cruz which had begun to be called Pánuco, after Grijalva had discovered a river there. Álvarez de Pineda had sailed down from Florida, observed the mouth of the Mississippi, and knew the size of Garay's claim. What these documents of which the notary spoke were it is hard to say.

Cortés returned post-haste to the coast with a hundred men, leaving the rest of his army at Cempoallan under the command of Pedro de Alvarado and Gonzalo de Sandoval (to the irritation of Alonso de Ávila, who looked on himself as the senior commander after the *Caudillo*).[25] Cortés benignly suggested that these intruders return to the ship and invite their commander to visit Villa Rica. La Loa said that he could not possibly do such a thing.[26] Cortés thereupon had them all arrested. They were soon persuaded to join his army. Among them were Andrés Núñez, a carpenter, and Maese Pedro, a harpist.

Several others of Garay's expedition landed soon afterwards. They too were tricked into surrender. Álvarez de Pineda sailed off. He had known Cortés in Santo Domingo. So he knew from experience that, once in authority, the captain from Medellín was not likely to be easy to outmanoeuvre.

Cortés then returned to his army, probably taking one or two of Garay's men with him, and leaving the rest with Escalante. The expedition set off again on 16 August. The next day it apparently reached a point close to what is now Jalapa, then probably closer to the sea than is the modern town.[27] The authorities there had been warned by Montezuma to look after the visitors. Perhaps the Spaniards stayed a day or two before moving to the south, as part of a detour in order to avoid the steepest point of the Cofre de Perote. Their road lay through Coatepec (some way from the present town of the name) and then through the Mexican fortress town of Xicochimalco, which was built in a good defensive position some miles higher up from the pretty modern village of Xico.[28] There also they were well received, though entrance was only possible on foot.[29] They then proceded to Ixguacan[30] and climbed along the edge of the Cofre de Perote over a pass to which they gave the name of Nombre de Díos. The path is easily traceable in the late twentieth century but is not much travelled. It was, and is, a lonely, cold journey, the mist comes down long before the top is reached, and the traveller imagines that he is leaving the tropics for Scandinavia. Several of Cortés' Cuban Indian servants died of the cold.[31] Cortés sent Alvarado ahead as an advance guard with a hundred and fifty men.[32]

The path eventually flattened out and, at first sight, the new landscape must have seemed a welcome relief after the bleak mountain paths. At least here would have been some rows of maguey cacti, those essential all-providers of old indigenous society, capable of surviving in any climate and on all soils, giving thorns as needles and nails, juice for fermentation as *pulque*, and fibre for cord. Here Alvarado rejoined Cortés. But the crossing of the plain ahead was worse than the climb. The area was dominated by the salt lake. There was no fresh water. The land was tributary to Mexico. But no crops seem to have been produced.

Cortés sought to avoid this barren zone by travelling round it to the north. Whether he considered, and rejected, going to the south is unclear. It might have been shorter, but there would have been other obstacles. None of the accounts, not even any of the many denunciations of Cortés, discuss this, nor the reason for it.

The route to the north, to begin with, was also austere. The accounts describe three days without water or food.[33] Then the expedition turned west through Altotonga, Xalacingo, Teziutlan and Tlatlauquitepec. These towns are identifiable today (though they are on slightly different sites). Unlike the route from Jalapa to the lake, they lay along good roads. These settlements were each said to have over three hundred inhabitants. At Xalacingo, the Castilians were presented with a golden necklace, some cloth and two girls.

After Tlatlauquitepec, the expedition turned south and, having travelled along a ridge, found themselves in mountainous country. There was another high pass, the Pass of La Leña, the Firewood Pass, and then a long march through a narrow, but beautiful, valley to the town of Zautla. It is impossible to know the reason for this further deviation, for such it seems: was it a desire to face the chief in Zautla? Or the other towns lower down the valley towards Tlaxcala? Was it a deliberate diversion by the guides? Or perhaps the way along the ridge which now appears the most sensible route (past the modern towns of Xonocatlan, Cuyuaco, and Ocotepec) then seemed inappropriate, because it lay too close to the west shore of the salt lake. The last explanation is probable.

The last stage of the journey to Zautla today may not, however, be very different from what it was in 1519. There is a path but it is no more than that, until it joins the river Apulco in the valley. The winding way through the forest of pine trees seems interminable. Cortés arrived there, however, about 24 August, not much over a week after leaving Cempoallan, though it must have seemed the longest week in the lives of those concerned.[34]

The chief of Zautla, Olintecle, was the first person of substance whom the Castilians had met since they had left Cempoallan. This potentate, a tributary of the Mexicans, received the conquistadors warmly. Presumably on Montezuma's instructions, he gave them both lodgings and a modest amount of food.[35] The pleasure of sleeping under a roof again for the first time since leaving Villa Rica was modified for the Castilians when they saw, in a square of the town, one of those remarkable racks of human skulls which were normal in front of Mexican temples. Thigh bones and other choice parts of human bodies were also shown.[36] Having observed this chilling sight, Cortés asked Olintecle if he were a vassal of Montezuma. That chief seemed surprised: was there anyone who was not a vassal or a slave of Montezuma? Was not Montezuma the ruler of the world?[37] No doubt Olintecle had been to Tenochtitlan as a secret guest and had watched, hidden by a famous rose-coloured screen, the great sacrifices at fiestas. Cortés repeated his now familiar sermon about the superiority of the Christian religion and spoke of the interests of the King of Spain. He asked Olintecle to desist from human sacrifice, and from allowing his subjects to eat human flesh. He said that Montezuma would shortly become a vassal of Charles V, as would all the people of that land. He did not suggest how that remarkable achievement would be secured; but he did suggest that Olintecle should himself instantly become a vassal, an arrangement which, he insisted, would be much to his benefit. If he did not, he might be punished. Cortés begged Olintecle to give him gold as a sign that he had been received into the service of King Charles and Queen Juana.

Olintecle said it was true that he had some gold, but he would give none of it to Cortés until Montezuma so ordained. Probably on the advice of Fr. Olmedo, Cortés decided against a challenge. He merely said that he would soon be asking Montezuma to order him to hand over his gold. Nor did Cortés set up a cross and a picture of the Virgin Mary: Fr. Olmedo thought such an action premature.[38]

Olintecle's intransigence was probably due to the existence of a Mexican garrison in Zautla.[39] That chief told Cortés that Montezuma had thirty major vassals, each of whom commanded 100,000 men; that he sacrificed 20,000 men a year; and that he lived in a place which was both the best defended and the most beautiful in the world.

While staying at Zautla, a mastiff belonging to Francisco de Lugo barked most of the night.[40] The people of Zautla asked some of the Cempoallans accompanying the Castilians whether it was a lion or a tiger, or just an animal to kill Indians. The Cempoallans explained that the Castilians took dogs with them in order to kill anyone who annoyed them. The people of Zautla also asked about the horses and the guns. On being told that the horses could catch anyone whom they ran after, and that the guns could kill at a distance anyone the Castilians wished, Olintecle apparently remarked warily, "Well, they must be gods then." The native allies, the Totonacs, did nothing to impair this interpretation. Olintecle did in the end give Cortés some golden presents of rather low quality: three necklaces, four pendants, and some lizards cast in gold, as well as some cloth and maize. He added four Indian women to make bread.[41] Some chiefs from nearby towns also visited Cortés out of curiosity. They too gave him girls and necklaces. Olintecle himself was not short of the first of these: he had thirty wives and a hundred maids.[42]

From Zautla, Cortés sent four Cempoallan chiefs to Tlaxcala with an instruction to warn that city of his impending arrival. They took letters of greeting and tokens of peace: a red hat of taffeta, "such as was then fashionable", a sword, and a crossbow. The messengers were to say that Cortés was coming in the name of the King of Castile in order to assist Tlaxcala in her admirable struggle against the tyranny of the butcher Montezuma. Cortés added a short sermon about the supremacy of the Christian God, but that was probably in a letter which the Tlaxcalans would not have been able to read.[43]

Cortés spent several days in Zautla in these uneasy circumstances. Apparently there was a festival at which Olintecle sacrificed fifty men with abundant bloodshed. Cortés did not speak of witnessing this spectacle. The townspeople also carried Cortés and his friends round on their shoulders or in hammocks.[44] Before starting off again the *Caudillo* sought advice from Olintecle about the route to Mexico. That chief suggested going by way of Cholula. Mamexi, the chief of the Cempoallans who were accompanying Cortés, insisted that that would be fatal. He continued to urge that it would be best to go by way of Tlaxcala. For it was in that city that the Castilians could expect to meet friends.[45] The two towns, however, were not alternatives. Cholula was further than Tlaxcala. From where they then were, there was no real possibility of avoiding Tlaxcala.

The Castilians certainly had no alternative, so far as their immediate journey was concerned, other than to move on down the valley of the river Apulco to Iztaquimaxtitlan, a locally important mountain town, with a Mexican garrison and several thousand families. Cortés commented extravagantly that the chief's fortress was "better than any one might find in Spain".[46] Once again, on Montezuma's insistence, Cortés and his expedition stayed at the expense of the chief. He was one of those who had visited the conquistadors at Zautla and given them girls and necklaces.

This hospitality to the Castilians must have been ruinous for the local lords and their townsmen. No doubt the reserves of maize kept against famine and drought had to be used. The experience would have made the famous sojourns of Queen Elizabeth at great houses in England seem modest.

Cortés waited at Iztaquimaxtitlan for the return of the messengers whom he had sent to Tlaxcala. There was no sign of them.[47] He therefore set off down the valley, accompanied by over a thousand local soldiers.[48] A few miles south they found themselves facing a stone wall nine feet high and twenty paces wide, running several miles across the valley from one mountain top to another. There was a gate but, like certain Renaissance fortresses in Europe, there was a right turn within it. A battlement about a foot and a half high lay on the top of the wall. This was the provincial border which the people of Iztaquimaxtitlan had built against Tlaxcala. Walls of any sort were rare in old Mexico. The barrier must indicate the fierceness of the feeling between Tlaxcala and Mexico. The spot where Cortés encountered it was probably at a place called Atotonilco. The Castilians thought this fortification pointless.[49] Perhaps it did have more a symbolical than a tactical use. Still, symbols were important in European wars too.

As they passed through this obstacle, Cortés again referred to his favourite slogan of Constantine: "Gentlemen: let us follow the banner, the sign of the Holy Cross, and by this we shall conquer."[50]

They travelled on. Cortés and a few horsemen were in front. They had gone beyond the site of what is now the town of Terrenate, and were probably on the slopes of the mountain Matlalcueyatl, when two of the horsemen in front met a small squadron of about fifteen Tlaxcalan scouts. These began to flee when they saw the horses. Cortés, catching up with them, tried to reason with them and say, by signs, that he was interested in negotiation. But the Indians would not stop till the horsemen overtook them. From there they called out to the main Tlaxcalan army, which was lower down the valley. Using their obsidian-bladed swords, the Indians killed two horses, one belonging to Olid, and wounded three others.[51]

At this, a much larger body of Tlaxcalans came up: more than 100,000 said Andrés de Tapia, with whom, as with most of his companions, accurate figures were not a strong suit.[52] Whatever the number, most had their faces painted to give them a terrible grimace. That vision, the sheer numbers of the enemy, and the sight of their wild leaps in the air, as well as the sound of their war cries, caused some of the Castilians to fear greatly. Several insisted on confessing to Fr. Olmedo or to Fr. Díaz.[53] But the rest of the horsemen had by then come up. These captains, among them Alvarado and Ávila, Sandoval and Lugo, dealt with the Indians severely, killing a number – anything between sixteen and sixty men – and causing the rest to fall back.[54]

Cortés had the dead horses carefully buried to prevent his enemies discovering anything about their anatomies. Even so, he realised that the Tlaxcalans now knew that horses at least were mortal.[55]

This victory of a handful of horsemen against a large number of Indians was not simply the achievement of the horses and their riders. It was, as usual, a consequence of Indian tactics. They had a tradition of head-on combat. Only the front rank could fight. When that front rank was cut down, the next followed, then the third. Provided that their opponents had the stamina to maintain themselves, there was no reason why a handful should not be able to dispatch hundreds, or even thousands. Artillery was also effective in this respect. Killing from a distance seemed dishonourable to the indigenous peoples. Such niceties were lost on the Castilians, for whom it did not matter how an enemy was killed, provided that he died.[56]

The Tlaxcalans, in common with the Mayas at Potonchan, and indeed in common with the Indians of the whole region, were of course less interested in killing their enemies than in capturing them for sacrifice: to find yet one more "star" to be sacrificed to the sun to nourish that fire with blood. This was a fatal limitation. Then their swords of obsidian blades, though initially damaging, quickly broke against the steel, the swords as well as the armour, of the Europeans. Those steel swords of the Castilians were immensely effective, whether wielded by foot soldiers or by the few horsemen. Finally, the indigenous peoples had no idea of military discipline. The conquistadors were far from being Prussians. But they knew how to obey orders.

This was, of course, the first real battle which Cortés had fought since Potonchan. Though it was a victory, the loss of the two horses was a blow. More serious still was the realisation that it was necessary to fight at all. The Totonacs had given Cortés the impression that the Tlaxcalans would make admirable allies for the Castilians. Now, however exaggerated the conquistadors' estimates of numbers, Cortés and his captains understood for the first time that the Indians could assemble a great array against them.[57] The captains' apprehension was heightened by the return, shortly afterwards, of two of the four Cempoallan ambassadors whom Cortés had sent to Tlaxcala. These emissaries explained that the men who had fought with the Castilians came from some of the autonomous Otomí communities in the east of the state and were not from Tlaxcala proper. The Tlaxcalans would like to pay for the dead horses, they said.

The Castilians dressed their wounds with fat obtained from a dead Indian: they had no oil. They then continued on their way. That night, probably 31 August, the expedition slept in the open, by a stream, near a place known later as La Noria. Still short of food, they dined off baby dogs from the nearby town.[58] They were about twenty miles from Tlaxcala.

After Tenochtitlan, Tlaxcala was the most interesting place in old

Mexico. It was geographically tiny, probably even smaller than the modern small state of Tlaxcala. It was densely populated. The population derived from three origins; the Pinomes, the earliest known inhabitants of the region, who were looked on as barbarous and ignorant; the Otomí, also despised as barbarians, whose language was considered savage, but who were prized as fighters; and the Tlaxcalans proper, of Chichimec origin, who spoke Nahuatl, and who had come down from the northern mountains at much the same time as the Mexica had arrived in the Valley of Mexico. Indeed they too were supposed to have been led to found their capital where they did because of being shown the spot by a bird: in the Tlaxcalans' case, a white heron. The last-named group were those who had created, and who maintained, the political structure of the place. The total population of Tlaxcala in 1519 was perhaps about 150,000.[59]

The traditional attitude in Mexico towards the Otomí is summed up in a passage in the Florentine Codex. The Mexica were supposed to address the Otomí as idiots: "Now art thou an Otomí . . . O Otomí how is it that thou understandeth not? Art thou perchance an Otomí? . . . A real Otomí, a miserable Otomí, a greenhead, a thickhead, . . . an Otomí blockhead, an Otomí."[60] The Florentine Codex, reflecting a Mexican view, insisted that the Otomí spent too much time thinking. Actually these comments were inappropriate. For the Otomí were brave, resilient and produced some good, if simple verse. Thus:

> The River goes, goes;
> Never stops.
> The wind blows, blows;
> Life passes;
> Never returns.[61]

Or:

> In the sky a moon
> In your face a mouth;
> In the sky, many stars,
> In your face only two eyes.[62]

Otomí women were said to paint their breasts blue, to be gaudy dressers, and to have been the originators of a practice much taken up among the Mexica, the flaying of an enemy's skin, and then the wearing of it ceremonially: "At Texcalopan, a noble Otomí woman was preparing maguey fibres at the river bank. She flayed a Toltec named Xiuhcozcatl. Then she wore his skin. For the first time there began the wearing of the Toltec skin . . ."[63]

Tlaxcala was in fact less a state than a grouping of small cities linked in a military federation hostile to the Mexica. There were about two hundred settlements which might just be called towns. Tlaxcala itself, a little to the north of the modern city of that name, was divided into four districts. Maxixcatzin, lord of one of these regions, Ocotelolco, was the military leader of the whole federation. He and Xicotencatl, the lord of Tizatlan, another of the four districts, were the joint political leaders of the whole region.[64] Both were in 1519 of a great age. Some chroniclers even argue that it was Maxixcatzin who had proposed to the *cihuacoatl* Tlacaelel the idea of a "flowery war" back in the 1440s.[65] If that is improbable, he was certainly alive at the time when those conflicts intensified. They and the leaders of the other two districts – Temilotecatl, lord of Tepeticpac, and Citlalpopocatzin, lord of Quiahuiztlan, were chiefs of separate dynasties in which succession, unlike with the Mexican emperors, went from father to son.[66] The line of ancestry in all four districts went back about seven generations. Thus Tlaxcala had had its present shape since the fourteenth century.

To begin with, Tlaxcala had been an important commercial city. Its traders were to be seen on the Pacific as on the Gulf of Mexico. Like the Mexica, the Tlaxcalans aspired to greatness. Their god Camaxtli had told them that they were destined to rule the world.[67] But in the early fifteenth century their commerce had brought them into enmity with the Mexica, who had effectively restricted their activities. They had become poor. They had no cotton of their own and hence no clothes of that commodity. Nor had they salt: something which they must have resented even more, because of the proximity of the salt lakes of Alchichica, in the control of the Mexica. There were no precious stones in Tlaxcala, no beautiful feathers, and no gold. The consequence of that strange convention, "the wars of flowers", was that, between about 1450 and 1510, Tlaxcala avoided absorption into the Mexican empire. But its economic isolation seems to have been increased. The Tlaxcalans had a reputation for untrustworthiness. Thus they had encouraged the people of Cuetlaxtlan to resist the Mexica. But they had stood aside when the Mexica attacked the Cuextla. They were not loved. Sometimes they were admired.[68]

The Tlaxcalans maintained a high morale. The Mexican empire surrounded them; but they persuaded themselves that they were free. They cultivated their land in a way which recalled Europe: most of it was worked by labourers who paid a rent in kind to lords who, in turn, retained the basic natural rights, such as water and the use of the forests. Several times the Tlaxcalans had withstood Mexican armies, which had been always far larger than those they themselves could field. Not only were they free, but they had developed a habit of consultation between the towns of their territory, which caused Cortés, extravagantly, to compare them to the free republics of Genoa or Venice (which he did not know from experience).[69] Peter Martyr even more fancifully compared Tlaxcala with "the Roman Republic before it degenerated into a despotic monarchy".[70] The reaction of Pope Leo X, to whom this comparison was addressed in a letter, is not recorded. Venice and Genoa were predatory. But they scarcely competed with Tlaxcala in respect of human sacrifice. At the latter's annual feast in March, eight hundred prisoners were said to be regularly sacrificed to the god Camaxtli at the temple of Matlaluege twelve miles outside the city. Afterwards the limbs were eaten with chilli.[71]

There was also a doubt about the real independence of Tlaxcala. Montezuma told Andrés de Tapia in Tenochtitlan that he could have conquered Tlaxcala whenever he wanted. But he preferred to keep it apparently free, as a quail in a cage, so that his people would not forget the practice of war and so that they would have enough people available to sacrifice. This was denied bitterly by the Tlaxcalans. They were probably right. The relation might at one time have been as Montezuma said it was, but the wars of the last years before the conquistadors came seem to have been real enough. By 1519 the Mexicans would have liked to have conquered Tlaxcala if they could have done so. Their failure to do so, indeed, was one reason for their undoing. Probably the explanation given by Montezuma to Tapia was merely the excuse which the Mexica gave themselves for their failures.[72]

Tlaxcala was not the only territory within the reach of Tenochtitlan which had maintained its independence of the Mexica. There was the little republic of the Yopi on the Pacific coast in what is now the state of Guerrero. There was Metztitlan in the sierras of the north-east; and there were the Chinantla, a hill people in the sierra between the Valley of Mexico and Oaxaca. But the Tlaxcalans were far the most important of these peoples, and the only one capable of giving the Mexica real trouble.

17

To leave none of us alive

"And we knew for certain that they came determined to leave none of us alive."
Bernal Díaz on the battle against Tlaxcala

WHEN THE CEMPOALLAN emissaries of Cortés arrived at Tlaxcala in late August 1519, they were taken to something like a general council of the leaders, so that they could deliver their message. They did so. They were given food and held under guard. The Tlaxcalan chiefs then discussed the Castilian question.

Maxixcatzin spoke in favour of accepting the offer of peace put forward by the strangers. Like many Tlaxcalans, he apparently believed that these newcomers might be gods, and peace seemed a fitting response.[1] The mercantile interests in the community supported him. But this view was opposed by the military commanders, headed by Xicotencatl the younger. His father Xicotencatl the elder was joint political leader with Maxixcatzin. But he was old and blind, and seems, at this time, to have allowed his son to speak in his stead. Then Temilotecatl, the lord of the third district, proposed a strategy which would have allowed the Tlaxcalans to give a welcome to the Castilians, in a guarded fashion, but to delay any formal arrangement. Xicotencatl the younger would meantime prepare a large army, mainly of Otomís, which would surprise the intruders when they were unprepared. If Tlaxcala won, there would be the usual banquets with a sacrifice of prisoners. If they lost, the authorities could blame their Otomí subjects. This devious scheme was enthusiastically supported by the meeting as a whole.

The first engagement with the horsemen was thus in no way an accident. The attackers were Otomí from Tecoac. It had been carefully planned so as to enable Tlaxcala to find out as much as possible about the nature of the Spaniards.

At another meeting, after the first battle, the leaders decided, as has been seen, to offer to pay for the dead horses. That was not out of regret, but a device to discover how the Castilians valued their horses.

Cortés, therefore, was facing wily antagonists. According to the Codex Ramírez, the Castilians had relied until this point on a guide, a Mexican, who expected that they would be destroyed by the Otomí.[2]

After Cortés and his men had rested overnight by the stream near Terrenate, they set off at sunrise. There seems to have been some discussion about tactics, in which the rank and file participated: thus it was thought best that, if attacked, the horsemen would ride forward fast, seeking to scatter the enemy, holding their lances upright rather than horizontal, in order to prevent their owners from being seized.

The Castilian expedition soon found themselves at a village where they met the second two Cempoallans whom Cortés had earlier sent to Tlaxcala as messengers. They were in tears. They said they had been tied up ready to be sacrificed and eaten. But they had escaped.[3]

Not far from there another army of Indians had appeared. Once again they were Otomí. Cortés approached them peacefully. Cortés then began himself to read out a *Requerimiento*.[4] On this occasion he did this helped by Marina and Aguilar, as well as in the presence of his notary, Diego de Godoy. But it was notably ineffective. The explanation as to who the Pope was, the relation between him and the King of Spain, and the offer of vassalship was not received with the slightest attention. The Otomí attacked with arrows and spears flung by *atlatls* (spear-launchers). The Castilians advanced and battle ensued: "*¡Santiago y cierra España!*", the old battle cry in engagements against the Moors, rang out against the unfamiliar hillsides.[5] After several hours' furious battle, the Spaniards and their allies forced the Otomí back, and advanced. But this was a trap, since they found themselves in an ambush. Xicotencatl had arranged for a far larger number of Otomí to remain on both sides of the ravine into which they had entered. Cortés estimated that these new enemies numbered the magic figure of 100,000.[6] His biographer, to whom he often later talked, wrote of "an infinite number of Indians"; while Díaz del Castillo (as usual more modestly) spoke of 40,000.[7] All these comments must be exaggerated.[8]

The ancient Mexicans, and here again the Otomí and Tlaxcalans resembled the lords of the valley, were fascinated by the idea of an ambush. But not as a method to strike from a position in hiding. That would have been dishonourable. The aim was to be able to confront the enemy more dramatically.[9]

The Otomí in this battle made great efforts to capture one of the Spanish horses. In this they were in the end successful, seizing a mare (owned by Juan Núñez Sedeño) being ridden by Pedro de Morón who was himself badly wounded. Morón, one of the Velázquistas anxious to return home from Vera Cruz, died several days later. The loss of a mare was of course a serious blow to Cortés, and he was the more distressed when later he heard that it had been sacrificed by the Tlaxcalans, along with the red taffeta hat: probably the priests in Tlaxcala saw the latter as something like the tuft of feathers, kept together by a red leather band, the *tecpillotl*, which the Mexica usually gave to a lord with whom they had decided to fight.[10]

The Castilians finally fought their way along the ravine, Diego de Ordaz on his horse being the first through, as he emphasised at an enquiry which he organised in his own interest two years later.[11] Much assistance was given on this occasion by the Totonac allies. The six guns, the forty crossbowmen and the five or six arquebusiers made a profound impression on the Otomí. The death of several Otomí leaders at the beginning of the battle also had a considerable effect. For the Indians looked on the death of a commander, with the consequent disappearance of the standard attached to his back, as equivalent to a defeat and sometimes abandoned the battlefield when that occurred.[12]

Cortés and the Spanish expedition spent that night on a hilltop called Tzompachtepetl. There was a small temple there with idols – soon to be christened Victory.[13] Here the expedition was to spend two embattled weeks, short of both supplies and morale, drinking rain water, eating beans, and sporadically fighting.[14]

Next day the Otomí did not sally out. Cortés sent another message of peace. Then, leaving Ordaz in command in the camp, he rode out himself with about half his force, two hundred Spanish foot soldiers and several hundred Indians, pillaging and burning, and taking numerous prisoners.[15] Both Juan Álvarez and Francisco Aguilar later, and separately, said that, in this expedition, the Castilians perpetrated many unnecessary cruelties, such as cutting off noses, ears, arms, feet and testicles, as well as throwing priests down from the tops of the temples.[16] Bernal Díaz, however, insisted that the outrages were committed "by our allies, who are a cruel people".[17] Probably both were responsible. So far as Cortés was concerned, the evidence seems to suggest that this activity was embarked upon coldly, in order to cause fear. Shaken by the resistance of a people whom he had expected to be helpful if not friendly, and angered by the difficulty of obtaining food, he took his revenge on civilians. It was Cortés' first such proscription. It was presumably reported to the Tlaxcalans in tones of incredulity. Even the Mexica never practised such things. Cortés probably had the memory of the effectiveness of similar tactics in Hispaniola and Cuba in mind.

When Cortés returned at night, he received the reply of the Tlaxcalan captains, which was simply that their full answer would come the next day. Cortés and his men spent the night apprehensively: most slept fully dressed and armed, ready for a night attack which did not, however, occur. Many made their confessions and prayed with the priests to avoid defeat. In the morning they were surprised to be sent a substantial amount of food by the Tlaxcalans: three hundred turkeys, and two hundred baskets of maize cakes. These gifts were not, however, intended as charitable offerings. The idea of the Tlaxcalans was: "Once they are filled up with food, let us attack and then we shall eat them and, in that way, they will pay us for the turkeys and cakes. We shall then learn why it is that they came here. If Montezuma is responsible for sending them, let him set them free. If they have come out of their own foolhardiness, let them pay . . ."[18] Cortés thought that the bringers of this food were spies, interested in having a good look at his camp.[19]

The Tlaxcalans assembled their army on the plain in front of the Castilians' position on its hill. Their numbers seemed "large enough to eclipse the sun", one conquistador, Fr. Aguilar, put it.[20] Of course, those who wrote of the affair afterwards, including Cortés, exaggerated.[21] But the Tlaxcalans certainly put out the best army that they could muster: these were not merely Otomí. They assembled in feathers and war paint, in wooden, leather and cotton armour, their weapons as usual obsidian-bladed swords, bows and arrows, lances and slings. Their troops were arranged in squadrons. Each was attended by drummers – using the long *teponaztli*, a cylinder of wood laid sideways and struck by rubber-tipped mallets – as well conch blowers.[22] It was a fine array. A battle then took place. Cortés himself, apart from saying that he was attacked by 149,000 men (an interestingly precise figure), was later reticent about the occasion, devoting only a few lines to the biggest battle that he had undertaken and probably the most difficult one that the Castilians had yet fought in the Indies.[23] Other writers were more informative. Perhaps Bernal Díaz best explains the reason for his commander's silence in "this dangerous and perilous battle". For the Castilians passed several difficult moments. Presumably Cortés did not like the idea of remembering such a thing. "We were in considerable confusion," Bernal Díaz went on. Cortés' orders could not be heard. The hail of stones from the Indian slings, the sharp javelins, and the obsidian-bladed swords seemed for a time seriously threatening. "Only the simple use of steel swords" saved the Castilians, Bernal Díaz recalled.[24]

There were, though, several other reasons for the Spanish victory. In addition to the same things which a week or so before had turned the day (swordplay, horses, the Indians' interests in prisoners not corpses, and the use of "fiery lightning" from the guns), the crowding of the Tlaxcalans made them prone to panic. Cannon balls, even if inaccurately aimed, caused havoc when they fell into the middle of a crowd. There were also divisions among the Tlaxcalans: the two main military leaders, Xicotencatl the younger and his deputy, Chichimecatecle, were jealous of one another. Then the Castilians had received detailed and unequivocal instructions: not only were horsemen to hold their lances short, and make for the enemies' eyes, but swordsmen were to aim at the bowels of the enemy, while musketeers and crossbowmen were to use their supplies slowly.

Even so, when the Tlaxcalans did in the end retire from the battlefield, it was obviously to the great relief of the conquistadors, "whose arms were weary from killing Indians".[25] Though as usual they had lost few killed (probably only one or two outright), about sixty men and all the horses were wounded.[26] That night the Castilians again slept by the little tower on the top of the hill of Tzompachtepetl. Once more, they looked after the wounded by using the fat of dead Indians.

The following day, Cortés embarked on another punitive expedition, this time burning ten towns, one of them with a population of over three thousand, and killing many Indians.[27] Once more his motive seems simply to have been to shock the people by fear into surrender. He then returned to his camp on the hilltop – just in time, apparently, since the Tlaxcalans were mounting another attack. This second day's battle seems to have been much like the first, with the same inconclusive results.

About this time, Cortés received the visit of more emissaries from Montezuma in the shape of five or six chiefs, accompanied as usual by a large number of servants. The Emperor, they reported, rejoiced at the great victory of the Castilians over the Tlaxcalans. He was also delighted that the Castilians were now so close to his city. He sent presents of a thousand castellanos' worth of gold, some cotton clothes and several good featherwork pieces. Montezuma also passed on the message that he would be delighted to become a vassal of the Spanish king. Cortés was to say how much tribute he thought appropriate. Montezuma promised to pay that every year in, for example, cloth, gold, silver, or jade. But there was one stumbling block. Montezuma begged Cortés not to come to Mexico. It was not that the Emperor would not have been delighted to see these visitors. But the road was bad, it lay through rough land, and, furthermore, his city was lacking in provisions. He would not like the Castilians to suffer.[28]

These emissaries also told Cortés not to trust the Tlaxcalans under any circumstances, since they were traitors, and would surely kill them. Cortés replied that he was determined to go to Tlaxcala. He was privately delighted to find that the Mexica were on such bad terms with the Tlaxcalans. "Every kingdom divided against itself will be brought to desolation" ("*Omne regnum in se ipsum divisum desolabitur*"), he remarked in Latin, quoting, approximately, from St Mark.[29]

The Tlaxcalans held another general meeting after these setbacks. There was again a dispute. Xicotencatl the younger accused his colleague Chichimecatecle of unskilled generalship. The latter replied with a refusal to go on fighting, and with a threat to Xicotencatl. The priests were summoned. They insisted that events were showing that the Castilians were men, not gods: after all, they ate turkeys, dogs, bread and fruit. Their guns did not produce lightning, nor was Francisco de Lugo's dog a dragon. The Cempoallan ambassadors, meantime, who, like all the

Totonacs, insisted still that the conquistadors were gods, had apparently indiscreetly told the Tlaxcalans that the visitors' powers waned after dark. In consequence, Xicotencatl the younger prepared a night attack. He first sent fifty of his friends to study the Castilians' camp. As a pretext, they explained that they were thinking of negotiating peace. They brought with them four miserable old women, whom, they suggested, the Castilians might be interested in having to sacrifice and eat. Cortés said that he had come to see them especially to entreat them on behalf of Christ and of the King of Spain not to carry out human sacrifices any more. He also said that he and his friends were men of flesh and blood, not gods, and should be taken seriously as such.[30]

These emissaries were not much good at espionage. The Cempoallan Teuch realised that they were spies. Cortés also noticed their "spying manner and want of frankness".[31] He had one of them taken aside and questioned. Under this interrogation the man confessed that Xicotencatl was planning to attack the camp that night. The plan was, he said, to set fire to the Spanish huts and then attack. Five others of these inadequate spies agreed with the first man interrogated. Cortés then seized all the messengers, and cut off the right hands of some of them, the thumbs of others and, according to one conquistador, the ears and noses of others, which sad trophies were then tied round their necks.[32] He then sent them back to Tlaxcala with the message: "Tell your chiefs that it is unworthy of brave soldiers and upright citizens to stoop to such odious stratagems . . . we are ready to receive you in battle at any hour . . . by night or by day".[33] Such conduct as Cortés' was unusual among the conventions of war in old Mexico; but it was not unknown. For example, in an early battle against Xochimilco the Emperor Itzcoatl cut an ear off every captive.[34]

The Tlaxcalans did not seem excessively disturbed by the treatment of their agents but continued to prepare to attack that night. The Castilians were, as they promised, ready for them, and indeed attacked first, before night had properly fallen. Once again, the sight of the horses and the noise of the cannon had their effects. Cortés had bells placed on his horses and that sound seemed uncanny.[35] The Mexica described the Tlaxcalans as "completely overwhelmed. . . . [The Spaniards] speared them, they were pierced with spears. They turned their guns on them. They shot them with iron bolts. They shot them with crossbows . . . great numbers of them were destroyed."[36] The fighting was brief. The Tlaxcalans fled through the maize fields back to their city.[37]

After this engagement, Cortés remained in his camp without moving for several days. Like Fr. Olmedo and many of his men, he had fallen ill with a fever. He took several pills of camomile which he had brought with him from Cuba.[38] These had little effect. What did seem to cure him, at least temporarily, was an attack by three large companies of

Indians on the third day. He mounted, went out and again fought all day. The next day he seemed to be better.[39]

It seems to have been the night after this that Cortés went out again into the country, with a hundred foot soldiers and all the horsemen, as well as some Indian allies. They had not gone far before a mysterious event occurred: Cortés' horse fell; then five other horses; and all refused to go further. Cortés sent them back to the camp where they soon recovered. The *Caudillo* was urged to return by some of his followers, for it was, so they said, an evil omen. Cortés, with unquenchable but on this occasion absurd optimism, insisted that the refusal of the horses was, on the contrary, a good sign. He and his colleagues continued on foot, somewhat losing their bearings.[40] Before dawn, Cortés attacked two towns, where many again were killed. At dawn he fell on a bigger town, apparently Tzompantzinco.[41] Many Otomí warriors were sleeping there. Through his interpreters, Cortés managed to persuade the leaders of the community that he intended no harm. He asked them to provide him with much-needed food. The rumour of Cortés' variation of conduct spread through the nearby villages. It effected better propaganda for him than his other, brutal expeditions. But his reputation now was one of unpredictability. Gods, of course, behaved similarly.[42]

The Castilians then returned to the camp. There was relief, since Cortés had been away longer than had been expected. Many had assumed that he had been killed or captured: that he had, in short, been shown to have been a "Pedro Carbonero", to recall a Spanish warrior who in the previous century had gone unwisely far into Moorish territory, where he had been killed with all his men.[43]

But pleasure at the return of Cortés soon turned to a different mood. Though miraculously few conquistadors had died in action since leaving Cempoallan, many had died of wounds or had succumbed to disease: forty-five, according to Bernal Díaz; fifty-five since leaving Cuba, according to Alonso de Grado.[44] Cortés did not deny these figures. The men were cold, there seemed to be little food, and several were ill. People began to wonder what would be the outcome of all this fighting. If Tlaxcalans could fight so well, how would the Castilians fare against the surely much more formidable Mexica? No one knew what was going on at Vera Cruz. Cortés' plans were obscure. That overweening confidence which he himself had felt when fighting the first battle against the Mexica near the coast had evaporated. If he had mentioned again that his intention was to take Montezuma dead or alive, he would have been mocked. Once again, those who had left families, houses and Indians back in Cuba were naturally the most eloquent. The leader of these dissenters was the *alcalde mayor* of Vera Cruz, Alonso de Grado, one of the most senior of Cortés' companions. God, he accepted, had hitherto helped the expedition, but it was surely unwise to tempt Him too far. He suggested returning to Vera Cruz, and building a ship to be sent to Cuba to ask for help. He personally thought it a pity that the boats had all been destroyed. Neither Alexander the Great nor Caesar, he said, to mention heroes on the mind of all self-respecting hidalgos at that time, had ventured to throw such a small force as Cortés' army against such a large population as evidently existed in Mexico.[45] He spoke as the owner of a property and Indians in Hispaniola. "May God take me to Castile!" was the theme of his speech.

Cortés spoke successfully against this mood. He had, he said, confidence that war against Tlaxcala had already ended. He also defended the destruction of the ships. He thought that, if they returned to Vera Cruz without going to Mexico, their Totonac allies would turn against them: "So, gentlemen, if one way is bad, the other is worse." It was better to die in a good cause, he concluded, than to live in dishonour (the quotation, a favourite one of his, was from *The Song of Roland*).[46] This statement held off mutiny for the moment. But it was obvious that some such feeling could spread unless a victory were obtained over the Tlaxcalans very soon. The memory of Pedro Carbonero was again invoked to characterise the expedition. The Castilians knew that if they were defeated and captured, they would suffer even worse than he had.[47] (According to his chaplain, Cortés quoted four proverbs in this oration: "Where goes the ox who will not draw the plough?"; "You are seeking a cat with five feet"; "Wherever we go, we shall find three leagues of bad road"; and, his favourite, "The more the Moors, the greater the spoil".)

Fortunately Cortés did not have long to wait before he was temporarily satisfied.

For in Tlaxcala a prolonged discussion was under way as to whether or no the war should be continued. Two soothsayers were sacrificed in order to concentrate the minds of the leaders. Maxixcatzin and, now, Xicotencatl the elder argued fiercely for peace, though Xicotencatl the younger continued to plead for war. But the defeats had shocked everyone. The fact that most of those killed were Otomí greatly disturbed the Tlaxcalans. For the Otomí had the reputation of being resolute fighters: Yet the Spaniards treated them as nothing. "In no time – in but the flutter of an eyelid they destroyed them."[48] The achievement of peace was delayed several days.[49] But in the end, the two elder leaders won the argument.

Xicotencatl the younger then went to Cortés' camp asking forgiveness for his people having taken up arms against the Castilians.[50] He is said to have added: "Be not astonished that we have never desired an emperor, have never obeyed anybody, and dearly love liberty, for we and our ancestors have endured great evils, such as no salt and no cotton clothes, rather than accept the yoke of Montezuma and the Mexica . . . but we now promise to obey your commands, if you admit us to your alliance."

He said that Tlaxcala had no gold or silver; but they wished all the same to become friends. They were even ready to become vassals of the King of Castile. At the same time, food arrived in the Spanish camp. Feathers, incense and slaves accompanied it. The messengers bringing these things said: "If you are of those gods who eat flesh and blood, eat these slaves, and we shall bring you some more; if you are benevolent gods, see this incense and these plumes; if you are men, take these turkeys, cherries and berries."[51] The Castilians were also invited to stay in Tlaxcala, the invitation being accompanied by the usual courtesies: "You have tired yourselves, you have laboured, O lords. But you have come and reached your poor home." Tlaxcala in short was at the Castilians' disposal.

Cortés replied rather harshly that the people of Tlaxcala were themselves to blame for the difficulties which they had encountered. He had come to their land thinking that he was going to meet friends. The Cempoallans had assured him that that would be the case. He, Cortés, had sent messengers to them to tell the Tlaxcalans of his peaceful intentions. But they had attacked him and killed two horses. Many days' fighting had followed. But he happily pardoned them. He repeated that he was a man and not a god. He also said that it was important that the peace would be a lasting one. Xicotencatl said that, of course, he realised the need for that. He and his colleagues would even be ready to remain with the Castilians as hostages. Cortés then agreed, after some days, to go to Tlaxcala.[52]

The Mexican emissaries who had spent much of the battle with the Castilians asked Cortés to wait a little longer before he carried out the last part of this undertaking and set out for Tlaxcala: until, indeed, they had received a further message from Montezuma. Cortés agreed, first, because he was still suffering from fever; second, because he realised that there was a chance that what the Mexicans had said about the untrustworthiness of the Tlaxcalans might be true.[53]

Within six days the Mexican emissaries received a reply from their emperor. Montezuma again warned the Castilians against having anything to do with Tlaxcala.[54] The people of Tlaxcala were poor and did not possess a good cotton cloth. As friends of Montezuma, the Spaniards would be robbed. The Emperor accompanied this advice by some more presents: three thousand pesos' worth of gold, two hundred pieces of cloth.[55] Cortés had, however, by then determined to accept the invitation of the Tlaxcalans. The following day the leaders of that people came to visit him and, presenting him with golden jewels and stones, repeated the invitation to go and stay with them. Cortés dismounted from his horse, made a deep bow, embraced Xicotencatl the elder, and made an elaborate speech saying that he wished to guarantee their liberty. He not only accepted their invitation but accompanied them. The Tlaxcalans even carried the Spaniards' guns. Feasting and celebrations followed.[56]

During these days, Montezuma, though continuing to be concerned by the approach of the mysterious intruders, would have been affected primarily by the knowledge that the time was approaching the month known in Mexico as the "sweeping of the roads". The festival then was dedicated to Toci, "our grandmother". The reference to sweeping meant an allusion to the coming of winter rains, and those rains marked the beginning of the season of war. The symbolism and the pageantry were elaborate. There would be four days of dancing before the House of Song, the dancers would circle round the female slave who had been chosen to represent Teteo Innan, "the mother of the saved". She would be first teased, then adorned, then sacrificed. Her body would be ceremonially flayed, and her skin would then be worn by a priest who would chase the warriors before he himself inaugurated the season of war. The Emperor would also run with the warriors, and then would present insignia to the knights of the eagle and jaguar in their quetzal plumes. Probably Montezuma carried out these duties this year with a heavy heart. He must have feared that the war on which he might soon have to engage would be the reverse of flowery.[57]

Perhaps it was now that Montezuma commissioned some further works of art: for example, a depiction of the "binding of the years", with a skeleton-like head of the god of death. True, 1519 was very definitely not a year when there was supposed to be such a binding, a new fire ceremony. But perhaps, Montezuma may have supposed, the priests' calculations had been askew, and the calendar should be changed to fit the arrival of the mysterious visitors. Droughts had altered dates of ceremonies of new fire in the past. In this sculpture there was seen a spider falling from the sky. The spider was the symbol of the Tzitzime, monsters of destruction who were expected to come down when the world came to an end. Montezuma, a pious man, was ready for almost anything.[58]

18
This cruelty restored order

"Cesare Borgia was accounted cruel [but] this cruelty of his reformed the Romagna, brought it to unity, and restored order and obedience."
Machiavelli, *The Prince* (1513)

CORTÉS AND HIS expedition entered Tlaxcala on 18 September 1519.[1] They were warmly received by its leaders, dressed in red or white material made from henequen or maguey fibre: they had, it will be remembered, no cloth because of the Mexican blockade. Priests in white hoods also came out to greet the Castilians, with their usual baskets of live coals, in honour of the god-like visitors. These men made their customary disagreeable impression on the conquistadors: like all the other priests whom they had seen, their hair was long, tangled and clotted with blood. Their nails were also horribly long.[2]

The Castilians were lodged by the lords of Tlaxcala in some "very pretty houses and palaces" near the main temple.[3] Food was made available for the expedition, including for the Totonacs and other Indian allies. Even the dogs and horses were given their share of the turkey and maize.[4] The Castilians knew very well that the Totonacs' role in the previous battles, in fighting as well as in other assistance, had been fundamental. "Had it not been for them," one of Cortés' intimates, Francisco de Solís, baldly testified later about these battles, "we should not have won"[5] (the soldiers of Iztaquimaxtitlan had returned home once they saw that the visitors had made peace with the traditional enemy of the Mexica).

Cortés and his men passed twenty days in Tlaxcala. This stay was as important in the history of the conquest of Mexico as any pitched battle. For the expedition rested. The complaints of the previous days among the homesick Castilians disappeared once they realised that they had again overcome a large army, with no losses to speak of. The welcome of the Tlaxcalans seemed genuine. The city impressed them: Cortés himself said that he thought it was, as he later told the King, "much larger than Granada".[6] In fact it was probably not as big as that town, and its single-storey, flat-roofed buildings could scarcely have been of comparable beauty. But of course the mixture of originality and similarity was the most remarkable element. There were markets every day, where, Cortés added, with his usual exaggeration, "as many as 30,000 people would come to buy and sell".[7] Above all, Cortés thought, "they are such an orderly and intelligent people that the best in Africa cannot equal them."[8] So much for the will of Isabel the Catholic! The *Caudillo*'s comment will sound a little illogical from a commander who had killed so many so ruthlessly; but perhaps he could persuade himself that those who died had been principally Otomís.

Here for the first time the Castilians saw the way of living of the inhabitants of the temperate zone of Mexico. They would have noted with approval the clothes of the Tlaxcalans as they swiftly walked the clean streets: men with cloaks of maguey fibre tied in a familiar knot on the right shoulder, almost as if they were Romans, worn over loincloths (*maxtlatl*), the indispensable item of male wear of all classes, usually with flaps at both front and back. They would have seen the almost equally essential hip-cloth, a square of material divided along the diagonal line, worn round the waist, and tied at the side. They would soon have realised that most types of known clothing were used: a special version of kilt, as well as cloaks, open-sewn and close-sewn garments, even clothes enclosing the limbs, somewhat like trousers, such as the grand war costumes.[9] They would have appreciated too the women in their white skirts of maguey fibre, the basic female dress, with tunics (*huipilli*) worn over them as a rule, though poor women usually left their breasts bare, and though there would have been as few women in the streets of Tlaxcala as in Seville: their place was in the home. Perhaps they saw the women weaving in the patios inside blocks of houses. At night, they would have observed, even in the palace where they were living, Tlaxcalans lying under cloaks.

Cortés received information about the route to Tenochtitlan. His expedition was at this time well over halfway from the sea to that city. They had to cross the mountains before they reached there. The Florentine Codex gives an impression of the exchanges between the conquistadors and the Tlaxcalans. The former asked: "Where is Mexico? What manner of place is it? Is it still distant?" The Tlaxcalans would reply: "It is not far distant, it can be reached in three . . . days, it is a very good place, [the Mexica] are very powerful, they have very brave warriors who go conquering everywhere."[10]

But the most important element in Cortés' stay at Tlaxcala was that, during these days, the *Caudillo* established a lasting alliance. This association was based on what seems, surprisingly, to have turned into friendship between himself and the two aged leaders, Maxixcatzin ("ring of cotton") and Xicotencatl ("ring of the wasp") the elder. Xicotencatl the younger, with his coarse and spotty face, did not share his father's enthusiasm for the foreigners. He had been the commander of the army whom Cortés had beaten in the field. He did not believe in the benefit of any alliance with these outsiders. But for the moment those reservations ceased to matter. When the country was at peace, his father and Maxixcatzin dominated Tlaxcala.

Cortés managed, through force of personality, to inspire, in Maxixcatzin and Xicotencatl *père*, something like respect. Apart from Columbus' ephemeral relationship with Guacanagarí in Hispaniola, it was the first time since 1492 that any Castilian commander had even tried to establish an alliance with leaders of an Indian community, much less achieve one. This feat of Cortés' shows him to have been a consummate politician. Cortés confirmed his success partly by his insistence to his followers that they take nothing except what was given to them, and partly by his ban on their going to certain parts of the city, such as the temple. But he also seemed convincing to the Tlaxcalans when he said that he had come in order to help them.[11] They in return thought that they could use him for their own purposes.

"The courtesy and affection with which the leaders of the Tlaxcalans spoke" was also impressive.[12] They seemed to understand what they were saying when they agreed to be vassals of the King of Spain.[13] The truth is that they were so hostile to the Mexica that they would make almost any concession (which, of course, could be easily gone back upon) to find a reliable ally against them. Their leaders must also have become realistically aware of the Spaniards' strength in combat. According to both Bernal Díaz, and the Tlaxcalan historian Camargo, Xicotencatl the elder insisted that one of their gods had told them, through their priests, that men would come from distant lands in the direction of the rising sun to subjugate and govern them. If the Spaniards were indeed these people, they, the Tlaxcalans, rejoiced, for they could see that they were good and brave.[14] Perhaps the leaders of the Tlaxcalans refined or repeated (or even invented) this myth to give themselves confidence against the Mexica, or to enable them to secure the support of their own people (for example, those who had sided with Xicotencatl the younger) for their hospitality to the newcomers.

The Tlaxcalans wished to cement the alliance by an exchange of presents. But, again, because of the Mexican blockade (a useful excuse for all inadequacies) they had little to give except food and girls.[15] Camargo wrote of "three hundred beautiful and well-adorned slave girls" being presented.[16] To these were added one or two daughters of the leaders of Tlaxcala. These Cortés accepted, and shared them out among his men – the captains taking the noblewomen. The Tlaxcalans thought that their daughters would thereby help to breed a new race of warriors.[17] In return, Cortés sent to Cempoallan to bring back some of the things which he had left there: cloaks, cloth, salt, and so on. When they arrived, these things were very well received since, suffering a permanent Mexican blockade, the Tlaxcalans "lacked everything".[18]

Cortés then thought better of his acceptance of the girls. Probably he had talked again to Fr. Bartolomé de Olmedo. He said that, though he appreciated them, he would like the slaves to work for Marina; and the rest, those of good birth, for the moment to remain with their parents. The Tlaxcalans asked the reason. Cortés replied that the King of Castile would like his hosts to throw away their idols and abandon human sacrifice. He showed them pictures of the Child Jesus and of the Virgin Mary. If they wanted to be brothers to the Castilians, and if they desired the Castilians to accept their daughters, they should start worshipping the Christian God and abandon their idols. If they did not do so, they would, unfortunately, go to hell when they died, and burn there for ever. The new master race would in those circumstances never be created.

Maxixcatzin and Xicotencatl, though they attended a mass of thanksgiving for peace conducted by Fr. Juan Díaz, predictably replied with a question: how could they think of abandoning their gods? What would their children and their priests say? The populace would rise in protest. At this, Fr. Olmedo told Cortés not to press the matter: "I would not like you to make Christians by force. Wait," he wisely said, "till they gradually feel the weight of our admonitions." Several of those to whom Cortés talked regularly, such as Lugo, Velázquez de León and Alvarado, agreed with Olmedo. In time the Tlaxcalan leaders said that they thought that they might become Christians, but only after they had seen more of Spanish customs.[19] The Castilians in the meantime persuaded their hosts to clean one of their temples, remove the idols there, and put the place at the disposition of the Christians. They naturally put there pictures of the Virgin and a cross. According to the seventeenth-century comment of a descendant of Montezuma, this was done against the advice of Fr. Olmedo and Fr. Juan Díaz.[20]

In the next two weeks Cortés talked ceaselessly of the benefits of Christianity. The historian Camargo reported a long, evidently romanticised, exchange between the leaders of Tlaxcala and Cortés about the purposes of the latter's expedition, and about the latter's provenance. Were they sons of gods or of men? Cortés in reply dwelt on the relation of the Christian religion to the temporal power. He denounced human sacrifice. He also repeated that the Castilians were human beings just as the Tlaxcalans were, with the difference that they were Christians.[21]

The legend is that eventually Cortés inspired the four main lords of Tlaxcala – that is, Maxixcatzin and Xicotencatl the elder, and also their fellow lords, Citlalpopocatzin and Temilotecutl – to accept baptism and to receive, at the hands of Fr. Juan Díaz, the Christian names of Don Lorenzo, Don Vicente, Don Bartolomé and Don Gonzalo. The conversion of a great many Tlaxcalans is then supposed to have followed: those who were to be called Juan were baptised one day, those to be known as Pedro the next, followed by numerous Juanas and Marías.[22]

There is, however, no statement before about 1550 that this dramatic event occurred at this time.[23] This lack of evidence indicates that the idea is as fanciful as that which suggested that, at the place where the four lords of Tlaxcala first received Cortés, a cross miraculously appeared.[24] The notion of the Christian God as yet one more deity, powerful no doubt but not unique, did not disturb the leaders of this city. But the Christian notion of a jealous God with no rivals, who requires all the love and devotion of the convert, was not something which could be communicated through interpreters by Cortés and his two spiritual advisers. It seems certain too that, if such a conversion had occurred then, the Dominican Fr. Aguilar (who long before he became a friar was a conquistador on this expedition) would have recalled it. Yet in his memoir he says nothing of it. Nor indeed did Cortés boast of it: which of course he would have done had it occurred. On the other hand, the Tlaxcalan leaders seem to have been impressed by Cortés' preaching.

The well-born girls of Tlaxcala were, however, probably baptised before they were delivered to Cortés' captains. Thus Tecuelhuatzin, a daughter of Xicotencatl, was christened "Doña María Luisa" and was given to Alvarado; Maxixcatzin's daughter, "Doña Elvira", went to Juan Velázquez de León; while three other girls were happily received by Sandoval, Olid and Ávila.[25] From then on, all the senior commanders seem to have had indigenous girls attached to them; Cortés, of course, with Marina, included. Within a few weeks, many ordinary soldiers seem to have found girls too. *Mestizos*, "race of warriors" or no, were not slow to follow.

Throughout this stay Montezuma's ambassadors remained in Cortés' company. Cortés continued to treat with them, since he was still hoping to be able "to reach Tenochtitlan without fighting".[26] For that reason Cortés continued to listen to their daily expressions of astonishment that the Castilians should wish to stay with the Tlaxcalans, a people poor, wicked, thieving and treacherous. Montezuma on one occasion during these days begged the Castilians to come without delay to Tenochtitlan: that was to prevent them staying with the Tlaxcalans any more. Every day the Mexican ambassadors would go to the *Caudillo* and tell him that they should leave Tlaxcala as soon as possible, and go to Cholula, where the leaders were Mexican allies. Every day, contrariwise, the Tlaxcalans would insist that they should avoid Cholula, for the best route to Tenochtitlan was by way of Huexotzinco, where the people were friendly to them.[27]

Cortés in the end decided to take the Mexicans' advice to go to

Cholula. But he also accepted the offer of new bearers and warriors from Tlaxcala to accompany him. By this means he contrived once again to be courteous to both sides. In addition, he arranged to send two of his followers to look at the city of Tenochtitlan before he set off for there himself. They were also if possible to speak to the "great Montezuma". The two men selected were Pedro de Alvarado, at that time Cortés' closest lieutenant, and Bernardino Vázquez de Tapia, the well-connected conquistador from Oropesa who had been Grijalva's standard-bearer.

It must have been an extraordinary journey. The two men travelled the sixty miles (as the crow flies) to Tenochtitlan on foot: Cortés would not spare any horses. The sight of two armed Spanish conquistadors, probably dressed in some traditional armour, tramping with swords through the Mexican countryside for the first time in history, must have been an astonishing one in the Indian villages through which they passed. They travelled, of course, in company, with Mexican guides. The Tlaxcalans were suspicious of the adventure and, according to Vázquez de Tapia, made several attempts to kill them *en route*. The journey must have been disagreeable. For the Mexicans often thought that the two Castilians were not walking fast enough and, at some parts of the journey, pulled them along. They went first to Cholula, on the same altitude as Tlaxcala at the foot of the mountains, then to the south of the volcano Popocatepetl, and finally to Texcoco opposite Tenochtitlan on the great lake.[28] There they apparently met a delegation from Tenochtitlan, including a son of Montezuma, and Cuitláhuac, the lord of Iztapalapa, that brother of the Emperor who had been most opposed to allowing a visit from the Castilians. Cuitlahuac said that Montezuma was ill and "so we could not go in". Vázquez de Tapia said later that he thought that, among those Indian lords whom he met at Texcoco, one might have been Montezuma in disguise.[29] From this reconnaissance, the Spaniards must have learned at least that their friends had not exaggerated when they talked of the size of Tenochtitlan.

Cortés meantime mounted his expedition to Cholula. He decided on this several days before leaving Tlaxcala and sent messengers ahead to that effect. Probably his reason for going to Cholula was strategic: he did not want to leave between himself and the sea a place as powerful as Cholula appeared to be.

The people of Tlaxcala warned Cortés again that there were certain to be plots against him in Cholula.[30] The streets in that city, they said, had already been blocked so that, once inside it, the conquistadors could be easily captured. The Cholulans had stored stones on the flat roofs of their houses ready to attack the expedition from above.[31] Cortés was also assured that one of the commanders of Tlaxcala – perhaps a brother of Xicotencatl the younger – was conniving with the Cholulans in a plot to kill all the Castilians.[32] He heard this from Alvarado, who himself had heard the story whilst in bed with María Luisa. Cortés had the treacherous commander secretly strangled,[33] and then sent Cristóbal de Mata with some others to reconnoitre. They returned with some minor Cholulan lords, who excused themselves for their non-attendance on Cortés: they said that they had been ill.

Cortés took an arrogant stand. They must come back within three days bringing senior lords worthy of treating with the representatives of the King of Castile, or otherwise he would look on Cholula as in open rebellion: a remarkable statement, even in the age of the conquistadors. For the Cholulans could scarcely be rebels, not having yet agreed to become vassals. It is true that there was as usual a precedent: King Alfonso XI of Castile had told the Pope that the kingdoms of Africa belonged to Spain "by our royal right".[34] The Mexica themselves also considered all independent peoples to be rebels if they happened to live near them since they, the Mexica, had taken on the mantle of the Toltecs. So anything which the Toltecs had ruled was looked on as theirs. The people concerned were "in rebellion" if they did not obey the Mexica.[35]

These menaces of Cortés' had some positive effects. Some senior lords of Cholula did visit Cortés' army. They attributed their earlier reluctance to fear of Tlaxcalan treachery. Cortés said later that they readily agreed to take an oath of vassaldom to the King of Spain, in the presence of his notary Godoy: no doubt, along with many others, they looked on this oath as being able to be cancelled when necessary.[36]

The distance between Tlaxcala and Cholula is twenty-five miles. Cortés and his army left the former haven on 12 October, being accompanied by many Tlaxcalans. Perhaps the figure ran into thousands.[37] The lords of Tlaxcala gave Cortés some chilling advice: if he were going to meet the Mexica in battle, he was to be sure to kill all he could, "leaving no one alive; neither the young, lest they bear arms again; nor the old, lest they give good advice".[38]

The first night after leaving Tlaxcala the expedition bivouacked in open country. Cortés slept in a ditch near the river Atoyac. The next day several leaders of Cholula with a large escort came forward to meet the Castilians, bringing maize and turkeys.[39] They feared, they said, that the expedition had been told many things unfavourable to Cholula. Cortés, they tried to insist, should not believe such stories. Some of their priests also appeared carrying braziers. They proceeded to fumigate Cortés and his captains with incense distributed from bowls. Others blew conch shells and played flutes.[40] These dignitaries were dressed in sleeveless cotton robes, some closed at the front like surplices, with cotton fringes at the sides.

Cortés gave his usual sermon about the iniquity of idols, the evils of human sacrifice, and the benefits of worshipping the Christian God. The Cholulans replied that they could hardly be expected to abandon their deities the moment that the Castilians arrived in their territory.[41]

That night the expedition entered Cholula and were lodged well, some food being made available for them. How much food is a matter of controversy. Andrés de Tapia reported the food to have been adequate to begin with.[42] But Cortés said that, even at the beginning, it was sparse, and it became more and more so every day.[43] Cortés' majordomo, Joan de Cáceres, recalled that "when they asked for maize for the horses, they were given water; and, when they asked for grass, they brought something else and little of it".[44] The Tlaxcalans and Totonacs, meantime, mostly lodged outside the city, but some – Cortés reported the improbable figure of five thousand – were allowed to enter it, since they were carrying the Castilians' cannon and other equipment: a most injudicious concession.

Cholula had been inhabited for a thousand years. It is said that, in early days, there was for a long time a tyranny there of an Olmec people from the tropical zone near Coatzacoalcos. But at the end of the thirteenth century, it seems, certain leaders came from Tula, expelled the Olmecs, and inaugurated the cult of Quetzalcoatl, whose temple was on the site of the modern church of San Francisco and the Capilla de los Reyes. Inside there was apparently the large statue of Quetzalcoatl already referred to, with a long beard: a thing rarely achieved in old Mexico till old age (though Quetzalcoatl on the Hamburg box also has a beard).[45] Quetzalcoatl, in Cholula, was associated especially with the cycle of Venus, the morning star. There was also a well-sited temple to Huitzilopochtli.

Cholula's biggest pyramid, housing the temple to Tlaloc, can still be seen. It was higher than the pyramid in Tenochtitlan (120 steps to 114), and covered over 500,000 square feet: it was, therefore, the largest pyramidal structure in the world. It was surrounded by numerous other shrines. These places of worship made Cholula one of the most important religious centres in all America. A Spanish official in the 1580s said that the two rulers of Cholula had to validate the rulers of the whole region and that it was the Rome or the Mecca of its world and day; and, if that must have been an exaggeration, the story certainly points to the significance of the town.[46]

In his account of the conquest, Andrés de Tapia, who later had an *encomienda* near Cholula, wrote that the Spanish expedition was now told of the part played by Quetzalcoatl in Cholula. He says that that "principal god" was a man who had lived in former times and had founded the city. This "Quetzlquate" had told the citizens not to sacrifice men; only quail. Tapia added that the god was said there to wear a white robe like a friar's and over it a mantle of red crosses adorned with green stones.[47] It will be seen that the robes described were not very different from what the priests of Cholula were said by Cortés to have worn, and that, unlike some later embroiderers of the Quetzalcoatl myth, Tapia did not say that the god was white, nor that he was bearded, nor that he was expected one day to return.

As to the population, Fr. Aguilar said that Cholula had 50,000 or 60,000 houses; adding that these had solid roofs and freshwater wells.[48] In another, better, statistic, a Spanish councillor in Tenochtitlan later stated that the Cholulans could send some 25,000 men to war.[49] These figures suggest a population of about 180,000 to 200,000. That seems rather a high figure, but it is likely that there were more inhabitants there than anywhere else between Tenochtitlan and the sea. Cortés himself said that, since Cholula was "very towered", it was "more beautiful than anything in Spain".[50] He observed four hundred and thirty towers (pyramids, that is) from the summit of the great pyramid (one more of his disturbingly precise figures). Bernal Díaz thought that Cholula resembled Valladolid: in those days at least a compliment.[51] Cholula had an immense market, especially renowned for featherwork, for pottery and for precious stones: Montezuma was said to insist on eating only from the fine Cholula ware, which was much superior to similar Mexican work.

The city was ruled by two men: one, Tlaquiach, a temporal ruler, the other, Tlalchiac, a spiritual one. These lived in houses attached to the temple of Quetzalcoatl.[52] The names of these potentates indicated "lord of the here and now" and "lord of the world below the earth".[53] They were supported by four other lords from whom, in the Mexican style, the successors to the first two leaders would naturally come. The people of Cholula spoke Nahuatl, and they acknowledged the suzerainty of the Mexica, to whom they paid tribute.[54] They were, however, proud; as well they might be, since they could not conceive circumstances in which they would not be protected by the god Quetzalcoatl in the event of danger.[55]

The Mexican ambassadors, meanwhile, made another attempt to dissuade Cortés from continuing on the road to Tenochtitlan. Montezuma, they said, would die of fear if the Castilians arrived. Anyway, they insisted, the road henceforth was impassable. It would be impossible to find provisions on the way. Montezuma's zoo was full of fierce animals or reptiles, such as alligators, which would tear the Castilians to pieces if they were let loose.[56] Cortés continued to be unimpressed. Presumably by now Alvarado and Vázquez de Tapia had arrived back, and their commander had a picture of the landscape which he would have to cross.

It is difficult to be certain now what happened next in Cholula. It is obvious that the city either found it difficult to provide the army of Cortés with food or did not want to. The first may be the most likely explanation. At all events, on the third day, the citizens only brought wood and water.[57] Fr. Aguilar recalled that the Tlaxcalans had to be asked to help to find food.

The leaders of the city still refrained from coming to see Cortés. Cortés sent for Tlaquiach, the temporal lord. That dignitary said that he was too ill to go out.[58] Members of the expedition noticed that, just as they had been warned in Tlaxcala might happen, streets of the town were indeed beginning to be blocked up. Stones were being piled on roofs.[59] Some Tlaxcalans and Cempoallans reported that the Cholulans were conniving with the Mexica, and with some of the expedition's Cuban servants, to kill the Spaniards.[60] Then it was said that preparations had been made for an ambush of the Castilians when they left Cholula. A "noblewoman" of Cholula is said to have told Marina that Montezuma's army was close by and that, if she wanted to escape death, she ought to hide with her. In future she could live with her and marry her son.[61]

In this increasingly suspicious atmosphere, Cortés, therefore, sent for two priests who were in the great temple near at hand. He asked them why everyone was so nervous. Receiving no answer he asked them to send once again for Tlaquiach. This time, he came. Cortés asked him the same question. This lord was embarrassed. He eventually said that Montezuma had given orders that no help should be given to the Spanish.[62]

Cortés again summoned the two priests. He asked them whether they really knew what was going on. Their tongues apparently loosened by a handsome gift of jade, and by torture, they said that the condition of their city's nerves was the fault of their ally Montezuma.[63] That emperor knew that the Castilians were on their way, but he could not decide what to do about the matter. Every day he was of many minds. One day he was considering a peaceful reception of the expedition. The next day he was thinking of having the entire force killed. That was probably an accurate picture of Montezuma's state of mind.

In any case, the priests continued, 20,000 warriors (or perhaps 2,000, one cannot help thinking) had been assembled and were waiting on the road to Mexico. The Mexica, the priests said, had planned an ambush as the conquistadors left the city on the way to the mountains. To further that end, the Cholulans were going to offer many hammocks with bearers to help the Castilians on their way. Once all their enemies were stowed in the hammocks, they would be carried off live to Montezuma. The aim, of course, was capture, not death. Twenty Castilians would be left for the Cholulans to sacrifice at home. The houses near the ambush, the priests explained, were already stocked with long poles, cord and leather collars to enable the conquistadors to be led, bound, up to the capital of Mexico.[64] Most of the women and children of Cholula had been removed from the town in order to avoid being caught in the fighting; and seven victims had already been sacrificed to Huitzilopochtli, the god of war, so that the gods would be benign.

Cortés held a discussion with his captains. Some (Grado perhaps, possibly Ordaz) thought that they should retreat to Tlaxcala; others thought that they should replan their route to approach Mexico through the friendly town of Huexotzinco. Others still (probably Alvarado, Olid, Sandoval) were in favour of a pre-emptive attack. The Tlaxcalans, scarcely knowing what they were supporting, agreed with, and perhaps urged, this recommendation.[65]

The last point of view carried the day. Cortés prepared an exemplary punishment, having first asked his Indian allies to put a certain sign (probably a flower) in their headdresses so as to be certain of being recognised if fighting began.[66]

The *Caudillo* asked the lords of Cholula to go to the courtyard of the temple of Quetzalcoatl – their normal place of assembly – so that he could take leave of them before he left for Mexico.[67] Over a hundred of them, including Tlaquiach, came, unarmed.[68] The doors of the courtyards were then closed by the Spaniards. Cortés asked why the Cholulans should want to kill him and the rest of the Spanish expedition when all they had done had been to warn them against idols and human sacrifices. He knew, he said, that the country outside the city was full of Mexican warriors. The chiefs of Cholula admitted it, but, they said, Montezuma had ordered it. Cortés then made an allusion, as was his wont, to the laws of Spain which, he said, decreed that treason of this nature should not go unpunished. For that crime, the lords of Cholula had to die.[69]

An arquebus was then fired as a signal and, in two hours, the Castilians, with their Tlaxcalan and Cempoallan allies, killed not only the hundred or so lords but many more who had gathered near the courtyard (Cortés himself said that three thousand were killed).[70] There was indeed much stabbing, slaying and beating of people.[71] The Tlaxcalan and Totonac allies then sacked the town, burning the most important houses and temples. The temple of Huitzilopochtli (the god whose presence emphasised Mexican suzerainty) was set on fire and burned for two days, according to Andrés de Tapia.[72] Many priests threw themselves from its summit to avoid capture or death at the hands of the Tlaxcalans.[73] The Indian allies plainly revelled in the opportunity, as one conquistador, Martín López, remarked years later, "to prove themselves such good vassals of King Charles".[74] Only after two days did Cortés call off the sack.[75] Many people were made prisoner and taken to Tlaxcala to be sacrificed. The few Cholulans who had collaborated with the Castilians were spared. The *Caudillo* then once again gave his familiar sermon, ordering the priests who remained to whitewash their temples so that he could set up there crosses and pictures of the Virgin. He ordered the destruction of all the idols of Cholula, an order over which the priests delayed: understandably, as Fr. Olmedo told Cortés. Cortés did not press the matter.[76]

The spoils were considerable. In Cholula there had been much gold, many precious stones, and remarkable featherwork.[77] The Castilians also found prison cages in Cholula built of thick wooden bars. These were full of Indians, some of them children, who were being fattened for sacrifice. They were freed.

According to the historian Juan Ginés de Sepúlveda, with whom Cortés discussed the matter years later, there was one further exchange between Cortés and the few remaining leaders of Cholula. Cortés returned to the square where some of the survivors were being held as prisoners and castigated them for their perfidy. They in turn again blamed Montezuma and begged Cortés' pardon. They said that, if he accepted their apology, they would thenceforth serve him. They would also arrange that the people who had fled would come back. Cortés thought that he had already punished the city adequately, and had done enough to terrify the population (he himself used the word "*atemorizar*"). He freed two leaders, and some who had fled returned. Then he freed the others, saying that he hoped that they would all conduct themselves well in future.[78]

This massacre at Cholula was one of the most controversial events in Cortés' life. Argument about it has never ceased. Las Casas gave the event publicity in his famous polemic, *La Brevísima Relación de la Destrucción de las Indias*. He insisted, for example, that the purpose of the massacre was simply to reduce the capacity of the Indians to resist by terror.[79] They did this, he argued, as a matter of policy. He recalled the similar massacre at Xaragua in Hispaniola and at Caonao in Cuba. Las Casas even suggested that Cortés recited, from his rooftop as he watched, a then famous ballad:

> Nero from the Tarpeian Rock
> Looked down on burning Rome
> The old people and children screamed
> But all sorrow the emperor spurned.[80]

It is most improbable that that could have occurred. Yet the thrust of Las Casas' argument must have been correct. Even Cortés' own friends, such as Juan González Ponce de León (a son of the discoverer of Florida, Ponce de León), at a hearing in the *Caudillo's residencia*, agreed that it was "suitable to carry out the said punishment in order to put fear into the land".[81] Francisco de Flores, another friend, and perhaps a native of Medellín, certainly an Extremeño, said that the "punishment" was appropriate to secure the pacification of the land.[82] Alonso de la Serna said that the action "caused such fear that no one dared to commit such treason again".[83]

A comment on these events made in 1581 by Gabriel Rojas, then the Spanish *corregidor*, was that the Indians of Cholula said that they had had no intent of "treason" against the Castilians. All "that they had been guilty of was that they had not provided the Spanish with the necessary food" (Rojas added that that was not to be believed).[84] Others, including Fr. Motolinía, have insisted that there was a plot of some kind.

To argue otherwise would be to suggest a degree of collaboration as well as invention in Cortés' and Díaz del Castillo's accounts of this affair, which is a little difficult to credit: Cortés talks of the Tlaxcalans having found barricades, stones on roofs, roads closed, and others with holes in them.[85]

So probably there was a conspiracy (though there is no knowing whether anything would have come of it); probably it was inspired, and to some extent arranged, by the Mexica; perhaps the people of Cholula, being as historically minded as most people of the region, recalled that their legends said that they had first established themselves by treacherously killing giants who had lived there before.[86] Probably the rumour of the plan was leaked to the Tlaxcalans, who seized on it as an excuse to get the Castilians to destroy an enemy city; and Cortés, recalling the effectiveness of similar massacres in Hispaniola and Cuba (as Las Casas recalled), seized on the chance to achieve "propaganda of the deed".[87] As Cortés' own majordomo, Joan de Cáceres, put it, it was "a punishment" ("*castigo*") which would have a deterrent effect.[88] The men of the expedition were at this time probably more nervous, more weary, and more disoriented than their memorialists record. Perhaps they were tired of unfamiliar food. Perhaps Cortés felt that he needed to give them a battle and, once it began, it was impossible to stop – if only because the Tlaxcalans saw an opportunity for revenge; though it seems likely that in practice that revenge was on a scale altogether new, and bore little relation to the kind of "massacres" which had occurred in the past. As to the Spaniards, perhaps Cortés had intended only to kill a few of the leaders of Cholula. But once the bloodshed had begun, something like blood-lust may have taken over and hundreds were killed. None of the conquistadors involved seem to have wanted to speak much about the matter afterwards.

Cortés had then next to deal with the Mexican ambassadors who, "half dead with fear", had been quivering in their lodgings during these events.[89] Cortés told the ambassadors that the chiefs of Cholula had attributed these acts of treachery to Montezuma. Since this showed that Montezuma did not keep his word, the Castilians, he said, had changed their plans. He had thought of going to Tenochtitlan in peace, as a friend. Now, he said icily, he intended to enter Montezuma's land in war, doing harm as an enemy.

The frightened ambassadors said that they had known of no encouragement by their emperor of the Cholulans to act in any way against Cortés. They asked if they could send a messenger to Montezuma to discover the truth. Cortés, pretending to be mollified, agreed.[90] A messenger then travelled the sixty miles to Tenochtitlan with great speed. When they knew what had transpired, the Emperor and the city returned to their mood of panic: It was no longer a time of calm. The common folk were in uproar. "There were frequent disorders. It was as if the earth quaked, . . . as if the surface of the land circled in tumult."[91] One consequence was certain: there could be little support now for the idea that Cortés was a reincarnation of Quetzalcoatl, the temperate god. No such reincarnation would surely have acted so brutally in the courtyard of that god's own temple. If god he were, Cortés was a god of war or brutality; perhaps Tezcatlipoca, perhaps even Huitzilopochtli.

Even more alarming, Quetzalcoatl had been inactive. The conch shell trumpets of his priests had sounded, but the god had done nothing. Not only had he left the Cholulans to their fate but he had allowed his holy house to be broken into, his priests murdered, his effigy apparently destroyed: at all events we hear nothing more of it. The news of this must have been catastrophic. Nothing was now certain, since nothing had been shown to be sacred.

The messenger of the Mexican ambassadors returned to Cholula from home in six days, with men carrying ten plates of gold, fifteen hundred cloaks of cotton, and a good deal of food.[92] Montezuma apologised profusely to Cortés for the alleged rebellion. He himself had had nothing to do with it. The fault lay with the leaders of the local Mexican garrisons (at Izúcar and at Acatzinco), who had been friendly with the lords of Cholula. He then said again that he would send anything to Cortés that he liked if only he would not come to Mexico. His difficulty was that he could give the Castilians nothing to eat since everything had to be carried into the town by bearers.[93] Cortés sent back one of his devious replies: he too had a difficulty. That was that he had to send an account of Montezuma and his kingdom to his own monarch, King Charles. Montezuma then himself returned an equally devious reply saying that, if Cortés did come to Tenochtitlan, he would be delighted to see him.[94] But he immediately busied himself with thinking of a new way to prevent such a thing.

Another new world of great cities and towers

"Another day the said Ordaz came [back from the volcano] and said that he had been staggered by what he had seen, saying that he had seen another new world of great cities and towers and a sea, and in the middle of it a very great city had been built and in truth it appeared to have caused him fear and astonishment."
Fr. Aguilar, *Relación breve de la conquista de la Nueva España*

MEXICO-TENOCHTITLAN IS ONLY fifty miles from Cholula as the crow flies. The two cities are both about seven and a half thousand feet above sea level. But between them, the high mountain chain, of which the volcanoes Iztaccihuatl and Popocatepetl are the peaks, stands as protection and obstacle. Several paths ran across these mountains: one, to the south of Popocatepetl, had been followed by Alvarado and Vázquez de Tapia on their visit to Texcoco; a second, to the north of Iztaccihuatl, follows the river Atoyac from Huexotzinco almost to its source and then descends, following another stream, to pass near Chalco. That has been the main road from Mexico to Veracruz throughout most of modern history. A third, more leisurely, route lies some way to the north, past Lake Apan and descending to the Valley of Mexico near Otumba. A fourth pass, the most difficult one, lies between the volcanoes. Even today it is for much of the way merely a track, passing through lost villages beyond Cholula, before reaching, at just under 13,000 feet, the col which is now known as the Pass of Cortés: for it was by that route that the conquistadors made their first approach to Tenochtitlan. Cortés chose this way as the one least likely to be expected, and therefore blocked, by the Mexica.

Cortés probably left Cholula on 1 November 1519. He now lost his first Indian allies, the Totonacs from Cempoallan. They returned home loaded with presents from Cortés, many of these having been originally given by Montezuma. Instead of these *naturales*, Cortés had now perhaps a thousand Tlaxcalans, only too anxious to assist their new allies: helping to carry or pull their cannons as the Totonacs had done previously, and making their tortillas – a task presumably performed by some of the three hundred girls given to Cortés by Maxixcatzin and Xicotencatl (and which Cortés had given back).[1] There was also the little group of Mexican ambassadors and their attendants.

On leaving Cholula, Cortés sent ten scouts ahead under Diego de Ordaz to look at the volcano Popocatepetl which at that time was smoking dangerously. Popocatepetl had erupted several times in recent years, the last occasion being 1509. A volcano was to most of the conquistadors a new sight. But some of the men on the expedition might have seen Etna or Vesuvius. One or two might have seen the volcanoes in the Canary Islands.

At all events, when Ordaz drew near the summit of Popocatepetl, a cloud of smoke was coming out from it, going straight up "like an arrow".[2] Hot rock was being thrown out. All the same, Ordaz nearly reached the top, being "two lances' distance" from it, but the smoke and cold as well as the rock and ash drove him back. (No modern traveller would attempt the last part of the ascent, in the snow, without crampons; and if Ordaz's version is true, the lances must have been astonishingly long.) Ordaz certainly returned with useful information about the best way to the great lake, interesting stories of the rocky surface of the recently emitted lava, as well as, his companion Gutierre de Casamori improbably reported, some icicles.[3] Ordaz had seen the lake and the cities of the Valley of Mexico spread far below him in the translucent air: "another new world of great cities and towers and a sea and, in the middle of it, a very great city".[4] Perhaps he thought of the tempting view of Naples which King Alfonso saw from above in a famous ballad, and whose capture he knew would lose him thousands of men. Exactly so too had the Cid and his men

> admired Valencia, how it spreads before them
> and beyond it the sea, and there the *huerta* vast and well planted,
> and all manner of things to delight them,
> and they raised their hands and gave thanks to God,
> for this gift so good and great . . .[5]

Ordaz later caused the smoking volcano to appear on the coat of arms for which he received permission in 1525.[6]

The main expedition meantime left Cholula in good heart. It must have been encouraging to observe how there was neither quarrelling nor fear on the journey up to the pass.[7] Velázquez de León now seemed as content to accompany Cortés as Ordaz did. The memory of the Governor of Cuba was forgotten.

To the Mexica the Castilians *en route* seemed a fearful sight. Sahagún's informants remembered how they came all together in a great assembly . . . "stirring up the dust. Their iron lances, their iron halberds, glistened from afar, and their iron swords moved in a wavy line as if they were a water course . . ." Their iron shirts and helmets jangled. And what some of them wore was all iron, they rode as if they had been turned into iron, "gleaming, hence they caused astonishment," they aroused great fear . . . "And their dogs went ahead. They went before them. At the vanguard they came, in the lead. They came at their head. They came panting", their noses in the air, their nostrils distended, the foam dripping from their mouths . . .[8]

On the first day out from Cholula the expedition reached Calpan, a substantial town which had once been allied to Huexotzinco. Several lords from the latter place came to see Cortés there and, like those of Tlaxcala, advised him against going to Tenochtitlan, on the ground that that city was too powerful to conquer. But they said that if, against all their advice, the Castilians persisted in their journey, they should realise that, when they got to the top of the pass between the volcanoes, they would find two roads: one blocked by felled trees, cacti and other undergrowth, the other clear. They should take the route which was blocked, since the Mexica would be sure to be preparing an ambush in the other one.[9] Having delivered this advice, the messengers of Huexotzinco must have returned home with pleasure at the realisation that they had avoided a Castilian visitation. They thus would have given especial thanks to their deity, Camaxtli, preparations for whose festival on 15 November must have been under way.

The next day the expedition started early, marched ten miles, climbed another few thousand feet and, a little before midday, reached the ridge between the volcanoes. This was where the god Quetzalcoatl was said, in one account, to have halted in his flight from Tula, and where his dwarfs and hunchbacks froze to death.[10] It was also where, a few years before, a diplomat from Huexotzinco had composed a poem when on his way to ask for help from the Mexicans against Tlaxcala:

> I climb; I reach the height,
> The huge olive-green lake,
> Now quiet, now angry,
> Foams and sings among the rocks . . .[11]

This verse suggests that, from the pass at that time, the view of the lake must have been uninterrupted by trees. But that poem must have been written in the spring. In November there is often cloud, rain and mist. It was probably thus on that 2 November 1519. Neither Cortés nor any other Castilian seems to have had any memory of a view of Tenochtitlan and its lake from the ridge between the volcanoes. The weather must have been to blame.

The conquistadors did, however, see the fork in the road, as the people of Huexotzinco had told them that they would. One way ahead was blocked, as had been foretold; the other was clear. Cortés silkily asked the Mexican emissaries why there were two roads, one blocked. Those long-suffering servants of Montezuma, unable to influence their fellow travellers, and fearful of their lives when they should eventually reach Tenochtitlan, explained that the blocked path had been so left to dissuade people from going along it, since it was windy, less direct, and with bad stretches on it. Cortés insisted on going by that path, however, ordering the Tlaxcalans to move the trees and other obstacles which had been laid across it. They made short work of these things. Cortés' army then started down that path.[12] It began to snow slightly before the expedition reached the town of Huehuecalco. But there was there an enormous refuge, where the expedition could pass the night and where food had been stored: perhaps for the use of a Mexican army on one of its journeys to a "flowery war".[13] A substantial guard was mounted, which, according to Cortés, was necessary since there might have been an attack.[14]

Here Cortés favoured some local Indians, who came politely to see him, with yet one more of his pitiless addresses: "You should know that those who are with me never sleep at night; and, if they do sleep at all, they do so a little during the day. At night, they are in arms and, whoever they see walking about or entering the camp, they kill; and there is nothing that can prevent this. Make this known, therefore, to your people and ensure that, after sundown, nobody comes to where we are since, if they do, they will die. And it would distress me if people died."

Despite this warning, some local Indians could not restrain themselves out of curiosity from trying to see what the Castilians did at night. They were killed, as Cortés promised, with nothing more being mentioned of the matter.[15]

The following day the weather was better. The Castilians were able to see, from the top of the sierra, much of the Valley of Mexico: the blue lake about ten miles from them, with the indication of a large city twice as far away as that; many other villages, with smoke rising upwards from the houses; and green, cultivated fields of maize and beans which were produced in the rich area nearest to where they were. If the legends of the valley have any validity, the then small tribe, the Mexica, would, two hundred and more years before, have seen much the same scene, if from another direction.[16] The exhilaration of the conquistadors was naturally tinged with apprehension; and there were some who thought, even then, that they should return to Tlaxcala till they were more numerous.[17] Such negative thoughts made no headway, however, with Cortés. His expedition was, by this time, in the territory of the Chalca, whose main city, Chalco itself, lay on the south-east inlet of the lake system.

The Chalca had been companions of the Mexica during the early days

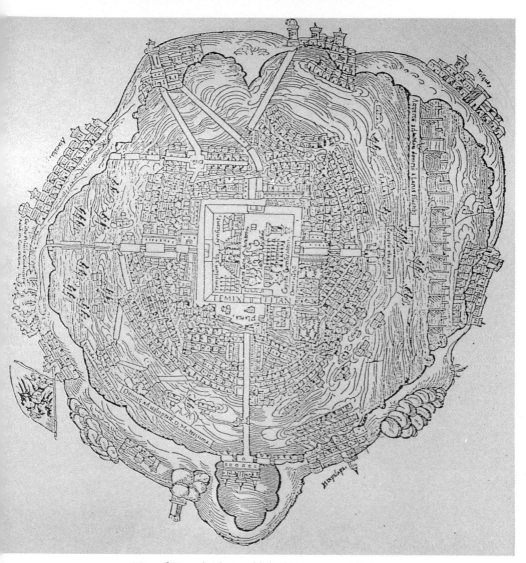

Map of Tenochtitlan, published Nuremberg, 1524,
with the first Latin edition of Cortés's second letter to
Charles V. Cortés is said to have inspired it. But the
designer was probably German. It may have influenced
Albrecht Dürer in his design for an ideal city

Beliefs 1 *(below left)* An important goddess of the Mexica was Coyolxauhqui, who probably stood for the moon. Her colossal stone head was intended to terrify; *(below right)* Xipe Topec, "the flayed lord," stood for fertility. The god of the goldsmiths, he is seen here wearing the skin of a sacrificial victim; *(foot)* the Mexica also had faith in portents, such as comets, here seen by Montezuma II from a rooftop

SANTA·MARIA·DLOSREMEDIOS

Beliefs 2 *(left)* The conquistadors prayed to, and put up, many statues of the Virgin Mary, of which the Virgin of los Remedios, in the cathedral of Seville (*c.* 1400), was a favourite of Cortés; *(below)* Alejo Fernández' The Virgin of the Sailors (1514), showing Columbus, (on the far left), perhaps Bishop Fonseca, "Minister of the Indies", and a *nao*, one of the ships which conquered the world

Ideals The hero of the
Mexica was an eagle
warrior (*c.* 1500)

That of the Spaniard
was a knight, depicted
by Christoph Weiditz
(*c.* 1528), on the kind
of horse which was
used in the Americas

Sacrifice and control *(below)* Human sacrifice, to ensure compliance with the rules of society, was the climax of Mexican ceremonies, here depicted in the Codex Magliabecchiano *(c.* 1540); *(foot)* Castile was largely ruled by noblemen in castles, such as that of Medellín, in Extremadura, birthplace of Hernán Cortés

Wheels of destiny and fortune *(right)* The Mexica believed life to be predetermined, according to an elaborate calendar of which this stone one *(c. 1480)* is an example; *(below)* the Spaniards looked on the wheel of fortune with almost equal awe (a Flemish tapestry, detail, made for the coronation of Charles V of 1520. See page 413)

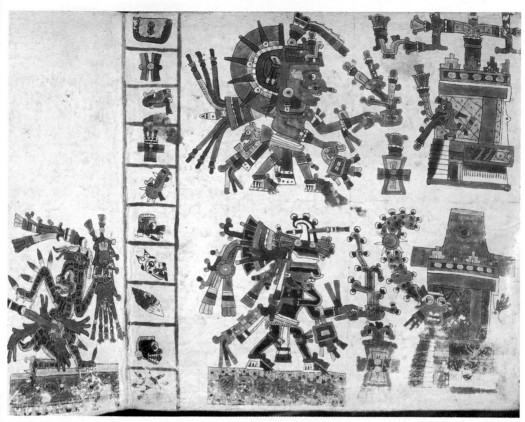

Glyphs and letters *(above)*
The Codex Cospi is a rare example of a pre-conquest Mixtec painted manuscript; *(right)* the Spaniards had the great advantage of the Latin alphabet. This manuscript, a Spanish royal judgement of 1488, mentions Martín Cortés, father of Hernán, in line 12

"A man born in brocade." Hernán Cortés painted *c.* 1528 by Christoph Weiditz, the only portrait done from life (in that painter's *Trachtenbuch*); *(inset)* A print of Cortés aged 63 just before he died

of migration. With Xochimilco, their land was the richest agricultural area of the Valley of Mexico.[18] The Chalca were said to have taught the Mexica how to draw *pulque* out of the maguey cactus.[19] They are associated with a style of sculpture which was both earlier and softer than that of the Mexica whom they probably influenced in that dimension too. Later they resisted the Mexica, fought them, and were defeated. Their tribute had, to begin with, included the provision of both stone and labourers to build or rebuild parts of Tenochtitlan. As tributaries, they had in 1519 to provide substantial quantities of goods: eight hundred large cloaks twice a year; and, once a year, two warriors' costumes with shields, six wooden bins of maize, two of beans, and two of sage.[20]

Just inside Chalca territory, the Castilians were met by yet another delegation from Montezuma. This was led by a nobleman named Tziuacpopocatzin. He had been instructed by Montezuma to dress as the Emperor and to pretend to be him. Montezuma seems feebly to have thought that the Castilians might be happy to withdraw, once they had, as they supposed, seen the object of their curiosity.[21] He was followed by certain of those magicians in whom Montezuma had previously placed confidence. He also carried presents: golden streamers, quetzal feathers, golden necklaces. The Castilians were pleased to receive these. Sahagún's sources described their reaction: When they were given the gifts, [they] "appeared to smile, to rejoice exceedingly. Like monkeys, they seized upon the gold. It was as if then they were satisfied, sated and gladdened. For in truth they thirsted mightily for gold, they stuffed themselves with it, and starved and lusted for it like pigs. They went about moving the golden streamer back and forth, and showed it to one another all the while babbling. What they said was gibberish . . ."[22]

The Castilians were at first impressed by Tziuacpopocatzin. They asked their Tlaxcalan allies: "Is this perhaps Montezuma?" The Tlaxcalans told them that it was not. They then asked the Mexican the same question. He replied: "Yes, I am your servant. I am Montezuma." The Castilians laughed and Cortés apparently said: Go home, why do you lie to us? Whom do you take us to be? You cannot mock us, nor make us stupid, nor flatter us, nor become our eyes, nor trick us, nor misdirect our gaze, nor turn us back, nor destroy us, nor dazzle us, nor cast mud in our eyes. You are not he! The indigenous sources add that Cortés continued: Now, Montezuma cannot hide from us. He cannot take refuge from us. Where after all can he go? Is he perhaps a bird that he can fly away? Or can he burrow under the earth? Is there somewhere a mountain pierced by a hole which he can enter? . . . We shall see him. We shall not fail to look him in the face. We shall hear what he has to say.[23]

The magicians, meantime, who had been sent with Tziuacpopocatzin, were as useless as their predecessors had been when Cortés was still on the coast. Worse than that, they are said to have had a disagreeable experience. On their return from the Castilian camp they (so they told Montezuma) came across a drunken man from Chalco. He was bound with eight ropes across his chest. He said to them: "What have you come here to do? What do you want? What would you still like Montezuma to do? Has he perhaps come to his senses? Is he now filled with a great fear? For he committed a great fault. He abandoned the common people. He destroyed men . . ."

The magicians told Montezuma that they quickly made the drunken man a shelter with branches; then an earth pyramid; finally, a straw bed. But he would not look at those things. He told them instead to look at the lake and said: "Why do you stand wanly there? There will be a Tenochtitlan no longer. It is gone for ever. Turn about, look what is going to befall the Mexica." They did turn and apparently saw all the temples, palaces and the houses burning. Everywhere there was fighting. They concluded that the drunken man from Chalco must be the mischievous god Tezcatlipoca – who, Montezuma may anyway have thought, was playing an important part in the unravelling of all these affairs.[24] When they turned back to ask more questions, the man had vanished. They went back to Tenochtitlan and related their experiences to Montezuma, who replied, in an unhinged manner: "What can we do? . . . We are finished . . ." Perhaps we shall climb up the mountains, perhaps we shall flee . . ." Unlucky are the poor old men and the old women. And the children, who have no understanding, where may they be taken? Where in truth can one go? For now we have taken the medicine . . ."[25]

Whatever may be said of the experience of the magicians, it is at least possible that these men had had recourse to sacred mushrooms, some of which grew on the slopes which they were so reluctantly descending. Their visions, like those of Montezuma and others earlier reported, sound similar to modern experiences of the hallucinogen.[26]

Montezuma again met his supreme council. Among those present were as usual the Emperor's brother, Cuitláhuac, and his nephew, Cacama, the King of Texcoco. There was a further long discussion as to whether or no to receive the Castilians; and, if so, how. Both Cuitláhuac and Cacama were now against the idea. So were most other lords. They thought that they should fight the strangers every inch of the way to Tenochtitlan. In fact Montezuma himself seems to have for a time taken a more forthright line: "We must not hide nor flee nor show cowardice, and let us not imagine that the Mexican glory is going to perish here. We are now resolved to die in defence of Tenochtitlan," he is supposed to have remarked. If he did so, the mood did not last.[27] He was soon thinking again that he "ought to receive them, have them as guests, give them presents".[28]

By this time in Tenochtitlan, the festivals of late October, the Mexican month of Tepeilhuitl, would have been concluded, as would the making from amaranth seed of little figures of mountain gods (always held to stand for water). Women representing those deities and a man standing for a serpent would have been sacrificed, after a procession with singing and dancing. Mexico was beginning to settle down to six dry months. The fact that the Spaniards were observed as coming from the mountains would have seemed auspicious to some: perhaps they were messengers of the rain god Tlaloc, not Quetzalcoatl (the Mexica thought that there were as many little Tlalocs as there were mountains and, for that reason, at special occasions sacrificed children to impersonate them: painting them blue to suggest water and, on occasion, shutting them up in a sacred cave to die).[29]

The inexorable, and, to the Mexica, still inexplicable movement of Cortés towards Tenochtitlan continued. The expedition moved down the hillside without turning aside to inspect any of the numerous Mexican mountain shrines which dotted the slopes of those mountains. They passed forests of oak, with some alder, acacia and cypress. They probably saw many of the whitetail deer which constituted, as the Castilians would soon find out for themselves, most of the supply of meat in old Mexico.[30] Occasionally, through the trees, there would in the distance be bright visions of lilac and of yellow fields. The day following that when Cortés left the pass, his expedition reached the bottom of the path, on the level of the Lake of Mexico, and spent the night at the town of Amecameca.[31] This was one of numerous cities probably settled in the thirteenth century by tribes of Chichimec nomads (of whom the Mexica were the last to arrive). Amecameca had been the only site where the predatory nomads forced out an indigenous population.[32] Most of these cities were by now ruled by royal families of Toltec descent, and so were distantly related to the Mexican monarchs. At Amecameca, whose inhabitants probably numbered three thousand, Cortés and his men were quartered in "some very good houses" belonging to the lord of the place. The latter dignitary, probably a cousin of Montezuma, gave Cortés all the food that he needed, some gold, and forty slave girls, "well dressed and well painted", according to Fr. Durán.[33] The *Caudillo* accepted these gifts without the hypocrisy which attended his reception of similar presents at Tlaxcala.[34] The expedition seems to have remained at Amecameca two nights, those of 3 and 4 November.[35]

Cortés heard there with satisfaction several further complaints by the local people of how Montezuma's tax gatherers robbed them of their possessions. Cortés said that he could not free them immediately from those burdens, but that he hoped eventually to do so. These chiefs also assured Cortés that it was obvious to them that the Mexica were intending to kill all the Castilians soon after their arrival. Cortés cheerfully discounted this and replied that he had to go into the city in order to explain to Montezuma what the Christian God had commanded.[36]

The following day the Castilians moved on and stopped the next night at Chalco, the first city which they saw on the edge of the lake, though on a small backwater of it. The population there was about double that of Amecameca, and so perhaps reached six thousand. Here apparently, during the night, Cortés had to scatter, with a few shots from his arquebuses, a number of canoes which one of his followers described as being "full of spies". Perhaps they were merely full of the curious.[37]

While Cortés was in this town, Montezuma held another council in Tenochtitlan with among others the kings of Texcoco and Tacuba. He must have been disturbed by the presence of Cortés in Chalco. For that town had rebelled more often than any other of the tributary cities since their conquest.[38] Had not a poet from there long ago written:

> Meditate upon this thing, O princes of Chalco
> O princes of Amecameca:
> A cloud of shields hangs over our houses
> A rain of darts!
> What was the judgement of he who gives life? . . .
> In the fields of the bells,
> In the field of battles,
> Here in Chalco the yellow dust,
> The houses, have begun to smoke . . .
> O thou who reignest amid reed mace,
> O Montezuma, O Nezahualcoyotl,
> Thou who destroyest the land,
> Have pity . . .[39]

But they had not done so. Montezuma II, great-grandson of the Montezuma in the poem, must have known that, over two generations, hatred of the Mexica had seethed beneath the surface in Chalco.

Montezuma spoke now apparently in the following curious terms to the kings of Texcoco and Tacuba: "O mighty lords, it is fitting that we the three of us should be here to receive the gods and, therefore, I wish to find solace with you and also to bid you farewell. How little did we enjoy the realms which were bequeathed to us by our ancestors! They, mighty kings and lords as they were, left this world in peace and in harmony. But woe is coming to us! How do we deserve this fate? How did we offend the gods? Who are these men who have come? Whence have they really come? Who showed them the way? There is only one remedy: we must make our hearts strong to bear what is about to happen. For they are at our gates."

Several lords are said to have wept in anguish. Then Montezuma again reproached the gods for having brought upon their peoples such a fearful fate. Then "he went out into the city and wept in public, abundantly, over the arrival of these foreigners. He begged the gods, the familiar gods, to have pity on the poor, the orphans, the aged, and those who would surely soon be widows. He then drew blood from his ears, arms and shins, and offered it to the gods. . . ."[40] These lachrymose proceedings did not prevent Montezuma from thinking further about the possible deception and even murder of the visitors. But the Emperor obviously felt a nameless sense of dread as to what would happen. The reaction was comprehensible since the year was still, after all, 1-Reed, bad for kings. In addition, it was unclear what the strangers would do. If they were treated as ambassadors, would they behave as ambassadors?

Montezuma continued to try and stave off the moment of their arrival. Whilst Cortés was at Chalco, the Emperor sent another delegation. This was headed by four Mexican chiefs who as usual brought gold and cloth.[41] The Emperor, they said, was very sorry not to have come to greet Cortés himself. But unfortunately he was ill. They, on the other hand, were at the Castilians' disposal. Montezuma was concerned at the hardships which they had endured in coming so far to see him. He had already sent to Cortés much gold and jade for the Christian king, and for the gods in whom he knew the Christians to believe. He now once again begged Cortés not to come to Tenochtitlan. There really was no food for them. The road to it was atrocious. The best way of coming was by canoe. That was dangerous. All his people were protesting against the idea of having the Castilians to stay. If Cortés were only to go home, Montezuma again promised that he would deliver him regular tributes of gold every year, deposited wherever Cortés specified.[42]

Cortés, offering his usual presents of glass beads, said that he was surprised that Montezuma could be so inconsistent. Now that he and his army had travelled so far, and were almost in sight of Tenochtitlan, how could they possibly return? Actually, if it were left to him alone, he said, in his usual deceptive way, he might consider going back, out of consideration for Montezuma's feelings. But if he were to do that, he and his men would be considered cowards. Cortés was determined to come and see Montezuma, since the King of Castile had ordered him to do so. He was required to give that monarch an account of what was happening. But of course if, after he had entered the capital, the Castilian presence seemed inappropriate, he would return whence he had come. As for food, which he understood might be a genuine concern for the Mexica, Cortés insisted that he and his men could survive on little of it.[43]

The Castilians spent the next night at Ayotzingo, only about five miles from Chalco. Here they found so much human filth that they assumed that a Mexican army must be at hand preparing to attack them.[44] Early the next morning they left, and were soon once again approached by four

Mexican chiefs. They said that Cacama, Montezuma's nephew and the King of Texcoco, was on his way to see them. And so he was. Borne on a litter richly worked in green feathers, with silver borders and golden bosses, he gave a most contradictory message: "Malinche," he said, addressing Cortés appropriately (master of Marina),[45] "here we have come to place ourselves at your service and to give you all that you may need for yourself and for your companions, and to arrange for you to settle in your home, which is our city. For so the great Montezuma, our prince, has ordered, and he asks your pardon once more that he has not come in person, it is on account of ill-health, and not because of ill-will."[46]

Cortés made a speech in reply and offered Cacama three pearls as a present: treasures apparently kept for an occasion of this kind (probably they came from the island of Margarita, off Venezuela, and had been supplied to Cortés in Cuba by Juan Riberol, the Genoese agent in the Indies of the Seville silversmith and pearl-merchant Juan de Córdoba, with whom the *Caudillo* already had dealings).[47] The Castilians travelled some way in Cacama's company. Cacama, though hostile to Cortés by instinct, and with none of Montezuma's spiritual hesitations, had enough of the traditional sense of Mexican hospitality to know that someone who claimed to be the ambassador of a foreign monarch had to be properly received. What he did not know, of course, was that the King of Castile had no idea what Cortés was doing, no knowledge indeed of who Cortés was, and had given him no mission.

The expedition now passed by the little town of Mixquic, the capital of a tiny nation, the Mixquica, which had been conquered by the Mexica before the end of the fourteenth century. Mixquic seemed to have been built half on the water, with many towers; "the most beautiful city which we had until then seen".[48] There was much *chinampa* farming nearby. Here Cortés learned that the way to Tenochtitlan was clear. The way would be by a causeway, built as a punishment the previous century by the men of Xochimilco. There were no difficulties about it.[49]

About four miles beyond Mixquic they reached the beginning of a causeway – in width "as long as a lance" – which led to an island where the city of Cuitláhuac had been built. That was the capital of another small people (totalling say three thousand) whom the Mexicans had conquered early on in their rise to power. Though there were so few of them, there were those who considered that that city might have been the site of legendary Azatlan.[50] The lords begged Cortés to pass the night there. He was tempted to do so. But the Mexican guides wanted them to press on along another causeway to the peninsula of Culhuacan. Cortés accepted. He was fearful lest the Mexicans cut the causeways before he reached his destination.[51]

These towns – Mixquic, Cuitláhuac and Culhuacan – were the

founders of the culture of the Valley of Mexico. The last-named, which had once defeated and then been defeated by the Mexica in the early days, was a very special dependency. The old royal house of Tula was said to have fled to Culhuacan after the fall of its city. Even now the monarchs of Culhuacan were held to be of their blood. They could still command respect, though not obedience, from the monarchs of other cities. In 1519, a daughter of Montezuma was married to Tezozomoc, Culhuacan's lord.[52] The Mexica, after being expelled from Chapultepec, had for a time lived at Tizapan, a town on the mainland which was then a dependency of Culhuacan. They often referred to themselves as the Culhua, because of their first monarch Acampichtli's Culhua (hence Toltec) blood. Approaching this territory, Bernal Díaz found the landscape of pyramids ("towers"), causeways and water before him so strange that he recalled that "it was as if it had come from the pages of *Amadís de Gaula*".[53] The statement, though much quoted, suggests that Bernal Díaz, fellow citizen though he might be of the author, had forgotten, or even had not read, *Amadís de Gaula*, since, in that romantic book, there are few descriptions of towers and cities of beauty.[54] On the other hand, King Perion in *Amadís* is represented as having had a dream in which "someone he knew not who entered his chamber by a secret door and, thrusting a hand between his ribs, took out his heart and threw it into the river". Was that a prophecy of Tenochtitlan written in Medina del Campo?[55]

That night the conquistadors lodged in the Culhuan city of Iztapalapa, on the edge of the lake facing Tenochtitlan. The elders of that city, including Cuitláhuac, Montezuma's brother, the lord of the place (he had the same name as the nearby city), had come out to meet them, near "the Hill of the Star", an extinct volcano, a place of great importance in Mexican lore, where, every fifty-two years, the fire ceremony took place solemnly and dramatically to "bind the years" and inaugurate a new "century" – the last time being in 1507.[56] It seems that the famous Toltecs had used the Hill of the Star as their capital before they went to Tula. Hence the sanctity of the site.

Iztapalapa was said to have a population of about 12,000 to 15,000 people, half the houses being on stilts over the water, half on the land.[57] It was only five miles as the crow flies from Tenochtitlan, whose remarkable buildings could be plainly seen in the distance. Cortés thought that the two-storey houses where they lodged were "as good as the best in Spain from the point of view of masonry". There were splendid rooms of stone, with roofs of cedarwood, and the courtyards covered with cotton awnings. He and his companions were also much impressed by the flowers, the pools of fresh water, the orchard with its large fishpond, and the kitchen gardens; Bernal Díaz noticed how canoes were able to enter the garden through a special gate.[58] From here, Cortés would have seen the ten-mile dyke of Nezahualcoyotl built north from

Iztapalapa. It bypassed Tenochtitlan to reach the northern shore of the lake at Atzacualco. This dyke, inspired by Nezahualcoyotl, had been built in the 1440s as a safety measure to avoid the flooding which had caused such damage before that date.[59]

The next day, 8 November, Cortés started along the main causeway to Mexico-Tenochtitlan in an elaborate order:[60] four horsemen in traditional European armour in front (probably Alvarado, Sandoval, Olid and Velázquez de León), then the standard-bearer (Cristóbal del Corral), then a contingent of infantry with drawn swords, led by Diego de Ordaz on foot, then a few more horsemen in cotton armour with lances. In the next contingent there were crossbowmen, quivers at their sides, also with cotton armour, their heads encased in helmets, with plumes on top. There followed the last of the horsemen, followed by the arquebusiers. Cortés rode at the rear, surrounded by a small group of horsemen and some more standard-bearers. Presumably there then came Cortés' personal staff, headed by his majordomo, Joan de Cáceres. Behind these were the Indian allies, dressed and painted as for war, some carrying burdens with them, others dragging two or three lombard guns probably on the wooden carts made by Diego Hernández on the coast.[61]

This remarkable array made their way along the causeway first westwards from Iztapalapa. On their left lay the peninsula of Culhuacan, with at first Mexicalzingo, the smallest of the four cities of the Culhúa, consisting of perhaps three thousand families, to be seen to the south. This Iztapalapa causeway, "a lance's length above the level of the water" (as well as in width),[62] stretched about two miles till, a mile short of the town of Coyoacán, it joined the main north–south causeway which ran from just next to Coyoacán to Tenochtitlan. Before they turned north, the Castilians would have seen the sizeable towns of Coyoacán and Huitzilopochco, with their "very good houses and towers".[63] From this point, the conquistadors were a mile and a half from the first houses of the capital. The excitement which they felt must have been intense. But Cortés insisted on an air of imperturbability.

Coyoacán had been one of the Tepanec allies of Azcapotzalco before the Mexican conquest in the 1420s. It had been destroyed by the Mexica and turned into a large garden city of private estates in the hands of the Mexican nobles. Much of the old population had become slaves. In 1502 the Emperor Ahuítzotl, in one of his last acts of authority, had had the lord of Coyoacán strangled for offering the unwelcome advice that it would be unwise to divert the waters from nearby Huitzilopochco.

The great broad causeway led the Castilians at last to their destination. It was probably about the same height from the ground as the Iztapalapa causeway, and about a hundred and forty feet broad (or twice the width of the previous one) – so that, Cortés said, eight horsemen could ride along it abreast.[64]

Montezuma, in a feeble attempt at showing that, symbolically, he did not wish to welcome the visitors, apparently told the citizens of these places not to go out and watch the foreigners' arrival: so the countryside was therefore empty but, on the roads and on the water, his orders seem not to have been carried out.[65]

The Castilian expedition naturally made an immense impression. Sahagún later described how the horses kept turning, moving back and forth repeatedly, pawing the ground during any halt, jingling and sweating, sometimes neighing, their riders looking at everything on every side with the greatest attention; how the great dogs ran ahead, sniffing at unfamiliar scents and panting; how Corral, the chief standard-bearer, walked by himself, waving his banner back and forth, making it circle, then tossing it from side to side. Sometimes, in the gentle breeze, it would stiffen and raise itself as if it were a man. Sometimes Corral would fling it up, turning, and allow it to billow. The Mexica were much impressed by the steel swords and lances, both of which flashed brightly. The crossbowmen and arquebusiers were to be seen wielding their weapons and making as if to test them. Behind Cortés, the Indian allies made noises as if preparing for war, shrieking, hitting their mouths with their hands, whistling and shouting. Presumably the Tlaxcalans wore their traditional half-red, half-white cloaks.[66] Their pleasure in entering the city of their enemies as if in triumph must have been limitless.

If the lake dwellers were fascinated, Cortés and his men also felt awe. For in front of them lay a city as large as any that anyone in his party had seen – though Naples and Constantinople, with over 200,000 people each, ran Tenochtitlan close. One or two of Cortés' men might have seen those cities: the "Italian" veterans; and the Greeks, such as Andrés de Rodas. But most of them had never seen any city bigger than Seville. In the Old World, only the cities of China (which of course no member of the expedition knew) would have greatly exceeded the capital of Mexico in size. The Castilians were also impressed by the vast number of canoes which they saw on the lake, many of them large, some carrying up to sixty people, and all hollowed out of tree trunks. Many were paddled close to the causeway to allow their owners to have a good look at the visitors.[67] The conquistadors thought that the numerous stucco-covered pyramids, with temples on top, platforms for the display of the shrines of the gods, on the islands as well as in Tenochtitlan, were, in the words of Fr. Aguilar, "castellated fortresses, splendid monuments . . . royal dwelling places! Glorious heights! How marvellous it was to gaze on them . . . all stuccoed, carved and crowned with different types of merlons, painted with animals, covered with stone figures . . . !"[68]

The Castilians must, however, also have been disconcerted by the fact that, though the causeway was wide, there were stretches in it where it gave way to bridges of wooden beams, which obviously could be removed.

The purpose was primarily to allow passage by canoes from one side of the lake to the other. But a secondary intention had always been defensive; and this latter intent surely might soon be put to use.

About a mile and a half short of the main gate, the expedition reached a place known as Acachinanco, the point where the houses of the city began and the causeway ended. This was the traditional place for greeting returning heroes: it had been there, for example, that the Emperor Ahuítzotl had welcomed the "vanguard merchants" when they had travelled to distant places. Here too was a spot known as Malcuitlapilco, "the tail end of the file of prisoners", where the line of those due for sacrifice at the inauguration of the Great Temple in 1487 had stretched.[69] It must have been approximately at the site of the modern hermitage of San Antonio el Abad.[70] Here another causeway ran off south-west to Coyoacán. Here too was a strong fort with two towers each ringed by a wall four feet thick and with what seemed to Cortés to be merloned battlements. A crowd of richly dressed Mexican noblemen came out to greet the Castilians. They as usual did this by placing a hand on the ground and kissing it. They did not look at the *Caudillo*: only, as had become normal in relation to rulers, at the ground. Cortés said that he waited an hour there till they had all done that. They then went on together to Tenochtitlan.[71]

Montezuma, despite everything, had finally decided to greet Cortés, in company with his counsellors. Whatever doubts he might have had about the intentions of Cortés, or his status as a man or a god, the Mexican tradition of hospitality really made this essential: "This was the custom among the Indians: they accommodated strangers and always gave them good lodgings."[72] Even the Mexica themselves had received such treatment during their legendary wanderings. One precedent must have seemed ominous: King Achitometl of Culhuacan had given the Mexica similar hospitality, on their long peregrination. But like Montezuma he had entertained them because he feared them.[73]

Montezuma came forward on a litter with a canopy of green feathers and much gold and silver embroidery, and fitted with jade. It was carried by noblemen. Other noblemen busied themselves sweeping the ground in front. A man walked before the Emperor carrying a stick to mark his authority.[74] Montezuma himself probably wore an embroidered cloak, with a green feathered headdress and, on his feet, gold-decorated sandals, the upper parts of which were studded with precious stones. The litter was decked with flowers, cacao blossom, wreaths, garlands, and golden neck bands. The Emperor was well prepared with presents. His welcome was given first by another group of lords, assembled in two columns down the street. All also were well dressed, each differently. Among them were Totoquihuatzin, King of Tacuba, and Cacama, King of Texcoco, as well as Itzquauhtzin, the elderly Governor of Tlatelolco.

They also performed the ceremonial of kissing their hands after touching the earth. They swept the ground and spread cloaks in front of them. All except for Montezuma (and probably Cacama and Cuitláhuac) were barefoot.[75]

Montezuma descended from the litter. Cortés dismounted from his horse, and went forward to greet the Emperor. He made to embrace him "in the Spanish fashion" (a hug, presumably) but attendants stopped him. He did shake him by the hand.[76] Montezuma greeted him. His words were translated by Aguilar and Marina, though possibly (as earlier noticed) the latter did not fully understand what Montezuma was saying, since her own Coatzacoalcos dialect may have been far from Montezuma's more elegant language.[77] According to Cortés and other Spanish witnesses, these greetings were formal. Cortés apparently said: "Art thou not he? Art thou Montezuma?" To which Montezuma simply replied: "Yes, I am he." (The more dramatic welcome which Fr. Sahagún describes as occurring on the causeway seems to have taken place later.)[78] But we must assume that Montezuma, having girded himself to welcome Cortés, would have used common Mexican salutations such as "I bow down to you" or "I kiss your feet", ending with the equally usual "That is all".[79] Such welcomes were easily recognisable in Spanish terms, assuming that they were adequately translated. When Cortés spoke to Montezuma, he took off a necklace of pearls ("diamonds of glass", Cortés described them), apparently perfumed by musk, and placed it round the Emperor's neck. Montezuma motioned to a servant to give Cortés in return two necklaces of red snails' shells, from which hung eight shrimps made of gold, almost certainly intended to be associated with Quetzalcoatl.[80]

None of the Castilians would have admired the polished stone labret with on it the blue figure of a humming bird which the Emperor wore on his lower lip. Nor would they have approved his large ear-plugs and turquoise nose-ornament. But they could not fail to have been awed by the fine feather headdresses which both the Emperor and the nobles wore, as by the jaguar costumes of the senior warriors, with the animals' heads over their own.[81]

Montezuma asked his brother Cuitláhuac to remain with him while he led the way into the city. All the noblemen in the two columns followed, pressed the earth with their hands, and greeted Cortés. None looked at Montezuma. The whole assembly walked slowly back down the broad, straight street, lined, to begin with, by houses of whitewashed adobe, and then by palaces. The roofs were filled with people who showed admiration of what they saw.[82] "Who could count the multitude of men, women and children which had come out on the roofs, in their boats on the canals, or in the streets, to see us?" apostrophised Bernal Díaz years later, adding, in terms familiar to all readers of novels, "It all passes before my eyes as if it were yesterday."[83]

Cortés and his men were taken to the palace of Axayácatl, the home and headquarters of Montezuma's father, the emperor before last. This may have been the only large lodging available; but it was an action imbued with symbolism. Even though the Mexica did not worship their ancestors, they respected them. At this, the conclusion to their extraordinary journey, the arquebusiers let off a discharge, filling the air with acrid smoke.[84] The artillery was also fired to mark the triumph which all felt, if only temporarily, at having arrived in the city.[85] Doubtless the few Valencians in Cortés' army rejoiced especially at such a familiar celebration. The Valencian Rodrigo Borgia similarly marked his arrival in Rome as Pope Alexander VI. Very loud noise, especially of fireworks, has always characterised Valencian celebrations. These volleys astounded the Mexica.

Axayácatl's palace appeared to Cortés a "large and beautiful house" just off the main square.[86] It seems to have been originally built for Montezuma I, and was probably constructed by workmen from Chalco as part of the tribute which they paid after their defeat; indeed, perhaps by female workers from Chalco, if it be true that those battles had left few men alive.[87] It must have been large to have accommodated Cortés' retinue. Montezuma led Cortés to a big room facing the courtyard and proposed that he sit on a large throne. There he left him. He said that he should wait there until all his men were properly quartered – including the Tlaxcalans and Cholulans.[88] "Malinche," he said, making use of the title which all Mexica used for Cortés, "you are in your own house. So are your brothers. Rest."[89] He would return after dinner. Food was then brought: turkey and tortilla, as usual, but also grass for the horses, and women to make tortillas.[90]

This palace, wrote Fr. Aguilar, "was a wonder to behold. There were innumerable rooms inside, antechambers, splendid halls, mattresses of large cloaks, pillows of leather and tree fibre, good eiderdowns, and admirable white fur robes, as well as well-made wooden seats. The attendance too was something which befitted a great prince and lord":[91] or, it might be said, a man "born in brocade".

Montezuma did return later, after dinner, to the palace where Cortés was staying, as he had promised he would. He then made a speech. Cortés reported ten months later what he said when, perhaps with the help of Marina and Aguilar, he was describing the occasion in a letter to Charles V. But he had then an important point to make: that Montezuma had made an astonishing act of submission, which he, Cortés, looked on as a formal one, entitling him to regard later hostile actions of the Mexica as being as rebellious as those of the people of Cholula.

Cortés said that Montezuma began with a repetition of the words of welcome usual on all formal occasions in Tenochtitlan: "Our lord, you must be tired, you have experienced fatigue, but you have arrived at your city . . ." Part of the warmth of Montezuma's welcome derived from the natural good manners for which the Mexica were well known. Indeed, the heart of the very expression already cited ("thou hast endured fatigue") was used on all sorts of occasions.[92] Was Emerson right to say that politeness is virtue gone to seed? Or was Goethe more correct to insist that there is no outward form of courtesy which does not have a most profound moral formation? In the case of the Mexica, the latter must be right. Perhaps the greeting, though, was the warmer because Montezuma was genuinely dazzled by the brilliance, the energy, the self-confidence, and the power of the Castilians which he had now seen for himself. The Spaniards' approach to religion, king, country and family may seem conventional to the modern age. But to the tightly controlled Mexica the visitors must have appeared outlandish on a grand scale. Probably Montezuma would have wished to seem friendly towards such a monarch as Charles V who was able, at a distance, to command the loyalty of such men. One king often feels fellow feeling for another.

These statements of Montezuma, given the slowness of the translation, might have appeared to Cortés to show that the Emperor was willing to accept not only the friendship but the suzerainty of Charles; or, more probably, that the expression of friendship could be so twisted as to make it seem, without overt mendacity, that Montezuma had made such concessions. The Castilians knew that the expression "*esa es su casa*", "this is your house", does not always mean what it appears to. There is less than might at first sight seem between a statement which might say "Tell your king I am his most obedient and humble servant" – a phrase which means nothing formal – and "Tell your king that I am his loyal vassal" – a statement which could mean a cession of authority.[93]

What Montezuma said next is a matter of controversy. It is thus necessary to interrupt the narrative to discuss the sources (recalling an earlier discussion of Montezuma's motives). Cortés, writing ten months later to Charles V, said that Montezuma recognised, in his speech in November 1519, that the *Caudillo* and his *santa compañía* incarnated lost gods or leaders, whose return he had both expected and feared. Cortés reported Montezuma as admitting that the Mexica had been, in the beginning, foreigners, and had been led to the Valley of Mexico by a lord whose vassals they had then been. Then, Cortés went on, Montezuma described how "the lord who brought us, the Mexica, to Tenochtitlan went away to his native land. After a long time, he returned and found the people whom he had led had married locally, had had children, and had built towns in which to live. When he wished to lead them onwards, they were reluctant and did not even wish to recognise him as their leader." So he went away again: "And we have always held that those who descended from him would one day come back . . . and take us as vassals."[94] Montezuma did not now mention Quetzalcoatl (or at least was not remembered, or translated, as having mentioned Quetzalcoatl). So, Montezuma went on, still according to Cortés, since the Castilians came from the east where the sun rises, and because they had talked of a great king (Charles) who, so he understood, had heard of them (the Mexica), he considered that he (Charles) was their natural lord.[95] Montezuma was said by Cortés to have added: "So be assured that we will obey you and hold you as our lord, in the stead of that great lord. In that there will be no mistake or deception of any kind. And in all the land which I hold in my power you can command as you will, for you will be obeyed. And since you are in your native country and in your own house, enjoy yourself and rest from the labour of your journey and your battles." Montezuma is then represented by Cortés as saying that he knew all about the Spanish battles at Potonchan and against Tlaxcala; and that, contrary to what he supposed Cortés had been told on the way to Tenochtitlan, he, Montezuma, was no god but a mortal – to prove which point he raised his clothes to indicate his humanity; equally, he wanted to point out that it was untrue that the palace's walls were of gold (as, again, he supposed that Cortés had been assured). They were stone, lime, and adobe, as were most buildings in that city.[96]

This account by Cortés was reflected, naturally, in the biography which he helped to inspire by his later chaplain, López de Gómara: who in the 1550s recounted the occasion in much the same terms, though he caused Montezuma also to say that he recognised Cortés and the Castilians to be mortal men, that their horses resembled Mexican deer, and that even their guns recalled Mexican blowpipes. Charles V's official historian, Sepúlveda, who later talked to Cortés, added the refinement that Montezuma had said that he realised the King of Castile was "of the lineage of their own old leader".[97]

Several other conquistadors who wrote of this affair differ somewhat in their accounts. Bernal Díaz, for example, who also wrote in the 1550s, but in Guatemala not Spain, recorded the speech quite shortly: Montezuma, he said, insisted that "now that he had us with him, he was at our service, and would give us all that he possessed; and that it was surely true that we were those of whom his ancestors had spoken, when they talked of men who would come from where the sun rose to rule over those territories".[98] Fr. Aguilar, another eyewitness, who wrote in El Escorial in the 1560s, being in 1519 a soldier, went further even than Cortés in describing the abasement of Montezuma. He said that Montezuma announced himself before a notary, no less, to be the King of Castile's vassal; declared that he would serve him as he would his own lord; that the Castilians were most welcome, for they had come home, and that his ancestors had always said that armed, bearded men would one day come out of the sunrise, who were not to be fought against, since they were the future lords of the earth. Fr. Aguilar added that

Montezuma "believed us to be immortals and called us *teules*, that is gods".[99] Aguilar may, however, have been confusing this occasion with another one in January 1520 which will be discussed later.

A third conquistador, Andrés de Tapia, reported nothing of this speech at that time but describes it as having been made, in much the same terms, a few days later, after Cortés had discovered a secret hoard of gold.[100]

None of the witnessses for or opposed to Cortés in the *residencia* against him said anything about this occasion. But then they were not asked to.

There was also mention of this occasion in most late sixteenth-century works. Thus Fr. Sahagún (who described Montezuma's speech as having been made on the causeway) wrote that, after the usual conventional welcome ("O our lord, thou has suffered fatigue, thou hast endured weariness"), Montezuma said dramatically, "Thou hast come to govern thy city of Mexico. Thou hast come to descend upon thy mat, upon thy seat, which, for a moment, I have watched for thee, which I have guarded for thee. For thy governors are departed." Montezuma then listed the emperors of Mexico who had preceded him and added: "O that one of them might . . . marvel at what to me now hath befallen, at what I see . . . I by no means merely dream . . . I do not see in my sleep, I do not merely dream that I see thee, that I look into thy face. I have been afflicted for some time. I have gazed at the unknown place whence thou hast come – from among the clouds, from among the mists. . . . The rulers departed maintaining that thou wouldst come to visit thy city, and that thou wouldst come to descend on thy mat; and now it hath been fulfilled."[101]

It seems, finally, that the lost so-called Crónica X, probably written by a Mexican, in Nahuatl, in the 1530s, included some speech of Montezuma's along these lines. For all the works which are held to derive from it include such a statement, though in less dramatic terms than those of Sahagún. Fr. Durán, for example, suggested that, in addition, Montezuma not only said that he had been an interim steward of the kingdom which Cortés' father Quetzalcoatl had abandoned, but (on the evidence of Fr. Aguilar, who was there) accepted to be both a vassal of the King of Spain and a Christian; while the Codex Ramírez, which also derived from the Crónica X, stated that Montezuma merely declared himself to be at the service of the King of Spain, and that all his treasure was at the disposal of Cortés.[102]

Let us leave aside the small matters: whether Montezuma greeted the Spaniards on the causeway; whether there was a notary present on the occasion of the speech; and to what Montezuma was alluding when he said that he was a mortal and that his palace was not made of gold. This speech of Montezuma's, along with another later one, has been described as "apocryphal";[103] as constituting "very probably fiction";[104] or as reflecting a "mythical historical anachronism".[105] It has been suggested that Cortés allowed the *Nunc Dimittis* to influence his style in phrasing the report of that section of the speech where Montezuma insists that he is a mortal not a god.[106]

Cortés was ruthless, imaginative and devious. His temperament was that of quicksilver. Yet it is difficult to believe that he invented the speech in the sense of writing it all, with no reference to what was said. Montezuma did, after all, subsequently accept abasement at Castilian hands. He must at this first meeting have shown something which went beyond the customary if extravagant courtesy. Some surprising element of submission may have been implicit in the Mexican emperor's conduct from the occasion of his first meeting with Cortés: the visual propaganda of the Spanish array and the knowledge of the brutalities at Cholula must have counted a good deal.

Had Cortés been as inventive as some have argued, he would surely have been denounced later by his own comrades. Cortés' letter to the King, describing what happened (the Second *Carta de Relación*), was published in 1522 by the German printer, Jacob Cromberger, in Seville. It had a wide circulation. Many people, including many conquistadors, read it. Had there been a real difference of opinion as to what happened, there were enough men alive who would have known the truth, and who subsequently came to hate Cortés, to have made it difficult for any mendacity to have remained undenounced. One of the two interpreters on this occasion, Fr. Gerónimo de Aguilar, gave evidence against Cortés in the latter's enquiry in 1529. By then an enemy of Cortés, he would not have hesitated to accuse his one-time *caudillo* of an untruth about anything as important as this – had it occurred.

Nor could Bernal Díaz and Aguilar have conspired with Cortés to give a single story. Díaz wrote in the 1550s, after Cortés was dead, in Guatemala. Aguilar wrote when a monk in the Augustinian monastery of El Escorial in the 1560s. It strains credulity to think that either would have agreed to collaborate with Fr. Sahagún, then in Mexico, and others who went to great trouble to collect what they thought were honest, indigenous impressions of what transpired.[107]

It is certainly possible that, by the 1560s, the myth of Montezuma's submission was so established that it was unquestioningly accepted, even by people who had been present, and who might have been expected to have known a different story. But Bernal Díaz was nobody's man. He wrote among other things in order to bring the figure of Cortés down to size.

The alleged concessions by Montezuma to Castilian suzerainty can be explained by Cortés' special, probably wilful, abuse of the customary courtesy of the Mexicans: even of the remark that Montezuma's treasure was at the disposal of the Castilians. Cortés' excuse for suggesting that

Montezuma made these concessions was that he had been exceptionally polite. He probably seized on Montezuma's speech with the determination of a man who has seen that his opponent has committed a mistake in chess. Cortés was not innocent in using the words of Montezuma in this way. But in his reporting he probably did not depart so far from the reality of the Emperor's remarks as has been supposed.

At all events, it must be likely that Cortés replied with dignity through Marina and Aguilar: "Have confidence, Montezuma, fear nothing. We love you greatly. Our heart is today well satisfied. We see you face to face, we hear you. We have wished for a long time to see you, to hear you speak in person."

The Mexican emperor and nobility were, like Teudile and the Totonacs on the coast, probably as surprised by the appearance of Marina as interpretress as they were by the horses and the guns. They would have been informed about the existence of Marina from their agents with Cortés on the way. But they had not seen her or heard her at work. As with the spokesmen on the coast, they would have been amazed, since she was a woman.

Whatever was or was not said by Montezuma and Cortés, the public mood among the Mexica was obviously different from what the Emperor conveyed. For no one of any standing could have avoided realising that the Spaniards, having arrived at Vera Cruz in the year 1-Reed, Quetzalcoatl's year, had chosen to enter the capital on the day 1-Wind, the sign of Quetzalcoatl in his capacity as a whirlwind. But they may have had a different version of the significance of Quetzalcoatl under this sign from that of their emperor. It was a sign as well regarded by robbers as by wizards. The latter were expected to use their opportunities on this day to hypnotise their victims while asleep, establish themselves in their houses, eat the stores, violate the women and, acting as robbers also, steal the treasure.[108] Thus the mood was "as if everyone had eaten stupefying mushrooms, as if they had seen something astonishing. Terror dominated everyone, as if all the world were being disembowelled. People went to sleep in terror."[109] The flutes and whistles which the Mexica played to themselves in their houses would have been muted. There was usually singing and dancing every evening in the state schools where the humble were educated. No doubt on 8 November there was silence.

Yet at midnight the conches would have sounded, as they always did, from the top of the Great Temple and on the little shrines in the mountains; and, unseen by the Spaniards, the priests both in the city and in the distance would have bled themselves to ensure that, Castile or no, in a few hours the sun would rise again.[110]

IV
Cortés and Montezuma

20

An image of Quetzalcoatl

*Those wizards were called Temacpalitotque . . . when they wanted to rob a
house they converted themselves into an image of Ehecatl or Quetzalcoatl,
and up to fifteen or twenty of them who understood this went dancing to
where they were going to rob, being guided by one who carried the image of
Quetzalcoatl, and another who carried the arm, from the elbow to the hand,
of a woman who had died in her first childbirth . . .*
Florentine Codex, Book x

I F THE NIGHT of 8 November 1519 was unusually quiet for Tenochtitlan, the dawn of the 9th was probably normal. An early riser among
the conquistadors would have seen boys hastening in the dark along
the streets near the Palace of Axayácatl with coals to add to the braziers on
the top of the pyramids, or girls carrying tortillas for the priests to eat.
They might have seen merchants returning in canoes with their goods
from far away: they always came before dawn, in order to avoid
publicity. Everyone would have heard the priests themselves greet the
new day by blowing on conch shells. Later, the expedition would have
heard the beating of a drum on the top of the round temple of
Quetzalcoatl to mark the rising of the sun, the triumphant revival of the
"turquoise prince, the soaring eagle": the beginning of the working day.

That new day must have led Cortés and his companions to speculate
about their position. In later life, Cortés implied that, by the mere act of
entering Tenochtitlan, he had captured the empire. That was a retrospec-
tive judgement.[1] He may have planned to do that. But the dangers of his
position at the time seemed, in that unpredictable and, as it appeared,
half-magic city, severe.

For the moment, all demands made by the Castilians were immediately
met: for white tortillas, turkeys, eggs, fresh water. The horses were fed
grain, and everything else that their masters requested. They were
bedded down with flowers.[2] The dogs were equally well treated. Even in
a large city, and one accustomed to visitors, the demands caused by the
necessity of feeding the strangers must have been considerable. But for
the moment, these caused neither resentment nor trouble. The extra
requirements were met from reserves.

Cortés and his followers spent several days resting and seeing the sights
of the city, in the company of Montezuma's attendants.[3] Of course, most

of the conquistadors were provincials who had never lived in a capital, and for that reason their expressions of amazement were the greater. They were thus as much astonished by the grid of narrow streets, hardly big enough for two people to walk abreast, as they were by the broad avenues, of well-beaten earth, which had canals in the middle and walkways on both sides. They observed with appreciation the great houses with their large courtyards and gardens, many of which were cultivated with fruit and vegetables as well as flowering trees. They saw the constant flow of people in and out of the houses, which even a hard-bitten conquistador such as Diego de Ordaz thought superior to those at home.[4] They realised that all the buildings had flat roofs, and that the characteristic dwelling place was a walled or fenced compound which surrounded a number of separate habitations with a congeries of small rooms which gave on to an open patio: not wholly unlike living conditions in Seville, they would have thought. (The average lodging housed ten to fifteen persons. That too would have seemed recognisable to a Sevillano of the early sixteenth century.)[5] The Spaniards would perhaps have looked into some of the houses of the ordinary Mexicans and seen how "they have usually no furnishings or clothes other than the poor garments which they wear, one or two stones for grinding maize, some pots in which to cook the maize, and a sleeping mat of reeds."[6] Every house had some terracotta figurine of a god, and all well-to-do houses had many such images, in stone or wood. These houses were of adobe brick, the roofs made from maguey leaves or pine, the floor either of clay or some volcanic conglomerate. Walls were plastered with mud. There would be a lot of smoke, especially in the morning, when the women would be preparing the tortillas for the main meal of the day: for the chimney was no more known there than it was in Castile. The hearth was in every house the centre of activity. The three stones on which the logs were burned were sacred. Later in the day the Mexican women would be observed weaving: their constant task, whatever their age and class.

In better houses, lime plaster and stucco were much used. The conquistadors would have seen that sometimes two small families connected by blood lived together.[7] They would have noticed that the houses of the rich were often ornamented, much as in Spain successful families placed their coats of arms above their doors. They might have been surprised to see how, especially on the outskirts of the city, the streets were interspersed with allotments, often *chinampas*, on which the families nearby grew their fresh vegetables (most families even without these gardens grew flowers, on their roofs or in their courtyards, while many had a turkey, a parrot, some rabbits and perhaps a dog, all being fattened to be eaten). The Spaniards would have seen the innumerable sellers of steaming chocolate, the favoured drink of the Mexican upper class, and heard both men and women continually rattling gourds of several kinds in preparation for some festival ahead.

Of course the visitors had spent two weeks in Tlaxcala and some of these sights would have been familiar to them. The Mexica and the Tlaxcalans wore much the same dress, except that even the upper class in Tlaxcala were obliged by the Mexican blockade to wear cloaks of maguey fibre rather than the cotton which was favoured by the Mexica. The Spaniards were presumably now familiar with the local cloaks tied in a knot on the right shoulder, worn over loincloths. But among the Mexica these would differ in colour and design according to the class of the wearer. They would soon have remarked the little differences of dress which in Tenochtitlan, though not in Tlaxcala, indicated noblemen (tassles, embroidery, fringes – and greater length of clothing). Probably there were more women in the streets of Tenochtitlan than in Tlaxcala.

There was in fact no shortage of prostitutes in the city, perhaps descendants of some vanquished tribe. The Florentine Codex described a typical one: how "she parades, she moves lasciviously . . . she appears like a flower, looks gaudy . . . views herself in a mirror . . . she bathes . . . she goes about with her head high, [she is] rude, drunk, shameless, eating mushrooms. She paints her face, variously paints her face, her face is covered with rouge, her cheeks are coloured . . . rubbed with cochineal . . . she arranges her hair like horns [a fashionable style of hair arrangement]" . . . finds pleasure in her body . . .; and "she waves at one . . . beckons with her head . . ."[8]

Such other women as would have been seen in the street would have tied their hair with braid or with coloured ribbons, would not (normally at least) have painted their faces, having been warned against such an indulgence by their mothers; but they might have dyed their hair dark blue with indigo (the numerous conquistadors who found Indians as mistresses would discover too that many women in Tenochtitlan, especially if Otomí in origin, tattooed or painted their bodies too, with elaborate designs, for erotic purposes).[9]

Some of those whom the conquistadors saw in the streets would be wearing paper loincloths only. These would be men or women who had confessed sins (adultery, for example) to Tlazolteotl, goddess both of confession and of carnal love, and were doing penance for them, singing and dancing in public (Tlazolteotl, "she who eats filth" – that is, sins – was also "the one who takes away the defilement"). Since only one confession was allowed in a lifetime, most of these penitents would have been elderly: a second confession led to a public stoning to death. At night the Spaniards would have seen the same sights as in Tlaxcala: men and women sleeping on mats under cloaks, sometimes using covers of feathers, which seemed "similar to . . . woollen cloth, like our fur hats".[10]

The activity must everywhere have seemed remarkable. The lakeside, for example, would have been dotted with snarers of birds, with nets over their wooden frames, as well as fishermen, busy with harpoons or spear-throwers (*atlatls*, as also used in war). The sound of the paddles of innumerable canoes dipping rhythmically into the water of the lake must have seemed to some Sevillanos a reassuring reminder of the Guadalquivir.

The Castilians must too have seen dancing, for there was so much of it: not just ceremonial dancing at festivals but flower dances, dances of subject peoples, dances on stilts, even dances of cripples, dances by torchlight, dances in the rain, traditional dances and brand new ones, dancing every night in torchlight, in public places and in private houses.[11]

The conquistadors can be forgiven if they thought that they had reached an exotic version of Venice: a city of which they would have heard, but probably not visited: not just "another Venice" but a "great Venice"; even "Venice the rich".[12] They would have realised the importance of religion in Mexico, but found the manifestations of it, even the mathematics, both alarming and complex.

Bernal Díaz noticed that not only were there for sale loads of human excrement to help with the manufacture of salt and the curing of skins and to serve as a fertiliser, but that "on all the roads, they have shelters made of reeds or straw or grass, so that the people can retire when they wish to do so, and purge their bowels unseen".[13] The lake was used as a sewer, though that may not have been effective since the outflow, though it did exist, was modest. Rubbish was also transported by canoe to remote places on the edge of the city, to assist in the further extension of the terrain.

What the Mexica thought of the Castilians is impossible to know: but as well as feeling admiration, interest and fear, they could hardly have avoided noticing that, for most Castilians, a bath was a rarity. The Mexica were always washing, in water obtained through the aqueduct, or in the lake, and would often go to the popular baths in the numerous stone steam houses (where birching, with grasses, or massage was also available). They would wash their hair in them with soap made from the pulp of avocado, the fruit of the soap tree or the roots of the *saponaria americana*.[14] The Mexica would have seemed to the Spaniards as conscious of the need for baths as had been the Moors. The conquistadors on the other hand probably smelled strongly. (A prayer to the goddess of water, Chalchiuhtlicue, "she of the skirt of gems", companion of the rain god Tlaloc, would often have seemed desirable.)

The followers of Cortés, men born in Seville or Medellín, in Cuéllar or in Medina del Campo, would have realised above all that they were in the heart of a prosperous, clean, tidy community. The armies of street sweepers, those who kept the canals clean, the men who placed braziers at night at regular intervals, those who collected human excrement for fertilisers or to cure leather – all seemed remarkably well organised.

Of one further element, both similar to and contrasting with what they knew in Europe, the conquistadors must have been especially aware. Those who first wrote of what they saw, including Cortés, described the distinctive pyramidical temples of the Mexica as mosques, *"mezquitas"*, and compared the Mexican costume to that of the Moors.[15] These conquistadors were, after all, men of a generation used to the idea of conquest of another culture, if not by their fathers in Granada, then by the great-grandfathers of their great-grandfathers in Seville and Córdoba. The word "conquistador" was one used by the Castilian victors against Islam. Vestiges of El-Andalus were everywhere to be seen in Spain. Had not the German traveller Thomas Münzer written in 1492 in respect of Seville: "Even now there remain many monuments and traces of the old regime"?[16] The church of San Salvador in Seville was still the main mosque, barely touched. Some of the walls of the new cathedral in Seville had been parts of another mosque. One did not have to visit Granada (none of the expedition came from there) to know of beautiful Moorish gardens, for the Alcázar in Seville (reconstructed by Pedro the Cruel) was a favourite royal dwelling.

This memory of another conquered civilisation pervaded Spanish confidence, in the improbable circumstances of being in Tenochtitlan. For a Castilian conquistador, there could not have been much difference between a gold labret of Mexico and gold earrings from, say, Jaen; between the embroidered textiles of El-Andalus and those of Texcoco; or between the excellent glazed bowls of the caliphate found in the valley of the Guadalquivir and those of Cholula. The market in Tlatelolco recalled the *souk* in Granada. For Cortés, the memory of the conquest of El-Andalus had been maintained by the shadow of the great castle of Medellín (originally built by the Moors: had not the ferocious Countess Beatriz imprisoned her son in the Moorish well?), as by the presence of an active Moorish minority, whose annual November fair was held in a street close to where he had himself been born. In Cortés' childhood, a Moor, Mahomet Rondé y Maray, had had a small vineyard close to the Cortés' family's own on the river Ortigas.[17] If Islam could be conquered, why not Huitzilopochtli?

No doubt Cortés and his expedition were at all times conscious that they possessed the advantage of a true religion. Some, above all Cortés himself, saw too that, to that benefit, the capacity for writing offered another mark of superiority.[18] The Mexica communicated often, by word of mouth; but Cortés was always writing notes, of command or merely of information. To an *escribano* as he was – the word indicates the nature of the mission – his advantage in possessing an alphabet must have seemed obvious.

Cortés could not have known what his next step would be: "take Montezuma dead or alive" had sounded well as a promise when at the coast. As a policy in Tenochtitlan it must have seemed extreme. The size of the city, the number of the Mexica, and the character of the protection afforded by the drawbridges must have concentrated Cortés' mind. Three hundred Castilians and a few thousand untrained and unpredictable allies with whom he could not communicate directly were scarcely a powerful combination among a population of at least 50,000 adults. Montezuma, whatever verbal concession he may or may not have made, seemed too to have a substantial bodyguard.[19]

Cortés soon found out how large the city was; how it was divided into four quarters, with Tlatelolco constituting a fifth one;[20] how large avenues meeting in the central square separated these districts; how each quarter had its own main temple, the headquarters of the district governors;[21] and how these districts were themselves divided into smaller zones, whose relation to the older divisions of the tribe, *calpultin*, is learnedly disputed, though it is certain that they also each had a temple as something like a civic centre.[22] But the *Caudillo* was slower to discover the size of Montezuma's empire. He knew that it reached to the Gulf of Mexico. He took some time to appreciate that it also extended to the "Southern Sea". He thought that the territory was nearly as big as Spain: a calculation which overestimated the enterprise, for the empire of Mexico seems to have been about 125,000 square miles, in comparison with Spain's size of about 300,000.[23] But the total area with a culture comparable to that of old Mexico, that is, including Tlaxcala, Michoacan and Yucatan, would have given this "new world" half a million square miles.

The day after their arrival in the Mexican capital, Cortés and several intimates paid a visit to Montezuma in his palace on the other side of the great square, in front of the temple. He went with four captains: Velázquez de León, Diego de Ordaz, Pedro de Alvarado and Gonzalo de Sandoval, the two first representing, as it were, the followers of Governor Velázquez; and the two last his own friends. They were accompanied by five soldiers (Bernal Díaz among them, according to his own account).[24]

The palace of Montezuma, the *tecpan*, was a new building. Before the present reign, and the rebuilding of so much of the city after the flood of 1502, the emperors had lived where Cortés and his expedition were lodged. The new palace from outside seemed to have been built of marble, but it was in fact of alabaster, jasper and black stone shot through by veins of red and white. The exterior seems to have been decorated with depictions of eagles and jaguars.[25] Inside, many ceilings were of wood, well finished, and sometimes carved to represent the branches of trees. The interior walls were often painted. Over the main door, the symbol of the rabbit showed the day when the palace had been finished. The ground floor was the administrative centre of the empire. It included workshops for craftsmen, comprising potters, goldsmiths and feather-workers. It was, therefore, vast: indeed, it covered nearly six acres, and had at least a hundred big rooms, including offices, centres of worship, kitchens, and rooms for many members of the family and retainers of different sorts. The floors were often covered by mats, while the grander ones had been allocated cotton, rabbit fur and feathers. One room was painted with scenes of the beauties of Mexico.[26] The second floor of the building was the Emperor's dwelling. Servants, sycophants and petitioners, as well as treasurers, majordomos and accountants, thronged three large courtyards, in one of which there was a fine fountain. The atmosphere seemed to the conquistadors uncannily Mediterranean in character.[27]

Fires burned throughout the night in this palace in copper braziers. Servants took it in turns to feed them with wood. This society without candles relied on torches from these braziers; to allow one to go out would have been a crime, as well as a bad omen. One brazier stood in the hall of the palace, another in a courtyard which served as a waiting room. A third was in the room where Montezuma slept.[28] There were many wooden sculptures and screens. Much featherwork and many cloaks were held in stores. In rooms or dependencies off the main palace, there were numerous special agencies: for example, the House of Song, where groups of Mexicans could be found constantly dancing, either for pleasure or in rehearsal for some great event; and the Cloud Serpent House, a magnificent dressing-up cupboard, where instruments and costumes were kept for every conceivable ceremony, secular or sacred, popular or military.

Montezuma received the Castilian delegation courteously, putting Cortés on his right on a mat. The Emperor usually sat on a seat made of a bundle of reeds woven into a regular throne, with a back (though it is possible that that had been replaced by a famous temple stone, a sculpture of complexity, which Montezuma had had made to mark the last New Fire ceremony of 1507).[29]

Through Marina and Aguilar, Cortés then gave a polished version of his usual speech on the benefits of Christianity. He said that the Christians worshipped the one true and only God. He explained that the son of God, Jesus Christ, had suffered death and passion on a cross to save the world. This Christ had risen from the dead three days after his execution and had then gone to heaven. He and His Father had created everything. As for the beings which the Mexica looked on as gods, these were, in Cortés' opinion, devils. Their looks were bad and their deeds worse.

Cortés also explained the Christian story of the creation and how Christians believed that all men were brothers, being descendants of Adam and Eve: including the Mexica. The very next year Paracelsus would put forward his heretical theory that there had been two creations, one in the West as well as one in the East.[30] But Cortés knew nothing of that (any more than he could have known of the activities in Germany of the still obscure monk of Wittenberg, Martin Luther).

Cortés hoped that Montezuma would soon end his sacrificing of other Indians precisely because all, priests and victims alike, were brothers. His king, said Cortés, would soon send over men many times more holy than himself: a first allusion to the friars, Franciscans or Dominicans, whom, from his experience in the Caribbean, Cortés wanted to encourage (as opposed to priests, such as Fr. Juan Díaz). Cortés perhaps also explained that he had come to Tenochtitlan not only to present the respects of his own monarch but to establish whether the Mexica or the Tlaxcalans were responsible for the disputes between them.[31]

Montezuma listened carefully to these extraordinary remarks in the interpretation of Aguilar and Marina. How much we wish that we knew what mistakes they made, what shades of meaning they added or subtracted!

One of the Emperor's nephews then produced some golden jewels and ten loads of fine cloth each for Cortés and his four captains. To the soldiers with Cortés he gave two gold necklaces and two loads of cloaks. It was obvious that the Emperor had informed himself about Castilian ranks and classes before deciding as to which presents to give.[32] Montezuma also gave Cortés many beautifully embroidered cotton cloaks which Cortés thought were remarkable, "considering that they were not silk" (the qualification betraying his continuing preference for that commodity).[33] According to Bernal Díaz, Montezuma then repeated what he had said in his speech of welcome: namely, that he regarded it as certain that the Castilians were those whom the ancestors of the Mexica had predicted would come from the direction of the sunrise. He attributed his previous reluctance to receive the Castilians to bad advice.[34]

Cortés and his entourage then left with the friendly words: "Already it is your time for dinner." Presumably he had heard the rustle of footmen, as well as the familiar noise of plates being prepared. Montezuma thanked Cortés for his visit. As the Castilians left, they saw the Emperor indeed beginning to dine.[35] Afterwards, Cortés said to his followers: "We have done our duty, considering it is the first attempt."[36]

Two or three days after their arrival in Tenochtitlan, the *Caudillo* visited the market at Tlatelolco, of which he had probably heard much from conquistadors in his party who had seen it already.

The size of this emporium astonished the Spaniards. Cortés thought that the great arcaded space in which the market was established was twice the size of the great square of Salamanca.[37] Others in his party who claimed to have been in Constantinople, and all over Italy including Rome, said that they had seen nothing like it.[38]

Of course the conquistadors saw this market through Castilian eyes, and compared it with what they knew in Castile. No doubt they underestimated the ceremonial activity implicit in all exchange of goods. All the same, Tlatelolco was the centre of Mexican commerce. It was the greatest trading place in the Americas.[39] It had been founded in the reign of Cuauhtlatoa, a king of Tlatelolco of the mid-fifteenth century who, the Tlatelolca insisted, had really been responsible for victories falsely attributed by history to Montezuma I, Emperor of Mexico at that time. It was there that trading in fine cotton cloth first began, as in many other things.[40] There too several of the incidents had happened which had led to the, for the Tlatelolca, disastrous wars of 1475 with the people of Tenochtitlan.[41] That defeat of 1475 had led the emperors of Mexico to close the great temple of Tlatelolco, but they had not dared, or wished, to touch the market.

Every day, thousands came to exchange goods. Usually they were bartered. Only if there was a disgreement about a value did the traders have recourse to cocoa beans or cloaks.[42] For this reason, the market at Tlatelolco (and, therefore, all the smaller markets in the country as a matter of course) was not concerned primarily with profits, in the classical sense; it was rather an easy method of redistribution smiled on by the authorities.[43] Market day was every five days. Twice as many visitors came then as on other days. The distinguishing mark of the place seemed to the Castilians, as did so many other things in old Tenochtitlan, to be that there was "much order".[44] The authorities looked after the management of the market for the good of the people so that they should not be harmed, abused, nor deceived, nor even disdained. Directors were appointed to ensure that no one cheated each other and to establish how articles might be priced and sold.[45] Three judges sat within the market and instantly made their decisions in disputes. If someone tried to sell goods known to have been stolen, he would be executed; unless he told from whom he had bought them. Every product had its own selling area; just as, as Bernal Díaz reflected, occurred in the great market of Medina del Campo.[46] The place seems to have been as much a source of pleasure as markets were in the old world: it was "so inviting, and so appealing and gratifying ... that great crowds attended".[47] Many goods came there which had been imported by private persons from outside the empire without explicit governmental permission. The government seems indeed to have had only a tenuous control over the commerce carried on, except in respect of gold and copper, where taxes were levied at the market stall where they had not previously been imposed on the producers.[48]

There were about fifty different sections for the sale of precious metals, pottery, clothes, food, knives, stones, and housing materials, such as mats, whitewash and even roofs. Manufactured and raw materials were also separately sold. Full-time and long-distance merchants exchanged luxuries, and innumerable small families, whose main task was to look after their farms, sold their maize cakes (*tamales*) or maize porridge. There were stalls where birds, animals and skins were sold. Salt and cotton cloaks were the most sought-after products. They too of course had their zones.[49] Cortés said that there was a sector which sold cotton on a more elaborate scale than obtained at the silk market in Granada.[50] All goods were sold by number and size rather than weight – for weights were unknown in old Mexico: gold dust, for example (all imported, since there was no gold in the Valley of Mexico), was sold in goose quills[51]. Many sections of the market provided services: for example, haircutting. There was another department where slaves were sold, tied to poles by collars, much as the Portuguese in Lisbon tied the slaves of Guinea. Prices varied: If the slave was not highly skilled as a dancer, his price was thirty large cloaks; but if he danced well his price was forty.[52] Canoes full of human excrement were disposed of to tan skins.[53] The market at Tlatelolco, like most great markets, was a haunt of prostitutes and gamblers.

A large pyramid, with a temple to Huitzilopochtli on top, dominated the market. This stood at one side of the square.[54] It had been reopened by Montezuma after thirty years of neglect following the war between Tlatelolco and Tenochtitlan in the 1470s. During those years, it had been a public lavatory and a rubbish dump. But Montezuma needed the support of the merchants (*pochteca*) whose headquarters were in Tlatelolco. So he favoured them. He even permitted them the honour of going to war again on behalf of his Triple Alliance. They still had to pay tribute as if they were a conquered people.[55] They also had a military governor (*cuauhtlatoani*) appointed by Montezuma rather than an independent monarch; the same man had filled the position for forty years, since the 1470s. But the temple had been reopened.[56]

Cortés returned to Tenochtitlan, and to the Great Temple there.[57] Before this monument he and his colleagues halted, seeking no doubt, in the style of hidalgos, not to seem to be surprised. The edifice, 113 steps up in two parallel staircases, was built at too steep an angle for easy climbing, that is, forty-five degrees: "higher than the cathedral of Seville", Cortés insisted, with his usual competitive sense.[58] (The Giralda in Seville was, however, then about 260 feet high; the pyramid 150 feet.)[59] The pyramid in Tenochtitlan was actually not as high as that of Cholula, and its size, 250 feet square, made it also considerably smaller than the Temple of the Sun at Teotihuacan which, of course, Cortés did not know.[60] Like most temples of the region, it had at its summit a platform of stone, on which stood two sanctuaries, one, to Tlaloc, to the north; the other to Huitzilopochtli, to the south. These two gods, of rain and of the sun, the forces which determine the prosperity of the earth, were thus joint objects of devotion on the summit of a temple built by a people which had once been nomadic and now was sedentary.[61] Each shrine had its own idols within, and outside some guardian idols too. The existence of the two sanctuaries reflected a now long-ago compromise between the priests of Tlaloc, who had been in the valley before the Mexica arrived; and those of Huitzilopochtli, the god of the Mexica.

The pyramid in its construction was probably supposed to recreate the, to the Mexica, sacred hill of Coatepec ("serpent mountain"), birthplace of Huitzilopochtli, perhaps even the earth itself. It symbolised the celestial order of the Mexica: for it was built on four platforms. The three lower platforms each comprised twelve sections. The top pyramid was the thirteenth and smallest. On it stood the temples. Both pyramid and shrines were new. They had only been inaugurated in 1487, in the sumptuous ceremony already discussed. But this new monument had been built over four older edifices constructed at intervals since the foundation of the city.

As with all important places of this nature, this temple had its permanent staff of black-dressed priests (and some priestesses), the lobes of their ears in tatters from their having taken so much blood from them in minor acts of sacrifice, their hair uncombed and knotted, their faces ashen from fasting and offering blood (most priests took blood from themselves as penance at least once a day).[62] From their necks, many of these priests hung as pectorals the conch shells with which they would mark the dawn and dusk. Cortés reported that no women were allowed entry into these temples, but he was misinformed: perhaps he did not identify the priestesses in their black robes; indeed they played a minor part.[63]

Montezuma escorted his visitors on this part of their tour. Some of the priests helped him climb the "jade steps", as this staircase was symbolically called – the steepness was to ensure that the dead bodies of victims fell without hindrance. But Cortés refused to allow the priests to assist him or his comrades, though he was probably at least in light armour. He began the climb without help, passing, or even stepping on, the monumental relief portrait of the dead and fractured Coyolxauhqui, the sister of Huitzilopochtli, which was set in the stone floor just in front of the pyramid ("Huitzilopochtli's dining table"), and on to which the bodies of those sacrificed above landed after being thrown down the ceremonial stairs.[64] Cortés, passing the frog sculptures on the side of the temple, as the victims of thousands of sacrifices who had preceded him up (and dead, down) those alarming stairs had done, could have had no clear idea as to what awaited him.

At the top, Montezuma remarked: "You must be tired from the climb." This phrase was, as we have seen, an obligatory piece of Mexican courtesy. Cortés replied that he and his friends were "never tired": a boast which must have seemed as inappropriate as it was churlish, especially to the sweating Castilians beside him.[65] His and his fellow conquistadors' first sight at the top would have been the polychrome reclining figure of a *chacmool*, divine messenger between priest and god; and their second, the green execution stone (*techcatl*), in front of the shrines.[66] They would, of course, have seen the thatch-roofed shrines set at the back, to the east of the platform, each being crowned by "a beautiful battlement of small black stones . . . all in perfect order and pattern, the entire frame stuccoed in white, with red paint".[67] Cortés seems to have thought that the shrines were "very pretty".[68] The sanctuaries were guarded by two stone figures, covered with turquoise and mother-of-pearl jewels, with gold masks, belts of snakes made of gold, and necklaces of human heads, also in gold.[69] One of these two figures seems to have been Coatlicue, the earth goddess ("serpent skirt", Huitzilopochtli's mother), the greatest of known Mexican sculptures, with two intertwined serpents as her head.[70] Above both sanctuaries, presumably in the centre, there was a colossal greenstone (diorite) head of Coyolxauhqui, incarnation of night, whose dismembered effigy in relief had been at the bottom of the staircase. The shrine of Huitzilopochtli was encircled by stone butterflies, to mark the sun; that of Tlaloc by shells, standing for water.

Montezuma enjoyed eminences. He often had himself carried to the summit of Chapultepec, past the bas-reliefs of his predecessors (and now of himself) carved there, to see the superlative view from the summit.[71] He, with pride, pointed out to his guests the sights of Mexico: the two cities below, joined by causeways, with their teeming markets and straight streets, many of them with canals; the big houses with their flat roofs, on which were often gardens;[72] the many secondary pyramids crowned by lesser temples; the great menagerie, such as was then only kept in Europe by a few Italian princes (and then on a smaller scale), in which Montezuma kept sacred animals, such as jaguars, especially important for the royal family; the often exotic vegetation and bright colours; the causeways to the north, south and west; the lovely lake, its surface covered by canoes; the towns, great and small, on the further side of the water; in the distance, the sierra, with the majestic volcanoes; and the col between the volcanoes, over which Cortés had himself passed, with his "*santa compañía*". The clear air and cloudless blue sky would at that time of year have seemed to the conquistadors as invigorating as the sheer splendour of the scene.

Cortés, impressed but determined not to show it, suggested to Fr. Olmedo, who had accompanied him, that now might be the moment to see if Montezuma would allow the Castilians to build their church on this vantage point. The idea was not quite ridiculous: Montezuma had himself had built a special temple (the *Coacalco*) within the temple precinct to accommodate the gods of conquered peoples. But Fr. Olmedo was doubtful. The idea seemed precipitate. Cortés instead requested to be shown the sanctuary. Montezuma asked the priests to usher them in.

It seems that the conquistadors went into the southernmost shrine, that to Huitzilopochtli. Here there were apparently two altars, one presided over by Huitzilopochtli himself, the other being dedicated to the mysterious and elusive figure of Tezcatlipoca. This was the first time that Castilians had seen these alarming idols close to. Probably in the dark they would even now have seen little more, to begin with, than the carved designs on the bottom of the sculptures – designs which were intended to be, as it were, buried in the gloom. They would have seen the eyes of shining stones. Huitzilopochtli carried a golden bow in his left hand, and golden arrows in his right, to recall that he was god of war and hunting. Hanging round his neck were other golden objects depicting the faces of men, and silver ones representing their hearts.

Behind the effigies of the principal gods was a smaller granite figure of something which appeared to be half man, half lizard, covered with a cloak and precious stones. In front of the idols were braziers. In these there were the still warm hearts of captives who had been sacrificed earlier in the day. The walls were, as usual, splashed and encrusted with blood. The smell was strong. Priests were to be seen in the shadows mournfully beating a large upright drum, a *huehuetl*.

The Spaniards were evidently disturbed to see these to them dreadful figures, whose purpose was of course to terrify, though they were practically never seen except by priests. Since the idols themselves do not survive, there is some doubt about what they were made of: both Cortés and his friend, Andrés de Tapia (who climbed up some months later), said that the main statues were made of seeds kneaded together by the blood of sacrificed humans, Tapia adding for good measure that this was of children. But the chronicler Fr. Durán wrote that Huitzilopochtli was made of wood, and was seated on a blue wooden bench as if it had been a litter; while, he said, in the northern sanctuary, Tlaloc was to be seen in stone, adding: "his face was very ugly, like a serpent with huge fangs".[73]

Cortés said to Montezuma: "I do not understand how such a great lord and wise man as you are has not realised that these idols are not gods, but bad things, called devils. So I hope you will allow us to place our sign of the cross here as well as a picture of the Virgin Mary and you will see how afraid your gods will be." The priests present were annoyed. Nor was Montezuma at all pleased. He said: "Had I known that you would say such dishonourable things, I would not have shown you my gods. We hold these beings to be good, they bring us health, water and good crops, rain and, when we need them, victories, and so we have to sacrifice to them. I request you not to say other things like that to their dishonour."[74]

Cortés seems to have made some kind of apology: a rare thing for him. His biographer López de Gómara recounts a beautiful speech which he says that Cortés then pronounced; but it sounds more like fiction than history.

What perturbed Montezuma was probably not Cortés' presentation of the Virgin Mary as a candidate for enthronement; it was the exclusivity of Christianity which upset him, as indeed it might have distressed an ancient Greek or Roman. Cortés and the Castilians went down and left Montezuma praying.

Perhaps the Emperor prayed for the poor: O lord consider those who lie on the floor of life, "those who are on the ground, those who know nothing, the poor, the miserable, the useless, those who rejoice not, the discontented, those who do not have the necessities of life."[75] But it is more likely that, at this dark moment in the history of the Mexica, he recalled a prayer uttered at his inauguration as emperor sixteen years before: O master, O our lord, O lord of the nigh, of the near . . . open my eyes, open my heart, advise me, set me upon the road . . . inspire me, animate me, for thou makest of me thy seat, I am as thy flute . . . let me not become proud, let me not become quarrelsome, may I not make sport of the common folk, Master incline thy heart . . . .[76] Probably he also held some sacrifices as atonement for the sin which he had committed in allowing his curious guests to come to the temple.

Cortés on his return to the seat of the old emperors decided to insist on building a chapel in the Spanish quarters. Up till then mass had been held in improvised circumstances. Montezuma agreed that that should be done, and provided the necessary help: carpenters, masons, and painters. Within two days a Christian sanctuary had indeed been established in the palace. Thereafter mass was heard regularly.[77] The fact that Cortés had to ask Montezuma about this modest move suggests that the Emperor had not as yet conceded his vassaldom in any sense in which Europeans understood the word.

During the building of the chapel, Alonso Yañez, one of Cortés' carpenters, came upon signs that a door in a room of the palace had recently been blocked up. Cortés had it opened. Inside there was a series of rooms in which, in wickerwork chests, the Spaniards found a colossal store of gold, in the form of jewels and idols, plumes, and some objects of jade. There seem to have been several gold plates and cups, four of the former large.[78] This method of concealing things was a frequent one in old Mexico.

Word of this treasure spread in the Castilian camp. But Cortés decided to keep the news from Montezuma.[79] Later he did inform the Emperor, who told Cortés that he could keep the gold, but asked him to leave the feathers, the property of the gods. The Castilians did not mind. Their eye had not become attuned to the splendour of Mexican featherwork. Gold was their prime consideration.

Cortés himself was probably the conquistador with the best artistic eye. His letters to Charles V showed some capacity for appreciation of art: "What greater grandeur can there be," he wrote, for example, a few months later, "if a barbarian lord such as this can produce images in gold, silver, stone and feathers of everything which exists in his domain and which, in the case of silver and gold objects, bear such a remarkable likeness to the original that no jeweller anywhere else in the world could do any better? . . . And the objects made of feathers could not be more beautiful, had they been made of wax or embroidered."[80] Here, as very often, Cortés was correct in his assessment. But these works of art would not move his emperor as much as he hoped.

21

Bees and spiders make works of art

*"The mere fact that the Mexica produce beautiful objects is no indication of
their moral goodness. Certain small species such as bees and spiders make
works of art such as no human being can make comparably . . . Nor can the
fact that the Mexica have streets, houses, kings and so on prove anything,
because it only serves to show that they are neither bears nor monkeys and do
not lack reason entirely. But on the other hand, nobody does anything on their
own, they are completely at the disposal of their king, and this is not the result
of force but done in a voluntary and spontaneous way: a sure sign of a servile
temperament."*
Ginés de Sepúlveda, *Democrates Alter* (1544)

IDLENESS AFTER THE great effort of the long march up from the coast
sat ill with the Castilian army. Amazement at the character of the city
was giving way to apprehension. Several captains, including those
who had gone with the *Caudillo* to visit Montezuma – Diego de Ordaz,
Velázquez de León, Pedro de Alvarado and Sandoval – went to see their
commander. The Tlaxcalans, many of whom seem still to have been in
Tenochtitlan, had told them that they would never be able to escape from
the city and carry off all the jewels and gold of which they had laid hold;
and that the Mexica were planning to kill them.[1] Several Spaniards began
to talk of being caught in a "spider's web".[2] Ordaz said that he had seen
from the roof how easily the Mexica could cut off their retreat, simply by
raising the drawbridges. The Spaniards had no boats in which to flee the
city. Several allies had warned that destruction would await them if they
went to Tenochtitlan. Who knew, too, what was really in the mind of the
Mexican Emperor under the veneer of courtesy and subservience?[3] The
interpreter Gerónimo de Aguilar said that he had been assured by the
Tlaxcalans that the Mexica were ceasing to be friendly.[4] Perhaps that was
just because the novelty of the visit was wearing off. But perhaps the
impression reflected something more serious. Looking south from the
roof of the Palace of Axayácatl, Cortés thought that one or two bridges
had already been raised on the causeway on which his expedition had
entered.[5]

At the enquiry into his conduct in 1529, Cortés himself said that:
"After a few days, seeing the size and the strength of the city, and the
many people who, whenever they wanted, could have killed him and
those with him, without any defence being possible, he [that is, Cortés
himself] sought a means of ensuring security . . ."[6] Given that Cortés
had already told the King of Spain that he was going to secure the person

of Montezuma, dead or alive, some such plan as he now carried through had probably existed in Cortés' mind since Vera Cruz. Fr. Aguilar, in his memoir, however, insisted that Diego de Ordaz thought of seizing Montezuma as a hostage; and that, to begin with, Cortés argued that it could not be done, because Montezuma had accepted to be a vassal of the King of Spain.[7] But Ordaz may have been simply expressing what he knew privately was already in Cortés' mind.

Cortés was apparently weighing up the advantages of striking now against Montezuma when he received bad news from the coast. The Tlaxcalans told him that Juan de Escalante, his lieutenant at Villa Rica de la Vera Cruz, and six other Castilians, with many Totonacs, had been killed. Qualpopoca, Montezuma's representative at Nauhtla (Grijalva had christened it "Almería"), fifty miles up the coast from Vera Cruz, had demanded, on behalf of the Mexica, the usual half-yearly tributes from certain places near Cempoallan. These primarily Totonac towns had refused to pay tribute on the ground that "Malinche had forbidden it". Qualpopoca had threatened reprisals. Escalante had sent messages to the Mexica telling them not to rob or in any other way annoy those towns. The Mexica took no notice. So Escalante, in the style of Cortés, set off with his local allies to challenge Qualpopoca. He demanded gold. Qualpopoca refused to deliver it. A battle ensued, close to Nauhtla-Almería. During the fighting Escalante was deserted by his allies, and had eventually to withdraw in some disorder (not without burning the town first), mortally wounded, leaving behind as prisoner a certain Juan de Argüello, a corpulent Leonese. Argüello was sacrificed and his head, a large head, it seems, with a black curly beard, was sent to Montezuma as a trophy.[8] Montezuma was terrified at the sight of this present. He ordered it to be sent to some city other than the capital. Perhaps it went to Tula to be buried alongside Grijalva's ships' biscuits.[9]

Cortés thereupon decided to use the incident at Almería as "a pretext" for the high-handed, audacious and probably long premeditated move of which Diego de Ordaz had talked.[10] There was a strategic justification: to avoid losing the help of the Totonacs a striking action was needed.

Cortés sought an audience with Montezuma on 14 November. He went as usual accompanied by several senior captains (Alvarado, Sandoval, Velázquez de León, Lugo, and Ávila), and with about thirty other men, all armed – as well as the interpreters Marina and Gerónimo de Aguilar.

On arrival in Montezuma's throne room, Cortés began to banter with Montezuma, as he had done before. The Emperor, with no sense that anything untoward was going to occur, offered Cortés some jewels, and one of his daughters as "a delicious fruit". He also proposed several noblemen's daughters for Cortés' men. Cortés expressed his gratitude but, just as on a previous occasion in Tlaxcala he had said that he could not take as a consort someone who was not baptised, he said now, equally sententiously, that he could not, under Christian law, take the daughter of Montezuma as a wife, since he already had one (this was the first time that Catalina Suárez de Cortés had been mentioned by the *Caudillo* since leaving Santiago de Cuba).[11]

Cortés then changed the subject sharply and said that he was astonished that Montezuma should have sent his captains at Nauhtla against the garrison which he, Cortés, had left at Vera Cruz. He had done everything possible to help Montezuma. But now the opposite of what he had desired had transpired. Precisely the same chain of events had occurred at Cholula, he icily observed. He then showed Montezuma a letter from Pedro de Ircio on the coast which purported to implicate the Emperor in the deaths of the Castilians.[12] Cortés said that he was willing to forgive everything if Montezuma would accompany him, without a fuss, to the Castilian lodgings. But if he were to cry out, or make any noise at all, his captains would immediately kill him.[13] With a characteristic comment, the *Caudillo* made out that he was doing the least which could be expected, putting the blame for the proposal on his friends. He insisted that, if Montezuma would not do as he demanded, the captains who were with him would become "annoyed".[14]

Montezuma was terrified at this. The prospect of Juan Velázquez de León, with his large black beard and deep voice, being annoyed, was disagreeable. Yet the alternative was equally appalling. He said, quite fairly: "My person is not such as can be made a prisoner of. Even if I would like it, my people would not suffer it."[15] An argument ensued –lasting most of the day according to Cortés' majordomo, Joan de Cáceres, over four hours according to Tapia, and half an hour according to Cortés.[16] The Emperor insisted that he had himself never ordered any attack on the conquistadors at the coast. He would send immediately to find out what had happened. If anything had gone wrong, the guilty would be punished. With that he took a small figurine representing Huitzilopochtli from his arm (apparently on a bracelet), and sent messengers to the coast to carry out an enquiry.[17] Cortés said that he wished to send with Montezuma's men three of his own; and Francisco Aguilar, Andrés de Tapia and Pedro Gutiérrez de Valdelomar also set off.[18]

But "the captains" by this time had become nervous. Velázquez de León said that Montezuma had to choose: either he came with them; or he would be killed there and then. Montezuma asked Marina what Velázquez had said. Marina replied that she advised Montezuma to go with the Castilians to their lodgings without any trouble. She said that they would honour him appropriately. If he did not so act, she was sure that he would be killed. Montezuma proposed his son and two daughters as hostages in order that Cortés might be able to avoid offering such an affront. What would his councillors say if he were taken away a prisoner?

Cortés insisted that there was no alternative to the Emperor coming with them.[19] Montezuma would have to stay with the Castilians until the truth were known about the events at Almería. In the meantime, he could carry on the administration of his empire from the Palace of Axayácatl.[20]

Montezuma agreed ultimately to accompany Cortés. Why and how he managed to escape his guards is not quite clear. But it is obvious that his decision derived from a mixture of fear of and fascination for Cortés. He insisted that he was going not because of the threat of force but out of goodwill. He told his guards, advisers and relations that he had been talking to the god Huitzilopochtli, who had told him that it would be good for his health to live a while with the Castilians. Thus it was decided. He went across the town on a litter carried by his noblemen.[21] Several of these men asked if they should fight the Castilians. Montezuma repeated that he was going to spend a few days with the strangers out of friendship.[22] Cortés himself gave out that he had many interesting things to say to Montezuma about the nature of the Christian deity.[23] Though "in the style of a prisoner", as Cortés put it some years afterwards, Montezuma continued to rule his empire.[24] But his status must have been obvious to his people, since a Castilian armed guard remained with him day and night.[25] Indeed the historian Ixtlilxochitl recalled that everyone in the city was terrified at such an astonishing act by Cortés.[26]

It was a brilliant *coup de main*: an example of Cortés' supreme dexterity;[27] a confirmation of the Renaissance view that great audacity can win great prizes. Nothing in the ideology of the Mexica, nothing which Montezuma could have learned at the *calmécac* suggested that he should have made such an abject surrender. Indeed, sermons from old men would surely have been in his mind counselling the opposite. If Montezuma was hoping to practise some subtle deception, it was well disguised.

Bartolomé de Las Casas later asked Cortés "by what law" he had made Montezuma prisoner. Cortés replied, with one of those quotations which seemed to spring so easily to him, and which convinced Las Casas that he was a "good Latinist": "*Qui non intrat per ostium fur est et latro*" ("Anyone who does not enter by the front gate is a thief and a robber"). Cortés added: "Let your ears hear what your lips say."[28] At which, all present dissolved into laughter, except Las Casas who, he said, wept at the further evidence of Cortés' insensitivity.[29]

But the fact was that this action, whether recently suggested by Ordaz, or whether long planned, was the critical one in the history of the expedition. The kidnapping, for so it seemed to be, gave Cortés a strategy. He would allow Montezuma to continue to govern the empire. But he, Cortés, would govern Montezuma.

Cortés never seems to have doubted the justice of his invasion of Montezuma's territory. He believed that he was thereby doing a service to the Church, to the King and, in the long run, to the Mexica to whom he hoped to offer both a new political and spiritual world.[30] Years later an impression of what may at this time have been in his mind was reflected in a dialogue written by an acquaintance, the philosopher Ginés de Sepúlveda, in his *Democrates Alter*.[31] Thus in this work of imagination we find a certain Leopoldo asking if it "conformed to justice, and to Christian piety, that the Christians should have made war on innocent mortals from whom they had received no injury".

Sepúlveda, speaking through his character Democrates, said: "To understand, you must know the condition and dignity of these men [that is, the Indians] . . . especially the most prudent and valiant of them, the Mexica . . . Well, when Montezuma discovered that Cortés wanted a kind of conference in Tenochtitlan, Montezuma tried to avoid it. Despite all his machinations, he could not do so. Then, as a prisoner of fear, he received Cortés, with his escort of 300. Cortés . . . despising the cowardice, the inactivity, and the crudeness of the people, by using terror obliged the King and the princes to accept the yoke and the dominion of the King of Castile. He also put the same Montezuma in prison, leaving the whole city in a state of such alarm that they were unable to try to liberate their monarch."[32]

Montezuma seems in fact soon to have become accustomed to his gaolers. Such adaptations often occur in the history of kidnappings. But the Emperor liked not only Cortés but also the guards, since they made him laugh.[33] He particularly approved of a page of Cortés, a boy called Orteguilla, who had already learned a little Nahuatl. From him, Montezuma learned something of Spain and its habits, and Orteguilla learned a great deal more about the nature of the Mexican regime, which he passed on to Cortés.[34] Cortés too talked to Montezuma ceaselessly about God the Father, the King of Spain, and the complex relation between the two.[35]

Montezuma was accompanied as a prisoner in the Palace of Axayácatl by Itzquauhtzin, the elderly governor of Tlatelolco, and perhaps by some others in his supreme council.[36]

Most noblemen of Mexico were neither deceived nor amused. Many refused to go and see Montezuma in his "prison". The citizens of Tenochtitlan continued to provide food and water for the visitors and for their animals. But they did not listen much more to their emperor: "no longer was he heeded".[37] Perhaps the majority of informed citizens thought that Cortés had hypnotised Montezuma into tranquillity, and was busy stealing – just as robbers articulating the sign 1-Wind might be expected to do.

The crisis was great, for the Emperor was essential to the direction of Mexican society. The Emperor was not just "he who commands", but also the "heart of the city", a "quetzal feather", "a great silk cotton tree", and a "wall, a barricade", in whose shade people took refuge. His words were looked upon as "precious jades", and he was also supposed to speak on behalf of the gods, of whom he was "the seat, the flute, the jaws, the ears".[38] His task was not only to govern the Mexica but, so it was supposed, to keep alive the universe itself. Now he was, physically, in the hands of a wholly unpredictable group of visitors about whom no one knew anything: whether they were gods or demons, ambassadors of a great power or, simply, terrorists like the Chichimecs.

The change in the Emperor's standing of course brought great anxiety: "Fear reigned," wrote Fr. Sahagún, on the basis of his numerous informants, "as if everyone had lost heart. Even before it grew dark, all huddled in frightened, awed, and thunderstruck groups. All slept in terror."[39]

No doubt people quoted old poems:

> We only came to sleep
> we only came to dream;
> it is not true, no it is not true
> that we came to live on earth.[40]

Tenochtitlan was even more perturbed after the return from the coast of Montezuma's messengers with Qualpopoca and his sons as prisoners, with fifteen other Mexican leaders. These men were delivered to Montezuma who, weakly, handed them over to Cortés. Qualpopoca told Cortés that he was indeed Montezuma's vassal but insisted that, in fighting Escalante, he had not been acting that day on Montezuma's orders. Later, probably under torture, he contradicted himself, and said that he had been so acting. Cortés went to Montezuma and told him that he thought that he must be guilty of having ordered the actions. But even if he were, he, Cortés, was now so fond of him that he would not have him harmed for all the world.

This technique, of kindness varied with brutality, secured Montezuma's continued co-operation. For immediately after these pleasant words to Montezuma, Cortés ordered Qualpopoca, with his sons and the fifteen other Mexican noblemen, to be put to death by burning in the square before the Great Pyramid.[41] The fire was made by using a pile of wooden arrows and sword holders taken from the armoury of the palace: a useful way both of inspecting and damaging the arsenal and of humiliating Montezuma.[42] The Emperor was taken to witness the execution. Cortés had him placed in irons to "prevent an uproar".[43] The Mexicans observed the burning in complete silence.[44]

Burning to death as a method of execution was at that time practised often in Europe, especially for those condemned by the Inquisition. In Cuba, Diego Velázquez, probably with Cortés present as his secretary, had burned alive the Taino chief Hatuey in 1511. Among the Mexica, burning to death was also used as a punishment for those who drank *pulque*, or committed adultery, whilst still in the state public school, the *calmécac*.[45] The demonic Tlacaelel had devised the so-called "Divine Hearth", on which he had sacrificed the captives from Cholula in 1467.[46] Nezahualpilli had had his unfaithful queen burned alive in 1499. Montezuma II is said to have begun to use the "Divine Hearth" as a punishment more indiscriminately. All the same, the harshness of this punishment, the speed with which it was executed (probably the prisoners died without benefit of hallucinogens), and the seniority of the victims made the death of Qualpopoca seem shocking. Somewhere, surely, Montezuma must have told himself, "thou wilt need the eagle warrior, the ocelot warrior" to escape the great trial which was developing in the history of his people.[47] Yet still he hesitated.

Cortés had the irons removed from the Emperor's ankles and, according to his own account, told Montezuma that he could now go free. But the latter, by then frightened because of the reputation which he realised that he had acquired among his own people, preferred, like a wild bird caught by humans, to remain with his captors for the time being.[48] He told Cortés that his going "might permit certain chiefs . . . to induce him . . . to do something against his will . . ." prejudicial to the Castilian cause.[49] Whether or no Cortés' account of his own willingness to free Montezuma is correct, the sight of the ruler in distress while one of his lieutenants was being brutally killed must have marked a further stage in the decomposition of his regime.

But that decay was not explicit. For some weeks yet, uncanny for both the Castilians and the Mexicans, Montezuma continued to seem to rule. He had his baths, his elaborate meals, the constant presence of his superior chiefs, his discreet meetings with his special women. He as usual rose at midnight to observe from the roof of the palace the North Star and the Great Bear, the Pleiades and other constellations, and to offer his blood to them. He saw innumerable suitors, and nominated judges, taking care that "they were not drunkards, nor likely to be bribed, nor to be influenced by personal considerations, nor impassioned in their judgements".[50] He prayed. He gave banquets. He sometimes went out of the city with the Castilians to hunt birds, or to fish, or merely to look at the country – no doubt visiting one or other of the properties which he possessed in different cities. There would be hawking, hunting with blowpipes (painted instruments with gold mouthpieces, which fired balls of baked clay) or bows and arrows, or snaring with nets; and Montezuma would return "gaily and contentedly", Cortés reported, to the apartments assigned to him. Jesters continued to tell Montezuma jokes, "laugh-giving and marvellous jugglers" made logs dance on the soles of their feet, maimed dwarfs leapt and danced, while singers performed to the accompaniment of flutes, drums, rattles and bells.[51] Sometimes Montezuma would visit his zoo, and see the jaguars, the ocelots, and the deformed humans. Sometimes he would watch the popular ball game (*tlachtli*), though he probably did not again, as he had been used, himself put on the hip guards and the belt in order to play, in the polished stucco courts, against his nephews and cousins.[52]

The popularity of this game in old Mexico is shown in the tribute of 16,000 rubber balls sent annually to Tenochtitlan by the Gulf cities – balls which must have semed one of the most astonishing of the novelties of Tenochtitlan to the Castilians, whose experience would have been confined to those made of feathers, or leather.[53] It was a game favoured especially by the nobility who, when not at war, played it incessantly. When they were too old to play, they bet on it – great sums it would seem, judging from the descriptions of the piles of cloaks, breech clouts, greenstone labrets and golden earplugs which were placed in the ball courts as wagers.[54] As with most things in old Mexico, it was not exactly what it seemed; it was more ceremony than mere entertainment, more a re-creation than recreation. From its court, astronomical observations were made.[55]

Montezuma often gave jewels, and girls, to his Castilian guards. The guards in turn treated Montezuma with respect. Once, two of them, a sailor named Trujillo and a crossbowman named Pedro López, broke this rule and were rude, and they were duly punished by the *Caudillo*.[56]

The city meantime was returning to something like normality. Nightly the dancing and the singing continued in the state schools, nightly the conch trumpets sounded from the pyramids and in reply from the nearby mountains, nightly there would be parties lit by torches in palaces and often also in huts. The conquistadors would see people carrying presents, of flowers or tortillas, for it was considered offensive when visiting someone not to give them something. The *calpullec*, the leader of each district, went every day to the time-honoured meeting place, the *calpixcalli*, where he would await the instructions of the Emperor's officials.[57] The courts made their judgements; and the regular life of the ordinary Mexican continued, with its two meals, one in the morning, the other when the sun was at its hottest, with tortillas as the main item on both occasions, now and then varied with fish or game, or perhaps amaranth soup. Tribute continued to reach Tenochtitlan at regular intervals, except presumably from the tributaries on the coast which had been "liberated" by Cortés.

Montezuma also continued to make sacrifices. Cortés deplored but could not prevent them. He pretended not to notice.[58] The festivals had to go on; and a Mexican festival without a sacrifice would have been like a Spanish one without a bullfight. Montezuma would have thought that, unless there were sacrifices, the world would end.

Thus the hunting fiesta of the month of "Precious Feathers" (Quecchol) gave way to the more important "Raising of the Banners" (Panquetzaliztli). There followed Atemoztli, "Descent of Water", and Tititl, "Ritual Teasing of Women". Of these, Panquetzaliztli had a major sacrifice of captives as part of the celebration.

Priests continued "noisily to turn the pages of the illuminated manuscripts", and diviners continued to predict, from the conjunction of dates, the destinies and the characters of newborn children. Diviners would refer to the sacred book of days, the *tonalámatl*, as a mirror and would say daily to their customers, You have come to see your reflection.[59]

Despite the appearance of continuity, Montezuma's own character, however, seemed to change. The pride, arrogance, harshness which had previously characterised him seemed to vanish. The new Montezuma was pliable, undecided, and subservient, if perhaps, underneath, subtle and untrustworthy.

As for the Castilians, they too for many weeks lived a normal life, insofar as that was imaginable. Cortés heard mass daily in his quarters and ordered his men to do the same. When the wine ran out about Christmas time, there were merely prayers.[60] Cortés often played Mexican games with Montezuma. There was, for example, *totoloquí*, a game played with small pellets of gold. There was *patolli*, a game of dice played on a black mat, with a scoring board in the form of a cross: the counters were black beans, with a numerical symbol inscribed on them. It was similar to backgammon.[61] Unlike the ball game, it was popular in all classes, and some people lived (and died) from gambling on it. Conscientious parents discouraged their children from playing.

In these games between Spaniards and Mexicans, Alvarado would sometimes keep the score on behalf of the Emperor. He would even cheat on his behalf. Montezuma, in common with his people, loved gambling.[62] If Cortés won, he would give his winnings to nephews of the Emperor; if Montezuma won, he would give his gains to the Castilian soldiers. Cortés also taught Montezuma the art of the crossbow.[63] Montezuma would often say how he "loved Cortés as a brother".[64] Sometimes he would talk of how he governed the Mexica: it was now that he explained that they had "to be treated not with love but with fear. One had to have order in government."[65] Sometimes Fr. Olmedo would give the Emperor instruction in the Christian faith. Perhaps Montezuma's polite enthusiasm was mistaken by that Mercedarian for real interest.

The adventurers of the *santa compañía*, meantime, became accustomed to Mexican food, and Mexican hours. Thus they would have become used to waiting for breakfast till about ten o'clock, when they would have maize cakes (*tamales*), probably sweetened with honey or sharpened by pimiento, and served on black or red earthenware plates from Cholula.

They would drink cocoa, sweetened with honey, in a painted gourd. Like their hosts they would dine when it was too hot to go out; and, while most Mexicans had to be content with maize cakes, beans, and tomatoes, the Spaniards would doubtless have been regularly offered venison, dog, turkey or game (pheasant, partridge, boar, iguana, duck and one or other of the forty types of water fowl found on the lake). They would surely have been offered thistles and rats with sauce, newts, eggs of water fly, tadpoles, ants, frogs and agave worms, though the silence on the subject of those who wrote memoirs does not suggest they appreciated them. But they seem to have discovered that larvae of salamander was as good as eel, and that lake scum had the taste of Manchegan cheese.[66] Many would, of course, have missed the red wine of Spain and even its salt beef, and suffered accordingly. No one seems to have liked *pulque* (even if it can, in the judgement of Jacques Soustelle, taste of cider). Cortés presumably was treated regally: water for him to wash in would be brought in gourds by women who would have anointed their bare feet with incense from copal and probably dyed them blue.

The Mexicans had rather austere table manners: "Do not make faces when you eat, do not eat noisily and without care like a glutton . . ." they were told as children, "if you drink water, do not make a noise, sucking it in: you are not a little dog. Do not use all your fingers . . . but only the three fingers of your right hand."[67] Those who had learned such rules at the *calmécac* would not have felt altogether at home with the Spaniards' manners which, like their washing, could scarcely have been up to the Mexican standard.

The memoir-writers are silent too as to whether the Castilians were offered any of those famous hallucinogenic products such as the *peyote* cactus or sacred mushrooms. Though later friars discussing the *naturales'* interest in such things were disapproving, the conquistadors coming from Extremadura could hardly have found them a surprise: thorn apple, mandrake and belladonna were all used to similar ends in the European countryside, if no doubt with less sensational results.[68] Some of those Castilians who had acquired the habit in Cuba would have smoked tobacco after dinner, as the Mexican lords did, with painted pipes of reed or baked clay (the tobacco in Mexico was usually mixed with charcoal and liquidambar resin).

Gambling, encouraged by the leaders, was rife: though no cards had been brought, Pedro Valenzuela, an elderly conquistador from Palencia, painted beautiful packs of cards on skins used for drums.[69] Other diversions were provided by the three hundred or so Mexican women whom Montezuma had provided as servants (*naborías*).[70] Cortés, as well as maintaining his association with his interpretress Marina, apparently also enjoyed the affections of both a daughter ("Doña Ana") and a niece

("Doña Elvira") of Montezuma, despite his censorious remarks about the idea a few weeks before.[71]

To be sure, Cortés had his difficulties: for example, adverse news came of Alonso de Grado, whom he had sent down to succeed Escalante as commander of the garrison in Vera Cruz. Grado was said to be living like a lord, gambling, eating well, whilst demanding both jewels and pretty women from his Totonac neighbours. Cortés, who remembered Grado's challenge to him during the Tlaxcala campaign, suspected him of preparing to treat with Diego Velázquez if and when that governor should try to interfere in Cortés' activities in Mexico. The young friend of Cortés from Medellín, Gonzalo de Sandoval, was appointed in his place. His unenviable first task was to send back Alonso de Grado in chains to Tenochtitlan under the escort of Pedro de Ircio – where, after being roughly greeted by Alvarado, he was put in the stocks for two days.[72]

One action of Cortés was second only in importance to the kidnapping of Montezuma. This was his decision some time in November to seek to make up for his exposed strategic position by arranging to build ships which would, as he himself said, "be capable, whenever we might wish it, of taking three hundred men and the horses to the mainland".[73]

He discussed this question with his captains. They proposed a certain Martín López of Seville as the most promising person to supervise any such construction.[74] López suggested the building of brigantines, ships which could be propelled on the lake either by sail or by oars (or even paddles). He made plans and agreed to supervise the undertaking, since, though he had never before built ships, he had with him servants who understood the craft.[75]

This Martín López was no ordinary shipwright since, then aged twenty-four, born in the parish of San Vicente in Seville, he was descended from a famous medieval knight, Pedro Álvarez Osorio, one of the first settlers of Seville after its liberation by St Ferdinand.[76] He also had some blood of the Ponce de León family. He had carried a good deal of equipment: "two pipes of wine, three or four boxes of cloth, and much extra stores" had been put on board his ship when setting out for this new land, as well as the brothers Pedro and Miguel La Mafla, who were skilled carpenters.[77] Several poor conquistadors had regularly dined with him at his expense. Martín López was an excellent choice for the building of the ships, since he was a "very skilful and intelligent man", several of his friends insisted in a later lawsuit, "a person willing to go anywhere and do anything, at any hour of the day or night".[78]

Cortés commissioned Martín López to build four brigantines. The latter assembled a small team of craftsmen (the blacksmiths Pedro Hernández and Hernán Martín, the sawyers Diego Hernández and Sebastián Rodríguez, the carpenter Andrés Núñez as well as the La Mafla brothers). Sandoval sent up from Vera Cruz much material from the grounded ships: chains for anchors, sails, rigging, pitch; and another compass.[79] Some native carpenters were also provided by Montezuma, who was led to believe that the boats were for pleasure. Wood was cut from near the lake, among the oak trees of Texcoco, and the cedars of Tacuba.[80] In the end, the boats turned out to be a little under forty feet long. Each was capable of carrying four bronze cannon and seventy-five men.[81] López's expenses (which seem never to have been paid) for the four vessels totalled two thousand pesos – presumably including a fee for himself, and payment to the craftsmen.[82]

Montezuma was invited on to one of these vessels as soon as they were complete. He and Alvarado, with several other Castilian captains (Velázquez de León, Olid, Ávila), crossed the lake to go hunting on the little island of Tepepolco (later El Peñón del Marqués) near Iztapalapa.[83] They travelled with numerous soldiers as escorts. Several guns were taken, managed by the Italian veteran Mesa. Montezuma enjoyed himself. Hunting, normally with bows and arrows, but also with traps, had a high status among the Mexica. The practice was usually carried on for skins, fur, and food, but a royal hunt also concerned itself with the capture of animals for the zoo. Montezuma did not appear to have been perturbed to see that the brigantines with their sails travelled much faster than his best canoes. The expedition served Cortés as a trial for the ships.[84] Thereafter, the brigantines cruised continually. The conquistadors gained priceless information about the lake's character, its vegetation, its harbours, and its depths.

They thus came to realise that there were, in fact, five linked lakes in the valley, not one big one: to the north, the two called Xaltocan and Zumpango; in the centre, that of Texcoco; and, to the south, Xochimilco and Chalco. They discovered how shallow the lakes generally were (six to ten feet at most), and how during only about half the year all the lakes were interconnected. They learned how Lake Texcoco was at the lowest point, and thus the destination of all drainage. Lakes Xochimilco and Chalco were about ten feet higher than Lake Texcoco. The first of these drained into Lake Texcoco all the year round and was, therefore, fresh (there were also many small springs on the shores there). Lakes Xaltocan and Zumpango were also higher than Lake Texcoco but only drained into it seasonally. They were, therefore, more saline than the other smaller lakes.[85]

The salinity too must have caught the attention of the conquistadors, since a stretch of the eastern shore was given over to the making of salt: a fact that someone soon told Peter Martyr, in Spain, for he is shortly found passing on to Pope Leo how "they make it hard, conveying it into trenches into the earth to thicken it and, being hardened and congealed, they boil it, and afterwards make it into round lumps".[86]

The Mexican empire continued, during most of this period, to function normally: tribute flowed; and long-distance merchants maintained their commerce. In both *urbs* and *orbis*, "harmony and order", as Cortés in one of his positive moods admiringly put the matter, was maintained.

22

Something must be done for the Lord

*"I promise on my word as a gentleman . . . that it appeared to me that the
Marquis gave a superhuman leap and balanced himself taking the bar so that
it hit the eyes of the idol and so removed the gold mask, saying: 'Something
must be done for the Lord.' "*
Andrés de Tapia, in his *Relación, c.* 1539

THE MEXICAN EIGHTEEN-MONTH year began in February. So
January, a time of frost and drought, marked the end of the old
year. The main anxiety in early 1520, as in most years, was
whether, and when, the rains would come. Thus we must picture the
Mexica, including those with whom the Spaniards were in constant
contact, to have been primarily concerned with, say, prayers to the
"benign wizard" Tlaloc:

O lord, our lord, O provider, O lord of greenness,
Lord of Tlaloc, Lord of the sweet-scented marigold, Lord
    of Copal!
The gods, our lords, the Providers,
The lords of rubber, the lords of the sweet-scented marigold,
The lords of Copal,
Have sealed themselves in a coffer, they have locked themselves
    in a box,
They have hidden the jade and the turquoise and the precious
    jewels of life,
They have carried off their sister, Chicomecoatl, the fruits of the
    earth,
And the Crimson Goddess, the chilli.
Oh, the fruits of the earth lie panting.
The sister of the gods, the sustenance of life,
Feebly drags herself along.
She is covered with dust, she is covered with cobwebs,
She is utterly worn and weary.[1]

The Mexica did not, however, now have only such traditional

anxieties. For their acceptance of the Castilians as visitors was brought to an end by quarrels with them over religion; and then over that perennial source of bloodshed in the New World, gold. There was also the question of who really was in control of the empire: the Mexica or the Castilians and their allies.

The quarrel over religion derived from the question of sacrifice. Cortés continued, over the games of *totoloque*, and the engaging conversations after dinner, to talk of the "things of God"[2] and to insist that Montezuma abandon sacrifice and the consumption of human remains. The conquistadors were capable of almost every brutality; but cannibalism, even ritual cannibalism, shocked them. The tearing out of a man's intestines with a pike was one thing. But the stewing of a foot was an insult to God. Cortés' demands to bring this custom to an end had no effect. Then, falling back on a technique which he so often used, of giving the credit (or the blame) for an initiative to others, he said that his "captains" were anxious to see this reform introduced. They also still wanted to place a crucifix and a picture of the Virgin at the summit of the Great Temple. As time went on, it would become evident, he thought, how beneficial it would be for the Mexican souls. Montezuma said: "O Malinche, how can you want us [the Mexica] to lose the whole city?" He added, "Our gods are very annoyed with us, and I don't know if they would even stop at your lives were we to do as you ask".[3]

Cortés then changed the subject and asked Montezuma to tell him which were the gold-producing areas of the empire. The Emperor did so. Probably a special summary of the sources of this tribute was made; or Montezuma permitted the Spaniards to consult one already in being. The conquistadors had noticed that careful accounts were made of everything brought in, and maintained by an official whom they nicknamed "Tapia" (perhaps because he looked like a dour royal inspector named Tapia in Hispaniola). "In Montezuma's income books," reported Bernal Díaz, "we looked up which were the provinces from which he drew gold as tribute, and where there were mines, cacao, and cotton cloaks . . ."[4]

Gold, as has been noted, meant less to the Mexica than it did to the Castilians. It was a newer commodity to them than either feathers or jade. Had Cortés asked for the whereabouts of the Mexican supply of those items, even of paper, he might have received a less satisfactory answer (paper was an essential element in innumerable festivals, as well as being necessary for such things as the very tribute rolls of which Díaz spoke). All the same, Montezuma concealed the sources of some gold-supplying provinces.[5] He said that most gold came from Zacatula, a Mixtec area in the central south, in what is now Oaxaca. Not far from there, there was Malinaltepec, a Chinantecan zone controlled by the Mexica, also in the central south. Three further places were

Tututepec, in the south-west, in what is now Guerrero; Coatzacoalcos, on the Gulf of Mexico; and Tochtepec, in what is now southern Oaxaca.[6] There was also a promising zone to the north-east, in what became known as Pánuco. In all these places, gold was obtained by the placer, or panning, method: the metal was washed from auriferous streams and rivers, much as would occur in the gold rushes of the nineteenth century in California. It was then treated in a three-legged crucible, a process which was plainly an early form of smelting.

As to the working of the gold, the Mixtecs were the most accomplished of the indigenous peoples. Their territory constituted a labyrinth of small monarchies. Though they had been mostly conquered by the Mexica, their rulers were permitted a free rein. Like the Tarascans, the Mixtecs seemed culturally and politically less "advanced" than the Mexica: they had no great city, and no central authority. But they produced admirable polychrome pottery; they were specialists in carving jade, onyx, shell and stone; and they were also very talented goldsmiths, who made gold ornaments of a delicacy rarely equalled, the style deriving from imitations of paintings in codices. Mixtec ornaments indeed looked as if they were drawings translated into gold.[7] Their beautiful bells, their rings, and their reliance on cosmic symbolism for themes, made their products unique. This jewellery, which began to be produced about AD 1000, and which Mexican tradition insisted originated in Tollan, may have been at first an import from the south; even from Peru.[8]

To the first of these zones of opportunity, Cortés dispatched Gonzalo de Umbría, who was one of those sailors whom the *Caudillo* had punished during the events at Vera Cruz in May. Indeed his toes were supposed to have been cut off. Whatever happened to Umbría's feet, they now must have much improved, though presumably he led this expedition on horseback. On the way to Zacatula, he and his friends saw fortified buildings which Cortés later fancifully reported to be "stronger and better built" than the castle of Burgos.[9]

To the region near Coatzacoalcos in the south-east, Cortés sent Diego de Ordaz with ten Castilians, in search both of gold and of a new harbour. He found a little (fifty pesos' worth) of the precious commodity. As to the harbour, the river Coatzacoalcos was so broad, and apparently without a current, that at first it seemed a possible strait to the "Southern Sea" – one of the things in which, of course, the *Caudillo* was really interested. But Ordaz reported that the channel became a normal river within a few miles of the sea. The strait would have to be found elsewhere.[10] Ordaz also busied himself with founding a fortified farm near what is now San Miguel de Malinaltepec, in order both to establish a Castilian presence (and so formally capture the territory), and to grow maize, cacao and beans, and raise ducks.[11]

For the moment Cortés neglected some of the places mentioned to him by Montezuma. But he did send to Pánuco both Andrés de Tapia and Diego Pizarro, a relation through his mother (of whom we know little more than his name), perhaps with a view to seeing whether there had been a repetition of a landing there by Garay, the Governor of Jamaica.[12]

The expeditions seem, on Montezuma's instructions, to have been well cared for by local people. The extraordinary mark of the journeys is that these foreigners travelled in perfect safety. The Spaniards even received many presents of jewels and gold: countless small figurines, models of birds, and grotesque animals designed as earplugs, labrets, collars, earrings and brooches.

Umbría returned from the Mixtec zone with the information that in central Oaxaca, and towards the east coast, there certainly were gold mines. Tapia and Pizarro similarly returned from the north-east, with some thousand pesos' worth of gold, as well as bringing the comforting information that the people there were very willing to speak adversely of the Mexica, who were cordially hated. Ordaz returned without any certain knowledge of a good harbour, but he did have some presents for Cortés. Tochel, a chief near Coatzacoalcos (not far from Potonchan, the scene of Cortés' first military victory), was, he reported, very willing to give homage to the King of Castile. He said that he would in future pay tribute.[13] Another farm was founded to the south of Tenochtitlan, the territory of the Chinantla, in the region of the Zapotecs, by Hernán de Barrientos who, entirely alone, seems to have remained in control of an establishment there for over a year.[14]

Cortés resolved the matter of supreme authority in Tenochtitlan to his satisfaction early in 1520. Whether the resolution was seen as such by Montezuma must, however, be a matter for doubt.

Cortés had frequently insisted that Montezuma should accept the King of Spain as his lord. But the need to ensure this formally seems to have become acute as a result of an attempt at resistance some time near the end of 1519 by Cacama, King of Texcoco: against both his uncle Montezuma and against the foreigners who seemed to have captured Montezuma's soul.

There are conflicting stories: but the most acceptable derives from the historian of the royal family of Texcoco, Fernando Alva Ixtlilxochitl. Normally pro-Spanish, or at least pro-Christian, that late sixteenth-century writer gave the impression that the upheaval flowed from a single act of intemperance by Cortés. According to this account, two of the many younger brothers of Cacama, Nezahualquentzin and Tetlahuehue-quititzin, were showing to certain Spaniards the power, the wealth and the grandeur of Texcoco. They had reached the house of the late monarch Nezahualcoyotl when a messenger arrived from Montezuma. The messenger took the first of these two princes aside and said that the Emperor hoped that he would treat the Castilians well and give them all the gold which he had. The Castilians misunderstood the messenger's behaviour. They assumed that double dealing was afoot. Nezahualquentzin was seized, and taken to Cortés, who ordered him hanged for conspiracy. Montezuma intervened, weeping, and nothing was done.[15] But the incident infuriated Cacama who, having long subordinated himself to his uncle, moved into open rebellion. Perhaps the burning of Qualpopoca had been the turning point which caused Cacama to see the folly of his earlier appeasement. At all events, he now reproached the Mexica for their acceptance of the Spanish demands. He secretly left Tenochtitlan, because he thought that the Mexica had no spirit for resistance, at least under Montezuma. He returned to his own city and plotted to release his uncle, and all the Mexican nobility, from the servitude which they had assumed. Ixtlilxochitl, Cacama's brother and one-time rival for the throne, told him that he agreed that something should be done. He suggested a meeting in the nearby wood of Tepetzinco. From there they could arrange jointly to blockade the city of Tenochtitlan. The journey there necessitated going by canoe. Cacama agreed to go with his brother. He entered a canoe with Ixtlilxochitl and another brother, Coanocochtzin. Cacama should have known that Ixtlilxochitl's enmity to Montezuma had made him in effect an agent of Cortés. When they set off, the canoe did not make for Tepetzinco but for Tenochtitlan, where Cacama was delivered a prisoner to Cortés.[16]

Another version of the story has it that Cacama arranged a meeting with the lords of Coyoacan, Tacuba, Iztapalapa, Toluca and Matalcingo to plan to overthrow Montezuma and destroy the Castilians. They reached an agreement to rebel but could not decide who should be heir to Montezuma. The lord of Toluca, who had a reputation as a warrior, saw that he would be passed over. He complained to Montezuma. Montezuma, finding his own position threatened, so the story goes, told Cortés. Cortés then suggested a joint Castilian and Mexican attack on Texcoco. Montezuma refused collaboration. Cortés next tried to persuade Cacama to take a favourable attitude to the Castilians. Cacama said that he did not want to hear any more of Cortés' flatteries. He wished that he had never known Cortés. There were further such exchanges. Cacama insisted to Montezuma that the Castilians were not so much gods as wizards who, by witchcraft, had stolen his uncle's strength and bravery. He urged the Mexica to make war. He believed that the conquistadors could all be killed in an hour. A short time afterwards, the Mexica would be eating their flesh. But before anything like a plot could be hatched, Cacama was kidnapped at a beautiful house on the lake, and thereafter kept a prisoner alongside Montezuma.[17]

Whichever of these stories one believes, it is evident that Cacama ended in Cortés' hands. He, the lord of Toluca, the lord of Iztapalapa, the King of Tacuba and some others were all imprisoned by Cortés. They were soon attached to an iron chain left over from the anchor chains of ships grounded at Vera Cruz. Cacama's brother, Conacochtzin, was named King of Texcoco.

This was by no means the end of the tragic tale of Cacama. Cacama later sought to make things up with Cortés – presumably to gain his freedom. He therefore told Cortés to send some men to see his majordomo in Texcoco. That official would hand over a new supply of gold. Cortés accordingly sent Rodrigo Álvarez Chico, Vázquez de Tapia and some others across the lake. They returned with 15,000 pesos in gold, without counting many gold shields and much clothing. Alvarado told Cortés that he believed that there must be even more gold in Texcoco. Cortés sent back Cacama, in irons, with Alvarado to deliver some more. They did not return. Cortés dispatched Vázquez de Tapia, with Rodrigo Rangel, to Texcoco to recall the ex-king, Alvarado and such gold as had been gathered. When they got to Texcoco, they found that Alvarado had tied Cacama to a stake and was having him burned with hot brands from a fire. He had thereby extracted another 8,000 or 9,000 pesos.[18]

The suggestion that Cacama was burned sounds too detailed to be an invention; yet one witness at the enquiry against Alvarado (Pedro Sánchez Farfán) said that he saw Cacama arriving back at Tenochtitlan safe and sound, with no damage to him whatever.[19] Alvarado himself insisted that he had not burned Cacama; if any bad treatment occurred, it was "a result of the trouble and teasing which Cacama had offered to the Spaniards, and to intimidate him". He added, "After that, they gave me some labrets of little value."[20] Another witness at that same enquiry (Cristóbal Flores) said that he had heard that Cacama had been tortured to say where the gold was. But he had not seen it himself.[21]

It was this "rebellion" of Cacama which seems to have persuaded Cortés to regularise once and for all the position of the Spanish in Mexico. As his chaplain, López de Gómara, later put it, "Had there been many Cacamas, I do not know how it would have turned out."[22]

According to both Cortés and his friends, the Caudillo one day persuaded Montezuma to summon the leading lords of the Mexican empire. Probably this was early in January 1520. They came. Joan López de Jimena, one of the Castilian witnesses of this occasion, later spoke of this gathering as a "junta".[23] Probably these lords were those already in the palace, that is those who had been chained up by Cortés some days before. The meeting occurred in the room where Montezuma was being held prisoner. A number of Castilians were present: apart from Cortés and his notary, Pero Hernández, there seem to have been Orteguilla, the page, and several other conquistadors: Juan Jaramillo, Andrés de Tapia, Alonso de Navarrete, Alonso de la Serna and Francisco de Flores, as well as Joan López de Jimena. According to Francisco de

Flores,[24] Montezuma then related to his lieutenants (perhaps for the first time) the legend of how their lands would be subjugated, controlled and governed (*soyulgadas, mandadas e gobernadas*) by a great lord who would come from the east and bring great benefits. The testimony of Flores was that Montezuma, having said that he had accepted to be a vassal of Cortés acting on behalf of the King of Spain, asked all the lords present if they would be the same; and "all replied to Montezuma . . . that they agreed to be vassals and Flores believed that the concession was made in the right form, since Cortés had, as usual, a notary with him."[25] Alonso de la Serna and Juan Jaramillo also thought (and later stated on oath) that the lords had accepted Montezuma's request. Alonso de Navarrete said that "all replied to the said Montezuma, and this witness did not understand what they said but that it seemed, according to the interpreters, that they accepted and took for good what Montezuma had asked".[26]

Cortés, according to his own account, made a speech in which he too recalled the ancient writings which had predicted that the Mexica were destined to become subject to a great lord from afar, and that he, Cortés, had been sent by that lord. Montezuma, so this story went, replied that the leaders of the Triple Alliance did not wish to make any complaints, that they were glad to have been born at a time when they could see Christians and hear about the King of Castile, and that they would happily give homage to that monarch and live under his protection, and, as Joan de Cáceres, Cortés' majordomo put it, "be his slaves".[27] Andrés de Tapia agreed that the proceedings fell out thus. By that time he himself had learned a little Nahuatl, and for that reason he was able, he said, to see that the interpreters did interpret accurately. He saw Montezuma, he said, give his obedience to the King of Castile, and he saw all the lords who were there agreeing with him, and "each one of them accepted to be vassals of His Majesty".[28] Joan López de Jimena said that he had heard the interpreter Aguilar say that the lords had accepted by writ (*auto*) the said argument: that is, obedience and vassalage.[29] The official historian of the reign of Charles V, Ginés de Sepúlveda, writing in the 1550s, presented this series of exchanges, as might be expected, in its most stark form: even representing, in his fine Ciceronian Latin, Montezuma as saying that he was sure that "the Spanish soldier had arrived with the authority and the aid of the gods to reclaim the rights of the ancient monarchy".[30]

Montezuma was also said by both Tapia and Cortés to have given his oath with many tears. After a brief suspension of the meeting (due to the tears), the Emperor, the kings and then the nobles, according to Alva Ixtlilxochitl, gave brothers, daughters, and children to the Spaniards as hostages to guarantee the solidity of their oaths.[31] Cortés may have been influenced in this audacious action by the knowledge that, after St

Ferdinand had conquered Seville in 1248, the Mahommedans of the city made a formal concession of their mosques to the Castilians. He was of course a lawyer, and saw the benefit of a legal justification for his actions. He then sought to console the Mexicans, and assured them that he would always treat them well. He even told Montezuma that they together would soon set about conquering a bigger empire than the present Mexican one.[32] This was an idea calculated to please Montezuma, as perhaps it did. It may well have represented, if fleetingly, a genuine ambition of Cortés: why should not Montezuma's army, with Cortés' weapons, conquer China – which everyone believed to be near at hand?

Cortés also told these Mexican lords that, since they were now vassals of King Charles, they ought to complete the process of transformation and become Christians. Montezuma already seems to have known some prayers, such as the Our Father, the *Ave Maria*, and the Creed (of course in Latin). For someone brought up in a *calmécac*, as he had been, learning by heart presented no difficulty. But the Emperor seems to have decided, tactfully and no doubt tactically too, that he would like to wait till Easter.[33]

The key to these remarkable exchanges was, as the historian Oviedo pointed out fifteen years later, that Montezuma was said (by Cortés) to have followed this oath with so many tears that even the *Caudillo* and his friends wept. Oviedo, who had a sensibly sceptical frame of mind, wrote that, "If what Cortés says or wrote really happened, the good faith and liberality of Montezuma in yielding his sovereignty and obedience to the King of Castile acting merely on the cunning words of Cortés seems to me a very extraordinary thing for him to do. And the tears which he shed when Cortés made his speech and threatened him, while stripping him of his power . . . seem to me meant or indicated something different from what he and they said . . . for the allegiance which is sworn to princes is usually something given with laughter and song and music and mirth, as a sign of pleasure, and not with mourning and tears and sobs, especially when he who gives the allegiance is a prince".[34]

The reality of this scene has been questioned. Like Montezuma's speech made on the night of Cortés' arrival in Tenochtitlan, it has been dismissed as being no more than another work of fiction written by Cortés in his role as great story-teller. But Cortés was not the only witness to what happened. There were at least six other conquistadors who were present at the time and who gave evidence, in the 1530s, at the *residencia* against Cortés, and whose accounts broadly confirm Cortés'. They spoke on oath. Not all of them were friends of Cortés. Alonso de la Serna in particular differed later from Cortés on substantial points. If they were all lying, it would argue a considerable conspiracy which would surely have been unearthed, and made much of by Cortés' real enemies who, by the date concerned, were numerous and active.

In fact, as happened often, Cortés in his account probably neither lied, nor told the whole truth. He persuaded the Mexica to accept his scheme by the use of menaces. Montezuma, under the influence of fear and charm, still desired to please. The other lords were, as has been seen, chained and could do little other than accept. The Mexicans, a distinguished modern historian put it, accepted Cortés' demands "out of superstition or terror".[35] We need not insist that Cortés lied in his account of the events. That seems to be too unsubtle. Why lie when one can bully?

The question as to whether the interpreters Marina and Aguilar were able to ensure that Montezuma understood the nature of "vassalage" is also important. Juan Cano, a conquistador who later married the beautiful Tecuichpo, Montezuma's daughter by his official wife, once said that he thought it uncertain whether Montezuma had understood the ceremony because of the inadequacy of the interpretation.[36] All the same, on a later occasion, he corrected himself and, though by then no friend of Cortés, said firmly that Montezuma had handed over his dominions voluntarily to Cortés.[37]

In outline, after all, the concept of "vassalage" in the Spanish sense was not so far from what the Mexican lords' relation was to Montezuma for the thing to be incomprehensible. The word may be complicated in all its variety of senses, and impossible to understand fully outside the local context. Yet if Montezuma wept, he must have done so because he understood, largely, what the words meant. Many years later, a grandson of Montezuma petitioned to be made a grandee of Spain. He said that, had Montezuma possessed other new worlds, he would certainly have renounced them in favour of the King of Spain.[38]

The significance of these scenes was that they enabled Cortés to claim first, that Montezuma had accepted the King of Spain as his lord; and second, therefore, that any action designed to resist his expedition could be castigated as rebellion. Thus a legal frame of a sort had been built round his adventure. This was the scheme of things first tested at Cholula. There were medieval and even recent precedents for his action: for example, an occasion when the Spaniards crushed a rebellion on the Canary Island of Gomera in 1488 by saying that the *guanches*, the natives, had deviated from "their vassals' path" to their lord.[39]

This ceremony, farce though it may seem, also gave Cortés a good excuse to make yet more demands for gold. A few days later, for example, Cortés spoke of the heavy expenses incurred by the King of Castile in his Italian wars and other enterprises. It would, therefore, be good if everyone in Mexico could contribute something to these essential costs.[40] Montezuma seems to have appreciated the requirement. Despite the insolence of this request, the Emperor sent out a new delegation of officials to insist on a special delivery of gold. Italy would be served.

Adventures into the interior were one thing, those in Tenochtitlan itself another. In order to satisfy what Montezuma seemed to accept was a legitimate demand, Andrés de Tapia and some others of Cortés' friends were taken by the Emperor's men into the so-called House of Birds, the *Totocalli* (approximately where the church of San Francisco was later built, and thus close to the palace where the conquistadors were lodged).[41] Cortés had seen this zoo early on during his time in Tenochtitlan: he had indeed gone into raptures over the tiles, the lattice work, the elaborate attention paid to the birds and animals kept there.[42] With the large number of tropical birds, the atmosphere must have been enchanting. The conquistadors were there shown one more vast collection of gold in plate, bars, and jewels. Tapia told Cortés. The *Caudillo* took the whole treasure into his own quarters.[43]

There were also in the House of Birds many cloaks and much featherwork. But, as usual, the conquistadors paid less attention to these things: as Sahagún put it, "the Spaniards demand gold! And Montezuma led them to the *Totocalli*, the treasure house, and there were brought out all the brilliant goods, quetzal fans, shields, golden discs, necklaces, golden nose crescents, golden leg bands, golden arm bands, golden head bands . . . all the gold was torn out from these things, detached . . . and the Spaniards melted it into bars . . . Of the green stones, *chalchihuites*, they took as much as was good for their eyes and the rest was taken by men of Tlaxcala . . . The Spaniards looked eager and content. They clapped each other on the back, as if happy . . . they scattered everywhere, bustled everywhere, as if greedy and covetous, they took goods which were exclusively Montezuma's . . ."[44] Much of the tribute paid over many years to the Mexican empire was thus delivered to the strangers.

Marina seems by now to have completely thrown in her lot with the Spaniards. At all events, after these insolent actions, she went on to a rooftop, perhaps that of the very House of Birds, and, adding insult to injury, called down: "O Mexica, come here. The Castilians have suffered great fatigue. Bring here food, fresh water, all that is required. For they are now . . . tired and exhausted. They are in need." When nothing happened, Marina asked them, "Why do you not wish to come? It appears that you are angry." But "the Mexica remained silent and inactive. They were weak with fear. They looked on the Castilian presence as if a fierce beast lay there – as if the land were dead." In the end, they brought the food, but "in dread, they left it on the ground, all ran back . . . like sparks flying . . ."[45] Sahagún later sought to justify Cortés' actions in looting this palace as a way of satisfying his restless captains.[46] But he was not uninterested in profit himself.

While the expeditions into the interior and the amassing of gold in the city were under way, and while Cortés still felt masterfully in command of his captive's throne and empire, the matter of the sacrifices in the Great

Temple came up once more.[47] Andrés de Tapia testified, and later wrote, that he and Cortés and some others happened to be walking in the courtyard before the Great Temple. This, with its numerous towers, was the most important place in Tenochtitlan. It was large: perhaps thirteen hundred feet square, with numerous sacred buildings surrounding it (some of these were functional: for example, the cell where the child victims to Tlaloc were kept; or the larger adjoining one for adults which was also used as a kitchen where the limbs of sacrificed victims were cooked).[48] There were also the skull racks, the two round stones on which certain war captives fought gladiatorial combats, springs used for sacred purposes, and a rock garden in which the god Mixcoatl was believed to live in spirit.

It can hardly have been that these conquistadors were merely passing the time of day in that place. Some design must have been previously conceived. At all events, according to Tapia, Cortés suggested to him that he go to the top of the steps of the pyramid, and examine the shrines there.[49] Tapia went up, escorted by some astonished priests: no Mexican would have dreamed of going there unasked. At the top of the pyramid, this intrepid conquistador walked through a curtain of hemp on which many bells were hanging – that is, into one of the two supreme shrines, presumably that to Tlaloc: that would account for the difference in his description of what he saw from what had been observed on an earlier visit by Cortés.[50] He observed the goggle-faced stone Tlaloc and a companion, not identified. At the nape of each neck hung another face shaped like a skinned human head. As in the shrine to Huitzilopochtli, observed some months earlier by Cortés, both idols were smeared with blood, in some parts two or three inches thick. Ugly though the effigy of Tlaloc seemed, he was, of course, the creator of beauty:

> Whence come the intoxicating flowers,
> intoxicating songs?
> Fine songs come only from him who is in heaven
> Only from his home come the flowers . . .[51]

Cortés had followed Tapia up, "to pass the time of day", as Tapia surprisingly put it in his memoir, with about ten Castilians, as well as some more priests, who had heard the ringing of the bells. The *Caudillo* asked the priests for the immediate establishment there of effigies of Christ and of the Virgin Mary, and the washing of the walls to free them of blood. The priests laughed and said that, if such a thing were done, the whole empire, not just Tenochtitlan, would rise against the Spaniards. Cortés sent one of his men to go to where Montezuma was being held and to ensure that he was well guarded. He also ordered some thirty or forty men to come to the temple. But even before these had arrived, the

Caudillo had begun to break the idols: "Annoyed by what he had heard, he seized a bar which was there and began to hit the stone idols. And I promise on my word as a gentleman, and I swear by God that it is true, that it appeared to me that the Marquis [i.e. Cortés] gave a superhuman leap and balanced himself taking the bar so that it hit the eyes of the idol and so removed the gold mask, saying: 'Something must be done for the Lord.' "[52] Even though Cortés insisted that he had merely been passing the time of day, it would seem certain that this was a calculated action, that his anger was feigned, and that he had sent Tapia up the pyramid first in order to reconnoitre.

Montezuma quickly heard of these activities. He sent to ask Cortés to allow him to come there and, for the moment, to do no further damage to the idols. Cortés agreed.[53] When he arrived, Montezuma weakly suggested putting his gods on one side in the shrines, and the Castilian ones on the other. Cortés refused this almost Anglican compromise. Montezuma said that he would do everything that he could to meet Cortés' demands, providing he would allow the Mexica to take their deities wherever they wanted. He apparently added that, though they, the Mexica, were not natives to the valley, it was a long time since they had come there. So it was possible that they had made one or two mistakes in their beliefs.[54] Cortés, who had come so recently, might be better informed. Cortés agreed with Montezuma's plan, saying of the gods which he had begun to destroy: "They are only stone. Believe in our God who made heaven and earth, and, by His works, you will know who the Master is."[55]

Three or four days later, it seems, several hundred priests came with ropes and some rollers, such as Europeans used for beaching ships. They went to the top of the steps with maguey mats and mattresses. They made of these a long bed, on which to put the idols (presumably both Tlaloc and Huitzilopochtli) so that they would not break. They then lowered the idols, and a "sacred bundle" of other objects associated with the cult, carefully down planks which they had previously greased, holding on by rings to the ropes: "They did this with such great harmony and so silently that it amazed our people, for they would usually do nothing without shouting . . . One or two pieces of the idols fell off, and they enveloped these in the folds of their cloaks as if they had been relics of some saint."[56]

At the bottom of the steps, the idols were put on to litters, and were carried off by priests and noblemen to a place where they were never seen again by the Castilians. No one would ever tell where they were kept, "even for money".[57] They seem to have been hidden in a shrine in Montezuma's palace, then in the palace of a Mexican nobleman named Boquín in Azcapotzalco; and afterwards they vanished.[58]

After the departure of the idols, Cortés had the shrines at the top of the pyramid cleaned. Some of the interior walls were knocked down to make room for a bigger church. While engaged in these works, the Castilians, in a space behind the other gods, found a life-sized subsidiary effigy of Huitzilopochtli made of maize and other vegetables, held together by blood. This effigy was taken out during festivals and decorated with gold and other precious stones, but, at other times, was left unadorned. In that condition it was even more alarming.[59] The Castilians made no mistake about this idol. It was destroyed.[60] The jewels were seized. Only some gods which had been embedded into the walls were allowed to stay where they were.[61] The Spaniards also discovered gold tucked into crevices at the top of the pyramid. This had been introduced alongside the ashes of Montezuma's predecessors. It was usually buried at the level of the highest step of the temple. Their successors then raised the staircase by two steps.[62]

Christian effigies of the Virgin Mary and of St Christopher were established on top of the Great Pyramid of Tenochtitlan soon after. (The cult of St Christopher was widespread in Europe in the late Middle Ages. As patron of travellers, his place in Tenochtitlan seemed appropriate. The Mexica must have been confused by the large number of minor deities whom the Christians seemed to worship: not just St Christopher, but St Antonio for lovers, St Hubert against rage, St Benito for erring husbands, and so on.)

The Spaniards celebrated. A *Te Deum* was sung, while Fr. Olmedo and Fr. Juan Díaz, at the head of a procession of armed Christians, slowly mounted the steps of the temple. Mass was thereafter celebrated (wine had been obtained from Vera Cruz). Not long after, some Mexicans came with wilting green stalks of maize, hoping that the Christian deities would bring them the rain which was needed. Cortés was once more lucky: it rained the next day.[63]

Cortés reported that from then on sacrifices ceased: "In all the time that I remained in the city I did not see a single living creature killed or sacrificed."[64] It may very well not have occurred in the Great Temple. But it must have continued in small temples. What Cortés' eye did not see, he could assume did not happen. What he did ensure was another arrangement, as in Cempoallan, whereby the "servants of the devil", as he continued to regard Mexican priests, looked after the Christian altar: Cortés "ordered an old soldier to be stationed there as guardian", and he asked Montezuma to order the priests "not to touch the altar, but to keep it swept and to burn incense and keep wax candles burning there by day and night, and to decorate it with branches and flowers".[65] Again as in Cempoallan, the priests were presumably instructed how to make candles, the most acceptable of Spanish imports to the Indies.

Oviedo the historian commented in 1540 on this extraordinary occurrence: "I consider it a marvellous thing," he wrote, "that Montezuma and the Indian nobles should view with great patience this treatment of their idols and temples. That they were dissimulating was proved later on when they saw how few the foreigners were. Time disclosed what the Indians in general had in their hearts . . ."[66]

In the early part of 1520, the expedition held a financial stock-taking.[67] The gold which had been gained, both from presents and from items seized, was estimated at 160,000 pesos. The Royal Fifth was, therefore, named as 32,000 pesos. This was exclusive of gold and silver jewellery, which in turn must have been worth, said the *Caudillo*, another 75,000 pesos or more.[68] A fifth of the remainder of the first amount of gold (128,000 pesos), which Cortés took for himself, would have been 25,600 pesos.[69] That left for distribution 102,400 pesos. But Cortés' had then to reimburse himself for his expenses, including the sailors' wages, the ships, the food and the horses. Money had also to be allocated to the two priests on the expedition, to Cortés' agents in Spain and the seventy men left behind at Vera Cruz. These subtractions left little to be divided. Some money was in fact distributed, and one or two soldiers seem to have been satisfied.[70] Senior captains such as Andrés de Tapia received five hundred pesos.[71] Ordinary soldiers were offered a hundred pesos. Most of them looked on that as an insult. Cortés apparently soothed them with some secret payments.[72] All the estimates were arrived at after the gold, including most of the jewels, had been melted down, in accordance with practice; indeed, in accordance with the law, though Cortés could not have known that, on 14 September 1519, in Barcelona, provision had precisely been made for the melting down of gold, "since, without melting down, it is impossible to know its weight or estimate its value".[73] No doubt the Mexicans were surprised at the destruction of their artefacts, though they do not seem to have made any complaint: the only indigenous leader in the Indies known to have done so was the son of Comogre, a chief in Panama, who reproved Balboa for melting down gold masks.[74] (Cortés had brought with him several specialists such as Antonio de Benavides to perform these duties.)

The figure for the booty – 160,000 pesos – was later challenged. Cortés' enemies estimated that there had been at least 700,000 pesos.[75] In a lawsuit in 1529, Cortés was even said to have been given a total of 800,000 pesos' worth of gold, feathered things, cloths and silver by Montezuma.[76] The truth of these long-ago accounts is never likely to be discovered.

In comparison with what other conquistadors had been accumulating (and giving to the Crown) these were large sums. Ponce de Léon, for example, in his property in Puerto Rico, accumulated, in the thirteen years 1509 to 1521, just under 22,000 pesos, of which he sent just under 4,000 to the King.[77]

There were other disputes. Alvarado, in the enquiry against him a few years later, was accused of having seized 30,000 pesos, as well as feathers, jade, cloth and cacao, with no Royal Fifth paid.[78] Then Velázquez de León and Gonzalo de Mexía, treasurer of the army (and responsible for seeing that the men of the expedition received their fair share of the booty) quarrelled over a set of gold plates that the former had had made by goldsmiths at Azcapotzalco (many captains had made similar commissions). Mexía claimed a fifth of the cost for the Crown. Velázquez said that Cortés had given him the gold from which it was made and so no fifth was payable. The two drew swords. They fought. Both were wounded. Mexía was also later said to have "lost" 3,000 pesos.[79]

Cortés imprisoned both these conquistadors in chains in a chamber near Montezuma's. The Emperor heard Velázquez de León groaning at the heavy chains which he had to carry around when he moved. Finding out through the page Orteguilla what had happened, Montezuma asked Cortés to be merciful (a remarkable transformation in the character of the unbending Emperor). Cortés assented; he first sent Velázquez de León to Cholula for more gold and then ordered him to follow Ordaz and found a city at Coatzacoalcos.[80] This was not the only time when Montezuma intervened on behalf of a Castilian whom Cortés wished to punish.

Mexía remained in confinement a little longer. He was angry. He allowed himself to say that "Hernan Cortés does not content himself to take the authority of the Community, but wants to take over that of the King also." Cortés heard of this remark and, in consequence, held Mexía for many days in "a small hut without seeing anyone".[81] Cortés said later that the explanation for Mexía's imprisonment was that he had embezzled certain funds. Mexía, an Extremeño, who had once been a favourite of Cortés, never forgave him for this.[82]

Some time in March 1520 the page Orteguilla went to Cortés. He told him that Montezuma wished to see him. Orteguilla added that he had noticed several secret discussions between Montezuma and his lords which suggested that some kind of plot was being contemplated. Cortés went with Olid and four other captains, as well as the two interpreters, to the Emperor. Montezuma seemed that day to be a new man. His gods, so long silent, had apparently now told him to make war on the Castilians, on the ground that they had stolen gold and other things, imprisoned himself and other lords, as well as imposed a Mary and crucifix in their holy places.[83] Montezuma said that, since he had become fond of the Castilians, he wished them to leave before they were attacked. He told the *Caudillo* to ask anything of him that he wanted before leaving. He offered Cortés himself two loads of gold and one each for each of his men.[84] In this statement he made no mention at all of the lost god or lost leader who had disappeared in the past, nor of the legend that he would return to rule the empire; nor did he speak of the oath which Cortés insisted that he took. He did not mention King Charles of Spain.

One reason, probably, for Montezuma's new self-assertion was that his own people were at last seeking to persuade him to expel, or kill, the Castilians, because of the affronts which they had been given, despite receiving them so well.[85] They were beginning, for the first time perhaps in the history of the empire, to question the judgement of their ruler. Even more important, on what the conquistadors thought of as 14 February, a new Mexican year had begun. The fatal 1-Reed, bad for kings, had given way to 2-Flint, a far more promising time.

Flint, *tecpatl*, was associated calendrically with beginnings and origins. The flint knife (and mention of flint usually meant a knife) was identified with the birth of the Mexica. The first flint knife was said to have fallen out of the night sky on to Chicomoztoc, the mythological Hill of the Seven Caves, conceived of as the Mexican place of origin. From that knife, sixteen hundred gods had sprung. The flint knife was also a symbol for the Mexica themselves. 1-Flint was associated with Huitzilopochtli. 2-Flint was a less good year than that, but it was vastly superior to 1-Reed.[86] Propitiation of Quetzalcoatl was no longer necessary.

What was necessary, in the meantime, was a suitable appeasement of Tlaloc, the rain god. He had to be given food, precious objects, people, children (small, like the little Tlalocs who were believed to wait on the chief god of that name), in a series of festivals.[87] The children had to cry, in order to indicate to the god exactly what was required; and to achieve this, their nails were often drawn out and thrown into the lake where they would be eaten by the lake monster Ahuítzotl, who usually lived from the nails of drowned persons.[88] Sometimes, it seems that the children were the offspring of noblemen, though probably the latter could escape the duty by offering slaves.[89]

The second month of the Mexican year, Tlacaxipeualiztli, literally "the Flaying of Men", from 6 March to 25 March, meantime, was marked by very elaborate ceremonies indeed, to celebrate the spring equinox. Montezuma must have been anxious to participate in them. They included a gladiatorial contest where eagle and jaguar warriors fought captives armed only with feather-edged swords; the wearing of the skins of the slave impersonators of at least nine gods (including Quetzalcoatl); the sacrifice of captives by the god Xipe Totec, represented by the mysterious Youallauan, "the Drinker by Night" (because it was at night that rain first came); and a dance, in which Montezuma was expected to wear the skin of a captive enemy lord.[90] If the Emperor was a prisoner and unable to perform these things, what would happen to the rain?

Perhaps too Montezuma had begun to grieve at the imprisonment and suffering of his nephew, Cacama. Cortés' charm, which had won such victories, may have waned. Perhaps most important of all, the task of feeding two or three thousand guests daily (including the Tlaxcalan allies) was becoming onerous, even for the rich Mexica.[91]

By this time too the Mexica seem to have made some important military moves which they kept secret from the Spaniards. Thus earlier in the year, messengers had been sent by some members of the administration to tributary monarchs to ask them to send military aid and other help to Tenochtitlan, so that they could expel the intruders. The initiative for these moves must have come from someone of the council of the realm who had remained out of prison, and who had been able to communicate privately with Montezuma – who we must suppose was seeking to co-ordinate all the initiatives which he had set in train. Among those who came to help was Cuauhtémoc, a young cousin of Montezuma, who had been lord of Ixtatecpan and who had now been for some time in an administrative or political capacity in Tlatelolco.[92] A serious effort was thus under way to assemble a new Mexican army, even though the season for war, as laid down in the calendars, had passed, and though the whole chain of command had been interrupted by the Castilians' imprisonment of the Emperor.[93]

Cortés replied to Montezuma that, though the Castilians could, of course, leave Tenochtitlan, he could not unfortunately leave the territory, since he had no ships. He therefore asked Montezuma to control his followers if possible, until he had built three ships on the coast. He wondered whether Montezuma could provide him with carpenters to assist. Montezuma was delighted to do this. He also told Cortés to take his time over leaving. There was no hurry. His enthusiasm at expecting soon to see the back of his uncomfortable guests was modified, however, when Cortés told him that, of course, if the Castilians were to abandon the land, he would insist on taking Montezuma to see the King of Castile.[94]

The plan to make the ships went ahead. Cortés asked that same Martín López, who had made the brigantines on the Lake of Mexico with the carpenter Alonso Yáñez, to go down to Cempoallan and begin work about the middle of March. Indian carpenters cut the wood needed, on the slopes of Mt. Orizaba, and carried it to the "shipyards" at Vera Cruz. Cortés' plan was that he would soon have at least one ship to carry gold and other treasure back to Spain.[95] He also wanted to send a ship to Santo Domingo to buy more horses, men and arms, in order to consolidate his conquests. Surely he never contemplated at any stage a withdrawal from Tenochtitlan. According to his own account, he told the carpenters: "Comply by building these ships ... Cut enough wood. In the meanwhile, God, our Lord, in whose business we are engaged, will provide men, help and a remedy so that we do not lose this good country ... work as slowly as you can, but appear to be doing something, so that they do not suspect ..."[96] One ship was soon near completion on the river Actopan near Cempoallan.[97] All the same, the building of the ships was to keep Montezuma happy; or, at least, guessing.

Whatever plan Cortés had, or did not have, for these ships was, however, transformed by disturbing news, in early April. A Cuban Indian in the employ of Alonso de Cervantes, probably an Extremeño, who had been with Sandoval on the coast, came to report that what seemed to be a Spanish ship had appeared off the coast near Villa Rica de la Vera Cruz. Most of Cortés' army thought that reinforcements had arrived, as a result of the efforts in Spain, on behalf of Cortés, of the *procuradores*, Montejo and Portocarrero. But the *Caudillo* was less sanguine. Perhaps the new Castilians had come from Diego Velázquez, and in anger.

V

Cortés' Plans Undone

23
The King, our lord, is more King than other Kings

*"The King, our lord, is more King than other Kings: more King because he has
more and greater realms than others; more King because he alone on earth is
King of Kings; more King because he is more naturally King since he is not
only King and son of Kings but grandson and successor of seventy and more
Kings and so loves his realms as he does himself . . ."*
Dr Ruiz de la Mota, at Santiago de Compostela, April 1520

THE APPEARANCE OF Pánfilo de Narváez's fleet off the coast of
Mexico in April 1520 was the consequence of the departure from
there, nine months before, of Alonso Hernández Portocarrero and
Francisco de Montejo.

Those two conquistadors, it will be remembered, left for home on the
Santa María de la Concepción as *procuradores*, representatives, of the
newly founded town of Villa Rica de la Vera Cruz. Their pilot was the
experienced Antonio de Alaminos, their master the same Juan Bautista
who had sailed with Cortés from Cuba to Vera Cruz. The ship, Cortés'
flagship, had been the last vessel of any size on the Mexican shore. It
carried treasure, and documents of the first importance. The mission of
the *procuradores* was to persuade the young King of Spain, Charles, to
recognise Cortés as governor and captain-general of the new territory;
territory which he had, of course, not yet conquered. They had been told
by Cortés to go directly to Spain. Speed was essential. Alaminos had,
therefore, determined to travel north of Cuba and then along the Gulf
Stream. He had discovered this route six years before, when with Ponce
de León's expedition to seek the Fountain of Youth. To find the Gulf
Stream might seem a fair compensation for failing to encounter that
sacred spring.

Alaminos' plan was then to turn north-east through the Lucays, as the
Bahamas were then known, before setting off on the long haul across the
Atlantic. Diego Velázquez later wrote crossly to his friend, Bishop
Fonseca, that that was a dangerous route which should not have been
taken.[1] Yet very soon it became the conventional way of travelling to
Spain from Cuba and Mexico.

Montejo persuaded his companions to stop in Cuba on the way home.
That was against Cortés' orders. But it was understandable: Montejo had

a property at Mariel not far off the route. Portocarrero, too, was said to have been ill.[2] Having taken an unconscionably long time since leaving Vera Cruz (presumably they travelled via Yucatan), they anchored off Cuba at Mariel on 23 August, and took on board water, cassava bread, and pigs.[3] They stayed for three days, during which Montejo busied himself organising his affairs. During this stay, one of Montejo's servants, Francisco Pérez, caught a glimpse of the treasure which they were taking home to Spain. There was "an infinite amount of gold, so much indeed that there was no other ballast than gold".[4] He exclaimed later that he had never seen such riches. Montejo is supposed to have sworn this individual to secrecy. But in the circumstances he could hardly have expected that that promise would be kept.[5] Perhaps Montejo really wanted to spread the word abroad about the kind of wealth available in Mexico in order to encourage Cuban settlers to go there. Montejo's loyalties seem a little divided: should he keep his old friend Velázquez informed? Or should he be loyal to his new one, Cortés? The best course would seem to be to keep in touch with both. Cortés would have done the same in similar circumstances. At all events, Francisco Pérez was sent by Montejo's administrator to Santiago to see Velázquez. There were, he told the Governor, 270,000 or even 300,000 castellanos in gold on board his master's ship.[6]

Diego Velázquez had passed the first six months after Cortés had finally left Cuba without much complaint. He was, as has been seen, swift to anger but swift to forgive. He had, it is true, confiscated Cortés' and some other conquistadors' property in Cuba.[7] Cortés' wife Catalina must have suffered. That was all. The modest Cuban sugar harvest, meantime, had ended, some more gold had been found, some more tobacco had been successfully harvested, and the Governor's little court in Santiago had survived. The native population had continued to fall. But the economic consequences had been offset by a continued trade in slaves with Pedrarias in Castilla del Oro. Velázquez had learned to be thankful for small mercies.

His only concern had been caused by the developments in Hispaniola that winter and spring. The weak Jeronymite friars had lost their power in December 1518. Their place was taken by a judge, Rodrigo de Figueroa, who became supreme magistrate. An Extremeño, and a relation of the Count of Feria (like Vasco Porcallo), he was to Velázquez an unknown quantity. He arrived from Spain in the summer of 1519. One of his missions was to conduct an enquiry into his predecessors' actions. By a declaration that "there were two types of Indian . . . those who accepted both Christianity and Castilian suzerainty; and those who resisted one or the other, and who could therefore be killed as Caribs", he showed himself, fortunately to Velázquez's mind, to be in spirit neither a Las Casas nor a Cisneros.[8]

A second, more disquieting thing was the news that, inspired by general discontent in the face of the exactions of the civil servants, in particular those of Velázquez's old friend, the royal treasurer, Miguel de Pasamonte, and influenced by the similar developments in Castile, a meeting of representatives (*procuradores*) of settlers from all parts of Hispaniola had met in January almost as a parliament of the island.[9] Pasamonte, it is true, had secured a new licence from the Crown in June to capture slaves in Venezuela, in order to serve a sugar mill which he had in mind.[10] But the political situation looked distinctly uneasy.

But good news had also come. This was (as earlier noticed) that Pánfilo de Narvaéz, Velázquez's second-in-command in the conquest of Cuba, and for the time being at home in Spain, had in April obtained from the Crown all the decrees (*reales cédulas*) which Velázquez needed in order to conquer Yucatan and the territory which he now knew, confusingly, to be sure, as "Culúa".[11] Velázquez's personal representative in Spain, Fr. Benito Martín, had at the court in Barcelona gained for him real independence from Diego Colón – though it is improbable that he would have known that by August.[12] In that month itself Fr. Martín had secured royal approval for the nomination of Pablo Mexía, a citizen of Trinidad, and a friend of his, as he was of Velázquez, as factor of the two "new islands" of Yucatan and Cozumel.[13]

But Velázquez's satisfaction was short-lived. For suddenly here, with the news of Montejo's arrival, was evidence that "Cortesillo" had found a colossal sum of money and other fine objects. He seemed to have unimaginably grand prospects. Cortés' action in sending an "infinite" amount of gold direct to the Crown, bypassing Velázquez himself, seemed an unparalleled act of insolence. It was also a personal injury, by one whom he, the Governor, had looked upon as a follower of his own for many years (*criado mío de mucho tiempo*). Velázquez had had confidence in Cortés, he wrote to Rodrigo de Figueroa, in Santo Domingo. That was why he had given him the command instead of to one of many other deserving people, including some of his own relations.[14] Now look what return he had been given!

Consumed by a desire for vengeance, determined to lay his hands on the gold, and to stop Cortés in every way possible, Velázquez first sent Gonzalo de Guzmán, an old benefactor of Cortés in Hispaniola as it happened, with Manuel de Rojas, a fellow citizen of Cuéllar (and a nephew by marriage), to hold up Montejo and Portocarrero on the high seas.[15]

But Guzmán and Rojas failed to find their prey.[16] Alaminos had already led the messengers of Cortés through the Bahamas. So on 7 October Velázquez turned to the law. First he organised a small enquiry in Cuba, on the usual lines, with thirteen questions put to ten witnesses who under oath sustained the Governor's view of the iniquity of Cortés' conduct.[17] In these hearings much detail was offered about the voyage of Montejo and Portocarrero: how the gold on board was more than anyone thought; and how the treasure included two wheels of gold and silver.[18] Velázquez and his friends also launched a legal attack on Montejo and Portocarrero, requiring them to be detained for defrauding the King.[19] Guzmán set off for Spain on 15 October in order to initiate proceedings.[20] He took with him an official letter to Bishop Fonseca telling him what had happened. This begged that bishop to thwart the designs of Cortés.[21] Velázquez accompanied that letter with a private one to Fonseca going a little more deeply, and more passionately, into the behaviour of Cortés. The Governor even asked Rodrigo de Figueroa in Hispaniola to write to the King about Cortés' "rebellion".[22]

Velázquez also planned an expedition to pursue and punish Cortés. He thought for a time of leading it himself. But his enthusiasm for such journeys at his age was modest. In addition, in October, smallpox reached Cuba in the form of an epidemic.

This visitation was the first outbreak in the New World of a European disease on a large scale. It seems to have originated in Sanlúcar de Barrameda and other places in south-west Spain in 1519.[23] It was carried to Hispaniola. There it had a calamitous effect. The small number of Indians who had survived in Hispaniola had no defence against it. The disease had been the final blow to the Jeronymite friars. They confessed to failure in their mission when a third of the Indians whom they had arranged to move to new villages died.[24] In May 1519, officials in Santo Domingo had to report that most of the Indians in the island were dead of smallpox. By the end of 1519 the disease had essentially put an end to the indigenous population.[25]

By November of that year the epidemic had reached Cuba. Here too the population collapsed. So did the Cuban production of gold which had depended on Indian workers. According to his own account, Velázquez felt that, in these circumstances, his responsibility was to stay in Cuba and remain with his people rather than go to Yucatan and "Culúa".[26] That statement was probably true. Velázquez had many faults, but he did have a sense of public service. The direction of an expedition to face Cortés would have been a good excuse, had he wanted one, for not staying in a disease-racked land.

Velázquez, therefore, chose Pánfilo de Narváez, just back from Spain, to organise an army to bring Cortés to his senses.[27] Pedrarias in the Castilla del Oro had shown how to cope with upstarts. He had had Balboa executed the previous January. Narváez would hang Cortés.[28]

Ignorant of the details of Velázquez's reaction but aware of its likely character, Portocarrero and Montejo had reached home, Sanlúcar de

Barrameda, by the mouth of the river Guadalquivir, at the end of October 1519. They may have taken off some gold privately there, but were in Seville by 5 November.[29] They were not immediately received as the heroes of a new discovery. Indeed, no sooner had the *Santa María de la Concepción* docked alongside the quay in Seville than Juan López de Recalde, Bishop Fonseca's protégé who was the accountant at the Casa de la Contratación, confiscated the treasure which they had carried. He also seized 4,000 pesos of gold which they had brought for their own expenses in Spain and those of Cortés' father, Martín.[30] It was Diego Velázquez's chaplain, Fr. Benito Martín, who had inspired this high-handed action. Presumably he had heard something from Velázquez during the previous spring about the way that Cortés had departed from Santiago; and a boat from Cuba, captained by a certain Covarrubias, had arrived in Seville at almost the same time as that of the *procuradores*. (Though it brought letters from Velázquez, it is hard to believe that it had beaten the *procuradores* in speed. Further, it included some gold sent by Andrés de Duero to Cortés' father – an interesting sign that even people in Governor Velázquez's circle thought it worthwhile to keep their connections with the new *Caudillo* of "Culúa".)[31] At all events, Fr. Martín requested the Casa de la Contratación, the regulatory body in Seville, to send the *Santa María de la Concepción* back across the Atlantic to Diego Velázquez, and to give authority to the Governor to punish Cortés.

This plea was not immediately heard. For Castile in the late autumn of 1519 was on the edge of chaos. The young King had been elected Holy Roman Emperor in June. The King-Emperor's new Chancellor, Mercurino Gattinara, a Piedmontese of learning, vision and intelligence, was ambitious for Charles to re-unite Christianity, under a single crown. He had advised Charles to prepare for this destiny in Germany, the heart of his empire. But the rumoured new departure of the monarch was causing not so much unease in Spain as fury.

In these circumstances it was easy enough for the experienced Bishop Fonseca to control the politics of the Indies just as he had done for a quarter of a century. Anything which promised continuity was to be welcomed. It is true that he had not maintained the bland Aragonese, Lope de Conchillos, as his secretary. Perhaps some inbuilt sense of self-preservation had told him that further protection of such an unpopular *converso* might be imprudent. The previous year a strong wave of anti-Semitism had swept through the court after a rumour had suggested that the Inquisition might be reformed.[32] Neither did Fonseca nor his new secretary, Francisco de los Cobos, a protégé of Conchillos but an "old Christian" from Ubeda, near Jaén, set about granting *encomiendas* or *repartimientos* in the Indies to themselves or their home-based colleagues, as Conchillos had done in 1514 (it would have been hard to find enough Indians in the West Indies to form an *encomienda*). Nor again did Fonseca and his associates permit themselves the falsification of royal documents such as they had carried out without hindrance during the last years of the reign of King Ferdinand.[33] But the power of the Bishop remained. Los Cobos, clever and self-made, was as ambitious and as persistent a bureaucrat as Conchillos. Friends of Fonseca's could still count on being nominated to places of influence. The King, except for his concern for the voyage which he himself had financed, in August, of the Portuguese Magellan from Sanlúcar to seek a passage round the world, continued to show little interest in the Indies.

By November 1519, Fonseca had managed to arrange the establishment, on a more or less permanent basis, of a group within the Council of Castile, with himself presiding, to deal expressly with matters relating to the empire in the Indies: thus at the end of March 1519 the documents of the Council of Castile were still speaking of "those of the royal council who understand things of the Indies".[34] By September, something close to the future Council of the Indies was in being, though it was still in a fragmentary shape, had no buildings, no permanent officials, and no formal approval.[35]

The Emperor, meantime, trusted Fonseca so much as to commission him to organise the large fleet which would the next year carry him and the court to the Low Countries.[36]

These developments seemed to be a consolidation of Fonseca's position. But the atmosphere in Spain was opposed to a real consolidation of anything. In most places in the heartland of Castile, between the Douro and the Tagus, *procuradores* from the towns were seeking to assert their influence on royal policy.

Though the Emperor was not especially interested in the Indies, the Chancellor, Gattinara, had time for them.[37] Indeed he seemed to have time for everything. He sought to give the Holy Roman Empire, which he was now being called upon to serve, a practical form. So far as the Indies were concerned, Gattinara made it evident that Fonseca's place was only held on sufferance. Fonseca might remain in day-to-day control of matters relating to the Indies. But what had happened once under Cisneros might, Gattinara seemed to imply, by the mere fact of his own supervisory role, happen again.

Those interested in changing the way that the Spanish dominions in the Indies had hitherto been managed were busy those days. For example, the historian Oviedo, a one-time settler in Castilla del Oro, presented proposals to Fonseca for the establishment in Santo Domingo of a "priory fortress" of the Order of Santiago, with a hundred knights to patrol the confines of the empire, and to prevent both brutalities and indiscipline. Fr. de Las Casas was suggesting to Diego Colón (who still believed that he had permanent rights over all the Americas) a revised version of one of the ideas in his memorandum to Cisneros of two years before: namely, a similar series of fortresses every hundred leagues along the north coast of South America. These would be "happy zones", where Indians would be protected rather than traded, raped or kidnapped.

Fonseca would have liked to have had Cortés' representatives in Seville hanged as rebels as soon as he knew what they were trying to do.[38] But both Gattinara and the Bishop of Badajoz, Dr Pedro Ruiz de la Mota, almoner to the Emperor Charles since his days in the Netherlands, a member of the Council of Castile, and president of the *cortes* (parliament) of that kingdom, as well as Francisco de los Cobos, the royal secretary, were impressed by the quantity, as well as the quality, of the gold which, they understood, Cortés had sent. They, and others in the court, began to talk of how pleased they were that a "new world of gold" had been discovered. Fonseca therefore temporised. From his own point of view, that was unwise. For Portocarrero and Montejo of course spoke of what they had seen. So did Alaminos and other members of the crew of the *Santa María de la Concepción*. The confiscated gold, and other treasures, which they had brought from Mexico was shown in the Casa de la Contratación. Fernández de Oviedo, the historian, about to set off for Hispaniola, saw it a few days before the end of 1519: "There was a great deal to see," he ruminated, as if he were a modern visitor to an exhibition.[39] Opinion in Seville, though as preoccupied as anywhere in Castile by the political upheavals then taking shape, was entranced by the evidence of Cortés' discovery of a rich kingdom. Perhaps this was at long last the equivalent in the Indies of the kingdom of Prester John.

Montejo and Portocarrero now made common cause with Martín Cortés, Cortés' father, who seems to have come to live in the capital of Andalusia for the time being, in a house in what had once been the Jewish quarter near Santa María la Blanca[40] – perhaps to be in touch with his son's adventures, of which he may by now have been informed by letter; perhaps to avoid the constant vexations in Medellín. One of the Cortés family's friends (an enemy of the Count), a septuagenarian, Juan Núñez de Prado, had been involved in a charge of murder a year or so before.[41] The only serene aspect of the scene was that Medellín, along with most of Extremadura, seems not to have been concerned in the great troubles about to explode in connection with the revolt of the *comuneros* (in that region only Cáceres and Plasencia would be seriously implicated). Perhaps the territory had already suffered too much from civil wars in the late fifteenth century.

Martín Cortés and the *procuradores* had long discussions in Seville that winter. As no doubt requested by Cortés, they entered into contact with some prominent merchants: Fernando de Herrera from Medellín; Juan de Córdoba, the silversmith and pearl dealer who had been a friend of Columbus and had been one of those concerned with loading the fleet of Ovando in 1502 (indirectly he may have sold to Cortés the pearls which he had given to Cacama); and Luis Fernández de Alfaro, the sea captain who had arranged Cortés' original journey to Santo Domingo, and was now a merchant. These men agreed to send back the *Santa María de la Concepción* to the "new lands" with the goods asked for by Cortés in a memorandum: wine, oil, flour, even underclothes, as well as six mares to be bought in Santo Domingo. Juan de Córdoba and Fernández de Alfaro set about founding a "Yucatan company" for trade in "Yucatan".[42] The *procuradores* and Martín Cortés also borrowed money, presumably on the strength of their confiscated treasure, from a certain Licenciado Juan de la Fuente in order to finance further merchandise.[43]

During all this time in Seville, the *procuradores* moved about freely, while the officials in the Casa de la Contratación made no move to arrest them as they easily could have done. Though those functionaries were old appointees of Fonseca, perhaps some sense of the need to turn a blind eye, even to those whom Fonseca opposed, may have moved them, out of an instinct to preserve themselves in uncertain times. The *procuradores* were protected by Portocarrero's uncle, Licenciado Céspedes, who was at the time judge of the Gradas (that is, magistrate at the market) in Seville: a most useful connection. Meantime their chief enemy, Fr. Benito Martín, had made his way as fast as possible to consult Bishop Fonseca, who had himself set out from Barcelona in order to start to organise the King's fleet in Corunna.[44] Fr. Martín's journey was paid for by drawing on money which had been confiscated from the *procuradores* by the Casa de la Contratación.[45] Gold from Mexico was thus entering the Spanish economy.

Some time in January Montejo and Portocarrero also set off from Seville for the court, which, because of the plague in Barcelona, had been established at Molins del Rey, some miles outside that capital. These *procuradores* had to travel across a country which at that time seemed a continent and was almost in open rebellion in some of the places through which they had to pass. By the time that Portocarrero and Montejo, now with Cortés' father Martín, reached Barcelona, the court had left for Burgos. The Emperor had, however, performed some important business relating to the Indies. He had, for example, heard Las Casas' account of the evils of the Castilian treatment of the Indians in the Caribbean; which, if it was a tenth as violent an oration as Las Casas himself represented it to have been, must have made a strong impression on him.[46] Charles had also issued a decree asking for the treasure which Montejo and Portocarrero had brought from the New World to be handed over by the Casa de la Contratación in Seville to Luis Veret, the keeper of the royal jewels. More important still, he even sent a friendly message to Cortés' emissaries, saying that he was pleased to hear of their arrival, ordering them to go to the court, "the place where I shall be" ("*a donde yo estoviera*"),[47] and asking them to bring with them the Totonac

Indians and to treat them well. Charles spoke of these Totonac slaves as chiefs, rather than victims intended to be sacrificed. He especially asked that, since they had apparently come with no warm clothes, they should be dressed well, in velvet coats "of some good colour", as well as cloaks of scarlet, simple jackets, with stockings and shirts of gold thread. Some good horses too were to be procured in order to carry these prize Indians to the royal presence.[48]

The moderate tone of these letters, and the fact that the monarch was induced to express pleasure at the thought of meeting the *procuradores* (whom, remarkably, he even referred to as such), was a clear indication that Fonseca's power was waning. The influence behind the change must either have been Las Casas directly, Gattinara, or Francisco de los Cobos.

These letters seem to have been brought back to Seville by Fr. Benito Martín, who then set off post-haste for Cuba by the first ship to give his chief, the Governor, the news that the *procuradores* of Vera Cruz had arrived, and that Francisco de Montejo was conducting himself more as an emissary of his new master, Cortés, than an ally of his old one, Velázquez.

Meantime, Charles V did not cease his attention to Indian matters even though he was on the road: a letter to Diego Velázquez about the recent death of Amador de Lares, chief accountant of the island of Cuba, and once one of Cortés' friends, was dispatched from the monastery of Santo Domingo de Calzada, three days short of Burgos.[49]

Cortés' party had much to do in Barcelona, even though the King had left, for they there established contact with Francisco Núñez, a cousin of Cortés, and a nephew of Martín. He was the son of that Inés Gómez de Paz, Martín Cortés' half-sister, in whose house the young Cortés had stayed when in Salamanca in his teens. Like his father, Francisco Núñez was a lawyer. He joined the friends of Hernán Cortés. He travelled on with the others to Burgos.[50] The *procuradores* also succeeded in meeting in Barcelona that immensely experienced royal counsellor, Lorenzo Galíndez de Carvajal, historian, lawyer, and native of Plasencia in Extremadura, who through the Monroys was also a cousin of Cortés. He had written a report in 1503 for the Crown on the reorganisation of the state bureaucracy: a brave thing for anyone to do.[51] His annals of the reign of Ferdinand and Isabel are not without value. His support for Cortés was swiftly gained, partly because of his connection with the Monroy family; partly no doubt by learning from the *procuradores* of the reality of the Mexican wealth. Extremeños usually supported one another, and Galíndez de Carvajal had interested himself in the feuds in Trujillo (where his father had lived, and which was a mere forty miles south of Plasencia), on the side of the Altamirano family: with whom, of course, Cortés was connected through his mother. Galíndez was a dry man and one critical of the corruption with which Fonseca had been associated. So his support for the projects of his distant cousin may not have had to be gained by bribery.[52]

Burgos was also an illusion so far as the friends of Cortés were concerned. The court had always been peripatetic. It would remain so under Charles V. Even his Habsburg grandfather Maximilian had not had a fixed capital. By the time that Montejo, Portocarrero, Martín Cortés and Núñez had reached the city, Charles and the court had moved on to Valladolid. The brevity of the visit to Burgos had infuriated the citizens there. They had supposed that the *Cortes* of Castile would meet. But Charles had summoned the meeting for Santiago de Compostela: a decision which astonished even his friends. Had not San Isidore predicted that the day when the *Cortes* met in Galicia the kingdom would be doomed?[53]

The royal departure from Burgos, indeed, had the characteristics of flight. The King was short of time: that was why he did not even receive the three Jeronymite fathers who had returned to Spain after their unhappy time in Santo Domingo in January 1520 (they went off angry to their monasteries).[54] The Emperor wanted to leave as quickly as possible for Germany which he thought needed him more. By his own standards he was right: "those knaveries of Luther", as Diego de Ordaz would describe the German Reformation, were clearly more of a challenge to the Habsburgs' imperial mission than were the town councils of Castile.[55] Then though elected Holy Roman Emperor, Charles could not call himself by that title until he had been crowned: a ceremony planned for Aix-la-Chapelle in the summer.

Montejo and Portocarrero, accompanied by Martín Cortés and Núñez, caught up with the court at Valladolid. They were far from alone. For there also, *en route* for Santiago, were the increasingly assertive *procuradores* of thirty important cities belonging to the *Cortes* of Castile. There also was the Council of Castile. Hernán Cortés' *procuradores*, perhaps feeling that their assumed title rendered them somewhat suspect in the eyes of the monarch, presented to the Council a petition from Cortés' father. This asked for the release of the funds which they had brought from Vera Cruz and which had been embargoed in Seville. Similarly, Martín Cortés requested the Crown to release the *Santa María de la Concepción* in which the *procuradores* had returned to Spain so that it could be filled with supplies which Cortés had sent money to buy. He asked the Crown too to confirm the appointment of Cortés as governor and chief magistrate of the new territory, "until the country's conquest was complete".[56] The petition showed that Hernán Cortés was going to try to capture the whole of Mexico, not just settle on the coast. The text was no doubt written by Licenciado Francisco Núñez. But the information which it contained of course derived from Montejo or Portocarrero.

The petition might easily have been lost among the vast amount of documents which the Emperor was receiving every day. The Emperor spent much of his time in Valladolid dealing with such affairs as the appeal of Pedro Girón, husband of Mencia de Guzmán, daughter by his first marriage of the late Duke of Medina Sidonia, who was claiming the vast lands of that dukedom on behalf of his wife, threatening that, if he did not obtain justice, he would go and take it himself.[57] Meantime, not far away, in Salamanca, a group of Franciscans, Dominicans and Augustinians collaborated with the councillors of that city to produce an agenda for the forthcoming *Cortes* which would turn into a programme for the revolution of the municipalities of Spain.[58] The most important item was that the Emperor should not go to Flanders. But also – and that attention to things of the Indies must have surprised the monarch – the friars demanded that the Casa de la Contratación should not be removed from Seville (certainly not to the Low Countries); and that the salaried jobs relating to the Indies as well as to Castile should not be given to foreigners – by which, of course, the petitioners meant not to Flemings.

The Emperor, the prince in whose name Cortés spoke so often to uncomprehending Mexicans so far away, and in such unpromising circumstances, was then just twenty years old. He seemed unimpressive. Adrian of Utrecht had been unable to teach him Latin. He still could not speak Spanish, though he understood it. He seemed a callow, if serious, youth. He was short of stature, his face was pale, and his eyes were motionless. Due to a defect in his long (and from so many portraits well-known) jaw, his mouth hung open much of the time: so much so that, when passing through Catalayud the previous year, a workman had gaily come up to him and said, "Lord, shut your mouth, the flies of this country are naughty."[59] He was so reserved in manner, so slow in speech (even in the French which he spoke naturally) that his mental capacity was questioned: after all, his mother was Queen Juana . . .[60] His reserved dignity had made an impression in England, where he had gone on a state visit at the age of thirteen. But the English were easily impressed. The Spaniards wanted a king who was more than a mere incoherent Burgundian nobleman.

Yet though Burgundy seemed to limit the Emperor, Burgundy had also made him. To Burgundy, he and Europe owed his high principles, his chivalric bearing, his style of life as a great international prince, his grand etiquette, and that sense of obligation to fight for his honour which was embodied in the code of the Order of the Golden Fleece.[61] That was all in the future. For the moment it was hard to picture him as the focus of allegiance, loyalty and vassaldom in Tenochtitlan.

But the New World was firmly placed on the agenda, so to speak, of Castile that spring in Valladolid. First, on 3 March, after mass (it being a Sunday), the court was able to admire for the first time both the marvellous works of art which Cortés had sent from Mexico and the Totonac Indians who had accompanied those objects. The treasure had been brought up in carefully made wooden boxes from Seville by Luis Veret, keeper of the royal jewels. They were displayed in the Convent of Santa Clara. So were five Totonac Indians, three men and two girls, all now elegantly dressed in bright colours, as the King had curiously requested, by well-known tailors and jewellers of Seville: the documents suggest that blue and green velvet had been added to Charles' request. Mounted on mules, provided with gloves against the Castilian winter (five pairs carefully noted as having cost a hundred and twenty maravedís)[62] and escorted by Domingo de Ochandiano, a nephew of the treasurer of the Casa de la Contratación, they must have been exhausted on arrival, since not only had the journey from Seville been long, but they, to begin with, had set out for Valencia, only turning north at Linares when they realised that the monarch was heading for the north-west not the east.[63] From the documents available it seems, though, that the monarch had not yet himself seen the treasure.

Three persons who did see the treasures at Valladolid wrote their impressions: the papal legate, Giovanni Ruffo di Forli, the Archbishop of Cosenza; Bartolomé de Las Casas; and Peter Martyr.

The Archbishop did not take to the Indians. He found the girls short of stature, disagreeable and unprepossessing in appearance, even if one of them had successfully learned Spanish. He was shocked to see how the bodies of the men were pierced and cut all over. Like most Europeans, he found the placing of a labret in the lower lip disconcerting. On the other hand, he was pleased when he was told that the Indians would like to become Christians. He admired the great wheels of gold and silver and the other jewels. The books which had been part of the treasure also pleased him. He was glad to know that the script in them was "probably Indian".[64] What script that could have been is, however, a mystery.

Las Casas also saw the Indians and the treasure at Valladolid, as he recorded in his *History*. He commented extensively, and said, "these wheels were certainly things to be seen".[65] But he made no comment on the Indians. (He also said that he saw the treasures the same day that the Emperor saw them; but the Emperor did not see them till he reached Tordesillas. After many years, such a mistake is comprehensible.)

Peter Martyr, discerning courtier that he was, was more enthusiastic than anyone. He wrote in a letter to Pope Leo X: "If ever artists of this kind have touched genius, then surely these natives are they. It is not so much the gold nor the precious stones that I admire as the cleverness of the artists and the workmanship which must exceed the value of the material . . . In my opinion, I have never seen anything which for beauty could more delight the eye."[66] He was especially interested in the books which Cortés had sent. Martyr had been to Egypt, and knew of Egyptian achievements with papyrus. Here was something comparable. He noted, "They do not bind them as we do, leaf by leaf, they extend a single leaf to the length of several cubits, after having pasted a certain number of square leaves one to the other with a bitumen so adhesive that the whole seems to have passed through the hands of a most skilful bookbinder."

The impact of the letter of Martyr was considerable. Leo X, the Medicean pope, probably had it read aloud, as was his custom, at a dinner with his cardinals and his sister. It was soon published: certainly before the end of 1520. Many people no doubt saw the exhibition in Valladolid. But far more read or heard of what it presented through the letter of Martyr. The event marked the beginning of a new fashion for what Martyr elsewhere called these "rich and truly Elysian lands".[67] In particular, knowledge of Mexican "books" as well as gold thus came to Europe.

Alas, we know nothing of what the Indians who had come to Spain thought of their hosts. Montaigne, in his essay on cannibals, reported a conversation through interpreters with some native Brazilian Indians in 1562. They expressed surprise that such strong men as the royal Swiss guard should accept such a weak child as Charles IX as King of France; and they were also impressed by the inequality of French society.[68] Charles V might have excited similar astonishment; and the contrasts of old Spain might have seemed formidable too. But in 1520 there were no adequate interpreters, the Indian who claimed to have learned Spanish does not seem to have talked much, and no exchanges are recorded.

The exhibition was not only an occasion for the court to become apprised of the treasures of Mexico. It was also a chance for the *procuradores* to get to know the court. Martyr and Las Casas talked at length with them, as did the former with the pilot Alaminos.

The second event which may have helped to transform European attitudes to the new Elysium was an account of Grijalva's journey, written by Fr. Juan Díaz, the priest on the expedition, as he was on Cortés'. It was published on 7 March.[69] This *Itinerario* was widely read. Its publication had been arranged by Fr. Benito Martín, Velázquez's agent in Spain, who thought that it would show how it had really been the governor's nephew Grijalva who had discovered the new land and first heard of the new kingdom. This scheme misfired. The publication awoke public interest, but it made Cortés' activities seem even more fascinating.

Ten days later, on 17 March, a third event occurred in respect of the world's attitude to Mexico: a pamphlet was printed by the well-known Friedrich Peypus in Nuremberg, which gave an account of the expeditions of Fernández de Córdoba, Grijalva and – for the first time – Cortés. This publication, *Ein Auszug ettlicher Sendbrieff*, etc., purported to have been taken from letters received by the King. The writer's information could also have come from Alaminos or some of the crew of the *Santa*

María de la Concepción.[70] One of the pamphlet's interesting accusations was that the Mexica staged at least five thousand human sacrifices of children every year. All the same, Peypus insisted that the Mexica would be assiduous Christians when and if they were taught.

By this time the Emperor had left Valladolid. Indeed, he was chased out of it. The councillors of the city had proposed sitting with representatives of all social classes, the radical programme of the monks of Salamanca was communicated to the councillors. The city was alive with rumours. It was said that Charles was proposing to go to Tordesillas, seize his mother Juana (imprisoned there) and take her to Germany. The great bell of the church of San Miguel was rung by mistake. That was a customary signal for a disaster. Several thousand citizens came out with sticks and stones. They made for the palace. Charles fled, not without a scuffle at the southern gate of the city, and in torrents of rain. He then did go to Tordesillas, some twenty miles to the south-west.[71] So did the court, the members of parliament, the friends of Hernán Cortés, and the Totonac Indians in their velvet suits. There the King at last saw in his rooms all the things which had been sent to him from Yucatan: including the three Indian men and the two Indian girls. Finding that they were suffering from the cold, he asked that they be sent back as soon as possible to Seville.[72] There is no proof that Charles now saw Cortés' *procuradores*, his father and his legal adviser. But it is probable that he did, even if only formally and distantly. The interview, assuming that it occurred, was almost certainly made possible by the intervention of Cortés' supporter and kinsman, Galíndez de Carvajal, the Extremeño member of the Council of Castile. The greeting made, these representatives of Cortés could subsequently establish good relations with the Council.[73]

The Emperor and the court set off for Santiago on the next stage of the long journey to Corunna and to Fonseca's fleet planned there. The treasure, like Cortés' delegation, accompanied him. The Totonacs went back to Seville.

The royal journey must have been inconvenient. The King stopped at fourteen places on the route: some of these overnight halts (Benavente, Astorga, Ponferrada, Sarria) may have been adequate for a court; others (Villapando, Bañeza, Mellide) could scarcely have been so, even if the second part of the journey lay along the road of St James, so that some kind of lodging would have been available. From Astorga, it is pleasant to notice, Charles sent a special message to Seville reminding the Casa de la Contratacíon to "try very hard to make them [the Totonacs] happy".[74] The evident interest of the King inspired Domingo de Ochandiano, the escort of the Indians, to buy for them new woollen gloves, cloaks, and even a pony, on their way back to Seville, as well as to arrange for their shirts to be washed.[75] All the same, one of his charges (who had acquired by now the name of Systan) died, and was buried in Seville, while the others (they by then were called Tamayo, Carlos, and Jorge) were sent back, not to the country of the Totonacs, but to Cuba, the fief of Diego Velázquez, in a boat captained by a Sevillano, Ambrosio Sánchez. They seem to have arrived there, but thereafter they disappeared, perhaps contributing a drop of Totonac blood to the already mixed population of Cuba.[76]

The court reached Santiago de Compostela on 26 March. The monarch was received with "much fish, fruit, wine, and all the necessary things"[77] by Bishop Fonseca, who was a master of organising such celebrations, and remained there for five weeks, till 3 May.[78]

The *Cortes* of Castile was inaugurated by its president, the Bishop of Badajoz, Dr Ruiz de la Mota, the monarch's almoner, who made a truly astonishing speech in the King's presence, in the monastery of San Francisco. He ignored the tumults in Castile and the high state of expectation among the members of the *Cortes*. He said that "the King our King is more King than other kings". The King was not like other kings, since Spain represented only a third of his inheritance (*"un tercio de vuestro pan"*). He was king of kings, being the descendant of seventy kings. He regretted that the people of Spain seemed sad. But the King had been elected Emperor. He had accepted the charge, and had to go to be crowned. Why? For ambition? On the contrary. For the glory of Spain. Just as that country had long ago sent Trajan, Hadrian and Theodosius to rule in Rome, now the "empire had come again to seek its emperor in Spain". The Bishop added that "our King of Spain" had become not only King of the Romans but "Emperor of the World", an echo of thoughts current in the day of Charles V's grandfather, Ferdinand, who was sometimes seen by certain Franciscans, affected by the work of the medieval Abbot Joachim de Fiore, as "the last world-emperor".

The speech most helpfully, so far as the friends of Hernán Cortés were concerned, contained a reference to the "other new world of gold which had been made for the Emperor, and which, before the days of the Emperor had not existed (*"otro nuevo mundo de oro fecho para él, pues antes de nuestros días nunca fue nascido"*): a fine piece of exaggeration.[79]

The King then spoke: he was sorry to leave; he would return in three years; and no public function in Castile would be fulfilled by foreigners. The *Cortes* was not impressed, but in the end it voted the taxes required. The speech of the Bishop left it uncertain whether he was talking, and the Emperor was thinking, of Christendom as the empire; or whether they had political aims in view. The debate continues among historians. For the *procuradores* of Castile, the consequence had been a large subvention to enable the Emperor to pay off some of the loans contracted with German bankers in order to capture the imperial title. For the *procuradores* of Villa Rica de la Vera Cruz, the mood in

Santiago became suddenly favourable. There is nothing that an administration short of money appreciates so much as "another new world of gold".

At Santiago, on 30 April, after the *Cortes* had concluded its main work, the *procuradores* were received by the Council. It must have been now, too, and now only, that the letters from Cortés to the Emperor were handed over.

Those of the Council of Castile "who occupied themselves with the Indies" were an important group of men. They included Cardinal Adrian of Utrecht, the King's learned and pious ex-tutor and now Bishop of Tortosa; Gattinara, the imperial chancellor; Jean de Carondelet, the Archbishop of Palermo, the most prominent of Charles' surviving Flemish courtiers; Antonio de Rojas, Archbishop of Granada; Hernando de Vega, *comendador mayor* of Castile, married to Blanca Enríquez de Acuña, a cousin of the late King Ferdinand – and the man who (*in absentia*, of course) had received the largest single share of Taino Indians in the redistribution of Albuquerque in Hispaniola in 1514;[80] and, of course, Bishop Fonseca.

Several civil servants were also present. Among them was Dr Diego Beltrán, who had already worked for some time in or around the Council of Castile, after having spent the twelve years from 1504 to 1516 as the director of the Casa de la Contratacíon in Seville. (He would in 1523 become the first salaried member of the Council of the Indies.) There was also Luis Zapata, a tiny man who had been a favourite of King Ferdinand. The list was completed by Licenciado García de Padilla; Licenciado Francisco de Aguirre; Cortés' cousin Lorenzo Galíndez de Carvajal; a royal clerk, Juan de Samano, who so often in those days wrote the monarch's letters; and, almost certainly, the royal secretary Francisco de los Cobos.[81] The occasion must have been a difficult one for the *procuradores* from Vera Cruz but, thanks to the advocacy of Francisco Núñez and the support of Galíndez de Carvajal, they emerged from the test very well.

Montejo and Portocarrero were asked many questions. The first-named showed himself on this occasion to be no friend of Diego Velázquez. For example, he accepted that the ships which Cortés had wrecked were old. He also insisted that Cortés had spent more money fitting out the fleet to Yucatan than Velázquez had. Portocarrero said that Cortés had paid for more than two-thirds of the cost of the fleet (while Velázquez had supplied three ships, Cortés had supplied seven).[82] Both said that the Governor of Cuba had done no more for the expedition than a merchant would by selling his goods. They made a good impression.[83]

The Council also apparently saw Gonzalo de Guzmán, who echoed Fonseca's accusation that the friends of Cortés were no more than "fugitives, thieves and traitors".[84] Fonseca still wished to have Cortés condemned as a rebel, and hanged. But the day had passed when that bishop's word was law. His star was indeed in decline for many reasons; even though his brother Antonio, the commander of the militias, had been named captain-general of Castile during the King's absence.[85]

The Council in the end delayed any decision about the nomination of Cortés as governor or chief magistrate in Mexico. "Both punishment and reward are postponed till both parties are heard," Peter Martyr reported.[86] But they did allow Martín Cortés, Portocarrero and Montejo to use the money which they had brought from Mexico, apparently in any way that they saw fit: for example, to provide new supplies for Cortés, as also to prepare for their defence of Cortés in any civil case which might be brought against him by Velázquez. A specific instruction was sent by the King on 10 May to the officials in the Casa de la Contratación, making this clear, and was confirmed on 14 May.[87] Further, the delay implied that the Council accepted that it was necessary to decide between Cortés and Velázquez as if they had been on an equal footing. Cortés was not named, as he and his father wished, captain-general, but he was informally referred to as "captain of the island of Yucatan".[88] No doubt, in reaching these judgements, the Council was influenced by the mood in Santiago.

Even more important in the Council's decisions, probably, was the realisation that the treasure sent by Cortés was likely to be very useful: as early as 10 April, indeed, the accountant of the Casa de la Contratacíon, López de Recalde, had been ordered to send to the viceroy of Majorca a thousand ducats of the gold which Portocarrero and Montejo had brought.[89] Money was also to be made available from the same source to the Bey of Tunis, one of the Castilian tributaries on the coast of North Africa.[90] It may be assumed that the prudent secretary, Los Cobos, drew the attention of both King and councillors to this promising side of Cortés' activities.

This was, therefore, close to a victory for Cortés' friends. The suggestion that Diego Velázquez might be reduced to bringing a civil case against Cortés was a concession of the greatest importance. Cortés' representatives had probably distributed money skilfully among the civil servants. Dr Diego Beltrán, who, in the past, would have always supported Fonseca (his benefactor in earlier days), had to confess, many years later, during an enquiry into the affairs of the Council of the Indies, that he had received money from Cortés.[91] Not surprisingly, therefore, Carvajal would later write harshly of him in a letter to Charles V, saying that neither his lineage, nor his way of living, made him suitable to be the councillor of a lord, much less of an emperor.[92]

The Council continued to discuss matters during the last few days before the Emperor and the court left on 20 May. The Crown made concessions. For example, there was a decree indicating that the monarch accepted that no office of the Crown (including those which affected the Indies) should henceforth be given to foreigners.[93] Las Casas received permission to found a peaceable colony at Cumaná in Venezuela. Diego Colón secured an extension of his mandate (in return for a loan to the King).[94] The public suit begun against Pedrarias in Darien was (unfortunately, no doubt, for the Castilians, as much as for the Indians) delayed. On 17 May, the Council decided formally to postpone indefinitely the whole question of Cortés' status.[95]

Charles may have left Spain without having himself ever read Cortés' letters.[96] But he did take with him much of the treasure, including Montezuma's two great wheels of gold and silver. It also seems that, in the end, four thousand pesos of the gold sent by Cortés from Mexico helped to finance the royal fleet.[97]

Long before this, Diego Velázquez had taken what he supposed would be decisive action against the rebel *Caudillo*. He had gathered together all the men he could and sent them off, under the leadership of Pánfilo de Narváez, to the new territories. Narváez was a typical conquistador of the second generation. Born about 1475, or nearly ten years before Cortés, in Navalmanzano, near Velázquez's birthplace of Cuéllar, he was probably a childhood friend of that governor. He had left for the Indies about 1498.[98] He made money in Santo Domingo before going as second-in-command first to Juan de Esquivel in Jamaica and then to Velázquez in Cuba. Tall and robust, fair (like Alvarado), with a great red beard, and a voice which sounded "very deep and hoarse as if it came from a vault", according to Bernal Díaz, Narváez was carelessly brutal in most things; and sometimes brutally careless.[99] He was conventional and gave an air of being prudent; but of that there is little evidence. After the massacre of Caoano in Cuba, Narváez, sitting on his horse, asked Las Casas: "What do you think these Spaniards have done?" as if he himself had had nothing to do with the matter. "I offer them, and you, up to the devil," was Las Casas' reply. That was always his attitude, Las Casas went on, after such events: "He would sit without saying or doing anything himself, as if he were made of marble, leaving the impression that, if he had wished it, he could have stopped the killing."[100] He was, from Velázquez's point of view, an appropriate person to lead the expedition to Mexico. But from the angle of difficulties which he might encounter both with the Indians and with Cortés, he could not have been less suitable. He had been in Spain in 1518 when Velázquez had asked Cortés to lead the third expedition to the new territories. All the same, the Governor had borrowed some money from him to help pay his own share of Cortés' costs.[101]

Narváez had some experience of the court in Castile. He and the Governor's cousin, Antonio Velázquez de Borrego, had indeed been *procuradores-generales* of Cuba from 1515 to 1518. But he had failed his constituents, for he had made no progress towards approval of their request for free trade between all the Spanish colonies of the Indies. With Antonio Velázquez, he had made a point of challenging Las Casas, accusing him of "talking of what he knew nothing", and recommending the neglect of his report.[102] Velázquez had granted him a substantial *encomienda* in Cuba with a hundred and fifty-nine Indians. But he was in no way satisfied with that.

Narváez sailed from Cuba in March 1520. As will be seen, he had many well-known Caribbean adventurers with him, drawn by the prospects known to be opening up in this new land. But he had one senior companion whom he greatly wished that he was without: Licenciado Lucás Vázquez de Ayllón, a judge in Hispaniola who had been sent by the *audiencia* in Santo Domingo to prevent fighting between Spaniards: between, that is, Narváez and Cortés.

The place of Vázquez de Ayllón in this expedition was unexpected. Vázquez, a native of Toledo, had originally been one of the many *converso* protégés of Bishop Fonseca. Aged fifty, he had played an important part in the tragic history of Santo Domingo since, coming out to the Indies in about 1504, he had been the judge responsible for supervising the partition of Indians in that island in 1513. He himself was among the most important *encomenderos* of the island.[103]

In December of the previous year, 1519, the senior officials in Santo Domingo had been told that Velázquez was collecting men to act directly against Cortés, as well as trying to pursue him through the institutions in Castile.[104] Merchants, miners and ranchers were being assembled to be sent to the "new lands". Cuba was likely to be defenceless. Juan Carrillo, the public prosecutor in Santo Domingo, suggested to the *audiencia*, the supreme authority there, that they should send someone to stop these preparations.[105] An enquiry was held between 3 January and 8 January 1520, before the new judge and *de facto* governor of Hispaniola, Rodrigo de Figueroa, who had authority by law over Velázquez.[106] On 15 January, Figueroa prudently stated that it was not to the benefit of the Crown that there should be fighting between two Spanish leaders. He instructed Vázquez de Ayllón to go to Cuba with two ships and a small staff (the *alguacil*, chief constable of Santo Domingo, Luis de Sotelo, and the *escribano* of the *audiencia*, Pedro de Ledesma) and stop Narváez's expedition.

Ayllón was a man with harsh views. Thus in 1517 he had insisted that the Indians of Hispaniola had no capacity for living on their own. Nor had they acquired the art of living in association with the Spanish. The implication of a long memorandum influenced by Ayllón and written by the Jeronomite friars in 1517 was that the Indians were rather lucky to be offered slavery.[107] He was, however, the embodiment of the idea of discipline and loyalty to Castile.

Ayllón did not want to go to Mexico, partly because, as a protégé of Fonseca, he was probably really in sympathy with Narváez. But he was nothing if not obedient to superiors. He did as he was bid. He arrived at Trinidad in Cuba on 24 January. He caught up with Narváez's fleet at Xaragua (the modern Cienfuegos). He abruptly ordered Narváez not to go to Mexico. Narváez brushed him aside and said that he did not recognise in Ayllón someone who could give him orders. Both parties then set off in the worst of humours for Narváez's point of rendezvous, Guaniguanico, off the south coast of the island, in separate ships.

The two met again, this time with Velázquez present, on Narváez's ship. Ayllón formally notified Narváez and Velázquez of his powers. They refused to listen. Ayllón's clerk, Pedro de Ledesma, all the same read out his instructions, which included the caution that it was most inadvisable to take so many men away from Cuba since that would diminish the royal rents in the island. That was true.[108] There seem to have been only ten Spaniards left in Trinidad.[109] Further, the question of how to deal with Hernán Cortés seemed to Ayllón to be best left to the Emperor. Ayllón gave Velázquez a copy of his regulations on 18 February. Two days later, he ordered Narváez to comply with these rules on pain of a fine of 50,000 ducats. He suggested that Velázquez dismantle the expedition and merely send a few supply ships to Cortés, as well as some discreet people to go and talk quietly to him, in order to dissuade him from rebellion. As to the rest of the fleet, why not send it on a voyage of discovery to, say, Cozumel?[110]

But Narváez's plans were too far advanced for postponement. Two friends of Velázquez, that same nephew by marriage Manuel de Rojas who had tried to intercept Montejo and Portocarrero, and Vasco Porcallo, who had enlisted with Narváez, insisted that Velázquez's authority was superior to Ayllón's.[111] Orders were given to proceed. Ayllón, obstinate and affronted, decided to take his two ships to accompany Narváez.[112] From being a potential ally, Narváez converted Ayllón into an enemy. Ayllón was intelligent, experienced, and well connected, as well as corrupt, snobbish and heartless. Narváez similarly offended the notary Pedro de Ledesma, also another natural ally, for he had been a strong proponent of the idea of keeping Indians as perpetual slaves.[113] (Ledesma had been a notary in the *residencia* in Santo Domingo against the humane judge Zuazo during the regime of the Jeronymites.)[114]

In Seville, meantime, Martín Cortés, despite the rebellions in Castile, was able to sell the *Santa María de la Concepción*, apparently with the captain Juan Bautista still engaged on it, for 30,000 maravedís: a sum equivalent to six times his annual income;[115] while Cardinal Adrian busied himself, among other things, with the completion of the arrangements for the nomination of a bishop for Yucatan (which he felt quite happy referring to as "Carolina"), in the person of Fr. Julián Garcés. In a letter of September 1520 Adrian asked Governor Velázquez, as governor of the "islands" of Culhuacan and Cozumel, to ensure his safe conduct to his see, and to guarantee his income along the usual lines.[116] Martín Cortés' sale was actually contrary to his son's explicit instructions, but he would compensate for this by sending him not only the food and clothes for which he had asked but a quantity of weapons also.[117] The details of these arrangements are obscure, partly because of the disordered circumstances of Castile at the time. But it seems probable that the merchants Juan de Córdoba and Luis Fernández de Alfaro were, by the sale of the ship, able to finance another larger vessel which would soon sail to "the new golden land" under the captaincy of Juan de Burgos, with a substantial quantity of armaments as well as cloths. Most of these men in Seville were *conversos* who had worked for years in partnership with Genoese traders. This meant that Cortés had henceforth at his disposal the best commercial network in Spain.

24

A voice very deep and hoarse as if it came from a vault

"Narváez seems to have been about forty-two years old, tall and strong-limbed, with a large head and a red beard and an agreeable presence and a voice and conversation very deep and hoarse as if it came from a vault."
Bernal Díaz on Pánfilo de Narváez

PÁNFILO DE NARVÁEZ left Cuba on 5 March 1520, with about nine hundred men on eleven *naos* and about seven brigantines.[1] He had with him many conquistadors whom Cortés and his comrades had known for years, either in Hispaniola or in Cuba.[2] The decline in population in both those islands had made the possession of Indians in *encomiendas* there an unreliable investment. Many of those with Narváez were hoping to renew their fortunes in the new lands. Cortés alleged that "most of Narváez's men had been forced to come with him for fear that, if they had refused, Velázquez might confiscate the Indians which he had earlier granted them". A few had indeed been were forcibly conscripted.[3] But otherwise Cortés' comment was far from the truth.

Characteristic of the adventurers with Narváez was Juan Bono de Quejo, born in San Sebastián but later resident in Palos. Now in his middle forties, he, like Alaminos, had been with Columbus on his disastrous fourth voyage. He had been too a captain of a ship with Ponce de León in his discovery of Florida in 1513.[4] After 1515 he had been concerned in trading, first, Indian slaves and then pearls from the Venezuelan coast to Cuba, with financial support from Genoese traders, such as the Grimaldi brothers. His expedition to Trinidad for slaves in 1516 was held to have been especially disgraceful: "Juan Bono, *malo*" ("John Good, bad")[5] was the simple burden of Las Casas' attack. He had been a favourite of Bishop Fonseca ever since he testified against Diego Colón in a lawsuit of 1513.[6] There also came Andrés de Duero, Velázquez's secretary but Cortés' friend. Conditions in Cuba must have been bad indeed if so comfortably placed an individual should venture out on such a journey. Another distinguished expeditionary was Leonel de Cervantes, member of a noble family from Extremadura. He claimed to have been honoured in wars in Italy as a *comendador* of the Order of

Santiago, though there is some doubt about that (his grandfather Diego, a councillor in Seville, was a cousin of Bishop Fonseca).[7] There was also Gerónimo Martínez de Salvatierra, a loud-mouthed coward from the province of Burgos, who came as quartermaster (*veedor*); and a nephew of Diego Velázquez, the Governor, with the same name and some of the same genial qualities (though he had been accused of killing in the street a certain Juan de la Pila, and the question was unresolved).[8] Another captain was Francisco Verdugo, Diego Velázquez's brother-in-law, and that magistrate (*alcalde*) of Trinidad in Cuba who had been so unexpectedly helpful to Cortés eighteen months before. Also present was Gaspar de Garnica, the friend of Governor Velázquez who had been charged the year before to kidnap Cortés at Havana. There even came the chief constable of Cuba, Gonzalo Rodríguez de Ocaña. Yet another volunteer with Narváez was Baltasar Bermúdez of Cuéllar, Velázquez's nephew by marriage, who had been asked by the Governor to captain the expedition which Cortés had afterwards led. There also came, with Narváez, Juan González Ponce de León, son of the discoverer of Florida and a man who himself had assisted in the conquest of Puerto Rico in a series of astonishing adventures.[9] Narváez thus had with him an "old crowd" of Caribbean conquistadors, of an experience as long as their reputation was dubious.

As with the expedition of Cortés and most others in the New World at that time, about a third of Narváez's expedition seems to have come from Andalusia. Eight and twenty per cent respectively appear to have been from Extremadura and Old Castile.[10] Narváez's captains were mostly from Old Castile, as was Velázquez's administration in Cuba. Some *conversos*, new Christians, also came: one was Bernardino de Santa Clara, whose father or uncle had been royal treasurer in Hispaniola; another was Hernando Alonso, a sixty-year-old blacksmith from Niebla, near Huelva, who was married to Beatriz, a sister (surely illegitimate) of Diego de Ordaz.[11] Narváez's commissary, or chief supplier of goods, was Pedro de Maluenda, a well-known merchant from an important *converso* commercial family from Burgos. He seems to have acted both for Narváez and for himself.[12]

Many of the expedition abandoned wives and property in Cuba: Narváez arranged for his wife, María de Valenzuela, to manage his estates.[13] Doubtless, some of these conquistadors left Cuba with relief because of the outbreak there of smallpox. But others must have done so with anxiety because of the threat so posed to their families: even though most Castilians, if they reached maturity, had become immune to the disease. No sense that they might be taking a fatal germ with them was in anyone's mind.

In order to provision this expedition Diego Velázquez apparently seized much cassava bread without paying for it from citizens of Havana. He sent too a great many Cuban Indians, despite having prohibited their going with Cortés.[14]

Narváez set off across the Straits of Yucatan and made first, as usual with Spanish adventurers in that zone, for Cozumel. There he rescued eighty men from an expedition who had been shipwrecked there, under the command of a Salamantino friend of Diego Velázquez, Alonso de Parada. He afterwards left most of them to establish a colony in the now much-visited island.[15] The native population there was soon decimated. That was the consequence of the arrival of smallpox. No one grasped the dimension of this tragedy, whose full significance indeed only became apparent later.

Narváez then followed the coast west and south, as Hernández de Córdoba, Grijalva and Cortés had done. The weather was unreliable and they made slow progress. By 7 April, Easter Saturday, they were still only at the mouth of the so-called Grijalva river. There they landed, again as Grijalva and Cortés had done. They found Potonchan and the towns near the sea empty. The few Indians with whom Narváez was able to get in touch were hostile and ready for war. This, as the new commander happily noticed, was a result of the bad treatment which they had received from Cortés when he had passed that way. Juan Bono de Quejo said that the *naturales* whom he had seen on the river Grijalva were transfixed with fear lest Cortés had returned.[16] Narváez swore that he himself would be more tolerant than his predecessor. He told the *naturales* that, since they were vassals of the King of Spain, they had to be well and honourably treated.[17]

A day or two later, Narváez set off for San Juan de Ulúa. His expedition took ten days to cover these three hundred miles, since they met a severe storm as soon as they set off. One ship was lost, forty men were drowned (including Cristóbal de Morante, the captain of the lost vessel, who had owned one of the three ships which had sailed with Hernández de Córdoba). Six other ships were damaged.[18] Narváez did not reach San Juan till 19 April.[19] Much to his irritation, the judge from Hispaniola, Vázquez de Ayllón, had already arrived there three or four days before.[20] On board one of his two ships, a sure sign of the times so far as confidence in the future of Mexico was concerned, was a merchant, Juan de Herrera, with merchandise for sale entrusted to him by a colleague from Santo Domingo, Juan de Ríos, who acted on behalf of a firm from Burgos[21] (he sold everything which he had to Pedro de Maluenda, and died soon after).[22]

Ayllón had received an unexpected visitor. This was Francisco Serrantes, a ship's carpenter who had been with Cortés in Tenochtitlan, and had then accompanied Cortés' cousin, Diego Pizarro, to the province of Pánuco. But he had stayed there in order to found a farm, taking the decision himself with an independence of spirit which had not at all pleased Cortés, who was told of it by Pizarro. For this reason,

Serrantes had become a fierce critic of Cortés. Apparently hearing from rumours on the coast of the approach of Narváez, he made certain to be present at San Juan when the new expedition arrived.[23] Serrantes went out to see Judge Ayllón in a canoe, in order to tell all he knew about the achievements of Cortés and the character of Tenochtitlan: how Cortés had received much gold; how he had taken his own fifth; how the rest of the money had been badly divided; and how Cortés had no intention of obeying Velázquez or anyone else but was waiting for the reaction of King Charles to his *procuradores'* proposals. He described Tenochtitlan vividly, and said that he thought that, should it be necessary, Cortés would be able to secure 50,000 Indians to fight against Narváez.[24]

Ayllón very responsibly did not keep this interesting news to himself. He sent Serrantes to Narváez, who was still off shore. To Narváez, Serrantes told the same story. Serrantes said that, if Narváez wanted to establish a colony, the best place would be near Coatzacoalcos, rather than where they had landed, since the soil was better down there. Narváez paid no attention to that recommendation but, of course, he took in everything that Serrantes had said. He then went in a small boat to visit Ayllón.

Narváez said that he would land all his men the next day. Ayllón counselled against that idea. He said that it was sure to create trouble with the Indians. Narváez said he had to land his expedition because his ships were so damaged. He did indeed go ahead as he had planned, and put into practice a long-previously drawn-up scheme to establish a town which he intended to call San Salvador, approximately on the site of the present city of Veracruz, some forty miles south of Cortés' first settlement at Villa Rica.[25] He named magistrates and councillors, much as Cortés had done in similar circumstances. Baltasar Bermúdez became chief magistrate (*alcalde mayor*).[26] Other magistrates included Francisco Verdugo, who had the same office in Trinidad, Cuba. Councillors included most of Narváez's captains: Salvatierra, Juan de Gamarra, and two nephews of Diego Velázquez, Pedro and Diego Velázquez the younger. They set about building houses, a church, a plaza, and a prison, in the usual style.

Narváez made every effort to be kind to the Totonacs and others whom he met. This must have been difficult for him, for no one was more consumed with a sense of his own superiority and with a greater contempt for indigenous peoples. The same went for some of his captains, such as Juan de Gamarra, survivor of several brutal expeditions when with Pedrarias in Castilla del Oro. But the size of Narváez's force, and the evident superiority of it to Cortés', impressed the Totonacs. After a few days Narváez proclaimed, through his town crier, that Cortés and his party were bad men who had come to rob and to take prisoners; and that he, Narváez would soon go up to Tenochtitlan and release Montezuma.[27] This statement was not universally popular among the

Castilians. Narváez's own treasurer, Bernardino de Santa Clara, for example, insisted that it was scandalous so to speak against Cortés when it was plain that the land was peaceful.[28] Further, while many people in Cortés' expedition had set off ignorant of their commander's aims, not everyone on Narváez's expedition was clear what their own leader's plans were either.

To begin with, Narváez's stay in the region of San Juan de Ulúa was as peaceful as Cortés' had been. The Indians brought bread, chickens and beans without complaint for over three weeks.[29] The Totonacs seem to have accepted Narváez with the same enthusiasm with which they had previously accepted Cortés.

Such restlessness as there was came from Narváez himself. He became quickly aware of divisions in the camp as to how to face Cortés. Ayllón still considered Narváez's refusal to obey him as an offence to the *audiencia* in Santo Domingo and made no secret of his opinions. Worse, the judge started to speak favourably of Cortés. He even wrote a letter to that captain, stating his position.[30] Narváez meantime made himself unpopular among his followers because he kept for himself the presents which the local chiefs gave to him, just as they had given similar things to Grijalva and to Cortés.

Narváez decided that Ayllón was responsible for the growing disaffection. That judge's presence was indeed a little odd. So Narváez had the "municipal officers" of San Salvador seize Ayllón and place him, with his servants and his clerk Pedro de Ledesma, on the ship on which he had come, and instructed the master to take him back to Cuba.[31] Some of Vázquez de Ayllón's supporters were put on another vessel and sent off with him.[32] Two other of Narváez's conquistadors were seized and imprisoned for speaking well of Cortés: first, Gonzalo de Oblanca, a Leonese hidalgo, who died in less than a week after fretting in the discomfort of a makeshift tropical prison; and Sancho de Barahona, probably from Soria, who lived to fight (and testify in lawsuits) another day. Five friends of Vázquez de Ayllón then abandoned Narváez's camp and went to that of Sandoval, Cortés' representative on the coast, on the ground that the judge had been treated disrespectfully.[33]

Ayllón did not go to Cuba. That judge told the master of his ship, Juan Velázquez, and the sailors, that if they took him there, he would have them hanged. If, on the other hand, they were to take him to Santo Domingo, he would see that they went free. Ayllón was more effective in persuading simple sailors to do his bidding than he was proconsuls. They set off for Santo Domingo. The journey was atrocious. They experienced "many previously unknown torments and dangers". At last they reached a small port, San Nicolás, in the west of Hispaniola. From there, Ayllón walked the three hundred miles to Santo Domingo. It was a most unpleasant journey. When he reached civilisation, his anger found its outlet. He sent back letters to Spain castigating Narváez's and Velázquez's behaviour towards him. The affront, he insisted, was to the Crown, as well as to his own person. These letters, as will be seen, greatly assisted the friends of Cortés in Castile.[34]

Narváez was, meantime, somewhat cheered by the arrival in his camp of four defectors from that of Cortés. These included Cervantes "*el chocarrero*", Velázquez's jester. The others were all men who had been with Pizarro and Serrantes in Oaxaca. All, as well as Serrantes, enjoyed a short-lived fame as they spoke with equal vividness of the marvels of Tenochtitlan and the iniquities of Cortés.[35] They acted, it seems, as interpreters for the newly arrived Castilians with the Indians, though it is scarcely possible that their Totonac was adequate for such a test.[36]

A fifth defector never reached Narváez. This was Cristóbal Pinedo, an old servant of Narváez, who had gone to Mexico the previous year with Cortés, and who, hearing (in a way shortly to be discussed) that his old master had landed, left that capital, without permission, to join him.[37] Cortés sent Indians from Mexico, probably Mexicans, to retrieve him before he reached the coast.[38] They overtook him, and Pinedo resisted arrest. In the mêlée, the escaping Castilian was killed. His body was brought back to Tenochtitlan in a hammock.[39] Cortés would later be accused not only of having connived at the murder of Pinedo but, through that action, foolishly allowing the Mexica to know that, after all, the Castilians were mortals, not gods. Cortés denied both these charges, saying that, long before that, the Indians in Mexico had known that "we are all mortal and, since our father Adam sinned, we all have to die".[40] Cortés also denied knowing that the Indians would kill Pinedo.[41] But Gerónimo de Aguilar, the interpreter, testified that he had heard Cortés order certain Indians to bring back Pinedo; and, "if they were unable to persuade him to return, to kill him".[42]

Cortés' chief representative on the coast was, of course, his companion from Medellín, Gonzalo de Sandoval, at Villa Rica de la Vera Cruz, a day's ride north of San Juan de Ulúa. It does not appear as if he received the news of Narváez's arrival very quickly – which seems strange, considering how fast the news had reached Serrantes, who was further away. Perhaps this delay was an indication of how Totonac opinion swayed with the wind. But as has been seen, Cortés himself received a message from Alonso de Cervantes, who was on some unrecorded errand to the coast, that a vessel had been seen off San Juan. This was presumably one or other of the two ships of Vázquez de Ayllón, who, as has been seen, had arrived first.

From Tenochtitlan, Cortés sent five of his army (Diego García, Francisco Bernal, Sebastián Porras, and Juan de Limpias, under the direction of Francisco de Orozco, a one-time captain of artillery in Italy) to find out who it was who had arrived on the coast and what their intentions were. He told his men to divide up after crossing the mountains which protect Mexico from the sea: one group was to travel by the northern route, as Cortés had himself done; the other was to go to the south via the modern Orizaba. If they found no one moving up from the coast, they were to go to where the newcomers had landed and, disguised, discover everything they could. At the same time, Cortés' two outstanding expeditions in the south-east, one led by Velázquez de León in Coatzacoalcos, the other by Rodrigo Rangel in Chinantla, were ordered to be ready to move on to Vera Cruz if necessary.[43]

But nothing more was heard for a fortnight. The person who did receive news quickly was Montezuma.

The Emperor's agents seem always to have been alive to the possibilities of further incursions on the coast. The news of Narváez's arrival reached Montezuma in the form of a cloth, on which had been painted eighteen ships, five of them wrecked and crushed on to the sand. This was before the fleet reached San Juan. Then another messenger brought another cloth which gave the news that some ships had reached that port.[44]

Montezuma did not tell Cortés immediately about these messages. Instead he had direct communication via runners with Narváez. That conquistador made it plain that he and Cortés did not see eye to eye. Learning from Serrantes and others what had transpired at Tenochtitlan, he even told Montezuma that the expedition with Cortés was composed of bad men; he, Narváez, had come to capture them, and to release Montezuma.[45] He, unlike Cortés, had no interest in gold. Once he had freed Montezuma, and captured Cortés, he would leave the country. Perhaps in consequence, Montezuma's messenger to Narváez (a man from Tenochtitlan who had been christened "Cortés" by the *Caudillo*) said, on his own authority, that Narváez was welcome. He passed on a message of complaint from Montezuma against Cortés who, he said, had made him a prisoner and treated him very badly.[46] According to one witness at Cortés' enquiry, Montezuma now said that he wanted Cortés killed or captured. He sent food, cloth and gold and instructed his men at the coast to provide Narváez with food. He also sent a golden medallion.[47] The Emperor's affection for Cortés, if it had ever been more than superficial, his vassaldom to Charles V, his aspiration to be christened at Easter seem all to have been forgotten.

Narváez in reply, presumably after consulting his captains, said, contradicting his earlier statements, that he had been sent to Mexico at the command of the King in order to colonise (*poblar*) the land, and that he would release Montezuma, give him back what had been stolen from him, and would not kill anyone.[48] He suggested that the two of them should exchange names: he, Narváez, would call himself Montezuma; Montezuma would thenceforth be known as Narváez.[49] This bizarre proposal derived from a usage which had often pleased native leaders in Hispaniola.

Montezuma in the end found it impossible to keep from Cortés the secret of Narváez's arrival. Perhaps he thought that Cortés would punish him if he discovered the news independently. Montezuma showed Cortés the painted cloths and urged him to leave Tenochtitlan.[50] He said to Cortés that he could see that the Castilians were not all united, and did not all have the same lord. He pointed out that now there were many ships available, so "You will have no need to build ships . . . you can all return together to Castile and there need be no further excuses." Cortés had already heard from Cervantes about the arrival of the two ships but seems to have been taken by surprise by the news of the others. He replied that the Castilians did all have the same lord, but that the new people who had arrived were probably bad people. They might be Basques (*vizcainos*): people who bring bad luck to the land because they would steal whatever there was.[51]

Cortés instantly realised that it was more likely that the intruders on the coast would be agents of Diego Velázquez rather than people direct from Spain. Still without direct information, Cortés next dispatched his friend and confessor, Fr. Bartolomé de Olmedo, with a letter to whoever it was who had landed on the coast. He hoped that the unknown arrivals would "let me know who they were and, if they were true vassals of the kingdom and of Your Highness [this was written in a later letter to the King], to write to say whether they had come to this country with Your Highness' instruction to settle it and remain in the land, or were going on, or had to return; adding that if they needed anything, I would provide them with whatever was in my power . . . but if they refused to tell me who they were, I required them on Your Majesty's behalf to leave your countries at once and not to disembark. I said that, if they were to persist, I would march against them with all the force that I had, both Spanish and natives."[52]

Cortés added that he hoped that Narváez would neither interrupt nor prevent his missionary work in converting the Indians.[53] At the same time Cortés sent Andrés de Tapia, now one of his closest confidants, to confer with Sandoval at Villa Rica. Tapia reached Villa Rica de la Vera Cruz in three and a half days, walking by day and being carried in a hammock by Indians on foot by night.[54]

By the time that Tapia reached Vera Cruz, Sandoval had already struck the first blow of Cortés' expedition against Narváez. He had first called together all the people in the as yet far from completed port, and told them to swear that they would accept no other governor than Hernán Cortés. Then he sent away his wounded and sick, as well as one or two old men, to Papalotla, fifteen miles inland in the foothills of the sierra.

A day or two later a delegation from Narváez arrived at Villa Rica de la

Vera Cruz, in the shape of a notary, Alfonso de Vergara, a priest, Fr. Antonio Ruiz de Guevara, and Antonio de Amaya, who appears to have been yet one more relation of Diego Velázquez. They carried letters from Narváez addressed to various members of Cortés' expedition, seeking to lure them to support their commander.[55] Three other Castilians and some Cuban Indians were with this little party. They were not met by anyone. Sandoval remained in his house.

The newcomers first went to the new church in order to pray. It was still a most primitive edifice and open to the winds. They then went to Sandoval's house. That too must have been little more than a large hut. They gave that conquistador a friendly salute. Fr. Guevara said that they had come on behalf of Narváez, who had arrived in the territory as captain-general on the appointment of Diego Velázquez. He suggested that Sandoval should immediately give himself up to Narváez. Cortés and his friends, he said, were traitors. Sandoval told Guevara that, had he not been a priest, he would have had him beaten for using such language. He said that they should go immediately to Mexico-Tenochtitlan, where they would find Cortés firmly established as "captain-general and *justicia mayor* of New Spain".[56] Here, he added, "we are all better servants of His Majesty than Velázquez and Narváez are".

Assuming that Sandoval did speak of New Spain, this was the first time that the expression was used: the usage became common in the next few months, as a result of a decision by Cortés. The prosperity of the place as well as certain physical similarities between it and old Spain inspired the name. "New Spain", not "New Castile": now that the kingdoms of Castile and Aragon were one, what had previously been a geographical expression could be positively employed, at least by imperialists abroad.[57]

Fr. Guevara then told the lawyer Vergara to read aloud the formal papers which he had with him which insisted that Cortés submit himself to Narváez. They were probably papers written by one of Velázquez's lawyers and signed by that proconsul. Sandoval boldly said, "If you read those papers aloud, I shall have you given a hundred lashes." Sandoval added that he had no knowledge as to whether the notary Vergara was a royal notary or not, nor whether the papers which he had were copies, or the originals. If he were not a notary, he would have no right to read out such a document even if it were genuine.[58] Vergara hesitated.

Guevara, a proud man, was angry: he said to Vergara, "How is it that you are negotiating with these traitors? Bring out the decrees and read them aloud."

Sandoval straightaway ordered his men to arrest Guevara's party, and take them as prisoners to Tenochtitlan. Some Totonacs who were working on building the fortress at Vera Cruz put them in some of the wooden cases built especially for porters (*tamemes*), and carried them on their backs swiftly to the city on the lake under the command of the *alguacil* of Villa Rica, a native of Burgos, Pedro de Solís ("Behind the door Solís", as he was known, because he was always secretly looking at what was going on in the street). They travelled without stopping and, in four days, reached Tenochtitlan, having been much astonished at the towns and people which they had managed to glimpse *en route*: they did not know, reported Bernal Díaz, whether they had been enchanted or were dreaming.[59] They reached their destination before either Fr. Olmedo or the five other messengers sent by Cortés had returned.[60]

Cortés dealt cleverly with these astonished visitors, whom he released. He went out of Tenochtitlan to greet them and organised a banquet for them. With his usual capacity for placing the blame for anything untoward on someone else, he criticised Sandoval for treating them roughly. He lodged them well. He then saw them quite alone.[61] From them Cortés discovered all that he needed to know about Narváez's expedition: the position of Licenciado Ayllón; the numbers of men; and the identity of the commanders. Not only that, but, in the space of two days, he had, by clever presents, promises and bribes, virtually won these visitors over to his side. The astonishing sight of Tenochtitlan reinforced Cortés' persuasion. Guevara and Vergara admitted that Narváez was not universally popular among his captains and suggested that Cortés would do well to give them some gold or chains of gold: for, as the proverb had it, "presents make nonsense of troubles" ("*dádivas quebrantan peñas*"). Cortés responded to this suggestion. Indeed, as well as giving these men gold for themselves, he gave them more for others. He thus began to buy the affections of Narváez's army. Whatever papers these visitors had with them, they did not produce them, so that, in the enquiry against him years later, Cortés was able to say truthfully that he "never knew that Narváez carried any provisions of His Majesty nor did that fact come to his notice. Had he, Cortés, seen them, or known what they contained, of course he would have obeyed them . . .; though, if His Majesty had known the truth [of what was going on in Mexico] he would not have issued any such provisions . . ."[62]

After two or three days, Fr. Ruiz de Guevara, Amaya and Vergara were sent back to Narváez.[63] They were accompanied by a servant of Cortés' named Santos, with a mare loaded with gold.[64] This party, when it reached the coast, found, of course, that Fr. Olmedo had arrived and that Narváez had read Cortés' first letter to him; and that Salvatierra, Narváez's lieutenant, had even chided his commander for so lowering himself. But others in the camp had been impressed by Fr. Olmedo's stories. Now Guevara, Amaya, and Vergara too described the size and wealth of Tenochtitlan. Many who heard them themselves began to long to go to the Mexican capital. Here at last was Eldorado! How wonderful to escape the mosquitoes and the heat of the coast! To find oneself in a mountain Venice, with undreamt-of riches and beauty! How worthy such an expedition was of those who had read their romances of chivalry! Guevara insisted that Cortés had at his disposal the richest city in the world, that it was a terrestrial paradise, and that he would give gold to all who supported him.[65] Santos began to distribute his presents. People began to suggest that Narváez should reach an agreement with Cortés. The country was surely big enough for both of them. Narváez was angry to hear all this and determined not to listen. He continued to busy himself with building his town of San Salvador and, by the early summer, had about eighty or ninety houses there, together with a church of timber.[66] But Ruiz de Guevara and Vergara, as well as Santos, were also by then busy distributing Cortés' gold. Perhaps 1,000 castellanos went to Narváez's chief of artillery, Rodrigo Martínez; 1,500 pesos to Francisco Verdugo; and an undefined sum to Baltasar Bermúdez.[67]

Narváez meantime sent his flagship back to Cuba on 4 May, primarily in order to report to Velázquez. The ship also carried private letters from Narváez's men. So news of what was happening was quickly passed from mouth to mouth in that island: how Cortés was living in a great city similar to Venice; how he was at peace with the Indians – indeed, lived in affection (*amor*) with them; how he was rich in gold and silver; and how Narváez and his men had not a penny to their names, and were seeking revenge on Cortés and a share for themselves.[68]

Cortés' letter to Narváez, courtesy of Guevara, apparently said that he was delighted to know that an old friend, from Hispaniola as from Cuba, had arrived. But he was astonished that he had not written; even more that, as he knew, Narváez had written to several members of his, Cortés', expedition, seeking to persuade them to rise against their commander. He expressed amazement too that Narváez had taken the title of captain-general and had appointed councillors and magistrates, since the land concerned belonged to the King, and had already been formally colonised.[69]

To this letter Narváez sent no reply. Cortés learned that his five original messengers had been captured by Narváez and that the Totonacs had decided to side with the newcomers: even Cortés' first ally, Tlacochcalcatl, the fat chief of Cempoallan, had bowed to the attraction of power.[70]

Faced with these signs that Narváez, in his position of apparent superiority, had no intention of seeking a compromise, Cortés had a meeting with his closest friends to discuss what should be done. Cortés asked their advice. They cautiously enquired, "What, Señor, does it seem to you that we should do?" Cortés replied: "Death to him [Narváez] and to anyone who argues about the matter."[71] They agreed that they should set off to attack Narváez as soon as possible. Fortune, after all, favoured the brave.

25

To cut off Don Hernando's ears

"One of those said in front of the said Narváez that they ought to cut off Don Hernando's ears and eat one of them."
Andrés de Tapia, in testimony at the *residencia* against Cortés

AT THE BEGINNING of May 1520 Hernán Cortés seemed to be in a weak position. He had divided his small force into four: he had only about two hundred men in Tenochtitlan, Velázquez de León and Rangel had in the interior about a hundred and thirty men each, and there were another hundred with Sandoval on the coast. It is true that Montezuma and an undetermined number of Mexican lords were prisoners. But it was unclear how long that could last. Montezuma now seemed altogether more resilient than he had been a few months before. Easter, 8 April, had come and gone.[1]

But Cortés had no hesitation about going down to the coast to face and, if necessary, to fight Narváez. He sent instructions to both Velázquez de León and Rangel to join him at Cholula, knowing that the order was a major test of his political capacity, since the first of those two commanders was not only a kinsman of Diego Velázquez but a brother-in-law of Narváez. The latter might be supposed to have been in touch with him, as indeed he had been.

Cortés set off at the beginning of May from Tenochtitlan with eighty or so men, most of them in cotton armour such as the Mexica wore.[2] Alvarado, at that time incontestably Cortés' second-in-command, had with him a hundred and twenty men – a tiny number to maintain Montezuma a prisoner and defend the Spanish quarters.[3] But he had with him a number of Indian allies, mostly Tlaxcalans. The Castilians left behind were required to swear on a missal that they would obey Alvarado, and be loyal to him.[4] The reason for this was that Alvarado's men included many who, rightly or wrongly, were suspected of disloyalty to Cortés. An important role was reserved to Alonso de Escobar, captain of one of the ships which left Cuba in 1518 with Cortés, and at that time supposed to be a Velazquista. He had been won over by Cortés and was now placed in charge of all the gold and jewels which the expedition had accumulated: apparently 132,000 pesos in gold already in bars, and perhaps another 100,000 in jewels.[5]

Cortés, before he left Tenochtitlan, warmly embraced Montezuma. He did not yet know that Montezuma had been in touch directly with Narváez. He said that he had to go to the coast to deal with Narváez and his "Basques"; for, if he did not, the Totonacs and the Mexica on the coast would be treated badly.[6] Montezuma showed sadness, but Marina the interpretress insisted that that attitude was pretended. The Emperor offered 100,000 warriors to fight if necessary, as well as 30,000 to carry equipment.[7] Cortés sternly said that all he needed was the help of God. He asked Montezuma, or rather his priests, to look after the picture of the Virgin in the Great Temple, and to ensure that she was always surrounded by flowers and wax candles: presumably by that time there were Mexicans who could make them; just as there were Mexican priests willing to perform the duties asked of them.[8] Montezuma promised to do this, to provide Alvarado and those who were left behind with all that they might need, and to guard closely everything left behind which belonged to the Spaniards: or to the King of Castile.[9] Montezuma begged to be told if these new people on the coast turned out to be hostile. If they did, he, Montezuma, would send warriors to help drive them away.

Cortés set off for the sea over the route between the volcanoes, which he knew from his passage in the other direction in November.[10] Arrived back in Cholula, Cortés sent a message asking the Tlaxcalans for four thousand men. But nobody there had any wish to fight again against Castilians. Instead, they sent twenty loads of turkeys. Undaunted, Cortés wrote to Sandoval in Villa Rica asking him to meet the expeditionary force before they reached the coast.

Cortés waited at Cholula till he was joined by the two hundred and sixty men, under Rangel and Velázquez de León. The latter showed Cortés a letter which Narváez had sent him asking for his support.[11] Velázquez de León had decided not to waver in his loyalty to Cortés. This was of course a great relief to the *Caudillo*. So now, with a respectably sized force of about three hundred and fifty, Cortés set off again in light order. For the first time since leaving Cempoallan the previous year, he took no servants. He seems also to have left behind his cannon and arquebusiers in Tenochtitlan, though not his crossbowmen. The only Indian locality which offered any help was the city of Huexotzinco which, thanks to the diplomacy of Pero González de Trujillo, offered four hundred men.[12] But Cortés did not accept the proposal.

Narváez had now moved up the coast with his army from "San Salvador" to Cempoallan, where he established himself as the guest of the same fat chief, Tlacochcalcatl, now very nervous, who had befriended

Cortés. Narváez confiscated the Spanish goods which Cortés had given him the year before. The chief naturally complained. Narváez's *veedor*, Salvatierra, expressed his astonishment at the fame which they were finding Cortés had acquired. "Cortesillo" had been remembered in Cuba as a person of the utmost insignificance.[13]

About two days after leaving Cholula, Cortés came upon Fr. Olmedo with a small band of men, returning from Narváez. That amiable friar described what was happening at the camp by the sea: how Licenciado Ayllón had been expelled to Cuba; how Narváez had suborned the chief of Cempoallan; how Narváez and Montezuma had exchanged presents; how Narváez had said that he would capture Cortés himself and free Montezuma; and how it seemed that Narváez intended to conquer the whole territory for himself.[14] He said that Narváez had been rude and dismissive to him, though he had been able to give away some presents and letters to people whom he thought could be influenced: men such as Andrés de Duero.

The news of Montezuma's relation with Narváez of course angered Cortés. It had indeed a decisive effect on his subsequent attitude towards the Emperor. But he had scarcely had time to absorb the information when, at Quechula, he came upon another delegation from Narváez. This consisted of Alonso de Mata, a notary from Quintana Rico (Santander), Bernardino de Quesada, from Baeza, whom some describe as also a notary,[15] and several others. They had the same instructions from their commander that Fr. Ruiz de Guevara and Vergara had had. Alonso de Mata, bravely but imprudently, challenged Cortés as if he had been a bailiff's officer imposing a fine. Taking letters from his pocket, he began to read. Cortés interrupted and asked Mata to show his authority as a King's notary. Mata said that he was unable to do that because he had left his important papers in the camp. In fact, he seems to have been an ordinary notary (*escribano*), not an *escribano del rey*. Cortés had all of them arrested, and kept them some days under guard. He said that he did this because they were bent on causing scandal in his army. They were soon released with presents and smooth words: to such an extent that, like Fr. Ruiz de Guevara, they returned to Narváez's camp full of praise for Cortés.[16]

Cortés moved on towards the coast by the favourite route of the Mexica, via Orizaba, which took him to the west of the mountain now called by that name. The army then reached Tanpaniguita (between Huatusco and Cempoallan, about twenty-four miles from the latter).

It seems that here Cortés took the precaution of distributing among his men some gold which had been brought from the south-west by Rodrigo Rangel. The aim was, of course, to keep everyone in good spirits in the event of fighting against fellow Spaniards, to whom, as several members of his own expedition knew, Cortés had also distributed gold. The sum shared out may have been anything between 5,000 and 15,000 pesos.[17]

Cortés also hinted rather rashly at all kinds of benefits which would follow a defeat of Narváez. He seems to have been free with his suggestions that, after the conquest of Mexico, many of his friends would become dukes, counts, or lords with other honours.[18]

At Ahuilizapan (Orizaba) Cortés welcomed back to his banners those spies whom he had first sent to discover the meaning of Narváez's landing, and who now had either been released or had escaped. They were able to supply further intelligence about morale in Narváez's "San Salvador".[19]

Delayed here by heavy rain, Cortés sent one of his Extremeño friends, Rodrigo Álvarez Chico, and Pero Hernández (the notary), with an imperious demand to Narváez, under the threat of various formal penalties, that he submit himself to the *Caudillo*'s orders. If Narváez had special orders from the King, well and good. But if he had not, he should call himself neither captain-general nor *justicia mayor*, nor exercise any of the functions of those offices, under pain of punishment. Cortés also insisted that those who had come with Narváez should present themselves before him. If they did not, he would proceed against them. Narváez merely imprisoned the messengers.[20]

Cortés seems to have done this only to give himself a legal justification for the military action upon which he was now determined. It was, as it were, a *Requerimiento*. For the Castilians in the age of the conquistadors, law governed civil war as well as conquest. His messengers were fortunate only to be imprisoned.[21]

There were still, however, some further intrigues to be played out before swords were drawn. Some of these were little actions of espionage, such as Sandoval's dispatch of some Castilian soldiers to Narváez's camp dressed as Indians. They had the satisfaction of selling some plums to Narváez's deputy Salvatierra and stealing two horses.[22] Then Narváez took another initiative. Cortés' old friend, Andrés de Duero, with Fr. Ruiz de Guevara and another priest of Narváez's, Fr. Juan de León, and some servants, appeared in Cortés' camp. Duero suggested a meeting between the two *caudillos*, Narváez and Cortés. There would be ten men on each side. Cortés seems to have toyed with the idea.[23] But Fr. Olmedo warned Cortés to keep away from such an arrangement.[24] Narváez's plan had been to hide a group of horsemen, led by Juan Yuste, behind a hill near where the meeting was planned. They would have fallen on Cortés and killed or captured him as soon as the "discussion" began.[25] A most unconvincing defence was later made by the friends of Narváez against the accusation that he planned to kill Cortés at the rendezvous: first, that the statement that Narváez had suggested such a meeting was untrue; and second, that any properly constituted authority had the right to arrest any malefactor at any time: Cortés was precisely such a person.[26]

Duero also carried a letter from Narváez with what he thought of as a compromise. Cortés would hand over to Narváez his command over the territory which he had discovered; Narváez would give Cortés ships in which to go away with his men wherever he wished.

Cortés gravely said that, if such a proposal came from the King, he would show it to the magistrates and councillors of Villa Rica de la Vera Cruz. He naturally could not answer for their likely reaction.[27]

Nothing of course came of this. Of Narváez's three negotiators, Fr. Ruiz de Guevara had already been won over by Cortés; Andrés de Duero still had a financial interest in Cortés' success; while Fr. Juan de León was already showing that he too was subornable.

Duero returned to Narváez's camp while Cortés was reinforced further by the arrival of Sandoval, Tapia, and about sixty men from Vera Cruz. Sandoval's original fifty had been reinforced by Pedro de Villalobos and some of those deserters from Narváez who had disliked that conquistador's treatment of Licenciado Ayllón. In addition, a soldier of experience in Italy, a certain Tovilla, appeared from Chinantla. He had persuaded Indian carpenters to make some long lances tipped with copper points, at Cortés' request.

Cortés sent Fr. Olmedo back to the coast with another letter to Narváez. This had a different tone from his earlier communications. He wrote much as he later told the King that he had conducted himself: how he had taken many cities and fortresses, how he had captured Montezuma, the supreme lord of the territory, and how he had found much gold and many jewels. Cortés asked Narváez and his captains to explain their aims and say in what way he, Cortés, could help them. If they refused to state their intentions, Cortés would have to require them to leave the territory; and, if they did not do so, he would proceed against them, and capture, or kill, them as if they were foreigners entering the realm of his lord and king. Cortés secured the signature of this letter by his captains and by a large number of ordinary soldiers.[28]

Fr. Olmedo took this new unyielding message back to Narváez, in the company of Bartolomé de Usagre, one of Cortés' original companions (an Extremeño) who, he had discovered, had a brother as one of those in charge of Narváez's artillery. They delivered the letter to Narváez without mishap. Narváez thought of arresting both Fr. Olmedo and Usagre. But he was dissuaded by Andrés de Duero. He instead suggested that Usagre the gunner should invite his brother Bartolomé to dine and discover exactly what was being planned by Cortés. Though the guests did perhaps communicate intelligence of interest to Narváez, they were also able to meet, in the company of this brother of Usagre's, several others who had in Cuba been friends of Cortés: for example, Bernardino de Santa Clara, who had already criticised Narváez's attitude to Cortés. More of Cortés' gold was cleverly spent by Fr. Olmedo in bribing

Narváez's captains. For he carried letters of Cortés to several of them: Salvatierra, Juan de Gamarra, Juan Yuste and Baltasar Bermúdez (all senior captains and *regidors* of "San Salvador"), to each of whom the *Caudillo* offered 20,000 castellanos should they join him. Juan Bono de Quejo, a year later, said that the camp of Narváez was soon awash with gold believed to have come from Cortés.[29]

Narváez again wished to detain Olmedo. Andrés de Duero said that, as ambassador of Cortés, and a priest, he should instead be asked to dine. Narváez gave the invitation. The two met before dinner. Olmedo made a most deceptive speech, saying that Narváez had no more loyal servant than himself and that the captains of Cortés were all ready to establish relations with Narváez.

Until now, Olmedo had not had the opportunity of giving Cortés' most recent letter to Narváez. Narváez asked him for it. Olmedo said that he had it in his lodgings, though in fact he had it on him. He used the pretext of going to retrieve the letter from his lodgings as a way of talking to numerous captains, with whom he returned to their leader. He then read out Cortés' letter. By this ruse he managed to ensure that everyone of importance heard of Cortés' proposals. Narváez and Salvatierra exploded with rage. But the damage was done. Several captains laughed.

The next move in these Byzantine exchanges was another visit to Cortés from Andrés de Duero. This time he was accompanied by Bartolomé Usagre on his way back. They were followed by a certain number of Cuban Indians. They described how Fr. Olmedo was conducting himself in the camp of Narváez.

The real purpose of Duero's second visit was probably for him to remind Cortés that in Cuba in 1518 they had made an arrangement to share the profits of the expedition. Cortés recognised his contract with Duero. He said that, when Narváez was dead or a prisoner, he and Duero would be the joint rulers of New Spain, and would divide up all the available gold between them. With that, Cortés loaded the Cuban Indians with presents for their masters. Cortés suggested that Duero negotiate with Bermúdez to take over the leadership of Narváez's army. (Bermúdez had accepted some of Olmedo's or Guevara's presents and so was considered by Cortés to be susceptible.) Duero agreed to negotiate with Bermúdez. Saying goodbye to Duero, Cortés said, "And mind that you do what you say you are going to do; or otherwise, by my conscience, within three days, I shall be with all my companions in your camp, and the first man to be put to the lance will be yourself." Duero laughed. He said that he would not fail to help Cortés.[30]

A final emissary from Cortés was Juan Velázquez de León. He set off to Narváez's camp with a sailor, Antón del Río.[31] This captain, as has been mentioned before, had been usually seen as a protégé of his kinsman, Governor Velázquez. Narváez had written to him asking him to join him. So Cortés knew that he would be well received. That turned out to be true.[32] Velázquez de León's jewels were particularly admired. But Velázquez de León said that he had only come to see whether Narváez would make peace. "What, make peace with a traitor?" laughed Narváez. Velázquez indignantly said that Cortés was no traitor but a faithful servant of the King. This was Narváez's opportunity to try and bribe an opponent into alliance. He did so by offers of command, not of money. He suggested to him that, after Cortés was dead or a prisoner, Velázquez de León should captain all Cortés' men with the title of second-in-command. It was Cortés' own proposal to Duero, in reverse. Velázquez de León said he could not betray Cortés. Narváez then decided to arrest his visitor. Once again he was talked out of a forceful idea by Duero, Bermúdez, and the disloyal priests, Ruiz de Guevara and León. Instead, as in the case of Olmedo, Narváez asked him to dine, in the expectation that he might perhaps be a mediator. Velázquez de León was related to several captains besides himself in Narváez's army. Perhaps old memories, the tropical night, and the influence of wine from Guadalcanal, of which Narváez's expedition had plenty, might make him amenable. Before dinner, too, Narváez paraded his men before Velázquez.[33] He fired his guns to impress the Indians who had gathered round the camp. He publicly promised money for Cortés dead or alive, just as Cortés had sworn to capture Montezuma. Teudile, Montezuma's by now thoroughly confused governor at Cuetlaxtlan, apparently gave Narváez cloaks and gold, in the name of his emperor. He even pledged his services.[34]

Narváez's plan to seduce Velázquez did not work any more than the similar one had done with Olmedo. Summer nights inspire quarrels as well as embraces. A quarrel between Velázquez de León and his kinsman Diego Velázquez, the nephew of the Governor, threatened the honour of the family. A duel was narrowly avoided. Both disputants were equally aggrieved, each certain that they represented the true heritage of the family of Velázquez: perhaps the spirit of the legendary medieval knight, Ruy Velázquez, about whom many ballads had been written. Velázquez de León was asked to leave the camp instantly.[35] He did so, setting off back to Cortés, having accomplished nothing in the way of a compromise, and being accompanied by Fr. Olmedo, as by Antón del Río. Before he went, Velázquez de León apparently gave another thousand pesos to Narváez's gunmaster, Rodrigo Martínez, to stop up the touchholes of Narváez's cannon with wax.[36]

One estimate suggested that, by the time Velázquez de León left Narváez's camp, there were a hundred and fifty people under Narváez's command who were well disposed to Cortés.[37] Some seem to have written to Cortés to that effect.[38] Neither Cortés nor Narváez had had at any time any idea of compromise. All these meetings and messages were merely manoeuvring for a superior moral position.

Velázquez de León and Olmedo found Cortés' men resting on the bank of what is now called the river Antigua, only a few miles from Cempoallan. They brought a final letter from Duero to Cortés. Cortés had it read aloud to his captains, who in theory constituted the muncipal council of Villa Rica de la Vera Cruz. It told Cortés to be careful since he was surely leading his men into a slaughterhouse. Cortés then seems again to have asked his captains for their advice. That turned out once more, as it had been before they left Tenochtitlan, to be "whatever *you* think". Cortés then quoted a Castilian proverb, "Let the ass die or whoever spurs him, it is the same thing."[39] He then made a speech in what Bernal Díaz describes as "such a charming style, and with sentences so neatly turned, that I am assuredly unable to write the like, so delightful was it, and so full of promises". Cortés was revealing himself as much a brilliant politician as a military leader. He once again explained how Diego Velázquez had sent him as the commander – though of course he recognised that there were others among his hearers who would have been just as effective. He had the previous year wanted to go home to Cuba and render an account to Diego Velázquez of what they had seen. But the army had urged him to stay and found a city. That done, the city itself had named him captain-general and *justicia mayor* until the King decided otherwise. Of course, the land was so good that it would be proper to give it to an infante or a *gran señor* . . .

Cortés added that he believed that all his followers were determined not to abandon his enterprise until they saw the royal signature on a document requesting them to do so. He recalled the hardships and the dangers of the journey. Then he spoke of Narváez. He had outlawed Cortés and his men as if they had been Moors. What a tragic error! Of course, he knew that the followers of Narváez were four times more numerous than those of Cortés. But they were not as used to arms as his own men were, and many were disloyal to their own captain. Some were ill. He, Cortés, had an idea that God would give them victory. Then he quoted again one of his favourite sayings (from the *Song of Roland*): "It is better to die for a good cause than live in dishonour." So he said, "Our lives and honour are in your hands and in those of God."[40] Cortés was then lifted on to their shoulders by some of his men, who would not put him down until he insisted. They shouted, "Long live the captain who has such good ideas."[41] The evening was enlivened by scurrilous stories from Velázquez de León and Fr. Olmedo about the incoherence in Narváez's camp. Narváez's numerous unsuccessful dinners probably came in for ribald comment. Olmedo was a good mimic and even made fun of himself.[42]

Cortés now arranged his men in five companies: first, sixty under his cousin, Diego Pizarro, would seize the artillery; second, eighty, under Sandoval, would go to seize Narváez and kill him if he resisted[43]

(Cortés' written order to Sandoval styled him "chief constable of New Spain").[44] Velázquez de León, with a third group of another sixty conquistadors, would seize his own cousin, with whom he had quarrelled, Diego Velázquez the younger. Ordaz, with a fourth company of perhaps a hundred soldiers, would lead a mission to capture Salvatierra. Finally, Cortés, with the rest, would remain to be called to wherever they might be especially needed.

The army then settled to sleep, though the rain, and the sense of anticipation before what was obviously going to be a battle, prevented much rest.[45] Cortés promised 1,000 castellanos to the first man to lay his hands on Narváez, while the second, third and fourth would receive respectively 600, 400 and 200 pesos.[46]

Narváez, meantime, had proclaimed open war against Cortés. One of those with him had suggested that they should cut off Cortés' ears, and eat one of them;[47] a pleasing compromise, it might be thought, between the least pleasing habits of Spain and of Mexico.

Narváez organised his artillery, horsemen, arquebusiers and cross-bowmen in flat territory a mile from Cempoallan.[48] But the rain came on heavily. After some hours, Narváez's captains, soaked to the skin and weary of waiting for an attack which half of them thought would never come, and which many hoped might be successful, decided to return to Cempoallan. These captains left their horses and other equipment outside the town. The friends of Narváez were so self-confident as to be unable to envisage any setback. Narváez in particular would not believe that Cortés was only about three miles away, even when one of his scouts told him so. The chief of Cempoallan, who both knew and feared Cortés, told them that, when they least expected it, the *Caudillo* would attack. But Narváez's captains, Bono de Quejo and Salvatierra, laughed, and asked: "Do you take 'Cortesillo' to be so brave that, with the three cats which he commands, he will come and attack us just because this fat chief says so?"[49]

Narváez took what he thought were good precautions for the night: he established himself in the shrine on the top of the main temple; twenty cavalrymen were below in the patio; there were crossbowmen on the upper platform of the temple to guard him, and his three most important lieutenants, Salvatierra, Bono de Quejo and Gamarra were also there. Cannon had been placed in front of the improvised barracks. The army of Narváez went to sleep. A herald first announced amidst cheers that, if an attack were launched, 2,000 pesos would be offered to anyone who killed either Cortés or Sandoval: a higher fee, it will be seen, than that offered by Cortés for the death of Narváez.[50]

The battle so long feared and prepared now came. It was Whitsun: the night of 28–29 May 1520.[51]

Cortés had explained to his men that Narváez was probably expecting them at dawn. Since it would be difficult to sleep, it might be as well to start before. They left their camp in darkness, their movements muffled by the rain.[52] Just short of Narváez's camp they came across Narváez's two sentries, Gonzalo Carrasco and Alonso Hurtado. The latter fled, the former was captured. Cortés himself half strangled Carrasco to get information from him. Carrasco explained that Narváez's cavalry and other armaments were outside Cempoallan, while Narváez himself, with his captains and most of his men, were sleeping in the precinct of the temple. Since the plan of the centre of Cempoallan was well known to Cortés from his own stay there a year before, this told him all he needed.[53]

Sandoval set off instantly with his sixty men for that site. The rain must have stopped; for Cortés later remembered the fireflies, "which looked just like the matches of arquebuses".[54] "Fireflies in the night" was an expression used by the Mexica to denote poems: their enemy saw the words more prosaically.

Just short of Cempoallan, the horses and the equipment were left behind in a ditch under the care of the page Juan de Ortega, in company with Marina. The expedition heard mass. Fr. Bartolomé de Olmedo read the general confession. The men knelt in the dark forest by the river.[55]

The sentry Hurtado, meantime, had run back fast to his camp. He made his way to where Narváez was sleeping in a thatch-covered shrine on top of the great pyramid. This sentry ran up the steps of the pyramid, woke the commander-in-chief, and said that Cortés was on his way.[56] So Narváez rose, sat on his bed, and began to dress and arm himself. He had probably thought that, in the end, Cortés would hesitate before attacking him.[57] After all, though there had been one or two quarrels in Hispaniola and Darien between different groups of conquistadors, a pitched battle between two parties of Castilians had not previously occurred in the Americas. Perhaps Narváez had expected a surrender.[58] Juan Bono de Quejo said later that Narváez had not wished to fight Cortés, since he was God-fearing, and also because he looked on Cortés (with whom he had been in Santo Domingo as in Cuba) as his son.[59]

Narváez called out to his friends to prepare themselves. One of his men, Alonso de Villanueva, heard the cry, "To Arms", and knew that it was Narváez who called. But Juan de Salcedo (a conquistador who had married Cortés' Cuban mistress) heard Cortés' men shouting, "¡Viva el Rey, Spiritu Santo!"[60] Villanueva made his way to the pyramid. There he saw that Sandoval and Andrés de Tapia, with their men, had already arrived. They had silently climbed the steps of the pyramid, and had pushed past the guards outside Narváez's quarters without difficulty. On the small platform on top of the pyramid, they began to fight with Narváez and about thirty of his men, who had been sleeping nearby.[61] Narváez was wielding a great two-handed broadsword, a *montante*, which he swung with dexterity but, in the dark, without much effect.

Sandoval and his men forced him and his friends back into one of those inner rooms in Mexican temples where the idols were usually kept, and which were more difficult to penetrate. There was also some fighting on the steps of the pyramid. Narváez's standard-bearer, Diego de Rojas, was badly wounded, as was the young Diego Velázquez.[62]

On the top of the pyramid, Narváez's men were in confusion, and struck out blindly and at random.[63] After some wild moments, Narváez was heard to shout out, "Holy Mary, protect me, for they have killed me and destroyed my eye." One of Sandoval's pikemen, Pedro Gutiérrez de Valdelomar, a man from Illescas near Toledo, had in fact extracted Narváez's right eye.[64] Sandoval was heard shouting that he would burn the shrine if Narváez did not surrender. With no reply forthcoming, Martín López, Cortés' tall shipbuilder, "he of the launches", set fire to the thatched roof.[65] With flames encircling them, Narváez and those with him gave themselves up to Pedro Sánchez Farfán (who later claimed the prize which Cortés had offered for seizing Narváez). The fire burned Narváez's feet.[66]

Blood gushing from his eye, Narváez demanded a surgeon; Cortés' friends (Ávila, Sandoval and Ordaz) were unmoved. They said, "Go to the devil" or "Traitor" and "other very injurious words". Narváez was taken to Cortés, who said, "Traitor, troublemaker [revolvedor], you have received better than your deserts." Narváez answered: "In your power I am and, for the love of God, don't let these gentlemen kill me." Cortés then told Sandoval to look after the prisoner. Narváez's own surgeon, Maese Juan, was then found.[67]

Narváez kept his most important papers under his shirt. Alonso de Ávila, with the help of Sandoval and Diego de Ordaz, tore them from that place.[68] Narváez called out: "All bear witness to me that Alonso de Ávila has taken from me the provisions of His Majesty."[69] Alonso de Ávila said later that these papers were not important, merely a few old letters rather than royal instructions ("no son sino unos papeles"). He immediately gave them to Cortés.[70] But several friends of Narváez later swore that the papers had included Velázquez's instructions.[71] Narváez was held in irons with Salvatierra, Gamarra and some others in one of the temples, while Cortés turned his attention to dealing with the rest of his enemy's army.[72]

Narváez's gunners had been firing some of their guns but, in the darkness, the shots went high. The wax placed in the mouths of the cannon as a result of Velázquez de León's bribe to the master gunner Martínez must have helped the attackers. So did the fact that, in the rain, the gunpowder was wet.[73] Pizarro and his men mastered the guns in the confusion. As for the cavalry, Cortés succeeded in arranging to cut the girths of many of Narváez's horses. Their riders fell to the ground immediately they mounted. Several horses cantered out of the camp alone.[74] All the horses were soon captured: "stolen", as it was later put by Narváez's friends.[75] But now the cry, "Viva Cortés and his victory", rang through the camp.[76] Still a number of supporters of Narváez held out in one temple under the direction of the wounded Diego Velázquez the younger.[77] This shrine had been converted into a makeshift chapel with a picture of the Virgin.[78] Cortés battered it with Narváez's own artillery, thereby showing that not all the powder could have been dampened. Cortés said that he would kill all the prisoners unless these men surrendered. They welcomed the chance to give up, and abandoned their arms.[79] The accusation that Cortés had attacked a church was, however, not quickly forgotten.

After it became generally known that Narváez had been captured, all his now directionless captains also happily surrendered. Cortés received them with tolerance. As previously mentioned, he knew most of them and asked them to forget the recent past as soon as they could. Both sides rejoiced. Sitting in a chair in his armour with over it a long orange robe (perhaps a present from Montezuma), Cortés regaled them with tales of the riches of Tenochtitlan.[80] A black jester of Narváez's, named Guidela, said ironically of his master, "The Romans never performed such a feat" (this recalls the jester of Charles the Bold, Duke of Burgundy who, after the defeat in the battle of Granson, remarked, "Well, sir, we are well Hannibalised this time"). Cortés went to see Narváez in his captivity. The latter said to him: "Well, Captain Cortés, you must consider it a great thing to have beaten me and made me a prisoner." Cortés replied gravely that his victory was thanks to God and to the brave men whom he had fighting for him; to capture Narváez was, on the contrary, he added churlishly, but perhaps accurately, "one of the least things which he had done in New Spain".[81] Narváez seems to have henceforth entertained much respect for Cortés: who, he later told Francisco de Garay, Governor of Jamaica, happily fitting into the fashionable mode of classical allusion, was showing himself "as lucky in his undertakings as Octavius, in his conquests as Caesar, and in overcoming difficulties as Hannibal".[82]

Cortés moved fast to benefit from his victory. He sent Francisco de Lugo to San Juan to order the masters and pilots of the ships in which Narváez's army had sailed to come and see him at Villa Rica de la Vera Cruz. Cortés then appointed Alonso Caballero, who had been one of Narváez's masters, but was also an old friend of his own, as "admiral" in charge of these ships (he came from a *converso* mercantile family of Sanlúcar de Barrameda).[83] He ordered him to unload all equipment; and much wine, flour and bacon, as well as cassava bread was also put on shore. This formed an invaluable reserve for Cortés' army. Cortés then had most of the ships beached, as he had had his own ships beached the previous year. All equipment was taken ashore, including sails and rudders. Other goods in the ships concerned were also seized as booty of war: including clothes and gold.[84] He left two ships which he planned to send to Jamaica to buy mares, calves, sheep, chickens and goats. The sailors demanded wages. Cortés promised to pay them: it does not seem that this undertaking was fulfilled, at least not for many months. Cortés therefore had a new constituency of critics with which to cope.

This victory was not expensive. Probably fifteen of Narváez's men were killed, and two of Cortés'.[85] These deaths included (either in action or from wounds) the standard-bearer Rojas, a young captain, Fuentes, probably the young Diego Velázquez, and Alonso Carretero, one of those who had left Cortés for Narváez. Several were wounded, including Narváez, of course, but also Escalona (another fugitive from Cortés), and Tlacochcalcatl, the chief of Cempoallan, knifed when he got in the way of the battle.[86] Cervantes el chocarrero was severely beaten by the victors.

A Mexican historian has commented that Cortés' triumph was due more to the use of gold than of steel.[87] Cortés' bribes were certainly intelligent. But his tactic of surprise, his determination, the experience of his men, their loyalty to him, all counted too. Narváez's men were lulled by the superiority of their numbers into an utterly misleading sense of confidence.

Cortés soon set all the prisoners free except for Narváez and Salvatierra. He gave back their arms and horses on condition that they joined his army. All expressed themselves delighted to return with him to the "richest city of the Indies".[88] Cortés' generosity was unpopular among some of his own old captains: Alonso de Ávila said sourly that the Caudillo was clearly interested in emulating Alexander the Great, who always showed greater favour to those whom he had defeated than those who had fought on his side.[89] Cortés was unimpressed by this classical allusion. He replied, "Those who do not wish to follow me need not do so: the women of Castile, after all, breed soldiers." Ávila replied: "They may breed soldiers, but what we need here are captains and governors."[90] But Cortés was determined to make good use of the doctors and other specialists who had come with Narváez. There were notaries public, too, who were able to tell precisely how the Caudillo should address the new King-Emperor Charles: no longer "Your Highness", but "Your Caesarian Majesty".[91]

Cortés was nevertheless firm in insisting, through a herald, that all those who had been with Narváez had thenceforth to accept him as captain-general and justicia mayor.[92] At the same time he dismantled Narváez's little town of San Salvador, including the church, and conscripted all who had settled there into his army.[93] Finally, in order to avoid further criticisms from his old friends, such as Ávila, he sent Narváez's captains up to Mexico on foot. These men were Salvatierra,

Pedro de Aguilar, Antonio de Amaya, Juan de Ayllón, Juan de Gamarra and Juan de Casillas – in fact nearly all of those who had been sworn in as officers and councillors of Narváez's ill-fated new town of San Salvador.

These men were angry. They were "people of good breeding and men of honour not accustomed to walk on foot".[94] That turned out the least of their worries. Halfway to Mexico, somewhere near Tepeaca, in a gorge, they, with about forty others, including some of Cortés' men who were accompanying them as guides, were all captured or killed by Mexicans and Texcocans.[95]

The chief of Cempoallan, though injured, was eager to make things up with Cortés. He offered him his house in which to stay. But Cortés preferred to remain in the house of "Doña Catalina", the ugly niece with whom he had lodged the previous year. There, it seems, the victory was royally celebrated.

Cortés next sent Juan Velázquez de León with a hundred and twenty men (including a hundred of Narváez's) back to continue to settle the coast beyond the river Pánuco – a measure which surely would prevent the Governor of Jamaica, Francisco de Garay, from further intervention; while Diego de Ordaz would go with another hundred and twenty men (again including a hundred of Narváez's army) to Coatzacoalcos to establish another colony.[96]

These men had already set out, and the rest of the two armies were still recovering, when Botello Puerto de Plata, a gentleman from Santander, "a Latin scholar, an honest man who had been in Rome and was said to be a magician",[97] went to Cortés to tell him: "Señor, don't delay here long, because you should know that Pedro de Alvarado, your captain, whom you left in the city of Tenochtitlan, is in great danger, since they [the Mexica] have made war against him and have killed a man, and are trying to climb into our quarters by ladders, so that it would be good if you went back quickly."[98] It was said that a demon had informed Botello of this news. It was more likely to have been a Tlaxcalan messenger. For Cortés had not decided how to react to this piece of "soothsaying" when four chiefs from Tenochtitlan appeared. They came from Montezuma, weeping, with the same message, except that they said that the fighting had been caused by Alvarado, who had killed and wounded many Indians at a festival for which Cortés himself had given permission.[99]

26
The blood of the chieftains ran like water

Some climbed the wall; they were able to escape. Some entered the calpulli;
there they escaped. And some escaped among the dead; they got in among
those really dead, only by feigning to be dead. They were able to escape. But if
one took a breath, if they saw him, they killed him. And the blood of the
chieftains ran like water . . .
Florentine Codex, Book xii

IT WILL BE recalled that in Tenochtitlan, Cortés had left behind Pedro de Alvarado, "Tonatio", "the Sun", with about a hundred Castilians. Alvarado had with him several well-known conquistadors such as Francisco Álvarez Chico, and Bernardino Vázquez de Tapia, as well as Fr. Juan Díaz, with the Mexican from Coatzacoalcos, Francisco, as interpreter. Alonso de Escobar, a Velazquista whom Cortés had won over at Vera Cruz, had been left to look after all the treasures which had been gathered in the six months in the capital.

The departure of "Malinche" for the coast of course had excited expectations among the Mexica. The mood in the streets and squares near the Spanish quarters was volatile. Rumours abounded. So did questions: had Cortés died? Who were these mysterious "Basques" who were said to have arrived? The difficulties came to a head during the celebration of the feast of Toxcatl.[1]

This was one of the most important of Mexican festivals. During earlier generations it had been just one more plea for rain, and associated with the god Tezcatlipoca. Then, like many other festivals, it had become attached to (or rather, captured by the priests of) Huitzilopochtli.[2] The climax was the sacrifice of a young man personifying Tezcatlipoca. The victim would have been selected at the end of the festival of Toxcatl the previous year for his beauty of appearance and demeanour. Since then he would have lived almost as if he had been a god.

Montezuma asked Cortés before the *Caudillo* left Mexico for permission to hold this fiesta. He received it.[3] Several days before the festival was due to begin, Montezuma again requested permission to hold it, this time asking Alvarado. Alvarado again gave authority: with the proviso that there should be no human sacrifices.[4] Several Mexicans asked if they could, for the festival, put back the image of Huitzilopochtli in the shrine on the great pyramid. Alvarado refused that request.[5]

During the last days before the opening of the festival, Alvarado's Castilians seem to have been fed with all sorts of apprehensions by their Tlaxcalan allies, many of whom had bitter memories of previous fiestas of Toxcatl, when the Mexica had sacrificed many of their people.[6]

The first sign of trouble was when the Mexica suddenly stopped providing the Castilians with food. A girl who used to do their washing, and who had said that the conquistadors had to eat, was found hanged.[7] The Castilians concluded that this was to frighten the other servants from continuing to work for them. Food thereafter was bought in the market by one of Alvarado's followers, Juan Álvarez. The situation was not ideal but it was manageable.

Then one morning Alvarado went out into the main square before the Great Temple. It was there that most of the celebrations concerned in the fiesta were due to take place. Alvarado saw fine canopies over the precinct, and stakes in the ground, and one bigger one in the main temple. He asked for an explanation. He was told, presumably by a Tlaxcalan, that they would be used to tie up the Castilians and sacrifice them. The big stake was for Alvarado himself.[8]

Alvarado also claimed that he saw several sacrifices being carried out, but that is improbable: a sacrifice was a solemn ceremony, not an occasional gesture.[9] One conquistador, Álvaro López, later testified, however, that he saw many pots, pans and axes being prepared, and that he observed the Indians saying that they were getting ready to cook and eat the Spaniards with garlic.[10]

Alvarado, excessively nervous, next came upon women putting the finishing touches to a figure of Huitzilopochtli which, as usual at this festival, was built on a frame made of sticks and filled with dough of amaranth seed. The whole had been kneaded together with the blood of recently sacrificed captives. The figure had been given serpent-shaped earrings in turquoise mosaic and a nose of gold. It had been dressed elaborately; a breech cloth covered its private parts. The god had been given two cloaks: one of stinging nettles, another of severed heads and human bones. It also had a jacket, on which were painted depictions of human limbs and genitals. The god's head was pasted with feathers, the face painted in stripes. Its right hand bore a paper banner dipped in blood and a shield of reed work, while, in its left hand, it held four arrows to recall that it was, of course, the god of war. The decoration was especially elaborate that year, since all the young . . . the "seasoned warriors" were as if determined to show and exhibit the feast to the Castilians.[11] Dough was an especially prized substance. The gods in the form of amaranth seed were represented thus as the food of men; while men, as blood and hearts, were the food of gods.[12] Effigies of Tlaloc and Tezcatlipoca were also there. All three were on litters.

Present too were girls who had fasted twenty days, and men who had lived on almost nothing for a year. The captains of Mexican wars, conquerors of Soconusco or cities near Cempoallan, were all getting ready, dressing up and painting themselves. Sacrificial victims were also being prepared; for despite Cortés' (and Alvarado's) prohibition, those rites certainly continued.[13]

Alvarado talked to one of these captives. This individual assured him (the Greek conquistador Andrés de Rodas was also present) that the Mexica were going to replace the pictures of the Virgin in the temple with a new effigy of Huitzilopochtli.[14] Alvarado's men had seen ropes and other gear being made ready to hoist the deity to the top of the pyramid. Alvarado's informant said that the priests had tried already to remove the "reredos" of the Virgin.[15] One of Alvarado's men, Alonso Lopes, saw black fingermarks on that painting – clearly an indication that a priest had been at work there, since those holy men usually painted themselves black.[16] The implication was that the "reredos", if indeed it was that, had miraculously resisted being moved by the Mexicans. Perhaps it was, however, firmly fixed into the wall by nails; which the Mexicans had not known before.

Alvarado came upon three more Indians who, with their heads shaved, were sitting in new clothes in front of each of the idols, and tied to them, apparently ready to be sacrificed. He took them back to his quarters under guard. Presumably they were captured prisoners, and certainly could not have been Mexican. All the same, in the Palace of Axayácatl, they were tortured, by having burning evergreen oak logs placed on their stomachs, to force them to tell what was being planned. One refused to make any confession. After torturing him a long time, the Spaniards gave up, and threw him to his death off the roof of the palace. One of the others confessed (through, of course, the inadequate interpreter Francisco) that, in ten days, the Mexica were going to rise against the conquistadors.[17] Vázquez de Tapia testified later that Alvarado also took two relations of Montezuma and had them tortured. They too told of likely risings.

These confessions are difficult to take seriously. For Alvarado had asked the interpreter such questions as, "Francisco, do they say that they are going to make war in ten days?" "Yes sir" was the inevitable reply.[18]

Alvarado then went to "that dog of a Montezuma who doesn't treat me as he used to". Describing what he had heard, Alvarado asked him to prevent all these disagreeable eventualities.[19] But the Emperor said that, being imprisoned, he could do nothing. Alvarado's nerves were kept on edge by the accusations of a converted Texcocan, "Don Hernando", who insisted that the Mexica were soon going to kill him and all the other Castilians.[20] The Mexica, he said, were preparing ladders with which to scale the palace in order to release Montezuma. Another Tlaxcalan said that the Indians were already boring holes in the rear walls of the palace. Alvarado feared that they would soon be able to enter by that means.[21] He might have been forgiven had he thought that the return of the god Huitzilopochtli to the temple would be the signal for the rebellion. Alvarado himself said later that Montezuma's attendants in the Palace of Axayácatl were found to have clubs ready with which to kill the conquistadors; and, under the Emperor's bed, they found a gilded one.[22]

The mood of anxious anticipation in Tenochtitlan on the eve of the fiesta was thus extreme. The sight of the city en fête must have been as inspiring to the Mexica as it was disconcerting to the Castilians. Alvarado's men in Mexico were few, they were not the most resourceful of the conquistadors in the country, and their morale was low. Alvarado was nothing like so subtle a leader as Cortés. Meantime, Cortés was about to face, on the coast near Vera Cruz, a larger group of Spanish warriors whose leader, whatever his private hesitations may have been about fighting Cortés, had told Montezuma that Cortés and his men were criminals on the run. Cortés had persistently humiliated both Montezuma and his nephew Cacama. The Spaniards had behaved brutally, on many occasions. The Mexica were proud: and, when every allowance is made for the fact that the concept of honour was different in old Mexico from what it was in Spain, any people with the slightest sense of self-esteem would have been seeking an opportunity for a reassertion of their old independence.

Yet there is no evidence for a plot. The Codex Aubin recorded a conversation between Montezuma and his chief of armaments, Ecatzin ("General Martín Ecatzin" as he was later referred to in Spanish texts), who was supposed to have warned the Emperor against the Spaniards and, recalling what they did in Cholula, to have said, "Let us hide our shields in each wall" (that is, the wall of the temple in which the main celebrations would occur). But Montezuma is supposed to have said: "Are we then at war? Have confidence."[23] The fact was that, with Montezuma imprisoned, it was difficult to mount any opposition to the Spaniards. The collective will ruled, and the collective will was decided upon by the Emperor. Without him, there was no one to take an initiative.

Cortés' insistence afterwards was that, had it not been for Narváez, order would have reigned in Tenochtitlan. It is a view which has something to it.[24]

The likely explanation for what now transpired is that the Tlaxcalans, and perhaps some Texcocan enemies of the Mexica, persuaded the jumpy Castilians that a plot was indeed under way. Then Francisco Álvarez Chico, one of Cortés' intimates, insisted to Alvarado that the Spaniards should attack before the Mexicans attacked them.[25] Alvarado was impetuous as well as nervous: he was exactly the kind of leader to suppose (or be persuaded) that, if fighting were inevitable, it would be as well to fight on his terms.[26] He was a gifted commander, as decisive as he was brave. Like Cortés he was ruthless. But his inclination was to anticipate trouble. Cortés' inclination was to circumvent it. (The accusation that Alvarado was suddenly moved by a desire for the ornaments of the nobility while they danced seems unlikely: he and his friends had already accumulated a good deal of gold).[27]

The first days of the fiesta passed without danger. The traditional dances were held at the sacred places of the city. The beautiful youth called on to impersonate the god Tezcatlipoca was now introduced to his eight attendants.[28] With a long head, wide mouth, straight nose and eyebrows close to the eyes, he incarnated the Mexican physical ideal.[29] His attendants had been elaborately prepared. They had fasted for a year. Then "Tezcatlipoca" had his long hair cut. He was given the dress of a "seasoned warrior", who had taken four prisoners. He was also presented with four beautiful women, each with the name of a goddess, including one who was allocated the name of Xochiquetzal, "flowery plume", goddess of love.

The "god" was given a flute and a conch. He was painted, decorated with flowers and feathers by the priests, and prepared for his sacrifice. This was to be held as usual on the fourth day of the festival at the temple of Tlacochcalco on the island of Tepepulco in the middle of the lake near Iztapalapa.[30] The sacrifice had to look as if it were willingly offered – and indeed as usual in these rituals some degree of co-operation must have been forthcoming. No doubt the god was usually given a special supply of "obsidian water" (*pulque*) or sacred mushrooms. The essential thing was that, though he would be guarded while he was being rowed over to the island in a canoe, he had, willingly, to walk up the steps of the pyramid there without being dragged. He had, also willingly, to stand on the platform at the top of the stairs, to turn round, to gaze at the lake, and then to break his flute. His sacrifice followed. It was supposed to stand for life on earth: "For he who rejoiceth, who possesseth riches", who seeks and covets our lord's [Tezcatlipoca's] sweetness, his gentleness, his riches and prosperity thus ends in great misery. "For it is said, none comes to an end here upon earth with happiness, riches and wealth."[31] A horn would be blown. Then the flutes of the new Tezcatlipoca, already chosen for the next year, 1521, would be heard all over the city.

The whole sacrifice was designed to stand for the fragility of love, the evanescence of beauty, and the speed with which grandeur fades.

The moment that the new Tezcatlipoca's flutes were heard, dancing was to begin in the precinct of the Great Temple. In 1520, this probably occurred on 16 May.

The effigy of Huitzilopochtli was left at the foot of the steps of the great pyramid. Those who fasted took the lead. They were followed by the captains. These dancers wore elaborate cloaks interwoven with rabbit fur and feathers, over loincloths of embroidered cotton. The dancers' sandals of ocelot skin had soles of deerskin, and were fastened by leather thongs. Above their ankles, they wore more ocelot skin as greaves, hung with golden bells. To the small tufts of hair on their otherwise shaven heads, they attached feather tassels. These noblemen also wore necklaces of jade or shells, bracelets of gold on their upper arms, bands of shell supporting their feather plumage, while, at the wrist, soft leather bands dangled, set with jade. They wore earplugs in their ears, nose jewels in their nostrils, and labrets of amber or crystal, carrying kingfisher feathers.[32] They were adorned with feathers of many colours, ornaments and paint.

The most important musical instruments were drums. Two sorts were as usual employed. One, the *huehuetl*, was large, made like European drums of a well-carved piece of hollow wood, with a painted deerskin or a piece of *amatl* paper stretched over the top, and played by hand, not with sticks. The second drum was the *teponaztli*, a horizontal drum, also carved, beaten with a rubber-tipped mallet. A special reddish wood with black veins was customarily used.[33] Music was also provided by flutes, bone fifes, and conches.

When the noblemen began to dance, one song followed another, the informants of Sahagún recalled, "rising in waves". There were probably about four hundred dancers, and several thousand Mexica standing at the side, probably clapping or participating in some other way. The main dance was the serpent dance.[34] This was often seen at fiestas, not just at that of Toxcatl. The dancers were all men, since women never danced in public. Holding hands, they danced – "so wildly that it was amazing" – in big concentric rings round the drums. Anyone who sought to leave the dancing without permission was pressed back by attendants with pine cudgels. Discipline had to be maintained till the end. The slightest mistake or deviation from the traditional steps (as in the playing of the music) led to punishment.[35] Dancing among the Mexica, as Fr. Motolinía would later put it, was not just an amusement, not just a rite, it was a way of desiring the favour of the gods, "by serving them and calling upon them with one's whole body".[36] The Mexican dances were, the conquistadors had decided before this, "better than the Zambra of the Moors", the best dance that the people in Spain knew at that time.[37] Some Mexican dances were, however, offensive to good Christians: for example, the *cuecuexcuicatl*, a "ticklish or scratching dance", used with "so many wriggles and glances and indecent coquetry" that it seemed "a dance for wanton women and susceptible men", as Fr. Durán was prudishly later to comment.[38]

The dancers at this fiesta were led by "Titlacauan", a shadow of

Tezcatlipoca, who would have grown up alongside his sacrificed companion, and now stood for the dark and unruly side of the god. He too would, according to the plan, be sacrificed later.[39] He was accompanied by most of the leaders of the Mexica, including many relations of Montezuma, the aristocracy of the country.

The Mexicans noticed the arrival of the Castilians in armour, with their swords and shields, led by Alvarado. But they did nothing. How could they? Once the dancing had begun, after all, a collective ecstasy would seize the Mexicans, every movement obeying the laws of ritual. They continued to dance, and to sing sacred songs, praising their gods, and begging them to provide them with peace, children, health and wisdom. Some festive dances, after all, went on for many hours. Dancers would in certain circumstances be allowed to withdraw in order to eat and rest, and then return.

Some of the Spaniards and their Indian allies – certainly there were Tlaxcalans among them – moved to block the three entrances of the precinct: the Eagle gate in the smaller palace; the gate of the Reed; and the gate of the Obsidian Serpent. About ten Spaniards were posted at each.[40] Alvarado and others of his men mixed with the crowd. Perhaps Mexica who noticed them saw them in the role of those wildly dressed buffoons who were supposed sometimes to weave in and out of dancers, to afford comic relief.[41]

Alvarado had divided his men into two groups: sixty to guard Montezuma and kill many of his attendant lords; the other sixty to come to the temple and kill the Mexican nobility who would be taking part in the dancing. Vázquez de Tapia insisted at the *residencia* against Alvarado in 1529 that he said that Alvarado should not do this since it was evil; but no one else supported him. No other witness recalled that Vázquez de Tapia had said anything.[42] Fr. Juan Díaz, who might have been supposed to express the voice of mercy, seems to have been notably quiet.

When the gates of the temple were well closed, Alvarado gave the order, "*¡Mueran!*" ("Let them die"). His men then fell on the dancers, beginning with a young captain, who had been designated the leader of the day.[43] His importance in the ritual would have been made obvious by the space which others would have left around him while he danced. The Castilians then turned on the priests who were playing the drums. The informants of Sahagún are vivid: "They surrounded those who danced . . . they went among the drums. They struck off the arms of the one who beat the drums . . . and, afterwards . . . his neck and his head flew off, falling far away. . . They pierced them all with their iron lances, and they struck each with the iron swords. Of some, they slashed open the back and there their entrails fell out. Of some, they split the head, they hacked their heads to pieces. Their heads were completely cut up. And of some, they hit the shoulder . . . they struck in the shank . . . on the thigh. Of some, they struck the belly, and then the entrails streamed forth . . ."[44] One of the Castilians, Núño Pinto, also struck off the golden nose of the effigy of the god Huitzilopochtli.[45]

After killing most of the dancers, Alvarado turned his attention to the spectators. None of the Mexicans had any weapons. They were taken completely by surprise. None of them had ever seen steel swords in action before, though some may have heard of them from the Otomí, who had fought the Castilians on behalf of the Tlaxcalans. Some Mexica climbed the walls and managed to flee. Some entered the so-called tribal temple and escaped that way. Some feigned death: "The blood of the chieftains," wrote Fr. Sahagún, who must have talked with survivors of the engagement, "ran like water, it spread out slippery and a foul odour rose from it . . ." The Spaniards went everywhere looking in the tribal temple, they ransacked every temple.[46] One of the priests then sought to rally the Mexica: "Mexicans, are we not going to war? Have confidence . . ." They then attacked the conquistadors with pine sticks; which unsurprisingly made little headway against the swords of Toledo.[47]

Juan Álvarez, meantime, had been in the city on his daily mission trying to find food. Bringing what he could back to the Palace of Axayácatl from Tlatelolco and elsewhere, with no doubt Tlaxcalan bearers, he saw Indians streaming wounded out of the temple precinct. Then he saw Castilians running out too: among them Alvarado, who ordered everyone to withdraw instantly to their quarters. Álvarez asked, "What about our food?" Alvarado replied, "The devil take the food, for we have taken action. As the Indians did not take the first step, we have done so ourselves" ("*comenzamos nosotros los primeros*"). Álvarado then told Álvarez that "two or three thousand Indians are dead". That showed that "he who begins the battle, wins" ("*el que primero acomete, vence*").[48]

The fighting soon became general in the streets around the temple. A general appeal for war to the Mexica was made. The drums on top of the great pyramid were beaten. All males were summoned by the leaders of their *calpultin* (that is, such of them who had survived the massacre) to go to the armouries (at each of the four entrances to the temple precinct), where they would receive weapons.[49] Some Mexican leaders were found who were able to direct a counterattack. They made a general appeal: O Mexica, O chieftains, hasten here, let us prepare our weapons, shields and arrows, hasten here, already many chieftains have died. They have been shattered, destroyed, put to death, O Mexica, O chieftains.[50] Alvarado himself was wounded on the head by a stone.

Back in their quarters, the Castilians found that their compatriots guarding Montezuma had also played their part in the butchery, for they had killed many of the lords who were surrounding the Emperor, including Cacama, the King of Texcoco. Almost all those lords whom the Castilians had attached in January to a chain of iron seem to have died.

Montezuma himself and those of his companions who survived the murdering, such as his brother Cuitláhuac, Itzquauhtzin, the governor of Tlatelolco, and perhaps the deputy emperor, the *cihuacoatl*, were now held in chains.[51] Alvarado, covered with blood from his wound, went to Montezuma and had the effrontery to say to the poor Emperor, "See what your people have done to me." Montezuma replied: "Alvarado, if you had not begun it, my men would not have done this. You have ruined yourselves and me also."[52]

The Mexica outside pressed forward again and again, seeking to climb into the palace, and trying to set fire to the door. The Tlaxcalans showed their loyalty to their Spanish allies by "damping their own cloaks and placing them over the flames". Either this day or the next the four brigantines, including the one on which Montezuma had gone hunting, were burned, thereby cutting off Alvarado from the possibility of escape by water, and greatly damaging all Cortés' plans.[53]

The fighting continued. The Castilians made no headway, despite using cannon and crossbows. On one occasion the main cannon at the door of their quarters failed to ignite. It went off by mistake at an unexpected if convenient moment.[54] At another point the Indians claimed later to have seen not only a vision of a woman of Castile – presumably the Virgin Mary – but also the unmistakable figure of St James on his famous white horse. It was probably María de Estrada, a *conquistadora* of great energy, accompanied by one of Alvarado's mounted comrades, such as Francisco Álvarez Chico.[55] A Mexican was supposed to have said: "If we had not been frightened by Mary and St James, your palace would by this time have been destroyed, and you yourselves cooked, though you would not have been eaten; for we tried your flesh the other day and it tasted bitter, so we should have thrown your carcasses to the eagles, lions, tigers and snakes, who would have eaten you for us." The same Mexican went on, "All the same, if you do not free Montezuma soon, you will be properly killed and then cooked with chocolate. We shall do this because you seized our Montezuma, and touched him with your filthy hands – Montezuma, our lord and god, who feeds us. Why does not the earth swallow you up, you who steal the gods of others . . .?"[56]

When even these miraculous occurrences had no effect, Alvarado returned to Montezuma and, placing his knife at his chest, told him to order his men to call off the battle.[57] So Montezuma went on to a roof with Itzquauhtzin, the Mexican governor of Tlatelolco. The Emperor did his best to persuade the Mexica to call off the battle.[58] Itzquauhtzin also spoke. He too seems to have been conciliatory. He said, O Mexica, hear! We are not the equal of the Castilians. Let "battle be abandoned. Let the arrow and shield be stilled. Unhappy are the poor old men and women, the common folk, those not yet of understanding, who toddle who crawl, who lie in cradles, those yet untrained." For this reason your ruler says 'may battle cease': for they have placed irons on his feet.[59] This apparently had some effect. The battle did die down for a time.

It is possible that the prisoners would not have acted in this way if Montezuma had not heard, from his agents at the sea, of Narváez's defeat at Cortés' hands.[60]

Many Mexicans were reluctant to cease fighting. They realised, rightly, that this was their opportunity to finish with the newcomers. So, some sporadic fighting continued during the following days. But they still had not, and could not, evolve a leader. The nation which lived in "harmony and order" could not easily produce individual chiefs. That did not prevent there being outrage at Montezuma's craven attitude: one man was heard to say: "What saith Montezuma, O fool? Am I not one of his warriors?"

Montezuma never recovered his authority after this. For the Mexica, as well as the conquistadors, realised subsequently that Vázquez de Tapia was right when he said that, had Montezuma not done as he was asked, all Alvarado's men would have been killed.[61]

When in Mexico people were killed in battle, there was always a mass cremation of the bodies of the dead in the square in front of the main temple. But before that, there would be private wakes for four days. Old friends would go to the house of the dead man, and offer the body presents. A dog might be brought, to symbolise Xolotl, the companion of the Mexican in his hunting days, and be ceremonially killed, so that the dead man in the underworld might have a companion. The body would be given the insignia, paint and hairstyle of the dead warrior's favourite gods. After the cremation, locks of the dead man's hair would be taken home, an urn filled with his ashes, and eventually these ashes would be taken either to the hill Yohualichan near Culhuacan, or to Teotihuacan; or, if the person were important, placed in crevices in the Great Temple. Eighty days' mourning would then follow. During this time, widows were forbidden to wash. At the end of that time, they would scrape off the dirt accumulated, and give it, wrapped in paper, to a priest.[62] It would be foolish to suppose that at this time any of these traditional customs could have been abbreviated. On the contrary, they were probably carried through with especial attention.

Alvarado was in a difficult position. There was no more carrying in of food to him and his men. Any Mexican seen taking tortillas to the Castilians was instantly killed – though Juan Álvarez was still apparently able to go out sometimes and bring back food, since he knew where to go.[63] The canals were made dangerous, several bridges were pulled up, and the streets were made impassable, just in case Alvarado should be thinking of trying to escape.

The city remained frenzied. The nights were filled with the lamentations of women and children in mourning, which seemed to resound against the mountains. The noise, an indigenous source reported, "should have made the stones weep; eight to ten thousand men torn to pieces who had done nothing to deserve that fate . . ." These wails were ritualistic, no doubt, but, equally certainly, they represented a real sense of outrage that Montezuma's guests should have conducted themselves so atrociously.

Alvarado had after all killed the flower of the Mexican nobility: all men who had come through the *calmécac*, who had learned to be proud of their land, their method of government, their people's astonishing achievements, their rituals and their gods, their poetry and their dances, their flowers and, no doubt, their sacrifices.

The festival of Toxcatl so brutally over, the priests would have been preparing themselves for the month of Etzalqualiztli. This was the culmination of the dry season. During this time, the priests usually took over the capital. They were customarily permitted to insult and maltreat anyone they met as they gathered reeds for seats to be used at the ceremonies ahead. Captives, slaves, and children were sacrificed, their hearts thrown into a whirlpool of the lake known as Pantitlan. Slaves decked out as "servants of Tlaloc", their eyes enlarged with paint, would go round from house to house, begging to be fed from a dour stew which was supposed to symbolise that there was nothing in that season to eat. Then the rains began, about the end of May.[64]

27

As a song you were born, Montezuma

"As a song you were born, Montezuma
As a flower you came to bloom on earth . . ."
Angel Garibay, *Historia de la literatura nahuatl*

CORTÉS WAS MAKING his way back from Vera Cruz to Tenochtitlan, his forces strengthened by the best men, new horses, and good equipment from Narváez's army. He had left Narváez himself in prison at Vera Cruz in the charge of Francisco de Saucedo, *"el pulido"*, Juan Rodríguez de Escobar, and Francisco de Terrazas.[1] Before he received that worrying message from Tenochtitlan, he had dispatched Velázquez de León and Rodrigo Rangel, each with about 400 of Narváez's force, to the new places for colonisation where they had been before the battle of Cempoallan. But now he had sent quickly to ask those captains to meet him again at Tlaxcala, as soon as they could arrange it.

Cortés arrived at that city with his men weary and exhausted. They were short of food since, once again, as on his first journey, the area of the salt lake had proved most inhospitable. Several men were close to death from hunger or thirst.[2] Two members of Cortés' original army, a Portuguese, Magallanes, and Diego Moreno, procured food for the commander from the prosperous city of Tepeaca on the west road between Tenochtitlan and Vera Cruz. The leaders of Tlaxcala held their breath. They knew of the setback to the Spaniards, and their own people, in Tenochtitlan, but they had committed themselves too profoundly to Cortés to be able to withdraw from their alliance. Xicotencatl the younger was no doubt insisting that he had foreseen everything, but his comments at this moment do not seem to have been recorded.

At Tlaxcala, Cortés was joined by Velázquez de León and Rangel, with their men. Though Cortés left behind a small garrison at Tlaxcala under the direction of a certain Juan Páez, it must have been with well over a thousand Spaniards, as well as about twice that number of Tlaxcalans, who perhaps had been given rudimentary military training by Alonso de

Ojeda and Juan Márquez, that eventually Cortés again reached the great lake in the Valley of Mexico.[3]

On the way, everyone had been struck by the complete absence of either observers or spies. The country seemed empty. Cortés had anticipated the formation of an army against him. But there was no sign of it.[4]

The expedition stopped a night at Texcoco where understandably, no one greeted the conquistadors with any enthusiasm. The chiefs seemed to have made themselves absent. The exception was Ixtlilxochitl, who still looked on himself as Cortés' ally. From him, Cortés learned that the garrison in Tenochtitlan under Alvarado was still in being.[5] The *Caudillo* thereupon sent a message to his deputy by canoe. But before this boat had returned, another canoe came from Tenochtitlan with two of Alvarado's men, the notary Pero Hernández, and a youth named Santa Clara. They explained that Alvarado and his men were nearly all alive. Only five or six had been killed. But, they said, they were surrounded, and could only secure food at great risk and at a high price.

Hernández and Santa Clara also brought a message from Montezuma. The Emperor insisted that what had happened had grieved him as deeply as it must have done Cortés. He was in no way responsible. He begged the *Caudillo* not to be angry. He hoped that he would come and live again in the city as before.

Cortés then took his expedition round the north side of the lake, so as to approach the Mexican capital from the west, planning to enter by the shortest causeway, namely that of Tacuba. This journey was partly one of reconnaissance: to see what that terrain was like, should it be necessary to fight there. Also, the other causeways seemed already to have been cut.

At Tacuba certain local leaders approached Cortés. They were anxious to be on good terms with him. They suggested: "Lord, stay here in Tacuba, or in Coyoacán, or in Texcoco, and send for Alvarado and Montezuma to come here, because, here on the mainland, in these meadows, if the Mexica rise against you, you would defend yourselves better than in the city"[6] This was intelligent advice, but Cortés refused to accept it. Instead, the following morning, 24 June, the day of St John the Baptist, he and his cavalcade rode into the capital, the horses cantering, with many cannonades and much gunfire, "making a happy noise", as a celebration of their victory and their return.[7] They "came stirring up clouds of dust, their faces covered and ashen with dust . . . caked with earth," recalled Fr. Sahagún.[8]

On their way, the Spaniards saw a dead Mexican hanging from a tree, before a piece of level ground, on which there was also a large pile of bread, with several hundred turkeys eating it. On the causeway, the horse of Pedro de Solís caught and broke its hoof between two beams on one of the bridges. The Castilian soothsayer Botello, whose morale and standing were those days high, naturally saw both these events as ominous.[9]

When they reached Tenochtitlan, the Castilians met something worse than omens: silence. The population had hidden itself. No one came out to greet them: "The Mexica decided thereafter that they would not be seen but would hide . . . they would speak no more but only spy out of entrances, openings in walls, and holes with which they had pierced the walls . . ."[10] Probably part of the quiet in the city was explained by the need for eighty days' mourning. But the silence gave Tenochtitlan the air of being one of those days when a Mexican army had been defeated, and the population had been given orders to boycott the surviving soldiers. This was normally a time in Mexico when there was a flower festival, with banquets and feasts, while girls, garlanded with flowers, would wait on a sacrificial victim supposed to stand for Huixtocihuatl, the salt goddess, who herself was usually included among the little Tlalocs, the attendants on Tlaloc. Presumably by this time the ceremony must have been over; if not, it must have been annulled.

The increase in size of the Castilian army meant that Cortés' men needed additional lodgings. They were offered these by Montezuma in the nearby temple of Tezcatlipoca. The rest remained, as before, in the Palace of Axayácatl.[11]

Alvarado and his men were naturally delighted to see Cortés. They had nearly starved. They were in no condition to resist a new attack. The market was closed. They had been short of water but recently had dug a well in the courtyard which gave them a modest supply. Alvarado gave an explanation to the *Caudillo* of what had happened. The cause of the trouble, he said, was that Cortés had put the portrait of the Virgin Mary and a cross in the temple of Huitzilopochtli. Some Indians had tried but failed to move these symbols of Christianity. Alvarado had discovered from several Tlaxacalans that, after the festival, Mexicans were in consequence planning to attack him. He had decided to forestall that attack.[12] Cortés said: "But they tell me that they asked your permission to hold the ceremony and the dances?" Alvarado said that that was so, and that he had then fallen on the Mexican leaders so that they would not attack him later. Cortés replied that that was very badly done and that it had been a great madness.[13]

Alvarado suggested to Cortés that he pretend to be angry with him, even threaten to arrest and punish him, thinking that Montezuma and the Mexicans might thereby be placated; might even plead for him.[14] But Cortés did not want to do this. He was never able to give Alvarado a reprimand. For some time he seems to have been in real doubt as to who had been responsible for the massacre.[15] He later always attributed the events to Narváez and his intrigues with Montezuma.[16] As to Alvarado, Cortés still valued his qualities; among which, loyalty to himself was not the least important. But Alvarado never again occupied the same place of pre-eminence as, more or less, second-in-command, *"segunda persona"*.

That position was now generally filled by the more reliable, industrious and less flamboyant Sandoval.

Montezuma also greeted Cortés on his return. He must have thought that, with all his faults, the *Caudillo* could be trusted not to be rash as Alvarado had been. But Cortés refused to speak to him.[17] Montezuma returned to his quarters in despair. His pride was damaged. He again became frightened, just as he had been before the first arrival of the Castilians, and sent a message once more begging Cortés to leave the city. Cortés said that he would not speak to "that dog of a Montezuma unless he gave him 20,000 castellanos".[18]

Montezuma continued to ask Cortés to go and see him. The *Caudillo* continued to decline the invitation. Several of Cortés' captains (Veláz-quez de León, Lugo, Olid, Ávila) asked him to soften his anger. Cortés was reluctant: "Why," he asked, "should I be moderate to a dog who had secret relations with Narváez and does not even give us anything to eat?" Had not Montezuma even sent a gold medallion to Narváez when pretending to be on good terms with Cortés? So the *Caudillo* even refused to acknowledge a son of Montezuma, though that prince came to see him with an affecting plea.[19]

The real reason for Cortés' anger was, of course, that his master plan, to win Tenochtitlan without fighting, and to hand over the Mexican empire to the Emperor Charles V as a working enterprise, had plainly now failed. He had to devise not just a new strategy, but a new plan of campaign. The most important innovations which Cortés had insisted upon during his previous stay in Tenochtitlan admittedly had remained: thus St Christopher's picture was still in the Great Temple: it was even seen there on 24 June by Juan González de León.[20] Cortés might have with him most of Narváez's men and horses, as well as his own old force.[21] All the same, the world for Cortés was quite different at the end of June from what it had been in early May.

It was also different for Montezuma. His loss of self-esteem because of Cortés' neglect was considerable. Montezuma, it has already been suggested, had the kind of affection for Cortés which victims of kidnappings often develop for their captors. The wound afforded by Cortés was thus doubly difficult to bear. Having handed over his will to Cortés in the winter, he could scarcely now live without attention from him. Montezuma's standing among his own people had of course fallen absolutely as a result of the massacre in the temple precinct. The result was that there was a vacuum of power among the Mexica. Most of the alternative leaders of the people had been killed. No one could take the initiative to find a new ruler. The tradition, in a rule-bound society, did not exist for improvisation. "What, do you think the empire is a dovecote that students can flutter about where and when they want?" a civil servant once expostulated to a young writer in Vienna in the nineteenth century. How much more difficult was it to envisage a new emperor being found in Mexico when the old one was still alive!

In the event the Mexican cause was inadvertently helped by Cortés. He was angry that the market in Tlatelolco had been closed. Perhaps the reason was mourning. But not only was it inconvenient not to have the resources of that emporium at his army's disposal; Cortés' own standing among Narváez's people sank, when it became clear that he could not show them the riches of that famous square, which he had extolled as bigger than that at Salamanca or Medina del Campo, and "richer than Granada". He had also told the new recruits that they could sleep peacefully. But the day after he had said that, he had to admit that most bridges over the canals were being raised.[22] The silence with which he had been received also seemed a personal defeat for him.

Cortés demanded through Marina that Montezuma order the market to be opened. Montezuma said that he could do nothing. The best thing would be to allow one of those lords who were still with him to go and do that. Cortés said that, for this purpose, Montezuma should choose whomsoever he wanted. Montezuma selected his brother Cuitláhuac, the lord of Iztapalapa. That prince had always from the beginning opposed letting the Spaniards into Tenochtitlan. Cortés perhaps did not know that, or did not care. At all events, Cuitláhuac was allowed to leave his captivity in the Palace of Axayácatl.

As soon as this prince was free, he began urgently to organise the Mexican resistance. Whether he was formally elected emperor of the Mexicans at this time is obscure. It is also unclear whether Montezuma realised the implications of what he was doing. But thenceforward the Mexica possessed a warlord.[23]

The very day that Cuitláhuac was freed, 25 June, a Castilian soldier came back from Tacuba, whence he had been ordered to escort a number of Indian girls, including a daughter of Montezuma, who were said to belong to Cortés ("*eran de Cortés*") and who had, for some reason unknown, been left in Tacuba when Cortés had gone off to face Narváez.[24] The Mexicans fell on this little expedition, seized the girls, and wounded the Castilian: had he not abandoned the girls, he would probably have been captured and sacrificed. Alonso de Ojeda and Juan Márquez were said also to have been attacked when they went out to buy provisions.[25] The same day Cortés sent a messenger, Antón del Río, the sailor who had accompanied Velázquez de León into Narváez's camp, to go to tell the people at Vera Cruz that the Spaniards under Alvarado and he himself were safe. Del Río expected to be able to reach Vera Cruz on foot in three days. But after half an hour, he returned. He had not got through. He had been attacked, beaten and wounded. All the Mexicans in the city, he said, were preparing for war. Cortés' earliest nightmare on his first visit to Tenochtitlan was being realised: he was surrounded.[26]

Cortés next sent out the stolid Diego de Ordaz with three hundred men, some arquebusiers, a few horses, and most of the crossbowmen. He was accompanied by Juan González Ponce de León, the son of the explorer of Florida. Perhaps he wanted both to examine the situation, and to calm the Mexica without fighting. More likely it was to show the flag.

Ordaz had not got far along the street leading to the causeway to Tacuba before he too was attacked by Mexicans throwing stones from the rooftops. Four or five Castilians were killed and nearly all the rest, including Ordaz himself, hurt.[27] The Mexica followed Ordaz back to the Palace of Axayácatl, hurling stones and shooting arrows. They again set fire to that building. The smoke and heat presented a serious difficulty until earth, or parts of walls and roofs, were thrown on to the flames. A breach in the wall was also made. The Mexica could have entered this had it not been for the crossbowmen and arquebusiers posted there.[28] Those who later talked to Fr. Sahagún testified to the effectiveness of the crossbowmen: "They sighted well along the iron bolts . . . which seemed to fly whirring and humming. Great was their whirring. Not purposelessly did the arrows fly . . . And the arrows too were well aimed."[29]

More than eighty of Cortés' men were wounded, including Ordaz and Cortés himself. Even after dark the Mexicans continued to shout from the roofs of nearby houses at their now unwelcome guests, who were busy mending breaches in the walls and dressing wounds.[30] Two Italians in Cortés' forces, using oil, Scotch wool and, as the wounded thought, charms, worked wonders with those who were hurt.[31]

These battles lasted several days, the only variation being that the Castilians started going out every dawn in order to try and secure the nearby houses. But this availed them little since, when they returned at night to the Palace of Axayácatl, usually with many people wounded and one or two dead, the Mexica would recover those buildings. Juan González Ponce de León led a successful sally to capture Montezuma's palace. But he afterwards withdrew. The conquistadors began to seem besieged by water. Ordinary water was, however, short since the Spaniards had nothing to drink except for what they obtained from the fetid and salty improvised well in the main patio.[32] Stones were constantly thrown into the Castilian quarters from nearby roofs so that the conquistadors had to walk along the edges of the courtyards to avoid being struck.[33] Possession of cannon no longer made much difference. True, the Castilians found that their lombards and culverins had scarcely to be aimed, for it was simple enough to fire into the middle of the Mexica. But this made no noticeable difference since, though every cannon shot probably killed ten, or even twenty, Mexicans, the gaps were immediately filled.[34] Superior technology did not count in street battles.

Soldiers who had fought in Italy against the French or the Turks said, with a trace of exaggeration, surely, that they had never known such battles; nor had they seen such bravery as was shown by the Mexica.[35] The Mexica also used psychological warfare: every night, their conjurers would arrange that Castilians looking out of the windows would see frightful things: sometimes a head would be seen walking round attached only to a foot; human heads would be seen jumping; sometimes decapitated corpses would roll round groaning. A soldier temporarily imprisoned in the improvised church in the Palace of Axayácatl told his guards that he had seen dead men jumping about and his own body on the altar.[36] These visions no doubt articulated the alarming Mexican ghost, Night Axe, a headless body which would traditionally reel about a haunted room, its open chest suddenly snapping closed with a fearful noise.[37] Night Axe had a distressing effect, particuarly on Narváez's men: they hurled maledictions. How happy they had been in Cuba before they had been so foolish as, first, to follow Narváez, and then Cortés![38]

The Mexica were themselves fighting a different kind of war from what they were accustomed to. For street fighting, at least on the scale made necessary by the war in their own city, was unknown to them. Further, they had not had the time, perhaps had not had the inclination, to prepare the elaborate offensive methods in which in the past they had set such store. In these new battles, the soldiers, if they had shields, did not delay till their wives had completed a hanging border of feathers; they did not adorn themselves with golden necklaces, nor did they place special faith in tunics of "princely feathers", or white heron feathers. They did not disdain such things and, from time to time, the leaders did so adorn themselves, to encourage their men. But in general all just fought as best they could, without many orders, but with instinctive discipline, with general guidance from Cuitláhuac and the few other leaders who had survived Alvarado's massacre.

On 26 June Cortés had the idea of building an early version of a tank: a square wooden war machine, a *mantelete*, or mantle, which would shelter twenty or twenty-five men, including arquebusiers and cross-bowmen, and some carrying pikes, axes, and iron bars. This mechanism had often been used in siege warfare in the past in Europe. The plan was that these machines would be borne by bearers on their shoulders, as if they were floats carrying the Christ and the Virgin during a procession at Holy Week, into the middle of the Mexican crowd of warriors. Shooting could then begin through apertures and loopholes. This would allow hidden sappers to destroy houses and walls.[39] Three or four were begun during the night of 26–27 June.[40] The aim was less to secure a Spanish escape from the city than to ensure a safe zone around the Palace of Axayácatl.

Before these machines were put to the test, a most difficult moment occurred. Cortés saw about twelve Mexicans well dressed with plumes and devices, decorated with gold and silver, and carrying shields plated with gold. These men seemed to be directing their compatriots. One of them was being treated by the others with reverence. Cortés assumed that that one was Cuitláhuac. He requested Marina to ask Montezuma who these men were. Montezuma was vague. He said that he thought that they seemed to be his relations, among them the lords of Texcoco and Iztapalapa. That last lord was of course Cuitláhuac. But the Emperor said that he did not believe that, while he was alive, the Mexica could elect a successor to himself.[41] Cortés then asked Montezuma, with Aguilar and Marina, to go again to the roof of the palace to talk to those in the Mexican crowd whom he had recognised.[42] Montezuma at first refused. He had been humiliated by Cortes' neglect and said: "What more does Malinche want of me? I neither wish to live, nor to listen to him, for to such a pass have I come because of him." Cristóbal de Olid and Fr. Bartolomé de Olmedo then spoke to Montezuma in the old affectionate terms, and convinced him that it was right to try and address his people. He agreed, though pointing out that the request had come very late in the day.[43]

As so often in trying to recall the events of those days, opinions differ as to what happened next. It seems, though, that Montezuma was taken to the roof by the "*comendador*" Leonel de Cervantes, and Francisco Aguilar (the future Augustinian monk and writer).[44] The two Castilians, perhaps with others, sought to guard the Emperor from the onslaught of stones by holding shields over him. Montezuma then either planned to make, or made, some kind of appeal to the Mexica (Cortés in his letter to the King about these events says that Montezuma was hit by a stone before he began to speak).[45] According to some observers, there was a moment of silence among the Mexica at the sight of Montezuma, as he called down to his friends and cousins. He probably tried to say again that he had come to live with the conquistadors on his own initiative, and that he could return to his own palace when he wished. There was, therefore, no reason for war. The Castilians had even promised to leave the city.[46]

Some sources say that the Mexican captains made a spirited and determined reply. The Codex Ramírez, for example, said that one of the young cousins of Montezuma, Cuauhtémoc, apparently in command of Tlatelolco, demanded, "What is that which is being said by that scoundrel of a Montezuma, whore of the Spaniards? Does he think that he can call to us, with his woman-like soul, to fight for the empire which he has abandoned out of fright . . . We do not want to obey him because already he is no longer our monarch and, indeed, we must give him the punishment which we give to a wicked man."[47] (The Mexica were educated to equate womanliness with cowardice, just as the Spaniards were.[48] They made the same mistake in respect of homosexuality. Still, this very Spanish-sounding speech may reflect the reality of what was said.) Bernal Díaz, who was present, reported, however, that, after the usual courtesies, the Mexican captains said that they had indeed elected Cuitláhuac as their new lord; that the war had to be carried on; and that they had sworn not to stop fighting till all the Castilian intruders were dead.

At all events, Montezuma's speech or attempt at it was followed by a shower of stones discharged at the roof on which he was standing. The guards could not protect him. It seemed "as if the sky was raining stones, arrows, darts and sticks". The Emperor was hit three times – on the chest, says Fr. Aguilar – and hastily taken below.[49]

The Castilians tried to treat the wounds of Montezuma. But he seems either to have refused to be treated, or to have had no wish to live longer.

The fighting meantime continued. There may have been another exchange between Cortés and the Mexica, presumably through Marina (who, it seems, now knew enough Castilian to be able often to interpret on her own, without the help of Aguilar). Cortés proposed peace, but in arrogant terms. The Mexica must know, he said, that the reason why he had not destroyed the city already because of its rebelliousness and obstinacy was on the petition of Montezuma. Since they no longer had Montezuma to respect, they should lay down their arms and become his own friends. They replied with dignity that they would never lay down their arms until they were free and avenged. But if Cortés remained in the city, they preferred war with him to peace. They insisted that they would kill him if he did not leave.[50]

This defiance stimulated Cortés to further adventures. First, on 28 June at dawn, he led his three war machines out of the Palace of Axayácatl and made for one of the bridges. Behind the new weapons marched many crossbowmen and arquebusiers. There were also four cannon, hauled by Tlaxcalans. But though the cortège reached the bridge for which they were aiming, the defenders were so many, and the stones thrown from the rooftops so large, that the engines were put out of action, and the Spanish were unable to advance a step from there. So they retreated after fighting all the morning, dragging back their new weapons.[51] That night Cortés also went out of his fortress and, catching the Mexicans unawares (for they did not as a rule fight at night), set fire to many of the houses from which stones had been so successfully thrown at his army.

Next day, Cortés turned his attention to the temple of Yopico next to his quarters. This was being used as a fortress, and its height had been of value as a lookout post, as well as a convenient place from which to fling stones on the Castilians.[52] This temple was a temple for the cult of the earth, with at the bottom a sunken hole within the inner chamber. That was a receptacle for the dried skins of sacrificial victims left as symbolic seed husks after the spring festivals, in particular the feast of Xipe Totec who, patron of the goldsmiths, with a golden shield and cloak, was especially associated with this temple. Probably here was the famous stone of the sun, which remains the best-known symbol of Mexican culture.

The Castilians set out for this monument, with their siege engines now repaired. Cortés implies that he had only a handful of men with him but he probably had at least forty, led by Pedro de Villalobos.[53] There were numerous short engagements with Mexica throwing stones from the top storeys of nearby houses. The Castilians nevertheless reached the foot of the pyramid, by which time the engines had been virtually destroyed, though they had enabled the conquistadors to get as far as they did. Cortés had the temple surrounded and then stormed. There followed a prolonged battle on the steps. The crossbowmen, the arquebusiers, and then the infantrymen with swords gradually mounted.[54] A great many Mexica were there, some with long pikes, with points as sharp, thought Cortés, as those of the Castilian lances. He and his men, at some cost, in men killed and wounded, made their way upwards. There were several setbacks.[55] Cortés, from his own account at least, fought ceaselessly, even though a wound the previous day had prevented him using his left hand. It seems also that he narrowly escaped being thrown from the top of the pyramid by two Mexicans.[56]

"What a fight it was," recalled Bernal Díaz, "it was certainly something to see our men all running with blood and covered with wounds."[57] It was all hand-to-hand fighting, much of it on the vertiginous steps. At the top the conquistadors set about the idols in their usual fashion, pushing them violently down the steps, burning those which they could not move, and thrusting priests after them: "like black ants they tumbled down", recalled one of Sahagún's informants.[58] They took two high priests, however, as prisoners. The Castilians themselves seem, for the first time, to have lost about twenty dead in this risky outing. "It was not the day to be in bed", commented González Ponce de León, who had thrown numerous priests off the summit.[59]

There seems then to have been one more discussion about the possibility of peace between Cortés and the Mexica. Cortés spoke from the top of the tower. He spoke in as elevated a way as usual: he wanted peace because it distressed him to see the damage being done to the city. But the Mexica, with their new leaders, were no longer disposed to accept that kind of rhetoric, even if they could understand what Cortés said. As soon as the Castilians had left their land, one spokesman is supposed to have said, they would stop the war. Otherwise, they would fight to the death. They tried to persuade Cortés to abandon the Palace of Axayácatl and make for Tacuba. But he thought, rightly no doubt, that that idea was a plot to enable them to be cut off on the causeway, and then be killed at the Mexica's leisure. The Mexica are also said to have pointed out that, even if 25,000 Mexicans died for every Castilian killed, the latter would be destroyed in the end.[60]

So the fighting continued, and the Castilians that night set about burning the houses leading towards the only causeway which they had seen, from the top of the temple, was still open, namely that to Tacuba, to the west. Even there, some of the bridges on the way had been destroyed. But Cortés ordered some of his Tlaxcalan allies to fill them in with debris from burned houses and walls.

Montezuma, meantime, seems to have died the next morning, 30 June. According to the Castilians, his death was due to the wounds caused by the stones thrown.[61] He asked Cortés to look after his three daughters: particularly his eldest daughter whom he looked on as his heir – though that was not a usual thing for a Mexican emperor, who was customarily succeeded by a brother or a cousin not a child, and very definitely not by a woman.[62] He can only have been referring to his private possessions. Montezuma, mesmerised by Cortés to the end (perhaps particularly at the end, when he had no one else to turn to), was later said by the *Caudillo* not only to have asked for his daughters to be baptised but to have said that if, by good fortune, he should live, and if God were to give him victory over those who had surrounded the palace, he would show more publicly (*largamente*) the desire he had to serve His Majesty the King of Spain.[63] By that time, Cortés seems to have forgiven Montezuma for his dalliance with Narváez: he continued to argue that Narváez had been entirely responsible for making it possible for Cuitláhuac to launch "a very brutal war against Montezuma and myself"; and to believe that Montezuma was not himself in any way implicated in the fighting by the Mexica.[64]

A later story insisted that Montezuma had asked for Christian baptism before he died, and that indeed he received it.[65] This cannot be true. Had it been the case, it is inconceivable that Cortés and others would not have spoken triumphantly of it. It is more likely that, though offered the last sacraments, Montezuma preferred to spend the last half-hour of his life with his own gods.

There is a contrasting but even stronger rumour, namely that Montezuma was murdered by the conquistadors.[66] Though anything is possible, and though neither mercy nor gratitude played a part in the conquistadors' outlook, this too is improbable.

On the other hand, Cortés seems to have followed Montezuma's death by having all those lords who were left with him killed there and then: at their head, Itzquauhtzin, the Tenochtitlan-appointed governor of Tlatelolco. These lords could have numbered about twenty or thirty.[67] One who seems to have died now was the *tlacatectal*, Atlixcatzin, a son of the late Emperor Ahuítzotl, who may have been the most likely candidate to succeed Montezuma. Their deaths freed the Castilians from the trouble of having to guard them. There were more men available for combat. Aguilar gave a vivid picture of the scene: "Some of the Indians who had not been killed carried out the bodies. After night fell, about ten o'clock, such a large number of women came carrying burning torches and braziers and fires as to cause terror. They came to look for their husbands and relations who were dead in the porticos . . . and, as the women recognised their relations and kinsmen (a thing which we who were watching on the roof saw with clarity), they threw themelves on them with grief and sadness, and began a weeping and a lament so great that it threw us into fear and terror; and he who writes this said to his companion [probably Leonel de Cervantes], 'Have you seen the hell and the lament down there? For if you haven't seen it, you can do so from here.' And never in the whole war . . . did I have such fear as that which I received when I heard that terrible lament."[68]

Cortés sent to tell the high priest, the *cihuacoatl*, that Montezuma had died, to say how grieved the Castilians were at this, and how they hoped that the Emperor would be buried as the great king that he had been, while his heirs were busy negotiating a peace.[69] The Castilians apparently pushed the body of Montezuma out of the gate, to be delivered to the Mexica.

If the *Caudillo* spoke of "burial", he would have been showing his ignorance, since cremation was the usual way in Tenochtitlan of disposing of the bodies of emperors, nobles, great warriors and indeed most people. Cremation was a sign that the spirit of the dead man or woman would rise to live in heaven with the sun. Burial was the lot only of a restricted category: women who died in childbirth, those who were drowned, and those who died of gout, leprosy and dropsy: that is, those who were taken away by the gods of rain or of water.

The funeral of an emperor in Mexico was as a rule a great occasion. For days women would cry strangely by slapping their hands over their mouths. The dead man would be dressed in his finest clothes. A piece of jade would be placed in his mouth, to symbolise a heart which would last for ever. The body would lie in state, and as many as twenty other bodies would also be prepared. The late Emperor's private priest, his jesters, dwarfs, hunchbacks and other servants would be sacrificed to serve the dead man in the next world, and they would probably be joined by some of his favourite concubines who might voluntarily give themselves up to accompany the Emperor on his dark journey. Perhaps a hundred prisoners would also be sacrificed. Rulers of nearby cities would be invited to the cremation, including those from enemy places such as Tlaxcala. In the main square, a priest dressed as the spirit of the underworld officiating, the corpse of the Emperor would be placed on a "divine hearth".

After eighty days' mourning (the same time as for an ordinary

Mexican), during which there would be several sacrifices, an effigy of the Emperor, with some genuine remains (his hair, for example) would be burned, in a ceremony which repeated the first one, though on a smaller scale.[70]

In the case of Montezuma, the traditional ceremonies seem to have been suspended, because of the unprecedented circumstances of his death, and also because of the discredit into which he had fallen at the end. All we hear is that "they took Montezuma's body in their arms and carried him to Copulco and laid him on a pyre and set fire to it. Flames roared up. Montezuma's body lay sizzling and it smelled foul as it burned." Some of course recalled Montezuma's old reputation before the Castilians had arrived, as butcher, inflexible high priest, determined reformer, successful general and disciplinarian: "This evildoer", he terrified the world. "In all the world, there was dread of him. When anyone offended him" a little, he slew him. Many he punished only for an imaginary evil.[71] The governor of Tlatelolco, Itzquauhtzin, on the other hand, seems to have been cremated honourably in the temple courtyard there.[72]

Montezuma was a tragic figure. An inflexible man in early life, who even made a virtue out of inflexibility, he lost power by an unprecedented and unforeseeable act, his kidnapping in November 1519. That converted him into a passive instrument. As happens often in such circumstances, he seems to have become enamoured of his captors, above all Cortés. This affection caused him to seem a coward. It was impossible to see, in the terrified, sometimes giggling, emperor in the Palace of Axayácatl, the powerful autocrat of ten years before. But many such transitions occur in characters, often positively, with age. Whether the myth of Quetzalcoatl, or Tezcatlipoca, or any other deity, did or did not exercise a decisive influence over Montezuma's judgements we may never know. But he was exceptionally superstitious, even for a Mexican. He certainly seems, at the very least for a time, to have toyed with the idea of identifying Cortés with a lost lord who vanished into the east. But this identification did not necessarily implicate Quetzalcoatl. Perhaps he at least subconsciously used the supposition that he was facing the reincarnation of Quetzalcoatl as a justification for his indecision. Probably he did make some kind of concession, as an act of temporary appeasement, to Cortés' demand to him and his lords to accept the supreme authority of Charles V. No doubt he also believed that what was given away under duress could be gone back upon when the occasion demanded. In March 1520, at the time when he requested Cortés to leave the country, some of his courage had returned, perhaps because of the nature of the new year, 2-Flint. In the end, after Alvarado's massacre, he could see that no further negotiation was possible for him. Rejected by his own people, he had to resign himself to being no more than a puppet of the invaders.

28
Fortune spins her wheel

"Fortune spins her wheel and, to great happiness, much sadness succeeds"
Bernal Díaz on the *"noche triste"*, 1520

THERE WAS BY now a growing feeling among the Castilians that it was essential to leave Tenochtitlan, come what may. They had little food, little gunpowder for the cannon, and the walls of the Palace of Axayacatl were riddled with holes. Out of those many Tlaxcalans who had come back with Cortés on June 24, fewer than a hundred remained.[1] The water which they had to drink continued fetid. The astrologer Botello told Alonso de Ávila that the spirits with whom he was magically in touch had informed him that, unless they left that night, they would all be killed.[2] These views were made known to Cortés by Ávila. Pedro and Gonzalo de Alvarado, Rodrigo Álvarez Chico, and Diego de Ordaz also told Cortés that they supported the idea of leaving. Cortés at first said that he would "sooner be cut to pieces than leave the city".[3] In withdrawing from Tenochtitlan, he would, he knew, be bound "to lose a great deal of the gold and jewellery which had been given to him".[4] The *Caudillo* joked to Tapia that, if they were short of cannon balls, they should make some out of the gold and silver which they had in such quantity.[5] For the idea of withdrawal was intolerable to Cortés. Had he not promised to give the city to the King? And to God, come to that? But eventually, with reluctance, he agreed that there was no alternative.[6] The combination against his judgement was for the first time composed of audacious men, rather than, as in previous arguments, timid friends of Governor Velázquez. Botello too had been in Rome. He was an astrologer to be respected.

Cortés decided to leave that very night, and by that causeway to the west, to Tacuba, over which the Castilians had already fought and come to know. Several captains had represented that it was best to go at night because the Mexicans did not like to fight in the dark.[7] Others thought that, by muffling the horses' hooves, they would escape undetected.

Others still thought that the plan should be to build movable wooden bridges which could be placed over the breaches, one by one, and thereby secure a sure passage to the mainland.

The plan was made to leave the Palace of Axayácatl at midnight. In the vanguard there would be Sandoval, Ordaz, Francisco Acevedo, Antonio de Quiñones (a man from Zamora whom Cortés had come greatly to trust in recent weeks), Tapia, and Lugo, with about two hundred men whom Cortés called "valiant and young". They were no doubt mostly Cortés' own men, rather than those of Narváez, though the distinction was becoming blurred. With them would go a small gathering of appropriate companions, Marina and Luisa, Cortés' mistress and Alvarado's, as well as the priests Fr. Olmedo and Fr. Díaz.[8] Cortés would follow with the bulk of the army, Alonso de Ávila and Olid being in positions of tactical command. There then would follow the surviving Tlaxcalans, with those prisoners who had not already been killed, among them Chimalpopoca, son of Montezuma, and two daughters of that monarch, "Doña Aña" and "Doña Leonor".[9] Finally, there would be Velázquez de León and Pedro de Alvarado, in command of the rear, with sixty horsemen. Just behind Cortés, there would be Alonso de Escobar and Cristóbal de Guzmán, Cortés' majordomo, in charge of the gold.[10] Cortés at first thought of riding with the rearguard. But Alvarado dissuaded him. He said: "It is better that you go with the vanguard, because there will be more resistance there and, seeing you there, everyone will fight better."[11]

The question as to what to do about the treasure occupied the conquistadors' last hours in the Palace of Axayácatl. Cortés himself, in a letter reporting these events to the King, said that the King's gold was placed on a mare to be escorted by trustworthy servants. He otherwise allowed everyone to help themselves to what remained of the rest of the gold: which they did by filling the bags which they had with them.[12] Most of this gold had been melted down and was in the form of bars.[13] One soldier, Gonzalo Ruiz, for example, said later that he took three bars of gold, worth about 600 pesos, and that 50,000 pesos' worth was distributed in this way.[14] The Castilians gave all the quetzal feathers which they had been given or accumulated since they had reached Tenochtitlan to the Tlaxcalans.[15]

Many people observed something of these arrangements: thus Alonso de Villanueva saw, in a room of the palace, a great pile of gold which he later heard was loaded on to a mare.[16] Martín Vázquez saw the gold being actually loaded on to the mare.[17] Tapia saw eight straw boxes and another eight or ten wooden boxes being loaded on to the mare.[18] Andrés de Duero saw a mare standing loaded with boxes which "they said were full of gold . . . belonging to their Highnesses [the King and Queen Juana]".[19] It was also later argued that much time was spent in saddling the mare and loading her.[20] Then Andrés de Monjaraz said that he saw Velázquez de León with a mare weighed down with gold, which Alonso Pérez told him belonged to the King.[21] Fr. Juan Díaz saw Alonso de Escobar taking charge of the gold "in the absence of the treasurer".[22] Others said that a servant of Cortés' own, Terrazas, was made responsible for the royal treasure.[23] Rodrigo de Castañeda said that he saw Cortés taking great care of his own treasure, summoning the notary Pero Hernández to testify that 300,000 pesos' worth was carried away in bundles by Tlaxcalans, under the command of a chief named Calmecahua.[24] A question in a later enquiry directed against Cortés suggested that the *Caudillo* had made off with 45,000 pesos belonging to the King.[25] Diego de Ávila, a witness always hostile to Cortés, said that he heard Cortés telling Pero Hernández to leave behind the King's gold and only take his, Cortés'; and Hernández then saddled three horses with this treasure.[26] This gold was in flat bars of a little under a foot long by two inches broad, and half an inch thick: the right size to fit under Spanish armour.[27]

Cortés later himself explained that he ordered the "four or five trustworthy Spaniards" with whom he had left all the gold to devote their attention to saving the treasure of the monarch and not to worry about his own share.[28] Though this is to run ahead of the narrative, Benavides, the smelter of the expedition, said, two months later, that the Castilians originally took 132,400 pesos.[29] Cortés later said that he saved 75,000 pesos of his own.[30] All these statements may be misleading: more, probably, was lost than anyone recounted.[31]

According to Juan Jaramillo, an Extremeño conquistador, Cortés found yet another mistress the night before they left: a certain "Doña Francisca", a sister of Cacama.[32] But he also prayed to the Virgin of Los Remedios: a combination of actions which might suggest a tranquil soul.

The conquistadors' retreat began quietly at midnight on 1 July 1520, in a mist or light rain, no one speaking.[33] One captain, Francisco Rodríguez Magariño, and sixty assistants, carried a portable wooden bridge made of beams and planks in which all placed as much faith as if it were a secret weapon.[34] It was laid across the first of the gaps in the causeway, that on the edge of the city, which was called Tepantzinco. Sandoval had the responsibility for organising the carriage of more wood to be placed across other gaps in the causeways. All these beams were obtained from ceilings in the Palace of Axayácatl.[35]

Most of the expedition had crossed the first four bridges, all those within the confines of the city, and were about to begin to cross the lake proper when a woman going to get water saw them.[36]

This woman called out, "Mexica, come quickly, our enemies are leaving. Now that it is night, they are running away! As fugitives!" In reply, a few minutes later, a man, presumably a priest, shouted out from the top of the temple of Huitzilopochtli, "Mexican chiefs, your enemies are leaving, run to your canoes of war."

No Mexican seems to have thought that the conquistadors would leave by night. But now the drum of war on top of the great pyramid was sounded. The male population of Tenochtitlan, roused from sleep, ran to take their canoes to the main waterway: "The canoes of war sped like arrows, the paddlers paddling fast and placing themselves in order." They fired so many arrows that it was as if "a lobster had reached its breeding ground".[37] The Mexica were, it seems, organised against the Castilians by Tlaltececatzin, a prince of the Tepanecs.[38] In the confusion of a night attack, and perhaps in their anger, they seem to have ignored their ancient tactic of seeking to capture, not to kill. All the sources indicate that, though some were captured, many Castilians were killed in the fighting – usually by being hit on the back of the head, the same way that criminals were killed.[39]

Despite these attacks, the vanguard of the Castilian column, as well as Cortés and his companions in the second section of the retreat, managed to reach the mainland at a village called Popotla, just short of Tacuba. All had to swim across the last two channels which had been opened up in the causeway since their last reconnaissance. Leaving a few fortunate soldiers there, with Marina, "María Luisa", Olmedo and Fr. Díaz, under the command of Juan Jaramillo, Cortés returned to the flawed causeway with five horsemen (Olid, Sandoval, Ávila, Morla and Gonzalo Domínguez), to assist those immediately behind him.[40] This was, however, easier planned than done, since the entire causeway was then under attack on both sides from innumerable canoes. All the bridges were up, the beams thrown across by the Castilians broken, half the Castilian army was floundering in water, the chaos was unspeakable, and many men had either been killed or were drowning. The cannon, many of the horses, and much of the gold was lost. Alonso de Escobar, the mare with the royal gold, and the treasures of the Mexican empire "did not appear again".[41] Pedro Gutiérrez de Valdelomar said that he found himself for a moment behind that horse on the causeway but then lost sight of it.[42] Its memory would haunt the Spaniards for years to come.

The main disaster occurred at the Toltec canal, "the bridge of the massacre", as it was described by Francisco de Flores. This was the second cut in the causeway after leaving the city (approximately on the modern site of St Hippolytus' church). The bodies of the dead seemed for a time to fill the breach: "All fell in there". The Tlaxcalans, the Spaniards, their "horses, some women, dropped there. The canal was completely filled with them . . . And those who came . . . last . . . crossed over only on men, only on bodies."[43] Of course in these circumstances horses, like cannon, were useless.

The only thing that does seem certain about this black night for the Castilians is that those who set off with gold weighing them down were more likely to be killed than those who had no more than their cotton armour.[44]

Cortés, and most of his captains, seem to have fought endlessly, bravely but ineffectively.[45] At one moment, the *Caudillo* himself fell into the water and was surrounded by a group of Mexica who (being usually good swimmers – no doubt better than the conquistadors) would have carried him off, for triumphant sacrifice of course, had it not been for the timely assistance of Cristóbal de Olea and Antonio de Quiñones.[46] The one Spanish woman among the combatants, María de Estrada, was also said to have astonished everyone with her remarkable and successful swordplay but, this time, the Mexica did not think that she was the Mother of God.[47] Otherwise, Fr. Juan Díaz was no doubt right when he sourly recalled, some years later, that "no one at the moment was interested in anything except saving his own skin".[48] Some, however, such as Ruy González, a conquistador who had come with Narváez, later insisted that they had done much to help others, and cited that in their claim for a coat of arms.[49]

In the darkness, noise and confusion, Velázquez de León and Alvarado lost control of the rearguard. The latter even later admitted that the confusion was such that "he could no longer captain his men".[50] His horse was killed; but, he said, he fought on till he was alone. He was accused later of vaulting over a third breach in the causeway, the cut of Petlacalco. Far from being considered at the time an act of heroism, the action figured in the enquiry against him as a jump away from his responsibilities, thus deserting his men as well as escaping the enemy. But this "leap of Alvarado" never occurred.[51] That conquistador walked over the breach, he himself said, on a beam, and then managed, with difficulty, to jump on the back of the horse of Cristóbal Martín de Gamboa, master of the horse to Cortés.[52] Cortés of course welcomed him when he saw him, but asked, "Where are the people with whom I left you?" Alvarado replied: "Señor, all of them are here and if some are not, forget them."[53] That was a most misleading report.

Alvarado was more fortunate than his fellow commander of the rearguard, Velázquez de León, another of those not seen again (Juan Jaramillo said that he had remained with the King's gold).[54] Nor was any more heard of Francisco de Saucedo, *el pulido*, Botello the soothsayer, Lares the great horseman ("Lares *el jinete*"), or Cortés' servant Terrazas. Montezuma's son, Chimalpopoca, who had been held a prisoner by Cortés, was killed, as was his sister, "Doña Ana".[55] Some of the Mexican lords who had become part of Cortés' entourage also died at the hands of their compatriots: for example, Xiuhtototzin, governor of Teotihuacan, who had taken the side of the pretender Ixtlilxochitl in the war for the throne of Texcoco.[56] Two other sons of the late King Nezahualpilli were also said to have been killed, and probably several of his daughters, one of whom, "Doña Juana", had been apparently the mistress of one of Cortés' fellow countrymen from Medellín, Juan Rodríguez de Villafuerte.[57]

Some of those in the rearguard did manage to reach land: for example, Francisco de Flores.[58] But several realised that they could not make their way along the causeway, and decided to turn back to their old quarters. Those who got there are supposed to have held out for a day or two, to have been captured, to have suffered terribly from hunger, and then to have been sacrificed.[59] It was also said that as many as 270 Castilians had in the confusion not even been told of the decision to leave Tenochtitlan and remained in their quarters, to be eventually also captured and sacrificed.[60] Alonso de Ojeda, who had been allocated the task of rousing them, may have forgotten to call some of the ex-followers of Narváez in the temple of Tezcatlipoca.[61]

The numbers of Castilians killed must have been somewhere between the figure of 400, the Mexican estimate (including, they said 200 horsemen, an impossible figure since there were only 100 horses when they started out),[62] and the 1,170 spoken of by Juan Cano, one of those present.[63] Martín Vázquez was probably right when he testified in 1525 that 600 Spaniards were killed or lost that night.[64] Perhaps the Tlaxcalans lost several thousand.[65]

Cortés showed himself at his best after this reverse. He never displayed for a minute any sign of weakening in his resolve eventually to recapture the Mexican capital and hence the Mexican empire. His determination had a touch of madness about it in these circumstances. But that is what a man possessed by a daemon inevitably offers. That is why men follow him. Cortés made clear that he was still determined to subdue this "rebellion" of the Mexica, as he continued, however bizarrely, to call it. He still had with him most of those on whom he had relied in the early stages of the expedition: the Alvarados, Olid, Sandoval, Tapia, Ordaz, Ávila, Grado, Rangel. Many of those who died had been men from Narváez's expedition. Neither Marina nor Gerónimo de Aguilar, the essential interpreters, were hurt. Immediately after he had reached land from the causeway for the second time, Cortés asked too if his shipbuilder, Martín López, that "very skilful and clever man" as his friends described him, who had built the brigantines, and who had been building ships at Vera Cruz just before the arrival of Narváez, had survived the night. The answer was "yes" but that he had been badly wounded. Cortés asked personally about no other single person. He said, "Well, let's go, for we lack nothing" ("*Vamos, que nada nos falta*").[66] That was an extraordinary statement not merely of the *Caudillo*'s will to survive, but of his determination to return and conquer. In a campaign of this nature, such sang-froid counts for everything.

The *Caudillo*, like all men of his time, knew very well the myth expressed in the story of the wheel of fortune. Peter Martyr, after talking with some who had experienced these events in Mexico, wrote to the pious Pope Adrian VI, "Fortune like a tender nurse smiles on us; her wheel turns and her caresses are turned into blows . . ."[67] "Fortune spins her wheel bringing up her cups, some full, some empty," remarked Celestina, in the dialogue of that name. The same goddess Fortune came to the mind of Bernal Díaz when, years later, he was writing of this battle. Cortés must have felt at this moment outside Tenochtitlan, surrounded by a beaten band of exhausted men, as if that blind deity had caused the wheel to be spun sharply against him. But he did not lose heart. He thus inspired others in his company to wish to survive and conquer too.

At that very moment, midsummer 1520, a magnificent tapestry depicting indeed the wheel of fortune, in a series entitled "Honours", was being woven in the workshop of Pieter van Aelst in Brussels, to commemorate the forthcoming coronation of the Emperor Charles V. The goddess Fortune, eyes suitably blindfolded, rides across the heavens on a charger, scattering roses with her right hand and throwing stones with her left. Below her is her famous wheel, propelled by a servant. Above are the attributes of empire: crown, sword, sceptre. To her right – that is, among the fortunate – there are galleons. Julius Caesar, that popular hero of the day, is depicted being rowed to the shore. He is dressed as Cortés would have been dressed; and he is praying.[68]

VI
The Spanish Recovery

29

The sweetness of death by the obsidian knife

May his heart not falter in fear. May he savour the fragrance, the sweetness
of death by the obsidian knife . . . May he desire, may he long for, the flowery
death by the obsidian knife . . . may he savour the sweetness of the darkness,
the din of the battle, the roar of the crowd . . .
Prayer for the prisoners, in the Florentine Codex

THE CASTILIANS' DEFEAT "on the bridges" at Tenochtitlan was the
biggest setback suffered up till then by the Europeans in the New
World. The Mexica, of course, did not realise that. But when they
placed the bodies of the dead conquistadors in rows, to look "like white
reed shoots, or white maguey shoots", or even "white maize ears", they
thought that they had seen the last of the intruders. As well as the
mountains of bodies, of men and of horses, they found substantial
numbers of swords, hilts of swords, crossbows, lances, and arquebuses.
There were bolts for crossbows, arrows, steel arrow heads, helmets,
corselets, bits of chain mail, breastplates and backplates, gorgets and
shields of wood, leather and iron. There were saddles and bits of horse
armour, chamfrons, drinking horns and knives for eating, daggers and
halberds, as well as one or two pieces of the new fashionable fluted
armour from Germany. There were innumerable gold bars, pieces of jade
and necklaces, all returned to their old owners from the mud of the lake.
In the mud, too, there must also have been documents: Velázquez's
instructions to Cortés, documents establishing the municipality of Villa
Rica de la Vera Cruz, papers seized by Grado and Ordaz from Narváez.
Among the bodies of the Tlaxcalans and other Indian allies there were
innumerable feather headdresses and cloaks.[1]

The Mexica who took prisoners were presumably rewarded by being
allowed as usual to cut their hair in a special way in honour of the
achievement. Those who had captured a prisoner single-handed would at
a ceremony have their faces painted with red ochre, their temples dabbed
with yellow, and be given an orange cloak with a striped border and a
scorpion device.[2]

The Mexica arranged the temples once more, picked up the dirt, the
rubbish and, in some streets, the rubble. They began to try to settle back,

as it were, to normal life. Preparations were presumably made for "the great festival of the lords", which always came at the end of June, in Huey Tecuilhuitl, the seventh month. As in past years, the ruler, Cuitláhuac on this occasion, would be seen to be preparing to give away food from the great grain store (the *petlacalco*) to the people, for this was a time of food shortage, and some of the maize in store was usually distributed at this time. Normally this occasion was a celebration of the power of the Emperor. His generosity with maize served to indicate also his dominant role.

After a victory, there was also usually a fine dance at night at the foot of the Great Temple. Lit by braziers and torches held by young men, "captains and other brave men used to war", victors of the "battle of the bridges", danced as usual in threes, two warriors and a woman from the so-called "companions of the unmarried soldiers" – prostitutes, whose standing in society seemed on these occasions much enhanced. All wore turquoise discs in their ears, the senior warriors wearing bird-shaped labrets or waterlilies, the girls with their hair loose, and wearing embroidered skirts. No doubt Cuitláhuac himself came to take part in the sacred celebration on this occasion.[3] The Spaniards would look back on the defeat as *"la noche triste"*, the sad night. But the Mexica saw it as the night of triumph.

Some captive Castilians were no doubt proposed for sacrifice, alongside Cholulans, Tlaxcalans and men from Huextozinco[4]. The first probably included some of those who had figured among the leaders of the expedition led by Cortés: perhaps Alonso de Escobar, who had guarded the mare with the King's treasure; possibly Juan Velázquez de León, whose eyes at birth had opened to see the great castle of Albuquerque in Cuéllar and now (if indeed he were sacrificed and had not been killed) would close for ever beneath the brilliant blue sky over Tenochtitlan. After these conquistadors' "precious eagle cactus fruits", as hearts were called, had been professionally extracted from their breasts by flint knives[5] and their heads cut off, their bodies would have been thrown down the steep temple stairs, just as (as the priests believed) the god Huitzilopochtli threw down his sister Coyolxauhqui from the mountain.

It is far from clear whether the capture of the Castilians was considered a great triumph, as the capture of Tlaxcalans was; or whether they were classified with the lowly Huaxtecs of the coast. The latter seems probable. In that case, the victims might not have been offered any of the "obsidian wine" (*pulque*) or hallucinogens in order to soothe their brains before death.

Nor is there any certainty that these Castilians "died like a flower", as the Mexica spoke of those who met death gallantly. The silence among chroniclers on these things suggests that, after this battle, some of the traditional rites affecting prisoners may have been forgotten. For example, a captor in the past had looked on himself as the prisoner's father. He it was who would hand him over to the "prisoners' hall", a cellar of the royal palace, before sacrifice. There, prisoners would be treated in luxury until the hour came for the fatal ceremony. Perhaps these things, in the heat of the moment, were waived. Were these prisoners longitudinally painted with red and white streaks, as was normal for victims? Were they persuaded to carry little paper flags to identify themselves as candidates for the block? And were they dragged up the steps by their hair since they surely did not make the ascent willingly? One must assume that afterwards, as was always the case, the hearts of these men, Spanish and Indian alike, were placed in the stone "eagle bowl" (*cuauhxicalli*), and that the captor dined off one of the thighs, while the other was eaten in the palace. If there were several captors, as there may have been "on the bridges", the bodies of the captives taken were divided. The first of the captors took the right thigh. The second captor took the left. The third took the right upper arm. The fourth took the left one. The fifth took the right forearm. The sixth took the left forearm.[6] Probably the torsos were either handed over to the animals in the zoo or taken for consumption by vultures on a remote part of the lake.[7] Their heads, and the captured horses' heads too, would, of course, be displayed in the skull rack.

The Mexica would not have pitied these Castilians. They had, by dying on the sacrificial stone, become "companions of the eagle", who would normally for four years sit in attendance on the sun itself, singing war songs and enacting mock battles, before being reincarnated as humming birds. But these privileges may not have been allocated to the prisoners of the *noche triste*.

Despite this air of triumph, the damage caused to the Mexican empire by the conquistadors had been great. The unquestioning loyalty of the people to the Emperor, for example, was no more. The subject peoples on the coast had rebelled with astonishing enthusiasm. There were doubts about deliveries of tropical products from the Totonacs. The flower of the nobility, the priesthood, and the warrior class had been murdered by Alvarado. Morale had been shaken by the successes of a tiny number of conquistadors, with their devastating weapons. Two leading monarchs of the Triple Alliance which had managed the empire for years had died violently. So had Montezuma's uncle, the long-lasting military governor of Tlatelolco. Much of the city of Tenochtitlan had been burned. The beautiful gardens of the houses between the Palace of Axayácatl and the lake had been ruined. That "harmony and order", to the preservation of which the Mexica had dedicated so much, had been devastatingly disturbed.

It was true that there was now a new, apparently valiant monarch:

Cuitláhuac, brother to Montezuma. He had certainly inspired a great victory. So the eventual enthronement of this new leader on the imperial mat seems to have been traditional. Like his predecessors, Cuitláhuac would have been led, dressed only in a loincloth, up the doom-laden stairway of the main temple, escorted by two noblemen; like his predecessors, he would have seen this near-nakedness as a symbol of a return to simplicity; like his predecessors, he would on the platform have been painted black by a chief priest and then dressed in a dark "sleeveless jacket. And they had him carry on his back his tobacco gourd with green tassels". They veiled his face, they covered his head with a green cloak . . . They put on him his new "sandals with green toes and placed in his hand his incense ladle, also painted with [representations of] the skulls of the dead."[8] He would have heard the high priest's reminder that "the order of things your forebears left was not established in a single day", and he would then, to the sound of shell trumpets, have retired into the armoury for four days' fast and meditation.[9] These four days would have been interrupted by two more visits to Huitzilopochtli's shrine, where incense would have been burned, and where the Emperor would offer his own blood, drawn off with cactus spikes. He would then emerge refreshed, it was assumed, for the burdens of monarchy as well as the celebrations of a coronation, in which the King of Texcoco would insert a green emerald in his cousin's nose, dress him with bracelets and anklets of gold, and lead him to the eagle seat: a throne decorated with eagles' feathers and ocelot hides. A long procession would follow, ending at that temple of Yopico which Cortés had stormed next to the Palace of Axayácatl. That visit was to symbolise communion with the earth. There would be sacrifices of quail, and of incense, and the Emperor would again draw off his royal blood.[10]

All was not yet over. The Emperor would then return to the palace, and there would be a ceremony of speeches. The kings of Texcoco and Tacuba would begin, other leaders would also speak. The Emperor would hear of his ancestors, there would be exhortations to wisdom, courage, austerity: "And now O lord, O our lord, our lord of the nigh, of the near, causeth the sun to shine, bringeth the dawn. It is thou: he pointeth the finger at thee, he indicateth thee. Our lord hath recorded thee . . . entered thee in the books. Now verily it was declared, it was determined above us in the heavens, in the land of the dead, that our lord places thee on the reed mat, on the reed seat, on his place of honour. The spine, the maguey, of thy progenitors, of thy great-grandfathers, which they planted . . . which they placed in the earth as they departed, sprouteth, flowereth . . ."[11]

In normal times there would then have been a war. The Emperor would (in theory) bring many captives home to Tenochtitlan. They would be sacrificed at a great ceremony of confirmation, with a great dance. The dance may have occurred in 1520, though that is not certain, but there was no celebratory war. How could there be?

The whole sequence of events was usually intended to mark the monarch's identification with the city, and its monuments; for its people, the aim was to offer them ceremony to symbolise Tenochtitlan's place in the world.

The new emperor would, equally traditionally, have been able to call on a wide range of advisers. For a wise man was, the Mexica knew, "a light, a torch that does not smoke", and "a mirror pierced on both sides", being, after all, one who "knows what is above us and in the region of the dead". A Mexican wise man could not only "comfort the heart", but "give remedies, and heal everyone".[12]

The trouble was that wise men were more concerned with omens, naming the right days to take such and such an action, than making military preparations; or imagining exactly what the Castilians would do next. A definition of a wise man was one who took with him the "black and red ink, the manuscripts, the pictures". That was what wisdom was.[13]

The main question which had to be addressed by the wise men was whether the late Montezuma II had been right in suggesting, by all his remarks and actions, that the Mexica had indeed reached the fatal day, 4-Motion, when the cycle of the Fifth, the Mexican, Sun would end; and when they had to anticipate a final earthquake, after which all would die.

All the evidence is that the wise men, the priests, and the new emperor rejected such a fatalistic conclusion. The Spaniards were difficult people. But they were not gods. The Mayas had fought them, successfully, at Champoton. The Mexica had fought them "on the bridges". They could be fought again if necessary. They could die. They could be beaten.

We should imagine the Mexica celebrating the defeat of the Castilians with feasts both public and private: the latter would have resembled those feasts given by merchants. Thus, "Paths were adorned, the courtyard prepared, the ground levelled . . . reed tips were arranged . . . and draped . . . Some plucked and removed the feathers from birds, and dressed them . . . slew, singed and dressed dogs; or prepared and cooked meat," braising it in pots. "Some ground and powdered tobacco and, with a heavy straw, filled tubes with it . . . they made *tamales* using dried grains of maize; they made white ones, with beans forming a sea shell . . . some carried and drew water . . . some broke up ground" and pulverised cocoa beans. Some mixed them into chocolate . . . some cooked stews and roasted chilli.[14]

When the guests eventually arrived there would be "great congregating . . . trampling, shoving, and crowding".[15] Then "all took their respective places, the houses were entered." How familiar seems another report: "There was disorder and scattering about, there was wandering and there were disputes, ... rushing about like fools, hurrying, hastening, and unrest. [Then] came the tobacco servers ... the flower servers ... They arranged before them bowls with tobacco tubes. They sat smoking, inhaling the fragrance. All smelled it ... "then came the chocolate server [he who made it foam and froth]. He made for each one the sticks with which the chocolate was beaten, whereby the chocolate was consumed." Probably there was turkey and dog, perhaps, as at lavish merchants' feasts, served together. Then for a short time "all sat relaxed, watching, all sat content in the place of lingering, in the banqueting place ... And when it was dark," the old men and women drank wine [that is, *pulque*] ... The wine server ... served the wine, perhaps white, or watered, or honeyed ... It was carried ... in jars ... So there was singing ... songs of sadness and tears. . . And some did nothing else but sit content and rejoicing, laughing and making witty remarks, making others burst with laughter as if their sides were sore. They sat exhausted with mirth ... It was as if the dogs were barking." In the house of each nobleman there was "singing and rejoicing . . ."[16] Doubtless there were jokes about the Castilians: their absurd demands for gold, their hypocrisy, their pale goddess, their hideous horses and their smell.

But none of these parties were wise. For the enemy was still in the neighbourhood. Cuitláhuac made no immediate effort to pursue the Castilians whom he must have supposed were broken for ever.

At the first place on land where the expedition rallied, beneath what became known as "the Tree of Sorrows" in Tacuba, Cortés had made clear, in a speech to his injured army, that he was not thinking, for a moment, of regarding the defeat on the *noche triste* as being any more than a tactical setback.[17] With a great show of calm, he insisted that he still proposed eventually to deliver Tenochtitlan as a prize to the King of Spain. In the short run, the surviving Castilians would make for Tlaxcala and, as he hoped, recuperate there in the company of friends. Now that his original plan of capturing the city without a fight, but through intimidation, exercised from above, had failed, he would find an alternative, making more use of the long-resentful tributaries of the Mexica. No doubt at the moment his plan was inchoate. It needed time, ruthlessness and, of course, good luck to be able to succeed. But the goddess Fortune would surely look warmly on him again soon after his reverses. Even in those first days after the defeat on the bridges, some plan must have been developing in his mind.

On the night of the withdrawal, Cortés was, of course, downcast. He was even observed with tears in his eyes. He had with him about four hundred men and only thirty horses.[18] Nearly all were wounded. He recovered enough, however, to tell the Tlaxcalans that he was not grieving out of lack of spirit, but from emotion that Santiago himself, and a benevolent God, had saved him; and because of the loss of so many dear comrades and friends. He himself had no fear of the Mexica. So far as his own life was concerned, he valued it at nothing, since if he were to be killed there would never be a lack of Christians to subjugate the Mexica; for, in the end, the law of the evangelists would, he knew, be established in the land.[19]

With that assurance, Cortés and his company set off before dawn along the north shore of the lake, by the route that he had returned, only a week before, after his triumph over Narváez.[20]

The first night after the retreat, the Castilians rested a while in a temple at Otoncalpulco, or, as it became known later, when a church was built there, the Virgin of Los Remedios, "of the Divine Assistance" – so named, as was for a time the island of Yucatan, after the Madonna in the cathedral of Seville to whom Cortés prayed before leaving the Palace of Axayácatl.[21] The Castilians were constantly attacked, though not in a co-ordinated way. Having rested some hours, they again set off at midnight, that is in the early hours of 2 July.

The Spaniards spent the rest of the day on the way to Teocalhueycan with Tlaxcalan guides. Those still capable of fighting were in the front and rear, with the wounded in the centre, and a small guard on each side. This was a march of a mere five miles. The slow pace was rendered inevitable by the condition of the wounded, and by the constant sniping (with stones, and bows and arrows) from Mexica in the neighbourhood. The expedition halted for the night at "a tower and fortified house" in Teocalhueycan, on the top of a rounded hill, and protected by a barrier of rocks. The people of the town were Tepanecs who, conquered by the Mexicans in the 1430s, had suffered from the attentions of Montezuma. So the chief offered comfort in the usual polite Mexican way: "Our lords the gods have become weary: let them rest; may peace be with them; may they restore themselves . . ." Thus the Castilian horses received fodder; the soldiers water, maize, tortillas, turkeys, eggs, *tamales* and various squashes. This support was as psychologically heartening as it was materially beneficial.

At one moment Cortés believed himself lost. "Villafuerte," he demanded of a fellow citizen of Medellín, "which is the way?" Rodríguez de Villafuerte pointed out the correct route.[22]

The following day Cortés made for Tepotzotlan, a lakeside town about fifteen miles to the north. Though the people there were also Tepanecs, and had nothing in common with the Mexica to whom they had to pay tribute, the population had fled to the mountains on hearing that the Castilians were coming, leaving everything behind – including their reserves of food. The Castilians dined, and then slept in the palace, "all crowded and heaped together . . . quite frightened".[23]

The third stop in this calvary for the conquistadors was Citlaltepec, another lakeside town dependent on Zumpango, whose limestone

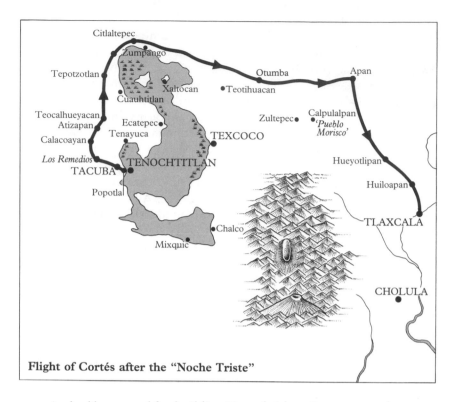

Flight of Cortés after the "Noche Triste"

quarries had been used for building Tenochtitlan. On the way, there were more sporadic attacks. Again there was a temple with a round tower in which to pass the night. Once more there were no people; and, this time, no food.[24] Then they continued to the east of the lake. On the way there were the usual sporadic attacks, in the course of which Cortés was wounded by stones which hit him on the head. At one point, the Mexica killed the horse of Cristóbal Martín de Gamboa – presumably that on which he had saved Pedro de Alvarado on the *noche triste*. There were consequently rations of meat for the first time since that defeat.[25]

So the journey went on, under Mt. Aztacuemecan, and past several menacing villages. Sometimes grass was the only food. The Castilians kept going, often travelling very few miles a day, always under attack. Several of their number died daily of wounds. They seem now to have been reduced to three hundred and forty soldiers, nearly all wounded in some way, and twenty-seven horsemen.[26] Just beyond the famous Teotihuacan (whose ruins they could not see, since they were then covered with bushes and trees), they began to climb towards the northernmost pass over the mountains towards Tlaxcala, and reached a town called Otumba. In happier days, this place had been known for the obsidian found nearby, and for a story of how its governor, accused of a crime, composed a poem on his way to be judged by the King of Texcoco,

Nezahualcoyotl: on his arrival he recited it to the King, who pardoned him forthwith.[27]

Here at last the new emperor, Cuitláhuac, having followed the Castilians in their retreat, appears to have decided to finish with Cortés and the conquistadors once and for all. So he had mounted a large force.[28] He did not commit himself to commanding this army, however, but gave over that position to his deputy, the *cihuacoatl*.

The battle was exhausting for the conquistadors. As usual, the Mexica, with their obsidian-bladed swords, fought to capture and not to kill. So there were few Castilian fatalities. But the sheer numbers of the Mexica tired the already wearied ranks of Cortés' army. They fought hand to hand for hours.[29] The small band of surrounded Castilians seemed to have no chance of breaking out: "Truly our enemies ... were innumerable," wrote one observer;[30] and "We could resist but feebly," said Cortés in his report, "since we were tired and nearly all of us wounded and fainting from hunger."[31] By about noon, after several hours' constant fighting, Cortés perceived that his men were flagging badly; "Our spirits were low," recalled Gaspar de Garnica, a Vizcayan, one of Velázquez's friends who had come to "New Spain" with Narváez.[32]

A decisive action was, therefore, necessary if the effort of the retreat were not going to seem wasted. Cortés himself provided it. He had seen for some time in the distance several Mexican captains, in glittering feathers. Contemporary accounts do not tell whether they were wearing the compressed quetzal feather insignia, the black and white feather sun insignia, or some other fine costume from the great wardrobe of Mexican military tunics.[33] But they were resplendent. Leaving Ordaz in command of the infantrymen, Cortés took five horsemen (Sandoval, Olid, Alonso de Ávila, Alvarado and Juan de Salamanca, who came from Fontiveros near Ávila) to attack this group with lances. They rode straight at, and through, the undisciplined ranks of the Mexica and overwhelmed the surprised Mexican leaders.[34] Mexican war costumes, cumbersome as well as heavy, were designed to overawe. They often came in five colours (to symbolise the four cardinal directions, and the centre). But these things had no effect on the Castilians. The *cihuacoatl* was knocked to the ground by Cortés, while Juan de Salamanca killed him with his lance, sweeping up his fine commander's plumes and standard for the benefit of Cortés who, however, tossed these trophies back to Salamanca.[35] It was the loss of the standard as much as, or even more than, the loss of the leader, which counted adversely for the Mexica.[36] This was partly due to the psychological effect, but the Mexican standard, mounted tightly on the back of the leader, on a bamboo frame, also indicated to the army where it was going. Its disappearance spelled confusion.[37]

Cortés' own mount on this adventure was said to have been an untrained carthorse.[38] The great lady of Cortés' army, María de Estrada, of Seville, once again fought in this battle with a lance in her hand, as if she were one of the most experienced soldiers in the world.[39] Bernal Díaz gave credit to the dogs: "with what fury the dogs fought", he commented, so showing that many of them had escaped the disaster of the *noche triste*.[40] The Mexica lost this engagement since they were badly organised. They were incapable of dealing with an attack in open country by mounted men, however weary.

The Mexican force retired in disorder at a moment when they were not far short of their second triumph over the Castilians. Otumba is always, deservedly, held to rank among the most famous battle honours of Cortés. It is a word which decorates his statue in the main square of Medellín. There should also be a statue there to the horse of Castile. For if ever that animal turned the day in a battle, it was on this occasion.

According to his own first account, Cortés lost two fingers of his left hand at Otumba. But though the rest of what he described as happening to him in this battle seems to be approximately true, that appears to have been exaggerated.[41] A later account by Cortés himself suggests that he was merely wounded in his left hand so that he could not properly hold the reins of his horse.[42]

The Mexican defeat at Otumba enabled Cortés to continue his slow journey across bleak country towards Tlaxcala. It caused a new crisis among the Mexica. Two factions took shape in Tenochtitlan. One was a group which wished to act harshly against all friends of the Castilians – anyone who had had anything to do with them during their long stay in the city; the other group were the survivors among the old councillors of Montezuma. There seem to have been disputes between the two factions for some days. The advocates of an unforgiving line emerged successful. Several of Montezuma's old friends and family were apparently put to death, including some of his children.[43] Then, under Cuitláhuac's leadership, the Mexica gave themselves over to the festival of Huey Tecuilhuitl. The populace set about, once again, adorning the idols with feathers, mosaic masks, and necklaces.[44] The Mexica were unable to concentrate on the threat facing them. After all, the season for fighting, the winter, was still far off. The Castilians, furthermore, were still in retreat.

Those conquistadors, meantime, spent the night after Otumba at Xaltepec, a town from which they could see the beginning of the mountains of Tlaxcala, where they believed that they would be safe.[45] On 9 July, only ten days after the "tragic night", they crossed the mountains and made a long trek slowly up to Hueyotlipan, the first town in the kingdom of Tlaxcala, where they were instantly made welcome.[46] This greeting was a great relief to them – above all, to Cortés, who otherwise might not have been able to maintain himself as leader of a disheartened, exhausted, hungry and wounded army, many of the men being lame and the few arquebusiers and crossbowmen being out of both powder and arrows. In Hueyotlipan, the Castilians were offered food and rest for three days. Cortés' old friends, Maxixcatzin, Xicotencatl the elder and Chichimecatecle, the second most important Tlaxcalan military commander, came to greet them.[47]

The army was still at Hueyotlipan nursing its wounds when Cortés issued a most unpopular proclamation: everyone who had saved gold in the retreat should, under pain of death, hand it in to him or to Pedro de Alvarado.[48] The purpose was to replenish the expedition's coffers. It is not clear how successful this demand was, nor exactly what happened to the gold concerned. In 1529 it was alleged that 45,000 pesos were so recovered and that Cortés took it all for himself.[49] Diego Holguín, a witness at an enquiry organised by Diego Velázquez the following year in Cuba, said that Cortés later had some people hanged for not delivering what they had. There is no other evidence of that. All the same, much gold did remain in the private effects of many Castilians.[50] The *Caudillo* himself certainly had money a few months later to send to some of his followers in Spain. The demand of Cortés was unpopular, and fired yet another of the little rebellions which had given such trouble to this enterprise.

There had, meantime, been a lengthy discussion in Tlaxcala as to how to treat the Castilians on their return from Tenochtitlan. This had been inspired by a message from Mexico. Cuitláhuac sent six ambassadors with presents of cotton, plumage and salt. They promised other favours to the Tlaxcalans if they were to refuse to help Cortés. The oldest of the Mexicans presented the gifts. Then he and his companions were conducted to the presence of the Tlaxcalan lords. This emissary pointed out that the Mexica and the Tlaxcalans had the same ancestry, the same language, and the same gods. They had common interests. It was true that, in recent years, they had been divided by religious questions. But it was time to return to older, more peaceful times. Possibly the ambassador recalled the remarks of the Mexican messenger when trying to persuade the Tlaxcalans to come to Ahuítzotl's coronation: "There are times when one must be an enemy, but there are others when one must heed the natural obligations which exist between us."[51] The strangers, said the Mexicans, were a menace to both peoples, for they had committed excesses, stolen the riches of the country, sought to reduce great monarchs to the status of vassals, and violated temples. The Mexica offered a perpetual alliance: presumably similar to that which they had with Texcoco and Tacuba.[52]

Xicotencatl the younger wanted to agree. He had never abandoned his unrelenting hostility to Cortés. Perhaps, as Fr. Aguilar suggested, he had been supplied with special presents by the Mexica.[53] He urged the Tlaxcalans to kill all the Castilians as soon as possible, something which he thought could easily be done, in view of "their beaten condition".[54] His father and Maxixcatzin were, however, in favour of maintaining the previous year's alliance with Cortés. It would not be right, they apparently argued, to visit such cruelty and treachery on men in such need, and to whom they had sworn friendship such a short time before. The two sides almost came to blows. In the end Maxixcatzin won the argument by vividly recalling the habitual treachery, the continual cruelty, and the customary arrogance of the Mexica. Despite his great age, Maxixcatzin pushed Xicotencatl the younger downstairs. So it was that he and his colleagues went to the Castilians, with the welcome which Cortés so much appreciated.[55] According to Fr. Aguilar, who had been among those who had survived the *noche triste*, Maxixcatzin greeted Cortés with these words: "May your lordship be most welcome. Already, as you know, I told you the truth before you went to Mexico and you did not wish to hear me. But now you are in your own house, you have come where you can rest and recover from your labours." As usual, turkey and tortillas were produced in abundance.[56] The Mexican ambassadors left in haste and secrecy.

There was, however, a quid pro quo. The chiefs of Tlaxcala drove what they intended to be a hard bargain with Cortés in return for helping him so substantially. First, they wanted the Castilians to guarantee to hand over Cholula to them. Second, they required, after the eventual defeat of the Mexica, to be allowed to command a special fortress to be built in Tenochtitlan which they would man, and so, as they thought, be guaranteed for ever against an attack by the Mexica. Third, they wanted to divide with the Castilians any booty which was gained. Fourth, they wanted perpetual freedom from paying tribute to whoever ruled in Tenochtitlan.[57] Cortés agreed to all these terms. In consequence he was well received after three days in Hueyotlipan.[58] To secure the services of the Tlaxcalans, it was worth paying almost any price: the enquiry against Cortés in 1529 was right to insist that "if the natives of Tlaxcala had risen against the Spanish, they [the latter] would have all been killed, because many Spaniards were wounded and had been badly injured".[59] Many, including Cortés' chief smelter of metals, Antonio de Benavides, would testify that, had it not been for the Tlaxcalans, "no Spaniard would have escaped the Mexica because there was nowhere else to go".[60]

The Castilians were even better received in Tlaxcala than in Hueyotlipan, though the town was in mourning for the many from there who had "died on the bridges".[61] The expedition stayed twenty days – the same length of time that they had stayed the previous year: perhaps that was because the Tlaxcalans had only enough food in their reserve for that length of time. During these twenty days, Cortés and many others, who, like him, were suffering from wounds, mostly recovered. About four more Spaniards, however, died of injuries.[62] Others took longer to be cured.

Rebuffed by the Tlaxcalans, Cuitláhuac made a serious effort to find another ally. He approached the Tarascans. He sent ten messengers to see Zuangua, the *cazonci* (monarch). The messengers carried elaborate presents (turquoise, green feathers, round shields with gold rims, blankets, bells and large obsidian mirrors). Thus the Tarascans grimly realised that the Mexica were in need. The messengers said: "Our Lord of Mexico[63] sends us ... to report to our brother, the *cazonci*, about the strange people who have taken us by surprise. We have met them in battle and killed some 200 of those who came riding deer, and 200 of those who were not mounted. Those deer wore coats of mail. They carried something which sounded like clouds, which, making a great thundering, kills all those whom it meets ... They completely broke up our position and killed many of us. They are accompanied by people from Tlaxcala."[64]

The *cazonci* considered, and consulted. "What shall we do?" he asked his advisers. "This message which they have brought me is serious.[65] We never used to know that other peoples existed ... [yet] what purpose would I have in sending my soldiers to help Mexico? For we have always been at war when we approach each other, and there is rancour between us ... the Mexicans are very astute when they talk and very artful with the truth.[66] We must take care lest it be a trick ... they may want to have vengeance on us by killing us through treachery."

So the *cazonci* merely gave the messengers presents in return: blankets, gourd dishes, leather war jackets.

A little later he heard from some Otomís that there had indeed been a terrible battle in Tenochtitlan: the city was "foul with the smell of dead bodies".[67] He asked some more questions, and said: "Never have we heard from our ancestors of the coming of other peoples. If [they] knew of it, they did not make it known to us. Where would they come from but from the heavens? ... And the deer ... what are they?"

So the cautious Zuangua sent messengers to Mexico in order to make further enquiries. The Mexica welcomed them. They even took them to the top of a mountain, beyond Texcoco, perhaps Iztaccihuatl (had it been Popocatepetl, the name would surely have been mentioned). There they pointed, far below them, to a long flat clearing, where the Castilians were.[68] The Mexica suggested the Tarascans make a formal alliance against these intruders. These men of Michoacan would go one way; the Mexica another; and the Castilians would be caught between them: "Why should we not be successful, since everyone runs away from the people of Michoacan, who are such good archers?" The Mexica were thinking of the Tarascans' copper-headed arrows.

On hearing this story, the *cazonci* was once more doubtful: "For what purpose are we to go to Tenochtitlan?" he asked. "We might go only to die, and we know what they would say about us afterwards. Perhaps the Mexica would betray us to these new people, and be responsible for having us killed. Let the Mexica do their own killing . . . let the strangers kill the Mexica because, for many years, they have lived in the wrong way." The *cazonci* obscurely complained that, for a long time, the Mexica had not brought wood to their temples, only songs: "What good are songs by themselves?" Then he went on to ask why the strangers should have come to Mexico without a cause. Obviously, some god must have sent them. The *cazonci* finally said that the Tarascan people should work to ensure that they carried out the gods' work well and, in that case, the gods would not be angry with them. But they certainly would not help the Mexica.[69] The *cazonci* was confident that his people's superior metallurgy would enable them, and him, to remain above the battle so far as Tenochtitlan was concerned. With that decision, he probably sealed the fate of the kingdoms of old Mexico.

Thus the new Emperor Cuitláhuac was unsuccessful in his approach to the Tarascans. He then began to make desperate initiatives: for example, he announced that he would remit all tribute for a year from any town which killed Castilians or expelled them from their territory.[70] But this offer did not seem any more effective than his scheme for alliances.

Down in the valley at Tlaxcala, and of course ignorant of the Mexica's dealings in the mountains behind him, Cortés was affected by four problems. First, he had to send back a messenger to Vera Cruz to describe what had happened in Tenochtitlan, without saying how many had been killed. Instead he asked for any soldiers and ammunition available to be sent up to him. He similarly ordered Alonso Caballero, his "admiral" in command of the ships on the coast, to take extra care to prevent anyone leaving for Cuba. Seven men came up from the sea to reinforce him, with some supplies, under the command of a certain Pedro Lencero, who had been one of his original followers. But all these men were ill, either with liver complaints or swellings on their bodies. The phrase "the aid of Lencero" passed briefly into the vocabulary of those days to indicate a useless piece of help.[71]

Second, news came of another setback. Cortés had earlier left behind at Tlaxcala some sick servants, silver and some clothes. Just before leaving for Tenochtitlan in June, Cortés had sent back to the sea one of his captains, Juan de Alcántara, both to fetch some supplies, and to take back from Tlaxcala what Cortés had left there. Alcántara gathered these treasures and stores and set off for the sea, with about forty-five foot soldiers, five horsemen, including one of Narváez's captains known as Juan Yuste, sometime *regidor* of Narváez's ill-fated municipality of San Salvador, and about two hundred Tlaxcalans. They carried 2,000 pesos' worth of gold in two chests, as well as 14,000 pesos in small pieces of gold which had been brought to Tenochtitlan by Velázquez de León. This force was, however, ambushed and all its members killed on their way from Tlaxcala at Calpulalpan (a place subsequently known as Pueblo Morisco), some miles to the west of Hueyotlipan.[72]

Following the disaster which had befallen Salvatierra and the others of Narváez's expedition near Tepeaca, this was the second calamity suffered by the Castilians in the course of a week or two, not to speak of the major tragedy of the defeat on the *noche triste*. The knowledge of the events at Pueblo Morisco seems to have been among the factors which led Cortés to determine, in subsequent weeks, to follow a particularly violent campaign of "punishment" against the tributaries of the Mexica to prevent such "crimes" – the crime being that of killing Castilians after the people concerned had accepted to be vassals of King Charles.[73]

Next, Cortés had to reprimand one of his own men, Juan Páez, whom, on the way to Tenochtitlan, before 24 June, he had left behind in Tlaxcala. When they heard that the fighting had begun in the city of the lake, the Tlaxcalans had offered 100,000 men to Páez in order to rescue Cortés in the Mexican capital. But Páez had said that he had strict orders to stay where he was. It was not the last time that a commander would seek to maintain obsolete instructions in order to justify cowardice.[74]

The fourth matter which came to a head in Tlaxcala was another protest by the Castilians, among whom there were now many who once again wanted to return to the coast or even to Cuba. This was, of course, an attitude of mind held by many from the beginning, especially among those known to have been friends of Diego Velázquez. But their protests had been silenced after the astonishing successes of the latter part of the previous year. Now those who remained among them were beginning to make common cause with the survivors of Narváez's expedition. The leader of the protests this time was the usually taciturn Andrés de Duero, Cortés' old friend and Velázquez's, who had accompanied Narváez. He, and his comrades, did not trust the Tlaxcalans as Cortés did. He had no confidence that the conquistadors could defeat the Mexica. Duero was furious that the gold which some of them had managed to lay hold of on the night of the *noche triste* had had to be given up on Cortés' orders. The restlessness of these men was compounded with fear. They said that "their heads were broken, their bodies rotting, and covered with wounds and sores, bloodless, weak, and naked. They were in a strange land, sick, and surrounded by enemies."[75] They seem to have made a written demand to Cortés along these lines:

"Very magnificent sir, the captains and soldiers of this army, of which your excellency is General, appear before you and say to you that the deaths, damages and losses which we have suffered while in the city of Tenochtitlan, whence we have just come, as well as on the road from there, are well known to you. Most of our men and horses are dead. The artillery is lost, our ammunition is exhausted, and we are lacking in everything with which to carry on the war. In addition, in this city, where we seem on the surface to have been given a good reception, and shown good will, we have found for certain that they are trying to reassure us (and others) with pretended words and deeds in order to lull us into a state of false security, and then, when we least expect it, they will attack us and finish us off . . . We cannot believe that these Indians will keep faith or promises with us, nor go against their own people and their neighbours in our defence. The enmity and war between them in the past will turn to friendship and peace so that, together, they may be more powerful against us and so destroy us. Of all this, we have seen and understand the beginnings . . . Besides we see that Your Excellency, our leader and general, is badly wounded. The surgeons say that your wound is dangerous and they fear that you may not survive. All these things, if Your Excellency will examine them, afford good reasons for us to abandon this city, and not wait for a worse conclusion to our affairs than exist at the present. We are also informed that Your Excellency, without taking into consideration the urgent and sufficient reasons to put a stop to the conquest, intends to go ahead and continue the war, a plan which, if put into effect, will lead to our destruction. We therefore ask and beg Your Excellency and, if necessary, demand . . . that you leave this city with all the army and set off for Vera Cruz, so that what is most to the service of God and His Majesty can be determined best. May Your Excellency not delay in this, since it would cause us much damage if our enemy were to close the roads, take away our food, and fight us cruelly, in such a way that we could not thereafter defend ourselves . . . We therefore require you, in the presence of our notary, to give witness of this; and we make formal claim against Your Excellency and your property for all the damage, deaths and losses which may occur if you do not do as we suggest."[76] Andrés de Duero, who knew from long experience with Velázquez how to write such documents, was probably the author of this skilful one.

Cortés answered this new challenge with his usual aplomb. According to his own account, he "said that to show the natives, especially those who are allies, that we lack courage would turn them against us the sooner; after all, 'Fortune always favours the brave'.[77] Furthermore, we are Christians who trust in the great goodness of God, who will not let us perish utterly nor allow us to lose such a great and noble land which has been or is to be subject to Your Majesty . . . Nor could I abandon so great a service [to Your Majesty]," Cortés went on, in his report to the King, "as continuing the war . . . I determined, therefore, that I would, on no account, go across the mountains to the coast. On the contrary, I told them that, disregarding all the dangers and work that might lie ahead of us, I would not abandon this land for, apart from being shameful to myself and dangerous for all, it would be great treason to Your Majesty; rather, I resolved to fall on our enemies wherever I could and oppose them in every possible way."[78] Cortés' chaplain, López de Gómara, added certain things which one must suppose that the *Caudillo* told him years later; for example, that he said: "What nation which had ruled the world had not at least once been defeated?" and "What famous captain went home because he had lost a battle?" and "Is there not one among you who would not take it as an insult to be told that he had turned his back?" He also said, impertinently, considering his agreement with them, that "The Tlaxcalans prefer slavery amongst us to subjection to the Mexica." As for his own wounds, he considered himself cured.[79]

Thus Cortés made a straightforward appeal to that sense of honour which he knew the Castilians had at the back of their minds.[80] As usual his eloquence was successful. The rebellion was stilled. But Cortés was taking no chances. He immediately proceeded with a new campaign on the insistence, as at Cholula and in Tenochtitlan itself, of the Tlaxcalans.[81] This was to be waged in the province of Tepeaca.

30
It was convenient to impose the said punishment

"It was convenient to impose the said punishment for the pacification of the land and as the thing was so new it was appropriate to have done what was done and much more, in order to put fear into the naturales so that they did no hurt to the Spaniards . . ."
Francisco de Flores, testimony in *residencia* against Cortés

TEPEACA WAS A hilltop fortress and the centre of tribute for the Triple Alliance in the flat region stretching from the volcano Popocatepetl to the slopes of Mt. Orizaba. In the previous century, it had long resisted incorporation into the Mexican empire. The subsequent sacrifice of a large number of victims to Huitzilopochtli must still in 1520 have been well remembered by its older citizens. Tepeaca lay on what was really the best route between Tenochtitlan and the sea at Vera Cruz. Hence the strategic benefit of winning it to the cause of the Castilian-Tlaxcalan alliance (as Cortés' expedition was turning out to be) was considerable.[1] The economic character of the place can be gathered from seeing the list of the tribute which had to be paid annually to Tenochtitlan: 4,000 loads of lime, 4,000 loads of thick canes, 8,000 loads of canes for arrows, and 200 frames for carrying goods on one's back.[2] The city was ruled, as was Tlaxcala, by four co-equal lords.[3]

Cortés wanted a striking victory over one of Tenochtitlan's most useful dependencies for several reasons: first, for the effect on other allies; second, because of the damaging consequences for the morale of Tenochtitlan itself; third, to preserve the character of the alliance with Tlaxcala; and fourth, to put to work his faction-ridden force, in which the men of Narváez were scheming with the remaining friends of Diego Velázquez to constitute an internal opposition.

The idea of such a campaign was the Tlaxcalans', the Iagos of the Spanish expedition. More than one witness in the enquiry subsequently mounted against Cortés said in Cortés' defence that, if they had not moved against Tepeaca, then Tlaxcala would have risen against the Castilians, and the expedition would have been at an end.[4] It will be remembered too, from the discussion of events at Cholula in 1519, that, as Cortés and others, such as Francisco de Flores, freely admitted, a contrived use of terror played a part in the Spaniards' psychological calculations.

The pretext for Cortés' action in 1520 was the murder at Quechula, in the neighbourhood of Tepeaca, of the twelve or so captains of Narváez whom Cortés had dispatched to Tenochtitlan on foot – most of the municipal council of Narváez's foundation of San Salvador, as the *Caudillo* put it rather disingenuously. The people of Quechula were assumed, from being tributaries of Tenochtitlan, to have become vassals of the King of Spain; so, of course, by the *Caudillo's* definition, what they had done constituted rebellion.[5] (The emphasis on a form of law in these circumstances is the most curious part of this campaign. At once touching and ridiculous, the modern observer, like Las Casas in hearing of the *Requerimiento*, does not know whether to laugh or to weep.)

Cortés wanted to investigate, he told the people of Tepeaca, the reason for those deaths. He also wanted to know, he said, why there were so many Mexica living in Tepeaca and its nearby towns[6] (the probable explanation was that the Mexican conquest of Tepeaca seventy years previously had been accompanied by a ferocious proscription and that the empire still feared a rebellion).

After their twenty-day rest, the bulk of the army followed Cortés towards Tepeaca about 1 August. With some additions from Villa Rica, the expedition probably now numbered a little more than five hundred Castilians, about seventeen horse, and six crossbowmen. Cortés left behind in Tlaxcala several wounded men. He also left Alonso de Ojeda and Juan Márquez to continue to train or work with the Tlaxcalans.[7] Since they were on their way to fight a people which had been for years an enemy, the Tlaxcalans sent with Cortés at least two thousand of their own warriors, as eager for provisions as for booty.[8] The army was accompanied by another Tlaxcalan leader, Tianquizlatoatzin, and several sons of Xicotencatl, but not the famous Xicotencatl the younger. He must be assumed to have been sulking in his tent after the defeat of his arguments in favour of acting against Cortés.

The distance from Tlaxcala to Tepeaca was only about forty miles, as the crow flies, in a south-westerly direction. But in order to reach the latter town, it was best to make a deviation several miles round the eastern slopes of Mt. Matlalcueye (Malinche). Thus the expedition camped the first night after leaving Tlaxcala at the Tlaxcalan city of Tzompantzinco. The second night was spent at Zacatepec. A skirmish occurred with Mexica and Tepeacans, who seemed quite opposed to any compromise with the conquistadors.[9] On the fourth day after leaving Tlaxcala, Cortés stopped at Acatzinco, a town which had a governor subordinate to the rulers of Tepeaca.

Here Cortés sent a message requiring the Tepeacans to explain their attitude to the Spaniards and asking why the captains of Narváez had been killed. The Tepeacans sent a defiant reply, saying that they demanded a retreat by the Castilians; or else there would be a banquet at which Castilian flesh would be the *pièce de résistance*. This was the occasion for Cortés to turn, as usual in these circumstances, to his notary, Pero Hernández; who was instructed to draw up a statement saying that, though the Mexica had sworn fealty to the King of Castile, they had all the same killed eight hundred and seventy Castilians and sixty of their horses, and so they and their allies would have to be sold into slavery.[10]

Two days later, the Castilians attacked Tepeaca. The battle was fought in a maize and maguey plantation outside the town. The small number of Castilian horse had the same kind of dazzling effect that it had had before the unsuccessful fighting in Tenochtitlan. The Tlaxcalans fought with much energy too to capture Tepeacans to be taken off as slaves – slaves in the fairly moderate Mexican sense rather than the harsh European one. About four hundred were killed.[11] Cortés moved into the centre of the town, the local *tlatoani* offered formal fealty to the Emperor Charles V, and, on 4 September 1520, Cortés founded there, in the centre of the hilltop fortress, a new town of his own, to be known, a distant echo of the frontier in Andalusia before the fall of Seville, as Segura de la Frontera.[12] A city council composed of Cortés' friends was formed.[13] In the act forming this body a special denunciation was made of blasphemy and gambling: actions which must have seemed insipid in comparison with the killings which attended the fall of the city.[14]

For the proscription after the battle was severe. Cortés enslaved the wives and children of those who had been killed either in the battle or afterwards: a departure from previous practice.[15] Most of these new slaves were branded on the cheek.[16] They were sold for ten pesos, and became slaves in the European or Caribbean sense, in that they were completely the property of their masters, who were in most instances Spaniards. Their children were also to be looked upon as slaves. Some Tepeacans were also torn to pieces by dogs: the word "*aperrear*" coming into odious use again. Others were lanced or piked to death in an indiscriminate fashion.[17] Cortés continued to employ the useful fiction that the people had rebelled. As to branding, it was a punishment used in Spain: thus in 1484 the inquisitor-general Torquemada decreed that anyone who failed to substantiate a claim made for a confiscated property should receive one hundred lashes and be marked with a hot iron on the face.

Cortés' Tlaxcalan allies were said by the *Caudillo*'s Castilian enemies to have sacrificed and eaten many corpses of the defeated. The first rumour that this occurred was heard after the fighting at Zacatepec.[18] But after Tepeaca, Cortés seems to have turned a blind eye to this practice. The Tlaxcalans wanted their pound of flesh in a way that Shylock would not have recognised; and Cortés needed their help.

Many accusations were subsequently made. Thus in an enquiry the following year in Cuba, Diego Holguín and Juan Álvarez, both at this time with Cortés, said that, after the killing of the enemy, the *Caudillo* allowed the Tlaxcalans to take away as many pieces to eat as they desired – roasted or cooked in other ways.[19] Diego de Ávila said that Cortés invited the Tepeacans to go to the rooftops; he had many thrown over into the square, where the Tlaxcalans took them off to be eaten.[20] Near the Castilian camp there were said to have been chopping blocks and butchers' shops where the carcasses of men from Tepeaca were dressed for eating.[21] Rumours abounded that at least one Castilian ate Indian flesh too.[22] Bono de Quejo said that the bodies of dead Indians were given to Mexican dogs, and that then the dogs were eaten by the Tlaxcalans.[23] Both he and Diego de Vargas stated that they had heard it said that many Castilians carried dead Tepeacans to the butchers' in Tlaxcala and exchanged them for chickens and cloth; and that the Tlaxcalans gave lavish parties "where the Mexica were eaten".[24] Bono de Quejo, always quick to pick up rumours adverse to Cortés, also claimed that he had heard it said that a Castilian ate an Indian's liver.[25] None of these stories is adequately supported: they read as if Bono de Quejo and his colleagues at the enquiry of 1521 had recalled too vividly Vespucci's account in which he described seeing in Brazil salted human flesh hanging in a butcher's shop.[26] On the other hand the conquistadors were hungry: Juan Ruiz testified in 1525 that if they managed to get hold of a slice of dog, they gave thanks to God.[27]

Cortés then set about conquering the entire province around Tepeaca. His treatment of the cities there was similar to what he had effected in Tepeaca. Nor did he do everything himself. Thus Cristóbal de Olid was said to have deceived the people of Quechula in a scandalous manner. This city was among the few in old Mexico to have walls. On reaching it some days after the battle at Tepeaca, Olid found the people in the fields, the men armed. He told the Indians not to fight the Castilians, since they would be sure to be killed if they did. The people of Quechula decided that discretion was the better part of valour, laid down their arms, and came to speak to the Castilians. Olid ordered Domingo García de Albuquerque to escort the entire population to Cortés in his camp at Tepeaca. Cortés had all the men, about two thousand, it was said, put on one side and killed; perhaps four thousand women and children were enslaved.[28]

There were said to have been similar atrocities in Izúcar, a town which also accepted fealty to the Emperor Charles V once the Mexica there had been killed, enslaved or dispersed. Several other towns (Tecamachalco, Acapetlahuacan) seem to have been reduced much as Tepeaca and Quechula had been – slaughter, enslavement, branding and probably an opportunity offered for sacrificial cannibalism by the Tlaxcalans afterwards;

others, such as Huexotzinco and even Cuetlaxtlan, all offered their submission to Cortés without a fight.[29] Cortés was accused by his enemies of having killed anything between 15,000 and 20,000 people in Tepeaca and its surroundings – while the "Jews of Tlaxcala", as Diego de Vargas described the allies in 1521, were given the same number to sacrifice and eat.[30]

Though these figures are doubtless exaggerated, this campaign was at once the most tedious, the most brutal, and the most important of Cortés' in New Spain. In the course of it, he won over half the country, he destroyed Mexico's links with the sea to the east, he finally cut the Mexica off from much-prized tropical vegetables and fruit and, by inspiring fear, he caused thousands of Indians to support him, and to accept to be vassals of the King of Spain (whatever they understood by that to them strange formulation).[31] He also established a secure base.

In respect of these events, Cortés himself wrote a report which, when taken into account with the accusations made against him, went far to admit the brutalities. He said that "when we crossed the border [into Tepeaca, that is into the Mexican empire from Tlaxcala], many of the natives came out to fight us, and defend the road as best they could from strong and dangerous positions. Not to give an account of everything which befell us in this battle, which would take too much time, I will only say that, after we had completed our demands for peace on Your Majesty's behalf and with which they had not complied, we made war on them, and they fought many times against us. With the help of God and the royal good fortune of Your Majesty, we always routed them and killed many, without their killing or wounding a single Spaniard . . . and within twenty days, we had pacified and subdued many towns and villages and the lords and chieftains had come forward and offered themselves as His Majesty's vassals . . . I have driven from those provinces many of the Mexica who had come to help the people of Tepeaca make war on us and to ensure that they did not become our allies . . ." On the question of slavery, he said, "In a certain part of this province [that is near Zautla] . . . where they killed ten or twelve Spaniards, the natives have been very warlike . . . I made certain of them slaves, of which I gave a fifth part to Your Majesty's officers, for they are all cannibals . . . I was also moved to take those slaves so as to strike fear into the [Mexicans] and also because there are so many people there that if I did not impose a great and cruel punishment they would never be reformed . . ."[32]

Other Spanish writers gave more bland accounts. Bernal Díaz (being ill in Tlaxcala) relates almost nothing of these actions except that Cristóbal de Olid was nearly persuaded to turn back by some of Narváez's men whom he had with him. Fr. Aguilar seems to have been especially forgetful, writing in the 1560s, about the brutal events in which he participated forty years before: "Tepeaca gave fealty to the Spanish king without offering resistance," he curiously says, "From here the captain sent out officers and men to treat for peace and persuade the people to break their alliance with the Mexica and accept that of the King. Many towns did so, offering themselves peaceably, and they were well treated by the captain and his officers who would not permit themselves anything taken by force but only asked to be given food, which they did willingly. In this manner many provinces and towns were pacified and gave fealty to the King and others came from far away to offer themselves peaceably . . ."[33]

Perhaps the sacrificial eating of flesh by Tlaxcalans was made by Cortés' enemies to seem as if it were cannibalism on a large scale.[34] But there obviously was much bloodshed. Cortés was, it seems, determined to create a zone in the centre of Mexico which would obey him unquestioningly. To ensure this, there was no action which he was not prepared to countenance. Until his defeat at Tenochtitlan, Cortés had conducted himself generally well so far as the Indians were concerned (Cholula apart), in comparison with other conquistadors. In Tepeaca and in the campaign based on that town once he had captured it, Cortés allowed himself, out of calculation, to observe once more that, in certain circumstances, terror can be successful. Vengeance for the "noche triste" must also have played a part.

As for the sacrifices and banquets by the Tlaxcalans, Cortés probably did ignore what was going on. Similar politic oversights have happened in European wars of the twentieth century.

Cuitláhuac was, meantime, doing his best to restore the morale, the defences, and the strength generally of the Mexican empire. The ruined teocalli (Great Temple) was rebuilt, while the idols were returned to their old sanctuaries. Streets, houses and causeways were also restored. Cuitláhuac celebrated his inauguration as emperor in September, the event coinciding approximately with the fiesta of Ochopaniztli ("Sweeping"). Castilian prisoners as well as Tlaxcalans probably served as victims. The skulls of those sacrificed were as usual hung on the great skull rack, the tzompantli. Because the Mexica thought that the horses of the conquistadors would be frightened to see the skulls of other horses, men's heads and horse's heads were carefully affixed alongside each other. The Spanish Virgin and the effigy of St Christopher had, of course, been removed from the Great Temple.

But none of this was very warlike. The Mexica had tried diplomacy unsuccessfully. They seemed to have realised that, while Cortés was alive, he would be a threat. Lacking a policy, however, they seem to have allowed themselves to live in a fool's paradise. Opulence was thought more important than defence. Even so, some things were done. New fortifications were built. Long lances were cut, of the same kind that Cortés had had made for use against the cavalry of Narváez. Yet no one knew when they would be needed.

∗

Cortés used his establishment of the base at Tepeaca/Segura de la Frontera as an occasion to take stock of his legal position. Thus a statement was drawn up on 20 August which, by the well-tried method of a carefully prepared questionnaire and replies from selected members of the expedition, formally recorded the efforts which he had made to preserve the gold of the King at the time of the flight from Tenochtitlan. The document also placed the blame for the tragedy of the *noche triste* squarely on Narváez.[35]

Following this, a number of Cortés' friends were prevailed upon to direct to him a request that, considering that Narváez and Velázquez had caused such havoc in Mexico, their property in Cuba and Santo Domingo should be confiscated. Though this request was formally supported by four prominent conquistadors,[36] and supported in principle by nine others (including one member of Narváez's expedition),[37] Cortés could have had no illusion as to the likelihood of it being successful as it stood. What he probably had in mind was a justification for seizing Narváez's ships and other goods.

Cortés drew up a third document which, in September, described the events of the last year and a half since he had arrived in Mexico. This was a joint letter from the army signed by the 534 Spaniards who were with him at Tepeaca.[38] Its purpose was to say that they all believed that it would be advantageous for Cortés to remain as captain and *justicia mayor*, as named by the municipality of Vera Cruz in 1519. Diego Holguín in 1521 insisted that Cortés arranged with some of his friends (Juan de Sarmiento, Domingo García de Albuquerque, newly named to be *procurador* of Segura, and Cristóbal del Corral, a councillor of the same place) to collect the signatures of most people. These men, Holguín said, went from house to house telling the conquistadors that they should sign a white paper which they were carrying round without apparently indicating what it was.[39] Diego de Vargas said that he was, on two occasions, walking past the lodgings of Domingo García de Albuquerque when he was asked by him to sign various documents which he could not read to identify what they were (the second time he did not sign).[40] Fear usually dictated submission: the rumour was even spread in the camp that it had been publicly proclaimed in Seville (perhaps by that judge of *las gradas* there, Alonso de Céspedes, who was an uncle of Alonso Hernández Portocarrero) that anyone who said that Cortés was a traitor would be hanged.[41]

A fourth paper was also produced, in early October, on the petition of a Basque lawyer, Juan Ochoa de Elizalde, whom Cortés had begun to use for his purposes, about the costs which Cortés had had in relation to the expedition to "Yucatan" in the first place (Ochoa was the son of a businessman of Guipúzcoa, and he himself had lived in Santo Domingo before taking part in the conquest of both Puerto Rico and Cuba).[42] This was designed to put Cortés' case against Velázquez in the event that the matter were to be examined in Spain. Once again there was a questionnaire and fourteen witnesses.[43] Though the expedition in Mexico had learned that King Charles I of Spain had become the Emperor Charles V of the Holy Roman Empire and King of Germany, they still had no information about the more important matter (to them) of the activities of the two *procuradores* of Vera Cruz, Francisco de Montejo and Alonso Hernández Portocarrero.

Finally Cortés wrote a second report (*Carta de Relación*) to the King in Spain, giving him an account of his activities during the previous fifteen months (since in fact his previous letter had been directed to him, along with that of the municipality of Vera Cruz). Cortés signed this new report on 30 October but may have changed his mind about when to send it home to Spain. Perhaps he was telling the truth when he reported later that bad weather delayed the dispatch of the letter till March 1521, when it was in the end sent in the care of a friend from Medellín, Alonso de Mendoza.[44]

Cortés' letter has already been mentioned when discussing the campaign of Tepeaca. It spoke of his defeat at Tenochtitlan as a temporary setback. He wrote, apparently without consultation of others, and without any other preparation, of his idea that the Emperor Charles V should look on himself as also Emperor of "New Spain", to use the name for Mexico which Cortés now also formally launched. The concept of empire was new to the thoughts of Castile. Her thinkers and officials only thought in terms of one emperor in Christendom, the Holy Roman one whose title was usually confirmed by coronation by the Pope.[45] The Pope sometimes spoke of Christendom as an empire.[46] Bishop Ruiz de la Mota, as we have seen, did talk of Charles becoming "emperor of the world", in his strange speech at Santiago de Compostela in April. To say, as Cortés now did, that "one might call oneself emperor of this kingdom with no less merit than of Germany"[47] was a leap into unknown intellectual territory; and, as some would say, an inappropriate leap, as well as an extraordinary one, since neither Castile nor Spain constituted an empire. They remained a collection of kingdoms. Here, as in other ways, Cortés showed himself a man of the Renaissance. For the idea of the universal empire of Rome was a preoccupation of Italian authors.

So too of course was that concern with glory of which Cortés also spoke in this letter. Cortés wrote that, had he died in the enterprise, he would have achieved "honour enough" ("*harta gloria*"); and added that, with his struggles to come, he would gain "the greatest prize and honour that until our times any generation had ever won" ("*la mayor prez y honra*").[48] It is fruitless to speculate whether these were more Renaissance goals than those which might have been sought by the Cid.

With this letter Cortés apparently also sent a rough map of Tenochtitlan. This much-published document was a most inadequate representation, and grossly underestimated the size of both city and lake. Yet it has interest. One modern scholar thought that certain spellings suggested that Cortés himself might have drawn it. It is more probable that it was drawn by a German on the basis of ideas sent by Cortés.[49]

Finally this letter was correctly addressed to Charles V as "sacred Majesty" and "Emperor", not merely as "most high and most powerful lord". Cortés had learned of the reality of the changing Spanish circumstances from some lawyer whom he had encountered among Narváez's men. He now knew too much, also, to continue to associate with the King the name of Queen Juana, to whom jointly he had addressed his earlier communications.

While Cortés was thus, legally and politically, preparing a defensive position in relation to Spain, he was also making evident his plan to carry back the war offensively against the Mexica. He showed this most conclusively by a decision again to set about building ships, brigantines, which could change the balance of power on the lake. He may have had something like that in mind as early as the night of the *noche triste* when, it will be remembered, he asked if Martín López still lived, to receive the positive news that he did. At all events, in September or October 1520, Cortés again charged López with a task of shipbuilding, though this time a far larger operation than either of the other works which he had carried through before.[50] He instructed him: "Proceed at once to the city of Tlaxcala with your tools and everything necessary, and seek a place where you can cut much wood – oak, evergreen oak and pine – and fashion it into the pieces necessary to build thirteen brigantines."[51]

A naval blockade had assisted King Ferdinand III in his siege and capture of Seville in 1248.[52] Probably, as was suggested by Andrés de Tapia in a later lawsuit, López himself suggested the idea of "entering the city by water".[53] López was a direct descendant of Pedro Álvarez Osorio, one of the heroes of the liberation of Seville by St Ferdinand. He may, therefore, have gained the idea from family history.

López left Tepeaca for Tlaxcala with several assistants – including his servants, the La Mafla brothers, a cousin of his, Juan Martínez Narices, and a number of craftsmen.[54] Several of these had worked on López's previous brigantines and the ship at Vera Cruz, which had been left unfinished at the time of Narváez's landing. López went to much trouble and expense in securing adequate food, including oil, wine, cheese and other provisions for his men ("white and red wines from Vera Cruz", said Lázaro Guerrero, one of the workers concerned):[55] supplies for which he paid himself and for the cost of which he subsequently sued Cortés; since, if at any time, Cortés "gave them something, taken from the Indians, it was a matter of giving them something one day, and nothing for twenty, so that they practically had to maintain them-selves".[56] The wood was cut on the slopes of the peak of Malinche and then transferred to Tlaxcala. No doubt many Tlaxcalans were concerned in this imaginative operation. So were the people of Huexotzinco: at least they claimed forty years later to have been.[57] The timbers of a brigantine left at Vera Cruz were transported to Tlaxcala to act as a model for the builders. These were brought up by the Tlaxcalans, who also perhaps carried bolts and other tackle from the ships destroyed on the beaches of Cempoallan. They moved the wood from the hillside to Tlaxcala, and then to the banks of the river Zahuapan just below the town of Tizatlan.

López was the motor of the undertaking: one of his workers, Lázaro Guerrero, said of him later that "he toiled in everything connected with their [the brigantines'] construction, all day long, and often, with the aid of candles, after dark and before dawn, working himself and directing and encouraging other workmen with the zeal of a man who compre-hended the urgency of the matter".[58] It was he who conceived such schemes as damming the river Zahuapan to form a small lake when, in the dry season (February), he wanted to test whether the boats floated. He too must have decided on the size of the ships: a little over forty feet long, just as the ones which he had built before on the lake of Mexico had been, except for the "flagship" which would be forty-eight feet.[59]

On arriving at Tlaxcala, Martín López found Cortés' ally, even his friend, Maxixcatzin, suffering from smallpox: indeed, on his death-bed.[60] He was very old. But the disease from which he was suffering was new.

This epidemic of smallpox had begun, so far as the New World was concerned, in Hispaniola. There, at the end of 1518, it had been enough to give the *coup de grâce* to the by then tiny native population. It had made the mildly benign reforms of the Jeronymite fathers seem both late and irrelevant.[61] By late 1519, the plague had spread to Cuba. The incidence of it there, as has been suggested, had been so great as to persuade Velázquez to remain at home (an indication either of his public spirit or his sloth), and so leave the ill-fated expedition against Cortés to be commanded by Pánfilo de Narváez. Narváez, or possibly Alonso de Parada, took smallpox to Cozumel. It did not become an epidemic till they left. But then the Mayas of Yucatan thought that the evil gods of illness, the three children Ekpetz, Uzannkak and Sojakak, took the new disease from place to place at night.

The destruction in Yucatan was great. King Hunyg and his eldest son Ahpop Achí Balam died that winter. So did another potentate, Vakaki Ahmak. The description of the disease does not actually sound like smallpox. But the results were similar: "First they became ill with a cough. They suffered from nosebleeds and illnesses of the bladder. It was truly terrible, the number of dead . . . little by little bleary shadows and black night enveloped our fathers and grandfathers, and us also, O my lord." The chronicler Francisco Hernández Arana, a grandson of King Hunyg, added: "Great was the stench of the dead . . . half the people fled to the fields, where the dogs and vultures devoured their bodies."[62]

The first case of smallpox in New Spain proper seems to have derived from one of Narváez's black porters, Francisco de Eguía, in Cempoallan.[63] The disease spread to the family in the house where he had lodged, then from one Indian family to another, from one town to another, from one people to another. The unfortunate Totonacs, who had made themselves Cortés' first allies, were decimated. The disease infected the hot zone, then spread inland. In many places whole households died not only because they had no experience of, and hence no immunity against, this disease, but because the Indian custom, when ill, was to bathe, as a cure. The Indians would take cold baths after hot ones. They used bitumen: to be rubbed with which "divine medicine", people came to the temples from all parts; probably they employed *pulque* which they used on open wounds; all to no avail.[64] Mexican diseases had in the past been the consequence of bad food or an absence of food.[65] The Mexica suffered too from gout, cancer, paralysis; they went lame and blind; they had stomach disorders; their glands might become inflamed. They had treatments for all these infirmities, some of them making use of the same hallucinogenic plants which priests and sorcerers used for their divine undertakings. Hallucinogens and tobacco were also used to reveal to doctor or patient the cause of an illness: the black magic which must have caused it. But old Mexico did not know viruses.[66]

Skin diseases did exist. They might be sent by the god Macuilxochitl ("five flower") who punished those who broke the rule of sexual abstinence during a time of fasting by inspiring venereal diseases, piles, and boils. For the rites celebrating the goddess Xochiquetzal ("flower quetzal feather") everyone was supposed to wash in the river; those who did not might also expect to suffer "pustules, leprosy and malformed hands".[67] Other skin diseases were believed to be afflictions sent by the gods Tezcatlipoca or Xipe. No doubt some Mexica thought that the coming of this disease proved that Cortés must have been at least in touch with those deities, even if he were not their incarnation (Xipe was supposed to punish people by bringing blisters, pimples, festering and eye diseases). A special fortune-teller, a *tlaolchayauhqui*, was asked, as usual, to determine the cause of the new disease by observing the pattern of grains of maize or beans scattered on a white cotton cloak. On this occasion he must have been baffled.[68] The old remedies must have been tried: "The core [of the sore] is removed with a pine resin and squashed black beetles are spread there."[69] But smallpox resisted the beetle, not surprisingly, and the disease was accompanied by a sense of gloom which the Mexica described as the loss of their soul.

If disease was in Mexico believed to have been sent from the gods as a punishment for a blasphemy, the implication of the epidemic was that many crimes must have been committed. But what had they been? If that question was answered properly, appropriate penance could be offered: banquets with the correct menus for the right gods, pilgrimages to appropriate remote sites while carrying lighted braziers on one's head, or some kind of blood-letting. An opossum's tail could be sacrificed, as was sometimes considered right. Twelve hundred plants were employed for medical treatment in old Mexico. Surely one of them could have been effective.[70]

Yet town after town became depopulated. In many streets there was no method of collecting the corpses. Officials, anxious above all to avoid catching the disease themselves, buried corpses, if they could, by having houses brought down on top of the bodies.[71] The smell was almost as bad as the despair, the suffering far greater than anything which the conquerors had previously wrought. Those who did not die but had caught the disease frightened the survivors merely by showing the pits all over their faces and bodies. In some places half the population seems to have died.[72] Then famine often followed. This was partly because when the women in a house fell sick there was no one to grind the maize (to suggest that the men should have performed that task would have been like asking the Castilians to eat human beings).

The disease reached Chalco in the Valley of Mexico in September 1520, and remained there seventy days, beginning to devastate the prosperous lacustrine community. Kings and noblemen died as swiftly as farmers and serfs did. Smallpox reached Tenochtitlan by late October.[73]

Of course the disease spared neither friends of the Mexica nor their enemies – nor even friends of the Spaniards. Thus in addition to Maxixcatzin in Tlaxcala, Cuitláhuac, Montezuma's successor as Emperor of Mexico, was struck down by the epidemic. He died quickly, even his name quickly forgotten. Indeed, his character, looks, and personal condition are quite unknown. All we know of him is that he was against the idea of being encouraging to the Castilians before they arrived; that he inspired an extraordinary attack at night on the retreating conquistadors; that he failed to follow up his success; and that he was an unsuccessful diplomat. He left a wife, Papantzin, a daughter of Nezahualpilli, King of Texcoco, one son, Axayactaztin (who in old age was an informant of the historian Ixtlilxochitl), and two daughters.[74] Some writers have alleged that Cuitlahuac also married the beautiful but very young Tecuichpo, daughter of Montezuma, but if this occurred it probably only did so formally.[75]

Totoquihuatzin, the King of Tacuba (Montezuma's father-in-law), the King of Chalco, and then the *cazonci* of the Tarascans, Zuangua, in far off Tzintzuntzan, were among others who died.[76]

The miraculous character of this epidemic was that, while it killed Indians, it seemed to spare the Castilians.[77] The Mexica naturally thought that the visitation of the disease was a punishment by angry gods. The intimation of divine partiality towards the conquistadors was a confirmation that, if they were not gods, they were at least superhuman, giants of a kind, bound to triumph.[78] No doubt most of the Castilians survived since, by the age of twenty-five or thirty, an Extremeño or a Sevillano would have developed an immunity to this disease. They would already have been through many epidemics, not just smallpox, at home.

Evidently the smallpox was enough to ruin not only the arrangements for the celebration of the harvest festival of 1520 but the harvest itself. Maize was left ungathered. One goddess associated with the harvest festival was Atlan Tonnan, who was supposed to be both the giver and the curer of skin diseases. Her incapacity, or unwillingness, to deal with this crisis must have caused a further decline in Mexican morale.[79]

The Castilians do not seem to have realised the damage caused among the Indians by this disease. Certainly Cortés, in his third report to his king and emperor – the "double emperor", in his way of putting the matter – mentioned the epidemic but did not appreciate the devastation.[80] Yet the book of Chilam Balam de Chumayel, written in Yucatan, which became affected some months earlier, talks of the disease as if it had been the real turning point in the history of the Americas. In speaking of the old days before 1519, that work states: "There was then no sickness; they had no aching bones; they had then no high fever; they had then no smallpox; no stomach pains; no consumption . . . At that time people stood erect. But then the *teules* arrived and everything fell apart. They brought fear, and they came to wither the flowers . . ."[81]

One of the consequences of the disease was that, in the region of Tepeaca and the central plain, where he had now effectively established his political control, Cortés began to be looked upon as a kind of kingmaker. When the lord of a place died, it was Cortés who would suggest who should succeed him. Thus when the lord of Izúcar succumbed to smallpox, Cortés decided that his successor should be a nephew of Montezuma.[82] The same occurred at Cholula, where the few lords who had survived the massacre of the previous year died of the pox.[83] The *Caudillo* was maturing from being the leader of a band of guerrilla warriors into the patron of a great alliance. Cortés' position in Mexico was thus transformed by his time in Tepeaca/Segura de la Frontera.

The goddess Fortune had begun to smile again in other ways on Cortés. For example, he started to receive external assistance. Thus six small expeditions reached San Juan de Ulúa or Villa Rica in these weeks. First, there was a ship from Cuba captained by Pedro Barba, carrying thirteen soldiers and one mare. It had been sent with a supply of cassava bread by Diego Velázquez to succour Narváez, of whose disaster he had not yet heard ("There is less news here than in Santo Domingo or in Seville," complained one merchant in Santiago de Cuba in July 1520 in a letter to Castile). Velázquez, who had temporarily established himself in Trinidad in Cuba, must have thought that Barba, his representative in Havana, was reliable. Barba, it will be remembered, had been to Yucatan with Grijalva. On board he carried a letter from Velázquez to Narváez instructing him quickly to send Cortés as a prisoner to Havana. But Barba had always been friendly with Cortés, to whom he had sold five hundred rations of bread in 1518.[84]

At Villa Rica, Cortés' "admiral", Alonso Caballero, lured Pedro Barba to surrender and sent him up to Segura. There Cortés took him aback by greeting him with warmth, and immediately made him captain of his crossbowmen. He gave him other responsible work in the subsequent engagements.[85] He never revived his loyalty to Velázquez.

Another small vessel from Cuba which anchored off Villa Rica was captained by Rodrigo Morejón de Lobera, a conquistador born, like Bernal Díaz, in Medina del Campo. He was similarly tricked by Alonso Caballero. Morejón, with his eight soldiers, six crossbowmen, and a mare, went up to Segura, with, as it turned out, much twine useful for new bowstrings.

A third expedition to reach Villa Rica was one led by Diego de Camargo. He had set off earlier in the year as part of another fleet organised by the restless Governor of Jamaica, Francisco de Garay, to carve out for himself an interest in the, to him, apparently mythical land of Pánuco, which to Cortés was merely the hot territory near the coast to the north of Villa Rica. Like the expedition of 1519, which had discovered the river Mississippi, it was led by Álvarez Pineda. The party left Jamaica with a hundred and fifty men in three ships, with seven horses and some guns, as well as material with which to begin to build a fortress. But though they had landed and begun to build a new Castilian city, they were defeated by the local Indians. They re-embarked, but one of the three ships sank. Álvarez Pineda, veteran of innumerable journeys in these seas, died offshore, as did many others. Camargo, the commander, arrived at Villa Rica, with nearly all the ship's company ill. These sixty nevertheless went up to Cortés at Tepeaca and joined his expedition without any hesitation: better by far a war of conquest on land, these Castilians no doubt considered, than a voyage of discovery by sea.[86]

Fourth, a ship was sent by Garay to relieve Álvarez Pineda. This was captained by Miguel Díez de Aux, a hearty, arrogant, rich and fat

447

conquistador, who had been a bosom friend of Garay ever since they had together found a colossal deposit of gold by a happy chance in the River Ozama in Hispaniola twenty years before. Díez de Aux had been one of the first colonists in Puerto Rico where he had been constable, *alguacil mayor*, and factor of San Juan. He had received a much-prized royal concession in 1511, which entitled his wife Isabel Carrión, from Cáceres, to take, and use, silk clothes in the Indies.[87] Miguel Díez was one of the few Aragonese to venture to the tropics.[88] Now he sailed down the coast, saw no sign of any Spanish ship in that mysterious Pánuco which Garay thought was his promised land, and anchored off Villa Rica. From there he and his fifty soldiers and seven horses went up to Tepeaca to be warmly welcomed by Cortés, who had known Díez de Aux in Hispaniola. Despite being well over forty, Díez de Aux was an asset to the expedition: he had a gift for making friends with those whose rival he had once been.[89]

A fifth vessel was captained by Francisco Ramírez the elder, who also came from Garay, with forty soldiers, ten horses and many crossbows and other arms.

Yet one more source of help was a large ship belonging to Juan de Burgos which reached Villa Rica from the Canary Islands. In fact the ship had come from Spain, and had been sent on the request of Cortés' business friends in Seville, as well as his father. It was laden with supplies, including muskets, gunpowder, crossbows, and crossbow bolts, as well as several horses. Burgos, a Canary Islander (Isleño), and the master of the ship, Francisco de Amedel, with one or two other adventurers, came up to Texcoco and for a time attached themselves, with their invaluable equipment, to Cortés' force.[90]

These ships added about another two hundred men to the expedition. But the men concerned were in the invidious position of being disliked by both the first wave of conquistadors who had come with the *Caudillo* in 1519, and by the survivors of those who had come with Narváez. They were, therefore, known by all kinds of derisive nicknames, such as "clumsy cuts" (*lomos recios*), or "little saddles" (*los de los albardillas*).

On the occasion of the arrival of one of these ships, the story was brought to Cortés that on board there was a royal investigator. Cortés is supposed to have commented, "Let the caravel be welcomed, and congratulated, and, whoever the investigator may be, to his letters, let us give letters . . . and let no one come to whom we do not give plenty of beatings as we gave to Narváez!"[91] The words may be untrue; but they probably express the *Caudillo*'s mood.

Cortés also himself sent two expeditions to purchase new equipment. The first of these, of four vessels, set off for Hispaniola, under Francisco Álvarez Chico and the clever Alonso de Ávila, in order to buy more horses, crossbows, guns and powder, as well as, if possible, to secure more men. They travelled in one of the ships which Cortés had commandeered from Narváez. The *Caudillo* wrote to the president of the *audiencia* there, Rodrigo de Figueroa, with an account of what had transpired in Mexico; and with a request that at least he should not obstruct him, even if he did not wish to assist.[92]

A similar expedition went to Jamaica to buy mares. This was led by Francisco de Solís, one of Cortés' intimates, though a Montañes, from Santander, a man with two nicknames: one, "of the orchard", *de la huerta*, and the other, "of the silk jacket", *del chaquete de sede*, a combination which suggests agricultural and urban qualities rarely united in a single individual.[93] Cortés did not communicate with Cuba, where the Governor and others were becoming frantic for lack of information. That island was in poor shape. One merchant reported in the summer of 1520, exaggerating of course, that on the island there were no men, and no Indians in the mines, only women.[94]

Finally, Cortés organised an expedition in New Spain itself to safeguard his supplies and communications. Two hundred soldiers with twelve crossbowmen and twenty horsemen were led north by the reliable Sandoval in December, into the territory through which they had passed just before they had fought the Tlaxcalans the previous autumn. Cortés thought it was necessary to secure Zautla and Xalacingo, on the road from Vera Cruz to Tlaxcala, which had both recently had new Mexican garrisons. They made the road dangerous on the northern route from Mexico to Vera Cruz.

After several skirmishes, Sandoval rejoined Cortés in thirty days, having secured the fealty to the Emperor Charles V of the lords of these two places (Zautla probably was still ruled by the Castilians' old host, Olintecle), and having recovered a number of bridles and saddles which they found had been stolen from them on their previous journey there. They also returned with a "great spoil of women and boys" branded as slaves, with only eight wounded Castilians and with the loss of three horses. These successes in the north of Tlaxcala had the same effect as the campaign that Cortés had waged to the south and west of Tepeaca. Several other towns previously doubtful about their loyalties came in and sued for peace in return for homage to the King-Emperor of Spain.[95] Whether the leaders of these communities had the slightest knowledge of how their declarations would be later used by Cortés is most doubtful. For the moment homage seemed merely to imply a verbal undertaking to pay tribute to Cortés rather than to Mexico.

Given his new mood of confidence, Cortés had no hesitation in allowing several members of his expedition, mostly captains who had come with Narváez, to return to Cuba. There had continued among these men to be resentment against Cortés' high-handed attitude to people who had accumulated gold in Tenochtitlan. Some were saying that Cortés himself had been seen ordering gold marked with the royal arms of Spain without having the Crown's permission.[96] Others accused Alvarado of taking the gold which his comrades had won gambling rather than proceeding against them (gambling of course being formally illegal); and then, when a certain Gonzalo Bazán had protested, he had had him whipped. (Alvarado in his enquiry in 1529 admitted having Bazán whipped, but said he had done so because he was a blasphemer, had played with marked cards, and told scabrous stories.)[97]

Among the men who were sent home to Cuba were Cortés' old collaborator Andrés de Duero, the spokesman of the rebels at Tlaxcala, as well as both Baltasar and Agustín Bermúdez, men who had been offered by their kinsman, Velázquez, and had rejected, the leadership of Cortés' expedition two years before. Others who left were Juan Bono de Quejo, the brutal expeditionary to Trinidad of 1513, and Bernardino de Quesada, that notary whom Narváez had sent up to Cortés after the latter had arrested Ruiz de Guevara. They also included Leonel de Cervantes, "el comendador", who promised Cortés that he would come back to New Spain with his seven daughters and marry them to conquistadors (he kept the promises), and some who, like Juan Álvarez, would give testimony at an enquiry into Cortés' activities which Diego Velázquez would arrange the following year, and for which historians, if not Cortés himself, have been later grateful.[98] Cortés sent back with these men food (salted dog, maize, turkey), gold (including a good deal with Andrés de Duero, perhaps to be transferred to Cortés' father in Spain), jewels and letters, including one of the last to his wife Catalina and her brother Juan Suárez; the jewels and gold coming from what he had saved at the noche triste. But all these men went down to Vera Cruz, where they remained several months awaiting permission to leave.

Freed, as he assumed, of potential conspiracies from these Narvaecistas, Cortés was able to concentrate on the next stage of his campaign against the Mexicans. He intended to plan his strategy in detail at Tlaxcala where he proposed to spend Christmas 1520 in the company of his allies, as of his master shipwright Martín López. Cortés left Francisco de Orozco, the Italian veteran who had been throughout in command of the artillery, at Tepeaca with sixty men. He himself set off on 13 December for Tlaxcala. He went via Cholula with the horsemen, but the foot soldiers, led as so often by Diego de Ordaz, went direct.[99]

My principal intention and motive in making this war

"And now I insist in the name of His Majesty that my principal intention and motive in making this war and the others that I have made is to bring and reduce the said naturales *to the said knowledge of our holy faith and belief . . ."*

Cortés' military ordinances, Tlaxcala, 22 December 1520

CUITLÁHUAC, THE UNKNOWN emperor, who died of smallpox, was succeeded in Tenochtitlan by his cousin, Cuauhtémoc, a son of his and Montezuma's uncle Ahuítzotl, the emperor before Montezuma. This prince, as the Spanish memorialists rightly call him, was at the time in his mid-twenties. The Spanish writers give appealing impressions of him. They describe him as graceful in both figure and face, with a long head, cheerful countenance, but "grave eyes, which never seemed to waver". He was more white of skin than most Mexicans.[1] He was determined and brave. He had already had successes in war.[2] But he was also as ruthless as were his enemies. Thus he apparently had Montezuma's son Axoacatzin killed, perhaps several such sons, in Turkish style: the purpose was not simply to remove potential rivals (for the throne in Mexico never passed from father to son) but to remove potential spokesmen for a policy of appeasement towards the Castilians.[3]

Cuauhtémoc's mother was Tiacapantzin, heiress of Tlatelolco (daughter, that is, of Moquihuix, the last king there).[4] Until he was grown up, Cuauhtémoc had apparently lived at Ixcateopan, in what is now the state of Guerrero, and which was inhabited by the Chontal Maya. But he seems to have returned to Tenochtitlan some years before the arrival of the Castilians.[5] He then seems to have become the leader of the people of Tlatelolco at a very young age.[6]

The choice of the electors fell on Cuauhtémoc since, young, brave and determined, he was seen as the natural leader of the Mexica in the new and extraordinary circumstances. Presumably the choice was restricted. Many members of the imperial family had died, as Cuitláhuac had done, from smallpox, or in the massacre in the temple precinct, or in the interfamily violence following the battle of Otumba. But Cuauhtémoc had proved himself in the fighting following Alvarado's massacre. According to one source, it had been he who had thrown the fatal stone which had injured Montezuma: if so, an action of far-reaching symbolic significance.[7] This reputation for valour had done much to remove the sense of bad luck suggested among the Mexica by Cuauhtémoc's name: which in Nahuatl means "the setting sun" or "the falling eagle". In addition, he represented the interests of Tlatelolco. That seemed important to those concerned to defend the twin cities.[8] All the same, it is odd that the Mexica, so preoccupied by symbolism, should, in this crisis, have chosen as an emperor a man with Cuauhtémoc's name. Presumably the electors supposed that it would save them precisely from the inglorious end which it seemed to predict.

Cuauhtémoc, it is to be presumed, had been through all the usual education normal for a member of the Mexican upper class: the years at the *calmécac*, with its strict rules, the regular drawing of blood with agave thorns for penance, the deliberate hardening of the body against cold, the learning by heart of the songs of the gods and other texts, the manual work in the temples, the acquisition of calendarial, historical and traditional learning.[9] Equally, we must presume that the formal election of Cuauhtémoc was accompanied by the same kind of speeches made in the past by the leaders of the realm who assembled in the square before the Great Temple.[10] The leaders would have been new but the speeches would have been the same. Thus Coanacochtzin, the King of Texcoco, who was ex officio a senior elector, probably asked his colleagues to choose a mirror in which we will be reflected . . . a mother who will carry us on her shoulders and a prince who will rule. The electors surely also told Cuauhtémoc, as King Nezahualpilli had told his co-electors in 1502 (when Montezuma had been chosen), that they were rich feathers from the wings of those splendid turkeys, the past kings, jewels, and precious stones fallen from the throats and wrists of those royal men . . . Behold, the eyebrows and the lashes, which have fallen from the courageous sovereigns of Mexico . . . extend your hands to the one who pleases you! "Now thou art deified," Cuauhtémoc would have been told, "although thou art human, as are we, although thou art our friend, although thou art our son . . . no more art thou human, as are we, we do not look to thee as human . . . [the god] speaketh forth from thy mouth, thou art his lips, his jaw . . . his tongue . . . his ears."[11]

Then Cuauhtémoc, dressed in priest's robes, would have been taken to the effigy of Huitzilopochtli, just as Cuitláhuac had been only months before. He would have offered the god incense, while conch shells were blown. The four principal advisers would similarly have offered incense. The accepted ritual would have been repeated.

A new king was also found for Tacuba, in the shape of Tetlepanquetzatzin, son of the old king, and a brother-in-law of Montezuma. A lesser version of the same ceremonies would have accompanied his inauguration.

Cuauhtémoc was elected as a spokesman of unrelenting opposition to the Spaniards. He had raised his voice against them. He had criticised Montezuma for his policy of appeasement. He was married to a daughter of Montezuma: indeed, the evidence is that he married two of them: first, a princess apparently called Xuchimatzatzin, who must have been adult, as he was, and by whom he had children;[12] secondly (presumably this wedding was not consummated), Tecuichpo, at this time merely eleven years old, Montezuma's legitimate daughter by his chief wife, and known to have been the favourite of her father. A later husband of this princess (and who could give better evidence?) said that she went through all the formalities of marriage with Cuauhtémoc, including the tying together of the ritual knot between the bride's blouse and the bridegroom's cloak, and presumably the laying of the sacred piece of jade and quetzal feathers in the marriage bed to symbolise the children to be born to them.[13] No doubt this marriage was a political strategem of the kind which in similar circumstances would have been practised in Europe. (It was said that both Atlixcatzin, the *tlacatecatl*, who had been killed in May or June, and who once had been thought of as a possible heir to Montezuma, and Cuitláhuac had been through the same ceremony with Tecuichpo.)[14]

Cuauhtémoc's mission was to fight but it was also, like that of his predecessor, to seek allies. Thus he, like Cuitlahuac, sent messengers to nearby monarchs. But they were still hesitant about helping him: either because they feared Cortés; or because they hated Mexico.

Typical of what happened was in relation to the Tarascans. Cuauhtémoc, like Cuitláhuac, sent ambassadors to the new *cazonci*, Zincicha, at Tzintzuntzan to ask for help. Zincicha was as suspicious of Mexican intentions as his father Zuangua had been. He said, "We know what their real interest is. Let the ambassadors follow my father to the other world and present him there with their petition." The Mexican ambassadors were informed of this response. They said: "If it has to be done, let it be done quickly." Zincicha sacrificed them. He had no intention of helping his people's old enemies.[15] Similar embassies met similar responses. Cuauhtémoc came to realise that the old sway of the Mexica had depended on fear. But that fear was dying.

Further, and despite the military nature of his education, Cuauhtémoc was scarcely ready for the conflict which lay ahead. No Mexican, however brave and astute, could have been. For they, like Cuauhtémoc, had always lived by rules. To those who recall how the French general staff failed to meet the challenge of the Germans in 1940, the experience will not be unfamiliar: *"L'un est affaire de routine et de dressage; l'autre, d'imagination concrète, de souplesses dans l'intelligence et peut-être de caractère . . ."*[16] The Mexican case was a more extreme example of living according to regulations. Cortés, on the other hand, was even by Spanish standards ruthlessly unconventional. He now was planning something unfamiliar to the whole idea of Mexican warfare: a siege, and a siege in the European style, with a blockade. He was making no plans for a battle. No arrangements would be made for the great eagle and jaguar warriors to meet Cortés and his captains in single combat. The entire Mexican population would be put under pressure. There would be a deliberate weakening of the enemy by seeking to cut off their food and their supply of water. Cortés still desired to take the beautiful city of Tenochtitlan without a fight; and then to offer it "as a jewel, as a feather" (as he might have put it had he been a Mexican) to his distant emperor. He must have been disturbed to know how much damage had been caused to the buildings near the Palace of Axayácatl during the fighting there the previous June. Further destruction, he hoped, could be avoided by his new strategy.

Perhaps in these methods we should see a Cortés no longer concerned to echo tactics proven in wars against the Moors; but one determined to reflect new techniques; had not the Great Captain, Hernández de Córdoba, gained his first triumph at Atella in 1495, where Montpensier's army had been defeated by a combination of partial attacks and careful entrenchment? Was not the same true too of Cerignola where, in 1503, the enemy had been induced to charge upon a well-prepared Spanish position? True, the Italian *condottiere* Fabrizio Colonna had sarcastically said, in respect of the latter battle, that the victors were "a ditch, a parapet and an arquebus".[17] But what did it matter provided the Spanish standard waved on the enemy citadel at nightfall? Cuauhtémoc did not seem to make a comparable adjustment.

In these months of late 1520, Cortés was in Tlaxcala laying his plans with skill. Thanks to the ships which had arrived in the late summer and autumn he now had eighty crossbowmen and arquebusiers, and forty horses. He had eight or nine field guns, though he was a little short of powder. He had altogether (that is, including the musketeers and crossbowmen) five hundred and fifty infantrymen, whom he assembled in nine companies of sixty men each.[18] The leaders of these units seem to have been Alvarado, Olid, Sandoval, Gutierre de Badajoz, Verdugo, Rodríguez de Villafuerte, Ircio, Andrés de Monjaraz and Andrés de Tapia. It will be seen that earlier captains, such as García de Albuquerque, Lugo, Ordaz and Ávila, had fallen out of the magic circle of command. The Extremeño superiority was slightly less marked: in addition to Cortés, there were Alvarado, Sandoval, Badajoz, and Rodríguez de Villafuerte. There were two Andalusians (Ircio and Olid), a Basque (Monjaraz), a Castilian (Verdugo), and a Leonés (Tapia, who, however, may have been Extremeño by blood).

Then there were the allies. Cortés grieved much at the death from smallpox of his chief ally of the previous year, Maxixcatzin, of Tlaxcala. Yet Xicotencatl the elder was almost as reliable. He was soon, with "the greatest ceremony", baptised as "Don Lorenzo de Vargas". Maxixcat-zin's twelve-year-old heir (a child of extreme old age) was baptised as "Don Lorenzo".[19]

Cortés received the offer of a large Tlaxcalan army. Numbers as usual are difficult to estimate: López de Gómara wrote that Cortés was offered 80,000 men, "mostly wearing feathers", but the *Caudillo* only wanted a quarter of that figure, since he was uncertain how to feed so many.[20] In fact, he probably took with him 10,000 Tlaxcalans, who mostly ended up being bearers or servants attached to the Castilian soldiers.[21] The Tlaxcalan commander was Chichimecatecle, that deputy to Xicotencatl the younger who had quarrelled with him after the actions against the Spaniards the previous year. He became a Christian before they set out. It must have become evident to him and his men that they were now embarked upon a far more serious engagement than they or their ancestors had ever known before. They responded with energy and dedication. The prospect of destroying the Mexica was intoxicating. Given their arrangement earlier with Cortés, they probably looked on the conflict as their great war against the Mexica, in which they had managed to find some skilful technicians to assist them in the fighting; perhaps afterwards to be rejected, and sent home, with all their Virgins and St Christophers.

The entire expedition, both Castilians and Tlaxcalans, assembled in the square in front of the main temple of Tlaxcala. Cortés, dressed in a short garment of velvet, spoke to them.[22] No doubt what he said bore some relation to what he claimed, in a letter to the King in May 1522, to have propounded: how the Castilians were fighting against a barbarian people; how, in order to serve the King, they had to protect their lives; and how they had powerful allies. The Castilians, Cortés insisted, had a just and good cause.[23] The Mexica, he said, were in rebellion. That argument, of course, depended for its validity on the meeting between Cortés and Montezuma with the latter's lords the previous January. Cortés had no intention of going back upon the famous concession said to have been made there.

But the principal reason for the war, the *Caudillo* claimed, was to preach the faith of Jesus Christ, "even though," he added with unusual if accurate candour, "at the same time it brings us both honour and profit: things which very rarely can be found in the same bag."

The speech ended with another nice statement of how the service to God and King could be combined with enrichment for those taking part: "For the business of Mexico is all these things."[24] Cortés then caused his herald (*pregonero*), Antón García, to read out a statement of purposes and rules for the conduct of the war which his new secretary, Juan de Ribera, "the one-eyed", a native of Ribera del Fresno in Extremadura, perhaps a remote relation of his own, had written for him.

This document first denounced the veneration of the idols. The purpose of the war against Mexico was to give to the local people "a knowledge of our holy faith", as well as to "subjugate them, under the imperial and royal yoke and dominion of His Majesty, to whom, legally, the lordship of these parts now belongs". The aim of Cortés could not have been expressed more directly. It was conquest. The months of subterfuge about intentions were over.

There followed seventeen instructions. The most important of these were that blasphemy by a soldier was to be punished by a fine, of which a third would go to the first brotherhood of Christ (a religious club of lay well-wishers at that time in formation). There was to be no duelling. No one was to laugh at the captains. No one was to sleep except where quartered. On the march, everyone was to keep together. When fighting began, no one was to hide in the baggage: an extraordinary instruction which presumably betrayed something of what had occurred in the recent past. No women were to be violated. No one was to put cities to the sack "without the permission of Cortés and the consent of the municipality of Villa Rica de la Vera Cruz" – that useful corporation which could be conjured up whenever necessary to make a point, and then forgotten as its "councillors" rode through territories distant from it. Such a sack would not come till after victory and the expulsion of all enemies from the town concerned. There were instructions as to when drums were to be played, how discipline was to be maintained, and how no one was to rob any Indian. All gold and silver, pearls and precious stones in any way obtained, featherwork, cloth, and slaves were to be taken to Cortés, who would subtract the Royal Fifth. There were to be fixed prices for horseshoes, as for clothing, since scandalous charges had recently been made for both commodities. Finally, there was a ban on gambling: with an exception which seemed unjust; for, in Cortés' own lodgings, cards could be "moderately" played.[25]

The *Caudillo* also made a speech directed at the allies: in which he reassured them that they would soon be free of Mexican servitude. He pledged himself again to secure for them many benefits in return for their support.[26]

Though Cortés was setting off with a force similar in size if perhaps superior in quality to that with which he had gone to Tenochtitlan about fourteen months previously, his strategy was now different from what it had been before. In 1519 he had hoped to impose his personality on Montezuma and use him as a puppet. Now he planned to defeat Montezuma's successor in battle.

The critical element in the *Caudillo*'s scheme to reduce Tenochtitlan admittedly remained incomplete: namely, the completion of the brigantines. When Cortés left Tlaxcala for Tenochtitlan on 27 December 1520, Martín López was still working on these vessels on the river

Zahuapan. Cortés' plan, even whilst still in Tlaxcala, was to establish a base for himself at Texcoco, on the eastern shore of the Lake of Mexico. There he would wait till the brigantines could be brought overland (in pieces) and assembled there. This tactic was in its way as breathtaking as Cortés' plan of campaign: he knew that, even despite the smallpox, the labour force would be available for such a colossal effort. Almost the only equivalent is Lord Kitchener's construction of a railway to the Sudan to beat the Mahdi.

Cortés' expedition spent their first night away from Tlaxcala at Texmelucan, a town close to the modern San Martín Texmelucan, which formerly belonged to Huexotzinco.[27] They then moved up to cross the mountain range which shelters the great lake by a pass now known as that of the River Frío, among the headwaters of the River Atoyac, about halfway between the "pass of Cortés" (over which the expedition had travelled in November 1519) and the yet more northerly pass of Xaltepec-Apan (the route Cortés had taken in retreat in June 1520).[28] This central pass was then "steeper and rougher than the other entrances" to the Valley of Mexico. Cortés supposed that he would find the Mexica unprepared and therefore that they would offer little resistance there.[29]

In this appreciation Cortés was not quite correct. The expedition did spend the night of 28 December on the pass in cold weather with no interference: a night in the open at over twelve thousand feet in December would be a trial for anyone.[30] But next day they found the path onwards blocked by recently felled trees. There were minor ambushes.[31] The vanguard, led by the son of the explorer Ponce de León, formed the distinct impression that they had an enemy behind every tree. But the Tlaxcalans removed the obstructions. In a short time, the Castilians were once again marvelling at the view of the lake, the distant sight of Tenochtitlan, and the great activity which lay below them.

This time Bernal Díaz did not evoke the precedent of *Amadís de Gaula*. He most have known that what lay ahead was a struggle fiercer than any envisaged in those high-flown pages. Instead, he recorded that all those who had been on the previous expedition were sad at the recollection of those of their comrades who had died since their last entry into the Valley of Mexico. All swore, he said, never again to leave that promised land unless they did so victorious. With that somewhat tautological resolution taken (for if they did not win they could scarcely expect to live), they moved on happily, "as if we were on a journey of pleasure". They could see that the Mexica were busy sending up smoke signals to warn of their arrival. But on the night of 29 December nothing stopped the expedition from reaching Coatepec, a small town which was the centre of a densely populated little province ruled by a *calpixqui* appointed by Texcoco.[32] (According to legend, Coatepec had been an early settlement of the Mexica. Once they had built a fine city,

Huitzilopochtli ordered them to leave. The Mexica were reluctant, an attitude supported by Huitzilopochtli's sister Coyolxauhqui, "she of the golden bells". Huitzilopochtli decapitated Coyolxauhqui on the ball court, and the Mexica continued their journey.)

During the night, Ixtlilxochitl, the brother of both Cacama and Coanacochtzin, kings of Texcoco, and the disgruntled rival of both for the throne of that people, came to Cortés and confirmed his intention to fight on his side against Mexico, giving him a golden chain as a sign of peace. Thereafter Ixtlilxochitl was a persistent and at times influential ally of the Castilians, though it was never clear how many men he had at his disposal: it seemed sometimes a large household, sometimes an army.[33] He too, like the Tlaxcalans, probably assumed that the expedition was his, and that he was fortunate to find such helpful military advisers in the shape of the Castilians.

The horsemen whom Cortés as usual sent ahead came back to him the next day, 30 December, to say that they had seen an array led by seven lords from Texcoco coming forward carrying golden banners of peace. The lords soon made their appearance. Their leader addressed Cortés: "Malinche, our lord and king, Coanacochtzin, sends to say that he covets your friendship. He is waiting for you peacefully in Texcoco. The squadrons who have been waiting in the ravines to attack you on your way down were sent by Cuauhtémoc and have nothing to do with us." They then offered Cortés the golden banners. Cortés welcomed this peaceful greeting and of course accepted the present. But both he and his captains believed the show of friendship to be a ruse. After all, Coanacochtzin, brother and successor of Cacama, was Cuauhtémoc's friend and ally.

That night Cortés and his expedition slept at Coatlinchan, an old city five miles from Texcoco to which it was then subject. The Texcocans would have liked the Castilians to have remained there. But Cortés' whole strategy depended on being in their city, with its easy access to the lake. So the next day he pressed towards there as soon as he could.

The Castilians were uncertain how they would be received in Texcoco. Until the end, they believed that combat was likely. Yet the chiefs who had come from Coanacochtzin had promised quarters for them in the centre of the city. These indeed had been prepared, as Cortés discovered when, the following day, 31 December 1520, he reached the city at noon. The palace of Nezahualpilli, where these preparations had been made, was in the heart of the place. It was so large that, Cortés thought, twice as many men as the Castilians had with them could have stayed there. But otherwise the welcome in Texcoco was ominous. For there was no one in the streets.[34]

Cortés did not wish to provoke trouble. So he caused his herald to tell the invading army to keep to their lodgings under pain of death.[35] He also sent Alvarado and Olid, with a small detachment, to climb the great temple. From there they had a good view of the lake. To their alarm they could see much of the population moving out of the town in canoes across the lake. The news soon came that Coanacochtzin had also fled to Mexico.[36]

This flight angered Cortés. He, therefore, permitted a sack of the city. As had occurred during the Tepeaca campaign, the few men found were killed, and the women and children were declared slaves, to be sold by public auction.[37] Ixtlilxochitl claimed to have tried to prevent these brutalities. But the Tlaxcalans were uninterested.[38]

Texcoco was, of course, the second city of the Mexican empire. The place covered 1,100 acres and had a population of about 25,000 people.[39] Her rulers, closely related to those of Tenochtitlan, also looked back to a mythical founder who, only about ten generations before, had led their ancestors out of the caves and woods to live by the lake. Their history was more peaceable than that of the Mexica: thus on several occasions the informants of Sahagún were able to report of such and such a Texcocan monarch, much as Austrians did of their Frederick III, "Ruled seventy years. Nor did anything happen in his time."[40] Texcocans looked back to the philosopher and poet-king Nezahualcoyotl, "the Harun-al-Rashid of the New World", a prince who not only toyed with the idea of a single god, but who would walk the streets of his capital disguised in order to "see the weaknesses and needs in order to remedy them".[41] He built several beautiful gardens, including one a few miles to the south-east, at Tetzcotzingo, where his gardeners sought to acclimatise plants from all over the region, where there was an outdoor theatre, and where the King had been used to sleep in a high round bedroom, with a remarkable view over the lake. This pleasure dome contained many of the beautiful rock sculptures for which the Mexica were well known: one was a large carved circular stone basin.[42] Nezahualcoyotl held competitions in music and poetry here, and listened to birds in cages, brought from remote regions, their song being so loud that it was impossible to speak.[43] (Some of the *ahuehuete* trees in these gardens can still be seen.)

Many of Texcoco's numerous fine buildings were as beautiful as those in the "Great Venice" on the lake. Several of them had patios, around which the principal rooms were arranged, as in Andalusia. A few were built on terraces. Some of these houses, including probably that in which Cortés and his expedition were lodged, were built on a frame of timbers so large "that no industry or human force could be thought to have put them in their place". That enabled them to have halls a hundred and twenty feet or more square, for these great timbers were supported by wooden pillars on stone bases.[44] Most of them had been washed with white bitumen on the outside: "Anyone who saw them from a distance might, unless forewarned, think that he was looking at little hills covered with snow."[45] A contemporary plan showed the layout of one of these buildings, with, in the centre of the main courtyard, two braziers, whose maintenance was the responsibility of subject towns.[46] The great temple was higher by four or five steps than that in Tenochtitlan.[47] The land adjacent to, and farmed by, Texcoco was fertile, being crossed by many streams. Texcoco's place in the Mexican empire had been important: the great kings of Texcoco, Nezahualcoyotl and Nezahualpilli, father and son, had together reigned a hundred years and had usually given good advice to their cousins, the emperors across the water. Those kings had also rallied with zest to the Mexican wars of conquest.[48] Indeed, some chroniclers attributed to Texcoco some of Mexico's conquests and even at one time a senior partnership in the Alliance.[49] If enthusiasm for poetry and art, not to speak of elegance of language, were a mark of superiority among nations, the reputation would have been deserved. The city was known for its textiles and for its pottery, in particular its round cups, from which to drink chocolate. Those who worked these things lived, as their fellows did in Tenochtitlan and Tlatelolco, in special quarters. An early fifteenth-century king of Texcoco had encouraged potters to come there from other places. Now they were organised in something like guilds.[50]

Texcoco's high level of living derived partly from the system of imperial tribute. Fifteen designated towns were responsible for the needs of the palaces and the temples for six months, and another fifteen had the same duty for the other six months.[51]

The Castilians remained in Texcoco for three days with no one coming to see them. The fear caused by the bloodshed directed at the men, and the enslavement of the women and children, evidently acted as a ferocious restraint. The conquistadors fed themselves by raiding the reserves in Texcoco, which were far from substantial: a fact which suggested that the Texcocans' withdrawal had been long planned.[52] So the Tlaxcalans passed the time setting fire to two beautiful palaces, both once belonging to the late King Nezahualpilli, thereby destroying the royal archives of the Texcocan and Mexican kingdoms which, with their maps, codices and genealogical records, had been kept there.[53]

Despite this vandalism, it was still possible for the Castilians to find a puppet monarch to act in the place of Coanacochtzin. The choice fell on one of his many bastard brothers, Tecocoltzin. But that prince survived only a month. Cortés then had recourse to a boy, Huaxpitzcactzin, another younger, and also illegimate, brother of the late ruler. This boy, like Tecocoltzin also, was optimistically named "Fernando Cortés". He was to be completely under Castilian influence, having Antonio de Villaroel (from Medina del Campo) as his tutor, and Pedro Sánchez Farfán (from Seville) with the bachelor Ortega (probably from Ecija) as his guards.[54]

After three days, the lords of two Texcocan towns, Huexotla and Coatlinchan (where the Spanish had spent the night before arriving at Texcoco), and one in Chalco (Tenango), came to see Cortés. They wept in his presence. They said that, in the past, they had fought against Cortés unwillingly, on the orders of the Mexica. They begged Cortés to forgive them. Thenceforth they would do everything which he commanded. Cortés did not know exactly to what they were referring, but presumed (rightly) that it had been they who had mounted the minor attacks on him on his way down from the pass of the River Frío. So he firmly stated, through Marina, that he believed that he had in the past treated these cities well. But he understood that the women and families of the citizens of the towns of these lords had fled to the hills. If the lords and their towns wished to be friends, they had to bring them back. The lords were displeased.

Cuauhtémoc was also displeased to hear of these negotiations, as of course he soon did. He sent messengers telling these lords that they ought to side with him in what looked like being a war, and that they should therefore go immediately to Tenochtitlan. The Castilians, he said, were certain to be defeated. The lords concerned seized these messengers and brought them to Cortés. Cortés, though he realised that the Mexica intended war, was now anxious to present himself to those few who remained of the people of Texcoco as a man of peace, for he still hoped to use them as allies, and their territory as his base. So he sent messages to Cuauhtémoc through these lords. He wanted to be a friend of the Mexica, as he had been before. The chiefs with whom he had fought the previous year were dead. The past should, therefore, be forgotten. He, Cortés, did not wish to fight them, for he did not wish to have to destroy their lands and cities. With that he sent the messengers to Tenochtitlan. The lords of Coatlinchan and Huexotla were pleased. From then on they worked with Cortés who, in the name of the Emperor Charles V, gravely pardoned them for their past misdeeds.[55]

One reason why Cortés was well received in these cities was commercial. The merchants of the region were sophisticated. But in recent generations, they had been prevented by the Mexica from trading as they liked, and in particular with the tropical regions. Tenochtitlan and Tlatelolco had insisted on a monopoly. So to buy goods from the region of Vera Cruz, the merchants of Coatlinchan had had to work through the Mexica.[56] This monopoly was now threatened. The agents of this change were certain to be popular.

32

They were all lords

"I made a sign that I wished to talk to them . . . and asked them why they were mad and wanted to be destroyed. I asked if there was among them some senior lord of the city because I wished to speak to him. And they replied that the entire multitude of people prepared for war which I saw there were all lords."

Cortés, Third Letter to Charles V, 1522

BEFORE CORTÉS RECEIVED any reply to his message to Cuauhtémoc, he began a journey of reconnaissance round the lake. His immediate purpose was to find food for his Tlaxcalan allies. But, for military reasons, a tour was also desirable. He knew the north of the lake. But apart from his journey across the causeways when arriving in Tenochtitlan for the first time in November 1519 he was ignorant of what happened to the south. So leaving about three hundred and fifty Castilians at Texcoco under Sandoval (who increasingly appeared in the role of second-in-command, if technically still described merely as constable, *alguacil*), Cortés set off with two hundred men (eighteen mounted, ten arquebusiers, and thirty crossbowmen) and with what was said by chroniclers to be about three to four thousand allies. Olid and Andrés de Tapia were jointly lieutenants of this expedition. They made their way along the south-east and then the south of Lake Texcoco to the strategically important town of Iztapalapa, once the fiefdom of the late emperor Cuitláhuac, where, the year before, the expedition had spent their last night before moving on to the causeway, on the last stage of their journey to Tenochtitlan.[1]

The march from Texcoco to Iztapalapa was twenty miles. When the Castilians approached the latter city, the people came out to face them in arms. As it seemed possible that the action might be difficult, the Mexica took a dramatic decision: a little way to the north of the town, they made a breach in the dyke of Nezahualcoyotl leading to Atzacualco, which divided the salt from the sweet lake. This led to a rush of salt water from the eastern part of the lake of Texcoco into the fresh water in the smaller, western portion of it. The aim was to flood Iztapalapa (two-thirds of the place was built over the water), and drown the Castilians.

The Mexica thought that this drastic measure would destroy the

Castilian offensive. But it did not do so. Cortés and his allies rode into the pretty city, killed a great many people, expelled the rest of the population, and then withdrew before the water there became so deep that they could not escape. Had the Castilians spent the night at Iztapalapa, as they had planned, they would have been drowned. As it was, they lost most of their gunpowder for their arquebuses. Cortés started to overstate the number of those whom he killed: a sure sign of the developing savagery of the conflict. But he blamed the Tlaxcalans for the slaughter of the local people: "The Indians, our allies, seeing that God had given them victory, only understood that they should kill and sack." Ixtlilxochitl, Cortés' Texcocan ally, here fought something like a duel with one of the chiefs of Iztapalapa, who had been charged to eize him and take him alive to Tenochtitlan. After Ixtlilxochitl had captured his opponent, he had him tied hand and foot and burned him alive on a "divine hearth". Only one conquistador died.[2]

The expedition in the end spent the night in the open near the town. When they awoke, they saw that the water from the west lake was flowing into the other. The two lakes were now approximately level. The lake to the east was full of Mexican warriors in canoes, expecting to capture the whole expedition. Cortés then returned to Texcoco, fighting most of the way. The Mexica assumed that this was a defeat for the Castilians. They themselves never willingly retired from positions once attained. The surmise cheered them, though the conclusion was falsely based.[3]

The next few weeks were spent similarly. For example, the lords of Ozumba and Tepecoculuco, both Chalco towns, and then the lord of Mixquic, the city which the Castilians had, the previous year, thought of as "little Venice" ("Venezuela"), on the southern lake shore, came to ask Cortés for his forgiveness, and to discuss the possibility of becoming vassals of the Christian emperor whom Cortés served. Cortés delivered to the lords a reprimand for their disloyalty in the past and then agreed to their request.[4]

But nothing was yet certain among these lakeside towns. Thus the lords of Coatlinchan and the other places which had submitted to Cortés in January 1521 told the *Caudillo* that they were being threatened by the Mexica. For those towns had begun to cut maize for the Castilian expedition. Their farmers had been attacked in the fields by the Mexica, who needed those products themselves, either as confiscations or in the form of tribute. Cortés dispatched some small units (fifty Tlaxcalans, say, with perhaps three or four Castilians) to try and protect the fields.

The lords of Chalco and Tlamanalco now sent word that they too would like peace with Cortés. But they said that they could not do as they wished because they still had their Mexican garrisons.

The offer of peace from Chalco seemed a really important change. Cortés, therefore, sent Sandoval and Francisco de Lugo, with a force of the same size as he himself had taken to Iztapalapa, to "remove the Mexica". Outside Chalco, in maize fields whose produce the Mexica definitely did not want to lose, Sandoval fought several difficult battles, but as usual emerged successful, with few losses. The Tlaxcalan allies apparently fought especially well in these engagements, perhaps as a result of rudimentary training in methods of European war by Alonso de Ojeda the previous winter. Afterwards they were able to seize some of the cotton cloths and the salt of which their long dispute with the Mexica had deprived them.

Chalco was then re-established, formally at least, as an independent city with no need to pay tribute to Mexico for the first time for half a century. The alteration was striking. A lord from that city insisted on returning to Texcoco with Sandoval to thank Cortés in person. That lord also said that their recent lord, who had died, like so many others, of smallpox, had wished Cortés to install his sons as lords of Chalco, since he apparently had known that men with beards would come from beyond the sunrise to rule these territories. Cortés gladly performed the acts of inauguration: the elder son became lord of Chalco; the younger, of Tlamanalco and Ayotzingo.[5]

After this battle, Cortés sent eight Mexican prisoners (whom Sandoval had taken at Chalco) to Cuauhtémoc in order to suggest peace; in which case, he, Cortés would pardon him. But no answer came. Cuauhtémoc was determined to fight Cortés to the finish, with no concessions, though he was prepared to make as many tactical offers as were necessary to the empire's subject towns for the remission of tribute in return for a continuing alliance against the interlopers. But none seem to have responded positively. The leaders of all of them were dazzled by the thought of the possible fall of the Mexica, as they were by the magnetism of Cortés and his friends.[6]

At the end of January Cuauhtémoc seems to have been formally inaugurated as emperor.[7] He busied himself reinvigorating the defences of Tenochtitlan, making ready the capital for a battle for which there was no precedent: deepening channels beneath bridges, making strong entrenchments, preparing darts and missiles, and even making long lances to which the Mexica could attach some of the swords which they had captured from the Castilians the previous year.

Like all Mexican monarchs, Cuauhtémoc began his reign with a military initiative. But there was nothing ritualistic about his campaign down the east side of the lake. It was designed to punish the cities such as Coatlinchan which had established good relations with the Castilians. Two lakeside towns were on this occasion persuaded to support the Mexica. Cortés, however, once again set out and, with two hundred foot soldiers and two small field guns, scattered his enemies. He afterwards burned the buildings of these allies. The leaders of both then came, as so many others had done, to apologise to Cortés, and to beg him to let them alone thereafter, undertaking never to have anything more to do with the Mexica. Cortés did pardon these men. He still needed allies.

By the end of January Cortés assumed that the brigantines would be ready. So he sent the ever-reliable Sandoval by the northernmost route to Tlaxcala to bring these secret weapons to Texcoco on the backs of Tlaxcalan bearers.

The constable (*alguacil*) thereupon set off, with a small force of Castilians and Texcocans, on the way stopping to afford exemplary punishment to the town of Calpulalpan, known to the Castilians as Pueblo Morisco, on the border of Tlaxcala and Texcoco. This place was known for the Mexica's execution of forty-five Castilians under Juan de Alcántara who had been ambushed there on the way to Vera Cruz during the siege the previous year. When he captured their temple, Sandoval found all the signs of sacrifice: the skins of horses and the blood of Castilians, while, in the prison, there was a message on the wall: "Here the unhappy Juan Yuste was held prisoner": Yuste, who may have come from the serene town of that name in the Sierra de Gredos, had accompanied Narváez and had been designated a magistrate in the shadowy settlement of San Salvador founded by Narváez.[7] He had been named by Narváez to command the treacherous ambush against Cortés near Cempoallan which never matured.

There was never any criticism of Sandoval's action. Campaigns are won by punishment as well as war.[8] Before setting out, Sandoval apparently asked Cortés: "What shall I do if the Indians of the Pueblo Morisco come out talking peacefully?" Cortés is said to have answered: "Even if they come out peacefully, kill them."[9]

Sandoval then went on with thirty men towards Tlaxcala. But he had only reached Hueyotlipan when he met Martín López, the organiser of the building of the brigantines, and the Tlaxcalan commander, Chichi-mecatecle. Two thousand bearers were bringing food to Texcoco, but another eight thousand were carrying planks and timber shaped and cut for assembly into brigantines.[10] So Sandoval and a file of bearers six miles long entered Texcoco about 15 February, with drums being beaten and conch shells sounded, and with cries both inspiring and curious: "*¡ Viva, viva el emperador, nuestro señor!*"; and the even stranger combination, "*¡ Castilla, Castilla, y Tlaxcala, Tlaxcala!*"[11] The feat of carrying boats so far across country was a remarkable one almost without precedent. But even more astonishing was the dedication of the Tlaxcalans to the struggle against their Mexican cousins. It showed that it was not only the Dutch who knew that "the less we differ, we more we hate".

Those Castilians who had been left at Texcoco during all these expeditions around the lake, under Cortés or under Sandoval, had already been busy either digging, or organising the digging, of channels in which the brigantines could be taken down from Texcoco into the lake itself. The next few weeks were spent in completing the channels and assembling the boats. "Do the work well and look to me for rewards," Cortés often said to the men working on these boats (though that promise, like many made in war, would be forgotten).[12] Among those occupied in these tasks was Hernando Alonso, the sixty-year-old *converso* blacksmith, who had come to New Spain with Narváez and who, having survived the *noche triste*, and the death of his wife Beatriz de Ordaz (from a fever) during the Tepeaca campaign, was reported to have "hammered many nails into the brigantines".[13]

Cuauhtémoc, meantime, had another indication of Cortés' tactics in February when the *Caudillo* decided on a second journey of reconnaissance, this time round the north side of the lake. Once again, Cortés set off with Alvarado, Olid and about half his army – twenty-five horse, three hundred foot, six small field pieces, together with a large number of Tlaxcalans.[14] They were attacked the first day, but to no effect. On the second day, having slept in the open, they entered Xaltocan, a town which had been built on an island off the coast. It was then ruled by the *tlatoani* of nearby Guautitlan. Once the Otomí capital, the Tepanecs, with the Mexica then acting as their mercenaries, had captured it in the late fourteenth century. The Mexica had controlled it for many years. Now they sought to protect it in the most obvious way by destroying the causeway to it. But the plan was betrayed by two Indians, probably Otomís. These men told Cortés where an old causeway still half existed. The Castilian infantry were able to get across the lake there and to sack the town, surely treating it more harshly than the previous conquerors had done. They returned to the mainland to spend the night on the edge of the lake, again in the open.[15]

Next day Cortés reached the western side of the lake at Guautitlan itself, which seemed large and beautiful, if empty: the people had fled either into the nearby hills or to Tenochtitlan.[16] There was neither food there nor activity.

Two more cities which suffered a Castilian visitation had also once been Tepanec fiefdoms: first Teneyuca, on the shore, to the north of Tenochtitlan; and then the old Tepanec capital, Azcapotzalco, the goldsmiths' city. At Teneyuca they presumably saw and passed by the elegant pyramid which seems to have been a replica of that which they had come to know at Tlatelolco. At Azcapotzalco, the goldsmiths' workshops would probably have been ransacked but, though the Castilians knew all about their riches from their earlier stay in Tenochtitlan (had not Velázquez de León among others ordered gold plate to be made there?), there is no mention of them. Perhaps the goldsmiths had successfully hidden everything. This city was known as a place where there were two *tlatoani*, one Tepanec and one Mexican. But neither was present on this visit of Cortés. Nor were there to be seen any of the slaves for the selling of which the market at Azcapotzalco was well known.

Finally, on the fifth day after leaving Texcoco, the Castilian expedition reached Tacuba, the third, smallest, and least important member of the Triple Alliance, which, with Tenochtitlan and Texcoco, made the Mexican empire what it was. This was Cortés' goal.

Tacuba was on the landward side of Tenochtitlan's western-facing causeway. It was of course there that Cortés had retreated after the *noche triste*. Though small, it was the main Tepanec city and so might have been expected to have rallied to the anti-Mexican cause. For that people had not forgotten their defeat by the Mexica ninety years before. Few people forgot anything in the Valley of Mexico. Yet no such recall of ancient emotions had been forthcoming the previous year. Nor was it so in 1521. The reason no doubt was the close connection between the (imposed) kings of Tacuba and the Mexican royal house: the new king Tetlepanquetzatzin had been Montezuma's first brother-in-law. So instead of the Castilians being received in peace, there was heavy fighting before the Castilians entered the town and lodged in a large house which they remembered from their dark night there the previous year. The Tlaxcalans then busied themselves with their favourite pastime of burning the rest of this to them long-hostile city, "as a punishment for helping Mexico".[17]

The following day Cortés returned to the causeway where so many of his friends had died. It had been rebuilt. The Mexica who, of course, had come to know all his movements, tried by taunts to draw the Castilians on to a point where, from lake and land, they could be surrounded. The conquistadors indeed rode farther than they should have done. They were well within range of stones cast by Mexican *atlatls* from the rooftops. Several Castilians were killed before Cortés who, at one moment, believed himself lost, ordered a retreat in bad order.[18]

Cortés spent six days in Tacuba. He fought there many skirmishes. Several times he made succesful sallies along the causeway, improvising new tactics for this method of fighting, and seeing how different it would be were he to have brigantines to assist from the waterside. The Tlaxcalan allies shouted loudly and often at their old enemies inside Tenochtitlan. They made a traditional style of preparation for war as it had been fought between Tlaxcala and Tenochtitlan in the old days. With banners, feathers and paint, "it was certainly a thing to see" ("*sin duda una cosa para ver*"). The feathers waved, but the war was serious.

Cortés had some exchanges with the Mexica. Indeed that was one of the main purposes, he subsequently said, of his coming to Tacuba. He hoped to persuade Cuauhtémoc to talk. But that was not easily arranged. The Mexica were at least as proud, in their way, as the Spaniards. On one occasion the Mexica shouted along the causeway: "Come in, come in and take your pleasure!" and again, "Do you think that there is another Montezuma to let you do what you please?" "Are you mad?" Cortés asked one morning. "Do you wish to be destroyed? Is there not a lord of the city [*algun señor principal*] to whom I can speak?" A Mexican replied in terms which should have roused some admiration among the Castilians: "We are all lords [*todos los que veis son señores*], so you can say what you want to any one of us." One of Cortés' men shouted that the Mexica would die of hunger. A Mexican replied that, when they needed food, they "would eat the Castilians and the Tlaxcalans". One of the Mexica threw Cortés some maize tortillas in contempt, saying, "Take and eat this, if you are hungry. We are in no need of it."[19]

Having seen again at first hand the strategic position of Tacuba, Cortés returned to Texcoco by the way that he had come, stopping at Guautitlan and Acolman, fighting most of the way with determined if badly organised Mexica. There was one ambush near Acolman – it must have been close to Teotihuacan – where Cortés and his horsemen startled a large body of Indians into a general retreat. The Castilians rode down the enemy with their lances. The *Caudillo* recorded the exhilarating victory as "a most beautiful thing".[20] Had not Achilles dealt just so with the Trojans?

Cortés' return to Texcoco coincided with more offers of vassaldom on the part of towns discontented with Mexican rule (for example, several from the coast north of Villa Rica, such as Tuxpan, Matalcingo, and Nauhtla). But it was hard for Cortés to offer the support which the towns said that they needed in return. Even the far more strategically important Chalco and Tlamanalco continued to call out for help after their formal adherence to the Castilian cause, but many of the Spaniards were wounded, exhausted, or merely weary from always wearing armour.[21]

It was about now that the *Caudillo* faced a new and dangerous threat to his authority. A soldier named Rojas told him that a number of conquistadors – nearly three hundred, according to Cervantes de Salazar – were planning to kill him and put one of the company commanders, Francisco Verdugo, Diego Velázquez's brother-in-law and sometime mayor of Trinidad (in Cuba) in his place. The leader of the plot was a friend of Narváez and Velázquez, Antonio de Villafaña, a native of Zamora who had been treasurer on Grijalva's expedition, and who had accompanied Narváez to New Spain. He had the post of treasurer of the goods of the dead – a task which sounded almost Mexican in its style but was all the same of much importance among the Castilians, all of whom had heirs, even if they did not always have possessions.[22] The plan of Villafaña was that, while Cortés was dining with his captains and favourites (Alvarado, Lugo, Olid, Tapia, Sandoval, Marín and Ircio), a letter would be brought to him purporting to be from his father.

While Cortés was occupied with reading this forgery, he and his close friends would be stabbed to death (it was important to distract the attention of Cortés since, like all Spanish knights, he always dined with his sword ready). In Vera Cruz, Narváez himself would escape to Cuba on a caravel belonging to his ex-commissary, the *converso* from Burgos, Pedro de Maluenda (though Maluenda himself had begun to work with Cortés by this time as commissary).[23]

When the soldier had told Cortés of this somewhat Roman conspiracy, the *Caudillo* went instantly with Sandoval and some others to Villafaña's quarters. Sandoval as *alguacil* arrested the conspirator and seized from him a list of persons who had agreed to support him. Villafaña was tried before the muncipality: the quartermaster Olid, the *alcaldes* (Marín and Ircio), and Cortés as *justicia mayor* officiated. Villafaña was condemned to be hanged: a penalty which was instantly carried out, after the prisoner had confessed to Fr. Díaz.

Cortés cleverly gave out that Villafaña had at the time of his arrest swallowed the list of plotters, and pretended thereafter that he did not know who had been against him. In fact, the confiscated list named fourteen prominent enemies, whose names Cortés never revealed but whose identities it would have been easy to guess. These men continued to conspire but most left for Cuba in a few weeks. Verdugo, however, said that he knew nothing about Villafaña's schemes. That may just have been true: beneficiaries of conspiracies do not always support those working on their behalf.[24]

The only other casualty of the plot was Diego Díaz, master of a ship belonging to Juan Bono de Quejo, who had agreed to take Narváez and some others back to Cuba for a fee of three hundred pesos. This sailor was tried (by the municipality of Villa Rica under the presidency of Alonso de Ávila), and condemned to be hanged.[25]

Cortés then appointed a bodyguard for himself under a trusted friend, Alonso de Quiñones, also like Villafaña a native of Zamora, who had come to notice when he saved Cortés during the retreat from Tenochtitlan on the *noche triste*; and it was said that thereafter Cortés slept always in a coat of mail.

About the same time, one more expedition joined Cortés from the coast. This, the seventh since the retreat from Tenochtitlan, was a little party from Santo Domingo sent as a result of the efforts of Francisco Álvarez Chico to interest opinion there in Cortés' activities. One settler in Santo Domingo who had listened to Cortés' emissary with attention had been Rodrigo de Bastidas, an experienced conquistador who had begun life as a businessman in Triana, and who had in 1500 discovered the Gulf of Uraba, in company with the famous pilot, Juan de la Cosa. One of the few men of that time to be given a good character by Las Casas in his history, Bastidas was all the same a trader in slaves from the mainland,

and the owner of an *encomienda*, with a few Indians and much land and cattle in Hispaniola.[26] He had carried out the first systematic search for pearls on the north coast of Venezuela in 1505.[27] He must have known Cortés before 1510. He was now chief collector in Santo Domingo of the tax known as the *almojarifazgo*, he was one of the three leading shipbuilders of his island, and was also in partnership with the richest Genoese financiers in Seville. Bastidas was facing economic difficulties because of the collapse of the population in Santo Domingo, as well as of events at home.[28] Probably one or other of the successful Genoese merchants by then established in Hispaniola shared the costs and risks of this assistance to Cortés: one of them, Jacome de Castellón, was turning the sugar mill at Azúa, where the *Caudillo* had spent so much of his twenties, into a successful enterprise. The Genoese did much to finance the establishment of other parts of the Spanish empire. It would have been surprising if they had had no interest in the affairs of New Spain.[29]

At all events Bastidas was responsible for fitting out an important expedition of succour for Cortés which, in three ships (a *nao*, the *María*, of a hundred and fifty tons, and two smaller caravels), included many arquebuses, a large store of gunpowder and swords, not to speak of two hundred men, sixty horses, and a Franciscan from Seville, Fr. Pedro Melgarejo de Urrea.[30]

The latter brought some papal bulls (*bulas de cruzada*), whereby the men of the expedition might absolve themselves if they had done anything during these wars which they should have confessed. As might be expected, the good friar in consequence later returned rich and prosperous to Spain.[31] But before that he had become a close friend of Cortés who may for a time have used him as a confessor instead of Fr. Bartolomé de Olmedo.

One of Bastidas' ships was captained by a young adventurer from Burgos, Gerónimo Ruiz de la Mota, a member of yet one more *converso* family, son of a councillor of that city, a first cousin of the then influential Bishop of Badajoz, Charles V's almoner, and himself sometime chamberlain to Diego Colón.[32] Another arrival was a Basque, Hernán de Elgueta, who created a stir by riding up from Vera Cruz on a chestnut mare. There also apparently came to New Spain at this time Cortés' brother-in-law and old partner, Juan Suárez.[33]

But the most important of all the new men who came with Bastidas' party was Julián de Alderete, a man born in Tordesillas (where there remains a remarkable Alderete tomb in the church of San Antolín), and who had been appointed by the authorities in Hispaniola to be Cortés' official treasurer. Alderete had once been *camarero* (steward) to Bishop Fonseca. That background seemed menacing to Cortés. But in truth his presence, if tedious, told the *Caudillo* that the authorities in Santo Domingo had begun to appreciate the importance of what he was doing.

Alderete was dazzled, too, by the view which he gained of Mexico from Texcoco. For a time, he was a humble admirer of Cortés. He subsequently became a focus for dissent. In the beginning, though, he must have given Cortés useful information about politics at home: for example, how Queen Juana was kept so badly in the castle in his own city.[34]

Cortés also learned from these men that "all the men in the islands [that is the Caribbean] were eager to serve him, but Velázquez had prevented many from doing so".[35] The growing success of Cortés' expedition was an obvious magnet for poor Castilians, in Hispaniola and in Cuba too, whether or no they had land there. But the latter island was suffering from the effect of Velázquez's ban on trade with "Yucatan". As late as February 1521, still no one in Santiago had received news as to what had happened to Narváez's expedition: the Sevillano merchant Hernando de Castro even thought that he must have triumphed.[36]

Just after the arrival of Alderete, Cortés' second letter to the Emperor Charles V, as well as some of the gold and other presents which he had gathered together after the *noche triste*, was dispatched to Spain in the care of Alonso de Mendoza, a fellow countryman of Cortés. Mendoza had been a quartermaster of Cortés' in Cuba before the expedition. He was accompanied by Diego de Ordaz, that Leonés who had begun as a firm Velazquista and was now a supporter of Cortés, and by Alonso de Ávila, that candid captain whom Cortés respected but did not like. Neither Ordaz nor Ávila had excelled in recent fighting (though Ordaz had commanded a company in the Tepeaca campaign). The latter had always been a poor horseman, and Cortés had promoted men younger than him to positions of command. Cortés judged Ávila to be better at negotiation than at war. The two left on 5 March 1521 on a ship belonging to Mendoza, Ordaz carrying five hundred pesos of gold given him by Cortés for his expenses.[37] They took with them the party of disaffected conquistadors whom Cortés had sent down from Tenochtitlan to Vera Cruz the previous year. They apparently went first to Yucatan, then to Matanzas, on the north coast of Cuba. There the recalcitrant members of the expedition were set down. Ordaz found that his property in Trinidad on that island had been confiscated by Velázquez.[38] They went thence to Santo Domingo, where Alonso de Ávila disembarked in order to attend to some further needs of Cortés and where the presents being sent back to Spain were publicly exhibited, being seen by, among others, Judge Zuazo.[39] Zuazo, a sober observer of considerable experience, must have been told some tall stories by one or other of the conquistadors, probably Ordaz, since he wrote a sensational letter to his old chief, Fr. Luis de Figueroa, on the subject. He explained that the Mexica were all sodomites, that they ate human flesh, and did not believe in God. He described some high mountains to the south-west of Tenochtitlan, where giants of "marvellous stature" lived. A bone from one of them was being carried back to Spain by Ordaz. He added one of the wildest tales of those days: beyond these mountains "there is a great house or monastery of women where there is a principal whom the Spaniards call the lady of silver . . . This lady has so much silver that the pillars of her house are made of it."[40] Presumably this was a roundabout allusion to Michoacan, where there was indeed silver, and to the *cazonci*, who must have been perceived as a woman.

In addition to telling good tales, Ordaz arranged a legal enquiry into his achievements in the fighting in New Spain, in order to contest the confiscation of his land. That delayed his departure for Seville, though not Mendoza's, till after the end of September.[41]

The presents shown in Hispaniola were intended to excite the interest of old Spain. They included three warriors' costumes with feather bodies and fierce animals' heads – a good combination for anyone who had wanted stories in old romances to come true; double-faced cloaks of feathers arranged so smoothly as to seem like skin; shields of gold and of ocelot skin; "a giant's bone"; some wood carving; and various jewels of gold shaped as butterflies, bumblebees, stuffed birds, and foliage.[42] Three Indian men and girls were also sent.[43] Presents were designated not only for the King but for other people whom Cortés thought might be helpful to his cause: Doña María, for example, the wife of Diego Colón, and a sister of the Duke of Alba. As one of the *Caudillo*'s enemies said, Cortés wanted to be confirmed as Governor of New Spain, and knew that there were many paths to the fulfilment of that ambition.[44]

This ship was said to have carried 4,000 pesos for their majesties, and 25,000 for the Cortés family, to be split between his wife, the forgotten Catalina, and his parents. Another 30,000 pesos were reserved for other friends and supporters in Cuba and Spain. Yet another 30,000, belonging to other conquistadors, was said also to have been on board the ships.[45] There were, however, accusations in Cuba later that there was still more gold on board; 100,000 pesos at least,[46] perhaps 140,000.[47] If so, it was no doubt intended for bribes at home. Some thirty loads of grain (from maize) were also carried – the first commercial export of Mexico for Europe.[48]

Finally, in addition to Cortés' so-called second letter, Mendoza's expedition to Spain also probably carried a document in which the *Caudillo* made a request to the King to send friars and priests to help the conversion of the Mexica.[49]

Back at the lakeside, Cortés had by now followed his enemies in seeking the assistance, or at least the neutrality, of the Tarascans. Some time in February he apparently sent a small delegation to Michoacan. There, several horsemen, probably led by Francisco de Villadiego, arrived at Tzintzuntzan either at the end of the month or in early March.

They were well received by the *cazonci* Zincicha, who had just confirmed his own position by killing his brothers, on the advice of a nobleman named Timas. As earlier remarked, the Tarascans had an excellent metallurgical tradition, but they were in other ways inferior to the Mexica: the latter never tired of pointing out that the male Tarascans did not wear loincloths, but instead had something close to a skirt; cloaks were unknown; and the women, despite the relative cold, did not wear tunics but usually went about with bare breasts.[50]

To impress the Castilians the *cazonci* organised a hunt. Five deer were also presented to the visitors, who were then dressed as local gods, much as Grijalva and Cortés had been arrayed on their arrival in Vera Cruz: wreaths of gold were placed on their heads, blankets on their bodies, and round shields with gold edges on their arms. They were offered *pulque*, bread and fruit. The Castilians said that they wished to trade things such as the fine green plumages which they had brought. The *cazonci* expressed enthusiasm but gave orders that no one should trade privately with them. The Castilians presented ten pigs and a dog to the *cazonci*, saying that the dog could guard his queen. They then left, the *cazonci* giving them traditional Tarascan presents such as blankets, gourd dishes, and leather war jackets.

The *cazonci* was unimpressed by both the dog and the pigs: "What are these things?" he asked. "Are they rats?" He had them killed. Before leaving, the visitors also asked for girls from among the *cazonci*'s relations. He gave them. Villadiego and his friends slept with them on their way back to Tepeaca. The Indians who travelled with the Castilians thereafter called them "*tarascue*", which meant "sons-in-law" in Purepeche (the language of Michoacan, and the real word for the people). The Castilians adopted the name for the people: "Tarascans" the people of Michoacan have been ever since.[51]

Sandoval, meantime, had by now returned to the eastern shores of the lake, where, in several weeks of skirmishing and negotiating, he and his deputy and friend, Luis Marín, the Sanluqueño of Genoese origin, won over, punished, and received homage from many other small towns. A Mexican army was frequently said to be massing, the people of the lake cities were constantly worried, yet, in the space of only a few weeks, the web of Mexican authority in this part of the great valley had been loosened, with Cortés beginning to play the part of the paramount power, and the Tlaxcalans playing that of sepoys.

The most important of these minor campaigns of Sandoval was in March. This took him into a temperate zone to the south of the volcano Popocatepetl, and nearly as far as Cuauhnahuac (Cuernavaca: the Castilians gave the place the latter name as a rough rendering of what they believed to be the Mexican one), almost due south of Tenochtitlan on the other side of the mountains. That city had, as its *tlatoani*, a member of the

Mexican royal family, who took precedence over the other nineteen lesser *tlatoani* in the province of Tlalhuic. The Tlalhuica, who spoke a Nahuatl dialect, had sent substantial tribute to the lord of Texcoco. There was a Mexican garrison. The region was densely inhabited in 1521, though, probably, like most other districts of the empire, it had been hard hit by smallpox the previous year. The Mexica prized Cuernavaca, because of the cotton grown there; and they regarded it as strategically important, since it was on the road to Xochichalco, a sacred city with a legendary history of beautiful sculpture. Its name indicated "flower", and was said to have been the site of the lost paradise of Tamoanchan, "mist land of turquoise". There the Mexican calendar was supposed to have been invented. There was a tree too to mark where the gods were born, and where the sacred mushrooms and indeed most of life derived.[52] A Nahuatl poem insisted that

> In Tamoanchan
> On the flowery carpet
> There are perfect flowers
> There rootless flowers . . .

Another insisted that those who entered this paradise

> Forever live in the springtime
> Nothing ever fades
> All is ever blooming
> All is freshly green
> All is ever green[53]

Tamoanchan, with its nine rivers, its delicate skies, and apparently its nine heavens, was dedicated to Quetzalcoatl, who was believed to have lived there before going to Tula.[54] The place was the site of one of the most curious of Mexican festivals, in which all the gods were asked (in the person of priests) to visit the goddess Xochiquetzal, goddess of love and pregnancy. An impersonation of the goddess was sacrificed, a priest put on her skin, flowering trees were set up in whose branches little boys dressed as butterflies and birds scrambled about, while below the priest-gods pretended to shoot them with blowguns.[55] Such celebrations were probably still, even in 1521, a preoccupation among the Mexica.

Tamoanchan seems in many legends to have been considered the same place as Tlalocan, where the great rain god Tlaloc lived. Fishermen were said to find jade fish in its lovely rivers.

With two hundred men, twenty horse, a dozen crossbowmen and some arquebusiers, supported by some thousand allies from Chalco and Tlaxcala, Sandoval's expedition of Castilian armed men made for the lodge gates of this enchanted land. They first reached Oaxtepec, a dependency of Cuernavaca, via Tlamanalco and Chimalhuacan. Beyond the second of these cities, they found a Mexican army. It was easily dispersed by Sandoval's horsemen. There was a similar engagement at Yecapixtla. At the last-named, Sandoval sent a message along the lines of what his leader Cortés would have done: a request for the people of the town to expel their Mexican garrison if they did not wish him to make war against them. The reply was equally characteristic: the Castilians might come when they liked, for the people of Yecapixtla were looking forward to feasting on their flesh. The Castilians would provide many suitable sacrifices for their gods. The chief of Chalco, who was with Sandoval throughout the campaign and probably advised him on the directions to take, said that this answer could only mean that a large Mexican force had gathered there. Some of those in Sandoval's force were opposed to any further action. But the Sanluqueño Luis Marín insisted that a retreat without defeating the enemy would be to invite trouble. Sandoval agreed, and led the Indian allies from Chalco and Tlaxcala in storming the town. He then returned to Texcoco having lost only one man and gaining much spoil, especially, so it was said, good-looking girls.[56]

No sooner had Sandoval returned than messengers came from Chalco that 20,000 Mexica had arrived in battle array, and that the leaders of that town begged for more help. Cortés was angry that Sandoval had not completed the task of pacifying the towns of the lake. He sent him back to fight at Chalco. But before he arrived, the Chalca showed that they had at last lost their fear of the Mexica. Without Castilian help (though with some assistance from Huexotzinco), they had at least held their old tyrants to a stalemate. This battle was the most sure sign yet that the Mexica, even under the leadership of Cuauhtémoc, "falling eagle", had entered on a time of decline.[57]

Castilian help, however, was needed to save Chalco from another Mexican army about ten days later, on 25 March. On that occasion, Sandoval remained there several days. He brought back to Texcoco about forty Mexican prisoners. Cortés interrogated them. He gleaned from them some information about Cuauhtémoc's intentions: above all, that he seemed to be planning a war to the finish. He asked if there were some among them who would take a message to Cuauhtémoc, saying again that he hoped that the Mexica would submit and become vassals of the King of Spain, as they had been before. For he, Cortés, did not wish to destroy them, but to be their friend, and lead them towards Christianity. The messengers feared that, if they returned with such a message, they would be killed. But in the end two prisoners did go back, escorted part of the way by five horsemen.[58] Cuauhtémoc's only reply was to make another attempt to attack Chalco. The fate of the messengers is unknown. So after celebrating Easter (on 31 March in 1521), Cortés, with three hundred men and twenty-five horses went off on 5 April to defend that city. He spent the night at Tlamanalco. But the Mexican threat next day seemed to have melted away.

When Cortés reached Chalco, however, he told his new allies there that he had no intention of remaining with them. He wished to make another round of the lake to the south, a more thorough journey than that which he had undertaken when he had first arrived at Texcoco, seeing for himself some of the towns which had been conquered, provisionally only, as he feared, by Sandoval. He was determined to bring the Castilian peace to the region. Perhaps his plan to revisit the southern flank of the Mexican empire partly arose from a desire to impress the King's treasurer, Julián de Alderete, and his companion, Fr. Melgarejo, both of whom went with him, as did tried captains such as the Alvarado brothers, Tapia, and Olid. Sandoval remained in command in Texcoco.

The journey was also intended, like that of Sandoval, to penetrate far to the south of the lake, enter the territory of the Xochimilca, whose loyalties were uncertain, and then perhaps capture Cuernavaca, before returning to the lake at Xochimilco itself. Cortés would go back then to Texcoco via Tacuba and Acolman. His knowledge of the Valley of Mexico would thus be considerable before he set about Tenochtitlan itself.

The early stages of this ambitious plan were carried through successfully. From Chalco, the expedition went first to Chimalhuacan, south of Amecameca.[59] A large number of allies joined Cortés from Chalco, Texcoco and Huexotzinco. Bernal Díaz estimated the numbers at 20,000, and said, "in all our expeditions, I had never known so many warriors from our friends . . . they came to gorge themselves on human flesh if there were battles" – just as it had always been in Italy, some veterans of that country grimly recalled, where armies were followed by crows, kites, and other birds of prey, which lived from dead bodies left behind on the battlefields.[60]

After sleeping at Chimalhuacan, the enlarged force moved on towards Cuernavaca. On the way they met the elusive Mexica, who had established themselves in Xochimilca territory, on a knoll at Tlaycapan, a rocky height in the middle of the plain between Chimalhuacan and Oaxtepec, though nearer the latter. Cortés rashly ordered a direct assault by four captains: Juan Rodríguez de Villafuerte (increasingly one of Cortés' intimates, and another native of Medellín, though his name would have suggested to any hidalgo a strong Salamanca connection); Francisco Verdugo (ex-*alcalde* of Trinidad and the intended innocent beneficiary of the Villafaña conspiracy); Pedro de Ircio; and Andrés de Monjaraz. These men led about forty or fifty soldiers against the Mexican position. Cortés' standard-bearer, Cristóbal del Corral, led another party of about sixty infantrymen up the steepest part of the hill.[61] But the assault failed, several Castilians were killed, and the expedition spent the night in the plain listening to the enemy drums and conches in rather difficult circumstances, since they could find no water.[62] The King's treasurer, Alderete, was far from impressed, though he proved his own worth as a crossbowman.

The next day, things went better for the Castilians, since an attack on a second hillock was successful. The Mexica on the first hill surrendered because they too needed water. After being refreshed by a spring on this second hill, Cortés apparently received the acceptance of obedience to the King of Spain of both groups of defenders – though in what form must be a matter of doubt: but certainly enough for Cortés to be able to treat them as rebels, should they change their minds.[63] After this victory, the expedition rested two days, and continued downhill to Oaxtepec, whose leaders gave themselves up without a fight. This was a fertile region, full of flowers as well as fruit and vegetables, then as now, being at 4,500 feet, already almost in the temperate zone. Here too was the finest of the Mexican botanical gardens, which had been begun by Montezuma I, who had filled it with rare trees and shrubs brought from the coast. The expedition bivouacked here. Cortés, Sandoval, the King's treasurer Alderete and Bernal Díaz all declared this "orchard", as they described it, the most beautiful which they had seen: "A better orchard they had never seen in Spain . . . There were arbours and . . . an infinite number of fruit trees".[64]

During these engagements, Fr. Melgarejo had also begun to make a mark on the expedition: "He showed such courage and zeal that he was present at every engagement with a crucifix in his hand . . . He preached to the army on numerous occasions, no small task, for the most difficult thing was to keep our men calm and in control, for many were the opportunities for them to be covetous, cruel to the Indians, and disobedient to their captain. The spirit of this saintly friar was very necessary in order to teach them salutary doctrines . . ."[65]

The next towns on the way to Cuernavaca were Yautepec and then Xiutepec.[66] A large force of Mexica fled from the first place only to be caught and mostly killed in the second, where, Cortés himself says, "we lanced and killed many; we found the people there unprepared, because we arrived before their spies . . . many women and children were taken and the rest fled. I stayed there two days, thinking that the lord would come, and present himself as Your Majesty's vassal, but he did not do so; so, when I left, I set fire to the town. [But] before leaving, some people from the town where I had been before, Oaxtepec, came to ask my pardon, and said that they wished to become vassals of Your Majesty".[67]

On 13 April, Cortés left early for Cuernavaca. On the last stage to this important centre, the expedition, like many later travellers, stopped first at Teputzlan (Tepotzlan). It was a place known for its *pulque* drinking. Its patron god, Tepoztecal, was the god of alcoholic excess. The town remained in the memory of the conquistadors, despite the regulations against such indulgences, as one where they "found some excellent Indian women".[68] The town was, and is, known for the fine mountain temple just outside it, built by Ahuítzotl, Montezuma's predecessor, as a symbol of authority.[69] The Spaniards then set off for Cuernavaca, which they found surrounded by ravines. This town, only finally subdued for the Mexica by Ahuítzotl, was also renowned as a site of the cult of Xochiquetzal, the goddess who, as has been seen, was associated at Tamoanchan with love. Probably these local cults seemed at the same time dangerous and enticing to the puritan Mexican conquerors.[70]

There was no way of entering the town save by the bridges, which the inhabitants had already broken. Once again, though, local Indians were persuaded to betray their city: they told Cortés that, a little way away, there was a passage where horsemen could pass; and, at the same time, some (Olid, Tapia) crossed over one of the broken bridges. Others crossed the ravine by means of fallen tree trunks. Taken by surprise, the defenders fled, though not before half the town, including the temple built by Ahuítzotl, had been mysteriously burned. The city fell thereafter without much difficulty; the Castilians established themselves in another beautiful orchard belonging to the *tlatoani*, and there too, they found excellent spoils of cloth and "more admirable women".[71] The local chiefs subsequently came in and gave themselves up, offering obedience to the to them mysterious Charles V, of whom Cortés never ceased to talk. Some slaves were taken, probably more in order to put fear into the minds of the natives than because they were needed.[72]

Cortés must have liked this city since afterwards he established there a palace and the centre of a vast *encomienda*. Fr. Durán said that, even in his time, it was one of the most beautiful places in the world ("had it not been for the heat").[73] It was rich in cotton. But at the time Cortés did not allow his force to linger there since, the very next morning, they all set off back towards the Lake of Mexico, making for Xochimilco, crossing the mountains, probably following a path close to the present road from Cuernavaca to the city of Tenochtitlan. The distance between the two cities as the crow flies is about fifty miles. Though Cortés left early, he decided to spend the night halfway to Xochimilco in some farm buildings in a pine forest. It was both cold and without drinking water.[74]

The next battle, of Xochimilco, was much more difficult than the *Caudillo* had expected. This city was an island in the lake, about half a mile from its southern shore. The Xochimilca had once been a powerful tribe. They had been an ally of the Tepaneca. Then they had been conquered in the late fifteenth century by the Mexica. Their lands had been seized. Both they and those who worked them had been divided among the conquerors. Much of the population, like that of Coyoacán nearby, had been condemned to perpetual slavery. Among their tasks had been the building of the causeway to Tenochtitlan. Another may have been the provision of the colossal greenstone (diorite) head of Huitzilopochtli's sister Coyolxauhqui, for the dedication of the Great Temple in 1487 – a head to be fashioned in the guise of Xochimilco's own goddess Chantico: an added humiliation.[75] Tribute was regularly paid to Tenochtitlan, much of it in the form of vegetables and flowers, grown on the *chinampas* along the southern shore of the lake.[76] In recent years, the Xochimilca had acquired a new reputation, as master lapidaries.[77]

The town was also known because of a tale that Montezuma, hunting in some gardens nearby, had committed the solecism of picking an ear of maize which had already formed. The farmer complained: "Lord, you who are so powerful, how can you steal an ear of corn from me? Does not your own law condemn a man to death if he steals an ear of maize?" Montezuma is said to have rewarded the man for his bravery in so speaking by making him the lord of Xochimilco.[78] Perhaps if the story is true, he was still there, known apparently as Yaomahuitzin, when the Spaniards arrived.

The Spanish attack was, to begin with, a direct one. The crossbowmen and arquebusiers destroyed the defences and, after an advance across the causeway, most of the city was captured. Thereafter the Xochimilca pursued a delaying tactic, suing for peace while waiting for help from the Mexica. In the evening the Mexica came, and sought to cut off the Castilians, by attacking the causeway where Cortés and his men had entered. This ruse was fruitless, thanks yet again to the horses. But the Mexica were far from beaten. Many of them carried especially well-adapted lances with captured Toledo blades on the end of them. Others had two-handed Castilian *montantes*, swords of the sort that Pánfilo de Narváez had favoured, and which had been captured at "the battle of the bridges". The Castilian advance guard, led by Cortés himself, was surrounded, the *Caudillo*'s horse, "El Romo" ("snub nose"), foundered and the *Caudillo* was thrown. Had the Mexicans been content to kill him, they would surely have succeeded. But they were, as usual, fatally (for them) anxious to seize him for sacrifice. In the end, Cortés was saved by an unknown Tlaxcalan and Cristóbal de Olea, a curly-haired conquistador from Medina del Campo known for his quickness. Several Castilians were, however, captured. These men (they included Juan de Lara, probably a Cordobés, and Alonso Hernández) were sacrificed by Cuauhtémoc, their legs and arms being distributed through nearby towns to demonstrate how the Mexica were winning the war.[79]

That night the Castilians spent in Xochimilco. But it was scarcely a night of rest. The crossbowmen spent it feathering their arrows. The arquebusiers were out of powder, and hence could not sleep. Cortés was busy supervising his Indian allies, whom he had ordered to fill in the gaps in the causeways with rubble from the destroyed houses: a technique which he had begun to use the previous year in Tenochtitlan.

Next day a major onslaught was launched by the Mexica both on land and by water. Cortés and several of his captains climbed the pyramid of Xochimilco. The temple there was dedicated to the goddess Chantico. As in other temples dedicated to her, the central room at the top of the fatal staircase was pitch black, having no windows, being entered through a tiny door through which the priests would surreptitiously creep. Cortés had no time, however, to investigate these secrets, for, from the temple platform, he and his captains could see what they calculated to be 12,000 Mexicans, in perhaps a thousand canoes, making for them, calling the battle cries "Mexico, Mexico", and "Tenochtitlan, Tenochtitlan".[80] Wave after wave of attacks followed by land and by sea.

Those on land were held by the Castilian horsemen, who were able to move at will across the filled-in causeway. The waterborne attacks could also be resisted effectively by crossbow. The Castilians and their allies set fire to the houses in the city, except for those in which they had established themselves. Much loot was obtained in the form of cloth and gold. When, on the third day of being in this city, Cortés decided to move on, he gave instructions for all this to be left behind. His men protested and, in the end, accompanied by that essential fruit of war, along with the baggage and the wounded, the expedition set off for Coyoacán, the horsemen divided between the rear and the vanguard.[81]

The battle of Xochimilco had been unexpectedly hard, but from it the Castilians learned several important lessons: particuarly that, when the Mexica left gaps in causeways, they could get the Tlaxcalans to fill them in: well enough for horses to pass easily across. This had not been realised during the previous year's stay in the capital.

Coyoacán was a town eight miles away to the north-west on the edge of the lake, the place from which the south-west spur of the main causeway to Tenochtitlan began. It was ruled by a Tepanecan monarch named Coapopocatzin, and was a centre for the collection of tribute for the Triple Alliance. Cortés might have expected a friendly welcome. For had not a recent king of Coyoacán been murdered by the Mexican emperor Ahuítzotl for giving him good advice about the consequences of his water policies? But the people were wary. When the *Caudillo* reached there on 18 April, the town was deserted: the people and the chiefs had left for Tenochtitlan. He therefore established himself in the vast house of Coapopocatzin, and remained there for two days. His followers made themselves busy, destroying idols and burning temples, looking after the wounded, making arrows for the crossbowmen, examining the exact line of the causeways, and discussing possibilities for a camp there during the proposed attack on the capital.[82]

From Coyoacán Cortés made haste to return to Texcoco along the west and north side of the lake, a route which by this time he of course knew. He passed, but did not stay at, Tacuba, though there was fighting there. On the way he sought to prepare an ambush for a small Mexican force. But in the end he himself was ambushed. He escaped unharmed, yet he lost two pages, Pedro Gallego, a Sevillano, and Francisco Martín Vendabal, a Basque. Both were captured and, presumably, sacrificed. Downcast, Cortés took the new arrivals, the royal treasurer Alderete and Fr. Melgarejo, to look at Tenochtitlan from the summit of the temple there. They were naturally carried away with the grandeur of the place. But Cortés remained sad at the loss of his pages. Licenciado Alonso Pérez, probably the only real university graduate in the army (apart from the priests), said to the *Caudillo*, "Señor, do not let your excellency feel sad, for such things happen in war; and it will never be said of your excellency:

> Nero from the Tarpeian Rock
> Looked down on burning Rome."[83]

Cortés replied to this piece of lawyerly unctuousness that he, Pérez, must have seen how many times he had sent to the Mexica asking them to make peace. He was not only grieving over the pages but at the thought of the bloodshed which would have to come before the Castilians would be able to establish their mastery over Tenochtitlan, "though, with the help of God, they would soon set to work".[84]

The army then returned to Texcoco around the north of the lake. They carried out at least one successful assault on a Mexican force and Cortés claimed to have killed "over one hundred chiefs, all brilliantly arrayed" in feathered costumes.[85] Probably the Mexica again thought that they had fended off an assault. In fact Cortés had carried out a successful if difficult reconnaissance in preparation for his siege.

The Mexica may have been as busy with the festival of the month Etzalqualiztli as with the preparations for war. The priests at this time of year always went to bathe ceremonially in the lake. The "priest of the precious stone" would announce: "This is the place of the serpents' anger, the flight of the wild duck, the murmur of the white rushes." All the priests would then leap into the water, imitating, as they splashed, the cries of ducks, ibis, and herons. The same actions were repeated for four days in succession. "Speaking hoarsely, they mimicked the birds . . . some spoke like ducks babbling . . . some imitated water ravens . . . some like kingfishers."[86] It seemed a different planet from that on which Martín López and his friends were meticulously preparing the brigantines. Yet it was the same lake.

VII
The Battle for Tenochtitlan

33
Remember the bold hearts

"O Brave Mexicans, you have seen how all our old subjects have rebelled against us! Our enemies used to be Tlaxcala, Cholula and Huexotzinco but now we must also face Texcoco, Chalco, Xochimilco and even Tacuba. All the latter have abandoned us and gone to join the strangers. So remember the bold hearts of the Mexica-Chichimeca, our ancestors who, though few in number, dared to enter this land . . ."
Speech of Cuauhtémoc, according to Fr. Durán

CUAUHTÉMOC, WITH HIS fellow new monarchs, Tetlepanquetzatzin and Coanacochtzin of Tacuba and Texcoco, had with care and skill been fortifying the beautiful capital. Tenochtitlan still stood in all its majesty. But the empire was in ruins. The loss of Chalco was a catastrophe. The knowledge that other cities in the Valley of Mexico and around the lake, not to speak of those in the *tierra templada,* such as Oaxtepec, Cuernavaca, and Huexotzinco, had made their peace with Cortés was an earnest of what might follow. Texcoco had been brutally treated by "Malinche". Perhaps because of the fear so caused, collaboration with him there was growing. Already Tenochtitlan was suffering from lack of tribute: not just an end to the delivery of cloaks, precious stones, and gold, but a shortage of the variety of food to which the Mexica had become used. Few supplies, for example, could have reached Tenochtitlan from the rich coastal zone since the previous autumn.

The idea of war in the early summer, and real war too, flew, as it had in 1520, in the face of convention. The Mexica at that time were usually busy planting. The festivals in those months were all concerned with the need to propitiate the gods of fertility. The challenge to these routines lowered Mexican morale. So of course did other unconventional tactics of the Castilians (killing their enemy; not making prisoners; fighting at night; fighting without announcements).

The Mexica do not seem to have curtailed their usual ritual activities except insofar as they had to in consequence of a loss of essential ingredients for offerings, by the suspension of tribute or lack of personalities to officiate because of smallpox. They may even have intensified some ceremonies, in order to propitiate the gods. Some new works of art, in greenstone, seem to have been commissioned: for example, the sculpture known as "the *pulque* drinker", with, appropriately, given the times, a skeletal mouth.[1] Another product of these months may have been a ceramic tripod plate with an intertwined eagle and jaguar: an exhortation perhaps to the knights of those two orders to remain together to the death.[2] Cuauhtémoc may too have commissioned an especially beautiful greenstone statuette of Quetzalcoatl, with exquisite bas-relief figures (now in Stuttgart). The statuette has, on its base, glyphs which were signs of disaster: 4-Wind, the date of a previous destruction of the world by hurricanes sent by Quetzalcoatl; and 9-Wind, referring to the nine levels of hell, a date held to be "completely and utterly malign". One interpretation of this effigy is that it was intended to show Quetzalcoatl as star of the night carrying the sun down to hell.[3] The aim would presumably have been to prevent such things from occurring by a prior, ceremonial depiction of it, in stone.

During the weeks before Cortés launched his blockade of the city, Cuauhtémoc mounted one more major diplomatic offensive, promising remission of tribute to numerous old subject cities. But the resentment against the empire continued to be strong. The once subject peoples sensed that the end of the empire was at hand. Perhaps they thought that the hour of the Tlaxcalans was imminent. Cuauhtémoc failed to move the ex-tributaries with the idea that they had as much to lose as Mexico from a Castilian victory. Would it not really be a Tlaxcalan victory? The Tarascans in Michoacan in particular continued to refuse to help.

Cuauhtémoc may also have made some tactical mistakes. Thus he filled Tenochtitlan with soldiers and weapons. But he left the city short of food.[4] This error may have occurred because he had no emergency means of finding essential and simple supplies. In addition, he had no real idea of what the Castilians were planning. He knew from his spies that Cortés expected to use boats. For that reason he had arranged sharp stakes to be stuck into the floor of the lake in the approaches to the city. For that reason too he had instructed his people to make ready their own fleet of canoes. The Mexica had been using canoes for warlike purposes for several generations. But they were not used for sea battles so much as for transporting men from one side of the lake to the other.[5] The notion of an amphibious siege was unknown to the Mexican experience, even though the Mexica would have recalled that, in 1428, their own defeat of their predecessors as masters of the valley, the people of Azcapotzalco, had also been in consequence of a siege. But the eventual assault had been by land.[6] Indeed, any idea of a long, defensive war, or a war lasting more than a few days, was unusual. In the past the Mexica had sallied out to fight and, after due warnings and ritual, put their fortune to the test, in a pitched battle. Probably Cuauhtémoc thought that his enemies would make a frontal onslaught.

Of course the Mexica appealed to their gods: to give them victory or, merely, to help them. But the priests seem to have been frightened. They said that the gods had become mute, or had died, since these new men, divinities as they might be or not, had come to take away their strength. Cuauhtémoc apparently had made a speech to his chief followers: "O Brave Mexicans, you have seen how all our old subjects have rebelled against us! Our enemies used to be Tlaxcala, Cholula and Huexotzinco but now we must also face Texcoco, Chalco, Xochimilco and even Tacuba . . . So remember the bold hearts of the Mexica-Chichimeca, our ancestors who, though few in number, dared to enter this land and to conquer it . . . therefore, O Mexica, do not be dismayed or be cowardly. On the contrary, strengthen your chests and your hearts . . . and . . . do not scorn me because of my youth."[7] As usual before battles, the surviving nobles no doubt danced, sang and probably, to enhance their courage, consumed mushrooms, the *peyote* cactus, the seeds of the datura or of morning glory. "Remember the bold hearts" was the essential injunction. The brilliant past had to be allowed to cast its light over the dark present.

There was no standing army in old Mexico. The soldiers were labourers, *macehualtin*, or serfs, *mayeques*, who, though trained at school in some martial arts, received no pay, and who normally looked to booty to compensate them for the time taken away from their fields, or whatever ordinary activity, as craftsmen for example, they carried on. These soldiers were still organised by the *calpultin*, grouped in companies of about one hundred men, each with their separate standards.[8] The leaders of the *calpultin* were responsible for making ready each unit, arranging with the women the necessary weapons, the uniforms, and the food. There was, however, a corps of professional officers and guards. The former were all noblemen, or those who, in the past, had achieved some distinction in fighting. The officers constituted a military council to advise both the Emperor and his generals. The knightly orders were also professionals and, of these, two, as has been seen, the jaguar and the eagle knights, were open only to noblemen. The other orders, the Otomí and the *Quachic*, were formed of men of all classes who had vowed never to retreat in battle.

Cuauhtémoc must be imagined consulting all these leaders, and whatever tactics were decided upon must have been jointly their responsibility.[9] But there was no suggestion by anyone that the new strategies of the invaders should be met by radically new policies by the Mexica: for example, by using as weapons of war the flint knives employed for ceremonial sacrifices in old Mexico. No one suggested that the little wheels, occasionally used for toys in old Mexico, might be adapted for carrying equipment.

The sense that the old days were over was also widespread. It was said that Cuauhtémoc's preparations were completed during the winter by throwing the remains of the treasure of Montezuma into a deep part of the lake, Pantitlan, where there was a whirlpool.[10] Those few noblemen who had survived both Alvarado's massacre of the previous summer, and the smallpox of the previous autumn, must have felt inclined to listen again to the sad poems of Nezahualcoyotl:

> I Nezahualcoyotl, I ask you:
> Is it true we have roots in the earth?
> Surely we are not forever here?
> Only for a time are we here!
> Though you are carved in jade you will break
> Though you are made of gold you will crack
> Though you are a quetzal feather you will wither
> Only for a time are we here.[11]

No such melancholy reflections characterised Cortés and his bearded soldiers. Castile in America was not the France of Villon. The brigantines were ready. The allies were waiting for their revenge on the empire which had extorted so much from them. The Tlaxcalans, the Totonacs, the Chalca, and the other allies (including even the Cholulans and the Huexotzinca) were blind to the intolerance of the Castilians. They even seem indeed to have been increasingly drawn to them because of their ruthlessness, their physical strength, their charm, their energy; and especially their apparent imperviousness to disease.

The allies must have been impressed too by the skill with which Cortés had organised the brigantines' construction. Thousands of men from towns near Texcoco, in relays, and directed by Ixtlilxochitl, had, after all, been inspired by Cortés, or by Martín López, to dig from Texcoco itself a channel twelve feet deep and twelve feet wide of about a mile and a half to the shore of the lake: "a very great work and one to marvel at", as Cortés himself said.[12] López still was evidently working "like a slave" from dawn till night.[13] The assembly of the vessels was done inland in order to safeguard them from Mexican sabotage. Had this work been performed on the lake front, the Mexica, with their thousands of canoes, might have hampered, or thwarted, the enterprise.[14]

Twelve brigantines were launched on 28 April. Flat-bottomed, with both sails and paddles, able to manoeuvre through the shallow lake without risk of being grounded, each could carry about 25–30 men.[15] The flagship, the *capitana*, was about 65 feet (32 cubits), the others 50 feet (27 or 28 cubits), that is, a little longer than had been previously envisaged.[16] Each carried, in its bows, a small bronze cannon, which probably had been sent from Seville and brought by Juan de Burgos. But the *capitana*, the admiral's ship, on which Cortés himself and Martín López expected to sail, carried heavy iron cannon. Half these ships had one mast, half had two.[17] To any experienced European sailor, the sight of these vessels might have recalled a navy of the Roman empire. If so they were a triumphant concession to classical history entirely worthy of the Latin-quoting *Caudillo*.

But Texcoco was not only a naval arsenal. In May 1521, the city seemed a workshop comprising a great variety of activity. Lances and swords were being sharpened. Pedro Barba, commander of the cross-bowmen, busied himself with ensuring that his men were well provided for, not only with arrows and arrowheads, but with spare bowstrings, spare nuts, and spare paste with which to repair arrows (they used some local Mexican glue, *zacotle*, which some specialists pronounced better than that of Castile).[18] Armour was polished and refitted. Commanders discussed with Cortés the likely tactics of the enemy.

Cortés had made an appeal to his Indian allies to send as many men as possible for the assault on the city. These were less for fighting than for auxiliary service. He asked those concerned to be present within ten days. He also requested certain cities to provide wooden arrows with copper warheads, on the model of those from Castile. The allies responded remarkably. For years they had mouthed criticism of the Mexica: the Tlaxcalans saw them as a "people who seem born never to rest, to leave anyone in peace".[19] The Otomí affected to consider that there was "none who can surpass the Mexica in evil".[20] Now the moment had come to test how far these remarks were real or ritualistic. The required arrowheads were in fact forthcoming in eight days. These peoples had committed themselves so far to friendship with the Castilians that they knew that, if they were to live, they would have to win.

Cortés' strategic plan comprised a variety of sanctions. The main element in the plan was to starve Tenochtitlan, by cutting off the supplies of the city by destroying the canoes and by occupying the causeways. No risks would be taken with Castilian lives. Few commanders in history have been so reluctant to lose men as was Cortés. So everyone at the time appreciated the importance of the brigantines.

Hence the launching of the ships was an occasion celebrated with music, the firing of cannon, the unfurling of flags, as well as shouts of exaltation from both the Indian allies and the Castilians. Fr. Olmedo celebrated mass at the water's edge.[21]

Soon after this, Cortés held a rally of his troops. The different allied peoples stood in regiments with banners unfurled, with their bows and arrows, swords, javelins, spears, lances and, not to be forgotten, whistles. Once again the cries of "*Viva* the Emperor, our lord!" and "*¡Castilla Castilla, Tlaxcala Tlaxcala!*" were echoed by feather-clad indigenous leaders.[22] It was said that in old Mexico an individual's home could be identified from an analysis of the placing on his body of his self-sacrificial scars.[23] The variety of such puncturing in this array must have been considerable.

Cortés now gave one of his homilies which, through Marina, seems to have been as usual eloquent. He recalled the ordinances which he had drawn up in Tlaxcala. He described how successful he had hitherto been with so few men. He insisted that the Castilians were fighting in order to spread the Christian faith. He pointed out how his political purpose was to submit "again" to the King of Castile the people and the lands which had "rebelled". Cortés believed that he had, in this oration, so animated his men that they were indeed once more ready to "conquer or die".[24]

The number of the allies is impossible to determine. Cortés himself said that he had 50,000 from Tlaxcala alone and that his total army numbered 150,000. His chaplain and biographer López de Gómara spoke of 60,000 Texcocans and 200,000 others. Responsible modern writers have added up different contributions to give an overall total of over 500,000.[25] All these estimates must surely be gross exaggerations. Neither the Mexica nor the Castilians had any method of accurate counting of hordes of men. Nevertheless, in the battles which lay ahead, Cortés clearly had a large number of men available to perform the essential quartermaster's work, such as building temporary lodgings, bringing food, filling in ditches, making bridges, and also burning the houses of the enemy. The Texcocans (from the villages nearby as well as a few from the city) and the Tlaxcalans were in the lead, the former being anxious to prove a new-found antagonism towards the Mexica, the latter determined to finish with their enemies once and for all. Thousands of people from other towns became suddenly aware that the Mexica might indeed soon be destroyed, and so, anxious to show themselves on the side of the new masters of the valley, declared themselves warriors.

The Texcocans and Tlaxcalans had established commanders directing them, in the shape of Ixtlilxochitl and Chichimecatecle, who sought to organise this unexpected mass of new volunteers for the fighting against the Mexica.[26] Ixtlilxochitl seems to have made use in Texcoco and its dependent towns of a well-established call to work, or arms, a kind of conscription which, using *calpultin* or the equivalent, was well tried in the Valley of Mexico, and was probably employed by most cities then existing there.[27]

Only one Indian leader among Cortés' allies seems to have had doubts about his people's decisions. This was Xicotencatl the younger, the free-thinking commander who had led the Tlaxcalans against Cortés in October 1519 and who, since then, had been overruled by his aged father and the now dead Maxixcatzin. He was in 1521 again one of the senior Tlaxcalan commanders. He had answered Cortés' call for men and, with his colleague and one-time rival Chichimecatecle, had brought several thousand Tlaxcalans to Texcoco. Just before the main operation against Tenochtitlan was due to begin, Xicotencatl abandoned his men and, with some of his friends, went home to Tlaxcala. Cortés sent some Texcocans and two Tlaxcalan captains to persuade him to return. Xicotencatl gave a hostile reply to the messengers, regretting that his father and Maxixcatzin had ever accepted Cortés as a friend. Cortés then sent to Tlaxcala Alonso de Ojeda and Juan Márquez, the two Castilians who had helped to train the Tlaxcalan troops, with orders to bring back the rebel in all haste. They did so. Cortés ordered Xicotencatl hanged in view of all the Indians in Texcoco. Pedro de Alvarado petitioned unsuccessfully on Xicotencatl's behalf. Perhaps there was enough of Alvarado himself in Xicotencatl's character to give Cortés' confidant some sense of fellow feeling. Moreover, Alvarado's mistress, "María Luisa", was Xicotencatl's sister. This was not the only occasion when Alvarado, often dismissed as pitiless, intervened in what he considered a just cause. Once Cortés ordered a Spaniard named Mora to be hanged for stealing a turkey from some Indians; the man would have died had not Alvarado cut the rope.[28]

The Indians were naturally distressed, but evidently Cortés performed this action, as others have done in similar circumstances, *pour encourager les autres*. Diego Camargo, the historian of Tlaxcala, wrote that the flight of Xicotencatl from the battle array in Texcoco had nothing to do with politics but derived from an *amour* being pursued by the alleged rebel with a beautiful girl in Tlaxcala. It was also said that Cortés only acted the third time that Xicotencatl was absent. Yet everything suggests that the *Caudillo* would have been happy to have hanged this Tlaxcalan leader even if he had merely gone fishing.[29]

The Castilians are, of course, much more easily numbered than the allies. Cortés had, as a result of recent reinforcements, now nearly ninety horsemen, about a hundred and twenty crossbowmen and arquebusiers, about seven hundred infantrymen, three large iron guns and fifteen small ones (on the brigantines), without, however, quite enough gunpowder: ten quintals only.[30] Nearly every soldier had equipped himself with well-quilted body armour, neck guard and leggings, as well as a steel headpiece, shield and sword (much of this equipment, not just the cannon, derived from the cargo which reached Mexico with Juan de Burgos). Instructions were given that no one was to sleep unless he were both armed and had on his sandals; that no one was to go to any nearby village for food; that no gambling was allowed for horses or for arms; and that no one was to mistreat allies or seize any loot. The penalty for sleeping on guard duty, as for desertion, was, as in most armies, death.

At the end of the sixteenth century, a rumour was propagated, for reasons difficult now to divine, by Fr. Sahagún, that about now Cortés met Cuauhtémoc at Acachinanco, the small fortress halfway along the north–south causeway between Iztapalapa and Tenochtitlan. It was said that Cortés explained why he had to wage war, and that Cuauhtémoc gave no reply except that he accepted the conflict. There is no evidence for this parley. Such a thing would have become known had it occurred. Like the conversation of Mary, Queen of Scots, with Queen Elizabeth, as described by Schiller, no doubt it should have happened, but almost certainly it did not.[31] What seems more probable is that Cortés may have sought to cause a schism in the ranks of the Mexicans by inviting the people of Tlatelolco to betray their allies of Tenochtitlan: an approach to which there was no response.[32]

In the final assembly, Cortés organised his forces into four divisions: three to fight on land, the fourth to be under his own direction on the brigantines. The three terrestrial commands were under the now experienced captains, Pedro de Alvarado, Sandoval, and Olid; two Extremeños and one Andalusian. Of these, Alvarado and Olid were in their middle thirties, as was Cortés, while Sandoval was still in his early twenties. Each commander had about twenty-five to thirty horsemen, fifteen crossbowmen and arquebusiers, together with a hundred and fifty foot, and a substantial number of Indian allies,[33] Cortés had three hundred Castilians for the brigantines, twenty-five men in each, and about six crossbowmen and arquebusiers too.[34]

Alvarado's deputies were his brother Jorge, Gutierre de Badajoz, and Andrés de Monjaraz (two Extremeños and a Basque). He also had with him Fr. Juan Díaz, Bernal Díaz, and his mistress, "María Luisa" of Tlaxcala.[35] Olid had as his lieutenants Andrés de Tapia, Francisco Verdugo and Francisco de Lugo (a Leonese and two Castilians); whilst Sandoval had in that capacity Pedro de Ircio and Luis Marín (a Sevillano and a Sanluqueño). All these commanders, like Cortés and Alvarado, no doubt had mistresses close at hand.

The three divisions were ordered to hold the three main entrances to the city of Tenochtitlan: Alvarado, Olid, and Sandoval were placed respectively on the Tacuba, Coyoacán and Iztapalapa causeways. The fourth causeway, that to the hill of Tepeyac, to the north, on which stood a well-known shrine of the mother goddess, was left open, a "silver bridge" along which Cuauhtémoc and the Mexica might perhaps be tempted to retreat following the pressure of the siege.[36] Cortés would have found it easier to fight on the mainland instead of on "that great fortress on the water".[37]

As for the brigantines, the captains seem to have been appointed not only from the ranks of those with naval experience. Some probably received their commands for political reasons (for example, Ruiz de la Mota, the cousin of the Bishop of Badajoz). About half of these captains were men who had been with Cortés since he first landed at San Juan de Ulúa in 1519.

The *Caudillo* had hoped to have enough volunteers to crew these craft by which he set such store. But these were not forthcoming. The work seemed hard, dangerous and ungallant. Cortés therefore appointed to the ships all those who had been sailors and then, even more high-handedly, anyone born in the Andalusian ports of Palos, Moguer, Triana, Sanlúcar de Barrameda or el Puerto de Santa María.[38]

Cortés again addressed his force in the *plaza* of Texcoco. He explained that he had much faith in the brigantines since, with them, the Castilians would be able to destroy the enemy canoes, and shut the Mexica up within their canals. The Mexica, he thought, could no more live without canoes than without eating. He commended the victory to God, for, he said, the war was His.[39]

On 22 May Alvarado and Olid left for the north to establish bridgeheads at the Tacuba and Coyoacan causeways. Olid had the largest force of Texcocans with him, that now being led by Tetlahuehue-quititzin, one of the many sons of the late King Nezahualpilli. It had been agreed that Sandoval should leave a few days later for Iztapalapa; and then Cortés himself would set off with the brigantines.

The first stage of the Castilian attack on Tenochtitlan was unedifying. Alvarado and Olid had been ordered to stop the first night at Acolman, a Texcocan city close to Teotihuacan, which had a *tlatoani* of its own, and which is now renowned for its lovely Augustinian monastery, built in the 1540s with an outside pulpit and remarkable wall paintings. It was known at the time as a place where fat little castrated dogs could be bought for eating; but also as a city of "medium healthfulness and . . . night dews".[40] In Mexican lore, it was also held to be the place where men and women were first created, as a result of a magical bowshot by the sun.[41] Somewhere near this famous site, Alvarado and Olid quarrelled as to where their two columns should sleep. The soldiers of the two columns began to threaten one another. The difficulties were only settled as a result of the pleading of Fr. Melgarejo and Luis Marín, who were sent up for the purpose by Cortés as soon as the news was brought to him.[42]

There was, happily, no dispute between the commanders when they stopped the next two nights at, first, Citlaltepec and then Cuauhtitlan, on the north and north-west shores of the lake, before reaching Tacuba, "at the hour of vespers" on the third day after leaving Texcoco. At Tacuba, the two columns established themselves in the house of the King in which, a few weeks before, Cortés himself had stayed. Alvarado's Tlaxcalans immediately went to inspect the causeway to Tenochtitlan. They skirmished sporadically there with the Mexica for several hours before night fell.

Next day, after a mass celebrated by Fr. Juan Díaz, Alvarado's priest, the two commanders left Tacuba. With a small force of horsemen, they rode to the other side of a bay, where, on the hill of Chapultepec, the "hill of the grasshopper", they seized the spring which, through the great aqueduct, had, since the days of Montezuma I, supplied Tenochtitlan with water.[43] They broke the conduits there, so that henceforth the Mexica had to depend on the small supplies of fresh water obtainable through wells in the capital.[44] Chapultepec had been where Huemac, last king of the legendary Tula, had killed himself. There the Mexican kings had often had themselves carved in stone. There the Mexica had spent a time before reaching Tenochtitlan. But, symbolically important, it was also the scene in ancient history of the Mexica's worst previous defeat when, before they had reached Tenochtitlan, their king Huitzilihuitl had been taken to die in slavery at Culhuacan. There is a vivid picture in the Codex Vaticano showing the Tepanecs in Chapultepec seizing the Mexican women.[45]

Cortés when he had conceived of this tactic may again have recalled a Spanish precedent. The same action had been carried out when King Ferdinand's forces under the Marquis of Arcos had besieged the Moors in Ronda in 1485. He had cut the water supply which came from a spring at the foot of a gorge.

Alvarado and Olid spent a few days seeking to level the causeway on the way to Tenochtitlan: not actually that one on which they had returned in disarray the previous year, but that more northerly one which passed over the island of Nonoalco. But they made little progress for, as they should have anticipated, they were attacked by Mexicans in canoes fighting from both sides. About thirty Castilians seem to have been wounded, by some of the devastatingly well-directed Mexican stones. Next day Olid set off, however, with his Texcocan allies, to go some five miles south to his agreed post at Coyoacán, leaving Alvarado at Tacuba, where he would remain many weeks, from time to time trying to fill in the ditches repeatedly dug in that causeway, which he wished to make good for his horses. Olid soon found that the same defensive digging of ditches was being pursued on the causeway from Coyoacán. For several days there was also sporadic fighting in the countryside, as both Olid's and Alvarado's men seized what maize they could from the farms which lay between their two headquarters, frequently lancing the peasants whom they caught unawares.[46]

Then, on 31 May, Corpus Christi day, Sandoval set off from Texcoco with his column for Iztapalapa.[47] The distance of the march could hardly have been less than twenty-five miles. But by nightfall, he and his large number of allies were established in the houses where the expedition of Cortés had lodged on two previous occasions. They were attacked by a small Mexican garrison while they were arriving, but these men soon withdrew when they saw the size of Sandoval's force, with its Indian allies. After they had retreated, smoke signals were seen on the top of the nearby hill of Huitzilopochtli, el Cerro de la Estrella, as the Spanish would soon call it. These were interpreted as calling together all the Mexican canoes.[48]

On 1 June, finally, the sails were raised on the brigantines. The condition of the lake had been permanently affected by the Mexican action some months previously in opening the causeway of Nezahualcoyotl during the fighting at Iztapalapa. It was, therefore, possible for the commanders of the Spanish fleet to treat the whole lake as a single battlefield.

Cortés himself left no record of his thoughts as his remarkable new ships glided across the beautiful sheet of water, using both oars and sails, making for the projected site of Sandoval's new headquarters at Iztapalapa. But the splendour of the scene, the clarity of the air, and the daring of the enterprise on which he was engaged surely must have caused him to reflect on the astonishing turn of events which had brought him to the brink of such achievements. With Cortés on the flagship was Martín López, the genius behind the building of the vessels, as apparently pilot-major for the fleet.[49] Behind this fleet was the chief Texcocan general, Ixtlilxochitl, with what his descendant the historian fancifully claimed to be 16,000 Indian canoes.[50]

Cortés was diverted from sailing straight to help Sandoval at Iztapalapa since he saw that, on the small, high, and rocky island of Tepepolco about three miles offshore, many Mexicans had gathered and were busy making signals with smoke to their compatriots in Tenochtitlan. The place obviously served as a centre of intelligence. It also played an important part in Mexican ritual. For example, it was on its summit that, on the fourth day of the fiesta of Toxcatl (the fiesta so savagely interrupted by Alvarado in 1520), the man designated as the god Tezcatlipoca would present himself, "willingly", and have himself sacrificed at the temple of Tlacochcalco. Cortés landed a hundred and fifty men, climbed the main hill, overwhelmed the fortifications, and killed all the inhabitants except for the women and children: "a most beautiful victory", he reported.[51]

After this triumph, Cortés reported, "over five hundred canoes . . . made for us. I re-embarked the brigantines but remained where we were. They halted two crossbowshots from us." Two worlds for a moment faced each other across the lake in silence.

Cortés said that "he was most intent that this first encounter should result in a great victory and would be achieved in a way as to inspire much fear of the brigantines, for the key to the war lay with them. And it pleased God," he went on "that, as we were watching one another, a land breeze came which was very favourable to attacking, and I ordered the captains to break through the fleet of canoes and follow them so as to shut them up in Tenochtitlan. Finally, the brigantines rammed many Mexican canoes."

But in fact not everything went according to plan. When this wind came, the flagship led the Spanish fleet. The Mexica paid special attention to this vessel – no doubt because they saw Cortés on it, and because they recognised it from its size as being important. But before the fighting had begun, its captain, Rodríguez de Villafuerte, allowed the ship to ground. This individual was Cortés' fellow citizen of Medellín, a man who was described, in the *residencia* into Cortés' affairs, as "a very temperate friend of Cortés".[52] But he also had the reputation of being "an undependable man of little knowledge".[53] It certainly seems as if it was in that latter role that he now conducted himself. Large numbers of Mexica swarmed over the ship. Rodríguez de Villafuerte gave the order to abandon the vessel. Martín López refused to follow this distressing instruction. With a small number of close friends, he fought back, cleared the deck of Mexicans with a feat of swordplay and then, observing a captain of the Mexica in feathers and plumes a short way from him in his canoe, killed him with a shot from a crossbow. Where Cortés was during this fight is not clear. But López obviously carried out a remarkable act of individual heroism. Cortés' failure to mention it, or indeed to pay attention in his letters to the King to any of López's achievements, shows that the *Caudillo*, whatever his godlike qualities, was certainly not free from human jealousy.[54] López thereafter seems to have acted as commander to the whole fleet of brigantines, despite the continuing formal precedence of Rodríguez de Villafuerte.[55]

This occurrence was not apparently much noticed at the time. Cortés described the battle as the triumph that it soon became: "As the wind was very good," he wrote, "we broke through an infinite number of canoes and killed or drowned many in them: a most remarkable sight. And in this chase we followed three leagues [say six miles] until we shut them up in the capital." Much of the success was due to the skilful use of the little bronze guns which each brigantine had on board and whose explosions caused fear as well as deaths. The crossbows and the arquebuses were also instrumental in killing innumerable Mexica. Sandoval at Iztapalapa said later that nothing in the world "gave him such joy as to see all thirteen sails with a fair wind over the water scattering the enemy".[56] Cortés' chaplain later added, presumably after talking to Cortés himself, "This was a notable victory and was the key to that war, because we were now masters of the lake, and the enemy had been greatly frightened and felt lost. They might," he added, "not have suffered so if they had not been so numerous, for they got in each other's way – nor would they have been so quickly defeated had it not been for the weather . . ."[57]

This victory caused Cortés to change his plans. He had expected, after assisting Sandoval at Iztapalapa, to go on to Coyoacán, and combine there with Olid. But instead he went instantly to the fortress of Xoloc at a point on the main causeway from Iztapalapa and Tenochtitlan known as Acachinanco. He thus was the first to make use of the opportunity created by the Mexica themselves to cross the old dyke of Nezahualcoyotl. In the evening of this same day, he landed on the causeway with thirty men to seize the two small stone temples at Xoloc. Once again, Martín López was the first into the fray: he jumped from the flagship on to the well-built road with the Castilian standard, shouting,

"Victory, victory for the King of Spain!"[58] A violent fight ensued but the Castilians carried the day. This was partly because Olid, assisted by brigantines guarding him from the east side, had thrust up from Coyoacán. Cortés then landed his three "big iron guns", and discharged one of them along the road to the north, causing no damage but much alarm.[59] Even so the water on both sides of the causeway continued to be full of canoes, and the cannon could not be fired any more since the gunner had allowed all the powder on Cortés' brigantine to be ignited (Cortés sent another brigantine to Iztapalapa to bring him, as a reinforcement, the powder which Sandoval had there). One Castilian who believed that he greatly distinguished himself on this day was the carpenter Diego Hernández who, according to his own later account, showed a remarkable capacity for throwing cannon balls into the enemy ranks, in Mexican style, causing "as much damage as if he had been a gun".[60]

The battle continued well into the night, a new counterattack being launched by the Mexica at midnight, an unusual hour for them, since they disliked fighting in the dark. In the Mexican mind, nights were full of monsters: dwarf-like women with flowing hair or death's-heads which ran after travellers, not to speak of the footless, headless creatures which rolled menacingly on the ground, such as the Castilians had seen during the attacks on the Palace of Axayácatl the previous year. Fierce animals were said to loom at crossroads. But on this night the dark was for the Mexica filled with worse monsters. For several other brigantines joined Cortés, each of them firing their cannons at the Mexican canoes, while the crossbowmen and arquebusiers on board them were also active. In the end, the Mexica withdrew and left the Castilians to an uneasy but triumphant sleep. Cortés had expected to sleep that night at Coyoacán. But instead he remained at Xoloc. His ever-attentive household established itself there with the usual comforts. Meanwhile, the captains of the brigantines made plans for the following day: to find out where the canals were deep or straight or narrow . . . and where they were twisting and winding[61], and, eventually, to prepare to cut off the Mexica from all food and water, as well as from possible assistance from the few cities still loyal to them.

This landing halfway up the main causeway was an improvisation which, following the amphibious action at Tepepolco and the naval victory, showed the capacity of Cortés for quick changes of plan.

Alvarado had been less unconventional. He had sent foot soldiers cautiously along the causeway of Nonoalco towards the capital, leaving his horsemen on dry land to protect the rearguard, thinking that some of the nearby towns might attack from behind.

In both these actions, Cortés and his captains had been well seconded by Indian allies: Ixtlilxochitl in particular appears to have been always at Cortés' side.[62]

Cuauhtémoc, realising the tactics of the enemy, divided his defence into four divisions to face the Castilians in four directions: on the northern causeway to Tepeyac which had, as yet, seen no action; towards Tacuba against Alvarado; against Cortés, Olid and Sandoval at Acachinanco; while a fourth division remained to defend the place against any landing of the enemy from a brigantine. Cuauhtémoc himself was paddled from place to place in a canoe to supervise the defence.[63] Enraged by the deaths of so many of his people, and angry because so many once good allies (Chalco, Texcoco) had abandoned him, he had determined not to show any weakness. Women were ordered to take up the swords of their husbands when they died. There was something close to total mobilisation.

The following morning, at dawn, Cortés sent for reinforcements from Olid's division at Coyoacán, and about fifty soldiers, seven or eight horsemen, and fifteen crossbowmen and arquebusiers joined him at Xoloc. Just as they arrived, the Mexica launched an attack down that road from the capital. There were also attacks on both sides of the causeway from canoes. The Mexica came shouting so loudly that Cortés remarked drily that it sounded as if "the world was coming to an end".[64] But he gained the advantage, since, by temporarily opening a bridge just to the south of Xoloc, he made it possible for some brigantines to move to the west side of the lake. Four went through and then, keeping close to the causeway, they, with the others on the east side, assisted the foot soldiers and horsemen to fight their way north towards the capital. The Castilians crossed one channel whose bridge had been removed, by using a brigantine as a stepping stone. When on the north side of it, with guns and horses, they drove back the Mexica to the first houses of the city. Some brigantines were carefully paddled into the city past the stakes which had been set in the water to obstruct them. The crews of these vessels set fire to houses in the south of the city, thereby opening a new and drastic dimension to the war. If Cortés felt any pangs of regret because he had reached that same spot on the causeway where, eighteen months before, he had first been greeted, with courtesy, by "the great Montezuma", he kept them to himself.

The four brigantines on the west side of the north–south causeway then set off to support Alvarado who seemed embattled with his division on the short Nonoalco causeway which, of course, ran west–east. Two other ships set off to assist Sandoval at Iztapalapa. With their help, and using the vessels more or less as bridges across an interrupted and sabotaged causeway, that conquistador transferred his division to Coyoacán; while Olid now changed his seat of operations to Xoloc.

After the successes of the first day of the siege, the next weeks were slow, painful, and difficult for the Castilians. The Mexica were quick to think of ways of dealing with new threats. On the causeways, they dug breastworks, they made use of hidden pits, they used their new lances with Toledo blades at the end of them, they even adapted Castilian scythes to military use, they flung javelins and, of course, they continually used bows and arrows. On Alvarado's front, most of the Castilians were wounded. Those who had horses did not want to risk them in battle.[65]

The fighting on the north–south causeway was also far from immediately decisive. Every day the Tlaxcalans or other allies filled in holes or breaches in the causeway which the Mexica had made overnight. This process, it will be recalled, had been tried at the battle for Xochimilco some weeks before. Then, escorted by brigantines on either side of the causeway, the Castilians would press forward as far as the first houses of the city, killing many Mexica. They would retreat at night to their camp at Xoloc. The Mexica would then return down the causeway, dig up the holes, and force the Castilians (or, rather, their Indian allies) to get to work again on this road the following day. The brigantines, it is true, continued to constrain the canoes of the Mexica. Cortés was thus in control of the lake. Often, too, the brigantines would penetrate the city, and their crews would burn the houses on either side of the canals.[66] But they too found progress slow, for there seemed to be an unlimited supply of Mexica to attack them with stones, darts and arrows.

There is just a touch of the bizarre about these battles: all day there was fighting, but the Castilians neither made much progress nor lost many men. The explanation must be that the brunt of the battle was borne in these early days by the Indian allies. Cortés continued to be as cautious with his own men as was Montgomery, say, with his army in the Second World War.

Alvarado reported to Cortés that the Mexica were regularly moving in and out of Tenochtitlan along the north causeway which led from Tlatelolco to the hill known as Tepeyac. Presumably they were bringing supplies. That was far from Cortés' desire: had they fled altogether along that route, he would have been pleased. But he was not happy that food should thus *enter* the blockaded city. So he sent Sandoval from Iztapalapa round via Coyoacán and Tacuba to that northern road, and gave him orders to block the path there. After some skirmishing on the Iztapalapa–Coyoacán section of his journey, Sandoval eventually arrived with twenty-three horse, eighteen crossbowmen and about a hundred foot soldiers. He later had three brigantines assigned to him. When he had established himself, Tenochtitlan was quite surrounded.[67]

By these decisions, in some ways improvised and unforeseen, Cortés had changed the nature of his siege. No longer did the Mexica have a silver bridge along which to escape, even had they wanted one. By permitting the brigantines to burn houses in Tenochtitlan, the destruction of the city had begun. Tenochtitlan was not an open city, nor were the conquistadors aesthetes or architectural historians. Yet Cortés had revelled in its "sumptuousness". He had been hoping to hand over to the

Emperor Charles V a jewel, not a ruin. This marked the second fearful major change in his policy: the first being when, after his return to the city in June the previous year, he realised that he could not expect to win Tenochtitlan without a battle.

In order to try and bring matters to a head as quickly as possible, without more damage being caused, Cortés resolved, after another ten days, about 10 June, to make a co-ordinated drive as far as he could into the heart of Tenochtitlan. He took command of all the two hundred foot which had been allocated in the original division of the army to Olid. He had also, of course, the support of brigantines on both sides of the causeway. He gave orders to Alvarado and Sandoval in the west and north to meet him near the main temple or the Palace of Axayácatl, where the Spaniards had had their quarters in 1520. So Cortés set off. Behind the Castilians on the causeway came an army of what he described as 80,000 Indian allies, though, in practice, it would be surprising if the figure attained a tenth of that. Still, even that would have constituted a considerable army.

The drive was at first successful. Cortés reached the end of the causeway just in front of the Gate of the Eagle, on which stood the figures of an eagle, an ocelot and a wolf, and which marked the entrance to the city.[68] There, a large bridge had been raised. But brigantines carefully placed as pontoon bridges enabled Cortés and a body of horsemen and infantry to cross into the city. The allies then busied themselves with knocking down the nearby houses and using the rubble thereby obtained to fill in the breach.

Once over that first obstacle, the Castilians pressed due north into the city, approximately along the line of the straight street now known as the Avenida José María Pino Suárez. There were further defences: a barricade, and another bridge over a canal had been raised. The latter was defended by a large earthwork of adobe and stone. This last must have been near the crossing of San Antonio de Abad with the present street of Fray Servando Teresa de Mier. Cortés ordered two guns to be fired down the street at the earthwork. The consequent shock gave the Castilians enough time to force the canal and capture it. The Mexica fled back towards the square of the Great Temple. The Castilians pressed on again and, after crossing a bridge (that over the aqueduct) which the Mexica had not thought to raise (they had not dreamed that Cortés would penetrate so far), soon found themselves at the edge of the square. Here, Cortés again set up one of his guns and caused it to fire several shots, causing much damage, as he reported. The Mexica fled again, to the temple enclosure. The Castilians pursued them. They too reached the enclosure for the first time since they had left it the previous July. But here, however, Mexican numbers told. When they saw that the horsemen had returned to their quarters, they drove the Spaniards not only out of the temple enclosure, but out of the square itself into the straight street which led to the causeway. The Mexican obsidian-edged *macuauhuitls* and sticks seemed for once the equal of Castilian swords. Cortés had to leave behind the gun which he had fired into the square. The Mexica dragged it to the lake and threw it in. They had no gunpowder and could not work the mechanism.[69] But then several Castilian horsemen went back to the square and, at dusk, Cortés was able for a time to reoccupy the temple enclosure.[70]

The hour then being late, Cortés now ordered a withdrawal. This was the signal for great attacks by the Mexica who dropped, or threw, innumerable stones from the rooftops, so that, though the street was broad, it was scarcely possible to avoid being hit. The Castilians in retreat set fire to many houses so that, the next time they entered, they would not find themselves facing this particular terror from above.[71] These acts of reprisal further limited Cortés' hope of handing over a "great Venice" in its pristine state to his far-off king.

Similar attacks had been launched on this day by Alvarado and Sandoval in the west and north, though they did not get anywhere near the centre of the city.[72] They too were restrained by traditional Mexican weapons, with bows and arrows as well as spears being effectively used in the defence. When the two commanders gave the order for retreat, they were still some three and four miles respectively from the centre of the city.

By this time so many houses had been burned and turned into rubble in the outskirts of the city that it was almost impossible for the Mexican canoes to operate. This meant, Cortés thought, that he could release several brigantines from guarding the camp at Xoloc. He sent three of these on permanent assignment to Alvarado and Sandoval, with instructions to cruise day and night in order to prevent food from being carried into the city. This was largely a successful blockade, though, within a week or so, the Mexica managed to trap two of these brigantines and kill their commanders, Pedro Barba and Juan Portillo.[73]

Meantime the numerous Indian allies, from Cholula, Tlaxcala, Texcoco and Huexotzinco, were busy filling in the holes in the causeway and even in the roads inside Tenochtitlan: a day or two before, a new force of such allies had been brought from Texcoco, while substantial numbers from Xochimilco and even some Otomí peoples from the north separately came to offer themselves as vassals of the King of Spain, begging Cortés' forgiveness for having delayed so long in doing so. Cortés on this occasion was benignly forgiving. About the same time, the Chalca and the Xochimilca also offered all kinds of assistance to Cortés, including food (fish and cherries) as well as canoes. They even offered to build houses on the causeway as temporary refuges for the Castilians.[74] Ixtlilxochitl, the Texcocan, presented himself as the intermediary between Cortés and all these people.[75]

On 15 June, Cortés made another major attack of the same sort as that of the 10th. He had done nothing very much in the way of operations for some days. So, not surprisingly, he found that the Mexica had again made breaches all along the causeway. But once again his brigantines closed in on both sides, once again the allies crossed the gaps by boat, once again the Castilians (some of them swimming despite their cotton armour) broke into the city across a gap in front of the Gate of the Eagle, and once again they destroyed an earthwork near what is now the intersection of the Calle Fray Servando Teresa de Mier. Once again too they made their way to the main square, though on this day they met with far greater opposition than they had done previously. The numbers, the stamina, and the discipline of the Mexica seemed remarkable.

After this engagement, the Castilians again retired, and this time the counterattack was less effective, since the allies had made good the entire broad street so that horses could gallop along the length of it.

The evident determination of the Mexica to fight to the death persuaded Cortés of two bitter truths: first, that he and his comrades would gain little or nothing back of the gold and other riches which they had lost in the *noche triste*; and second, far more important, that, given the Mexican resistance, there was no alternative but to, as Sepúlveda would put it in his History with his usual candour, "destroy the city".[76] This last decision, Cortés said, "weighed on my soul, and so I tried to find a way whereby I might frighten them [the Mexica] and cause them to recognise their errors and the harm they would come to".[77] As a warning, Cortés instructed the captains of several brigantines to make their way up the appropriate canal and set fire not only to the great Palace of Axayácatl where they had been quartered the previous year, but also Montezuma's House of Birds. This grieved the Mexica but, all the same, they did not hesitate to continue the war. An outrage, as modern generals have discovered, as often stiffens resistance as ends it. So it was that Cortés and his captains, in the words of Fr. Sahagún, decided to do away completely with the Mexica.[78]

Years later, Cortés was asked about his strategy. The question was raised as to whether he had shown himself unnecessarily destructive. He was defended by several of those who had been with him. For example, Luis Marín insisted that, if Tenochtitlan had not been razed to the ground, it could not have been taken. For if the Castilians had not destroyed most buildings which they captured, the Mexica would have returned to them at night, in such a way that another battle would have been necessary for the same place the following day. Cortés' method, he thought, had been the only way of gaining the city.[79] Alonso de Navarrete agreed that, had it not been destroyed, "the city would not have been gained, or at least not so quickly, or at least with much more labour"; Juan López de Jimena said that it was both "convenient and necessary to act thus because there were large buildings in the city from which the Mexica could maltreat the Spaniards from the rooftops"; "it was necessary so to act," stated Gaspar de Garnica (one of Velázquez's associates who had come with Narváez), "because one could see the damage which would have been caused by the enemy if the buildings had not been pulled down"; "in order to win the city, it was necessary to demolish it," said Rodríguez de Escobar; and others said the same.[80]

Yet the cost was terrible. Tenochtitlan was not destroyed by chance. It was the consequence of a deliberate policy, carefully and methodically carried through, with all the forcefulness of European war, and with no care for the ruin of a masterpiece of urban design. The Tlaxcalans were jubilant. Perhaps also Ixtlilxochitl advised Cortés to have no qualms about what he was doing.[81] Probably all non-Mexica were happy at the thought of razing Tenochtitlan. All the peoples of the valley wanted to settle scores with the Mexica. Only the Castilians seem to have had any regrets at all for the policy which their commander had decided upon; and those regrets were muted.

One change was immediately noticed as a result of Cortés' new policy: in addition to the noise of gunfire, the shouting of the Mexican war cries, and the neighing of horses, there was also the sound of the destruction of great buildings by fire, the smell of dust, and the shrieks of men and women caught in falling masonry.

The day following Cortés' second penetration to the temple precinct, his army returned to the city in the early hours, before, as they hoped, the Mexica would have been able to reopen the breaches. But still, overnight, holes had been dug, and the Castilians had the same difficulties as before. The majority of the army had to swim across the breach between the end of the causeway and the Gate of the Eagle. Once in the city, however, they were in a better condition than they had been before, since the Mexica were less able to attack from rooftops now that most of the houses along the street to the main square had been gutted. Having made the point that they were able to go to and from the main square almost at will, the Castilians again withdrew. Some of Cortés' captains thought that he should there and then establish the camp in that square. But Cortés recalled to them how, the previous year, he had been caught inside Tenochtitlan. He therefore refused: in addition, the establishment of such a camp would have necessitated the Castilians having to fight all and every night. They would also have been unable to guard the bridges. That would have been dangerous had they needed to escape. In addition, there remained many buildings near the main square which could still have been used by the Mexica as fortresses.[82]

Cortés instead decided to pursue this series of attacks by attrition: to enter the city in the same way every day and attack the inhabitants every time in three or four different places. He did this, always escorted at the beginning by brigantines and after some days, in late June, by canoes supplied by the allies. By 20 June Cortés was not stopping at the main square, but instead was passing through it, and turning to the left down the street which led to the Tacuba causeway, so that he could soon effect a junction with Alvarado.[83]

That commander's attacks had also continued unabated. Each day his force, like the *Caudillo*'s, would advance along his causeway in regular order. They were attacked with persistence but they always made headway. Yet the Mexica always seemed to have reserves ready to throw into the battle to prevent the advance being fast and, at the end of the day, the Castilians would find it still essential to retreat to their camp where their wounds could be treated with oil and, if necessary, bandaged; where they could dine off tortillas, vegetables, and tuna, the fruit of the nopal cactus which comes into season about the middle of June; and where many of the soldiers, including Alvarado, would sleep with their indigenous mistresses. During the night, a relief force of Mexica, probably many of them women, would come out and again dig up all the breaches which the Castilians would have filled.[84]

On 23 June, the vanguard of Alvarado's division went too far, several brigantines were impaled on posts in the water, and the attack had to retreat in disorder, finding that one of the breaches in the causeway which they had crossed earlier had not been properly filled. They left at least five Castilians alive in enemy hands to be sacrificed. Had it not been for the last-minute use of horsemen and cannon, the disaster would have been greater. Alvarado later claimed that he had swum to the help of some of those cut off, and that, if he had not done that, they too would have died.[85]

Cortés was naturally disturbed at this news when it reached him. He sent a letter to Alvarado telling him that he should never leave an opening in the causeway unfilled. He was always to fill in gaps with, for example, adobe or timber obtained from the houses which they had destroyed. He added that the horsemen should, as a matter of course, sleep on the causeway, and keep their mounts saddled and bridled.

Alvarado himself nevertheless always returned to the city of Tacuba at night, in order, as he claimed, to ensure a proper supply of crossbows and other equipment. But it was said, and he was subsequently accused in his *residencia* of exactly that, that he went there primarily in order to sleep with "María Luisa".[86]

A second setback dates from this period of late June. Two brigantines were paddling down some of the back canals when one, captained by Cristóbal Flores, became temporarily grounded. It was attacked by the Mexica. Fifteen of the Castilians on board seem to have been captured, and many of the others were severely wounded. The ship was freed, it is true, by men from the second brigantine, captained by Gerónimo Ruiz de la Mota, and was refloated.[87]

By this time, Cortés seemed, however, in an overwhelmingly strong position. He had the backing of almost all the cities round the lake. Huitzilopochco, Culhuacan, and Mixquic, for example, had seen how the war looked likely to be determined, and they too sought to save themselves, as they supposed, by offering fealty to the Emperor Charles V. These local people mixed freely with the Spaniards in their camps, many coming to serve them, others to steal, some to eat, many to gape, and others still to build more huts along the line of the causeway to Cortés' headquarters.[88] A thousand or so slept there, while many more did so at Coyoacán, which became the first of the vast shanty towns for which Latin America has subsequently become known. On one occasion Cortés persuaded several thousand of these people to set off from Coyoacán for Tenochtitlan in canoes, attack that capital from several different directions, and then burn buildings and do all the damage that they could.[89] Probably by now the sheer number of allies was, however, an embarrassment to both Cortés and Alvarado, since they could not easily tell them what to do in action. Filling in breaches in causeways and waiting at the table were different matters: and the Spanish captains seem to have continued to dine in style every day, even if the fare was unvarying.

When Cortés entered the city on 23 June, he found that the Mexica had staged a considered withdrawal from the area between the now ruined Gate of the Eagle and the main square. Several members of his army began to clear the route west towards Tacuba. Cortés went to see Alvarado by brigantine, and saw how much progress he had made along the causeway. He was impressed, and decided that, after all, he did not have to reprimand Alvarado for his rashness in pressing an attack which had led to casualties (as has been said, Cortés found it hard to reprimand Alvarado: a serious weakness). Alvarado told him that he soon planned to move his camp to a small square inside Tenochtitlan. They would leave behind their Indian breadmakers, as well as the Tlaxcalan allies, the horsemen and presumably their ladies, at Tacuba.

So by the end of June, final victory seemed to be close. Cortés thought that Cuauhtémoc was certain soon to surrender. The Castilians had conquered half the capital. Alvarado, Sandoval and Cortés were about to link their forces. The supply of food brought in from the countryside to the Mexica was as much a thing of the past as the water supply from Chapultepec. Many of the intensely cultivated *chinampas* actually within the city, on which so many families depended for fresh fruit and vegetables, had been lost or destroyed. Equally, the brigantines interrupted, and often prevented, the fishing and low-scale hunting which had occupied so much of the time of the average man from Tenochtitlan, and which contributed so greatly to his table. In ensuring the blockade, the thousands of canoes from the allies were beginning to play almost as important a part as the brigantines. The Mexica, it is true, still had stores of maize, assembled against drought or famine in the past. There were wells. But these did not prevent the need for strict rationing.

There were also, as it turned out, difficulties among the Mexica. Two more of the sons of Montezuma, Axayaca and Xoxopehualoc, led a group of noblemen who would have liked to have begun negotiations with the Castilians. Cuauhtémoc apparently had them executed. In reprisal, some of their followers seem to have killed the high priests of Huitzilopochtli and Tezcatlipoca. These murderous divisions exposed one more weakness in the Mexican regime.[90]

Yet for the Castilians there were still many troubles ahead.

34
A great harvest of captives

One heard the cry: 'Mexicans, now is the moment! Who are these savages?
Let them be flung out of here!' ... At that time the moment began for
catching men. Many from Tlaxcala, Acolhuacan, Chalco, Xochimilco were
captured. There was a great harvest of captives, a great harvest of dead.
Florentine Codex, Book xii, Chapter 25

T HE MEXICA CONTINUED to show astonishing resilience. Every
night they re-dug the ditches in the causeways which the Spaniards
or their allies had filled in the previous day. They still seemed able,
day after day, to withstand heavy attacks on three fronts. They were able
to adapt themselves to facing the horses, the guns, even the steel swords
with skill, and then were able to inflict far more damage than the
Spaniards could have supposed possible with their obsidian-edged
weapons, their stones, their arrows, and even their clubs or sticks. They
rarely killed, it is true. Their weapons were not made for that. But they
wounded often. They were able to hold up the Spanish and allied
advances remarkably, still making it impossible, after a month of the
siege, for the Spaniards to move down a street whose buildings they and
their friends had not previously cleared or burned.

One explanation for the resilience was that the education at the
calmécac was showing its benefits. When boys set out for those schools,
their fathers would say: "Listen, you are not going to be honoured, nor
obeyed, nor esteemed, you are going to be looked down upon,
humiliated, and despised. Every day you will cut agave thorns for
penance, and you will draw blood with those spines and you will bathe at
night, even when it is very cold ... harden your body."[1] It is true that
the education in the *telpochcalli* had a less severe syllabus. Still, it was, all
the same, an education in collective action. Everything was done there to
prepare the boys for war: not, it is true, the kind of war being experienced
in Tenochtitlan, but still war; for which rhetoric had prepared their
minds.

In both institutions, pupils would have learned by heart songs about
past combats, long-dead warriors, legendary victors in Homeric conflicts.
In 1521 the Mexican education showed its merits.

It is very possible that the Mexica were also sustained by drugs. The favourite drug of the Chichimecs, for example, was the *peyotl*, a little white truffle-like cactus: Those who ate or drank it [presumably powdered, with water] saw either appalling or ludicrous things. This drunkenness lasted two or three days, then vanished. This plant sustained them [the Chichimecs], gave them courage for battle, destroyed fear, and kept them from thirst and hunger. It was said that it preserved them from all danger.[2] Sacred mushrooms may also have been eaten: the sensations caused as a result often enhanced bravery to wild levels.

On most days, anyway, in late June 1521, Cortés led attacks at dawn into the Mexican capital and, in early morning mist so characteristic of the lakeside at that season, burned more houses and palaces. After the allies had filled in the canals, the Castilian horsemen would appear, "winding, wheeling, twisting about". All would withdraw at dusk. Cortés hesitated to go further than the central square and the temple precinct for fear of being cut off. The same policy was followed by both Sandoval and Alvarado with their divisions. Yet every night the Mexica would still dig up the ditches in the causeways. Their ancestors had built the city. They would preserve it; or perish in the attempt.

Cortés consulted his captains as to whether to attempt another combined offensive with Alvarado and Sandoval, asking them as well as his own forces to thrust, for example, to the marketplace at Tlatelolco.[3] If that square were taken, the Mexica would have little to defend. Divided, they would have to choose between surrendering and dying of hunger and thirst.

Cortés was wary of this scheme. After all, even if the Castilians were to establish a headquarters in the square of Tlatelolco, they could easily be surrounded. There seemed no shortage of numbers among the enemy. To reach Tlatelolco, it was necessary to cross one of several broad causeways which, however wide, could be interrupted. In the square, no brigantines could assist them. Besiegers might become besieged. But Cortés' captains (particularly Verdugo, Olid, Tapia, Lugo and the standard-bearer Corral) kept pressing the idea. Alvarado and his captains insisted that they wanted to beat the laggardly men of Cortés to the square. They were joined in the advice by Alderete, the King's treasurer, who said that the whole camp favoured the idea, as he did too. Cortés took this recommendation seriously, more so, perhaps, than he should have done. So eventually, and against his better judgement (at least according to this report), Cortés agreed to go ahead with a combined attack on 30 June.[4]

Before this attack could come to anything, there was an important, if, even now, not altogether comprehensible change in the position of the Mexica. This affected the relative strengths of Tenochtitlan and Tlatelolco. Hitherto most of the fighting had been done by the men of Tenochtitlan. It had been the houses of Tenochtitlan which had burned.

The northern city, suburb and dependency of Tlatelolco and its people had been almost untouched. This indifference was the culmination of years of insolence on the part of the rulers of Tenochtitlan. The people of Tlatelolco complained: Tenochtitlan "did not seem to know that they, the Tlatelolca [too], were Mexica". The people of Tlatelolco had had to pay tribute to their imperial neighbours ever since their conquest in 1473: every year, eighty war costumes, eighty shields, 64,000 cloaks, and over six hundred baskets. They resented it.[5]

Now Tenochtitlan needed Tlatelolco: its manpower, its site, the energy of its people. Cuauhtémoc made an appeal to Tlatelolco for help. Its leaders agreed to help the Emperor. But they seem to have insisted on a price. Henceforward Tenochtitlan would have to give up their management of the empire. Cuauhtémoc might remain the general in command of the forces fighting the Castilians. But thereafter Tlatelolco would dominate.[6] This was acceptable to Cuauhtémoc, presumably because of his Tlatelolcan blood (it will be remembered that he was a grandson of Tlatelolco's last king) and because he had been a leader of that city when he returned to the Valley of Mexico before becoming Emperor.[7]

Cuauhtémoc moved his headquarters to a building known in Tlatelolco as Yacacolco (approximately where the church of Santa Ana now stands). The effigy of Huitzilopochtli was taken from the Great Temple of Tenochtitlan to Tlatelolco. The armies then moved to Tlatelolco too. The remainder of the population in Tenochtitlan also did what they could to withdraw there also. Cortés tried to take advantage of these changes, of which he was brought news. He sought a meeting with the leaders of Tlatelolco. When he found some means of communicating with them, he said, "Why seek the greater misery of perishing with them when they have made such fools of you?" But the Tlatelolca did not contemplate surrender. They instead thought that their hour of glory had come.[8]

For a few days this even seemed to be possible. First, Tlapanecatzin, one of the Tlatelolcan leaders, captured a Castilian banner. Surely this was a harbinger of triumph?

Second, Cortés' new joint offensive ended badly. Cortés had written to Sandoval and Alvarado to tell them of the plan to establish a camp in the market of Tlatelolco. Sandoval was to join Alvarado. But he was to leave behind his horsemen on the mainland, and give the impression that he was breaking camp altogether. That would enable the cavalry on what had been looked on as his causeway to lure the Mexica in the north of the city into an ambush. Alvarado would, meantime, advance from the west, in collaboration with Sandoval's infantrymen.

Cortés divided his own troops. They would drive up the southern causeway in the normal way. Once inside Tenochtitlan, they would divide into three. One column, headed by Alderete, with seventy foot soldiers and seven or eight horse, would move up the main street which the Castilians by now knew so well, first to the main square before the temple precinct, and then north-west to Tlatelolco. They would be supported by a large number of allies to fill in the breaches which Cortés knew would have been made in the streets.[9] Andrés de Tapia, with Jorge de Alvarado, would, with a similar array, advance from the road which led east–west to the Tacuba causeway. Cortés himself would travel north along a narrower road, with about a hundred foot soldiers and eight horse, as well as another large contingent of allies. Each of them would of course have to cross the large waterway which divided Tenochtitlan from Tlatelolco, but would do so at different points.[10]

Mass was said at Xoloc by Fr. Bartolomé, the brigantines set off, the canoes of the allies followed, the Castilians crossed by the now ruined Gate of the Eagle. Their main force divided, as planned, into three. Cortés' column captured two new bridges and two barricades on his route. He crossed into Tlatelolco. His pace was then slow because Tlatelolco did not have the broad avenues, nor the quadriform division into *barrios*, which marked Tenochtitlan.[11] Nor did he know the streets so well. Then Cortés found himself facing a strong Mexican counter-attack, and was forced to halt. He returned to check that the breaches remained filled in, to find that one substantial one, that used by Alderete's column, had either not been done adequately or had been immediately dug up by the enemy. However it happened, instead of the big ditch between the two cities being filled with masonry, wood and earth, there was a gap ten or twelve paces wide in which water already stood eight feet deep. Cortés later blamed Alderete for this mistake; Alderete placed the responsibility on Cortés. It seems more likely that the Mexica themselves had contrived the idea by a brilliant piece of commando-style work after Alderete's column had passed.[12] At all events, in a few seconds, the tide of battle had turned against the Spaniards.

Alderete's men were also being forced backwards by the sheer weight of Mexican opposition. The retreat suddenly became a rout as the unexpected obstacle of the new breach caused chaos. In the crowded street, the conquistadors could use neither guns nor horses. The press was continuous, the Indian allies panicked, while the triumphant Mexica, having realised what had happened, sent round their canoes to the gap in the route. There, their crews tried to capture as many of their enemies as they could, as one after another of the Castilians and their allies leapt into the water, intending to swim to the far side. Cortés himself was so busy fighting, at least according to his own account, that he did not notice his own danger. Once again, as "on the bridges" and at Xochimilco in February, the Mexica could surely have killed him had it not been for their institutionalised wish to secure him live for the benefit of the sacrificial stone. That so-much-desired capture could probably have been attained, had it not been (again as at Xochimilco) for the efforts of Cristóbal de Olea, the clever swordsman from Medina del Campo. Once more, he saved Cortés by cutting off the hands of those Mexica who had seized him. But this time he himself was struck down and killed after he had saved his commander. Thereafter Cortés' chief bodyguard, Antonio de Quiñones, secured his survival, insisting that he had a duty to retire, since, if he did not save himself, the expedition would be lost.[13] Earlier, Cortés saved Martín Vázquez from capture: an action which no doubt explains why that conquistador from Llerena could always be relied upon to testify afterwards in the *Caudillo*'s favour.[14]

In these confused battles the Mexica also had their heroes. Most of them, in this phase of the fighting, were from Tlatelolco. One hero in particular was Ecatzin, who belonged to the Otomitl, the military order comparable to the eagle and jaguar knights, composed of men sworn never to retreat. Ecatzin was an outstanding propeller of large stones, the "weapons" which had been causing the Castilians most damage. He passed among the Mexican fighters sometimes in the glittering uniform which was his right, in view of past prowess, but sometimes disguised as an ordinary soldier: always with his head uncovered, as was the order's custom.[15]

The curious thing about this Mexican victory is that no source speaks of Cuauhtémoc himself being concerned in this fighting. He seemed the remote emperor, the man who took decisions, but his own part in the conflict appears to have been nonexistent. He was never criticised. But it is an irony that in a nation organised for war, its supreme commander should have seemed to be above the battle.[16]

Without the loss of Cortés, the damage to the attackers was bad enough: "There was a great harvest of captives, a great harvest of dead."[17] The Castilians killed must have been about twenty, including Olea. But probably over fifty – fifty-three, according to several sources – were captured, including Cristóbal de Guzmán, Cortés' chamberlain who had been with him throughout the expedition. Two thousand Indian allies were said to have been killed too. One cannon and one brigantine were lost.[18]

Alvarado and Sandoval had, meantime, been making slow progress along the streets just within the city towards the western causeway. They operated separately, though they were in touch. As usual the numbers of Mexica delayed progress. Towards evening, the leaders of both these Spanish columns separately saw new Mexican forces approaching them. They were carrying the severed, bloody, but still bearded heads of recently killed Castilian prisoners. Flinging these prizes in front of them, the Mexica said to Alvarado's troops, "Thus we shall kill you, as we have killed Malinche and Sandoval." To Sandoval's forces, they said the same, though substituting the name of Alvarado for that of Sandoval.

As the Mexica shouted these threats, the Castilians heard, in the distance, the sonorous sound of drums, trumpets and horns, indicating that some prisoners were about to be sacrificed. The drums and trumpets were so loud as to suggest, once more, that the world was coming to an end, as Cortés again put it, using an expression of which he was fond.[19]

Alvarado, Sandoval, Lugo, and Tapia, as well as the commanders of the brigantines in the lake, all saw, in the distance, from the Tacuba causeway, that "our comrades . . . were being carried by force up the steps of the great temple" – probably the temple in Tlatelolco. They were, of course, naked.[20] "When they got them up to the little square in front of the shrines of the gods," wrote Bernal Díaz, in a famous passage, "we saw them place plumes on their heads and, with things like fans, they forced them to dance before the god Huitzilopochtli . . . then they placed them on their backs on some stones . . . and, with large flint knives, they sawed open their chests, and drew out their palpitating hearts and offered them to the gods . . . they kicked the bodies down the steps and Indian butchers, who were waiting below, cut off the arms and legs and flayed the faces and prepared them afterwards as a kind of glove leather with the beards still on, for use in drunken fiestas, while the bodies were eaten with *mole* . . . and the stomachs and guts they threw to the tigers, lions and snakes which were kept in the wild animals' zoo."[21] The ceremony of sacrifice was, of course, designed to be seen from afar. In the Graeco-Roman tradition, spectators look down at the stage. In old Mexico, the public were intended to look up.

The Florentine Codex described how, on this horrifying occasion for the Castilians, some captives wept, some sang, and "one went crying out while striking his mouth with the palm of his hand". Then when they reached Cuauhtémoc's headquarters at Yacacolco, they were made to stand in rows. One by one the multitude went to the pyramid where they were sacrificed. The Spaniards went first . . . [then] the allies . . . They strung up the heads of the Spaniards on the skull rack . . . they also strung the heads of four horses.[22]

Slowly the extent of the defeat became known to the Castilian commanders. Sandoval and Lugo went by boat to Cortés' camp to find out what had happened there, while Cortés sent Tapia by land with three other horsemen (Juan de Cuéllar, Guillén de la Loa, and Diego Valdenebro) to Alvarado's camp for the same purpose. In the end Sandoval went on to Alvarado. At least it became known that the commanders were still alive. Some degree of trilateral control was thus re-established. But that was all. The continuous and, to the Castilians, terrifying noise of drums and horns, and the groans of the wounded made this one of the worst moments of the expedition.

Immediately most of the Indian allies disappeared. One moment they were present, filling in causeways, hauling guns, serving and carrying food. The next moment they seemed to have vanished. Over the next few days, support from the cities around the shore of the great lake faded. The myth that the newcomers could never be defeated had evaporated. Only a few of the allies remained: Ixtlilxochitl, and about forty of his Texcocan relations; one chief from Huexotzinco, also with about forty men, in Sandoval's camp; and Chichimecatecle and two younger sons of old Xicotencatl, with about forty Tlaxcalans. But these were nothing compared with the vast host which had been present previously. For a few days in early July 1521, most of the population in the Valley of Mexico probably thought that the empire of the Mexica would soon be revived. Had not Xicotencatl the younger predicted, before he had been hanged, that, in the end, the Mexica would kill all the Castilians?[23]

For four days the conquistadors remained in their camp, guarded by the brigantines on both sides of the causeway, but forced to hear the continuous sound of sacrifice, celebration, and exaltation. An unofficial healer, Juan Catalan, an artilleryman, moved about the camp, muttering prayers over wounds. Several Castilian women established themselves in Cortés' camp as nurses: Isabel Rodríguez, for example, who was said to have a legendary touch with the wounded; and Beatriz de Paredes, a *mulata* who not only nursed but on occasion fought in the place of her husband, Pedro de Escoto.[24]

This was Cuauhtémoc's opportunity. He sent messengers to the chiefs of Chalco, Xochimilco, Cuernavaca and elsewhere with the flayed heads of his captives, as well as their hands and feet. He sent several horses' heads too. He assured those lords that half the invaders had been killed and that the rest had been wounded. After all, he was able to insist, Huitzilopochtli had not abandoned the Mexica. Cuauhtémoc pointed out how the Indian allies of Cortés had fled overnight. He said that he was learning from captured crossbowmen how to use the bows of the Europeans; even that he had secured five crossbowmen to fight for him. That arrangement did not turn out very well: when the battles began again, these Sevillanos – they apparently included Cristóbal de Guzmán – were ordered to shoot their bows at their countrymen. That they did. But they always shot in the air and every arrow fell harmless. The Mexica tore them apart.[25]

Every day brought news of "rebellions", as Cortés called them, of people who he had supposed, or persuaded himself, were firmly in his camp. But a different kind of intelligence came from the chiefs of Cuernavaca. They had accepted Castilian rule when Cortés had been there in the spring. Recently they had been attacked by an army from the nearby sacred city of Malinalco. They wanted help. The news particularly disturbed Cortés, for Cuernavaca was the key to the communications with the gold-producing country in what is now the state of Oaxaca. Further, as a matter of policy, Cortés tried never to turn down a request for help from an important Indian ally.[26]

So he dispatched Andrés de Tapia, with eighty foot and ten horse, south across the mountains of Ajusco, and instructed him to take such action as he thought right to restore the loyalty of Cuernavaca to him and the Spanish Crown. This seems to have been a turning point in the campaign. Tapia conducted his campaign with remarkable success. In about ten days, he drove the chiefs of Malinalco to take refuge in their magnificent, but remote sanctuary.[27] Malinalco, a magical site in the hills west of Cuernavaca, was devoted to the cult of the jaguar and eagle warriors. Its temple, carved out of the rock in Montezuma's time three hundred feet up from the valley, had (and has) its entrance shaped as the jaws of a serpent. Sorcerers were supposed to learn their craft there.[28] It had been there, according to legend, that Malinalxochitl ("maguey flower"), the beautiful sister of Hutzilopochtli, had led a group of dissident Mexica on their way south from Pátzcuaro, and had lived conspiring there ever since.[29] Psychologically Cortés was right to take the threat from that place seriously.

A similar expedition led by the tireless Sandoval was a few days later sent in support of the Otomí against Matalcingo, whose leaders had plainly been influenced by the sight of the flayed heads of Castilians sent by Cuauhtémoc.[30] He also defeated a potentially dangerous force from Tula which the Emperor had been expecting would attack Cortés in the rear. Similarly Alonso de Ojeda was dispatched for more supplies to Tlaxcala; and these came, being escorted by Pedro Sánchez Farfán and his wife María de Estrada.[31]

By the middle of July, the Castilians realised that Cuauhtémoc had not used the opportunity of his victory on 30 June to carry the war into their camp. He mounted no attack. Probably this neglect was from exhaustion. The Mexica were short of food and water. The brigantines, though about five had been lost, were still in control of the lake. The blockade was still in place even if the canoes of the allies had been withdrawn. The Tlaxcalan allies were returning. It began to seem, and not only to the Castilians, that the victory of 30 June had been the Mexica's last throw.

This interpretation seemed confirmed when, seeing that the Castilians were still resting after their setbacks, busy coping with their wounds, Chichimecatecle and a small force of Tlaxcalans made a raid into the city, with no Castilian participation. An exploit of this nature had not been performed before. The Tlaxcalans aquitted themselves well. Their bowmen attacked and captured a bridge, they pursued the enemy into the city, and a considerable battle followed, before the Tlaxcalans, following the Spanish example, made a strategic retreat at nightfall with many prisoners. The psychological effect of this on the Castilians, the Tlaxcalans and the other allies was considerable.[32]

35
Such mad dogs

"Although the enemy saw that they were being hurt, they were such mad dogs that we could by no means prevent their pursuing us"
Cortés, Third Letter to the King

FOR A MOMENT the expedition of Cortés in June 1521 had believed that they were about to experience a second *noche triste*. The sight of the sacrifice of their companions appalled them. But the successes of Tapia and Sandoval restored morale. By mid-July the conquistadors were beginning to make tentative new attacks into the city along the same routes as before.

The work of filling in the breaches was for a time performed by the Spaniards themselves. They received violent responses, with the defenders ever more anxious to seize the Castilians alive. But it became apparent that the Mexica were finding it harder than before to send these squadrons in relief. They also seemed less effective than they had been in the past in reopening the canals and causeways at night after the Castilians had withdrawn. This cannot be attributed to the greater skill of the Castilians in filling in the breaches. The explanation must have something to do with Mexican fatigue, their shortage of food, and their poor supplies of water. They did stage one night attack on the camp of Alvarado, but it was easily foiled.[1] Cortés seemed meantime to be possessed of renewed energy. In Alvarado's camp, Bernal Díaz said that the *Caudillo* "was always writing to us to tell us all what we were to do and how we were to fight".[2]

The rainy season had now begun. Every afternoon at four o'clock the downpour was heavy. But this did not prevent the Castilians from resuming their activities of before 30 June, knocking down houses and burning them, as well as filling in canals. But since the rains made these things harder than they would otherwise have been, they did them with a difference. They determined to raze all the houses in the streets along which they had been in the habit of advancing, and to fill in for good the canals which they crossed, no matter how long it took them to do it. The

Tlaxcalans and other allies began once again to carry out these services. Pedro Sánchez Farfán and António de Villaroel, guards to the young puppet king of Texcoco, also brought back a substantial number of Texcocans. A few people from Huexotzinco and Cholula came too.

The Mexica continued to fight bravely, and to reoccupy at night territory which they had lost in the day. But quite suddenly, from about the middle of July, they ceased to open up the breaches in the causeway.[3] There is no indigenous explanation, nor even mention, of the occurrence. The fact is that men were becoming scarce. Cuauhtémoc's only innovation was to seek to conceal his increasing shortage of men by using women as warriors, and dressing them accordingly.[4] Such a thing would in the past have been unheard of: women's umbilical cords belonged to the hearth.

To shortage of men was soon added an extreme scarcity both of water and of food. In the middle of the month, Alvarado's column reached the spring which had afforded the Mexica a modest supply of brackish water. They dstroyed it. The water thereafter available to the Mexica was from the lake It was foul: "Many died of a bloody flux," recorded the Florentine Codex.[5] As for food, the reserves of maize and other supplies were by now almost all consumed.

Other sources of revived confidence for the Castilians derived from the arrival of new gunpowder, crossbows and even soldiers. These were sent up from Vera Cruz following the landing there of a ship which had been part of Ponce de León's recent expedition to Florida in search of the Fountain of Youth.[6]

Another reinforcement was made possible by Francisco de Montano, a native of Ciudad Real who had originally come to New Spain with Narváez. He was lieutenant to Gutierre de Badajoz, who commanded a company under Alvarado. With gunpowder running low, Montano volunteered to climb to the rim of the crater of Popocatepetl. There, with remarkable sang-froid, he arranged to lower himself by a chain to find sulphur, which, when obtained, made a substantial contribution to Cortés' gunpowder. Cortés, recording the event, said that the Indians thought it a great thing to have done. Indeed it was, since no one in the twentieth century would venture such a climb in the summer, without crampons. The feat had, however, been done by the Indians, if in very difficult circumstances: for the Mexica had seen how "that place . . . is filled with enormous clefts like the mesh of a net, or like a grating, or like latticework. Between one abyss and another, two men can walk abreast. And that smoke, thick and evil, escapes from those clefts. Clefts, one next to the other, like rugged crags!"[7]

Some communication meantime had begun again between the Mexica and the conquistadors. The former seem in a roundabout way to have again suggested that peace should be made on condition that the

Castilians leave the country. Cortés did not take the offer seriously. He suspected it of being simply a ruse because his enemies needed food. All the same, any contact seemed a step forward. During this abortive negotiation, apparently, an old Mexican, on the Mexican side of a canal which at that time divided the two forces, drew certain provisions out of a knapsack and ate them slowly, in full view of the Castilians, to leave the impression that there was no lack of food in the Mexican part of the city.[8] That propaganda was an act of bravado: already the shortages were such as to cause the Mexica to eat straw and grass. Even the gnawing of wood and of mud bricks began to play a part in the life of that once luxurious people.[9]

A day or two later, when the Castilians were once again making for the now battered great square, just short of the precinct of the Great Temple, the Mexica passed a message telling them to halt since they desired peace. Cortés ordered his men not to attack, and asked for Cuauhtémoc. The Mexica said that he had been sent for. But this initiative seems to have been another ruse. The Mexica were still far from wanting to make peace. Once they had the Castilians off their guard, they launched another attack with javelins, stones and arrows.[10] It is, however, possible that the contradictory actions reflected confusion within the Mexican camp, and that different commanders were taking different decisions.

Soon after this the Castilians captured three prominent Mexicans. Cortés sent them to Cuauhtémoc to propose peace. They were to say that Cortés personally had great respect for Cuauhtémoc, if only because of his being so closely related to his old friend Montezuma. But what a tragedy it was that so great a city should be destroyed! He, Cortés, knew that it had been "the most beautiful thing in the world".[11] Now Cortés realised that the Mexica had neither food nor water. Cortés would pardon everyone if only Cuauhtémoc would surrender. He assumed that he had had bad advice from his gods and priests. Cortés attributed his foolish conduct to his youth.[12]

Ixtlilxochitl now took prisoner his own brother, Coanacochtzin, the King of Texcoco, who had been acting in some capacity as a general with the Mexican forces.[13]

Cuauhtémoc apparently held a conference of his captains and other advisers at his headquarters in Yacacolco. Though angry, it seems that he was himself now in favour of making peace. He said that he had already tried everything that he could think of to win the war and had changed his manner of fighting several times. But the Spaniards had always outwitted him. He met unexpected opposition to his ideas. His captains were adamant. They told him that, under no circumstances, should he negotiate with "Malinche", who, they insisted, was quite untrustworthy. That peace of which Cuauhtémoc talked was, they said, imaginary. They added that it was better that they all should die than put themselves in the power of those who would make slaves of them, or torture them for their gold. To support this Numantian attitude, the priests promised that the gods would, in the end, bring victory.[14] None of them ventured the thought that the Mexica's world was at an end, that the predicted last act in the Legend of the Suns was about to be fulfilled, and that the Fifth Sun, the Sun of Movement, was about to die. That school of thought had been discredited by Montezuma and his foolish courtiers. Their successors were of sterner stuff.[15]

Perhaps even more telling, the people of Tlatelolco were busy accusing their colleagues and cousins of Tenochtitlan of cowardice. For the withdrawal *in extremis* of the Mexican emperor and his household to the once despised city of merchants, Tlatelolco, did not seem to have achieved a common cause between the two cities. Indeed, the retreat appears to have revived the old bad relations which had been cleverly soothed by Montezuma II. The *Anales de Tlatelolco* almost leave the impression that the troubles between Castile and Mexico were scarcely worse than those between Tenochtitlan and Tlatelolco.[16]

Now every day was bringing new victories to the Castilians. Thus, on 22 July Cortés and Sandoval carried out a spectacular ambush with horses hidden in a palace in the main square: they fell on the Mexica as they streamed out of their hiding places to attack the Castilians in a feigned retreat.[17] The next day, at dawn, Cortés and his allies captured or killed many Mexica, including women and children, who had come out of Tlatelolco, now the only Mexican redoubt, in search of food[18] (had the Mexica been cannibals pure and simple, they would, with so many bodies about, have been well supplied with meat).[19] On 24 July, the whole stretch of the road to Tacuba was conquered, so that Cortés and Alvarado could communicate direct, and by land. The old palace of Cuauhtémoc himself was burned that day by the Tlaxcalans.[20] On 27 July, early in the morning, Cortés, while still at Xoloc, saw smoke rising from the top of the pyramid of the temple at Tlatelolco: a sign that, at last, Alvarado, after a long battle against merchants and women, as well as soldiers, had captured the marketplace there. Thereafter, he and his horsemen could gallop round it.[21] Gutierre de Badajoz, accompanied by the hero of Popocatepetl, Francisco de Montano, now Alvarado's standard-bearer, had fought their way up to place the flag of Cortés, with its blue cross on a yellow background, on top of the temple: an achievement which one chronicler insisted was the most important event in the history of the siege.[22]

Alvarado was, however, again forced to retreat, after prolonged fighting in the arcades which surrounded the square. It was not till the following day that he and Cortés were able to ride round the square of Tlatelolco, seeing the surrounding roofs full of the enemy. The place was so large that no damage could be done from those vantage points. Cortés himself climbed the steps of the great temple. As well as seeing the heads of Christians who had been sacrificed in recent weeks, he could observe that seven-eighths of the city was in Castilian hands.[23]

Several remarkable feats of arms are associated with this stage of the war: thus the Mexica taunted Hernando de Osma with cowardice by waving a captured Spanish sword. Osma went to avenge the insult, riding through a crowd of enemies. The standard-bearer of Cortés, Corral, showed great energy in extricating himself from a fall behind enemy lines. Rodrigo de Castañeda, a Montañés, a native of Santander, dressed himself in Mexican clothes and had great success with the crossbow at close range.[24]

There were Mexicans too whose courage was legendary. Dressed in eagle or jaguar costume, many leading captains wielded their obsidian-edged swords and lances with great skill. Of course they found that their feather headdresses excited derision rather than awe among the Castilians. But those ancient costumes seem to have had their usual effect upon the allies. Often escorted by flute players, the Mexica were always, even in their weakened state, a match for the Tlaxcalans.

The sang-froid of their enemies continued to astonish the Castilians. For example, the Mexica taunted the Tlaxcalans for burning the city. If the Mexica won, they said, they would require the Tlaxcalans to rebuild the city. Even if the Castilians gained a victory, they would surely also force the Tlaxcalans to do so.[25]

Cortés was now once more approached by Mexican leaders, and told that Cuauhtémoc wanted to speak to him across a canal. Cortés went to the appointed place. But a message came that Cuauhtémoc had forgotten that he might be killed by crossbows. Cortés offered guarantees of safety. He also seems to have suggested to the Mexica that they celebrate one of their regular festivals: ironically, after all, Miccailhuitontli, the festival of dead children, was usually commemorated about 8 August. The Mexica rejected the appropriate proposal.[26] Cortés said that, if Cuauhtémoc were to surrender, he would be allowed to govern as the emperors had always done in the past, provided, presumably, that he accepted to be a "vassal" of Charles V. A message came from Cuauhtémoc that he would give Cortés his reply in three days. But still all the Mexican captains were in favour of fighting on to the end. The proponents of reaching an accommodation with Cortés were all dead or in hiding. At the end of three days, the Mexica once again launched a major attack which the Castilians still found difficult to hold. The eloquence of Cortés seemed for once ineffective.

Cortés established himself in a tent, with a crimson canopy, on a roof on top of a house which had belonged to a Tlatelolcan nobleman named Atzauatzin. This was in the Amaxac district. He contemplated the appalling scene beneath him with horror. There is no reason to doubt the assertion of Charles V's semi-official historian Sepúlveda that by now the

Caudillo seriously desired a Mexican surrender, with no further bloodshed.[27] Yet the zone controlled by the Mexica, if small and ruined, still seemed well organised for defence. They might have very few men. They still had stones ready on their roofs.

The heroic resistance of the Mexica was beyond the recent experience of anything in Spain or Italy. The last Moorish king, Boabdil, had loved Granada, but he had not preferred to see it destroyed rather than give it up to King Ferdinand. Cortés now had no doubt about ultimate victory. The allies had almost all returned to his support. But all the same, there still seemed to be difficulties ahead. The Castilians, for example, were again suffering from a shortage of gunpowder.[28]

In this mood, Cortés allowed himself to be influenced by a certain Sotelo, a Sevillano, who had been in Italy with the Great Captain. He suggested to the *Caudillo* the idea of building a big catapult to fling stones or cannon balls into the heart of Cuauhtémoc's redoubt. The idea of a "new weapon" always attracts commanders at a loss as to how to finish a war; even if catapults could hardly be called new – the Carthaginians had relied on them. But an ex-comrade of the Great Captain had always to be listened to in a Castilian army. Cortés gave Sotelo every encouragement. He was not averse to introducing another element of terror into the battle. Perhaps the shock of the catapult would cause a recognition of the need for surrender. Diego Hernández, the carpenter who had made the first carts in New Spain so long ago at Cempoallan, and who had laboured with López on the brigantines, did the work.[29] The catapult was built. It was placed on top of the pyramid whose temple was dedicated to the god Momoztl. But the carpenters, experienced though they were, failed to make it work. The carefully prepared large stones slid from the mechanism. Cortés escaped from having to admit failure in front of the allies by saying that he had been moved to compassion at the thought of the damage that the catapult might do, and so did not want to use it.[30]

The Mexica continued to refuse negotiations. The enormity of what was happening, the prospect of complete defeat, the suspicion that the end of their history as long predicted might be upon them, seems to have frozen them into a kind of courageous folly. Cortés and Alvarado had no alternative, as it seemed to them, other than to set about the capture of Tlatelolco step by step. The report on this stage of the war by Cortés to Charles V a year later reads like a catalogue of evils: "we again entered the city and found streets full of starving women and children"; and "we killed or made prisoners of over 12,000".[31] Each day, Cortés later wrote, "we expected them to sue for the peace which we desired as much as our own salvation; but we could not induce them to do it." Alvarado took the lead in most of these battles. He drove with his horsemen into one of the last quarters of Tlatelolco held by the Mexica. Difficult though it is to believe, given the weakness of the defenders, the fighting was again fierce. Then Cortés allowed the allies to kill or capture the survivors: many were no doubt sacrificed and eaten.[32]

Cuauhtémoc's reply to Alvarado's new attack was to name a quetzal-owl warrior. This nomination was usually the final action of the Mexica at war. The action had in the past always brought them victory. The feather costume was that worn by the conqueror Ahuítzotl, Cuauhtémoc's father and Montezuma's·predecessor as emperor. The *cihuacoatl*, Tlacotzin, made a rousing speech: he invoked the power and the darts of the god Huitzilopochtli, he recalled the great past of the Mexican people.[33] How often in the past had hardened warriors quailed before the sight of such a hero!

According to the informants of Sahagún, the Castilians were at first indeed astonished at the sight. The body of the warrior was quite hidden beneath the birds' feathers, which had been skilfully assembled on a cloth or frame. The plumes, gold and other decorations were so grand as to make it seem "as if a mountain burst. The Castilians fought as if they had seen something inhuman . . ." In the subsequent fighting, three men (probably allies, not Castilians) were apparently captured by the quetzal-owl. They were instantly sacrificed by Cuauhtémoc in person. The Castilians even seemed for a moment to withdraw. But an isolated act of valour could not alter the reality of the siege: the quetzal-owl, fighting with his spears and arrows, was observed for some time from a distance by his compatriots in the middle of the fray. Then, reported the Florentine Codex, "he dropped from a terrace", and was seen no more. Then, little by little, the Mexica "drew back along the walls, little by little they retreated".[34]

Maize became so sought after in Tlatelolco that slaves were exchanged for a mere two handfuls of it; while a handful of gold was said to have been given for a day's supply of corn: out of this trade, several of the lacustrine cities, of course, prospered.[35]

But the Mexican leaders still did not give up. There seemed a contrast between their attitudes and those of prisoners interrogated by the Castilians. The prisoners gave the impression that everyone wished to surrender. Yet the mechanism of surrender could not be invoked by humble men. That had to be contrived by the leaders. Humble men would follow their leaders' orders. One of those captured by Cortés told him that he did not understand why the *Caudillo* (whom he seemed to believe to be the sun who could go round the earth in twenty-four hours) did not kill them all and so end their suffering. That would enable them to go to heaven and live with Huitzilopochtli.[36] In Nahuatl, "the verb to die can mean to marry the earth".[37] The prospect was not unappealing to the suffering people.

One prisoner made at this stage by Cortés was a prince of Texcoco who had remained loyal to the old order, one of the many sons of the late King

Nezahualpilli. Cortés sent this individual back to Cuauhtémoc to try and persuade him to come to terms. Cuauhtémoc sent him to be sacrificed, and ordered a new counterattack. His exhausted and half-starving warriors still had enough energy to prevent the Castilians from bringing the siege to an end immediately.[38]

When Cortés returned from Xoloc to the centre of the city one day in early August, he found that many allies had spent the previous night in the main square. They were waiting like wolves to fall on the surviving Mexica and their remaining belongings. Cortés asked across a barricade in Tlatelolco: why did not Cuauhtémoc now come and speak to him? Even now if he accepted peace he would be well received. The Mexica wept, went away, and returned to say that Cuauhtémoc could not come then, because it was already late. But he would come the following day. Cortés gave orders that the next day a platform such as the Mexica used on ceremonial occasions should be put in the main square. Food was laid out.[39]

But still there were prevarications. When Cortés went the following day to Tlatelolco, Cuauhtémoc sent five prominent persons instead of himself. Cuauhtémoc, they said, apologised, but he was ill, and was also afraid of appearing before Cortés. But they for their part would do everything which the Castilians asked of them. Cortés received them joyfully, and gave them food and drink. He told them that Cuauhtémoc need fear nothing. If he were to surrender, he would suffer no indignity, nor would he be held as a prisoner. The Mexica returned to their headquarters and then came back, bringing cotton cloths as presents for Cortés. They now said that on no account would the Emperor come to see Cortés. It was pointless to discuss the matter further. Cortés argued with them. Surely Cuauhtémoc could see that they were being well treated. So would they not go back and try once more to convince him? They promised to do so. They agreed to meet the following day.[40]

There were yet further postponements. First, these same five Mexican leaders did come to see Cortés as planned. They asked him to go to the marketplace of Tlatelolco. There, they said, Cuauhtémoc would meet him. Cortés went there. He waited four hours. Nothing happened. Angry, Cortés instructed Alvarado to attack again. That conquistador this time broke easily through the Mexica's last defences with his horsemen. The Indian allies, mostly Tlaxcalans, followed him into the narrow streets there.[41] They killed – women and children as well as "warriors" – with a ferocity which shocked the Castilians. Cortés thought that "no race has ever practised such fierce and unnatural cruelty as the *naturales* of those parts".[42] All the later accounts agree that the Spaniards sought to prevent their allies from carrying out a massacre, but were unsuccessful.[43] Everywhere, there were to be seen broken bones, ruined houses, roofs fallen in, houses stained with blood, unburied bodies in the street. Cortés returned to his camp at Xoloc, glad to leave the smell of dead bodies, and the sight of starving Indians. The Spaniards said that they or their allies killed or captured 40,000 that day.[44]

When night fell on this 12 August 1521, the rain was heavy. The Mexica claimed later to have seen what they took to be a portent: a flame like a ball of jasper appeared in the sky: "it seemed like a whirlwind, it went spinning and revolving, like a coppery wind." It circled round the remains of the dyke of Nezahualcoyotl, travelled towards Coyoacán, and then was lost in the middle of the lake.[45] Whatever judgement is made about the earlier portents in the sky and elsewhere which so disturbed Montezuma, this was no doubt a post-conquest rationalisation of what the Mexica later thought ought to have happened. For there seems to be no confirmatory astronomical evidence for the phenomenon.

Cuauhtémoc realised that defeat was inevitable. But he was unable to make the gesture of surrender. It is true that some weeks earlier he had thought of a negotiation with the Castilians. But it is improbable that that would really have achieved anything which Cortés could or would have accepted. Also the subsequent weeks had seen destruction on an unimaginable scale. Cuauhtémoc did not have in him the capacity to negotiate peace now. All his education prevented it. Surely, he had been trained to suppose, in the end, the gods would save him and the remains of his empire. He called on the last prisoners to be delivered to him. He personally carried out the necessary sacrifices (as he saw them to be), so that none should be left for the Castilians; nor, above all, for the Tlaxcalans.[46] He held a final meeting, at a place called Tolmayecan, between himself and the remaining leaders of Mexico: Tlacotzin, the *cihuacoatl*; Petlauhtzin, the *tlillancalqui* (the holder of that office whom Grijalva and Cortés had known in 1518 and 1519 had probably been killed); Motelchiuh, that *uitznahuatl* who two years before had led a mission to Cortés at Vera Cruz; Coyoueuetzin, the *tlacochcalcatl*, or commander of the army; Temilotzin, the *tlacatectal*; and Auelitoctzin, the chief justice; and other officials.[47] The difficulty which the Western reader must find in a recital of their names should not lead him to overlook the significance of their offices. Present too was Tetlepan-quetzatzin, King of Tacuba.

There seems to have been an unreal discussion as to the type of tribute which might be offered to the Spaniards; and, more relevantly, "how we should yield" ourselves to them.[48] Cuauhtémoc now accepted that the Mexica could fight no more. But he himself was not going to surrender. He told his advisers that he would leave the city. No doubt once again the Mexica (and probably the Indian allies) recalled how Azcapotzalco had fallen in 1428 after a siege of over a hundred days, how Maxtla, the king of that city, had been killed in a bath, and how the population had been destroyed by the Mexican conquerors (indeed it had been said that "not a house had been left standing").[49] The Castilians, brought up on the memory of the Celts' last stand at Numancia, as of Guzmán el Bueno's famous gesture at Tarifa, should have felt at home.[50]

The priests were no help. The *tlacochcalcatl*, Coyoueuetzin, said, "Let us consult our neighbour, the priest of Huitznauac". But that priest merely said: "Noble lords, hear what we anticipate. Only four days remain till we shall have passed eighty days since the beginning of the war. Thus says the oracle of Huitzilopochtli: nothing will happen."[51] The Mexica, he predicted, would be saved on the eightieth day. A reading of the illuminated books suggested it. In consequence, the next day the war began again.

As Alvarado was preparing to re-enter Tlatelolco, the Emperor was making ready to set off by canoe. He would not surrender. He would leave secretly. That was impossible. Weeping women saw him: Now goeth the young king Cuauhtémoc, now he goes to deliver himself to the 'gods', they intoned.[52] The Emperor was probably seeking to escape to the other side of the lake. He may have been intending to make for Azcapotzalco, where the effigy of Huitzilopochtli seems to have been taken. There, he might have tried to raise again the standard of the Mexica against the Castilians. With him in his canoe travelled Tetlepanquetzatzin, King of Tacuba, a soldier, Teputzitoloc, and Yaztachimal, his page. There was a boatman, Cenyaotl.[53]

Cortés was, meantime, maintaining his pressure. He went up into the city on the morning of 13 August accompanied by men bearing three heavy guns. He conferred with Alvarado and Sandoval. It was agreed that the firing of an arquebus would be the signal for the divisions of Alvarado and of Cortés (the last led by Olid) to enter the ruins of Tlatelolco, and to drive the remaining Mexican fighters to the water's edge. There, Sandoval would be waiting for them with the remaining brigantines (probably eight). Everyone had instructions to look for Cuauhtémoc: "we need him alive".

Before the battle began again, the Mexica brought the *cihuacoatl* to see Cortés. That potentate told the *Caudillo* that Cuauhtémoc preferred to die rather than give himself up. Cortés said coldly that if that were the case, all the Mexica would be killed.

Cortés watched the Castilian forward movement from his crimson-canopied tent on the rooftop in Amaxac. He sat there with Luis Marín, Francisco Verdugo and some others. From there they could see Alvarado's men entering the last Mexican district of Tlatelolco, without meeting any resistance.

The end of the conquest of Tenochtitlan moved even Cortés' heart to some degree of remorse: for when Alvarado's men entered the streets of Tlatelolco, that morning of 13 August, the day of St Hippolytus, the patron of horses (an appropriate day considering the assistance overall that those animals had afforded the conquerors), the Castilians could see such privation that "it was beyond our understanding how they could endure it . . . Countless men and women came towards us and, in their eagerness to escape, many were pushed into the water where they drowned . . . we came across piles of dead and were forced to walk over them."

The Indian allies, above all the Tlaxcalans, however, had no mercy. Cortés had given new orders to abstain from killing citizens. But they killed a large number, Cortés himself said, many being sacrificed. Cortés later commented: "There was not one man among us [Castilians] whose heart did not bleed at the sound of these killings."[54]

Most Mexica surrendered on this day without seeking to fight. Sandoval swept with his brigantines into the moorings where the Mexican canoes were kept.[55] Some fifty large ones (the *piraguas*) were observed. Many Mexican leaders were taking to these boats. They were putting on board as much gold and other treasure as they had left, as well as women, children and some stores.

One of the brigantines was commanded by García Holguín, an Extremeño captain, from Cáceres. A hidalgo, he was one of those whom Diego Velázquez had once considered for the command of the expedition instead of Cortés. He had had some difficulties with Cortés, for he had been overheard saying that the *Caudillo* served neither God nor the King.[56] Now he had his great opportunity. He observed that one of the canoes among those still afloat "appeared to be carrying persons of rank". He gave chase. He ordered the rowers to stop. They did not do so. He prepared to bombard them with his cannon. They signalled to him not to do so because they had distinguished passengers on board.[57] Cuauhtémoc, for it was he, was apparently still prepared to fight. But, seeing that the Spaniards had so many more men, he finally surrendered himself – though not, formally, his city.[58] García Holguín drew up alongside. One of those under his command, Juan de Mansilla, a conquistador from Old Castile, secured Cuauhtémoc and Tetlepanquetzatzin.[59]

These triumphant Castilians then set off to take their prisoners to Cortés. Sandoval overhauled García Holguín and told him, as his commander, to hand over his prisoners. García Holguín refused. There followed an unedifying dispute which Cortés himself had to soothe by sending Luis Marín and Francisco Verdugo to calm the two parties. They did so. It was they who, in the end, brought Cuauhtémoc before Cortés – on the roof of the house of Atzauatzin.[60] Cortés, ever anxious to show his humanist education, or his memory of popular ballads, told García Holguín and Sandoval that their quarrel put him in mind of a similar quarrel between Marius and Sulla over the capture of Jugurtha, King of Numidia.[61]

The conversation between these three Extremeños in the ruins of Tenochtitlan about Jugurtha, Marius and Sulla, in the presence of the uncomprehending Cuauhtémoc, adds a final bizarre if certainly classical note to the history of the conquest. (Of course the reference was inappropriate, for Sulla and Marius were men of a different level to Sandoval and García Holguín. But the commander-in-chief of the Roman forces had been Caecilius Metellus, father of the founder of Medellín.)

Cortés then received Cuauhtémoc as an emperor in a theatrical if appropriate ceremony. Cuauhtémoc made a speech along the following lines: "Ah, Captain, I have done everything in my power to defend my country and keep it out of your hands. And since my luck has not been good, I beg you to end my life. That would be just. And with that you can finish with the Mexican kingdom since you have destroyed and killed my city and my vassals."[62] Cortés answered affectionately, through Marina and Aguilar, whose roles in achieving victory had been so considerable. He said that he esteemed the Emperor the more for having defended the city with such courage. He only wished that Cuauhtémoc had made peace before so much had been destroyed. Now he suggested that he should rest. Thereafter, "he would be able to rule over his empire as before".[63] According to his own account he told Cuauhtémoc that he should "fear nothing".[64] All these reassurances were, alas, deceitful. The best that can be said for them is that it is improbable that Cuauhtémoc took them seriously.

Cortés next asked after Cuauhtémoc's wife, the daughter of Montezuma. The Emperor replied that she had been left in his last lodgings in the care of the Castilians. Cortés had her brought. That was done. Cortés received her, and those with her, with gallantry. He gave orders for her and her companions to be looked after well and, of course, well guarded.[65]

After these dramatic moments, the Castilian soldiers, says Bernal Díaz, seemed to become deaf, for, day after day, the long siege had been persistently punctuated by shouts, music, horns, drums and the noise of falling buildings. Now for the first time for months, Tenochtitlan was silent. Even the conch trumpets ceased to sound at night. An old Mexican prayer ran: Master, O our lord, our city is a baby, a child, perhaps it has heard . . .[66] The unbelievable had happened. Tenochtitlan, marvel of the world, had fallen, just as Tollan and Teotihuacan had fallen so long ago.

It rained heavily. There was thunder. The Mexica had always thought that that was the breaking of the jugs in which the little blue Tlalocs, the gnomes in attendance on the great Tlaloc, used to keep the rain. Those spirits lived in the mountains, surrounded by treasure, always feasting. The evidence of their survival must have been the only encouraging sign of the times for the defeated people.

There was one more formal meeting the following day between Cortés and the leading Mexicans. Most of the Mexican lords who had been among those consulted in the end by Cuauhtémoc were present. Cuauhtémoc sat in a royal cloak of quetzal feathers but it was dirty. Coanacochtzin and Tetlepanquetzatzin sat in humbler cloaks of maguey fibre, bordered by radiating flowers. But they too were dirty – as was ritually correct after a defeat.[67] The Mexica remember the Castilians pressing their noses with handkerchiefs ("fine white cloths"). The overpowering smell of death offended them.[68]

Here the victory was, as it were, confirmed. The Mexica were not asked to sign any document. Nor did Cortés read the famous *Requerimiento*. But the meeting formally marked the end of the siege and of the war.

There was a discussion about gold. Cortés asked: "What of the gold?" A good deal was then presented: armbands, helmets, discs, even flags. It had all been put into canoes when the Mexican leaders had begun to flee by water. Cortés then asked: "Is this all?" The *cihuacoatl* then said, surely the Castilians had taken the rest of the gold of Mexico when they had left the capital the previous year? Cortés answered that all had been lost in the *noche triste*: "You forced us to drop it there. You will produce it all," he added menacingly. The *cihuacoatl* then said that it had been the Tlatelolca who had fought the Castilians that night. They must have taken it. Cuauhtémoc corrected this misinterpretation. All the same, a dispute seems to have begun between the captives who came from Tenochtitlan and those who came from Tlatelolco. Marina again interrupted, on Cortés' request: "The captain asks, is this all? Quite all?" The *cihuacoatl* then said that perhaps some of the common people had taken away the gold after the *noche triste*. It would be sought. Marina then told him: "You will produce two hundred pieces of gold this size." She moved her hands in a large circle. The *cihuacoatl*, pursuing his previous train of thought, said: "Perhaps some poor woman put it into her skirt." He nervously added that he was certain that Cortés would find this treasure in the end. The chief justice, Auelitoctzin, then said that Montezuma had possessed all the gold of the Mexica, and that he had given it to the Castilians.

The armistice was concluded. But that discussion would be renewed.[69]

For the defeated, the days immediately after the fall of Tenochtitlan were atrocious. The Tlaxcalans, the Texcocans, and other allies killed indiscriminately. The city was full of unburied bodies. The smell was fearful. There was still no food and no drinking water. Cuauhtémoc, in captivity, asked Cortés to permit all Mexicans still alive to be allowed to go to the neighbouring towns on the lake. The *Caudillo* agreed and, for some days, the causeways were full of these hungry, dirty, smelly, sick refugees, of all ages. They left behind their homes: still smoking ruins.

"There is no house left to be burned and destroyed," Pedro de Maluenda, Narváez's commissary, who was now working with Cortés, wrote to his associate in Cuba, Hernando de Castro: he added that "to go down from Tenochtitlan to Vera Cruz is like travelling from hell to heaven".[70] Women fled half naked, barely covered with rags. But the rumours spread that many were hiding gold and precious stones somewhere on their bodies. The conquerors prowled everywhere: "even in women's nostrils they looked for it."[71] Women were said to have concealed gold in their bosoms or their skirts, men to have done so in their breech clouts or their mouths. This caused many Castilians to set about the women. Some women tried to make themselves look inconspicuous by dressing in rags or putting mud on their faces. This stratagem was not very successful.

The only loot found by the conquistadors was the women themselves. Many of them, whose husbands or fathers had been killed, were only too glad to go with the victors, and so assure themselves at least of the chance of food. Tlaxcalan women and others had served the Castilians' needs in these respects in the past. Now they had Mexica.

The conquistadors similarly seized men to act as messengers, servants and runners. Many of these were branded.[72] Cortés established guards at the city gates to prevent both Mexica and Castilians taking away gold illegally. But there was not much gold forthcoming; neither for the King nor for soldiers.

The discrepancy, invention and exaggeration which characterised the estimates of observers throughout the campaign continued, as might be expected, into the summaries made of the losses of this siege. Thus Cortés' chaplain and friend, Fr. López de Gómara, would suggest that the Castilians lost only fifty killed and six horses, while the Mexicans lost 100,000, "not including those who died from hunger and disease".[73] That chronicler also attributed, no doubt rightly, many of the deaths of the defenders to "our Indian friends, who would spare the life of no Mexican, no matter how they were reprimanded for it". The Florentine Codex said that over 30,000 Texcocans died in the fighting, and "over 240,000" Mexica, including almost all the Mexican nobility.[74] Ixtlilxochitl put the Mexican dead at 240,000. Bernal Díaz thought that the Castilian losses were between sixty and eighty, while Fr. Durán estimated that, at the end of the battle, about 40,000 Mexica killed themselves by throwing themselves into canals with their children and wives.[75] Later chroniclers made other calculations, though only Fr. Juan de Torquemada thought that the Castilians lost more than Díaz estimated. His figure was "less than a hundred".[76] But Cervantes de Salazar and later Antonio de Herrera both thought that fifty was right for the Spaniards.[77] A sensible estimate is hard to make. Perhaps 100,000, as given by López de Gómara, would be right for Mexica killed in fighting. A hundred at least might be a sensible guess for the Castilians in a hard siege which lasted nearly three months. Probably the Castilians lost nearly a thousand men killed in the two years since they reached Mexico, out of a total of about 1,800 in all who came to the country between 1519 and 1521.[78] The difference between the numbers of conquistadors and Mexica dead may be held to indicate the superior fighting skill of the former. But it also shows the hatred felt by the allies for the Mexica; as well as the fighting techniques of the latter, who sought to wound and capture, never to kill.

The Mexica commemorated their defeat with a lament:

> It was called the jaguar sun.
> Then it happened
> That the sky was crushed.
> The sun did not follow its course.
> When the sun arrived at noon,
> Immediately it was dark;
> And when it became dark
> Jaguars ate the people . . .
> The giants greeted each other thus:
> 'Do not fall down, for whoever falls
> Falls forever.'[79]

As for the Castilians, Cortés ordered a banquet to mark the victory. This was held the day after the fall of Tenochtitlan, in the house of the lord of Coyoacán. Wine had been brought up from Vera Cruz: another ship had recently arrived from Spain. There was pork from Santo Domingo. There was no shortage of Mexican turkey and maize bread. All those captains and soldiers who "had done well" were invited, though how the distinction was made between them and those who had not done well is not clear. How "well" had Verdugo done? And Fr. Díaz? But there were few niceties. Drinking was heavy. When the guests arrived at the banquet, barely a third of those invited could find room to sit down. After dinner, brave men walked on the tables, and could not find their way into the patio. Several conquistadors fell down the steps into the street. Speeches were made by soldiers saying that they looked forward to owning horses with golden saddles. Crossbowmen insisted that, in future, their arrows would be tipped with gold. When the tables were taken away there was gambling – and dancing. The few women who had been with the expedition came into their own: María de Estrada, for example, the extraordinary *conquistadora* whose valour at the battle of the bridges on the *noche triste* had inspired such admiration; and Francisca, the sister of Diego de Ordaz. The two girls called "la Bermuda" were there. These adventurous women went gaily to dance with men still in their quilted armour.[80]

Next day there was a mass. A long procession of conquistadors followed a picture of the Virgin Mary and the cross to a high point overlooking the lake and the ruins of the city. A *Te Deum* followed.[81]

The sense of triumph felt by Cortés at these moments was touched with melancholy. Time and again in his account of the last stages of the siege he had used phrases such as "we could not but be saddened by their determination to die".[82] There was the destruction of Tenochtitlan to consider: for the prospect of capturing the beautiful city, of which he had heard tell when still at Vera Cruz, had surely fired his imagination. Now it was rubble. Sacred books had been destroyed in hundreds. Cortés had organised the complicated siege, he had inspired the brigantines, he had built an unlikely alliance with the Indian subject peoples through clever diplomacy. He had even made an alliance between Extremeños and Castilians. He had seen friends killed. He had won a great victory with modest losses to his own men. His fellow conquistadors had fought bravely, against what seemed, in the beginning, to have been great odds. For a time he and his friends seemed to have been looked upon by some Mexica at least as being reincarnations of deities. But in the end, to be honest, it had been the Mexica who had fought like gods.

VIII
Aftermath

36

The general exodus

"And so the march goes on: the general exodus.
Who among the nobles, the princes, the kings,
Shall not leave us at last, abandoned like orphans?
Be sad, O princes!
Does no one ever come back from the Place of Wonder?
Does no one return from the No-Returning?"
  "Only Flowering Death", tr. Irene Nicholson, *Firefly in the Night*

CORTÉS HAD CONQUERED an empire. He had used well his talents for flattery, for courtesy, for eloquence, for swift decision, for improvisation, for deviousness, for sudden changes of plan. His will and courage in adversity had been decisive. He had used terror coldly and effectively. His ambition to achieve something astonishing should have been satisfied.

Cortés had also performed this task making use of men of his own choice. The leading captains had been Extremeños. The two most important of these, Alvarado and Sandoval, had probably been known to Cortés since he had been a child in Medellín. The *Caudillo* had been constantly sustained by a strong group of other men from that part of Spain, either as captains or as members of his household: Rodrigo Rangel, Rodríguez de Villafuerte (both of whom came from Medellín), the other Alvarado brothers, García de Albuquerque, the Álvarez Chico brothers, Juan de Cáceres, Alonso de Grado, his cousin Diego Pizarro, and García Holguín. Beside them, the few leaders from Castile proper (Tapia, Ordaz, Ávila, Fr. Bartolomé de Olmedo, Verdugo, Lugo) or Sevillanos and Andalusians (Sánchez Farfán, Martín López, Fr. Juan Díaz, Olid) had never managed to establish anything like a clique in the command (as suggested earlier, Tapia may anyway have been an Extremeño by blood). The triumph was thus very much one achieved by hidalgos of lower Extremadura, even if they had been substantially assisted by several merchants and sea captains from Seville (Juan de Córdoba, Pedro de Maluenda, Juan de Burgos, Cortés' "admiral" Alonso Caballero, and Luis Fernández de Alfaro), most of whom were *conversos*.

Yet something essential was missing. Neither Cortés nor anyone else in New Spain knew what their own emperor thought of them. Though at this time a journey from Spain to the West Indies took about two months, it was two years since Cortés' *procuradores* had set off for Spain. Cortés wrote a quick letter home in August 1521 explaining that he had conquered the city, leaving a longer account for later. That note only reached Spain in March 1522, and it is not clear how it reached there.[1] For months more there was silence. Cortés believed that he had accomplished a triumph. But fame needs recognition, applause, flattery, the approval of dukes, the smiles of infantas, recognition by others in the waiting rooms of power.

The reality was certainly obscure.

In May 1520, the King-Emperor Charles, it will be remembered, had set off from Spain for his Burgundian dominions, leaving the friends of Cortés with the hope that their suit might prosper. Charles went via England to Flanders, finally to Brussels, carrying with him not only his court, but many officials, and most of the treasure given him by Cortés, including the famous wheels of gold and silver, which had so impressed Peter Martyr and Las Casas, and many others, when they had seen them in Valladolid.

Charles V did not abandon Spain out of feckless neglect of his patrimony. In Germany he faced the major crisis of Western Christendom. In the summer of 1520, Pope Leo declared Luther a heretic and decreed him excommunicated unless he recanted. In the autumn, Luther launched his "Appeal to the Christian Nobility". The Emperor, young though he was, was persuaded that his duty was to save the unity of Christianity. He had too to be crowned. That would be at Aix-la-Chapelle on 23 October.

But Charles also left behind a crisis in Spain – a more serious one than any such upheaval that the country had experienced since the formation of the Castilian kingdom in the thirteenth century.[2] This revolt of the "*comunidades*" in Castile was, at one level, a protest against the threat of standardised political forms, which seemed to be demanded by the "Flemish" court around the new king-emperor. At another level, it was a desire for the recovery of primitive political units: even an anticipation of that federalism which has never since been entirely absent from the Spanish political agenda. As with many revolutions which seem to be aiming at a new future, the councillors of the main municipalities of Castile, the *comuneros*, were attempting to recover what they thought of as old liberties. Partly the *comuneros* were embarking on a fiscal revolt for selfish reasons. Partly they were rallying ancient towns against new encroachments by the Castilian sheep pasturage monopoly, the Mesta. Many leaders joined the rebels out of disenchantment with the government or men favoured by it (that seems the case with Peter Martyr's correspondent and ex-pupil, the cultivated Marquis of los Vélez, *adelantado-mayor* of Murcia).[3] Others saw the movement as a bid for freedom, a method of ending poverty, even a way of achieving in Castile the system of free cities which had for so long characterised Italy.[4]

Cortés' *procuradores* were brushed aside. They could make no headway with their suit, any more than could their opponents, the friends and agents of Diego Velázquez. Had Montejo and Hernández Portocarrero been foolish enough to suppose that they could influence Bishop Fonseca, they would have been hard put to find him. In the summer of 1520, that prelate was on the run. His brother Antonio was the commander of the Castilian royal armies. But that did not help the Bishop; nor indeed his niece, that Mayor Fonseca whom Diego Velázquez had once talked so freely of marrying: her and her husband's house in Medina del Campo was burned down by angry crowds that year, as a protest against the Fonseca family.[5] Nothing indeed shows the character of the crisis in Spain in those years so much as the fact that while Mayor's house burned, her sister, María, also once considered a possible bride by Velázquez, was the wife of the Marquis of el Cenete, who (because of a family quarrel about property) had become a leader of the rebels in Valencia.

The Bishop of Burgos, meantime, fled his bishopric. Accused by the rebels of making money out of his public offices, he was moving secretly from curacy to curacy in his diocese, fearful for his life until given shelter in Astorga, on the way to Santiago, by the marquis of that name. Equally, his new assistant in respect of imperial affairs, the Madrileño *converso* Luis Zapata, minuscule if mellifluous, an old favourite of King Ferdinand's, had fled his office in Valladolid disguised as a Dominican.[6] Other members of the Council of Castile were being accused of crimes: Dr Beltrán and García de Padilla, for example, were charged with having bought their posts in 1516.[7] The pious Adrian of Utrecht, the Constable of Castile, Iñigo de Velasco, and the Admiral of Castile, Fadrique Enríquez, the three royal regents, would also have been hard to find, as they tried to maintain some notion of royal authority (the promotion of Velasco and Enríquez to serve as regents alongside Adrian was a wise, if tardy, move of the Emperor's). There was a moment in 1520 when Adrian was alone in Valladolid with neither troops nor money. By contrast, Queen Juana had had a brief moment of triumph, from which she was unwilling to profit, when the *comuneros* laid the Crown of Castile at her feet.

The *audiencia* in Hispaniola might send back letters from Santo Domingo on the subject of Narváez's rough treatment of Licenciado Ayllón.[8] Diego Colón, when he returned to Hispaniola in November 1520, might dispatch the honest judge Zuazo to begin a *residencia* in Cuba against Diego Velázquez. Magellan, in these months, might be moving through the straits which bear his name into the Pacific (as the "Southern Sea" became swiftly known). Las Casas might be setting out once again for the Indies with yet another new plan for a Christian empire. Cortés might be preparing for his great assault on Tenochtitlan. But no one took any notice. The reports about these occurrences in the Americas made no impact on a Castile which had turned brutally on itself.

Yet there was some communication of a different nature between the separate parts of Charles' empire, the new and the old. First, far from the tumults of Castile, an exhibition was mounted at the Hotel de Ville in Brussels of the strange treasures which Cortés had sent back as presents to the Emperor through Montejo and Portocarrero. By a fortunate chance, Albrecht Dürer, then at the height of his powers, was in Brussels at that time, on a "large-scale sales trip", as his biographer put the matter.[9] Like Martyr, Las Casas, Oviedo and the papal nuncio in Spain, he wrote of his impressions: "I have seen the things which they have brought to the King out of the new land of gold," he noticed, using the same phrase employed six months earlier by Bishop Ruiz de la Mota, "a sun all of gold, a whole fathom broad, and a moon, too, of silver of the same size, also two rooms full of armour and the people from there, with all manner of wondrous weapons, harness, darts; wonderful shields; extraordinary clothing, beds and all kinds of wonderful things for human use, much finer to look at than prodigies. These things are all so precious that they are valued at 100,000 guilder. In all the days of my life, I have seen nothing which touches my heart so much as these for, among them, I have seen wonderfully artistic things, and have admired the subtle ingenuity of men in foreign lands. Indeed, I do not know how to express my feelings about what I found there."[10]

Dürer's comments were important since, a protégé of the Archduchess Margaret, the Emperor Charles' aunt and mother-substitute, what he said might, through her, reach the Emperor himself (though the Emperor had looked at these Mexican objects in Tordesillas).[11] Dürer as son, and son-in-law, of well-known goldsmiths, once himself apprenticed to the goldsmith Wohlgemuth, knew what he was talking about when he praised the gold. He was at Aix-la-Chapelle when the Emperor was crowned on 23 October. Perhaps he talked to Charles about the exhibition in Brussels.[12] What seems a little strange is that Dürer never painted, nor drew, anything inspired by these sights. He had drawn a Brazilian in 1516, as well as a rhinoceros brought to Europe for the King of Portugal from Africa, though he never saw it himself. Yet these treasures in which he seems to have been so interested left no trace in his work.[13] The reason may be that Dürer's efforts were at that time chiefly concentrated on securing from Charles V a continuance of the pension which the Emperor Maximilian had paid him.[14] It may be too that Dürer was so captivated by Erasmus, whom he met now for the first time, that he had no time for further emotions. Nor, it has to be allowed, did the objects seem to have made much impact on the Emperor Charles; whose silence on the whole matter of his empire in the Indies was the most remarkable omission from his memoirs.

But his sister the Archduchess retained some of the treasures, which were given to her by Charles and by the courtier la Chaulx.[15] Her court painter, Jan Mostaert, did paint a dramatic picture, a year or two later, of what has seemed to some to be a Mexican battle, even if it is usually known, unduly innocently, as "A Picture with a Colonial Theme".[16] Another reminder of the conquest of Mexico may be a painting of the Virgin of the Palm (or Victory) which was completed that very year for the cathedral of Amiens: a fierce battle can be seen between dark-skinned Indians and Europeans in armour on the edge of an imaginary lake and on the steps of a fantastic cathedral.[17] The architect of the palace of the Prince-Bishop of Liège, Erard de la Marck, was probably also influenced by what he saw in Brussels to sculpt the faces of Mexicans at the top of some of the capitals.[18] Perhaps it was now too that Charles gave some of these objects to his brother the Archduke (and Infante) Ferdinand, who retained them for so long at his castle of Ambras near Innsbruck.[19]

A few months later Peter Martyr published his first impressions of New Spain, *De Insulis nuper repertis*.[20] Dedicated to Dürer's benefactor, the Archduchess Margaret (whom Martyr had known when she lived in Spain married to the Infante Juan), this work, written in Latin, had a considerable circulation. It included, no doubt to the satisfaction of Fr. Benito Martín, Velázquez's agent, the text of Fr. Juan Díaz's *Itinerario*. But there was also an account of Cortés' voyage up until July 1519, based on information gleaned by Martyr from Portocarrero and his companions. There too was Martyr's own impression of the same golden and silver wheels. As usual, no doubt, good Latinists were offended by the haste with which Martyr wrote. His Latin was rough. But the publication was a literary event of importance.[21] Martyr had also written an enthusiastic private letter to his ex-pupils, the marquises of los Vélez and of Mondéjar, on 7 March 1520. In that he described Tenochtitlan as "Venice the rich"; and discussed at length such matters as cocoa beans and human sacrifice.[22]

The combination of the writings of Martyr and the descriptions of Dürer continued the process of changing the mood towards America at the court of Charles V back to what had first been thought of it: namely, that it was, after all, "a new land of gold", full of extraordinary things, exceeding the romances in their fantasy. The news tilted the balance of influence still further away from Diego Velázquez, who seemed increasingly a man of the past generation. The artistic impact of Mexico, like that of the Indies generally, continued, however, to be modest: cultured Europeans, still busy shedding the influence of the Middle Ages, were in no mood for "barbarism".[23]

The diffusion of these views, and the knowledge of the magnitude of the task which Cortés had set himself, did not, however, prevent yet one more political recovery of Bishop Fonseca, after the re-establishment of traditional authority in Spain. The *comuneros* were defeated at Villalar in April 1521. The same month, Queen Juana was restored to her odious gaoler, the Marquis of Denia, who kept her alone in a dark room in Tordesillas for the next thirty years. By the end of April 1521, Fonseca, with the diminutive Luis Zapata, was back in control of the Indies (he was also appointed a judge to deal with the crimes of those accused of having sympathised with the *comuneros* in his own old diocese of Palencia). The Bishop not only secured the imprisonment of Cortés' *procurador* and friend Alonso Hernández Portocarrero, on the trumped-up charge of having seduced a certain María Rodríguez eight years previously, before he first went to the Indies; but he soon persuaded the exhausted regent, Adrian of Utrecht, to appoint one of his, Fonseca's, protégés, Cristóbal de Tapia, the royal inspector (*veedor*) at Hispaniola, to take over the government of New Spain from Cortés.[24] The charge against Porto-carrero seems the more scandalous when it is realised that his colleague, Montejo, had once committed much the same sin, since he had seduced Ana de León, in Seville: yet he went free, a clear indication that Fonseca hoped to win over that Salamantino.[25] Portocarrero never emerged from prison. For he died there soon afterwards.[26]

The instructions to Tapia were couched in strong terms against Cortés. He was charged with greed, ambition, and disobedience. But at the same time Narváez was accused, in even stronger terms, of having failed to accept the instructions of Licenciado Lucás de Ayllón. After all, men such as Ayllón should be treated "as if they were our ministers". Both Cortés and Narváez were to be sent home for judgement to Spain.[27]

Tapia, inspector, *veedor*, of Hispaniola, had gone to the Indies with Ovando in 1502. A tailor's son from the parish of Omnium Sanctorum in Seville, he had begun life as page to Bishop Fonseca during his time as archdeacon in that city. So had his brother Francisco, now a magistrate in Santo Domingo. Another brother, Juan, a citizen of Buenaventura in Hispaniola since 1514, accompanied Narváez against Cortés. Tapia seemed to have a gift for survival, for he had emerged triumphant after a serious clash with Governor Ovando in 1510.[28] He had a business sense and, as well as being an official, he was a keen investor in the early sugar industry in Hispaniola.

Adrian distrusted Fonseca. It is surprising that he agreed to the appointment of Tapia. But his elegant mind was then on other things. April 1521 saw Luther's great speech at the Diet of Worms and his denunciation by Adrian's one-time pupil, the Emperor Charles. Much was happening in the Church to whose interests he, Adrian, was devoted. The revolt of the *comunidades* had also shaken him, even if that crisis was over. There was too that month a serious bread riot in Seville, in which the people of the poor quarter near the Calle de Feria seized arms from the Duke of Medina Sidonia's palace and took as their standard of revolt a green Moorish banner which had long been preserved in the church of Omnium Sanctorum, the parish where Tapia had been brought up.[29] Adrian's attention must have been far away from matters relating to the Indies.

This instruction for Tapia does not seem to have reached Santo Domingo till the late summer.

One other European document treated of New Spain that same month of April 1521: that was a bull of Pope Leo X, *Alias Felicis*. Having already insisted that Indians be properly treated in the New World, this bull authorised two Franciscans to go to the new country (Leo was surely roused to this concern by the letters of Martyr.)[30] These Franciscans were Fr. Jean Glapion, a Flemish confessor of the Emperor and famous preacher, and Fr. Juan de los Angeles, a Spanish aristocrat, brother of the Count of Luna (he was born Francisco de Quiñones). But though they went to Spain, from Rome, they took a long time to arrange to leave it. Indeed, Glapion died before setting out, and Fr. de los Angeles became General of the Franciscan order. Delays thus attended the spiritual mission.[31]

By the autumn of 1521, meantime, Antonio de Mendoza and Diego de Ordaz had arrived in Seville from New Spain. They came separately, because of the latter's desire to testify about his own achievements to a court in Hispaniola (and perhaps also to buy pearls for subsequent sale in Spain: the little group of three ships on which Ordaz travelled carried 484 marks' worth of pearls).[32] They presumably met again in Seville. Mendoza had carried Cortés' second letter to the Emperor Charles V to Spain, along with some treasure, and other material. They had not been present at the fall of Tenochtitlan, which occurred after they had left New Spain. But they knew all about that city, its size, its wealth and its grandeur. They were the first in Castile to speak of it from experience, though they did not know that it was being destroyed. Their stories must have kept Seville agog.[33]

Ordaz and Mendoza arrived in a Spain recovering from civil war. Seville itself had been the scene of some fighting. The continuing uncertainty enabled Cortés' new messengers to hide much of the gold which they were privately bringing for Cortés' family, as for the financing of Cortés' cause in Spain. They left the rest of it in the Casa de la Contratación in Seville. They narrowly avoided arrest there, but were able to go up to talk to Cortés' father in Medellín, which had remained free from disturbances in the revolution of the *comunidades* (Mendoza came from Medellín, and so would have wished to go there anyway). They established relations with Francisco Montejo; perhaps with Portocarrero, in gaol. The three (Mendoza, Ordaz, and Montejo) then made their way to see the regent Adrian, who had established himself in Vitoria. They may have been accompanied by Martín Cortés and Francisco Núñez. In Vitoria, they apparently gave Adrian the letters from Cortés. As a result of his reading of these, and in consequence of the impression they personally left, Ordaz and Mendoza gained permission to charge Bishop Fonseca with prejudice against Cortés. Adrian had been displeased at what was told to him about the activities of Fonseca at Seville. Thereafter he seems broadly to have taken the side of the friends of Cortés against both Fonseca and Diego Velázquez. He must also have been influenced by the stories of what had occurred in Mexico told by Licenciado Lucás de Ayllón who had travelled back in the same ship as Ordaz from Hispaniola. The accidental coincidence of Ayllón and Ordaz on the ship, with the influential Burgos businessman, García de Lerma, must have led to an important exchange of news about New Spain which was afterwards of great value to Cortés.[34]

Still, the only sign of activity among the friends of Cortés for the rest of 1521 was a petition by Cortés' father Martín for the return of four thousand pesos which he had sent to Licenciado Céspedes, the uncle of Portocarrero, in Seville, as expenses earlier in the year.[35] Perhaps that money, though, had helped to pay for the supplies sent to Cortés in the ship of Juan de Burgos, which had made such a difference to the campaign on the lake in its last stages.

Meantime the Council of Castile seems to have taken a further step towards the regular construction on a permanent basis of a committee of its members to be known as the Council of the Indies, even though formally it did not come into being till later.[36] Someone who went to Mexico in the winter of 1521-2 (perhaps Alaminos, who returned there, perhaps Juan de Burgos) must have told Cortés that it existed, for Cortés himself is found using the expression in May 1522.[37]

Adrian could have taken a definite decision about Cortés' claims and demands. Had he been Cardinal Cisneros, he would have done so. But he was not, and did not. He moved his court, such as it was, from Vitoria to Saragossa in March 1522. His enquiries into the situation in New Spain continued. Meantime the question of his interest in Cortés' position was thrown into doubt by an utterly unexpected occurrence: after the sudden death in December of Leo X, the last great pope of the Renaissance, Adrian was elected to the throne of St Peter in January 1522.

The affair astonished Europe: first, because the Emperor had played little part in seeking to influence the conclave to vote for the man who had been the dominant influence (after the Archduchess Margaret) in his own childhood; second, because the college of cardinals had for once chosen as head of the Church of Rome a conscientious, kindly, and serious man "generally esteemed for his piety".[38] That piety which was such an important part of Charles V's personality had its roots in Adrian. "We hold it for certain that God Himself has made this election," the Emperor Charles wrote to Lope Hurtado de Mendoza.[39] But this decision in Rome could have only a negative effect where the suit of Cortés was concerned. Adrian's place in dealing with the affairs of the Indies was taken by Francisco Pérez de Vargas, Treasurer of Castile, a corrupt official, protégé of the Duke of Alba, known as the man sent to take over all Cardinal Cisneros' goods immediately after he died, and as one who had accumulated more money from his public offices than most of his colleagues put together.[40]

Adrian remained a few months more in Saragossa. One further benefit occurred in respect of Cortés. Charles de Poupet, Seigneur de la Chaulx, a close Flemish adviser of Charles V (he had used to sleep in his bedroom), came to Spain in order to tell Adrian how pleased the Emperor Charles was at his election.[41] No doubt his real purpose was to find out something of the new Pope's plans in Rome. But being a friend of the Archduchess Margaret, an observer of how the Mexican jewels had been appreciated when exhibited the previous year at Brussels, and a shrewd judge of financial priorities, la Chaulx was a convinced supporter of Cortés. His presence in Spain turned out to be wholly positive for the *Caudillo*'s cause.

Adrian left for Rome in August 1522. He did not enjoy himself as Pope. His piety was mocked. The plague was attributed to him. He commissioned few works of art. Cellini recorded that he was asked to do practically nothing in this papacy, in comparison with what had happened during the reign of Leo X.[42] The Italians laughed at how he asked the chapter of the Cathedral at Saragossa for the jawbone of St Lambert (they even laughed when Adrian soon died from drinking too much beer).

By the time that Adrian left for Rome, Cortés, neglected and ignored, had been *de facto* ruler of the Mexican empire for a year. That had been a time marked by six things: the physical recovery of the conquerors; the beginning of reconstruction; a ruthless pursuit of gold; persecution; the eclipse of much of the old religion, but the remarkable survival of the rest of it; and the beginning of the colonisation of places in New Mexico other than Tenochtitlan.

The physical recovery was easy enough. Cortés himself, with much of his army, soon left the great camp on the causeway at Xoloc. He established himself in a palace at Coyoacán, where he had stayed the previous spring, and which had belonged to the *tlatoani* of that city, who was unceremoniously moved out. There he set up his temporary government of the empire.[43] Rodríguez de Villafuerte, his loyal but incompetent friend from Medellín who had nearly lost the flagship in the first battle of the lake, became the Castilian governor of the almost deserted Tenochtitlan.

So far as the administration of the Mexican empire was concerned, Cortés tried to keep to old principles: dominance would be assured by governing through the old monarchs, the *tlatoani*, as tributaries. In this respect, Cortés followed a policy such as he must have learned from memories, passed on by word of mouth, of how Christian conquests in Extremadura and Andalusia were at first managed. Thus it became accepted that "in order to escape a visit from the Castilians", each chief in the province of Texcoco, say, had to pay 60,000 pesos a year in gold. In addition, he had to deliver specified quantities of maize, turkey and other game. Other chiefs in the old empire received the same treatment, with the tribute to be paid decided upon, no doubt, by a study of Montezuma's *Matrícula de Tributos*. In principle, Cortés sought to permit most provinces to "enjoy real liberty . . . with old customs intact, except for human sacrifices".

But Castilian control became, perhaps had to become, both direct and absolute. The local *tlatoani* might often continue to function. But the old Mexican imperial organisation had collapsed. A Castilian substitute for it was necessary. Cuauhtémoc was left formally as ruler of Tenochtitlan. A cousin, Auelitoctzin, hitherto chief justice of Tlatelolco, was given control of that city. Tetlepanquetzatzin was left formally in control of Tacuba, but he was a prisoner. There was already a new young "Don Fernando" as ruler of Texcoco. In fact none of these men counted. Cortés kept Cuauhtémoc in prison in Coyoacán, and began to use his cousin Tlacotzin, the deputy emperor, or *cihuacoatl*, as *de facto* Mexican governor. Tlacotzin, anyway more equipped to deal with domestic administration, held this task of collaboration for several years. Under his direction, acting under the overall Castilian authority, life in Mexico began falteringly to recover.[44] Franciscans such as Fr. Toribio de Benavente ("Motolinía") would later complain that in these years the "demons continued to be served and honoured. The Spaniards," he grumbled, "were content to build their houses and they seemed happy enough that no human sacrifice occurred in public. But many took place in secret and in the suburbs of Tenochtitlan. Thus idolatry lived in peace . . ."[45] This judgement may have exaggerated the real position, for numerous members of the old royal house had begun to make their peace with the conquerors. Many became Christians. Several less important *tlatoani*-ships, Christianised, survived for generations.[46]

The resultant confusion, perhaps the outrage, was expressed in a poem which seems to be of the time:

> Who are you, sitting beside the captain-general?
> Ah, it is Doña Isabel, my little niece!
> Ah, it is true, the kings are captives . . .[47]

Whether demanded as tribute, under proper legal forms, or in any other way, the shortage of food was severe. The fields in the Valley of Mexico had not been sown during 1521. Thus during the the last part of that year, and much of 1522, the lack of maize was so great that even the Castilians encountered hardship.[48] There had hitherto been only a minuscule amount of trade from Spain and Hispaniola, and none from Cuba. So there was no wine, nor clothes, nor flour.[49] The suffering of the indigenous population in the Valley of Mexico, already severely hit by the epidemic of smallpox, must have been considerable, and this may have continued for years. Beyond the valley, in Tlaxcala, Cholula, Oaxaca, and Vera Cruz, living was much better.

In the absence of news from Castile, or even of any clear reasons why there was none (Cortés could have known little of the rebellion of the *comuneros*), it was natural that the *Caudillo* should have behaved as if he had been a viceroy, or even a king. He obviously said extravagant things in those first days after the conquest. For example, he was heard to remark, in the presence of many, that he would like to make thirty or forty dukes or counts, and put the people of New Spain under their control.[50] Vázquez de Tapia heard him say that if the King were to send men to take over New Spain, and if some of those in the country wanted to accept those men, he, Cortés, would hang a dozen of them to keep the rest quiet.[51] Some said that Cortés had the habit of touching his captains (Olid, Sandoval, Corral) on the shoulder with a sword, and, in royal style, saying, "God and the apostle Santiago make you a good knight."[52] He was similarly supposed to have said that "even if the Infante Don Fernando [the future Emperor of Austria] should come as governor, I would not yield to him the governance of the country".[53] (The mention of that prince, who had been brought up in Spain, was daring, since there had been a strong group of courtiers in Castile, by now dispersed, who had hoped that he might have become their king instead of Charles.) On another occasion Cortés was supposed to have said: "The country which we have won is ours and, if the King does not give it to us, then we shall take it."[54] Others said that they had heard Cortés insisting on being called "Highness". Friends of Cortés were heard to say that they had taken an oath not to give the country to the King unless he, Cortés, were made governor of it. Gonzalo de Mexía, the discredited treasurer of the army, once said aloud that "despite everything, Don Hernando will not be content with the responsibility for running the country, he will want to carry off the King's whole authority".[55]

All these remarks seem to have been the understandable comments of a conqueror who had achieved, by any standards, a remarkable victory, and seemed not to be appreciated at home. There is no evidence at all that Cortés contemplated a unilateral declaration of independence. What he wanted was royal favour: to enable him to live as a duke, a patron of the arts, a great employer of men, a collector of women as of jewels, a friend of princes. A great deal of evidence was presented in his favour at the enquiry against him, as well as the testimony against him. Francisco de Terrazas, for example, said that he had never known Cortés show himself other than the most enthusiastic supporter of the Crown.[56] Juan de Ortega recalled that Cortés, in his house in Coyoacán, had a Flemish painting on wood of Charles V, the Queen, and the King's brothers and sisters, and that "he always took off his hat to it when he passed".[57]

A measure of reconstruction began soon after the fall of Tenochtitlan. Here Cortés did make use of the imprisoned ex-Emperor Cuauhtémoc: first, to secure the collaboration of the Mexica to repair water pipes from Chapultepec to the city; second, to clear the ruined streets of dead and rubble; and third, to ensure that some Mexica would go back and live in what remained of the ruined capital, particularly in the northern suburbs which had been less damaged than the southern ones. A new temporary harbour on the east side of the city facing Texcoco was built. Pedro de Alvarado, always ready to serve Cortés in minor undertakings as well as grandiose ones, was named *alcalde* of the docks. All the same, until the end of 1521, Cortés and his friends all expected that the old city would eventually be abandoned.

Repression continued sporadically for many weeks after August 1521. It is clear neither how this was decided upon, nor why precisely certain people were killed. Probably there was no principle. But the list of those hanged after the fall of Tenochtitlan included two out of the four *tlatoani* of the four cities of the ancient principality of the Culhua: Macuilxochitl, *tlatoani* of Huitzilopochco; and Pizotzin, *tlatoani* of Culhuacan.[58] In Tenochtitlan, the high priest of Huitzilopochtli and the priest of Xipe Totec were also hanged (on the way to Mazatlan, in northern Oaxaca).[59] Several Mexican leaders were thrown to the dogs: for example, the *tlacatecatl* (military commander) and the *tlillancalqui* (Keeper of the House of Darkness) of both Tenochtitlan and Cuauhtitlan.[60] There must have been hundreds of others, their deaths unrecorded.

The repression, however, soon became indistinguishable from the frenzied search for gold.

This presented the most difficult problem. Most conquistadors were in New Spain in the first place because they wanted wealth. But there was little of it available. As earlier mentioned, individual Spaniards looked for it, usually unsuccessfully, in numerous brutal ways. With increasing restlessness, the scarcity of food, and the lack of communication from Castile, it came to be believed that Cortés had seized all the gold that there was. Cortés' palace in Coyoacán was surrounded by a whitewashed wall. Lampoons began to be scribbled on it. One day the statement appeared there that Cortés had given his own soldiers a worse defeat than the one which they had given the Mexica. Next day there came the comment: "How sad will my spirit be till Cortés has given back all the gold which he has taken." Cortés was for a time prepared to enter into the spirit of the thing. Thus he himself one day wrote the phrase "A blank wall is the paper of fools." But he soon became angry at the constant denigration of his achievements.[61] Perhaps, though, he had indeed hidden away a fortune: Juan de Ribera, Cortés' later disloyal secretary, would tell Peter Martyr in Spain in late 1522 that Cortés had a secret treasure of three million pesos.[62]

Some conquistadors were finding bills rather than treasure. The expedition of Cortés had been a venture of private enterprise. Thus men such as Maese Juan, Narváez's surgeon who had stayed with Cortés throughout the expedition after the battle of Cempoallan, and the druggist, Murcia, were demanding exaggerated sums for their services during the campaign. Two of Cortés' friends, Bernardino de Santa Clara, the *converso* planter of Cuba, and García Llerena, were appointed as arbitrators to fix prices on goods sold and also on services for doctors. They gave orders that, in the event of people having no money to settle these accounts, they would have a grace in which to pay of two years.[63]

Other conquistadors kept on saying that Cortés was seeking personal power in Mexico. Why otherwise had he set up a foundry for the manufacture of new artillery? Was this not likely to be used more against the King's officials than Indian rebels?[64]

The constant restlessness of the conquistadors was echoed by the demands of the royal officials, headed by the King's treasurer, Julián de Alderete. He too wanted gold: for himself, as for the Crown. In the end, therefore, Cortés agreed that, once more, the chief prisoners should be summoned and examined as to where "the treasure of Mexico" might be found. No one seems to have realised that much of the gold, the amber and jade, the feathers and other treasures of old Mexico, had been in the warehouses not of the Emperor but of the *pochteca*, the long-distance merchants. Private enterprise was more advanced in old Mexico in some ways than it had been in old Spain.

Those who came to Cortés' meeting included Cuauhtémoc; Tlacotzin, the *cihuacoatl*; Motelchiuh, now the majordomo of Tenochtitlan, that commander who had long ago visited Cortés at Cempoallan; Tetlepan-quetzatzin, the King of Tacuba; Oquitzin, the *tlatoani* of Azcapotzalco, the goldsmiths' city; and Panitzin, *tlatoani* of Ecatepec, a Mexican town on the mainland just north of Tenochtitlan. Through Marina, Cortés asked these lords the whereabouts of the gold of Mexico. They replied that all that they had had been placed in Cuauhtémoc's canoe, and thus it had already passed to the Castilians. There were some further arguments as to where, if it had been so, the gold could have gone and whether, indeed, there had been any. The Mexica were adamant that there was no more. The Castilians insisted that there must be. A golden statue of

Huitzilopochtli, for example, was known to have existed. Where was it?

Given the silence of the Mexican leaders, Alderete insisted that Cuauhtémoc and the King of Tacuba be put to the torture to provide information about the whereabouts of the missing gold.[65] Cortés said later that he had been against this inhumanity but was powerless to prevent the King's treasurer from going ahead with it.[66] He told Andrés de Tapia, for example, that the action always weighed heavily upon him. Francisco de Terrazas told the same story, as did Salcedo, who said that Alderete especially went to Cortés' house to request permission.[67] Several conquistadors, it is fair to add, are said to have thought that Cortés did not want to put pressure on Alderete, because he believed that the treasurer, if thwarted, might endanger his own possession of stolen gold.[68] This cannot represent the whole truth. Cortés was at that time quite strong enough to have prevented Alderete from doing something of which he did not approve.

This inhumane action also ran directly against the promises which Cortés had made to Cuauhtémoc when he had surrendered to him.

Cuauhtémoc was tortured by being tied to a pole and having his feet (perhaps his hands) dipped in oil, which was then set alight.[69] The poor Emperor tried to hang himself first.[70] The Castilians similarly treated Tetlepanquetzatzin, King of Tacuba. The latter kept his eye on Cuauhtémoc in the hope that he would have mercy on him and say something or give him leave to say what he knew. But the Emperor looked at him fiercely, and is supposed to have painfully said: "Am I enjoying some kind of delight or bath?"[71]

Despite the later comment of one conquistador (Martín Vázquez, a friend of Cortés) that the Emperor gave away nothing,[72] the brutality was evidently severe. Cuauhtémoc thereafter was crippled, and walked with a limp. The wounds of the King of Tacuba, Tetlepanquetzatzin, were apparently worse.

Cuauhtémoc in the end confessed that the gods had told him some days before the fall of the city that defeat was inevitable. He had given orders for such gold as there was to be thrown into the lake. He made no other statement. Castilian divers went to look in the lake at the place where Cuauhtémoc said that the gold had been dropped. They found a few ornaments, but nothing substantial. Probably if there had been such a jettisoning of gold, it would have occurred months before the end, as indicated earlier. In the ruins of Cuauhtémoc's palace, the Castilians did, however, come upon a large golden disc comparable to the one given to Cortés by Montezuma.[73] One beautiful jade head was discovered.[74]

The Castilians also interrogated several Mexican priests about gold lost in the *noche triste*. Where, for example, were the eight large bars of gold which had been assembled in Montezuma's palace before the conquistadors set off on their flight that night and which had apparently been left in the hands of Ocuitecatl, Montezuma's majordomo, who had died in the smallpox epidemic? Out of eight bars only four had appeared.

The consequence of all this brutality and grubbing round for gold was unsatisfactory for all concerned. The new sum available was estimated as being between 185,000 and 200,000 pesos[75] (174,000 would be melted down between 25 September 1521 and 16 May 1522).[76] The sum paid to the Crown as the Fifth was decided as 37,000 pesos. Cortés then took 29,600 pesos as his Fifth of the rest.[77] The total available for distribution was, therefore, a little less than 120,000 pesos – which, divided among, say, 750 men, would have left everyone with about 160 pesos each. This seemed to be so tiny a sum in comparison with the extraordinary dangers experienced that some soldiers indeed, philanthropically or ironically, suggested that the whole should be divided among those who had lost limbs, or were lame, or paralysed, or burned with powder, or, indeed, among the families of the dead. There were, it is true, slaves, other booty, and certain gold objects and jewellery which were in theory subject to being *quintado*. Many of the jewels were in Cortés' judgement "so remarkable that they could not be described"; and therefore should not have been melted down.[78] But they seem to have been so treated, and valued, accordingly, at the equivalent of 125,00 pesos.[79]

Even worse, some special payments were made to the senior captains. Some of these were a little curious: thus 6,000 pesos went to Francisco de Montejo (to be kept for him though he was away in Spain, and though his share in the campaign had been minimal), 3,000 each to Julián de Alderete and Alonso de Ávila, 2,000 each for Diego de Ordaz, Antonio de Quiñones, Cortés' bodyguard, and Licenciado Céspedes, Cortés' lawyer in Spain (presumably on behalf of Portocarrero, his nephew); and 1,500 to Juan de Ribera, Cortés' secretary, and to Fr. Pedro Melgarejo.[80] A later lawsuit suggested that the "true captains" of the *santa compañía*, Alvarado, Sandoval, Olid, and Martín López, only received 400 pesos each – though most people assumed that they would have been able to seize a great deal more (this does not seem to have been the case in respect of López).[81] One of Cortés' new close associates, Diego de Ocampo, of Cáceres, brother of the circumnavigator of Cuba, received 6,000 pesos: a sum difficult to explain unless the money was intended indirectly for Cortés himself.

After those payments, the horsemen in the expedition received eighty pesos; crossbowmen, arquebusiers and other special forces gained between fifty and sixty pesos; the rest less.[82] Everyone thought these sums ridiculous: after all, that was a time when the purchase of a mere sword cost fifty pesos; and a crossbow sixty.

Some of the sums were paid in the light of money invested in equipping the expedition. But this led to bad blood. This was not only because Cortés was thought to have taken so much, but because the real total available was supposed to have been much more than 200,000 pesos; perhaps indeed 380,000 as Bernal Díaz suggested, without any evidence.[83] García del Pilar, one of Cortés' enemies but a man who had been quick to learn Nahuatl, said, in the *residencia* against the *Caudillo*, that a Mexican, by then named "Juan Velázquez", had once taken him to the island of Xaltocan where he had seen a room full of gold, and told him that he could take what he wanted, before Cortés took the rest.[84] Another witness, Marcos Ruiz, said that he saw this same "Velázquez", with other servants of Cortés, laden down with gold intended for the *Caudillo*.[85] Several other witnesses at Cortés' *residencia* said that they had seen that Cortés had a private place for melting down gold in his house, and that he had hired Indians to work for him there, no doubt making gold bars out of jewels which were not declared to Alderete.[86] This accusation was denied fiercely: the Indians who went into Cortés' house were said (by Cortés' friends) to be servants bringing fruit to Doña Marina.[87] Then there was once a great fiesta in Cortés' house, at which certain Castilian girls were present. Cortés wished to give them presents. He went to his room and was seen to open four large Flanders chests full of gold bars and jewels.[88] Francisco de Orduña, in 1522 an ally of Cortés but a few years later an enemy, testified in 1529 that Cortés ordered his lawyer, Ochoa de Lexalde, to bury on his behalf the equivalent of about 12,500 or 14,000 pesos in bars.[89]

Some extra gold was received from Texcoco. Though that city under the generalship of Ixtlilxochitl had been ultimately an ally of Cortés, the ex-monarch Coanacochtzin had been an enemy to the end. He was a prisoner. The sores caused by having to wear irons round his ankles troubled him greatly. His brother, Ixtlilxochitl, told Cortés. Cortés genially said that he should ransom him. Ixtlilxochitl sent Cortés all his gold. Cortés said that it was not enough. Ixtlilxochitl secured all the gold which the family had in four hundred houses and the ransom was raised. The gold seems to have gone direct to Cortés.[90] A little later, García del Pilar said that he had seen some of Ixtlilxochitl's men in the province of Oaxaca selling human flesh. They improbably explained that they had to do this in order to buy gold to give to Cortés.[91]

Some conquistadors are said to have been paid in the old Mexican commodity of exchange, cocoa beans: but it is hard to believe that the average Castilian was much impressed by a payment in a currency which was also used as a drink.[92]

37
The songs and voices scarcely ceased

"The seventh plague was the construction of the great city of Mexico in which in the first years more people were working than in the building of the temple of Jerusalem . . . and they had the custom to work singing and talking and the songs and voices scarcely ceased by night and by day . . ."
Fr. Motolinía, *Historia de las Indias*

DETERMINED TO PREVENT the unrest at the poor rewards for the victory from turning into rebellion, Cortés sought to give his men a *raison d'être* by sending some of them to found new communities. Thus in October, Sandoval was dispatched south with an expedition to Tustepec. Having established a small settlement there, he went on to Coatzacoalcos, near the mouth of the river of that name, which seemed a possible alternative to Vera Cruz as a port. Then Francisco de Orozco, Cortés' commander at Tepeaca/Segura de la Frontera since the previous year, was ordered to go to Oaxaca, known, from Montezuma's *Matrícula de Tributos*, to be the main gold-producing region of Mexico. Diego de Pineda and Vicente López went to conquer Pánuco, that flat and hot region to the north of Villa Rica near the coast which so mesmerised Francisco de Garay, the Governor of Jamaica. Cortés' sometime steward, Rodrigo Rangel, went down to Villa Rica to reinforce Pedro de Ircio, who had become Cortés' governor there. Juan Álvarez (perhaps the one-time pilot of that name) was dispatched to Colima; while the incompetent Juan Rodríguez de Villafuerte made for Zacatula on the Pacific coast. Cristóbal de Olid set off for the independent kingdom of Michoacan. A little later, Pedro de Alvarado, "Tonatío", was sent to Tututepec, a Mexican garrison town near the Pacific coast which controlled the Tlapanecan community of Ayotlan. The emphasis on new conquests showed the frontier spirit of these conquistadors: after the capture of Seville, Granada; after Tenochtitlan, the Pacific; after the Pacific, China. "In my opinion we must move on," as the Cid would have said.[1]

But before these expeditions had achieved their aim, and indeed in some cases before they had set off, Cortés was faced with the most serious challenge to his authority since the coming of Narváez. This occurred as a result of the arrival on the coast at Vera Cruz of the inspector of Hispaniola, Cristóbal de Tapia, whose instructions from Fonseca to take over power in New Spain had come from Castile in the late summer of 1521.

The *audiencia* of Hispaniola had not been enthusiastic about Tapia's instructions. They were more anxious to make progress with the enquiry (*residencia*) which, as has been noticed, had been embarked upon by the judge Alonso de Zuazo against Diego Velázquez in Cuba: even if Zuazo himself was under the threat of a similar enquiry in Santo Domingo.[2] The *audiencia* had told Tapia not to go to New Spain, since they could see that his arrival at that time would "break the thread" of the Mexican conquest.[3] Tapia had brushed these doubts aside because he knew that his instructions had been signed by Fonseca and his colleagues; including Adrian of Utrecht.

Tapia reached San Juan de Ulúa with a small staff in early December 1521. He immediately commended himself to the local councillors at Villa Rica, such as Jorge de Alvarado (who had just taken the place of Rodrigo Rangel as Cortés' representative). Tapia showed his instructions and letters to all whom he found at Vera Cruz. They thought that they were in order. But since the greater part of municipal government in New Spain lay with Cortés, they wisely said that Tapia should consult the *Caudillo*. Tapia wrote to Cortés saying that he had come to New Spain as governor in the name of the King. He hoped to see Cortés soon, though he could not set out as yet himself, since his horses were ill from the journey across the Caribbean. Could Cortés arrange a meeting?[4] He, Tapia, would be delighted to go up to Tenochtitlan; or, perhaps, Cortés might prefer to meet him near the sea.

Cortés had heard of Tapia's arrival before his letter reached him. He would have remembered Tapia perfectly well from his time in Hispaniola. Once again Cortés played a game of municipalities. He ordered Sandoval to go directly from Tustepec down to "Medellín", on the coast near Vera Cruz and, though it was still the purely Totonac town of Nauhtla, with no Spanish inhabitants at all, formally constitute a municipality there, with a full paraphernalia of (presumably absentee) councillors and magistrates. He himself took the opportunity to form a municipality in Tenochtitlan. Thus, with Villa Rica de la Vera Cruz and Segura de la Frontera, there were now four Castilians towns in New Spain. Tapia would have to reckon with all of them.[5]

Cortés then wrote to Inspector Tapia a friendly letter saying how glad he was that he had come. Had they not once lived next door to one another in Hispaniola? He, Cortés, could not think of anyone better equipped to govern New Spain than Tapia. He suggested that they should meet in Texcoco.[6] But Tapia had also written to the King's treasurer, Alderete, telling him of his instructions. Alderete showed this letter to Cristóbal de Olid. Olid, by now restless at Cortés' leadership and the modesty of his own profits, agreed to accept Tapia as governor. The two of them went to talk to Francisco Verdugo and other surviving old friends of Diego Velázquez. (Alderete had recently quarrelled with Cortés, since he had said that the *Caudillo* only gave gold to those whom he liked. Cortés had said that he lied. Alderete had put his hand to his sword at this comment, but had left the house. Alonso de Ávila, as he left, had told Cortés that his biggest error had been to have received Alderete in the beginning.)[7] They all agreed that, if Cortés were to refuse to see the new governor, and were to show signs of not obeying him, they would raise a rebellion.[8] The news of this little plot inevitably reached Cortés, as all other such conspiracies had done in the past. He instantly changed his mind about seeing Tapia at Texcoco. He abruptly took away Olid's staff of office as lieutenant-governor of Tenochtitlan.[9] Then he wrote again to Tapia saying that, since the conquest was not yet complete, and since any change might excite the Indians, he would, on second thoughts, send down Fr. Pedro Melgarejo de Urrea to describe everything that had happened, to examine the decrees brought by Tapia, and to work out a good plan for the future; and Fr. Pedro, now a close friend of Cortés, set off.

A little later, Cortés received a letter from the municipality of Villa Rica de la Vera Cruz, describing what had transpired and also explaining that their delay in putting the new governor's orders into effect had annoyed Tapia, who then "attempted certain scandalous things" – probably selling merchandise which he had brought with him.[10] Cortés brushed this letter aside, and wrote back saying that he was proceeding to go down to the sea himself. At this, those who were formally, if somewhat eccentrically, *procuradores* of the municipalities of Tenochtitlan, Segura and Vera Cruz, but who were in Coyoacán, represented to Cortés that, out of regard for the safety of the whole of New Spain, he should not leave the Valley of Mexico. If he did, the Mexica would surely revolt. They would think that Tapia was another Narváez. Instead of the *Caudillo* going, they said, they would travel down themselves to see Tapia.

These *procuradores* were, of course, Cortés' allies: Vázquez de Tapia, a counsellor of Vera Cruz; Cristóbal del Corral, councillor of Segura de la Frontera and, for a long time, the standard-bearer of the expedition; and Pedro de Alvarado, chief magistrate of Tenochtitlan. Cortés, with his now practised air of yielding reluctantly to a proposal which he had almost certainly thought of himself, accepted this plan, and formally gave up any thought of leaving Coyoacán.[11]

Tapia met the other leading conquistadors of New Spain at first at Jalapa and then, on 24 December, at Cempoallan, where Narváez had lost his eye eighteen months before.[12] These conquistadors were Pedro de Alvarado, appearing on behalf of the new municipality of Tenochtitlan; Corral, for Segura/Tepeaca; Monjaraz, for "Medellín"; and Francisco Álvarez Chico, Jorge de Alvarado, Simón de Cuenca, and Vázquez de Tapia for Vera Cruz. Sandoval, Diego de Soto, and Diego de Valdenebro appeared on behalf of Cortés himself.

These conquistadors must have made a powerful impression on Tapia. He probably had known several of them from ten years or more before in Hispaniola. Then they would have appeared modest men, with aspirations no doubt, but nothing much in the way of achievements. Pedro de Alvarado would have seemed merely the promising kinsman of his fellow *encomendero*, the crusty Diego de Alvarado of Santo Domingo. Now Pedro, like the others with him, was an experienced man who had seen triumphs and tragedies. These conquistadors had won victories in what must have seemed to themselves heroic circumstances. They were at the height of their self-confidence. They might seem to be outlaws in old Spain. But in New Spain they were as paladins.

They adopted a polite but determined attitude. They read Tapia's instructions carefully. They recognised that these had been issued at Burgos on 11 April last. They even kissed these instructions, and placed them on their heads, since they were decrees of the King of Spain. But as to carrying out what was in them, they said that they would have to appeal to the King. They insisted that Tapia knew nothing of the political reality of New Spain. They argued that, despite his legal training, Tapia was inadequate to be Governor. That office required special qualities. They knew, of course, that Fonseca, Bishop of Burgos, was hostile to all of them; and, indeed, that he kept giving inadequate orders to favour his friend, Diego Velázquez, who had as surely misinformed the King about conditions in New Spain. It was probably Alvarado and Sandoval who took the lead in all these discussions on Cortés' behalf.

The inspector at first tried to insist that these *procuradores* of the new cities of New Spain had no standing, and again urged obedience to his provisions. But again the *procuradores* insisted (untruthfully, so far as is known) that Tapia's arrival had already caused an upheaval. How much more trouble would be caused by his taking over of power?[13] Tapia was physically not in a strong position to take any action against this demonstration by the *procuradores*. Perhaps he had already received a bribe from Fr. Melgarejo not to cause too much trouble. Perhaps indeed a bribe for doing nothing was what he expected from his journey to New Spain.[14] In fact, he did shortly agree to return to Hispaniola and await there the appeal of the conquistadors to the Crown. In order to ease further this happy conclusion to what might have been a dangerous business, he was given some African slaves and some horses. He asked for a notarial note of the discussion; and this was provided by Alfonso de Vergara, a notary who had come to New Spain with Narváez. It had been he who, in such different circumstances, had, in the spring of 1520, gone to call on Sandoval and asked him to surrender to himself, as the representative of Diego Velázquez.

Tapia was preparing to leave when Alonso Ortiz de Zúñiga, also originally one of Narváez's men, appeared as the agent of the King's treasurer, Julián de Alderete (Ortiz de Zúñiga had had permission of Cortés to leave Mexico).[15] He brought letters to Tapia from Alderete. It is not known what these contained. But, on reading them, Tapia changed his mind about leaving and said that he would like to stay in New Spain as "a private citizen" until he received further instructions from the King.[16] Cortés' friends were, of course, not going to accept such an artful procrastination. Francisco Álvarez Chico, as lieutenant-governor of Villa Rica, gravely gave Tapia an order to embark there and then, as something advantageous to the King. Tapia tried to delay further on the pretext that he had to sell some slaves. Sandoval said that he would send him home to Santo Domingo in a canoe if he did not get on his ship immediately. Bernardino Vázquez de Tapia then forced him to embark. Sandoval watched the ship from the shore to ensure that it did leave.[17]

This done, the *procuradores* went back to Coyoacán to tell Cortés of their achievements: at hearing which "Don Hernando showed much pleasure and happiness".[18] Thereafter, though, Cortés treated harshly those who had received Tapia well. Olid, once one of his favourites, never received back his staff of office as lieutenant-governor of Tenochtitlan (though Cortés still sent him to Michoacan); and Jorge de Alvarado lost his position on the town council at Villa Rica.[19] Pedro de Alvarado told his brother that he was "a pig and a fool", and would not call him brother any more.[20] Ortiz de Zúñiga was not allowed to embark for Santo Domingo, as he had planned, was taken back to Coyoacán, and was kept in an improvised prison for three months. Francisco Verdugo apparently suffered similarly. In the charges against Cortés in the *residencia*, it was said that thereafter Cortés started to hate these men and sought to destroy them.[21] Equally, he spoke roughly to Alderete, who had shown such sympathy for Tapia's position. He was never on good terms with him again.[22] Something of a mania seems to have seized hold of Cortés. García del Pilar who, after hearing of Tapia's arrival, had merely said, "Now we have a new government," was also apparently imprisoned.[23]

The affair of Tapia left Cortés, all the same, in a stronger position than he had been before. He even felt able to send for Narváez, and show him the remains of Tenochtitlan. Many flatteries passed between them: Narváez, for example, with the courtesy which came easily to him, recalled Cortés' remark to him after capture, and said: "*Señor capitán*, the least of the things that you and your valiant soldiers have done was to capture me." Cortés replied sententiously: "The only cause is that of God and our great Caesar."[24]

Scarcely had Tapia returned to Santo Domingo than a ship arrived from Cuba captained by that old, discredited but determined Caribbean conquistador, the Biscayan sailing master, Juan Bono de Quejo. He had come to New Spain, it may be remembered, with Narváez. Having survived the *noche triste*, he had been among those friends of Narváez (and Diego Velázquez) permitted to return to Cuba in early 1521. Bono de Quejo had given much hostile evidence against Cortés at Velázquez's enquiry in June 1521.[25] Now he returned, apparently assuming that Cristóbal de Tapia was in power. He had with him dispatches and documents for Tapia from his and Tapia's mutual benefactor, Fonseca, the Bishop of Burgos.[26] They included promises of "singular benefits" (said Bernal Díaz) to those who accepted Tapia as governor. He even had with him letters signed by the Bishop with the names of the addressees left blank: Bono de Quejo could direct them to whom he wished. There was a letter too for Cortés, promising him great favours if he would give way peacefully to Tapia.

Cortés pretended to be angry. He even suggested that these interventions by Bono de Quejo (and Fonseca) were stimulating some talk among his friends at that time of forming a rebellious "*comunidad*", as had been done in Castile, "in order to maintain order until Your Majesty is informed of the truth".[27] Still, it was fortunate for the *Caudillo* that Bono de Quejo arrived in January 1522 rather than in December 1521, when he could have created serious trouble. As it was, he remained for a time in Mexico. He still seems to have been a frequent visitor to Cortés' dining table in the late summer, even suggesting that he, Cortés, like Velázquez might like to marry one of Fonseca's nieces: a proposal as out of date as it was inappropriate for a married man.

There was a postscript to this business which was most satisfactory to Cortés. Tapia, it will be recalled, had been advised by the *audiencia* in Santo Domingo not to go to New Spain, because it would "break the thread" of the conquest there. When he arrived back, he was in a measure of disgrace. Further, the *audiencia* now came out explicitly on Cortés' side. They gave permission to Cortés to conquer all New Spain, a licence which, though tardy, was by the nature of things vague, and could be held to cover almost anywhere to which Cortés wished to direct his attention. They gave him a licence to brand slaves, such as he had requested through Alonso de Ávila; and they said that, so far as they were concerned, he could allot Indians to conquistadors in *encomiendas*, just as had occurred in Hispaniola itself, Cuba, and Jamaica. These instructions were to remain valid until such time as the King in Castile should decide differently. The *audiencia* had written to the King, it seemed, about those matters, but not to Bishop Fonseca, since they were too annoyed at his nomination of Cristóbal de Tapia to New Spain.

Ávila, who had remained in Santo Domingo since being left there by

Antonio de Mendoza and Diego de Ordaz on their way home the previous year, had returned to New Spain with this news (he was still in Santo Domingo in September 1521, for he was to be found there giving evidence on behalf of Diego de Ordaz).[28] The decisions of the *audiencia* had been his triumph, for he had been working towards that end ever since he had arrived in Hispaniola. Whether it was also a triumph for the bribes which he effected on Cortés' behalf it is impossible now to say positively. But the assumption must be that some Mexican gold changed hands and that the *audiencia* and others were excited by the stories of Mexico told by Ávila and Ordaz.

Cortés was always grateful to Ávila for these services. By April 1522 Ávila had become *alcalde mayor* or chief magistrate of Mexico. Though this is to anticipate, he was, later in the year, the beneficiary of one of Cortés' first grants of *encomienda*, becoming the master and, in theory, the moral guide of thousands of Indians in Cuauhtitlan, a Tepanec city on the lake, just to the north of Tenochtitlan. But though Cortés was grateful to Ávila he still never brought himself to like him. Perhaps Ávila's Castilian origins disturbed him: he had been born in Ciudad Real. Cortés seems only to have felt at ease with Extremeños. Ávila's frank, arrogant, quarrelsome and direct nature was also unappealing to Cortés. Though the *Caudillo* appreciated his services, he always kept him at a distance.[29]

The importance of Ávila was seen in April 1522 when, precisely as chief magistrate, he presided over an enquiry (*probanza*). The aim was to investigate the appeal by Cortés against the nomination of Cristóbal de Tapia. All the witnesses duly said that, had Tapia become governor, the gains of the conquest would have been lost: he was the wrong man to govern a country such as Mexico at such a time.

Witnesses were also questioned about the expeditions of Grijalva and Hernández de Córdoba. The purpose of these arcane discussions was to secure the rejection of the claim which Juan de Grijalva had made to have discovered the territory on behalf of his uncle Diego Velázquez, and to emphasise the earlier claim made by the now dead Francisco Hernández de Córdoba in the name of the King. Six of those who testified in 1521 said that they had seen the latter jump to land and claim the territory. If the conquistadors had enough time to discuss such things, their control over Mexico must have been secure.[30]

Once inspector Tapia had been satisfactorily dispatched, Cortés returned to his projects of exploration, and the journeys which had been planned before. His purpose was to complete his triumph over a city with the conquest of a country. The most important of these projects were: Alvarado's journey to Tututepec, in the south-west towards Oaxaca; Sandoval's to Coatzacoalcos; and Olid's to Michoacan.

Alvarado left Tenochtitlan with about two hundred men, forty horse and two small cannon. After a characteristic series of negotiations, acts of treachery, and impetuous ventures, he founded a city temporarily, if confusingly, known as Segura de la Frontera (the other Segura, at Tepeaca on the way to Villa Rica, was abandoned about then, and its population removed to the new city). Alvarado subsequently developed an interest in that region (later in the year, Cortés granted him a large *encomienda* there).[31]

After Tututepec, Alvarado journeyed further to the south to establish a Castilian presence at Tehuantepec, a remote but rich province of the Mexican empire, on the isthmus, whose *tlatoani*, a Zapotec, but related to Montezuma, had submitted to Castilian control the previous year.[32] This was a heroic journey with much suffering, even for the commander-in-chief. In Tehuantepec, Alvarado imprisoned the *tlatoani*, since he suspected a plot. He crushed a suspected Castilian conspiracy, hanging two of his own men (Salamanca and Bernaldino) to discourage others.[33] He sent Cortés a substantial supply of gold deriving from this expedition. Cortés apparently kept it himself. An unseemly lawsuit followed between them on the matter in 1528.[34]

Sandoval, having dealt firmly, if roughly, with the people of Tustepec, went down, as planned, to the region of Coatzacoalcos. No Spaniard, perhaps no Mexican at that time, realised that this was the site of the "mother culture" of the whole region, where high civilisation took shape in the Americas.[35] The great Olmec sites, with their colossal dark heads with the faces of screaming babies, were covered with dense vegetation. It was, however, as Cortés had already discovered, a heavily populated territory. It lay just beyond the south-eastern boundary of the Mexican empire so far as tribute was concerned. So Sandoval was actually seeking to extend the size of the old empire, rather as Cortés had suggested to Montezuma that they would do together during that pleasant period when they were both in Tenochtitlan. Diego de Ordaz had, however, been in the region in 1520, as had Rodrigo Rangel and Juan Velázquez de León. They had established good relations with the *naturales*, so that there was, to begin with, no hostility.

All the same, those *naturales* greatly disliked the idea of a permanent Castilian settlement. Sandoval had to fight before he set up his city, complete with municipality, about ten miles from the mouth of the river Coatzacoalcos. He called it "Espiritu Santo": it was founded the day after the feast of Espiritu Santo; and that was also the name of the city where Sandoval had used to live in Cuba.[36]

As soon as the city was founded, Sandoval made divisions of land and Indians among those conquistadors who had said that they would live there: among them, Luis Marín, the Sanluqueño of Genoese origin who was his great friend and whom Cortés had used several times for keeping peace between conquistadors; Bernal Díaz, the chronicler; Diego de

Quetzalcoatl *c.* 1500, the plumed serpent, Mexican god of wind, of intellect and education, possibly once a king of Tollan, whom Cortés was probably for a time thought to reincarnate

Spain in 1517 *(anti-clockwise from right)* Poor Queen Juana, already incarcerated as mad; the regent Cisneros, as happy with the smell of gunpowder as that of incense; King Charles, then only seventeen, later the Emperor Charles V; Bartolomé de las Casas, historian and propagandist on behalf of the indigenous peoples; Bishop Fonseca, "Minister for the Indies"

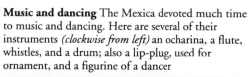

Music and dancing The Mexica devoted much time to music and dancing. Here are several of their instruments *(clockwise from left)* an ocharina, a flute, whistles, and a drum; also a lip-plug, used for ornament, and a figurine of a dancer

Games The Mexica had games with rubber balls. They also juggled with logs of wood on their feet. The bird recalls how much the Mexica needed feathers for mosaics. All sketched from life by Weiditz *c.* 1528

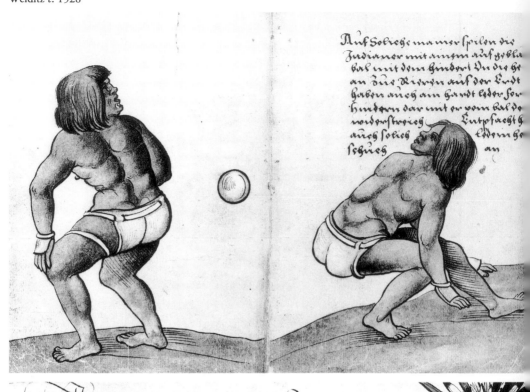

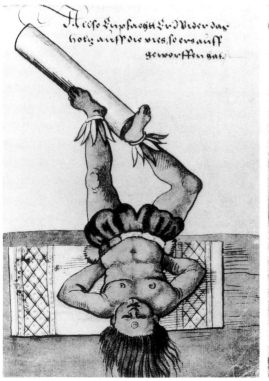

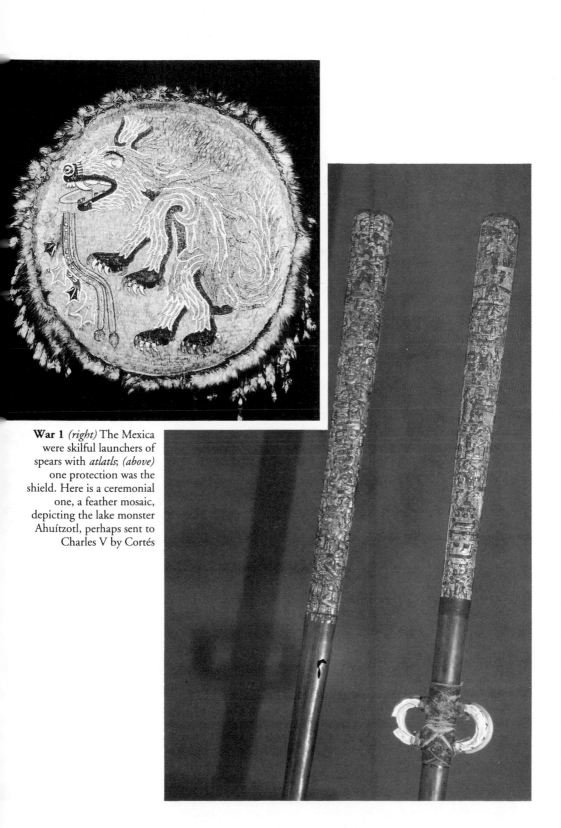

War 1 *(right)* The Mexica were skilful launchers of spears with *atlatls*; *(above)* one protection was the shield. Here is a ceremonial one, a feather mosaic, depicting the lake monster Ahuítzotl, perhaps sent to Charles V by Cortés

War 2 The weapons of Mexica (none of their flint blade swords survived) were nothing in comparison with the arquebus *(right)*; the crossbow *(centre)*; the culverin *(below)*; and above all the Toledo blade *(far right)*, said to have belonged to Gonzalo Fernández de Córdoba

War 3 The Spaniards had two secret weapons: brigantines *(left)*, which they built so as to besiege Tenochtitlan by water; and smallpox *(below)*, which killed thousands

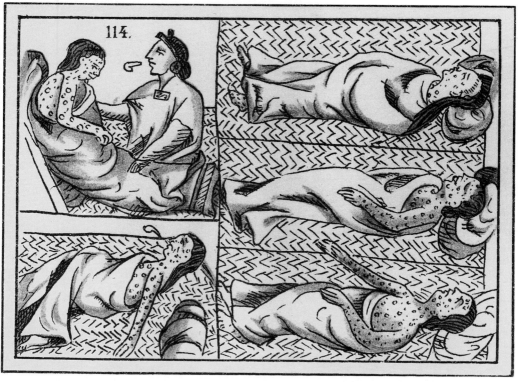

Consequences *(below)* The turkey, Mexico's contribution to the European dinner table, seen in a tapestry based on a painting by Bronzino; *(left)* the face of a Mexican seen at the top of a capital in the Prince-Bishop's palace at Liège, in a courtyard called a "Praise of Folly in stone" (*c.* 1525); *(below left)* the pulque drinker (*c.* 1521, see page 486), of whom there were thousands after the Conquest, for the remaining Mexica took to drink; *(foot)* a golden pendant representing the sun, one of the few jewels to survive from those which, melted down to make bars, debased the Spanish currency

Godoy, the notary from Pinto; Francisco de Lugo, one of the original horsemen, from old Castile, who had been with Cortés since the beginning; and one or two other men who would soon be listed among Cortés' enemies, such as Gonzalo de Mexía, ex-treasurer of the army, and Pedro de Briones, a boastful Salamantino (he untruthfully said that part of his ear had been lost in the Italian wars), who was later hanged as a mutineer.[37] These grants were informal, and later had to be confirmed. They were, however, the first such given in New Spain.

There were also several expeditions north to Michoacan. The first after the conquest was led in February 1522 by a certain Parrillas, who went in search of food. There followed two more, by Antonio Caicedo and Francisco de Montano (he of the volcano).[38] Montano, one of Narváez's men, originally from Ciudad Rodrigo, established a good relation with the *cazonci*.[39] Finally there was a more serious expedition led by Cristóbal de Olid in the summer of 1522. Olid arrived in the Tarascan capital, Tzintzuntzan, with Andrés de Tapia and Cristóbal Martín de Gamboa, at the head of a force of about twenty horse, twenty crossbowmen and a hundred and thirteen infantrymen.[40] Cortés' nomination of this insensitive soldier (whom he had reason to distrust because of his disloyalty in the *affaire* Tapia) to such a place was an example of his occasional lack of judgement as great as his constant faith in Alvarado. The mere prospect of facing Olid, at all events, terrified the *cazonci*, who, instead of organising a resistance, fled to Uruapan. He even pretended for a time that he had drowned himself in Lake Pátzcuaro.

The Tarascans, as they were now known for the reasons previously touched on, were impressed by the Castilians. They called them "*tucupacha*", gods, or "*teparachua*", "big men" or, even, "*acaececha*", "people who wear hats". They thought that the curious clothes which they wore must be the skins of dead men, such as their own priests wore sometimes in fiestas. They thought that the horses were similar to those models of deer which they made out of amaranth seed, with tails and manes, during the fiesta of Cuingo. They supposed for a time that the horses must talk; for the Castilians talked to them. They also imagined that their own goddess Cueruahaperi, mother of all the gods, had given to the Castilians the seeds and wine which they brought. But though they were impressed, they were fearful. Hence the desire of the *cazonci* to hide.[41]

This cowardice stimulated Olid's greed. He gave the Tarascans a show of firepower. He sacked the *cazonci*'s palace, looking for gold. He had the idols thrown down from the temple. The *cazonci* then inopportunely returned to Tzintzuntzan. He made a formal acceptance of the Castilian presence, though this seems to have fallen short of vassaldom. He was genuinely surprised at the conquistadors' interest in gold: "they must eat it if they like it so much," he reflected.[42] Olid sent the *cazonci* to Tenochtitlan, together with several loads of gold and silver. That monarch travelled as a visitor, even if he feared that he was a prisoner. He spent four days in Tenochtitlan. He was fêted and entertained, so much so that he returned to Michoacan as a more or less willing Castilian puppet, though he retained a show of independence: "The Spaniards certainly are generous," he is supposed to have said, "I could not believe it." Thus he remained docile until, some seven years later, he was killed during the expedition of Nuño de Guzmán, whose savageries would make those of Olid seem mild.

Olid himself moved towards Colima, in a westerly direction, having recruited a substantial number of Tarascan soldiers to form part of his army.[43] This extra mission was given by Cortés to Olid since those whom he had previously dispatched in that direction, Juan Álvarez and Juan Rodríguez de Villafuerte, had failed to establish a Castilian presence there. Colima, a more modest version of the polity at Michoacan, was also the centre of a large number of semi-independent towns, mostly speaking languages which now appear lost.[44] Olid succeeded in pacifying the region. But a rebellion broke out when he left. Sandoval was dispatched there (a mission which in turn led to a rebellion in Coatzacoalcos, put down by Luis Marín).[45] That in turn opened the way first to a colony at Colima in 1523; and then, even more important for what Cortés wanted now to establish, a harbour and shipbuilding yard at Zacatula, on the Southern Sea (the Pacific was still generally so called).

The discovery of the Southern Sea at four separate places was one of the great achievements of the winter of 1521–2. The first sighting was made at Zacatula. This city was the centre of another region of heavily populated independent city states, speaking many languages. Like Coatzacoalcos, it lay outside the zone of tributary demands of both Tenochtitlan and Michoacan. Francisco Álvarez Chico explored the coast between there and Acapulco in early 1522. The story that, at Ciguatlan, there was an island inhabited by Amazons, alas, turned out not to be true.

Sandoval built a settlement. It soon became the Villa de la Concepción de Zacatula. Carpenters, blacksmiths and sailors, as well as anchors, sails, cordage, and rigging, arrived from Vera Cruz. There was plenty of local wood, and three caravels and two brigantines were built, the first "to discover, the second to follow the coast".[46] There were several aims: the most important being to find the strait which was still widely held to lie between the Caribbean and that Southern Sea. Most explorers were so devoured by this ambition, Peter Martyr wrote to the Duke of Milan, "that they risk a thousand dangers".[47] But by now Cortés may have guessed that there was no such thing. His purpose was to open another way to Cathay, which, despite Magellan, was still thought to be close at hand. Perhaps China itself could be conquered. How else are we to explain Cortés' undertaking to Charles V in 1522 that his plans for the Southern Sea were "greater than anything else in the Indies", and that his designs would make the King "lord of more kingdoms and realms than up till now in our nation we have heard of"?[48] In 1524, he would write to the Emperor that his adventure in the Southern Sea, whether or no through a strait, would "prove a very good and very short route from the Spice Islands [*la Especería*] to your realms".[49]

The most significant journey in these months was that of Cortés himself to the east in the region of the river Pánuco. Perhaps it was true that, as his critics said, he decided to move into that territory because of his fear lest his old friend and enemy, Garay, should make yet another expedition there.[50] Cortés also saw a strategic need to protect the Caribbean ports of Villa Rica de la Vera Cruz and San Juan de Ulúa. There had been a dangerous indigenous rising beyond Tlaxcala at Tututepec,[51] which Cortés put down: defeating the so-called rebels in what seems to have been a pitched battle at Acasuchtitlan. He afterwards sold some of his captives as slaves to pay the cost of the twelve horses killed.[52] Like Michoacan, Zacatula and Espiritu Santo, Pánuco had not been a tributary of the Triple Alliance. The whole area, like most of these new territories, was a congeries of small city states which in the past had come together to resist outside conquerors. The Huaxtecs, who may have numbered a million or so at the time of their first contact with the Castilians, fought well and consistently against Cortés.[53] They were to give him and subsequent conquistadors much trouble.

This campaign occupied Cortés during much of early 1522. There were several pitched battles, several moments of anxiety, and some gruesome discoveries: for example, in a temple in a beautiful town on a lake, they found the flayed heads of numerous Castilians, trophies from the Huaxtecs' defeat of one of Governor Garay's expeditions. But in the end a Castilian colony was set up at San Esteban del Puerto: a town which can just still be recognised as the place which is called Pánuco today.[54] Pedro Vallejo, one of the new men promoted by Cortés in these days, became Cortés' lieutenant there, when the main expedition returned to Mexico.

Cortés later argued that, because of this expedition, he was able to hand over to the Crown a large and fertile region. Yet, he complained, he had received no compensation for his costs, on the ground, it was said, that he had only gone there in order to thwart Garay. Cortés said that he had spent over 30,000 pesos; and that there had been no spoils.[55]

A remarkable characteristic of all these expeditions was the participation in them of Indians, lords as well as soldiers: Tlaxcalans, Texcocans but also Mexica. The Indian leaders were permitted to ride horses, use Castilian dress, and to take the Castilian rank of captain. Cortés even allowed them to be called "Don" – though it was not formally his right to give that permission. These men played an important part in the pacification of the outlying provinces of what would soon become the viceroyalty of New Spain. They were more than the sepoys of the new empire; for, in two or three generations, their descendants became, in habits and speech, indistinguishable from the grandchildren of conquistadors. Cuauhtémoc seems to have shown some support for these campaigns. Thus he gave what was said to be 15,000 troops. A cousin of his own apparently even commanded them.[56]

As significant as these forays, Cortés had already decided, by the beginning of 1522, to rebuild Tenochtitlan, and to do so on its old site. This decision was controversial. That was partly because Cortés changed his mind. At first he had said that the city would be depopulated and that any Mexican who sought to settle there would be hanged. At that time he had thought only of building a fortress where his invaluable brigantines could be effectively guarded and also command the lake, should it ever be necessary to defend the city (this construction may have had something to do with his wish to fulfil his pledge of two years before to the Tlaxcalans, whom he otherwise treated distantly). Thus two strong towers were constructed as watchtowers for possible use in a defensive war. Between them, there was a building with three naves, for the brigantines, and an outlet on to the lake.[57] The works involved for this enterprise were begun before the end of 1521. Those who worked on it were Mexica, under the direction of Tlacotzin, the *cihuacoatl*, with Castilians concerned in the planning. The architecture was agreeably *mudéjar* in style.

Then in January or February 1522, before indeed he set out for Pánuco, Cortés took the decision to rebuild the capital. He later told the King that he "debated with himself as to whether to establish another town within the circuit of the lakes . . ." but it seemed "to us that it was well to rebuild . . ."[58] The reasons were partly strategic: if the Mexica had been able to withstand the Castilians so long, surely, if there were to be a need, the Castilians could maintain themselves there too. There was also a psychological reason: *not* to have rebuilt would have left the ruins of the old city as a monument to Mexican grandeur.[59] He thought that, if he had not built the capital at Mexico-Tenochtitlan, the Indians might have rebelled.[60] But perhaps there was for him a deeper personal reason. He wanted to re-create one of the wonders of the world whose glories he had so often described in letters home to Spain.[61] No city in old Europe, he had thought, was finer than Tenochtitlan had been: it would be reconstructed on an even grander scale.[62] Cortés the prince of the Renaissance would create something which would make even Venice seem a village.

Cortés' decision was later criticised. Thus Vázquez de Tapia, in 1522 a friend of Cortés but by 1529 one of his enemies, said that everyone except

Cortés himself would have preferred to have seen the new capital at Coyoacán, Tacuba or Texcoco. Vázquez even said that he believed that Cortés placed the capital on its old site because he would be able more easily to defy the royal authorities. Others attacked Cortés in 1529 on this score.[63] But in 1522 these critics were less articulate than they were seven years later: if, indeed, they raised their voices in the former year at all. Such opposition which was heard then came from soldiers who thought that it would be better to build on dry land, in a healthy place, near the mountains, with water always available.[64]

During the winter of 1521–2, the rebuilding was already being planned. Alonso García Bravo, a soldier from Ribera who had come to New Spain with Diego Camargo in 1520, was asked by Cortés to drew up a plan, the so-called *traza*.[65] García Bravo was no more a professional architect than Martín López had been a shipwright. His efforts at construction had hitherto been confined to helping with the fortress at Villa Rica, and building a palisade (*palenque*) to act as a hospital for sick soldiers. That was how Cortés decided that he was a good "geometrician".[66] The *traza* followed to some extent, at least for the centre, the line of streets and waterways of the old city. Those streets had been reconstructed after the flood of 1501. The old layout was adhered to, though it is unclear whether the new architects had anything in the way of a plan of it. The centre of the city would be reserved for the Castilians and the outskirts would be for the *naturales*. Lots were allocated for different functions: cathedral, prison, governor's palace, markets, monasteries and so on, as well as the division into blocks, *manzanas*, to be offered to persons who said that they wished to finance a building. There was discussion as to the appropriate whereabouts for the new slaughterhouse, the granary, the fountains, the bridges, and causeways, not to speak of sewers, water conduits and minor squares. The façades of all buildings were planned by the architects who, inspired by Cortés himself, insisted on uniformity. This was to be a classical city. Plans for buildings which did not conform to the general pattern were rejected. Some years later we hear of houses having been "built so regularly and evenly that none varies a finger's breadth" along the straight road leading to Tacuba, with an open canal down its centre.[67] Perhaps García Bravo had some personal experience at home in Castile of one or other of the towns there which had been built on a grid plan. He undoubtedly acted as if he did.[68]

The scheme of García Bravo was Roman in ambition. Thus water was not only a municipal responsibility, but would be piped to individual buildings: such a thing never occurred in those days in Castile. Paving would be the responsibility of the householder, and so would the maintenance of gutters and cleaning. Avenues were planned to be fifteen yards (fourteen *varas*) wide, while some canals were made broader and deeper than they had been before. The four *barrios* for the indigenous population round the *traza* would be much the same in dimension as the old four quarters of Tenochtitlan. But to each old name there was now a Christian prefix: San Juan Moyotla, Santa María Zoquiapan, San Sebastián Atzacualco and San Pablo Cuepopan.[69] Individual Mexican chiefs were given responsibility for rebuilding these *barrios* and then repopulating them. Tlatelolco would survive as Santiago Tlatelolco, and its market would be re-created, while the big Tezontlalli canal, dividing Tlatelolco from Tenochtitlan, would be re-dug.

The reconstruction began early in 1522.[70] So did allocations of building sites. Once again the latter gave rise to controversy. The *Caudillo* was accused of having been particuarly generous to his friends and mean towards his enemies in this distribution. He was also said to have allocated to himself as many as fifty blocks. Some criticism was also directed later at the towers which Cortés and Alvarado built on their palaces (for there was a law in Castile against towers being built without permission, and that was assumed to apply in New Spain).[71] Cortés' palace was on the site of the old one of Montezuma: he found an architect in the shape of a certain Juan Rodríguez, but the builders were apparently from Chalco, Huexotzinco, Tepeapuloco and Otumba: the same places from which the Mexica in the past had brought in masons to build their great palaces.[72] One more complaint about the *Caudillo* was that, despite his constant attendance at mass, he was slow about building a church. Instead, he had a little chapel in a porch, next, it was said, "to a room where Indians, blacks, and dogs slept, and where he had his stables".[73]

Still, what most impressed during the early days of rebuilding Mexico-Tenochtitlan was the herculean size of the operation. Were there really 400,000 Mexicans at work there by the spring of 1523, as Ixtlilxochitl said, usually working under the direction of Texcocans as foremen and the general supervision of yet one more prince of Texcoco, Don Carlos Ahuaxpitzatzin, and the ex-*cihuacoatl*?[74] Figures, as we know, cannot be trusted in the sixteenth century. But at all events, many *naturales*, from all parts of the Valley of Mexico and beyond, worked very hard, and very long. The imagination of the remaining Mexica was grasped by the knowledge that Montezuma's surviving son, "Don Pedro Montezuma", as he was by now known, was responsible for supervising the reconstruction of one district. All these men collaborated with the conquerors in a way which made the task of Cortés far easier than he could have supposed would be possible.

The Franciscan Fr. Motolinía (who reached the city in 1524) said that more people were working on this great enterprise of rebuilding than had worked on the Temple of Jerusalem;[75] and "There was such a great fervour," he wrote, "that the labourers sang, and the songs and voices scarcely ceased at night." No project of building in Europe in the sixteenth century remotely approached this undertaking in size, ambition and splendour.

The speed with which the Mexica adapted to European techniques was a surprise. Everything new, from nails to pulleys, candles to steel knives, carts to screws, seemed attractive to them. The use of carts was especially interesting: for in the building of the new city, the wheel – articulated in wheelbarrows as well as in carts – was first put to use in a society which might be said to have needed it. Soon too there would come an even more important method of movement: the mule, the great engine of Mexican society for the next four hundred years.[76] No doubt Mexican civilisation had before 1518 already been a "mosaic of borrowed habits" – borrowed from the Toltecs and the Mayas, the Otomí or the Totonacs. But nothing made such an impression as the European innovations. "They are friends of novelties," commented Luis Marín and Martín Vázquez, two of Cortés' friends.[77] Herodotus found the Persians to be good at learning other men's techniques. The Mexica were equally adept.

Soon Mexican souls would similarly be captured by the European mendicant friars. In the months immediately following the fall of the old empire, the average Mexican labourer, however, was at a loss. He no longer received the instructions to which he was used to tell him about favourable moments for planting and harvesting. The conch shells were silent. The illustrated books were neglected, and indeed many had been burned. Work lacking a ceremonial frame was work without a sanction.

The clause in Adam's will which excludes France

"I would like to see the clause in Adam's will which excludes France from the division of the world."
King François I of France

CORTÉS STILL HAD no clear message from the King, and no exact knowledge of what had been happening in Castile. He would have learned (through the pilot Antonio de Alaminos, for example, or from some others who sailed from old to New Spain in 1521) that the reason for the King's earlier silence was his absence in Flanders and his active pursuit of that "Caesarian" role of which Cortés himself had spoken in several documents.[1] But it was now three years since Montejo and Portocarrero had left Vera Cruz; and it was a year since the battle of Villamar had put paid to the ambitions of the *comuneros*. How could it be that there had been no letters from the Crown, whose realm Cortés, as he told himself as well as others, had so expanded?

So Cortés sent more letters home. First there was another, a third, *Carta de Relación*, letter of report. It was signed at Coyoacán on 15 May 1522. It differed in its direction from the second letter sent from Segura de la Frontera, just as that letter from Segura did from the first letter, the one from the municipality. Thus Cortés addressed it to the "very high and most powerful Caesar and unconquered lord, Don Carlos, Emperor, always Augustus and King of Spain, our Lord". It gave a full account of the capture of Tenochtitlan. It was one of the most vivid pieces of Spanish writing of the century. The King's treasurer, Alderete, Alonso de Grado and Vázquez de Tapia endorsed it as giving an honest account.[2] There was also another, private, letter, from Cortés to the Emperor (he knew that the *Carta de Relación* would be published), whose main point was this reflection: "What I would like to make known to your Highness is that I have now been . . . more than three years in this land. I have always written and advised your Majesty, and your Council of the Indies, of those things which are much concerned with your service; and, up till now, I have never had any reply to these things. The cause I believe has been either that my letters have not been received . . . or the neglect of the people who look after my affairs . . ."[3] Finally, there seems to have been a third letter which suggested that Cortés should explore at his own cost the whole of the Pacific coast, in return for receiving one tenth of the wealth obtained, and a lordship over three islands discovered.[4]

These letters were accompanied by an astonishingly large treasure, whose dimensions suggest that the *Caudillo* had been far from direct in his dealings with his own followers. Cortés decided to send this to Spain under the guard of his reliable, if complicated, comrade, Alonso de Ávila, and Antonio de Quiñones, his own bodyguard in the last part of the war in Mexico. They would take about 50,000 pesos in gold, many jewels, including pearls the size of filberts, much jade, some reputed bones of giants (perhaps they were dinosaurs), and three live jaguars (described by Cortés as tigers).

The list of recipients was as remarkable as that of the presents. Here was Cortés, the man "born in brocade", playing the part of the Maecenas of the New World. No other conquistador had been able to put himself in such a role. Indeed, it is doubtful whether such a vast hoard of treasure had ever been sent back to Europe from beyond the seas. The Crown would receive the lion's share: its fifth was a little over 9,000 pesos.[5] But in addition every member of the Council of Castile who dealt with Indian matters was remembered. First and foremost there was Bishop Fonseca. He might have been a deadly enemy of Cortés. This was not the time to recall such things. After all, Fonseca, for all his prejudices against adventurers, was interested in the arts. Nor did Cortés forget Bishop Fonseca's brother, Antonio, the discredited commander of the Castilian army during the recent revolt, the man who burned Medina del Campo. Cortés of course sent a present to Bishop Adrian, whose importance as regent of Castile he must have known, though he could not have expected that he would by then have been named Pope.[6] There figured on the list Fadrique Enríquez, the Admiral of Castile, and Iñigo Fernández de Velasco, the Constable, both of whom had been added to the regency in the summer of 1520 in order to prevent the revolt of the *comuneros* from becoming a revolution. There was the Bishop of Palencia, Dr Pedro Ruiz de la Mota, a cousin of one of Cortés own captains of the same surname, and that orator who in 1520, as president of the *Cortes* of Castile, had talked of Charles V as "emperor of the world". No one would have been surprised to find on the list that perpetual courtier, the *comendador mayor* of the Order of Santiago, Hernando de Vega, who was married to a cousin of the late King Ferdinand, and whose demands on Indian treasure have been described by a hostile modern historian as "insatiable".[7] Even the shadowy officials of the Casa de la Contratación (Sancho de Matienzo, Francisco Pinelo, and Juan López de Recalde, respectively treasurer, factor and accountant of that body), who had done all they could to thwart Cortés for years, were not neglected. Several royal secretaries were included (for example, Dr Luis Zapata, the tiny civil servant loved by Ferdinand the Catholic, and in consequence sometimes known as the "little king").[8] There was also the rising star of the royal bureaucracy, Francisco de los Cobos, though, interestingly, Cortés included neither Lorenzo Galíndez de Carvajal nor Dr Diego Beltrán, who would shortly become the first paid employee of the Council of the Indies: Cortés' *procuradores* had already secured their support. Important Castilian noblemen were also favoured: for example, the Duke of Alba, nephew by marriage of Diego Colón, and that official's best friend at court. The *Caudillo* also included in his list the turbulent Count of Medellín, the lord of Cortés' own town, who had a position at court, as well as his son and heir Juan. Local politics not affection determined this gift. The one major omission in this list was the absence of any one of the Flemish counsellors by now so influential with the King; not even the imperial chancellor, Gattinara, figured.

Cortés' presents to Fonseca were characteristic of all these offerings: two specially made cloaks in the style of a bishop's robe, one in blue, with a heavy gold border, the collar with elaborate plumes and a white border; the other in green, with a collar decorated by masks; four ornamental shields, one with a ruby in the middle; several parrots reconstructed with real feathers and gold beaks; a large cricket made of feathers; not to speak of a coat of arms of large green feathers, with golden quills, also presumably made by Indians since the conquest.[9]

Many churches or chapels were also favoured. The *Caudillo* must have been well advised – by Fr. Melgarejo, perhaps, or Olmedo, or even Alderete – for the recipient sites were subtly chosen, even if their number would have caused any austere court to be disturbed. Thus there were two favoured places in Seville: first, the chapel of La Antigua, in the cathedral, with its beautiful Virgin with the rose in her hand – where, just when Cortés had left Spain, the Cardinal Archbishop Diego Hurtado de Mendoza had raised the roof in order to establish his own tomb there (the painting of the Virgin of la Antigua was done in the early fifteenth century on what had been in fact the old wall of the mosque, whilst it was still being used by the Christians as a church. It has been much retouched during its history, but it is to be assumed that the rose was already there when Cortés was in Seville); and second, the great Carthusian monastery of Las Cuevas, "the best after that at Pavia," commented Thomas Münzer, with its lovely gardens, its noble orchards just outside the walls of Seville on the west bank of the river Guadalquivir, where the body of Columbus then lay (it afforded the friars, wrote Andrea Navagero, Venetian ambassador, "a fine jumping-off place for their journey to heaven").[10] These two bequests to Seville were perhaps tactical. They did not reflect Cortés' own tastes. He might himself have preferred to give presents to the Virgin of los Remedios rather than that of la Antigua. But la Antigua, judging from her use as a name for ships at this time, as for towns in the New World, was the most popular Virgin in Seville. Columbus had given the name to one of the Leeward Islands on the route from Spain to Hispaniola – a name which of course it still bears.[11]

Cortés did not forget the chapel of St Ildefonso in the cathedral at Toledo, built by the warrior primate of that name in the days of Alfonso VIII, nor the convent of Santa Clara at Tordesillas, where (as Julián de Alderete would have told Cortés) the tomb of Felipe el Hermoso currently stood, an object of desire for his ever-grieving widow, Queen Juana. In Ávila a present went to the Dominican monastery of St Thomas, a royal residence built, it was said, on the profits of confiscations from expelled Jews. It too was the site of a tomb, that of the still much-regretted Infante Juan, the Catholic king's only son (a tomb humbly built by the Prince's treasurer, Juan Velázquez de Cuéllar, a cousin of the Governor of Cuba). The gift to Toro was to Nuestra Señora del Portal, in the "Colegiata", a famous romanesque church which was a favourite shrine of the powerful Deza and Fonseca families. (Cortés may have been told that by his new majordomo, Diego de Soto, a native of Toro). So it went on: in Burgos, the donation was to the Chapel of the Crucifixion, whose locally famous Christ was at that time held to have been made, quite in the Mexican mode, of stuffed human skin, though it has since turned out to be of buffalo hide, with human hair; in Ciudad Real, the gifts were for San Francisco, presumably on the advice of Alonso de Ávila, who came from there. The Jeronymite monastery of Guadelupe, especially favoured by Extremeño conquistadors, the cathedral of Santiago de Compostela, the cathedral of San Salvador in Oviedo and, of course, Medellín (the new monastery of San Francisco, founded in 1508 by the Count of Medellín just outside the town, on the banks of the Río Ortigas, not far from Cortés' father's own vineyard), were all supported by the *Caudillo*. Each place had a special significance for Castilian political and ecclesiastical life. The cathedral of San Salvador, Oviedo, for example, not only housed one of the shoes of St Peter and one of the jars which held the water that Jesus changed into wine, but was the site of the tombs of the kings of Asturias. The church was so famous that in the fifteenth century the city itself was often spoken of as San Salvador rather than Oviedo.[12] As with the list of presents to persons, there were some omissions: nothing for Salamanca, nothing for Valladolid, the two cities where it is to be presumed Cortés learned the art of living.

All this treasure travelled with Ávila and Quiñones on the first two vessels. But there was a third ship, the *Santa María de la Rábida*, accompanying them, captained by Juan Bautista, who had commanded Cortés' *nao* in 1518, Montejo's in 1519, and who had returned, perhaps with Alaminos, on another vessel, the *San Antonio* at the beginning of 1522.[13] On this vessel, there was Cortés' founder of metals, Antonio de Benavides, and Juan de Ribera, Cortés' secretary, who had learned some Nahuatl.

The expedition had with them several documents as well as Cortés' letters: a new power of attorney for Martín Cortés, the *Caudillo*'s father, as well as some more money for him.[14] The "municipality of Mexico" also apparently sent a letter to the King about the "great services" of Cortés. One paragraph of that letter requested the dispatch as soon as possible of bishops and monks to assist the conversion of the country. New Spain, they added, would be undoubtedly lost were Tapia to be confirmed as governor. The municipality requested the King not to allow Bishop Fonseca to interfere in the administration of New Spain. For that would "break the thread" of many matters relating to the conquests.[15] (Fonseca had ordered Ysaga, the new accountant in Cuba, and Juan López de Recalde, his equivalent in the Casa de la Contratación in Seville, not to send any arms to help Cortés.) It also hoped that the King would ensure that Garay stayed in Jamaica until Cortés' conquest in Pánuco was complete. To have two captains there was dangerous. The letter begged the King not to send any more lawyers to New Spain, for they would turn the country upside down. Finally, the writers hoped that the King would withdraw Velázquez from Cuba, and punish him for trying to have Cortés killed. This letter was clearly Cortés' in spirit, even if the pen was not his.

Most of the treasure was on the main vessels with Quiñones and Ávila. But Ribera and Benavides apparently had with them on the *Santa María de la Rábida* copies of the main letters and money for Martín Cortés, as well as some Indians and minor items of featherwork and jewellery.[16] The boats set off on 22 May.

This journey was disastrous. First, the King's treasurer, Julián de Alderete, converted during the *affaire* Tapia into an enemy of Cortés, was also on board. He had left Cortés on bad terms, having allegedly said to the *Caudillo*, "O cursed traitor, I cannot suffer more. I must go to Castile, to tell the emperor our lord."[17] Alderete fell ill soon after the ships left Vera Cruz, and died near Havana; poisoned, according to some; because of a bad salad eaten the night before sailing, according to others.[18] Then, halfway across the Atlantic, one of the jaguars got loose, killed two sailors, and savaged a third before leaping overboard.[19]

Next, after a reasonable journey across the Atlantic, Antonio de Quiñones, Cortés' bodyguard, was stabbed to death in a brawl on the island of Terceira, in the Azores. There had apparently been an argument over a girl.[20]

Finally, halfway between the Azores and Spain, the little fleet was attacked by a French pirate, Jean Fleury from Honfleur, operating with six ships under the general direction of France's master seaman of that time, Jean Ango, of Dieppe. Ango, probably apprised of the riches of the "new land of gold", having learned of Cortés' earliest presents to Charles V, shown at Brussels in 1520, ordered Fleury to lie in wait. Fleury seized the main treasure ships, and carried them, Alonso de Ávila, the treasure, and all the presents on board, to Dieppe.[21] Fleury was a precursor of innumerable pirates who used the French wars with Spain as an excuse for robbery on the high seas: he was also one of the most effective.[22] François I gave the justification: "I would like to see the clause in Adam's will which excludes France from the division of the world."[23] Thus the great benefactions of Hernán Cortés were lost. Thus France enters the modern history of Mexico.

We can catch a last glimpse of these presents in 1527. In that year, Ango gave a fête at his remarkable new Renaissance house, the "manoir", at Varengeville outside Dieppe. People even came from Paris. There was a masque entitled "Les Biens", composed by a great sailor of his, Jean Parmentier, who was also a man of letters.[24] All the riches of the earth were symbolically depicted. Heroes of antiquity passed by dressed in strange costumes which were surely those stolen from Cortés and his Spanish beneficiaries. There was Alexander the Great, for example, on a dais described as having been made by Indians (appropriately, since Cortés had begun to see himself as a new Alexander). Before him stood a half-naked page with plumes, holding a two-handed sword.[25] Thereafter, except for a purchase by Admiral Philippe de Brion Chabot of a large piece of jade which he thought was an emerald, the treasures of Cortés altogether vanished.[26] Perhaps one day in the still surviving gardens of Varengeville some trace of these riches will be found. Perhaps though their sale helped Ango to finance in Dieppe the rebuilding of the church of Saint-Jacques; or enabled him to hire Italian artists to give Varengeville its Italian medallions of himself, his wife, the King and the Queen.[27] But most of the gold was no doubt melted down, the turquoises prised out of their settings, and the feathers allowed to disintegrate in some disused cupboard at Varengeville.

Some reminder of what was so farouchely disposed of can probably be seen in the figures of Ango's chapel in that church of Saint-Jacques, as well, perhaps, as in one of the masks around the colossal tomb of the Cardinal d'Amboise in Rouen, completed in these years: Ango was a protégé of that archbishop.[28] There is also a possibility that the Cardinal d'Amboise's friend, the ecccentric Cardinal Bishop of Liège, Erard de la Marck, allowed himself to be influenced by some of Fleury's, or Cortés', treasure in the plumed masks on the capitals of his columns in his new episcopal palace begun in 1526: an *In Praise of Folly* in stone, it has been engagingly described.[29]

When the news of the loss of this great treasure fleet reached Cortés, probably early in 1523, he was of course thrown into the most profound gloom. The "gentlemanly corsair" of Cuba in 1518 had been out-manoeuvred by a real professional. How wise Isabel the Catholic had been when she had declared the French to be "a people abhorrent to our Castilian nation"![30] All Cortés' presents had been calculated nicely to win him friends. They were also an expression of his achievement.[31] This disaster would lead to discussion for the first time of the idea of treasure fleets being escorted in a convoy.[32] But such things were too late for the *Caudillo*.

The third ship on the expedition, the *Santa María de la Rábida*, however, did manage to escape the attentions of the French; so Juan de Ribera, Antonio de Benavides, and Juan Bautista reached Spain on 8 November.[33]

An absolute monarch

Gonzalo de Mexía, about Cortés, *c.* 1524

OW THE CONDITION of Castile was as different in the autumn of
1522 from what it had been when Ordaz and Mendoza had
reached home a year earlier, as it had then been from the time of
the arrival there of Montejo and Portocarrero in 1519. On 1 March 1522,
the news had come of the fall of Tenochtitlan, a brief report of which
event was printed as a postscript to Cromberger's edition to Cortés'
second *Carta de Relación* (that written in Tepeaca) in September of that
year.[1] Then in May the new Pope Adrian, though preoccupied with his
plans to meet the challenge of Luther (he had made his astounding
promise to reform the hierarchy of the Roman Church), suggested that
he had not forgotten the affairs of the Indies when he issued a bull at
Saragossa, repeating the decision of his predecessor to provide friars of
the mendicant order, "and in particular the friars minor of regular
observance", for Mexico (Adrian only left for Rome on 7 August and
entered that city on the 29th).[2]

In June, the King-Emperor Charles, on his way back from Germany,
demonstrated that he too had absorbed the significance of the discovery of
Mexico when he apparently showed his brother monarch Henry VIII in
England some of Montezuma's treasures.[3] On 16 July Charles arrived at
Santander. He went from there to Palencia, where he received information
about the Indies – not simply from Bishops Fonseca and Ruiz de la Mota, but
from the letter of Cortés of 30 October 1520 and the other short one, now lost,
which had arrived in March 1522.[4] The Emperor reached Valladolid, which he
treated as his Spanish capital, on 25 August.[5] He was to remain in Spain for
seven years: the longest period that he would stay anywhere.

That summer the Emperor was busy reorganising the different
councils and subcommittees of his Spanish realm, making the Council of
Castile smaller, dismissing many people and appointing others. The

Council of the Indies was on the point of being regularised as a special institution: Dr Diego Beltrán would in May 1523 be nominated a life member of it, its first salaried civil servant.[6] Charles confirmed Pope Adrian's desire to deprive Bishop Fonseca of the automatic right of jurisdiction in the case of Cortés. Fonseca seems to have been reprimanded for keeping back information about Cortés and his requests.[7] His protégé, the long-standing treasurer of the Casa de la Contratación in Seville, was relieved of his functions as a result of the accusations of his new colleague, the factor Aranda.[8] Charles appointed a special committee to advise him on the matter of Cortés. Fonseca was not a member of it.

The members were: the Grand Chancellor, Mercurino Gattinara, who was now, after the recent death of the Prince de Cröy at Worms, the Emperor's supreme councillor; two Flemish councillors, la Chaulx and de la Roche.[9] There was also the inevitable Hernando de Vega, *comendador mayor* of the Order of Santiago; Lorenzo Galíndez de Carvajal, of the Royal Council of Castile, cousin of Cortés, lawyer and historian; and Francisco Pérez de Vargas, the Treasurer of Castile.[10] These men met in Gattinara's lodgings in Valladolid.[11]

Neither Cortés nor Velázquez could have been quite sure, nor satisfied, with a committee of these men. La Chaulx and Galíndez de Carvajal were likely to support Cortés. Vargas, corrupt though tolerant, and Hernando de Vega, prince of sinecures and distant benefices, were equivocal. So was de la Roche. But all in Spain would have realised that Gattinara would have the dominant voice.

The men of this committee would have read the letters to the King from Cortés and other members of the expedition. They would also have studied those from Velázquez, Ayllón and Tapia. They would have looked at other papers from the *audiencia* at Santo Domingo and from Cuba, including those deriving from the enquiry which the Governor had set on foot there in June of the previous year. No doubt they would have seen a letter from the treasurer of Hispaniola, Miguel de Pasamonte, in January 1520, which told the King that if Cortés were guilty of rebellion, he should be punished to discourage others from committing the same crime. But they saw also papers brought from New Spain by Ordaz: for example, the statements signed in 1520 by numerous conquistadors at Tepeaca in favour of Cortés.[12] Perhaps they had on their desks the report of the discussion in Mexico chaired by the now imprisoned Ávila. They must have listened to the numerous persons by then in Spain who knew something of the matter at stake between Velázquez and Cortés. Thus they surely saw Diego Velázquez's relations from Cuéllar, Manuel de Rojas and Bernardino Velázquez, as well as Andrés de Duero, Cortés' old partner, Velázquez's old secretary and a veteran of the *noche triste*, now back in Spain. They would have talked to the energetic chaplain to Velázquez, Fr. Benito Martín, recently returned from Cuba; and they also seem to have received Martín Cortés, Diego de Ordaz, António de Mendoza, Francisco de Montejo and Francisco Núñez, Cortés' cousin and lawyer. Perhaps the committee were influenced in their judgement by the sense of triumph which filled Spain after El Cano returned to Sanlúcar de Barrameda with the *nao Victoria* in September, with its cargo of cloves from the Moluccas, having been round the world for the first time, even if the great captain Magellan had died long before. They must have been affected by the presents of gold which had been brought back from Mexico even if the leaders of the last journey home had lost most of it to the French; as has been seen, in 1520 there had been some useful allocations of the first consignment of Cortés' gold, in Majorca and in Tunis, while, in the winter of 1522, Mexican gold had been directly used for the prosecution of the King's European interests: a troop of soldiers in San Sebastián were paid in consequence in November.[13] A certain confidence began to pervade Spain in late 1522 after the question of the *comunidades* had been finally resolved, and after the relatively mild treatment of those guilty of rebellion.[14] Patrons were beginning to support new philanthropic ventures.[15] The committee were surely influenced by Peter Martyr's arguments in favour of Cortés: that scholarly Italian presented him, after all, as a "great man" – and one who, properly handled, would bring the Crown much money.[16] They were probably most affected by the fact that Diego Velázquez had gone against the orders of the *audiencia* in sending Narváez to Mexico. They were certainly critical of Narváez for imprisoning, and disobeying the orders of, Licenciado Ayllón. They presumably saw Ayllón himself.

At all events, and not without some hesitations about what they had heard of Cortés' character, the committee reached a decision favourable to the *Caudillo*. It was true that the committee thought that Cortés should repay Velázquez what he had spent on the fleet in 1518. But all other disputes between the two were to be settled at a court of justice. Above all, Velázquez was told not to meddle in Cortés' affairs any more, and ordered to suffer the indignity of an enquiry into his conduct.[17]

The Emperor, on hearing of these decisions, on 11 October 1522, formally appointed Cortés *adelantado* (say, commander-in-chief with political responsibilities), *repartidor* (distributor) of Indians and, above all, captain-general and governor of New Spain, confirming everything which the *Caudillo* had claimed in the service of the Crown.[18] A decree of 15 October instructed the new captain-general about the treatment of the Mexica and other Indians, the question of grants for *procuradores* and, indeed, arrangements for a regular colonial system.[19] In appointing Cortés to these positions, the Emperor wrote a letter to the *Caudillo* which spoke warmly and enthusiastically of his achievements.[20] At the same time Ordaz was received into the Order of Santiago.[21] Perhaps Charles was elated by the news of the success of another great enterprise.

Though pious and responsible, he was always impressed by stories of great feats of arms – as is suggested by his enthusiasm for chivalric novels such as the Burgundian Olivier de la Marche's *Le Chevalier Délibéré*.[22]

Few at the time noticed a second decree of 15 October, which named four persons to assist Cortés in his government: Alfonso de Estrada, said to be an illegitimate son of the late King Ferdinand, as treasurer; Gonzalo de Salazar, as factor; Rodrigo de Albornoz, as accountant; and Pedro Almíndez Chirino, as inspector. These then unknown men, all of them Castilians, would, in the end, give Cortés as much trouble as Velázquez and Narváez had done. Albornoz was allocated a secret code with which to communicate to the Council of the Indies since, even then, that body was afraid of what they described as Cortés' "crafty clevernesses, burning avarice and almost obvious taste for tyranny".[23]

An order of 20 October fixed salaries for Cortés and his staff. The range is interesting. Thus, while Cortés as captain-general would receive 366,000 maravedís a year, the chief magistrate would receive 100,000, while doctors, apothecaries and surgeons would be allocated 30,000. Foot soldiers would get 11,832. But the new major royal officials would be paid no less than 510,000 maravedís a year, an indication of the trouble that lay ahead. It would not have escaped Cortés' notice that the sum stipulated for him was the same as that granted twenty years before to Ovando when he set off for Hispaniola, and also to Pedrarias when he left for Castilla del Oro. When all account is taken of Ovando's and Pedrarias' standing at court, Cortés' achievements would seem to have merited more.[24] Still, the president of the royal council, Antonio de Rojas, Archbishop of Granada, was at that time receiving only 350,000 maravedís, Dr Diego Beltrán 100,000, and the chief pilot of Seville 50,000, together with 25,000 maravedís as expenses.[25]

But when Ribera, Benavides and Bautista finally arrived at Sanlúcar de Barrameda, and then Seville, in November 1522, they found a country which had recognised Cortés' achievements and was ready to honour him. The very day that they had reached Spain, Cortés' second letter, dated 30 October 1520 (accompanied by a short note saying that victory had been attained), was published by Cromberger in Spanish in Seville. Previously its publication had not been authorised because of opposition from Fonseca. The new emissaries were able, of course, to supplement that letter with the third one from Cortés, which described the siege and fall of Tenochtitlan. Ribera and Benavides were soon talking to the great gossip Peter Martyr about what they had themselves seen and felt, to the benefit of that scholar's readers, at that time and later. A digest of Cortés' letters was soon printed, beautifully, in Milan, by the same brothers Calvo, no less, who had published both Boccaccio and Luther.[26] There could scarcely have been a greater compliment to the *Caudillo*. Ribera presented the letters which he had with him to the appropriate officials: thus Cortés' proposal to discover the Pacific at his own cost was received by Dr Diego Beltrán (he suggested that discussion of the idea be postponed).[27]

It was some time in the early winter of 1522 when (probably in Seville) Ribera went to see Martyr. Also present were the papal legate, Marino Caracciolo, and the illustrious Venetian ambassador, Gasparo Contarini. Caracciolo was hotfoot from dealing with the Elector of Saxony over the matter of Luther. But he had always had an interest in the New World, ever since he had been secretary to Cardinal Ascanio Sforza: in which capacity he had received Martyr's first letters about Columbus.[28] Contarini on the other hand was probably at that time preparing the first draft of his famous essay in praise of his own country, *The Commonwealth and Government of Venice*.[29] Ribera, despite bringing what Cortés would have considered treasures of the second rank, displayed to the diplomats an astonishing collection of pearl necklaces, rings shaped like birds, vases, earrings, chains of gold, as well as plumes, shields, helmets and obsidian mirrors of "exceptional beauty" (Martyr's words), bordered with circles of gold and painted green. Then Ribera exhibited cotton cloths, clothes of feathers and rabbit's hair, as well as some painted maps. Finally a Mexican, dressed in a tunic made of feathers, a cotton loincloth, a handkerchief hanging from his belt, wearing beautiful sandals, gave a realistic impression of single combat in a Mexican battle, using a *macuauhuitl*, without, however, the obsidian blades. He carried a shield of reeds covered with gold, bordered by ocelot skin, the centre being of a fine plumage. He showed how to capture an enemy and, in dumb show, carried out a sacrifice (the "enemy" was a slave). The worldly-wise and experienced Italians left amazed, certain that they had seen a vision of a new world, and one whose capture by Cortés reflected credit on both the Emperor Charles V and Pope Adrian.[30]

The news of the decision of the Emperor took an unconscionably long time to reach Mexico. That seems to have been because it had been agreed by Cortés' own friends in Spain that two of the *Caudillo*'s cousins, Rodrigo de Paz, son of that Francisco Núñez and Inés de Paz with whom the *Caudillo* had lodged as a boy in Salamanca, and Francisco de Las Casas, a relation through the Pizarros, should be the bearers of the good tidings. They went also to Cuba where they had to bring the bad news to Diego Velázquez. Paz and Las Casas delayed in Spain for many weeks, while other old friends and relations of the new captain-general prepared themselves to seek their fortune in the shadow of the great man whom they dimly remembered as an unpredictable youth nearly twenty years before.

Cortés himself was, of course, already captain-general in Mexico in all

but name. Indeed, in one sense he even had the name, as granted to him in
1518 by the municipality of Vera Cruz. Between his dispatch of his famous
letter of May 1522 and the arrival of the news of his nomination as supreme
magistrate, sixteen months elapsed, during which time he determined the
general lines of the government of New Spain. For example, he finally
embarked upon grants of *encomiendas* to conquistadors (and to some
Mexicans of high birth). Though many *encomiendas* would change hands
later, the arrangements which Cortés embarked upon in the summer of 1523
set the pattern for Mexican land- holding.

Cortés had, in the past, presented himself as a critic of the arrangement
whereby Indians in the Caribbean were handed over to the care of
conquistadors. Younger sons of impoverished families from poor parts
of Castile were far from being ideal persons to preside over a cultural,
technological and spiritual revolution. Cortés knew too (as he told the
King) that the Indians of New Spain were "of much greater intelligence
than those of the other [*sic*] islands. Indeed," he added, "they appeared to
us to possess such understanding as is sufficient for an ordinary citizen to
conduct himself in a civilised country."[31] He saw that it would be a
serious matter to compel these people to work for the Castilians as the
Tainos had been forced to do in the Caribbean. Yet unless there were
some economic bond between the two races, the conquistadors would
not be able to maintain themselves.

Cortés said that he tried to think of alternatives to the *encomienda*. But
in the end, once again, he allowed it to seem at least that his army
influenced him. Here were hundreds of men who had risked everything
to help him conquer a great empire! Could they be expected to be
satisfied with a reward of fifty or sixty pesos in gold? Like other
conquistadors they wanted land, responsibility, wealth, position, even
"sumptuousness". Thus in the early summer of 1522 Cortés embarked
on a policy intended to satisfy them. He was, he says, almost forced
("*casi forzado*") to deposit the lords and natives of the place into the
hands of the Spanish.[32] So, he told the King in his letter of May 1522, he
was going to do so: "Until a new order is made, or this one confirmed,"
he wrote, "the aforementioned chiefs and natives will serve the Castilians
with whom they have been deposited in all that they may require for their
maintenance. This conclusion was reached on the advice of persons who
have considerable knowledge and experience in this land [who these
could have been apart from those who profited, such as Alvarado,
Grado, Olid and Vázquez de Tapia, is difficult to see]. In addition,
nothing better could be devised, either for the maintenance of the Spanish
or for the safety and good treatment of the Indians . . . I entreat Your
Majesty to approve this . . ."[33] The first Bishop of Mexico, Juan de
Zumárraga, later wrote that Cortés took his decision after talking to the
King's treasurer, Julián de Alderete, as well as others (that must

have been before May 1522, for Alderete died that month).³⁴ This method of handing out men as well as land was similar to what had been done in Andalusia, Extremadura and Murcia during the *Reconquista* there. But in Mexico there were no knightly orders to take a share.

The first *encomenderos* were then chosen, in April 1522. Between then and the middle of 1523, the *Caudillo* "enfeoffed" hundreds of them. Most of the territorial units reflected roughly the boundaries of old Indian lordships. By a year after that, in 1524, he had distributed most of the population of central Mexico "*in depósito*", as the phrase was, to himself, to his companions-in-arms and to a few Mexicans who had become Christians (for example "Doña Isabel" and "Don Pedro Montezuma", the children of the late emperor). Each native town was placed under the protection of a conquistador whose task was to ensure that his charges became both Christians and vassals of the Spanish King: "to indoctrinate them in matters of the Holy Catholic faith with all the vigilance and care possible and necessary".³⁵ In return for this work, the *encomendero* was entitled to their services and tribute.

The first *encomienda* seems to have been given in respect of Cholula in April to a certain Gonzalo Cerezo, of whom nothing else is recorded: the odds must be that the concession was to someone else, and Cerezo held it in his name: probably to Andrés de Tapia, who subsequently held it.³⁶ The first major concession near Tenochtitlan was the town and population of Xochimilco, allocated to Alvarado in August 1522.³⁷ The goldsmiths' town of Azcapotzalco went to Francisco de Montejo, the still absent *procurador* of 1519. Coyoacán was held by Cortés himself, as were Ecatepec, Chalco and Otumba. Alonso de Ávila, despite being in prison in France, received a large *encomienda*, in the shape of Cuauhtitlan, Zumpango, Xaltocan, and some other communities to the north of the lake. Francisco Verdugo, even though he was a barely concealed enemy of Cortés, received Teotihuacan, while Verdugo's nephew Juan de Cuéllar received Chimalhuacan; Martín López, Tequixquiac; Martín Vázquez, Xilotzingo; and the bachelor Ortega, Tepotzotlan. "Don Pedro Montezuma", Montezuma's son, in a politically tactful move, received Tula (Tollan). Even rather modest conquistadors such as the *converso* blacksmith, Hernando Alonso, received an *encomienda*, at Actopan, sixty miles north of Tenochtitlan, though he was not at all happy with it.³⁸ Six towns (Cuitláhuac, Culhuacan, Huitzilopochco, Iztapalapa, Mixquic, and Mexicalzingo) were reserved for the provisioning of the new city of Mexico- Tenochtitlan. But at the beginning Cortés seems to have used these towns mainly to service his own interests.³⁹

Later the Mexica, who swiftly mastered Spanish litigation, would show themselves adept at exploiting the rules of these arrangements by taking their *encomenderos* to court, and charging them with all kinds of breaches of the law, such as neglecting their religious responsibilities.

The plans must have seemed to them like a tougher version of ancient practices. The tribute gatherers of Montezuma sometimes collected for the conquistadors. But the latter were much more demanding than their predecessors.[40]

One reason why Cortés favoured the idea of *encomiendas* was vividly shown by his own allocations. In the later enquiry against him, it was persistently said that he had allocated himself "a million souls": even "a million and a half".[41]

Cortés was also alive to the possibility of economic development. He therefore tried from 1522 onwards to arrange for the import of European domestic animals (cattle, pigs, sheep, goats, asses, mares) from the West Indian islands. These he obtained from Hispaniola and Jamaica, since, as a result of his continuing feud with Velázquez, Cuba was still closed to him. He sent to Spain for sugar cane, mulberries (for silk worms), vines, olives, as well as wheat and other plants. His aim was to liberate the new realm of New Spain from dependence on the islands of the Caribbean (the effect in the Antilles was to make for such shortages that the ranchers there sought to prevent cattle being exported).[42] Cortés even desired to make New Spain self-sufficient in silk. By 1525 Peter Martyr would note that wheat was already doing well.[43] Pigs as ever flourished, as they had in Cuba in the first days after Cortés had arrived there with Velázquez. These new foods consequently available were much welcomed in Mexico, especially by the Mexicans who were much less rigid in sustaining old diets than the Spaniards were. Pork in particular was said to have been sought after by what remained of the old upper class, since it had a slight taste of human flesh.[44]

Cortés also did his best in these months to encourage conquistadors who had served with him to bring to Mexico their wives, daughters and other ladies.

The *Caudillo* believed that the mendicant friars held the secret of the tranquillity of such a large population. So he was pleased, therefore, to be able to welcome, at the end of August 1523, still before he received his official approval as governor, three volunteer Flemish Franciscans. These were Johann van der Auwern, Johann Delckus and Pedro de Gante. The first had been a professor of theology in Paris, the second claimed Scottish ancestry, while Pedro de Gante, the most important of these three, was an intellectual admirer, as well as a neighbour, of Erasmus. Personally of legendary beauty, he had a mental perspective broader than anyone else in New Spain at that time. That vision was precisely what was needed. Whether or no he was, as was rumoured, an illegitimate son of the Emperor Maximilian, he brought something of the Renaissance world of the latter emperor to his grandson's newest domain.[45]

So began fifty years of the domination of the mendicant orders. Many more friars came in the next ten years, from the Dominican and

Augustinian orders, as well as the Franciscan. These men, often as intelligent as they were devout, founded the Church in Mexico, carrying out conversions by the thousand: one of the most remarkable triumphs of Christianity, even though no doubt many conversions were superficial – leaving the converts in a state of "nepantilism", to use a word which a modern historian has coined to describe a state suspended between a lost past and a present incompletely understood.[46]

The friars especially impressed the Tarascans. They were amazed that they dressed so differently from the other Castilians, supposing for a time that they were dead men, and that their habits were shrouds. They thought that, when they went to bed at night, they became skeletons, went down to the other world, and found women. They also thought that holy water was used in order to divine the future.[47]

One further act of imagination by Cortés at this time was his skilful move into the manufacture of both gunpowder and artillery. The former continued to be made from sulphur obtained by baskets lowered into the volcano Popocatepetl. Cortés' artillery was made possible by the discovery of iron near Taxco, a zone of Chontal-speaking Indians to the south-west of Cuernavaca. This territory was first subjugated in 1522 by Miguel Díez de Aux and Rodrigo de Castañeda. Copper was available from Michoacan. Francisco de Mesa, who had been in charge of the manipulation of the guns during the campaigns, with Rodrigo Martínez, who had been in charge of the artillery of Narváez, started making guns soon after the fall of Tenochtitlan. It was formally illegal to make guns without a royal licence. But Cortés insisted that it was essential.

In later years several of those involved predictably declared that they were convinced that Cortés had started this industry not for the possible use against Mexica and other Indians, but to have some artillery of his own to fight the Crown if the King did not make him governor. Indeed, Alonso Pérez testified that he had heard the friends of Cortés say just that. There is, however, no other evidence for it, and it seems improbable.[48]

Two serious crises, however, occurred for Cortés in these last months before he received the news of his official approval as captain-general. The first followed the sudden, unannounced, and unexpected arrival in June or July 1522 of his wife, Catalina Suárez, in a ship from Cuba, at a small landing place known as La Rambla, near Ahualco (the present Santa Ana), in the River Ayagualulco, just east of Coatzacoalcos. On board was not only Doña Catalina but her sister, and her brother, Juan Suárez, who had once been Cortés' best friend, and who had gone back to Cuba after being present at the last stages of the siege of Tenochtitlan. He now returned with his wife "la Zambirana", as well as numerous maids whom Catalina presumably thought that she would need as vicereine of a new empire. This party was warmly greeted by Sandoval, in whose territory the landing occurred. They were then escorted to Mexico by Francisco de Orduña. There Catalina was equally warmly greeted by Cortés. She was borne into Tenochtitlan on the naked shoulders of Cortés' bodyguard: an honour which Orduña himself considered inappropriate.[49]

This unexpected arrival must have been unwelcome to Cortés, since he then had several mistresses, apart from his principal friendship with Marina: indeed, "an infinite number of women" were said to live, or to have lived, in his house, most Mexican, a few Castilian. Some, so witnesses in the enquiry against Cortés would later insist, as if that were the greatest scandal, were blood relations of one another – both Indian and Castilian.[50]

Catalina was nevertheless installed as the first lady of the land by Cortés in his house in Coyoacán.[51] Cortés may have had something else on his mind at that time. For it was about then that Marina gave birth to his eldest son, whom he christened Martín, after his father, and to whom he later became much attached.[52] A maid, Ana Rodríguez, later testified, however, that Cortés and Catalina lived as man and wife.[53]

Several months later, on All Saints' Day, there was a banquet in Cortés' house: a large dinner, followed by dancing. Catalina seemed lively and in good health.[54] There was some banter between Catalina and one of Cortés' friends, Francisco de Solís ("of the orchard" or "of the silk jacket"). They were talking about the employment of Indians. Catalina said, "I promise you that, before many days, I will do something with my Indians which no one will understand."[55] Cortés said, apparently joking: "With *your* Indians? I do not want to hear anything about *your* things."[56] Catalina felt abashed and then ran to her room. Perhaps she had claimed an interest over Indians which she should not have done. She dropped in at the chapel. There she met by chance Fr. Bartolomé de Olmedo. Cortés stayed a little time more with his guests and then retired also.

In the middle of the night, the *Caudillo* called his majordomo, Isidro Moreno, and his treasurer, Diego de Soto. Catalina was dead.[57] Moreno and Soto went to the room, sent for the chambermaids and dispatched a message to Catalina's brother, Juan Suárez, telling him his sister had died. But they added the mysterious qualification that he was not to come to see her body, because they thought that his "pestering" had killed Catalina. They also sent for Fr. Olmedo to console Cortés. The maids then ran into the room. Most of them later testified things adverse to Cortés' reputation: implying that he had strangled or smothered her; for example, Juana López said that she had seen the broken beads of a necklace on the floor. Ana Rodríguez, who knew Catalina to have been jealous of Cortés' Mexican ladies, said that Catalina had said, on her way to bed, that she wished God would take her from this world. Other maids insisted that there were bruises on the neck of Catalina; that Catalina's head had gone blue, and that the bed had been wetted. María Hernández, who claimed to have known Catalina for ten years, said that Cortés often threw her out of bed. Catalina had once said to her, "One day you will find me dead from the way that I live with Don Hernando."[58] Violante Rodríguez, evidently of a literary disposition, said that the event was just like what happened to the Count of Alarcos in the old ballad of that name.[59] Cortés was said to have insisted, against the advice of Fr. Olmedo, that the body of his wife be put in a coffin, nailed up and buried. No one else saw her body after she died.[60]

Accusations soon began against Cortés. In the enquiry into his behaviour to which repeated reference has been made, this matter was lavishly aired. Several witnesses, such as even Gerónimo de Aguilar and Juan de Tirado, explicitly declared that Cortés had murdered his wife.[61]

It is impossible to decide exactly what did happen that faraway November night in Coyoacan. Several modern historians have supposed that Cortés strangled Catalina in a fit of anger because she complained about his mistresses.[62] The manner of her death does not sound very like the "asthma" which it was stated to be by Bernal Díaz. Nor does "mal de madre", a disease of the womb characterised by terrible pains in the stomach, sound probable, though Catalina's death was suggested to have been so caused by several witnesses on Cortés' behalf, as by Catalina's nephew, Juan Suárez de Peralta.[63]

The case for Cortés was stated by many people. Thus Suárez de Peralta said that Catalina was known to have had a bad heart, and had had heart attacks in Cuba. Her sisters Leonor and Francisca died similarly.[64] Other witnesses testified (in another case) that Catalina had had many illnesses in Cuba, and that she had there been looked on as "a delicate woman", even "constantly ill".[65] Juan de Salcedo said that he remembered a time in Baracoa, in Cuba, when Catalina had seemed to be dead and Cortés had had to revive her with a bowl of water.[66] Cortés himself explained the bruises as being caused by his efforts to shake her into wakefulness. Alonso de Navarrete said that it was common knowledge that Catalina had a bad heart,[67] Juan Rodríguez de Escobar and Juan González de León said that she had fainted and nearly died two weeks before, at a visit to a farm owned by Juan Garrido (famous as one of the first free black Africans to pass to America and, even more, as the first "Spaniard" to plant wheat in Mexico),[68] while Gaspar de Garnica, a friend of Diego Velázquez's, said that Catalina's bad health showed in her face.[69] As to seeming insensitive about the death, Ortega said that he afterwards saw tears come to Cortés' eyes when talking about her.[70] Gonzalo Rodríguez de Ocaña saw Cortés grieving because of her death, as did Alonso de la Serna.[71] Cortés pointed out in 1534 that "it is not to be believed, nor likely that, while the marquis was sleeping with his wife in the chamber, and there were other rooms and apartments close to ... where the women servants of his wife, and the pages and servants of the marquis were, that he could strangle his wife without it being noticed . . . there would have been noise."[72]

No doubt Cortés was capable of murder. His actions at Cholula and Tepeaca show him to have been entirely capable of brutality, though those were actions of war. One witness, Andrés de Monjaraz, said that he had seen two or three Indians hanging in Coyoacán because they had assaulted Marina.[73] But Cortés does according to his lights seem to have been a serious Christian. This was admitted rather curiously even by his enemies: for example, a certain Marcos Ruiz said that he held Cortés to be a good Christian who went regularly to mass; but he thought that he did not fear God, for he held it for certain that he had killed Catalina.[74] More important, Cortés was subsequently supported, in the enquiry into his conduct, by well-known Franciscans, such as the saintly Fr. Motolinía and Fr. Pedro de Gante, as by Fr. Juan de Zumárraga, first bishop of Mexico, in a letter to the Emperor. Pedro de Gante, Motolinía and Luis de Fuensalida did not answer the questions in the *residencia*'s questionnaire about Catalina; but they did answer some other questions. It is inconceivable that they would have done so had they believed Cortés to have been guilty of murder. "As to those who murmur against the marquis," Motolinía wrote to Charles V in the 1550s, "God rest him; and those who try to blacken and obscure his deeds, I believe that, before God, their deeds are not as acceptable as those of the marquis." He went on, "Although as a human being he was a sinner, he had the faith and performed the works of a good Christian, and a great desire to employ his life and property in widening and increasing the work of Jesus Christ . . . he would confess with many tears and receive communion devoutly, putting his soul and property in the hands of his confessor."[75] Another monk who supported Cortés in a similar enquiry was Fr. Martín de la Coruña, the apostle of Michoacan.[76]

The most probable eventuality is that when Cortés went to Catalina's room, she upbraided him for his mistresses. Perhaps he was nettled, and seized her by the neck, intending to give her the same shaking which he gave to that spy of Narváez before the battle of Cempoallan in 1520. At that point Catalina perhaps had a heart attack and died. Cortés tried to shake her further into life. Failing to do that, he realised that a finger of accusation would be pointed at him. He therefore sought to keep subsequent proceedings as brief as possible. The fact that Cortés never showed any remorse is perhaps one more reason for thinking him innocent of murder.

The issue continued to dog Cortés. The criminal charge was dropped, but Catalina's mother, "la Marcayda", continued with a civil case, as did her descendants. Nearly one hundred years afterwards, money was still being paid by Cortés' descendants to the great-grandchildren of his first mother-in-law.[77]

The second crisis facing the *Caudillo* related to yet another attempt by Garay, the Governor of Jamaica, to establish himself in Pánuco. Why that proconsul supposed so persistently that that hot but fertile region to the north of Vera Cruz would lead him to fortune and happiness is interesting. Could he have realised that the region was rich in cotton? Was he drawn there by the legend of its abundant food and of the licentious behaviour of its people. The Huaxtecs fascinated the Mexica because of their love of strong drink; indeed, because of their cult of *pulque*. El Tajín, between Nauhtla and Pánuco, was the site of a famous pyramid. But the conquistadors were not concerned with such things. The Huaxtecs had perfected three-dimensional sculpture of curious implications, and had initiated the great ball games of the region. But Garay could scarcely have known of these diversions. The oil which has made modern Mexicans give the area a grudging respect was then neither prized nor known. Perhaps the determined, if ageing, Governor of Jamaica supposed that the Fountain of Youth might be discovered there rather than in Florida. Perhaps he thought that the famous strait leading to the Southern Sea could be found in Pánuco. Perhaps he had an instinct which told him that, in this last unknown region of the eastern coastline of the Americas, there would be untold prizes.

At all events, Garay could not allow the matter to leave his mind. Thus in 1521 he received permission from Spain to settle the country, with its affectionate (*amorosas*) people – permission granted at a time when Fonseca could more or less make up his own mind about that kind of matter.[78] Garay went to Cuba to concert his own efforts with those of Diego Velázquez. There it was already known that Cortés was very prosperous. Rumour had it that he was mysteriously in alliance with that fabulously rich "lady of silver" ("*la señora de la plata*") of whom Judge Zuazo had written, and who, beyond the mountains to the west of Tenochtitlan, owned great palaces and mines.[79]

By June 1523, Garay had organised a large fleet: nine *naos*, and three brigantines, with 145 horse and 850 Castilians, as well as some Jamaican Indians. He carried 200 musketeers and 300 crossbowmen. He stocked the ships with merchandise and placed himself in command. Surely, he supposed, the failures of the previous expeditions derived from lack of good leadership. Cortés wrote to Jamaica encouraging Garay to come, adjuring him to bring as big a force as possible, and insisting that, if he did get into difficulty, he, Cortés, would come and help him.[80] Garay was unimpressed. He thought Cortés' offer to be treacherous. He had known him in the past, having been chief magistrate of Santo Domingo when Velázquez had set off with Cortés for Cuba in 1511.[81]

In late July, Garay reached the Río de Palmas, to the north of Pánuco (he went there to avoid Cortés in Pánuco proper), and founded a city which he had the temerity to name "Garayana".[82] Councillors and magistrates were appointed. The designations were grand. A Mendoza was appointed governor of the colony (Alonso, nephew of the royal equerry, Alfonso Pacheco). A Figueroa was associated with him. A cousin of the Duke of Alba, Gonzalo Oraglio, was appointed magistrate. This would be no ordinary colony. It would be a colony for aristocrats.[83] Garay then moved overland towards Pánuco. The journey was long, the heat overpowering, the mosquitoes appalling, the forest trackless, the suffering terrible. There were many desertions. Men walked desperately away from the expedition into the jungle, never to be seen again. Morale collapsed. Garay sent his lieutenant Gonzalo de Ocampo to San Esteban to greet Cortés' representative, Pedro Vallejo. Ocampo was an experienced man in the Indies, having lived for many years in Hispaniola, where he had an *encomienda*. So Vallejo welcomed him with pleasure, but sent a letter to Cortés asking for instructions. He also told Garay that he could not feed so many at San Esteban. Garay thereupon regrouped at Tacaluca. Garay unwisely told the Indians there that he had come to punish Cortés for having harmed them. This ill-judged remark led to an affray between Garay's men and Vallejo's, in which the latter, more experienced in the land and climate, emerged triumphant.[84]

But this was already September. On 13 September 1523, Rodrigo de Paz and Francisco de Las Casas at last arrived in Mexico and delivered the decree of October 1522, naming Cortés captain-general and governor. They also brought a royal decree of the previous April requiring Garay not to settle in Pánuco, but to go down to Espíritu Santo or, better, beyond it.[85]

This news could not have arrived at a more appropriate moment. Cortés said that he kissed His Majesty's feet a hundred thousand times.[86] There was, among the friends of Cortés in Tenochtitlan, "much happiness and many celebrations".[87] The *Caudillo* was able to write to Garay announcing that the Crown had given him authority in the whole region. He dispatched Pedro de Alvarado, Gonzalo de Sandoval, and a new confidant, Diego de Ocampo, brother of Garay's lieutenant, to go to Garay to discuss the future. They were accompanied by Francisco de Orduña, a convenient notary, who was able formally to demand that Garay obey the royal decree.

Since his men were melting away through desertion or death, Garay had no alternative but to do so. His ships were soon seized by Vallejo (including one captained by the now forgotten Juan de Grijalva), and his guns by Alvarado. In those humiliating circumstances, he went up to Mexico as the guest of the new governor-general who showed him, so he said, "such hospitality as I would have shown my brother". A plan was made for Garay's son to marry an illegitimate daughter of Cortés, Catalina.[88] All the same Garay died of a stomach complaint after dining with Cortés on Christmas Day: perhaps partly from grief caused by the death of his son at the hands of Indians. Alonso Lucas, one of Cortés' friends, heard Garay calling out in the night. Going into his room, he heard the poor Governor of Jamaica shouting: "Without doubt I am mortal."[89] Meanwhile Garay's men on the coast were busy killing Indians. But many Castilians, including Pedro Vallejo, subsequently died as a result of raids in reprisal.[90]

Cortés' triumph was now complete. He was legally in command at last. It was true that the Crown, among other proposals for the good treatment of Indians, had prohibited the *encomiendas* which he himself had originally criticised – on the ground that they had in the West Indies led to "bad treatment and too much work".[91] Cortés had also been asked to rescind any grants which he might already have made before the document reached him. The Indians of Mexico were to be left in "entire liberty". But the *Caudillo* would appeal against that provision. That appeal was tacitly accepted, in the light of the realities to which Cortés had pointed. Garay's sudden death enabled Cortés' enemies later to accuse him of yet another murder. But few rational people took that accusation very seriously. Even Cristóbal Pérez, *alguacil* to Garay, said that his leader died of pleurisy.[92]

No one can say how the *Caudillo* would have behaved if Cristóbal de Tapia had in 1522 or 1523 been again appointed governor. Perhaps there would then have been a risk of a unilateral assumption of independence. But it is most improbable. What Cortés coveted was royal favour, not enmity: a man "born in brocade" would not have wished to be monarch of a remote province. He wanted to be the Emperor Charles' vicar. By the Emperor's decision in 1522 the risk, or benefit, of independence was anyway avoided.

Cortés' enemies were all by now dead or discomfited. Cristóbal de Tapia was in Hispaniola, in semi-disgrace. Narváez was still in confinement, though he would soon be released by an act of Cortés' own, characteristically princely, grace. Bishop Fonseca was no longer in favour in Castile. The new city of Tenochtitlan was already half built. Cortés could surely look forward to a long career as a great, benign, philanthropic, and rich proconsul.[93] Hispaniola, Cuba and Jamaica were beginning to empty of Castilian settlers, as the glittering opportunities of New Spain became evident to all.

Cortés had begun too to act the part of viceroy: one of Garay's senior officials, Cristóbal Pérez, described to Peter Martyr how, in 1523 or 1524, the *Caudillo* usually dressed in black silk; and how "his attitude is not proud, except that he likes to be surrounded by a large number of servants, I mean attendants, stewards, secretaries, valets, ushers, chaplains, treasurers, and all such as usually accompany a great sovereign. Wherever he goes, he takes with him four native lords on horseback. The magistrates of the town concerned, and soldiers, armed with maces to exercise justice, precede him. As he passes by, everyone prostrates themselves, according to an old custom. He accepts such greetings affably, and prefers the title of *adelantado* to that of governor, both having been conferred on him by the Emperor" (the word *adelantado* had a good Castilian ring about it, as Cortés would have known from his childhood. Had not an *adelantado* of Castile once been received in splendid style in Medellín?).[94] On Cortés' lips, there would often be a Latin tag or a classical allusion; or (and that would please his comrade Alvarado more) a line from a half-forgotten ballad. "The suspicion that Cortés did not pay homage to the Emperor," went on Pérez, was baseless: "Neither he nor anybody else has ever noticed the slightest sign of treason in him."[95] He was, however, happy for people to compare him with Caesar or Alexander; and to live as "an absolute monarch".[96]

Yet Cortés knew when to humble himself, at least in public. Thus in 1524, in the summer, twelve more Franciscans, headed by Fr. Martín de Valencia, arrived in Vera Cruz and walked the two and hundred and seventy miles to the capital. They reached Vera Cruz on 13 May and Mexico-Tenochtitlan on 18 June. It was a terrible journey. "One of the twelve", Fr. Toribio de Benavente (Motolinía), described having to cross twenty-five streams in just over six miles. The climate was harsh, either excessively hot or excessively dry, the friars were attacked by mosquitoes at the coast, and snakes and insects at other stages.

Cortés, who had long been demanding the dispatch of monks, in order that the temporal conquest of Mexico might be completed by a spiritual one, received these new apostles outside the city, on his knees.[97] Afterwards this moment was remembered as the time when "faith began".[98] The minister-general of the Franciscan order, Fr. Francisco de los Angeles, had said farewell to "the twelve" with a sermon which ended with the words: "The day of the world is already reaching its eleventh hour; you are called by the Father of the family to go to the vineyard."[99]

The leader, or "custodian", of this party, Martín de Valencia, came from a small town, Valencia de Don Juan, in a remote part of the kingdom of León. He had been especially chosen as the chief of a section of the Franciscan order, that of St Gabriel of Extremadura, a devoted reformist section of the brotherhood, founded at the end of the previous century by a certain Juan de Guadalupe. The section had undertaken, in Spain and now in Mexico, to pay particular attention to prayer and to the example of St Francis. All "the twelve" came from that provenance, all were dedicated, and all had spent some time in preparation for their task at the monastery of Santa María de los Angeles, in the the Sierra Morena.[100] With this preparation, they set about the business of destroying old temples and idols with incomparable will and energy.

As for the Indians, in these post-conquest days of Cortés' triumph,

Cuauhtemoc remained a prisoner, with some other Mexican lords who had survived the battles and the immediate aftermath of the war. But Don Pedro Montezuma, the late emperor's son, and the sometime deputy-emperor, the *cihuacoatl*, assisted the conquerors in the rebuilding of the capital, and played other roles which later generations would have referred to as "collaborationist". Many Mexican princes and noblemen who survived made formal obeisance to Christianity and were baptised: it even seems possible that Cuauhtémoc was among them.[101] The Tlaxcalans and other Indian allies realised soon that their collaboration with the Castilians was not going to lead to their own succession to the Mexica as masters of the valley. But debilitated by disease, as by losses in conflict, they were in no condition to do more than complain: Ixtlilxochitl of Texcoco seems to have accompanied Cortés on most of his journeys. A modest attempt at rebellion in 1523 was repressed.[102]

A remarkable conversation was held in late June 1524 between some Mexican priests and the newly arrived Franciscans.[103] The Mexicans made a moving defence of their old religion and old gods. Those gods, they insisted, had given the old monarchs "courage and the capacity to rule". Their own forefathers had commended those gods. They had said:

> These are the gods through whom there is life.
> These have given us our rewards
> At the time
> At the place
> Which was yet all in darkness.
> And they said, as they went,
> Those gods: "Give us our sustenance
> And whatever can be drunk
> Whatever can be eaten:
> Our food
> Shelled corn
> Beans
> Amaranth . . ."

The Franciscans asked the Mexica to conform to Christianity. The priests asked, in a dignified manner: "Is it not enough that we have already lost? That our way of living has been lost, has been annihilated? . . . Do with us what you please. That is all we answer, all that we reply to your breath, your words, O our lords! . . ."[104] They accepted their catastrophe realistically. They were not looking for pity. They wished only to be forgotten. Huitzilopochtli was, it seemed, destroyed as completely as Tenochtitlan, Montezuma, and the Mexican warrior army. Cortés would soon have a daughter by Montezuma's favourite daughter. What remained of the old society was expressed only in an elegiac verse:

> Sweet flower of cacao bursts open with perfume;
> The fragrant flower of *peyote* falls in a raining mist.
> I the singer I live. My song is heard, it takes root;
> My transplanted word is sprouting;
> Our flowers stand up in the rain.[105]

Epilogue

"The departure continues
All make their exit.
Princes, lords, nobles,
Leave us orphans.
Feel melancholy, O lords!
Perhaps someone will return;
Perhaps someone will come back
From the land of the shadows . . ."

Attributed to Axayácatl, Emperor of Mexico, c. 1477[1]

AFTER THE CONQUEST, a shrine to the Sevillana Virgin of Los Remedios, with her Sienese smile and in a golden skirt, was established on top of the great pyramid in Cholula. With its one hundred and twenty steps, it was in mass the biggest pyramid in the world. The new divinity was appropriately placed, given the importance of Seville and Sevillanos in the conquest. But it was only the most striking of the new manifestations. For the Franciscan friars, whose "call to the vineyard" in Mexico was described in Chapter 39, and their Augustinian and Dominican colleagues who arrived soon after, carried out an astonishing feat in converting hundreds of thousands, probably millions, of Mexican Indians to Christianity. Fr. Motolinía, one of the twelve Franciscans, describes having baptised over 300,000 people himself. Pedro de Gante baptised "often 4,000 in a day, sometimes 10,000". The great "open chapels" of Mexico remain as witnesses to these endeavours.[2]

These efforts had precedents among the Moors after the conquest of Granada.[3] But the documents suggest that at least on a superficial level the success in Mexico was more remarkable: Fr. Jacobo de Testera, then custodian of the Franciscan mission, later commissar-general for the Indies (brother of the chamberlain to François I, King of France), wrote in 1533 how some of those whom he had baptised "sang plainsong and played the organ and performed counterpoint, made songbooks and taught others music . . ."[4] (The mention of this interesting man, who designed a pictographic catechism, should recall how many of the early Franciscans in New Spain were Frenchmen, thereby beginning a long history of fruitful Franco-Mexican collaboration.)[5] The Indians' love of music made it very easy to recruit church musicians, who quickly learned to read, and write, religious music. The eight canonical hours of Franciscans were easily substituted for established Mexican rules. Rising regularly at night to perform penance was not new. Mexican flutes played Spanish canticles. Hymns were even written by Indians in Nahuatl in the 1530s. A Tlaxcalan composed a mass and put it to a Gregorian chant with "rare ingeniousness".[6] Julián Garcés, who eventually became the first bishop of Tlaxcala, wrote to Pope Paul III in 1535 praising the intelligence of the Mexican Indians, insisting that they were neither turbulent nor ungovernable, but reverent, shy and obedient to their teachers. The idea that they were incapable of receiving the doctrines of the church "surely had been prompted by the devil".[7] "May the Holy Spirit dwell in your very honoured dear souls, dear ladies," a great-grandson of Montezuma is found writing in 1587 to relations in Iztapalapa, themselves of royal Mexican blood.[8]

The conquerors had by then covered the country with a network of monasteries, churches, shrines, and parishes – first Franciscans, then Augustinians and Dominicans, finally secular clergy. Processions at Corpus Christi and in Holy Week, as well as masques, such as an annual battle of Christians and Moors, had become popular. The turning point of the history of the Mexican church was, however, when the Virgin Mary herself was supposed to have appeared, with a dark skin, on 9, 10 and 12 December 1531, to a newly baptised Indian, "Juan Diego", on the hill of Tepeyac just to the north of Tenochtitlan. Thus began the cult of the "brown Virgin", "*la virgen morena*", of Guadalupe, recalling the monastery of Guadalupe in Spain, and establishing that the Indians too could have their divine heroines.

Yet this conversion of the Indians was a patchwork. In 1527, a young Tlaxcalcan, Cristóbal, was tortured and killed by his father, Acxotecatl, for trying to convert him to Christianity.[9] In the late sixteenth century, Fr. Durán was honest enough to see that Mexicans, while formally attending Christian festivals, seemed, underneath, to be celebrating pagan ones. The secret practice of ancient religious rites, without, it would seem, human sacrifice, continued for many years.[10] So did the rites associated with the sorcerers and fortune tellers, the sacred mushrooms and the *peyote* cactus. The goddess Cihuacoatl was said to have eaten a child at Azcapotzalco in the 1530s. Even in the eighteenth century, certain Indians conceded the dignity of gods to certain old men "in whom they have the greatest confidence. After offering them gifts in their ceremonies of cult and adoration, they ask for rain, for the sun to shine . . ."

Fighting, meantime, continued sporadically with frontier Indian tribes, particularly the Chichimecs, and there were Christian martyrdoms, the first being that of the Franciscan Fr. Juan Calero, killed in 1541 by recalcitrant Indians near Tequila.[11]

There were also some public denunciations of the new regime by old priests. Instances can be found for many parts of the country. Thus some senior Indian converts in Coyoacán publicly washed their heads: so renouncing their baptism.[12] The case of the trial of Don Carlos Ometochtl, lord of Texcoco, yet one more brother of the ill-fated Cacama, in 1540, was as much religious rebellion as political protest, as his accusers knew and as his words suggest: "If I saw that my ancestors and fathers conformed with this law of God, perhaps I would keep and respect it. But, brothers, keep and hold on to what our ancestors had . . ."[13] (Don Carlos was executed). Both that trial and an earlier one of "Don Juan", lord of Matlatlan, in the Sierra de Puebla, may have been simply the result of conservatism: Don Carlos surrounded himself with concubines, drank *pulque*, and had neither destroyed his local idols nor converted his sons to Christianity. Nor did he seem to be in any hurry to build a parish church.[14] Similarly, prayers to the rain god Tlaloc and the vegetable goddess Chicome Coatl continued to be made in the seventeenth century:

> Come here
> Giver of things with the day sign 1-Water
> Already the giver of things has arrived!
> Now come to deposit the giver of things
> Who is princess Chicomecoatl . . .[15]

Nor were these acts of defiance the only ones. The Maya in Yucatan did not fully (if at all) accept the Spanish empire till the end of the seventeenth century. Other indigenous people, such as the Yaqui, of the north-west, continued their opposition into the eighteenth century.

The first sixty years after the conquest of Mexico were astonishing in respects other than the spiritual. It has been noticed how Cortés' friend, Martín Vázquez, pointed out in 1535 how quick the Mexicans were in imitating European ways. They not only carried out the orders of friars but anticipated them in building the innumerable great monasteries (many with schools attached) and churches which architecturally still dominate Mexico: even when today they house schools, government departments, museums or hotels, they stand as silent witnesses to one of the most colossal achievements of the Roman church.

The Mexica adapted fast in other ways. Nahuatl and other indigenous languages soon began to use Latin script. Mexicans, with Spanish Christian names, entered into litigation lustily, adapting their own practices to Spanish forms in a sophisticated manner. They also welcomed the wheel enthusiastically. Of course, they might one day have developed the latter themselves for technological purposes: had there not been toys with wheels in Oaxaca and in Pánuco?[16] But it might have taken a long time. It has been seen how the Mexicans found the mule, the ox, the pulley, the nail and the screw as welcome as they did the candle.

They also found the new steel point on their digging sticks equally beneficial.[17] The use by the Mexicans of Spanish techniques was one reason why *chinampa* agriculture expanded during the sixteenth century.[18]

Yet the Spaniards imposed tributes which appear to have been nearly everywhere heavier than what had been paid to the Mexica by their tributaries. Enslavement of numerous Indians, forced labour extracted from others, the execution of leaders, the destruction of native monuments, sculptures and books as works of the devil, as well as the trauma of military defeat, destroyed the morale not only of the remaining Mexica but of most of the peoples of the valley. Most native traditions declined as the Spaniards hired talented Indians to work in their way, and on their projects.[19] Only indigenous pottery maintained a life of its own after the conquest, becoming more elaborate and interesting as Spanish motifs were combined with old designs. Perhaps that was because the possession of pottery was not thought to be idolatrous, as was that of idols, sculptures and books.[20]

The grand tragedy of the Mexican conquest by the Europeans was not the destruction of Tenochtitlan. However atrocious that must seem, cities can be rebuilt. Nor was the disaster vested in the brutality of the conquistadors. The combination of an increasingly enlightened administration at home (at least in theory) and the persistence of the friars would have mitigated the savageries within a generation. As it was, the teaching at Santiago/Tlatelolco was already by the 1540s creating European-educated Mexican-born aristocrats and even intellectuals: the Latin talked by some of the Indian-born graduates of that school was the wonder of the empire. It is true that some of the measures taken by the Spaniards on religious grounds had a harmful effect on diet: for example they discouraged both the Mexican dog and amaranth seeds because of their association with ancient rites, and thereby cut off the Indians from a source of protein.[21] They also overfished the lake.

The real cataclysm derived from a different sort of catastrophe which no one had foreseen, which the Castilians had not wished or expected, and for which there had been no portents. This was demographic in character. The calamity derived primarily from the diseases from the old world which caused havoc among a population which had no capacity for resistance. It is true that despair was caused by the death of the old gods and beliefs; as by the ceaseless demands of the conquistadors for gold and other precious metals, causing a partial abandonment of the old economy and consequent famines. These were important reasons for the decline of population in Mexico, as had previously occurred in the Caribbean. Fr. Motolinía and Judge Zorita, excellent sources, considered them to be decisive. But the real significance of those things was surely that they made the Mexicans much less able to withstand the waves of infections which came close to destroying them.[22]

The numbers of those who lived before the conquistadors arrived in what became New Spain are discussed in Appendix I. Let us suppose, though, that Judge Zorita's estimate is roughly correct. His figure for the population of the country in the 1560s was 2.6 million and, by implication, that in 1518 would have been about 8 million.[23] Even with the decline at that level, the transformation was appalling. Throughout the accounts, *relaciones*, of Mexico made on the orders of Philip II, there are sober stories of towns dying and villages being deserted. The smallpox of the 1520s gave way to measles (1531–2), plague (if that was what was described as *mazlazahuatl*), *cocoliztli* (probably a kind of influenza, 1545 and 1576), whooping cough, and mumps.

Had it not been for these diseases, the history of Mexico might have been closer to that of British India than that of New Spain:[24] a small colonial class of masters (150,000 seem to have come to New Spain from the old world in the first half of the sixteenth century, nearly half from Andalusia)[25] intermarrying with a large, intelligent native population.

The diseases were especially destructive among the old upper class of Mexico, insofar as it survived. This was probably because they mixed with the Spaniards most. The effect was greater than that of the Black Death, the import from Asia which had so greatly affected Europe in the fifteenth century.

As inadequate exchange, as happened in the West Indies but on a far larger scale, sheep, cattle and horses were imported, and bred at a great pace. So did European crops (wheat above all) and European weeds: wild white-flowered clover, thistles, bracken, sedge, dock leaves were common by the late sixteenth century: even intoxicating growths such as nightshade. A botanical historian has argued that clover was another very successful conquistador.[26]

Against this background of disease and decline, a succession of remarkable ecclesiastics, and some others, tried for different reasons to give an account of what old Mexico had been like before it died: Fr. Olmos, Fr. Motolinía, Fr. Bernardino de Sahagún, Fr. Diego Durán, and Judge Zorita, to mention only the earliest, worked very hard to produce, more or less scientifically, their fascinating accounts.

At the same time, after some unedifying disputes in the late 1520s, when the history of the country in its savagery, cynicism and frivolity, seemed like that of a small Italian city in the Dark Ages, Mexico became a viceroyalty. Grandees named in Castile set off regularly for nearly three hundred years to manage a strange, closed, beautiful kingdom, which curiously combined the eccentric and the conventional. Foreign travellers, even English pirates, were unusual. New Spain sent much silver home to Europe, to be displayed in fine forms on tables of mahogany from Nicaragua, at which cigars from Cuba were smoked, and the ravages of syphilis, another product of the New World, discussed.

The events discussed in the earlier part of this book came eventually to be looked upon as a legend, and the personalities as mythical.

So it would seem right to show what happened to those individuals who played an important part in the history of the conquest. To consider the Indians first, Cuauhtémoc, a tragic prisoner for four years, was hanged by Cortés in 1525, on the accusation that he had been concerned in a rebellion. He died on the latter's expedition to Honduras. It was alleged, on dubious evidence, in 1949 that his remains had been found in Ichcateopan, in the province of Guerrero in Mexico.[27] By his first wife Xuchimatzatzin ("María"), Cuauhtémoc is said to have left an infant son, improbably known as "Diego de Mendoza Austria y Moctezuma", to whom Cortés granted an *encomienda* in 1527, and Charles V a coat of arms in 1541, and who himself later had three children named, biblically, Melchor, Gaspar and Baltasar, from whom many descend.[28]

Of the children of Montezuma, the beautiful Tecuichpo lived on into the 1550s, married (after the death of Cuauhtémoc) to three conquistadors in succession: Alonso de Grado, whom Cortés had made responsible for investigating accusations of cruelty towards the Mexicans, and who died in 1527; Pedro Gallego de Andrade; and finally, Juan Cano, after Andrade had died suddenly in 1530. She had a daughter, Leonor, by Cortés, born some time after her marriage to Gallego, by whom she also had a son. By Cano she had five children, of whom two, daughters, took vows of poverty, and entered the convent of La Concepción in Mexico. Tecuichpo later took to the courts, as has been seen, to try and improve her condition. Cortés, however, had in 1526 given her Tacuba, some surrounding villages, and about twelve farms as an *encomienda*. By the late sixteenth century this was the largest surviving *encomienda* in the Valley of Mexico. She should not have been poor, though she did not live in the style of the favourite child of a monarch, to which status she had been brought up. She was said by her husband to have given such a good example that "quiet and repose" were implanted in the minds of her fellow Mexicans.[29]

Among other descendants of Montezuma there were some cases of distress. Thus Diego de Moteçuma (Montezuma) was found telling his nieces in 1598 that he would inform King Philip II about "all the grandchildren of Montezuma who are in poverty".[30] Meanwhile, the heroine, or villainess, of the conquest, Marina, the interpreter, whose translations were so important but of whose accuracy in that function we shall never be certain, lived on till 1551, married to Juan Jaramillo, and leaving a daughter by him as well as a son by Cortés.[31] The other children of Montezuma, Cacama and other rulers of the Valley of Mexico became generally hispanicised, the family of the counts of Moctezuma survived many generations in Spain, and, though the line is now extinct, their palace, called after them, is, perhaps suitably (considerng the role of Extremeños in their overthr >w) the provincial archive of Cáceres, not far from the house of García Holguín, the commander of the brigantine who arrested Cuauhtemoc. One grandson of Montezuma, Don Luis, seems to have given the authorities in Spain a few moments of disquiet in the 1570s, on the ground that he might have revived his claim to the Mexican throne. But nothing came of it except rumour and suspicion.[32]

As for the Spanish, Diego Velázquez died of fury, it was said, in 1524, before a *residencia* could be completed against him. Though he died poor, he left money for three hundred masses for his soul in the church of San Francisco at Cuéllar, as well as for some other pious works in the convent of Santa Clara in that town – the costs to be paid for by, rather surprisingly, "income from Ulúa".[33] There is no evidence, alas, that, from one of his innumerable nephews to be found in Cuba in the early 1520s, there descended that Juan Velázquez, father of Jerónima Velázquez, who, in Seville, gave birth, in 1599, to Diego de Silva Velázquez, the painter, usually known by the same name as the Governor.[34] But just one allusion to Mexico can perhaps be seen in the latter's most famous painting: in "Las Meninas", one of the maids of honour on the left of the picture is shown offering to the princess a small piece of then fashionable Mexican pottery.[35]

Most of Cortés' companions remained, and died, in Mexico. Alvarado continued his brutal career of unconcern for human life in numerous parts of the growing empire, became the first governor of Guatemala, and obtained both the sought-after title of *adelantado* and the Order of Santiago which he had in his youth pretended already to have; he was killed in 1541, still in his late forties, while leading a campaign against Indians near Guadalajara, from wounds caused by falling from his horse. Pánfilo de Narváez, released from prison in Mexico, made his way to Spain and then led another expedition to find the Fountain of Youth in Florida, where he died horribly.

Olid was executed as a rebel in 1525. Montejo went on to become the first *adelantado* and governor of Yucatan: the conquest of which was continued by that son whom he had with him in Mexico, and by his nephew. He was accompanied by Alonso de Ávila, after his release from his French prison. Diego de Ordaz embarked on a journey to the river Marañón, the great tributary of the Amazon, which conquest would also have given him control over the Pearl Coast, had he not died in mid-Atlantic in 1532. Unlike many Spaniards of those days, Ordaz admired the Mexicans' featherwork, and a request for some of it was sent in one of his last letters to Francisco Verdugo in 1529 ("send me some good feathers, and a dozen mirrors").[36] Ávila, Vázquez de Tapia, Andrés de Tapia, and Martín López all settled in Mexico, none of them (except Andreś de Tapia, always Cortés' ally) thinking that their services had been as appreciated as they should have been, and so devoting much of their lives to litigation proving the worth of their past actions. Fr. Juan Díaz seems to have been killed by Indians when breaking up some idols.[37] Fr. Olmedo died early, in 1524, much regretted, it is said, by Indians as well as by conquistadors. No less than eight of Cortés' expedition entered holy orders: five became Franciscans, one, Aguilar, a Dominican. Another, Gaspar Díez, became a hermit in Mexico and lived to be told by Bishop Zumárraga to lead a less austere life.[38]

As for the *Caudillo* himself, his nomination as governor and captain-general of New Spain in 1522, and his acceptance of those offices a year later, marked the apogee of his life. He was still under forty. But though he was admitted into the Order of Santiago in 1525 and received a grant of arms, little turned out well for him thereafter.[39]

Even when busy laying the foundations of the government of New Spain, its agriculture and its property-holding, which lasted for three hundred years, he was restless. Using the rebellion of Cristóbal de Olid as a pretext, he embarked in 1524 on a journey to Honduras. Olid had been executed by Cortés' own friends before he set off, though he did not know it.

Cortés gaily set off with a cavalcade of several thousand. This included Indian kings and jugglers, Franciscans and dancers, harpists and jesters, horses and artillery. It was the greatest such procession which Mexico had ever seen, a happy band, apparently, of brothers of all races. Two years later, a small group of under a hundred returned alive to Mexico-Tenochtitlan, after appalling hardships in the jungle, on the edge of unknown seas, crossing innumerable rivers with the greatest difficulty, facing disease, hunger, thirst, solitude, and mutiny.

Then when Cortés did return to the capital in the middle of 1526, he was shocked to find how the city had been ill-governed in his absence by the very royal officials sent to Mexico at the same time as the confirmation of his governorship. Assuming that Cortés was dead, they had tortured and murdered his first cousin Rodrigo de Paz. All who had defended his interests had suffered.[40]

Immediately the *Caudillo* was back, in the summer of 1526, a judge came from Spain to set in motion a commission of enquiry, a *juicio de residencia*, against him. The judge, Luis Ponce de León, died, after eating bacon, it was said, at Cortés' table. A second magistrate, the elderly Marcos de Aguilar, who had spent years in Hispaniola, died immediately afterwards. Gossips, such as the Dominican Fr. Tomás Ortiz, of course suggested that Cortés had caused both to be poisoned. People now remembered the sudden but so convenient deaths of Catalina Cortés, of Francisco de Garay, and of Julián de Alderete.

Though the master of the vast estates which as governor and captain-general he had allocated to himself before leaving for Honduras, Cortés was now without influence. He heard from friends in Spain that his enemies, some new, some old, were influencing the court against him. He resolved to return home to put his case personally to Charles V. He wished to be able to govern, in the Emperor's name, the great territory which he had won for him, and to embark, with royal backing, on expeditions into the Southern Sea.

The *Caudillo* therefore set off for home in March 1528 with his intimates Gonzalo de Sandoval and Andrés de Tapia. He travelled as Montezuma might have done. With him were three sons of Montezuma (Don Martín, Don Pedro, Don Juan), a son of Maxixcatzin of Tlaxcala (Don Lorenzo), a descendant of the kings of Tlatelolco, a son of the King of Tacuba, and the lords of Culhuacan, Tlalmanalco, and Cuitláhuac. He had an escort of other noble Indians, some "with skins more white than Germans".[41] One of the Indians came from Cempoallan. There were also jugglers and acrobats, some dwarfs and hunchbacks. The Indians totalled about forty.[42] Did not the Count of Benavente have an elephant which someone had sent him from India? Cortés did as well with his jaguars, an armadillo, some pelicans, and an opossum. Columbus had had in his presentation at Barcelona a parade of natives and very little gold. Cortés would have many feather headdresses and cloaks, fans, shields, obsidian mirrors, as well as turquoise, jade, gold and silver, some of it as jewels. It was one of Cortés' great public shows, in which he took so much pleasure. Cortés may or may not have been a great Latinist. But he knew what constituted a Roman triumph.[43]

This cortège arrived at Palos after a voyage of forty-two days, in early May 1528. There Sandoval fell ill and died. On his deathbed that victor of a hundred battles in Mexico was too weak to prevent a thief making off with his gold. Cortés went first to the monastery of La Rábida where legend, though not historical evidence, says that by chance he met his distant cousin, Francisco Pizarro, then setting off to conquer Peru. He went then to Medellín, where he found that his devoted father had died eighteen months before. He greeted his mother and went to Guadalupe to give thanks to the Virgin of Extremadura, and to present her with a scorpion in gold, long preserved in the treasury there. He moved on to see the Emperor, that monarch who had figured so often in his speeches to the Mexicans, the "emperor of the world" in Bishop Ruiz de la Mota's expression, in whose name Cortés had done everything. He found the court in June at Monzón, a summer capital of Aragón. There he met the great men of the kingdom and also the shadowy bureaucrats: the chancellor Gattinara, the royal secretary Los Cobos, Dr Beltrán, the president of the Council of the Indies, Dr García de Loyasa, as well as the deputies of the *Cortes* of Aragón.[44] Most of these men would have read and appreciated copies of his letters from Mexico, for Cromberger in

Seville had printed them. Many of his enemies, such as Bishop Fonseca, had died. Cortés' triumph seemed assured.[45]

Charles V received Cortés with what seems to have been genuine enthusiasm. He took him by the hand immediately he knelt before him, raised him to sit at his side, made him a marquis (of the Valley of Oaxaca), granted him a twelfth part of the profits of all his conquests, accepted that he should have an *encomienda* of 23,000 vassals, thereby making him one of the richest men in the Spanish empire. Charles was entranced by a display of dancing performed by Cortés' Indians at Valladolid. He confirmed him too as captain-general of Mexico, though not as governor: an *audiencia* headed by one of Cortés' enemies, Nuño de Guzmán, had been allocated that task. It was therefore unclear what Cortés' duties would be. He was named also "governor of the islands and territories which he might discover in the Southern Sea" – though the concession was much less than he had asked for in 1522.[46]

Charles V also blessed Cortés' new marriage with Juana, daughter of Carlos, Count of Aguilar, a niece of the Duke of Béjar, Alvaro de Zúñiga, *justicia mayor* of Castile, one of the most powerful men in the kingdom – and especially powerful in northern Extremadura. She was well connected in every way, having not only Enríquez, Mendoza, and Guzmán blood, but was also a great-niece of that Juan de Zúñiga, grand master of Alcántara by whose rural academe at Zalamea de la Serena the young Cortés may have been influenced. Juana brought Cortés a substantial dowry: 10,000 ducats.[47] The Duke of Béjar, with the three hundred horses in his stables and his income of 28,000 gold florins, must have seemed to Cortés an ideal benefactor. Only six noblemen in Spain were richer than he.[48] When, later, Cortés fell ill in Toledo, the King visited him: an unheard-of honour. Charles also forgave Cortés for taking a seat in the royal pew in the chapel there, in front of most grandees. Cortés was drawn by the German artist Christoph Weiditz, apparently on the suggestion of the Polish ambassador, Juan Dantisco, as he was known in Spain. So was his escort of Mexicans.[49] As in 1520, the King showed concern for the welfare of these Indians, and once again arranged special velvet clothes for them.[50] (Charles V had received several Mexican noblemen in 1526. They were granted *encomiendas*.)[51] Some of these Indians seem to have remained in Europe, and were presented in various parts of Charles' domains.[52]

Cortés then returned with his new wife, his mother and 400 others to Mexico. He left Seville in the spring of 1530, and arrived at Vera Cruz on 15 July. Most of his Indians had left earlier, by royal command; three died, some remained. One, Benito Mazutlaqueny, was sent to Rome in the meantime: Pope Clement VII gravely said that he thanked God that such countries as New Spain had been discovered in his day, and promptly legitimised three of Cortés' bastard children.[53] Back in

New Spain, Cortés was refused entry to his house in the capital since his *residencia* was under way. His mother died at Texcoco before she could properly appreciate the size of her son's achievement. The *Caudillo* went to his property in Cuernavaca where he built a palace, and where he established a sugar mill, introduced slaves from Africa, and grew wheat, vines, and olives.[54] Much time was taken up defending himself against accusations of profiteering during the conquest, of killing Indians unnecessarily, of murdering his wife and others. Cortés even had to face an argument by Andrés de Monjaraz that in 1521 he had attacked the beautiful town of Oaxtepec without first reading the *Requerimiento*.[55] The hearings in the Mexican court, the long questionnaires and the answers by innumerable witnesses stretched on for many years, enriching notaries, providing priceless information for historians who choose to use it. But the affair was embittered by the presence of many old comrades of Cortés who, out of disappointment or envy, turned against him. Who exactly was where on the night of the *noche triste*? What really occurred in the Palace of Axayácatl when Cortés secured from Montezuma the concession of powers? How precisely did Catalina "la Marcayda" die? Cortés was even accused, by a fellow veteran, Rodrigo de Castañeda, of wishing to preserve temples and idols on his properties in defiance of the policy of the Franciscans to destroy them. Meantime the first *audiencia* in New Spain, of narrow men presided over by the cruel Nuño de Guzmán, gave way to a bench of high-minded clergymen; and that gave way in 1535 to the first viceroy, Antonio de Mendoza, a great courtier as well as a great administrator, member of the most enlightened family of Castile, but a man who had no hesitation in retaining Cortés in a secondary place.

Cortés embarked on great expeditions to the Pacific. He failed to find the famous strait linking that ocean with the Caribbean: indeed he must by then have realised that it did not exist. He perhaps thought that he would reach the Moluccas, and even discover, close at hand, a little to the north, China itself.[56] He devoted great sums of his own money to these enterprises, and discovered, and named, California, presumably after that Queen Califia who figured in one of the then fashionable romances. Once more he took great risks, suffered great privations, lost half his men. But he never found a short cut to China.

He quarrelled with the viceroy over these Pacific journeys, and returned again to Spain in January 1540 to plead his cause. By then he was in his fifties. His achievements were half forgotten. A prosaic era had set in. People no longer remembered the name of "El Clavero" Monroy, and recalled the first years of the conquests in America, if at all, with distaste. Cortés' letters, so successful in the 1520s, were by then prohibited. They had anyway caused people both to fear and to envy him. The *Caudillo* offered to help the Emperor capture Algiers, but his advice was not taken, though he and his son were present at (and survived) that inglorious affair. He now wearied the Emperor with his demands. Once at the court in Barcelona, he yet again complained that his merits had not been recognised. Charles sharply intervened to say: "Stop vaunting your merits when you have been speaking of a province which is not yours but that of another" – meaning, of course, Diego Velázquez.[57] Cortés realised that he was not needed. Men of his quicksilver mind were no longer popular at the Spanish court.

From the angle of a Spanish civil servant, a *letrado* educated in Salamanca, in an age of administration, Hernán Cortés was too much his own man. He had established *encomiendas* without (and then explicitly against) royal approval. There were many question marks about his conduct: the convenient disappearance in Mexico of so many enemies seemed a little alarming, all too Italianate a series of coincidences. Cortés' clever outmanoeuvring of Velázquez, Narváez, Tapia and Garay might be forgiven him because of his eventual victory over the Mexica. No one ever mentioned Alvarado's massacre of the Mexican noblemen, though everyone knew that Cortés had not reproached him for the action. Yet a man as clever as Cortés showed himself to be would always remain an uneasy subject of the Crown. Though Cortés had been meticulous in treating Indians after the conquest, the events at Cholula and Tepeaca suggested a capacity for astonishing ruthlessness. So did the torture of Cuauhtémoc. Surely Cortés was infinitely richer than he declared himself to be. Surely he had not always remembered the Crown's fifth of all profits. In becoming lord of so many towns in Mexico, was not Cortés seeking a degree of independence which was no longer a possibility in Spain itself, even to a great nobleman: even to the Count of Medellín?

Aware that he had passed his prime, Cortés in the mid-1540s wisely went to live out the remainder of his life in Seville, or near it, sometimes going to the court, and known for his participation in interesting *tertulias*, or private discussions. He exaggerated both his poverty and his age in a letter to the King in 1544. His last years were, like those of Columbus, passed in disillusion. He died just outside Seville, at Castilleja de la Cuesta, in a house still standing, on 2 December 1547, at the age of sixty-two, leaving behind in Mexico a great legend, a vast property, colossal wealth, and numerous children. He had among his possessions two brocade-covered beds which, after his death, went to a Florentine merchant, Jacome Boti, in return for the annulment of a mortgage in Seville.[58]

Cortés' remains have been moved several times, though less dramatically than those of Columbus. They were first to lie in San Isidoro del Campo, at Santiponce, a village just outside Seville, in two separate places in the same church (1547–50, 1550–66). They were then taken to San Francisco in Texcoco (1566–1629); to San Francisco in Mexico (1629–

1794, though there was an exhumation in 1716 when the church was rebuilt); and, finally, to the church of Jesus Nazareno in Mexico – in which last site, the bones have been both hidden, in 1823 and 1836, and, in 1946, exposed.[59]

The artistic impact of the conquest of Mexico, like that of the whole of the Americas, continued to be insignificant in Europe. Historians of art are hard put to find much indication of the effect in the sixteenth century: apart from the previously mentioned stone Mexicans in the episcopal palace in Liège, and a mask on a bishop's tomb in the cathedral of Rouen. Mexico for Europe was a place for curiosities, not artistic achievement. The pieces of featherwork acquired by Cosimo de' Medici were seen as artefacts, not works of art: an attitude which lasted till the twentieth century. A Mexican obsidian mirror owned by an English eccentric, John Dee, was known as the "Devil's Looking Glass".[60] Even economically, New Spain seemed of little importance for thirty years. The supply of gold was much less than that from other places incorporated into the Spanish Crown. Potatoes from Peru, tobacco from Cuba seemed more important than what Mexico had to offer. Charles V kept little to remind him of these American adventures: even if his abdication (an unheard-of action for a king) may have been prompted by Lisuarte's abdication as King of England in *Amadís de Gaula*.[61] Only after he died did the great silver mines of New Spain, making use of the new process involving mercury, begin to offer new wealth on a splendid scale.

Perhaps, it will be said, the disappointments in Cortés' later life were no more than were deserved by a man who had destroyed a civilisation, even if he had sought not to do so, but to offer his King a new prize. Yet by the standards of Spain of his time, Cortés' achievements were astonishing. It may be argued that if Cortés had not carried through his conquest, someone else would have done so. That cannot be proved. The conquest of 1520–1 required Cortés' capacity and determination to win over the Indians: above all the Tlaxcalans. Had it not been for their help, as porters, as quartermasters, and in providing a sanctuary, the expedition would have foundered. Had that occurred, who is to say that the Mexica under Cuauhtémoc might not have acquired the use of Spanish weapons, and perhaps learned to use horses? Even allowing for the onslaught of smallpox, they might have maintained a determined opposition until Spain became weary of conquering. Perhaps they would have embarked upon their own version of the Meiji era in Japan. One Spanish proconsul in the Philippines offered to Philip II to conquer China. The offer was typical of the old Andalusian frontier spirit. The idea was turned down by the prudent king. He might have done the same in respect of a Mexico rejuvenated under a well-prepared line of emperors.

The word which best expresses Cortés' actions is "audacity": it contains a hint of imagination, impertinence, a capacity to perform the unexpected which differentiates it from mere valour. Cortés was also decisive, flexible, and had few scruples. A nineteenth-century Extremeño said of Cortés' kinsman, "El Clavero" Monroy, that he was "quick in talk, skilful and daring in execution, full of threats in war which suddenly turned into decisive blows: in no way suffering from bad weather, vast distances, dangers or reverses": not unlike his kinsman Hernán Cortés.[62] One does not have to be a believer in any special theory that great men dominate history to see at once that Cortés' combination of intelligence and prudence, bravery and originality were decisive in the extraordinary events in Mexico between 1519 and 1521.

In 1524 Cortés sent a model silver cannon as a present to Charles V. The silver came from Michoacan. He called it "the Phoenix". On it he had had inscribed:

> This was born without equal
> I am without a second in serving you
> You are without equal in the world.[63]

The gift was an extravagant one, as jealous men in Spain were not slow to point out. But it was, as the German traveller, Thomas Münzer, would have agreed, "sumptuous". On this occasion, the present reached Spain. It was, however, soon melted down for the silver.

The name of the cannon had its irony; for Cortés had levied a tax named "the Phoenix" on all gold and silver produced in Mexico, in order to make up for the losses on the disastrous journey home of Ávila and Quiñones. Yet it was a good name: a new, and eventually an extraordinary, society, with its own magic, would rise from the ashes of old Tenochtitlan.

Glossary

Nahuatl

Pronunciation: "ch" and "x" as in English "sh"; "hu" before a vowel as "w"; "z" as "s"; vowels as in Spanish; "l" at end of word (e.g. Nahuatl) is hardly pronounced.

amatl: paper made from the bark of the wild fig

atlatl: a dart or spear-thrower

Aztlan: "white place of herons"; legendary original home of the Mexica

Aztec: people of Aztlan

calmécac: school for the upper class

calpisqui: (plural, *calpixque*) steward whose task was to collect tribute

calpulli: (plural *calpultin*) districts or clans in Mexico-Tenochtitlan. The head of one of these was called a *calpullec* (plural, *calpulleque*)

Chicomoztoc: "the Seven Caves", a possible place of origin of the Mexica

chinampa: a platform of logs, branches and reeds covered with silt etc., either floating on the lake or, more likely, secured to the muddy bottom of the lake, and on which intensive agriculture was carried out

cihuacoatl: "snake woman", goddess; but also deputy emperor for domestic activities

ezhuacatl: "he who claws blood", one of the top four advisers to the Emperor from whom his successor would normally be chosen

huehuetl: large vertical drum whose mouth is covered with stretched skin

huey tlatoani: emperor, or senior king

huipil: (plural *huipilli*) a long blouse worn by women

macehual: (plural *macehualtin*) worker

macuauhuitl: a wooden sword edged on both sides with sharp obsidian

mayeque: lowest class above slaves; serf

Mexica: the Mexicans

Mexico: "in the navel of the moon"

Nahuatl: the common language of most of the peoples in the Valley of Mexico *c.*1519

pilli: (plural, *pipiltin*) the Mexican upper class, the "nobles"

pochteca: long-distance merchant

tamale: maize cake

tameme: bearer

telpochcalli: school for the majority

Tenochca: people of Tenochtitlan (as opposed to Tlatelolca, people of Tlatelolco)

Tenochtitlan: "place of the prickly pear"

teponaztli: a horizontal drum carved from a log

tlacatecatl: "he who commands the warriors", one of the top four advisers of the Emperor from whom the successor would normally be chosen

tlacochcalcatl: "head of the house of javelins", one of the top four advisers of the Emperor from whom the successor would normally be chosen

Tlatelolca: people of Tlatelolco

Tlatelolco: "place of many mounds", city of Mexica to the immediate north of Tenochtitlan

tlatlacotin: slaves

tlatoani: (plural *tlatoque*) literally spokesman, in effect king, lord

tlatocan: supreme council, e.g. of war

Tlaxcala: "place of maize cakes"

tlillancalqui: "keeper of the house of darkness", one of the top four advisers of the Emperor from whom the successor would normally be chosen

tonalámatl:	book of destinies, that is, a kind of almanac made of *amatl* on which were painted the signs of the divinatory calendar of 260 days
totocalli:	aviary
tzompantli:	skull rack

Spanish

adelantado:	commander with political functions
alcalde:	magistrate
alguacil:	constable
encomienda:	a grant of people for a conquistador to look after (hence *encomendero*, a conquistador so favoured)
probanza:	legal statement
procurador:	representative
regidor:	councillor
residencia:	a judicial enquiry into an official's conduct
veedor:	inspector

Appendices

Appendix I: The population of old Mexico

To estimate the population of Mexico before the coming of Cortés, like that of the rest of the Americas before 1492, is complicated. For Hispaniola, see Chapter 5, note 45.

The evidence of the period is contradictory. That has not prevented propaganda figures from being shamelessly used.[1] When in the eighteenth century the history of these things began to be written, the population of old Mexico was discussed in relation to the views held by the historians concerned of the nature of the conquest. Thus Clavijero, the Jesuit, who, in his bitter Bolognese exile in the 1770s, began to create the idea of a Mexican identity, talked in terms of a population of thirty million;[2] while William Robertson insisted that the Spanish exaggerated the size of the indigenous population in order to enhance the nature of their achievement in conquering it.[3] Similar attitudes have marked historians ever since. But the attitudes, though similar, have not been exactly the same: thus those who explicitly or implicitly denounce the conquest favour high figures. They can thus allow it to seem that the Spanish were responsible for the largest demographic disaster in history; for it is incontestable that the population of Mexico was down to about two or three million by 1558. The friends of the Spaniards tend to favour low figures.

In the twentieth century, the debate has veered between estimates by the minimalists, of about four million, and by the maximalists, of thirty million. Thus Karl Sapper, a great German scholar, who then passed as a maximalist, in 1924 spoke of Mexico having a population of twelve to fifteen million.[4] Alfred Kroeber in 1939 thought that the cultivable land of Mexico would then be able to support ten million, from which he deducted a fifth for the fact of antiquity. So he thought in terms of eight million,[5] while Julian Steward, in an essay of 1949 in the *Handbook of South American Indians*, like George Kubler, the great architectural historian, in 1942, both gave low figures.[6] Angel Rosenblat, in his summary of the native population of old America, in 1954, estimated that Mexico had 4,500,000 people in 1518, the whole double continent in 1492 a little more than 13,300,000.[7]

Meantime the maximalists, the "California School", were preparing their counterattack. Using primarily estimates made by friars (especially Motolinía) for the number of converted natives, and the military estimates of the conquerors, Lesley B. Simpson, one of the greatest of United States historians of Mexico (author of the brilliant *Many Mexicos*), and Sherburne F. Cook, professor of psychology at the University of California, argued to begin with that that region had 9,030,000 people "at contact".[8] In 1957 Cook, with this time Woodrow Borah, the distinguished professor of Latin American history at Berkeley, considered sixty-four Mexican towns for which reasonably good population figures for 1552 and 1570 could be established. They found that, though the epidemics then had been less disastrous than earlier, between those dates there was an average fall in population of 3.8 per cent. By applying that proportion to Cook and Simpson's overall estimate for 1565, and extrapolating backwards, they reached a figure for central Mexico (that is, the territory between the isthmus of Tehuantepec and the Chichimec frontier) in 1520 of 25.3 million. They described this figure as "a calculation of theoretical significance only and . . . presented simply as one possible way of approaching the problem".[9]

Though they soon increased their estimate to thirty million (by using not only the technique of extrapolation in reverse, but also tribute estimates – the *Matrícula de Tributos*, the Codex Mendoza and the "Scholes document"), they later returned to an estimate for 1519 of 25,200,000.[10]

These scholars were, of course, suggesting that there had been in the sixteenth century a demographic catastrophe of unprecedented dimensions. Their techniques seemed so professional that their figures held the field for some time. Henry Dobyns, in a well-known article, for example, supported Cook and Borah and in 1966 even went further, in suggesting also that Clavijero's figure of thirty million was probably correct (his methods were pleasantly broadbrush).[11]

But the wheel of fortune turned. William T. Sanders, in a fine article published by William M. Denevan, in his collection of articles with different conclusions,[12] demolished the methods of Cook and Borah: the tribute lists were approximations and unrelated to population; different peoples received different treatment from the Mexicans; the tribute was levied in kind; Texcoco and Tenochtitlan both levied tribute but Borah and Cook used only the Tenochtitlan tribute list; the authors assumed that there was the same proportion of tax-exempt persons in 1519 as in 1548; there were disagreeements between the three sources about the rates of tax; and the tribute, not being a tax, was unrelated to capacity to pay. Sanders then introduced his own technique, based on observation of the conditions in the Valley of Teotihuacan (for example, the study of "occupational debris" and the capacity of specific acreage of agriculture to support people), itself deriving from a special study made in the 1960s by Pennsylvania State University. He estimated a population for central Mexico in 1519 of 11.4 million (Denevan, his editor in this book, decided diplomatically to give his own estimate of 18.3 million, as the average between the highest and the lowest figures!).[13] At about the same time Pedro Armillas estimated that the southern lake chinampa zone covered 28,000 acres[14] – a territory which Sanders thought might support about 17,000 people with a per capita maize population of 160 kilos. The total number of those living from drainage agriculture might, he thought, have been 300,000, to include the population of Texcoco and its cultivated plain.[15] Carlos Rangel, in his famous polemic *Du Noble Sauvage au Bon Révolutionnaire*, then made an inspired criticism: how could so many people feed themselves in Tenochtitlan? He thought that the most plausible estimates suggested that the Mexican empire only consisted of a million people.[16] Two historians from Bordeaux (Henri Enjalbert and Serge Lerat) made the same point.[17]

But the maximalists were not to be beaten so easily. Cook died in 1974. He had done a lot more work before that and, in 1979, Borah was able to publish a long essay which was their joint work in the third volume of *Essays in Population History: Mexico and the Caribbean*. In a learned and, from many points of view, admirable chapter, they suggested that their 25,200,000 Mexicans before Cortés arrived could have been supported by the cultivation of 10 to 15 per cent of the available land. With this response, these one-time "revolutionary" demographers seemed to have settled the matter.[18]

But this stability was short-lived. Sanders, heading his "Basin of Mexico" survey project, in 1979 argued that the Basin of Mexico had a population of between 800,000 and 1,100,000, of whom half, he thought, lived in Tenochtitlan. He and his team thought that the total carrying capacity of the area (area of cultivable land, production per hectare, etc.) was 1,250,000.[19] Rodrigo Zambardino, in a brilliant if neglected essay in 1986, suggested that the very methods of Cook and Borah could be used to find a lower figure. Zambardino based his critique on the fact that if Borah and Cook had been right to argue for a population of a little over twenty-five million for central Mexico in 1519, the average density of population would have been 125 per square mile (49 per square kilometre) over the whole area of 2,000–3,000 square miles in the Valley of Mexico. But that density of population would be superior to that of China and Japan. So in fact Borah and Cook were insisting on a density greater than any in the world at that time.

Borah and Cook, Zambardino pointed out, had two techniques: one based on the pictographic records of the Triple Alliance; the second deriving from extrapolating estimates from later years. Both methods were, he argued, faulty. The first only used four regions out of eleven. For another three regions of old Mexico, Borah and Cook merely added 10 per cent to the figures estimated for 1532. For two more regions the Californians assumed that the population had the same relative weighting in 1518 as in 1568. For the final two regions the figures for 1568 were simply projected backwards to 1518 on the basis of tribute data for one province. So in six of the regions the estimate of 1963 was either arbitrary or had a very low level of validity.

As for the first four regions, the conversion of tribute figures into values, and that converted into population figures, was obviously open to many errors. Zambardino thought that Borah and Cook's own figures, for example, could be interpreted as giving a figure of either 2.2 million or twenty-eight million. In the end, Zambardino suggested a figure of six million, with variants perhaps making for a possible level of five or ten million.[20]

The consequence of this controversy has been that several scholars recently have avoided commitment to any figures (for example, Inga Clendinnen, though she did accept "more than 200,000" for Tenochtitlan).[21] But Professor van Zantwijk, without having been able to see Zambardino's article, talks of central Mexico as having "at least 20 million people".[22] That figure was repeated by Mary Ellen Miller in *The Art of Mesoamerica*, as by Frances F. Berdan and Patricia Rieff Anawalt in their article, "The Codex Mendoza", in *The Scientific American*, (June 1992).[23] But the confusion attending the subject is expressed by the fact that in that excellent article the authors say that 10 per cent of the population lived in Tenochtitlan – that must be two million; but on the very next page they say that the population of that capital was perhaps 200,000.

The whole controversy, as Rosenblat rightly says, recalls the remark of Delbruck that if Herodotus had been right and Xerxes had had 5,283,220 people in his army, the tail of the army would still have been on the Tigris at the moment that its head had reached Thermopylae.[24]

As for the special case of Tenochtitlan: Cortés himself merely said that he thought it was as large as Seville and Córdoba.[25] None of the other members of his expedition ventured an estimate, and it was not a subject which was ever mentioned in the hearings of the *residencia* against him. His biographer, López de Gómara, presumably on Cortés' own evidence, estimated that there were 60,000 houses in the city.[26] The Anonymous Conqueror estimated 60,000 "people": perhaps a mistranslation for "*vecinos*" ("householders") by the Italian to whom we owe the survival of that document.[27] Oviedo talked of the city being as big as Seville and Cordoba.[28] Many other late sixteenth-century writers said the same: none based their estimates on any data. Most thought in terms of 50,000 residents. It was an estimate which has led subsequent historians (for example Vaillant) to multiply it by five or so to cover an "average household" and so reach the figure of 300,000 people.[29] Las Casas as usual spoke in large numbers: a million inhabitants living in 50,000 houses.[30]

No other interesting estimates were given till the twentieth century. Then Manuel Toussaint, Federico Gómez de Orozco and Justino Fernández studied sixteenth-century maps of the city and in 1938 suggested a figure of 60,000 for Tenochtitlan in an area of 7.5 square kilometres.[31] But Jacques Soustelle, in La vie cotidienne des Aztèques, in 1955, estimated anything between 500,000 and a million in a city of 80,000–100,000 households.[32] Borah and Cook in 1963 estimated 235,000 for Tenochtitlan, 125,000 for Tlatelolco.[33] Then Borah by himself in 1976 proposed that the area of both Tenochtitlan and Tlatelolco was sixteen square kilometres.[34] William Sanders meantime thought that the produce of the chinampas could have supported 150,000 to 200,000 people.[35] In 1970, Edward Calnek, having demolished the idea that the so-called maguey map was a part of Tenochtitlan, said that that city was twelve square kilometres large. For that area he also estimated 150,000 to 200,000 people.[36] Later, William Sanders, with Jeffrey Parsons and Robert S. Santley, in their admirable study, estimated that the population of the basin was about a million in 1518, that of "Greater Tenochtitlan" 500,000, and that of the entire lacustrine population half a million.[37] In 1980, Miguel León-Portilla gave the low figure of 70,000 for the capital.[38] In 1986 José Luis de Rojas, a Spanish historian of great assiduity, after a careful examination of nearly all past estimates, including all the above, seems to have decided that it was impossible to decide between 200,000 and 300,000 in a city sized 13.5 square kilometres.[39] Nigel Davies suggested 150,000.[40] Inga Clendinnen, though, as noticed above, thought that over 200,000 would be right, as did Eduardo Matos Moctezuma and Patricia Rieff Anawalt and Frances F. Berdan.[41]

All that can really be said of these last fifty years of research and speculation is that there have been many brilliant calculations but that, in the end, nobody can be shown to have made anything more than an inspired guess. It is certain that the population, when statistics began to be gathered, in the late 1540s, and even more the late 1560s, was less than what it was in 1518. Judge Zorita thought that about 1568 the population was not a third of what it had been at the time of the conquest. Since the population was then 2.6 million, a population of eight million might seem obvious. But Zorita guessed, as everyone later has done.[42]

Nicolas Sánchez Albornoz in 1976 sensibly summed up the situation when he said that Tenochtitlan was "the largest city on the American continent . . . the precise size is still disputed, but it was unusually large for that age."[43] I do not think that that statement can be improved upon.

Appendix II: A summary of Montezuma's tribute

Source: the Codex Mendoza (1545), a good copy of the contemporary *Matrícula de Tributos* (c.1511–19). The measurements must be approximate because of different interpretations of the original glyphs. The payments were made every eighty days, that is, 4½ times a year.

Featherwork, etc.

war dresses	625
war tunics	40
headdresses	466
standards	200
shields	665
feathers	33,680
sacks of down feathers	20
royal badges	2
fans	4
bird skins	320
live eagles	2

Clothes

cloaks of cotton or fibre	123,400
loincloths	8,000
women's tunics and skirts	11,200

Agricultural produce

bins of maize	28
bins of beans	21
bins of sage leaves	21
bins of purslane	18

baskets of mixed maize flour and cacao	160
baskets of sage leaves	160
loads of red cacao	160
loads of cacao	820
bales of cotton	4,400
chilli (loads)	1,600
canes	16,000
canes for spears	32,000
canes for smoking	32,000
loading frames for bearers	4,800
logs	4,800
large planks	4,800
small planks	4,800
baskets of refined copal	3,200
baskets of unrefined copal	64,000
cakes of liquidambar	16,000
pots of liquidambar	100
pans of yellow varnish	40
bags of cochineal	65
pots of bees' honey	2,200
balls of rubber	16,000

Manufactures

reams of maguey paper	32,000
pottery bowls	1,600
gourd bowls	17,600
pottery cups	800
stone cups	800
rush seats	8,000
rush mats	8,000
crates	800

Minerals

turquoise masks	10
turquoise necklaces	1
turquoise mosaic discs	2
turquoise, pans of small stones	1
turquoise, packets of stones	1
jadeite necklaces	21
jadeite large beads	3
gold-mounted crystal lip plugs	40
amber lip plugs	44
pieces of amber	4

loads of lime   16,800
loaves of refined salt   4,000

Gold

shields   1
diadems   2
necklaces   2
tablets   10
discs   60
bowls of gold dust   60

Copper

bells   80
axeheads   560

Miscellaneous

deerskins   3,200
ocelot skins   80
conch shells   1,600

Appendix III: Mexican calendars

Two calendars were used. The first, the *xihuitl*, was the 365-day one, made up of 18 "months" of 20 days, together with five extra days known as *nemontemi* which came at the end of the year. Each month was probably associated with the moon, and celebrated with fiestas. The order of the months was the same throughout Central Mexico though there were variations as to with which month the year began. Both months and days were named and numbered. Each year was apparently called after the last day of the last month. Days began at noon, not midnight. The Mexica did not have what Alfonso Caso calls a "Julian correction", or leap year, but probably had another means of adjustment.

The months and their European equivalents for 1521–1522 (for 1519 or 1522 they were a day later), were, in Mexico–Tenochtitlan: Izcalli (Resurrection), Jan. 24–Feb. 12; Atlcahualo ("They leave the water"), Feb. 13–Mar. 4; Tlacaxipehualiztli ("Flaying of men"), Mar. 5–Mar. 24; Tozoztontli ("Short watch"), Mar. 25–April 13; Hueytozoztli ("Long watch"), April 14–May 3; Toxcatl ("Dry thing"), May 4–May 23; Etzalcualiztli ("Meal of maize"), May 24–June 12; Techuilhuitontli ("Small feast of the lords"), June 13–July 2; Hueytecuilhuitl ("Great feast of the lords"), July 3–July 22; Tlaxochimaco ("Flowers are given") or Miccailhuitontli ("Small feast of the dead"), July 23–Aug. 11; Hueymiccailhuitl ("Great feast of the dead") or Xocotluetzi ("The fruit falls"), Aug. 12–Aug. 31; Ochopaniztli ("Sweeping"), Sept. 1– Sept. 20; Pachtontli ("Little Spanish moss") or Teotlelco ("The arrival of the gods"), Sept. 21–Oct. 10; Hueypachtli ("Big Spanish moss") or Tepeilhuitl ("Feast of the mountains"), Oct. 11–Oct. 30; Quecholli ("Flamingo"), Oct. 31–Nov. 19; Panquetzaliztli ("Raising of flags"), Nov. 20–Dec. 9; Atemoztli ("The water falls"), Dec. 10–Dec 29; Tititl

("Shrunk or wrinkled"), Dec. 30–Jan. 18; and Nementemi, Jan. 18–Jan. 23.

The years were indicated by four of the day signs: Reed, Flint, House and Rabbit. A "century", at the end of which there was a ceremony of renewal ("the tying of the years", for which see Ch. 1 and Ch. 10), was, therefore, every fifty-two (four times thirteen) years. The thirteen European years 1511–1523 were:

1511: 6-Reed
1512: 7-Flint
1513: 8-House
1514: 9-Rabbit
1515: 10-Reed
1516: 11-Flint
1517: 12-House
1518: 13-Rabbit
1519: 1-Reed
1520: 2-Flint
1521: 3-House
1522: 4-Rabbit
1523: 5-Reed

(1993 is 7-House, and 1994 8-Rabbit.)

The second calendar was the *Tehalpohualli* a word meaning "count of days": a cycle of 260 separately named days. These names were composed of a figure and a word. The numbers ran from 1 to 13, and there were twenty words which composed 13-day signs (as below). When the names were used up, number 1 began again, but with a different sign. There would thus be 260 day signs in this cycle. The book in which this calendar was painted was called a *Tonalamatl*. Numbers were represented by dots. One of these calendars in Western script would look thus:

Alligator (Cipactli)	1	8	2	9	3	10	4	11	5	12	6	13	7
Wind (Ehecatl)	2	9	3	10	4	11	5	12	6	13	7	1	8
House (Calli)	3	10	4	11	5	12	6	13	7	1	8	2	9
Lizard (Cuetzpallin)	4	11	5	12	6	13	7	1	8	2	9	3	10
Snake (Coatl)	5	12	6	13	7	1	8	2	9	3	10	4	11
Death (Miquiztli)	6	13	7	1	8	2	9	3	10	4	11	5	12
Deer (Mazatl)	7	1	8	2	9	3	10	4	11	5	12	6	13
Rabbit (Tochtli)	8	2	9	3	10	4	11	5	12	6	13	7	1
Water (Atl)	9	3	10	4	11	5	12	6	13	7	1	8	2
Dog (Itcuintli)	10	4	11	5	12	6	13	7	1	8	2	9	3
Monkey (Ozomatli)	11	5	12	6	13	7	1	8	2	9	3	10	4

Grass (Malinalli)	12	6	13	7	1	8	2	9	3	10	4	11	5
Reed (Acatl)	13	7	1	8	2	9	3	10	4	11	5	12	6
Jaguar (Ocelotl)	1	8	2	9	3	10	4	11	5	12	6	13	7
Eagle (Cuauhtli)	2	9	3	10	4	11	5	12	6	13	7	1	8
Buzzard (Cozcacuauhtli)	3	10	4	11	5	12	6	13	7	1	8	2	9
Movement (Ollin)	4	11	5	12	6	13	7	1	8	2	9	3	10
Flint (Tecpatl)	5	12	6	13	7	1	8	2	9	3	10	4	11
Rain (Quiahuitl)	6	13	7	1	8	2	9	3	10	4	11	5	12
Flower (Xochitl)	7	1	8	2	9	3	10	4	11	5	12	6	13

Modest regional differences, the significance of certain divisibilities, the nature of certain gods associated with special days and nights, the role of lucky and unlucky days, etc., all the life's work of the professional interpreters (*tonalpohualli*), are indicated clearly and expertly by Alfonso Caso in his essay, "The Calendrical System of Central Mexico", in the *Handbook of Middle American Indians*, vol. 10 (Austin, 1971), 333–48, on which this Appendix is based.

Appendix IV: Spanish money c.1520

The Spaniards at the time of the Conquest of Mexico employed many denominations with no clear rules of practice. Pesos, castellanos, ducats and maravedís were all used. The usual coin was a maravedí, a copper coin equal to a ninety-sixth part of a Spanish gold mark, which in turn was equivalent to 230.045 grams.

1 real = 34 maravedís
1 ducat = 375 maravedís
1 peso = 450 maravedís
1 castellano = 485 maravedís

A *sueldo* (from *solidus*) was a tiny sum (*sou*), perhaps no more than a way of saying that.

Appendix V: Cortés' ladies

LEONOR PIZARRO: an "Indiana" of Cuba. Later married to Juan de Salcedo. Cortés had a daughter by her

CATALINA "LA MARCAYDA": Cortés married her in Cuba in 1514. She died in Mexico in 1522

MARINA (MALINALI): interpretress, by whom Cortés had a son, Martín, born 1522

ELVIRA DE HERMOSILLA: later married Juan Díaz de Real, later still Lope de Acuña

TECUICHPO, "DOÑA ISABEL": daughter of Montezuma. Cortés had a child by her

"DOÑA ANA", "DOÑA INÉS": daughters of Montezuma, killed in the *noche triste*

"DOÑA ANA", daughter of Cacama, later married Juan de Cuéllar

"DOÑA FRANCISCA": daughter of Cacama, killed in the *noche triste*

JUANA DE ZÚÑIGA, niece of the Duke of Béjar. Cortés married her in 1528 and had several children by her

Genealogies

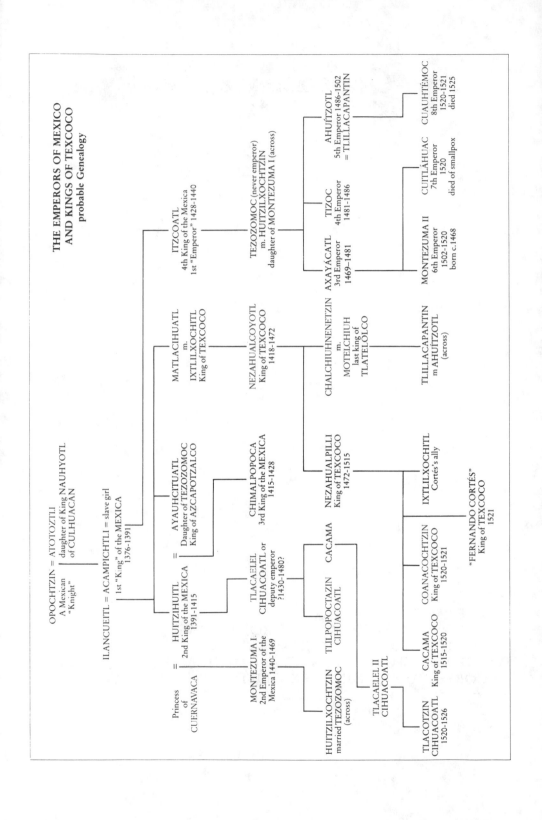

THE EMPERORS OF MEXICO
AND KINGS OF TEXCOCO
probable Genealogy

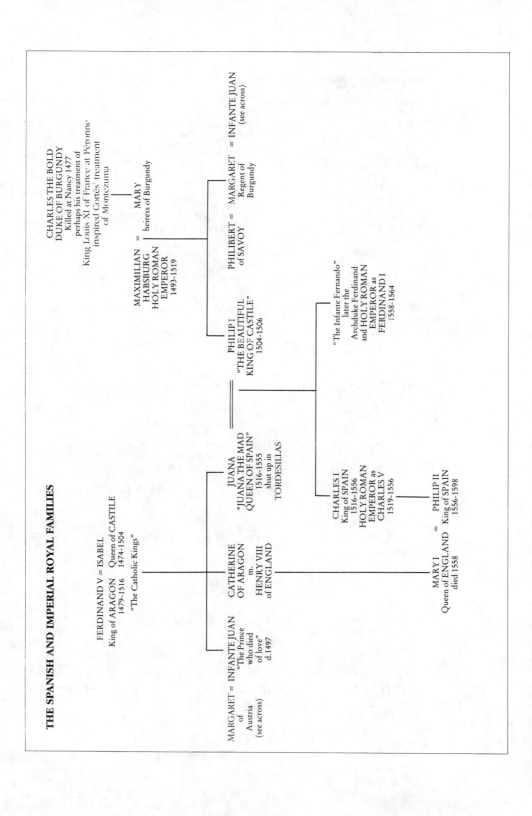

THE SPANISH AND IMPERIAL ROYAL FAMILIES

CHARLES THE BOLD
DUKE OF BURGUNDY
Killed at Nancy 1477
perhaps his treatment of
King Louis XI of France at Péronne
inspired Cortés' treatment
of Montezuma

MARY
heiress of Burgundy

MAXIMILIAN =
HABSBURG
HOLY ROMAN
EMPEROR
1493-1519

PHILIBERT = MARGARET = INFANTE JUAN
of SAVOY   Regent of   (see across)
            Burgundy

PHILIP I
"THE BEAUTIFUL
KING OF CASTILE"
1504-1506

"The Infante Fernando"
later the
Archduke Ferdinand
and HOLY ROMAN
EMPEROR as
FERDINAND I
1558-1564

FERDINAND V = ISABEL
King of ARAGON   Queen of CASTILE
1479-1516   1474-1504

"The Catholic Kings"

JUANA
"JUANA THE MAD
QUEEN OF SPAIN"
1516-1555
shut up in
TORDESILLAS

CATHERINE
OF ARAGON
m.
HENRY VIII
of ENGLAND

CHARLES I
King of SPAIN
1516-1556
HOLY ROMAN
EMPEROR as
CHARLES V
1519-1556

MARGARET = INFANTE JUAN
of   "The Prince
Austria   who died
(see across) of love"
             d.1497

MARY I = PHILIP II
Queen of ENGLAND   King of SPAIN
died 1558   1556-1598

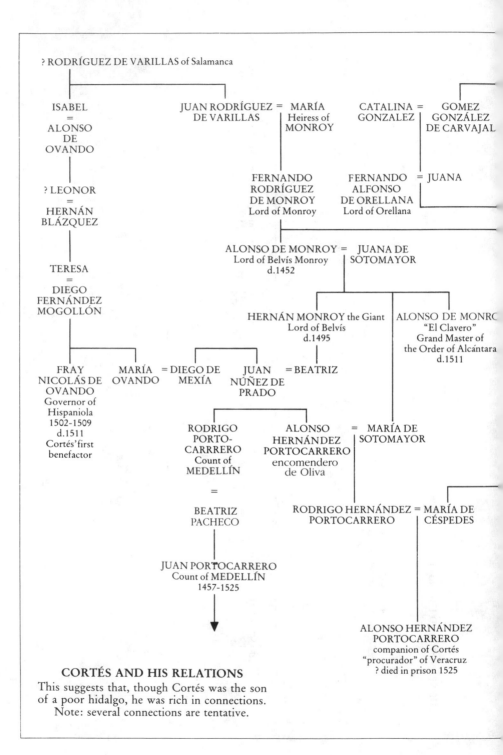

? RODRÍGUEZ DE VARILLAS of Salamanca

ISABEL
=
ALONSO
DE
OVANDO

JUAN RODRÍGUEZ = MARÍA
DE VARILLAS | Heiress of
MONROY

CATALINA = GOMEZ
GONZALEZ | GONZÁLEZ
DE CARVAJAL

? LEONOR
=
HERNÁN
BLÁZQUEZ

FERNANDO
RODRÍGUEZ
DE MONROY
Lord of Monroy

FERNANDO = JUANA
ALFONSO
DE ORELLANA
Lord of Orellana

ALONSO DE MONROY = JUANA DE
Lord of Belvís Monroy | SOTOMAYOR
d.1452

TERESA
=
DIEGO
FERNÁNDEZ
MOGOLLÓN

HERNÁN MONROY the Giant
Lord of Belvís
d.1495

ALONSO DE MONRO
"El Clavero"
Grand Master of
the Order of Alcántara
d.1511

FRAY
NICOLÁS DE
OVANDO
Governor of
Hispaniola
1502-1509
d.1511
Cortés' first
benefactor

MARÍA = DIEGO DE
OVANDO   MEXÍA

JUAN   = BEATRIZ
NÚÑEZ DE
PRADO

RODRIGO
PORTO-
CARRRERO
Count of
MEDELLÍN

ALONSO   = MARÍA DE
HERNÁNDEZ | SOTOMAYOR
PORTOCARRERO
encomendero
de Oliva

=

BEATRIZ
PACHECO

RODRIGO HERNÁNDEZ = MARÍA DE
PORTOCARRERO | CÉSPEDES

JUAN PORTOCARRERO
Count of MEDELLÍN
1457-1525

ALONSO HERNÁNDEZ
PORTOCARRERO
companion of Cortés
"procurador" of Veracruz
? died in prison 1525

CORTÉS AND HIS RELATIONS

This suggests that, though Cortés was the son
of a poor hidalgo, he was rich in connections.
Note: several connections are tentative.

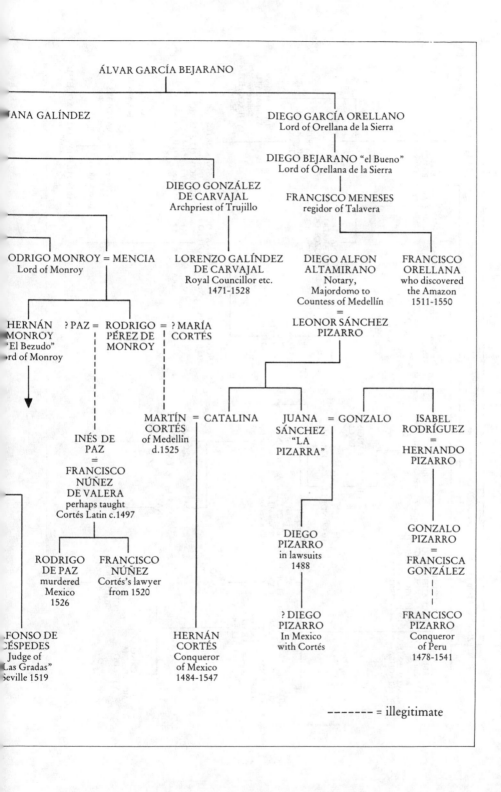

ÁLVAR GARCÍA BEJARANO

_ANA GALÍNDEZ

DIEGO GARCÍA ORELLANO
Lord of Orellana de la Sierra

DIEGO BEJARANO "el Bueno"
Lord of Orellana de la Sierra

DIEGO GONZÁLEZ
DE CARVAJAL
Archpriest of Trujillo

FRANCISCO MENESES
regidor of Talavera

_ODRIGO MONROY = MENCIA
Lord of Monroy

LORENZO GALÍNDEZ
DE CARVAJAL
Royal Councillor etc.
1471-1528

DIEGO ALFON
ALTAMIRANO
Notary,
Majordomo to
Countess of Medellín
=
LEONOR SÁNCHEZ
PIZARRO

FRANCISCO
ORELLANA
who discovered
the Amazon
1511-1550

_HERNÁN   ? PAZ =   RODRIGO = ? MARÍA
MONROY   PÉREZ DE   CORTÉS
"El Bezudo"   MONROY
_rd of Monroy

INÉS DE
PAZ
=
FRANCISCO
NÚÑEZ
DE VALERA
perhaps taught
Cortés Latin c.1497

MARTÍN = CATALINA
CORTÉS
of Medellín
d.1525

JUANA = GONZALO
SÁNCHEZ
"LA
PIZARRA"

ISABEL
RODRÍGUEZ
=
HERNANDO
PIZARRO

RODRIGO
DE PAZ
murdered
Mexico
1526

FRANCISCO
NÚÑEZ
Cortés's lawyer
from 1520

DIEGO
PIZARRO
in lawsuits
1488

GONZALO
PIZARRO
=
FRANCISCA
GONZÁLEZ

_FONSO DE
_ÉSPEDES
Judge of
_Las Gradas"
_eville 1519

HERNÁN
CORTÉS
Conqueror
of Mexico
1484-1547

? DIEGO
PIZARRO
In Mexico
with Cortés

FRANCISCO
PIZARRO
Conqueror
of Peru
1478-1541

------- = illegitimate

THE TRANSFORMATION OF THE MEXICAN ROYAL FAMILY

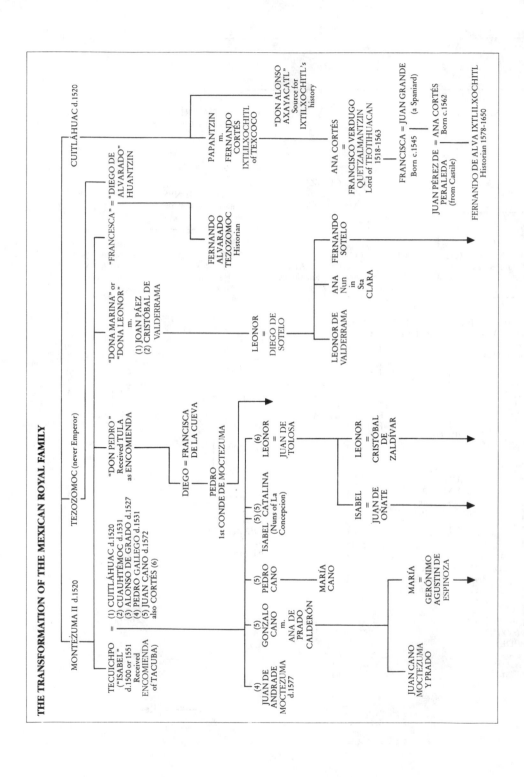

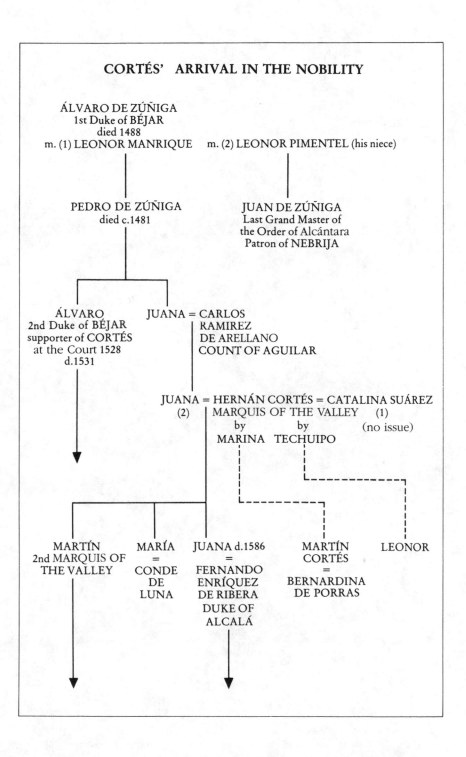

CORTÉS' ARRIVAL IN THE NOBILITY

ÁLVARO DE ZÚÑIGA
1st Duke of BÉJAR
died 1488
m. (1) LEONOR MANRIQUE   m. (2) LEONOR PIMENTEL (his niece)

PEDRO DE ZÚÑIGA
died c.1481

JUAN DE ZÚÑIGA
Last Grand Master of
the Order of Alcántara
Patron of NEBRIJA

ÁLVARO
2nd Duke of BÉJAR
supporter of CORTÉS
at the Court 1528
d.1531

JUANA = CARLOS
RAMIREZ
DE ARELLANO
COUNT OF AGUILAR

JUANA = HERNÁN CORTÉS = CATALINA SUÁREZ
(2)   MARQUIS OF THE VALLEY   (1)
        by   by   (no issue)
      MARINA   TECHUIPO

MARTÍN
2nd MARQUIS OF
THE VALLEY

MARÍA
=
CONDE
DE
LUNA

JUANA d.1586
=
FERNANDO
ENRÍQUEZ
DE RIBERA
DUKE OF
ALCALÁ

MARTÍN
CORTÉS
=
BERNARDINA
DE PORRAS

LEONOR

Unpublished Documents

In the preparation for this book many interesting papers were found. Most of these were in the Archivo de las Indias, in Seville, and most derived from the enquiry taken against Hernán Cortés known as the *residencia*, which began in 1529 and never properly ended. There were, however, other such documents in the Archivo de Protocolos in Seville, and in the Archivo General de Simancas.

Some of these documents which seem of special interest are published here.

1 *Cortés' father Martín Cortés in Medellín: a royal judgement*

Don Fernando and doña Isabel etc. to you, our *corregidor* of the city of Trujillo, and to your mayor in office, greetings and grace: may it be known that Diego Pizarro,[1] resident of the town of Medellín, in his own right and in the name of Alfonso Robles, his brother, gave news of their petition, which he presented in person before us in our council, saying that they and Pero de Merino and Martín Cortés and Yucaf Salinas, residents of the said city of Medellín, during the month of January past, made a certain bid [*puja*] in respect of the *alcabalas*, *tercios* and other taxes and customary dues of the said town of Medellín for the present year with certain conditions, qualifications and undertakings by common agreement, which for the most part were heard before a notary, in consequence of which they made a division and a declaration of the said revenues . . . and they said that Juan Portocarrero, Count of Medellín, and other persons under his command, had seized these revenues from them . . . and made them many other attacks and insults and injuries and they said that they had demanded the Count to make amends but he had said that he did not want to do so . . . in consequence of which we ask you to look at the petition which has been made to us . . . in such a way that henceforth Diego Pizarro and his brother do not receive any more harassment, nor injury, and so that they never have further reason to appeal to come to us nor send to complain before us . . . Given in the town of Ocaña, 18 August 1488 . . .

(Archivo General de Simancas: Registro General del Sello, August 1488)

2 Cortés' grandfather Diego Alfon Altamirano: part of a contract

It has been long known that Cortés' maternal grandfather was Diego Altamirano, majordomo to the Countess of Medellín. But a document found in the archives of the Medellín family now in the Archivo de Medinaceli shows that he was also a lawyer:

I Diego Alfon Altamirano, notary [escrivano] and notary [notario] of the King our Lord in all his lands, kingdoms and territories, present myself [indecipherable] with the other witnesses and when my lord the count consents here to be present, I ask the said count to tell the said notary to write down the truth . . . Diego Alfon Altamirano.

(Archive Medinaceli, Medellín: leg. 1, document 9, unnumbered folio, apparently 1488)

3 Cortés' journey to America, 1506: a contract

For the background to this document, see Chapter 9, note 86.

Let it be known to all who see this letter that I, Hernando Cortés, son of García Martínez Cortés, resident of Don Benito, a territory of Medellín,[2] consent and know that I must give and pay to you, Luis Fernández de Alfaro,[3] resident of this city [of Seville], master of the nao which God protects and which has the name of San Juan Bautista, now in the port of Las Mulas on the river Guadalquivir, in this city (whether you exhibit this letter publicly or whether you in your power show this letter to anyone), eleven pesos of assayed and marked gold [honze pesos de oro fundido e marcado] which are given in return for a passage and maintenance which you agree to give me in the said nao from the port of [Sanlúcar de] Barrameda to the isle of Hispaniola, to the port of the town of Santo Domingo, this journey which the said nao is about to make . . . the said eleven pesos of gold I undertake to give and pay you in the said island of Hispaniola . . .

(Archivo de Protocolos, Seville: oficio iv, lib. iv, 29 August 1506)

4 A letter from Cortés in Mexico, 6 July 1519

This letter should be read in connection with Cortés' dispatch of two *"procuradores"*, Francisco Montejo and Alonso Fernández Portocarrero, to Spain from Vera Cruz in July 1519. The letter seems not to have been previously known. It is not, alas, the so-called lost "first letter" of Cortés to the King (see page 218). But it is the earliest surviving letter written by Cortés from Mexico, being dated four days before the so-called Carta del Regimiento, the letter of the municipality of Villa Rica de la Vera Cruz.

Let all who see this letter know that I, Hernando Cortés, captain-general and chief justice of these islands newly discovered for their highnesses, consent and know that I give and grant with all my power . . . to you Juan Bautista, master, resident of the island of Fernandina, and resident of this town in which I am at present, so that you are master of the *nao* called *Santa María de la Concepción* which at present is registered ready to make a journey in the bay and port called San Juan of this island, and so that you go to the kingdoms of Castile, to the port of las Mulas in the river Guadalquivir, of the city of Seville, and there you discharge the jewels of gold and silver, and the other things which are being sent to their highnesses, handing them over to Alonso Fernández Portocarrero and Francisco de Montejo who will be setting off for those parts, and, that done, you should careen [*adobar*] the said ship and do everything else necessary for your return to this island, you remaining all the time as master; and if it appears to you necessary that you dismiss some sailor or cabin boy from the said *nao*, you can do it, and for that you should promise to give them the wage or wages, which may appear to you necessary, until you have brought back the said *nao* to the bay and port of San Juan, or whatever port of this said island you direct.

Further, I accept and consent with all my power so that if Martín Cortés my father and the *licenciado* Alonso de Céspedes[4] can send and stock in a short time the said *nao* with those things in a way which I by my memorandum have asked them to and so that you can consider this there in consequence [*para que alla nos detengays a cabsa de los susdicho*] you can in my name take or may take in exchange for whatever quantity of maravedís is necessary up to a sum of a thousand ducats on the said *nao* or merchandise . . . and if, because of the long voyage that there is from Spain to these parts, it is necessary for you to stop briefly in the island of Fernandina, you can in my name take the said maravedís in exchange to whichever of the said ports of Fernandina you like . . . though the said *nao* must not be detained there nor the merchandise discharged . . . [Most of the rest of the letter continues with a discussion as to how Juan Bautista would be responsible for the cost of losses] . . . and if necessary I relieve you and your crew of that clause of the law *"judicius yste judycatum solin"* with all its accustomed clauses and for a surety I sign this and I guarantee my person and goods, furniture and property, which I possess now and will possess in future. This letter is signed in Villa Rica de la Vera Cruz of this island newly discovered and named Qulna,[5] Wednesday 6 July, in the year of Our Lord One Thousand Five Hundred and Nineteen years, witnesses present being Anton Alaminos,[6] chief pilot, and Cristóbal Sánchez, master, and Pablo de Guzmán, and Joan de Cáceres[7] being in this town, and the said Hernando Cortés, captain-general and chief justice . . .

(Archivo de Protocolos, Seville: oficio iv, lib. iv, f.3743, 1519)

5 *Montezuma's concession of power, 1520*

In the course of the *residencia* taken against Hernán Cortés, those defending Cortés were asked (question 98) what they recalled of the occasion in early 1520 when, according to him, the Mexican emperor, Montezuma, was said to have conceded powers to the King of Spain. Some ten witnesses gave answers. One of these was Francisco de Flores who, like so many of Cortés' intimates, was an Extremeño: perhaps from Medellín, perhaps from Fregenal de la Sierra. He fought throughout the campaign in Mexico, being a companion of Alvarado in the retreat from Mexico-Tenochtitlan during the *"noche triste"*.

Going one day with the said don Hernando to see the said Moctezuma, just as we used to do on many other occasions, accompanied by the interpreters [that is Gerónimo de Aguilar and Marina], he [Cortés] made to the said Moctezuma many arguments telling him things of God, and how the Emperor our lord, the greatest lord in the world, had sent him to see these parts, and how all the Spaniards which had come with him as well as he himself were vassals of the Emperor our lord, and his servants, and various other things which this witness does not have fully in his memory at the moment . . . and one day with don Hernando talking thus with these arguments, the said Moctezuma was listening with many principal lords [*muchos principales, e señores de la tierra*] to whom the said Moctezuma said many things among which he had known for a long time and had had information from his ancestors and from elderly lords that they had from the evidence of holy writings [*sus scrypturas*] that these parts had one day to be subjugated, commanded, and governed by a great lord who lived in the land where the sun rose and from which all the people of the land would receive thereby a very great benefit and that now it appeared that all was fulfilled, as had been told and revealed to him in secret, according to the news and splendours of the emperor our lord, who had been talked of by the said don Hernando, being from the part where it had been said that he would come, that he now saw that it was he, he who had come to command and govern everything ... and that, knowing this, he had given his lordship to the said don Hernando [*el avia dado su señorio al dicho don hernando*] in the name of his majesty, and that he asked them all that, just as all their ancestors had been loyal vassals, friends and vassals that they would do likewise ... this and other similar things were said by the said Moctezuma to the said lords and principals who were there and who were there in a considerable number and all replied to the said Moctezuma and most of them said that he who ruled them had done well, and so they themselves accepted it as good, and therefore offered obedience to his majesty and gave themselves as his vassals [*e quedaban la obediencia a su magestad, e se davan por sus vasallos*] ... and this witness believes that as a result the said ordinance was agreed formally since the said don Hernando always had with him a notary to be present at things which occurred ...

(Francisco de Flores: AGI, Justicia, leg. 223, p. 2, his evidence being in ff.511–84)

6 *New evidence about the death of Catalina*

Catalina Suárez, Cortés' first wife, died in mysterious circumstances three months after her arrival in Mexico, in November 1522. Many questions were asked about her death, and the matter was taken up as something close to a murder enquiry against Cortés.

Among those who testified at the enquiry into Cortés' activities, the *residencia*, were Juan de Salcedo. He had been a business associate of Diego Velázquez, had married Leonor Pizarro by whom Cortés had had an illegitimate child before he left Cuba, and had arrived in Mexico with Pánfilo Narváez. After the conquest he was given the *encomienda* of Tenancingo. Asked about Catalina he replied:

that he knew and saw that she was very ill of *mal de madre*, and that she many times fainted in consequence and fell to the ground, and that this witness knows of it since one day when they were in Baracoa which is in Cuba, already they were wanting to dine, when an Indian in the said marquis' service came in crying out and saying that her mistress was dead; and this witness and the said marquis went to see what was happening, and they found the said Catalina as if dead on the ground, with no pulse, so much so that this witness believed her dead, and he took her in his arms and put her on a bed, and the said marquis carried water and flung it in her face in such a way that after having fainted more than an hour she revived, returning to her old self ...

(AGI, Justicia, leg. 224, p.1, f.660v–722r)

Another witness who testified on this matter was Juan González Ponce de León, son of the discoverer of Florida, who was credited, when his son Diego received a coat of arms in 1558, with being in 1521 the first man to the top of the main temple of Tenochtitlan. He received an *encomienda* in Actopan, in the modern state of Hidalgo, in company with the Jewish *converso* blacksmith, Hernando Alonso. Gonzalez Ponce de León said that:

he and some others being in Coyoacán went with Catalina [a few days before she died] to the orchard of Juan Garrido, and walking there she felt so strongly an attack of a bad heart or *mal de madre* that she fell fainting to the ground, and this witness felt her pulse many times and she appeared dead and very cold, and as a result of the use of water and onions which he pushed up her nostrils after more than an hour and a half she returned to herself as if she had been dead, and this witness and others present had much concern for her, and thus they took her to the lodgings of the said marquis . . .

The visit to the farm is of interest, for Juan Garrido was not only the first free black African to pass to New Spain, but he has been held to have been the first to plant wheat in the Americas.

González Ponce de León also said that:

the night when she died this witness saw the said Catalina Xuáres seated at the table with the said marquis and with other gentlemen [*caballeros*] and she was looking ill [*mal dispuesta*], and this witness and Juan Xuares brother of the said doña Catalina were standing behind her, looking at a letter and some golden jewels, and her said brother asked her why she was not dining, and this witness said that, with such a desire for such jewels, she would not want to dine, but she said that it was not that but that she had the illness which had come upon her in the orchard [*no era sino que tenia el mal que le avia dado en la huerta*] when this witness and the others were with her, and that night at midnight she died, and this witness believed that she died of that illness, as indeed is public and notorious . . .

(AGI, Justicia, leg. 224, p.1, f.722r–89v)

7 Cortés, art and loyalty

Juan de Hortega, from Medellín, another witness for Cortés, came out to New Spain in 1523 as part of the group of Extremeños who sought to profit from their countryman's triumph. He became almost immediately a magistrate (*alcalde ordinario*) *in Mexico*, and received an *encomienda* in Tepozotlan.

He testified about Cortés' personal intentions, and said that:

one day, entering Cortés' room, he saw a piece of wood painted in the Flemish way [*una tabla pintada de Flandes*] in which there was painted the figure of His Majesty, and the Queen, and the infantas and the King of Hungary his brother, and this witness saw it well, being the said don Hernando in the said bedroom and passing the picture he took off his hat, and this witness, wishing to see the said board in order to look at the portraits which were there depicted [*esculpidas*], opened a window and saw the said wood and asked the said don Hernando what the pictures were, and he said that it was the figure of His Majesty and the infanta as this witness said, and that he had brought it painted in the beginning and thereafter this witness saw that every time the said don Hernando passed before the said figures in the said picture he would take his hat off . . .

(AGI, Justicia, leg. 224, ff.152r–89r)

8 *Diego Velázquez's punishments*

Cortés was at first the protégé, then the enemy of Diego Velázquez. This document (dated 1524), from the *residencia* taken against Velázquez, shows that he was often at loggerheads with him, before of course he went to Mexico:

Pero Péres, protector of the estate of Diego Velázquez [replied] . . . to the ninth question. I say that, if the said *adelantado* agreed to cards being played on the island, it was at the beginning of the settling of the island, and not afterwards, because he punished it and he penalised Alonso de Esteve and Alonso de Mancelo, mayor, and Gonçalo Rodrigo de Ontano and Juan de Çia and Francisco Medina and Pero Péres and Hernando Cortés and Francisco Carmona on several occasions, and many other people because they did play . . .

(AGI, Justicia, leg. 49, f.15)

Chapter Notes

Sources cited often are referred to by abbreviations. Otherwise, the reference is indicated as follows: the full title of a work is given at its first mention; thereafter, the book, article, or other source is shown by citing, in square brackets, after the author's name, the chapter in which the work was first mentioned; then the note number. Thus Garibay [1:13] means that the full title etc., of the work by Garibay will be found in Chapter 1, Note 13. The abbreviations below refer to the editions of the work used: not necessarily the best.

Abbreviations

AEA:	*Anuario de Estudios Americanos*
AGI:	Archivo General de Indias
AGN:	Archivo General Nacional (Mexico)
AGS:	Archivo General de Simancas (Simancas)
AHN:	Archivo Histórico Nacional (Madrid)
APS:	Archivo de Protocolos, Seville
BAE:	*Biblioteca de Autores Españoles*
BAGN:	*Boletín del Archivo General de la Nación*, Mexico
BRAH:	*Boletín de la Real Academia de la Historia*, Madrid
C:	Hernán Cortés, *Cartas de Relación, Historia 16*, Madrid 1985, ed. Mario Hernández.
Camargo:	Diego Muñoz Camargo, *Historia de Tlaxcala*, ed. Germán Vázquez, Madrid, 1986
C de S:	Francisco Cervantes de Salazar, *Crónica de la Nueva España*, The Hispanic Society of America, Madrid, 1914
CDI:	*Colección de documentos inéditos relativos al descubrimiento, conquista y organización de las posesiones españoles en América y Oceania*, 42 vols., Madrid, 1864 onwards, ed. Torres de Mendoza, Joaquín Pacheco and Francisco Cárdenas
CDIHE:	*Colección de documentos inéditos para la historia de España*, ed. M. de Navarrete, Madrid, 1842, 113 vols.
CDIU:	*Colección de documentos inéditos relativos al descubrimiento,*

	conquista y organización de las antiguas posesiones españoles de Ultramar, Madrid, 1884– 1932, 25 vols.
Cline's Sahagún:	*Conquest of New Spain* of Fr. Bernardino de Sahagún, 1588 revision, translated by Howard Cline with intr. by S. L. Cline, Salt Lake City, 1989
Cod. Ram:	Códice Ramírez
Conway:	Conway papers either in Aberdeen (Aber.), Cambridge (Camb.), Tulsa (Tul.), or Library of Congress, Washington (L of C)
D del C:	Bernal Díaz del Castillo, *Historia verdadera de la conquista de la Nueva España*, 2 vols., ed. Miguel León-Portilla, 2 vols., Madrid, 1984
DIHE:	*Documentos inéditos para la Historia de España*, Madrid, 1953–7
Docs Inéditos:	*Documentos inéditos relativos a Hernán Cortés y su familia, Publicaciones del Archivo General de la Nación* (Mexico, 1935), Vol. XXVII
Durán:	Fr. Diego Durán, *Historia de las Indias de Nueva España*, 2 vols., ed. Angel Garibay, Mexico, 1967
ECN:	*Estudios de Cultura Nahuatl* (Mexico)
Epistolario:	Francisco Paso y Troncoso, *Epistolario de Nueva España 1505–1818*, Mexico, 1939–42, 16 vols.
FC:	Florentine Codex, *The General History of the Things of New Spain*, by Fr. Bernardino de Sahagún, tr. Charles E. Dibble and Arthur J. Anderson, 12 vols., some revised, School of American Research, University of Utah, New Mexico, 1952 onwards. References to Vol xii are to the 2nd ed. 1975 unless otherwise stated.
G:	Francisco López de Gómara, *La Conquista de México*, ed. José Luis Rojas, Madrid, 1987
García Icazbalceta:	Joaquín García Icazbalceta, *Colección de documentos para la historia de México*, 3 vols., 1858–66, reprinted 1980
HAHR:	*Hispanic American Historical Review*
HM:	*Historia Mexicana*
HMAI:	*Handbook of Middle American Indians*
Inf. de 1521:	*Información hecha por Diego Velázquez sobre la armada que costeó*, an inquiry made in Santiago de Cuba, June 1521, published by Camilo de Polavieja, in *Hernán Cortés*: see below under Polavieja (it was also published in CDI, XXX, but page references are to Polavieja)
Inf. de 1522:	*Información de 1522, Mexico*, under the presidency of Alonso de Ávila, published in *BAGN*, 1938, t. ix, no.2
Inf. de 1565:	*Información recibida en Mexico y Puebla, el año de 1565*, Mexico, 1875; published as Vol. 20 of the Biblioteca Ibérica
Ixtlilxochitl:	Fernando Alva Ixtlilxochitl, *Historia de la Nación Chichimeca*, Madrid, 1985. For the same author's *Decimotercia Relación*, there is no general abbreviation
J. Díaz, et al.:	This is a collection of testimonies of eye-witnesses, viz. J. Díaz, Andrés de Tapia, Bernardino Vázquez de Tapia, and Francisco Aguilar, in *La Conquista de Tenochtitlan*, ed. Germán Vázquez, Madrid, 1988
JSAP:	*Journal de la société des américanistes de Paris*
Las Casas:	Bartolomé de Las Casas, *Historia de las Indias*, 3 vols., M. Aguilar, Madrid, 1927
MAMH:	*Memorias de la Academia Mexicana de la historia*

Martínez, *Docs*:	José Luis Martínez, *Documentos Cortesianos*, I (1518–28), II (1526–46), III (1528–32), IV (1533–48), Mexico, 1990, 1991
Martyr:	Peter Martyr, *De Orbe Novo*, tr. with notes by F. A. MacNutt, London, 1912
Muñoz:	Juan Bautista Muñoz collection, Real Academia de la Historia, Madrid
Oviedo:	Gonzalo Fernández de Oviedo, *Historia General y Natural de las Indias*, 5 vols. (Vols. 117 to 121 in *BAE*), ed. Juan Pérez de Tudela, Madrid, 1959
Polavieja:	General Camilo de Polavieja, *Hernán Cortés, Copias de Documentos existentes en el archivo de Indias ... sobre la Conquista de Méjico*, Seville, 1889
RAMH:	*Revista de la Academia Mexicana de la Historia*
R de I:	*Revista de Indias*
REE:	*Revista de Estudios Extremeños*
Rel. de Michoacan:	*Relación de las ceremonias y ritos y población y gobierno de los Indios de Michoacan*, 1541, tr. by José Tudela, with intr. by Paul Kirchhoff, Madrid, 1956
Res (Rayón):	Ignacio López Rayón, *Documentos para la historia de México*, Mexico, 1852–3. Documents from papers relating to the Residencia against Cortés.
Res vs Alvarado:	*Proceso de residencia instruido contra Pedro de Alvarado y Nuño de Guzmán*, ed. Ignacio López Rayón, Mexico, 1847
Res vs Velázquez:	Residencia tomada a Diego Velázquez, 1524, in AGI, leg. 149
RHA:	*Revista de la Historia de América*
RMEA:	*Revista Mexicana de Estudios Antropólogicos*
Sahagún:	Fr. Bernardino de Sahagún, *Historia General de las Cosas de Nueva España*, ed. Juan Carlos Temprano (Madrid, 1990, 2 vols.)
Sepúlveda:	Juan Ginés de Sepúlveda, *Historia del Nuevo Mundo*, ed. Antonio Ramírez Verger, Madrid, 1987

Minor Abbreviations

Ch.	chapter
cit.	cited
ed.	edition: edited by
f.	folio
fn.	footnote
intr.	introduced by
leg.	legajo
lib.	libro
N.F.	Neue Folge
n.s.	new series
p.	pieza, i.e. piece (in archives)
R.	Ramo, i.e. section (in archives)
r.	recto (in folio pages)
tr.	translation; translated by
v.	verso (in folio pages)
vol.	volume

Preface

1 *JSAP*, n.s., xxxix (1950).
2 Francisco Cervantes de Salazar, *México en 1554*, ed. Eduardo O'Gorman (Mexico, 1963), 64.
3 Durán, I, 260.
4 V. S. Naipaul, *The Overcrowded Barracoon* (London, 1972), 196.
5 Miguel León-Portilla, *Aztec Thought and Culture*, tr. (Norman, 1963), 177; Rudolph van Zantwijk, *The Aztec Arrangement* (Norman, 1985), xvii.
6 W. H. Prescott, *History of the Conquest of Mexico* (London, 1849), II, 439.
7 W. H. Prescott to Count Adolphe de Circourt, 19 November 1840, in *The correspondence of William Hickory Prescott*, ed. Roger Wolcott (Boston, 1925), 176.

Chapter 1

1 Fray Toribio de Benavente ("Motolinía"), *Historia de las Indias de Nueva España*, in García Icazbalceta, I, 177.
2 The first published text to speak of Mexico Tenochtitlan, *Newe Zeitung von dem Lande das die Spanier funden haben . . .* (probably Augsburg, early 1522), calls it a "great Venice" (*HAHR*, 1929, 200).
3 This was *tezontle*. Francisco de Cervantes in Tenochtitlan 1519 told Licenciado Vázquez de Ayllón in 1520 that there were *"Treynta casas de cal y canto fuertes"* (Polavieja, 81).
4 A recent estimate of Felipe Solís Olguín, "Mexico-Tenochtitlan, capital de la Guerra y los lagos de jade", in *Arte Precolombino de México* (Madrid, 1990), 100, gave 250,000.
5 Sahagún said that there were 78 sacred buildings but that cannot be so in the area concerned. No doubt Soustelle, and Eduard Seler, were right to think that this was the number of such edifices in different parts of the city (Jacques Soustelle, *La vie quotidienne des Aztèques à la vielle de la conquête espagnole* (Paris, 1955), 45, and Eduard Seler, cit. E. Hill Boone, *The Aztec Templo Mayor* (Washington, 1987), 37, fn. 13).
6 Miguel León-Portilla, *Precolombian literatures of Mexico* (Norman, 1969), 87.
7 Gift of Cortés, 1526 to Alonso de Grado and Isabel, daughter of Montezuma, AGI, Justicia, 181, cit. Amada López de Meneses, "Tecuichpoctzin, hija de Moctezuma", in *R de I*, 1948, 471–95.
8 Durán, II, 335–6; Alonso de Zorita, *Breve Relación de los señores de la Nueva España* (Madrid, 1992), 36.
9 I follow Soustelle in translating the Mexican term *Huey tlatoani*, literally high spokesman, as Emperor. I translate *tlatoani* as king or lord. For the numbers of polities, see Edward Calneck, "Patterns of Empire Formation in the Valley of Mexico", in George A. Collier, et al., *The Inca and Aztec states 1400–1800* (New York, 1982).
10 R. H. Barlow, "The Extent of the Culhua Empire" (Berkeley, 1949), 71.
11 The word "mosaic" is that of Soustelle [1:5], 20.
12 FC, ix, 48. See Jacqueline Durand Forest, "Cambios económicos y moneda entre los aztecas", *ECN*, ix (1971).
13 Camargo, 85. For Nahuatl, see Soustelle [1:5], 135, and Angel Garibay, *Historia de la literatura nahuatl* (Mexico, 1953, 2 vols.), I, 17. In the 18th century, Lorenzo Boturini thought Nahuatl "superior in elegance to Latin" (cit. León Portilla, [Preface:5]; while Fr. Clavijero, though less enthusiastic, thought that "spiritual matters could be well expressed in Nahuatl" (Francisco Javier Clavijero, *Historia Antiguo de México*, ed.

Mariano Cuevas, Mexico, 1964, 239). Classical Nahuatl of the 16th century does not survive. Dialects do (e.g in Milpa Alta, near the city of Mexico).

14 About 200 Nahuatl poems exist. Held in the memory (perhaps helped by some kind of pictographic guide with cues), they were (no doubt not always faithfully) written down after the conquest.

15 Garibay [1:13], I, 90.

16 Garibay [1:13], I, 29.

17 Zorita [1:8], 107: see Victor Wolfgang von Hagen, *The Aztec and Maya Papermakers* (New York, 1943), 12.

18 Alfredo López Austin, *La Constitución Real de México-Tenochtitlan* (Mexico, 1961), 141; Fernando Alvarado Tezozomoc, *Crónica Mexicayotl* (Mexico, 1949), 137.

19 Office holders can be seen in Fernando Alvarado Tezozomoc, *Crónica Mexicana* (Mexico, 1975), 268–9. By the 16th century the electoral college seems to have consisted of 13 high dignitaries; district officials; some serving and retired generals; and leading priests. There was no poll: as in surviving Nahuatl villages (and as with the PRI), in the 20th century, a name "emerged". Tezozomoc says that there were 14 electors.

20 Durán, II, 249.

21 León-Portilla speaks of this in "Mesoamerica before 1519", in *Cambridge History of Latin America*, ed. Leslie Bethell (Cambridge, 1984), I, 21.

22 FC, viii, 61. For these leaders, see Glossary.

23 See Ross Hassig, *Aztec Warfare* (Norman, 1988), 142; Rounds, "Dynastic succession and the centralisation of power in Tenochtitlan", in Collier, et al. [1:9], 70; Nigel Davies, *The Aztecs* (New York, 1973), 43; and Virve Piho, "Tlacatecutli, Tlacacochtecutli . . ." *ECN*, x (1972).

24 Nigel Davies, *The Toltec Heritage* (Norman, 1980), 340; for Tizoc, see Juan de Torquemada, *Monarquía Indiana* (Mexico, 1975), I, 185.

25 López Austin, *The Human Body and Ideology* (Salt Lake City, 1988, 2 vols.), I, 68–9.

26 Angel Garibay, *Vida económica de Tenochtitlan* (Mexico, 1961), 15; FC, vii, 23.

27 Ross Hassig, *Trade, Tribute and Transportation* (Norman, 1985), 121; van Zantwijk [Preface:5], 125–50; and Miguel Acosta Saignes, "Los Pochteca", *Acta Antropológica* (Mexico, 1945).

28 Durán, I, 38.

29 *Codex Mendoza*, ed. James Cooper Clark (London, 1938), I, 89; FC, iv, 3 and i, 200–4.

30 FC, ii, 3; vi, 171–2.

31 "El Conquistador Anónimo", in García Icazbalceta, I, 373. All these weapons were ancient in the Valley of Mexico: the bow, like fire, was probably brought from Asia by the original Americans between 35,000 BC and 8000 BC, when they came from Asia on the prehistoric land bridge now severed by the Bering Straits. See Edward McEwen, Robert L. Miller and Christopher A. Bergman, "Early Bow Design and Construction", *Scientific American*, June 1991. The Mexican bow was up to five feet long with either deerskin thong or animal sinew as a string. The arrows had a variety of points (obsidian, flint, bone) and were not poisoned. There were other versions of both sword (including a four-edged variety) and spear (one with three prongs).

32 Durán, II, 236.

33 Montezuma I to Tlacaelel, in Tezozomoc [1:19], 322.

34 Miguel León-Portilla, *Ritos, sacerdotes y atavíos de los dioses* (Mexico, 1958).

35 Durán, I, 165, 217; Tezozomoc [1:19], 539–40. Hassig [1:23], 60, thought that, "in an ordinary offensive war", a city of 200,000 might muster 43,000 warriors, if every male between 20 and 50 were called up.

36 "We did not seek trouble, they incited us" (Durán, II, 357).

37 Durán, II, 26, thought of the Mexica as Jews; see Alfonso Caso, "El Aguila y el Nopal", in *MAMH* v, no.2 (1946), 102.

38 FC, vi, 214.

39 Zorita [1:8], 163.

40 The appropriateness of this word is discussed by López Austin [1:18], 150.

41 FC, viii, 75–7.

42 H. B. Nicholson, "Religion in prehispanic Central Mexico", *HMAI*, 10 (Austin, 1971), 99 (the best general survey); Michel Graulich, *Mythes et rituels du Méxique ancien préhispanique* (Brussels, 1982), 85–6. See Gordon Brotherston, "Huitzilopochtli and what was made of him", in Norman Hammond, *Mesoamerican Archaeology: new approaches* (London, 1974).

43 Durán, I, 18–19.

44 The best introduction is Christian Duverger, *La conversion des Indiens de la Nouvelle Espagne* (Paris, 1987), 113.

45 Motolinía [1:1], 33–5.

46 Nicholson [1:42], 408–30.

47 *Historia de los mexicanos por sus pinturas, c.* 1535, in *Nueva Colección de Documentos para la historia de México*, ed. Joaquín García Icazbalceta (Mexico, 1941).

48 As quoted by Miguel León-Portilla, *Cantos y Crónicas del México antiguo* (Madrid, 1986). The difficulty of judging this cult is that all that is known of it derives from this king's by then Christian descendants, anxious to suggest that their ancestor was *en route* for his Damascus.

49 Angel Garibay, *Veinte himnos sacros de los nahuas* (Mexico, 1958), 53.

50 Camargo, 155.

51 FC, x, 192.

52 Alfonso Caso, *La religión de los Aztecas* (Mexico, 1936), 7–8. Still, Fernando Alva Ixtlilxochitl, great-grandson of this monarch, wrote, in the late 16th century (cit. Miguel León-Portilla, *Los antiguos mexicanos* (Mexico, 1961), 137) that his ancestor "held to be false all the gods adored in this country".

53 A text of 1547 describes how *"le diable abeusoyt leur faisant manger quelque herbe qu'ils noment nauacatl"*, *Histoyre du Mechique*, ed. Édouard de Jonghe, *JSAP*, n.s., xi (1905), 1, 18. Motolinía [1:1], 25, has a similar description. See Francisco Hernández, who said that these mushrooms produced "temporary dementia", and "immoderate laughter", while another variety produced all kinds of visions and demons (*Obras Completas*, Mexico, 1959, II, 396.) For commentary, see Mercedes de la Garza, *Sueño y alucinación en el mundo nahuatl . . .* (Mexico, 1990), 63. The chief hallucinogen-giving mushroom was the *Psilocybe Mexicana*. The peyote cactus is *Lophophora Williamsii*. The morning glory is *Ipomea Violacea*. Other plants inducing hallucination included the mescal bean and *salviaheimia* (which was said to enable people to recall events of years earlier). See Richard Evans Schultes, "Hallucinogens in the Western Hemisphere", in Peter Furst, *Flesh of the Gods* (New York, 1972), 2–11. V. P. and R. G. Wasson (*Mushrooms, Russia and History*, New York, 1957) think (286) that "the whole corpus of surviving pre-conquest artistic expression should . . . be reviewed on the chance that divine mushrooms figuring therein have hitherto escaped detection." Christian Duverger, *L'esprit du jeu chez les aztèques* (Paris, 1978), 107, suggests that the North American Indians brought the taste for these from Siberia and that the Mexica found the practice in the valley when they arrived.

Chapter 2

1 FC, x, 196: "who are the uncouth people?"

2 Patricia Rieff Anwalt and Frances F. Berdan, "The Codex Mendoza", *Scientific American*, June 1992, 45.

3 FC, ix, 1-2.

4 Zorita [1:8], 112; Soustelle [1:5], 50.

5 See López Austin [1:18], 99-109, and, for the defence, *Códice matritense: Real Academia de la Historia* (Mexico, 1952), 78, 80.

6 Zorita [1:8], 130.

7 Letter of Gerónimo López, 25 February 1545, on the basis of what Montezuma told Cortés, *Epistolario*, iv, 170.

8 *Codex Mendoza* [1:29], I, 91.

9 FC, x, 1-7.

10 FC, x, 1-7, 15-16. This Codex (II, 157) gave a vivid picture of the festival of Uahquiltamalqualiztli, when *pulque* was allowed: "All showed that they had drunk wine . . . with ruddy faces crying out short of breath, with glazed eyes all mingled one with another. There were disputes. All circled and milled about. Becoming more and more intense, all crowded and pressed together, elbowing each other. All took one another by the hand. They were bemused . . ."

11 *HAHR* (1929), 199.

12 Durán, II, 313.

13 Zorita [1:8], 15.

14 Paul Kirchhoff, "Land Tenure in Ancient Mexico", *RMEA*, xiii (1952), 351-61; H. R. Harvey, "Aspects of Land Tenure in Ancient Mexico", in *Exploration and Ethnohistory*, ed. H. R. Harvey and H. R. Prem (Albuquerque, 1984).

15 See Charles Gibson, *The Aztecs under Spanish Rule* (Stanford, 1964), 320 and 557 fn.113; Pedro Armillas, "Gardens on swamps", *Science* (1971), 174; Jeffrey Parsons, "The role of chinampa agriculture in the Food Supply of Aztec Tenochtitlan", in *Cultural Change* . . . ed. Chas. E. Cleland (New York, 1970); also Jeffrey Parsons, et al., *Prehispanic settlement in the southern valley of Mexico* (Ann Arbour, 1982).

16 This was 9,000 hectares. Pedro Armillas [2:15], 653, suggested that 2.4 acres of this kind of land would feed 20 people.

17 Hassig [1:27], 51.

18 Ixtlilxochitl, 123; 9. Teresa Rojas Rabiela, "Agricultural Implements in Mesoamerica", in Harvey and Prem [2:14], finds three types of hand tools and one operated by foot.

19 FC, x, 41-2.

20 In their letter to Charles V of 6 July 1519, the municipality of Vera Cruz commented, "they grow many chickens which . . . are as big as peacocks" (C, 66).

21 "*por todos los pueblos e provincias de su reino se habian de sembrar* **por fuerza** . . . *e habia veedores* . . ." (my emphasis) (*Epistolario*, IV, 169-70). William T. Sanders, et al., *The Basin of Mexico* (New York, 1979), 239, drew attention to this. Armillas [2:15], 660, thought the same: "the pattern of chinampa expansion . . . betokens control at a higher political level". The implication of the letter in the *Epistolario* is that this innovation occurred under Montezuma II.

22 Figures in Codex Mendoza, analysed by N. Molíns Fábregas, "El Códice Mendocino y la Economía . . ." in *RMEA*, xiii (1952-3), 2 and 3.

23 Sanders [2:21], 486, gave figures which suggests that venison accounted for only 1% of diet in comparison with a far higher percentage in the (remote) past.

24 Oviedo, IV, 248-50, on the basis of interviews, said, surely inaccurately, "these are the poorest people . . . in these Indies".

25 Zorita [1:8], 140.

26 Ixtlilxochitl, 204.

27 FC, x, 55.

28 FC, iv, 114; x, 16.

29 André Emmerich, *Sweat of the Sun and Tears of the Moon* (Seattle, 1965), xix.

30 Motolinía [1:1], 212.

31 W. F. Foshag, "Mineralogical studies in Guatemalan jade", Smithsonian Misc. Collection, 135 (Washington, 1957), 5.

32 FC, iv, 7, 19.

33 FC, iv, 144; H. B. Nicholson [1:42], 433.

34 Both the Cod. Ram., 64, and "Relacion de la Genealogía", in *Varias Relaciones de la Nueva España*, ed. Germán Vázquez (Madrid, 1991), 118, say that Acampichtli married 20 Mexican women who were "nobles, daughters of the lords of the territory . . . and from them descended all the lords"; presumably daughters of leaders of the *calpultin*.

35 *Códice matritense de la Real Academia*, viii, f.168, quoted by León-Portilla [Preface: 5], 168.

36 FC, x, 166.

37 Christian Duverger, *L'Origine des Aztèques* (Paris, 1987), Ch. II.

38 Both Paul Radin ("The Sources and Authenticity of the History of the Ancient Mexicans", *University of California Publications in American Archaeology*, XVII (1920), 1–150), and Duverger [2:37], 344, argued that Montezuma I was the inventor, with Tlacaelel.

39 Edward Calneck, "Patterns of Empire Formation . . ." in Collier, et al. [1:9], 51. See Enrique Florescano, in *HM*, 155, (1990), 101–25 and 607–62.

40 H. B. Nicholson [1:42], 433.

41 See Robert Stevenson's admirable *Music in Aztec and Inca Territory* (Berkeley, 1968). No tunes of antiquity are known.

42 Durán, I, 151.

43 "Los Primeros memoriales compilados en cuatro capítulos por Fray Bernardino de Sahagún como Fundamento . . ." ed. Paso y Troncoso (Madrid, 1905), 54 r., cit. Thelma D. Sullivan, "Tlatoani and Tlatocoyotl in the Sahagún manuscripts", *ECN*, xiv (1980), 225.

44 Durán, II, 235.

45 For the sacrifice as a game, see Duverger [1:53], 134.

46 *"Toutes les foys qu'ils gagnoynt quelque bataille, lui sacrifyont le meilleur esclave que prenoynt . . ."* (*Histoyre du Mechique* [1:53], 14).

47 See Miguel León-Portilla, "Tlacaelel y el sistema electoral . . ." in *Toltecayotl* (Mexico, 1980), 293–9. The Cod. Ram., 326, says that the Emperor "did nothing more than Tlacaelel advised him".

48 Durán, II, 171, calls him "bold and cunning . . . the devilish inventor of cruel and frightful practices". But see *Tlacaelel*, by Antonio Velasco Piña (Mexico, 1979).

49 This was the Codex Telleriano, quoted in *Codex Mendoza* [1:29], I, 37.

50 Van Zantwijk [Preface: 5], 208–20, gives a fine analysis. Motolinía, in a letter to Charles V, spoke of 80,400 being sacrificed in 1487 (*CDI*, II, 254). Durán, II, 340, has much the same number, on what he implies was the authority of what is now called the Crónica X. Chimalpahin spoke of 16,000 Zapotecs, 24 Tlapanecs, 16,000 Huexotzinca, and 24,000 Tzuihcoluaca (*Relaciones originales de Chalco, Amecameque*, Mexico, 1965). Cortés told Charles V that the figure was 3,000 or 4,000 a year (C, 67); Bernal Díaz calculated 2,000 (D del C, II, 455). Sherburne Cook calculated (in "Human Sacrifice and Warfare . . .", *Human Biology*, XVIII, May 1946) that if each victim were dispatched in two minutes, and if the sacrifices were to continue for four days (priests working in relays), 11,520 sacrifices could have been managed. One should have the same hesitation in accepting such figures as those for dead killed in battle. Walter Krickeberg, *Altmexanische Kulturen* (1956), 220, suggested 20,000. Woodrow Borah, surely exaggerating, proposed 15,000 a year for Tenochtitlan; and 150,000 for all Central Mexico. Burr Brundage, *The Jade Steps*

(Austin, 1985), 252, suggested between 4,000 and 16,000; Duverger [1:53], 221, seems to accept 4,000.

51 Tapia, in J. Díaz, et al., 108–9.

52 Bernard Ortiz de Montellano, "Counting skulls", *American Anthropologist*, 85 (1983), 403–4. A conquistador who talked to Fr. Durán said that the heads were so many that he could not count them (Durán, I, 23).

53 Durán, II, 300.

54 FC, ii, 42–5.

55 See Juan Alberto Román Berreleza, "Offering 48: Child sacrifice", in E. Boone [1:5], 135.

56 Paul Westheim, *Arte antiguo de México* (Mexico, 1985), 195.

57 The subject is discussed in Oswaldo Goncalves de Lima, *El Maguey y el pulque en los códices mexicanos* (Mexico, 1956), 202.

58 Durán, I, 140–1. See Francis Robicsek and Donald M. Hales, "Maya Heart sacrifice", in *Ritual Human Sacrifice in Mesoamerica*, ed. Elizabeth Hill Boone (Washington, 1984), 40–87.

59 Durán, II, 341.

Chapter 3

1 See Geoffrey W. Conrad and Arthur A. Demarest, *Religion and Empire: The Dynamics of Aztec and Inca Expansionism* (Cambridge, 1984), 70; and Warwick Bray, "Civilising the Aztecs" in J. G. Friedman and M. J. Rowlands, *The evolution of social systems* (London, 1977), 373.

2 So too was Cacaxtla, between Tlaxcala and Cholula, only 80 miles east of Tenochtitlan, whose beautiful murals were painted c. AD 790.

3 FC, III, 1.

4 See René Millon, Bruce Drewitt and George Cowgill, in *Urbanization in Teotihuacan* (Austin, 1973); Zelia Nuttall's ed. of *Relación de Teotihuacan* (*Official Reports on the towns of Tequixistlan, Tepechpan, Acolman, and S. Juan Teotihucan sent by Francisco de Castañeda to HM Philip II and the Council of the Indies 1580*), Papers of the Peabody Museum, xi, 2 (1926), 68; and Enrique Florescano, "Mito e historia en la memoria nahua", *HM*, 155 (1990), 622.

5 FC, vi, 43 and 81.

6 Miguel León-Portilla (ed.), *Cantos y Crónicas del México Antiguo* (Madrid, 1986), 169.

7 FC, vi, 93.

8 Sanders, et al. [2:21], 82.

9 Durán, II, 226.

10 Sanders, et al. [2:21], 184, suggested that the population may have been 175,000 in the Valley of Mexico in 1250, and was a million or 1.2 million in 1519.

11 Inga Clendinnen, *Aztecs* (Cambridge, 1991), 19.

12 Figures deriving from Codex Mendoza worked out by N. Molíns Fábregas, "El Códice mendocino y la economía de Tenochtitlan", *RMEA*, xiii (1952–3), 2–3, 315.

13 Among the dyes used were red from cochineal, red ochre, and red earth; blue from turquoise; yellow from yellow ochre.

14 Hassig [1:27], 145; D del C, I, 146, 177, gives these hours, the weight being two *arrobas* (that is, about 50 lb). Durán, II, 367, wrote of "a million Indians every eighty days". See Frances Berdan, "Luxury Trade and Tribute", in Boone [1:5], 163.

15 About 20 toys with wheels have been discovered. See Duverger [1:53], 162.

16 Sahagún, II, 587. Francisco Hernández [1:53], has a description of paper-making at Tepotzlan. See von Hagen [1:17], 35–6. His chapter (iv) on the myth that paper was made from the maguey cactus is revealing. Of these records, the *Matrícula de Tributos* (c.1519) is in the Archaeological Museum, Mexico. A copy, the Codex Mendoza, made c.1545 for the viceroy of that name, is in Oxford. A third piece of evidence is *Información sobre los tributos que los Indios pagaban a Montezuma, año 1554*, published by France V. Scholes and Eleanor Adams, in *Documentos para la historia de Mexico colonial* (Mexico, 1957). See also R. C. E. Long, "The payment of tribute in the Codex Mendoza", *Notes on Middle American Archaeology and Ethnology*, no.10 (Washington, 1942); and R. H. Barlow, "The periods of tribute collection in Moctezuma's empire", in the same, no.23 (1943).

17 Durán, II, 339.

18 See Edward Calnek, who, in "The Sahagún texts as a source of sociological information", in *Sixteenth century Mexico: the work of Sahagún*, ed. Munro Edmondson (Albuquerque, 1974), 202, thought that these could number tens of thousands by the early 1500s.

19 Ixtlilxochitl, *Obras*, II, 127. I owe this reference to Nigel Davies [1:24].

20 Durán, II, 214.

21 Patricia Anwalt, "Custom and Control: Aztec sumptuary laws", *Archaeology*, 33, 1, 33–43, has doubts about the efficacy of these rules; see J. Durand-Forest, *ECN*, 7 (1967), 67.

22 Zorita [1:8], 194.

23 Cod. Ram., 120, gives Montezuma's orders.

24 Durán, I, 226.

25 Samuel Ramos, *El perfil del hombre y la cultura de México* (Mexico, 1963), 35: much the same as the judgement of Alfonso Caso, in *The Aztecs: People of the Sun*, tr. (Norman, 1958), 96–7: the Mexica, he said, "lacked a progressive ideal which would have enabled them to conceive of life as something more than the invariable meticulous repetition of ceremonies in honour of gods . . ."

26 They may have descended from emigrant Mixtecs. See Donald Robertson, *Mexican Manuscript Painting in the Early Colonial Period* (New Haven, 1959), 138.

27 Sahagún, II, 119.

28 Zorita, *CDIHE*, II, 105; and C. de Molina, in *Actas del Cabildo de Mexico*, 54 vols., 1889–1916, xxiii. 144–5, cit. Gibson [2:15], 221.

29 Van Zantwijk [Preface:5], 27.

30 Frances Berdan, *The Aztecs of Central Mexico* (New York, 1982), 41. See Fred Hicks, "Mayeque y calpuleque en el sistema de clases . . .", in Pedro Carrasco and Johanna Broda, *Estratificación social en la Mesoamérica* (Mexico, 1976), 67; and Pedro Carrasco, "Los Mayeques", in *HM*, 153 (1989), 121–61.

31 *"Aunque los mataran o vendieran, no hablaban . . ."* Sebastián Ramírez de Fuenleal, President of the Audiencia (1532), in *CDIHE*, XIII, 256.

32 The controversies are summarised by Yoloti González Torres, "La esclavitud entre los Mexica", in Carrasco and Broda [3:30], 78.

33 FC, xi, 270.

34 FC, iv, 11.

35 Tezozomoc [1:18], 117–21; for this dispute, see R. C. Padden's brilliant if negative *The Hummingbird and the Hawk* (New York, 1967), 45.

36 Victorious generals received a share of the tax on what was sold in the part of the market allocated to them. This was evidently an assertion in the lost Crónica X, as argued by R. H. Barlow, in *RMEA*, vii (1945), 1, 2 and 3. See also Barlow's "Tlatelolco como Tributario de la Triple Alianza", in *Tlatelolco a través de los tiempos* (Mexico, 1945), IV, 20–34.

37 The word "Tarascan" was a Spanish adaptation of a Purépccha one. See *Rel. de Michoacan*; and J. Benedict Warren, *La Conquista de Michoacan* (Norman, 1985), Ch. I. For the campaign, see Hassig [1:23], 186–7.

38 This was a phrase in the Crónica X, as quoted in Durán, II, 284.

39 The Mexica, Texcocans, and even the Tlaxcalans, considered themselves Chichimec in origin. In heroic mood, they so called themselves: which by the 16th century they were not.

40 Durán, II, 359; Hassig [1:23], 119.

41 Durán, II, 236.

42 Fred Hicks, "Flowery War in Aztec History", *The American Ethnologist*, February 1979. Nigel Davies, in *The Aztec Empire* (Norman, 1987), 238, pointed out that something similar occurred in Papua, Borneo and even New Zealand: war for heads, not territory.

43 She was said to have had many lovers, whom she had killed after they had made love to her. She had statues made of them, and dressed these elaborately. One day, she unwisely gave a current lover a jewel given to her by Nezahualpilli. Nezahualpilli arrived one night at her rooms, found her in the company of three men, saw the jewel and the statues, and had all four executed (Ixtlilxochitl, 195).

44 Ixtlilxochitl, 218–19.

Chapter 4

1 A Jamaican woman was found by Cortés in 1519 in Cozumel. See Ch. 12.

2 Fray Toribio Motolinía, *Memoriales*, ed. Joaquín García Icazbalceta (Mexico, 1905), 155; G, 313.

3 Motolinía, in García Icazbalceta, I, 65.

4 Sahagún, I, 341.

5 "He had news of the arrival of the Christians from merchants who had been to the fairs on those coasts", Fernando Alva Ixtlilxochitl, *Decimatercia Relación* (Mexico, 1938), 7.

6 For these colonies, see Ch. 5. See too Ryszard Tomicki's "Las profecías aztecas de los principios del siglo XVI y los contactos maya-españoles ..." (*Xochipilli*, Madrid, 1, 1986).

7 FC, ii, 33–4.

8 These portents appear in one form or another in most 16th-century accounts: e.g. FC, xii, 1–3; *Historia de los mexicanos por sus pinturas* [1:47], 254: Camargo [1:13], 179–83; Domingo ... Chimalpahin, *Séptima relación*, tr. Rémi Siméon (Paris, 1889), 181; Cod. Ram., 128; *Codex Aubin (Código de 1576)*, tr. Charles Dibble (Madrid, 1963); and Torquemada [1:24], I, 324. The last-named work tells of the vision of Princess Papantzlin, sister of the Emperor, who returned, shaken, from the dead, having seen Spaniards in hell.

9 *Rel. de Michoacan*, 231–6; Camargo [1:13], 183–4; see Diego Landa, *Relación de Yucatan*, ed. A. M. Tozzer (Cambridge, Mass., 1941), 42–3, especially fn. 214.

10 Durán, II, 459. The same story is in the Cod. Ram., 126.

11 Ixtlilxochitl, 212–13.

12 Durán, II, 459.

13 FC, iv, 151–69. See Ignacio Romerovargas, *Moctezuma el magnífico* (Mexico, 1963, 3 vols.), I, 141, for suggestions of 3 eclipses of the sun, 9 comets and several aurorae borealis in the reign of Montezuma II.

14 Francesco Flora and Carlo Cordiè, *Tutte le Opere di Niccolò Machiavelli* (Milan, 1949), I, 214.

15 Jacob Burckhardt, *The Civilisation of the Renaissance in Italy* (London, 1945), 315.

16 Montaigne, *Oeuvres complètes* (Paris, 1962), 690.

17 This interpretation was pursued with learning by Felipe Fernández-Armesto, in "'Aztec' auguries and memories of the conquest of Mexico", in *Renaissance Studies*, 6 (1992), 287–305. He points to the "thunderbolts without noise", the light and the chariots in the sky, the prodigies, and the frenzied woman in Lucan, in Josephus, as in Plutarch – many of which authors, he shows, were in the library of Santa Cruz in Tlatelolco by the 1540s. Josephus was particularly popular. See also Tzvetan Todorov, *La conquête de l'Amérique* (Paris, 1982), 97, who suggested that, in late 16th-century America, the present could only become intelligible if one could be certain that it had been foretold.

18 M. Minnaert, *The Nature of Light and Colour in the Open Air* (New York, 1954). Mexico is within the belt of the aurora borealis.

19 Codex Vaticanus A (Rome, 1900) for 1489; A. Aveni, *Skywatchers of Ancient Mexico* (Austin, 1980), 26, as in FC, vii, for 1496; and for 1506, Lorenzo Galíndez de Carvajal, *Anales Breves del Reynado . . .* , in *CDIHE*, XVIII, 316; and D. K. Yeomans, *Comets: a Chronological History of Observation, Science and Folklore* (Wiley, 1991), appendix.

20 Aveni [4:19], 96.

21 Tezozomoc [1:19]; Davies [1:24], 127, warns, "it is not . . . possible to say for certain whether Montezuma ascended the throne in 1501, 1502, or 1503".

22 Aguilar, in J. Díaz, et al., 181; Cod. Ram., 118.

23 Cod. Ram., 121; *Codex Mendoza* [1:29], I, 41; Durán, II, 407.

24 Sahagún so speaks of the reaction at the time of his funeral; Durán, loc. cit., wrote, "he was the greatest butcher who ever lived".

25 FC, viii, 42.

26 So he told Cortés (Gerónimo López, in *Epistolario*, X, 168).

27 Aveni [4:19] discusses.

28 Durán, II, 398, 414: the reaction of those who chose him.

29 300–400, according to Cortés (C, 140), though figures of that *Caudillo* are often imaginative.

30 *Codex Mendoza* [1:29], II, 69.

31 Chimalpahin [4:8], 225; Tezozomoc [1:18], 125 and 151.

32 Tezozomoc [1:18], 149–58, gives the names of nineteen children (and descendants). Oviedo, iv, 262, speaks of 150 as something he had heard. See Luis Cuesta and Jaime Delgado. "Pleitos Cortesianos en la Biblioteca Nacional", *R de I*, January–June 1948, where the main children are discussed. Juan Cano insisted that his wife Tecuichpo, Montezuma's "favourite daughter" (see Epilogue), was the Emperor's heiress, no doubt for legal reasons of his own.

33 See C, 112; D del C, I, 322–9; FC, viii, 3; *El Conquistador Anónimo*, in García Icazbalceta, II, 382; Miguel León-Portilla, *Crónicas Indígenas, La visión de los vencidos* (Madrid, 1985), 76. See too Davies [1:23], 206–37.

34 FC, ix, 91.

35 Esther Pasztory, *Aztec Art* (New York, 1984), an admirable study.

36 Durán, II, 439, recalled seeing in the 1550s remains of these idols in the streets.

37 Tezozomoc [1:19], 683–4. Tezozomoc was son of Francisca Moctezuma, daughter of Montezuma II, by Diego Huantzin, a nephew of the last emperor. He was born about 1525, and owned such documents of his family which could be saved from the siege of Tenochtitlan.

38 Another version of this story is that the majordomo heard of what was said by this informant through an eavesdropper.

39 *Historia . . . por sus pinturas* [1:47], 254.

40 This magician was Martín Ocelotl who, after the conquest, became rich. Baptised in 1526, he would, with his brothers, be charged by the Spaniards of leading a movement against Christianity. He was accused, at his trial in 1536, of having boasted that Montezuma had had him cut up, but that he survived by becoming magically whole again. He was sentenced to be imprisoned by the Inquisition in Seville in 1537 but on the way there his ship sank. See Luis González Obregón, "Procesos de indios idólatras y hechiceros", in *Publicaciones del Archivo General de la Nación*, 3 (1912), 17–35; and, for commentary, see Jorge Klor de Alva, "Martín Ocelotl: clandestine cult leader", in D. G. Sweet and Gary B. Nash, *Struggle and Survival in Colonial America* (Berkeley, 1981).

41 Tezozomoc [1:19], 684.

42 Durán, II, 500.

43 Durán, II, 485.

44 R. H. Barlow [1:11], 91, fn.1; Tezozomoc [1:19], 684 fn. It probably was at the present site of Boca del Río.

45 Tezozomoc, [1:19], 684 fn.; Durán, II, 506; FC, ii, 168.

46 Tezozomoc, [1:19], 684–5; Durán, II, 505–7.

47 Tezozomoc, [1:19], 685. What follows derives also from Durán (who used the same Crónica X), II, 507, and FC, xii, 5–7. I have assumed that what Tezozomoc said happened now occurred a year later.

48 FC, xii, 5.

49 FC, xii, 6, and Sahagún II 952.

50 See the stone standard-bearer, with six rows of beads round his neck, in the Museum of Anthropology, Mexico.

51 Most of this derives from Duran, II, 507, but Tezozomoc has the same story.

52 FC, xii (1st ed.), 5–7.

53 Durán, II, 267.

54 FC, xii; Cod. Ram., 131; Cline's Sahagún, 37. Durán, II, 507, says that, as early as this, Montezuma began to think that the stranger might constitute a god, especially the god Quetzalcoatl. See Ch. 14.

55 Todorov [4:17], 112.

56 Durán, II, 514, 525.

Chapter 5

1 *O rey Don Hernando y Doña Isabel*
   En vos comenzaron los siglos dorados;
   Serán todos tiempos nombrados
   Que fueron regidos por vuestro nivel
Cancionero de Juan del Encina, Salamanca, 20 June 1496, ed. E. Cotarelo (Madrid, 1928).

2 Hassig [1:27], 57. For the sail, see Ch. 7., fn 17. "*Canoa*" was a Caribbean word, as were "*cacique*", "*pulque*" "*maguey*" and "*maiz*".

3 Durán, II, 128.

4 Tezozomoc [1:19].

5 See S. K. Lothrop, *Archaeology of Southern Veragua, Pánama*, Peabody Museum, Memoirs, IX, No. 3, 1958; and Doris Stone, *Introduction to the Archaeology of Costa Rica* (San José, 1958).

6 Emmerich [2:29], 145.

7 Graulich [1:42], 68–9; Pasztory [4:35], 102.

8 Las Casas, III, 173; Carl Sauer, *The Early Spanish Main* (Berkeley, 1966), 212.

9 *CDI*, XI, 428. Stevenson [2:41] argued that the *teponaztli* had reached Hispaniola.

10 Irving Rouse, *The Tainos* (New Haven, 1992), 56–7.

11 They were called turkeys because they were first imported into Spain, and then England, at a time when the mainland of America was supposed to lie off the Asian coast. Cf. *"granturco"*, the Italian word for maize, a consequence of a similar mistake. See Hugh Honour, *The New Golden Land* (London, 1975), 39.

12 Cristóbal Colón, *Textos y documentos completos*, intr. Consuelo Varela (Madrid, 1982), 293; Fernando Colón, *The Life of the Admiral Christopher Columbus* (tr. Benjamin Keen, New Brunswick, 1992), 231; for the identification of the place, see Mauricio Obregón, *Colón en el mar de los Caribes* (Bogotá, 1992), 235–6.

13 Ramón Ezquerra, "El viaje de Pinzón y Solís al Yucatan", in *R de I*, XXX (1970), 217–38. Documents relating to the voyage can be seen in *CDI*, XXII, 5–13, and XXXVI, 210–21.

14 Ponce de León came from a Sevillano family but was born in Santervás de Campos in the modern province of Valladolid. He was probably one of the 21 illegitimate children of the Count Juan Ponce de León and, therefore, half-brother of the (also bastard) Marquis of Cádiz ("the Ulysses of the war against Granada"). See V. Murga Sanz, *Juan Ponce de León* (San Juan, 1971), 23. One of his sons by Beatriz de Luna would be a companion of Cortés, Juan González (Ponce) de León, for whose life see AGI, Mexico, leg. 203, no. 19. For the journey, see S. E. Morison, *The European discovery of America: the Southern Voyages, AD 1492–1616* (New York, 1974); and Aurelio Tío's excellent "Historia del descubrimiento de la Florida o Beimeino y Yucatán", in *Boletín de la Academia Puertorriqueña de la Historia*, II (8) (1972), 81–2. Tío argues that Montezuma first got wind of the Castilians as a result.

15 See Michael Closs, "New Information on the European Discovery of Yucatan", *American Antiquity*, 41, (1976), 192–5.

16 Martyr, I, 400 (letter to Pope Leo X).

17 Peter Boyd-Bowman estimated that, of Spanish emigrants to the New World between 1505 and 1518, 40% were Andalusian, 18% from Old Castile, 14% from Extremadura, 8% from New Castile, 7% from León, and 6% Portuguese or Basques (*Índice Geobiográfico de más de 56 mil pobladores de América en el siglo xvi*, Mexico 1985). Pieter Jacobs Auke points out that Boyd-Bowman, Bermúdez Plata, and even Chaunu, neglect illegal passages and traffic from cities other than Seville: in the early 16th century there was a trickle of emigration from Corunna, Bayona (Galicia), Avilés, Laredo, Bilbao, San Sebastián, Cartagena, Málaga and Cádiz. José Luis Martínez, with the same percentages as Boyd-Bowman, estimated a total of Spanish emigration to the Indies between 1493 and 1519 as 5,481; 2,172 from Andalusia, 987 from Old Castile, and 769 from Extremadura (*Pasajeros de Indias*, Mexico, 1984).

18 Marie-Claude Gerbet, *La noblesse dans le royaume de Castille* (Paris, 1979), 367, argued that, among the 353 Extremeños who went to the Indies between 1509 and 1518, 32 (9%) were hidalgos.

19 Luis Arranz, *Emigración española a Indias* (Santo Domingo, 1979).

20 Diego de Ordaz to Francisco Verdugo, 23 August 1529, AGI, Justicia, leg. 712, cit. Enrique Otte, *Nueve Cartas de Diego de Ordaz*, in *HM*, 53 and 54, v, xiv, July–September and October–December 1964, 114; Francesco Guicciardini in *Viajes de Extranjeros por España y Portugal* (Madrid, 1952), 614.

21 Las Casas, III.

22 Eleven ducats was the rate in 1506; the equivalent of 4,125 maravedís, a year's income for an unskilled workman in, say, a workshop in Seville.

23 Marcel Bataillon, *Erasme et Espagne* (Paris, 1937), 65, fn.1.

24 Jocelyn Hillgarth, *The Spanish Kingdoms, 1250–1516* (2 vols., Oxford, 1976), II, 424.

25 In Jehan Wauquelin's *Histoire du bon roy Alexandre* (Paris, written c. 1448).

Alexander's real exploits were eclipsed by legend. See J. Huizinga, *The Waning of the Middle Ages* (London, 1924), and *Circa 1492* (Washington, 1991), 122.

26 The first printed book in Spain described a synod in the diocese of Segovia. It was produced by Juan Parix of Heidelberg, for Bishop Juan Arias Ávila, in 1472.

27 Huizinga, referring to any printed book, in *Erasmus of Rotterdam* (London, 1924), 65. See also Irving Leonard, *Books of the Brave* (New York, 1964).

28 Aguilar, in J. Díaz, et al., 204.

29 Bataillon [5:23] wrote of Santillana's *Proverbs*: "Few books were so popular in Spain at the time when Erasmus published in Venice his treasury of quotations ..." For publication dates, see *Catálogo de Incunables* (Madrid, 1988–90).

30 Julio Valdeón Baruque, "España en vísperas del descubrimiento", *Historia 16*, 198, 26. For López, see *Publicaciones del Archivo General de la Nación*, Vol. XII (Mexico, 1927), 328.

31 *The Poem of the Cid*, bilingual ed. (London, 1984), 86.

32 *Amadis of Gaul*, ed. and tr. R. Southey (London, 1872), III, 181.

33 J. Huizinga [5:25], 19.

34 Varela, ed. [5:12], 302.

35 Recalled 1536 by Fernán Yáñez de Montiel, of Huelva, in Juan Gil, *Mitos y Utopías del Descubrimiento*, (Sevilla, 1989), I, 47.

36 Víctor Pradera, *El Estado Nuevo* (Madrid, 1941), 276.

37 Antoine de Lalaing, "Primer viaje de Felipe el Hermoso", in *Viajes* [5:20], 483.

38 Pierre and Juliette Chaunu recorded 186 ships to Santo Domingo, 12 to Puerto Rico, 14 to Cuba (*Séville et L'Atlantique, 1504–1650* (Paris, 1956, 10 vols.), II, 12–101.

39 Martyr, I, 103–4. Despite Irving Rouse, *The Tainos* (New Haven, 1992), the most complete study remains S. Loven's *Origin of the Tainan Culture* (Göteborg, 1935). See also Rouse and José Juan Arrom, "The Tainos", in *Circa 1492* (Washington, 1992), 509–13; and *La Cultura Taína* (Madrid, 1991).

40 The best study of Ovando's expedition is J. Pérez de Tudela, *Las Armadas de Indias y las orígenes de la política de colonización 1492–1505* (Madrid, 1956), 192 ff.

41 See Ursula Lamb, *Fray Nicolás de Ovando, Gobernador de las Indias* (Madrid, 1956), 27; also Robert S. Chamberlain, *The Castilian background of the repartimiento-encomienda* (Carnegie Institution, Washington, 1939), 39.

42 Oviedo, II, 103; Las Casas, II, 27.

43 Luis Arranz, *Don Diego Colón* (Madrid, 1982), I, 111.

44 Quoted in Morison [5:14], 157.

45 This was at the time of the *repartimiento* of 1513. See *CDI*, I, 50–236. The size of the population of Hispaniola in 1492 is a controversial issue. I have adopted the modest estimate of Angel Rosenblat in, for example, *The native population of the Americas in 1492*, ed. William M. Denevan (Madison, 1976), 48–9. Like Rosenblat, I accept that there was a demographic disaster, but I do not believe it to have been on the scale sometimes suggested. Charles Verlinden, "Le repartimiento de Rodrigo de Albuquerque à Hispaniola en 1514" in *Mélanges offerts à G. Jacquemyns* (Bruxelles, 1968), suggested 55,000–60,000. Frank Moya Pons, "Datos para el estudio de la demografía aborigen en Santo Domingo", in *Estudios sobre política indigenista española en América* (Valladolid, 1977), III, 15–18, thinks in terms of 400,000. Arranz's examination of the issue in *Repartimientos y Encomiendas en la Isla española* (Madrid, 1991), 30–64, is convincing. Rouse eschews a figure.

Las Casas (in numerous citations; see Rosenblat op. cit. 48–9) spoke of Hispaniola having a population of 3 million in 1492. Oviedo thought of 1 million, as does Zambardino in *HAHR*, 58 (4) (1978), 700–712. Judge Zuazo gave 1,1430,000. Pierre Chaunu, "La Population de l'Amérique Indienne" in *Revue Historique* (July–September 1969), gave 3 million. S. Cook and W. Borah, *Essays in Population History, Mexico and the Caribbean, Vol. I* (Berkeley, 1971), 408, allowed themselves, surely with grave risk to their great reputations, 7–8 million. An excellent study by David Henige, "On the contact population of Hispaniola: history as Higher Mathematics", *HAHR*, 58 (2) (1978), 217–37, disposes of Borah and Cook, concluding that "it is futile to offer any numerical estimates at all on the basis of the evidence before us". Most demographic historians have neglected the Spanish archives used by Arranz.

46 Rouse [5:39], 161.

47 José María Pérez Cabrera, "The Circumnavigation of Cuba by Ocampo", in *HAHR*, 18 (1938), 101–5.

48 Sauer [5:8], 189.

49 Martyr, II, 52.

50 Juan Ginés de Sepúlveda, *De Orbe Novo (Historia del Nuevo Mundo)* (Madrid, 1987), 80 (he was Charles V's official historian); I. A. Wright, *The Early History of Cuba* (New York, 1916), 15.

51 These imported Indians were not legally slaves but permanent servants, *naborías perpetuas*, unlike the natives of Hispaniola who were supposed to work two-thirds of the time.

52 Alfonso de Zuazo to the Prince de Croy (Chièvres), 22 January 1518 in *CDI*, I, 316: "*E pidióles que le diesen oro, si no que los quemaría ó los appearearía . . .*"

53 "Totalitarian transpersonalism" in politics, "caesaropapist regalism" in religion and total corruption in economic life is how Giménez Fernández characterises the place in those days.

54 *Brevísima Relación de la Destruyción de las Indias*, ed. José Alcina Franch, in *Las Casas, Obra Indigenista* (Madrid, 1982). It was written in 1542 to inform the future Philip II.

Chapter 6

1 Felipe Fernández-Armesto, *Columbus* (Oxford, 1992), 153.

2 Las Casas, I, 318–19; II, 383–5.

3 Quoted in Lewis Hanke, *The Spanish Struggle for Justice in the Conquest of America* (Philadelphia, 1949), 27.

4 See Eloy Bullón Fernández, *Un colaborador de los Reyes católicos: el doctor Palacios Rubios* (Madrid, 1927), 121.

5 Aristotle, Book IB, in Ernest Barker's ed. (Oxford, 1946), 11–18.

6 See Juan López de Palacios Rubios, *De las islas del mar*, ed. Silvio Zavala and Agustín Millares Carlo (Mexico, 1954), cit. D. A. Brading, *The First America* (Cambridge, 1991), 80.

7 L. B. Simpson prints the text in *The Encomienda in New Spain* (Berkeley, 1929).

8 Hanke [6:3], 23.

9 Bullón [6:4], 136.

10 Palacios Rubios' mockery is noted by Oviedo (III, 31–3), who talked to him in 1516.

11 Las Casas, II, 581.

12 "*dijieron que el papa deviera estar borracho . . .*", Martín F. de Enciso, *Suma de geografía* (Seville, 1519), hiii v. This was when he had been with Pedrarias in 1515. See María del Carmen Mena García, *Pedrarias Dávila o "la ira de Dios"* (Seville, 1992), 65.

13 Mena García [6:12], 43. The first *Requerimiento* is in AGI, Panamá, leg. 233, lib. 1, 49–50. There are several English translations. e.g., in *Documents of West Indian History, 1492–1655*, ed. Eric Williams (Trinidad, 1963), 59–61.

14 See Claudio Guillén, "Un padrón de conversos sevillanos (1510)" in *Bulletin Hispanique*, LXV (1963), 79; Américo Castro, *De La Edad Conflictiva* (Mexico, 1961), 264; and Francisco Morales Padrón, *Historia de Sevilla* (Seville, 1989), 99. Rafael Sánchez Saus, *Caballería y linaje en la Sevilla medieval* (Cádiz, 1989), 137, suggests a French origin. But a good way to disguise ancestry was to give the family foreign roots. In the late 17th century, a boy was asked in Spain by a monk what his name was. The answer was "at home Abraham, Father. Outside it, Francisquito".

15 Fray A. de Remesal, *Historia general de las Indias Occidentales, BAE* (Madrid), I (1964), 142.

16 Raymond Marcus, "El primer decenio de Las Casas en el Nuevo Mundo", *Ibero-Amerikanische Archiv*, v, 21, N. F., 1977, 107.

17 Alcina Franch [5:54], 149.

18 Las Casas, II, 495.

19 Las Casas, III, 58–61; Manuel Giménez Fernández, *Bartolomé de Las Casas* (Seville, 1953 and 1960, 2 vols.), I, 51 (a masterpiece to which I am indebted).

20 Las Casas, III, 75–80.

21 There is no modern biography of Cisneros. But see Rosario Díez del Corral Garnica, *Arquitectura y mecenazgo. La imagen de Toledo en el renacimiento* (Madrid, 1987), 60–77.

22 Las Casas, III, 90.

23 Giménez Fernández [6:19], II, 553.

24 Wright [5:50], 70.

25 Las Casas, III, 89–97. Simpson [6:7], 191–205, gives Ximenez's instructions to the priors. Figueroa was prior of La Mejorada, near Olmedo (Valladolid), and a favourite retreat of Queen Isabel; Manzanedo was prior of Monta Marta, Zamora; Santo Domingo was prior of San Juan de Ortega, Burgos; while Salvatierra was an intimate of Figueroa. Zuazo was a protégé of Palacio Rubios. In the University of Valladolid, Zuazo's birthplace is given as Pardiñas, near Segovia. See Ana Gimeno Gómez, "Los Proyectos de Alonso de Zuazo en búsqueda del estrecho", *Actas del Congreso de Historia del descubrimiento* (Madrid, 1992, 4 vols.).

26 Zuazo to the Emperor, 22 January 1518, *CDI*, I, 310.

27 See their enquiry of leading settlers in *CDI*, XXXIV, 201–29, and Emilio Rodríguez Demorizi, *Los Dominicanos y las encomiendas de la Isla Española* (Santo Domingo, 1971), 273–354.

28 Their reports are in *CDI*, I, 347–70, and XXXIV, 279–86. A letter of Manzanedo to Charles V is in Manuel Serrano y Sanz, *Orígenes de la Dominación Española en América* (Madrid, 1918), 567–75.

29 Zuazo [6:26], 312.

30 He later became interested in pearl and slave trading; Pasamonte to Charles V, 10 July 1517, in Serrano y Sanz [6:28], 558.

31 Rosenblat, in Denevan [5:45], 56.

32 Serrano y Sanz [6:28], 567–75.

33 Las Casas, II, 449.

34 Galíndez de Carvajal, *CDIHE*, XVIII, 384–5. For the Velázquez family (to whom the Loyolas were connected through the Velascos), see Caro Lynn, *A college professor of the renaissance* (Chicago, 1937), 225–6, and Alonso de Santa Cruz, *Crónica de Carlos V* (Madrid, 1922–5), ii, 126. For the Infante Juan, see Oviedo's *Libro de Cámara del Príncipe Don Juan* (Madrid, 1870). For St Ignatius' years with Velázquez at Arévalo, see Leonard V. Matt and Hugo Rattner, *St Ignatius of Loyola* (London, 1956), 9–10. Juan Velázquez resisted, arms in the hand, the grant of Arévalo, Madrigal and Olmedo, to the King's stepmother, Germaine de Foix. For Sancho Velázquez, see José Antonio Escudero, "Los Orígenes de la Suprema Inquisición", in A. Alcalá, et al., *Inquisición*

española y mentalidad inquisitorial (Barcelona, 1984), 100.
35 See Balbino Velasco Bayón, *Historia de Cuéllar* (Segovia, 1974).
36 He could scarcely have served in Naples, as suggested by Gonzalo de la Torre de Trasierra in *Cuéllar* (Madrid, 1896), 2nd part, 217.
37 Oviedo, II, 112.
38 Las Casas, II, 168–9.
39 Las Casas, II, 452.
40 Levi Marrero, *Cuba, economía y sociedad* (San Juan, 1972), 30.
41 Las Casas, III, 470.
42 For the indigenous population, see Marrero [6:40], 56. A sensible figure might be 80,000. Las Casas was with Narváez on this journey – apparently as a foot soldier – and left an account in III, 486–7. One householder, he wrote, described how only 1 in 10 Cubans survived after 3 months. This was typical of his use of figures.
43 Baracoa, Santiago de Cuba, San Cristóbal de la Habana (at first on the south, not the north coast), Trinidad, Sancti Spiritus, San Salvador de Bayamo and Puerto Príncipe. The last-named was later moved from the shore to the inland site which it now has, with its name changed to Camagüey. There was also a settlement at Xagua (Cienfuegos).
44 "Relación de Alonso de Parada in 1527", in *CDI*, XL, 265.
45 *Inf. de 1521*, in Polavieja, 304. He was a bad judge of good behaviour.
46 Las Casas, II, 450. In the *residencia* against him, after his death, he was accused of having permitted too-lavish banquets to be given for him: see AGI, Justicia, leg. 49, f.112.
47 Las Casas, II, 476.
48 *CDIHE*, I, 196–200; also Ruth Pike, *Enterprise and Adventure* (Ithaca, 1966), 103.
49 François Chevalier, *Le Tabac* (Paris, 1948).
50 For this court, see Gabriel Maura, *El Príncipe que murió de amor* (Madrid, 1953). A royal instruction of 1516 told Cuéllar and a colleague, Andrés de Haro, to hand over the gold which they had in their control (AGI, Indif. Gen., leg. 419, lib. 6, f.30, quoted in Giménez Fernández [6:19], I, 487). For the Infante's excessive lovemaking, see Charles V's letter of 1542 to Philip II, in Karl Brandi, *The Emperor Charles V* (tr. London, 1949).
51 Las Casas, II, 475.
52 Las Casas, II, 476, described him as "only one cubit in size but sensible and very silent and wrote well". For Duero, see AGI, Indif. Gen., leg. 419, lib. 8, ff.36v.–37, and lib. 10, f.289.
53 See map at the back of Velasco's *Historia de Cuéllar* [6:35].
54 Velázquez's *repartimiento* and those who benefited can be seen in *Epistolario*, II, 128–31.
55 Application to bring in three slaves was granted, 22 March 1518. See *Epistolario*, I, 36.
56 The flavour of this trade can be gathered from the letters of Hernando de Castro to Antonio de Nebreda, published by Enrique Otte in "Mercaderes Burgaleses en los inicios del comercio con México", *HM*, July–September 1968.
57 Fr. Mariano Cuevas (ed.), *Cartas y otros documentos de Hernán Cortés nuevamente descubiertos en el Archivo General de Indias* (Seville, 1915), 330; see "Relación de . . . Parada" [6:44], 260.
58 Columbus and Garay had married two of three sisters, Felipa and Ana. A third sister, Briolanja, first married Miguel Moliart, a Valencian, later a Florentine, Francesco de' Bardi.
59 Giménez Fernández [6:19], II, 316.
60 For the Esquivel family, see Sánchez Saus [6:14], 167–76.
61 Martyr, II, 324, 346–8; Las Casas, III, 207.
62 Morison [5:14], 505, described him as young, valiant and enterprising but Las Casas called him the most ruthless of all the conquistadors. Nor was he very young.

63 Oviedo, II, 103.

64 Sancho Velázquez derived from Olmedo or from Arévalo, no distance from Cuéllar, and his father's name was Diego (Mgr. Murga Sanz, *Historia documental de Puerto Rico, Juicio de Residencia de Sancho Velázquez . . . 1519–1520*, Seville, 1957, xcviii).

65 "*Ríos de oro mui ricos*": letter of Núñez de Balboa, 20 January 1513, in Angel de Altolaguirre, *Vasco de Balboa* (Madrid, 1914), 19. See also Demetrio Ramos, "'Castilla del Oro', el primer nombre dado oficialmente al continente americano", *AEA*, XXXVII, 5–67.

66 See table in Edward Cooper, *Castillos señoriales en la corona de Castilla* (2nd ed. Salamanca, 1991, 2 vols.), Vol. II, 1034.

67 Their departure from Seville was described by Alonso de Zuazo in a letter to Croy (Chièvres), January 1517, cit. Sauer [5:8], 248–9.

68 Las Casas, II, 565.

69 This conquistador thus echoes the actions of Giovanni Maria Visconti who too was "famed for his dogs" – not for hunting, but for tearing humans apart.

70 Zuazo [6:26].

71 See David Radell, "The Indian Slave Trade and Population of Nicaragua in the Sixteenth Century", in Denevan [5:45], 67.

72 Hanke [6:3], 9.

73 See Mariano Alcocer Martínez, *Don Juan Rodríguez de Fonseca* (Valladolid, 1926), and Adelaida Sagarra Gamazo, "La formación política de Juan Rodríguez de Fonseca", in *Actas del Congreso* [6:25], I, 611–42.

74 Martyr, I, 67.

75 Tomás Teresa León, "El obispo don Juan Rodríguez de Fonseca, diplomático, mecenas y ministro de las Indias", *Hispania Sacra*, 13 (1960), 251.

76 Teresa Jiménez Calvente, "Elio Antonio de Nebrija", *Historia 16* (1992), 132.

77 Las Casas, III, 252.

78 "Get the reward for telling the good news to Dr Matienzo that, in his abbacy, there is gold" was the injunction of Hernando de Castro in a letter to Alonso de Nebreda, Santiago de Cuba, 31 August 1520, in Otte [6:56], 123.

79 Ernest Schäfer, *El consejo real y supremo de las Indias* (Seville, 1935, 2 vols.), I, 18–19; also John Parry, *The Spanish Seaborne Empire* (London, 1966), 57.

80 For example, Juan de Flandes, and Michael Zittow (an Estonian). See Teresa León, [6:75], 276–84; also *Reyes y Mecenas* (Toledo, 1992), 324–9.

81 Demetrio Ramos, in "El problema de la fundación del Real Consejo de Indias y la fecha de su creación", in *El Consejo de las Indias en el siglo xvi* (Valladolid, 1970), 11–48, warns against thinking that this Council of the Indies was formed as early as 1519. He points out that it did not have an office in Valladolid till 1524. Yet there are references earlier. Thus a letter of the King of 10 September 1521 (signed by Fonseca, Luis Zapata and Pedro de los Cobos) to Licenciado Zuazo talked of a *residencia* to be taken against Governor Velázquez in which he spoke of "*nuestro consejo de las Indias*" as if it had been a well-established entity (AGI, Indif. Gen., leg. 420, f.2). Martyr suggested that the council was "renewed" in 1524 (letter 800 to the Archbishop of Cosenza, in *Cartas sobre el nuevo mundo* (Madrid, 1990), 136). It seems that the Council had an informal being by 1520, even if it did not have a permanent base. See Ramón Carande, *Carlos V y sus Banqueros* (3rd ed., Madrid, 1987), I, 430–3. A *cédula* of 8 May 1523 (AGI, Indif. Gen., leg. 420, f.15) named Dr Diego Beltrán a life member of that body. Antonio de León, *Tablas cronológicas de los Reales Consejos* (Madrid, 1892), suggested that the Council was founded in 1511. Alcocer, in his life of Fonseca [6:73], said that the Council had been founded in 1517, but formally in 1524.

82 Giménez Fernández, "La juventud en Sevilla de Bartolomé de Las Casas 1474–1502",

in *Miscelánea de estudios dedicados a Fernando Ortiz* (Havana, 1956).

83 Giménez Fernández [6:19], 1, 28–32, has a good picture of this civil servant whose dependence on Fonseca, he infers, derived from the fact that he was a converted Muslim from Ibdes, near Catalyud.

84 The first painting is anonymous; the second probably the work of the Flemish Jan Joest of Calcar, one of the Bishop's protégés. Another, idealised, portrait can probably be seen in a panel of Alejo Fernández's "Virgen de los Navegantes", now in the Alcázar de Sevilla.

85 Fr. Antonio Guevara, *Epístolas Familiares*, in *BAE* (Madrid, 1850), vol. xiii, letter 41, 137–9, Segovia, 12 May 1523.

Chapter 7

1 *CDI*, XI, 428.

2 Wright [5:50], 71–2; see Marshall H. Saville, "The Discovery of Yucatan by Francisco Hernández de Córdoba", *The Geographical Review* (New York), vi, no. 5 (November 1918); and H. R. Wagner, *Documents and Narratives concerning the Discovery and Conquest of Latin America*, Cortés Society, n.s., 1 (Berkeley, 1942). Saville insisted that the expedition touched land on the Isla de Mujeres.

3 See Abel Martínez-Luza, "Un memorial de Hernán Cortés", in *AEA*, XXXXV supplement (1988), 8.

4 Francisco López de Gómara, *Historia de las Indias* (Mexico, 1965, 3 vols.), I, 244. The explorer of Yucatan is usually referred to as Hernández de Córdoba, while El Gran Capitán was Fernández de Córdoba, but Spanish Christian names and surnames beginning with F and H were interchangeable in the 16th century. Thus Cortés was Fernán (and Fernando) as well as Hernán (and Hernando). His name is spelled three different ways on one page in the inventory of the manuscripts in the Biblioteca Nacional, Madrid.

5 From the Greek *naus*, a ship with 1 or 2 masts in the middle ages, but, in the 16th century, mostly 3-masters and square-rigged. The *nao*, a "dangerous word", says Pierre Chaunu, was the typical ship of the age of discovery, basically Portuguese in design.

6 A brigantine or bergantine was a small, flat-bottomed ship, up to 40 feet long, equipped for both sailing and rowing. It usually had 2 masts, with lateen sails and between 8 to 16 banks of oars, on which there would be 1 or 2 oarsmen each. The main sections could be carried in pieces on larger ships and then assembled, when needed, on any coast where there was timber suitable for planking. A ship of this kind drew little water (18 inches probably) and was, therefore, suitable for going up rivers. It could be made to sail to windward and against currents. Ships of this type were much more roughly constructed than those of the same name in the 18th century. See Morison [5:14], 237, 551, 567. I shall call all these ships "brigantines", though "bergantine" may be more correct.

7 D del C, I, 67.

8 Chaunu [5:38], II, 72. The only study of Alaminos is that of Jesús Varela Marcos, "Anton de Alaminos: piloto del Caribe", in [6:25], II, 49. He explains why Alaminos does not figure on the usual lists of seamen on Columbus' fourth voyage.

9 *Cédula* of 4 July 1513, in Colección Muñoz, t. 80, f.126.

10 AGI, Indif. Gen., leg. 419. lib. 6, f.108: the Governor was licensed to "arm ships in order to discover islands close to Cuba".

11 Ramón Ezquerra, "Los compañeros de Hernán Cortés", in *R de I*, IX, (January–June 1948), 37–95.

12 Bernal Díaz said (D del C, II, 447) that he was son of Francisco Díaz del Castillo and María Díez (or Díaz) Renjón. But in the list of travellers to the New World in the AGI Sevilla, there is a Bernal Díaz from Medina del Campo who went to the Indies in October 1515 (6 months after Pedrarias left) and who was the son of Lope and Teresa Díaz of that city (Cristóbal Bermúdez Plata, *Catálogo de Pasajeros a Indias durante los siglos xvi, xvii, xviii*, Seville, 1940, I, 1509–34, 135). Presumably there were two Bernal Díaz from Medina del Campo in the Indies; and the chronicler must have missed the ship's register in Seville. See Carmelo Sáenz de Santa María, *Historia de una historia, Bernal Díaz del Castillo* (Madrid, 1984). Diego Díaz del Castillo, son of the chronicler, was granted a coat of arms in 1565 in honour of the achievements of his father (*Nobilario de conquistadores* (Madrid, 1892), 69–70).

13 "we were somehow related" (D del C, I, 85). He also claimed to be a "near relation" to Gutierre Velázquez, *oidor* in the 1550s of the Council of the Indies.

14 Las Casas, III, 126. But Cervantes de Salazar, who knew many conquistadors, said that the captain, not the pilot, chose the route. Diego de Landa, *Relación de las cosas de Yucatán*, ed. Miguel Rivera (Madrid, 1985), implied that, in his day (say 1560), the question whether Hernández de Córdoba sailed to procure slaves or to discover new lands was still being discussed.

15 Eye-witness accounts are those of Alaminos, who was examined by Peter Martyr in Corunna in 1520 (see Martyr, II, 6–11), and Díaz del Castillo (D del C, I, 16–20), who was on the expedition. Alaminos also gave an account of his activities in the *Inf. de 1522*, 230–4. Las Casas was a friend of Hernández de Córdoba who, he said, wrote him a letter on his deathbed (Las Casas, III, 125–31).

16 The goddesses were Aichel, Ixchebelix, Ixbunic and Ixbuneita (Landa [7:14], 44, 178).

17 For the sails, see D del C, I, 69, and commentary by Eulalia Guzmán, *La Conquista de Tenochtitlan* (Mexico, 1989), 160. Primitive sails were possibly used for boats on the sea, not on the lakes of Mexico.

18 Landa [7:14], 73. For carrying on the hip, see Tozzer's note 369 on p. 58 of his ed. [4:9] of Landa.

19 Where these beads were made is hard to know. Toledo, North Africa, Venice, Germany and Flanders seem all to be possibilities. The history of the European glass bead, which played such a part in the discovery and conquest of America, from its first presentation of one by Columbus to the "King" of Tortuga in December 1492, remains to be written.

20 Martyr, II, 7.

21 Landa [7:14], 41 fn. See discussion in Tozzer's ed. [4:9], 4, fns. 15–17.

22 *CDI*, XXVII, 303: here Martín Vázquez said in 1529 that the land reached was generally recognised to be "Tierra Nueva".

23 Yucatan continued often to be thought of as an island until *c.* 1530. Thus Francisco de Montejo in 1526 petitioned to be allowed to "colonise and bring to Our Holy Catholic faith the islands of Yucatan and Cozumel". Peter Gerhard, *The South East Frontier of New Spain* (Princeton, 1979), 3, points out that Yucatan is a great limestone plateau sticking out into the sea, with "many insular qualities". All the same, Martyr said already in 1521 that though it was not known whether "it was an island or not" it was "believed to be part of the continent" (II, 15). On 24 September 1522, the Venetian ambassador to Spain, Gasparo Contarini, a friend of Martyr's, wrote (probably on the information of Alonso de Mendoza, for whom see Ch. 39) that "Don Hernando . . . had found that Yucatan, which he had believed to be an island, was connected with the mainland which stretches westward" (Contarini to the Signory, 24 September 1522, *Calendar of state papers and manuscripts . . . in the archives and collections of Venice*, London, 1869, III, 1520–6). But Mercator's map of 1538 gave Yucatan a misleading connection with the

mainland. Sebastián Cabot's "planosphere" of 1544 was the first to depict it as it is.

24 Michael Coe, *Deciphering Maya Script* (New York, 1992).

26 France V. Scholes and R. L. Roys (with R. S. Chamberlain and Eleanor B. Adams), *The Maya Chontal Indians of Acalan Tixchel* (Washington 1948), 3.

27 Discussed in Linda Schele, "Human sacrifice among the classic Maya", in Boone [2:58], 7–45.

28 Landa [7:14], 54.

29 Scholes [7:26], 3. See Tozzer [4:9], 169–70.

30 See Ralph Roys in *HMAI*, I, 661. Gerhard [7:23], estimated 1,128,000 for 1511.

31 D del C, I, 70. Bernal Díaz emphasised such consultations whether or no they really meant anything.

32 The explanation naming "Ciuthan" was the report of Blas Hernández, a conquistador of Yucatan, in Landa [7:14], 41. Miguel Rivera's footnote on that page of his ed. discusses other possibilities for the origin of the word. Martyr reported the penultimate explanation, on the basis of Alaminos' stories to him; Bernal Díaz, the last.

33 "the said Francisco Hernández and this witness leapt to land ... and, before an *escribano*, the said Francisco Hernández, in the name of His Majesty and of himself as the discoverer of it, took possession of the said land" (Alaminos. in *Inf. de 1522*, 231). The *Inf. de 1522* aimed to underline that Hernández took possession in the name of the King, not of Velázquez.

34 For birds, see Landa [7:14], 176.

35 See Adolph Bandelier, *Art of war and mode of warfare of the ancient Mexicans* (Cambridge, Mass., 1877), 107–8.

36 Martyr, II, 9, speaks of cannon (as does Landa [7:14], 45), but the detonation must have come from arquebuses.

37 Martyr, II, 7, on the basis of Alaminos' testimony.

38 D del C, I, 82. The Grand Dragoman to the Sultan during Martyr's embassy was a sailor from Valencia wrecked on the Egyptian coast.

39 Landa [7:14], 72.

40 Alaminos told this to Oviedo (II, 114), who dismissed the story as a fable.

41 Patricia Anawalt, *Indian Clothing before Cortés* (Norman, 1981), 173–92.

42 Landa [7:14], 74.

43 Catalans have argued that they (Arnaldo de Vilanova's *Tractatus de Vinos*) invented the distilling process. That view is not universally shared. Salerno is a candidate.

44 Landa [7:14], 76.

45 Martyr, II, 9.

46 Emmerich [2:29], 121–3.

47 Angus MacKay *Spain in the Middle Ages* (London 1977), 82.

48 Martyr, II, 9.

49 Durán, I, 50.

50 Martyr (II, 9) said that the menu included wolf, lion, tiger, and peacock.

51 This theory was developed in relation to Cortés by Artemio Valle-Arizpe, *Andanzas de Hernán Cortés y otros excesos* (Madrid, 1940).

52 "We were afraid" ("*tuvimos temor*"): D del C, I, 73.

53 According to Landa [7:14], 54, fn.5, Champoton is Chakan Putun, where "Chakan" is a plain, "*put*" is to carry, and "*tun*" is stones. So Champoton is a plain to which stones are carried.

54 Hernández's instructions seem lost. Cortés' did include such a prohibition (see Ch. 11), though perhaps they were written with Hernández's action in mind.

55 Landa [7:14], 45. It was subsequently suggested that the Maya were led by a Spanish

"defector", Gonzalo Guerrero. But Guerrero lived in another part of Yucatan. The idea implies that the Mayas were incapable of winning any victories of their own. What Guerrero reported, however, may have been important.

56 Las Casas (III, 133) wrote, "Captain . . . Hernández went ashore . . . and many Indians came at them with their arms and a certain kind of metal hatchet [*ciertas hachas de metal*] with which they usually do their agricultural work."

57 Landa [7:14], 45.

58 D del C (I, 75–6) wrote that 50 were killed, Martyr, on Alaminos' evidence, 22, and Landa ([7:14], 45), 20. Martín Vázquez, in a *probanza* of 1539, on behalf of Bernal Díaz, said that 21 died. See Joaquín Ramírez Cabañas' ed. of *Historia Verdadera* . . . (Mexico, 1967), 575. Landa suggests that the two prisoners were sacrificed.

59 Martín Vázquez (AGI, Mexico, leg. 203, no. 5) said in 1525, "we escaped from the Indians by swimming in the sea" ("*escapamos de los yndios a nado por la mar*"), a rare indication that some conquistadors could swim.

60 Las Casas, III, 255. Hernández told this in a letter to Las Casas.

61 *CDI*, XXVII, 303.

62 "*otras tierras en el mundo no se habían descubierto mejores*": D del C, I, 82.

63 E.g., FC, x, 37–8.

64 D del C, I, 52.

65 See instruction of Velázquez to Cortés in 1518 (AGI, Patronato, leg. 15, R. 7).

66 The letter, dated 20 October 1517, is in *CDI*, XI, 556–9. Giménez Fernández [6:19], I, 672–3, interprets it as part of a *converso* conspiracy. This Santa Clara was a son or a brother of that treasurer of Hispaniola who, at a banquet in Santo Domingo on Corpus Christi Day 1507, had the salt cellars filled with gold dust.

Chapter 8

1 Summary by Cortés at the time of his *residencia*, *CDI*, XXVII, 304–5.

2 D del C, I, 106.

3 Ixtlilxochitl, 224.

4 This is Cortés' statement. According to one interpretation, he had expected to be paid back in slaves (Manuel Orozco y Berra, *Historia Antigua y de la conquista de México* (Mexico, 1880, 4 vols.), iv, 20).

5 The relationship is confirmed by Antonio Velázquez Bazán, a great-nephew of Velázquez, in a *Relación* ed. in *CDIHE*, IV, 232 (also in *CDI*, X, 80–8).

6 Antonio de Herrera, *Historia General de los hechos de los Castellanos en las Islas y Tierra firme del Mar Oceano* (Madrid, 1936), IV, 200; Las Casas, II, 479. Herrera, like the Velázquez family, was a native of Cuéllar.

7 *Epistolario*, II, 130.

8 For Bono see Las Casas, III, 106–9, Muñoz, 49, f.35, and Tío [5:14], 37.

9 Oviedo (II, 118), who may have had access to a journal kept by Grijalva. D del C (I, 37) gave 140, and Cortés (C, 6), 170. D del C describes the expedition as an eyewitness, but makes one or two omissions, etc., so that Wagner, and others, have thought that he did not go on the journey. They pointed out that, in a *probanza* of 1539, Díaz did not say that he had accompanied Grijalva, but only started to say later that he had when there were no survivors of the expedition to contradict him.

10 C de S, 11.

11 This story seems to come from Garcilaso de la Vega, cit. Adrian Recinos, *Pedro de Alvarado* (Mexico 1952), 11.

12 Several witnesses (Francisco Verdugo, Bernardino Vázquez de Tapia, Pedro de

Ovide, Rodrigo de Castañeda) testified at the *residencia* against Alvarado in 1529 to have heard him called *comendador*, wrongly, at the time (Res. vs Alvararado, 420–44). Pedro's cousin, Diego, went to the Indies in 1502, and was *alcalde* in Santo Domingo by 1518. He was a harsh man. He had complained to an enquiry of 1517 that the Indians in their hour of rest spent their time dancing. In order to prevent them overthrowing the government, he believed that they should be worked to exhaustion (AGI, Indif. Gen., leg. 624, R.1, ff.14–15). There is a genealogy of the Alvarados in the Libro de Genealogía, in the AHN, Madrid. One should not confuse two Diegos de Alvarado, one the *comendador* (died c. 1494 in Extremadura and for whom see Vicente Navarro, "Don Diego de Alvarado . . .", in *REE*, May–June 1960, 575–95), and the other the settler (alive in Santo Domingo, 1528). I have not yet established whether Pedro de Alvarado of Cuba, Mexico, etc., was that Pedro de Alvarado who, in 1495, presented a plea before the Council of Castile for the fulfilment of the *comendador*'s will in favour of his, Pedro's, father. Presumably that was not possible, since the Alvarado of the Indies would then have been only 10 years old (AGS, Registro General del Sello, 30 June 1496, f.105).

13 This is the description of D del C (II, 449). Maudslay's translation is here misleading. See J. Ignacio Rubio Mañé, *Monografía de los Montejos* (Mérida, 1930), 22, and the same's "Los padres del Adelantado Montejo", *Diario de Yucatan*, 10 April 1949.

14 See R. S. Chamberlain, *Conquista y colonización de Yucatán 1517–1550* (Washington, 1948), 17, and a *probanza* on the merits and services of Montejo in AGI, Escribanía de Cámara, leg. 1006A, p.2a.

15 D del C, II, 450.

16 C, 44.

17 Las Casas, III, 176.

18 D del C, I, 86.

19 Oviedo, II, 118.

20 C de S, 64. Milanese, Romans, and Florentines all still wore their hair long.

21 Oviedo, II, 118.

22 Andrés de Tapia (*"Relación de algunas cosas . . ."*, in J. Díaz, et al., 69) says 2,000, and López de Gómara, 3,000. For Cozumel, see S. K. Lothrop, *An Archaeological Study of East Yucatan* (Washington, 1924), 152–6.

23 This is the statement of Juan Díaz in his *Itinerario*. The earliest ed. of this book surviving is an Italian tr., ed. Venice, 1520 by Zorzi Rusconi Milanese, as an appendix to an account of a journey by Ludovico de Varthema, of Bologna, to the East and to Africa. Perhaps there was no original Spanish ed. and the Italian one derives from a manuscript. There are two abbreviated versions, one in Latin. Both, confusingly, add details which the original does not contain. The three versions are compared by Henry Wagner in *The Discovery of New Spain* (Berkeley, 1942). The ed. of J. Díaz used here is that ed. Germán Vázquez (Madrid, 1988).

24 Scholes [7:26], 52–3. Henry Wagner, *The Rise of Fernando Cortés*, (New York, 1944), 44–51, has a good chapter on Cozumel.

25 C de S, 64.

26 Oviedo, II, 32, 120.

27 J. Díaz, et al., 41.

28 See Tapia, in J. Díaz, et al., 41. By October 1518 the existence of the crosses, reported perhaps by Pedro de Alvarado, was known in Cuba. See Martínez, *Docs*, I, 51, fn.6.

29 Oviedo, II, 124.

30 One uncle of Vázquez was a professor at Salamanca, and had been a member of the Council of Castile. Another, Francisco Álvarez, abbot of a rich *convento* in Toro, had been inquisitor-general of Murcia. Vázquez de Tapia, now in his mid-twenties, like

Bernal Díaz and Montejo, had passed 3 years in Castilla de Oro with Pedrarias, with whom he had come out to the Indies in 1514. Then, like Montejo, he had obtained an *encomienda* in Cuba. He was later an enemy of Hernán Cortés, whom he pursued through law courts in two continents: see Guillermo Porras Muñoz, "Un capitán de Cortés . . .". *AEA* (1948).

31 The original Italian ed. (1520) of Díaz reads, "*dentro tenia certe figure d'ossi & de cenis e de idoli*" (M, iiv.). Wagner [8:23] insists, on the strength of a different spelling in the abbreviated versions of Díaz, that "*ossi*", bones, should read "*orsi*", bears, and that "*cenis*" must be a misprint for "*simie*", female apes. Martyr (II, 13) also talks of "*orsi*" made of terracotta. Yet all the early editions of Díaz's *Itinerario* (e.g. those of 1526 and 1535) have "*ossi*" and "*ceni*". "*Ceni*" may be a misprint for "*cemi*", devils.

32 Oviedo, II, 122.

33 Martyr, II, 14.

34 LANDA [7:14], 169.

35 J. Díaz, et al., 42; Lothrop [8:22], 14, suggested Tulum.

36 "*Habitada da donne che viveno senza homine. Se credi che siano de la stirpe de amazone*" (M, iiii v.). Germán Vázquez plausibly suggests (in J. Díaz, et al., 42, fn.20) that, because Oviedo did not copy this, and did copy most other things in Díaz, this sentence was written into the text by the Italian translator.

37 D del C, I, 44; Oviedo, II, 127.

38 *Provinciae sive regiones in India Occidentali noviter repertae in ultima navigatione*, a "copy" of Fr. Díaz's *Itinerario* tr. into Spanish, 1519, into English by Wagner [8:23].

39 D del C, I, 91.

40 Joan de Cuéllar, AGI, Justicia, leg. 223, p.2; Oviedo, II, 125–30; J. Díaz, et al., 45; and Martyr, II, 18. D del C (I, 43), spoke of 7 Spanish killed and over 60 wounded; the questionnaire in the *residencia* against Cortés spoke of 1 or 2 dead (*CDI*, XXVII, 306).

41 J. Díaz, et al., 45; FC, vii, 21.

42 Oviedo devoted a chapter (II, 130–1) of his history to Alaminos' mistakes of geography; Chamberlain [8:14], 14.

43 J. Díaz, et al., 4. The first Italian ed. of Fr. Díaz had "*desiderato*".

44 Scholes [7:26], 89.

45 As to whether there was, as suggested in Diego de Landa ([7:14], 54), a Mexican garrison at Xicallanco, see Davies [3:42], 143.

46 Marshall H. Saville, *The Goldsmith's Art in Ancient Mexico* (New York, 1920), 20.

47 D del C, I, 44–5.

48 Martyr, II, 16; J. Díaz, et al., 47; Las Casas, III, 183. The presents are listed in Oviedo, II, 133, presumably on the evidence of Grijalva's log.

49 Las Casas, III, 181.

50 J. Díaz, et al., 50; Oviedo, II, 137.

51 Perhaps Zelia Nuttall, "The Island of Sacrifices", *American Anthropologist*, n.s. 12, 1910, was right to say that it was Alvarado, who came from near Mérida, who made this identification. But it could not have been very like the arch of Mérida, for the Mexica did not have the method which the Romans had of building arches. Alvarado was not the only Extremeño on the expedition.

52 The family of Montejo were, in a *probanza* into his achievements in 1583, keen to point out that he was the first to land ("*el primer capitán que saltó a la tierra*"). See Joan de Cárdenas, *BAGN*, IX, 1, (January–February 1938), 101. Montejo, when he was granted arms, took a device of seven "*panes*" of gold and five flags.

53 Oviedo, II, 138; *CDI*, XV, 137. Bernal Díaz makes several confusing mistakes here; for example he talks of seeing white flags being raised on a "*río de Banderas*".

54 Martyr, II, 36. This was what Martyr said of Cortés' expedition, being no

doubt informed by Alaminos. Walled towns were rare in Mexico and the region.

55 Henry Brumar, "The Culture History of Mexican Vanilla", *HAHR*, 28 (1946); Alain Ichon, *La réligion des Totonaques de la Sierra* (Paris, 1969), 44–8.

56 R. H. Barlow [1:10], quoted from *Codex Mendoza* [1:29], 92. I have adopted Frances Berdan's rule about alleged "bunches" of feathers.

57 Frances Berdan, "The Economics of Aztec Luxury Trade and Tribute", in Boone [1:5], 171; Patricia Rieff Anawalt, "Memory Clothing . . .", in Boone [2:58], 174.

58 FC, x, 184–5; C, 66.

59 Durán, I, 243–4.

60 See Duverger [1:44], 66–7; Peter Gerhard, *A Guide to the Historical Geography of New Spain* (Cambridge, 1972), 360, 363.

61 *"él nos mostraba tanto amor que era cosa maravillosa"*: J. Díaz, et al., 132.

62 There is a list in G, 42–5. See also Martyr, II, 20–1, and Oviedo, II, 139.

63 Bernardino Vázquez de Tapia, in J. Díaz, et al., 133.

64 Motolinía [1:1], 144–5. See also Martyr as quoted above. For the translation of the word *teules*, see Chapter 13, fns. 39 and 40.

65 J. Díaz, et al., 52.

66 *". . . tienen harta política y habitan en casas de piedra y tienen sus leyes y ordenanzas y lugares públicos diputados para la administración de justicia"*: J. Díaz, et al., 57.

67 *"sopra vi he morto uno che e piu lucido e resplendente chel sole"* (last page of original text). This was Fr. Díaz, in J. Díaz, et al., 57, and is here as published in 1520. Martyr (II, 8) makes a similar allusion, but he must be copying Díaz's text.

68 Landa ([7:14], 89) pointed to the reason for this mistake.

69 J. Díaz, et al., 52; Martyr (II, 18–19), presumably on the evidence of Alaminos, agrees. D del C (I, 101) and Vázquez de Tapia (in J. Díaz, et al., 133), who had his own reasons for doing so, deny that Grijalva stopped his followers from establishing themselves at Vera Cruz – a factor of importance when it comes to judging whether or no there was a disposition on the part of Cortés' men to *poblar*, as the Spaniards put it, the next year.

70 This discussion is reported by C de S (79–81), who allegedly heard of it from "old conquistadors". See J. Díaz, et al., 52. Both Richard Kontezke, "Hernán Cortés como poblador de la Nueva España", *R. de I* (1948), 369, and Victor Frankl, "Hernán Cortés y tradición de las siete partidas", *Revista de la Historia de América* (1962) 33–4, take Alvarado's speech seriously.

71 Andrés de Duero, in *Inf. de 1521*, in Polavieja, 309.

72 "Culhúa" or "Colhúa" derives from "grandfather" in Nahuatl. "Culhuacan" is thus "the place of those who have grandfathers": thus a city with traditions. Culhúa came to be associated with Toltec urban dwellers in the Valley of Mexico as opposed to the Chichimeca nomads. See Davies [1:24], 23. Oviedo says that the day of the naming was 17 June.

73 G, 42.

74 G, 42–4.

75 G, 44.

76 Martyr, II, 16.

77 J. Díaz, et al., 52–3.

78 Baltasar Dorantes de Salazar, *Sumaria relación de las Cosas de la Nueva España* (Mexico, 1962), 189.

79 J. Díaz, et al., 53.

80 Oviedo, II, 141.

81 J. Díaz, et al., 54. Bernal Díaz says that the river was the Tonalá.

82 D del C, I, 104. Grijalva took 40 of these back to Cuba.

83 This claim was omitted in his first ed. See Sáenz de Santa María's ed. of *Historia verdadera* (Madrid, 1982), 33.

84 J. Díaz, et al., 55.

85 Oviedo, II, 147.

86 *CDI*, XXVII, 307.

87 This is the argument of Cortés (C, 47).

88 D del C, I, 102.

89 Las Casas, III, 193: Oviedo (II, 148) knew Fr. Martín and said that he went home in May.

90 *CDI*, XXVIII, 22.

91 In the *residencia* against Cortés, Alonso de Navarrete said that "Velázquez had much pain, and showed it, and said that in public, and said that he deserved as much for having sent an idiot [*bobo*] as captain" (AGI, Justicia, leg. 223, p.2, f.424v.).

92 In a report to Charles V, 1526.

93 C de S (78–9) said that Velázquez had always planned to send Olid.

Chapter 9

1 It was so referred to by the papal nuncio to Spain, in his letter of March 1520 to Pedro de Acosta, ed. in *HAHR*, 9 (May, 1929). The first "Bishop of Yucatan" was soon named, Fr. Julián Garcés, being referred to as "of La Carolina" (see Muñoz. vol. 58, f. 140v.).

2 Las Casas, III, 193; C de S, 388; Dorantes [8:78], 321; G,19.

3 Giménez Fernández [6:19], II, 1102.

4 *CDIU*, I, 114; see also questionnaire of 22 February 1522 to Vasco, in Muñoz, vol. 58, f. 274.

5 D del C, I, 111.

6 Velázquez was later accused of having Cortés as a favourite (AGI justicia leg 49, f. 27).

7 For Dávila see *CDI*, XXVIII, 16, and, if he was the same Francisco Dávila, Arranz [5:45], 502–6.

8 Dávila in the *residencia* against Cortés, *CDI*, XXVIII, 23: "Don Hernando Cortés wrote a letter to this witness telling him how Diego Velázquez was sending him as captain with certain ships to Yucatan whence had come the said Joan de Grijalva, and that he had accepted . . ." Cortés was known in his lifetime more as "Hernando" ("Don Hernando") than Hernán, but the latter has come to be used regularly.

9 The year of Cortés' birth is usually given as 1485. But I follow Wagner who ([8:23], 9) pointed out that an inscription next to a portrait of Cortés in Lasso de la Vega's *Cortés Valeroso* reads "*aetatis 63*"; which means, since he died in 1547, that he could not have been born later than 1484; and, in a petition to the Emperor of 1544, Cortés says that he was then aged 60. In AGI, Mexico, 203, no. 19, a hearing on the merits of Juan González de León, Cortés in 1532 swore that he was then over 50! It has also been supposed, following Cortés' own submission to the Emperor Charles V of 1541, in *CDIHE*, IV, 219, and echoed by López de Gómara, (G, 37), that Cortés went to Santo Domingo in 1504. But a document in the APS shows 1506 as the right year. See Document No. 1.

10 This assumes that Cortés' father was that Martín Cortés described as a simple *hidalgo* "*vecino de Don Benito, tierra de Medellín*", Don Benito being a town a few miles to the east of Medellín; and who is also described as an infantryman in 1489, 1497 and 1503 (AGS, Registro General del Sello, 27 November 1488, f.231 and later papers there). The identification of this Martín with the father of Hernán seems right since, in a bill of 1506 for Hernán Cortés' passage to the Indies, he is also described as "*vecino de Don Benito, tierra de Medellín*" (APS, *oficio* iv, lib. III, f.102).

11 Federico Gómez de Berrio,"¿Cual era el linaje paterno de Cortés?", in *R de I*, XXXI–XXXII (January–June 1948), 297–300; and the same's "Mocedades de Hernando Cortés", in *RAMH* (1952), 1 and 3.

12 See Leonardo Romero's intr. to Alonso Maldonado's *Vida e historia del maestre de Alcántara, Don Alonso Monroy* (Tarragona, 1978). For these wars, see Luis Suárez Fernández's vol. xvii (Ch. vi) of the history of Spain ed. by Menéndez Pidal. It seems possible that there was a blood connection between the Monroys, and therefore Hernán Cortés, and the paladin of French chivalry, Bayard. For this tantalising but unexplored genealogical morsel, see Manuel Villar y Macías, *Historia de Salamanca* (Salamanca, 1887), II, 61.

13 Two leaders from Medellín went to the war against Granada, the Count and his bitter enemy, Juan Núñez de Prado, both taking with them *"gente de Extremadura"* – of whom Núñez de Prado is the more likely to have been Martín Cortés' commander (Angel del Arco, *Glorias de la nobleza española*, Tarragona, 1899, 210, 211).

14 *"el Infante ... partiose para Medellín: y allí le vinieron nuevas ..."*; see Arnao Guillén de Brocar, *Crónica del serenísimo rey Juan Segundo ... corregida por Lorenzo Galíndez de Carvajal* (Logroño, 1517), f.xxxii v.

15 Celestino Vega, "La hacienda de Hernán Cortés en Medellín", in an annex of the *REE*, (1948); Fernand Braudel, *The Mediterranean*, tr. Siân Reynolds (London, 1972, 2 vols.), I, 458, classified the miserable as those who had less than 7,500 maravedís (20 ducats). One needed 56,000 (over 40 ducats) to be "reasonably" off. A textile worker in Segovia at this time would expect about 200 a month only (Ramón Carande, *Carlos V y sus Banqueros* (3rd ed., Barcelona, 1987) I, 180), and a worker in the vineyards during harvest only 35 maravedís a day. See Bartolomé Bennassar, *Valladolid au siécle d'or* (Paris, 1967), 295. In a declaration to Charles V of *c.* 1533 Cortés said that his father left him 400,000 maravedís of pasture: presumably land which could be sold for that (Martínez, Docs, IV, 70).

16 Evidence of Diego López, in a hearing in 1525 as to whether Cortés was entitled to be a knight of Santiago, in AHN (Santiago), published in *BRAH* (1892), 199, 220–1.

17 Las Casas' phrase was *"harto pobre y humilde aunque cristiano viejo y dicen que hidalgo"*; see Diego Soto y Aguilar, "De la diferencia que hay entre el hidalgo y el escudero", *Hidalguía*, III, 1955, 299–304, and other articles by that author in that journal.

18 Evidence of Diego López, Juan de Montoya, and Juan Núñez de Prado in AHN (Santiago). Juan de Burgos Colchero and Alonso Herrera testified similarly in respect of Hernán Cortés' son Martín that the family was neither Jewish nor *converso* nor Moorish. The coat of arms in the sketch of Cortés by Christoph Weiditz is sorted out by Miguel J. Malo Zozaya in "Revelador hallazgo en la heráldica cortesiana", *Norte* (Mexico), 3rd series, 242 (July-August 1971). When Hernán Cortés was granted a coat of arms in 1525, he was told that he could display it "beside the one which you have inherited from your ancestors" (Harkness collection, Library of Congress, 40).

19 Lucio Marineo Siculo, *De los memorables de España* (Alcalá de Henares, 1530), f.ccviii-ccxi. r. and v., in the section "De los claros varones de España", in *Historia 16*, x, 108, 98. There were several Italian Cortes, for example Antonio Cortes, bookseller of Florence; and a literary man of Rome, Paolo Cortese.

20 Morison [5:14], 198.

21 *"el padre e la madre del dicho Martín Cortés heran vesinos e naturales de la çibdad de Salamanca"*: AHN (Santiago), f.8 v. Núñez de Prado, who might have been a determined conquistador had he been 50 years younger, was a witness at the wedding of Gonzalo de Pizarro and Isabel de Vargas in Trujillo in the 1480s, and was 80 in 1525. He had once been expelled from Medellín by the Count but seems to have been mostly living in the town in

the 1490s. For his many complaints against the Count, see AGS, Registro General del Sello, Medellín, almost *passim* 1479–99.

22 Alfonso Figueroa and Dalmiro de la Goma, in *Linaje y descendencia de Hernán Cortés* (Madrid, 1951), speak of Martín Cortés without such a comment. I accept their view that Martín was the son of Rodrigo, not of Hernando, "El Bezudo". But Gómez de Orozco seems correct in his suggestion of illegitimacy in "¿Cual era el linaje paterno . . .?" [9:11]. See also D. A. Franco Silva, *El señorío de los Monroy*, and Elisa Carolina de Santos Canalejo, *Linajes y señoríos de la Extremadura*, both in *Hernán Cortés y su tiempo*, "Actas del Congreso del V centenario 1485–1985" (Mérida, 1987).

23 Altamirano is named as *"escribano e notario del rey"* in the Medellín papers (Medinaceli archive, Casa de Pilatos, Seville, leg. 1, doc. 9, f.15 [not numbered]: see Document 2). Juan Núñez de Prado, in the hearings in 1525 for Hernán Cortés' entry into the Order of Santiago, said that Altamirano had been *mayordomo* to Beatriz. For Trujillo, see Ida Altman, *Emigrants and Society: Trujillo in the sixteenth century* (Berkeley, 1989); and David Vassberg, who, in "Concerning Pigs: the Pizarros . . .", *Latin American Research Review*, (1978), xiii, 3, 47–62, shows that the conqueror of Peru was not necessarily a swineherd in his youth.

24 Evidence of Juan de Montoya in AHN, Santiago, 1525, ed. *BRAH*, 1892.

25 See Miguel Muñoz de San Pedro. "Doña Isabel de Vargas, esposa del padre del conquistador de Perú" (*R de I*, xxxxiii–xxxxiv, 1951, 9–28).

26 *"tan soberbios como pobres"* (Oviedo, V, 33). Among the Altamiranos was Fray Diego, a Franciscan who was early in Mexico and whom Cortés referred to as his cousin in a letter of 13 May 1526, *CDI*, XII, 367. See Anastasio López, "Los Primeros Franciscanos en Méjico", *Archivo Ibero-Americano* (1920), xxxvii, 21–3. For Diego Pizarro in Mexico, see Ch. 22.

27 Both Cortés' Altamirano and Pizarro ancestors beyond his grandparents remain to be traced. See Genealogy III.

28 Cooper [6:66], II, 1095–1100, prints much useful material.

29 See Andrés de Bernáldez, *Historia de los Reyes Católicos*, in *BAE*, III, 345, 594–5. Manuel Fernández Álvarez, *La sociedad española del Renacimiento* (Madrid, 1970), 71, says that, at the end of the 16th century, there were 616 householders (*vecinos*), in Medellín (548 taxpayers, 35 hidalgos, 31 clergy, 17 monks).

30 Information about Medellín between 1479 and 1520 can be found in Simancas in the Registro General del Sello and in Castilla: Cámara.

31 Vicente Barrantes, *Discursos leidos ante la Real Academia de la Historia* (Madrid, 1872), 37.

32 Luis Suárez Fernández, *Historia de España* ed. Ramón Menéndez Pidal (Madrid, 1970), xvii, 63.

33 Francisco García Sánchez, *Medellín, Encrucijada Histórica* (Cáceres, 1984), 117. The prominent Jews of Medellín were Samuel Almale, Abraham Zumael, Mosen and Samuel Corcas, Atiuin Alberi, and Cege Folloquines. Rabbis included Fioraine Almale, Simon Almale and Mosen Hadida, of whom the first was the Count of Medellín's tax farmer, the second his collector of rents. Folloquines converted in 1492 as "Luis González", Mosen Corcas as "Rodrigo de Orozco". The father of Abraham Zumael had been *mayordomo* to the Countess of Medellín, preceding Cortés' grandfather.

34 In Lorenzo Galíndez de Carvajal's *Anales* (*CDIHE*, XVIII, 258) we read: "8 of November 1475 at Dueñas [the town near Palencia where Ferdinand and Isabel married] they liberated Juan de Valladolid, *negro*, lord and mayoral of *negros y negras*, *loros y loras* [brown people, i.e. *guanches* from Canaries] who, by that time, by contract had already delivered a great quantity of such from Guinea to Seville . . ." For slaves in Extremadura, easily available because of proximity to Portugal, see Altman [9:22], 72.

667

35 See the famous picture of Nebrija teaching at Zalamea in the Bibliothèque Nationale, Paris. Also see Américo Castro, *La Realidad Histórica de España* (Mexico, 1962), 418.

36 See Owen Gingrich in his forward to Aveni's *Skywatchers of Ancient Mexico* [4:19], xi, and Harry Friedenwald's brief life of Zacuto (London, 1939). Expelled from Spain in 1492, from Portugal in 1497, Zacuto fled to Tunis, and died in friendly Damascus in 1525.

37 G, 35.

38 López, in AHN (Santiago, 1525). Juan Suárez de Peralta, *Tratado del descubrimiento de las Indias* (Mexico, 1949), 82, says that the church was Santa Cecilia, but that was not built in Cortés' youth; it may have been erected on the site of the synagogue.

39 Rafael Varón Gabai and Auke Pieter Jacobs, "Peruvian Wealth and Spanish Investments: the Pizarro family", *HAHR*, 67 (November 1987).

40 Vega [9:15], 389.

41 Gabai and Jacobs [9:39], 685.

42 I have come to see Núñez de Prado as the key to Cortés' relations' difficulties in and doubts about Medellín. He deserves a monograph.

43 The Count of Puñonrostro, brother of Pedrarias, married María Girón, sister of the Count of Medellín (Jesús Larios Martín, *Nobilario de Segovia* (Segovia, 1956), I, 92).

44 Cooper [6:66].

45 *Aquí yacen los señores Gutierre*
de Monroy y doña Constanza D'Anaya,
su mujer a los quales de Dios
tanta parte del cielo como por sus
personas y linajes merecían de la tierra . . .
Cit. M. Fernández Álvarez [9:29], 143.

46 Marineo [9:19], 100. Marineo was then himself at Salamanca. Others say Cortés was 14 when he went to Salamanca. It seems to be possible that this Inés went, perhaps widowed, to the Indies in 1513: no. 1452 in Bermúdez Plata's list (Cristóbal Bermúdez Plata, *Catálogo de Pasajeros a Indias durante los siglos XVI, XVII, XVIII*, Seville, 1940). Cortés spoke of Núñez as having been a notary in a reply of April 1546 to a suit brought against him by Núñez's son (Martínez, *Docs*, IV, 307).

47 Marineo [9:19], 100, was the first to say this. He was followed by Las Casas (II, 475); and López de Gómara (G, 36). But neither seem to have known of Altamirano's legal training.

48 Barrantes [9:31], 43, referred to Salamanca as "no Spanish Athens but an Extremeño university". Martyr, lecturing there with great success on Juvenal in 1488, thought highest of the theology school (see Nicholas Rounds, "Renaissance Culture in Fifteenth Century Castile", *Modern Language Review*, lvii, January–April 1962, 211).

49 "this witness studied some time in the school [*estudio*] where Cortés studied . . . and dealt with him a good deal and we both talked a lot" [9:25].

50 Las Casas, II, 475.

51 Josefina Muriel, "Reflexiones . . ." in *R de I* (1948).

52 "*Hacía ventaja en ser latino, solamante, porque había estudiado leyes en Salamanca y era de ellos bachiller.*" For Cortés' latinity, see José Luis Martínez, *Hernán Cortés* (Mexico, 1990), 849.

53 "he greatly enjoyed [*deleitaba mucho*] the Latin language" (Marineo [9:19], 100).

54 "he was a friend of reading when he had time but he was more inclined to arms" (C de S, 98).

55 "*desbaratar la barbarie por todas partes de España*" was Nebrija's expression.

56 See Caro Lynn [6:34], Ch. v.

57 Jerónimo Munzer, "Viaje por España y Portugal 1494–1495", in *Viajes* [5:20], 391.

58 "even now I have not forgotten the presents and kindnesses which you gave me in my

childhood" ("*aun no tengo oluidadas las mercedes y caricias q. Vm. me hizo en mi niñez*"):
Letter of 24 October 1524, in B. N. Mss. 10713, f.33, ed. José V. Corraliza, in *R de I, año*
VIII (December 1947), no. 30.

59 For the connection, at the same time close and tenuous, see Genealogy III.

60 "A Viriatus had Lusitania, a Hannibal had Carthage, an Alexander Greece, a Diego de
Paredes Extremadura . . ." (*BAE*, I, 392).

61 For Pedro de Monroy, apparently a *licenciado* (lawyer), see Muñoz de San Pedro,
Diego García de Paredes (Madrid, 1946), 424; also Marie-Claude Gerbet, *La noblesse
dans le Royaume de Castille* (Paris, 1979), 370.

62 María de Ovando married Diego Mejía, brother of Núñez de Prado, as his second
wife.

63 For the enterprise, see Pérez de Tudela [5:40], 200, 203.

64 Navagero, in *Viajes*, [5:20], 883-4. "Babylonia" passed as a synonym for Seville into
thieves' jargon of the time.

65 Münzer, in *Viajes* [5:20], 372-6.

66 Antonio de Lalaing, with Felipe el Hermoso in 1501, in *Viajes* [5:20], 473.

67 Galíndez de Carvajal, *Anales Breves del reinado de los reyes católicos*, in CDIHE,
XVIII, 304.

68 G, 36.

69 Las Casas, II, 154.

70 "set off [*se encaminó*] for Valencia" was López de Gómara's expression (G, 36).

71 Münzer, in *Viajes* [5:20], 339, said it was the "capital of the realm's commerce".

72 See *Joan Lluis Vives, Valentinus e seu Temps* (Valencia, 1992). Lalaing was also
there with Felipe *el hermoso* in 1501 (*Viajes* [5:20], 477); see also María Purificación
Benito Vidal, "La indumentaria valenciana en los años del 1470 al 1540" in *Joan Lluis
Vives*.

73 G, 36.

74 For his comparison of Granada with Tlaxcala, see Ch. 20: for the silk market in
Granada in 1501, see Lalaing, *Viajes* [5:20], 474, and Carande [9:15], I, 195, II, 321.

75 Suárez de Peralta [9:38], 82; for the notaries of Valladolid, see Bennassar [9:15], 365.

76 See Victor Frankl [8:71], 53-4; and John Elliott, "The Mental World of Hernán
Cortés", *Transactions of the Royal Historical Society*, Fifth Series, 17 (1967), 41-58.

77 It was not till 1548 that notarial activity became incorporated in Spanish faculties of
law. See Bernardo Pérez Fernández del Castillo, *Historia de la escribanía en la Nueva
España* (2nd ed., Mexico, 1988), 32.

78 Lorenzo Vital, the Venetian ambassador, in *Viajes* [5:20], 706.

79 The conjecture of Demetrio Ramos, in *Hernán Cortés* (Madrid, 1992), 33.

80 "*la mayor suntuosidad . . .*": Münzer, in *Viajes* [5:20], 390.

81 "*Tengo por mejor ser rico de fama que de bienes*": letter of 26 September 1526, in
Mariano Cuevas [6:57], 29.

82 "*como si naciera en brocadas*" (Las Casas, III, 200). Brocade was not unknown in
Medellín, for the Count bought silks and brocades from the Florentine merchants
Francesco Fabrini and Antonio Ridolfi (AGS, Registro General del Sello, 22 September
1490, ff. 137-138; and 23 December 1492, f.193), for whom see Consuelo Varela, *Colón y
los Florentinos* (Seville, 1988), 34. The Count was slow to pay.

83 This was the Rodríguez de las Varillas arms. See Malo Zozaya [9:18].

84 Leon Battista Alberti, "The Family", tr. Guido A. Guarino, in *The Albertis of
Florence* (Lewisburg, 1971).

85 Suárez de Peralta [9:38], 82.

86 See Document 3. The amended date gives Cortés 2 more years in his native Spain than
is usually assumed. López de Gómara states that Alfonso Quintero was the master of

Cortés' ship which, according to APS, *lib. del año* 1506, *oficio* vii, lib. 1, last page in the legajo, and Chaunu [5:38], II, 8, was in 1506 the *Trinidad*. It carried a cargo of clothes. The *San Juan Bautista* was captained by Sancho de Salazar. I assume that Cortés planned to go with Fernández de Alfaro, and then changed to Quintero.

Chapter 10

1 Marineo wrote an account of this journey, but confused the storm with one in 1519. Cortés may have had Extremeño relations in the Canaries; see Manuel Lobo Carrero, "Extremeños en Canarias" in *Hernán Cortés y su tiempo* [9: 22], 193.

2 It will be seen that though I have established a new date for Cortés' departure from Spain, I accept that the unreliable Quintero was his captain, as indicated vividly in, e.g., López de Gómara.

3 Fray Tomás de la Torre, *Desde Salamanca, España hasta Ciudad Real, Chiapas, diario del viaje, 1544–1545*, ed. Franz Blom (Mexico, 1945) 72–3, 113.

4 G,36; Pérez de Tudela [5:40], 248, speaks of a Pedro de Medina who was factor to an Aragonese merchant, Juan Sánchez de la Tesoría, for whom see Muñoz, vol. v, 72, ff.33 and 36 (he was brother of Alonso Sanchís, treasurer of Valencia, active in trading slaves from the Canaries). Sánchez de la Tesoría was, with the Genoese Riberol, responsible, in 1502, for the first private business between Europe and the Americas.

5 Miguel Muñoz de San Pedro, in an essay on Lizaur (*BRAH*, cxxiii (1948), 89), cites an unpublished 17th-century ms history of Brozas (*Noticias de las Brocas*), saying that Lizaur and Cortés became *"muy grandes amigos"*, and that the former later claimed to have done much for Cortés *"con el Comendador"* : i.e., Ovando.

6 The events at Xaragua (allegation of an Indian rebellion, Spanish "pre-emptive strike") were not dissimilar to those which would occur at Cholula. See Ch.18.

7 *"fue algo travieso sobre mujeres"*, wrote Díaz del Castillo (D del C, II, 420), who gained that judgement from hearsay. Juan Núñez Sedeño remembered Cortés as *escribano de Azúa* (*Docs Inéditos*, 194).

8 C de S, 99–101.

9 Oviedo disliked lawyers.

10 G, 10–11. Explanations of this disease include an "abcess"; a tumour (on his right leg); and syphilis (C de S, 98). For Nicuesa, see Angel de Altolaguirre, *Vasco Núñez de Balboa* (Madrid, 1914), ix.

11 Arranz ([5:45], 256) gave that figure for 1513 at the time of the *repartimiento* of that year; for the depopulation, see Hernando Gorjiri, of Azúa, in Muñoz, vol. 58, f.210.

12 The map, the oldest of the island, is in the University of Bologna and is published by Arranz, [5:45], 256; "Relación de . . . Parada," in *CDI*, XL, 261.

13 Zuazo to the Emperor, January 1518, *CDI*, 1, 311.

14 Pike [6:48], 132–3. The mill had not been finished by 1523, though; see *cédula* of 26 June 1523 in favour of Licenciado Ayllón.

15 The fraction had been decided during the wars with the Moors in the 11th century. The practice derived from the Moors' own custom. The Koran talks of it: "Know that whatever booty you take, the fifth of it is God's and the messenger's." See A. J. Arberry, *The Koran: an interpretation* (London, 1980), 201.

16 G, 39.

17 The letter of 1 April 1514 is in *CDI*, XI, 412–429.

18 "Relación de . . . Parada", *CDI*, XL, 261; Las Casas, II, 477.

19 The *cédula* which enabled Velázquez to make the division was dated 13 May 1513 (*CDIU*, VI, 2); Wright [5:50], 40–4.

20 D del C, I, 112.

21 From testimony in the suit of María de Marcayda in 1529 against Cortés.

22 See *Tributos y servicios personales de Indios para Hernán Cortés y su familia*, ed. Silvio Zavala (Mexico, 1984), 3.

23 *"tan bajo y tan humilde que del más chico criado que Diego Velázquez tenía quisiera tener favor"*: Las Casas, II, 476.

24 See evidence in *Tributos* [10:22], 2–7.

25 So he told Las Casas (Las Casas, II, 477).

26 D del C, I, 73.

27 Las Casas, III, 194.

28 *"su hacienda, y muy buena y tal que no había en la isla quien mejor la tuviese"* (*Probanza* of 1531, in *Docs Inéditos*, 2); *"una gran fortuna de oro"* was the expression of Sepúlveda, 93.

29 *CDI*, xxviii.

30 Wright [5:50], 74. Cortés' paternal great-grandmother was an Orellana. See Genealogy III.

31 Las Casas, II, 475. Although the Governor had recently punished him (probably by a fine) for gambling (see Documents).

32 See García del Pilar, in Res (Rayón), II, 216; "he heard mass devotedly though at the same time one saw many women in his house".

33 "that ninny [*nonada*] of a Cortesillo . . ." was Salvatierra's phrase in 1520 (D del C, I, 406).

34 *"un Hernando Cortés, natural de Medellín, criado mío de mucho tiempo"* (letter to Fonseca, 12 October 1519); and, in a letter to Rodrigo de Figueroa (17 November 1519), he spoke of "a certain Hernando Cortés, who always seemed to be prudent and who had been a long time in this island as my servant".

35 Suárez de Peralta [9:38], 82.

36 D del C, II, 420–1.

37 This derives from an examination in 1946 of his alleged bones by two separate committees. Eulalia Guzmán said that the bones showed both congenital and acquired syphilis: of which the first accusation is especially interesting, for syphilis was not known in Europe at the time of Cortés' birth.

38 Weiditz, born in Strasbourg, was a protégé of the Polish ambassador, Johnan von Hoeven (Johannes Dantiscus), who became friendly with Cortés. See the coloured illustration in *Das Trachtenbuch des Christoph Weiditz von seinen reisen nach Spanien (1529) und der Nederland (1531/32)*, intr. by Theodor Hampfe, Berlin 1927; and M. Jean Babelon, "Un retrato verdadero de Hernán Cortés", in *MAMH*, XIII (July–August 1954), 173–8. Neither Babelon nor Franz Blom, who also wrote of the picture, in *Hernán Cortés y el libro de trajes de Christoph Weiditz* (Tuxtla Gutiérrez, 1945), seem to have noted the colour of Cortés' hair in the painting.

39 *"resabido y recatado"*: Las Casas, II, 475. This medal, often reproduced, is in Paris.

40 *"el cabello algo rojo"*, in Marineo Siculo [9:20], 100. This distinguished humanist also wrote a eulogy of Bishop Fonseca (cited in Appendix 16 to an essay of Tomás Teresa León, in *Hispania Sacra*, 13, 1960, 52–4), so perhaps his judgement of virtue was not always reliable. But surely an Italian can be trusted in respect of colours?

41 *"la barba clara, el cabello largo . . ."*: G, 492.

42 *"las barbas tenían algo prietas y pocas y ralas . . . el cabello que en aquel tiempo se usaba era de la misma manera de las barbas"*: (D del C, II, 420. *"Prieto"* usually means very dark.

43 *CDI*, xxvii, 308. This account is much the same as that in G, 19, which was written with Cortés' help (C, 48).

44 Diego Velázquez to Figueroa, 17 November 1519, in Martínez, *Docs*, I, 99.

45 The text is in the AGI, Patronato, leg.15, R. 7. This was a copy made 13 October 1519, and sent to Bishop Fonseca with Gonzalo de Guzmán. It has been widely edited, most conveniently in Martínez, *Docs*, I, 45–57. The original was taken by Cortés to Mexico, and presumably lost in the retreat from Tenochtitlan in 1520.

46 Andrés de Duero, *Inf. de 1521*, 310; Ramos [9:79], 93, suggests Cortés' involvement.

47 See Nestor Meza, "La formación de la fortuna mobiliaria de Hernán Cortés", *Estudios sobre la conquista de América* (Santiago de Chile, 1971).

48 *Circa 1492* [5:39], 122.

49 José María Ots Capdequí, *El Estado Español en las Indias* (Mexico, 1941), 16–17. See also Silvio Zavala, *Las Instituciones Jurídicas en la conquista de América* (3rd ed., Mexico, 1988), 117–18.

50 Wright [5:50], 55.

51 Oviedo, II, 147.

52 The first Bishop of Mexico, Juan de Zumárraga, commenting on this, said that, with the appearance of Grijalva, the whole reason for Cortés' expedition vanished. So Cortés, "*por inspiración divina*", found another purpose: letter to Charles V, 29 August 1529, in *CDI*, XIII, 106.

53 "*las calendas de noviembre*", as it was characteristically put by Sepúlveda, 92.

54 Ramos [9:79].

55 AGI, Justicia, leg. 985, *Probanza de Antonio Sedeño*, question xxxi in the questionnaire, cit. Ramos [9:79], 59.

56 See map of 1511, printed with Martyr's *Decades* in that year; and Ptolemy's world map of 1548, printed in *AEA*, XLVII, 1990, 25.

57 This is Ramos' argument [9:79], 47–54.

58 D del C, I, 114.

59 *Cédula* of 29 December 1516 in *CDIU*, I, 69–70.

60 *CDI*, XXVII, 309. Other lenders to Cortés included Andrés de Duero, Pedro de Tieres (Jerez), Antonio de Santa Clara, and Jaime and Jerónimo Tria: the last two gave him together 4,000 pesos in cash, and 4,000 pesos in goods, the loans being secured on Cortés' Indians and other property. Vázquez de Tapia said that he invested his fortune in the expedition. In October 1520, Cortés said that he borrowed over 19,000 pesos (AGI, Patronato, leg. 15, R. 16); Martínez prints this in his *Docs*, I, 148–55).

61 Juan Jaramillo, evidence in *residencia* against Cortés, AGI, Justicia, leg. 224, p.1, f.464 v.

62 "I came with horses and arms and other things as a captain of a *nao* and of people, at my own cost . . ." Res vs. Alvarado, 86.

63 For Gómez de Alvarado, see *Libro de Genealogía*, under Pedro de Alvarado's petition to be admitted to the Order of Santiago, in AHN, Ordenes Militares (Santiago). He had property in Medellín. See AGS, Registro General del Sello, 8 August 1498, f. 121.

64 One witness at an enquiry held by Velázquez two years later described Alvarado coming back to explain "how friendly" Grijalva had been "with the lords and principals of the land" ("*quedaba muy amigo de los tecles e principales señores della . . .*"): Juan Álvarez in *Inf. de 1521*, in Polavieja, 250.

65 Cortés "*fizo lo que quiso*", Velázquez said in his will.

66 Las Casas, III, 194.

67 See Las Casas, III, 196. The rhyme went (D del C, I, 112):
A la gala de mi amo Diego, Diego,
¿Qué capitán has elegido?
Que es de Medellín de Estremadura,
Capitán de gran ventura.

Mas temo Diego no se te alce con el armada;
Que le juzgo por muy gran varón en sus cosas.

68 D del C, I, 113.

69 C de S, 82–3.

70 Cortés seems to have said this in his lost first letter, as cit. by Sepúlveda (93).

71 Las Casas, III, 194–5.

72 Información de los méritos de Francisco Rodríguez Magariño, in AGI, Patronato, leg. 54, no. 3, R.1.

73 John Elliott in intr. to Anthony Pagden's ed. of the *Cartas de relación (Letters from Mexico)* (London, 1972).

74 Hernández Portocarrero, La Coruña, 30 April, 1520, in AGI, Patronato, leg. 254, no. 3c, Gen. 1, R. 1, f.4 v.

75 The source for this is the son of the alleged murderer, Juan Suárez de Peralta [9:38], 34–5. The matter seems not to have been investigated. Perhaps only the family knew of it if it did occur. Suárez de Peralta was anxious to ingratiate himself with the Cortés family, but to say that one's father committed a murder when he did not seems extravagant even by 16th-century standards of sycophancy.

76 See the evidence against Cortés at his enquiry, in *CDI*, XXVII, 310–11. The figure of 30 pigs derives from the *Inf. de 1520* (see Polavieja, 153), a document drawn up on Cortés' insistence. Las Casas, III, 197, wrote that Cortés told him about what happened, either in Mexico in 1538 or in Spain in 1542. Cortés, in a letter in 1542 to Charles V, spoke of the incident (see letter in *CDIHE*, IV, 219).

77 See statement by this official at the *residencia* against Cortés (AGI, Justicia, leg.224, p.1, f.294 r.).

78 This anecdote was approximately confirmed by Cortés himself in the *residencia* against him in 1529 (*CDI*, XXVII, 311). It also appears in Las Casas, III, 123, as in G. 23. C de S (83–5) says the conversation took place on the quay.

79 This date was given in the *probanza* of a year later (4 October 1519, in Tepeaca).

Chapter 11

1 Evidence of Dávila, in *CDI*, XXVIII, 26; *CDI*, XXVII, 312. Its master was Pero González de Trujillo.

2 Verdugo would play a large part in Cortés' life, ending up, as occurred in respect of most of his friends, with a lawsuit against him.

3 Oviedo, II, 388. Pedro de Ordaz had settled down on a farm in Trinidad.

4 Francisco Verdugo, Velázquez's brother-in-law, was his nephew in a way that I have not established.

5 Diego Bardalés and Pedro López de Barbas, in Ordaz's *información* in 1521 (Santo Domingo), in *CDI*, XL, 91, 104. 17 letters of his to his nephew Francisco Verdugo the younger are in the AGI, Justicia, leg.712, of which 9 were published by Enrique Otte, in *HM*, XIV, 102–29, and 321–38. See Florentino Pérez Embid, "Diego de Ordás, compañero de Cortés", *AEA*, (Seville, 1950); and Ch. 2 of Demetrio Ramos' *El Mito del Dorado* (Caracas, 1973).

6 These debts, like those of Francisco de Morla, were inscribed by Andrés de Duero in "a book with a vellum cover" of which there was much talk in the Res vs Velázquez (AGI, Justicia, leg. 49, f.100).

7 Tirado vs. Cortés. in Conway, Camb., Add. 7284.

8 D del C, I, 118–19; *CDI*, XXVII, 313. See also Nuñez Sedeño's evidence to his own suit against Cortés many years later, in *Tributos* [10:22], 10. In that suit, the ubiquitous

witness Bernardino Vázquez de Tapia said that Ordaz asked Núñez Sedeño to join Cortés, on Velázquez's orders.

9 Diego de Coria, who remained a *"criado"* of Cortés for years (he so described himself at a hearing in 1532 against Núño de Guzmán), told this to C de S (157).

10 Sometimes described as "Gonçalo" and with his name spelled "Fernández Puertocarrero", he was son of Rodrigo Hernández Portocarrero and María de Céspedes (APS, *oficio* iv, lib. 1, f.274 v.). Rodrigo was a first cousin of the Count of Medellín but he also had Monroy blood. See Genealogy III and Miguel Muñoz de San Pedro, "Puntualizaciones históricas sobre el lineaje de Monroy" (*REE*, May–August 1965, 213–29), as well as Cooper [6:66], II, 1099. Rodrigo Portocarrero had lawsuits against the Count of Medellín. See, about a suit of 1504, Medellín papers (Casa de Pilatos) in leg.4, doc.30.

11 According to Bernardino Vázquez de Tapia.

12 AGI, Indif. Gen., leg.419, lib.5, f.183.

13 D del C, I, 117.

14 *CDI*, XXVII, 313. He seems to have done so when he reached Macaca.

15 The objects are listed in G, 42–5.

16 Juan de Cáceres in evidence to the *residencia* against Cortés, AGI, Justicia, leg.223, p.2, says it was on the north but, as Irene Wright says in "The Beginnings of Havana", *HAHR*, 5, 1922, it remains unclear when and why Havana moved.

17 *CDI*, XXVII, 315.

18 Tapia, in J. Díaz, et al., 68.

19 *CDI*, XXVII, 314; Tapia in J. Díaz, et al., 68; evidence of Martín Vázquez, in *CDI*, XXVIII, 121.

20 The Order of Merced was founded in 1218, half a military order, half mendicant, a small group but effective: "the Mercedarians are few but they conduct themselves well".

21 G, 50.

22 D del C, I, 126.

23 Tapia gave evidence in answer to question 22 of the questionnaire in the *residencia* against Cortés, AGI, Justicia, leg.223, p.2. He repeated it in much the same terms in 1541; see Tapia, in J. Díaz, et al., 84. Tapia, born in León, may have had connections with Extremadura; the Tapias were one of the main families of Trujillo. That would account for Cortés' reliance on him. An Andrés de Tapia is found as a resident of Medellín in 1492 asking the King for a safe-conduct, since he and another feared the Count of that city (AGS, Registro General del Sello, 23 June 1492, f.126).

24 Las Casas (III, 92) met Grijalva in Hispaniola in 1523, and told him of this talk.

25 Juan de Salcedo, in the *residencia* against Cortés, AGI, Justicia, leg.224, p.1. f.66ov. Salcedo had a property which he shared with Velázquez in Baitiquiri. Gómara says that Cortés and Velázquez were jointly appointed *"Capitán y armador"* (G, 47). The first surviving letter of Cortés to the King says that there was no new permission obtained (*"sin lo decir ni hacer nada a los padres Jerónimos"*). He did not know of the *démarche* of Salcedo.

26 The will of Velázquez is in *Epistolario*, I, document no. 59.

27 C, 49.

28 C, 48: Cortés' father Martín, in petition in 1520 to Charles V, spoke of his son as having paid for 7 ships and Velázquez 3 (Martínez, *Docs*, 102–3).

29 The questionnaire and the answers are in AGI, Patronato, leg.15. R. 16. The questionnaire alone is printed in Martínez, *Docs*, I, 148–65.

30 Angel Losada, "Hernán Cortés en la obra de Sepúlveda", in *R de I* (January–June 1948), 137.

31 Alaminos, in *Inf. de 1522*, 22.

32 Porras Muñoz, in *R de I* (January–June 1948), 333. See also Pedro V. Vives, "La conquista de Nueva España como empresa", ed. in *Historia 16* (December 1985).

33 Ots Capdequí [10:49], 16.

34 Ships were then measured by *toneles* (capacity) rather than *toneladas* (weight). There was a *Santa María de la Concepción* of 100 tons which left Spain for Cuba in 1516 under the captaincy of Juan del Castillo. It could be the same as Cortés' flagship though the duplication of names of ships makes for confusion.

35 Res vs Alvarado, 87.

36 The figure of 530 is derived from the evidence given independently at the *residencia* against Cortés in 1529 in *CDI*, XXVIII, 122 and *CDI*, XXVII, 316. Other sources have variants; for example, Velázquez, in a letter to the King, gave 600 (Muñoz, A 103, f. 157). Bernal Díaz gave 508, but 100 sailors on top of that figure. Tapia gave 560. López de Gómara (with Cervantes de Salazar following him) gave 550, of whom 50 were sailors. Oviedo spoke of 500 men and 16 horses. Martyr, who talked with Alaminos, also spoke of 500 soldiers. Cortés, in *Carta de Relación*, speaks of 400 men. The first published account of Mexico, "Ein Auszug . . ." (1520) also spoke of 400 foot soldiers (*HAHR* of May 1929).

37 A culverin was a large piece of muzzle-loaded artillery using a small-calibre shot; a falconet was similar but smaller.

38 D del C, I, 122; Hassig [1:23], 237. There are several in the Museo del Ejercito, Madrid, one said to have been used by Cortés.

39 D del C, I, 128.

40 See list of Ponce de León's crew to Florida in 1511, on which there were two black sailors, both called Jorge (Murga [5:14], 104).

41 Boyd-Bowman [5:17], 36, established the geographical origin of 383 out of the 500 or so of Cortés' men. There are interesting insights in Francisco Castrillo, *El soldado de la conquista* (Madrid, 1992). The names of those days are difficult to sort out. Sometimes men were known only by their nickname, sometimes by their place of origin, sometimes by a surname as well as a nickname. One could normally choose from the four surnames of grandparents.

42 Dorantes de Salazar [8:78], 320, gave the names of 9, though perhaps he, like Orozco y Berra, may confuse those who went with Cortés with those of the later expedition under Narváez.

43 Andrea del Castillo said in 1583, "I am no less a *conquistadora* than are the *conquistadores* . . ." and added, "often the leading women of my quality when they are found present in wars and conquests . . . with their special vision invigorate themselves and work well and serve their monarchs and lords with more energy and valour [than the men] . . .": "Méritos y servicios del adelantado D. Francisco de Montejo", published in *BAGN*, IX, 1 (January–February 1938), 87.

44 Son of a doctor, Ochaita, from Durango in Guipúzcoa, he had gone to the Indies in 1516. See José Castro Seoane, "El P. Bartolomé de Olmedo", *Misionalia Hispánica*, 6 (1949), 5–78. There is a statue to him in Olmedo's main street. For a short time in Fr. Olmedo's childhood, Bishop Fonseca had been Archdeacon of Olmedo: perhaps that influenced his decision to seek a new life in the Indies (Sagarra Gamazo [6:73], 624).

45 Vázquez de Tapia, in *CDI*, XXVI, 422.

46 The Greeks were Andrés de Rodas, Manuel and Juan Griego, Andrés de Mol, and Arbolenga; the Italians, the pilot Lucas, Juan Lorenzo, Sebastián de Veintemilia (all from Genoa), Juan el Siciliano, Tomás de Rijoles, and Vicencio Corcio of Corsica; the Portuguese included Gonzalo Sánchez, a certain Magallanes, Alonso Martín de Alpedro, Juan Álvarez Rubazo, Gonzalo Rodríguez, Gonzalo Sánchez, Diego Correa and Rodrigo Cavallo.

47 Baltasar de Mendoza, *alcalde ordinario* of Trinidad, in an *información* on 20 November 1520, said that he knew that Cortés "*sacó de esta isla, al tiempo que della*

partió, yndios . . . pero non sabe que cantidad que han llevado . . ." (*CDI*, XXXV, 60). In the same (*CDI*, XXXV, 63), Xoan de Valdecillo said that Cortés had taken 500–660 Cuban Indians. Juan Alvarez said the same, in *Inf. de 1521*, in Polavieja, 263, and it was one of the accusations against Diego Velázquez at the *residencia* against him that he had allowed this to happen (AGI, Justicia, leg.49, f.99). The Florentine Codex (FC, xii, 21) says that the Spanish were held to be gods, while the black men on the expedition were "dirty gods". There were then about 40,000 black slaves in Spain, a few hundred in the Caribbean. See Fernández Álvarez [9:29], 187.

48 Francisco de Icaza, *Conquistadores y pobladores de Nueva España* (Mexico, 1969, 2 vols.), I, 98. He may have come to Mexico in 1520.

49 Xoan de Estacio, in *información* of 20 November 1520, at Trinidad, *CDI*, XXXV, 74.

50 Lucas Fernández de Piedrahita, *Noticia Historial de las conquistas del Nuevo Reino de Granada* (Bogota, 1973, 2 vols.).

51 There were still two styles of riding in use in Spain: *a la brida*, the old Spanish style, with long stirrups, a low back to the saddle, which had a small pommel, and wings which pressed the rider's knees into the horse: and *a la gineta*, deriving from the Moors and taken up extensively, just, ironically, as the Spanish completed the *reconquista*. In the war against Granada, Angus MacKay *Spain in the Middle Ages* (London 1977), 149 tells us, there were 10 times more *jinetes* than men who rode the old way. By 1519, the style *a la gineta* was normal for Spanish *caballeros*; *"mi país se ganó a la gineta"*, wrote the Inca Garcilaso, in respect of the conquest of Peru in the 1530s. The same could have been said of Mexico. For this, see Robert Moorman Denhardt, "The Truth about Cortés's horses," *HAHR* 17 (1937), 525–35; and the same author's "The Equine Strategy of Cortés", *HAHR* (1938), 500– 55. R. B. Cunninghame Graham, *Horses of the Conquest* (London, 1930), gives details about saddles.

52 See Oviedo, II, 103, and J. G. Vanner, *Dogs of the Conquest* (Norman, 1983).

53 *"Muy de palacio"*, says Castro Seoane [11:44], 37.

54 "a man of social graces even if not a very good soldier", in Torquemada's expression.

55 See genealogy of Álvaro de Lugo (who married a sister of Juan Velázquez de Cuéllar), in Cooper [6:66], 447.

56 Evidence of Joan de Cáceres, in AGI, Justicia, leg. 223, p.2, f.227r.; see his recommendation of the King for his son, Diego, in AGI, Indif. Gen., leg.420, 22 July 1523. Cáceres declared himself unable to write at the *residencia* against Alvarado, 150.

57 *"a poner casa y a tratarse como un señor"* (D del C, I, 123), having been *"casi un compañero"*, as Núñez Sedeno put it in the suit of 1529.

58 Zavallos vs La Serna, in Conway, Camb., Add. Mss.

59 I deduce this from examining the statements of age made by the witnesses at the *juicios de residencia* against Cortés and Alvarado in 1529. The majority said that they were then *"de hedad de treynta años más or menos"*.

60 Diego de Vargas in *Inf. de 1521*, Polavieja, 289.

61 For Gamboa and Cáceres, see *Información de 1531*, in *Publicaciones del Archivo General de la Nación*, Vol. xii (Mexico, 1927), 22. For Suárez, see Icaza [11:48], no.130.

62 Fernando López Ríos, "Alimentación y dieta en las navegaciones", *Historia 16*, 198, 64.

63 Mexican cotton armour (*ichcahuipilli*) was made of unspun cotton tightly stitched between two layers of cloth and sewn with a leather border. Sometimes it was soaked in salt to make it stronger. Being about 2 fingers thick in various styles (sleeveless jacket, a jacket tied at the back, etc.,) they were usually strong enough to resist arrows and spears.

64 G, 50.

65 The grant of arms to Francisco de Montano (1540) suggests that Cortés' personal flag was a blue cross on a yellow background. But colours seem to have baffled these

conquistadors. Thus Tapia says that the flag had a red cross on a blue and white background (Tapia, in J. Díaz, et al., 67). Bernal Díaz (D del C, I, 114) says that it was a yellow flag on which the royal arms had been inscribed as well as a cross. He implies that all the ships had such a banner. Cervantes de Salazar (C de S, 107) says that the banner was black with blue and white signs, while Motolinía said that the cross was red on a black field, in the midst of blue and white flames (CDI, VII, 287). The words "*In hoc signis vincis*" can be found in Eusebius' life of Constantine.

66 CDI, XXVI, 458; Vázquez de Tapia's comment is in CDI, XXVI, 408.

67 Motolinía [1:1], 274.

68 "*. . . no tiene más consciencia que un perro*", in Otte [11:5], 320.

69 Article V of the Will of Cortés, for which see Martínez, *Docs*, 313–41.

70 Many efforts have been made to plumb the religious faith of Cortés: e.g. Fr. Fidel de Lejarza, OFM, "*El espíritu misionero de Cortés*", in *AEA*, VI (1949), 343–450.

71 Vázquez de Ayllón, in CDI, XXV–XXVI.

72 D del C, I, 126.

73 D del C, I, 173.

Chapter 12

1 For Alaminos' continuing important role, see Jesús Varela Marcos [7:8], 99–101.

2 G, 53.

3 This was Alvarado's account in the *residencia* against him (Res vs Alvarado, 62–3).

4 Both Rodrigo de Castañeda (Res vs Alvarado, 42) and Bernardino Vázquez de Tapia (Res vs Alvarado, 34) had been on Alvarado's boat and testified that they had seen him treating Indians roughly.

5 D del C, I, 127. The accusation that Alvarado had robbed several *pueblos* without cause was one of the accusations against him in his *residencia*. He denied it.

6 D del C, I, 127.

7 Martyr, II, 27.

8 Joan de Cáceres. in AGI, Justicia, leg. 223, p.2, f. 227; CDI, XXVIII, 124.

9 CDI, XXVII, 317; G, 54.

10 C, 123.

11 Martyr, II, 28.

12 G, 55.

13 D del C, I, 132.

14 G, 34.

15 See Tapia evidence in answer to question 43 of the questionnaire in the *residencia* against Cortés, AGI, Justicia, leg. 223, p.2; also in J. Díaz, et al., 69.

16 CDI, XXVII, 318.

17 Evidence of Vázquez de Tapia, CDI, XXVIII, 124.

18 CDI, XXVII, 319; Martyr, II, 28. Portable altars with pictures of Virgins were used both by the court and on ships.

19 This is López de Gómara's assertion, no doubt on the information of Cortés.

20 He probably mentioned this in his lost "first letter" as we learn from Sepúlveda, 83, where he talks of reading of it in Cortés' "*comentarii*", though it is unclear where Cortés saw it.

21 When granting land in 1526 to the children of Montezuma, cit. Josefina Muriel, "Reflexiones sobre Hernán Cortés", *R de I* (1948), 233.

22 CDI, XVIII, 124.

23 G, 55.

24 *CDI*, XXVII, 319; Tapia, in J. Díaz, et al., 70, says that they spoke of "three or four other bearded men".

25 Ordaz questionnaire, in *Inf. de 1521* (Santo Domingo), evidence of Diego Bardalés, Anton del Río, Pero López de Barbas, Gutierre González, and Alonso de Ávila, all of whom were present (*CDI*, XL, 78ff).

26 Evidence of Joan de Cáceres, AGI, Justicia, leg. 223, p.2.

27 G, 57.

28 Tapia in answer to question 48, AGI, Justicia, leg. 223, p.2.

29 Several witnessess at the *residencia* against Cortés were present, and answered about this in answer to question 49 in Cortés' main questionnaire: for example, Joan de Cáceres, Tapia, and Alonso de Navarrete, in AGI, Justicia, leg. 223, p.2, f.227 r., f.309 v. and f.424 v; see too Tapia, in J. Díaz, et al., 70–1.

30 Martyr, II, 31.

31 *CDI*, XXVII, 322.

32 Las Casas, III, 204.

33 D del C, I, 135.

34 See Cortés' own account in answer to question 51 in 1534, in *CDI*, XXVII, 322 (where Guerrero is wrongly given the name of "Morales"); see Germán Vázquez, in his intr. to Tapia, in J. Díaz, et al., 71–3. Since Chactemal is in the south-east of Yucatan, Guerrero could scarcely have been the instrument of the defeat of Hernández de Córdoba in the north-west, in 1517, as argued there. But he may have rendered other signal services to the Mayas.

35 See Alejandro Lipschutz, "En defensa de Gonzalo Guerrero, marinero de Palos", in *Miscelánea de Estudios dedicados a Fernando Ortiz* (Havana, 1956); and, more recently, Bibiano Torres Ramírez, "El odisea de Gonzalo Guerrero en México", in *Congreso* [6:25], 369–86. There is more material on the life of Guerrero who "lost his soul for an Indian girl", in Eligio Ancona, *Historia de Yucatan* (Barcelona, 1889, 4 vols.), I, 209–18.

36 *Y en Niebla con hambre pura*
otra madre a un hijo muerto
también sacó las asadura . . .

37 Las Casas, I, 123.

38 G, 61 (the cheese and the plate were said to have fallen from Alvarado's ship).

39 Tapia, in J. Díaz, et al., 74.

40 Question 53 in the *residencia* against Cortés (*CDI*, XXVII, 323) speaks of "a bitch which on the said little island [*isleta*] . . ."; Tapia, in J. Díaz, et al., 74; G, 64.

41 Vanner [11:52], 60.

42 Cortés questionnaire (question 53) and at least one witness (Joan de Cáceres, in AGI, Justicia, leg. 223, p.2) say that this looking for Escobar took 6 weeks. These texts are surely wrong.

43 *CDI*, XXVII, 325.

44 This figure is that of Martyr (II, 33), who talked with at least 3 members of the expedition the same year or in 1520. Cortés' *residencia* gives the figure of 80 (*CDI*, XXVII, 329).

45 Martyr, II, 33; G. 66.

46 Martyr, II, 34.

47 Rubber came from the *hule* tree which, if slashed, exuded thick white drops of resin. They were mixed, treated to harden, and were then used for many purposes.

48 Juan Álvarez, in *Inf. de 1521*, in Polavieja, 250.

49 Joan de Cáceres, in AGI, Justicia, leg. 223, p.2, f.227 r.; C, 55; G, 60.

50 Juan Álvarez, in *Inf. de 1521*, in Polavieja, 250.

51 *CDI*, XXVII, 324–5.

52 G, 67.

53 Ordaz's questionnaire in *Información de Diego de Ordaz* (Santo Domingo, 1521), and testimony of Diego Bardalés (who spoke of 40, 000), Gonzalo Giménez (he was among those who rescued Ordaz), and Alonso de Ávila, in *CDI*, XL, 74ff.

54 *CDI*, XXVII, 329.

55 *CDI*, XXVII, 325. Ramos [9:79], 67, argues that this was not the famous *requerimiento* of Palacios Rubios but one "custom-written" by one of Cortés' notaries.

56 Joan de Cáceres, in AGI, Justicia, leg. 223, p.2, f.227 r.

57 Diego de Vargas, in the *Inf. de 1521*, said that 300 Indians were killed, but the Indians themselves said the figure was 2,000: Álvarez, also in the *Inf. de 1521*, Polavieja, 271.

58 Joan de Cáceres, a crossbowman in this operation, in AGI, Justicia, leg. 223, p.2. f.227 r.; *CDI*, XXVIII, 130, 131, and *CDI*, XXVII, 325–9: Martyr, II, 33; G, 69–72; D del C, I, 142–3; and Juan Álvarez, in *Inf. de 1521*, in Polavieja, 257.

59 Mena García [6:12], 43.

60 D del C, I, 145.

61 In describing the battle for Tenochtitlan, Bernal Díaz comments (D del C, I, 454) that the Castilians at first made little progress *"aunque estuvieron allí diez mil Hectores, Troyanos y otros tantos Roldanes . . ."* Another citation of Roland is in D del C, I, 157.

62 D del C, II, 100.

63 Barbara Price, "Demystification . . .", *American Ethnologist*, 5, no.1, February 1978, 109.

64 G, 70.

65 *CDI*, XXVII, 329. Other sources give different names (e.g. G, 71, has Pedro de Alvarado and Alonso de Ávila instead of García de Albuquerque and Gonzalo Alvarado; D del C, I, 143, has Alvarado and Lugo) for these commanders. But the names in the text, given about 10 years later and under oath, seem likely to be correct. Probably Cortés was trying out different commanders to see how they conducted themselves.

66 Evidence of Rodrigo de Segura, who was wounded (AGI, Justicia, leg. 223, p.1, f.611 v.).

67 Cortés' majordomo Joan de Cáceres said (AGI, Justicia, leg. 223, p.2, f.227 r.) that there were over 30,000 against them.

68 The names of those allocated horses – not always their own – suggest who were emerging as leaders: Cortés, Olid, Pedro de Alvarado, Hernández Portocarrero, Escalante, Montejo, Ávila, Velázquez de León, Morla, Lares, Gonzalo Domínguez, Morón and Pedro González de Trujillo. Diego de Ordaz, no horseman, commanded the foot. The standard-bearer was Antonio de Villaroel.

69 *CDI*, XXVIII, 130–1.

70 Tapia was one of those who took the divine intervention seriously (J. Díaz, et al., 76). Sepúlveda, 102, suggests that Cortés mentioned the affair in his *"commentarii"*, that is, his lost first letter. Denhardt [11:51] points out that, according to Bernal Díaz, Morla's horse was a chestnut. So he must have borrowed someone else's.

71 200 appears in *La Carta del Regimiento* (C, 58), 800 was mentioned by the Indians themselves to Cortés, quoted in D del C, I, 151.

72 D del C, I, 152. It has been suggested that in encouraging his horses to neigh at an appropriate moment Cortés was emulating the way that Darius, in rather different circumstances, made himself Emperor of Persia – thanks to having read the then very popular *Epitome* of Justin, in which this incident figures.

73 The Nahuatl for "friend" is *teicniuh*, for "vassal" *temaceual*.

74 "and declared themselves and were received as vassals of his majesty": Joan de Cáceres, in AGI, Justicia, leg. 223, p.2, f.227r.; *CDI*, XXVII, 333.

75 Ramos stresses this side of Cortés' actions [9:79], 89.

76 Martyr, II, 35.

77 *CDI*, XXVII, 229–332: G, 65–9. There are also accounts in Martyr, II, 36; and in Tapia who, in J. Díaz, et al., has the account of Santiago. See Ixtlilxochitl, I, 227.

78 "This witness saw the breaking of, and did his part in breaking, the idols": Joan de Cáceres, in AGI, Justicia, leg. 223, p.2, f.227 r.; the same was said in the same enquiry by Juan Jaramillo: ibid, leg. 224. p.1, f.464 v.

79 It is now the finca El Coco, according to Enrique Cárdenas de la Peña, in *Hernán Cortés*, ed. Alberto Navarro González, (Salamanca, 1986), though Jorge Gurría Lacroix was sure that it was at Bellota, the archaeological ruin on the left bank of the river: *Cortés ante la Juventud*, ed. R. García Granados (Mexico, 1949).

80 Martín Vázquez recalled that "that Palm Sunday a solemn mass was said, and there was a procession and a cross was put up in the square" (*CDI*, XXVII, 333; also *CDI*, XXVIII, 32). Tapia also talks of the procession (in AGI, Justicia, leg. 223, p.2, f.309v., as in J. Díaz, et al., 77); G, 78; D del C, I, 156; C de S, 137.

81 The processions of Holy Week in Seville did not acquire their modern richness till the late 16th century. But some processions were always mounted, some brotherhoods existed, even if the manifestations at Carnival, Corpus Christi and the Assumption were more important than they are now. See Morales Padrón [6:14], 268–72; Antonio del Rocío Romero Abad, *Las fiestas de Sevilla en el siglo XV* (Madrid, 1991).

82 Tapia describes how the realisation came that Marina could be useful, in J. Díaz, et al., 78.

83 For Marina and Cortés, see evidence of Gerónimo de Aguilar against Cortés; "*el dicho Fernando Cortés se echó carnalmente con Marina la lengua e huvo en ella un hijo . . .*" (Conway, Camb. Add. 7286, 19). Dr Cristóbal de Hojeda said the same: "*el dicho Hernando Cortés . . . se hechaba con Marina, muxer desta tierra*" (*CDI*, XVIII, 494). Martín Vázquez said that "*el dicho Don Hernando Cortés la conquistó*" (*CDI*, XXVIII, 131). See also evidence of Diego de Ordaz and Alonso de Herrera in respect of a grant of the Order of Santiago to Martín Cortés *hijo*, in AHN (Santiago). Cortés' grandson by Marina acknowledged the relationship: "Mexico where he [Cortés] held his court and his house with the said Marina his grandmother [*aguela*]" (Cuevas [6:57], 290). For Marina, there is Germán Vázquez, *Malinali Tepenal, la mujer que conquistó Mexico* (Madrid, 1986), and now Ricardo Herren, *Doña Marina, Malinche* (Madrid, 1992).

84 Southern Nahuatl has no "tl" and "p" becomes "b". So the Spaniards rendered the name of the Mexican god Huitzilopochtli "Huichilobos". See Otto Schumann's arguments in L. B. Simpson's ed. of Gómara, *Cortés: the Life of the Conqueror by his secretary* (Berkeley, 1964), 100 fn.4.

85 She is often referred to as "Malinche". This derives from a misunderstanding. The word comes from "Malintzine", made up of the first part of Malinali and two other elements: the reverential "tzin" and the "e" which indicates possession. Thus the correct translation of Malintzine – and Malinche – would be "Lord of Marina" – which was used to indicate Cortés, not Marina. For this, see Germán Vázquez, fn.78 of his ed. of Aguilar (in J. Díaz, et al., 164). See also Orozco [8:4], iv, 110–11.

86 Thus when she passed through Coatzacoalcos many years later she forgave her mother for her act of treachery. The mother and stepbrother became Christians, as "Marta" and "Lázaro".

87 Camargo, 184. His account of Marina is, however, full of mistakes.

88 Joan de Cáceres speaks of her being used even at Potonchan (AGI, Justicia, leg. 223, p.2, f.227r.): "having interpreters [*lenguas*] and people who made them understand the truth . . . many of them . . . separated themselves quickly from that erroneous heresy [*aquella errónea secta*]" (C, 67).

89 Stephen Greenblatt, *Marvellous Possessions* (Chicago, 1992), 145, recalling that Nebrija had written that language had always been the companion of empire, points out that, in Marina, Cortés had found *his* companion.

90 FC, iv, 4. For the use of the word "christening", see Ch. 1.

91 *Cata Francia, Montesinos,*
    Cata París la ciudad,
    Cata las aguas del Duero,
    Do van a dar a la mar.

There are other versions. The ballad-writer may have substituted "Duero" for "Seine" because the first would have been understood better in Spain.

92 *"Que si sueldo del rey toma/ todo se puede vengar"*. See José Luis Martínez [9:52], 70, and Victor Frankl [9:76], who pointed out the significance of the rest of the poem, suggesting that Cortés, the "greatest statesman produced by Spain", consciously made himself directly dependent on the monarch, "the incarnation of the common good", as opposed to "egotistical commercialism", thereby showing himself the "maximum symbol of the continuation of the middle ages into the renaissance".

93 D del C, I, 157.

94 *"cuanto más moros, más ganancias"*. This proverb, about the Moors, was one of Cortés favourites (G, 139). The Spartan allusion is Euripides, Fragment 723 in Eramus' *Adagio*.

Chapter 13

1 Teudile also appears as Teutliltzin or as Tendile.

2 "They made much of Cortés according to their custom": G, 81. Sahagún and others say that, on this occasion, the Indians, on the orders of Montezuma, and as a mark of honour, dressed Cortés in the garb of Quetzalcoatl. Juan Álvarez, a responsible witness, aged 45 and certainly present in 1519, gave evidence in Cuba in 1521 that Cortés was dressed elaborately, but that this was 2 or 3 days later (Polavieja, 252). See below. Cervantes de Salazar also says (IV, 146) it was later. Las Casas (III, 217) says that two expeditions of Indians came to see Cortés on the water, bringing gold on both occasions. The idea that the local Indians had these rich clothes waiting for Cortés is not to be believed. Álvarez's account is the most reliable. He was an enemy of Cortés, and had nothing to gain from lying.

3 Hassig [1:23], 237.

4 "signs of love [*amor*]"; question 81 in Cortés questionnaire (*CDI*, XXVII, 334). Miguel de Zaragoza, lost during Grijalva's expedition, claimed to have told Cortés where to land and so avoid hostile Indians. This story is in Dorantes de Salazar [8:78], 189–90. That author was later a neighbour of Zaragoza.

5 Frances Berdan, "The Luxury Trade", in Boone [1:5], 169.

6 Anwalt [7:41], 3.

7 Juan Álvarez, in *Inf. de 1521*, 252.

8 Álvarez, *Inf. de 1521*, 252.

9 C, 117.

10 G, 83.

11 "They made many huts", *CDI*, XXVII, 334; Martyr, II, 36; Álvarez, in *Inf. de 1521*, quoted in Polavieja, 252.

12 G, 319.

13 This self-assumed "embassy" of Cortés can be seen in e.g. Ixtlilxochitl, 230.

14 D del C, I, 162.

15 *"estiércol"*: Las Casas, II.

16 D del C, I, 169.

17 FC, xii, 19.

18 G, 84–5; Tapia, in J. Díaz, et al., 79.

19 See note of José Corona Núñez, quoted in *Rel. de Michoacan*, 241.

20 Ixtlilxochitl, 229–30: G, 85.

21 G, 85; Ixtlilxochitl, 230; D del C, I, 168. This lieutenant was perhaps that same slave Cuitlapitoc who had come with Teoctlamacazqui. The suggestion (in a document first printed in García Icazbalceta, II, 1–24, and reprinted often, e.g. in Martínez, *Docs*, I, 60–76) that Cortés was greeted now by two Mexicans, Tlamapanatzin and Atonalctzin who, from hatred of Montezuma, offered themselves as vassals of the Emperor Charles V, seems to be a forgery.

22 Hassig [1:27], 51.

23 Durán, II, 517.

24 FC, xii (1st ed.), 20.

25 Sahagún II 958.

26 Durán, II, 249.

27 Sahagún I, 379, 384.

28 FC, xii, 19.

29 FC, xii (1st ed.), 19.

30 FC, xii, 21. But see Sahagún, II, 938, and Durán, II, 517ff. The timetable in both the Florentine Codex and Sahagún must be a little out because of the well-attested fact that Teudile sent messengers to Montezuma. Juan Álvarez says that, "after fifteen or twenty days . . . Montezuma . . . sent Cortés a wheel of gold and one of silver".

31 FC, iii, 17–20, for Huemac.

32 FC, xii, 21. Durán, II, 517 ff., and Tezozomoc insist that Huemac, last king of Tula, and a god also, controlled that site and that his permission had to be asked before Montezuma could make a plan. But he did get permission and was on his way when a priest saw him and shamed him out of the idea. Durán says that this attempt at flight occurred during the visit of Grijalva. See comment in Susan Gillespie, *The Aztec Kings* (Tucson, 1989), 159–60.

33 Cline's Sahagún(47) has the Spaniards themselves saying that that was their purpose.

34 Cod. Ram., 134.

35 Martyr, II, 60, writing in 1522 or early 1523, as a result of information from Montejo, Portocarrero, Alaminos or Juan de Ribera (for the latter, see Ch. 37).

36 Fr. Aguilar, in J. Díaz, et al., 165.

37 Marineo Siculo wrote in 1530 that the *naturales* of the coast, because of Cortés' good treatment, believed that he was "truly a god or a messenger of one" ([9:20], 102). The Códice Chimalpopoca (*Anales de Cuauhtitlan*), c. 1555, f. 68, said "they called them fêted, gods, *teules*, with the names which they gave to their gods: Four Wind, Tonatiuh (that is, the sun), Quetzalcoatl". A few years later some Yucatec Maya did greet some Spaniards under Alvarado as gods (*Anales de los Cakchiques*, ed. Adrian Recinos, Mexico, 1953, 121).

38 John Bierhorst, *Four masterworks of American Indian Literature* (New York, 1974), 327.

39 "*teules*, their name for gods or evil spirits" ("*su nombre como sus dioses o cosas malas*"): D del C, I, 297.

40 See Richard Townsend: "This force was pre-eminently manifested in the natural forces – earth, air, fire, and water – but was also to be found in persons of great distinction, of things and places of unusual or mysterious configuration": "State and Cosmos in the art of Tenochtitlan" (Dumbarton Oaks, Washington, 1979), 28.

41 Tezozomoc [1:18], 687. Eulalia Guzmán, in *Relaciones de Hernán Cortés a Carlos V sobre la invasión de Anahuac* (Mexico, 1958), 223, Romerovargas [4:13], II, 76, and, to a lesser extent, Wagner [8:23], 187–98, dismiss most of this as nonsense, since there was no pre-conquest evidence for a myth of return.

42 "we have always held that those who descended from him were bound to come [habían de venir] and subjugate this land and ourselves as vassals" (C, 117).

43 C, 116 and 128. This was question 98 in CDI, XXVII, 341–2.

44 "When Cortés arrived with the Spaniards, the people of the land received him thinking that he was Orchilobos" – the latter being what the Spanish, to begin with, called Huitzilopochtli: Oviedo, IV, 245–9. Oviedo said that he did not believe it.

45 FC, X, 190–1.

46 Ixtlilxochitl [4:5], 7.

47 H. B. Nicholson, Topiltzin-Quetzalcoatl (Ph.D., Harvard, 1957), 361, 412–13, 428–30. One of his conclusions(361) was that "the evidence for a widespread belief in his eventual return to reclaim his own, which materially influenced Motecuhzoma II in his initial dealings with the Spaniards, is very strong". Other conquistadors (Bernal Díaz, Fr. Aguilar) say that something like this occurred in Tenochtitlan in November. The Rel. de Michoacan records the surprise of the Cazonci (the king of that territory) that his ancestors had not told him of anything like the Spanish coming, though he does accept that some god must have sent the Spaniards. Other references to a myth of a god returning can be seen in Historia Tolteca-Chichimeca, ed. Paul Kirchhoff et al. (Mexico, 1976), ff. 10 and 33; Domingo ... Chimalpahin, 2nd Relación, in Silvia Rendón, Relaciones Originales de Chalca Amecaqucan (Mexico, 1965) f. 18r; and the Codice Chimalpopoca (Anales de Cuauhtitlan), as tr. in Bierhorst [13:38]. Maya views can be seen in Popol Vuh, ed. Adrian Recinos (Mexico, 1953), 220–3; and Anales de los Cakchiques [13:37], 62, 67, 79. See for discussion, León-Portilla, "Quetzalcoatl-Cortés en la conquista de Mexico", HM, XXIV, 1(1974). There is a negative summary in Gillespie [13:32], Ch. VI, while the positive case is put by David Carrasco in Quetzalcoatl and the Irony of Empire (Chicago, 1982).

48 Códice Chimalpopoca in Bierhorst [13:38], 28. But van Zantwijk [Preface: 5], 51, believes that the followers of Quetzalcoatl practised human sacrifice and introduced it to the Mayas.

49 Bierhorst [13:38], 15.

50 "the image of queçalcoatl which was in the said great temple made with a long beard [hecha de buelto y con barba larga] . . ." (Relación de Cholula, 1582, by Gabriel de Rojas, corregidor, ed. by Fernando Gómez de Orozco, Revista Mexicana de Estudios Históricos, I, 5, (September–October 1927).

51 Historia de los mexicanos por sus pinturas [1:47], 253. The temple, described by Durán (II, 333ff.), and discussed by Brundage ([2:50], 92), was where the archbishop's palace later stood. There was a courtyard in which Mexican farces were performed. See Angel María Garibay, "Poema de Travesuras", Tlalocan, III, 2 (1952).

52 "The Hamburg Box", in the Hamburgisches Museum für Völkerkunde, has the glyph for 1-Reed on it. It is discussed in Pasztory [4:35], 256. The same author's "El arte Mexica y la conquista española", ECN (1984), 110, raises the possibility that this bearded Quetzalcoatl could be Cortés.

53 H. B. Nicholson ([13:47], 8–19), dated this relief on the Cerro de Malinche, the only definitely pre-conquest depiction of Quetzalcoatl, as "fifteenth or early sixteenth century". Eloise Quiñones Keber, in "The Aztec Image of Topiltzin Quetzalcoatl", in Smoke and Mist, Studies in honour of Thelma Sullivan (Oxford, 1988), suggests that the Mexica carried out the relief in order to create a historical tradition and so prepare the way for the idea of their own monarchs being carved on the cliff in Chapultepec.

54 Códice Chimalpopoca, tr. Bierhorst [13:38], 37.

55 Discussing the suggestion by e.g. Eulalia Guzmán that the identification of Cortés with Quetzalcoatl was a "post eventum" fabrication by (for example) Tlatelolca determined to make a point of their own with Fr. Sahagún, David Carrasco ([13:47], 48)

wrote that "the belief in Quetzalcoatl's return, as shown in a number of . . . sources, had such a strong grip on the Aztec mind that, even decades after the events described, it was used to communicate the persistence of the Aztec commitment to certain cosmological patterns of destiny. While it is possible that the Tlatelolcans may have elaborated this belief, I do not think they could have fabricated it." A good study is Paul Kirchhoff, "Quetzalcoatl, Huemac y el fin de Tula", *Cuadernos Americanos* (November–December 1955). He argued that Quetzalcoatl as a ruler was contemporary with Huemac.

56 Códice Chimalpopoca in Bierhorst [13:38], 39. This method of vanishing, reminiscent of Moses in Egypt, persuaded Durán that the Mexica must be Jewish.

57 Luis Weckmann, *La herencia medieval de México* (Mexico, 1984, 2 vols.), I, 392.

58 *Anales de Tlatelolco*, ed. Heinrich Berlin, intr. Robert H. Barlow (Mexico, 1948).

59 *Historia de los mexicanos por sus pinturas* [1:47], 251.

60 Motolinía, in García Icazbalceta, I, 65.

61 This letter was dated 6 October 1541 (Oviedo, IV, 252).

62 E.g. Juan Cano's *Relación* of *c.* 1532; *Historia de los mexicanos por sus pinturas* (*c.* 1535); and *Histoyre du Mechique* (*c.* 1543).

63 Sahagún, II, 953. This was omitted by Sahagún in his ed. of 1585. See Cline's Sahagún, 34.

64 Cod. Ram., 131. The Codex Ríos (*c.* 1566–89), deriving from material assembled in the early 1560s, says the same. The suggestion that Quetzalcoatl was a *white* god appeared in 1596 in Gerónimo de Mendieta, *Historia Eclesiástica Indiana* (Mexico, 1870), 92; Tapia (in J. Díaz, et al., 95–6) said that he wore a white tunic, with red crosses.

65 FC, i, 11–12. These strangers would turn out to be the sons of Quetzalcoatl.

66 FC, i, 5. This identification was suggested by Martin Wasserman, in "Montezuma's passivity: an alternative view without post-conquest distortions of a myth", *The Masterkey* (1983), 85–93. The capricious nature of this deity is studied in van Zantwijk [Preface: 5], 128.

67 Nicholson [1:42], 402.

68 I have here used Thelma Sullivan's tr. in "Tlatoani", *ECN* (1980).

69 Thelma Sullivan in ECN iv (1963), 93.

Chapter 14

1 Sahagún said that the leader of the mission was a priest, "Yoalli ichan" (FC, xii, 10). D del C (I, 164) said that he was called Quintalbor and looked like Cortés.

2 Durán, II, 518–21. Durán presents this speech as made at the time of Grijalva's visit.

3 FC, xii, 13; D del C, I, 161; Martyr, II, 45–6.

4 Durán, II, 507–8. Durán also tells this tale of Grijalva's visit.

5 H. B. Nicholson identified the ruined statue in 1961. See his brilliant "The Chapultepec Cliff Sculpture of Motecuhzoma Xoyocotzin," in *El México Antiguo*, 379–444; and discussion in Pasztory [4:35], 127–8.

6 Pasztory [13:52], 110.

7 Everyone who accepts the story describes the events as occuring on Cortés' ship. The picture in the FC says so too. There would be no difficulty about this if the messengers had gone out to the ship on Cortés' arrival. But that could not have been so. The only reliable Spanish version, by Álvarez (*Inf. de 1521*, in Polavieja, 252), speaks, as stated, of the events as happening "two or three days" after the arrival.

8 Cline's Sahagún, 41.

9 Durán, II, 521.

10 Álvarez, in *Inf. de 1521*, in Polavieja, 252.

11 *Anales de Tlatelolco* [13:58], 149.

12 For Quetzalcoatl's dress, *Ritos, sacerdotes y atavíos de los dioses*, ed. Miguel León-Portilla (Mexico, 1961), 118–19.

13 Duverger [1:44], 247.

14 Álvarez testified: "within two or three days, the said principal lord came with many of the Indians and brought to the said captain fernando cortés a head like a dragon's of gold [*una cabeza como de dragon de oro*] and within it fangs [*colmyllos*] and palates [*paladares*] all of gold and on top a rich plumage and certain anklets of gold and silver . . . as is the custom among the lords of the said Indians . . . and they put these things on the said fernando cortés [*todo esto segund que es costumbre entre los principales de los dichos yndios se pusyeron al dicho fernando cortés . . .*]" (Polavieja, 252). The Florentine Codex (FC, xii, 12–15) says that the dress was that of Quetzalcoatl and that there was a green mask, not a dragon's head. Andrés de Duero, who was not present, but of course had been Cortés' partner, testified in 1521 that Cortés was given a golden alligator's head (*Inf. de 1521*, Polavieja, 310). The reason why Gómara and Cortés himself did not mention the event may be that the *Caudillo* made off with the jewels without reckoning them part of the rest of the booty from which the Royal Fifth would be deducted.

15 Duverger [1:44], 227.

16 *Anales de Tlatelolco* [13:58].

17 A lombard, like a falconet, was a swivel gun, often used on ships. It had a removable breechblock which resulted in a loss of power.

18 The best source for the Mexican reaction continues to be FC, xii, but I have as before also used material from Sahagún (both versions) where it is slightly different.

19 Hassig [1:23], 280. For a description which makes the House of the Eagle Knights sound as if it were the Metropolitan Club, Washington, see Durán, I, 106. It was excavated in the 1980s: see Augusto Molina Montes, "Templo Mayor Architecture", in Boone [1:5], 102.

20 For his poems, see Garibay [1:13], I, 102. He was Montezuma's father-in-law.

21 Durán, II, 321.

22 Discussed in Zorita [1:8], 143, 107.

23 López Austin [1:18], 95. There seem to have been several councils, whose chairmen were to be found in the Supreme Council, not unlike a modern state.

24 Tezozomoc [1:19], 388.

25 Guzmán [7:17], 98.

26 Donald Robertson, *Mexican Manuscript Painting of the Early Colonial Period* (Yale, 1959), 138.

27 Edward Calnek, "The Internal Structure of Tenochtitlan", in *The Valley of Mexico*, ed. Eric Wolf (Albuquerque, 1976), 289–90.

28 This discussion appears in Ixtlilxochitl [4:5], 8.

29 Cod. Ram., 135; Cline's Sahagún, 48.

30 *Anales de Tlatelolco* [13:58].

31 Joan de Cáceres says that he held them in his hands, and called them copper and silver (AGI, Justicia, leg. 223, p.2, f.227 v.) – an odd mistake for Cortés' majordomo. Cortés' questionnaire called them "plates". Oviedo saw them in Seville: "The gold one weighed 4,800 pesos, the silver one 48.50 marks. Each were 9 and a half palms in diameter [say 6 feet 6 inches], 30 in circumference [20 feet]" (Oviedo, IV, 10). For Dürer's description, see Ch.37, and for the Venetian ambassador's, Ch.23. That they had a wooden base is made clear by a document in AGI, Contratación, 4675, where they are described as wooden wheels on which gold and silver had been placed. New nails were needed in Spain to keep on the precious metals.

32 Emmerich [2:29], 140; Dudley Easby, "Fine metalwork in Pre-Conquest Mexico", in *Essays in Pre-Colombian Art and Archaeology*, ed. S. K. Lothrop et al. (Cambridge, Mass., 1961), 35–42.

33 Graulich [1:42], 57.

34 Cline's Sahagún, 49.

35 FC, xii, 21. According to Sahagún (in the Cline version, 49), the occurrence made the Mexicans think that "these are not gods like ours. They are heavenly gods. We should worship and appease them". But this may be an *ex post facto* argument.

36 FC, xii, 22.

37 G, 87.

38 *"una copa de vidrio de Florencia, labrada y dorada, con muchas arboledas y monterías que estaban en la copa . . ."* (D del C, 166). Maudslay tr. *"labrada"* as "engraved" (Díaz del Castillo, Maudslay ed., I (London, 1908), 145). But that may not be right. No glass to speak of was made in Florence at this time. It must have been Venetian. Within 20 years, though, the Florentines did make glass: a new activity inspired by Cosimo I. Perhaps Bernal Díaz saw some of it in the late 1540s. See Detlef Heikampf, "Studien zur mediceischen Glaskunst", in *Mitteilungen des Kunsthistorischen Institutes in Florenz*, XXX, Band 1986, Heft 1/2, 265–6.

39 Berdan [3:30], 38.

40 Ixtlilxochitl says that his ancestor of the same name also privately sent messengers to Cortés about this time to tell Cortés what a tyrant Montezuma was (Ixtlilxochitl, 232). No other source records such an initiative.

41 D del C, I, 170, anxious to emphasise the popular nature of the expedition, says that he was elected to this position by popular vote.

42 D del C, I, 117. This Gonzalo de Mexía (or Mejía) may have been connected with the Mejía of Cáceres, hence with the friend, probably benefactor, of the Cortés family, Juan Núñez de Prado, whose father and brother were named Mejía. So was the Alvarados' grandmother, causing them to have uncles of that name. Gonzalo is different from another of the same name, without the particule, nicknamed "Rapapelo, the plunderer", who was also on the expedition, grandson of a famous robber of the Sierra Morena, and who would be killed on Cortés' journey to Honduras in 1525.

43 FC, xii, 22; also Durán, II, 522.

44 D del C, I, 167.

45 D del C, I, 178–9. López de Gómara attributes this expedition to the leadership of Cortés.

46 Res vs Alvarado, 64.

47 These witnesses included Bernardino Vázquez de Tapia and Rodrigo de Castañeda. See Res vs Alvarado, 36.

48 Aguilar, in J. Díaz, et al., 205.

49 D del C, I, 173. Wagner suggests that the Spanish saw human sacrifice as an excuse for conquering the Indians – a view which led him to underestimate the practice. There were, however, many exaggerated accounts: for example, in *Newe Zeitung von dem Lande das die Spanier funden haben* of 1522, where 12 to 18 children are said to have been sacrificed before every battle, then eaten (*HAHR*, May 1929, 199).

50 Alaminos, in *Inf. de 1522*, 233.

51 "everyone came together and demanded that a settlement be made" (*"toda la gente se juntan e le requieren que se poblasen"*), in report of Portocarrero and Montejo, at Corunna, in AGI, Patronato, leg. 254, no.3c, Gen. 1, R. 1, f.4v.

52 But see Luis Navarro, in "El líder y el grupo en la empresa cortesiana", in *Hernán Cortés y su tiempo* [9:22].

53 This is the argument of Ramos [9:79], 104, who quotes Oviedo (II, 147) in support.

54 See the conversation reported by D del C (II, 173), which that chronicler says took place outside his hut with Portocarrero, Escalante and Lugo (not inside, for his companions there were "of the party of Velázquez").

55 ". . . and no more" (Garcia Llerena, *CDI*, XXVII, 203).

56 C, 60–1, puts this challenge as happening earlier; but the points made were the same. See *CDI*, XXVII, 334–5 for the texts of two of Cortés' questions (84 and 85) at his *residencia* which spoke of "the great disposition which there was to settle" ("*el grande disposición que había de poblar*").

57 G, 64. The source for the plotting is D del C, I, Chapters xli and xlii.

58 Martyr, II, 37; C de S, 141. The Álvarez Chico brothers were from Oliva, near Medellín.

59 C de S, 188–91, may have been informed about this by Vázquez de Tapia.

60 Francisco de Zavallos on behalf of Narváez, vs La Serna: Conway, Camb., Add. Mss., I, 59.

61 "until His Majesty was served", Joan de Cáceres put it (AGI, Justicia, leg. 223, p.2).

62 G, 66; C de S, 153.

63 Marrero [6:40], 108.

64 Manuel Giménez Fernández, in "Cortés y su revolución comunera en la Nueva España", *AEA* (1948), 91. See too the same author's *Las Doctrinas populistas en la independencia de Hispano América* (Sevilla, 1947), 15 ff. There is quite a bibliography on this subject: e.g., Silvio Zavala, *Hernán Cortés antes la justificación de su conquista* (Mexico, 1985).

65 "the said election was on the advice of all; and this witness gave his vote and counsel" ("fue la dicha elección de un parecer de todos; e queste testigo dió su voto e parecer en ello") (Vázquez, in *CDI*, XXVIII, 134; Tapia, in AGI, Justicia, leg. 223, p.2).

66 Sepúlveda, 111–12.

67 The *Carta del Regimiento* makes this clear (first letter of Cortés, C. 61).

68 Aguilar, in J. Díaz, et al., 165, points this out.

69 See the accusation of Andrés de Monjaraz, in *CDI*, XXVI, 540.

70 In a letter of 4 July 1519 (printed as Document 4), Cortés would call himself "*capitán-general y justicia mayor*".

71 As argued by García de Llerena, in *CDI*, XXVII, 203–4.

72 This was an accusation in the *residencia*. See *CDI*, XXVII, 8.

73 Partida II, Law I of Título X talks of "a muncipal council of all the men acting in common" ("ayuntamiento de todos los hombres comunalmente"): see Francisco López Estrada y María Teresa López García-Berdoy, *Las Siete Partidas* (Madrid, 1992), 173.

74 The connection with the *Siete Partidas* was developed by Frankl [8:70], who suggested a similarity between the language of the *Carta del Regimiento* ("it seemed to us desirable . . . for the pacification and concord between us, and to govern us well, it was convenient to name a man . . .") and the *Siete Partidas*, Título I, Law II.

75 C, 29.

76 Silvio Zavala (*Ensayos sobre la colonización española en América*, Buenos Aires, 1944, 211), suggested that there may have been a copy in the hands of the expedition to Mexico. If so, it would have been of the (large) Seville edition of the 1490s. Copies had certainly reached Hispaniola and probably would have got to Cuba.

77 This view is developed by Eulalia Guzmán, with her usual panache [7:17], 100.

78 "*sin las leyes se abían quebrantar por reinar, se han de quebrantar, le que ansí mismo decía Ceasar*": Vázquez de Tapia said in Cortés' enquiry that he had often heard the *Caudillo* quote that (*CDI*, XXVI, 424). So did Juan de Tirado (Res (Rayón), II, 40). Citing this, Oviedo (II, 148) quotes Cicero: "*Si violandum est jus, regnandi gratia violandum est.*" He recalled that Suetonius says the same in his life of Caesar. John Elliott [9:76], 46, thought that Cortés might have read the latter.

79 Martyr, II, 38, after conversation with Montejo and Alaminos, may have under-estimated the extent to which the desire to settle existed independently of the *Caudillo*.
80 Martyr, II, 37.
81 "the people had constituted themselves a town" ("*la gente había hecho pueblo*"): Martínez, *Docs*, 114.
82 Bernal Díaz says so. The fact is accepted by Giménez Fernández [14:64], 73.
83 Luis Marín, in *CDI*, XXVIII, 58.
84 G, 94.
85 Juan Álvarez, in *Inf. de 1521*.
86 D del C, I, 177.
87 G. 95.
88 Cf. Valdés, who said: "One has seen many republics without a ruler but never a ruler without a republic" (cit, Rogerio Sánchez, in his ed. of López de Mendoza's proverbs, Madrid, 1928, 17); Giménez Fernández [14:64] argued that these actions were a colonial anticipation of the Castilian revolution of the *comunidades* which would occur a year later. But, as Joseph Pérez says, the comparison is impossible to sustain.

Chapter 15

1 FC, xii, 25–6.
2 Godoy fought a duel in 1524 with the chronicler Bernal Díaz who, therefore, did not talk highly of him in his book.
3 Villa Rica de la Vera Cruz was at Quiahuixtlan from 1519 to 1525, when it was moved to Antigua. It went to modern Veracruz at San Juan de Ulúa about 1600.
4 *El Conquistador Anónimo*, in García Icazbalceta, I, 378.
5 D del C, I, 181; G, 123.
6 Gerhard [8:60], 365. Tribute paid by Cempoallan does not figure separately in the *Matrícula de Tributos*, but was merged with Cuetlaxtlan. The journey to Cempoallan is described in G, 95–6; D del C, I, 180–1; C, 123; Aguilar, in J. Díaz, et al, 88–9; and Ixtlilxochitl, 233. There is also a letter from a conquistador describing some of it, dated 28 June 1519, published by Marshall H. Saville, *Indian Monographs*, Vol.ix, No. 1 (New York, 1920).
7 14,000 was the comment of Montejo, Hernández Portocarrero, Alaminos, etc., in Seville in November 1519, to an unknown writer, who sent a letter, 7 November 1519, to Juan de la Peña in Burgos, published by Saville [15:6], 31–4.
8 Ixtlilxochitl, 233.
9 Zorita [1:8], 161.
10 Joan de Cáceres, AGI, Justicia, leg. 223, p.2, f.227 r.; G, 99–100.
11 Tezozomoc [1:18], 484.
12 Ixtlilxochitl, 234. For Medellín, see for example the commissioning of Licenciado Bernardo in 1493 (AGS, Registro General del Sello, 17 May 1493, f.383).
13 S. Jeffrey Wilkerson, "In search of the mountain of foam . . ." in Boone [2:58], 103; the *Carta del Regimiento* (C, 67) says: "some of us saw the sacrifices and those who did say that it is the most crude and frightful thing to see that they had ever seen". Bernal Díaz says the same: "every day they sacrificed in front of us three or four or five Indians" (D del C, I, 198).
14 Martyr, II, 43.
15 D del C., I, 123, implies a shorter stay.
16 G, 101–2
17 D del C, I, 185, says that there were only 5 Mexicans.

18 G, 105–6.

19 See *CDI*, XXVII, 338, for Cortés' question 93 in his *residencia* about the alliance with the Totonacs.

20 D del C, I, 188. It ("being built high up": *CDI*, XXVIII, 30) seemed similar to Archidona, near Málaga, which played an important part in the war against Granada. There is also an Archidona near Seville.

21 Ixtlilxochitl, 235.

22 I assume that the two delegations mentioned by G (107) and Durán (II, 525) as coming at this time were the same. There is a discrepancy between the advice that the two suggest that the visitors gave to Cortés: G suggesting a delay would be in order; Durán being more encouraging.

23 This town disappeared in the 16th century. It was probably close to Papalote de la Sierra, halfway along the modern road between Cempoala (Cempoallan) and Jalapa.

24 See *Nobilario* [7:12], 232–3, where the coat of arms granted to Zaragoza's son in the 1550s is shown, including "two pails on a verdant background".

25 D del C (I, 195–6) denies there was any battle here. But Diego Vargas, in the *Inf. de 1521*, suggests that there was much killing (Polavieja, 272). Martín Vázquez, in a *probanza* on his own conduct in 1525, spoke of "four or five days of fighting" (AGI, Mexico, leg. 205, no. 5).

26 D del C, I, 123.

27 Clendinnen [3:11], 52.

28 D del C, I, 201 See Richard Trexler, "Aztec Priests for Christian Altars", in *Scienze, credenze, occulte livelli di cultura* (Florence, 1983), 192.

29 I derive this from a note by Sr. Fernández de Castillo in Conway (Camb.).

30 C de S, 173. Referred to also as Salceda and Herrera Salcedo. Andrés de Tapia doubted whether there were as many as 70 men or more than 7 or 9 horses (AGI, Justicia, leg. 223, p.2, f.309). Bernal Díaz said there were only 10 soldiers and 2 horses. Cortés himself said that there were 7 to 9 horses. Ixtlilxochitl said 15. I incline to the higher figure as being more likely.

31 The Marini family were known as bankers. See Carande [9:15], I, 73, 76, etc. Felipe Fernández-Armesto [6:1], 13, points out that Andalusia was a "frontier land of Genoa as well as of Castile". For the Genoese in the region, see H. Sancho de Sopranis, "Los genoveses en la región gaditano-xericense . . .", *Hispania*, 8 (1949), 355–402. Luis Marín's services to Cortés may have included the confirmation of his seriousness to the Marinis and other Genoese, hence to all the forward-looking merchants in Spain. There also came on this expedition Pero Rodríguez de Escobar and Dorantes de Salazar.

32 Text in *CDI*, XXII, 38–52, and Vicente de Cadenas, *Carlos I de Castilla* (Madrid, 1988), 109–11, signed 13 November 1518, by the King, Cobos, the Chancellor, the Bishops of Burgos and Badajoz, as well as Zapata. For comment, see Mario Hernández Barba in his ed. of Cortés (C, 17). Las Casas (III, 231–2) has a summary.

33 "*adelantado diego Velázquez, lugarteniente de nuestro gobernador de la ysla Fernandina, capitán y repartidor della*" (see AGI, Indif. Gen., leg. 420, f.9).

34 See Giménez Fernández [14:64], 53, 77, 86; Las Casas, III, cxxiv.

35 He began to refer to himself as Abbot. See APS, 31 October 1519, oficio xv, lib. 2, f.391.

36 John Elliott, intr. to Pagden's ed. of Cortés' Letters [10:73], xx.

37 L. B. Simpson, in his tr. of López de Gómara, *Cortés, the Life of the Conqueror, by his Secretary* (Berkeley, 1964), has "delegates" (88), but the sense is other.

38 See Giménez Fernández [6:19], I, 147–76.

39 This is the letter, whose original is lost, of which there is a contemporary copy (c.1527) in the Codex Vindobonensis, Vienna, usually ed. as the first letter in Cortés' *Cartas de Relación*. It is formally the *Carta del Regimiento*, which last word should be translated "municipality".

40 This letter is described by Tapia, in J. Díaz, et al., 85. See Giménez Fernández [14:64], 94 fn., 172.

41 For example by Valero Silva, in *El legalismo de Hernán Cortés, instrumento de la conquista* (Mexico, 1965). Why, he asks, should Cortés have written a letter to the King, when he had nothing particular to say, and would have to have admitted his disobedience to Velázquez?

42 Bernal Díaz says that the letter was written independently of Cortés. Wagner [8:23], 8, 82, discusses. For Cortés' style, see Beatriz Pastor Bodmer, *The Armature of the Conquest* (Stanford, 1992), 63–100. Manuel Alcalá, *César y Cortés*, (Mexico, 1950), and Frankl [8:70] speculate as to whether the habit of placing verbs regularly at the end of sentences suggests a Latin education.

43 AGI, Justicia, leg. 223, p.1, f.1. It was first ed. by Robert S. Chamberlain: "Two unpublished documents of Hernán Cortés and New Spain", *HAHR*, 18, No. 4 (November, 1938). It is also printed in Martinez, *Docs*, 1, 77–85.

44 "They live more politically and reasonably than I have seen in these parts."

45 William Greenlee, *The Voyage of Pedro Alvarez Cabral to Brazil and India* (London, 1938), 29.

46 Fr. Prudencio Sandoval, in his *Historia de la vida y hechos del emperador Carlos V* (Madrid, 1955), 1, 123, argued that "majesty" was an innovation. The word had, however, been used by Juan II. See José Manuel Soria, *Fundamentos Ideológicos del poder real en Castilla* (Madrid, 1988), 120.

47 Tapia, in J. Díaz, et al., 85.

48 "I undertook [*certifiqué*] to Your Highness that you would have him a prisoner or dead, or a subject of the royal crown of your Majesty" (C, 82). This is from a letter which Cortés wrote in 1520 to the King – the so-called second *Carta de Relación* (C, 82). Oviedo also wrote of it: "and even offered in his letter to have Montezuma dead or a prisoner" (Oviedo, IV, 11). Perhaps he saw the letter. C de S, 177, refers to the first letter and also has this expression in it. Sepúlveda talked of Cortés' "*comentarii*".

49 See Abel Martínez-Luza, who, in "Un memorial de Hernán Cortés", *AEA*, XLV supplement (1988), 1–3, argued that a letter to Charles V usually dated 1533 by Fr. Mariano Cuevas [6:57], 129–40, was really written in 1522, and there Cortés talks of having mentioned the matter about "two years and a half before".

50 Martín Vázquez in answer to question 28 of the second questionnaire, in *CDI*, XXVIII, 239–40.

51 This hitherto unknown letter is published as Document 4 of this book.

52 Letter ed. by Saville [15:6]. Mention of a bedstead makes it suspect, for the Totonacs had none.

53 See John T. Lanning, "Cortés and his first official remission of treasure to Charles V", in *Revista de Historia de América*, 2 (Mexico, June 1938), 5–29.

54 Compare Cuba's (declared) output of 62,000 pesos of gold in the four years 1511–15, in which the King's Fifth was 12,347: Wright [5:50], 69.

55 Antonio de Solís, *Historia de la conquista de México* (Madrid 1849), 153–4, without evidence.

56 Otto Adelhofer, in his facsimile ed. of the Codex (properly *Vindobonensis Mexicanus I*), 11–12. This seems to have been given by the Emperor Charles V to his brother-in-law, the King of Portugal, who gave it to Cardinal Medici, subsequently Pope Clement VII. Adelhofer speculates how it reached Vienna. Zelia Nuttall, in her intr. (Cambridge, Mass., 1902) to the codex called after her, discusses how the book came to be in the monastery of San Marco in Florence. A description of the books appears in Martyr. See Ascensión Hernández de Léon-Portilla, "Tempranos testimonios europeos sobre los códices del México Antiguo", in *El Impacto del Encuentro de dos Mundos* (Mexico, 1987),

45–54. There are other candidates, among them the Maya Codex Dresden, the finest of all.

57 C, 137.

58 Pointed out by Maudslay in Appendix I to Vol. I of his ed. of Bernal Díaz [14:38], 300.

59 The list in the AGI was published by John T. Lanning [15:53], 24–2. See too that in C, 711–76; G, 123; Martyr, II, 45; and CDI, I, 461–72, tr. by Marshall H. Saville [14:31], 21, 35. See also Torre Villar [15:56], I, 1–21, 55–84.

60 These figures were well worked out by Wagner [8:23], 120–1.

61 C, 71.

62 For years it was in the Schloss Ambras, which belonged to the Infante, later Archduke and Emperor, Ferdinand. It seems to appear on an inventory of 1596 there. See Ferdinand Anders, "Der Federkasten der Ambraser Kunstkammer", in *Jahrbuch der Kunsthistorischen Sammlungen in Wien*, LXI (1965), 119–32.

63 D del C (I, 163) put the departure of the *procuradores* before the events about to be described. But since they both referred to the events concerned in Spain in 1520, as did Martyr, the order of what happened must have been the reverse.

64 Martín Vázquez, evidence in CDI, XXVIII, 134.

65 C, 68.

66 Andrés de Monjaraz, in *residencia*, CDI, XXVI, 541.

67 Alonso de Navarrete, in AGI, Justicia, leg. 223, p.2. f.424 v.: "I saw that the said don Hernando sentenced . . ."

68 Juan Álvarez, Tapia, Alonso de Navarrete, Pero Rodríguez de Escobar and Gerónimo de Aguilar all described seeing the sentences being carried out (Polavieja, 271; AGI, Justicia, leg. 223, p.2, f.309v.; ibid., f.424; leg. 224, p.1, f.378r.; and Res (Rayón), II, 200). An accusation in the *residencia* against Cortés (CDI, XXVII, 9) was that Umbría had his foot cut off, but it is often said that it was only his toes. Others (Luis Marín in CDI, XXVIII, 29) spoke of a "part of his leg". Francisco Verdugo and others in 1529 (e.g. Res, (Rayón), I, 389) said that they saw in 1520 how Umbría had "had his foot cut". This penalty was sometimes given to erring slaves. López de Gómara says that Umbría was merely whipped: which may have been true, since he afterwards led an active life.

69 Diego de Vargas, in *Inf. de 1521*, quoted in Polavieja, 272.

70 Juan Bono de Quejo saw it in April 1520 (see Polavieja, 292).

71 Polavieja, 253.

72 CDI, XXVII, 9.

73 Polavieja, 174. Other accounts of the conspiracy were given by Diego de Ávila in 1521 (Polavieja, 123); C, 51; Martyr, II, 62; and CDI, XXVI, 503. One witness in the *residencia*, Vázquez de Tapia (CDI, XXVI, 423), said that he thought that Escudero and Cermeño had both been whipped, not executed, and sent back to Cuba in the very brigantine which they had considered stealing. But so many others saw them hanging that that opinion is worthless.

74 CDI, XXVII, 205.

75 Cortés' words were, according to Tapia, who was there: "let them come to the coast and there break up" ("*vengan a la costa y romperlos*") (Tapia, in J. Díaz, et al., 81). Cortés himself said that he "declared the ships unsafe to sail and grounded them" (C, 52).

76 Portocarrero's declaration as printed in Martínez, *Docs*, I, 113. In the suit of Tirado against Cortés (1529), Gerónimo de Aguilar said that the "order was given to dismantle the foremasts and throw them overboard, so that they could not sail" (Conway, Camb., Add. 7284, 87).

77 Alva Ixtlilxochitl, 237, mentions the payments as matters of fact.

78 Evidence of Joan de Cáceres, AGI, Justicia, leg. 223, p.2, f.227; Cortés, he thought, believed them necessary on land.

79 "To end the gossiping, the intrigues and the conversations [*los chismes e los corrillos e*

las pláticas] which had been going on, especially among the friends and the servants of Diego Velázquez": Joan de Cáceres, in AGI, Justicia, leg. 223, p.2, f.227 r. Many witnesses in the *residencia* against Cortés praise this action of the *Caudillo* as having been essential.

80 Francisco de Terrazas, AGI, Justicia, leg. 223, p.2, f.424v., answer to question 89.

81 Pero Rodríguez de Escobar, AGI, Justicia, leg. 224, p.1, f.378, answer to question 90.

82 *CDI*, XXVII, 337. The Emperor Charles would one day bring himself to approve when, in his grant of arms to Cortés in 1525, he wrote: "seeing that your followers would not put out their full efforts in the dangers which might arise had the ships not been beached" quoted in Library of Congress, Harkness Collection, Vol.3, ed. J. Benedict Warren (Washington, 1974).

83 García de Llerena, in *CDI*, XXVII, 204, 205.

84 D del C, I, 215. Gonzalo de Badajoz, despite his name, came from Ciudad Rodrigo, but the idea would have been passed on in hidalgo circles in the Indies. For the classical precedent, without which no action by Cortés would have been complete, see the action of Agathocles, tyrant of Syracuse, when at Carthage in 310 BC, and commentary by Juan Gil, in "El libro greco-latino y su influjo en Indias", in *Homenaje a Enrique Segura*, etc. (Badajoz, 1986), 101.

85 Begun by Maestro Oliva and finished by Cervantes de Salazar, *Diálogo de la Dignidad del Hombre* (Alcala, 1546). The sentences are obscure. The key phrase is *"encendía a los unos y a los otros"* (*Epístola Nuncupatoria*, iiii and v). Cervantes changed his position in his book (C de S, 180–2). The next reference to burning is Juan Suárez de Peralta [9:38], 42, who, in the 1580s, spoke of "vivid fires".

86 Luis Marín (wrongly spoken of in *CDI*, XXVIII, as Luis Martínez), in the hearings of the *residencia*, said that he saw how the ships were sailed on to the coast, where they were lost.

87 Sepúlveda, 122–3. Juan the Surgeon (Juan Cirujano), a witness at a hearing in 1525 on the merits of Martín Vázquez, said that he did not know if Cortés had run the ships on the ground or if they had been really eaten by the *broma* (AGI, Mexico, leg. 203, no.5).

88 Half the sailors wanted to go back because they preferred sailing to fighting (G, 91).

89 "Don Hernando arranged to go into the territory and find out for himself . . . the grandeur of the said Moctezuma" (Cáceres, in AGI, Justicia, leg. 223, p.2, f.227).

90 Tapia, in J. Díaz, et al., 79–80. Ramos [9:79], 159, suggests that Cortés must have heard of the myth of a god who disappeared in the sea, but there is no evidence, and Cortés was always denying that he and his men were gods.

91 C,38. Bernal Díaz said both 23 and 26 July, Cervantes de Salazar has 26 July.

92 *CDI*, XXVI, 5–16. There is a paper in the AGI on this: Justicia, leg. 223, f.23. It is possible that this was the first time that the fifth for Cortés was mentioned, though Cortés himself testified that the plan was confirmed 3 times. See Polavieja, 151–2.

93 Wagner [8:23], 135.

94 The dubious "letter from a conquistador", ed. by Saville [15:6], was, however, dated Nueva Sevilla, 28 June 1519.

Chapter 16

1 Las Casas, III, 209.

2 I take the estimate made in Charles V's grant of arms to Cortés in 1525 as the "official" version: Library of Congress, Harkness Collection, Vol.3, ed. J. Benedict Warren (Washington, 1974). Cortés said that he took 350 foot soldiers, 1,000 Indians and fifteen horsemen. Ixtlilxochitl said that there were 1,000 porters (*tamemes*) and 1,300 Indian soldiers, with 400 Spaniards. López de Gómara said there were 400 Spaniards, 15 horses, 300

Indians, including some from Cuba, and 3 small guns. Díaz del Castillo says that only 60 were left behind at Villa Rica, but Cortés says 150 and 2 horse. Aguilar says 30–40 were left behind. D del C also said that 35 had died since leaving Cuba: a figure which appears nowhere else. One should not forget the 60 or so who came with Saucedo.

3 See Vidal [9:71], 210.

4 AGI, Justicia, leg. 223, p.2, f.227.

5 See Columbus' letter to the King: "Our people here is such that there is neither good man nor bad who hasn't two or three Indians to serve him . . . and . . . women so pretty that one must wonder at it" (cit. Fernández-Armesto [6:1], 133).

6 The Great Captain was renowned as having been the first to make decisive use of both small firearms and field fortifications.

7 Conway (Camb.), Add. 7292. Hernández later worked on brigantines on the lake of Mexico, and spent most of the rest of his life suing Cortés in order to recover the fees which he believed were due to him for these activities.

8 Joan de Cáceres, AGI, Justicia, leg. 223, p.2, f.227r.; Alonso de Navarrete, in op.cit., f.424v, pays a similar tribute.

9 Hassig [1:23], 64.

10 Cline's Sahagún, 73.

11 "*no reposaré hasta ver el dicho Montecuma . . .*" Tapia, AGI, Justicia, leg. 223, p.2, f.309v.

12 Magellan took 18 such clocks on his journey in 1520 (Morison [5:14], 163).

13 G, 356.

14 This comes from question 89 in Cortés' questionnaire in the *residencia* against him: "*disiendo a la xente e compañeros que va no le quedaba otro rremedio sino sus manos, e procurar de vencer e ganar la tierra, or morir*" (*CDI*, XXVII, 337).

15 I am grateful to Felipe Fernández-Armesto for his suggestions. D del C (I, 217) said that it was the soldiers to whom the example of the Rubicon occurred. Menéndez Pidal wrote, in his "¿Codicia insaciable? ¿Ilustres hazañas?" (*La lengua de Cristóbal Colón* (Buenos Aires, 1942), 98–9), "even men who had read little, such as Bernal Díaz, were drenched in ideas of glory and fame, such as they had read in old books" – or old ballads, one might add.

16 C, 67.

17 See *CDI*, XXVII, 229 ("*por voluntad e consentimiento general de todos los compañeros*").

18 C de S, 184. The Florentine Codex says the contrary, as quoted in León-Portilla [4:33], 75.

19 Durán, II, 527.

20 Hassig [1:23], 65, 73.

21 Gerhard [8:60], 141–2; Aguilar, in J. Díaz, et al., 69; Herrera [8:6], III, 360; and Torquemada [1:24], II, 282.

22 G, 94.

23 C de S, 331

24 G, 93.

25 Juan Álvarez, in *Inf. de 1521*, Polavieja, 266; D del C, I, 218.

26 Martyr (II, 643) said that the message was taken to Garay, who refused on his own.

27 D del C, I, 222. Maudslay, the translator of D del C (I, 211), thought, like Wagner ([8:23], 145), that a journey to Jalapa in a day was impossible; but, starting at 5 a.m. and ending at 9 p.m., 40 miles at 2½ miles an hour would not have been beyond conquistadors who had been resting for some time, and who had bearers to carry their equipment: even with an increase in height of 4,000 feet.

28 Also known as Sochochima, Sicuchitimal and Sienchimalen.

29 C, 87–8.

30 Now Izhuacan. Other renderings are Ceyxnacan (Cortés), Teoizhuacan, and Ixhuacan.

31 There is a late 16th-century description of this pass by Fr. Alonso Ponce (Madrid, 1875).

32 Aguilar, in J. Díaz, et al., 167.

33 For example, Ixtlilxochitl, 238, and Tapia, in J. Díaz, et al., 86.

34 Everyone called Zautla, the modern name, something different. Ixtlilxochitl and Cervantes de Salazar called it Zacatlan, Díaz del Castillo spoke of both Xocotlan and Castilblanco (because some Portuguese on the expedition thought it looked like a Castel Branco which they knew), Cortés called it Caltamí (C, 89), Tapia Çacotlan (in J. Díaz, et al., 86) and López de Gómara spoke of Zacotlan.

35 C, 89; G, 121; and Ixtlilxochitl, 238, spoke of the Spanish being received with rejoicing; D del C, I, 223, says that the Spanish were badly received.

36 D del C, I, 224 said that the skulls were so well arranged that he could count 100,000 of them. That is improbable. A rack of that many skulls 20 feet high would, at a skull every 6", be over 450 yards long.

37 C, 89; G, 121; Tapia, in J. Díaz, et al., 86, reports the same, as did Oviedo, who elaborately reported a conversation about the greatness of the two emperors.

38 D del C, I, 220–1, Ixtlilxochitl (238) and G (123) said that Olintecle allowed Cortés to throw down his gods from the top of the town's main temple, but the idea is inconceivable.

39 G, 122.

40 Bernal Díaz has "*lebrela*", greyhound, but mastiff must be the best translation.

41 D del C, I,224, and C, 89.

42 G, 120.

43 Camargo, 191, said taffeta (perhaps therefore from Córdoba). D del C (who was there), 226, said fluffy and woollen. The latter says that the messengers were sent from Xalacingo. Both C, 90, and Ixtlilxochitl, 238, say it was Zautla. Cortés did not go to Xalacingo after Zautla. It would have been absurd. Díaz del Castillo's description of this part of the journey is inadequate.

44 G, 121.

45 D del C, I, 225–6.

46 C, 89. This town is now on the map as Ixtacamaxtitlan. It is in the valley, not on the hill, but the remains of the old town can be seen. See Harry Franck, *Trailing Cortés through Mexico* (New York, 1935).

47 G, 97; C, 89.

48 C, 124.

49 C, 91; G, 123–4. See preface to Archbishop Francisco Antonio Lorenzana's ed. of Cortés' letters (Mexico, 1770), v-viii. The text reads as if the archbishop had seen it. There are in this area two Atotonilcos, one a substantial town near Tlaxco, the other a hamlet near Terrenate. It was probably at the latter that Cortés found the wall.

50 D del C, I, 229.

51 Aguilar, in J. Díaz, et al., 165; D del C, I, 229, speaks of 30 Indians.

52 Tapia, in J. Díaz, et al., 87. D del C, I, 229 speaks of a mere 3,000.

53 Aguilar, in J. Díaz, et al., 167.

54 C, 91–2; Ixtlilxochitl, 239; Martyr, II, 68–9, who no longer had the help of Alaminos, Montejo and Portocarrero, here copied Cortés almost word for word. Charles Gibson, *Tlaxcala in the 16th Century* (New Haven, 1952), says that this fight took place somewhere near Quimichocan, which I have not yet identified.

55 G (99) says that one of the Spaniards wounded later died, and gave the lower figure for the Indian dead. Cortés (C, 124) gave the higher figure.

56 See Inga Clendinnen, "The Cost of Courage in Aztec Society", *Past and Present*, 107 (May, 1985), 90.

57 Wagner ([8:23], 154) speaks of this skirmish as a turning point. I agree. Eulalia Guzmán says that it never occurred!

58 This detail derives from D del C, I, 230, as does the reference to the fat.

59 See Gibson [16:54], 9, 11, 13; Gerhard [8:61], 324–7. This calculation of 150,000 derives from a *relación* of 1544, in which Bartolomé de Zárate, a *regidor* of Mexico, said that, in the pre-Cortesian days, 20,000 warriors could be sent out: "*sacaba esta provincia 20,000 hombres de guerra*" (*Epistolario*, III, 136). Another report, sent to King Philip II of Spain, 15 December 1575, stated that, in 1521, 100,000 Tlaxcalans fought for Cortés, but this must be one of the usual exaggerated round numbers (printed in *Epistolario*, XV, 36–58).

60 FC, x, 178.

61 Tr. from Otomí by Miguel León-Portilla, in his *Precolombian literatures of Mexico* (tr. Norman, 1969), 95.

62 Garibay [1:13], I, 239.

63 Walter Lehmann, *Die Geschichte der Königreiche von Colhuacan und Mexico* (Stuttgart, 1938), 104, cit. Arthur Anderson, "Aztec Hymns of Life and Love", *New Scholar*, viii. 27. For the Otomí see FC, x, 174–84. Van Zantwijk [Preface: 5] thought that the Otomí might be ancestors of the Mexica.

64 Camargo, 123.

65 Ixtlilxochitl, 150–1; Juan Bautista Pomar, "Relación de Texcoco", in *Relaciones de la Nueva España* (Madrid, 1991), 74.

66 Camargo, 231.

67 Durán, I, 71–80.

68 Durán, II, 178.

69 C, 98. The *Conqu. Anón.*, in García Icazbalceta I, 388, compared the city to Granada and Segovia, "with a larger population".

70 Martyr, II, 77.

71 Motolinía, in García Icazbalceta, I, 59.

72 Tapia, in J. Díaz, et al., 93–4; Camargo, 148. Soustelle [1:5], 289, calls this the "Mexicans' fatal mistake".

Chapter 17

1 Camargo, 192, prints Xicotencatl's alleged speech.

2 Cod. Ram., 137; Cline's Sahagún, 54.

3 G, 126.

4 On previous occasions he had someone else read it out. But the text of the second *carta de relación* implies that he did this himself – with his interpreters (C, 92–3).

5 This cry does not mean "Santiago and close ranks Spain", but "Santiago and close in on the enemy!" It may have seemed out of date to many Spaniards but was less so to men from Extremadura for whom the Order of Santiago continued powerful.

6 C, 92–3.

7 C, 93; G, 127; D del C, I, 232. Vázquez de Tapia (in J. Díaz, et al., 138) said that, "in this place we stayed over 30 days, and each day there came at us over 80,000 warriors . . ."

8 J. Huizinga, *The Waning of the Middle Ages* (London, 1924), 215. He added, "men of the middle Age . . . could not for a moment dispense with false judgements of the grossest kind . . . it is in this light that the general and constant habit of ridiculously exaggerating the number of enemies killed in battle should be considered."

9 Clendinnen [16:56], 269.

10 Soustelle [1:5], 207.

11 Questionnaire in *información* of Diego de Ordaz (Santo Domingo, 1521), and evidence of Diego Bardalés, Antón del Río, Pero López de Barbas, and Gonzalo Giménez, in *CDI*, KL, 74ff.

12 Eulalia Guzmán [13:41], 131, insisted that there was no fighting. All that happened, she argued, was that Cortés killed a lot of people in various towns while looking for food. But Tapia, Vázquez de Tapia, Aguilar, and Díaz del Castillo all refer to these battles. Martín López, no friend of Cortés, testified in *Inf. de 1565* that, "when we entered the province of Tlaxcala, we had various engagements with the naturales . . ." They would not have joined in a conspiracy headed by Cortés to misreport history.

13 This was near Tecoatzingo (Teocacingo), and is now probably San Francisco Tecoac. When visiting the area in 1990, I was assured that this camp was at Tzompantepec.

14 Aguilar, in J. Díaz, et al., 169.

15 C, 93; questionnaire in *información* of Diego de Ordaz (Santo Domingo, 1521).

16 Juan Álvarez (who was present) in *Inf. de 1521*, Polavieja, 253; Aguilar, in J. Díaz, et al., 169.

17 D del C, I, 234: "*los amigos como son crueles . . .*".

18 This was G, 129. Ixtlilxochitl, 239. Cortés says that this event occurred later on.

19 C, 94.

20 Aguilar to Durán, II, 529.

21 Thus Cortés speaks of 149,000, Díaz del Castillo of 50,000, López de Gómara of 150,000.

22 G, 129–30.

23 C, 93.

24 D del C, I, 237: "*los hicieron conocer cuánto cortaban las espadas de hierro*".

25 D del C, I, 238.

26 See comment by Francisco de Flores, AGI, Justicia, leg. 223, p. 2, f. 511v.

27 C, 92; G, 130.

28 C, 95, G, 134, D del C, I, 265.

29 St Mark, III, 25; C, 99–100. Elliott [9:76], 44, points out that this was Cortés' only biblical quotation. But he often alluded to the Bible, e.g. C, 251.

30 Tapia, in J. Díaz, et al., 90.

31 Ixtlilxochitl, 239; C, 94.

32 Aguilar, in J. Díaz, et al., 169; where Germán Vázquez argues that the atrocities did not occur.

33 Martyr, II, 74; G, 106; D del C, I, 259–60.

34 Hassig [1:23], 115.

35 G, 134.

36 FC, xi (1st ed.), 27.

37 Martyr, II, 74.

38 D del C, II, 258.

39 G, 134; Tapia, in J. Díaz, et al., 88; C, 94.

40 C, 95; Aguilar, in J. Díaz, et al., 170.

41 Vázquez de Tapia (in J. Díaz, et al.,) gave an eyewitness account, prejudiced against Cortés; C, 96; Ixtlilxochitl, 240; G, 136.

42 Aguilar (who was with this expedition), in J. Díaz, et al., 171; D del C, I, 250. Ixtlilxochitl, 240, says this town had 20,000 *fuegos*, or households.

43 Tapia, in J. Díaz, et al.; G, 111.

44 D del C, I, 247.

45 D del C, I, 254.

46 *The Song of Roland*, verse 128, has "*Mielz voeill murir que hunte nus seit retraite*". The speech is summarised in G, 112, fulsomely in C de S, 226–7.

47 Tapia, in J Díaz, et al., 92.
48 FC, xii, 28.
49 Gibson [16:54], 21.
50 C, 96; D del C, I, 266.
51 Tapia, in J. Díaz, et al., 90, G, 131, and D del C, I, 252. Gómera's account impressed Montaigne; he discussed the offer in his essay "on Moderation".
52 Tapia, in J. Diaz, et al., 90; Martyr, II, 76; C, 93. Durán (II, 530) makes the curious suggestion that Cortés kidnapped the Tlaxcalan leaders. He did capture their souls, not their bodies.
53 C, 94; Ixtlilxochitl (240–2) reports a clash between the Mexican emissaries and the Tlaxcalans in which the latter accused the Mexica of establishing a brutal tyranny simply in order to eat and dress well.
54 Ixtlilxochitl, 241.
55 D del C, I, 271.
56 D del C, I, 264; Ixtlilxochitl, 244. Camargo, 194, also speaks of the pomp with which Cortés was received. Earlier, he neglects the fighting, apart from mentioning that, by mistake, a few Otomí on the frontier attacked Cortés as he was coming in from the north- east.
57 FC, ii, 110–11; Clendinnen [3:11], 201–3. There is no explicit description of this ceremony in 1519 but it must have occurred.
58 Pasztory [4:35].

Chapter 18

1 C, 98; G, 143. Jorge Gurría Lacroix, Códice "Entrada de los Españoles en Tlaxcala" (Mexico, 1966), has an impression of the late 17th or 18th centuries.
2 D del C, I, 276.
3 Aguilar, in J. Díaz, et al., 179.
4 Inf. de 1565, 114.
5 AGI, Justicia, leg. 224, p.1. f.95r.
6 Perhaps Cortés had read an account of the triumphant entry of the Spaniards into Granada in the letter of Peter Martyr to Cardinal Arcimboldo of Milan: "Alhambrum, proh dii immortales! . . ."
7 C, 98–9; Aguilar, in J. Díaz, et al., 172.
8 C, 98. According to Antonio Sotelo (Inf. de 1565, 188), Cortés wrote a letter to his friend Roberto Rangel on the coast describing his welcome at Tlaxcala.
9 See Anawalt [7:41], 61–80; and "Memory Clothing", in Boone [2:58], 180–8.
10 FC, xii (1st ed.), 29.
11 Aguilar, in J. Díaz, et al., 179.
12 D del C, I, 277.
13 Aguilar, in J. Díaz, et al., 179.
14 D del C, I, 274; Camargo, 192.
15 Camargo, 194, wrote of elaborate gifts made to Cortés by the Tlaxcalans but that seems improbable, considering their poverty. He was writing of course in the late 16th century to impress the Spanish Crown with reports of Tlaxcala's services.
16 Camargo, 195.
17 G, 118; Camargo, 197.
18 Ixtlilxochitl, 245.
19 Tapia, in J. Díaz, et al., 94; G, 146.
20 Diego Luis de Motezuma, SJ, Corona Mexicana (Madrid, 1914), 370.
21 Camargo, 198–208.

22 Camargo, 208.

23 Plate VIII of the Lienzo de Tlaxcala, dated c. 1550, shows the baptism of the four chiefs, with Cortés holding a cross and Marina looking on. Bernal Díaz stated this in a *probanza* on the services of Pedro de Alvarado in Joaquín Ramirez Cabañas' ed. of *La historia verdadera* (Mexico, 1967), 585. See also Camargo, who of course wrote c. 1576, 233.

24 These stories are discussed by Gibson [16:54], 31–2.

25 Camargo, 197. Alvarado would have a son and a daughter by María Luisa, "Don Pedro" and "Doña Leonor".

26 "*ir a México sin tener guerra*" (D del C, I, 279).

27 *Inf. de 1565*, 114.

28 Vázquez de Tapia gave the route as Cholula, Guaquichula, Tochimiloc, Tetela, Tenantepeque, Ocuituco, Chimaloacan, Sumiltepeque, Amecameca, and Texcoco.

29 Vázquez de Tapia, in J. Díaz, et al., 139–42. Alvarado never mentioned the matter. Cervantes de Salazar said that Alvarado went by himself with a servant (C de S, I, 290).

30 *Inf. de 1565*, 115.

31 C, 101. The *Inf. de 1565* confirms this. Camargo said that the Tlaxcalans sent one of their nobles, Patlahuatzin, to Cholula to explain that the bearded white strangers were fine people who would not do them any harm. But if they behaved foolishly, Cortés would destroy them. The Cholulans in reply detained the messenger, skinned his face and arms up to the elbows, and cut off his hands at the wrists, leaving them hanging down. In this disagreeable condition, he was sent home to Tlaxcala, where he soon died (Camargo, 212–13). Perhaps this story describes something which occurred in a previous war between these two cities. No Spanish source mentions it.

32 G, 148.

33 G, 148. Antonio Saavedra de Guzmán's *El Peregrino Indiano* (Madrid, 1580) has a similar story about the Indian girl at this time with Jorge de Alvarado – perhaps, as Wagner said, because Guzmán's wife was a granddaughter of Jorge.

34 C, 100; Felipe Fernández-Armesto, *Ferdinand and Isabella* (London, 1975), 147.

35 Ixtlilxochitl, 190.

36 C, 101–2.

37 Tapia, in J. Díaz, et al., 99, said 40,000. Cortés had 100,000 (C, 72); G, 125.

38 D del C, I, 278.

39 Ixtlilxochitl, 246, says that the "escort" was over 10,000 strong.

40 Reed flutes (*cocoloctli*) or ocarina-like globular flutes (*huilacapitzli*).

41 C, 103; D del C, I, 285.

42 Tapia, in J. Díaz, et al., 95; Ixtlilxochitl, 246.

43 C, 104.

44 Joan de Cáceres, AGI, Justicia, leg. 223, p.2.

45 *Relación de Cholula* [13:50], 161.

46 The same, 162.

47 Tapia, in J. Díaz, et al., 96; Tapia had an *encomienda* at Cholula after the fall of Tenochtitlan and presumably learned this then (Gerhard [8:61], 117).

48 Aguilar, in J. Díaz, et al., 174. Sepúlveda, though after talking to Cortés, says 20,000 (Angel Losada, "Hernán Cortés en la obra del cronista Sepúlveda", *R de I*, IX (January–June 1948), 127–62).

49 Relación de Bartolomé de Zárate, 1544, in *Epistolario*, III, 137.

50 C, 105 (this statistic inspired one of Prescott's most famous passages); Aguilar agreed on "the number of towers and towered temples" (Aguilar, in J. Díaz, et al., 174).

51 C, 105.

52 *Relación de Cholula* [13:50], 160.

53 Camargo, 210.

54 Gerhard [8:60], 114–17; Aguilar, in J. Díaz, et al., 89.

55 This is Camargo's loaded version (Camargo, 211).

56 G, 126.

57 Evidence of Martín Vázquez at the *residencia* against Cortés, in *CDI*, XXVIII, 184; D del C, II, 6.

58 D del C, II, 6.

59 Martín López, in *Inf. de 1565*, 115.

60 *CDI*, XXVII, 386; Tapia, in J. Díaz, et al., 96.

61 In reporting this the following year to the King of Spain, Cortés made his only reference to Marina: "the interpreter [*lengua*] which I have is an Indian girl from this land which I was given in Potonchan" (C, 73); G, 125; Tapia, in J. Díaz, et al., 96. Juan de Jaramillo remembered the incident with Marina (AGI, Justicia, leg. 224, p.1. f.464): eventually he would marry her.

62 D del C, II, 9.

63 Juan de Limpias Carvajal testified in 1565 that these men were tortured (*Inf. de 1565*, 176):"*por premio y tormentos que los hizo*".

64 D del C, II, 5.

65 Sepúlveda, who talked to Cortés of this, stresses the consultation (Sepúlveda, 141); *Inf. de 1565*, 113; Gibson [16:54], 22.

66 Ixtlilxochitl, 246.

67 Vázquez de Tapia in his evidence in the *residencia* against Cortés (*CDI*, XXVI, 417); FC, xii, 29; Ixtlilxochitl, 247.

68 Evidence of Andrés de Tapia in AGI, Justicia, leg. 223, p.2: "certain leaders rather more than one hundred in number, and he told them that he knew their treason".

69 Tapia, in J. Díaz, et al., 100.

70 C, 180; Sepúlveda (141) said 4,000, Alva 5,000, Gómara 6,000, and Vázquez de Tapia "over 20,000". Las Casas, in *De Thesauris in Peru* (Madrid, 1562, republished 1958), 310–11, said that Cortés revealed himself a "new Herod" who killed 15,000 innocents without mercy. One accusation in the *residencia* was that Cortés had "killed 4,000 without cause" (*CDI*, XXVII, 27). Aguilar said that 2,000 were killed, but insisted that they were those who carried the wood and the water to the Spanish lodgings. Rosa de Lourdes Camelo Arredondo, in her unpublished *Historiografía de la Matanza de Cholula* (Mexico, 1963), 119, pointed out that it is still not clear precisely who was killed.

71 FC, xii, 30.

72 Tapia, in J. Díaz, et al., 100.

73 Camargo, 212.

74 Martín López said in 1565 that these allies "*mataron mucha gente e servieron muy bien como buenos e leales vasallos de su majestad*" (*Inf. de 1565*, 116).

75 Tapia, in J. Díaz, et al., 99.

76 "until they begin to understand matters" (D del C, I, 295).

77 Ixtlilxochitl, 247–9.

78 Sepúlveda said that he met Cortés at a private discussion in Valladolid, probably between January and May 1542, when the Emperor was present (Sepúlveda, 142–3). The version in the text comes, however, from Losada in "Hernán Cortés en la obra . . .", [18:48], 140.

79 Las Casas, *Brevíssima Relación de la destruyción de las Indias*, in José Alcina Franch, *Obra Indigenista* (Madrid, 1992), 93.

80 This ballad is attributed to Velázquez de Ávila in the late 15th century. See *BAE*, X, 393–4. It was recited to effect by Sempronio in *La Celestina*. Velázquez de Ávila was probably a relation of Diego Velázquez de Cuéllar.

81 AGI, Justicia, leg. 224, p.1, f.722r.

82 AGI, Justicia, leg. 223, p.2, f.511.

83 AGI, Justicia, leg. 223, p.2, f.584v.

84 *Relación de Cholula* [13:50], 160.

85 C, 102; D del C, II, 9. It is confirmed by several witnesses in the *Inf. de 1565*.

86 Durán, II, 25.

87 Orozco [8:4], iv, 252, argued that the conspiracy was framed by the Tlaxcalans and that Marina invented the story of the old woman who tried to "save" her. Wagner accepted this interpretation ([8:23], 176), and pertinently asked what happened to the Mexican army said to be waiting to ambush the Castilians outside Cholula. Germán Vázquez in his ed. of Aguilar (J. Díaz, et al., 175, fn. 37) finds for Cortés.

88 "This punishment was known and was made public among the *naturales*" (AGI, Justicia, leg. 223. p.2, f.309 v.).

89 Martyr, II, 85.

90 C, 106. Both Tapia (in J. Díaz, et al., 98) and Díaz del Castillo have a contrasting view of this exchange in which Cortés is made to tell the Mexican ambassadors that he did not believe that Montezuma would stoop to try and kill the Spanish in an underhand way.

91 FC, xii (1st ed.), 30.

92 G, 133.

93 D del C, II, 26.

94 C, 106–7.

Chapter 19

1 Figures differ as usual: D del C, II, gave 1,000 Tlaxcalans, Cortés (C, 109) 4,000, López de Gómara and Ixtlilxochitl 6,000, while the *Inf. de 1565*, 73, says that Cortés had no Tlaxcalans with him.

2 C, 107.

3 "when he returned, he brought snow from the said sierra"; see questionnaire in *información* of Diego de Ordaz (Santo Domingo, 1521), and evidence of Gutierre de Casamori (*CDI*, XL, 74ff).

4 Aguilar in J. Díaz, et al., 176. The modern traveller would not be able to see anything of the lake because of the smoke-haze.

5 For the ballad about Alfonso, see *BAE*, X–XVI; for the Cid, see *Poem of the Cid* [5:31], 107, and *BAE*, X, 534.

6 C, 109.

7 Aguilar, in J. Díaz, et al., 176.

8 FC, xii (1st ed.), 30. I have taken into account the tr. of this passage in León-Portilla [4:33], 81, and Sahagún, II, 965.

9 D del C, II, 28–9.

10 This version of the myth derives from FC, iii, 35.

11 Angel María Garibay, *La Poesía Lírica Azteca* (Mexico, 1937), 39.

12 FC, xii, 37; Pedro de Solís, in the *Inf. de 1565*, said that the Tlaxcalans did the clearing, though an earlier witness in that enquiry had said that there were none such with Cortés.

13 C, 109.

14 C, 109.

15 Tapia, in J. Díaz, et al., 100.

16 For the view of the Mexicans, see Enrique Florescano, "Mito e Historia en la memoria nahua", *HM*, 155 (1989), 607.

17 Cod. Ram., 212.

18 Sonia Lombardo de Ruiz, "El desarollo urbano de México-Tenochtitlan", *HM*, 86 (1972), 131.

19 See illustration in Codex Boturini, in Pasztory [4:35], 200.

20 Barlow [1:10], 75; Davies [1:24], 11; Gibson [16:54], 15–16.

21 Cline's Sahagún, 61.

22 FC, xi (1st ed.), 31. The Greeks thought that the languages of non-Greeks were like "the fluttering of birds".

23 Cod. Ram., 138–9; FC, xii, 31–2, modified to fit what I render as Cortés' style of speech.

24 Cod. Ram., 139–40; Wasserman [13:66].

25 FC, xii, 34–5.

26 See Gastón Guzmán, in *The Sacred Mushroom Seeker*, ed. Thomas J. Reidlinger (Portland, 1990), 95, for the identification of *Psilocybe Aztecorum* with the *nanácatl* mentioned in *Histoyre du Mechique* [1:53], 18; and 92–5 for "sacred" mushroom eating.

27 Cline's Sahagún, 63.

28 Cod. Ram., 211–12.

29 Nicholson [1.42], table 4.

30 Sanders [2:21], 87; see his appendix, "Prehispanic meat consumption", 475.

31 C, 111. G, 136, speaks of the expedition spending this night at Tlamanalco.

32 Gerhard [8:61], 104.

33 Durán, II, 535, who says that these girls were presented to Cortés at Chalco.

34 C, 111. The gold was said to be worth 3,000 castellanos.

35 Domingo . . . Chimalpahin, *Octava relación* (Mexico, 1983), 145. Several chronicles based on the Crónica X, e.g. Durán and Cod. Ram., state that now Cortés went to Texcoco: Cortés was described as having been received in Texcoco by Ixtlilxochitl who said he had come to understand the mysteries of Christianity. He and his family thereupon became Christians – an event which drove his mother Yacotzin mad. The events described, if not invented, must have occurred during a later visit by Cortés to Texcoco – probably in 1524, as suggested by Ixtlilxochitl in *Decimatercia Relación* [4:5].

36 D del C, II, 31–2.

37 Tapia, in J. Díaz, et al., 101. The references to "when Cortés was at Chalco" may be to the province or state of that name, not the town.

38 See table of the 17 recorded rebel cities in Hassig [1:27], 94.

39 Garibay [1:13], I, 220.

40 Durán, II, 535.

41 C (110) and D del C (I, 307) say that this delegation was led by Cuitláhuac, brother of Montezuma, and that there were two such groups, one led by that prince, the other by Cacama.

42 Díaz del Castillo says that Montezuma offered to give 4 loads of gold to Cortés and one each to every member of his expedition if only he would stay away. But if a load (*carga*) means 50 lbs as it usually did, there could not have been that much gold in all Mexico.

43 D del C, II, 34; C, 111.

44 Aguilar, in J. Díaz, et al., 177. The identification of the town was the work of Germán Vázquez, who suggests that it had a factory of human dung.

45 See Chapter 12, above.

46 D del C, I, 309.

47 Enrique Otte, *Las Perlas del Caribe* (Caracas, 1977), 59.

48 Tapia, in J. Díaz, et al., 101.

49 Durán, II, 112. For *chinampas* here, see Pedro Armillas [2:15], 656.

50 Van Zantwijk [Preface: 5], 54–6. The evidence revolves round common personal names.

51 Tapia, in J. Díaz, et al., 101; G, 123.

52 Codex Chimalpopoca, *Anales de Cuauhitlan y Leyenda de los Soles*, ed. Primo Velázquez [Mexico, 1975), 61.

53 D del C, I, 311: "*parecía a las cosas y encantamiento que cuentan en el libro de* Amadís *por las grandes torres y cues y edificios que tenían en el agua*..." The expressions of Bernal Díaz seem to have been almost ritualistic: thus when Philip II went to England for the first time (in 1554), one of his followers said that Philip showed such enthusiasm for the gardens of Winchester where he lodged that he seemed to be somewhere of which "he had read in books of chivalry" (quoted in R.O. Jones, *The Golden Age: Prose and Poetry*, London, 1971, 54).

54 *Amadís de Gaula* (though it had an earlier, Portuguese origin) was written for publication by Garcí Rodríguez (or Gutiérrez) de Montalvo, councillor, *regidor*, of the commercial city of Medina del Campo. Medina del Campo was the town of the chronicler, Díaz del Castillo, whose father was also a *regidor* there. Presumably the "author" of *Amadís* was related to the other Montalvos of Medina, whose family tree is in Cooper [6:66], 447, and so was distantly related not only to Francisco de Lugo, one of Cortés' captains, but also to Velázquez de Cuéllar. One Montalvo of Medina del Campo, Francisco, had an *encomienda* in Cuba (Muñoz, vol. 72, f.124). The city was in the 1480s marked by anti-Semitic legislation. It is appropriate that this great market city, renowned for its lawyers, should have produced men who wrote two of the most famous books of the century.

55 *Amadís de Gaula*, tr. R. Southey (London, 1872), 6. See Ida Rodríguez Prampolini, *Amadises de América* (Mexico, 1948), and M. Hernández Sánchez-Barba, "La influencia de los libros de caballería sobre el conquistador", *AEA*, XIX.

56 For the ceremony, see Ch.1. The description by Sahagún is vivid: all were frightened and filled with dread, would the sun come out again or would the demons of darkness descend to eat men? Hence everyone ascended the terraces, all went on to the housetops... They placed the women in granaries for it was thought that if new fire were not drawn they would be turned into wild beasts and also eat men... They paid heed to only one thing: the summit of Uixachetectatl... Then, when the confirmation came that life would go on, all the people cut their ears and spattered their blood towards the fire. Another description is in Motolinía [1:1], 113.

57 Sanders [2:21] gives "10,000 or more".

58 Tapia, in J. Díaz, et al., 113; C, 82. Bernal Díaz (D del C, I, 311) said that the gardens were full of "roses and flowers", but the rose had not yet arrived in Mexico. The memory of the scene filled him with melancholy: "today all is overthrown and lost..."

59 C. Harvey Gardner, *Naval Power in the Conquest of Mexico* (Austin, 1959), 51–2.

60 As Aguilar puts it (J. Díaz, et al., 178), "the captain had ordered that the foot soldiers and the horsemen were in time".

61 FC, xii, 39–41.

62 Martyr, II, 89. This stretch of the causeway was said by Maudslay, on the evidence of Cepeda and Carrillo, to have been 5,200 *varas* long and 11 wide (Appendix A to his tr. of D del C).

63 C, 114.

64 A section of this was dug up in 1961 and the dimensions, varying between 135 and 145 feet in width, confirmed (Francisco González Rul and Federico Mooser, "La Calzada de Ixtapalapa", in *Anales*, INAH, 15, 113–19) quoted in Pasztory [4:35], 107.

65 Cline's Sahagún, 65.

66 FC, xii, 39–41; Hassig [1:23], 58. Wagner [8:23], 202, thought that Sahagún's description of the entry of Cortés derived from a painting. But Sahagún talked with survivors of the day on whom the sight must have made a great impression.

67 How many canoes? *Ein Schöne Newe Zeytung* of 1520, *HAHR* (1929), 208, suggested (perhaps on the evidence of Francisco Serrantes, for whom see Ch. 22) 70,000; Cervantes de Salazar suggested 100,000. There were canoes which could be operated by a

single man. Many were intended for about 6 warriors. They were in constant use for fishing, moving food and tribute. They were flat-bottomed, without keels, and narrower at the bow than at the stern. See Gardner [19:59], 54, for a summary of the evidence.

68 Aguilar to Durán in Durán, I, 20.

69 In Veytía, II, 243, in Muñoz papers, Madrid.

70 See map facing page 103 in Ignacio Alcocer, *Apuntes sobre la antigua México-Tenochtitlan* (Tacubaya, 1935), where the Calle San Antonio meets the Calle Pino Suárez, near the Calle Chimalpopoca.

71 Aguilar, in J. Díaz, et al., 170; C, 115; D del C, II, 40.

72 Durán, II.

73 The consequences had been unpleasant. In order to prevent the Mexica from settling down, Huitzilopochtli secured Achitometl's daughter as queen of the Mexica, had her sacrificed as "The Woman of Discord", flayed her, dressed a youth in her skin, and invited Achitometl to attend a ceremony in her honour: a visit which understandably caused that monarch to vow to kill all the Mexica (Durán, II, 42).

74 Aguilar, in J. Díaz, et al., 178. Alvarado, in the *residencia* against him, recalled how Montezuma "came out to receive us in peace". (Res vs Alvarado, 64).

75 Cortés says that all but Montezuma had bare feet, but it is inconceivable that the two other kings were so, as Eulalia Guzmán points out ([13:41], 211).

76 C, 86; D del C, II, 42.

77 Nicholson [13:47], 126.

78 For example, Aguilar, in J. Díaz, et al., 178; D del C, I, 319: Martín Vázquez, in *CDI*, XXVIII, in the *residencia* against Cortés: and Vázquez de Tapia. Sahagún, in his 1585 version (Cline's Sahagún, 680–9) omits all mention of Montezuma's speech. So did Tapia, while C de S, 274, also represents the speech as happening now.

79 For these salutations, see Arthur J. O. Anderson, et al., *Beyond the Codices* (Berkeley, 1976), 30.

80 A typical necklace of Quetzalcoatl was one of gold sea snails: "*caracoles marinos del oro*" (León-Portilla [1:34], 117–18). Fr. Díaz said that the present to Cortés was "a golden chain" (evidence in Res vs Alvarado, 126). See Mario Hernández's intr. to C, 113 (fn.18), 114. Cortés' present seems to have been a necklace of pearls and cut glass. D del C (I, 314) talked of pearls with wonderful colours.

81 Durán, I, 20; Aguilar told Durán in the 1560s of "the day when they entered the city and saw the height and beauty of the temples".

82 Aguilar, in J. Díaz, et al., 178.

83 "*se me representaba todo delante de mis ojos como si ayer fuera cuando esto paso*" (D del C, I, 314–15). Cf. the first line of *Treasure Island*.

84 FC, xii, 39; also Martín Vázquez, in *CDI*, XXVIII, 138.

85 Cod. Ram., 141.

86 For a long time it was supposed that this palace was to the north-east of the Temple but Ignacio Alcocer [19:70], 85–6, demonstrated that it must have been to the west, approximately on the site of the modern national pawn shop.

87 Burr Brundage, *A Rain of Darts* (Austin, 1972), 145.

88 Tapia, in J. Díaz, et al., 101.

89 D del C, I, 42; Aguilar, in J. Díaz, et al., 178.

90 C, 87.

91 Aguilar, in J. Díaz, et al., 180.

92 For example, a grandfather addressed his grandson thus: FC, vi, 183.

93 Having written the above, I was glad to find that the same thoughts had occurred to Eulalia Guzmán [7:17], with whose judgements I am rarely in agreement.

94 *"siempre hemos tenido que los que de él descendiesen habían de venir a sojuzgar esta tierra y a nosotros como vasallos"* (C, 117).

95 *"él sea nuestro señor natural"* (C, 117).

96 C, 116–17.

97 G, 164–6; Sepúlveda, 148, has almost the same account, if better written.

98 D del C, I, 316–17.

99 Aguilar, in J. Díaz, et al., 179–80.

100 Tapia, in J. Díaz, et al., 104.

101 FC, xii, 44. Sahagún's *Historia* in its original ed. is here much the same as a tr. of the FC (ii, 970–1). But his version of 1585 says that Montezuma spoke "with great reverence and goodwill" (Cline's Sahagún, 69).

102 Durán, II, 542. Aguilar told Durán that he did not see Montezuma baptised but thought that he had been. But Aguilar did not mention this dramatic event in his own later, and considered, memoir. Durán must have misunderstood.

103 Pagden in his ed. of Cortés [10:73], 467.

104 Miguel León-Portilla, in "Quetzalcoatl – Cortés en la Conquista de México", *HM*, XXIV, no.1, (1974), 35; see too Inga Clendinnen's phrase in "Fierce and unnatural cruelty", *Representations* (Winter 1991), 33.

105 Vázquez, in J. Díaz, et al., 180, fn.45. These commentaries began with Dr Eulalia Guzmán, who insisted that the speech was an invention of Cortés for his own purposes ([13:41], 216–33). Dr Viktor Frankl said much the same ("Die Cartas de Relacíon de Hernán Cortés und der Mythos der Wiederkehr des Quetzalcoatl", *Adeva-Mitteilungen*, Heft 10, November 1966, 12).

106 Guzmán [13:41], 211.

107 When Frankl writes [19:105], 16, of "the pseudo-historical work of the Christo-indigenous group of Sahagún", he injures nobody but himself.

108 See Pasztory [13:52], 115–17.

109 Orozco, the best of the Mexican historians on this subject, concluded that "religious sentiment, belief in predictions about Quetzalcoatl, and the most stupid of superstitions, threw the imbecile monarch at the feet of the invader and placed the Empire without a fight under the yoke of Castile" (Orozco [8:4], iv, 275). Cf. Octavio Paz (*México en la obra de Octavio Paz*, I, *El Peregrino en su Patria*, Mexico, 1987, 87), who called Montezuma's fascination with Cortés "a sacred vertigo".

110 FC, viii, 81.

Chapter 20

1 See text of Cortés' gift to the daughters of Montezuma, in Josefina Muriel, "Reflexiones sobre Hernán Cortés", in *R de I*, IX (January–June 1948), 229.

2 G, 168.

3 Ixtlilxochitl, 133; Tapia, in J. Díaz, et al., 102.

4 Ordaz to Francisco Verdugo, 23 August 1529, (Otte [5:20], 116).

5 Edward Calnek, "Settlement patterns and chinampa agriculture at Tenochtitlan", *American Antiquity*, Vol.37 (1972), 1, 111.

6 Oviedo, IV, 249.

7 See Pedro Carrasco, "Estratificación social indígena en Morelos durante el siglo XVI", in Carrasco and Broda [3:30], and a similar essay by Pedro Carrasco, "Family structure in sixteenth century Tepotzlan", in *Process and Pattern in Culture*, ed. Robert Manners (Chicago, 1964). Carrasco's evidence is not for Mexico and is post-conquest, but the moral holds for old Tenochtitlan.

8 FC, x, 55.

9 One text of Sahagún from an interview with an indigenous informant described the prostitute of old Mexico: "you are a harlot, a harlot. You come out to catch men. To wander about alone. You are talkative and restless. You are afflicted with sores and the itch. You beckon to men with your gestures . . . You fish for men . . . You paint your face with cochineal . . . You are wasting your time in the square . . ." (Angel Garibay, "Paralipómenos de Sahagún", *Tlacocan*, II, 2 (Mexico, 1947).

10 Aguilar, in J. Díaz, et al.

11 Soustelle [1:5], 173, and Brundage [2:50], 19, dwell on this side of Mexican life.

12 The first published text to speak of Mexico-Tenochtitlan, *Newe Zeitung von dem Lande* of Augsburg, 1522, spoke of it as "great Venice" (*HAHR*, (1929), 200). Martyr (II, 108, 192) said, in a letter to the Marquises of Los Vélez and of Mondéjar, that the Castilians called Tenochtitlan "Venice the rich". Sahagún said that Mexico was "another Venice" and that the Mexica, in knowledge and breeding (*policía*), were Venetians (Sahagún, 4). Tenochtitlan was even compared to Venice by Gasparo Contarini, Venetian ambassador to Spain, in a report to the Senate of his city, 15 November 1525, in Eugenio Alberi, *Relazioni degli ambasciatore veneti al senato*, ser. I, vol. II (Firenze, 1840). Sepúlveda, having met Cortés, described Tenochtitlan as "similar to Venice" (a city which he probably himself knew), "but almost three times bigger in both extension and population" (in *Democrates Alter*, published in *BRAH*, xxi, October 1892, *cuadernos* iv, 310).

13 See William T. Sanders, "Settlement Patterns in Central Mexico", in *HMAI*, X (1971), 7.

14 José Alcina Franch, et al., "El 'temazcal' en Mesoamérica", *Revista Española de Antropología Americana*, X, 1980.

15 C, 30.

16 Münzer, in *Viajes* [5:20], 372.

17 García Sánchez [9:33], 110.

18 This point is developed by Todorov [4:17], as by Greenblatt [12:89], 9–11.

19 According to Cortés' biographer, there were 600 *pipillin* present in the palace, each with 3 or 4 armed men; a total of 3,000 men (G, 145). *El Conqu. Anón.*, in García Icazbalceta, I, 179, suggests there were 1,000 guards.

20 These quarters were Moyotla ("place of the mosquitoes"), Teopan-Zoquiapan ("place of the god", that is the temple), Aztacualco ("beside the house of the herons") and Cuepopan ("place of the blossoming of the flowers"). Alfonso Caso, "Los Barrios Antiguos de Tenochtitlan y Tlatelolco", *MAMH*, XV, no.1 (1956), prints a further breakdown of the 5 quarters into 68 named districts: but there may have been 108.

21 Calnek [14:27], 297.

22 Edward Calnek, "The internal Structure of Tenochtitlan", in E. R. Wolf (ed.), *The Valley of Mexico* (Albuquerque, 1978), 323.

23 C, 137: "*era su señorío casi comó España*".

24 D del C, II, 55.

25 Lombardo de Ruiz [19:18], 152.

26 Durán, II, 413.

27 G, 148.

28 Martyr, II, 205.

29 Pasztory [4:35], 166–7.

30 Paracelsus thought that the new Indians had been found in out-of-the-way islands, such as no descendant of Adam would go to: "it is most probable that they are descended from another Adam". Perhaps they were born there "after the deluge and perhaps have no souls. In speech, they are like parrots." (*Philosophiae Sagacis*, Frankfurt, 1605, lib.1, c.11, vol.x. 110, cit. Thomas Bendyshe, "The History of Anthropology", in *Memoirs read before the Anthropological Society of London*, 1863, I, 353).

31 Cod. Ram., 141–2. He returned to this theme later.

32 G, 160.

33 On his first voyage, Columbus offered a coat of silk to the first man who sighted land. Perhaps Cortés remembered the magical ballad of Count Arnaldos who, hunting near the sea, saw a galley with silk sails: the sailor who commanded it was singing a magic song which caused the wind to drop, the sea to become calm, the seagulls to rest on the masts, the fish to come to the surface. The Count asked the name of the song. The sailor replied that he could only tell that to someone who went to sea with him (*BAE*, X, 153). Alvarado's uncle, the *comendador* of Lobón, had drawn an income from taxes at the silk market of Granada, so the place may have come up in conversation.

34 D del C, I, 320.

35 D del C, I, 321.

36 D del C, I, 319.

37 C, 132; *El Conqu. Anón.*, in García Icazbalceta, I, 392, said it was 3 times bigger.

38 D del C, I, 335.

39 A derisive view was expressed by Armando García Garnica in "De la Metáfora al Mito: la visión de las crónicas sobre le tianguis prehispánico", *HM*, CXXXIII (1984–5). But the next article in the same journal, Janet Long-Solís' "El abastecimiento de chile en el mercado de México-Tenochtitlan en el siglo xvi", gave the commercial side of the market its old standing.

40 Soustelle [1:5], 60.

41 Clendinnen [3:11], 48–9.

42 Las Casas, *Apologética historia sumaria* (Mexico, 1967), 68.

43 Sanders [2:21], 404–5, discusses. Those hired to sculpt the Emperor would receive (as we hear from Tezozomoc [1:18], 668) clothes, chillis, maize and slaves.

44 *El Conqu. Anón.*, in García Icazbalceta, I, 394.

45 FC, viii, 68.

46 See C. Espejo and J. Paz, *Las Antiguas Ferias de Medina del Campo* (Valladolid, 1908–12). The square where the markets of Medina used to be held is still to be seen, and still measures 200 yards square, though markets, surrounding houses and warehouses have long vanished. The notaries of Medina were famous: Queen Isabel used to say that if she had three sons, one would succeed her, one would become Archbishop of Toledo, and the third would become a notary in Medina del Campo.

47 Durán, I, 178.

48 Berdan, "Luxury Trade", in Boone [1:5], 179.

49 *El Conqu. Anón.*, in García Icazbalceta, I, spoke of only one metal, gold in quills, but Cortés (C, 132) spoke also of silver, lead, copper, brass and tin. But no brass, lead or tin has been found in Mexico. The "brass" was likely to have been copper. For the 50 sections, see FC, x, 63–94.

50 C, 133.

51 C, 105; D del C, I, 322. The fact that the Mexicans had measures but not weights was emphasised by Martyr, II, 206.

52 FC, ix, 46.

53 D del C, I, 323. A skilful analysis of all reports of this market, listing nearly 300 separate items (if looking on live turkeys as separate from dead ones) was made by José Luis Rojas, *México Tenochtitlan* (Mexico, 1986), 163–9. He presents (233–4) a list of nearly 100 names of those who did the selling.

54 Cline's Sahagún, 124; for a discussion, see Eduardo Matos Moctezuma, *The Aztecs* (New York, 1989), 205–8.

55 Durán, II, 419–20.

56 The pyramid resembled the pretty surviving one at Tenayuca. Their bases were similar:

see Antonieta Espejo and James Griffin, "Algunas semjanzas entre Tenayuca y Tlatelolco", in *Tlatelolco a través de los tiempos* (Mexico, 1944).

57 D del C (I, 333–4) seems to show that the Castilians climbed the pyramid in Tenochtitlan: "thus we left the great square [that is, the market in Tlatelolco] without seeing more, and we arrived at the great courtyards and enclosures where the great temple [*el gran cu*] was and, before arriving there, we had to traverse a great circuit of courtyards ..." This has been interpreted by some as suggesting that the visitors went up the pyramid of Tlatelolco. Despite new research on the size of the temple precinct at Tlatelolco (for which, see Matos Moctezuma [20:54]), that cannot be so, given the description of the view from the top, and given that the ashes or bones of Mexican kings were said to be in the building. This view is confirmed by Matos Moctezuma in "The templo mayor de Tenochtitlan", in Boone [2:58], 139, fn.2. See also Pasztory [4:35], 115.

58 C, 134 ("*la iglesia mayor de Sevilla*"). Tapia spoke of 113 steps, Bernal Díaz of 114.

59 Alcocer [19:70], 28, for Mexico; as for Seville, the old Moorish tower in 1500 had on it a small spire whose height was not so great as the present bell-tower with its "Giraldillo" of 94 metres. The pyramid was 46.56 metres high, while that of the sun at Teotihuacan, without reckoning the temples at the top of it, was 61 metres.

60 For the size, see E. Pasztory, "Reflections", in Boone [1:5], 457.

61 For this building, see Eduardo Matos Moctezuma, *The Great Temple of the Aztecs* (London, 1988).

62 Cecilia F. Klein, "Ideology of autosacrifice", in Boone [1:5], 355. Torquemada said that there were 5,000 priests attending this temple (Caso [3:25], 188–9).

63 C, 134.

64 Pasztory [4:35], 155. It was the sensational discovery in 1978 of this relief which led to the formation of the Proyecto Templo Mayor.

65 D del C, I, 333.

66 FC, ii, appendix. Early versions of this *chacmool*, and one of these stones, perhaps that which once served Huitzilopochtli, were excavated in 1978. See Matos Moctezuma [20:61], 142. Johanna Broda, in Broda, Eduardo Matos Moctezuma and Pedro Carrasco, *The Templo Mayor* (Berkeley, 1987), speculate on its use.

67 Durán, I, 19–20.

68 G (188) says so. He must have heard it from Cortés.

69 Tapia, in J. Díaz, et al., 107 (he went to the temple later).

70 Jorge Gurría Lacroix, "Andrés de Tapia y la Coatlicue", *ECN* lxxviii, 23–32.

71 Francisco de Salazar, *Dialogue* (1554).

72 Aguilar, in J. Díaz, et al., 182.

73 C, 137; Tapia, in J. Díaz, et al., 107; Durán, I, 81.

74 D del C, I, 336.

75 FC, vi, 4.

76 FC, vi, 18–20. Translation adapted to fit first person singular.

77 D del C, I, 340.

78 Fr. Aguilar so told Fr. Durán.

79 Tapia, in J. Díaz, et al., 102; G, 169; D del C, I, 341.

80 C, 123.

Chapter 21

1 Ixtlilxochitl, 250–1.

2 Aguilar insists on Ordaz's part. Bernal Díaz says that he went with the captains to make these points to Cortés (D del C, I, 341).

3 This is López de Gómara's account.
4 D del C, I, 343.
5 Tapia, in J. Díaz, et al., 102.
6 *CDI*, XXVII, 340.
7 Aguilar, in J. Díaz, et al., 182.
8 Juan Álvarez, in *Inf. de 1521* (Polavieja, 223); Aguilar, in J. Díaz, et al., 182; D del C, I, 344–6; and evidence of Juan de Tirado (who was wounded), in an *información* of 1525 (AGI, México, 203, no.3). Cortés wrote that Qualpopoca had said that he would offer homage to Charles V but needed an escort to help him through enemy territory. So, he went on, Escalante sent him 4 Spanish of whom Qualpopoca killed 2, the others escaping. Prisoners said that Montezuma had asked Qualpopoca so to behave (C, 88). Ixtlilxochitl (250) says that he had a letter which showed the affair was an invention of the Tlaxcalans.
9 D del C, I, 346. Cortés says (C, 118) that Montezuma was said to have asked how it was possible, seeing that the Mexica had several thousand men and the Castilians not much more than a hundred, that the former did not destroy the latter. The messengers from the coast said that that was because the Castilians had a great lady (*tecleciguata*) from home fighting for them. Montezuma was said to have been persuaded that that was Mary, the Mother of God.
10 Cortés' biographer (G, 193) wrote that the *Caudillo* explicitly stated that the affair of Qualpopoca was the occasion or pretext (*"la ocasión o pretexto"*) for him to do something which he had already conceived. Fr. Díaz, in the Res vs Alvarado (124) said that it was "after several days", and after the incident in Almería, that Cortés acted.
11 G, 194. This daughter was probably "Doña Ana", with whom Cortés later had an affair (see Muriel [20:1], 235). Several conquistadors testified later to having seen her in Cortés' room.
12 G, 193.
13 D del C, I, 348–50.
14 Tapia, in J. Díaz, et al., 102–3.
15 Tapia, in J. Díaz, et al., 103.
16 "the said reasoning [*razonamyento*] lasted the better part of a day" (AGI, Justicia, leg. 223, p.2, f.227); Tapia, in J. Díaz, et al., 103, and G, 194, said 4 hours.
17 Tapia, in J. Díaz, et al., 110.
18 Aguilar, in J. Díaz, et al., 182.
19 D del C, I, 348–50.
20 C, 120.
21 Martín Vázquez testified that he saw Montezuma being carried across the city (*CDI*, XXVIII, 140).
22 C, 121.
23 *CDI*, XXVIII, 14.
24 "as a prisoner" (*"a manera de preso"*). When giving land to the daughters of Montezuma in 1526, see appendix to Muriel [20:1], 241.
25 Tapia in answer to question 96 of Cortés' questionnaire said that he thought that the deception worked perfectly in relation to the Mexica (AGI, Justicia, leg. 223, p.2, f.309 v.).
26 Ixtlilxochitl [4:5], 9.
27 "*Maña*" was the word used by Alonso de Navarrete, in AGI, Justicia, leg. 223. p.2, f.424 v.
28 "*Oigan vuestros oidos lo que dice vuestra boca*".
29 Las Casas, III, 199–200: in 1540 in Monzón, when the court was there.
30 "On His Majesty's behalf, I passed to these parts with certain ships and people in order to pacify and settle and attract the people there to the dominion and service of the imperial Crown of His Majesty . . ." Hernán Cortés, *Donación de tierras de D. Isabel*

Montezuma, in AGI, Escribanía de Cámara, 178 A.

31 Sepúlveda met Cortés several times in the 1540s and discussed these things with him. See Sepúlveda [20:12], 311.

32 Sepúlveda [20:12], 311.

33 G, 193.

34 D del C, I, 390.

35 *CDI*, XXVIII, 141.

36 Sahagún, II, 971. That chronicler says that Cacama, the King of Texcoco and Tetlepanquetzatzin, as well as the majordomo of Montezuma, Topentemoctzin, were held.

37 FC, xii, 47.

38 FC, vi, with Thelma Sullivan's glosses in "Tlatoani and Tlatocayotl in the Sahagún manuscripts", *ECN*, 14 (1980).

39 FC, xii (1st ed.), 45.

40 *Sólo venimos a dormir:*
   Sólo venimos a soñar;
   No es verdad, no es verdad
   Que venimos a vivir en la tierra
quoted in Garibay [1:13], 1, 91.

41 C, 121; D del C; G, 178.

42 Tapia, in J. Díaz, et al., 110.

43 Cod. Ram., 221, and Tezozomoc [1:19], 36, reported Qualpopoca hanged, Juan Álvarez that he was shot to death by bows and arrows, as occurred in Chalco and at the Tlacacalli fiesta in honour of Tlacolteotl the earth goddess, but Cortés (C, 90), Ixtlilxochitl (254) and Bernal Díaz say that the punishment was by burning. The *Anales de Tlatelolco*, quoted in León-Portilla [4:33], 150, says that Qualpopoca was killed at the time of the massacre by Alvarado (see Ch. 26). Durán (II, 528) says that Montezuma had him torn to pieces.

44 G, 201.

45 FC, iii, 64.

46 500, according to the doubtless exaggerating Cod. Ram., 65–6, 125–6. For the "divine hearth", see Durán, II, 143.

47 For these warriors, see Hassig, 1:23.

48 Tapia, in AGI, Justicia, leg. 223. p.2, f.309 v.

49 C, 91–2.

50 Sahagún, II, 317.

51 FC, viii, 30.

52 The absence of surviving ball courts in central Mexico is explained by the buildings on their sites. Games were also played informally in open spaces as is football today. The rules of these games are discussed in Durán, I, 206.

53 See Vernon Scarborough and David R. Wilkcox, *The Mesoamerican Ballgame* (Tucson, 1991), 13, and analysis by Christian Duverger [1:44], especially 43–52.

54 FC, viii, 58. Once an emperor of Mexico bet the market in Tenochtitlan against a garden in Xochimilco: the emperor lost. Mexican soldiers went to greet the victor, threw flowers round his neck with a thong in them, and killed him.

55 The pun is Duverger's [1:44], 128: "*pour les aztèques la récréation doit toujours être une* re-création".

56 D del C, I, 358–9.

57 Torquemada [1:24], xiv, Ch. v. See Manuel Moreno, *La organización política y social de los Aztecas* (Mexico, 1931), 46.

58 Bernal Díaz (D del C, I, 363) says, "we could not at that time do anything other than

pretend about the matter" ("*no podíamos en aquella sazón hacer otra cosa sino disimular con el*").

59 FC, v, 152.

60 D del C, I, 340.

61 See FC, viii, 30, and the rules in Durán, I, 198. Pictures of a game between 4 players are in the Codex Magliabecchiano and, between 2, in Weiditz, *Trachtenbuch* [10:38], where the author says that the game reminded him of *morra* in Italy. The similarities with backgammon were discussed by A. L. Kroeber, in *Anthropology* (1948), 551. He thought in terms of a coincidence. But E. B. Tylor in 1891 thought that the mathematical probability of two such similar games being invented separately was low. There is an analysis in Duverger [1:44], 53–9, who sees a relation between *patolli* and *peyotl*, the white hallucinogenic truffle-like cactus.

62 See FC, iv, 94; Soustelle [1:5], 160.

63 "playing with a crossbow with the said marquis": Joan de Cáceres, AGI, Justicia, leg. 223, p.2, f.227r.

64 Tapia, answer to question 97 in AGI, Justicia, leg.223, p.2, f.309.

65 "Montezuma told the Marquís . . . that these people did not wish to be treated with love but with fear" ("*no se quería tratar por amor sino por temor*"), Gerónimo López, 25 February 1545, letter to the Emperor, *Epistolario*, IV, 168–9.

66 Sahagún listed 40 types of water fowl; D del C, II, 62. See too Soustelle [1:5], 150–1. G, 162, talked of the scum tasting like cheese: Cortés must have told him.

67 *Huehuetlatolli*, Documento A. cit. Garibay [1:13], I, 443.

68 Richard Evans Schultes and Albert Hofmann, *Plants of the Gods* (London, 1979), 26.

69 D del C, II, 141. This Valenzuela had been punished with Cortés and others for playing cards in Cuba (see Res vs Velázquez, AGI, Justicia, leg.49, f.21). Perhaps he also painted extra pictures of the Virgin needed for so many conquered temples.

70 C de S, 125.

71 Evidence of Vázquez de Tapia, in *CDI*, XXVI, 423, as of Mejía (Res (Rayón), I, 99) who, like Gerónimo de Aguilar, said that she was a daughter: "Cortés went with two sisters, daughters of Montezuma". Francisco Vargas, as well as the other witnesses, said that he saw "Doña Ana in Cortés' room in the palace" (Res (Rayón), II, 241–3).

72 Neither Cortés nor Alvarado would hear the end of complaints deriving from this. See Vázquez de Tapia's evidence in *CDI*, XXVI, 395, García Llerena's in *CDI*, XXVII, 218, and Francisco Davila's in *CDI*, XXVIII, 44–5; and the discussion of Grado in the Res vs Alvarado: Alvarado said that Grado, having been the accountant, had acquired much gold without having to have it *quintado*. Grado did well in the next few years, and his resentment only seems to have been fired afterwards. Cortés arranged for him to marry "Doña Isabel", the eldest, most beautiful, and favourite daughter of Montezuma. See *CDI*, XXVII, 358, for Cortés' questions 145 and 146 on this matter.

73 C, 132.

74 *Relación del conquistador Bernardino Vázquez de Tapia*, ed. Manuel Romero de Terreros (Mexico, 1939), 35–6. Antonio Bravo said (*Información de 1540*, in Conway (Camb.), Add. 7242) that López volunteered.

75 Tapia (alone of Cortés' inner circle) later spoke enthusiastically of López. See Conway (L of C), I, 45. Martín López, in *Inf. de 1565*, 118–19.

76 See his grant of arms in 1550, where it is shown that his genealogy led back to the gallant Osorio (see *Nobilario*, Conway (Camb.), Add. 7242, AGI, Escribanía de Cámara, 178, and Guillermo Porras Muñoz, *R de I* (January–June 1948). That made him distantly related to the Marquis of Astorga.

77 Questionnaire of 1534 in Conway (Camb.), Add. 8597.

78 Conway (L of C), I, 45, 139; the phrase was of the carpenter Diego Ramírez, in Conway (Camb.), Add. 7289, 797.

79 D del C, I, 378–81.

80 Ignacio de Mora y Villamil, "Elementos para la Marina", in the *Boletín de la sociedad mexicana de geografía y estadística*, Mexico, 1st epoch, ix, (1862), 301, quoted in Gardner, [19:59], 67.

81 AGI, Patronato, leg.57, R. I, no.1, ff.3, 4, 6, 7, 8, 17. There is a tr. in Conway (Aber.), 6–7, 10, 19, 23, 25.

82 Conway, (L of C) I, 45, 118.

83 D del C, I, 363–5.

84 The commander of the first brigantines seems to have been Francisco de Flores, in Información de los méritos y servicios de Francisco Flores, AGI, Mexico, leg. 203.

85 Sanders [2:21], 84–5.

86 Martyr, II, but Oscar Apenes in 1944 described the last signs of traditional salt-making in his "The primitive salt production of Lake Texcoco", *Thenos*, 9 (1) 25–40, cit. Sanders [2:21], 173.

Chapter 22

1 FC, vi, Ch. 8. tr. here by Thelma Sullivan in "Nahuatl proverbs, conundrums and metaphors, collected by Sagahún", in *ECN* (1963).

2 *"cosas de Dios"*: Francisco de Flores, in answer to question 57.

3 D del C, I, 389.

4 D del C, I, 325.

5 This is evident from Frances Berdan's analysis of the Codex Mendoza, the Matrícula de Tributos, and certain *relacionas geográficas*, in "Luxury trade and tribute", Boone [1:5], 167.

6 C, 122. The list of tribute in gold in the Matrícula de Tributos and in the Codex Mendoza records that, in the past, 560,000 pesos' worth were given to the Mexica every year – equivalent to almost two tons (Emmerich [2:29], 149, discusses). Barlow [1:10], 6–7, thought that the Matrícula de Tributos, a European book in form but indigenous in style, either might have been specially made for Cortés or that he had it with him that winter 1519–20.

7 Emmerich [2:29], xxii, 128–35, 139, argued that it was the shortage of gold in old Mexico which inspired such elaborate use of what they had. For a summary of what was found in the famous Tomb 7 in Monte Alban, see Alfonso Caso, "Reading the Riddle of Ancient Jewels", *Natural History* (New York), XXXII, 5, 464–80. Emmerich's Ch. xvi summarises the technology.

8 See Ronald Spores, *The Mixtecs in ancient and colonial times* (Norman, 1984), Chs. 1 and 2.

9 C, 122.

10 Max L. Moorhead, "Hernán Cortés and the Tehuantepec passage", *HAHR*, 29 (1949).

11 Questionnaire in *información* of Diego de Ordaz (Santo Domingo, 1521), and evidence of Diego Bardales, Antón del Río, Pero López de Barbas, Gonzalo Giménez, and Gutierre de Casamori (in *CDI*, XL, 74ff).

12 Andrés de Tapia said so (AGI, Justicia, leg. 223, p.2, f.309 v.); see *CDI*, XXVIII, 141, where it is stated that "four or six" or even "ten or twenty" Spanish set off in different directions; D del C, I, 375; C, 13. Diego Pizarro was probably a son or grandson of "La Pizarra", Cortés' aunt, who played a part in lawsuits in Medellín in the late 15th century: for example, in AGS, Registro General del Sello (28 July 1485), f.208, we see how "la Pizarra" was granted a surety for herself and her son Diego against the Count of Medellín.

13 *CDI*, XXVIII, 142; D del C, I, 376; C, 124.

14 See Howard F. Cline, "Problems of Mexican Ethno-History: the ancient Chinantla", *HAHR*, 37 (1957), 274–95.

15 Ixtlilxochitl [4:5], 10.

16 Ixtlilxochitl, 256.

17 D del C, II, 118: C, 127.

18 Vázquez de Tapia in Res vs Alvarado, 35–6; see too Ixtlilxochitl's *Sumaria Relación*, in *Obras Históricas*, ed. Edmundo O'Gorman (Mexico, 1985, 2 vols.), I, 389.

19 Sánchez Farfán's evidence is in Res vs Alvarado, 138. Sánchez Farfán was probably connected with the famous Farfán family of Seville lawyers.

20 Res vs Alvarado, 65.

21 Res vs Alvarado, 133.

22 *"Si hubiera muchos Cacamas, no sé cómo fuera . . ."* (G, 207).

23 "many lords came together" (*"se hizo la junta de muchos señores"*); Joan López de Jimena, answer to question 98 in AGI, Justicia, leg. 224, p.1. ff.12r–46v.

24 From evidence in Bermúdez Plata [9:46], he seems to have come from Medellín or from Encinasola, in the Sierra de Fregenal.

25 Evidence of Francisco de Flores, in AGI, leg. 223, p.2, answer to question 98.

26 Alonso de Navarrete, in AGI, leg. 223, p.2, ff. 425–511.

27 *"se daba por esclavo"*; Joan de Cáceres, in AGI, Justicia, leg. 223, p.2. The rest is Cortés' account in 1529 when he framed question 98 at his *residencia*, *CDI*, XXVII, 341–2. Tapia agreed that the proceedings fell out thus. In his letter to the King, of September 1520, Cortés said that the proceedings were begun by Montezuma, who made a speech in much the same terms as he was said to have spoken on 8 November (C, 128).

28 "Each of them individually [*Cada uno por sí*] offered themselves as vassals to His Majesty [*se dió por vasallo de su majestad*]"; Tapia, in evidence in AGI, Justicia, leg. 223, p.2.

29 Joan López de Jimena, in AGI, Justicia, leg. 224, p.1, f.1 r.

30 Sepúlveda, 158–9.

31 Ixtlilxochitl, 257.

32 Tapia, in J. Díaz, et al., 104. See also *CDI*, XXVII, 341–2, and XXVIII, 142, where Martín Vázquez testified the same.

33 "Montezuma . . . asked to be baptised but the matter was deferred until Easter" (Joan de Cáceres, answer to question 102 (*CDI*, XXVII, 344) in AGI, Justicia, leg. 223, p.2). Pero Rodríguez de Escobar said that he knew Montezuma asked for baptism, while Joan López de Jimena said that he thought he actually was baptised. Juan Cano said the same ("he converted to our Holy Faith without any resistance"), though that was in the late 1540s when he was trying to persuade the Crown (he had married Montezuma's daughter) to give him some of the royal Mexican gold (*Epistolario*, XV, 137–9). For Cano, a hidalgo from Cáceres, see Amada López de Meneses, "Un compañero de Hernán Cortés: Juan Cano", *REE*, (September–December 1965), and Altman [9:23], 140. Cano's uncle Diego had been with the historian Oviedo at the famous court of the Infante Juan (Oviedo, IV, 259).

34 Oviedo, IV, 42.

35 Silvio Zavala, "Hernán Cortés ante la justificación de su conquista", *Revista de Historia de América*, 92 (July–December 1981), 53.

36 "Origen de los mexicanos", in *Relaciones de la Nueva España* (Madrid, 1990), 153.

37 Juan Cano: "of his own will he gave himself up to the marquis of the valley in the name of Your Majesty, coming out to receive him in peace without any resistance and also giving him much gold" (letter to Charles V, 1 December 1547, in *Epistolario*, V, 62–3). Cano said that some of the gold had belonged to Tecuichpo's mother Tecalco.

38 *Historia del Emperador Moctezuma*, by P. Luis de Motezuma, Montezuma's grandson (*c.* 1560), cit. Silvio Zavala, *Las Instituciones Jurídicas en la Conquista de América* (3rd ed., Mexico, 1988), 320.

39 Fernández-Armesto [18:34], 158.

40 G, 186.

41 Cristóbal del Castillo, *Fragmentos de la obra general sobre la historia de los Mexicanos* (Florence, 1908), 106.

42 C, 138.

43 Tapia records this (J. Díaz, et al., 105). FC, xii, 48, says that Montezuma himself took the Spaniards to this place. Juan Álvarez, in the *Inf. de 1521*, says that Cortés seized the House of Birds himself (Polavieja, 194).

44 and 45 This is the text of Angel Maria Garibay K., Informantes de Sahagun, qu. León-Portilla [4:33]

46 Cline's Sahagún, 72.

47 I accept here the timing of Tapia, an eyewitness, rather than other sources.

48 Pasztory [4:35], 111-14.

49 Tapia, in AGI, Justicia, leg. 223, p.2, f.309. In his written account he says that it was a suggestion, not an order.

50 Matos Moctezuma [20:61], 65.

51 Angel María Garibay, *Poesía lírica Azteca* (Mexico, 1937).

52 *"A algo nos hemos de poner por Dios"* (Tapia, in J. Díaz, et al., 111). In Tapia's account in answer to a question in the *residencia* (that is, some years before this written *relación*), Cortés' phrase is represented as *"esto es honrra de Dios e ansy se ha de azer"*. Francisco de Flores has much the same phrase in his answer in the *residencia*. The story appears in Marineo's biography of Cortés, *c.* 1530 – five years before the evidence given at the *residencia*. Inga Clendinnen, in "Fierce and unnatural cruelty", insists that this incident was a fabrication. But as in other instances, it seems improbable that not only Cortés but Andrés de Tapia, Francisco de Flores, Martín Vázquez and others who answered the relevant question in the *residencia* against Cortés should lie, under oath. Tapia's *relación* is vivid, he certainly was a protégé of Cortés, but that did not mean he always did what Cortés demanded of him. That is shown by his appearance as a witness for Martín López, who was complaining of neglect by Cortés.

53 Francisco de Flores, who was with Cortés, could not remember Montezuma coming (AGI, Justicia, leg. 223, p. 2, f. 511v., in answer to question 102).

54 This was Cortés' account (C, 135).

55 Tapia, in J. Díaz, et al., 112.

56 Memorandum of Alonso de Ojeda, as reported in C de S, 344. (This Alonso de Ojeda is not to be confused with the discoverer of Venezuela of the same name, as pointed out by Gonzalo Miguel Ojeda, "Alonso de Ojeda in Mexico", in *MAMH*, LXX (1960), 113-24.) Flores gives a slightly different account, suggesting that the idols were merely wrapped up and taken away.

57 Alonso de Ojeda, in C de S, 344. Cortés (C, 106) says that he had the idols thrown down the steps. López de Gómara says the same (G, 174), but they both must be alluding to the dismantlement in the temples, not the taking of the idols. The accounts of Tapia, Flores, and Ojeda coincide in saying that, on the contrary, they were taken away. Either Cortés did not know what happened; or he did not wish to admit that the idols might still be held in secret. López de Gómara says that this event occurred when Montezuma and Cortés went to the temple after the former's kidnapping. D del C, I, 389, has a less dramatic account, merely stating that Cortés successfully sought permission to have the Christian images set up in the temple.

58 They were apparently later returned to Tenochtitlan, and later still taken to Tula where the trace was lost. Padden [3:35], 254–74 has a study of Bishop Zumárraga's search for them.

59 Durán has a vivid description, suggesting that this was the only statue to Huitzilopochtli in the temple.

60 García del Pilar, Res (Rayón), 215: "*estando en este dicha ciudad echó de un templo de los Yndios ciertos ydolos*".

61 Joan de Cáceres, in AGI, Justicia, leg. 223, p.2, f.227r.

62 Tapia, in J. Díaz, et al., 123.

63 Martín Vázquez (*CDI*, XXVIII, 144) says that he helped to remove the idols and put the Christian images in their place: "*queste testigo fué in ayuda de quitar los dichos ydolos e poner los dichos ymagenes*". Tapia in evidence to answer to question 102 recalled mass being celebrated in the temple. Francisco de Solís and Juan Jaramillo also saw the idols being removed. Ojeda's account is in C de S, 345.

64 C, 135.

65 D del C, I, 389.

66 Oviedo, IV, 48.

67 Once again Wagner is a good guide on these figures.

68 G, 186, gets the figures fitting together. Martyr says that "Cortés, after melting down the gold of Montezuma's chiefs into ingots, wrote the Royal Fifth as being 34,000 ducats".

69 In his *residencia* (*CDI*, XXVI, 427), Cortés was accused of having taken 25,000 pesos de oro at the first partition of the spoil without paying the Royal Fifth.

70 Thus in the *residencia* against Alvarado in 1529, Sánchez Farfán stated that he "saw how all the gold was melted down and how parts were given out to the comrades [*compañeros*], including himself [*y que a este testigo le fizieron su parte*]" (Res vs Alvarado, 113).

71 Tapia, in AGI, Justicia, leg. 223, p.2, f.309 v.

72 D del C, I, 385. Among these last was Luis de Cárdenas to whom Cortés gave 300 pesos. It did not stop him complaining against Cortés for years. See his letter to Charles V of 29 August 1527, in *CDI*, XL, 273–87.

73 Ley Primera, cited in Cadenas [15:32], 301–3. La Celestina says, in the dialogue of that name: "Fine gold, wrought by the hand of the master, is of greater worth than the material."

74 Sauer [5:8], 222.

75 E.g. by Salvatierra in the camp of Narváez (D del C, I, 413).

76 This was in Juan Tirado vs Cortés, in *CDI*, XXVII, 430.

77 21,938 and 3,939 are Murga's precise figures, in his *Juan Ponce de León* [5:14], 230.

78 Res vs Alvarado. In respect of cacao, Alonso de Ojeda said the same to C de S, 374.

79 García Llerena in *residencia* against Cortés, *CDI*, XXVI, 211; Martín Vázquez, in *CDI*, XXVIII, 154, and D del C, I, 386.

80 G, 205.

81 Vázquez de Tapia in *residencia* against Cortés, *CDI*, XXVI, 395.

82 Juan Jaramillo, evidence in AGI, leg. 224, p.1, f.464 v.

83 Montezuma was presumably referring not to Cortés' seizure of the treasure in the Teocalli but to the seizures, such as those of Ojeda and Alvarado, of 600 *cargas* of cacao (each of 24,000 beans), as chronicled by C de S, 107–8; or to the fact that Alvarado had carried out other thefts, as alleged by, for example, Rodrigo de Castañeda (Res vs Alvarado, 12–14) or Francisco Verdugo (Res vs Alvarado, 17).

84 D del C, I, 390–1.

85 G, 211.

86 For flint, see Debra Nagao, *Mexican Buried Offerings* (Oxford, 1985), 62–4.

87 FC, iii, 142.

88 FC, iii, 134.

89 Motolinía [4:2], 63.

90 FC, i, 39–40; ii, 44–57; viii, 86; Durán, I, 95–103.

91 Cline's Sahagún, 73, says that the Mexica were beginning to suffer hunger because of Spanish demands. G, 191, discusses this incident, again presumably on the evidence of Cortés himself. Díaz del Castillo also reports, but neither Cortés nor Tapia did.

92 This derives from José Francisco Chimalpopoca, 1768, allegedly a descendant of Cuauhtémoc, as cited by Josefina Muriel, "Divergencias en la biografía de Cuauhtémoc", *Estudios de Historia Novohispana*, I, 53–114. This excellent study establishes the wife of Cuauhtémoc as Xuchimatzatzin, daughter of Montezuma.

93 G, 212.

94 D del C, I, 391.

95 Statements of Fr. Juan Díaz, Fr. Bartolomé de Olmedo and Gonzalo de Alvarado, etc., at Segura, August 1520, in Conway (Camb.), Add. 7306, 24, 30.

96 G, 213.

97 Evidence of Clemente de Barcelona, in Conway (Camb.), Add. 7289, 497. In an *información* of 1544, Diego Ramírez, Hernán Martín, Rodrigo Nájera, and Andrés Martínez all said they had worked on these ships.

Chapter 23

1 Velázquez to Fonseca, 12 October 1519, in *CDI*, XXVII, 346.

2 D del C, I, 208. Mariel was in 1519 often known as Marién.

3 Luis J. Ramos, "El primer barco enviado por Cortés a España . . .", in *Hernán Cortés como hombre de empresa* (Valladolid, 1990), 63–76. The subject is also explored by Varela Marcos in his study of Alaminos [7:8], 110. The *procuradores* probably stopped in Yucatan.

4 See letter of Montejo's administrator, Juan de Rojas (whom I take to be one of the Velázquez-Rojas cousinhood), 11 September 1519, in *CDI*, XII, 155–60.

5 D del C, I, 208, says that Montejo sent a sailor explicitly to tell the Governor. But he was not there himself.

6 Velázquez to Fonseca, *CDI*, XXVII, 346.

7 This was explained by Martín Cortés to Charles in March 1520 (Cuevas [6:57], 4).

8 *CDI*, XI, 321.

9 Pasamonte had been the inspiration of the *repartimiento* of 1514 which had given much property in Hispaniola to royal officials and others living in Spain who had had no intention of ever going to the New World (see Arranz [5:45], and AGI, Santo Domingo, leg. 77, R.1, quoted in Giménez Fernández [6:19], II, 148ff.).

10 AGI, Indif. Gen., leg. 420, lib. 8, no.9 (19 June 1519, Barcelona).

11 Culúa was Culhuacan, one of the cities which the Mexica had conquered, but whose name, through its connection with Tollan, they sometimes used. See also Giménez Fernández [6:19], II, 274.

12 This was achieved in a roundabout way. There did not seem to have been a specific concession, but a decree dated 5 May 1519 spoke of Velázquez as "*Adelantado*, lieutenant of our governor of Fernandina, captain and redistributor of Indians . . ." (AGI, Indif. Gen., leg. 420, lib. 8, f.60). See Giménez Fernández [6:19], 1–58; in writing this chapter, I have pursued his references in the AGI as in the APS, and would never have found them without his lead.

13 AGI, Indif. Gen., leg. 420, lib. 8, f.109.

14 Velázquez to Licenciado Figueroa, in Martínez, *Docs*, 99.

15 Some texts suggest that this Rojas was Gabriel, but Gabriel, a brother of Manuel, conquistador of Peru, was then in Darien, and there must have been a mistake for Manuel.

16 *CDI*, XXVII, 346.

17 This enquiry, in Santiago de Cuba, 7 October 1519, is in *CDI*, XII, 151–209.

18 Evidence of Pedro Castellar, in *información* of Santiago (1519), in *CDI*, XII, 171: "*dos ruedas como de carreta, redondas, la una de oro, e la otra de plata . . .*"

19 *CDI*, XII, 204.

20 *CDI*, II, 435. He took with him a copy of the previous year's instructions to Cortés, dated 5 October, presumably that now in the AGI.

21 *CDI*, XII, 246–51.

22 This *información* is in *CDI*, XII, 150–204.

23 Información . . . del adelantado Rodrigo de Bastidas, 22 June 1521, Santo Domingo, in *CDI*, II, 373.

24 Sauer [5:8], 205.

25 "*viruelas . . . de que murieron todos los más de los indios . . .*" (Información de Bastidas, *CDI*, II, 373).

26 Velázquez to Figueroa, in García Icazbalceta, I, 390.

27 Velázquez had considered Narváez as the leader of the expedition as early as October, as his first letter to Fonseca suggested (*CDI*, XII, 250).

28 That that was the aim of Narváez was testified to by, for example, Leonel de Cervantes, "*el comendador*" (evidence of 3 September 1520 at Segura, Conway (Camb.), Add. 7806, 49). Alonso de Vilanueva said, "the said armada was organised by the said Diego Velázquez to take or kill the said Marquis"; *CDI*, XXVII, 486 (Cortés became a marquis, and was often so referred to).

29 Letters sent from Seville to Burgos by agents or servants to their merchant masters (e.g., Juan de la Peña), describe their arrival, with information about the discoveries. So does a note given to Gaspar Contarini, Venetian ambassador to Spain, ed. in *Calendar of state papers relating to English affairs in the archives of Venice* (London, 1869), III, 2878 (18 November 1519). Three of the letters to Burgos were published at the time in German, and republished by Marshal Saville, in *Indian Notes and Monographs*, ix, 1 (1920), 31–9. Another letter (apparently a copy of one of the others) was ed. as "Primeras Noticias de Yucatan" by Cesáreo Fernández Duro, in *Boletín de la Sociedad Geográfica de Madrid* (Madrid, 1885), xix, 336–42. Aurelio Tío [5:14], 67, insisted that Ponce de León, to whom Alaminos had been pilot in 1513, should have been known as the father of the Gulf Stream.

30 AGS, Castilla, leg. 110, f.76–99. The seizure is referred to by Martín Cortés in a memorandum of 24 June 1520, APS, oficio iv, lib. iii.

31 APS, oficio iv, lib. iv, 29 November 1519. This document is not in the folio indicated in the index (f.3565). A search for it has not been successful. I believe, though, that I am justified in stating the evidence as it is in the text from the summary, which runs: "Martín Cortés, resident of Medellín, recognises that he received from the treasurer Luis de Medina, *veinticuatro* [that is, councillor] of Seville . . . 102 pesos of gold which had been sent to him by Andrés de Duero in the *nao* of Covarrubias . . ."

32 See a letter dated 24 September 1519 from King Charles to the Pope, saying that his court in Flanders had "often been approached by these men offering much money as a bribe if only we were to get rid of the Inquisition" (AGS, Consejo de la Inquisición, lib. xiv, f.95, quoted in Giménez Fernández [6:19], II, 17). These tales were probably spread by the Dominicans.

33 Giménez Fernández [6:19], II.

34 AGI, Indif. Gen., leg. 420. lib. 8, f.46. This describes how Juan Fernández de las

Varas (a merchant who was an associate of the Genovese Grimaldis, a pioneer in slaving expeditions into *"islas inútiles"*, and an enemy of Fonseca) presented a complaint before "those of my Council who understand affairs of the Indies" (*"los de mi consejo que entienden en las cosas de las Indias"*). It was signed by Fonseca, Gattinara, Licenciado Zapata, and Licenciado García de Padilla.

35 AGI, Indif. Gen., leg. 420, lib. 8, f.127. This paper, a *cédula real,* was signed by Gattinara, Fonseca, Ruiz del Mota, Zapata and García de Padilla. In these arguments, I follow Schäfer ([6:79], I, 35), though, as earlier noted, Demetrio Ramos ("La fundación del consejo de Indias", in *El Consejo de las Indias en el siglo XVI* (Valladolid, 1970), shows that nothing formal was set up till 1524. The informal arrangements seem, however, to be confirmed by allusions in both Las Casas and Martyr, who became a member of "our council". I have also found a document in Seville (AGI, Indif. Gen. leg. 420) which, dated 10 September 1521, speaks of a discussion in the Council of the Indies (*"visto e platicado sobre todo en el nuestro consejo de las Indias"*).

36 Ramon Carande, *Carlos V y sus banqueros* (3rd ed., Barcelona, 1987), III, 36–7.

37 Schäfer [6:79], I, 48.

38 Las Casas says as much (III, 229).

39 *"todo era mucho a ver"* (Oviedo, II, 150, and III, 10). A letter from Seville of 3 November, but sent from "secretary Dedo" in Naples, to Venice, quoted in Marini Sanuto, *I Diarii,* (Venice, 1890), Vol.28, talks of *"tanto oro che è meraveglia"*.

40 APS, Libro del año 1519, oficio iv, lib. iv, f.3747: "I Martyn Cortés and I Fernando de Herrera, resident as we are of the villa of Medellín, being as we are in this city of Seville [*estantes que somos en esta çibdad de Seuylla*] . . ."

41 See Medellín papers (in Casa de Pilatos, Archivo de la Fundación Medinaceli), leg. 4, no.30, for the lawsuit of 1504; and Cooper [6:66], 1095–1100. The extraordinary life of Medellín in these years can be pursued in the AGS, Castilla, Cámara, leg. 106, 114, 116, 117, 120, 127, 129–30, 141, 151–3.

42 APS, oficio iv, lib. iv, f.3739, of 9 December 1519, and the same, f.3565, of 29 November 1519. For the *converso* merchant, Juan de Córdoba, who began his transatlantic trading in 1502, see Giménez Fernández [6:19], II, 963, and Ruth Pike, *Aristocrats and Traders* (Ithaca, 1972), 102. Pike also, 75, discusses judges of *las gradas.* The pearl-dealing of Córdoba and Luis Fernández de Alfaro can be followed in Otte [19:47], 67, 403, 421. Cortés in Hispaniola and Cuba may have remained in touch with these merchants.

43 APS, oficio iv, lib. iv, f. Reg. Indias, 34 (18 December 1519).

44 Manuel Giménez Fernández, "El Alzamiento de Fernando Cortés según las cuentas de la Casa de Contratación", in *RHA* (June 1951), 27.

45 AGI, Contratación 4675, lib. 1, f.113.

46 Las Casas, III, 321.

47 "wherever I am . . ." cit. Giménez Fernández [23:44], 28.

48 AGI, Indif. Gen., leg. 420, lib. 8, ff.173 and 175. The phrase is to be found after the list of the treasure in the Manuel de Tesoro in the AGI, Sevilla (*CDIHE*, I, 472).

49 AGI, Indif. Gen., leg. 420, lib. 10, 7 February, signed by Cobos, Zapata, García, and Gattinara.

50 His movements are chronicled in Núñez's later suit against Cortés, ed. in Cuevas [6:57], 257–69.

51 *"Avisos de lo que convendría hacerse para evitar algunos abusos en el gobierno"*, in *CDIHE*, LXXXVIII, 504–6.

52 See Genealogy III. For Carvajal, see Joseph Pérez, *La révolution des "comunidades" en Castille* (Bordeaux, 1970), 391–4. Núñez implied that he introduced Montejo, Portocarrero and Martín Cortés in Barcelona to Carvajal: "At the time I was there with

Doctor Carvajal" ("*a la saçon estaua yo allí con el doctor Caruajal*"), Cuevas [6:57], 261. Carvajal was an official for whom public expenditure seemed a crime: see his letter to Charles V, cit. Carande [9:15], II, 77, in which he implored that monarch "most humbly", with "as much insistence" as he could muster, not to spend money. All the same, he owned mines by royal grant of 1511 (Carande [9:15], II, 350).

53 Martyr, letter 667, in *DIHE*, 12.

54 Las Casas, III, 340.

55 Otte [11:5], 113.

56 Martínez, *Docs*, I, 102–4.

57 Martyr, letter 666 of 5 April 1520 to the marquises of Los Vélez and Mondéjar, in *DIHE*, 12. Charles said that if he did so act, he would be punished.

58 Pérez [23:52], 149.

59 Ramón Menéndez Pidal, *Idea Imperial de Carlos V* (Buenos Aires, 1941), 15.

60 Martyr, II, 38.

61 Brandi [6:50], 61. Plate 10 shows Charles in the Golden Fleece.

62 AGI, Contratación, leg. 4675, f.cxx v.

63 The tailors were Juan de Alcalá and Martín de Irure, the jeweller Beatriz Franca and the stocking-maker Juan de Murga. Giménez Fernández sorts all this out ([23:44], 37).

64 The letter of the Archbishop of Cosenza was to the apostolic protonotary, Pedro de Acosta. It was written in Spanish, 7 March 1520. It dealt with many things as well as Mexican matters, and was tr. into Latin by Fernando Flores of Fimbria (Femeren). It was ed. the next year as *Provinciae Sive regiones in India*, English tr. F. M. Carey, *HAHR*, (August 1929), 361–3.

65 Las Casas, III, 220.

66 Letter to Pope Leo X, 13 March 1520, Martyr, II, 45–6. This was ed. later in 1520. Martyr wrote a similar, if less enthusiastic, letter on 14 March to the marquises of Los Vélez and Mondéjar (in *DIHE*, 12, 18, also in *Cartas sobre el nuevo mundo*, Madrid, 1990, 106). Another communication from Valladolid was a letter by the Venetian ambassador, Francesco Corner, on 6 March. He described a "great moon of gold", as well as one of silver and, like everyone else, he was adversely impressed by the labrets of the natives. But he reflected the general mood when he reported that there was plenty of gold in their country ("*nel suo paese vi si trova oro et arzento assae*"): Sanuto [23:39], 375–6.

67 Martyr, II, 25.

68 Montaigne [4:16], 241.

69 The first publication of Díaz's *Itinerario* was in Italian, in Venice, on 3 March 1520. It appeared as an appendix to *Itinerario de Ludovico de Banthema bolognese ne lo Egypto, ne la Siria, ne la Arabia . . .* (Venice, 1520). Díaz's original text was lost. Modern versions of Díaz, e.g., J. Díaz, et al., *La Conquista de Tenochtitlan* (Madrid, 1988), are translated (back?) from the Italian.

70 This was ed. in Spain in 1842 and in English tr. by Ruth Frey Axe in *HAHR*, 9 (May, 1929), with notes by Henry Wagner. The only known 16th-century copy is that attached to the ms. copies of three of Cortés' letters in Vienna, in the "Codex Vindobensis".

71 Martyr, letter of 14 March 1520, to the marquises of Los Vélez and of Mondéjar, in *DIHE*, 12, 17.

72 Letter of the King, 9 March 1521, in AGI, Indif. Gen., leg. 420, lib 8, f.185, cit. Giménez Fernández [23:44], 39–40. This letter suggests that the King had not yet seen the treasures in Valladolid.

73 Herrera [8:6], dec. ii, lib. ix, ch. vii, says that the Emperor marvelled at the number of new provinces which, to God's glory, had been discovered, but the source for this story is unknown and it may be an invention. Ramos [9:79], 188–9, thinks that the

presentation never occurred. See also AGS, Estado, Castilla, leg. 7 (Cuentas de las Casa de Contración de los años 1515–21).

74 *"tratar muy bien para que estén muy contentos"* (AGI, Indif. Gen., leg. 420, lib. 7, ff.185–6).

75 AGI, Contratación, 4675, lib. 1, f.41v., cited Giménez Fernández [23:44], 41.

76 We know that they arrived in Cuba from a letter referring to Ambrosio Sánchez of 8 August 1520 from Hernando de Castro, a merchant in Santiago, to Alonso de Nebreda, Seville, ed. by Otte [6:56], 120, 129. Then they vanish into the anonymous unknown.

77 Alonso de Santa Cruz, *Crónica del emperador Carlos V* (Madrid, 1920), 225.

78 Manuel Foronda y Aguilera, "Estancias y viajes de Carlos V", *Boletín de la Sociedad Geográfica de Madrid* (Madrid, 1910).

79 Cortes de . . . León y Castilla, RAH, Madrid, 1882, vol. IV, 293–8. See Menéndez Pidal [23:59], 15, and Pérez [23:52], 156–8. Giménez Fernández [6:19], II, 343, says the speech was written by the Emperor's doctor, Luigi Marliani, now recently appointed Bishop of Tuy.

81 *CDIHE*, I, 486.

82 The statement of the *procuradores* is in AGI, Patronato, leg. 254, no.3, R.1. It is quoted in *Epistolario*, I, 44–50, as in Martínez, *Docs*, I, 109–13.

83 Martyr, II, 48.

84 Martyr, II, 48.

85 Giménez Fernández [6:19], II, 365.

86 Martyr, II, 49.

87 AGI, Indif. Gen., leg. 420, lib. 8, f.200. This was signed in Corunna by Los Cobos, Zapata and Carvajal. The confirmation of 14 May is referred to by Martín Cortés in APS, oficio iv, lib. iii, f.1943, of 24 June 1520.

88 "captain of the island of Culuacan" (AGI, Indif. Gen., leg. 420, lib. 8, f.200).

89 AGI, Contratación, leg. 4675, f.125 v.

90 *Cédula* of 19 April 1519, cit. Giménez Fernández [23:44], 50.

91 There was an enquiry (*residencia*) against the council in 1542. Beltrán confessed (AGI, Patronato, leg. 185, no.34) that he had received money from Pizarro and Almagro, as well as from Cortés ("I myself received the same, from . . . don Diego de Almagro and the marquis of the Valley . . ."). He was condemned to loss of his salary and his office, and fined. Ruined, he entered the Augustinian monastery of Nuestra Señora de Gracia, Medina del Campo, where he remained till he died.

92 *CDIHE*, I, 125. The letter is undated but must be later.

93 AGS, Estado, Castilla, leg. 2, f.8.

94 AGI, Indif. Gen., leg. 420, lib. 8, f.213 ff., and AGI, Contratación, leg. 4675, lib. 1, where payments are mentioned to Diego Colón to serve the loan.

95 AGS, Estado, Castilla, leg. 7, f.14. This meeting was the one where the council was referred to as *"lo de las Indias"*, as if the council was by then well established.

96 Las Casas says so (III, 340) and was present. He also says, mysteriously, that if Charles had read that letter, things would not have turned out so favourably for Cortés.

97 Ramos [9:79], 179, says that Fonseca ordered the Genoese financier Juan Bautista de Grimaldo to be paid this sum out of the Casa de la Contratación.

98 Frank Goodwyn, "Panfilo de Narváez", *HAHR*, 29, 150–6, for a bad short study.

99 Las Casas, II, 472.

100 Las Casas, II, 484.

101 G, 47.

102 AGI, Patronato, leg. 252, R.1, p.2: "Bartolomé de las Casas, a clergyman who . . . is a lightweight [*persona liviano*] of little authority and credit, who talks of what he knows nothing and has not seen".

103 Arranz [5:45], 532; Bermúdez Plata [9:46], 36; Giménez Fernández [6:19], I, 326–7.

104 They were told this by people (Alonso de Morales Martínez, Gonzalo de Montoro, etc.) who had been in Santiago de Cuba a month earlier (Polavieja, 22, 23).
105 Polavieja, 24.
106 AGI, Patronato, leg. 15, R.2, 10.
107 Giménez Fernández [6:19], II; I, 573–90.
108 Xoan de Valdecillo, in Trinidad, 21 November 1520, in CDI, XXXV, 61.
109 Joan Bernal, in CDI, XXXV, 65.
110 Ayllón's testimony at Trinidad, November 1520, is in CDI, XXXV, 79–90.
111 Evidence of Luis de Sotelo, in *información* of January 1520, in CDI, XXXV, 196.
112 Conway (Camb.), Add. 7253, vii, 10.
113 *CDIHE*, I, 476, 495.
114 Giménez Fernández [6:19], II, 309, fn. 859.
115 APS, Libro del año 1520, oficio iv, lib. iii, f.2984, of 15 September 1520, the sale being to Pedro de Soria, who probably soon went to the Indies, for he was found in Santiago de Cuba in 1521 (see letter from Francisco de Herrera to Alonso de Nebreda, 5 November 1522, AGI, Justicia, leg. 712, cit. Otte [6:56], 268, 270).
116 AGI, Indif. Gen., leg, 14, of 10 September 1520, signed in Burgos by the Cardinal, the Constable of Castile, Fonseca, Pedro de los Cobos and Licenciado Zapata.
117 For the shipload of guns, crossbows etc., and powder dispatched with Juan de Burgos, via the Canaries in the late summer or early autumn of 1521, see Ch. 31. This consignment is, however, touched on by a document in the APS (Libro del año 1520, oficio iv, lib. iii, f.2986, of 15 September 1520) before Manuel Segura, the same notary who had witnessed the contract for Cortés' original departure for America. There seems to be no mention of the departure of Burgos' ship in the records of the Casa de la Contratación, nor, that I have been able to see, in the APS. This suggests that the ship left furtively for the Canaries, then for Mexico. For Juan de Burgos, see Carmen Carlé, "Mercaderes en Castilla . . ." *Cuadernos de historia de España*, xxi–xxii (1954), 289. Presumably Córdoba and Fernández de Alfaro chose Burgos, a fellow *converso*, as their agent. A document in the APS for 1525 (oficio iv, lib. ii, f. 880) shows Fernández de Alfaro paid Juan de Córdoba over a million maravedís for goods sent, in 1520, in another *Santa María*, belonging to Francisco Caparrero (master, Juan de Salamanca), under the charge of Córdoba's son (or brother-in-law?) Juan de Herver, to "Yucatan". Giménez Fernández [6:19], 963, called Córdoba "the financier of Cortés".

Chapter 24

1 As usual, the sources disagree about the size of this force. Alonso de Villanueva, who came with Narváez, said that there were about 1,000 men with him (*CDI*, XXVII, 483). Diego de Avila, another companion of Narváez, in the *Inf. de 1521*, said that Narváez had 700 men with 80 horsemen plus artillery and crossbowmen (Polavieja, 203). The *Audiencia* of Santo Domingo, in a letter to the King of 30 August 1520, wrote of 600 men (*CDI*, XIII, 337). Cortés, in his own questionnaire of 1529, talked of 90 horsemen, 80 arquebusiers, 120 crossbowmen, and over 600 infantrymen. Díaz del Castillo spoke of 1,400 soldiers, in 19 ships, Cortés in his report to the King (C, 123), 800, and Aguilar said that Narváez had 100 horses (Aguilar, in J. Díaz, et al., 186).
2 Aguilar, in J. Díaz, et al., 186: "many knights, *hijosdalgos*, lords of Indians who, on the island of Cuba, had many excellent *repartimientos* . . ."
3 Xoan de Valdecillo, of Santiago, at an enquiry in November 1520, gave the names of Xoan Destacio, Porras, Medina, and Coblanca as having been embarked in irons (*CDI*, XXXV, 63–4). Xoan Destacio testified in the same enquiry and said that he tried

unsuccessfully to escape to the mountains to avoid being conscripted (*CDI*, XXXV, 71–2).

4 Murga [5:14], 105.

5 Las Casas, III, 157.

6 See his evidence in *Inf. de 1521*, Polavieja, 290; Giménez Fernández [6:19], I, 301, fn. 300. Paso y Troncoso published letters from the King to Diego Colón asking him neither to damage nor to hurt Juan Bono. They were signed by Conchillos (see *Epistolario*, I, 11–12). For Bono's cruel expedition to Trinidad of 1516, which snared 180 Indians, see Las Casas, III, 107, and Giménez Fernández [6:19], II, 327, fn. 964. There is a summary of his life in Otte [19:47], 133, fn. 650. For his command of the caravel *Barabola*, one of Ponce de León's ships in 1513, see Tío [5:14], 142. Bono would have seen Mexico or at least Yucatan, at that time, as Tío points out ([5:14],150).

7 John Schwaller, "Tres familias mexicanas", *HM* (1981), 183. See also AGI, Indif. Gen., leg. 133, no.3 for Diego de Cervantes.

8 AGI, Justicia, leg. 49, f.98 (Res vs Velázquez). Neglect to punish Diego the younger was an accusation against the Governor. But the Governor's friends said that the real murderer fled to the hills (Pero Pérez, on behalf of the Governor in the *residencia*, f.108).

9 AGI, Mexico, leg. 203, no. 19, Información de los servicios de Juan González Ponce de León.

10 Boyd-Bowman [5:17] identified 272 out of Narváez's 900.

11 Santa Clara must have been a substantial planter, for he received permission to take his silver out to Cuba in 1513 (see Muñoz, vol. 72, f.119). As for Alonso, see G.R.G. Conway, "Hernando Alonso, a Jewish conquistador with Cortés in Mexico", *Publications of the American Jewish Historical Society*, 31 (1928), 12. Bernal Díaz's statement that he married Beatriz was confirmed by Bartolomé González, a witness before the Inquisition in 1574.

12 Maluenda was a man of whom a partner said that he would prefer to have 90 dealings with him instead of 120 with someone else: a fraction which, if odd, is indicative ("*quiero más con él noventa que ciento y veinte con otro . . .*", Otte [6:56], 124). He was from a "notoriously *converso* family", originally from Catalyud, connected with the Santa Marías, and also a cousin of his correspondent, the Sevillano merchant Alonso de Nebreda (E. Domínguez Ortiz, *Los judeos conversos en España y América*, Madrid, 1992, 167–8).

13 Wright [5:50], 88.

14 AGI, Justicia, leg. 49, f.98 (Res vs Velázquez).

15 Parada had been a judge in Hispaniola. I take him to have been a member of the Sevillana family discussed by Cooper ([6:66], 1076).

16 Bono, in *Inf. de 1521* (Polavieja, 291); Ayllón in *Inf. de Trinidad*, November 1520, in *CDI*, XXXV, 90.

17 This was how question 18 in the *Inf. de 1521* was put, and how it was answered by Andrés de Duero (Polavieja, 310).

18 Both Hernando de Castro's letter (in Otte [6:56], 121) and Ayllón's account say that 6 ships were lost. In fact, they must only have been damaged if, as both agree, only 40 men died.

19 The date is evident from a letter from the merchant Hernando de Castro, in Otte [6:56], 121.

20 *CDI*, XXVII, 348.

21 AGI, Justicia, leg. 1004, no.5, R.21, cit. Otte [6:56], 111.

22 Otte [6:56], 113.

23 *Inf. de Trinidad* [24:16], 43–4.

24 Serrantes' (sometimes rendered Cervantes) evidence to Ayllón is in *CDI*, XXXV, 140–6.

25 Ayllón's account is to be seen in Polavieja, 39–49: Serrantes gave an account in reply to questions in 1521, for which see Polavieja, 80–3.

26 See Sepúlveda, 165.

27 *CDI*, XXVII, 345. One of Narváez's friends, Diego de Ávila, would the next year testify in Santiago de Cuba that his master had never wanted to fight Cortés but always wanted peace. That is hard to believe in view of the statement in the text (*Inf. de 1521* quoted in Polavieja, 203).

28 Evidence of Juan González Ponce de León, in AGI, leg. 224, p.1, f.722 r. He, a Salamantino, had written in 1517 to Francisco de los Cobos, describing the journey of Hernández de Córdoba.

29 Diego de Vargas, in *Inf de 1521*, in Polavieja, 274.

30 *CDI*, XXVII, 348. Luis Marín (*CDI*, XXVIII, 38) remembered Cortés saying that he had received it.

31 Diego Ginovés, a Genoese sailor on Ayllón's ship, in *Inf. de Santo Domingo*, 15 October 1520, in *CDI*, XXXV, 167. Other witnesses in this enquiry confirm this.

32 Juan de Salcedo, who was with Narváez, in AGI, leg. 224, p.1, f.660 v.; letter to the King, 10 November 1520, from the *Audiencia* in Santo Domingo, in Polavieja, 136–7.

33 *CDI*, XXVII, 356; CDI, XXVII, 43; and D del C, I, 169. These included Pedro de Villalobos, a Zamorano who afterwards distinguished himself with Cortés.

34 *Inf. de Trinidad* [24:16], 45–9.

35 These were Diego Ramírez; Hernando de Escalona, "*el mozo*"; and Alonso Hernández de Carretero.

36 Andrés de Monjaraz, in *CDI*, XXVI, 542; D del C, I, 395.

37 The defector's name is variously styled Pineda, Pinedo, and Pinelo.

38 That they were Mexicans was testified by Lorenzo Suárez in Res (Rayón), II, 284.

39 Gonzalo Mejía, in *CDI*, XXVI, 502.

40 C, 123.

41 Bernardino Vázquez de Tapia, in *CDI*, XXVI, 394; see Cortés' reply through García Llerena, in *CDI*, XXVII, 208.

42 In Tirado vs Cortés, Conway, (Camb.), Add. 7284, 88. Juan de Mansilla said that he saw Pinedo's body being brought back wrapped in a cloak. Vázquez de Tapia described him as coming back dead, with his crossbow.

43 C, 142; Andrés de Monjaraz, in Res (Rayón), II, 459.

44 Tapia, in J. Díaz, et al., 113.

45 Luis Marín in the *residencia* against Cortés says that he had heard Narváez so speak. See *CDI* XXVIII, 37. The same story is repeated in remarks of Cortés himself, in *CDI*, XXVII, 352.

46 Diego de Ávila, in *Inf. de 1521*, in Polavieja, 293.

47 Pedro Sánchez Farfán, in Conway (Camb.), Add. 7306, 41.

48 Diego de Ávila, a witness hostile to Cortés, in *Inf. de 1521* (Polavieja, 203–4).

49 Leonel de Cervantes, in Conway (Camb.), Add. 7306, 50.

50 Tapia, in J. Díaz, et al., 113.

51 Montezuma: "How is this? You have loyalties to different lords? You want to fight each other?" Cortés: "All of us have the same lord, but . . . the men who have come are bad people, Basques [*vizcaínos*]" (*CDI*, XXVII, 10). Other evidence of the conversation, by Gerónimo de Aguilar and Rodrigo de Castañeda, is in Res (Rayón), I, 221, and II, 184. "*Vizcaíno*" was a word used in the 16th century as a synonym for rustic, uncultured, people. Bernal Díaz, however, says (D del C, I 409) that Cortés insisted that the people concerned were Basques in the exact sense of the word. One or two were: for example, Bono de Queijo, Gaspar de Garnica, perhaps Antonio de Vergara. "*Vizcaíno*" was also used as a synonym for an old Christian, that is neither a Jew nor a Moor: a recollection

that, during the Muslim invasion, many true Christians had taken to the hills (see Albert Sicroff, *Les controverses des statuts de "pureté de sang"* (Paris, 1960), 277, fn. 55). Still, Basque ships were preferred by all. Had not Cisneros insisted on having them when he went to Oran in 1509?

52 *CDI*, XXVII, 350; C, 143.

53 Ixtlilxochitl, 259; *CDI*, XXVII, 350–1.

54 Tapia's own account, in J. Díaz, et al., 113. The distance is 270 miles. Tapia in answer to question 219 in Cortés' questionnaire (AGI, leg. 223, p.2, f.309 v.) said he had become very intimate with the *Caudillo* ("*amigo y muy familiar en sus secretos*").

55 C, 144.

56 D del C, I, 399. It is not clear whether this phrase could have been used then. Juan de Torquemada (*Historia de la Monarquía Indiana*, Mexico, 1972, II, 28) said that Grijalva had thought of the name, but there is no evidence for that. It occurred neither in Oviedo nor in Fr. Juan Díaz's *Itinerario*. It seems first to appear in a document in the *probanza* of 6 August 1520, 4 months later than this conversation between Sandoval and Ruiz de Guevara. Cortés wrote, in his second letter to the king, 30 October 1520, that he thought of the name – "New Spain of the Ocean Sea" – "because of the similarity between this land and Spain – its fertility, great size, and many other things". "New Spain", note, not "New Castile". Cortés' men included men from the whole peninsula, however few there were from Catalonia, Aragon or Murcia. Perhaps Cortés wanted to differentiate the territory from "Castilla del Oro", the colony directed by Pedrarias.

57 For medieval usages (e.g., *Anales Sagallenses*, AD 778: "*hoc anno domus rex Carolus perrexit in Spania*"), see J. A. Maravall, *El Concepto de España en la Edad Media* (Madrid, 1954), 135.

58 It is not clear whether Vergara had any serious "provisions". García de Llerena, a witness who always spoke in favour of Cortés, said, in the *residencia*, that he had letters asking people to go with him to Narváez (*CDI*, XXVII, 201).

59 Andrés de Monjaraz in evidence in *CDI*, XXVI, 541; D del C, I, 399–400.

60 Tapia gave evidence of these events (in answer to question 143 of the questionnaire of Cortés), having been informed by Sandoval.

61 Andrés de Monjaraz, *CDI*, XXVI, 542.

62 *CDI*, XXVII, 206.

63 D del C, I, 400–401. Several witnesses in the case of Tirado vs Cortés (1529) said that they saw Solís as the gaoler to Vergara and Guevara. There is a different story, reflected in the evidence in the *residencia*: Andrés de Monjaraz testified that he saw Pedro de Solís arriving at night, having left them with Pizarro, that relation of Cortés who had been in Pánuco. In another section of the *residencia* (*CDI*, XXVII, 108), it was said that Cortés, far from lodging the Spanish visitors well, shut them in a "*pierde amigos*" (dungeon). Diego de Vargas said in 1521 that Cortés had thought of having Amaya and Vergara hanged, but was dissuaded by Francisco de Saucedo, "*el pulido*" (Polavieja, 274).

64 "a man who, it is said, was called Santos, a servant of the said Cortés, had an Indian carry a load of gold weighing, it was said, 10,000 gold pesos" (Diego de Holguín, in *Inf. de 1521*, in Polavieja, 255).

65 Diego de Vargas, in *Inf. de 1521*, in Polavieja, 275.

66 Questionnaire in *Inf. de 1521*, in Polavieja, 175.

67 Diego de Vargas, in *Inf. de 1521*, in Polavieja, 206.

68 "many letters which they wrote from there". All seem to be lost (Otte, [6:56], 121).

69 C, 145–6.

70 C, 144, 146.

71 *CDI*, XXVII, 12.

Chapter 25

1 The change may have been principally to do with the fact that they were now living in the year 2-Flint.

2 Ixtlilxochitl, 259. For dates, see Wagner [8:23], 279–80. One of those present, Fr. Aguilar, said that they all went in cotton armour and only Cortés was on horseback. That is hard to believe.

3 Juan Álvarez (among those who were with Alvarado) and Diego de Ávila gave the figure of 120 at the *Información de 1520* (Polavieja, 209, 250). Cortés inaccurately said that he had left 500 men under Alvarado (C, 147), but by 1529 he seems to have accepted (*CDI*, XXVII, 363) a more modest number, 120; as did Martín Vázquez (*CDI*, XXVIII, 154). D del C (I, 123) said 80, and Tapia (in J. Díaz, et al., 114) only 50.

4 Francisco de Vargas, in Res (Rayón), II, 307.

5 Segura questionnaire, questions 1 and 2 (Segura, 1520), Polavieja, 133. Probably there was more.

6 Juan Álvarez, in Polavieja, 256.

7 Rodrigo de Castañeda, in Res (Rayón), I, 21.

8 See Trexler [15:28] for discussion.

9 C, 119.

10 No contemporary mentions the route, but it is discussed by Orozco [8:4], iv, 382.

11 C, 144.

12 Andrés de Monjaraz, in Res (Rayón), II, 48.

13 D del C, I, 406.

14 C, 148.

15 Juan Álvarez, in *Inf. de 1521*, quoted in Polavieja, 256.

16 Cortés does not speak of this party. See Tapia, in answer to question 132, Monjaraz, in *CDI*, XXVI, 543, and Cortés' question 132, in *CDI*, XXVII, 354; García de Llerena, in *CDI*, XXVII, 212; D del C, I, 41. Some witnesses say that these men were kept for some time in prison. See the evidence of Antonio Serrano de Cardona, Juan de Mansilla, and Andrés de Monjaraz, in Res (Rayón), I, 180–1, 247, and II, 49.

17 Juan de Tirado alleged the first, Andrés de Monjaraz the second; see Res (Rayón), II, 7, 49. The incident is mentioned as an accusation against Cortés in the *residencia* (*CDI*, XXVII, 11). Cortés denied it, weakly, through García de Llerena (*CDI*, XXVII, 20).

18 Aguilar, in J. Díaz, et al., 184.

19 Andrés de Monjaraz, in Res (Rayón), II, 49.

20 C, 150. Cortés places this event later for reasons which Anthony Pagden goes into in his ed. of Cortés' letters [10:73].

21 Evidence of Juan Mansilla, Res (Rayón), I, 248.

22 Andrés de Monjaraz said (Res (Rayón), II, 47) that these were Tapia, Diego García, Francisco Bonal, Francisco de Orozco, Sebastián de Porras and Juan de Limpias, but, if so, it is surprising that Tapia did not mention the adventure in his memoir. Nor is it clear how the others had escaped from Narváez.

23 Tapia in answer to question 124, AGI, Justicia, leg. 223, p.2, f.309 v. Cortés told Tapia that he would have been one of his 10.

24 Cortés' own letter (C, 124) says that it was the "treachery of one of Narváez's men" which revealed the plot, though, in his enquiry, Cortés says that Rodrigo Sánchez Farfán, who had also gone to Narváez's camp, advised him against the idea (*CDI*, XXVII, 352).

25 Alonso de Villanueva who came with Narváez later testified in support of Cortés to this effect (*CDI*, XXVII, 490).

26 F. de Zavallos, in La Serna vs Zavallos (1529), Conway (Camb.), Add. 7253, vii, 28.

27 C, 149; J. Tirado, in Res (Rayón), II, 9; *CDI*, XXVII, 352.

28 D del C, I, 414–15.

29 Juan Bono de Quejo, in Polavieja, 294: "this witness saw that, in the camp of the said pánfilo de narváez, many pieces of gold were floating about [*andaban muchas piezas de oro*] which were said to have come from the said fernando cortés . . ." Cortés said nothing about these last-minute negotiations.

30 D del C, I, 421.

31 *CDI*, XXVIII, 150; Díaz del Castillo, like López de Gómara, gave him the Christian name of Juan.

32 *CDI*, XXVII, 488.

33 Velázquez de León talked of this to Tapia, whose evidence is in reply to question 128 of the *residencia*, AGI, Justicia, leg. 223, p.2, f.309 v.

34 G, 224.

35 *CDI*, XXXV, 541.

36 Diego de Vargas, in *Inf. de 1521*, Polavieja, 276; Juan Álvarez said the same, in *Inf. de 1521*, Polavieja, 257. Diego de Ávila said that he saw the guns blocked up (*Inf. de 1521*, Polavieja, 203). For ballads about Ruy Velázquez, see *BAE*, XI, 439–57.

37 Diego de Vargas, in *Inf. de 1521*, in Polavieja, 276.

38 Diego Holguín, in *Inf. de 1521*, in Polavieja, 226. Holguín had been part-owner of a gold-mine with Antonio Velázquez de Cuéllar, of whose will he was a witness in 1517. He was a friend of the Velázquez family though, from his name, he must have come from Cáceres (APS, Libro del año 1517, oficio iv, libro ii, f.690; AGI, Justicia, leg. 49, f.100). For the Holguín family, see Miguel Muñoz de San Pedro, "Aventuras y desaventuras del tercer Diego García de Paredes", in *REE*, xiii (1957), 8ff.

39 Tapia, in J. Díaz, et al., 115; *CDI*, XXVII, 12.

40 This is D del C (I, 431–2), who was writing down what he remembered 40 years later. But the speech was described in much the same terms by Gerónimo de Aguilar in 1529, for which Res (Rayón), II, 186.

41 Tapia, in J. Díaz, et al., 115.

42 Olmedo was a man of Castile and probably knew many of Narváez's captains.

43 *CDI*, XXVII, 12.

44 "chief constable [*alguacil mayor*] of this New Spain"; D del C, I, 434. Tapia said that he saw the written order in Sandoval's hands (Tapia in answer to question 137).

45 Tapia, in J. Díaz, et al., 115. Díaz del Castillo says that Olid was in charge of the last of the companies.

46 Juan Álvarez, in *Inf. de 1521*, Polavieja, 259; Gerónimo de Aguilar said in 1529 that the sum was 500 pesos (Res (Rayón), II, 186).

47 Velázquez de León brought back this news (Tapia in answer to question 119).

48 *CDI*, XXVII, 216.

49 D del C, I, 430.

50 *CDI*, XXVII, 210.

51 This was Cortés' date but his timing is unreliable. See Eulalia Guzmán [13:41], 381, fn. 373 for a destructive criticism. But her suggestion that there was no fighting (a view derived from study of the Lienzo de Tlaxcala) is countered by a wealth of testimony from people opposed to Cortés, as well as from his friends, in innumerable lawsuits over many years.

52 Tapia, in J. Díaz, et al., 117; Juan de Mansilla said the attack was at 11 p.m., Juan Álvarez at 2 a.m. (Polavieja, 250, 276).

53 Juan de Tirado in Res (Rayón), II, 11. Carrasco (*Inf. de 1565*, 170) said later that Cortés threatened to have him hanged since "he did not want to tell the truth of what he was asked".

54 *"Andaban allí muchos cocuyos y pensaron las mechas de arcabuz"*, G, 225.
55 Juan Tirado, in Res (Rayón), II, 11; also Herrera [8:6], V, 393.
56 Gaspar de Garnica, in AGI, Justicia, leg. 224, p.1. f.46v.
57 Diego de Vargas in 1521, Polavieja, 275.
58 Wagner [8:23], 279, argues that Fr. Olmedo engaged in double-dealing and misled both Narváez and Cortés. But see Fr. Castro Seoane [11:44], for a more positive interpretation.
60 Juan de Salcedo, in AGI, Justicia leg. 224, p.1, f.722r.
61 Alonso de Villanueva, in *CDI*, XXVII, 493. See also *CDI*, XXVII, 216, where Cortés' defence was that the attack could not be considered a surprise because of the spy Hurtado's messages. There is an eyewitness account of what transpired, in Alonso Ortiz de Zúñiga, in *CDI*, XXVII, 126. Other accounts are those of A. de Mata, who especially remembered the pikes of Cortés' men (*CDI*, XXVI, 257).
62 C de S, 440.
63 La Serna in Zavallos vs La Serna, in Conway (Camb.), Add. 7253, 151.
64 D del C, I, 437; also interview of 1544, of Juan Cano, who was present, to Oviedo (IV, 264).
65 García del Pilar, in Res (Rayón), II, 204.
66 This was a question in the *Inf. de 1521*, Polavieja, 179. The tale of the feet is in the evidence of Francisco Zavallos, in Zavallos vs La Serna, 1529, in Conway (Camb.), Add. 7253, vii, 5.
67 Andrés de Monjaraz, in Res (Rayón), II, 51.
68 The capture of Narváez was described in 1521 by Diego de Ávila in the *información* of that year (Polavieja, 207).
69 Monjaraz, in *CDI*, XXVI, 545. This action was confirmed by witnesses in the case of Zavallos vs La Serna, e.g., Juan de Mansilla and Gonzalo Sánchez Colmenares, in Conway, (Camb.), Add. 7284, 87.
70 Bono de Quejo in *Inf. de 1521*, Polavieja, 279. See for other details of this battle (which Eulalia Guzmán [13:41], 383, said never happened) Monjaraz, Res (Rayón), II, 52; Alonso Ortiz de Zúñiga, Res (Rayón), II, 143; Gerónimo de Aguilar, Res (Rayón), II, 187; García del Pilar, Res (Rayón), II, 204; Juan de Marsilla, Res (Rayón), I, 364; Juan Tirado, Res (Rayón), II, 13; and Ruy González, Res (Rayón), I, 344.
71 E.g., Francisco Verdugo, in Conway (Camb.), Add. 7284, 73–86.
72 Aguilar, in J. Díaz, et al., 185; *CDI*, XXVI, 545.
73 Aguilar, in J. Díaz, et al., 185; Tapia, in J. Díaz, et al. 118.
74 Tapia, in J. Díaz, et al., 118.
75 For example, Diego de Vargas, in Polavieja, 276.
76 Tapia, in J. Díaz, et al., 119: *"¡Viva Cortés que lleva la victoria!"*
77 Bernardino de Santa Clara, evidence in Res (Rayón), II, 168.
78 Evidence of Diego de Vargas, in *Inf. de 1521*, in Polavieja, 277.
79 Juan Bono de Quejo, in *Inf. de 1521*, in Polavieja, 296.
80 D del C, I, 440.
81 D del C, I, 439.
82 D del C, II, 169.
83 Diego de Ávila, in *Inf. de 1521*, in Polavieja, 208; D del C, I, 443. The Caballero family played a large part in commercial life in Seville and Hispaniola. See their tomb in the *capilla del mariscal* in the cathedral in Seville. Discussed in Giménez Fernández [6:19], II, 1123, fn.3858, and Pike [23:42], 44.
84 Diego de Vargas, in *Inf. de 1521*, in Polavieja, 279.
85 Hernando de Caballos, in *CDI*, XXVII, 107; C, 152. Aguilar (J. Díaz, et al., 185) said that no one was killed, but he must have been misinformed. G, 225, gives 17 Narváecistas killed.

86 Diego de Vargas, in *Inf. de 1521*, in Polavieja, 290.

87 Orozco [8:4], iv, 403.

88 *"el más rico pueblo de Indias"* (G, 227).

89 D del C, 444–5.

90 D del C, I, 444.

91 *"Podíamos servir más a vuestra cesárea majestad . . ."* (C, 204).

92 Diego de Ávila, in *Inf. de 1521*, in Polavieja, 207; also Juan Bono de Quejo, in Polavieja, 297.

93 Diego de Ávila, in *Inf. de 1521*, in Polavieja, 181, 205.

94 Diego de Ávila, in *Inf. de 1521*, in Polavieja, 206; also Juan Bono de Quejo, in Polavieja, 296.

95 Diego Holguín, in *Inf. de 1521*, in Polavieja, 228; Diego de Vargas, in Polavieja, 278.

96 Questionnaire in Inf. de Diego de Ordaz (Santo Domingo, 1521), in *CDI*, XI, 85.

97 D del C, I, 463.

98 Aguilar, in J. Díaz, et al., 185.

99 D del C, I, 44.

Chapter 26

1 Chapter 24 of Book II of the Florentine Codex is devoted to this festival (FC, ii, 64–73).

2 Joan de Cáceres, Cortés' majordomo, said, in evidence at the *residencia* against Cortés in 1529 (AGI, Justicia, leg. 223, p.2, f.227 r.), that he had heard the Mexica say that they had arranged their fiesta in order to kill the Spanish garrison. This cannot be so since the festival concerned happened every year. Nor is it clear in what language Cáceres heard this.

3 *Codex Aubin* [4:8], 54. Other stories included (Sahagún, 973) that Alvarado had asked Montezuma to hold the fiesta because he wanted to see it, or that Cortés planned the massacre (Cod. Ram., 81).

4 G, 229.

5 Cline's Sahagún (xii, 19) suggests that Alvarado wanted to see the festival.

6 Ixtlilxochitl, 260, says that he saw a letter to this effect.

7 Guillen de Laso, in Res vs Alvarado, 118. Nuño Pinto in the same said that he saw the girl's body in the nearby canal. There is also testimony about the Indian girl by Andrés de Rodas, in the same, 113, by Francisco Martín Carpintero (who said that she was beaten up, *aporreado*, not hanged), in the same, 143, and by Alvarado himself, 64.

8 Alvarado's own account in the *residencia* against him (Res vs Alvarado, 65). Fr. Juan Díaz was with Alvarado at this time, and confirmed what Alvarado said (Res vs Alvarado, 126). So did Núño Pinto, Álvaro López and Andrés de Rodas (Res vs Alvarado, 134, 130 and 113).

9 "I was in the patio where Oechilobos was to be found, covered with a canopy of rich cloths and they were sacrificing many Indians in front of him, taking out their hearts . . ." (Res vs Alvarado, 66).

10 "This witness heard the Indians say that all the above was for killing Spaniards, and cooking them, and eating them with garlic" (Res vs Alvarado, 130).

11 FC, i, 156, and xii, 51. Durán, I, Chs. 2 and 4, gave a slightly different description of what usually occurred at this festival.

12 This image is that of Pasztory [4:35], 78

13 FC, xii, 54.

14 Res vs Alvarado, 66, 113.

15 These ropes were part of the usual procedure of raising Huitzilopochtli up to the temple. See FC, xi, 70, where the festival is described as it always was, that is not necessarily this special year: when they brought it [the figure of Huitzilopochtli] to the foot of the temple, they carried it up the [platform]. Cords fastened it to the four corners . . . they went stretching the cords that the platform might not twist them.

16 Res vs Alvarado, 130.

17 This account comes from Juan Álvarez, who was present and gave evidence as indicated in the *Inf. de 1521* (Polavieja, 260–2). The story of the torture, of which Alvarado did not speak, occurs too in Vázquez de Tapia's account in the Res vs Alvarado.

18 Vázquez de Tapia, in Res vs Alvarado, 37.

19 Vázquez de Tapia, in Res vs Alvarado, 37.

20 Alvarado in Res vs Alvarado, 66. Nuño Pinto and Andrés de Rodas both said that they heard this conversation also (Res vs Alvarado, 134, 144).

21 Res vs Alvarado, 144.

22 Res vs Alvarado, 67: confirmed by Andrés de Rodas, Fr. Juan Díaz, Nuño Pinto and Martín Porras in that enquiry, 113, 127, 134 and 143 respectively. Fr. Díaz said that the sticks were wands of office, *varas*, not clubs, *porras*.

23 "*¿Estamos acaso en guerra? ¡Que sea poca cosa!*" (Codex Aubin [4:8], 55).

24 *CDI*, XXVII, 221. This was part of Cortés' questionnaire and a great many witnesses in the hearings agreed with it.

25 Juan Álvarez, in *Inf. de 1521*, in Polavieja, 261.

26 Las Casas was of this view.

27 Sepúlveda, 168, in his "official" history for Charles V, however, says the opposite.

28 Sahagún (FC, ii, 65) gives a description of male perfection, as required for sacrifices, presumably for this one too: he had to be "like something rounded, like a tomato, or like a pebble, as if hewn from wood . . . no curly hair, rather, straight long hair . . . no scabs, pustules, boils . . . his nose should be well placed straight" – comparable to the famous eagle knight, suggests Mary Ellen Miller, *The Art of Mesoamerica* (New York, 1986), 214.

29 See the greenstone mask in the Dumbarton Oaks Pre-colombian collection, discussed in Pasztory [13:52], 154.

30 FC, xi, 68; Cod. Ram., 167–75.

31 FC, ii, 68.

32 This description of the dancers' costumes comes from the *Codex Mendoza* [1:29], 56. What a *tlatoani* might have worn can be glimpsed in the picture of Nezahualpilli, King of Texcoco, in f.108 of Jacqueline Durand-Forest's *Codex Ixtlilxochitl* (Graz, 1976).

33 See G, 148–9; *Codex Mendoza* [1:29], 56; *Circa 1492* [5:39], 557. About 20 drums survive: see Pasztory [4:35], 270, and Stevenson [2:41].

34 G, 208, says it was, but is it the same as the serpent dance? The Castilians called it an *areyto*, at that time a generic word for any Indian dance. See Ixtlilxochitl, 11.

35 Samuel Martí and Gertrude Kurath, in *Dances of Anahuac* (Chicago, 1964), 15, point out that Mexican composers, although they knew of more advanced instruments and scales from the south and the coast along the Gulf, continued to base their ceremonial music on a traditional 5-tone scale: flutes with 4 holes rather than the 5 possessed by older cultures.

36 Motolinía, *Memoriales* [4:2], 386.

37 G, 172. This must have been the judgement of Cortés. The Zambra used to be danced with Moorish flutes (*xabelas*) or instruments such as the lute. The gypsies danced this. Later on, it is possible that figure 17, "The Mexicans manner of dancing", in the Codex Tovar, may show the Fiesta Toxcatl, as proposed by Jacques Lafaye (*Quetzalcoatl et Guadelupe*, (Paris, 1974), 273). But the presence of eagle and jaguar warriors suggested to

Michael Coe (in *Circa 1492* [5:39], 571) that might not be so.

38 Durán, I, 193. Durán says that this dance was "similar to the sarabande", but that dance, long judged *risqué*, afterwards considered stately, seems to have come from Mexico. Possibly (see Stevenson [2:41], 227) it came in fact from the *cuecuexcuicatl*.

39 Ixtlilxochitl, 261.

40 G. 208.

41 Brundage [2:50], 18, discusses this.

42 Res vs Alvarado, 289. Alvarado said, as recorded in the proceedings of that same enquiry, that he was merely trying to prevent the Mexicans going up to the Great Temple with the effigy of Huitzilopochtli and that he was then attacked, but that cannot be true.

43 *Codex Aubin* [4:8], 55.

44 FC, xi (1st ed.), 53.

45 He said that he had "destroyed the idol" (Res vs Alvarado, 134).

46 FC, xii (1st ed.), 53; the Cod. Ram., 88–9, describes the scene almost in the same words. Durán (I, 21) talked to a conquistador (unnamed, but this time not Fr. Aguilar, then with Cortés), who said that he had killed "many Indians with his own hands".

47 This priest was described as one of Acatlyacapan (*Codex Aubin* [4:8], 56–7).

48 Juan Álvarez's evidence in *Inf. de 1521*, in Polavieja, 261–2.

49 Bandelier [7:35], 131; Hassig [1:23], 61.

50 FC, xii, 54.

51 FC, xii, 57.

52 Vázquez de Tapia, in Res vs Alvarado, 36–8.

53 Pero Hernández and Francisco Rodríguez, in an *información* of 1544 in Zacatula in relation to Martín López's suit against Cortés, quoted in Porrúa Muñoz, *R de I*, (January–June 1948); evidence of Diego Vadalés in *Inf. de 1565*, 44. After the burning, Francisco Rodríguez tried to rebuild one of these brigantines, and had nearly finished when other events obliged him to leave the city.

54 G, 210; D del C, II, 225.

55 The mythical appearance of the Virgin and of St James is in G, 230.

56 G, 231. It is not clear who was supposed to have said this.

57 Diego de Vargas, in *Inf. de 1521*, Polavieja, 280–1.

58 His appearance on the roof was attested by Alonso de Navarrete (AGI, Justicia, leg. 223, p.2, ff.424–511) and Juan Álvarez (evidence in *Inf. de 1521*, in Polavieja, 261), both of whom were there.

59 FC, xii, 57.

60 Aguilar, in J. Díaz, et al., 186.

61 *CDI*, XXVI, 396.

62 Brundage [2:50], 196–7, summarises.

63 Evidence in *Inf. de 1521*, Polavieja, 262.

64 Anderson [16:63], 20–1.

Chapter 27

1 Narváez would spend 2 years and more in confinement at the sea before returning to Spain in 1523 and setting out later for Florida.

2 C de S, 453, on the basis of information from Alonso de Ojeda

3 Pedro de Meneses (*Inf. de 1565*, 62) confirmed Ojeda's role. Cortés said that he left Tlaxcala with 500 foot and 70 horse (C, 154); Díaz del Castillo says 1,300 men, 96 horses and 80 crossbowmen.

4 Orozco [8:4], iv, 409.

5 Ixtlilxochitl, 261.
6 Aguilar, in J. Díaz, et al., 186.
7 Aguilar, in J. Díaz, et al., 186.
8 FC, xii (1st ed.), 59.
9 C de S, 123.
10 FC, xii, 59.
11 Orozco [8:4], iv, 410.
12 Juan Cano, who was present, to Oviedo (Oviedo, IV, 262).
13 D del C, I, 449.
14 G, 232; Camargo (216) says that Cortés told the Mexica – how, is unclear – that he had come to help them; that his followers in Tenochtitlan had been people of little experience, and had made a mistake; and that he would punish them.
15 C de S, 464.
16 See the statement by García Llerena in CDI, XXVII, 221.
17 Juan Álvarez, Inf. de 1521, in Polavieja, 262.
18 Juan Bono de Quejo, Inf. de 1521, in Polavieja, 299.
19 Cristóbal de Guzmán, who had seen the medallion (Conway, (Camb.), Add. 7306, 45); "the said Cortés turned his head so as not to see him" (Diego de Holguín, in Inf. de 1521, Polavieja, 233).
20 AGI, Justicia, leg. 224, p.1. f.722r.
21 D del C, I, 452.
22 Diego de Vargas, in Inf. de 1521, in Polavieja, 81.
23 Diego de Holguín, in Inf. de 1521, in Polavieja, 231; G, 210–11; Res vs Alvarado, 67.
24 D del C, I, 452.
25 C de S, 167.
26 C, 156; Aguilar, in J. Díaz, et al., 187.
27 Questionnaire in Información de Diego de Ordaz (Santo Domingo, 1521), CDI, XL, 86, and evidence of Gonzalo Giménez who was present (CDI, XL, 116). Also questionnaire of Juan González Ponce de León, in AGI, Mexico, 203, no. 19, 13.
28 D del C, I, 453; G, 233; C, 156.
29 FC, xii, 59.
30 C, 56. Díaz del Castillo said that there were 46 wounded, of whom 12 died of wounds.
31 Aguilar, in J. Díaz, et al., 188; this was presumably "Scotch cloth", a type of lawn but cheaper, said to have been made from the pith of nettles.
32 Alonso de la Serna, in AGI, Justicia, leg. 223, p.1, f.584v.
33 Aguilar, in J. Díaz, et al., 188.
34 C, 157.
35 D del C, I, 455.
36 Aguilar, in J. Díaz, et al., 190.
37 FC, iv, 157, 179; A. López Austin, "El Hacha Nocturna", ECN iv (1963).
38 D del C, I, 459.
39 D del C, I, 455; G, 233–4.
40 I prefer the dating of Cortés. Díaz del Castillo says 4; López de Gómara, 3.
41 C de S, 232–3.
42 C de S, 232–3, said that Montezuma offered the idea; so did C, 151. Everyone else (Aguilar, Diego de Holguín, Díaz del Castillo) says that Cortés asked him to go up to the roof. It seems more likely.
43 D del C, I, 459; Aguilar, in J. Díaz, et al., 189.
44 Juan Cano, in Oviedo, IV, 262. Cortés entrusted Montezuma, says Vázquez de Tapia, in J. Díaz, et al., 145, to "certain caballeros to look after and shield him".
45 C, 157; López de Gómara says the same and adds that the Mexicans did not see

Montezuma because the Spanish had covered him with a shield to protect him. Cortés did not know whether Montezuma had begun his speech or not. Vázquez de Tapia (in J. Díaz, et al., 145) and Aguilar (in J. Díaz, et al., 189) both say that Montezuma's speech could not be heard because of the large number of people. Aguilar adds that Montezuma's uncle, who had also been imprisoned, made the speech. In 1527, in his *"donación de tierras"* to Montezuma's daughters, Cortés said that Montezuma went to a window, where he was hit on the head by a stone. See appendix to Josefina Muriel [20:1], 31–2, 229–45.

46 Cervantes de Salazar's rendering of Montezuma's speech is, as usual, imaginative but probably imaginary. But what Montezuma may have said can be found in the Cod. Ram., 144; in D del C, I, 459; in Vázquez de Tapia, in J. Díaz, et al., 145.

47 Cod. Ram., 145; Ixtlilxochitl, *Sumaria relación de Obras Históricas de todas las cosas que han pasado en la Nueva España*, ed. Eduardo O'Gorman (Mexico, 1975), I, 390, says that Montezuma was hit; see also Ixtlilxochitl's *Decimatercia Relación* [4:5], 12.

48 For example, in the feast of Uei Tocoztli, the great vigil, painted girls in a procession would insult the boys whom they saw as they passed and, for any act of reticence on their part, would say, "Or perhaps you are only a woman as I am?" (FC, ii, 61).

49 Aguilar, in J. Díaz, et al., 189; *Historia de los mexicanos por sus pinturas* [1:47] 255; D del C, I, 459–60.

50 This speech derives from G, 235–6, which I have, however, rendered without including the obviously false references to Montezuma's death, which did not occur for some days. Eulalia Guzmán [13:41], 445, says the idea that Cortés made a speech of this kind is "pure fantasy".

51 C, 158.

52 Alcocer [19:70], 66–7, argued that this must have been the temple of Yopico dedicated to Xipe Totec rather than the Great Temple of Huitzilopochtli since it was close to the Palace of Axayacatl and, therefore, more damage could be caused from it. There is also the implication in Cline's Sahagún, 82, that it was not the Great Temple, for he reports that "the Mexicans . . . agreed . . . to fortify themselves in a [*sic*] very large and high temple". Cortés specifically says it was "the Great Temple", an identification made also by G, 236, and D del C, I, 456.

53 See grant of arms of 1527 to Pedro de Villalobos, where (*Nobilario* [7:12]) the citation is "you with forty men took the top of the high tower".

54 FC, xii, 62.

55 López de Gómara suggests that there were attempts on the temple over several days, but his timing must be wrong.

56 C, 158–9.

57 D del C, I, 457.

58 FC, xii, 61.

59 Aguilar, in J. Díaz, et al., 190; Información of González Ponce de León [27:27]. Cortés himself confirmed the comment in answer to question 15.

60 C, 160; G, 239; C de S, 472.

61 See for example evidence of Joan de Cáceres and Alonso de la Serna: "they threw a stone at his head from which he died" (AGI, Justicia, leg. 223, p.2, f.227).

62 Vázquez de Tapia, in J. Díaz, et al., 145. Cortés accepted this charge and looked after his daughters not only by seducing two more of them, and having a child by one, but also eventually arranging for all of them to have land and Castilian husbands.

63 This was stated by Cortés when in 1526 he handed over land to Montezuma's daughters, fulfilling his word to look after them, in Muriel, [20:1]. It is as difficult to distinguish between Montezuma's politeness and his opinions as it is between Cortés' protestations and his actions.

64 See Muriel [20:1], 242.

65 Camargo (217), and Cod. Ram., 146–7, say that Montezuma begged to be baptised before he died (though the latter also says that Montezuma was killed by the Spanish). This story of the baptism has no basis to it other than rumour ("many conquistadors whom I knew affirmed . . ." says Camargo, 234).

66 Nearly all the indigenous, or indigenous-based, sources – Durán, the Codex Ramírez, FC, xii, 65, Chimalpahín – say that Montezuma was stabbed to death or garrotted by the Castilians. Durán (II, 556) said that, after the Castilians had fled, the Mexican leaders went to Montezuma's chamber to deal with him "more cruelly than they had with the Castilians . . . they found him with a chain about his feet and five dagger wounds in his chest. Near him lay the bodies of noblemen who had been imprisoned with him." Orozco y Berra thought that Montezuma might have been killed by the Castilians, since he could be of no more use to them and that Cortés hoped to escape from the city while his funeral was being held ([8:4], 437). The *Anales Tepeanacas* say that Montezuma was only taken to the roof of the palace after being killed. Hence his silence!

67 Ixtlilxochitl, 12, on the evidence of "Don Alonso Axayácatl", son of Cuitláhuac, said that Cacama died now or a few days earlier or later, though the Castilians say he was killed in the retreat from Tenochtitlan.

68 Aguilar, in J. Díaz, et al., 191.

69 D del C, I, 460.

70 The funerals of Tizoc and Axayacatl are described in Tezozomoc [1:19] 454–7 and 571. See FC, iii, 43, fn.11, and Torquemada [1:24], 521; also Brundage [2:50], 200–2.

71 FC, xii (1st ed.), 64. Durán, II, 556, says that Montezuma's body was buried without ceremony, and that some of his children were killed too in order to extinguish the memory of his disastrous reign. The *Codice Aubin* [26:3], 58, says that the body of Montezuma was carried off by a legendary Apanecatl, who found it hard to find the right place to bury him. Juan Comas, in an article in *ECN*, vii (1967), shows that the so-called "cranium of Montezuma" in the Musée de l'Homme, Paris, is not.

72 FC, xii, 65.

Chapter 28

1 Juan de Najera, in *Inf. de 1565*, 83; G, 220.

2 Aguilar, in J. Díaz, et al., 190.

3 Gonzalo de Alvarado, in *Información de Segura*, 1520, in Conway (Camb.), Add. 7306, 22.

4 Question 6 of questionnaire of August 1520, Segura, in Conway (Camb.), Add. 7306, 6.

5 Evidence of Andrés de Tapia in AGI, Justicia, leg. 223, p.2, f.309.

6 Letter from the army of Cortés, August 1520, in García Icazbalceta, II, 429; the *probanza* of Tepeaca, 1512, also represents Cortés as acceding to his followers' requests (Polavieja, 134). So does Aguilar, in J. Díaz, et al., 190.

7 Alonso de Navarrete, in AGI, Justicia, leg. 223, p.32, f.424v.

8 Bernal Díaz, in a *probanza* of 1563 about Alvarado, on demand of Leonor de Alvarado, published as appendix to Ramírez Cabañas' ed. of D del C [18:23], 586.

9 C, 162.

10 This was the subject of a full-scale enquiry later at Tepeaca. See Polavieja, 132–5.

11 Francisco de Flores heard this: AGI, Justicia, leg. 223, p.1, f.511v.

12 C, 162; Cortés caused Llerena to say the same on his behalf in 1529: *CDI*, XXVII,

234–5; Oviedo, IV, 230; *Inf. de 1521*, Polavieja, 134; Cristóbal del Castillo [22:41], 103. In 1529, Gonzalo Mexía, who was treasurer in 1520, said that he heard Cortés saying, "call the comrades [*llamen a los compañeros*] and let each one of them take what he can" (*CDI*, XXVI, 470).

13 Camargo, 222.

14 Rodrigo de Castañeda, in Res (Rayón), I, 241; and Andrés de Monjaraz in Res (Rayón), II, 78, Alonso Pérez in Res (Rayón), II, 105, and Marcos Ruiz, in Res (Rayón), II, 122.

15 Cristóbal del Castillo [22:41], 103.

16 *CDI*, XXVII, 510.

17 *CDI*, XXVIII, 173.

18 Andrés de Tapia, in AGI, Justicia, leg. 223, p.2. f.309.

19 *Probanza* (August–September 1529), in G. L. R. Conway, *La noche triste* (Mexico, 1943), 10.

20 *CDI*, XXVII, 21.

21 *CDI*, XXVI, 546.

22 Fr. Díaz, in Conway [28:19].

23 Gonzalo Mexía, in Res (Rayón), I, 101; Vázquez de Tapia, in Res (Rayón), I, 67.

24 Camargo, 222. Question 53 in *Inf. de 1521*, related to the gold, in Polavieja, 132; D del C, II, 300. The gold on the mare was variously reported to have been worth 700,000, 400,000 and 300,000 pesos.

25 This was question 14 in the *Pesquisa secreta* against Cortés, (1529), in *CDI*, XXVI, 380.

26 Diego de Avila, in *Inf. de 1521*, Polavieja, 210.

27 In early 1981, a curved bar of these dimensions was uncovered near the line of the Tacuba causeway. This may have been one lost on this occasion.

28 Question 6 in questionnaire of 1520 in Conway, (Camb.), Add. 7306, 77. That was confirmed by Fr. Juan Díaz in Conway (Camb.), Add. 7306, 437. Similar versions were given by Rodrigo Álvarez Chico, Cristóbal de Olid, Bernardino Vázquez de Tapia, Gonzalo de Alvarado, Cristóbal de Corral, Fr. Bartolomé de Olmedo and Juan Rodríguez de Villafuerte (Conway (Camb.), Add. 7306).

29 Question 21 in questionnaire of September 1520 and reply of Alonso de Benavides, in Conway [28:19], 16.

30 *CDI*, XXVI, 432.

31 D del C (I, 464) says the figure lost was 700,000 pesos.

32 "when they left in flight, the said don fernando made love to a certain doña francisca, daughter of the lord of Texcoco" ("*se avía echado con una doña francisca*") (Res (Rayón), I, 264).

33 Sahagún reported that "it was raining, lightly raining as if it had been dew, they were light drops of rain, as when one irrigates, it was a very modest rain". Cristóbal Martín de Gamboa said it was "a dark and rainy night" (Res vs Alvarado, 139). Aguilar said that the rain was heavy and there was hail (J. Díaz, et al., 193).

34 See *Información de méritos y servicios* of this captain in AGI, Patronato, leg.54, no.3, R.1.

35 Francisco de Flores, in AGI, Justicia, leg.223, p.2, f.511v.

36 Gómara says that the alarm was given at the second waterway. Alfonso Caso, "Los Barrios Antiguos de México y Tlatelolco", *MAMH*, XV, no.1 (January–March, 1956), suggests that this was anywhere between the streets Zarco and Lázaro Cárdenas.

37 Cristóbal del Castillo [22:41], 103. The tale of the woman gathering water is to be found in FC, xii, 24, and Camargo, 220. The only Castilian source which mentions a warning cry was Aguilar, who speaks of a man calling out.

38 Ixtlilxochitl, *Decimatercia Relación* [4:5].

39 FC, xii, 35; Inga Clendinnen, "Fierce and unnatural cruelty", in *Representations*, 33 (Winter 1991).

40 Tapia, in evidence in AGI, Justicia. leg.223, p.2, f.309v.

41 Pedro Sánchez Farfán, in Conway (Camb.), Add. 7306, 38.

42 Tapia, in AGI, Justicia, leg.223 p.2, f.309.

43 FC, xii, 68.

44 Joan de Cáceres said that all who were loaded with gold died because they were easily cut off (*atajaron*) by the Indians (AGI, Justicia, leg.223. f.227r).

45 See Cortés own description in *CDI*, XXVII, 223, and the evidence of numerous witnesses at his enquiry, e.g., Martín Vázquez (*CDI*, XXVIII, 159) and Joan de Cáceres, in AGI, Justicia, leg. 223, p. 2, f. 250 v.

46 For the Mexicans as swimmers, see G, 246. Had they not gone swimming, in Lake Pátzcuaro, on their legendary "peregrination", only to have their clothes stolen by their god Huitzilopochtli? Cortés is known to have swum successfully for his life in Cuba, and so did Martín Vázquez, when with Hernández de Córdoba. But it must be doubtful whether, apart from the sailors, many conquistadors could swim.

47 This derives from a handwritten addition to Bustamente's copy of Camargo, 219.

48 Fr. Díaz, in Res vs Alvarado, 127.

49 See claim of 1 September 1530, in *Epistolario*, II, 6–7.

50 Res vs Alvarado, 68.

51 The leap of Alvarado, famous in Mexican folklore (described in, e.g., G, 242), was part of an accusation against Alvarado for deserting his men. Alonso de la Serna was with Alvarado but did not mention a leap in his evidence on the events.

52 Alvarado said this himself (Res vs Alvarado, 69) and it was confirmed in the same by Martín de Gamboa (Res vs Alvarado, 139); others saw it too.

53 Alonso de la Serna, in AGI, Justicia, leg.223, p.2, f.584. Pedro González de Nájera also heard the exchange (Res vs Alvarado, 28).

54 AGI, Justicia, leg.224, p.1, f.464.

55 Tezozomoc [1:18], 150.

56 Ixtlilxochitl, *Decimatercia Relación* [4:5], 12.

57 Tezozomoc [1:18], 124, implies that she was not killed on this occasion, for Rodríguez de Villafuerte is said to have had 2 children by her. Ixtlilxochitl, 263, says that she had been another of Cortés' mistresses.

58 Res vs Alvarado, 317.

59 Aguilar (in J. Díaz, et al., 193) said that there were 40 of them, as did certain Texcocans who talked to Cortés later in the year (D del C, I, 517); C de S, 100.

60 Juan Cano, who was present, should have been a good source, since he eventually married Montezuma's daughter, "Doña Isabel". He talked of this in 1544 to Oviedo (IV, 262).

61 Orozco [8:4], iv, 446.

62 *Rel. de Michoacan*, 123.

63 Cano's figure was given to Oviedo in 1544 (Oviedo, IV, 262). But Cortés, in his letter to the King of 1520, spoke of a mere 150; in the *probanza* of 1520, over 200: Vázquez de Tapia, in Res vs Alvarado, 38, had 680, but in the *residencia* against Cortés spoke of over 200 (*CDI*, XXVI, 397); Martín López's figure, of 600, was given in the *Inf. de 1565*. Bono de Quejo, Diego de Ávila and Diego Holguín in the *Inf. de 1521*, spoke respectively of "over 300", 600, and 400 (Polavieja, 299, 209, 334); question 51 of that *información* spoke of 500–600 (Polavieja, 182); the letter "of the army" of October 1520 to the King spoke of over 500 killed (García Icazbalceta, I, 427–36). The charges against Cortés in 1529 stated that 800 Spanish were killed and 200,000 Mexicans (*CDI*, XXVII, 18); Juan

Tirado, in Cortés *residencia*, (*CDI*, XXVI, 518), talked of 1,000 killed. D del C (I, 475) wrote of 860 (Ch. xxxviii). The Emperor, in his grant of arms to Cortés in 1525, spoke of 300 Spanish being killed, with 50 horse (that was also the estimate of Cortés' majordomo Cáceres); but, in a similar grant, to the son of Juan González de León, the Emperor spoke of 600 dead Christians.

64 AGI, Mexico, leg. 203, no. 5.

65 Camargo talked of 4,000 friends (Camargo, 220). Martín López said the same in *Inf. de 1565*, 116. Juan Cano spoke of 8,000, according to Oviedo.

66 Cit. by the royal notary at the time of the grant of arms to López, in Porrua Muñoz, "Martín López", *R de I* (1948), 328. Others, including Antonio Bravo, Andrés de Tapia, Andrés de Trujillo, Lázaro Guerrero, and Vázquez de Tapia heard the exchange. The last-named said: "this witness is of the opinion that Our Lord inspired him [Cortés] to believe that, by means of this Martín López, the city which was now lost might be regained." (Conway (L of C), Martín López papers, I, 45, 130).

67 Martyr, II, 126.

68 The tapestry is in the Palacio de San Ildefonso, La Granja. See Antonio Domínguez Ortiz, et al., *Resplendence of the Spanish Monarchy* (New York, 1991).

Chapter 29

1 FC, xii, 80.

2 For rewards, for captures, see for e.g. FC, ii, 44; and viii, 75–7.

3 FC, ii, 93–5.

4 FC, xii, 81, 75.

5 *¡Corazón mío, no temas:*
en medio a la llanura quiere mi corazón
la muerte de obsidiana . . . !
Garibay [1:13], I, 217.

6 FC, viii, 75; see Hassig [1:23], 40.

7 Tezozomoc [1:19], 333.

8 FC, viii, 62.

9 Zorita [1:8], 95.

10 FC, viii, 65; see Richard Townsend's brilliant "Coronation at Tenochtitlan", in Boone [2:58], 390–4.

11 FC, vi, 48.

12 *Códice Matritense de la Real Academia*, VIII, facsimile ed. f. 118r. and 118v., cited León-Portilla [1:6].

13 *Coloquios y doctrina cristiana con que los doce frailes de S. Francisco . . . convertieran a los Indios*, fascsimile ed. in Nahuatl and in Spanish, by Miguel León-Portilla (Mexico, 1986), 96–7.

14 FC, iv, 123–4.

15 FC, iv, 121.

16 FC, iv, 117–19.

17 This ceiba tree is still visible, if neglected and dusty.

18 Vázquez de Tapia, in *Relación de servicios*, (1547), in J. Díaz, et al.

19 Ixtlilxochitl, 264.

20 Comment of Joan de Cáceres (AGI, Justicia, leg. 23, p.2, f.227r.).

21 Durán, II, 554

22 FC, xii, 71; C. 164; Gerhard [8:60], 247; Alfredo Chavero, *Lienzo de Tlaxcala* (Mexico, 1892), plate 21. For Rodríguez de Villafuerte see evidence of Juan González in

información of that conquistador (Zacatula, September 1525), AGI, Mexico, leg. 203, no. 2.

23 C, 164; FC, xii (1st ed.), 73. The *Lienzo de Tlaxcala* [29:22], plate 22, depicts Marina here with a spear and a shield.

24 *Relaciones Geográficas del siglo XVI: Mexico*, ed. René Acuña (Mexico, 1986), 194–202; G, 223; FC, xii, 73.

25 C, 165; FC, xii, 74; *Lienzo de Tlaxcala* [29:22], plate 23.

26 These figures in Ruy González, letter to the King, dated 24 April 1553, *Epistolario*, VII, 34; Ortiz de Zúñiga (for the grass), in *Inf. de 1565*, 90.

27 Torquemada [1:24], I, 165.

28 I say "it appears", for Chavero, the editor of the *Lienzo de Tlaxcala*, thought that the Mexicans were an ill-organised mob, while Camargo (222) said that many of the "enemy" at Otumba were Texcocans who had gone there for a fiesta.

29 *"Pie a pie"*, according to Joan de Cáceres, in AGI, Justicia, leg. 223, p.2, f.227r.

30 Alonso de Navarrete, AGI, Justicia, leg. 223. p.2 f.424 v.

31 C, 166.

32 *"muy desmayada"* (AGI, Justicia, leg. 224, p.1, f.46 v.). Garnica was one of the many friends of Velázquez who became supporters of Cortés.

33 The most complete list of war-dresses is in the *Códice Matritense de la Academia de la Historia*, ed. Thelma Sullivan, in *ECN*, X (1972).

34 Francisco de Flores, AGI, Justicia, leg. 223, p.2, f.511. Aguilar, in J. Díaz, et al., 196, as one of the foot soldiers, observed the scene, as did Joan de Cáceres and Alonso de Navarrete. Juan Gil [15:84] suggests Cortés' action was a deliberate emulation of Alexander the Great against Darius at Issus.

35 Gonzalo Rodríguez de Ocaña, AGI, Justicia, leg. 224, p.1, f.294; D del C, II, 254; and Camargo, 221, also gives a vivid account. Salamanca used those plumes as an inspiration for his coat of arms when he was granted them in 1535 (*Nobilario* [7:12], 71). Ruy González, a native of Villanueva de Fresno, Badajoz, but all the same a supporter of Narváez, told the Emperor Charles V (*Epistolario*, VII, 34) that "we escaped only because they did not wish to fight, but to have their liberty . . . and the Mexicans did not follow us because they were afraid of those around and wished to guard their city, as tyrants are accustomed to do who fear everything and are certain of nothing. That is the truth, though some, to make themselves out valiant, have told a different story to Your Majesty." This was a hit at Cortés. All the same, Martín Vázquez, Navarrete, Rodríguez de Ocaña, Joan de Cáceres, García Llerena and many others in the *residencia* against Cortés confirmed the *Caudillo's* role (*CDI*, XXVII, 222, and *CDI*, XXVIII, 160). Plate 26 of the *Lienzo de Tlaxcala* [29:22] shows Cortés killing a naked Indian.

36 Clendinnen [3:11], 85.

37 Hassig [1:23], 58, 283.

38 Camargo, 225.

39 Camargo, 221.

40 D del C, I, 472.

41 C, 168; Juan Cano said that he often saw Cortés after this battle with all his fingers (Oviedo, IV, 263).

42 *CDI*, XXVII, 366.

43 This information was given by an indigenous informant to Torquemada [1:24], II, 229.

44 FC, xii, 81.

45 *Lienzo de Tlaxcala* [29:22], plate 27.

46 Martín López, in *Inf. de 1565*, 116.

47 *Lienzo de Tlaxcala*, [29:22], Plate 28, shows the kindly reception the Spanish had there. See too Ixtlilxochitl, 266.

48 Diego Holguín, in *Inf. de 1521*, in Polavieja, 235; Juan Álvarez in the same, 263.

49 *CDI*, XXVII, 22. This last charge was reflected by Diego de Ávila in 1521 (*Inf. de 1521*, in Polavieja, 210). Probably most of the gold was dispatched to Spain in the next ship which Cortés sent with Alonso de Mendoza.

50 Diego Holguín, in *Inf. de 1521*, 235. See discussion in *residencia* against Cortés, in respect of questions 189, 190, and 191, in the questionnaire in *CDI*, XXVII, 376–8, and the evidence of Gonzalo Mexía, Serrano de Cardona, Rodrigo de Castañeda, and Alonso Ortiz de Zúñiga (Res (Rayón), I, 101, 211, and 241: also, II, 163).

51 Durán, II, 324.

52 Ixtlilxochitl, 67; Orozco [8:4] iv, 470–1.

53 Aguilar, in J. Díaz, et al., 195.

54 Cline's Sahagún, 101.

55 Ixtlilxochitl, 269; Camargo, 267–8.

56 Aguilar, in J. Díaz, et al., 195; Ixtlilxochitl, 123. There is discussion of this in Orozco [8:4], iv, 470–2, but see also Herrera [8:6], V, 451–4; and Torquemada [1:24], II, 232.

57 These terms appear in the *Inf. de 1565*. Several (Spanish) witnesses then swore that Cortés had promised this, including Francisco de Montano, Pedro de Meneses, Alonso Ortega de Zúñiga, and Martín López ("he of the brigantines"), who said that he remembered the Tlaxcalans being told that they would be forever free of tribute if they helped the Castilians beat the Mexicans (*Inf. de 1565*, 120). The agreement is summarised in Camargo, 230. By 1565, Tlaxcala was paying a tribute of 8,000 *fanegas* of maize, say 12,000 bushels. The *Audiencia* of Mexico, in a letter of 15 December 1575 to the King, said that that was very little, considering how fertile Tlaxcala was (*Epistolario*, XV, 36–58). The original agreement was confirmed in 1585, but not maintained.

58 None of the Castilian accounts mention this agreement, but the *Inf. de 1565* is clear about it; the document is not a forgery, and several unbiased witnesses, including Martín López, swore to its validity.

59 *CDI*, XXVII, 503.

60 Conway, (Camb.), Add. 7306, 21. The same was said by Olid, Conway (Camb.), Add. 7306, 422.

61 Their arrival is illustrated in plate 29 of the *Lienzo de Tlaxcala* [29:22].

62 C, 144.

63 The *Rel. de Michoacan* (from which this account derives) says this was Montezuma. But, as Nicolás León pointed out (*Rel. de Michoacan*, 236fn.), this could not have been so, since the messengers were sent after the fighting in Tenochtitlan.

64 *Rel. de Michoacan*, 238.

65 The history and development of the Tarascans remains a largely neglected subject.

66 "*muy arteros a la verdad*"; "economical with the truth"?

67 *Rel. de Michoacan*, 239.

68 This could have been outside Tlaxcala or near Tepeaca, where the Castilians went next.

69 *Rel. de Michoacan*, 239–40.

70 G, 259.

71 D del C, I, 478.

72 The gold which Velázquez de León had received from various chiefs is mentioned in question 14 of the questionnaire of 22 August 1520 at Segura, quoted in Polavieja, 135.

73 *CDI*, XXVIII, 57.

74 Alonso de Sandoval, in *Inf. de 1565*, 163; C de S, 512; Torquemada [1:24], II, 232.

75 This summary derives from several witnesses in the *residencia*, e.g., Rodríguez de Ocaña, Gaspar Garnica, Juan de Hortega, in AGI. See also G, 228. Cortés, in question 163 in the questionnaire at his *residencia*, said that "the Spaniards were so terrified that all,

or at least most, wanted to set off for the port, to return to the West Indies" ("*la xente española estaba tan atemorrizada, que todos o los más, se querian ir al Puerto, para que se pasar a las islas*").

76 This is C de S, 516–17, and so approximate. But it reads as if the author had the text.

77 Cortés had said this before during this expedition. It was his favourite saying. It is, of course, in origin not a proverb but a quotation from Terence, *Phormio*, i, 4: "*fortes fortuna adjuvat*". It occurs in Polydore Virgil's *Adagia* of 1499 and Erasmus' *Adagia Chiliades* of 1508. Cortés could have picked it up from either of them; or from common parlance.

78 C, 169.

79 This speech is rendered by Sepúlveda (177) as if Cicero had pronounced it.

80 This assumes that Cortés did say something like this, and did not invent it in the 1540s, when the Castilian sense of honour had become even more intense than in 1520.

81 The Tlaxcalan hand behind this campaign is mentioned in the *residencia* (*CDI*, XXVII, 502). See too D del C, II, 271: "because they had come to rob their farms".

Chapter 30

1 For Tepeaca, see Gerhard [8:60], 286–9.

2 Barlow [1:10], 102.

3 Zorita [1:8], 89.

4 Ixtlilxochitl, 267. His source was an old Tlaxcalan. See too Gaspar de Garnica, AGI, Justicia, leg. 224, p.1, f.46v.

5 *CDI*, XXVII, 231–2; see too Joan de Cáceres in AGI, Justicia, leg. 223, p.2, f.223.

6 D del C, II, 271.

7 C de S, 526. Cervantes de Salazar had a memorandum from the first of these men, but no one else confirms their role. Juan Márquez is not otherwise identifiable.

8 Díaz del Castillo says 200, Ixtlilxochitl 4,000, but others (for example Diego de Ávila), who was there (in *Inf. de 1521*) 100,000 (Polavieja, 211). So much for the value of eyewitnesses.

9 Ixtlilxochitl, 270. Plate 31 of the *Lienzo de Tlaxcala* [29:22] depicts.

10 C, 123.

11 *CDI*, XXVII, 28.

12 There is a Segura de la Sierra between Badajoz and Seville, which many conquistadors (including both Cortés and the Alvarado brothers) must have known. It was just within the kingdom of Sevilla in the Sierra de Aroche, and then known as Segura de la Orden (de Alcántara). Its Jewish *aljama* contributed more than any other city to the war of Granada in 1491 (María Antonio del Bravo, *Los Reyes Católicos y los Judíos Andaluces*, Granada, 1989, 93–4). Another possible inspiration was Segura de Toro, between Plasencia and Bejár on the way from Mérida to Salamanca, at which Cortés may have stopped on the way to the latter city. It is improbable, but not quite impossible, that Cortés called the place after Manuel Segura, the lawyer who had been present at his own contract with Luis Fernández de Alfaro to go to the New World in 1506, and who was also present at the negotiations for loans, sales etc., in which his father Martín was concerned in Seville.

13 Pedro de Ircio and Luis Marín were magistrates; Cristóbal Corral, Francisco de Orozco, Francisco de Solís, and Cristóbal Millán de Gamboa were councillors, and Alonso de Villanueva was town notary (*CDI*, XXVI, 17–18). The document is in AGI, Justicia, leg. 223, p.1, ff.34–85.

14 *CDI*, XXVII, 20–1.

15 *CDI*, XXVII, 28.

16 Diego de Holguín, in *Inf. de 1521* (Polavieja, 237), said that they received the sign of "X". D del C, I, 489, says that it was simply a "G", for Guerra. In Seville at this time, slaves, though often treated as least as well as servants, were sometimes branded as a punishment, often with, on one cheek, the letter S and a line, for *esclavo*, on the other (Pike [23:42], 177).

17 García Llerena, in *CDI*, XXVII, 231: "if he sent several of the said Indians to be killed . . . and branded some others, it was in order to do what a good captain should . . ."

18 Accusations come from Diego de Ávila, in *Inf. de 1521*, in Polavieja, 211; also Vázquez de Tapia, in Res (Rayón), I, 58 ("many days he allowed the eating of human flesh"); Cervantes de Salazar says that the Tlaxcalans boiled 50,000 pots of human flesh.

19 As quoted in Polavieja, 236 and 263.

20 Polavieja, 211.

21 Polavieja, 212.

22 Diego de Ávila said he had heard Bartolomé Bermúdez say that it had happened; and Juan Bono de Quejo had heard the story too (in Polavieja, 300).

23 Polavieja, 300.

24 "publicly banquets were held by the said Indians" (Vargas, in *Inf. de 1521*, in Polavieja, 283). Juan Álvarez said that he had seen Indians summoning people to such parties but had never actually seen Christians eating Indians ("*ha visto a los dichos yndios caribes combidar a los cristianos que coman de aquella carne umana, pero no ha visto comer a ningund cristiano carne humano*", Polavieja, 264).

25 Bono evidence in *Inf. de 1521*, in Polavieja, 301.

26 See Anthony Grafton, *New worlds, Ancient texts* (Cambridge, Mass., 1992), 83, for these stories.

27 "Anyone who achieved a slice of little dog [*un pedaço de perro*], thought that he should give thanks to God" (AGI, Mexico, leg. 203, no. 5).

28 Vázquez de Tapia, in *residencia* against Cortés in Res (Rayón), I, 58–9. Cortés, in his defence, in the *residencia* said that he killed 500 Indians as a warning to others not to kill Spaniards on the road between Vera Cruz and Tenochtitlan (*CDI*, XXVII, 231–2). Rodríguez de Ocaña agreed (AGI, Justicia, leg. 224, p.1, f.294). Antonio Serrano de Cardona and Francisco Verdugo said the same. G, 254, has a different account. See *Lienzo de Tlaxcala* [29:22], plate 32, for a sad illustration.

29 C, 156. Cortés mentions Izúcar's wall, though he was probably not present at the fall. For the surrender of Cuetlaxtlan, see a statement by that city of 1580, in *Epistolario*, V, 41.

30 "and he agreed that those Jews of Tlaxcala [*los yudios de taxaltecle*] should carry off over 20,000 souls captive to be eaten and sacrificed" (Diego de Vargas, in *Inf. de 1521*, Polavieja, 282). The figure of 150,000 appears in a denunciation of Pero Pérez against Cortés: see Martínez, *Docs*, I, 175.

31 Joan de Cáceres, AGI, Justicia, leg. 223, p.2, f.227.

32 C, 169–70.

33 Aguilar, in J. Díaz, et al., 157.

34 Orozco [8:4], iv, 477, suggested that (perhaps out of hunger and privation) the Tlaxcalans ate flesh during this campaign without the persons concerned being sacrificed, thereby initiating a change in Indian practices (agreeing, in respect of Tlaxcala, with the Harmer thesis).

35 AGI, Patronato, leg. 5, R.15. This was a *probanza* made on the demand of Juan Ochoa de Elizalde, a notary acting for Cortés, and signed by Jerónimo de Alanís, a notary well known in Hispaniola who presumably reached New Spain with Narváez. It was ed. in part by García Icazbalceta, I, 411 ff., in full by G. L. R. Conway [28:19]. The witnesses were Pedro Álvarez Chico, inspector, Cristóbal de Olid, Vázquez de Tapia, factor of the

Crown, Andrés de Duero, Gonzalo de Alvarado, Juan Rodríguez de Villafuerte, and Diego de Ordaz, all councillors, Bartolomé de Olmedo, the Mercedarian brother, Juan Díaz, the priest, Cristóbal de Corral, Gerónimo de Aguilar, Pedro de Alvarado and Alonso de Ávila, of whom the last two were magistrates. These officials of Segura had their terms of office truncated, for the formal declaration of Segura's *cabildo* included the less important names listed earlier.

36 Alonso de Ávila as treasurer, Alonso de Grado (back in Cortés' favour) as accountant, Vázquez de Tapia, as factor, and Rodrigo Álvarez Chico as inspector.

37 The 9 were Alonso de Benavides, Diego de Ordaz, Gerónimo de Aguilar, the interpreter, Juan Ochoa de Elizalde, the lawyer, Pedro Sánchez Farfán, Cristóbal de Olid, Cristóbal de Guzmán, Pedro de Alvarado and Leonel de Cervantes, "the *comendador*", of whom only the last named had come with Narváez.

38 See AGI, Justicia, leg. 223, p.1, ff.12–22. It is ed. in García Icazbalceta, I, 427, together with the names. In the *residencia* against Cortés, García de Llerena said that everyone signed "without any omissions" (*CDI*, XXVII, 229) but Alonso de Villanueva, Francisco Verdugo and Bernal Díaz are only some of those who, perhaps because they were recovering from wounds in Tlaxcala, did not. Probably some refused to sign. Some must have got others to sign on their behalf since they could not write.

39 In *Inf. de 1521*, in Polavieja, 246–8.

40 Diego de Vargas, in *Inf. de 1521*, in Polavieja, 287.

41 Juan Álvarez, in *Inf. de 1521*, in Polavieja, 268.

42 John Schwaller, "Tres familias mexicanas del siglo xvi", *HM*, 122 (1981), 178.

43 The evidence in this *probanza* dated 4 October 1520 was used where appropriate when discussing the costs of the expedition. It is in AGI, Patronato, leg. 15, R.16, and Polavieja, 151–62. There were 14 witnesses and 32 signatories.

44 C, 181–2. Mendoza came from a family of hidalgos in Medellín which was often embroiled in difficulties with the Count. He seems to have gone out to Hispaniola in 1510, when he is mentioned in a letter from the King to Diego Colón (Muñoz, vol. 72, f.59). When he came to Mexico is uncertain. Perhaps he arrived with Salcedo. He would become an efficient assistant to Cortés in confidential affairs. This letter, like most such, was intended for publication. Juan Cromberger of Seville printed it on 8 November 1522.

45 See Mario Hernández's notes to his ed. (1985) of the *Cartas de Relación*; C, 81, fn.; and also, for Cortés' notion of empire, deriving partly perhaps from his attitude to Montezuma's method of rule, but also designed to keep out other adventurers from the West Indies, Victor Frankl's "Imperio particular e imperio universal in 'Las Cartas de relación de Hernán Cortés' ", *Cuadernos Hispanoamericanos*, 165 (1963). Frankl pointed out that Cortés later developed a notion of universal empire ("*monarca del mundo*") on the lines of what was suggested by Bishop Ruiz de la Mota at Corunna.

46 In the Bull of 1492, Alexander VI talked of the honour of God and "the propagation of the Christian Empire".

47 "*no menos mérito que el de Alemaña*" (C, 80): an astonishing sentence.

48 The Cid coveted "honour, consideration and wealth" (line 3413 [5:31]).

49 Alcocer [19:70], 13. F. Gómez de Orozco suggested Martín Plinius of Nuremberg as the cartographer (Ola Apenes, *Mapas Antiguos de México*, Mexico, 1947). Cortés referred to this map in his third letter (C, 198), and it was first published in Nuremberg in 1524, in a Latin edition of Cortés' letters. For the possibility that Dürer was inspired by it when working out his ideal city, see Ch. 39.

50 The date must have been before 30 October when Cortés signed his letter to the King.

51 This was in question 2 in an affidavit of 1528, in AGI, Patronato, leg. 54, R.2, ff.4–24. See Porras Muñoz, "Martín López, carpintero de ribera", *R de I*, (January–June 1948), 313. Various carpenters and craftsmen (who later testified) were present during this

conversation. Cortés says that he only ordered 12 brigantines (C,179–80).

52 Miguel Angel Ladero Quesada, *Historia de Sevilla, II: La Ciudad Medieval* (Seville, 1980), 18–19. That the "Great Captain" used ships in his siege of Taranto (1501–2) may also have influenced Cortés.

53 Conway (L of C), I, 45, 150.

54 Others were carpenters: Diego Ramírez, Alvar López, Diego Hernández, Martín Alabés, Clemente de Barcelona, and Francisco Rodríguez. There also came Lázaro Guerrero; Andrés Martínez; Hernán Martín and Pero Hernández, blacksmiths: Antón de Rodas, one of the Greek members of the expedition; and Andrés Núñez. Juan Gómez de Herrera did the caulking. Nearly all these men testified for López in 1529 in hearings to secure payment.

55 Conway, (Camb.), Add. 7289, 17.

56 AGI, Patronato, leg. 57, no.1, R.1, f.18 interrogatory (1544).

57 In a letter of 1560 to Philip II, published in Anderson, et al. [19:79], the council of that city protested against a tribute asked of them since among many other things they "had given the Spaniards wood and pitch with which they built their boats".

58 AGI, Patronato, leg.57, no.1, R.1, ff.18r., 21–21r., 44, tr. in Conway, (Camb.), Add. 7289, 67.

59 AGI, Patronato, leg.57, no.1, R.1, ff.2r–3v., tr. in Conway, (Camb.), Add. 7289, 84. See also López's evidence in *Inf. de 1565*, 120–1.

60 This is Cervantes de Salazar's story (C de S, 53–4). He adds that he asked for baptism. This is considered at a later point.

61 Las Casas, III, 244.

62 F. Hernández Arana, *Annals of the Cakchiquels* (Norman 1953), tr. Adrian Recinos, 115.

63 Ixtlilxochitl, 270. It may have begun to decimate Cempoallan, before the *noche triste*. See Francisco Guerra, "La logística sanitaria en la conquista de México", in *Hernán Cortés y su tiempo* [9:22], 412.

64 Durán, I, 52.

65 They may have had typhus (*typhus exanthematicus*), known in Mexico as *matlazahuatl*. See S. F. Cook, "The Incidence and Significance of Disease among the Aztecs", *HAHR* (August 1946).

66 FC, iv, 24, 128.

67 Durán, I, 156.

68 H. B. Nicholson [1:42], 440.

69 FC, x, 157.

70 Francisco Hernández [1:53], II.

71 Motolinía [1:1], 88.

72 FC, xii, 81.

73 Suárez de Peralta [9:38], Ch. xvii. Sahagún says that it began seriously in Tepeilhuitl, a month which started on 13 October.

74 Tezozomoc [1:18], 161.

75 Ixtlilxochitl, *Obras Históricas* (Mexico, 1975) (*Décima Relación*), I, 379. For the death of Zuangua, see *Rel. de Michoacan*, 245. The outbreak in Michoacan may have been due to Cuitláhuac's ambassadors' visit to the Tarascans. For the deaths in Tlamanalco, see Chimalpahin [19:35], 190.

76 See Rel. de Michoacan, 246.

77 "miraculously Our Lord killed them" (Vázquez de Tapia, in J. Díaz, et al., 148).

78 W. H. McNeil, *Plagues and Peoples* (Oxford, 1976), 207, argued, extravagantly, that Cortés would not have defeated the Mexica had it not been for this epidemic. The same emphasis is given by Alfred W. Crosby Jr., "Conquistador y pestilencia: the first new

world pandemic and the fall of the Great Indian Empires," *HAHR*, 47 (1967), 522.

79 Durán, I, 136, discusses this festival.

80 C, 188.

81 *Chilam Balam de Chumayel*, ed. Miguel Rivera (Madrid, 1986), 72.

82 D del C, II, 291.

83 C, 165.

84 Polavieja, 156. Hernando de Castro, merchant of Santiago, described this in a letter of 24 July 1520 to Alonso de Nebreda, Seville, ed. Otte [6:56], 117. Oviedo, II, 150, said that Diego Velázquez had reacted to the news of the defeat of Narváez by setting off himself for Mexico with 7 or 8 ships but that, after conferring with Licenciado Alfonso Parada off Yucatan, he went back. This seems to have been what Oviedo would have called a *"fábula"*.

85 D del C, II, 276–7.

86 D del C, II, 283; Morison [5:14], 517.

87 *Epistolario*, I, 21.

88 Boyd-Bowman [5:17] found only 32 Aragonese out of over 5,000 from the whole of Spain between 1493 and 1519.

89 D del C, II, 283.

90 D del C, II, 286; Burgos' ship was the delayed reply from Seville to Cortés letter of 6 July 1519 (Document 3). That it reached New Spain when Cortés was at Tepeaca is confirmed by Burgos himself in an *información* of 9 November 1525, in AGI, Mexico, leg. 203, no. 4. The financing, as has been seen, must have been by Martín Cortés, Luis Hernández de Alfaro, Fernando de Herrera and Juan de Córdoba, the pearl merchant, as well as Burgos himself. Burgos said (in the *información* cited) that he invested 6,000 castellanos of his own money on this enterprise without any return. His investment included 3 or 4 horses, 2 servants, and a black slave. He became an inveterate enemy of Cortés against whom he testified in several lawsuits. See APS (15 September 1520), lib. iii. f.2986.

91 *CDI*, XXVII, 30.

92 G, 237.

93 He was a witness for Cortés, 9 September 1534. D del C, II, 228; *CDI*, XXVII, 374.

94 Otte [6:56], 119.

95 C, 187–8; D del C, II, 281. Joan de Cáceres and Alonso de Mata who went with Sandoval gave evidence in the *residencia* (AGI, Justicia, leg. 223, p.2, f.227 r.). There was also a small expedition to Tustepeque, where Hernando de Barrientos had settled at Chinantla when a year before he had been sent with Diego Pizarro in search of gold.

96 Juan Álvarez, in the *Inf. de 1521*, in Polavieja, 123.

97 Res vs Alvarado, 69.

98 Others who left New Spain at this time included Francisco Velázquez, a hunchback relation of Diego; Gonzalo Carrasco, Narváez's spy at Cempoallan, whom Cortés nearly strangled the night before the battle of Cempoallan to get information from him; Melchor de Velasco; a certain Maldonado, who came from Medellín, and who was ill with syphilis; Diego de Vargas, who had property at Trinidad in Cuba; Luis de Cárdenas, a native of Triana, who had quarrelled with Cortés over what he saw as the mean division of gold; and Diego Holguín, for whom see Ch. 25, fn. 38 above. Of these, Álvarez and Cárdenas had come with Cortés. Bono, Vargas, Holguín and Álvarez would testify against the *Caudillo* in Velázquez's enquiry of 1521. For Cárdenas' later complaints against Cortés, see his letter to Charles V of 30 August 1527, in *CDI*, XL, 273–88.

99 D del C, II, 299; C, 164–5.

Chapter 31

1 D del C, II, 113. There seems to be a portrait, not from life, in Picture C of the Codex García Granados, in the Salón de Códices of the Anthropological Museum, ed. in *Tlatelolco a través de su tiempo*, VI (1945), 40. A serious study is Hector Pérez Martínez, *Cuauhtemoc, vida y muerte de una cultura* (Mexico, 1952).

2 See Torquemada [1:24], I, 16, for his war against Quetzaltepec and Iztactlocan.

3 Juan Cano told Oviedo of the death of Axoacatzin (Oviedo, IV, 260). The story of the killing of his 6 brothers is in Tezozomoc [1:18], 163. Tezozomoc was himself a grandson of Montezuma and so had an axe to grind. See also Juan Bautista Pomar, in *Relaciones de la Nueva España* [16:65], 24, and in the same, "Relación de la Genealogía", where it is said that the cause of the executions was that Axoacatzin and his brothers wanted to go in peace to Cortés in Tepeaca.

4 This is stated by Sahagún and most other indigenous sources of the era; Ixtlilxochitl gave her name. But Eulalia Guzmán, in her ed. of Cortés, [13:41], xxxvii, and in her *Vida y Genealogía de Cuauhtémoc* (Mexico, 1948), argued that Cuauhtémoc was a grandson of Ahuítzotl, not a son, and that his mother was Cuyauhtitlalli, daughter of the lord of Ixcateopan. This, with other controversial matters affecting Cuauhtémoc, is discussed in Josefina Muriel's "Divergencias" [22:92].

5 The "Anales de la Conquista de Tlatelolco en 1473 y en 1521", in *Tlatelolco a través de su tiempo*, V, (1945), tr. McAfee and Barlow, says that Cuauhtémoc had ruled Tlatelolco for 4 years before the conquistadors had arrived.

6 See Josefina Muriel [22:92], 66–6, for a presentation of the problems.

7 Cod. Ram., 145.

8 McAfee and Barlow noted that Cuauhtémoc was "above all lord of Tlatelolco . . ." ("Anales de la Conquista" [31:5], 39). This may go too far.

9 See FC, iii, 53–5; viii, 72, 76–7.

10 Soustelle [1:5], 89; FC, viii, 61.

11 FC, vi, 52–3.

12 Muriel [22:92], based on AGN (Mexico), R. Tierra, Vol. 1563.

13 Juan Cano to Oviedo (Oviedo, IV, 261). Cano, perhaps for legal reasons affecting himself, said that all the usual ritual was gone through in relation to this marriage. For Mexican marriage, see Warwick Bray, *Daily Life of the Aztecs* (London, 1968), 177.

14 Pedro Carrasco, "Royal Marriages in Ancient Mexico", in Harvey and Prem [2:14], clears up some of these problems.

15 *Rel. de Michoacan*, 255.

16 Marc Bloch, *L'étrange défaite* (Paris, 1957), 89.

17 Paulo Giovio, *Illustrium Virorum Vitae* (Florence, 1551), 253–5.

18 C, 191.

19 D del C, I, 510.

20 G, 263.

21 D del C, I, 513, and II, 28, where the chronicler says that he had at this time 3 strong Tlaxcalans as servants. Herrera ([8:6] V, 481), always happiest with big figures, says that the Tlaxcalans had 110,000 men to offer. López de Gómara spoke of 20,000

22 Herrera [8:6], V, 478.

23 It was the use of this phrase, which could have been a quotation from the *Siete Partidas*, which suggested to Silvio Zavala that Cortés had a copy with him of that work. See Silvio Zavala, *Ensayos sobre la Colonización Española en América* (Buenos Aires, 1944), 84.

24 "honremos a nuestra nación, engrandezcamos a nuestro rey, y enriquezámonos nosotros, que para todo es la empresa de México", (G, 262).

25 AGI, Justicia, leg. 223, p. 1, ff. 342–48, ed. in Cortés, *Escritos sueltos*, 1–23, and in Martínez, *Docs*, I, 164.

26 G, 263.
27 C, 192; D del C, I, 514.
28 It is where the modern main road runs from Mexico to Veracruz.
29 C, 192.
30 C, 192.
31 G, 264.
32 C, 193; Gerhard [8:60], 76.
33 Ixtlilxochitl, 272–3: Ixtlilxochitl, *Sumaria Relación*, in *Obras Históricas*, ed. Edmundo O'Gorman (Mexico, 1985), I, 391: "never, in the eighty days, when the Spaniards were in Mexico, was Ixtlilxochitl absent", (*"nunca, en ochenta días que los españoles estuvieron sobre México, jamás faltaron Ixtlilxochitl"*).
34 *CDI*, XXVII, 245–6.
35 *CDI*, XXVII, 243.
36 The Texcocans were said, in the *residencia* against Cortés, to have over 8,000 canoes (*CDI*, XXVII, 245).
37 Antonio Serrano de Cardona and Alonso de Villanueva, in the *residencia* against Cortés (*CDI*, XXVII, 385 and 519).
38 Ixtlilxochitl, 273: for the evidence against, see preceding fn.
39 Discussed in J.R. Parsons, "Settlement and Population History", in Wolf [14:27], 98.
40 FC, viii, 10; the obscure early history of Texcoco is discussed in Davies [1:24], 126–9.
41 Ixtlilxochitl, 165–6. Germán Vázquez, the editor of the most recent ed. of this work, compared this prince to the famous caliph (Ixtlilxochitl, 36).
42 Zelia Nuttall, "The Gardens of Ancient Mexico", *Annual report of the Smithsonian Society*, (1923), 409; Pasztory [4:35], 128–33.
43 A vivid account of this part of the campaign is in the Información of Ponce de León [27:27].
44 Ixtlilxochitl, 154.
45 Pomar, in "Relación de Texcoco", *Relaciones de la Nueva España* [31:3].
46 Martyr, II, 353. Aguilar (in J. Díaz, et al., 197) talks of the city having 80,000 or 100,000 houses. A recent estimate for the population was 12,500 to 25,000 by Jeffrey Parsons, while Fred Hicks suggested 100,000 for the kingdom of Texcoco (Davies [3:42] 46).
47 *"Mapa Quinatzin"*, illustrated in Pasztory [4:35], 203.
48 Motolinía [1:1], 119, 137.
49 In his time he and his son "conquered people everywhere" and "made war in all parts" (FC, viii, 9).
50 Ixtlilxochitl, *Sumaria Relación* [31:33] I, 326–7, and II, 187.
51 Berdan [3:30], 40.
52 Luis Marín, in *residencia* against Cortés, *CDI*, XXVIII, 63.
53 Ixtlilxochitl, 273. See Garibay [1:13], i, 26–7.
54 Ixtlilxochitl, *Sumaria Relación* [31:33], 396–7; Ixtlilxochitl, 276–7; see also Orozco [8:4], iv, 518.
55 C, 196–7.
56 Van Zantwijk [Preface: 5], 130

Chapter 32

1 C, 200.
2 Ixtlilxochitl, 278; G, 266–7; C, 197–8; D del C, I, 520–1.
3 G, 268.
4 G, 268; D del C, I, 522.

5 D del C, I, 527; C, 201; Chimalpahin [19:35].

6 D del C, I, 528–9.

7 *"aquí estuvo preso el sin ventura de Juan Yuste"*, C, 206; Juan Bono de Quejo, in *Inf. de 1521*, 294; *CDI*, XXVII, 233. Plate 41 of the *Lienzo de Tlaxcala* [29:22] shows Texcoco with the head of a horse looking out of a temple and two skulls on top: plainly "Pueblo Morisco". Several who accompanied Sandoval gave evidence at the *residencia* against Cortés: for example, Juan de Salcedo and Alonso de Navarrete.

8 "Without such punishments it is impossible to make war" (*"sin los semexantes castigos, no se puede facer la guerra)" CDI*, XXVII, 233). Readers of Kipling's *Kim* will recall the colonel who told his adjutant: "remember, this is punishment, not war".

9 *"Aunque os salgan de paz, los matad"*; question 26 in *residencia* against Cortés, *CDI*, XXVII, 20.

10 *Inf. de 1565*, 22, and 120, for López's evidence. Sandoval's second-in-command was Francisco Rodríguez Margariño. C de S, 594–8, enlarges on the role of Ojeda.

11 The date derives from question 6 of the suit of de la Peña vs Santa Cruz in Conway (L of C); D del C, I, 533.

12 Pedro Hernández, a blacksmith, 1529 (Conway, (Camb.), Add. 7289, 517). Cortés had a loan from López of 325 pesos which he repaid but he never gave him anything else.

13 Bartolomé González to Inquisitor Bonilla, 1574, cit. G.L.R. Conway, "Hernando Alonso, a Jewish conquistador with Cortés in Mexico", *Publications of the American Jewish Historical Society*, XXXI (1928), 9–31.

14 For this expedition, there seems, apart from C, 208–10, and D del C, I, 535, only one first-hand account, that of Antonio de Villanueva, in *CDI*, XXVII, 521–2. Cortés gave a figure of 30,000 Tlaxcalan auxiliaries, Bernal Díaz 15,000.

15 C, 208.

16 C, 208.

17 C, 209.

18 D del C, I, 539.

19 C, 209.

20 C, 210.

21 D del C, I, 541.

22 Diego de Holguín, in *Inf. de 1521*, in Polavieja, 233.

23 *CDI*, XXVI, 287–97 This is a *probanza* about Narváez's plan for flight, wrongly dated 1529, not 1521. D del C, II, 41–3, dates this plot as April, but others place it in January. Cortés says it occurred when they were preparing for the expedition against Tenochtitlan in Texcoco. February is likely, since Alonso de Ávila (who left for Spain at the end of that month) was invited to join the plot, but refused. He also presided at Vera Cruz over the trial on 16 February of Diego Díaz.

24 D del C, II, 43–5; C, 283–5; C de S, 34.

25 Diego de Vargas, in *Inf. de 1521*, in Polavieja, 286. There is a suggestion that Díaz was not hanged, but lived to fight on one of the brigantines in the siege of Tenochtitlan: thus Andrés de Monjaraz said that Licenciado Alfonso Pérez saved Díaz (Res (Rayón), II, 79). The same is given in *Información de los méritos y servicios de Diego y Fco. Díaz*, Paso y Troncoso collection, Museo Nacional, Mexico, quoted in Gardner [19:59], 149. But the text in *CDI*, XXVI, 297, like Vargas, is firm that he was hanged in 1521, in front of named witnesses. Díaz had been with Bono in the search for pearls off Venezuela before 1520.

26 Arranz [5:45], 224.

27 Otte [19:47], 102.

28 *Información de los servicios del adelantado Rodrigo de Bastidas* (Santo Domingo, 21 June 1521), in *CDI*, II, 376.

29 Pike [6:48], 141.

30 *Inf de . . . Bastidas* [32:28], 377. Witnesses described how they saw the ships leave.

31 D del C, II, 16. Estimates made for the numbers brought in this little fleet vary from under 200 to 400. For Fr. Melgarejo, see Atanasio López, "Los primeros franciscanos en Méjico", *Archivo Ibero-Americano*, vii (1920), no. xxxvii; Robert Ricard, "Note sur Fr. Pedro de Melgarejo, évangélisateur du Méxique", in *Bulletin Hispanique*, 25 (1923), 253–6, and the same's "Fr. Pedro de Melgarejo", in the same, 26 (1924/5), 68–9.

32 For the family see Schwaller [30:42], 171. The Bishop was an enemy of Bishop Fonseca. Gerónimo Ruiz de la Mota gave evidence to Cervantes de Salazar (C de S, 638).

33 In an *información* of 1526 (AGI, Mexico, leg. 203. no. 8), Alonso de Ávila testified that he had carried Elgueta in his ship from Hispaniola; presumably to Cuba.

34 Others who now joined the expedition of Cortés were Francisco de Orduña, a lawyer, also from Tordesillas; Antonio de Carvajal, perhaps a *placentino* (who would be known for his census of Michoacan); and a vain veteran of the Italian wars, named Briones.

35 G, 281.

36 Hernando de Castro to Alonso de Nebreda, in AGI, Justicia, leg. 712, cit., Otte [6:56], 137.

37 Ordaz to Francisco Verdugo, 22 August 1529, AGI, Justicia leg. 712, cit. Otte [11:5], 108.

38 Questionnaire and evidence in *Información de Diego de Ordaz* (Santo Domingo, 1521), *CDI*, XL, 88. Anton del Río said that Ordaz only learned in Yucatan of the confiscation (*CDI*, XL, 103).

39 See his letter of 14 November 1520, to the president of the Jeronymite priors, Fr. Luis de Figueroa, Prior de la Mejorada, in García Icazbalceta, I, 358–69.

40 Zuazo to Fr. Luis de Figueroa, in García Icazbalceta, I, 363. "The lady of silver" crops up afterwards often in these months, e.g., in *Ein Schöne Newe Zeitung* (*HAHR*, 1929, 203): a figure of romance in whom the Spaniards had good practical reasons for believing.

41 See *probanza* of Ordaz, in *CDI*, XL, 74–130. Avila was among those who testified. Mendoza was not. Probably he went straight on by the first boat to Spain. Ordaz waited till September when, with Licenciado Lucas Vázquez de Ayllón, *comendador* Cervantes, and some others (perhaps the Juan Álvarez who travelled was the same who gave evidence against Cortés at Diego Velázquez's *probanza* of June), he went on board a flotilla of 3 ships carrying pearls to Seville. See AGI, Contratación, leg. 2439, cit. Otte [19:47], 410.

42 These items were described by Licenciado Zuazo in his letter cited above (in [32:40], fn. 46), and also were mentioned in *Ein Schöne Newe Zeitung* (*HAHR*, 1929, 203). Wagner sorts out the relation between all these ([8:23], 327).

43 AGS, Cámara, Castilla, 7, ff.76, 95, 28.

44 Bono de Quejo, in *Inf. de 1521*, in Polavieja, 395; for Doña María, see the evidence of Holguín, who saw the ship sail, in Polavieja, 239.

45 Estimate of Juan Bono, in *Inf de 1521*, in Polavieja, 301.

46 Diego de Ávila, in *Inf. de 1521*, in Polavieja, 213.

47 Diego Holguín, in *Inf. de 1521*, in Polavieja, 238.

48 Diego de Ávila, in *Inf. de 1521*, in Polavieja, 238.

49 This was mentioned by Herrera [8:6], V, 469. Herrera may have been confusing this letter with a later one, or there may even have been a misprint.

50 FC, x, 189; Anwalt [7:41], 84–6.

51 *Rel. de Michoacan*, 241–7. In the original, illustration 44 shows the Spanish arriving on 3 horses. It is possible that this expedition was not till February 1522 but I think that there was another one then. The *Rel. de Michoacan* may telescope two expeditions into one.

52 FC, x, 190–1: see de la Garza [1:53], 57.

53 *En Tamoanchan*
    en alfombra florida

hay flores perfectas
hay flores sin raíces:
desde los tesoros preciosos
tú estás cantando . . .

Angel Garibay, *Poesía Nahuatl* (Mexico, 1964), I, 29. Other beautiful poems about Tamoanchan can be found in this work or in Garibay [1:13], I, 178.

54 See Pasztory [4:35], 42, for the influence of Xochicalco on Mexican art.

55 Discussed in Brundage [2:50], 62–4.

56 G, 274: C, 211.

57 D del C, II, 13.

58 C, 213.

59 C, 214. Not to be confused with Chimalhuacan, the city and hill near Texcoco, though it is frequently spelled the same. It is now San Vicente Chimalhuacan.

60 D del C, II, 18–19.

61 G, 276.

62 C, 215. This battle was called that of Yautepec (Oaxtepec) by Bernal Díaz, but it could not have been so. C, 215, Ixtlilxochitl, 282, and Orozco y Berra [8:4], iv, 541, suggest Tlayacapan as the correct place.

63 D del C, II, 25.

64 C, 216; D del C, II, 25. These gardens were still visible in the 1570s when the botanist Francisco Hernández visited them. See Zelia Nuttall [31:42], 453–4.

65 Joan de Grijalva, *Crónica de la Orden de NPS Agustín en la provincias de Nueva España* (Mexico, 1624).

66 Gilutepeque, according to Cortés. Now Juitepec.

67 C, 217.

68 D del C, II, 25.

69 Pasztory [4:35], 134–5.

70 Johanna Broda, "Las fiestas aztecas de los dioses de la lluvia", in *Revista Española de Antropología Americana*, 6 (Madrid, 1971), 245–327.

71 D del C, II, 26; C, 218.

72 Francisco Dávila in *CDI*, XXVIII, 64: "to give fear to the said Indians so that they might obey".

73 Durán, II, 23.

74 C, 218.

75 Pasztory [4:35], 153.

76 Gibson [2:15], 41–2.

77 FC, ix, 79–80.

78 Tezozomoc [1:19], 81–2.

79 D del C, II, 35.

80 C, 220; D del C, II, 28–36, claims Olea as one of his (many) relations.

81 C, 220–1.

82 G, 280–1; D del C, II, 36; C, 220–1.

83 This was the ballad which Las Casas said that Cortés had recited at Cholula.

84 D del C, II, 39. There was later a ballad about Cortés in these circumstances:
En Tacuba está Cortés
Con su escuadrón esforzado.
Triste estaba y muy penoso,
Triste y con gran cuidado,
La una mano en la mejilla,
Y la otra en el costado . . .

85 C, 223.

86 FC, ii, 77

Chapter 33

1 Also *pulque* beaker. This is in the Museum für Völkerkunde, Vienna.
2 In the Museo de Antropología, Mexico.
3 This green statuette is in the Wurttembergisches Landesmuseum, Stuttgart. See the discussion in Pasztory [13:52], 111–15, though she thinks that it could have been made even later than 1521. But after the conquest, sculpture could not be colossal, for it could neither be hidden nor moved.
4 Durán, II, 564, Josefina Muriel [22:92] questions whether this point is valid.
5 Van Zantwijk [Preface:5], 198.
6 Accounts of those faraway hostilities can be found in the *Anales de Cuauhtitlan*, in Bierhorst [13:38], and Tezozomoc [1:19]: see Davies [1:24], 314.
7 Durán, II, 563.
8 Durán, I, 85; Tezozomoc [1:19], 437.
9 Berdan [3:30], 103–4.
10 Durán, I, 88.
11 *"Yo, Nezahualcoyotl, lo pregunto:*
¿Acaso de veras se vive con raíz en la tierra?
No para siempre en la tierra:
sólo un poco aquí.
Aunque sea de jade se quiebra,
Aunque sea de oro se rompe,
Aunque sea plumaje de quetzal se desgarra.
No para siempre en la tierra:
sólo un poco aquí."
Cantares Mexicanos, f.17r., quoted in León-Portilla [1:48], 169.
12 Cortés in testimony 1532 [24:9].
13 Rodrigo de Nájera, in Conway, (Camb.), Add. 7289, 417.
14 Gardner [19:59], 123. Orozco y Berra ([8:4], iv, 526) says that on one occasion a commando unit of Mexica tried to burn the shipyard. In 1938, the town council of Texcoco put a monument where they believed that Cortés launched the brigantines.
15 Gardner makes a case for supposing that these vessels had paddles, not oars, in his excellent essay on the naval aspects of the war [19:59], 130.
16 Conway (Camb.), Add. 7289, 357.
17 López built 13 brigantines, but one, the smallest, was not finished, for it was overturned and flooded (Andrés López, in suit of Martín López vs Cortés, 1545, in Conway (L of C), 45, I, 94).
18 D del C, II, 44.
19 Herrera [8:6], III, 160.
20 *"Los mexicanos son sumamente malos. No hay nadie que sobrepase en maldad al mexicano . . ."* (Sahagún, ed. Garibay, Mexico, 1956, IV, 132).
21 C de S, 600–1, had an account from Gerónimo Ruiz de la Mota.
22 D del C, II, 48–9. Probably in early May, though Cortés said it was on 28 April.
23 Motolinía [1:1], 40.
24 C, 225. For Cortés as a strategist, see Colonel Eduardo de Fuentes Gómez de Salazar, *Estrategías de la Implantación Española en América* (Madrid, 1992), Ch.5.
25 See the analysis by Martínez [9:52], 318.
26 Ixtlilxochitl gave a list of Indian commanders.

27 See Charles Gibson, "Llamamiento General, repartimiento, and the Empire of Alcolhuacan", *HAHR*, 36, (1956).

28 Letter of Fr. Motolinía to Charles V, 1555, in *CDI*, VII, 289.

29 Camargo, 122, 124 fn., 154; D del C, II, 49.

30 These are Cortés' figures, in C, 225. Díaz del Castillo had similar figures: 84 horsemen, instead of 86, 194 crossbowmen and musketeers, instead of 118, and 650 infantrymen, instead of 700.

31 Cline's Sahagún, 106–8, gives Cortés' purported speech. This included, he says, the insistence that Cortés came to arbitrate between the Mexica and the Tlaxcalans (as if he had been a royal lawyer in the Extremadura of his youth); it discussed Alvarado's responsibility for the massacre in the temple; it said that Montezuma was killed by the Mexicans; and it ended uncompromisingly: "all these things you have done against us like idolatrous cruel people, devoid of all justice and humanity. Therefore, we come to make war on you as brutal unreasonable people, from which we will not cease till we avenge our grievances and overthrow the enemies of God, idolators who do not observe the law of neighbourliness and humanity with their fellow creatures." See also Torquemada [1:24], II, 273–5, and Martínez [9:52], 304.

32 *Anales de Tlatelolco*, in Léon-Portilla [4:33], 148.

33 Cortés in his letter to the King gave figures of 25,000, "over 20,000" and "over 30,000" for each of these 3 commands. They are unbelievable estimates.

34 C, 123; D del C, II, 123.

35 In a *probanza* brought by the daughter of María Luisa in 1563 (Ramírez Cabañas' ed. of Bernal Díaz, 563), it was said that Alvarado took this lady everywhere: "*el dicho Pedro de Alvarado siempre truxen en su companía a la dicha doña Luisa*".

36 There is in Spain a proverb: "If your enemy flees make him a bridge of silver". Its classical origin is shown by its inclusion in Erasmus' *Adagia*, vii: "*hostibus fugientibus pontem argentuem exstraendum esse*".

37 C, 234.

38 There are several lists of captains of brigantines. Díaz del Castillo and Cervantes de Salazar agree over the names of 8 (García Holguín, Pedro Barba, Juan Xaramillo, Gerónimo Ruiz de la Mota – Cervantes' informant – Antonio de Carvajal, Juan de Portillo, Juan de Limpias Carvajal (*el sordo*), and Pedro de Briones). But thereafter Bernal Díaz (D del C, II, 47) gave Francisco de Zamora, Juan Esteban Colmenero, Hernando de Lerma, Ginés Nortes, and Miguel Díaz de Aux; while C de S (637–8) had, for the outstanding names, Juan Rodríguez de Villafuerte, Francisco de Verdugo, Francisco Rodríguez Magariño, Cristóbal Flores, Rodrigo Morejón de Lobera and Antonio de Sotelo. The explanation for the two versions is presumably that the commands changed.

39 G, 283.

40 Nuttall [3:4], 75.

41 Angel María Garibay, *Épica Nahuatl* (Mexico, 1945) 17–18.

42 D del C, II, 53; C, 228–9.

43 The aqueduct ran along the lake on the east side of what became later the Calzada de la Veronica, turned at la Tlaxpana to follow the Calzada de Tacuba until it arrived approximately at the modern central post office, where canoes came to distribute water to the city. An underground pipe ran from there to the main temple.

44 S. Linné, *El Valle y la ciudad de México en 1550* (Stockholm, 1948), 25, points out that there must have been wells in Tenochtitlan, since it was a big city long before Montezuma I built his aqueduct from Chapultepec in the 1450s.

45 See "Chapultepec en la literatura nahuatl", Miguel León-Portilla, *Toltecayotl* (Mexico, 1980), 385–401.

46 C, 229.

47 This account follows the statement of Cortés who said that the siege lasted 75 days. Counting back from the day of the end of the siege, 13 August, 31 May must be the day of the beginning. But Díaz del Castillo wrote of 13 May as the opening day.

48 C, 229.

49 Many people testified that, from the other side of the lake, they saw Cortés setting off, e.g., Alonso de Arévalo, in Conway (L of C), I, 45, 78–82.

50 Ixtlilxochitl, *Decimatercia Relación*, 26.

51 C, 230.

52 *CDI*, XXVI, 476: "*amigo e persona muy piadosa del dicho Don Hernando Cortés*".

53 Ruy González so testified having served under him in Michoacan (AGI, Justicia, leg. 220, ff.142v.-143). He was later punished by Cortés for disobedience.

54 López's achievements are testified to by, for example, Francisco García, Gerónimo de la Mota, Andrés Truxillo, Andrés Bravo, Lázaro Guerrero, Antonio Cordero, Juan Griego, and Andrés López. The last-named said that he had been on a nearby brigantine "and seen the whole thing". All these statements can be found in AGI, Patronato, leg. 57. R.1, no. 1.ff. 20, 23, 32, 35, 40r., as in Conway (Camb.), Add. 7289. Oviedo never mentioned López, though he must have known of him, for he said that his achievement compared with that of Sesostris King of Egypt (Oviedo, IV, 113).

55 Rodríguez de Villafuerte remained the supreme commander: see his *información* in AGI, Mexico, leg. 203, no.2.

56 C, 231.

57 G, 287. Gardner [19:59], 165, quoted Captain Mahan: "strenuous, unrelaxing pursuit is . . . imperative after a battle" *Naval Strategy compared and contrasted with the principles and practice of military operations on Land* (Boston, 1911), 267.

58 López enquiry, 1540, in Conway (L of C), 45, I, 153.

59 C, 214.

60 C de S, 663. Salazar knew Hernández in later years.

61 FC, xii, 83.

62 Ixtlilxochitl, *Decimatercia Relación*, 25.

63 Durán, II, 564.

64 "*parecía que se hundía el mundo*": C, 233.

65 D del C, II, 61.

66 C, 234.

67 C, 234.

68 FC, xii, 85.

69 FC, xii, 88.

70 Ixtlilxochitl [4:5], 330–1, argued that, at this time, Cortés and Ixtlilxochitl (the writer's ancestor) climbed the pyramid of the Great Temple, killed a Mexican "general", attacked the gods, cut the head off Huitzilopochtli, seized the gold mask which he was wearing, and threw the remains of the god down 100 steps below. But there is no confirmation from any Spanish source of this dramatic happening (though Durán, II, 567, says that they captured the pyramid: as does the citation in *Nobilario* [7:12], 206–7, for a coat of arms for Juan González Ponce de León). Ixtlilxochitl's source was Alonso Axayaca, Cuitláhuac's son, and several native paintings.

71 C, 236–7.

72 C, 237.

73 C, 238; D del C, II, 668.

74 In 1563, the Governor, magistrates, and leading citizens of Xochimilco requested various grants from the King of Spain alleging services made during the conquest: provision of 12,000 warriors, 2,000 boats, food in abundance, and many men sent to assist

the expedition of Honduras, etc. (*CDI*, XIII, 293–301). About this time, however, according to FC, xii, 96, the Xochimilca, the people of Iztapalapa and those of Cuitláhuac (altogether lakeside peoples known as the "Chinamanecans") came and offered their services to the Mexica – an offer gratefully accepted. No sooner had they been assigned places in the defence, and the fighting had begun, than they turned against the Mexica, started killing them and carried some off as prisoners for sacrifice. The Mexica sent a fleet of canoes and captured many of them.

75 Francisco Rodríguez, in *Inf. de 1565*, 40, says that "the Tlaxcalans provided everything necessary . . . opening up the paths"; Ixtlilxochitl, *Decimatercia Relación*, 34.

76 Sepúlveda, 215.

77 "*Me pesaba en el alma*" (C, 240).

78 The decision was of course urged on the Spaniards by their allies.

79 "*si no se derrocára, no se podiera acabar de ganar a lo menos, tan presto*" (*CDI*, XXVIII, 49).

80 AGI, Justicia, leg, 223, p.1, f.424; leg 224, p.1, f.1r.; leg 224, p.1, f.46v.; leg.224, p.1, f.152r.

81 The historian Ixtlilxochitl says, "Cortés, with the agreement of Ixtlilxochitl and the other lords, ordered that all the houses which were captured should be razed to the ground [*todas las casas que se ganasen se derribasen por el suelo*] and this Ixtlilxochitl ordered the Texcocans to do": [4:5], 41.

82 C, 241.

83 C, 240.

84 "at night all the enemy natives would fortify themselves and make themselves strong again": Alonso de la Serna, in AGI, Justicia, leg. 223, p.2, f.584.

85 Cristóbal de Flores, in Res vs Alvarado, 136. G(298) said there were 3 such.

86 Res vs Alvarado, 44, 70–1.

87 C de S, 688; FC, xii, 99. Joan Tirado seems to have played a part in the rescue. The matter was cited in his patent of nobility (*Nobilario* [7:12], 127–9).

88 G, 123.

89 C, 242.

90 These events, revealed by Tezozomoc (*Crónica Mexicana*), were explored by Padden [3:35], 212. But Tezozomoc (*Crónica Mexicayotl*, 150) also says that these princes were killed on the *noche triste*.

Chapter 34

1 Sahagun I, 502–503.

2 FC, x, 173.

3 Cortés' text (C, 245) speaks of the square of Tenochtitlan but, from the context ("a square bigger than Salamanca"), it is obviously that at Tlatelolco which is meant.

4 C, 246, suggests that he committed himself against his better judgement. D del C, II, 76–7, suggests that Cortés was not so hostile to the plan as he reported himself to have been.

5 R.H. Barlow, "Tlatelolco como Tributario" [3:36], 33 summarises the evidence.

6 See *Anales de Tlatelolco*, in León-Portilla [4:33]; FC, xii, 91; see also discussion in Muriel [22:92], 86.

7 Bryan McAfee and R.H. Barlow, ed., "Anales de la conquista en 1473 y en 1521", *Tlatelolco a través de los tiempos*, V (Mexico, 1945), 39.

8 The Tlatelolca at this juncture badly need a careful study.

9 Both Cortés and López de Gómara say 15,000 to 20,000.

10 C, 248.

11 Calnek, in "The Internal Structure of Tenochtitlan", in E. Wolf (ed.), *The Valley of Mexico* (Albuquerque, 1976), 300.
12 Durán, II, 566, talks of a "false bridge".
13 C, 250.
14 For Vázquez, see his *información*, in 1525, AGI, Mexico, leg. 203, no.3.
15 FC, xii, 91–2.
16 Muriel [22:92], 94–5.
17 I have here used Garibay's translation from the Nahuatl, as ed. in León- Portilla [4:33], 132.
18 Figures for the dead and captured are as much matters of dispute for this battle as any other. Thus for the captured, the Florentine Codex has 53, Díaz del Castillo 66, López de Gómara 40, Cortés 35 to 40.
19 C, 252.
20 D del C, II, 86.
21 D del C, II, 86. FC, xii, 95, has a simpler, but none the less vivid, picture of the occurrence: "they stripped them, they took from them their arms and their cotton armour, and everything which they had on. They left them all naked. Then, when they were fully converted into victims, they sacrificed them, and their companions remained watching from the waters as to the way that they were given death." Cortés heard the drums preparing for the sacrifices, and smelt the copal resin used in the preparation of the victims, but seems not to have seen the acts of sacrifice.
22 FC, xii, 103–4.
23 D del C, II, 91.
24 C de S, 700–2. Beatriz Bermúdez mocked the retreating Spaniards.
25 Durán, II, 567. D del C, II, 94: Guzmán is said to have been sacrificed last.
26 C, 252.
27 C, 252. See Orozco [8:4], iv, 615.
28 Durán, I, 285; Pasztory [4:35], 136–8. It escaped Spanish attentions.
29 See, e.g., Durán, II, 30–1.
30 The Matalcinga were an ancient people, with an obscure history, from the neighbourhood of Toluca. See Davies [1:24], 135–9. Juan de Burgos accompanied Sandoval, as the *información* in his favour in 1525 showed, taking with him several horses, his Spanish servants and a black slave (AGI, Mexico, leg. 203, no. 4).
31 C de S, 700.
32 See G, 303, and C, 253.

Chapter 35

1 C, 256.
2 D del C, II, 95.
3 Ixtlilxochitl [4:5], 42: *"los enemigos nunca más la abrieron"*.
4 Durán, II, 568.
5 FC, xii, 104.
6 There had been 2 ships. The expedition had set off in February 1521. It had been defeated by the natives of Florida. One ship had returned to Cuba, carrying on board the mortally wounded Ponce de León; the other reached Villa Rica, to Cortés' benefit. See Murga [5:14], 236–40.
7 C, 285, 323. Durán, I, 163, thought Montano could not have performed this feat, yet he was awarded a coat of arms for having done so (Nobilario [7:12], 315–16). The grant of arms read, "Lacking powder, you went to seek sulphur which . . . did much to gain the city." See also a statement of services undated, where the same claim is made (*CDI*, XIII, 481).

8 C, 256. D del C, II, 108, says that 2 Mexican leaders began lazily to eat tortillas, cherries and turkey legs. But he was probably not present, and he puts this event as occurring a little later.

9 FC, xii, 104–5.

10 C, 258.

11 C, 257.

12 D del C, II, 98–9.

13 Ixtlilxochitl, *Decimatercia Relación* [4:5], 42.

14 D del C, II, 99–100.

15 Graulich [1:42], 77.

16 *Anales de Tlatelolco*, in Léon-Portilla [4:33], 68.

17 C, 258, 260.

18 G, 306.

19 Bernard Ortiz de Montellano, in "Aztec cannibalism . . .", *Science*, 613 (1976).

20 Ixtlilxochitl, *Decimatercia Relación* [4:5], 43.

21 Cline's Sahagún, 123; C, 60; FC, xii, 107.

22 Dorantes de Salazar [8:79], 184–8, insisted that Badajoz was the real conqueror of the Great Temple of Tlatelolco. This view is sustained by a questionnaire of 1537 about Badajoz's achievements: where it is implied that Badajoz, "with his people, were the first to enter the said Tatelulco[sic], and took the two towers which were called Ochilobos, and killed many people in them and, on the two towers, raised the flags" (in AGI, Mexico, leg. 203, and ed. in *Epistolario*, V, 15, 12–13). We learn of the actions of Montano and Mata from the grants of arms to these 3 conquistadors, in *Nobilario* [7:12], 313–15, for Badajoz (1527), and for Montano (1540). The coats of arms of these men depicted their great achievements. Badajoz was said to have lived for 118 years, mostly in poverty (*Nobilario* [7:12], 314).

23 C, 264.

24 Res (Rayón), II, 214.

25 C, 262.

26 Ixtlilxochitl, *Decimatercia Relación* [4:5], 44; Durán, I, 269–70.

27 Sepúlveda, 218.

28 C, 264; Hassig [1:23], 238.

29 Diego Hernández vs Cortés, 1531, in Conway, (Camb.), Add. 7285, 76. See also Diego de Corria and Francisco de Maldonado, in Conway (Camb.), Add. 7285, 89 and 92.

30 C, 265.

31 C, 266.

32 C, 265. Perhaps archaeological research will one day throw new light on the nature of the fighting in Tlatelolco in 1521. Already, Moctezuma Matos [20:54], 207, has noted, in excavation in the late 1980s, many skeletons and burial remains. The effect could be to reduce further the estimates of deaths.

33 FC, xii, 117. The dress does not figure in the list of arms and insignia of the Mexica in the Códice Matritense (Thelma Sullivan, "The Arms and Insignia of the Mexica", in *ECN*, (1972) 156–93). Presumably it was a minor variation of the 8 different types of quetzal costumes which do figure there.

34 Sahagún, quoted in León-Portilla, [4:33], 133.

35 Durán, II, 564.

36 C, 258.

37 Graulich [1:42], 66.

38 C, 266–7.

39 C, 267.

40 C, 268–9; Ixtlilxochitl, *Decimatercia Relación* [4:5], 46.

41 Ixtlilxochitl, *Decimatercia Relación* [4:5], 46.
42 C, 269.
43 Sepúlveda, 223.
44 C, 269.
45 FC, xii, 119.
46 *Anales de Tlatelolco*, in Léon-Portilla [4:33], 71.
47 FC, xii, 119.
48 FC, xii, 119.
49 Durán, II, 81.
50 But they might have heard, for example, the ballad "The Siege and Burning of Numancia":

Viendo el Scipio tan bravo y fuerte
Todos o no entregarse se dan muerte . . .

(*BAE*, X, 377).
51 *Anales de Tlatelolco*, in Léon-Portilla [4:33], 73.
52 FC, xii, 116.
53 FC, xii, 120. The Mexican sources forget about the King of Tacuba being in the boat, but the Spanish ones find him there.
54 C, 271.
55 C, 270.
56 Diego de Ávila, in *Inf. de 1521*, in Polavieja, 217.
57 Ixtlilxochitl, *Obras Históricas* [30:75] (*Décima Relación*), I, 277–78. Durán, however (II, 568) says that Cuauhtémoc was hidden in a small boat, escorted by a single rower, and was discovered and captured.
58 "*viendo que era mucha la fuerza de los enemigos, que le amenazaban con sus ballestas y escopetas, se rindió*": Ixtlilxochitl, *Decimatercia Relación* [4:5], 46. This is the site now of a pretty church, La Concepción. A plaque on it announces: "Here the Emperor Cuauhtémoc was captured and slavery began."
59 Muriel [22:92], 97.
60 FC, xii, 11.
61 D del C, II, 114. Jugurtha had earlier fought for the Romans at Numancia. It would seem likely that there was a ballad about that. There were one or two about Marius: one observing the ruins of Carthage; another about Marius, "the conqueror of the Cimbri". The latter does not notice that in fact the victor was delayed several hours by fierce fighting dogs, led by women. Plutarch talks of this in his life of Marius, which possibly Cortés knew.
62 Ixtlilxochitl, *Decimatercia Relación* [4:5], 47. G, 311 and D del C, II, 112, have similar speeches.
63 D del C, II, 112: "*a que mandará a Mexico y a sus provincias como de antes los solían hacer*".
64 C, 272. Ixtlilxochitl (*Decimatercia Relación* [4:5], 45) and G (311) said that Cuauhtémoc was persuaded by Cortés to call for the surrender of those of his men who remained fighting to lay down their arms; and that he went up to a high tower and made this appeal for surrender. That is improbable. As with other such events, Cortés would have mentioned the matter in his report of some months later to the Emperor.
65 Presumably that was Cuauhtémoc's long-standing wife, Xuchimatzatzin, not Tecuichpo.
66 FC, vi, 4.
67 FC, xii, 119; Durán, II, 289. A ritual humble reference which an emperor would make on his inauguration was that "the tatters, the miserable cloak, were my desert" (FC, vi, 42).

68 FC, xii, 123.

69 FC, xii, 215–16. It is possible that this conversation occurred later.

70 In AGI, Justicia, leg. 712, cit. Otte [6:56], 258–9.

71 *Anales de Tlatelolco*, in Léon-Portilla [4:33], 162.

72 FC, xii, 118: "very few", said Joan de Cáceres, "were those who misbehaved".

73 G, 311.

74 León-Portilla [4:33], 145.

75 Durán, II, 319.

76 Torquemada [24:56], II, 312.

77 See Martínez [9:52], 332, for a good discussion.

78 These calculations are well done in R. Kontezke, "Hernán Cortés como poblador del la Nueva España", *R de I*, IX, (January–June 1948), 366. He gave 600 for Cortés' original expedition, 12 for Saucedo's reinforcement, 157 for Garay's ships in 1520 (surely an exaggeration), 800 with Narváez (perhaps too few), 14 with Barba, 9 with Rodríguez de Lobera, 15 with Juan Burgos, 200 with Alderete, and 15 from Ponce de León's ship: 1,822 in all, estimating deaths of 800–900.

79 *Anales de Cuauhitlan*, in Bierhorst [13:38].

80 D del C, II, 117.

81 *Anales de Tlatelolco*, in Léon-Portilla [4:33], 70.

82 C, 233.

Chapter 36

1 That letter, lost, was summarised by the printer Jacob Cromberger for a postscript which he put at the end of his ed. of Cortés' second letter (that written in Tepeaca in 1520). That postscript, with the letter concerned, was ed. in Seville in November 1522. It made the letter even more exciting.

2 This crisis is brilliantly treated in Joseph Pérez's *La Révolution des "Comunidades" de Castille* (Bordeaux, 1970).

3 Pedro Fajardo, Marquis of Los Vélez, one of the most gifted men of his age, had been a page at the legendary court of the Infante Don Juan. He built the castle of Mula in order to overawe the townsfolk. A lawsuit began over his rights. It lasted 300 years.

4 See Pérez [23:52], 165–77. The war of the *comuneros* in Seville had the character of a fight inspired by the Ponces against the *conversos* protected by the Duke of Medina Sidonia. The leading *conversos* assembled to prepare their defence in the house of Juan de Córdoba, the silversmith turned merchant. See Giménez Fernández [6:19], II, 963.

5 Cooper [6:66], I, 135. Mayor had married Rodrigo Mexía.

6 Giménez Fernández [6:19], II, 900.

7 Pérez [23:52], 193.

8 AGI, Patronato, leg. 15, R. 2. nos. 12 and 13. The second of these documents was published in Polavieja, 136–7.

9 Erwin Panofsky, *Albrecht Dürer* (Princeton, 1943), 206.

10 Albrecht Dürer, "Tagebuch der Reise in die Niederlande, anno 1520", in *Albrecht Dürer in seine Briefe und Tagebüchern*. ed. Ulrich Peters (Frankfurt am Main, 1925), 24–5. There is a tr. of the Tagebuch by Roger Fry, ed. as *Record of journeys to Venice and the Low Countries* (Boston, 1913).

11 Massing, "Early European Images of America", in *Circa 1492* [5:39], 572.

12 Charles V celebrated his coronation by creating the rank of grandee of Spain.

13 Erwin Walter Palm, in "Tenochtitlan y la ciudad ideal de Durero", *JSAP*, n.s. 40

(1951), 59–66, suggested that the painter was influenced in his scheme for an ideal city (*Ettliche Underrate zu befestiegung der stet Schloss und Flecker*, Nuremberg, 1527, f. E. 1) by seeing Cortés' map of Tenochtitlan. It is possible.

14 Panofsky [36:9], 206.

15 *Inventaire des tableaux, livres, joyaux et meubles de Marguerite d'Autriche*, ed. Léon de Laborde (Paris, 1850). This includes a list of *"accoustremens de plumes, venuz des Indes présentées par l'Empereur à bruxelles le xxe jour d'aoust XV XXIII et aussi par monseigneur de la Chaulx"*.

16 Painted 1523–5, according to Edouard Michel, "Un tableau colonial de Jan Mostaert", in *Revue Belge d'Archéologie et l'histoire d'art*, I (Brussels, I 1931), 133. It is now in the Frans Hals Museum, Haarlem. Michel thought the influence on Mostaert was treasure seized in 1522 by Jean Fleury, a captain of Jean Ango of Dieppe (see Ch. 38). Ango's benefactor, the Cardinal d'Amboise, and the Prince-Bishop of Liège were in touch with one another at that time, so it is possible.

17 Honour [5:11], 21.

18 See André Chastel and Suzanne Collon-Gevaert, "L'art précolombien et le palais des princes-évêques de Liège", in *Bulletin de la société d'art et d'histoire de Liège*, XL (Liège, 1958), 73. Hugh Honour assumed that the inspiration came from what those Indians brought in 1528. The treasures of 1520 are also possible.

19 Julius von Schlosser, *Der Kunst- und Wunderkammern des Spätrenaissance*, (Leipzig, 1908). But Schlosser dates the presents 1524.

20 Peter Martyr, *De Insulis Nuper Repertis, simultaque Incolarum Moribus Enchiridion, dominae Margaritae divi Max. Caesar* (Basle, 1521). There seem to have been German and Italian editions in 1520. This became Martyr's *Fourth Decade*, the last work which he published in his lifetime.

21 McNutt's introduction to his trans. of Martyr, I, 46–7.

22 *DIHE* 12, 143–5.

23 This theme is brilliantly developed in Honour [5:11], 30.

24 Tapia had had a famous row with Ovando. In a *residencia* in 1509–10 against that governor, Tapia had been a witness: for which (the first colonial *residencia* for which material survives), see E. Rodríguez Demorizi, *El pleito Ovando-Tapia* (Santo Domingo, 1978) and Ursula Lamb, "Cristóbal de Tapia vs. Nicolás de Ovando", *HAHR*, 33 (August 1953). For Tapia and his sugar interests, see Mervyn Ratkin, "The Early Sugar Industry in Hispaniola", *HAHR*, 34 (February 1954). Lamb says that Tapia was a "distant relation" of the Fonsecas. Probably illegitimate if so.

25 D del C, II, 433.

26 AGI, Contratación, leg. 4675, lib. 2, f.164v. (11 November 1523). Papers dealing with 4,000 pesos embargoed in the Casa de la Contratación show that Portocarrero's interests were being looked after by his mother, María de Céspedes, since he was by then dead. It appears that these 4,000 pesos were used by the Bishop of Burgos for ships in Bilbao. See Muñoz, A/103, f. 307.

27 The text of Tapia's instructions (11 April 1521) is in AGI, Justicia, leg. 4. Lib. 1, ff.132–47. The document was signed by Archbishop Adrian, Fonseca, Zapata, Antón Gallo and Juan de Sámano (an assistant to Los Cobos charged to receive documents relating to the Indies until that official returned from Germany).

28 E. Rodríguez Demorizi [36:24].

29 Diego Ortiz de Zúñiga, *Anales eclesiásticos y seculares de la muy noble y leal ciudad de Sevilla* (Madrid, 1796), III, 325–6, cit. Pike [6:48], 18.

30 Mendieta [13:64], I, 15.

31 The fact that Glapion was nominated for this post shows the seriousness with which the Pope, and presumably the Emperor, took the mission at this time. For Leo, see

Ludwig Pastor, *The History of the Popes* (tr. Frederick Antrobus, new ed. Lichtenstein, 1969), viii, 459–60.

32 Ordaz sailed from Hispaniola at the beginning of October. Otte [19:47], 410, published the passenger list.

33 The best account available of what happened seems to be that of Solís [15:55], II, 235. It is obscure whence he gained his material but, in this instance, it seems to be correct. See also Louis Gachard, *Correspondance de Charles Quint et d'Adrien VI* (Brussels, 1859).

34 García de Lerma, a favourite merchant of Fonseca, slave- and pearl-dealer, may have been as important as Ayllón. He must have heard Ordaz's reports. See Emelina Martín Acosta, "García de Lerma en la inicial penetración del capitalismo mercantil en América" [6:25], II, 439.

35 *CDI*, XII, 285–7. This document is dated 1525. Internal evidence suggests 1522.

36 Demetrio Ramos, in *El Consejo de las Indias* [6:81], 34. Martyr was a *de facto* member of it in the early summer of 1522 (Martyr, II 200).

37 C, 123.

38 Cardinal Guilio de' Medici who proposed Adrian (and would succeed him): Pastor [36:31], ix, 23. But Charles le Poupet (la Chaulx) had made clear who the Emperor favoured.

39 Brandi [6:50], 167.

40 Martyr, II, 200; for Vargas, see Pérez [23:52], 129, 193, and Carande [9:15], II, 83.

41 Gachard [36:33], 24.

42 John Pope-Hennessy, *Cellini* (London, 1985), 27–8.

43 In the 1550s, the Indians of Coyoacán successfully sued Cortés' son for land usurpation as a result of this occupation. See *"Docs Inéditos"*, 381.

44 Diego de Ordaz told Martyr (Martyr, II, 176).

45 Motolinía [1:1], 26.

46 See the case of Coyoacán, where the development can be illustrated by a family tree (Charles Gibson, "The Aztec Aristocracy in Colonial Mexico", *Comparative studies in Society and History* (The Hague, 1, October 1959):

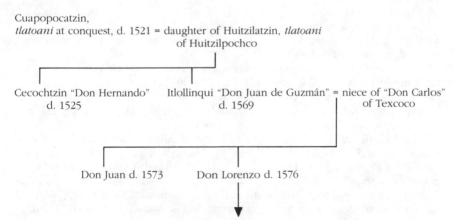

Cuapopocatzin,
tlatoani at conquest, d. 1521 = daughter of Huitzilatzin, *tlatoani*
of Huitzilpochco

Cecochtzin "Don Hernando"   Itlollinqui "Don Juan de Guzmán" = niece of "Don Carlos"
d. 1525   d. 1569   of Texcoco

Don Juan d. 1573   Don Lorenzo d. 1576

Last heir died in Spanish prison *c.* 1800 in lawsuit with Godoy

47 *¿Quién eres tú, quien te sientas junto al Capitán General?*
¡Ah es doña Isabel, mi sobrinita!
¡Ah es verdad, prisoneros son los reyes!

(*Cantares Mexicanos*, Biblioteca Nacional de México, quoted in Garibay [1:13], II, 94). This was, of course, Tecuichpo, known to the Spanish as "Doña Isabel", daughter of Montezuma, formerly married to both Cuitláhuac and Cuauhtémoc, subsequently married, in church, to 3 Spanish husbands one after another (Alonso de Grado, Pedro Gallego de Andrade, and Juan Cano). See Muriel [20:1], 229–45. Another Mexican princess who made a successful transition to Spanish life was Ana, daughter of Cacama, who married first Pedro Gutiérrez de Trujillo, and then Juan de Cuéllar, taking with her to both husbands the lands which her father had given her at birth. See the *Probanza* of 1531 of Juan de Cuéllar, in AGI, Mexico, 203, no. 11, including interesting evidence from Ana's relations.

48 Domingo ... Chimalpahin, *Séptimo Relación*, in Silvia Rendón, *Relaciones Originales de Chalco Amaquemacan* (Mexico, 1965).

49 Pedro de Maluenda to Hernando de Castro, 15 October 1521, in AGI, Justicia, leg. 712, cit. Otte [6:56], 258.

50 Letter of Luis de Cárdenas, 15 July 1528, in García Izcabalceta, II, 25–7.

51 Vázquez de Tapia, in *CDI*, XXVI, 424.

52 For example, Antonio de Villanueva, in Res (Rayón), II, 226.

53 Marcos Ruiz, in Res (Rayón), II, 117.

54 *CDI*, XXVII, 34.

55 Alfonso Pérez, García del Pilar, Juan Coronel and Francisco Verdugo, in Res (Rayón), II, 164, II, 218, I, 377, and I, 373.

56 AGI, Justicia, leg. 224, p.1, f.189.

57 Presumably Queen Juana, AGI, Justicia, leg. 224, p.1, f.152. See Documents, page 637.

58 *MS anónimo de Tlatelolco, 1528*, quoted in León-Portilla [4:33], 164; Gerhard [8:60], 178.

59 *Anales de Tlatelolco*, in Léon-Portilla [4:33], 76.

60 *MS anónimo de Tlatelolco, 1528* [36:58] quoted in León-Portilla [4:33], 164.

61 D del C, II, 125, says that the ringleaders were Juan Tirado, Gregorio de Villalobos and Juan de Mansilla.

62 Martyr, II, 277.

63 D del C, II, 123.

64 Juan de Mansilla, in Res (Rayón), I, 266.

65 Chimalpahin, *Séptimo Relación*, [36:48], implied that about 5 prisoners were tortured, but no one else does.

66 For example, question 200 in the questionnaire in his *residencia* asked about "that torment which was given to Guatinuca [*sic*] in order that he should say where the treasure of Montezuma was at the request of Julián de Alderete" (*CDI*, XXVII, 382).

67 Tapia, in AGI, Justicia, leg. 223, p.2, f.309; Terrazas, in AGI, Justicia, leg. 224, p.1, f.189; Salcedo in AGI, Justicia, leg. 224, p.1, f.660.

68 D del C, II, 122. Others who testified later that Alderete had taken the initiative included García Llerena (*CDI*, XXVII, 239–40); Martín Valdés (*CDI*, XXVIII, 180); and Luis Marín, present at the torture (*CDI*, XXVIII, 60). All said that the torture was "at the petition and request of the said Julián de Alderete". Alonso de Villanueva said that Alderete "importuned often" to have the ex-Emperor tortured (*CDI*, XXVII, 576–7) and that the torments were decided upon "against the wishes [*contra la voluntad*] of Cortés."

69 Cristóbal de Ojeda, a doctor charged by Cortés to look after the wounds, testified that the hands, as well as the feet of Cuauhtémoc, were burned ("*quemava los pies e las manos al dicho Guatimuza*"), in Res (Rayón), I, 126. Most writers suggest that this torment occurred immediately after the fall of Tenochtitlan. It is likely that it occurred now because of the time needed for Alderete's insistences to bear fruit. The Anales Tolteca-Chichimeca (Mexico, 1949) also say that the torture was in 1522.

70 "the said Guatimuza tied himself up on a tree in order to hang himself" ("*se colgó de un arbol para se ahorcar*") Francisco de Zamora, Res (Rayón), II, 303–4.

71 "*si estaba él en algun deleite o baño*" (G, 314). For a discussion of this phrase, and its link with "heroic" literature, see María Rosa Lida, "Estar en(un) baño, estar en un lecho de rosas", *Revista de Filología Hispánica*, III, (1941), 263.

72 Martín Valdés, in *CDI*, XXVIII, 180: "and this witness saw the torment given to the said Guatinuca; and he saw that he only gave what valued scarcely anything".

73 D del C, II, 123–4; G, 314.

74 Francisco de Zamora, Res (Rayón), II, 303–4.

75 Cortés' figure in his letters (C, 272) was in castellanos, so was López de Gómara's (G, 315). 200,000 pesos first appeared in a letter of Pedro de Maluenda, Narváez's and then Cortés' commissary, to Hernando de Castro in Cuba, in October 1521 (AGI, Justicia, leg. 712, cit. Otte [6:56], 258). But it also probably figured in a letter of Cortés written in late August 1521 and now lost, arriving in Spain on 1 March 1522, but mentioned in the postscript to Cortés' second letter published by Cromberger in Seville in September 1522. It was echoed in the evidence of Cortés' friends at the *residencia* (*CDI*, XXVII, 23).

76 *CDI*, XII.

77 185,000 minus 37,000 = 148,000; ⅕ of that last figure = 29,600.

78 C, 271.

79 G, 315.

80 Vázquez de Tapia's (biased) evidence, in *CDI*, XXVI, 411.

81 See the answers to question 13 in Santa Cruz's defence in De la Peña vs Santa Cruz, in Conway (L of C), I, 45, 77; for the last statement, see Cerezo evidence in Conway (L of C), I, 45, 109.

82 This was Díaz del Castillo's figure (D del C, II, 124).

83 See Pagden's note to C, 492.

84 *CDI*, XXVIII, 123. See AGI, Mexico, leg. 203, no. 9, for his Nahuatl.

85 Res (Rayón), II, 121.

86 E.g. in *CDI*, XXVI, 497.

87 *CDI*, XXVII, 237.

88 Res (Rayón), II, 222.

89 Res (Rayón), I, 449.

90 Ixtlilxochitl, *Decimatercia Relación* [4:5], 50–1.

91 Res (Rayón), II, 219.

92 This point is made by Pasztory [4:35], 208.

Chapter 37

1 Gerhard [8:60], 148; D del C, II, 127. For the frontier spirit, see Guillermo Céspedes del Castillo, "Los hombres de las fronteras", in *Proceso histórico al conquistador* ed. Francisco Solano (Seville, 1988), 37–9: "God is in Heaven, the King is in Castile, and I am here."

2 Wright [5:50], 92–3.

3 D del C, II, 131.

4 C, 278.

5 *CDI*, XXVII, 16–17.

6 Res (Rayón), I, 365.

7 Monjaraz, in Res (Rayón), II, 74.

8 *CDI*, XXVII, 227.

9 Res (Rayón), II, 143.

10 C, 279: "*había tentado algunas cosas escandalosas*". Andrés de Tapia suggested that he had (merely) been selling goods (*CDI*, XXVI, 30–6).

11 *CDI*, XXVI, 30.

12 Evidence of Andrés de Monjaraz, in *CDI*, XXVI, 547–8.

13 C, 275.

14 John Elliott, in his intr. to Pagden's ed. [10:73] of the *Cartas de Relación*, xxix; Ursula Lamb, "Cristóbal de Tapia vs. Nicolás de Ovando" [36:24].

15 Ortiz de Zúñiga later had a suit against Cortés and was a hostile witness at the *residencia* and other occasions. See *CDI*, XXVI, 126; *CDI*, XXVII, 126; and *CDI*, XXVIII, 100. Also Conway, (Camb.), Add. 7284, 36–45 and Add. 7286, II, 69.

16 Monjaraz evidence, *CDI*, XXVI, 548.

17 Andrés de Monjaraz said: "*Sandoval le echaría en una canoa por esa mar syno quería yrse en su navio como avía venido*" (Res (Rayón), II, 56); *CDI*, XXVII, 228; *CDI*, XXVI, 36–58.

18 *CDI*, XXVII, 19.

19 Evidence of Valdenebro, in Conway, (Camb.), Add. 7284, 15–16.

20 Evidence of Andrés de Monjaraz, in Res (Rayón), II, 57.

21 *CDI*, XXVI, 518. It was later alleged in Cortés' defence that Olid and Alderete, with over 100 seamen with whom they were in touch, made a plan to kill Cortés (*CDI*, XXVII, 227–8).

22 *CDI*, XXVII, 18.

23 *CDI*, XXVII, 231.

24 D del C, II, 132.

25 Polavieja, 290–308.

26 C, 294.

27 C, 295. Giménez Fernández, in his "Hernán Cortés y su revolución comunera en Nueva España", *AEA*, V (1948), implied that Cortés had already done this.

28 *CDI*, XL, 74ff.

29 D del C, II, 140, II, 291, II, 450; Gibson [2:15], 416.

30 *Inf. de 1522*, 113–23 and 230–4. There were 11 witnesses.

31 Gerhard [8:60], 149.

32 Gerhard [8:60], 264.

33 D del C, II, 159.

34 AGI, Justicia, leg. 1030, p.2. quoted in Wagner [8:23], 388: Cortés' answer is in Cuevas [6:57], ix.

35 The phrase was that of the painter Miguel Covarrubias.

36 Gerhard [8:60], 141.

37 Gerhard [8:60], 138; C de S, 805; Alonso de Grado and Licenciado Ledesma would also have an *encomienda* there.

38 *Rel. de Michoacan*, 246, and fn.

39 Cervantes de Salazar devotes much space to Montano's visit since Montano told him of it.

40 Evidence of Andrés de Tapia, AGI, Justicia, leg. 223, p.2, f.309 v.

41 *Rel. de Michoacan*, 264–6.

42 "*Débenlo de comer estos dioses por eso lo quieren tanto*" (*Rel. de Michoacan*, 260).

43 *Rel. de Michoacan*, 248–56. Gerhard [8:60], 343–53.

44 Gerhard [8:60], 78–82; see also Carl Sauer, "Colima of New Spain in the sixteenth century", *Ibero-Americana*, 29 (Berkeley, 1948).

45 D del C, II, 157.

46 C, 123.

47 Letter in *De Orbe Novo*, II, 283. See Pagden [10:73], 505, for a discussion as to why it was so widely supposed to exist.

48 *"señor de más reinos y señoríos que hasta hoy en nuestra nación se tiene noticia"* (C, 277).

49 C, 325.

50 Francisco Verdugo, a hostile witness, said he remembered going into Cortés' house, where the *Caudillo* had just learned of the arrival of some ships which he believed to be Garay's, and said: "we are going to Pánuco to throw that Garay out of the country" (Res (Rayón), I, 366).

51 The same name, but not the same place, as Tututepec in what is now Guerrero province, to which Alvarado had gone earlier.

52 G, 307.

53 Gerhard [8:60], 214, gave the figure of a million.

54 C, 297; D del C, II, 137.

55 C, 297.

56 Ixtlilxochitl, *Decimatercia Relación* [4:5], 389–90. See also a letter from Pablo Nazareo, in which it was stated that Cuauhtémoc, with his relation "Don Juan Axayaca", pacified Mexico, to prevent anyone from contradicting the Castilians, and then began to conquer other provinces (*Epistolario*, X, 109–29).

57 Cortés sent back to Spain a plan of this building, known as the Atarazanas of Mexico, but it does not seem to be extant.

58 C, 277.

59 George Kubler, *Mexican Architecture of the Sixteenth Century* (New Haven, 1948, 2 vols.), I, 70–1.

60 *CDI*, XXVII, 255.

61 G, 340.

62 C, 320.

63 Res (Rayón), I, 60–1: *"todos quisieran que fuera la población en Cuyuacán"*. Others who attacked the decision included Gonzalo Mexía, Rodrigo de Castañeda, Ruy González, Juan de Tirado, Marcos Ruiz, Domingo Niño, Antonio de Carvajal, and Alfonso Ortiz de Zúñiga.

64 Rodrigo de Castañeda, in Res (Rayón), I, 235: "healthier places nearer the mountains with more water and . . . where houses can be built without so much trouble".

65 See Manuel Carrera Stampa, "El Autor o Autores de la Traza", in *MAMH*, XIX (1960), 167–75, who argued that Bernardino Vázquez de Tapia was also involved in the delineation of the *traza*. See José R. Benítez, *Alonso García Bravo, planeador de la ciudad de México* (Mexico, 1933).

66 Replies of witnesses to question 9 in *probanza* of July 1561, in Mexico, cit. Carrera Stampa [37:65], 169, and Manuel Toussaint, *Información de méritos y servicios de Alonso García Bravo* (Mexico, 1956).

67 *Life in the Imperial and Loyal City of Mexico in New Spain . . . as described in the dialogues for the study of the Latin language prepared by Francisco Cervantes de Salazar (1554)*, ed. M. L. B. Shephard with notes by C. E. Castañeda (Austin, 1953), 38.

68 See Graziano Gasparini, *Formación Urbana de Venezuela*, (Caracas, 1991), Ch. 1.

69 As usual, there was a medieval precedent. Thus when King James the Conqueror captured Murcia in the 13th century, "the Muslim authorities asked me to divide the town as agreed . . . I said that, from the mosque and the Alcázar down to the gate facing my camp, should belong to the Christians" (MacKay [7:47], 63).

70 In May 1522, Cortés wrote that the building had already been under way for 4 or 5 months. An account of the rebuilding was given by Juan de Ribera (who left Mexico in May) to Martyr (II, 193).

71 Juan de Burgos, in Res (Rayón), I, 148.

72 Manuel Toussaint, "El criterio artistico de Hernán Cortés", *Estudios Americanos*, vol.1, no.1 (1948).

73 Joan de Tirado, in Res (Rayón), I, 39.
74 Ixtlilxochitl, *Sumaria Relación*, in *Obras Históricas* [22:18], 386.
75 Motolinía [1:1], 19.
76 See Braudel [9:15], I, 284, and references there, for a lyrical statement about the role of this wonderful animal, probably in use in Mexico by 1522.
77 Kubler [37:59], II, 421; "*e son amigos de novedades*", in evidence at the *residencia*, *CDI*, XXVIII, 52 and 167.

Chapter 38

1 Alaminos or Juan de Burgos must have informed Cortés of the state of political life in Spain.
2 A copy of this so-called "third letter" of Cortés is to be seen in AGI, Patronato, leg. 16, R.1, no.1, and was printed by Cromberger in Seville, 30 March, 1523.
3 Cortés, in Pascual Gayangos, *Cartas y Relaciones de Hernán Cortés al emperador Carlos V* (Paris, 1866), 26.
4 This letter was published by Fr. Mariano Cuevas, in his *Cartas y otros documentos* [6:57], 129–40, but is there dated 1533. As suggested earlier (in Ch.35), Abel Martínez Luza argues that this letter was written in 1522. Cortés sent another power of attorney to his father Martín, a copy of which can be seen in Muñoz, vol. 4. f.258.
5 This figure and the figure of 50,000 (of which 9,000 pesos was less than ⅕) derive from the sums done by Clarence Haring, for "Ledgers of the Royal treasurers in Spanish America in the sixteenth century", in *HAHR*, 2 (1919), 174–5.
6 The register of the ship, with an inventory of the gold and other objects, signed by Alderete, Grado and Vázquez de Tapia, on behalf of the "municipal council" (*cabildo*) of Mexico, is to be seen in Saville [14:31], 79–96. The list of goods has been often published, e.g. in Polavieja, 138–43, and Martínez, *Docs*, I, 242–53.
7 Giménez Fernández [6:19], II, 482. Vega was "*fundidor y marcador de oro*" of Cuba, but he also had property and Indians in Hispaniola, as earlier indicated.
8 Las Casas, II, 396 ("*el rey chiquito*").
9 Martínez, *Docs*, I, 245–6.
10 Munzer, in *Viajes* [5:20], 374; Navagero, in *Viajes* [5:20], 884. La Cartuja was the site of the great "Expo" of 1992.
11 In his will of 1524, Diego Velázquez gave money to the chapel of la Antigua, as to two other intended beneficiaries of Cortés: Guadelupe and Santiago de Compostela (*CDI*, XXXV, 520).
12 See the journal of the Armenian Bishop of "Arzendján", Armenio Mártir, in 1492, in *Viajes* [5:20], 424.
13 Chaunu [5:38], II, 130.
14 Martínez, *Docs*, 225–9.
15 This is Díaz del Castillo's summary of the letter, in D del C, II, 141. The letter does not seem to have survived. The fact that this expression about the thread was used now, as in Díaz's summary of the attitude of the *Audiencia* of Santo Domingo towards the nomination of Tapia, suggests that it was a phrase in common use.
16 D del C, II, 144–5, says that Alonso de Ávila sent the letters to Spain after his imprisonment.
17 Luis de Cárdenas, letter to Charles V, 30 August 1527, in *CDI*, XL, 276.
18 "*una ensalada que le dieron al tiempo que se quería embarcar*": evidence of Francisco de Orduña and Domingo Niño, Res (Rayón), I, 441, and Res (Rayón), II, 137. Orduña had become an enemy of Cortés since he had been punished for blasphemy (*CDI*, XXVIII, 127).

19 Martyr, II, 178.

20 French sources say that Quiñones was killed in action. See Antonio Rumeu de Armas, *Piraterías y Ataques navales contra las Islas Canarias* (Madrid, 1947), I, 32. Ávila said the same, in a letter to Charles V.

21 D del C, II, 143. Jean Fleury was captured in 1525 on another piratical expedition and hanged with his captains Michel Fère and Meziéres. He offered his captor, Martín Pérez de Irizar, 30,000 ducats to help him escape. Pérez refused and was made a nobleman as a result. Ávila remained a prisoner in La Rochelle for 3 years before being exchanged after the battle of Pavia (C de S, 752). See his letter to Charles V describing the battle, in Muñoz, A/103. Other letters about it can be seen in the same collection, ff.288–9.

22 For Fleury and Ango, see Eugéne Guénin, *Ango et ses pilotes* (Paris, 1901).

23 A. Thomazi, *Les flottes d'or* (Paris, 1956).

24 Parmentier discovered Fernambouc in 1520, travelled to China in 1529, and was killed in Sumatra in 1530. He translated Sallust and composed poems as well as masques.

25 Thomazi [38:23], 45; Charles de la Roncière, *Histoire de la Marine* (Paris, 1934), 249.

26 Martyr, II, 356.

27 Guénin [38:22], Ch. II.

28 For the frieze there is, unsatisfactorily, Pierre Margry, *Les navigateurs français* (Paris, 1867), 371; and, for the tomb, A. Chastel, "Masques méxicains à la renaissance", *Art de la France*, I, (1961), 299, as well as N. Dacos, "Presents américains à la renaissance", *Gazette des Beaux Arts*, LXXIII, (1969), 57–64, who doubts the Mexican inspiration of the tomb in Rouen, and considers the Liège capitals the only sure sign of Mexican influence. The tomb, whose details are the work of Arnoult de Nimègue (for whom, see Jean Lafond's *La résurrection d'un maître d'autrefois . . .*, Paris, 1942), was finished in 1523. For the connection, see Elizabeth Chirol, *Le château de Gaillon* (Paris, 1952), 245, in which she asks the question, "Ango, n'était-il pas le protégé de Georges d'Amboise?"

29 See Suzanne Collon-Gevaert, "Érard de la Marck et les palais des princes-évêques de Liége" (Liége, 1975). For the "intimacy" of the two cardinals, achieved during a French campaign against Venice, see J. de Chestel de Haneffe, *Histoire de la maison de la Marck* (Liège, 1898), 170.

30 Fernández-Armesto [18:34], 28.

31 Martyr, II, 365.

32 Martyr, II, 277–8.

33 Chaunu [5:38], II, 132.

Chapter 39

1 Probably written by Cromberger himself, the postscript (C, 181–2) states baldly how "Temixtitan" had been captured the previous August.

2 This bull, *Charissimo in Christo*, dated Saragossa, 9 May 1522, can be seen in Mendieta [13:64], 128–9.

3 Brandi [6:50], 169. I have failed to find an English source.

4 Wagner [8:23], 513, n.80, thought that the reference to the brigantines in the French tract, *Les contrées des iles et des paysages trouvés et conquis par le capitain du très illustre, très puissant, et invincible Charles, élu empereur romain* (Anvers, not dated but probably early 1523), proved that the author, and therefore probably Charles V, had seen the letter of March.

5 Manuel Foronda y Aguilera, *Estancias y Viajes de Carlos V* (Madrid, 1910), 24.

6 See *cédula* of 8 May 1523 (AGI, Indif. Gen. leg. 420, no. 15) naming Beltrán to be a life member of that body ("*agora y de aquí adelant para en toda vuestra vida seades uno de los de nuestro Consejo de las Indias*").

7 G, 344, said that Fonseca swore that the letters of Cortés would never see the light of day whilst he was alive. This would explain the disappearance of Cortés' first letter, if indeed Fonseca was unwise enough to say such a thing.

8 Giménez Fernández [23:44], 15.

9 Giménez Fernández [6:19], II, 781.

10 For Núñez on this committee, see Cuevas [6:57], 262. Ordaz was at this time in great difficulty, being accused of having illegally sold pearls in Lisbon (Muñoz, A/103, f. 307).

11 G, 328; in a house belonging to a certain Alonso de Argüello.

12 Martyr, II, 178; see a note by Juan Bautista Muñoz on a copy of the *Información de Segura* (Tepeaca), 4 September 1520, in his Vol.4, f. 250.

13 6,000 ducats were paid on 4 November 1521 in San Sebastián by the Genoese Nicolás de Grimaldo, for the war against François I, and he was reimbursed "with gold from Hernán Cortés and his *procuradores*" (Carande [9:15], III, 69). Carande's source was, I expect, Muñoz, A/103, f. 279v.

14 There were about 23 death sentences. About 20 people died in prison before they could be tried. Perhaps 100 *comuneros* finally paid with their lives for rebellion. As Pérez rightly comments [23:52], 633, this was not too harsh for a revolt which put the foundations of the state to the test. Compare the 20th century!

15 Thus José Gestos, in his *Historia y descripción de la sacristía mayor*, in the cathedral of Seville (Seville, 1892), 5, says that decoration of that sacristy began to be considered then.

16 Martyr, II, 200. Juan Dantisco, the Polish ambassador, would write in 1524 that "he had never seen the court so poor", in *Boletín de la Real Academia*, (1924).

17 AGI, Indif. Gen., leg. 420, lib. 8, ff. 314–15.

18 AGI, Justicia, leg. 220. p. 2. f. 128.

19 *CDI*, XXVI, 59–65.

20 This is in *CDIHE*, I, 97. See *CDI*, XXVI, 65–70.

21 Oviedo, II, 389.

22 Manuel Fernández Álvarez, "Hernán Cortés y Carlos V", in *Hernán Cortés, Actas del Primer Congreso Internacional Sobre . . .* (Salamanca, 1986).

23 The Latin ran "*contra Cortesii vafros astus et ardentem avariciam ac semiapertam tyrannidem formatae sunt*" (*De Orbe Novo*, 1527, 8th Decade, Ch. 10). There were 6 decrees (*cédulas*) on 15 October: the 3 mentioned in the text, one dealing with Cortés' salary, another discussing how much should be given to the conquistadors, and a final one about bridges and causeways. See texts in Beatriz Arteaga Garza and Guadalupe Pérez san Vicente, *Cedulario Cortesiano* (Mexico, 1949), 49–56.

24 For Ovando, see Pérez de Tudela [5:40], 206; for Pedrarias, see Mena García [6:12], 32; for the *piloto mayor*, see Schäfer [6:79], 21. The porter in the Casa de la Contratación received 10,000 maravedís a year (Schäfer [6:79], 48).

25 AGI, Indif. Gen., leg. 420, no. 15, for Beltrán.

26 Andrea Calvo, *News of the Islands and the Mainland*, tr., with notes, by Edward Tuttle (Labrynthos, 1985). Publication must have been between May 1522 and March 1523, when the Calvos fled Milan.

27 Martínez-Luza [7:3], 3–28.

28 Martyr, II, 245.

29 Felix Gilbert, "The date of the composition of Contarini's and Giannotti's Books on Venice", *Studies in the Renaissance*, 14 (1967), 172–84.

30 Martyr, II, 197. Ribera started speaking adversely of Cortés. He refused to hand over money intended for Cortés' father. A lawsuit ensued. Some years later (though not before he returned once to Mexico), Ribera died suddenly, as happened with remarkable regularity to the enemies of Cortés, at Cadalso, in a remote part of Extremadura, after eating a rasher of bad bacon.

31 C, 285.

32 *CDI*, XII, 474–5, and C, 285. See Silvio Zavala, "Hernán Cortés ante la encomienda", in *Hernán Cortés en su época* (Madrid, 1986), 77–85.

33 C, 285. The best introduction remains Gibson [2:15], Ch. 1 and Appendix I. See also Silvio Zavala, *La Encomienda Indiana* (2nd ed. Mexico, 1973) and, now, Robert Hemmerich, *The First Encomenderos of New Spain* (Austin, 1991).

34 Zumárraga to the King, 27 August 1527, in *CDI*, XIII, 107: "*a importunación de Julián de Alderete*".

35 Alvarado's *encomienda* in Jalapa, 24 August 1522, cit. Res vs Alvarado, 177.

36 Zavala [39:33], 323.

37 *CDI*, XIII, 293–4: Gibson [2:15], 433.

38 Conway, "Hernando Alonso . . ." [32:13], 13. Alonso, now a widower, later married the beautiful Isabel de Aguilar, daughter of a one-eyed tailor, whom he forbade to go to church during her menstrual periods: this was a charge against him which led to his condemnation and burning in 1528 for "secret jewish practices". He was the first Jew thus to be burned in Mexico.

39 Evidence of Rodrigo de Castañeda, in Res (Rayón), I, 235.

40 Henry Wagner tried ([8:23], 372–7) to compare tribute extracted from Tepetlaoztoc (Texcoco) in Mexican and Spanish times. So did José de la Peña Cámara in his *El Tributo* (Seville, 1934), suggesting that Indians gave 6 times more in the 1590s than they had under Montezuma.

41 See comments of Vázquez de Tapia, Gonzalo de Mexía, Ojeda, Juan Coronel, Francisco Verdugo, and Rodrigo de Castañeda (in Pesquisa Secreta, in AGI, Justicia, leg. 220).

42 José Matesanz, "Introducción de la ganadería en Nueva España", in *HM*, XIV, (April–June 1965).

43 Martyr, II, 357.

44 *Codex Magliabecchiano (Book of the Life of the Ancient Mexicans)*, ed. Zelia Nuttall (Berkeley, 1903), 72v.

45 Pedro de Gante himself once hinted at their relationship when he wrote to Charles V: "Your Majesty and I know well how we are so close as to have the same blood running in our veins". See Ernesto de la Torre Villar, *Fray Pedro de Gante*, in *Estudios de Historia Novohispana*, V, 9–77.

46 Miguel León-Portilla, "Testimonios nahuas sobre la conquista espiritual", *ECN*, xi (1974), 11–36. This theme is imaginatively followed by J. Jorge Klor de Alva, in "Spiritual conquest and accommodation in New Spain", in Collier, et al. [1:9], 345–62.

47 *Rel. de Michoacan*, 264.

48 Andrés de Duero, in Polavieja, 218.

49 Francisco de Orduña, in Res (Rayón), II, 309.

50 He was accused by Vázquez de Tapia of having "had relations with at least forty Mexican women" since 1519. That Marina had been used to live with him in his own house is clear from a remark of Cortés himself: thus, when accused of having a private foundry to melt down gold, he said that the Indians whom his enemies saw coming to his house, and whom they supposed to be metallurgists, "were bringing fruit, tobacco and other things to Doña Marina" (García Llerena, *CDI*, XXVII, 239).

51 Bernal Díaz says that Cortés was sorry to see her but did not show it. He must have learned that from hearsay, since he was himself enjoying the first years of his *encomienda* near Coatzalcalcos (D del C, II, 155).

52 Wagner [8:23], 407, showed that Martín must have been born between 19 July 1522 and 19 July 1523.

53 "*les vido fazer vida maridable como tal marido e muxer*" (*CDI*, XXVI, 322).

54 *"alegre e recoxada e sana, sin enfermedad alguna"*.

55 *"vo os promete que antes de muchos días, haré de manera que no tenga nadie que entender con lo mío"*.

56 *"con lo vuestro, señora, yo no quiero nada"*.

57 Isidro Moreno, in *CDI*, XXVI, 340.

58 *"Ay, señora, algún día me habeis de hallar muerta"*: *CDI*, XXVI, 349.

59 *Echóla por la garganta*
   Una toca que tenía,
   Apretó con las dos manos
   Con la fuerza que podía
(*BAE*, X, 227).

60 The evidence for all this is in the *residencia* (AGI, Justicia, leg. 220. ff. 316–42), but the testimony of Cortés' household was ed. in *CDI*, XXVI, 298 ff., including that of Ana Rodríguez, Elvira Hernández, Antonia Rodríguez, etc. Fr. Olmedo's advice was, according to Juan de Burgos, that Cortés should have the body examined by a doctor, with a lawyer, before it was put into a coffin (Juan de Burgos, in the *residencia* against Cortés, in Res (Rayón, I, 160–2).

61 Res (Rayón), II, 197 and 217.

62 For example, Wagner [8:23], 408 and Martínez [9:52], 561. There is also the denunciation by Alfonso Toro, *Un crimen de Hernán Cortés* (Mexico, 1922), and, effectively, a defence by Angel Altolaguirre, "Prueba Historica de la inocencia de Hernán Cortés en la muerte de su esposa", *BRAH* (1920), lxxvi.

63 Suárez de Peralta [9:38], 76–7. *Mal de madre (matrix)* was also called *Pasión histérica*.

64 Suárez de Peralta [9:38], 77.

65 See evidence of Francisco Osorio, Antonio Velázquez and Pedro de Xerez in *Docs Inéditos* no. xxvii, 34–78.

66 AGI, Justicia, leg. 224, p.1, f.722 r.

67 AGI, Justicia, leg. 223, p.2, f.511 r.

68 AGI, Justicia, leg. 224, p.1, f.789 v. and f.457 v. One of the first free Africans to establish themselves in Mexico, he was said to have been the first man to grow wheat there.

69 AGI, Justicia, leg. 224, p.1, f.94v.

70 AGI, Justicia, leg. 224, p.1, f.189r.

71 AGI, Justicia, leg. 224, p.1, f.378 r. and leg. 223, p.2, f.648 v.

72 Cuevas [6:57].

73 *"han echado con la dicha marina"* (Res (Rayón), II, 102).

74 Res (Rayón), II, 117.

75 Motolinía's letter of 1555 to Charles V, in *CDI*, VII, 254–89. An attempt to blacken the name of Motolinía was made by Nuño de Guzmán in 1529 by asking for evidence that he was excessively in favour of Cortés, for which see the questionnaire, questions 18 to 20, and testimony by Juan de Burgos, García del Pilar, Gerónimo Ruiz de la Mota, and Antonio Serrano de Cardona (*CDI*, XL, 468–570).

76 See evidence in "Juicio seguido por Hernán Cortés contra los Lics. Matienzo y Delgadillo" (1529), in the *Boletín del Archivo General de la Nación*, IX, 3 (July–August 1938), 403–40.

77 See report of the suit [39:65]; and also Francisco Fernández del Castillo, *Doña Catalina* (Mexico, 1926), 17.

78 This permission is in Martín Fernández de Navarrete, *Colección de los viajes y descubrimientos que hicieron por mar los Españoles desde fines del siglo XV* (Madrid, 1825–37), III, 147. Perhaps Garay's interest had been excited by Judge Zuazo: see Ana Gimeno Gómez's study of Zuazo's interest in the "strait" [6:25].

79 This mythical lady is mentioned in a letter dated 21 September 1522 of Francisco de Herrera in Cuba to Hernando de Castro then in Seville (in Otte [6:56], 275), and by Alonso de Zuazo, after seeing Cortés' treasure fleet of 1522 in Santo Domingo.

80 Andrés de Monjaraz, in Res (Rayón), II, 74-5.

81 E. Rodríguez Demorizi [6:27], 84.

82 Perhaps the river Palmas was the modern River Barbarena.

83 Martyr, II, 334,

84 Sancho Pizarro, Gonzalo de Figueroa, and Diego Ruiz de Carrión, in an enquiry carried out in December 1523 (CDI, XXVI, 77-135).

85 This was signed 23 April 1523 and read out at a meeting of the "municipality of Mexico" on 3 September 1523.

86 C, 304.

87 Evidence of Hernando Alonso Herrera and Gonzalo Sánchez de Colmenares, in Conway, (Camb.), Add. 7284, 53 and 60.

88 CDI, XXVII, 396. This was a daughter born in Cuba, probably by Leonor Pizarro.

89 "syn duda yo estoy mortal" (Res (Rayón), I, 284).

90 Cortés' account of the affaire Garay can be seen in García Llerena's evidence in reply to question 59 of the main questionnaire of the residencia against Cortés, in CDI, XXVII, 261-4. See also Cortés' questionnaire, questions 227-38, in CDI, XXVII, 395-7. There is much about Garay in Cortés' fourth letter and in Martyr, II, 331-45.

91 "mal tratamiento y demasiado trabajo". This was in a decree of 23 June 1523 (printed in CDI, XXIII, 353-68, as by Cardenas [15:32], 240-5) brought to Mexico at the same time as all the other decrees of the previous October. For the reception by the Crown of Cortés' letter about encomiendas, see Martyr's account in Martyr, II, 184.

92 Cuevas [6:57], xxv; Martyr, II, 350.

93 CDI, XXVI, 80; CDI, XXVI, 131; G, 311; CDI, XXVI, 521; C, 310.

94 Medellín papers, leg. 5, 30 (Archivo de la casa de Medellín, Casa de Pilatos). That Cortés preferred the title is confirmed by his use of it as his first title when he sought to become a member of the Order of Santiago (AHN, Santiago, cit. BRAH, 1892, 20-1, 191).

95 Martyr, II, 350-1.

96 "como rey e señor asoluto", in the words of Gonzalo de Mexía (Pesquisa Secreta, in AGI, Justicia, leg. 220.

97 Mendieta [13:64], I, 128, on the basis of a relation of Juan de Villagómez, at that time in Cortés' service.

98 "Aquí principió la fe" (Codex Aubin [4:8], 62).

99 Mendieta [13:64] I, 203-4. For Fr. Martín de Valencia, see his life by Fr. Francisco Jiménez, a companion of his, ed. in Archivo Ibero-Americano, xxvi(1926), 48-83.

100 For a good introduction, see Duverger [1:44], Ch. 1.

101 This subject is discussed in Muriel [22:92], 105-6. Tezozomoc, who was related to Cuauhtémoc, says that he was baptised, but only in 1525, just before he was hanged [1:18] 338-9.

102 There are hints of these obscure events in Ixtlilxochitl, Decimatercia Relación, 57, as in Motolinía [1:1], 20.

103 For the date see Duverger [1:44], 40.

104 Coloquios [29:13]. Mendieta had written of the meeting ([13:64], I, 130-1). The best study of the background is Duverger [1:44], 43-125. There is some doubt about the validity of this text which was obviously worked upon by Sahagún.

105 Cantares Mexicanos, quoted in Bierhorst [13:38], 62.

Epilogue

1 Miguel León-Portilla, "Axayacatl, poeta y señor de Tenochtitlan," *ECN*, vi (1966).

2 For Gande's letter, 27 June 1529, see García Icazbalceta, (1954), 103. There were then still "open chapels" in Seville; outside San Francisco and San Salvador. See Emilio Gómez Piñol, "Arquitectura y ornamentación en los primeros atrios Franciscanos" [6:25].

3 See Cisneros' speech about the conversion of 50,000 in 1500, cit. Hillgarth [5:24], II, 424.

4 *Cartas de Indias* (Madrid, 1877), 65; Duverger [1:44], 153.

5 For Tastera, see the article of Fidel Chauvet, *Estudios de Historia Novohispana*, III, 7–33.

6 Miguel León-Portilla, "Testimonios nahuas sobre la conquista espiritual", *ECN*, xi (1974); Motolinía [1:1], I, 210.

7 Cit. Robert Ricard, *La "conquête spirituelle" du Méxique* (Paris, 1933), 91.

8 Anderson, et al., [19:79], 199; letter of 9 October 1587, tr. from Nahuatl. See for an extended treatment James Lockhart, *Nahuas and Spaniards* (New York, 1991).

9 Camargo, 233–40.

10 Durán, in the 1560s, wrote, "The ancient beliefs are still so numerous, so complex, so similar to our own in many cases, that the one overlaps the other. Occasionally we suspect that they are playing, really adoring idols, casting lots about the future before our very eyes" (Durán, I, 5–6).

11 Mendieta [13:64] II, 738.

12 Juan Tetón, 1558, Archivo Capitular de Guadalupe, cit. León-Portilla [39:46], 31.

13 *Proceso inquisitorial del cacique de Texcoco* (Mexico, 1910), 49.

14 *Procesos de Indios idolatrías y hechiceros* (Mexico, 1912), 205–15.

15 Hernando Ruiz de Alarcón, Pedro Sánchez de Aguilar, and Gonzalo de Balsalobre, *Tratado de las idolatrías . . .* (Mexico, 1953), 102, cit. Anderson [16:63], 32.

16 Gordon F.Ekholm, "Wheeled toys in Mexico", *American Antiquity*, 11, no. 4 (1946); Res (Rayon), II, 68; Robert Lister in *American Antiquity*, 3 (1947), 185).

17 Kubler [37:59], II, 1221.

18 Armillas [2:15], 58.

19 George Kubler, "On the colonial extinction of the motifs of pre-Colombian art", in S. K. Lothrop, *Essays in precolombian art and archaeology* (Cambridge, Mass., 1961).

20 Pasztory [13:52], 104, 119.

21 Bernard Ortiz de Montellano, "Aztec Cannibalism: An Ecological Necessity?" *Science*, 200 (1978), 611–17.

22 Carlos Sempat Assadourián, "La despoblación indígena en Perú y Nueva España durante el siglo xvi . . .", *HM*, XXXVIII (1989), 420, warns against thinking that disease was the only reason.

23 Compare *Relación de Cholula* [13:50], where Gabriel Rojas, the *corregidor*, said that there were over 40,000 in the town in the past compared with 9,000 in 1582.

24 J. Klor de Alva, in Hugh Thomas, *The Real Discovery of America* (New York, 1992), 46.

25 This would be regarded as an underestimate by Juan Friede ("Algunas Observaciones sobre la realidad de la emigración española a América en la primera mitad del siglo XVI", *R de I*, XII (1952), 467–96).

26 Alfred W. Crosby, *Ecological Imperialism: the Biological Expansion* (Cambridge, Mass., 1986), 155.

27 Wigberto Jiménez Moreno, "Los Hallazgos de Ichcateopan", *HM*, XII (October–December 1962).

28 Muriel [22:92], 67.

29 *"Por su respecto y ejemplo mas quietud e reposo se imprime en los ánimos de los mejicanos"* (evidence of Juan Cano to Oviedo, IV, 260). For a study see Donald

Chipman, "Isabel Moctezuma: a pioneer of mestizaje", in Sweet and Nash [4:40], 1981.

30 Letter of 18 November 1598 to his nieces, in Anderson, et al. [19:79], 207.

31 In AGN, Hospital de Jesús, leg.285, expediente 99, f.152, her son Martín Cortés speaks in 1551 of her as living in a house belonging to Xoan Rodríguez Albaniz ("*en que bibe al presente Doña Marina*"). But a letter of Luis de Quesada, married to her daughter María (by Jaramillo), of 15 February 1552, speaks of her as dead in 1552. So much for Eulalia Guzmán's remark that nobody said when, where, and how she died ([7:17], 108).

32 See Georges Baudot, "Pretendientes al imperio mexicano en 1576", *HM*, LXXVII (1970), 42.

33 Oviedo, II, 150; Velázquez's will was drawn up in 1524, in Santiago, apparently proved in Cuéllar, 1530. The *residencia* heard before Licenciado Juan Altamirano (scarcely an encouraging name for the friends of Velázquez, though the relation with Cortés is not clear) began in June 1525 (AGI, leg. 49). Nothing shows more the change in the nature of the Spanish enterprise in America than this small-scale enquiry, with accusations about mules lent and not returned, and the illegal melting-down of tiny quantities of gold, compared with the colossal scale of the accusations later made against Cortés.

34 *Varia Velazqueña, Homenaje en el cuarto aniversario de su muerte* (Madrid, 1960), II, 303–77, publishes the painter's genealogy when applying for the Order of Santiago. This established that Jerónima Velázquez, the painter's mother, was daughter of Juan Velázquez and Catalina de Cayas (herself the daughter of Andrés de Buen Rostro), both of Seville. All the witnesses from Seville said that they knew Juan Velázquez, the painter's grandfather to have been *hijodalgo*, with the privilege of *blanca de carne* (a tax refund on meat bought: half a maravedí, *una blanca*, per pound purchase) and even "noble", along with Andrés de Buen Rostro. In the Libro de la Imposición de la Carne, 7 July 1600, Juan Velázquez and Andrés de Buen Rostro are both mentioned. But there the traces fade.

35 María Concepción García Sáiz and María Angeles Albert de León, "Exotismo y Belleza de una Cerámica", *Artes de México*, 14 (Mexico, 1991).

36 Otte [11:5].

37 Torquemada [1:24], I, 116.

38 D del C, II, 535.

39 The testimony of witnesses (Juan de Montoya, aged about 65, Diego López, aged about 50, Juan Núñez de Prado, then aged 80, etc.), relating to Cortés' entry in the Order of Santiago is in the *BRAH* xx–xxi (1893), 191–9.

40 A first-hand account of these years can be seen in the letter of Bishop Zumárraga to Charles V, 27 August 1529, in *CDI*, XIII, 104.

41 Oviedo, IV, 242 (on the evidence of Fr. Diego de Loaysa, who accompanied Cortés from Vera Cruz to Havana).

42 Howard Cline, "Hernando Cortés y los Indios Aztecas en España", *Norte* (Monterrey) 242, 61–70, also published in the *Quarterly Journal of the Library of Congress* (April 1969).

43 For the Count of Benavente's elephant, see Vital in *Viajes* [5:20], 752.

44 Amada López Meneses, "El primer regreso de Hernán Cortés a España", *R de I*, Año XIV (January–June 1954), 69–91. For the scorpion, see Marita Martínez del Río de Redo, "Joyas Coloniales románticas", in *Artes de México*, 165 (1960), 50, and Antonio Ramiro Chico, "Bibliografía de Hernán Cortés en Guadalupe", in *Hernán Cortés y su tiempo* [9:22], 720.

45 "La persona del marqués a sydo en esta corte y en toda España . . . muy tenida y estimada . . ." (AGI, Justicia, leg. 712, cit. Otte [11:5], 112).

46 *Cédula* of Charles V, 5 November 1529, in *CDIHE*, II, 401. For the dancing, see Esteban Palomera, *Fray Diego Valadés* (Mexico, 1968), which prints Valadés' *Crónica Mexicana*.

47 Antonio Muro Orejón, *Hernando Cortés, Exequias, almoneda e inventario de sus bienes* (Seville, 1967), 1. For the Duke of Béjar, one of the largest stock farmers in Spain, see Altman [9:23], 146. For an Extremeño it must have been very satisfactory to marry into his family. For the wedding at Béjar, see AGN, Hospital de Jesús, leg. 123.

48 Figures (for 1500) in Lalaing, in *Viajes* [5:20], 489–90.

49 The sketches are in the German Museum, in Nuremberg. See Hampfe, *Weiditz* [10:38]. Part of Dantisco's journals of his time in Spain were ed. in the *Boletín de la Real Academia* in 1924 and, more briefly, in *Viajes* [5:20], 791. The section covering 1528 and 1529 appears lost, perhaps destroyed in Leipzig in the Second World War.

50 AGI, Contratación. leg. 4673, B. ff.124 v.–127v., cit. Howard Cline, "Hernando Cortés y los Indios Aztecas en España", *Norte* (242), 58–70.

51 Gibson [16:54], 16. Surely these were the Indians whom Navagero saw in Seville showing themselves adept at flinging up pieces of wood with their feet and other marvels (*Viajes* [5:20], 851–2).

52 Honour [5:11], 61.

53 These children were Martín Cortés, son of Marina; Luis de Altamirano, son of Antonia Hermosillo; and Catalina Pizarro, daughter of a Cuban girl, known as Leonor Pizarro. For Cortés' return, see the manifest of the ships in Martínez, *Docs*, III, 116–31.

54 Charles Verlinden, "Cortés como empresario económico y la mano de obra esclava", *HM*, XXXVIII (1989), 771.

55 Res (Rayón), II, 68.

56 Martínez-Luza [7:3], 6.

57 Cortés told this "with great sadness" to Sepúlveda, who put it in his book (Sepúlveda, 113). But 3 letters from Cortés published by Rita Goldberg, *Hernán Cortés y su familia en los Archivos Españoles*, (Madrid, 1987), show him to have been interested in further adventures, even in the last year of his life, for he had then contracted a debt for arms, etc., with a Genoese, Julio Canova (unpaid till the 1570s).

58 For the will of Cortés, see Muro Orejón [Epilogue: 47]; and G. L. R. Conway, *Postrera voluntad y testamento de Hernán Cortés* (Mexico, 1940). The beds are described in Muro Orejón, 71. For Boti (presumably Botti), see Carande [9:15], I, 311–15. San Isidoro del Campo was a Jeronymite monastery, and its prior and some monks were in 1559 burned for secret Lutheranism ("Relación de las personas que salieron al auto de fe . . . Sept. 24. 1559", in British Museum, Add. MSS, 21, 447. f.93). For Cortés' possessions, see "Inventario of 1549", in AGN, Hospital de Jésus, leg. 28, expediente 39.

59 Francisco de la Maza, "Los Restos de Hernán Cortés", in *Cuadernos Americanos*, xxxi, I, (1947), 153–74.

60 Honour [5:11], 62.

61 R. O. Jones, *A literary history of Spain* (London, 1971), 50.

62 See Vicente Barrantes' "Discurso leido ante la Real Academia de la Historia", 14 January 1872. Both Elliott [9:76], 48, and Alfonso Figueroa y Melgar, *Algunas familias españoles*, 3 (1967), 723, note the similarity of this individual's character to Cortés, his first cousin twice removed.

63 *Aquesta nació sin par*
   Yo en serviros sin segundo
   Vos sin igual en el mundo.

Those who took this back were Francisco de Montejo (*el mozo*, future conqueror of Yucatan); Diego de Soto, Alderete's successor as treasurer; and Juan Velázquez de Salazar (in AGI, Justicia, leg. 126, no.5). Antonio de Oliver confirmed that the silver (adulterated) came from Michoacan: see *Inf. de Antonio de Huitsimingari* (AGI, Patronato, leg.60, ff.29 v.–30). Martyr, II, 399–400, for a description. For the classical inspiration of the verse (probably Justin), see Juan Gil, "Los modelos clásicos en el

Descubrimiento", in María de las Nieves Muñiz (ed.), *Espacio Geográfico, Espacio Imaginario* (Cáceres, 1993), 25.

Appendices

1 For a splendid study of the different figures given at different times by Las Casas for the population of Hispaniola in 1492, see David Henige, "On the contact population of Hispaniola: History as higher mathematics", *HAHR*, 58, 2, May 1978.

2 Francisco Javier Clavijero, *Historia Antigua de México*, 4 vols. (Mexico, 1945), Vol. 2, 561–70.

3 William Robertson, *The History of America*, 2 vols. (London, 1777), Vol. 2, 276 and 476 (note xlix).

4 Karl Sapper, "Die Zahl und die Volksdichte der indianischen Bevölkerung in Amerika vor der Conquista und in der Gegenwart", Proceedings of the 21st International Congress of Americanists, The Hague, 1924, Vol. I, 100.

5 Alfred Kroeber, *Cultural and Natural Areas of Native North America* (Berkeley, 1939), 166.

6 George Kubler, "Population movements in Mexico 1520–1600" in *HAHR*, 22, 606–43.

7 Angel Rosenblat, *La población indígena y el mestizaje en América*, 2 vols. (Buenos Aires, 1954), Vol. 1, 102.

8 Leslie B. Simpson and Sherburne Cook, "The Population of Central Mexico in the Sixteenth Century", *Ibero-Americana*, 31 (1948), 18–38.

9 Sherburne Cook and Woodrow Borah, "The rate of population change in Central Mexico, 1550–1570", *HAHR*, 37, 460.

10 Sherburne Cook and Woodrow Borah, "The aboriginal population of Central Mexico on the eve of the Spanish conquest", *Ibero-Americana*, 45, Berkeley, 88.

11 Henry Dobyns, "Estimating aboriginal American population", *Current Anthropology* (October 1966), 95–116, with comments by a wide variety of people.

12 William Sanders, in William M. Denevan (ed.), *The native populations of the Americas in 1492* (Madison, 1976).

13 Denevan [Appendices: 12], 291.

14 Pedro Armillas, "Gardens in swamps", *Science*, 174.

15 W. T. Sanders, "Agricultural history", in Eric Wolf (ed.), *The Valley of Mexico* (Albuquerque, 1976), 135.

16 Carlos Rangel, *Du noble sauvage au bon révolutionnaire* (Paris, 1976), 203, a book foolishly entitled in English *The Latin Americans* (New York, 1977).

17 Hachette, *Mexique Guatemala Guides Bleus* (Mexico, 1984), 87–8.

18 Woodrow Borah and Sherburne Cook, *Essays in Population History*, Vol. III (Berkeley, 1979).

19 W. T. Sanders, with Jeffrey R. Parsons and Robert S. Santley, *The Basin of Mexico: Ecological Processes in the Evolution of a Civilisation* (New York and London, 1979), 378–9.

20 Rudolfo A. Zambardino, "Mexico's population in the sixteenth century: demographic anomaly or mathematical illusion", *Journal of interdisciplinary history*, XI, 1 (Summer 1980).

21 Inga Clendinnen, *Aztecs* (Cambridge, 1991), 18.

22 R. van Zantwijk, *The Aztec Arrangement* (Norman, 1985), 285. This book was an enlarged version of a book published in Dutch in 1977.

23 Mary Ellen Miller, *The Art of Mesoamerica* (New York, 1986), 230; Frances Berdan and Patricia Anawalt, et al., "The Codex Mendoza", *The Scientific American* (June 1992).
24 In Denevan [Appendices: 12], 46.
25 Hernán Cortés, *Cartas de Relación*, ed. Mario Hernández (Madrid, 1985), 132.
26 Francisco López de Gómara, *La Conquista de México*, ed. José Luis de Rojas (Madrid, 1987), 180.
27 Joaquín García Icazbalceta (ed.), *Documentos Inéditos par la historia de México* (Mexico, 1980), vol. I, 391.
28 Oviedo, V, 44.
29 George C. Vaillant, *The Aztecs of Mexico* (Harmondsworth, 1973), 127, 137.
30 Bartolomé de Las Casas, *Apologética Historia de las Indias*, in *BAE*, XIII, 131.
31 Manuel Toussaint, Federico Gómez de Orozco and Justino Fernández, *Planos de la ciudad de México* (Mexico, 1938).
32 Jacques Soustelle, *La Vie Quotidienne des Aztéques* (Paris, 1955), 34.
33 Borah and Cook [Appendices: 10], 63.
34 In Denevan [Appendices: 12], 25, fn. 32.
35 In Denevan [Appendices: 12], 82, 148–9.
36 Edward Calnek, "The Internal Structure of Tenochtitlan", in E. Wolf (ed.), *The Valley of Mexico* (Albuquerque, 1970).
37 W. T. Sanders, et al. [2:21], 183–219.
38 Miguel León-Portilla, *Toltecayotl, aspectos de la cultura náhuatl* (Mexico, 1980), 252.
39 Jose Luis de Rojas, *México Tenochtitlan* (Mexico, 1986), 35, 84.
40 Nigel Davies, *The Aztec Empire* (Norman, 1987), 169.
41 Eduardo Matos Moctezuma, *The Great Temple of the Aztecs* (London, 1988), 15; Berdan and Anwalt [Appendices: 23].
42 *"los indios no son de las tres partes la una de los que solía haber"*: Alonso de Zorita, *Relación de los Señores de la Nueva España* (Madrid, 1992), 162.
43 Nicolás Sánchez Albornoz, *La Población de America Latina* (Madrid, 1976), 32.

Documents

1 Diego Pizarro was probably son of Juana Sánchez Pizarro, "la Pizarra", and so was a nephew of Cortés' mother, Catalina. See Genealogy III. The fact that Juana Sánchez Pizarro's father, Diego Alfon Altamirano, was a notary in the service of the Count of Medellín gives piquancy to this tale. On the other side of his family, Diego Pizarro was a first cousin of Gonzalo Pizarro, father of the conqueror of Peru.
2 The eccentricity of the spelling of Martín Cortés' name is explained by the general vagueness about spelling of the time. Martín Cortés is said to be "of Don Benito" since, presumably, his vineyard etc. was there.
3 Luis Fernández Alfaro, afterwards involved in the pearl trade of Venezuela, is discussed in the text. He became concerned in business to "Yucatan" in 1519, by which time he knew everything which was going on in the Caribbean. He was an essential link between Hernán Cortés and the world of Sevillano business. I wish I knew more of him. A loan of 60 pesos of gold was made to him in 1511 by Francisco Lizaur, the financial agent of Ovando, and friend of Cortés, as can be seen in the catalogue of the APS, *libro* for 1511, oficio 1 (Mateo de la Cuadra), lib. 1, f. 176 v.
4 Alonso de Céspedes, an uncle of Alonso Hernández Portocarrero, was judge *de las gradas* in Seville. He was looked on as a "colombista", being a friend of Diego Colón. He was another key figure in Cortés' finances.
5 That is, Culhúa.

6 He was the pilot of Cortés as of Ponce de León, Hernández de Córdoba, and Grijalva, as he was also on this vessel, the *Santa María de la Concepción*, on its return to Spain.
7 This individual was Cortés' majordomo and gave important testimony in the *residencia* against Cortés, in AGI, Justicia, leg. 223, ff. 207 r., 309 v.

Sources

Given the character of the Chapter Notes, it did not seem necessary to have an extensive bibliography listing sources consulted. But it did seem desirable to summarise the main sources for the study of the Conquest of Mexico. The first section lists material necessary for the understanding of the Mexicans. The second section lists sources about Spain and the conquistadors. For a full bibliography of the codices, see José Alcina Franch, *Códices Mexicanos* (Madrid, 1992).

Works of special value for the conquest are starred* .

Mexican Material

Acosta, José de, SJ, *Historia natural y moral de las Indias* (ed. 1590). Modern ed. in *BAE*, ed. Fr. Francisco Mateos (Madrid, 1954), and Edmundo O'Gorman (Mexico, 1962). Acosta's main source was Juan de Tovar, SJ (see Codex Ramírez), of whose work he incorporated a large chunk. He also used Durán (see below). He relied on the Crónica X, probably indirectly. No substantial value.

* Alva Ixtlilxochitl, Fernando de: *Obras Históricas*. First ed. Alfonso Chavero (1891). Best ed. Edmundo O'Gorman (Mexico, 1975, 2 vols.). Ixtlilxochitl was a *mestizo* descendant of the kings of Texcoco (see Genealogy IV). His works are a defence of them, are hostile to the Mexica, and were written in the shadow of the complaints which his family made against the Spaniards whom they had helped. Though he wrote in the early 17th century, he had first-hand informants, e.g., "Don Alonso" Axayacatzin, son of the Emperor Cuitláhuac, who gave him documents (the names of the informants are in O'Gorman's ed., I, 285–6). His works are: * (1) *Historia de la Nación Chichimeca* which figures as Vol.II of O'Gorman's ed. (and re-ed., Madrid, 1988 as *Crónicas de América*, 11, ed. Germán Vázquez); and (2) various *Relaciones Históricas*, figuring as Vol.I of O'Gorman's ed. of which several give information about the conquest: * (a) the *Decimatercia Relación, "De la venida de los Españoles y principio de la ley evangélica"* (this has been separately published, Mexico, 1938); and (b) Appendix 6 of the *Sumaria Relación de las Cosas de la Nueva España* (in pp.387–93 of O'Gorman, I).

Alvarado Tezozomoc, Fernando de: * (1) *Crónica Mexicana*, written in Spanish c. 1598 (ed. Mexico, 1878), new ed. Mexico, 1944. This is a conventional history which tells the story of Mexico to the arrival of Cortés or Grijalva; * (2) *Crónica Mexicayotl*. Annals in Nahuatl, begun 1609, tr. Adrián León (Mexico, 1949). Much of the book is a revised version of the *Crónica Mexicana*.

Tezozomoc was a son of Francisca, a daughter of Montezuma, who married her cousin Diego de Alvarado Huanitzin, son of one of Montezuma's brothers.

Anales de Cuauhtitlán: see **Codex Chimalpopoca**

* **Anales de Tlatelolco** or **Unos Anales históricos de la Nación Mexicana;** or, merely, **Anales**. MSS in the Bibliothèque Nationale (Bib. Nat.), Paris, probably 1524– 1528, in Nahuatl, by citizens of Tlatelolco, ed. in Spanish (1948) by Heinrich Berlin, summary by Robert H. Barlow (new ed. Mexico, 1980). Perhaps written by Pablo Nazareo, of Xaltocan, a nephew of Montezuma II and a pupil of the college of Tlatelolco. Facsimile ed. Ernst Mengin, *Corpus Codicum Americanorum Medii Aevi*, Vol. ii (Copenhagen, 1945).

The oldest historical narrative written by Mexicans using Nahuatl with Latin characters. Mexicans express feelings without self-hispanisation. In five parts, of which the last, "Relación de la conquista por informantes anónimos de Tlatelolco", is tr. in Spanish in Miguel León-Portilla, *La Visión de los vencidos* (Madrid, 1985), 148–64.

Anales Tolteca Chichimeca: See **Historia Tolteca Chichimeca**

Anónimo: Testimonio de la antigua palabra. Collection of addresses (*huehuetlatolli*), made by Miguel León- Portilla and Librado Silva Galeana, ed. as Crónicas de América 56 (Madrid 1990).

* **Cantares Mexicanos**, MSS in Biblioteca Nacional of Mexico. Probably a copy c. 1560 of an earlier transcription. 85 folios of poems in Nahuatl, used by Miguel León-Portilla in his *Cantos y Crónicas del México Antiguo* (Madrid 1986) and Garibay in his various editions of Nahuatl literature. Facsimile ed. Antonio Penafiel (Mexico, 1904).

* **Castillo, Cristóbal del,** *Fragmentos de la obra general sobre historia de los mexicanos*, written c. 1600, tr. from Nahuatl by Fr. José Antonio Pichardo and ed. Francisco Paso y Troncoso (Florence, 1908). A vivid description of the migrations of the Mexica. Castillo was probably pure Mexican. He hated the conquistadors.

* *Chilam Balam de Chumayel*. The most important of the books written by Mayas after the conquest. Probably written in the 17th century and put together by Juan José Hoil. Facsimile ed. Philadelphia, 1913. English tr. Ralph Roys (Washington, 1933). Ed. in *Crónicas de America*, 20 (Madrid, 1986), ed. Miguel Rivera.

Chimalpahin Quauhtlehuanitzin, Domingo Francisco de San Antón Muñón, *Relaciones originales de Chalco Amaquemacan*. This author, with his endless names, was a descendant of the kings of Chalco and was warden of San Antonio Abad, Mexico. His book, written in the 1620s, is anti-Mexican in tone. There is an ed. of the 6th and 7th *relaciones* tr. into French by Rémi Siméon, Bibliothèque Linguistique Américaine, Paris, vol.xii (1889), and of the 7th *relación* alone, into Spanish by Silvia Rendón (Mexico, 1935). A new ed. is Silvia Rendón, *Relaciones originales de Chalco Amaquemacan* (Mexico, 1965).

* Codex Aubin (also called **Códice de 1576**). In Bib. Nat., Paris, where it was ed. E. Leroix (1893) as **Histoire de la nation mexicaine depuis le départ de Azatlan** ... Belonged to José María Aubin. The best ed. is Chas. Dibble (Madrid, 1963). A screenfold collection of Mexican testimonies, including pictures, sagas, poems, etc., dealing with events from the departure from Azatlan to the conquest, to which there are interesting references. In style it is close to the Codex Borbonicus. It seems to have come from Tlaxcala. There is a *tonalamatl* (book of days and destinies).

Codex Azcatitlan (also called **Histoire Mexicaine**). Ed. by R. H. Barlow, *JSAP*, n.s., t.xxxviii, 101–35 (Paris, 1949). An incomplete text of 50 pages, giving a pictorial history of the Mexica, including their later conquests, from when they left Azatlan. In the 17th century in the collection of Boturini and, like the Codex Xolotl, passed to Aubin, thence to the Bib. Nat., Paris, where it now is.

Codex Badianus, *c.* 1551, a herbal written in Latin by Juan Badiano, an Indian from Xochimilco who taught at Santiago Tlatelolco, on the basis of a Nahuatl work by Martín de la Cruz. As useful for the mentality of the Mexica as for the Nahuatl language. Ed. as "The Badianus Manuscript" by Dr Emily Emmart (Baltimore, 1940). Spanish and facsimile ed. Mexico, 1964, ed. Dr Efrén del Pozo.

Codex Becker. 26-page Mixtec codex in Ethnographical Museum, Vienna. Owned by a Mixtec family till mid-19th century. Brought from Mexico by Philip Becker of Darmstadt. Facsimile ed. (Geneva, 1891) by Henri de Saussure as "Le manuscrit du cacique". Zapotec written in Spanish letters. Probably part of Codex Colombino (see below). New ed. by Karl Novotny (Graz, 1964).

Codex Bodley. Mixtec, *c.* 1521. In Bodleian Library, Oxford, which it reached early 17th century. Perhaps stolen by Earl of Essex in a raid on Portugal. The story of a princess, with genealogies of Mixtec rulers in Tilantongo and Teozacoalco. Ed. Alfonso Caso (Mexico, 1947).

Codex Borbonicus. Palais Bourbon (Assemblée Nationale), Paris. 36 large pages, two lost. Once in the Escorial. Reached Paris *c.* 1823. Facsimile ed. Paris, 1899, and Graz, 1974. The only screenfold Mexican book which dates from the era of the conquest. The Spanish notes on it added later. Perhaps designed in Iztapalapa or Culhuacan, on the basis of an older model. In part a *tonalamatl*, in part a pictorial account of the year's festivals.

Codex Borgia. This pre-Cortesian work is so called since it was in the collection of Cardinal Stefano Borgia in the late 18th century. Now in the Library of the Vatican, Rome. From Puebla or Tlaxcala. It describes the gods in control of the ritual calendar, and includes a *tonalamatl*. Facsimile ed. with intr. in Italian, Rome, 1898; also Mexico, 1963 and Graz, 1976. One of "Borgia Group" of MSS.

Codex Boturini (la Tira de la Peregrinación; Tira del Museo). Ed. Mexico, 1975. Screenfold MS painted Mexico *c.* 1535. Perhaps a copy of a pre-conquest work. Travels of the Mexica from Azatlan to the Valley of Mexico. It has a *tonalamatl*. In Museo Nacional de Antropológia, Mexico.

* Codex Chimalpopoca. This badly entitled document contains:
(a) **Anales de Cuauhtitlán,** also known as **Anónimo de 1570,** and **Historia de los reynos de Culhuacan y México,** written *c.* 1570 (see Robert H. Barlow, *HAHR*, 27, 520–6, and Garibay, *Literatura Nahuatl*, I, 27–8), tr. J. Bierhorst in *Four Masterworks of American Indian Literature* (New York, 1974). Its 68 pages include an account of Nezahualcoyotl in his youth; (b) **Breve relación de los Dioses y Ritos,** written by Pedro Ponce; and, (c) **Leyenda de los Soles** (also known as **el manuscrito de 1558**), a collection

of myths for reciting. Similar to Codex Mendoza. This perhaps includes work by some of Sahagún's witnesses; ed. Primo Velázquez (Mexico, 1945).

Codex Colombino. Museo Nacional de Antropológia, Mexico. Probably part of the same MSS as Becker. Mixtec. Appeared in court in 1717. Ed. Alfonso Caso and Mary Elizabeth Smith (Mexico, 1966).

Codex Cospi. Biblioteca Universitaria, Bologna. Mixtec, pre-conquest. A ritual painted screenfold MS such as existed in most temples or seminaries in the Mexican empire. Facsimile ed. Rome, 1898. It is called after the Marchese Cospi to whom it was given as Christmas present, 1665. He established a museum in Bologna (Museo Cospiano) which once included this. One of "Borgia group" of MSS. New ed. Carmen Aguilera (Puebla, 1988).

Codex Dresden. Maya, in the Dresden Sächsische Landesbibliothek, a 39-leaf screenfold painted *c.* AD 1000. The most beautiful and interesting of all the codices; mostly in black and red, but with some other colours. It contains auguries and predictions for agriculture. Many calculations and rituals are described. Allegedly from Chichen-Itza. Sir E. Thompson suggested that it was sent 1519 by Cortés to Charles V. In Vienna, 1739, when the librarian at Dresden bought it. Best ed. probably Graz, 1975.

Codex en Cruz. In Bib. Nat. Describes Cuauhtitlan, Texcoco and Mexico, 1402–1557. Three pages, probably once screenfold; each gives an account of a pre-conquest "century" (52 years). Pre-1557. Ed. (1942) by Charles Dibble, Mexico.

Codex Féjerváry-Mayer (Tonalamatl de los Pochtecas). So called from the Féjerváry family, who sold it to Joseph Mayer of Liverpool, who gave it to the Liverpool Musuem, where it now is. Probably Mixtec. It gives instructions for the merchants (*pochteca*). Ed. Paris, 1901 and Mexico, 1985, by Miguel León-Portilla. One of the "Borgia Group".

* Codex Florentino; and **Sahagún's Historia General de las Cosas de Nueva España.** Probably influenced by Pliny's Natural History. Fr. Bernardino Sahagún sought to give a picture of life under the Mexican ancient regime. He began work in 1547 and consulted surviving Mexicans, at Tepepolco in the 1550s, subsequently in Tlatelolco.

His consultants were all Mexicans who had taken Spanish names: Martín Jacovita, Diego de Grado and Bonifacio Maximiliano, from Tlatelolco; Alonso Vegeriano and Pedro de San Buenaventura, from Cuauhtitlan; Mateo Severiano, from Xochimilco; and Antonio Valeriano, from Azcapotzalco. These men may have remembered things badly; or deliberately distorted the truth because of bad feeling towards the conquerors; or their stories may have been transcribed badly by Sahagún, who had his own preconceptions. Yet Sahagún made elaborate efforts to cross- check his material.

The result is a wonderful book, the greatest of all the sources for old Mexico. The consultants were all ex-students of the *calmécac*, and would have learned old songs, legends, rules and speeches by heart. Sahagún said of his sources that they were "principal persons of good judgement, and it is believed that they told all the truth". His findings in Nahuatl are in the Codex Florentino (FC), so called because the original is in the Laurenziana Medicean Library in Florence. A facsimile ed. was published of this in 3 vols., by the Mexican government (Archivo General de la Nación) (Florence, 1979).

Earlier, less complete, but (to some) more authentic versions are in the two **Códices Matritenses**, one of which is in the library of the Royal Palace in Madrid. The other is in the RAH, Madrid. Facsimile eds. (of both) by Francisco del Paso y Troncoso (Madrid, 1905–6).

Sections of these last were ed. in Mexico from 1958 onwards: by Miguel León-Portilla (ed.), *Ritos, sacerdotes y atavíos de los dioses*; Angel María Garibay (ed.), *Veinte himnos sacros de los nahuas*; Garibay (ed.), *La vida económica de Tenochtitlan* (Mexico, 1961); and Alfredo López Austin (ed.), *Augurios y alusiones* (Mexico, 1969). Some differences between these texts and the Florentine Codex text are discussed in the appendix to *Ritos, Sacerdotes . . .* Some have even suggested that the informants were the real authors of the work. Sahagún used the material in the Codex Florentino as the basis for his "Historia general de las cosas de Nueva España". The first edition of this work was finished in 1579. Sahagún worked further on the text and produced a revised Spanish edition in which he devoted much attention to Book XII, on the conquest.

The first complete Spanish edition was that of Angel Garibay, *Historia general de las Cosas de la Nueva España* (ed. Porrúa, Mexico, 1956, 4 vols.). Another ed. is in *Crónicas de América*, 55a and 55b, ed. Juan Carlos Temprano (Madrid, 1990). It is to this that the few footnotes in this book alluding to this volume refer.

An English ed. of the Codex Florentino was published direct from Nahuatl, a real masterpiece of the translator's art, fully worthy of the original, by Charles Dibble and Arthur Anderson (Utah, 1953–82).

The only full ed. of the ed. of 1585 is that of Carlos María de Bustamante: *La Aparición de Nstra. Señora de Guadalupe . . .* (Mexico, 1840). An excellent English ed. of Book XII, translated from the Spanish, was published by S. Cline (Salt Lake City, 1989).

Codex Grolier. 11 pages of a Maya calendrical book, *c.* AD 1250, found in Chiapas, *c.* 1965, presented 1971 at the Grolier Club, New York, by Michael Coe, and now in a private collection in Mexico. Ed. Coe, *The Maya Scribe and his World* (New York, 1973).

Codex Huichapan. Otomí description of pre-Hispanic and colonial Mexico. Ed. Manuel Alvarado Guinchard (Mexico, 1976). It gives evidence independent of the chronicles based on the Crónica X (Acosta, Durán, Tovar, etc.) of the role of the mysterious Tlalcaelel in 15th- century Mexico.

Codex Ixtlilxochitl. Belonged to the historian Ixtlilxochitl. This is in Bib. Nat., Paris, (Mexican MSS, 65–71); facsimile ed. Graz, 1976. Some pictures seem part of Pomar's *Relación de Texcoco*. Probably a copy of Codex Tudela. In three parts, in different hands: (1) an illustrated account of the solar year drawn from same lost original as the Codex Magliabecchiano; (2) Europeanised pictures of Texcocan, Mexican and Tlatelolcan lords; and (3) a calendar of festivals.

Codex Laud (MS Laud Misc. 678). Either Mixtec or from Cholula. Probably a present to Charles, Prince of Wales, from the King of Spain (1623). Called after Archbishop Laud to whom it once belonged and who gave it to the Bodleian Library, Oxford, where it is now. Facsimile ed. Graz, 1966. Part of the "Borgia Group".

Codex Magliabecchianus. Mid 16th century. It belonged to Antonio Magliabecchi, librarian to the Medici; now in Biblioteca Nazionale, Florence. Partly pictures, partly Spanish 16th-century MS. Religious themes; ed. Rome, 1904. Tr., ed. and abbreviated, as *The Book of Life of the Ancient Mexicans*, by Zelia Nuttall (Berkeley, 1903). There is also an edition by Zelia Nuttall and Elizabeth Hill Boone at Berkeley (1983).

Codex Matritense del Real Palacio and **de la Real Academia** (Madrid). See **Codex Florentino.**

* **Codex Mendoza.** Original in Bodleian, Oxford. Compiled *c.* 1541 for Viceroy Mendoza. Tr "J", i.e., probably Martín Jacovita, Rector, Sta Cruz, Tlatelolco. It passed to the Bodleian via French pirates and André Thevet (see *Histoyre du Méchique*) and Richard Hakluyt. Facsimile ed. J.C. Clark (London, 1938, 3 vols.), and Patricia Rieff Anawalt and Frances F. Berdan (Berkeley, 1992, 4 vols.). This is (1) a history of Mexico from 1325; (2) a list of tribute from *c.* 400 towns, sent 1516–18; and (3) a picture of life in Mexico. Federico Gómez de Orozco, "¿Quién fué el autor material del Códice Mendocino . . . ?" (*Revista mexicana de estudios antropológicos*, 5, 1941, 43–52) names the author as Francisco Gualpuyogualcal.

Codex Mexicanus, Bib. Nat. de Paris, MSS nos. 23–4, ed. Ernest Mengin (in *JSAP*, XLI, fasc. 2, Paris, 1952). Diverse contents by several artists. Late 16th century.

Codex Nuttall (Zouche). Mixtec. It tells of the Mixtec dynasty of Tilantongo, beginning with the creation of the world, paying special attention to a famous ruler, 8-Deer. Intr. Zelia Nuttall, who describes how it left San Marco, Florence, for Lord Zouche's library. She says that this was one of two MSS sent by Cortés to Charles V, (the other may have been the Codex Vienna, 1, whose origin she believed "unquestionably" the same as that of the Nuttall). But Henry Nicholson suggested that it could have been taken home by Ordaz in 1521. Now in British Museum. Facsimile ed. Cambridge, Mass, 1902; also Mexico, 1974, and New York, 1975.

Codex Osuna. MS by several painters, *c.* 1565. Drawn up as part of an enquiry by an official named Valderrama. Owned by the Dukes of Osuna, now in the Biblioteca Nacional, Madrid. Contains material from Mexico, Tacuba, Tlatelolco and Tula. Chronicles debts.

Codex Peresianus (or **Pérez**), Maya, painted *c.*AD 1000; only a few pages. It appeared in Paris in 19th century mysteriously and is in the Bib. Nat. Religio- astronomical, with description of ceremonies.

Codex Porfirio Díaz. In Museo Nacional, Mexico. Cuicatlan, Oaxaca. Probably end 16th or early 17th century. On a screen. Published 1892 as part of celebrations for Columbus.

* **Codex Ramírez** (*Relación del origen de los Indios que habitan esta Nueva España, según sus historias*). Text by Juan de Tovar, SJ, a *mestizo*, who *c.* 1570–80 carried out an enquiry on behalf of the viceroy into the recent past. So named because discovered, in the ruined library of the monastery of San Francisco, Mexico, by José Fernando Ramírez, 1878. A series of fragments. Ed. first by Orozco y Berra, (Mexico, 1878). The first part is a history of the Mexica until the *noche triste*; the second a description of Mexican rites; the third an account of Texcoco written from the Texcocan angle and describing the conquest. The whole is a version of the *Segunda Relación* of Tovar. English tr. in Radin, "Sources and Authenticity of the Ancient Mexicans", *University of California publications in American archaeology and ethnology*, XVII, no. 1. New ed. as *Crónicas de América*, 32, intr. Germán Vázquez, (Madrid, 1987), entitled *Romances de los señores*.

Codex Ríos. See **Codex Vaticano A**.

Códice de Santa María Asunción. 80 pages, *c.*1540, now in Museo Nacional de Antropología, Mexico. It describes a *barrio* in Tepetlaoztoc, a town once dependent on Texcoco. The signature of a Spanish official, Pedro Vázquez de Vergara, is at the beginning and the end. See **Codex Vergara**.

Codex Selden. Acquired by the Bodleian Library from the estate of John Selden (d. 1654). Mixtec. Most pages completed before the conquest, some after it. It tells, among other things, the genealogy of the Mixtec family of Magdalena Saltepec. The story of 6-Monkey, who killed the murderers of her relations, shows that some women in old Mexico fought well. Ed. Alfonso Caso (Mexico, 1964).

Codex Sigüenza. A name sometimes given to A. Chavero's "Historia antigua de la conquista", published as Vol.I of *México a través de los siglos* (Mexico, 1887).

Codex Telleriano-Remensis. In Bib. Nat., Paris, Mexican MSS 385. Named after Archbishop Le Tellier of Reims, a 17th-century royal librarian, who owned it. It is a book-form complement to the Codex Vaticanus A, *c.*1550–63, and the first part seems a copy of the same lost work which inspired the paintings in Vaticanus A. It was ed. Lord Kingsborough in his *Antiquities of Mexico* (London, 1831), Vol.1. There is also an ed. Paris, 1899 and Mexico, 1964. It includes a *tonalpohualli*, a ritual section and a historical one.

* **Codex de Tlatelolco.** A MS on a long screenfold *tira* which could be made into a book, describing events in Tlatelolco between 1554 and *c.*1562, full of complaints about bills, published by R. H. Barlow, *Anales de Tlatelolco* (Mexico, 1947).

Codex Tró Cortesianus (or **Madrid**). Maya. The first part of it was found in the possession of Juan Tró, 1866; the second part is supposed to have been brought back by Cortés. Discovered in Madrid in 1880. The two were parts of the same MS. Compiled 15th century, perhaps near Tulum. 56 leaves. Apparently made in haste. In the Museo de América, Madrid. Religio-astronomical. Best ed. Ferdinand Anders (Graz, 1967).

Codex Tudela. In Museo de América, Madrid. Dated 1553. Named after José Tudela de la Orden, *c.*1950. A copy of part without illustrations was published as "Costumbres, fiestas, enterramientos y diversas formas de proceder de los Indios de la Nueva España", in *Tlacocan* 2, no. 1 (Mexico, 1945). This codex seems to have inspired Cervantes de Salazar's passages on Mexican customs. Facsimile ed. 2 vols. (Madrid, 1980).

Codex Vaticanus A. Vatican MS 3738, also named **Codex Ríos**, because presented by Fr. Ríos in Hispano-Italian. Book form. Compiled between 1566 and 1589, probably by a non-Indian artist, in Italy. It is thought to be a copy of the same lost MS as Telleriano-Remensis. This describes, first, the cosmic origins of Mexico (this section is probably a copy of a pre-Hispanic codex); secondly, it publishes a ritual calendar; and thirdly there is material from the conquest to 1563. See *Antiquities of Mexico*, ed. Lord Kingsborough, Vol.II (London, 1831) and reproduced in facsimile Rome, 1900 and Mexico, 1964.

Codex Vaticanus B. Mixtec or from Cholula. It has been in the Vatican library since the 16th century (MS 3773). Facsimile ed. Rome, 1896 and (ed. Ferdinand Anders), Graz, 1972. Like the Codex Borgia, it includes a *tonalamatl*. Part of the "Borgia Group".

Codex Vindobonensis Mexicanus I (or **Codex Vienna**), National Library, Vienna. Facsimile ed. by Otto Adelhofer, Graz, 1963. Perhaps, with Codex Nuttall, one of the two books sent by Cortés, July 1519. Probably given by Charles V to King Emanuel of Portugal, by him to Pope Clement VII, who left it to Cardinal Ippolito de' Medici, from whom it passed to Vienna. A pre-Hispanic Mixtec text. Primarily a detailed genealogy of Mixtec rulers. Not to be confused with that other so-called Codex Vindobonensis which includes Cortés' letters.

Codex Xolotl, in Bib. Nat., Paris, a picture book from Texcoco, amplified by Spanish prose, about the legendary leader of the Chichimecs, Xolotl. Perhaps *c.*1540. It describes early Chichimec and Texcoco history. It includes maps of the Valley of Mexico. It was used by Alva Ixtlilxochitl. It belonged to the Boturini collection, whence it passed to that of Aubin, thence to the Bib. Nat.; ed. Charles Dibble, *The Códice Xolotl* (Mexico, 1951).

* **Coloquio y doctrina cristiana** . . . MS found in 1924 in the Archivo Secreto de la Biblioteca Vaticana. Notes made 1524 of a discussion between the Franciscans and surviving Mexican priests. Perhaps distorted by Sahagún. 14 chapters found, another 16 had been destroyed; facsimile ed. Miguel León-Portilla, with Nahuatl and Spanish (Mexico, 1986).

"Crónica X": or **"la Crónica Primaria"**, a lost source so described by Robert Barlow ("La Crónica 'X'," *Revista Mexicana de Estudios Antropológicos*, VII (Mexico, 1945), 65–86). Probably written by a Mexican, in Nahuatl, with pictures, c.1536–9, used by Tovar for his history (1568–80), Durán (1581) and Tezozomoc (1598). Subsequently, Tovar probably used Durán for his second work (Codex Ramírez) and, later still, Acosta (Book vii). The "Crónica X" was obviously confused between the arrivals, a year apart, of Grijalva and Cortés at San Juan de Ulúa.

* **Durán, Fr. Diego**, *Historia de las Indias de la Nueva España*, written 1579–81, MS in Biblioteca Nacional, Madrid, in three sections: (1) *Ritos y ceremonias en las fiestas*, begun in 1570; (2) *Calendario*, finished 1579; and (3) *Historia de las Indias de Nueva España*, finished 1581, first published by José Fernández Ramirez, (Mexico, 1867–80, 2 Vols.). A good new edition ed. Angel Garibay (Mexico, 1967, 2 vols.). Both volumes tr. into English by Doris Heyden and F. Horcantes: *Book of the Gods and Rites and the Ancient Calendar* (Norman, 1971), and *The Aztecs* (New York, 1964), though, unfortunately, in the first of these two, cuts were made without indicating where.

Durán, a Dominican and, perhaps, according to Garibay, a *converso*, was influenced by living from childhood in Texcoco, later working there, as in Tlatelolco. He was both scholarly and imaginative, made extensive use of the "Crónica X", but firmly believed that the Mexica were a lost tribe of Israel.

Hernández, Francisco, *Obras Completas* (Mexico, 1959). A doctor from Toledo, he wrote a natural history of New Spain in the 1570s.

Herrera y Tordesillas, Antonio de, *Historia General de los hechos de los castellanos en las islas y tierra firme del mar océano*. This enormous work, inspired by Livy, was written 1605–15, when it was ed. New ed. by Antonio Ballesteros-Beretta and Miguel Gómez del Campillo (Madrid, 1934–57, 17 vols.). Vols.3–6 of this ed. cover Cuba and Mexico. Herrera used Cervantes de Salazar, Díaz del Castillo, Muñoz Camargo and Zorita. See Carlos Bosch García's essay in Iglesia's *Estudios*, 148–53.

* **Historia de los Mexicanos por sus pinturas**. Written c.1536, perhaps a preparation for the work of Fr. Olmos. Perhaps it was an interpretation of various now lost pictographic MSS: hence the title. In Austin, Texas. It was ed. by García Icazbalceta, in *Nueva colección de Documentos para la historia de México* (Mexico, 1886–92, 5 vols.), III, 1891, 228–62. Another ed. is that of Angel María Garibay, *Teogonía e Historia de los Mexicanos* (Mexico, 1973). Its 12 folios constitute an effort to reconstruct the history of the Mexica. Section I describes the origin of the gods, II the peregrination of the Mexica, while III is a cosmological and sociological study. Bad English tr. by Henry Phillips Jr., in *Proceedings of the American Philosophical Society* (May, 1883 – December, 1884).

Historia Tolteca-Chichimeca. An anonymous account in Nahuatl, with pictures, of the last days of Tollan etc. Composed in Cuauhtinchan, near Cholula, c.1545. Probably copied from a pre-Hispanic text and probably used by the compiler of Anales de Cuauhtitlan. Part of Boturini's collection, it is now in the Bib. Nat., Paris. Several facsimile eds., e.g., by Paul Kirchhoff, Lina Odena Güemes and Luis Reyes García (Mexico, 1976).

* **Histoyre du Mechique**, anon. Handwritten French fragment in Bib. Nat., Paris, probably by Fr. Olmos, in Spanish, tr. André Thevet, *c.*1547. It describes myths, including one about Quetzalcoatl; ed. Edouard de Jonghe in the *JSAP*, n.s. II (Paris, 1905), 1–41; ed. Garibay, with moderate Spanish tr., in *Tegonía e Historia de los Mexicanos* (Mexico, 1965).

Huehuetlatolli. There are at least five vols. with this name: (1) **Documento A**, MS in Bancroft Library, ed. in *Tlalocan*, i, no.1(1943–4) by Garibay. Sermons addressed to boys of the *calmécac* or the *telpochcalli*, and to adults on marriage, funerals etc; (2) there is a MS in Nahuatl by Fr. Olmos in Library of Congress. The first part was ed. Réné Simeon, in *Arte* . . . of Olmos (Paris, 1875): see below under **Olmos**; (3) a similar vol. in MS, in Nahuatl, in Biblioteca Nacional de Mexico; (4) another vol. in the Library of Congress, apparently by a disciple of Olmos, *c.*1550; (5) an ed. of Juan Baintesan, *c.*1599–1600.

* **Información sobre los Tributos que los Indios pagaban a Moctezuma: Año de 1554**. *Documentos para la Historia de México Colonial*, 4, ed. France Scholes and Eleanor Adams (Mexico, 1957).

* **Landa, Diego de**, *Relación de las cosas de Yucatan*. Written *c.*1566. Landa went to Yucatan as a priest in 1547. He later became Bishop. The *Relación* is a fragment of a lost larger work. It was ed. partially Paris, 1864, first ed. in Spanish, Madrid, 1881, ed. Juan de Díos de la Rada. Monumental edition by A. M. Tozzer, in English (1941), as Vol.xviii of the *Papers of the Peabody Museum of American Archaeology and Ethnology*. A new ed. in Spanish appears as *Crónicas de América*, 7, ed. Miguel Rivera Dorado (Madrid, 1985).

* **Lienzo de Tlaxcala**. This picture book was commissioned by Viceroy Luis de Velasco. Three copies were originally made. Two were sent back to Spain and lost. Fragments may survive. The third remained in the hands of the municipality of Tlaxcala, and was lost during the French occupation of Mexico in the 1860s. A copy had been made, however, and was ed. (Mexico, 1892) by Alfonso Chavero.

Mapa de Quinatzin. In Bib. Nat., Paris. A Texcocan history, it begins with the rule of Quinatzin, son of Tlotzin, and ends with Nezahualpilli. There is a panel depicting a Texcocan palace and a "quasi-cartographical, quasi-landscaping setting" (D. Robertson). 1542–6. Discussed by R. H. Barlow in *JSAP*, XXXIX (1950) and reproduced by Aubin, in *Mémoires sur la peinture didactique et l'écriture des anciens mexicains* (Paris, 1885).

Mapa de Santa Cruz. A map of the Valley of Mexico, *c.*1555–6; in Sigvald Linné, *El valle y la ciudad de México en 1550* (Stockholm, 1948).

Mapa Tlotzin. A similar document to the Quinatzin, it is also in the Bib. Nat, Paris, also of Texcoco, reproduced by Aubin in op. cit. (Tlotzin was father of Quinatzin.)

Matrícula de Tributos. A summary of payments made to Mexican empire, *c.*1519, perhaps made for Cortés. 15 folios, in library of Museo Nacional de Antropología. Facsimile ed., Mexico, 1990.

Motezuma, Pedro Diego Luis de (SJ), *Corona Mexicana*. The author was a descendant of Montezuma, he lived entirely in Spain, his work was finished 1686, and ed. Lucas de la Torre (Mexico, 1914). A pro-Indian polemic.

* **"Motolinía" (Fray Toribio de Benavente)**: * (1) *Historia de los Indios de la Nueva España*, written *c.*1541. Two 16th-century copies survive in the Escorial and in Mexico. It was ed. García Icazbalceta in his *Colección de Documentos para la historia de México*,

SOURCES

Vol.1 (Mexico, 1858). An outstanding work of great passion. English tr. by Fr. Francis Borgia Speck, SJ (Washington, 1959); (2) *Memoriales*, also written *c.*1541, MS now in Austin, Texas, ed. Luis García Pimentel (Mexico, 1903), and a critical ed. by Eduardo O'Gorman (Mexico, 1971). It is in places a mere repetition of the Historia. Motolinía is said to have written a larger **Guerra de los Indios**, apparently seen by Cervantes de Salazar, and perhaps by López de Gómara. The *Historia* and the *Memoriales* may have been, or were intended to be, part of it. One might cite as a separate work his **Carta al emperador Carlos V** (Mexico, 1944).

* **Muñoz Camargo, Diego**, *Historia de Tlaxcala*, written 1576–95, as part of a plea for good treatment for the people of Tlaxcala, but not ed. till 1870. New ed. (Madrid, 1988), by Germán Vázquez, with his usual excellent introduction, as *Crónicas de América*, 26. A second work is **Descripción de la ciudad y provincia de Tlaxcala de las Indias y del Mar Oceano para el buen gobierno y ennoblecimiento dellas**, published as Vol. 4 of his *Relaciones Geográficas del siglo XVI: Tlaxcala* by René Acuña (Mexico, 1984). This has 156 pictures, of which 80 came from the Lienzo de Tlaxcala.

Muñoz Camargo was a cattle-farmer, son of an early colonist, a friend of Cortés, and a Mexican. He married a Tlaxcalan, and wrote to defend Tlaxcala. He was probably financed by the municipal government of Tlaxcala. He used López de Gómara, perhaps Sahagún, but also some elderly local informants, including a man who had been a Tlaxcalan priest, and an unidentified conquistador, "*de los primeros desta tierra*". The value is modest, even when the author discusses Tlaxcala.

Olmos, Fr. Andrés de: *Arte para aprender la lengua mexicana.* This includes *huehuetlatolli* (sermons) collected by Olmos in the 1530s. Published Paris, 1875. See James Pilling, *The Writings of Andrés de Olmos, in the languages of Mexico, The American Anthropologist*, viii, i (1895).

Origen de los Mexicanos. A second essay written between 1530 and 1535, probably by the same Franciscan who wrote **Relación de la Genealogía** (see below under that title). Not to be confused with the Codex Ramírez, which is also sometimes called "Origen de los mexicanos". It was ed. García Icazbalceta, in *Nueva Colección* . . . , III, 281–308.

Plano en Papel de Maguey. A panel, showing part of a city with *chinampa* agriculture. Now expertly thought not a part of Mexico-Tenochtitlan. Probably before 1540. Perhaps a copy of a pre-conquest map.

* **Pomar, Juan Bautista**, *Relación de Texcoco.* He was son of a conquistador and a sister of the last kings of Texcoco. The book was finished in 1582 but, dedicated to the glory of Nezahualcoyotl and Nezahualpilli, was not published till 1890, being then ed. Joaquín García Icazbalceta, in *Nueva Colección* . . . , III, 1–69. A new edition was ed. Madrid, 1992, as Part I of *Crónicas de América*, 65, with an intr. by Germán Vázquez. Pomar consulted survivors of old Texcoco.

Popol Vuh. A history of the Quiché Indians. Written down by a Quiché in mid 16th century. A book written by an Indian for Indians. A most important work of Maya mythology. New ed. Adrian Recinos, 1947. English tr. Norman, 1950.

* **Relación de la Genealogía** . . . A short essay on the past of the Mexica done for Juan Cano *c.*1540. Written by an anonymous Franciscan, it was ed. García Icazbalceta, *Nueva Colección* . . . , 262–81, and also as the second part of *Crónicas de América*, 65 (Madrid, 1991).

* **Relación de Michoacan** (*Relación de las ceremonias y ritos y población y gobierno de los*

783

Indios de la provincia de Michoacan). Probably compiled 1541 by Fr. Martín de Jesús de la Coruña. Original in El Escorial. Facsimile ed. Aguilar (Madrid, 1956), ed. José Tudela, intr. by Paul Kirchhoff. An English tr. (Norman, 1970), though of a Spanish ed. of 1903, by Eugene R. Craine and Reginald C. Reindorf as "The Chronicles of Michoacan".

* **Relaciones Geográficas.** In the late 16th century King Philip II asked for a description of his empire. This was the origin of a series of *Relaciones Geográficas*, 1579–81. A summary of these, where they now are, where they have been published, etc., is in Manuel Carrera Stampa's *Relaciones Geográficas de Nueva España, siglos XVI y XVII*, in *Estudios de Historia Novohispana*, ii (1968), 233–61. See also Howard Cline, *The Relaciones Geográficas of the Spanish Indies 1577–1648*, in the HMAI, Vol. 12, I (Austin, 1972), 183–242. The best published collection is that of René Acuña, *Relaciones Geográficas del siglo XVI* (Mexico, 1982–8, 10 vols.).

Román y Zamora, Jerónimo, *Repúblicas de Indias: idolatría y gobierno en México y Perú antes de la Conquista*, (Madrid, 1897, 2 vols.).

Torquemada, Fr. Juan de, *Monarquía Indiana.* Written 1603–13. Published Seville, 1615, 3 vols. Cortés is described in it as God's instrument. According to León-Portilla, the "richest and best synthesis of the . . . Indian past available in . . . the seventeenth century". A facsimile copy of an ed. of 1723 was ed. Mexico, 1943, by S. Chávez Hayhoe. New edition of Miguel León-Portilla, 3 vols. (Mexico, 1975).

Tovar. See **Codex Ramírez.**

Unos Anales de la nación Mexicana. See **Anales de Tlatelolco.**

* **Zorita, Alonso de,** *Relación de los señores de la Nueva España.* Written 1566–70 by the then *oidor* of the royal *audiencia* of New Spain. Ed. García Icazbalceta, in *Nueva Colección* . . . , III (Mexico, 1891), and by Germán Vázquez (Madrid, 1992). It used lost MSS, perhaps that of Olmos. An excellent and fair-minded work. It gives special attention to the Mexican system of justice and land. Tr. into English, with a good intr., by Benjamin Keen, as *Life and Labour in Ancient Mexico*, (New Brunswick, NJ, 1963).

Spanish Material

I. Manuscripts

CAMBRIDGE

CAMBRIDGE UNIVERSITY LIBRARY

Conway Papers. See p. 787 for description.

LONDON

BRITISH LIBRARY

Add. MSS 21, 447

MADRID

ARCHIVO HISTORICO NACIONAL

Ordenes Militares: Santiago
Libros de visita de las Encomiendas, 1480–1515 (1234c, 1101c to 1109c)
Libro de genealogía

REAL ACADEMIA DE LA HISTORIA

Juan Bautista Muñoz collection.

MEXICO

ARCHIVO DEL NACION

Papeles de la Hospital de Jesús. These were papers of the Cortés family formerly in the hands of the conquistador's descendants

SEVILLE

ARCHIVO GENERAL DE INDIAS (AGI)

Contratación
leg. 4675, lib. 1 This contains documents relating to the treasure the Indians brought back from Mexico in 1519
lib. 2 This has information about Alonso Hernández Portocarrero
Escribanía de Cámara
leg. 178 A Documents of a lawsuit between descendants of "Doña Marina", daughter of Montezuma, and the Crown, 1681
leg. 1006 A *Probanza* of Francisco de Montejo
Indiferente General
leg. 419, lib. v Material relates to Alonso Hernández Portocarrero
leg. 420, lib. viii, ix and x. These files contain much material relating to Cuba, Diego Velázquez, etc., and the establishment of the Council of the Indies.
Justicia
leg. 49 *Residencia* against Diego Velázquez, 1524
leg. 220–5 *Residencia* against Hernán Cortés, 1529. These folios are very disorganised. The following summary is based on a paper by Teresa Alzugaray:
leg. 220, p.1 (584 folios), of which 8 (f.1 to f.5 and new f.1 to f.3) are preliminary papers relating to the king's setting-up of the *residencia* and the charges against Cortés. The secret enquiry (*pesquisa secreta*) is in f.3; the 38-question questionnaire attached to that follows (ff.5–9). Witnesses (ff.32–275) include Gonzalo Mexía, Cristóbal de Hojeda, Juan de Burgos, Antonio Serrano, Rodrigo de Castañeda, Juan Mansilla, Juan Coronel, Ruy González, Francisco Verdugo, Antonio Carvajal, Francisco de Orduña, Andrés de Monjaraz, Alonso Ortiz de Zúñiga, Bernardino de Santa Clara, Gerónimo de Aguilar, and García de Pilar. ff. 275–316 show the presentation of new witnesses.
ff.316–25 is the investigation of the death of Catalina, Cortés' wife; 326–8 has the questionnaire on the subject, and 328–42 the witnesses, including the maids and the majordomo Isidro Moreno.

ff.342–522 is the suit of Juan Tirado against Cortés (questionnaire and witnesses, some interesting, e.g., García Holguín, Gutierre de Badajoz, Juan Cano).

ff.526–42 are the charges against Cortés following the secret enquiry.

ff.548–54 is the reply to these by García de Llerena on behalf of Cortés.

p.3 (29 folios): appeals in Valladolid and Madrid, 1543–5 for the conclusion of the *residencia*.

p.5 (35 folios): documents exchanged 1526 between Cortés, Luis Ponce de León and Marcos Aguilar.

leg. 221

p.1 (318 folios): declaration by Cortés in response to the charges, with short replies by witnesses to the questionnaires noted above and below.

p.2 (30 folios): reply by Cortés to the *audiencia*, 1529–34.

p.3 (66 folios): charges, declarations and petitions. ff.58–66 is a petition by Alonso de Paredes in the name of Cortés to present other witnesses and a request for a delay. Cortés was granted two more years.

p.4 (76 folios): Cortés' questionnaires:(1) 380 questions; (2) 42 questions.

leg. 222

pp.1–4 (273 folios): consist of 101 charges against Cortés, followed by witnesses statements about it, and then replies (*descargo*) of Cortés (1531).

p.6 (353 folios): ff.1–4, power of attorney by Cortés to García de Llerena: ff.4–33 are Llerena's statements; ff.34–42 is presentation of witnesses re the replies, of whom the most important are by Juan de Salcedo, García de Aguilar, Alonso de la Serna, Alonso de Villanueva, Juan Altamirano, Luis Marín, Alonso de Mendoza, and García Holguín.

leg. 223

p.1 (401 folios): ff.1–41, copies of documents sent by Cortés to the king between 1519 and 1526; ff.41–51 is a questionnaire with 22 questions of 1520 (at Tepeaca/Segura); ff.51–85 are replies by witnesses, including Alonso de Benavides, Gerónimo de Aguilar, Sánchez Farfán, Leonel de Cervantes, Pedro de Alvarado and Sancho Barahona; ff.85–8 are declarations and documents of Cortés; ff.89–95 is another questionnaire of 1520 (15 questions) and witnesses presented by Cortés, of which the most important were Bernardino Vázquez de Tapia, Cristóbal de Olid, Andrés de Duero, Fr. Bartolomé de Olmedo, Diego de Ordaz, Alonso de Ávila and Fr. Juan Díaz; ff.127–198 contain papers relating to the arrival of Cristóbal de Tapia, some to Cortés' dispute with Velázquez. ff.198–258 relates to the *probanza* of Coyoacán of 1522, and includes questionnaire and witnesses; ff.259–321 includes papers, questionnaire (7 questions) relating to the coming of Francisco de Garay; ff.336–41 relates to Olid and Rodríguez de Villafuerte in Michoacan; ff.342–401 are copies of various orders, decrees, etc., of Cortés, 1520–4.

p.2 (480 folios): replies (1534) of Cortés' witnesses to the two questionnaires. The most important of these are Alonso de Villanueva, Luis Marín, Martín Vázquez, Alonso de Navarrete, Francisco de Flores, Xoan López de Jimena, Juan de Hortega, Gaspar de Garnica, Gonzalo Rodríguez de Ocaña, Pero Rodríguez de Escobar, Fray Luis de Fuensalida, Francisco de Santa Cruz, Rodrigo de Segura, Juan de Salcedo, Juan González de León, Alfonso de la Serna, Francisco de la Serna, Francisco de Solís, Juan Jaramillo, Andrés de Tapia, Joan de Cáceres, Francisco de Terrazas, Fr. de Toribio de Motolinía, Fr. Pedro de Gante, and Francisco de Montejo.

leg. 224.

p.1 (300 folios) (1534): continuation of testimonies as in p.2 of the preceding *legajo*.

p.2 (139 folios): declarations of some witnesses for the prosecution. The statements are from much the same witnesses as in leg. 220, p.1 (if not exactly the same) but the information is different.

p.3 (30 folios): various demands of Cortés against the ex-judges of the *audiencia*, Ortiz de Matienzo and Delgadillo.

p.4, R. 1 (93 folios): another suit of Cortés against the *audiencia*, in 1543, questionnaire with 9 questions, and 9 witnesses for Cortés: for the ex-judges, questionnaire of 11 questions, with 3 witnesses.

p.4, R. 2 (5 folios): further documents relating to the same suit.

p.5 (201 folios): statement made in support of the defence, Oaxaca, 1535–7, with questionnaire and witnesses.

leg. 225. In 8 *piezas*, consists of the *residencia* against Juan de Ortega *alcalde mayor* of Mexico, as a result of charges deriving from the *residencia* against Cortés.

Note: some of this material has been published in e.g.: (**a**) **Colección de Documentos Inéditos relativos al descubrimiento** . . . , *Vols.xxvi, xvii, and xxviii (Madrid, 1876–8);* (**b**) **Ignacio López Rayón, Documentos para la historia de México** *(México 1852–3, 2 vols.);* (**c**) *José Luis Martínez,* **Documentos Cortesianos,** *Vol. II, (Mexico, 1991); and* (**d**) *Polavieja. Though all are useful, they are incomplete. Many things were left out of the transcripts made in the 19th century, sometimes by mistake. Most of the material printed derives from witnesses who testified against Cortés. For a summary of the hitherto unpublished testimonies, see Martínez [9:52], 581, fn. 14.*

Some material from these legajos was also transcribed, and for the most part left in typescript, on the instructions of G. L. R. Conway, a British engineer who worked in Mexico. As with the other material mentioned in his collections (much of it taken from Patronato, leg. 57) copies of these can be seen in the Conway collections in the Library of Congress, Washington, the Gilcrease Institute of the University of Tulsa, and the University Library, Cambridge. The Conway collection in the University of Aberdeen seems to have nothing in it which is not in Cambridge. The only material in Tulsa which is not in either Washington or Cambridge, and which relates to the Conquest of Mexico, seems to be that numbered Box 82, which contains a suit by Francisco de Verdugo against Cortés in 1529–32 (168 folios). For summaries of the different collections, see articles by Schafer Williams, A. P. Thornton, J. Street and Ivie Cadenhead Jr., HAHR, 35(1955), 36(1956), 37(1957) and 38(1958).

leg. 295–6 *Residencia* vs Pedro de Alvarado and his lieutenants, (Santiago de Guatemala, 1535), 916 folios, in 5 *piezas*. Most of the interesting material seems to have been published by José Fernando Ramírez, *Proceso de residencia contra Pedro de Alvarado, ilustrado con estampas . . . y notas . . .* (Mexico, 1847).

leg. 699, no. 2 Suit, Seville, between Alonso de Nebreda and Hernando de Castro, merchants, 1525. Several letters from this *legajo* were ed. Enrique Otte, "Mercaderes Burgaleses en los inicios del comercio con México", *HM*, XVIII (1968).

leg. 712 Diego de Ordaz vs. Francisco de Verdugo before the Casa de la Contratación. Includes letters of Ordaz to Verdugo, of which 9 were ed. Enrique Otte, *HM* XIV (1964).

Patronato

leg. 15 This includes much useful material including a letter from Fr. Benito Martín to the King complaining of Cortés' conduct (R. 8), a copy made 1519 of Velázquez's instructions of 1518 to Cortés (R. 11), various *probanzas* relating to the costs of the expedition of Cortés (R. 16), material about Narváez, etc. (R. 17).

leg. 16 Mostly post-conquest material, but useful.

leg. 50, R 2 Contains material about Rodrigo de Bastidas in 1520.

eg. 57, R. 1–5 This contains a *probanza* of 1542 on the qualities of Martín Lóez. Much of this was copied on the instructions of G. L. R. Conway.

leg. 60 Has an interesting *información* of 1553 of Antonio Huitsimagari, son of the last *cazonci* of Michoacan.

leg. 75, no. 3, R. 1 Has an *información* of Bernal Díaz del Castillo in 1536. It was published as an appendix to Ramirez Cabañas' ed. of *La Historia Verdadera*.

leg. 86, no. 6, R. 1 About 300 folios which has much material about Pedro de Alvarado and Francisco de Alvarado. A *probanza* of Leonor de Alvarado from this *legajo* was published in *Anales de la sociedad de Geografía e Historia de Guatemala*, Vol. 13 (December 1938).

leg. 150, no. 2, R. 1 This has an *información* about the achievements of Gerónimo de Aguilar.

leg. 180, R. 2 This includes the *probanza* about the cost of the expedition of Segura, September 1520.

leg. 252, R. 1 Relates to Las Casas.

leg. 254 Doc. 3-C, R. 1, has the presentation of Cortés' case at Corunna by Portocarrero and Montejo, April 1520.

Mexico

leg. 203 This *legajo* contains *informaciones de méritos*, etc., about many conquistadors, made from about 1524 onwards. With one or two exceptions (e.g., Juan González Ponce de León), they are much less interesting than they promise to be. The most important relate to Juan Rodríguez de Villafuerte, Martín Vázquez, Francisco de Orduña, Juan de Burgos, Juan de Tirado, Hernán de Elgueta, Juan de Cuéllar, García del Pilar, Diego de Halcón, Diego de Ocampo, Lope de Samaniego and Gutierre de Badajoz.

ARCHIVO MEDINACELI (CASA DE PILATOS)

Colección Condes de Medellín

ARCHIVO HISTORICO PROVINCIAL

Archivo de Protocolos de Sevilla, in which there are many papers relating to Cortés, Martín Cortés, and their business associates (Luis Fernández de Alfaro, Juan de Córdoba, etc.), 1506–22. I was much helped by the splendid index published by the Instituto Hispano-Cubano relating to "Indian" matters.

SIMANCAS

ARCHIVO GENERAL DE LA NACION

Cámara de Castilla, legs. 106, 114, 116, 120, 127, 129, 130, 141, 151–3 These papers relate to Medellín, 1502–22.

Consejo Real, **leg.91** A suit of the Count of Medellín against the town of that name.

leg.112 (63 folios) Cortés vs Fernando Quintana, who built the fortress of Vera Cruz (1531–3).

leg.140 p.2, and p.4

leg. 141 p. 1–2: problems of the new town of Medellín (Nauhtla, Mexico).

Estado: Castilla The files examined related to the foundation of the Consejo de las Indias, and to *cédulas* applying to New Spain.

Registro General del Sello Papers relating to lawsuits before the royal court. There are many here which affect Medellín *c.* 1475–1500. The fine index is invaluable.

WASHINGTON

LIBRARY OF CONGRESS

Conway Papers

II. Main Published Documents

Actas del Cabildo de México, 1524 (Mexico, 1889–1916)

Colección de documentos inéditos relativos al descubrimiento, conquista y coloni-zación de las posesiones españoles en América y Oceania (Madrid, 1864 onwards 42 vols.), ed. Torres de Mendoza, Joaquín Pacheco and Francisco Cárdenas (*CDI* in sources)

* *Colección de documentos inéditos para la historia de España* (Madrid, 1842), ed. M. de Navarrete (*CDIHE* in sources)

* *Colección de documentos inéditos relativos al descubrimiento, conquista y organización de las antiguas posesiones españolas de Ultramar* (Madrid, 1884–1932, 25 vols.) (*CDIU* in sources)

Corraliza, José Ignacio, "Una carta familar de Hernán Cortés", *R de I*, VIII (1947) 893–5

Cortes de León y Castilla, Vol. iv (1520–5) (Madrid, 1882)

* **Cortés, Hernán, Escritos sueltos de,** Biblioteca Iberia, Vol. xii (Mexico, 1871)

Dantisco, Juan, Journal 1524–7: *el embajador polaco Juan Dantisco en la corte de Carlos V,* ed. A. Paz y Mella, *Boletín de la Real Academia Española* (Madrid, 1924–5), Vol. xii.

* *Documentos inéditos relativos a Hernán Cortés y su familia,* Archivo General de la Nación (Mexico), xxxvii (Mexico, 1935)

Fernández Duro, Cesáreo, "Primeras Noticias de Yucatan", *Boletín de la Sociedad Geográfica de Madrid,* Vol. xviii (1885)

Goldberg, Rita, *Nuevos Documentos y Glosas Cortesianos* (Madrid, 1987)

* *Hernán Cortés y Cristóbal Colón, Datos biográficos sacados del Archivo General de la Orden de Santiago,* in *BRAH,* xx–xxi (1892). This is a transcript of the material about Cortés' candidacy for the Order of Santiago of which the original is in the AHN, Madrid.

Icaza, Francisco A. de, *Conquistadores y pobladores de Nueva España* (Madrid, 1923). Re-issued Mexico, 1923. This volume consists of abbreviated versions of texts taken from the large number of statements of services (*méritos y servicios*) in the Archivo de Indias.

Icaza generally presented the most interesting material contained in the statements concerned, as I can testify, having examined many original texts. Numerous of these *informaciónes* have been separately published in a variety of publications to which there seems to be no index.

* *Información de 1522, Mexico,* under the presidency of Alonso de Ávila, ed. Edmundo O'Gorman, in *Boletín del Archivo General de la Nación,* Vol. ix, no. 2 (Mexico, 1938)

* *Información recibida en México y Puebla el año de 1565 a solicitud del gobernador y cabildo de naturales de Tlaxcala sobre los servicios que prestaraon los tlaxcaltecas a Hernán Cortés en la conquista de México siendo los testigos algunas de los mismos conquistadores, Biblioteca Histórica de la Iberia,* xx (Mexico, 1875)

* **Otte, Enrique:** *Mercaderes Burgaleses en los inicios del comercio con México, HM,* XVIII (1968), letters from Alonso de Nebreda and Hernando de Castro, 1524; and *Nueve Cartas de Diego de Ordás, HM,* XIV, 1–2 (1964)

* **Paso y Troncoso, Francisco,** *Epistolario de Nueva España 1505–1818* (Mexico, 1939–40, 16 vols.)

* **Polavieja, General Camilo,** *Hernán Cortes, Copías de documentos existentes en el archivo de Indias y en su palacio de Castilleja de la Cuesta sobre la conquista de Méjico* (Seville, 1889) (Polavieja in sources). The most important items are (a) a questionnaire of 106 questions, and 5 interesting witnesses' replies (Juan Álvarez, Diego de Ávila, Diego Holguín, Juan Bono de Quejo and Diego de Vargas), at the enquiry inspired by Diego Velázquez about Cortés' expedition, in Cuba, in June 1521 (*Información de 1521*); (b) a report made in 1520 in Santo Domingo about Cortés' and Velázquez's dispute; and (c) letters from Diego Velázquez to Spain, 1519

Saville, Marshall, "Earliest Notices concerning the Conquest of Mexico by Cortés", in **Indian Notes and Monographs,** ix, no.1, (1920). Three letters from Seville, 1520, one from Mexico

Three accounts of the Expedition of Fernando Cortés. Published originally as (a) *Ein Auszug Ettlicher Sendbrieff,* etc. (Nuremberg, 1520); (b) *Newe Zeitung von dem Lande das die Spanier funden haben,* etc. (probably Augsburg, 1522); and (c) *Ein Schöne Newe Zeytung,* etc. (probably Augsburg, 1523). Ed. Henry Wagner in *HAHR,* ix (1929)

* **Tributos y servicios personales de Indios para Hernán Cortés y su familia,** ed. Silvio Zavala, Archivo General de la Nación (Mexico), (Mexico, 1984)

III. Memoirs, Letters, Contemporary Accounts, etc.

* **Aguilar, Francisco de,** *Relación breve de la Conquista de Nueva España,* written *c.* 1565 by a conquistador who had become a Dominican monk, previously known as Alonso de Aguilar. The original is in the Escorial, first published in *Anales del Museo Nacional de México,* vii, (June, 1900). A recent edition is in *Crónicas de América,* 40 (Madrid, 1988). For English tr., see below under **Tapia.**

* **Cervantes de Salazar, Francisco**, *Crónica de la Nueva España*, written 1558–66 by the then Rector of the University of Mexico. First vol. dealing with the conquest ed. Madrid, 1914. For a destructive essay about this work, see Jorge Hugo Díaz-Thomé, in *Estudios de Historiografía de la Nueva España*, ed. Ramón Iglesia (Mexico, 1945), 17–41. Still, Cervantes de Salazar knew Cortés, and he had conversations with, and some statements from, old conquistadors (e.g., the mysterious Alonso de Ojeda, Alonso de Mata and Gerónimo Ruiz de la Mota).

* **Cortés, Hernán**, *Cartas de Relación*. The originals of Cortés' letters to Charles V are lost. But a copy, probably made in 1528, of all but the first, as well as a copy of the letter of the municipality of Vera Cruz of 1519 which substitutes for that letter, are in the National Library of Vienna, as the so-called Codex Vindobonensis, SN 1600. The second and third letters were ed. in Seville in 1522 and 1523, the fourth was ed. in Toledo in 1525, along with two *relaciones* by Alvarado and Diego de Godoy. The fifth letter was published only in 1858, in Vol.22 of the *BAE*. That was the first time that all the known *Cartas de Relación* were published together. A facsimile ed. of the whole collection in Vienna, including other material, was ed. by Chas. Gibson (Graz, 1960). A recent Spanish ed., to which chapter notes refer, is that of Mario Hernández, *Crónica de América*, 10 (Madrid, 1985). The best English edition, indeed far the best edition of all, is *Hernán Cortés, Letters from Mexico*, tr. and ed. Anthony Pagden, with intr. by John Elliott (Oxford 1972).

* **Díaz, Juan**, *El Itinerario de la armada del rey católico a la isla de Yucatan, en la India, en el año 1518* . . . An account of Grijalva's expedition. Written in 1519. The first ed. which survives is in Italian, published Venice, March 1520. First Spanish ed. García Icazbalceta, in *Colección de Documentos para la historia de México* (Mexico 1858), Vol.1. There is an excellent new Spanish ed., ed. Germán Vázquez, in *Crónicas de América*, 40 (Madrid, 1988). My references are to that edition. English trs. are by H. R. Wagner, *The discovery of New Spain by Juan de Grijalva* (Berkeley, 1942), and Patricia Fuentes, (see below under **Tapia**).

* **Díaz del Castillo, Bernal**, *Historia verdadera de la Nueva España*, written c. 1555, published 1632, critical ed. in Spanish, 1982, new ed. intr. by Miguel León-Portilla and Carmelo Sáenz de Santa María (Madrid, 1984). The only full English tr., sometimes with mistakes, is that by Alfred Maudslay (London, 1908–12, 5 vols.).

A *probanza* of the services of Díaz of 1539 contains material about the conquest. It includes evidence from Cristóbal Hernández, Martín Vázquez, Bartolomé de Villanueva, Manuel Sánchez Gazín, and Luis Marín. It was ed. in Ramírez Cañadas' ed. of *La Historia Verdadera* . . . (Mexico, 1939 3 vols.), III, 314–17. 7 royal decrees relating to Díaz are in *Epistolario*, VI, 28–36. There are several versions of Díaz's text. All seem to be true, prepared at different stages by the author himself. Díaz's detail is fascinating, occasionally wrong.

Dorantes de Salazar, Baltasar, *Sumario Relación de las cosas de la Nueva España*, written 1604, ed. José María de Agreda y Sánchez (Mexico, 1902). A ragbag of stories, rather favourable to the Mexicans.

El Conquistador Anónimo (The Anonymous Conqueror), *Relación de algunas cosas de la Nueva España* . . . *escrita por un compañero de Hernán Cortés*, first ed. 1538 in Italian as "Relatione di alcune cose della nuova Spagna . . . un gentil'homo del Signor Fernando Cortese". García Icazbalceta published it in *Colección de documentos para la Historia de México*, Vol.1. For English tr. see below under **Tapia**. Federico Gómez de Orozco, "El Conquistador Anónimo", *HM*, II (1952), 401–11, insisted that this was written by someone who had not been to Mexico, probably Alonso de Ulloa. Jean Rose, in a French ed. (Paris, 1970), tried to prove it genuine.

* **Fernández de Oviedo, Gonzalo,** *Historia General y Natural de Indias*: summary published 1526, Toledo; first part ed. Seville, 1535; Book XX of the second part, 1552. The whole was not ed. till 1851, Madrid, by José Amador de los Ríos. A new ed. was in the *BAE* (Madrid, 1959) by Juan Pérez de Tudela. Oviedo talked to many, including Juan Cano, and perhaps had access to a diary of his voyage written by Grijalva.

* **Las Casas, Bartolomé de:** (1) *Historia de las Indias*, written 1527–66, not ed. till 1875–6, though consulted in MS. The best ed. is by Juan Pérez de Tudela (Madrid, 1957), Vols. 95–6 in *BAE*. This unfinished work contains much first-hand material, since Las Casas knew Diego Velázquez, Narváez, Grijalva, etc, as well as Cortés. Of special value are Book II, Chapter X; and Book III, Chapters XXI–XXXII and Chapters XCVI–CXXIV; (2) **Apologética Historia,** *BAE* (Madrid, 1958), Vol. 105; (3) **Brevísima Relación de la destrucción de las Indias,** first ed. Seville 1552. There is a new Spanish edition, ed. Lewis Hanke and Manuel Giménez Fernández (Mexico, 1965, 2 vols.); (4) *De Thesauris de Peru*, in Latin, published 1557, ed. 1898 by Ramón Menéndez Pidal, has some Mexican allusions. (José Alcina Franch's edition, Las Casas, *Obra Indigenista*, Madrid, 1992, has a section dealing with Mexico, 63–115.)

* **López de Gómara, Francisco: La Conquista de México:** This is the second part of *Hispania Victrix*, a history of the Spanish conquest of the New World (ed. Saragossa, 1553). López de Gómara was Cortés' chaplain in the last years of his life. He talked to him about the work. It is Cortés' *apologia pro vita sua*: though the extent to which Cortés read the manuscript (if at all) is uncertain. Gómara used Cortés' letters to Charles V, including perhaps the lost first letter. He also made use of Tapia's account. For long banned and left un-republished in Spain, it was revived in the 19th century. A new Spanish edition is that ed. by José Luis de Rojas, in *Crónicas de América*, 36 (Madrid, 1987). There is a readable, although abbreviated, English tr. by L. B. Simpson, published as *Cortés The Life of the Conqueror* (Berkeley, 1964): the abbreviation relates to a section about Mexican life which the author took largely from Motolinía.

* **Marineo Siculo, Lucio, "Don Fernando Cortés, marqués del Valle",** in *De Rebus Hispaniae, Memorables de España* (Alcalá de Henares, 1530, facsimile Madrid, 1960). Republished in *Historia 16* (April, 1985), 95–104, with intr. by Miguel León-Portilla. This short essay is in effect the first biography of Cortés, being written by the Italian humanist who taught in Salamanca, and advised the court. He knew Cortés, and talked with some members of his expeditions.

* **Martyr, Peter,** *De Orbe Novo*, original ed. 1527. New ed. by Joaquín Torres Asensio (Madrid, 1892, 2 vols.), tr. by Francis Macnutt (New York, 1912, 2 vols.). New Spanish ed. Ramón Alba (Mexico, 1989). Martyr talked to several who had been to Mexico. These included Antonio Alaminos, Francisco Montejo, Alonso Hernández Portocarrero, Juan de Ribera and Cristóbal Pérez Hernán. His excellent reports were influenced by them.

A complete ed. of his letters tr. into Spanish was published in *Documentos Inéditos para la Historia de España* (Madrid, 1953–7), Vols. 9–12. Material about Mexico is in letters 623, 649, 650, 665, 715, 717, 763, 770–1, 782, 797, 800, 802, 806, 809. All these except 623 were ed. in *Cartas sobre el Nuevo Mundo* (Madrid, 1990).

Mendieta, Fr. Gerónimo de, *Historia Eclesiástica Indiana*, written 1573–96, ed. García Icazbalceta (Mexico 1870); new ed. by S. Chavez Hayhoe (Mexico, 1945, 4 vols). The best ed. is in *BAE*, Vols. 260–1, ed. Francisco Solar y Pérez Lila (Madrid, 1973). Mendieta denounced the *encomiendas*, praised the Mexicans and devoted much attention to the friars. So his works were not published in his lifetime.

Fr Antonio de Remasal, *Historia de las Indias Occidentales* . . . , 1620, new ed. in *BAE* (Madrid, 1964), ed. Carmelo Sáenz de Santa María. Books I and II have some useful material.

* **Sepúlveda, Juan Ginés de**, *De Orbe Novo (Historia del Nuevo Mundo)*. The official chronicler of Charles V, Sepúlveda met Cortés several times, and wrote his elegant book in the 1550s in Latin. Though largely based on Cortés' letters (including probably the lost first one), and López de Gómara, the book is very well written, and its judgements are often interesting, giving an impression of what was thought of the conquest towards the end of the reign of Charles. The first Spanish ed. was in 1976, the most recent was Madrid 1987, with intr. by Antonio Ramírez de Verger.

Solís, Antonio de, *Historia de la conquista de Mexico*. Written 1661–84, ed. 1684, modelled on classical historians, e.g., Livy. A successful book for 150 years. A defence of Spain. He hated Bernal Díaz. Though he followed López de Gómara, Cervantes, etc., there is some new material in the book. Numerous later eds. and trs.

* **Suárez de Peralta, Juan**, *Noticias Historicas de la Nueva España*. This book was written in the 1580s and ed. 1878 by Justo Zaragoza. A new ed. is published as *Tratado del descubrimiento de las Indias*, with intr. by Féderico Gómez de Orozco (Mexico, 1949). The author was a nephew of Cortés' first wife. The author sought to exalt Cortés and ruin the reputation of his father and his aunt.

* **Tapia, Andrés de**, *Relación de algunas cosas* . . . , written c.1545, an account by one of Cortés' friends. Much used by López de Gómara, it was first ed. by Joaquín García Icazbalceta, in *Colección de Documentos para la historia de México* (México, 1866), Vol. II. New ed. in *Crónicas de América*, 40, ed. Germán Vázquez. English tr. by Patricia de Fuentes in *The Conquistadors* (London, 1964). Tapia's text is a modified version of his evidence to the *residencia* against Cortés.

* **Vázquez de Tapia, Bernardino**, *Relación de Méritos* . . . A statement of services. First ed. by Manuel Romero de Torres (Mexico, 1939), with extra documentation, e.g., Vázquez's evidence in the *residencias* against Cortés and Alvarado. Re-ed. in *Crónicas de América*, 40, and tr.; see above under **Díaz**.

Index